Principles and Practice of

Marketing

THIRD EDITION

Principles and Practice of

THIRD EDITION

Marketing

www.jobber-marketing.com

David Jobber

Professor of Marketing, University of Bradford

McGraw-Hill Publishing Company

London   New York   Burr Ridge, IL   St Louis   San Francisco   Auckland   Bogotá
Caracas   Lisbon   Madrid   Mexico   Milan   Montreal   New Delhi   Panama   Paris
San Juan   São Paulo   Singapore   Sydney   Tokyo   Toronto

Published by
McGraw-Hill Publishing Company
Shoppenhangers Road, Maidenhead, Berkshire, SL6 2QL, England
Telephone: 01628 502500
Fax: 01628 770224
Website: www.mcgraw-hill.co.uk

British Library Cataloguing in Publication Data
A catalogue record for this book is available from the British Library

Library of Congress Cataloguing in Publication Data
The LOC data for this book has been applied for

Publisher	Andy Goss
Sponsoring Editor	Tim Page
Development Editor	Caroline Howell
Editorial Assistant	Catriona Watson
Senior Marketing Manager	Petra Skytte
Production Editorial Manager	Penny Grose
New Media Developers	Douglas Greenwood
	Alex Cane
	Veronique Elhorgha
Permissions Manager	Judith Spencer

Created for McGraw-Hill by the independent production company
Steven Gardiner Ltd TEL +44 (0)1223 364868 FAX +44 (0)1223 364875

McGraw-Hill

A Division of The *McGraw-Hill* Companies

Cover by DesignDeluxe
Printed and bound by Mateu Cromo, Madrid

ISBN 0 07 709613 4

The Author

David Jobber is an internationally recognized marketing academic. He is Professor of Marketing and Head of the Marketing Group at the University of Bradford Management Centre. He holds an Honours degree in economics from the University of Manchester, a Masters Degree from the University of Warwick and a Doctorate from the University of Bradford.

Before joining the faculty at the Bradford Management Centre, David worked for the TI Group in marketing and sales, and was Senior Lecturer in Marketing at the University of Huddersfield. He has wide experience of teaching core marketing courses at undergraduate, postgraduate and post-experience levels. His specialisms are industrial marketing, sales management and marketing research. He has a proven, ratings-based record of teaching achievements at all levels; his industrial management MBA module is one of the most highly-rated electives at Bradford. His competence in teaching is reflected in visiting lectureships at the universities of Aston, Lancaster, Loughborough and Warwick. He has taught marketing to executives of international companies such as Rhône-Poulénc, Allied Lyons, the BBC, Bass, Rolls-Royce, RTZ and Kalamazoo.

Supporting his teaching is a record of achievement in academic research. David has over 100 publications in the marketing area in such journals as the *International Journal of Research in Marketing, MIS Quarterly, Strategic Management Journal, Journal of International Business*

Studies, Journal of Business Research, Journal of Product Innovation Management and the *Journal of Personal Selling and Sales Management*. David has served on the editorial boards of the *International Journal of Research in Marketing, Journal of Personal Selling and Sales Management, European Journal of Marketing* and the *Journal of Marketing Management*.

Brief Contents

Contents

Case contributors

Case 1 Virgin Direct 2000
Susan Bridgewater, Lecturer in Marketing, University of Warwick

Case 2 Sylvan Ireland
John Faby, Professor of Marketing, University of Limerick, Ireland

Case 3 Heron Engineering
David Shipley, Professor of Marketing, University of Dublin, Ireland

Case 4 Weatherpruf Shoe Waxes
Graham Hooley, University of Aston

Consumer Behaviour Exercise 1
Understanding Consumer Decision Making
Richard Elliott, Professor of Marketing and Consumer Research, University of Exeter

Consumer Behaviour Exercise 2 The Symbolic Meaning of Brands
Richard Elliott, Professor of Marketing and Consumer Research, University of Exeter

Case 5 Winters Company
David Jobber, Professor of Marketing, University of Bradford

Case 6 Morris Services
David Jobber, Professor of Marketing, University of Bradford

Case 7 Marks and Spencer
David Cook, Senior Lecturer in Marketing, University of Leeds

Case 8 The Friendly Bank
David Jobber, Professor of Marketing, University of Bradford

Case 9 WP Forty
David Smith, Market Research Society, Chief Diploma Examiner

Case 10 Harveys Stores
Professor Gillian Wright, Professor of Strategic Management, John Moores University, Liverpool

Case 11 Repositioning Budweiser
Susan Bridgewater, Lecturer in Marketing, University of Warwick

Case 12 Automatic Vehicle Location
David Cook, Senior Lecturer in Marketing, University of Leeds

Case 13 Levi Jeans
David Jobber, Professor of Marketing, University of Bradford

Case 14 Müller Dairy UK
Julie Verity, Lecturer in Strategy and Simon Knox, Professor of Brand Marketing, Cranfield University

Case 15 Swatch
Colin Gilligan, Professor of Marketing, Sheffield Business School and Franz Weisbrod, Regional Export Manager, CompAir Rucklufttechnik GmbH

Case 16 Philips' Aqua Wave
Erik Van Hultink, Delft University of Technology, The Netherlands

Case 17 Hansen Bathrooms (A)
David Jobber, Professor of Marketing, University of Bradford

Case 18 Computron Inc., 1994
Dominique Turpin, IMD, Lausanne, Switzerland

Case 19 DHL Keeps Your Promises
Patrick De Pelsmacker, M. Geuens and J. Van den Bergh, University of Antwerp

Vignettes

Marketing in Action

e-Marketing

Preface

Marketing is a vibrant, challenging activity that requires an understanding of both principles and how they can be applied in practice. The Third edition of my book attempts to capture both aspects of the multidiscipline. Marketing concepts and principles are supported by examples of international practice to crystallize those ideas in the minds of students who may have little personal experience of real-life marketing.

My objective, then, was to produce a tightly-written textbook supported by a range of international examples and case studies. The third edition places a great emphasis on the use of the case study as a teaching method. In my experience, all types of students enjoy applying principles to real-life marketing problems. This is natural as marketing does not exist in a vacuum. It is through application that students gain a richer understanding of marketing.

Becoming a successful marketing practitioner requires an understanding of the principles of marketing together with practical experience of implementing marketing ideas, processes and techniques in the marketplace. This book provides a framework for understanding important marketing issues such as understanding the customer, marketing segmentation and targeting, brand building, pricing, innovation and marketing implementation that form the backbone of marketing practice.

Marketing does not exist in a vacuum: it is a vibrant, sometimes energy-sapping profession that is full of exciting examples of success and failure. Moreover, marketing practitioners need to understand the changes that are taking place in the environment. As the quotation which heads Chapter 5 says, 'Change is the only constant'. Marketing-orientated companies are undergoing fundamental readjustments to their structure to cope with the accelerating rate of change. If you wish to enter the marketing profession then an acceptance of change and a willingness to work long hours are essential prerequisites.

Marketing in Europe has never looked stronger. International conferences organized by the European Marketing Academy and national organizations such as the Marketing Education Group in the UK make being a marketing academic challenging, rewarding and enjoyable. We should always value the companionship and pleasure that meeting fellow marketing academics brings. The growth in the number of students wishing to study marketing has brought with it a rise in the number of marketing academies in Europe. Their youth and enthusiasm bode well for the future of marketing as a major social science.

Most students enjoy studying marketing: they find it relevant and interesting. I hope that this book enhances your enjoyment, understanding and skills.

Structure of the book

The book comprises twenty-one chapters organized into four parts:

Part I: Fundamentals of Modern Marketing Thought summarizes core marketing theory including the marketing concept and marketing planning, consumer and organizational buyer behaviour, marketing research and segmentation and positioning. The emphasis throughout is on the strategic development of a market-driven company committed to exceeding the expectations of its customers.

Part II: Marketing Mix Decisions focuses upon the development of effective strategies for pricing, promotion, product development and distribution. The text emphasizes that each element of the marketing mix should be developed within the context of the overall marketing strategy.

Part III: Competition and Marketing discusses the issues of competitive strategy, competitive advantage and the nature of competitive behaviour.

Part IV: Marketing Implementation and Application provides in-depth coverage of how to overcome resistance to marketing-led change, and analyses the various forms of marketing organization. This module also covers the special characteristics of service industries and their implications for marketing strategy, and particular issues associated with marketing in the global marketplace.

Taking into account its European readership, foreign currency conversion rates are given in appropriate places. These were accurate at the time of writing (2000). Obviously, changes since then may need to be taken into account.

New to this edition

As always, recent events are reflected throughout this book and all chapters have been updated with new conceptual material, illustrative examples and case studies. Here is a brief summary of the key content changes for this edition:

The Internet and e-marketing

A major new feature of this third edition is its focus on Internet and on-line marketing. This reflects the enormous interest in this aspect of marketing and its potential in revolutionizing the way in which marketing is practised. A full new chapter is devoted to the exciting developments in Internet technologies and on-line marketing. 'E-Marketing' boxed illustrative examples appear throughout the book to demonstrate the impact of the Internet on marketing today. The URL (web address) of organizations mentioned in the text have also been included in this new edition. Every chapter ends with an on-line marketing exercise to take full advantage of the educational potential of this medium.

Ethical marketing

The third edition also contains a greater focus on social responsibility and ethical marketing issues, which are of increasing concern to companies. These are introduced in the Marketing Environment chapter and, where appropriate, chapters conclude with a discussion of ethical issues in marketing. Thus, new sections cover ethical issues in marketing research, managing products, pricing, advertising, personal selling, direct marketing, Internet marketing, distribution, sales promotion and public relations.

Key marketing topics

Writing the third edition has provided the opportunity to expand the coverage of key marketing topics to reflect their importance in modern marketing management. Hence the following areas have been given special attention: managing service relationships, key account management, integrated marketing communications, branding and sponsorship.

How to study using this book

This book has been designed to help you to learn and to understand the important principles behind successful marketing. To check you really understand the new concepts you are reading about, work through the case studies, exercises and questions at the end of each chapter.

Case studies

The new edition contains forty-two cases and exercises as support material for classroom teaching. Twenty are new to this edition, having been commissioned from some of marketing's leading case writers. The new cases often feature well-known brands such as Marks and Spencer, Budweiser, Levi Jeans, Müller, Swatch, DHL, Mitsubishi, Wal-Mart, Eurocamp and British Airways. Two popular cases, Virgin Direct and First Direct, have been up-dated. Each chapter ends with two case studies. To cater for all requirements, there is a mixture of short and long cases.

Case-study analysis

The aim of this book is not to tell you what marketing is about. Rather I hope that the book will develop the skills you need to analyse marketing situations and make sensible recommendations. Your lecturers and tutors will select cases, which they feel are particularly relevant to the principles that they are teaching. At first the prospect of case analysis can seem daunting, particularly when the case is long and is full of unfamiliar facts and statistics. A sensible approach is to read the case fairly quickly to get an understanding of the broad situation and major issues covered. Follow this by a slower, more in-depth reading to extract the key details of the case.

The figures and discussion in each chapter can be useful in providing a framework for case analysis. Key questions to ask are such as: What are the important customer characteristics and behaviour patterns? How is the market segmented? How well is the company matching or exceeding customer expectations? Who are the competitors and what are their strengths and weaknesses? These are fundamental to understanding marketing situations.

To guide your thinking, most of the case studies end with questions. Your tutor may or may not decide to use these for case-study analysis. Above all remember that marketing is an inexact science: there are no unambiguously right answers. Marketing decisions are fraught with risk. For example, the success of a strategy may depend on how competitors react. Predictions of reactions should be built into the decision-making phase, but ultimately competitor response is uncontrollable and hence there can be no guarantee that a strategy will work in the marketplace. The best that can be asked of you is that you justify your strategy choice based upon a clear understanding of the major marketing issues that impinge upon the decisions.

Internet exercises

The Internet exercises are a new feature of this edition of my book. They are designed to support your learning by providing short exercises, which will help you develop a clearer understanding of marketing principles and practice. They should also help to make you aware of the richness of marketing information available on the Internet. Finally, they should help you relate the organizations, products and services you will encounter to your own experience as a consumer. I hope you find them interesting and useful.

Study questions

Study questions appear at the end of each chapter. These may be used by your tutors as essay subjects or as tutorial questions. Their aim is to test knowledge and understanding of marketing principles. Whether your tutor uses them as a formal part of their marketing teaching or not, you can use them to check how well you have assimilated the information and procedures discussed in each chapter. Allocate some time after reading each chapter to answering these questions. If you make notes you may find them useful when the time for revision comes.

To assist you in working through this text, we have developed a number of distinctive study and design features. To familiarise yourself with these features, please turn to the Guided Tour on pages xxii–xxiii.

You can also test your understanding and expand your knowledge by loading-up the accompanying Student CD-ROM, and exploring the on-line resources centre. For more information about the CD-ROM and On-line Learning Centre website, read the teaching and learning resources section on page xx.

Indexes and Glossary

For ease of reference and to help you in revising, towards the end of the text we have provided the following:

+ **Company Index**: all brands and companies featured in the text
+ **Subject Index**: all concepts discussed in the text

✦ **Author index**: all authors of articles, books, and other materials references in the text

✦ **Glossary**: a full list of all key terms used in the text with an accompanying definition.

Additional teaching and learning resources

We are always trying to improve the quality of this text and the supplementary resources that accompany it. For this edition, we have significantly expanded the range, quality and delivery of on-line resources to support both students in their studying, and lecturers in their teaching of marketing.

Student CD-ROM

Free with your copy of this book is a CD-ROM. This contains a range of electronic resources to help you study marketing, including:

✦ additional case material exploring ideas from the text in greater depth

✦ marketing plan template to help you develop successful strategies

✦ chapter-by-chapter Internet exercises, that allow you to self-test your understanding of marketing on the web

✦ web links that take you to Internet sites demonstrating E-Marketing in action

✦ topical and current marketing in the news features.

This has been designed to help you to better understand the concepts you read about in the text, so take time to explore the CD-ROM as you work through the chapters in the book. You will find all these resources and more on the textbook's On-line Learning Centre.

On-line learning centre

Please visit our on-line learning centre at www.jobber-marketing.com to gain access to an extensive range of materials for both students and lecturers. In addition to the resources featured on the CD-ROM, you will find chapter-by-chapter revision notes, self-tests, and a range of other useful extra material for your studies.

Remember to check the website frequently, as we will be regularly updating and adding to the material on this site.

Acknowledgements
for the Third Edition

I should like to thank my colleagues (past and present) at the University of Bradford Management Centre for their stimulating insights and discussions. I should also like to thank Ian Chaston from Plymouth Business School and Daragh O'Reilly, a colleague at Bradford, for their help in all things 'Internet'. And I shall never forget the work of the tireless Chris Barkby, Dee Dwyer, Lynne Lancaster and Jo Cousins at the University of Bradford Management Centre for typing the book. Many thanks to all of the case contributors for providing such a varied selection of cases and those of you who have reviewed previous editions of my book. I am also indebted to the Institute of Direct Marketing, the Institute of Practitioners in Advertising and the Market Research Society for supplying case material. Finally, my thanks go to Janet, Paul and Matthew who have had to endure my weekends of toil.

I would also like to thank the following people who took part in the market research for this edition:

Max Aiken, University of Wolverhampton
Roger Baty, University of Central England
Chris Blackburn, Oxford Brookes University
Rob Bradshaw, De Montfort University
Belinda Dewsnap, Loughborough University
Robert Duke, University of Leeds
Jane Martin, Warrington Collegiate Institute
Hans Ouwersloot, Maastricht University
Jill Ross, University of Teesside
Tuire Ylikoski, Helsinki School of Economics and Business Administration.

Finally, thanks to all those who contributed material to the CD-ROM and On-line Learning Centre:

Max Aiken, University of Wolverhampton
Sue Bridgewater, University of Warwick
Declan Fleming, National University of Ireland, Galway
John Goodfellow, University of North London
Nanne Migchels, Nijmegen University
Steve Storey, Sunderland University
Wonter Van Rossum, Utwente Univesity
Elaine Wallace, National University of Ireland, Galway.

Guided Tour

Part openings set the scene for each main area of study and a list of component chapters.

Learning objectives identify the primary topics covered and the skills you should acquire after studying each chapter.

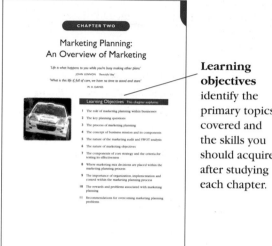

Study questions encourage you to review and apply the knowledge you have acquired from each chapter. These questions can be undertaken either individually or as a focus for group discussion in seminars or tutorials.

The **chapter summary** briefly reviews and reinforces the main topics you will have covered in each chapter.

Internet exercises provide an opportunity to test out your knowledge of important ideas on the Internet. They direct you towards interesting websites and provide questions to test your understanding.

Each chapter contains a full list of **references** so that if you wish, you can continue to research in greater depth after reading the chapter.

URLs (Internet addresses) point you towards the Internet sites of organizations mentioned in the text. If you want further useful Internet addresses to help you study marketing, go to www.jobber-marketing.com and have a look at the links sections.

Key terms are highlighted and explained in the text where they first appear, with summary definitions for all key terms compiled at the end of each chapter. A full glossary at the end of the book provides a further handy reference for your study.

Colour advertisements and **illustrations** throughout the book demonstrate how marketers have presented their products in real promotions and campaigns.

Look out for the steering wheel icon that directs you to the **Marketing-in-Action** boxes. These boxes provide additional practical examples to highlight the application of concepts, and encourage you to critically analyse and discuss real-world issues.

Graphs and tables are presented in a simple and clear design; the use of colour will help you to further understand and absorb key data and concepts.

Where you see the chequered flag icon, read the **E-Marketing** boxes. These examples illustrate real-life e-marketing, by demonstrating how organizations have used new technologies in their marketing strategies.

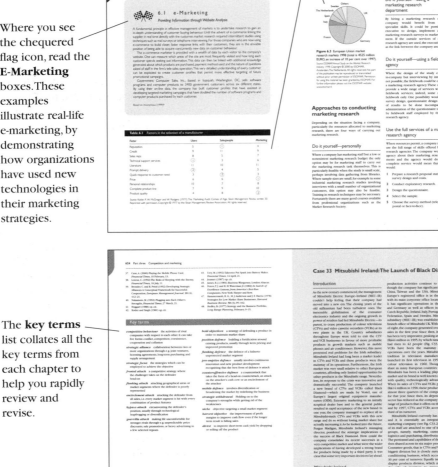

The **key terms** list collates all the key terms from each chapter to help you rapidly review and revise.

Each chapter concludes with two **case studies**. These up-to-date case examples encourage you to apply what you have learnt in each chapter to a real-life marketing problem. You can test yourself by trying out the **Case Questions** at the end of the study section.

Currency Conversion Table

The value of one pound sterling at the time of going to press was:

2.71	Australian dollars
22.54	Austrian schillings
66.07	Belgian francs
2.24	Canadian dollars
12.22	Danish kronas
3.61	Dutch guilders
1.64	Euros
9.74	Finnish markkas
10.74	French francs
3.20	German marks
558.14	Greek drachmas
11.44	Hong Kong dollars
1.29	Irish punts
3171.92	Italian lira
164.34	Japanese yen
5.58	Malaysian ringgits
3.42	New Zealand dollars
13.25	Norwegian kroner
328.37	Portuguese escudos
2.55	Singapore dollars
272.52	Spanish pesetas
14.17	Swedish kroner
2.47	Swiss francs
1.47	US dollars

PART ONE

Fundamentals of Modern Marketing Thought

CHAPTER ONE

Marketing in the Modern Firm

'Management must think of itself not as producing products, but as providing customer-creating value satisfactions. It must push this idea (and everything it means and requires) into every nook and cranny of the organization. It has to do this continuously and with the kind of flair that excites and stimulates the people in it

THEODORE LEVITT

Learning Objectives   *This chapter explains:*

1   The marketing concept: an understanding of the nature of marketing, its key components and limitations

2   The difference between a production orientation and marketing orientation

3   The differing roles of efficiency and effectiveness in achieving corporate success

4   The differences between market-driven and internally driven businesses

5   The dimensions of market-driven management

6   How an effective marketing mix is designed and the criticisms of the 4-Ps approach to marketing management

7   How to create customer satisfaction and value

8   The relationship between marketing characteristics, market orientation, adoption of a marketing philosophy and business performance

In general, marketing has a bad press. Phrases like 'marketing gimmicks', 'marketing ploys' and 'marketing tricks' abound. The result is that marketing is condemned by association. Yet this is unfortunate and unfair because the essence of marketing is value not trickery. Successful companies rely on customers returning to repurchase; the goal of marketing is long-term satisfaction, not short-term deception. This theme is reinforced by the writings of top management consultant Peter Drucker, who stated: [1]

> Because the purpose of business is to create and keep customers, it has only two central functions—marketing and innovation. The basic function of marketing is to attract and retain customers at a profit.

What can we learn from this statement? First, it places marketing in a central role for business success since it is concerned with the creation and retention of customers. Second, it implies that the purpose of marketing is not to chase any customer at any price. Drucker used profit as a criterion. While profit may be used by many commercial organizations, in the non-profit sector other criteria might be used such as social deprivation or hunger. Many of the concepts, principles and techniques described in this book are as applicable to Action Aid as to Renault.

Third, it is a reality of commercial life that it is much more expensive to attract new customers than to retain existing ones. Indeed, the costs of attracting a new customer have been found to be up to six times higher than the costs of retaining old ones. [2] Consequently marketing-orientated companies recognize the importance of building relationships with customers by providing satisfaction and attracting new customers by creating added value. Grönroos has stressed the importance of relationship building in his definition of marketing in which he describes the objective of marketing as to establish, develop and commercialize long-term customer relationships so that the objectives of the parties involved are met. [3] Finally, since most markets are characterized by strong competition, the statement also suggests the need to monitor and understand competitors, since it is to rivals that customers will turn if their needs are not being met.

Marketing exists through exchanges. *Exchange* is the act or process of receiving something from someone by giving something in return. The 'something' could be a physical good, service, idea or money. Money facilitates exchanges so that people can concentrate on working at things they are good at, earn money (itself an exchange) and spend it on products which someone else has supplied. The objective is for all parties in the exchange to feel satisfied so each party exchanges something of less value than that which is received. The idea of satisfaction is particularly important to suppliers of products because satisfied customers are more likely to return to buy more products than dissatisfied ones. Hence, the notion of customer satisfaction as the central pillar of marketing is fundamental to the creation of a stream of exchanges upon which commercial success depends.

The rest of this chapter will examine some of these ideas in more detail and provide an introduction to how marketing can create customer value and satisfaction.

The marketing concept

The above discussion introduces the notion of the marketing concept, that is that companies achieve their profit and other objectives by satisfying (even delighting) customers. [4] This is the traditional idea underlying marketing. However, it neglects a fundamental aspect of commercial life: competition. The traditional marketing concept is a necessary but not a sufficient condition for corporate achievement. To achieve success companies must go further than mere customer satisfaction; they must do it better than competition. Many also-ran products on the market would have been world-beaters in the mid-1990s. The difference is competition. The modern *marketing concept* can be expressed as:

> The achievement of corporate goals through meeting and exceeding customer needs better than the competition.

To apply this concept three conditions should be met. First, company activities should be focused upon providing customer satisfaction rather than, for example, producer convenience. This is not an easy condition to meet. Second, the achievement of customer satisfaction relies on integrated effort. The responsibility for the implementation of the concept lies not just within the marketing department. The belief that customer needs are central to the operation of a company should run right through production, finance, research and development, engineering and other departments. The role of the marketing department is to play *product champion* for the concept and to coordinate activities. But the concept is a business philosophy not a departmental duty. Finally, for integrated effort to come about, management must believe that corporate goals can be achieved through satisfied customers (see Fig. 1.1).

Unfortunately the realities of commercial life are such that there can be a conflict between the interests of suppliers and customers. Price fixing, for example, can raise profit levels while lowering customer satisfaction. Such anticompetitive activities can hinder the adoption of the marketing philosophy as the means to corporate prosperity. In France the supermarket chain Leclerc has mobilized the marketing philosophy to break down anticompetitive supplier activities, and to lower prices for its customers. Marketing in Action 1.1 describes the way in which Leclerc has married customer satisfaction with commercial success.

Marketing versus production orientation

There is no guarantee that all companies will adopt a *marketing orientation*. A competing philosophy is production orientation.* This is represented by an inward-looking stance that can easily arise given that many employees spend their working day at the point of production.

Production orientation manifests itself in two ways. First, management become cost-focused. They believe that the central focus of their job is to attain economies of scale by producing a limited range of products (at the limit just one) in a form that minimizes production costs. Henry Ford is usually given as an example of a production-orientated manager because he built just one car in one colour—the black Model T— in order to minimize costs. However, this is unfair

* This of course is not the only alternative business philosophy. For example, companies can be financially or sales-orientated. In the first case companies focus on short-term returns, basing decisions more on financial ratios than customer value; and sales-orientated companies emphasize sales push rather than adaptation to customer needs. However, we shall concentrate on the fundamental difference in corporate outlook: marketing versus production orientation.

to Mr Ford since his objective was customer satisfaction: bringing the car to new market segments through low prices. The real production-orientated manager has no such virtues. The objective is cost reduction for its own sake, an objective at least partially fuelled by the greater comfort and convenience that comes from producing a narrow product range.

The second way in which production orientation reveals itself is in the belief that the business should be defined in terms of its production facilities. Levitt has cited the example of film companies defining their business in terms of the product produced which meant that they were slow to respond when the demand to watch cinema films declined in the face of increasing competition for people's leisure time.[5] Had they defined their business in marketing terms—entertainment—they may have perceived television as an opportunity rather than a threat.

Figure 1.2 illustrates production orientation in its crudest form. The focus is on current production capabilities which define the business mission. The purpose of the organization is to manufacture products and aggressively sell them to unsuspecting customers. A classic example of the catastrophe that can happen when this philosophy drives a company is Pollitt and Wigsell, a steam engine producer which sold its products to the textile industry. They made the finest steam engine available and the company grew to employ over 1000 people on a 30 acre site. Their focus was on steam engine production so when the electric motor superseded the earlier technology they failed to respond. The 30 acre site is now a housing estate.

Marketing-orientated companies focus on customer needs. Change is recognized as endemic and adaptation considered to be the Darwinian condition for survival. Changing needs present potential market opportunities which drive the company. Within the boundaries of their distinctive competences market-driven companies seek to adapt their product and service offerings to the demands of current and latent markets. This orientation is shown in Fig. 1.3.

Marketing-orientated companies get close to their customers so that they understand their needs and problems. When personal contact is insufficient or not feasible, formal marketing research is commissioned to understand customer motivations and behaviour. Part of the success of German machine tool manufactures

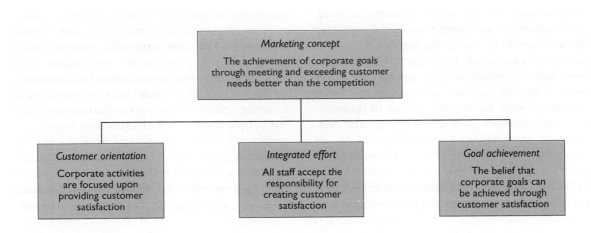

Figure 1.1 Key components of the marketing concept

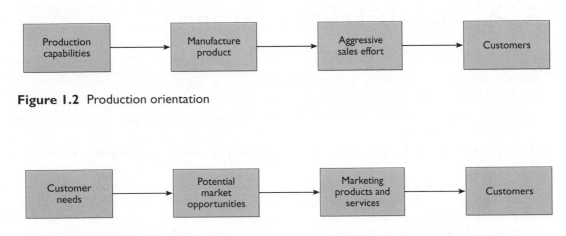

Figure 1.2 Production orientation

Figure 1.3 Marketing orientation

can be attributable to the willingness to develop new products with *lead customers*: those companies who themselves were innovative.[8] This contrasted sharply with the attitude of UK machine tool manufacture who saw marketing research only as a tactic to delay new product proposals and feared that involving customers in new product design would have adverse effects on the sales of current products. Marketing-orientation is related to the strategic orientation of companies. Marketing-orientated firms adopt a proactive search for market opportunities, use market information as a base for analysis and organizational learning, and adopt a long-term strategic perspective on markets and brands.[9]

Efficiency versus effectiveness

Another perspective on business philosophy can be gained by understanding the distinction between efficiency and effectiveness.[10] *Efficiency* is concerned with inputs and outputs. An efficient firm produces goods economically: it does things right. The benefit is that cost per unit of output is low and, therefore, the potential for offering low prices to gain market share, or charging medium to high prices and achieving high profit margins, is present. However, to be successful a company needs to be more than just efficient: it need to be effective as well. *Effectiveness* means doing the right things. This implies operating in attractive markets and making products that consumers want to buy. Conversely, companies that operate in unattractive markets or are not producing what consumers want to buy will go out of business, the only question is one of timing. The link between performance and combinations of efficiency and effectiveness can be conceived as in Fig 1.4. A company that is both inefficient and ineffective will go out of business quickly because it is a high-cost producer of products that consumers do not want to buy. A company that is efficient and ineffective may last a little longer because its low cost base may generate more profits from the dwindling sales volume it is achieving. Firms that are effective but inefficient are likely to survive because they are operating in attractive markets and are marketing products that people want to buy. The problem is that their inefficiency is preventing them from reaping the maximum profits from their endeavours. It is the combination of both efficiency and effectiveness that leads to optimum business success. Such firms do well and thrive because they are

1.1   Marketing in Action

Leclerc Applies the Market Philosophy

Leclerc is a French supermarket and hypermarket chain set up by Eduard Leclerc, who is recognized as the founding father of modern retail distribution in France. The chain's philosophy is based upon a highly original formula combining shrewd commercial sense with concern for the customer. The success of the chain owes much to the passionately held beliefs of its founder and his training in the church. His experience in retailing led him to believe that the interests of the consumer were not always being served by big business in France. His son, Michel, explains:

> France is dominated by big companies. But unlike Anglo-Saxon countries where these companies have stood for modern thinking, consumer rights and the exchange of liberal ideas, big companies in France have been the force behind protectionism against foreign countries and against competition. We wanted to prove that not only could we sell groceries cheaper but also leisure goods, health products and cultural items. Each time, we came against price fixing, regulations or restrictive practices which prevented us from selling cheaper. So we had to fight.

Their battles were fought in the law courts as well as the media. In total 1400 court cases were brought, some even going to the European Court of Justice. For example, battles were fought against fixed prices for petrol, and against chemists, who it was claimed held the monopoly in the distribution of cosmetics.

The campaigns made good publicity. Advertising backed up this image of the consumer's friend. 'Wanted—For Selling Cheaper' ran one poster campaign. The result was that the consumer believed that Leclerc stood for giving the biggest choice and the best prices. 'Honest, trustworthy', 'Defender of the consumer', 'You always pay less at the Leclerc check-out' and 'Everything is cheaper' are some of the comments that customers made.

By following a mission based upon putting the customer first Leclerc has created a clear *position* in the minds of its customers and has built its success by adopting the fundamental marketing principle of creating customer satisfaction. It is this formula that has established Leclerc as one of France's retail market leaders along with Intermarché and Carrefour.

Based on: BBC2 Television (1993);[11] Anonymous (1998)[12]

operating in attractive markets, are supplying products that consumers want to buy, and are benefiting from a low cost base.

A company which set out to establish itself as both efficient and effective is Virgin Atlantic. Innovations in service delivery (for example, personal televisions built into the seating) and low costs (for example, promotional expenditures are kept low by Richard Branson's capacity to generate publicity for the airline) mean that both objectives are achieved. Direct Line, the UK insurance company, has also achieved efficiency through eliminating the broker through its direct marketing operation, while becoming highly effective through its service excellence (for example, convenient motor repairs through its nationwide dealer network which eliminates the need to 'get two quotes', a fast telephone response facility which removes the need to fill in forms, and a car return service).

The essential difference between efficiency and effectiveness, then, is that the former is cost-focused while the latter is customer-focused. An effective company has the ability to attract and retain customers.

Market versus internally driven businesses

A deeper understanding of the marketing concept can be gained by contrasting in detail a *market-driven business* to one which is internally orientated. Table 1.1 summarizes the key differences.

Market-driven companies display customer concern throughout the business. All departments recognize the importance of the customer to the success of the business. In internally focused businesses convenience comes first. If what the customer wants is inconvenient to produce, excuses are made to avoid giving it.

Market-driven businesses know how their products and services are being evaluated against competition. They understand the choice criteria that customers are using and ensure that the marketing mix matches those criteria better than the competition. Internally driven companies assume that certain criteria—perhaps price and performance if the company is supplying industrial goods—are uppermost in all customers' minds. They fail to understand the real concerns of customers.

Businesses that are driven by the market base their segmentation analyses on customer differences that have implications for marketing

	Ineffective	Effective
Inefficient	Goes out of business quickly	Survives
Efficient	Dies slowly	Does well Thrives

Figure 1.4 Efficiency and effectiveness

Table 1.1   Marketing-orientated businesses

Market-driven businesses	Internally orientated businesses
Customer concern throughout business	Convenience comes first
Know customer choice criteria and match with marketing mix	Assume price and product performance key to most sales
Segment by customer differences	Segment by product
Invest in market research (MR) and track market changes	Rely on anecdotes and received wisdom
Welcome change	Cherish status quo
Try to understand competition	Ignore competition
Marketing spend regarded as an investment	Marketing spend regarded as a luxury
Innovation rewarded	Innovation punished
Search for latent markets	Stick with the same
Being fast	Why rush?
Strive for competitive advantage	Happy to be me-too

strategy. Businesses that are focused internally segment by product (e.g. large bulldozers versus small bulldozers) and consequently are vulnerable when customers' requirements change.

A key feature of market-driven businesses is their recognition that marketing research expenditure is an investment that can yield rich rewards through better customer understanding. Internally driven businesses see marketing research as a non-productive intangible and prefer to rely on anecdotes and received wisdom. Market-orientated businesses welcome the organizational changes that are bound to occur as an organization moves to maintain strategic fit between its environment and its strategies. In contrast, internally orientated businesses cherish the status quo and resist change.

Attitudes towards competition also differ. Market-driven businesses try to understand competitive objectives and strategies and anticipate competitive actions. Internally driven companies are content to ignore the competition. Marketing spend is regarded as an investment that has long-term consequences in market-driven businesses. The alternative view is that marketing expenditure is viewed as a luxury that never appears to produce benefits.

In marketing-orientated companies those employees who take risks and are innovative are rewarded. Recognition of the fact that most new products fail is reflected in a reluctance to punish those people who risk their career championing a new product idea. Internally orientated business reward time-serving and the ability not to make mistakes. This results in risk avoidance and the continuance of the status quo. Market-driven businesses search for latent markets: markets that no other company has exploited. The 3M's 'Post-it' product filled a latent need for a quick, temporary attachment to documents, for example. Internally driven businesses are happy to stick with their existing products and markets.

Intensive competition means that companies need to be fast to succeed. Market-driven companies are fast to respond to latent markets, innovate, manufacture and distribute their products and services. They realize that strategic windows soon close.[9] Dallmer, the chief executive of a major European company, told a story which symbolizes the importance of speed to competitive success.[10] Two people were walking through the Black Forest where it was rumoured a very dangerous lion lurked. They took a break and were sitting in the sun when one of them changed from his hiking boots to jogging shoes. The other one smiled and laughed and asked, 'You don't think you can run away from the lion with those jogging shoes?' 'No,' he replied, 'I just need to be faster than you!' Internally driven companies when they spot an opportunity take their time. 'Why rush?' is their epitaph.

Finally, marketing-orientated companies strive for competitive advantage. They seek to serve customers better than the competition. Internally orientated companies are happy to produce *me-too* copies of offerings already on the market.

Dimensions of market-driven management

What is required to achieve marketing orientation? Figure 1.5 summarizes some of the key dimensions.

Peters and Waterman's research stressed the importance of shared values and beliefs as a necessary prerequisite for successful marketing implementation.[13] Achieving this can be a problem for long-established companies that hitherto did not put the customer first. In general, changing attitudes is a hard-won battle. The second dimension concerns the skills in understanding and responding to customers. Peters and Waterman called it getting and keeping close to the customer.

Kohli and Jaworski interviewed 62 managers in marketing, non-marketing and senior management positions to gain an idea of what marketing meant to practitioners.[14] Their results stress the importance of market intelligence to an understanding of market orientation. They defined market orientation as 'the organization wide generation of market intelligence pertaining to current and future customer needs, dissemination of the intelligence across departments and organization wide responsiveness to it'. The starting-point of market orientation was intelligence gathering, which included not only customers' needs and preferences but also an analysis and interpretation of the faces that influence those needs and preferences. Information gathering was not the exclusive responsibility of the marketing department. Individuals and departments throughout the organization often gathered information informally, such as research and development

(R&D) engineers at scientific conferences and senior executives with trade journals.

Next, information needs to be disseminated throughout the company by formal and informal means. Kohli and Jaworski tell how marketing managers in two consumer products companies developed and circulated periodic newsletters to facilitate the spread of information. While in another manufacturing company a manager encouraged the process of dissemination by *storytelling*. She told stories about customers, their needs, personalities, and even their families. The idea was to have secretaries, engineers and production personnel get to know customers. Finally, responsiveness highlighted the need to select target markets, design and offer products and services that cater to current and anticipated needs, and producing, pricing, distributing and promoting those products and services in a way that customers value.

Third, a customer focus implies market-led strategies and the desire to meet needs better than the competition. However, as Davidson points out, the reality of the marketplace should be aligned with the assets (distinctive competences) of the company.[15] When looking to enter new markets, companies should be aware of their inherent corporate strengths and weaknesses. Organizational structure must reflect marketing strategy. As markets change, marketing strategy changes and the structure and systems may require modification to implement strategy. This may involve using new distribution systems, the introduction of marketing information systems, the development of customer-based sales and marketing organizations, the sharing of skills between

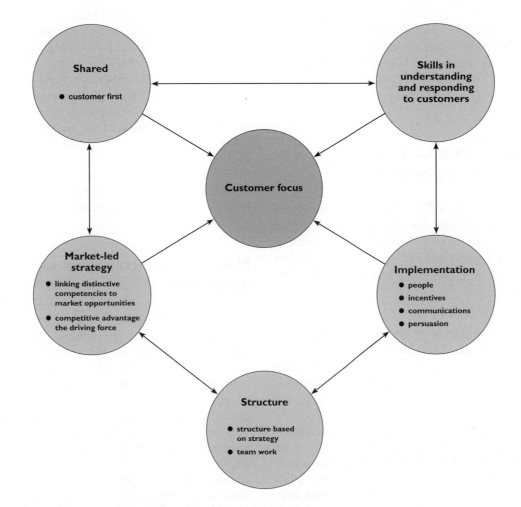

Figure 1.5 Key dimensions of market-driven management

business units, and between organizations through strategic alliances, and the breaking down of barriers between departments to foster innovation.[16]

The last dimension of market-driven management is implementation, which requires clear communication of strategy so that it is not undermined by those who deal with the customer at first hand. Kashani cites the example of the introduction by a French company of a CT-scanner in Germany.[17] The product was positioned with a premium price based upon advanced technology which conferred economic and psychological benefits to the customer. However, this strategy was being undermined by the salesforce, who were heavily price discounting when meeting customer resistance. The result was that the strategy was discredited and adoption in Germany was slow. Persuasion of the need to adopt the marketing concept may be necessary to change the value system within an organization. British Airports Authority uses financial incentives for staff to reflect its belief in a customer focus. Bonus payments are made based upon regular customer satisfaction surveys of passengers using his airports.

Limitations of the marketing concept

A number of academics have raised important questions regarding the value of the marketing concept. Three issues—the marketing concept as an ideology, marketing and society, and marketing as a constraint on innovation—will now be explored.

Marketing concept as an ideology

Brownlie and Saren argue that the marketing concept has assumed many of the characteristics of an ideology or an article of faith that should dominate the thinking of organizations.[18] They recognize the importance of a consumer-orientation for companies but ask why after 40 years of trying has the concept not been fully implemented? They argue that there are other valid considerations that companies must take into account when making decisions (e.g. economies of scale) apart from giving customers

exactly what they want. Marketers' attention should therefore be focused not only on propagation of the ideology but also on its integration with the demands of other core business functions in order to achieve a compromise between the satisfaction of consumers and the achievement of other company requirements.

Marketing and society

A second limitation of the marketing concept concerns its focus on individual market transactions. Since many individuals weigh heavily their personal benefits while discounting the societal impact of their purchases, the adoption of the marketing concept will result in the production of goods and services which do not adequately correspond to societal welfare. Providing customer satisfaction is simply a means to achieve a company's profit objective and does not guarantee protection of the consumer's welfare. This view is supported by Wensley, who regards consumerism as a challenge to the adequacy of the atomistic and individual view of market transactions.[19] An alternative view is presented by Bloom and Greyser, who regard consumerism as the ultimate expression of the marketing concept compelling marketers to consider consumer needs and wants that hitherto may have been overlooked.[20] 'The resourceful manager will look for the positive opportunities created by consumerism rather than brood over its restraints.'

Marketing as a constraint on innovation

In an influential article Tauber showed how marketing research discouraged major innovation.[21] The thrust of his argument was that relying on customers to guide the development of new products has severe limitations. This is because customers have difficulty articulating needs beyond the realm of their own experience. This suggests that the ideas gained from marketing research will be modest compared to those coming from the 'science push' of the research and development laboratory. Brownlie and Saren agree that, particularly for discontinuous innovations (e.g. Xerox, penicillin), the role of product development ought to be far more proactive than this.[22] Indeed technological innovation is the process that 'realizes' market demands which were previously unknown. Thus the effective exploitation and utilization of technology in developing new products is at least as important as market-needs analysis.

However, McGee and Spiro point out that these criticisms are not actually directed towards the marketing concept itself but towards its faulty implementation: an overdependence on customers as a source for new product ideas.[23] They state that the marketing concept does not suggest that companies must solely depend on the customer for new product ideas. Rather the concept implies that new product development should be based on sound interfacing between perceived customer needs and technological research. Project SAPPHO, which investigated innovation in the chemical and scientific instrument industries, found that successful innovations were based on a good understanding of user needs.[24] Unsuccessful innovations, on the other hand, were characterized by little or no attention to user needs.

Creating customer value and satisfaction

Customer value

Marketing-orientated companies attempt to create *customer value* in order to attract and retain customers. Their aim is to deliver superior value to their target customers. In doing so, they implement the marketing concept by meeting and exceeding customer needs better than the competition. For example, McDonald's global success has been based on creating added value for its customers which is based not only on the food products it sells but on the complete delivery system that goes to make up a fast-food restaurant. It sets high standards in what is called QSCV—Quality, Service, Cleanliness and Value. Customers can be sure that the same high standards will be found in all of McDonald's outlets around the world. This example shows that customer value can be derived from many aspects of what the company delivers to its customers—not just the basic product.

Customer value is dependent on how the customer perceives the benefits of an offering and the sacrifice that is associated with its purchase. Therefore:

Customer value = Perceived benefits − Perceived sacrifice

Perceived benefits can be derived from the product (for example, the taste of the hamburger), the associated service (for example, how quickly customers are served and cleanliness of the outlet) and the image of the company (for example, is the image of the company/product favourable?).

A further source of perceived benefits is the relationship between customer and supplier. Customers may enjoy working with suppliers with whom they have developed close relationships. They may have developed close personal and professional friendships and value the convenience of working with trusted partners.

Perceived sacrifice is the total costs associated with buying the product. This consists of not just monetary cost but the time and energy involved in purchase. For example, with fast-food restaurants, good location can reduce the time and energy required to find a suitable eating place. But marketers need to be aware of another critical sacrifice in some buying situations. This is the potential psychological cost of not making the right decision. Uncertainty means that people perceive risk when purchasing. McDonald's attempts to reduce perceived risk by standardizing its complete offer so that customers can be confident of what they will receive before entering its outlets. In organizational markets, companies offer guarantees to reduce the risk of purchase. Figure 1.6 illustrates how perceived benefits and sacrifice affect customer value. It provides a framework for considering ways of maximizing value. The objective is to find ways of raising perceived benefits and reducing perceived sacrifice.

Customer satisfaction

Exceeding the value offered by competitors is key to marketing success. Consumers decide upon purchases on the basis of judgements about the values offered by suppliers. Once a product is bought, *customer satisfaction* depends upon its perceived performance compared to the buyer's expectations. Customer satisfaction occurs when perceived performance matches or

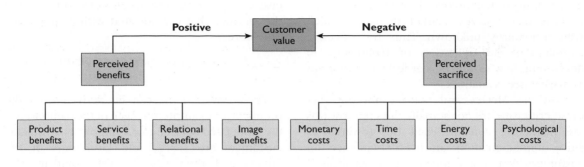

Figure 1.6 Creating customer value

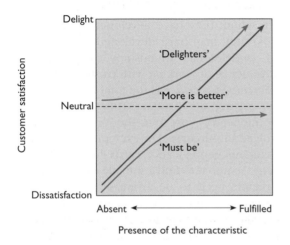

Figure 1.7 Creating customer satisfaction.

Source: Joiner, B.L. (1994) *Fourth Generation Management*, New York: McGraw-Hill

exceeds expectations. Expectations are formed through post-buying experiences, discussions with other people, and suppliers' marketing activities. Companies need to avoid the mistake of setting customer expectations too high through exaggerated promotional claims since this can lead to dissatisfaction if performance falls short of expectations.

In today's competitive climate, it is often not enough to match performance and expectations. Expectations need to be exceeded for commercial success so that customers are delighted with the outcome. In order to understand the concept of customer satisfaction the Kano model (see Fig. 1.7) helps to separate characteristics that cause dissatisfaction, satisfaction and delight.

Three characteristics underlie the model: 'must be', 'more is better' and 'delighters'.

'Must be' characteristics are expected to be present and are taken for granted. For example, in a hotel, customers expect service at reception and a clean room. Lack of these characteristics causes annoyance but their presence only brings dissatisfaction up to a neutral level. 'More is better' characteristics can take satisfaction past neutral into the positive satisfaction range. For example no response to a telephone call can cause dissatisfaction, but a fast response may cause positive satisfaction or even delight. 'Delighters' are the unexpected characteristics that surprise the customer. Their absence does not cause dissatisfaction but their presence delights the customer. For example a UK hotel chain provides free measures of brandy in the rooms of their adult guests. This delights many of its customers who were not expecting this treat. Another way to delight customer is to under promise and over deliver. For example, by saying that a repair will take about five hours but getting it done after two.[25]

A problem for marketers is that over time delighters become expected. For example, some car manufacturers provided small unexpected delighters such as pen holders, and delay mechanisms on interior lights so that there is time to find the ignition socket at night. These are standard on most cars now and have become 'must be' characteristics as customers expect them. This means that marketers must constantly strive to find new ways of delighting. Innovative thinking and listening to customers are key ingredients in this. Marketing in Action 1.2 explains how to listen to customers.

Developing an effective marketing mix

Based upon its understanding of customers, a company develops its *marketing mix*. The marketing mix consists of four major elements: product, price, promotion and place. These '4-Ps' are the four key decision areas that marketers must manage so that they satisfy or exceed customer needs better than the competition. In other words, decisions regarding the marketing mix form a major aspect of marketing concept implementation. The second module of this book looks at each of the 4-Ps in considerable detail. At this point, it will be useful to examine each element briefly so that we can understand the essence of marketing mix decision-making.

Product

The *product* decision involves deciding what goods or services should be offered to a group of customers. An important element is new product development. As technology and tastes change, products become out-of-date and inferior to competition so companies must replace them with features that customers value. The launch of the £40 000 Range Rover Vogue incorporated a new suspension system based upon 10 litres of microprocessed air.[26] Four air springs are operated by an electronic control unit under the right front seat which reads height sensors, road and engine speed, foot and handbrake, autotransmission level and door-closing switches. The air springs offer five different height settings varying

1.2   Marketing in Action

Listening to Customers

Top companies recognize the importance of listening to their customers as part of their strategy to manage satisfaction. Customer satisfaction indices are based on surveys of customers and the results plotted over time to reveal changes in satisfaction levels. The first stage is to identify those characteristics (choice criteria) which are important to customers when evaluating competing products. The second stage involves the development of measuring scales (often statements followed by strongly agree–strongly disagree response boxes) to quantitatively assess satisfaction.

Marketing research can also be used to question new customers about why they first bought, and lost customers (defectors) on why they have ceased buying. In the latter case, a second objective would be to attempt a last-ditch attempt to keep the customer. One bank found that a quarter of its defecting customers would have stayed had the bank attempted to rescue the situation.

One company which places listening to customers high on its list of priorities is Kwik-Fit, the car repair group. Customer satisfaction is monitored by its customer survey unit which telephones 5000 customers a day within 72 hours of their visit to a Kwik-Fit Centre.

A strategy also needs to be put in place to manage customer complaints, comments and questions. A system needs to be set up that solicits feedback on product and service quality and feeds the information to the appropriate employees. To facilitate this process front-line employees need training to ask questions, to listen effectively, to capture the information and to communicate it so that corrective action can be taken.

Based on: Jones and Sasser Jr (1995);[27] Morgan (1996);[28] White (1999)[29]

Shouldn't getting there
be as relaxing as being there?

Relax.

Our routes spare you

the driving and take you

to the heart of Holiday

France and Spain.

Relax.

Our award winning

service costs less

than you think.

Just call us or ask your

travel agent.

Brittany Ferries
as relaxing as being there

www.brittany-ferries.com   0870 900 0900

Brittany Ferries promote the benefit of relaxation

by 13 cm: high profile for wading or off road, standard for normal road use, low which automatically engages under 50 m.p.h., extended to regain traction when the bottom is grounded, and access for getting into and out of the vehicle. Sensors read each wheel 100 times a second for a ride of remarkable smoothness. These features have been built into the Range Rover because they confer customer benefits. For example, the new lower level for access was incorporated into the design because marketing research had discovered that women occasionally found it embarrassing to climb into the old version. Some motoring journalists have christened this the 'modesty' level. The illustration opposite shows how Brittany Ferries promote the benefit of relaxation during their crossing.

Product decisions also involve choices regarding brand names, guarantees, packaging and the services which should accompany the product offering. Guarantees can be an important component of the product offering. For example, the operators of the AVE, Spain's high-speed train capable of travelling at 300 km.p.h. are so confident of its performance that they guarantee to give customers a full refund of their fare if they are more than five minutes late.

Price

Price is a key element of the marketing mix because it represents on a unit basis what the company receives for the product or service which is being marketed. All of the other elements represent costs, for example, expenditure on product design (product), advertising and salespeople (promotion) and transportation and distribution (place). Marketers, therefore, need to be very clear about pricing objectives, methods, and the factors which influence price setting. They also must take into account the necessity to discount and give allowances in some transactions. These requirements can influence the level of list price chosen, perhaps with an element of negotiation margin built in. Payment periods and credit terms also affect the real *price* received in any transaction. These kinds of decisions can affect the perceived value of a product or service offering.

Promotion

Decisions have to be made with respect to the ***promotional mix***: advertising, personal selling, sales promotions, public relations, direct marketing and Internet and on-line marketing. By these means the target audience is made aware of the existence of a product or service and the benefits (both economic and psychological) that it confers to customers. Each element of the promotional mix has its own set of strengths and weakness and these will be explored in the second module of this book. Advertising, for example, has the property of being able to reach wide audiences very quickly. Procter and Gamble used advertising to reach the emerging market of 290 million Russian consumers. They ran a 12-minute commercial on Russian television as their first promotional venture in order to introduce the company and its range of products.[30] A growing form of promotion is the use of the Internet as a promotional tool. A key advantage is that small companies can expand the scope of their market at relatively low cost. E-Marketing 1.1 illustrates how the use of the internet can radically change the fortunes of a small business.

Place

Place involves decisions concerning the distribution channels to be used and their management, the locations of outlets, methods of transportation and inventory levels to be held. The objective is to ensure that products and services are available in the proper qualities, at the right time and place. Distribution channels consist of organizations such as retailers or wholesalers through which goods pass on their way to customers. Producers need to manage their relationships with these organizations well because they may provide the only cost-effective access to the marketplace.

Key characteristics of an effective marketing mix

There are four hallmarks of an effective marketing mix (see Fig. 1.8).

The marketing mix matches customer needs

Sensible marketing mix decisions can be made only when the target customer is understood. Choosing customer groups to target will be discussed in Chapter 6, which examines the process of market segmentation and target marketing. Once the decision about the target market(s) is taken, marketing management needs to understand how customers choose between rival offerings. They need to look at the product or service through customers' eyes and understand, among other factors, the choice criteria they use.

Figure 1.9 illustrates the link between customer choice criteria and the marketing mix. The starting-point is the realization that customers

evaluate products on economic and psychological criteria. Economic criteria include factors such as performance, availability, reliability, durability and productivity gains to be made by using the product. Examples of psychological criteria are self-image, a desire for a quiet life, pleasure, convenience and risk reduction. These will be discussed in detail in Chapter 3. The important point at this stage is to note that an analysis of customer choice criteria will reveal a set of key customer requirements that must be met in order to succeed in the marketplace. Meeting or exceeding these requirements better than the competition leads to the creation of a competitive advantage. Style is an example of a choice criterion and is used by Ericsson to create a competitive advantage, as the illustration overleaf shows.

The marketing mix creates a competitive advantage

A *competitive advantage* may be derived from decisions about the 4-Ps. A competitive advantage is a clear performance differential over the competition on factors which are important to customers. The example of the Range Rover Vogue launch is an example of a company using product features to convey customer benefits in excess of what the competition is offering. Variable height adjustment can therefore be regarded as an attempt to establish a competitive advantage through product decisions. Aldi, the German supermarket chain, is attempting to establish a competitive advantage in the UK by low prices, a key customer requirement of its chosen target group of customers.

Using advertising as a tool for competitive

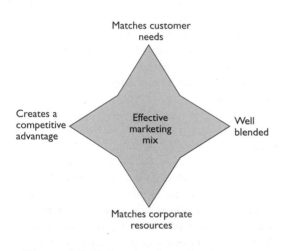

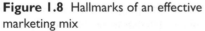

Figure 1.8 Hallmarks of an effective marketing mix

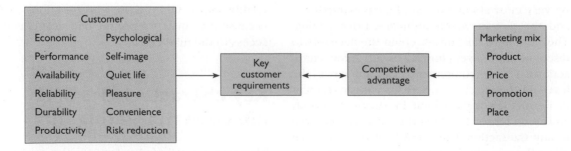

Figure 1.9 Matching the marketing mix to customer needs

advantage is often used when product benefits are particularly subjective and amorphous in nature. Thus the advertising for perfumes such as Chanel, Givenchy and Yves St Laurent is critical in preserving the exclusive image established by such brands. The size and quality of the salesforce can act as a competitive advantage. A problem that a company such as Rolls-Royce faces is the relatively small size of its salesforce compared to their giant competitors Boeing and General Electric. Finally, distribution decisions need to be made with the customer in mind not only in terms of availability but also with respect to service levels, image and customer convenience. Scotcade built up a successful mail order business with direct distribution of consumer goods—for example, clothing and accessories—by using Sunday magazines to advertise their products. This is an example of where the combination of two elements of the marketing mix were used together in a novel way to satisfy customer needs for convenience of purchase at a time when they were relaxed and had time to send for the merchandise.

The marketing mix should be well blended

The third characteristic of an effective marketing mix is that the four elements—product, price, promotion and place—should be well blended to form a consistent theme. If a product gives

 ### 1.1   e-Marketing

Promoting through the Internet

Through market research, Paul Smedley found that many people would like to buy high-quality chocolates but were unable to buy them within the UK. His initial idea was to import chocolates from mainland Europe and to sell these through mail order. However, during the business planning process, he found that mail order companies face certain restrictions concerning taking credit card payments over the telephone. His solution was to open a shop known as Sweet Seduction in Leamington Spa in the West Midlands of the UK and to run mail order as a part of the overall business operation.

The company advertised the mail order business through the shop, through flyers and direct mail shots. The business did not advertise on a national basis and hence the majority of the mail order sales came from customers in the immediate vicinity of the shop. Paul used a personal computer to prepare the company accounts, and through contacts with the local computer industry he became interested in the potential opportunities which might be available from exploiting the Internet. He established a dial-up Internet connection through the Internet Service Provider, Demon, and then worked with a consultant to develop software which would permit Sweet Seduction to sell chocolates over the Internet. As the company already had a PC, there was no need to purchase any new hardware other than a modem. Hence the additional expenditure was restricted to the payment of a rental fee for use of the Parallax site.

The launch of the website was accompanied by a national and local press campaign to make people aware of the website address, www.parallaxco.uk.seduct. The launch of the Internet site had a dramatic impact on the mail order business, bringing in both new customers and increased repeat purchase by existing customers. Within only a few months retail shop sales were overtaken by revenue generated from the mail order and Internet operation.

Based on: Lymer et al. (1998)[31]

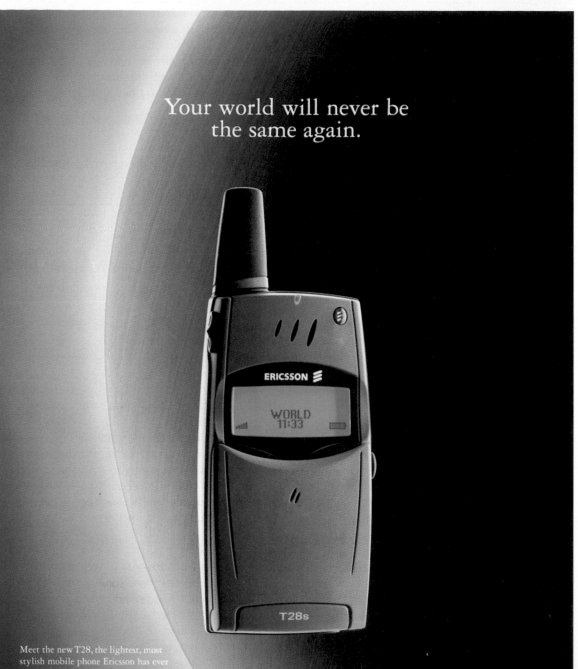

Style is an important choice criterion for brands that are conspicuous in use

superior benefits to customers, price, which may send cues to customers regarding quality, should reflect those extra benefits. All of the promotional mix should be designed with the objective of communicating a consistent message to the target audience about these benefits, and distribution decisions should be consistent with the overall strategic position of the product in the market-place. The use of exclusive outlets for up-market fashion and cosmetic brands—Armani, Christian Dior and Calvin Klein, for example—is consistent with their strategic position.

The marketing mix should match corporate resources

The choice of marketing mix strategy may be constrained by the financial resources of the company. Laker Airlines used price as a competitive advantage to attack British Airways and TWA in transatlantic flights. When they retaliated by cutting their airfares Laker's financial resources were insufficient to win the price war. Certain media, for example television advertising, require a minimum threshold investment before they are regarded as feasible. In the UK a rule of thumb is that at least £1 million per year is required to achieve impact in a national advertising campaign. Clearly those brands which cannot afford such a promotional budget must use other less expensive media, for example posters or sales promotion, to attract and hold customers.

A second internal resource constraint may be the internal competences of the company. A marketing mix strategy may be too ambitious for the limited marketing skills of personnel to implement effectively. While an objective may be to reduce or eliminate this problem in the medium to long term, in the short term marketing management may have to heed the fact that strategy must take account of competences. An area where this may manifest itself is within the *place* dimension. A company lacking the personal selling skills to market a product directly to end users may have to use intermediaries (distributors or sales agents) to perform that function.

To bring to life the opportunities associated with developing an effective marketing mix, Marketing in Action 1.3 examines the rise of IKEA; the Swedish-based retailer, to become an international force in stylish furniture.

Criticisms of the 4-Ps approach to marketing management

Some critics of the 4-Ps approach to the marketing mix argue that it oversimplifies the reality of marketing management. Booms and Bitner for example argue for a 7-Ps approach to services marketing.[32] Their argument, which will be discussed in some detail in Chapter 20 on services marketing, is that the 4-Ps do not take sufficient account of people, process and physical evidence. In services people often are the service itself; the process or how the service is delivered to the customer is usually a key part of the service, and the physical evidence—the décor of the restaurant or shop for example—is so critical to success that it should be considered as a separate element in the services marketing mix.

Rafiq and Ahmed argue that this criticism of the 4-Ps can be extended to include industrial marketing.[33] The interaction approach to understanding industrial marketing stresses that success does not come solely from manipulation of the marketing mix components but long-term relationship building whereby the bond between buyer and seller become so strong that it effectively acts as a barrier to entry for out-suppliers.[34] This phenomenon undoubtedly exists to such an extent that industrial buyers are now increasingly seeking long-term supply relationships with suppliers. Lucas (a UK components producer) as part of its Strategic Sources Review sought such partnerships with *preferred suppliers*. Lucas helps investment with such suppliers who in turn allow Lucas to understand their costs. Bosch, the German producer of industrial and consumer goods, conducts quality audits of its suppliers. These kinds of activities are not captured in the 4-Ps approach, it is claimed.

Nevertheless, there is no absolute reason why these extensions cannot be incorporated within the 4-Ps framework.[35] People, process and physical evidence can be discussed under 'product', and long-term relationship building under 'promotion', for example. The important issue is not to neglect them, whether the 4-Ps approach or some other method is used to conceptualize the decision-making areas of marketing. The strength of the 4-Ps approach is that it represents a memorable and practical framework for marketing decision-making and has proved useful for case study analysis in business schools for many years.

Marketing and business performance

The basic premise of the marketing concept is that its adoption will improve business performance. Marketing is not an abstract concept: its acid test is the effect that its use has on key corporate indices such as profitability and market share. Fortunately in recent years three quantitative studies in both Europe and North America have sought to examine the relationship between marketing and performance. The results suggest that the relationship is positive. We examine each of the three studies in turn.

Marketing characteristics and business performance

In a study of 1700 senior marketing executives published in 1985, Hooley and Lynch reported the marketing characteristics of high versus low performing companies.[36] The approach that they adopted was to isolate the top 10 per cent of companies (based on such measures as profit margin, return on investment and market share) and to compare their marketing practice with the remainder of the sample. The *high fliers* differed from the *also-rans* as follows:

1 More committed to marketing research.
2 More likely to be found in new, emerging or growth markets.
3 Adopted a more proactive approach to marketing planning.
4 More likely to use strategic planning tools.
5 Placed more emphasis on product performance and design rather than price for achieving a competitive advantage.
6 Worked closer with the finance department.
7 Placed greater emphasis on market share as a method of evaluating marketing performance.

Marketing orientation and business performance

Narver and Slater studied the relationship between marketing orientation and business performance.[37] Marketing orientation was based upon three measures: customer orientation, competitor orientation, and the degree of interfunctional coordination. They collected data from 113 strategic business units (SBUs) of a major

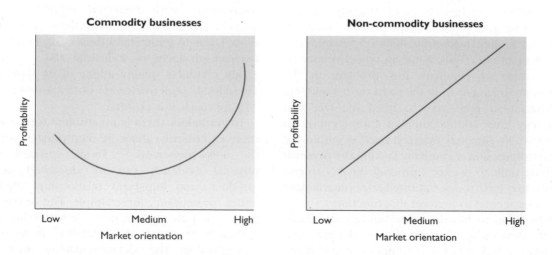

Figure 1.10 The relationship between market orientation and profitability

US corporation. The businesses comprised 36 commodity businesses (forestry products) and 77 non-commodity businesses (speciality products and distribution businesses). They related the SBU's profitability, as measured by return on assets in relation to competitors over the last year in the SBU's principal served market, to their three-component measure of market orientation.

Figure 1.10 shows the results of their study. For commodity businesses the relationship was

1.3 Marketing in Action

IKEA Expands Internationally

The success of IKEA, the Swedish-based furniture and home furnishings store, is impressive. In four decades it has grown from a single store in Sweden to become one of the most successful international retailers in the world. The first store outside Scandinavia opened in Switzerland in 1973. Since then IKEA has opened 70 stores around Europe and has expanded into 29 countries with 158 on four continents. It is now the world's largest furniture retailer. Its clean, simple designs have become fashionable around the world, making it one of the few retailers to sell products that are able to cross national boundaries.

Two factors make IKEA's growth even more remarkable. First, unlike most furniture retailers which have been badly affected by the recession, IKEA has proven recession resistant. Second, IKEA's sales per square foot are over 2.5 times the industry average. What are the bases of their success?

First, they have a clear marketing-orientated business philosophy. 'We shall offer a wide range of home furnishing items of good design and function at prices so low that the majority of people can afford to buy them.' The key has been to use huge volumes and simple self-assembly designs to keep prices low, while selling more stylish products than the competition. The products are based upon Sweden's strong design skills which produce products from furniture to household items such as crockery and linen. Variations in national tastes have been smoothed into a uniform, modern look. IKEA sell a range of 12 000 products that are all designed in-house but manufactured around the world. The combination of stylish products, an enormous range from which to choose, and inexpensive prices produces a powerful competitive advantage to middle-income people, particularly young homemakers, their primary target market segment.

IKEA augment their offering by providing a playroom for 3–7-year-olds, a children's cinema, baby-care rooms, and children's buggies to appeal to couples with young children. They provide a family restaurant (with Swedish specialities), a bistro and a Sweden shop selling such items as biscuits, jams and preserved fish to enhance the experience of shopping there. Finally, they cater for customers' needs by supplying a home delivery service, the possibility of buying or borrowing a roof rack, wheelchairs for disabled people, and a one-month no-nonsense returns policy.

The distribution policy is to build vast out-of-town stores which cater for regions. Their policy is one of cautious expansion. In 1992 IKEA had five stores in the UK; by 2000 this had grown to 10, with plans to open another 20. They attempt to penetrate one region successfully before moving on to the next.

IKEA is a classic example of how the marketing mix can be designed to meet customer needs better than the competition. Their strong competitive advantages are the bases of their success.

Based on: Lynn (1992);[38] Thornhill (1992);[39] Jones. (1996);[40] Anonymous (1999);[41] Baird. (1998);[42] Bring et al. (1999); [43] Clark;[44] Moss (2000)[45]

U-shaped, with low and high market-orientation businesses showing higher profitability than the businesses in the mid-range of market orientation. Businesses with the highest market orientation had the highest profitability and those with the lowest market orientation had the second highest profitability. They explained this result by suggesting that the businesses lowest in market orientation may achieve some profit success through a low cost strategy, though not the profit levels of the high market orientation businesses, an explanation supported by the fact that they were the largest companies of the three groups.

For the non-commodity businesses the relationship was linear, with the businesses displaying the highest level of market orientation achieving the highest levels of profitability and those with the lowest scores on market orientation having the lowest profitability figures. As the authors state: 'The findings give marketing scholars and practitioners a basis beyond mere intuition for recommending the superiority of a market orientation.'

The marketing philosophy and business performance

A study published in 1990 by Hooley, Lynch and Shepherd sought to develop a typology of approaches to marketing and to relate those approaches to business performance.[46] Based on a sample of over 1000 companies, they identified four distinct groups of companies, as shown in Fig. 1.11.

The *marketing philosophers* saw marketing as a function with the prime responsibility for identifying and meeting customers' needs and as a guiding philosophy for the whole organization: they did not see marketing as confined to the marketing department, nor did they regard it as merely sales support. The *sales supporters* saw marketing's primary functions as being sales and promotion support. Marketing was confined to what the marketing department did and had little to do with identifying and meeting customer needs.

The *departmental marketers* not only shared the view of the marketing philosophers that marketing was about identifying and meeting customer needs but also believed that marketing was restricted to what the marketing department did. The final group of companies—the *unsures*—tended to be indecisive regarding their marketing approach. Perhaps the term *stuck-in-the-middlers* would be apt for these companies.

The attitudes, organization and practices of the four groups were compared, with the marketing philosophers exhibiting many distinct characteristics. In summary:

1 Marketing philosophers adopted a more proactive aggressive approach towards the future.

2 They had a more proactive approach to new product development.

3 They placed a higher importance on marketing training.

4 They adopted longer time horizons for marketing planning.

5 Marketing had a higher status within the company.

6 Marketing had a higher chance of being represented at board level.

7 Marketing had more chance of working closely with other functional areas.

8 Marketing made a greater input into strategic plans.

The performance of the four groups was also compared using two criteria: a subjectively reported return on investment (ROI) figure, and performance relative to major competitors. The marketing philosophers achieve a significantly higher ROI than the remainder of the sample. The departmental marketers performed at the sample average, while the unsures and sales supporters performed significantly worse. The marketing philosophers performed significantly better than each of the other groups. Using the performance relative to competitors' criteria, the marketing philosophers again came out top, followed by the departmental marketers.

Hooley *et al*'s conclusion was that marketing should be viewed not merely as a departmental function but as a guiding philosophy for the whole organization. 'Our evidence points to improved performance among companies that adopt this wider approach to business.'[47]

What overall conclusions can be drawn from these three studies? In order to make a balanced judgement their limitations must be recognized.

They were all cross-sectional studies based upon self-reported data. With any such survey there is the question of the direction of causality. Perhaps some respondents inferred their degree of marketing orientation by reference to their performance level. However, this clearly did not occur with the commodity sample in the Narver and Slater study.[48] What these three separate studies have consistently and unambiguously shown is a strong association between marketing and business performance. As one condition for establishing causality, this is an encouraging result for those people concerned with promoting the marketing concept as a guiding philosophy for business.

Summary

Marketing achieves company goals by meeting and exceeding customer needs better than the competition. The focus is on giving extra value rather than widespread cost cutting. Marketing-orientated companies attempt to achieve not only efficiency but also effectiveness—the ability to attract and retain customers. They show customer concern throughout the business and encourage innovation so that new products can be developed to meet the needs of tomorrow's customers.

However, it should be recognized that the marketing concept has its limitations. It should not be regarded as an ideology; societal as well as individual considerations need to be taken into account, and the limitations of marketing research as a means of developing fundamentally new products should be acknowledged.

A key marketing task is to understand customer needs and develop a competitive advantage through marketing mix decisions. The marketing mix comprises the 4-Ps: product, price, promotion, and place. Implementing the marketing concept in organizations can be difficult but studies have shown that the rewards in terms of better business performance can be expected.

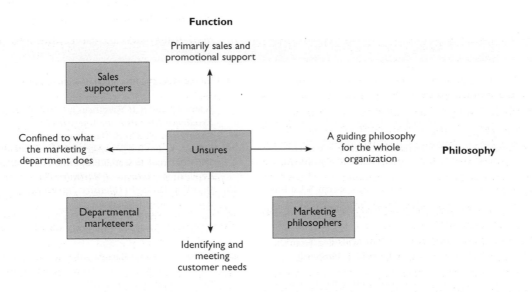

Figure 1.11 Marketing approaches.

Source: Hooley, G. J., J. E. Lynch, and J. Shepherd (1990) The Marketing Concept: Putting Theory into Practice, *European Journal of Marketing*, 24 (9), 11. Reproduced with permission

Internet exercise

Marketing concept

Sites to visit
http://www.virgin.co.uk
http://www.gucci.com
http://www.ikea.com
http://www.starbucks.com/

Exercise
Compare and contrast the four organizations' marketing orientation.

Study questions

1   What are the essential characteristics of a marketing-orientated company?

2   Are there any situations where marketing orientation is not the most appropriate business philosophy?

3   Explain how the desire to become efficient may conflict with being effective.

4   What barriers may a marketing manager face when trying to convince other people within an organization that they should adopt the marketing concept?

5   To what extent do you agree with the criticisms of the marketing concept and the 4-Ps approach to marketing decision-making?

References

1. Drucker, P. F. (1999) *The Practice of Management*, London: Heinemann.
2. Rosenberg, L. J. and J. A. Czepeil (1983) A Marketing Approach to Customer Retention, *Journal of Consumer Marketing*, **2**, 45–51.
3. Grönroos, C. (1989) Defining Marketing: A Market-Oriented Approach, *European Journal of Marketing*, **23** (1), 52–60.
4. Houston, F. S. (1986) The Marketing Concept: What It Is and What It Is Not, *Journal of Marketing*, **50**, 81–7.
5. Levitt, T. (1969) *The Marketing Mode*, New York: McGraw-Hill.
6. Parkinson, S. T. (1991) World Class Marketing: From Lost Empires to the Image Man, *Journal of Marketing Management*, **7** (3), 299–311.
7. Morgan, R. E. and C. A. Strong (1998) Market Orientation and Dimensions of Strategic Orientation, *European Journal of Marketing*, **32** (11/12), 1051–73.
8. Brown, R. J. (1987) Marketing: A Function and a Philosophy, *Quarterly Review of Marketing*, **12** (3), 25–30.
9. Abell, D. F. (1978) Strategic Windows, *Journal of Marketing*, July, 21–6.
10. Anonymous (1989) Fortress Europe, *Target Marketing*, **12** (8), 12–14.
11. BBC2 Television (1993) Hypermarketing. France Means Business series, 23 February.
12. Anonymous (1998) Global Powers in Retailing, Stores, 34–5.
13. Peters, T. J. and R. H. Waterman Jr (1982) *In Search of Excellence: Lessons from America's Best Run Companies*, New York: Harper and Row.
14. Kohli, A. K. and B. J. Jaworski (1990) Market Orientation: The Construct, Research Propositions and Managerial Implications, *Journal of Marketing*, **54** (April), 1–18.
15. Davidson, H. (1998) *Offensive Marketing*, Harmondsworth: Penguin.
16. Saunders, J. and V. Wong (1985) In Search of Excellence in the UK, *Journal of Marketing Management*, winter, 119–37.
17. Kashani, K. (1984) Managing the Transition from Marketing Strategy to Sales Force Action, *Journal of Sales Management*, **1** (2), 21–5.
18. Brownlie, D. and M. Saren (1992) The Four Ps of the Marketing Concept: Prescriptive, Polemical, Permanent and Problematical, *European Journal of Marketing*, **26** (4), 34–47.
19. Wensley, R. (1990) The Voice of the Consumer? Speculations on the Limits to the Marketing Analogy, *European Journal of Marketing*, **24** (7), 49–60.
20. Bloom, P. N. and S. A. Greyser (1981) The Maturity of Consumerism, *Harvard Business Review*, Nov.–Dec., 130–9.
21. Tauber, E. M. (1974) How Marketing Research

Discourages Major Innovation, *Business Horizons*, **17** (June), 22-6.

22. Brownlie and Saren (1992) op. cit.

23. McGee, L. W. and R. L. Spiro (1988) The Marketing Concept in Perspective, *Business Horizons*, May–June, 40-5.

24. Rothwell, R. (1974) SAPPHO Updated: Project SAPPHO Phase II, *Research Policy*, **3**.

25. White, D. (1999) Delighting in a Superior Service, *Financial Times*, 25 November, 17.

26. Samuel, J. (1992) Marketing Air Waves, *Guardian Weekend*, 3 October, 39.

27. Jones, T. O. and W. E. Sasser, Jr (1995) Why Satisfied Customers Defect, Harvard Business Review, November–December, 88-99.

28. Morgan, A. (1996) Relationship Marketing, *Admap*, October, 29-33.

29. White D. (1999) Delighting in a Superior Service, Financial Times, 25 November, 17.

30. Freeman, L. and L. Wentz (1990) P and G's First Soviet TV Spot, *Advertising Age*, 12 March, 56-7.

31. Lymer, A., A. Nayak, R. Johnson and B. Spaul (1998) UK Business and The Information Highway, ACCA Occasional Research Paper No. 23, Association of Chartered Certified Accountants, London, 41-3

32. Booms, B. H. and M. J. Bitner (1981) Marketing Strategies and Organisation Structures for Service Firms, in Donnelly, J. H. and W. R. George (eds) *Marketing of Services*, Chicago: American Marketing Association, 47-52.

33. Rafiq, M. and P. K. Ahmed (1992) The Marketing Mix Reconsidered, *Proceedings of the Marketing Education Group Conference*, Salford, 439-51.

34. Ford, D., H. Håkansson and J. Johanson (1986) How Do

Companies Interact? *Industrial Marketing and Purchasing*, **1** (1), 26-41.

35. Buttle, F. (1989) Marketing Services, in Jones, P. (ed.) *Management in Service Industries*, London: Pitman, 235-59.

36. Hooley, G. and J. Lynch (1985) Marketing Lessons from UK's High-Flying Companies, *Journal of Marketing Management*, **1** (1), 65-74.

37. Narver, J. C. and S. F. Slater (1990) The Effect of a Market Orientation on Business Profitability, *Journal of Marketing*, **54** (October), 20-35.

38. Lynn, M. (1992) Booming IKEA Conquers Britain's Middle Classes, *Sunday Times*, 13 September, section 3, 5.

39. Thornhill, J. (1992) IKEA's Logic Furnishes a Market Riddle, *Financial Times*, 20 October, 27.

40. Jones, H. (1996) IKEA's Global Strategy is a Winning Formula, *Marketing Week*, 15 March, 22.

41. Anonymous (1999) IKEA Sparks Border Clashes, *Marketing*, 26 August, 53.

42. Baird, R. (1998) IKEA Avoids Free Fall in Furniture Sector, *Marketing Week*, 15 October, 21.

43. Bring, J., J. Zaleski, P. Gediman and C. Abbott (1999) Leading by Design: The IKEA Story, *Publishers Weekly*, 19 July, 174.

44. Clark, A. (2000) Branching Out, *The Guardian*, 20 June, 30.

45. Moss, S. (2000) The Gospel According to IKEA, *The Guardian*, 26 June, 2.

46. Hooley, G., J. Lynch and J. Shepherd (1990) The Marketing Concept: Putting the Theory into Practice, *European Journal of Marketing*, **24** (9), 7-23.

47. Hooley, Lynch and Shepherd (1990) op. cit.

48. Narver and Slater (1990) op. cit.

Key terms

exchange the act or process of receiving something from someone by giving something in return

marketing concept the achievement of corporate goals through meeting and exceeding customer needs better than the competition

marketing orientation companies with a marketing orientation focus on customer needs as the primary drivers of organizational performance

production orientation a business approach that is inwardly focused either on costs or on a definition of a company in terms of its production facilities

effectiveness doing the right thing, making the correct strategic choice

efficiency a way of managing business processes to a high standard, usually concerned with cost reduction; also called 'doing things right'

customer value perceived benefits minus perceived sacrifice

customer satisfaction the fulfilment of customers' requirements or needs

marketing mix a framework for the tactical management of the customer relationship, including product, place, price, promotion (4Ps). In the case of services three other elements to be taken into account are: process, people and physical evidence.

product a good or service offered or performed by an organization or individual which is capable of satisfying customer needs

price (1) the amount of money paid for a product; (2) the agreed value placed on the exchange by a buyer and seller

promotional mix advertising, personal selling, sales promotions, public relations and direct marketing

place the distribution channels to be used, outlet locations, methods of transportation

competitive advantage a clear performance differential over competition on factors that are important to target customers

Case 1 Virgin Direct 2000: Market-Orientated Personal Financial Services

Virgin's entry into financial services

> You bought the record, you drank the cola, you took the aeroplane to New York, Richard Branson's Virgin empire is more than a casual assortment of consumer goods; in marketing terms, it is a whole way of life. But Branson's baby boomers are about to grow up. With all the pre-publicity of a Hollywood film premiere, Virgin is set to enter its least glamorous market: the personal equity plan.[1]

Ask any member of the Virgin Direct team why Richard Branson was interested in the financial services market and you will get the answer 'if an industry needs "sorting out", Richard Branson is interested in doing so'. The brand image of good service, good value for money and of challenging the status quo has led Richard Branson's Virgin Group to diversify into a variety of seemingly unrelated sectors. If the customers needs could be met better, then there is a challenge for the Virgin brand. In the words of Jayne-Anne Gadhia, operations director of Virgin Direct:

> The Virgin brand is about taking on the rest of the industry. It is a brand with personality. Richard Branson is seen by the public as a customers' champion, who is allowed to question how to do things better and differently.

In March 1995 the Virgin Group set up a joint venture with Norwich Union to enter the financial services market using the telephone as its distribution method. On entry into the market, Virgin stated its aims:

> to advertise itself as the friendly face in a world of financial cowboys. The combination of easy-to-understand products and low initial charges will soon be applied to pensions and life insurance, where public faith has been shaken by accusations of miss-selling and over-charging.[2]

The Virgin PEP was Richard Branson's attempt to attract new customers into a market that he felt was over-complicated. After experiences of trying to invest his own money, Branson said of the financial services market:

> My impression was that it was packed with hidden charges, pushy salesmen, poor performance and meaningless jargon. I couldn't believe it could all be so complicated, so I put together a team to do it better.[3]

Virgin Direct's target market can be broadly described as aged 35+, ABC1 adults. The company has a wide appeal and, while viewed as a young brand, has been particularly successful in attracting the older age groups. The opportunity created by an often ill-served customer cuts right across the demographic groups.

The managing director of Virgin Direct, Rowan Gormley, regards traditional financial services as product-oriented. They are concerned at creating clever products even though these are expensive and ineffective in meeting customers' needs:

> They create new options, new bells and whistles. Once these have been sold, they need to pay administration costs to run a massive number of variants. The customer is paying for this and for the sales force. Resources are going into keeping the business ticking over. Yet the fundamentals are so simple. Obviously we need to communicate with the customer. We do this via the telephone rather than by employing agents or a salesforce. And we take a jigsaw approach to products: no gaps, no overlaps. That way there is real value creation.

Virgin Direct's approach to financial services is that of a virtuous circle. Identify a genuine customer need, design products to meet that need, offered by a company that can be trusted. In this way the maxim that financial services must be sold, because they are not voluntarily bought, can be broken.

---

[1] Richard Wolffe *Financial Times*, 11 February 1995, Weekend Money: Putting the Pop into PEPs, 1.

[2] Tony Wood, Virgin Direct Marketing Director, quoted in Richard Wolffe, *Financial Times* (1995) 11 February, Weekend Money: Putting Pop into Peps—Virgin is about to expand into financial products but will sell them only by telephone, 1.

[3] Richard Branson, Head of Virgin Group quoted in Richard Wolffe, *Financial Times*, (1995) 4 March, 7.

An expanding portfolio of services

With its initial product, the Personal Equity Plan (PEP), Virgin made innovative use of index-tracking, a technique of investment which shadows the performance of the All Share stock market index, rather than using fund managers who pick and choose the companies in which they invest. At the time of its launch this was the lowest price PEP, with no entry and exit charges.[4] By July 1997, Virgin Direct managed over £1 billion on behalf of its 20 000 customers and the Virgin Growth PEP had established itself as the UK's most popular PEP. Virgin's entry into this market forced established firms to review their charges and brought a number of other non-financial services firms into the 'no-frills' sector.

Building on their early success, in June 1996 Virgin launched life insurance, health and critical illness plans and, on 1 November 1996, entered the pensions market. The introduction of these new, more complex financial products was a significant step. Virgin's PEP products were initially sold on an execution-only basis; customers made their own decisions about the suitability of the product based on the information provided. With a core product range in place, Virgin Direct introduced a service to advise customers about the best financial choices for their own particular circumstances. Although it is early days to judge the success of the move into life insurance and pensions, Virgin received 6000 phone calls a day during the launch of its pensions and has over twice the industry conversion rate from interest into purchase.

The Virgin experience

Virgin Direct has two main communication rules. The first is about what is said. Everything must be about the customer or for the customer. Statements of fact should be used, not claims. The second is about the way things are said; clear, straightforward, not patronizing, witty, surprising and different. Television has played a key role in communicating the Virgin message. However, a major challenge is that the target audience are light viewers of television. Therefore the thrust of advertising has been through poster campaigns

and in the national press. Messages include: 'Beware of the charges of the light fingered brigade' and 'Choose the wrong pension and you might be condemned to an extra eighteen months of hard labour'.

Part of Virgin Direct's strategy is to put the customer firmly in control by giving the information they need. If a customer rings to ask about PEPs, an information pack will be sent with a simplified application form which has already been filled in with as many details as possible to reduce the time required to fill it in. A follow-up call will check that the pack has arrived, but the customer will never be chased to return an application. This is part of Virgin's 'no pester promise', a response to the hard sell tactics traditionally associated with the industry. In its simplicity and clarity, Virgin Direct literature differs markedly from the complex financial formulae usually found and is one of the major tools in showing Virgin's different approach to the business.

The Call Centre is where the customers come into contact with the 'Virgin Experience'. The systems are designed to be user friendly and to offer quick quotes to customers. Every contact with the customer is important and is carefully thought through. When the caller gives his or her postcode, a database is called forward which provides details of any previous transactions with the firm. Virgin undertakes not to supply this database to anyone else.

It is quite usual in life insurance to have to go through several stages of form filling before a quote can be given. At this stage the customer has already invested significant time and effort, but may not even be eligible. Also, when needing to claim, the definitions are so vague that it may not be clear whether the person is covered.

To overcome this problem, Virgin Direct has introduced an expert system to allow the tele-operator to fill in the answers to a series of basic questions. In the majority of cases, this will result in an immediate quotation, although if there are some pre-existing medical conditions, this may be provisional pending a medical examination. Here again, Virgin have taken an innovative approach. Rather than telling the customer to go away, have a medical and then begin the process again, Virgin has a 'nurse on a motorbike'. If a medical is necessary, a date can be agreed there and then with the customer and someone will come to them to carry it out.

[4] *Financial Times* (1995) 4 October, Midweek Money: Branson Competes on Price—Bond Peps/Smart Money.

The launch of Virgin One

In October 1997, a year after the launch of pensions, Virgin Direct entered the retail banking market with the words:

> We are delighted to announce that we are taking on the banks and building societies. The newspapers have been talking about it for months, our competitors have feared it for ages and our customers have been asking for it for years. We have teamed up with the Royal Bank of Scotland plc to launch the Virgin One account which could change the way you manage your money forever.
>
> (Launch Announcement, October 1997)

The Virgin One account offered the combined features of a mortgage, loan and current account (see Appendix C1.1). Richard Branson said, on launch, that it was:

> set to turn personal banking on its head by breaking down the artificial barrier between savings and borrowings ... banking is inherently a very straightforward business: it astonishes me that it has been allowed to become so complicated.

This new form of banking was aimed at busy people 'who have got better things to do than to chase around trying to get a return on their money'. It set a new challenge to traditional banks and building societies through the five principles which were used to create the account:

+ One account, One statement and One phone number.
+ All borrowings at mortgage rate.
+ Your money works, you don't.
+ It's your money not ours.
+ You'll be treated as an adult.

By late 1998, one year after launch, Virgin One lending had reached the £500 million mark and had 5000 account holders.

Creating sustainable advantage

During 1997 Virgin Direct saw business grow dramatically. Funds under management passed the £1 billion mark. By late 1999 Virgin Direct had reached £2.1 billion in assets, employed 800 staff and reached around 300 000 customers (close to 50 per cent of the direct market). Underlying this success was Virgin's ongoing commitment to give customers what they want. Accolades include that 1998 Marketing Society's brand of the year in the finance category[5] and the 1999 Unisys Management Service Excellence award. Surveys show that 99.4 per cent of customers describe Virgin's service as good or excellent.

Complacency is not, however, a company failing. Said Rowan Gormley in September 1999: 'We believe we have until the end of 1999 to build a position for ourselves ... the rest of the industry is fighting back'.[6]

Appendix C1.1

Key features of the One account

Customers decide how much money they will need to meet their financial needs, including their mortgage, credit cards, other loans etc.

We'll agree a suitable credit limit with the customer. This is called their 'facility'.

They pay their monthly income into the account.

There is no tax to pay whilst the One account is in net debit. This is because the customer is paying back borrowings rather than saving.

The account can be used for all the usual financial transactions, including cash withdrawals, direct debits, cheque payments, Switch and Visa cards.

There's one rate of interest for the entire facility.

Interest will be calculated each day and charged to the account monthly.

Customers can run their One account over the telephone 24 hours a day, any day of the year.

Other important information:

Minimum facility is £50 000.

Customers must agree to use their home as security

The facility must be repaid on, or before, retirement.

All accounts will be held by the Royal Bank of Scotland.

This case was prepared by Susan Bridgewater, Lecturer in Marketing, University of Warwick.

[5] *Marketing Week* (1998) Brand of the Year: Virgin Direct, 23 April, 54.

[6] *MT* (1998) September.

Questions

1 Why were customers dissatisfied with traditional financial services?

2 In what ways does Virgin Direct meet customers' needs?

3 What major challenges must Virgin Direct face to sustain its competitive advantage in the direct financial services marketplace?

Case 2 Sylvan Ireland

Introduction

Mushrooms have been one of Ireland's agricultural success stories. Mushroom production throughout the island has grown from just over 15 000 tonnes in 1983 to over 83 000 tonnes in 1997. The total number of growers in the Republic of Ireland has risen from 330 in 1987 to 554 in 1998, with the largest concentration of growers in counties like Monaghan, Cavan, Roscommon and Mayo. It is estimated that grower numbers in Northern Ireland are in the region of 400. The bulk of Irish mushroom production is exported fresh to the UK where it is mainly sold via the major multiples. In 1991, it was estimated that the Republic of Ireland mushroom industry had a 36 per cent share of the UK retail mushroom business. Currently this share of market stands at 45 per cent. Sylvan Ireland is Ireland's leading manufacturer of mushroom spawn, the 'seeds' which are used to grow mushrooms. The key challenges facing the company is how to build and sustain its dominance of the Irish market.

Growing mushrooms and the mushroom industry in Ireland

Much of the success of the Irish mushroom industry is down to the organization of the industry which is characterized by specialization and outsourcing. Mushrooms are the fruit (like an apple) of the mushroom 'plant'. The body of the mushroom is called mycelium, which is a vast network of interconnected cells that permeates the ground and lives perennially. Mushrooms are grown from spawn, which is a pure culture of a mycelium on a solid substance such as cereal grains. The mycelium chosen for spawn production must be of first-class quality, that is, it must be healthy and show no signs of degeneration. Inoculation and growth must take place under sterile conditions to prevent infection and poor transport and storage can also severely damage the quality of the spawn. Spawn manufacturers sell their product to mushroom companies who produce mushroom compost. The spawn is then mixed through the compost, which is in turn sold to growers. A successful crop of mushrooms cannot be obtained from poor quality compost and nor will it be achieved unless there is a complete and rapid colonization of the compost by mushroom mycelium.

Irish mushroom growers use a system of growing in plastic bags and tunnels rather than the traditional tray system and the former has the potential to produce very high quality mushrooms at relatively low production cost. The type of mushroom produced is almost exclusively the white button mushroom (*Agaricus bisporus*). The outsourcing of the growing phase of the production process to a system of 'satellite' growers greatly improves the efficiency of the overall production system. Growing has a high labour content and strict discipline is required in picking and grading mushrooms. Mushrooms are grown in tunnels (or houses) that are usually 33.5 metres long and 7.0 metres wide. Floors are made of concrete and the tunnels are covered and insulated using polythene. The two basic requirements for mushroom growing are good compost and the right environmental conditions. The task of the grower is to concentrate on crop management from the day the compost is delivered until the house is emptied. The principal management factors that need attention are temperature monitoring, watering, carbon dioxide levels at different stages of the production cycle, humidity control, air movement and good hygiene practices to control pests and diseases.

After the mushrooms are picked and graded, they are sold to the mushroom companies who are responsible for marketing and distributing the crop, usually fresh to the UK retail sector but also for domestic consumption in Ireland and for sale in the processing industry. Ireland's leading company is Monaghan Mushrooms Ltd, which was founded in 1981 and is responsible for just under 50 per cent of Ireland's exports of mushrooms. Other leading competitors include Walsh Mushrooms in Co. Wexford and Carbury Mushrooms in Co. Kildare. Consolidation in the British retail sector is likely to create further downward price pressure in the future. Supermarkets have over 76 per cent of the retail trade in the UK with the big four, Sainsbury, Tesco, Safeway and Asda accounting for 66 per cent of the total. Traditionally, mushrooms have been an extremely profitable line of the supermarket fresh produce department. For example in 1996, prices in the region of £1.59/lb left significant margins for the retailer. Since then competition has intensified with prices falling to 99p/lb.

Sylvan Ireland

In 1986, Mel O'Rourke, who had been laid off from his job in Baileboro Co-operative decided to form a company manufacturing mushroom spawn. The company which was called International Spawn was set up using personal savings and funding provided by three Business Expansion Scheme (BIS) investors. International Spawn signed a technology acquisition agreement with L. F. Lambert Spawn Company based in Pennsylvania, which is the oldest spawn manufacturer in the USA. This agreement gave International access to a wide range of spawn strains and it began production in 1988. It marketed itself as Ireland's only supplier of mushroom spawn and emphasized the quality of its product and its level of technical support. In those days, Mel placed a strong emphasis on developing direct relationships with the growers. He travelled around the country, getting to know the growers and establishing a rapport with them. This strategy worked very successfully and by 1991, International Spawn had over 50 per cent of the Irish market. But then disaster struck. One batch of spawn which had been sent to Co. Wexford failed. This raised doubts over the quality of International Spawn's products leading to a 90 per cent drop in sales and significant cash flow problems for the growing company. However, International Spawn recovered from the problem. Quality control was tightened and the company's financial difficulties were alleviated when the state venture capital company, Nadcorp took a 30 per cent stake. The company also set up a sophisticated tracking system to minimize the effect of any such quality problems in the future. Now all batches of spawn that are sold to a composter are tracked through to the grower so that if there is a problem batch, International Spawn is able to identify which growers have this spawn and can take immediate action.

Sylvan Inc. built its first commercial spawn plant in Kittanning, Pennsylvania, in 1981. Since then, the company has grown rapidly to become the world leader in the supply of products and services to the mushroom growing industry. In 1991, Sylvan acquired Somycel S.A. based in Langeais, France, which at that time was Europe's largest spawn company. Subsequently, it purchased the Swiss-headquartered, Hauser Champignonkulturen AG in 1992 and has built spawn plants in the Netherlands, Australia and Hungary. It now manufactures spawn at seven locations and sells its products in more than 45 countries. It is the market leader in the sale of mushroom spawn in the United States, Canada, Holland, the UK, Belgium, Germany, Hungary, Scandinavia and Australia while having significant positions as well in Italy, France and South Africa. As well as a range of products including spawn, supplements, casing inoculum, grower supplies and pesticides, Sylvan Inc. provides extensive technical support including spawn strain selection, sanitation and pesticide programmes, disease identification and eradication and yield and quality improvements.

In May 1998 Sylvan Inc. acquired International Spawn and Sylvan Ireland was formed. Prior to this acquisition, Sylvan Inc. had targeted the Irish market through its distribution centre based in Co. Armagh, Northern Ireland. After the two companies came together, it was decided to consolidate production at International Spawn's old plant in Navan, Co. Meath. A £2 million investment programme is currently being undertaken at the plant to incorporate blender technology and to give Sylvan Ireland the most modern and advanced spawn manufacturing facility in the world.

Sylvan Ireland is the dominant spawn manufacturer on the Irish market with a 58 per cent market share. Its nearest competitor is Amycel with an 18 per cent share, followed by Le Lion with 12 per cent, Italspawn with 10 per cent and Eurosemy and Le Champion with 1 per cent of the market each. It provides a comprehensive range of mushroom spawn strains, including, white mushrooms 501, 2001, 130, A15, 512 and 806 and brown mushrooms 81 and 856. It has five customer support representatives, three based in Ireland and two in the UK. Whereas Sylvan Inc. had traditionally emphasized its technical expertise when dealing with the customer base, International Spawn had tended to be more commercial, relying on sales promotions such as the chance to win free tickets for major sporting events based on purchases of spawn products. Sylvan Ireland has continued with this approach and its promotional programme for 2000 offers growers the opportunity to enter into a draw for a free computer or a two-week mushroom growing course in Holland with every purchase of a Sylvan spawn strain. The major issue currently facing the company is how to build on its expertise and reputation to continue to be the Irish market leader in the face of growing competition.

This case was prepared by John Fahy, University of Limerick, Ireland. Copyright © John Fahy 2000.

This case is intended to serve as a basis for classroom discussion rather than to show either effective or ineffective handling of an administrative situation. The author gratefully acknowledges the assistance and support of the management and staff of Sylvan Ireland. The case was developed as part of the National Action Learning Programme, a pilot project under Article 6 of the European Social Fund and administered by the Irish Management Institute.

Questions

1 How would you characterize the business orientation of Sylvan Ireland?

2 What kind of marketing research would be useful to Sylvan Ireland?

3 How could Sylvan Ireland create more value for its customers?

CHAPTER TWO

Marketing Planning: An Overview of Marketing

'Life is what happens to you while you're busy making other plans'

JOHN LENNON   *'Beautiful Boy'*

'What is this life if, full of care, we have no time to stand and stare'

W. H. DAVIES

Learning Objectives   *This chapter explains:*

1   The role of marketing planning within businesses

2   The key planning questions

3   The process of marketing planning

4   The concept of business mission and its components

5   The nature of the marketing audit and SWOT analysis

6   The nature of marketing objectives

7   The components of core strategy and the criteria for testing its effectiveness

8   Where marketing mix decisions are placed within the marketing planning process

9   The importance of organization, implementation and control within the marketing planning process

10   The rewards and problems associated with marketing planning

11   Recommendations for overcoming marketing planning problems

In Chapter 1 we saw that commercial success follows companies who can create and retain customers by providing better value than the competition. But this begs the question 'Which customer?' The choice of which customer groups to serve is a major decision that managers have to make. Furthermore the question 'How should value be created?' needs to be addressed. This involves choices regarding technology, competitive strategies and the creation of competitive advantages. As the environment changes, so businesses must adapt to maintain strategic fit between their capabilities and the marketplace. The process by which businesses analyse the environment and their capabilities, decide upon courses of marketing action, and implement those decisions is called *marketing planning*.

Marketing planning is part of a broader concept known as *strategic planning* which involves not only marketing, but also the fit between production, finance and personnel strategies and the environment. The aim of strategic planning is to shape and reshape a company so that its business and products continue to meet corporate objectives (e.g. profit or sales growth). Because marketing management is charged with the responsibility of managing the interface between the company and its environment, it has a key role to play in strategic planning.

In trying to understand the role of marketing planning in strategy development the situation is complicated somewhat by the nature of companies. At the simplest level a company may market only one product in one market. The role of marketing planning would be to ensure that the marketing mix for the product matches (changing) customer needs, as well as seeking opportunities to use the companies' strengths to market other products in new markets. Many companies, however, market a range of products in numerous markets. The contribution that marketing planning can make in this situation is similar to the first case. However, there is an additional function: the determination of the allocation of resources to each product. Inasmuch as resource allocation should be dependent, in part, on the attractiveness of the market for each product, marketing is inevitably involved in this decision.

Finally a company may comprise a number of businesses (often equating to divisions) each of which serve distinct groups of customers and have a distinct set of competitors.[1] Each business may be strategically autonomous and thus form a *strategic business unit* (SBU). A major component of a corporate plan will be the allocation of resources to each SBU. Strategic decisions at the corporate level are normally concerned with acquisition, divestment and diversification.[2] Here, too, marketing can play a role through the identification of opportunities and threats in the environment as they relate to current and prospective businesses.

Despite these complications the essential questions which need to be asked are similar in each situation. These questions will now be discussed.

The fundamentals of planning

Planning can focus on many personal as well as business issues. We can produce a career plan, we can plan our use of leisure time, or we can plan for our retirement. In each case the framework for the planning process is similar and can be understood by asking the questions posed in Table 2.1. Let us first examine planning in the context of a person developing a career plan. Then we shall explain the process of planning in a business context.

The starting-point is asking the basic question 'Where are we now?' This may involve a factual statement and a value judgement as to the degree of success achieved against expectations. The answer will depend upon 'facts' as perceived by the individual. The next question 'How did we get there?' focuses on an analysis of significant events that had a bearing on the achievements and short-comings identified earlier. To illustrate the process so far the answer to the first question could be 'assistant brand manager in a fast-moving consumer goods company for five years with

Table 2.1   Key planning questions

1 Where are we now?
2 How did we get there?
3 Where are we heading?
4 Where would we like to be?
5 How do we get there?
6 Are we on course?

experience in developing advertising, sales promotion and new product variations'. Our self-assessment of this situation may be negative: five years is too long in this position. Our assessment of how we got there might include the gaining of an academic (degree) and professional qualifications and the use and development of personal skills which we assess are communicational and analytical.

The next question 'Where are we heading?' focuses on the future, given that we make no significant changes in our actions. If we proceed as we have done in the past, what are the likely outcomes? Our assessment of this may be that we proceed to brand manager status at our company in three years' time and product manager in ten. But 'Where would we like to be?' This question allows us to compare our prediction of the future with our aspirations. It is a key planning question. If our aspirations match our predictions based on current behaviour, we shall proceed as before. We are satisfied that we shall achieve brand manager status in three years and become a product manager in ten.

However, if we want to become a brand manager in one year and a product manager in five, we need to change behaviour. Our assessment of the situation is that current actions are insufficient to achieve where we would like to be. So we need to ask 'How do we get there?' We begin thinking creatively; we identify options that make sense in the light of our aspirations; we consider changing jobs; we ponder working more effectively; we assess the likely impact of working longer hours; we look at the methods of successful people in our company and analyse the reasons for their success. Out of this process we decide upon courses of action which give us a better chance of achieving our aspirations than current behaviour. Thus answering the question 'How do we get there?' provides us with our strategy. Finally after putting into practice our new actions we periodically check our position by asking 'Are we on course?' If we are, then the plan remains unaltered; if not, then we modify our plan.

In business the process is essentially the same in theory. However, the practice is much more complex. Businesses are comprised of individuals who may have very differing views on the answers to these questions. Furthermore, the outcome of the planning process may have fundamental implications for their jobs. Planning is therefore a political activity and vested interests may view it from a narrow departmental rather than a business-wide perspective. A key issue in getting planning systems to work is tackling such behavioural problems.[3] However, at this point in this chapter it is important to understand the process of marketing planning. A common approach to the analysis of the marketing planning process is at the business unit level (for example Day[4]) and this is the level adopted here.

The process of marketing planning

The process of marketing planning is outlined in Fig. 2.1. It provides a well-defined path from generating a business mission to implementing and controlling the resultant plans. In real life, planning is rarely so straightforward and logical. Different people may be involved at various stages of the planning process and the degree to which they accept and are influenced by the outcomes of earlier planning stages is variable.

However, the presentation of the planning process in Fig. 2.1 serves two purposes. First, it provides a systematic framework for understanding the analysis and decision-making processes involved in marketing planning, and second, it provides a framework for understanding how the key elements of marketing discussed in subsequent chapters of this book relate to each other. The stages in marketing planning will now be discussed in some detail, and finally they will be related to the basic planning questions given in Table 2.1.

Business mission

Ackoff defined *business mission* as

> A broadly defined, enduring statement of purpose that distinguishes a business from others of its type.[5]

This definition captures two essential ingredients in mission statements: they are enduring and specific to the individual organization.[6] Two fundamental questions that need to be addressed are: what business are we in and what business do we want to be in? The answers define the scope and activities of the company. The business mission explains the reason for its existence. As such it may include a statement of market, needs and technology.[7] The market reflects the customer groups being served; needs refer to the customer needs being satisfied, and technology describes the process by which a customer need can be satisfied, or a function performed.

The inclusion of market and needs ensures that the business definition is market-focused rather than product-based. Thus the purpose of a company such as IBM is not to manufacture computers but to solve customer's information problems. The reason for ensuring that a business definition is market-focused is that products are transient but basic needs such as transportation, entertainment, and eating are lasting. Thus Levitt argued that a business should be viewed as a customer-satisfying process not a goods-producing process.[8] By adopting a customer perspective new opportunities are more likely to be seen.

While this advice has merit in advocating the avoidance of a narrow business definition, management must be wary of a definition that is too wide. Levitt suggested that railroad companies would have survived had they defined their business as transportation and moved into the airline business. But this ignores the limits of business competence of the railroads. Did they possess the necessary skills and resources to run an airline? Clearly a key constraint on a business definition can be the *competences* (both actual and potential) of management, and the resources at their disposal. Conversely, competences can act as the motivator for widening a business mission. Asda (Associated Dairies) redefined their business mission as a producer and distributor of milk to a retailer of fast-moving consumer goods partly on the basis of their distribution skills which they rightly believed could be extended to products beyond milk.

A second influence on business mission is *environmental change*. Change provides opportunities and threats which influence mission definition. Asda saw that changes in retail practice from corner shops to high-volume supermarkets presented an opportunity that could be exploited by their skills. Their move redefined their business. Imperial Tobacco redefined their business (manufacturing and marketing cigarettes) in the early

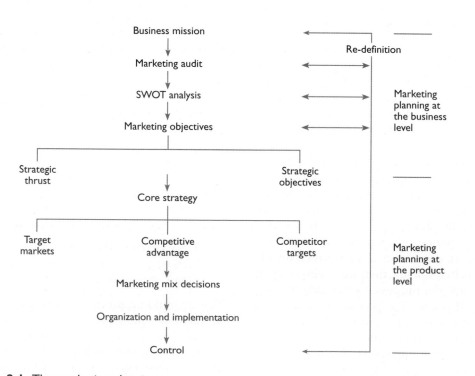

Figure 2.1 The marketing planning process

1960s partly as a result of the threat of the anti-smoking lobby.

The final determinants of business mission are the *background of the company* and the *personalities of its senior management*. Businesses that have established themselves in the marketplace over many years and have a clear position in the minds of the customer may ignore opportunities that are at variance with that position. The personalities and beliefs of the people who run businesses also shape the business mission. This last factor emphasizes the judgemental nature of business definition. There is no right or wrong business mission in abstract. The mission should be based on the *vision* that top management and their subordinates have of the future of the business. This vision is a coherent and powerful statement of what the business should aim to become.[9]

This is demonstrated by the growth of Ahold, the Dutch food retailer, and is discussed in Marketing in Action 2.1.

So far we have discussed business mission as a means of giving direction to an organization in the sense of deciding what activities to focus upon and where the boundaries of these activities lie. Campbell and Tawadey, however, view mission as a broader concept.[10] Based upon interviews with managers they developed the idea of mission in the context of a *sense of mission*. Businesses that have a sense of mission are clear about what they are doing and are enthusiastic about doing it. For example in the Body Shop, an international retailer of cosmetics, they found managers

2.1   Marketing in Action

Corporate Vision at Ahold

Ahold's chairman, Cees Van der Hoeven, has a clear vision of the future of the company. Its mission is to become undisputed leader among the multinationals which are competing in the increasingly global food distribution market. Its strategy reflects this goal. Recently, Ahold has engaged in major foreign takeovers and joint ventures in the USA, Spain, Eastern Europe, the Far East, Brazil and China. Its purchase of the US retailing chain Stop and Shop was the largest ever Dutch takeover.

Van der Hoeven has successfully communicated his vision to Ahold employees. He says, 'They understand the direction we are moving. This means a lot of questions don't have to be asked any more, and it creates a strong sense of togetherness'. Colleagues describe him as inspiring.

Indicative of Ahold's entrepreneurial approach is its move into the Far East. Despite the differences in consumer behaviour (less than two per cent of shoppers in the Asia Pacific region buy their food in supermarkets) Ahold has sealed partnerships with established retailers in Singapore, Malaysia, Thailand, Indonesia and China. Over 100 Ahold supermarkets have opened in the region within the space of six months under the names of the American Tops chain and the discount firm Bi-Lo.

Ahold is also a pioneer in the area of home shopping. Cees Van der Hoeven was proud to announce that after 15 years of experimenting with home delivery, its subsidiary Albert Heijn, the Dutch grocery market leader had finally moved into profit.

A further element of its strategy to expand in areas of economic growth and where the supermarket concept is in its infancy is its moves into Portugal, Poland and the Czech Republic. In all markets, Van der Hoeven recognizes the need to 'act local' by focusing on local customers, while taking advantage of the benefits of working on an international scale ('think global').

Based on: Business Portrait (1997);[11] Mitchell (1999)[12]

who bubbled with enthusiasm about their company and what it does. Their definition of mission is based upon four core concepts. Figure 2.2 describes their definition of mission which they term the 'Ashridge Mission Model'. Each of these concepts will now be described.

Purpose

This element of mission explains why the business exists; for whose benefit is the effort being exerted? One approach is to list the stakeholders associated with the company. These are the groups that come together through the company as a means of fulfilling their needs. Employees, customers, suppliers and shareholders are examples of stakeholders. Each has a stake in the success of the company. A stakeholder definition of *purpose* is based on the assumption that the company exists to serve the needs of its stakeholders and, therefore, the business mission should state what each will get out of the relationship. For example the mission might state that customers will get quality products at fair prices, and shareholders will get a high return on their investment.

Companies with a sense of mission strive for a higher ideal, however. They define purpose as some objective that is more important than any of the stakeholders' individual interests. In Marks and Spencer, one manager described their purpose as

being to raise the living standards for the average man or woman, while at the Body Shop the purpose was to encourage the sale of cosmetics that do not harm animals or the environment. The effect is to draw together stakeholders, particularly employees, by showing that they can commit themselves to the business not only because of financial benefits but also because the purpose of the business is worthwhile.

Strategy

Strategy is the commercial logic of the business and equates to our earlier discussion of business definition: what business are we in and what business do we want to be in? Strategy, in this sense, defines the boundary of the business and identifies the competitive advantages or distinctive competences that will enable the business to compete effectively in its chosen business domain.

Standards and behaviours

These are instructions about how employees should behave. The classic example is the Marks and Spencer standard of visible management. Board members, as a matter of routine, visit 25 stores on average every week. This behaviour is not optional: it is expected of them. Behaviour standards become the ways in which a company does business.

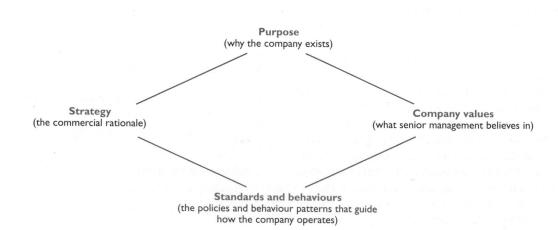

Figure 2.2 The Ashridge Mission Model.

Source: Campbell, A. and K. Tawadey (1990) *Mission and Business Philosophy: Winning Employee Commitment*, Oxford: Heinemann. Reproduced with permission

Company values

A key determinant of behaviour standards are the *values* that form the foundation of the organization's management style. Values are the justification of behaviour.

Many Japanese companies have used the value system to provide the motivation that has made them global leaders. They have created an obsession about winning at all levels of the organization that has projected them to become market leaders against strong, well-entrenched competitors. In 1970 Komatsu was less than 35 per cent as large as Caterpillar and relied upon just one product line—small bulldozers—for the bulk of its sales. By the late 1980s it had passed Caterpillar as the world leader in earth-moving equipment and had diversified into industrial robots and semiconductors. Canon, also, had drawn level with Xerox as a global manufacturer of photocopiers. Hamel and Prahalad term this obsession *strategic intent*, which becomes a central pillar of business mission.[13] Thus Kamatsu sought to 'encircle Caterpillar' and Canon set out to 'beat Xerox'. By specifically naming a major competitor the business mission is personalized and sets a target that drives personal effort and commitment.

The fusion of all four elements of business mission provides a sense of meaning to employees that inspires high levels of commitment and loyalty, and gives a common sense of direction. Research in large organizations in the UK found that mission statements were commonplace, and were seen as most valuable in giving leadership and motivating staff.[14] It represented an attempt to communicate senior management's beliefs about the company's distinctive competences to employees and to indicate the standards of behaviour expected from them. It provided managers with a common direction, and was used by new chief executives to lead the organization in a new direction. Research by Cox has indicated that mission statements may have an external role as well.[15] Although subsidiary to their internal use, they can also have the effect of informing, guiding and gaining commitment from suppliers and communicating reputation, quality and service levels to organizational customers.

To summarize, four characteristics are associated with an effective mission statement.[16] First, it should be based upon a solid understanding of the business, and the *vision* to foresee how the forces acting on its operations will change in the future. A major factor in the success of Perrier was the understanding that their business was natural beverages (rather than water or soft drinks). This subtle distinction was missed by major competitors such as Nestlé with grave marketing consequences. Second, the mission should be based upon the *strong personal conviction and motivation of the leader*, who has the ability to make their vision contagious. It must be shared throughout the organization. Third, powerful mission statements should create the *strategic intent* of winning throughout the organization. This helps to build a sense of common purpose, and stresses the need to create competitive advantages rather than settle for imitative moves. Finally, they should be *enabling*. Managers must believe they have the latitude to make decisions about strategy without being second-guessed by top management. The mission statement provides the framework within which managers decide which opportunities and threats to address, and which to disregard.

A well-defined mission statement, then, is a key element in the marketing planning process by defining boundaries within which new opportunities are sought and by motivating staff to succeed in the implementation of marketing strategy.

Marketing audit

The *marketing audit* is a systematic examination of a business's marketing environment, objectives, strategies and activities with a view to identifying key strategic issues, problem areas, and opportunities. The marketing audit is therefore the basis upon which a plan of action to improve marketing performance can be built. The marketing audit provides answers to the questions:

1   Where are we now?

2   How did we get there?

3   Where are we heading?

Answers to these questions depend upon an analysis of the internal and external environment of a business. This analysis benefits from a clear mission statement since the latter defines the boundaries of the environmental scan and helps

---

Table 2.2 External marketing audit checklist

Macroenvironment
> Economic: inflation, interest rates, unemployment
> Social/cultural: age distribution, lifestyle changes, values, attitudes
> Technological: new product and process technologies, materials
> Political/legal: monopoly control, new laws, regulations
> Ecological: conservation, pollution, energy

The market
> Market size, growth rates, trends and developments
> Customers: who are they, their choice criteria, how, when, where do they buy, how do they rate us *vis-à-vis*
> competition on product, promotion, price, distribution
> Market segmentation: how do customers group, what benefits do each group seek
> Distribution: power changes, channel attractiveness, growth potentials, physical distribution methods, decision-
> makers and influences

Competition
> Who are the major competitors: actual and potential
> What are their objectives and strategies
> What are their strengths (distinctive competences) and weaknesses (vulnerability analysis)
> Market shares and size of competitors
> Profitability analysis
> Entry barriers

decisions regarding which strategic issues and opportunities are important.

The internal audit focuses on those areas that are under the control of marketing management, whereas the external audit is concerned with those forces over which management has no control. The results of the marketing audit are a key determinant of the future direction of the business and may give rise to a redefined business mission statement. Alongside the marketing audit, a business may conduct audits of other functional areas such as production, finance and personnel. The coordination and integration of these audits produces a composite business plan of which marketing issues play a central role since they concern decisions about which products to manufacture for which markets. These decisions clearly have production, financial and personnel implications and successful implementation depends upon each functional area acting in concert.

A checklist of areas which are likely to be examined in a marketing audit is given in Tables 2.2 and 2.3. External analysis covers the macro-environment, the market and competition. The **macroenvironment** consists of broad environmental issues that may impinge on the business. These include the economy, social/cultural issues,

Table 2.3 Internal marketing audit checklist

Operating results (by product, customer, geographic region)
> Sales
> Market share
> Profit margins
> Costs

Strategic issues analysis
> Marketing objectives
> Market segmentation
> Competitive advantage
> Core competences
> Positioning
> Portfolio analysis

Marketing mix effectiveness
> Product
> Price
> Promotion
> Distribution

Marketing structures
> Marketing organization
> Marketing training
> Intra- and interdepartmental communication

Marketing systems
> Marketing information systems
> Marketing planning system
> Marketing control system

technological changes, political/legal factors and ecological concerns.

The *market* consists of statistical analyses of market size, growth rates and trends, and *customer analysis* including who they are, what choice criteria they use, how they rate competitive offerings and market segmentation bases; finally, *distribution analysis* covers significant movements in power bases, channel attractiveness studies, an identification of physical distribution methods, and understanding the role and interests of decision-makers and influences within distributors.

Competitor analysis examines the nature of actual and potential competitors, and their objectives and strategies. It would also seek to identify their strengths (distinctive competences), weaknesses (vulnerability analysis), market shares and size. Profitability analysis examines industry profitability and the comparative performance of competitors. Finally, entry barrier analysis identifies the key financial and non-financial barriers that protect the industry from competitor attack.

The internal audit allows the performance and activities of the business to be assessed in the light of environmental developments. *Operating results* form a basis of assessment through analysis of sales, market share, profit margins and costs. *Strategic issue analysis* examines the suitability of marketing objectives and segmentation bases in the light of changes in the marketplace. Competitive advantages and the core competences upon which they are based would be reassessed and the positioning of products in the market critically reviewed. Finally, *product portfolios* should be analysed to determine future strategic objectives.

Each element of the *marketing mix* is reviewed in the light of changing customer requirements and competitor activity. The *marketing structures* upon which marketing activities are based should be analysed. Marketing structure consists of the marketing organization, training and intra- and interdepartmental communication that takes place within an organization. Marketing organization is reviewed to determine fit with strategy and the market, and marketing training requirements are examined. Finally, communications and relationship within the marketing department and between marketing and other functions (e.g. R&D, engineering, production) needs to be appraised.

Marketing systems are audited for effectiveness. These consist of the marketing information, planning and control systems that support marketing activities. Short falls in information provision are analysed; the marketing planning system is critically appraised for cost effectiveness, and the marketing control system is assessed in the light of accuracy, timeliness (Does it provide evaluations when managers require them?) and coverage (Does the system evaluate the key variables affecting company performance?).

This checklist provides the basis for deciding on the topics to be included in the marketing audit. However, to give the same amount of attention and detailed analysis to every item would grind the audit to a halt under a mass of data and issues. In practice, the judgement of those conducting the audit is critical in deciding the key items to focus upon. Those factors which are considered of crucial importance to the company's performance will merit most attention. One by-product of the marketing audit may be a realization that information about key environmental issues is lacking.

All *assumptions* should be made explicit as an ongoing part of the marketing audit. For example key assumptions might be

✦ Inflation will average 5 per cent during the planning period.

✦ VAT levels will not be changed.

✦ Worldwide overcapacity will remain at 150 per cent.

✦ No new entrants into the market will emerge.

The marketing audit should be an ongoing activity, not a desperate attempt to turn round an ailing business. Some companies conduct an annual audit as part of their annual planning system; others operating in less turbulent environments may consider two or three years an adequate period between audits. Some companies may feel that the use of an outside consultant to coordinate activities and provide an objective, outside view is beneficial while others may believe that their own managers are best equipped to conduct the analyses. Clearly there is no set formula for deciding when and by whom the audit is conducted. The decision ultimately rests on the preferences and situation facing the management team.

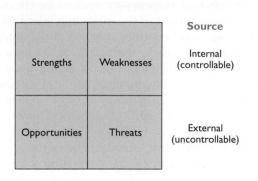

Figure 2.3 Strengths, weaknesses, opportunities and threats (SWOT) analysis

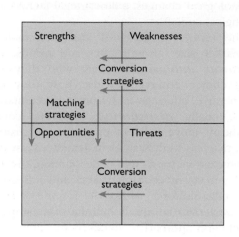

Figure 2.4 SWOT analysis and strategy development

SWOT analysis

A *SWOT analysis* is a structured approach to evaluating the strategic position of a business by identifying its strengths, weaknesses, opportunities and threats. It provides a simple method of synthesizing the results of the marketing audit. Internal strengths and weaknesses are summarized as they relate to external opportunities and threats (see Fig. 2.3).

A number of guidelines must be followed for a SWOT to be useful. First, not only absolute, but also relative strengths and weakness should be identified. Relative strengths focus on strengths and weaknesses as compared to competition. Thus if everyone produces quality products this is not identified as a relative strength. Two lists should be drawn up based on absolute and relative strengths and weaknesses. Strengths that can be exploited can be both absolute and relative but how they are exploited and the degree to which they can be used depends on whether the competition also possesses them. Relative strengths provide the distinctive competences of a business. An absolute weakness which competitors also possess should be identified because it can clearly become a source of relative strength if overcome. If all businesses in an industry are poor at after-sales service, this should be noted under weaknesses, as it provides the potential for gaining competitive advantage. Relative weaknesses should also be listed because these may be the sources of competitive disadvantage to which managerial attention should be focused.

Second, in evaluating strengths and weaknesses only those resources or capabilities which would be valued by the customer should be included.[17] Thus strengths such as 'We are an old established firm', 'We are a large supplier', and 'We are technologically advanced' should be questioned for their impact on customer satisfaction. It is conceivable that such bland generalizations confer as many weaknesses as strengths. Third, opportunities and threats should be listed as anticipated events or trends *outside* the business that have implications for performance. They should not be couched in terms of strategies. For example, 'to enter market segment X' is not an opportunity but a strategic objective that may result from a perceived opportunity arising from the emergence of market segment X as attractive because of its growth potential and lack of competition.

Once a SWOT analysis has been completed, thought can be given to how to turn weaknesses into strengths and threats into opportunities. For example a perceived weakness in customer care might suggest the need for staff training to create a new strength. A threat posed by a new entrant might call for a strategic alliance to combine the strengths of both parties to exploit a new opportunity. Because these activities are designed to convert weakness into strengths and threats into opportunities they are called *conversion strategies* (see Fig. 2.4). Another way to use a SWOT analysis is to match strengths with opportunities. These are called matching strategies and are discussed in Marketing in Action 2.2.

A company that benefited from a market audit and SWOT analysis was the ACT Group, a UK computer manufacturer and services business, more commonly known as Apricot Computers. As a result of such an analysis (with the assistance of Sir John Harvey-Jones) they concluded that their core strengths lay with computer services. Computer manufacturing, reluctantly, was considered non-viable in the face of strong Japanese and US competition. Apricot sold their computer assembly facilities to Mitsubishi Electric of Japan and concentrated on building their computer services operation. This effectively redefined their business mission. The result has been a thriving service business while production of computers has increased under Mitsubishi ownership. Apricot is Mitsubishi's world centre for workstations and open systems technology.

Marketing objectives

The results of the marketing audit and SWOT analysis lead to the definition of *marketing objectives*. Two types of objectives need to be considered: strategic thrust and strategic objectives.

Strategic thrust

Objectives should be set in terms of which products to sell in which markets.[18] This describes the *strategic thrust* of the business. The strategic thrust defines the future direction of the business. The alternatives comprise:

1   Existing products in existing markets (market penetration or expansion).

2   New/related products for existing markets (product development).

2.2   Marketing in Action
Matching Strengths to Opportunities

New opportunities can arise as a result of the changing market environment, for example those created by new technology, deregulation and demographic shifts. One way of choosing those opportunities to exploit is to analyse company strengths and select opportunities where those strengths can be used to create a competitive advantage. For example Next, the UK clothing retailer, saw an opportunity in the growing demand for telemarketing activities. One of Next's strengths was the fact that it had run its own call centres for more than a decade to service its own home shopping operation. The result is that Next has created a profitable business running call centres for other businesses.

Another example of how strengths can be used to exploit new opportunities is the move by Dixons, the UK's leading electrical goods retailer, into internet service provision. Two of Dixon's strengths were its credibility as a supplier of PCs and its large customer base. Dixons leveraged these strengths to exploit the growth in Internet usage by creating a free Internet portal, Freeserve. There was no need to advertise its service at huge expense because a large traffic of PC users already passed through its stores. All Dixons had to do was stick up posters in its stores and hand out a free CD-Rom to anyone who was interested.

The skill of both Next and Dixons was to identify things that they were already good at and could be exploited in new ways. By matching strengths to new opportunities both companies succeeded in creating attractive new businesses.

Based on: Jackson (1999)[19]

3 .Existing products in new/related markets (market development).

4 New/related products for new/related markets (entry into new markets).

These alternatives are shown diagrammatically in Fig. 2.5.

Market penetration This strategy is to take the existing product in the existing market and to attempt increased penetration. Existing customers may become more brand loyal (brand switch less often) and/or new customers in the same market may begin to buy our brand. Other tactics to increase penetration include getting existing customers to use the brand more often (e.g. wash hair more frequently) and to use a greater quantity when they use it (e.g. two spoonfuls of tea instead of one). The latter tactic would also have the effect of expanding the market.

Product development This strategy involves increasing sales by improving present products or developing new products for current markets. The Ford Mondeo which replaced the Sierra is an example of a product development strategy. By improving style, performance and comfort the aim is to gain higher sales and market share among its present market (especially fleet buyers).

Market development This strategy is used when current products are sold in new markets. This may involve moving into new geographical markets as Marks and Spencer has done in Europe, or by moving into new market segments as Apple did when they expanded their market (high penetration of the educational sector) to desk-top publishing.

Entry into new markets This strategy occurs when new products are developed for new markets. This is the most risky strategy but may be necessary when a company's current products and markets offer few prospects of future growth. When there ıs synergy between the existing and new products this strategy is more likely to work. For example, Heinz developed a new service 'Weight Watchers' to support a new range of low-calories brands targeted at dieters. This has proved very successful in both Europe and the USA in expanding sales beyond its traditional product lines of baked beans and soups.

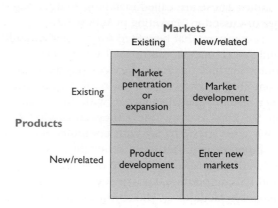

Figure 2.5 Strategic thrust: the generic options

Strategic objectives

Alongside objectives for product/market direction, **strategic objectives** for each product need to be agreed. This begins the process of planning at the product level. There are four alternatives:

✦ Build

✦ Hold

✦ Harvest

✦ Divest.

For new products the strategic objective will inevitably be to *build* sales and market share. For existing products the appropriate strategic objective will depend upon the particular situation associated with the product. This will be determined in the market audit, SWOT analysis and evaluation of the strategic options outlined earlier. In particular, product portfolio planning tools such as the Boston Consulting Group Growth-Share Matrix, the General Electric Market Attractiveness-Competitive Position Model and the Shell Directional Policy Matrix may be used to aid this analysis. These will be discussed in detail in Chapter 8 on managing products.

The important point to remember at this stage is that *building* sales and market share is not the only sensible strategic objective for a product. As we shall see, *holding* sales and market share may make commercial sense under certain conditions; *harvesting*, where sales and market share are allowed to fall but profit margins are maximized, may also be preferable to building; finally, *divestment*, where the product is dropped or sold, can be the logical outcome of the situation analysis.

Together, strategic thrust and strategic objectives define where the business and its products intend to go in the future.

Core strategy

Once objectives have been set, the means of achieving them must be determined. ***Core strategy*** focuses on how objectives can be accomplished and consists of three key elements: *target markets*, *competitor targets* and establishing a *competitive advantage*. Each element will now be examined and the relationship between them discussed.

Target markets

A central plank of core strategy is the choice of ***target market(s)***. Marketing is not about chasing any customer at any price. A decision has to be made regarding those groups of customers (segments) that are attractive to the business, and match its supply capabilities. To varying degrees the choice of target market to serve will be considered during SWOT analysis, and the setting of marketing objectives. For example, when considering the strategic thrust of the business, decisions regarding which markets to serve must be made. However, this may be defined in broad terms, for example, enter the business personal computer market. Within that market there will be a number of segments (customer groups) of varying attractiveness and a choice has to be made regarding which segments to serve.

One way of segmenting such a market is into large, medium and small customers. Information regarding size, growth potential, level of competitor activity, customer requirements and key factors for success is needed to assess the attractiveness of each segment. This may have been compiled during the marketing audit and should be considered in the light of the capabilities of the business to compete effectively

YOU'RE ONLY
YOUNG ONCE.
DAWDLING WON'T
MAKE IT LAST LONGER.

Don't do anything you may live to regret.
Like pass up the chance to experience 290 bhp
with the sun on your back and the wind in your hair.
For information call 0800 70 80 60 or visit www.jaguar.com

JAGUAR
THE ART *of* PERFORMANCE

An important part of marketing planning is target marketing. Here Jaguar target the wealthy young and young-at-heart in each specific target market. The marketing audit and SWOT analysis will provide the basis for judging our capabilities.

For existing products, management should consider their current target markets. If the needs of customers have changed, this should be recognized so that the marketing mix can be adapted to match the new requirements. In other cases current target markets may have fallen in attractiveness and products repositioned by targeting different market segments. The process of market segmentation and targeting is examined in depth in Chapter 7. An example of targeting is shown in the Jaguar illustration on the previous page.

Competitor targets

Alongside decisions regarding markets lie judgements about **competitor targets**. These are the organizations against which the company chooses to compete directly. Weak competitors may be viewed as easy prey and resources channelled to attack them. The importance of understanding competitors and strategies for attacking and defending against competitors is discussed in Chapters 17 and 18, which examine in detail the areas of competitor analysis and competitive strategy.

Competitive advantage

The link between target markets and competitor targets is the establishment of a competitive advantage. For major success, businesses need to achieve a clear performance differential over competition on factors that are important to target customers. The most successful methods are built upon some combination of three advantages.[20]

✦ *Being better*: superior quality or service.
✦ *Being faster*: anticipate or respond to customer needs faster than competition.
✦ *Being closer*: establishing close long-term relationships with customers.

Another route to competitive advantage is achieving the lowest rate cost position of all competitors.[21] Methods of achieving high profitability through cost control were discussed under 'generation and evaluation of strategic options'. Lowest cost can be translated into a competitive advantage through low prices, or by producing standard items at price parity when comparative

Figure 2.6 Testing core strategy

success may be achieved through higher profit margins than competitors. Achieving a highly differential product is not incompatible with a low cost position, however.[22] Inasmuch as high-quality products suffer lower rejection rates through quality control and lower repair costs through their warranty period they may incur lower total costs than their inferior rivals. Methods of achieving competitive advantages and their sources are analysed in Chapter 17.

Tests of an effective core strategy

The six tests of an effective core strategy are given in Fig. 2.6. First, the strategy must be based upon a *clear definition of target customers and their needs*. Second, an understanding of competitors is required so that the core strategy can be based upon a *competitive advantage*. Third, the strategy must *incur acceptable risk*. Challenging a strong competitor with a weak competitive advantage and a low resource base would not incur acceptable risk. Fourth, the strategy should be *resource and managerially supportable*. The strategy should match the resource capabilities and managerial competences of the business. Fifth, core strategy should be derived from the *product and marketing objectives* established as part of the planning process. A strategy (e.g. heavy promotion) which makes commercial logic following a build objective may make no sense when a harvesting objective has been decided. Finally, the strategy should be *internally consistent*. The elements should blend to form a coherent whole.

Marketing mix decisions

Marketing managers have at their disposal four broad tools over which they can match their offerings to what customers require. These marketing mix decisions consist of judgements about price levels, the blend of promotional techniques to employ, the distribution channels and service levels to use, and the types of products to manufacture. Where promotional, distribution and product standard surpass those of competition, a competitive advantage may be gained. Alternatively, a judgement may be made only to match or even undershoot the competition on some elements of the marketing mix. To outgun the competition on everything is normally not feasible. Choices have to be made about how the marketing mix can be achieved to provide a superior offering to the customer at reasonable cost.

A common failing is to keep the marketing mix the same when moving from one target segment to another. If needs and buying behaviour differ, then the marketing mix must change to match the new requirements. The temptation, for example, to use the same distribution outlets may be great but, if customers prefer to buy elsewhere, a new distribution system, with its associated extra costs, must be established.

Organization and implementation

No marketing plan will succeed unless it 'degenerates into work'.[23] Consequently the business must design an organization that has the capability of implementing the plan. Indeed organizational weaknesses discovered as part of the SWOT analysis may restrict the feasible range of strategic options. Reorganization could mean the establishment of a marketing organization or department in the business. A study of manufacturing organizations by Piercy found that 55 per cent did not have a marketing department.[24] In some cases marketing was done by the chief executive, in others the sales department dealt with customers and no need for other marketing inputs was perceived. In other situations environmental change may cause strategy change and this may imply reorganization of marketing and sales. The growth of large corporate customers with enormous buying power has resulted in businesses focusing their resources more firmly on meeting their needs (strategy change) which in turn has led to dedicated marketing and sales teams being organized to service these accounts (reorganization). Organizational issues are explored in Chapter 18.

Because strategy change and reorganization affects the balance of power in businesses, and the daily life and workloads of people, resistance may occur. Consequently marketing personnel need to understand the barriers to change, the process of change management and the techniques of persuasion that can be used to affect the implementation of the marketing plan. These issues are dealt with in Chapters 18 and 19.

Control

The final stage in the marketing planning process is *control*. The aim of control systems is to evaluate the results of the marketing plan so that corrective actions can be taken if performance does not match objectives. Short-term control systems can plot results against objectives on a weekly, monthly, quarterly and/or annual basis. Measures include sales profits, costs and cash flow. Strategic control systems are more long term. Managers need to stand back from week-by-week and month-by-month results to critically reassess whether their plans are in line with their capabilities and the environment.

Lack of this long-term control perspective may result in the pursuit of plans which have lost strategic credibility. New competition, changes in technology, and moving customer requirements may have rendered old plans obsolete. This, of course, returns the planning process to the beginning since this kind of fundamental review is conducted in the marketing audit. It is the activity of assessing internal capabilities and external opportunities and threats which results in a SWOT analysis. This outcome may be a redefinition of the business mission, and, as we have seen, changes in marketing objectives and strategies to realign the business with its environment.

So how do the stages in marketing planning relate to the fundamental planning questions stated earlier in this chapter. Table 2.4 shows this relationship. '*Where are we now and how did we get there?*' are answered by the business mission definition, the marketing audit and SWOT analysis.

Table 2.4 Key questions and the process of marketing planning	
Key questions	*Stages in marketing planning*
Where are we now and how did we get there?	Business mission Marketing audit SWOT analysis
Where are we heading?	Marketing audit SWOT analysis
Where would we like to be?	Marketing objectives
How do we get there?	Core strategy Marketing mix decisions Organization Implementation
Are we on course?	Control

'*Where are we heading?*' is forecast by reference to the marketing audit and SWOT analysis. '*Where would we like to be?*' is determined by the setting of marketing objectives. '*How do we get there?*' refers to core strategy, marketing mix decisions, organization and implementation. Finally '*Are we on course?*' is answered by the establishment of a control system.

The rewards of marketing planning

Various authors have attributed benefits to marketing planning.[25,26,27]

1 *Consistency*: the plan provides a focal point for decisions and actions. By reference to a common plan, decisions by the same manager over time, and by different managers should be more consistent, and actions better coordinated.

2 *Encourages the monitoring of change*: the planning process forces managers to step away from day-to-day problems and review the impact of change on the business from a strategic perspective.

3 *Encourages organizational adaptation*: the underlying premise of planning is that the organization should adapt to match its environment. Marketing planning, therefore, promotes the necessity to accept the inevitability of change. This is an important consideration since adaptive capability has been shown to be linked to superior performance.[28]

4 *Stimulates achievement*: the planning process focuses on objectives, strategies and results. It encourages people to ask, 'What can we achieve given our capabilities?' As such it motivates people to set new horizons for objectives who otherwise might be content to accept much lower standards of performance.

5 *Resource allocation*: the planning process asks fundamental questions about resource allocation. For example, which products should receive high investment (build), which should be maintained (hold), which should have resources withdrawn slowly (harvest) and which should have resources withdrawn immediately (divest).

6 *Competitive advantage*: planning promotes the search for sources of competitive advantage.

However, it should be realized that this logical planning process, sometimes called *synoptic*, may be at variance with the culture of the business which may plan effectively using an *incremental* approach.[29] The style of planning must match business culture.[30] Saker and Speed argue that the considerable demands on managers in terms of time and effort implied by the synoptic marketing planning process may mean that alternative planning schemes are more appropriate, particularly for small companies.[31]

Incremental planning is more problem-focused in that the process begins by the realization of a problem (for example, a fall-off in orders) and continues with an attempt to identify a solution. As solutions to problems form, so strategy emerges. However, little attempt is made to integrate consciously the individual decisions that could possibly affect one another. Strategy is viewed as a loosely linked group of decisions that are handled individually. Nevertheless, its effect may be to attune the business to its environment through its problem-solving nature. Its drawback is that the lack of a broad situation analysis and strategy option generation renders the incremental approach less comprehensive. For some companies, however, its inherent practicality may support its use rather than its rationality.[32]

Problems in making planning work

Empirical work into the marketing planning practices of commercial organizations has found that most companies did not practise the kinds of systematic planning procedures described in this chapter, and of those that did, many did not enjoy the rewards described in the previous section.[33] However, others have shown that there is a relationship between planning and commercial success (e.g. Armstrong and McDonald).[34,35] The problem is that the *contextual difficulties* associated with the process of marketing planning are substantial and need to be understood. Inasmuch as forewarned is forearmed, the following is a checklist of potential problems that have to be faced by those charged with making marketing planning work.

Political

Marketing planning is a resource allocation process. The outcome of the process is an allocation of more funds to some products and departments, the same or less to others. Since power bases, career opportunities and salaries are often tied to whether an area is fast or slow growing, it is not surprising that managers view planning as a highly political activity. An example is a European bank, whose planning process resulted in the decision to insist that their retail branch managers divert certain types of loan applications to the industrial/merchant banking arm of the group where the return was greater. This was required because the plan was designed to optimize the return to the group as a whole. However, the consequence was considerable friction between the divisions concerned because the decision lowered the performance of the retail branch.

Opportunity cost

Some busy managers view marketing planning as a time-wasting ritual which conflicts with the need to deal with day-to-day problems. They view the opportunity cost of spending two or three days away at a hotel thrashing out long-term plans as too high. This difficulty may be compounded by the fact that people who are attracted to the hectic pace of managerial life may be the type who prefer to live that way.[36] Hence they may be ill-at-ease with the thought of a long period of sedate contemplation.

Reward systems

The reward systems of many business are geared to the short term. Incentives and bonuses may be linked to quarterly or annual results. Managers may thus overweight short-term issues and under-weight medium and long-term concerns if there is a conflict of time. Thus marketing planning may be viewed as of secondary importance.

Information

To function effectively a systematic marketing planning system needs informational inputs. Market share, size and growth rates are basic inputs into the marketing audit but may be unavailable. More perversely, information may be wilfully withheld by vested interests who, recognizing that knowledge is power, distort the true situation to protect their position in the planning process.

Culture

The establishment of a systematic marketing planning process may be at variance with the culture of the organization. As has already been stated, businesses may 'plan' by making incremental decisions. Hence the strategic planning system may challenge the status quo and be seen as a threat. In other cases the values and beliefs of some managers may be hostile to a planning system altogether.

Personalities

Marketing planning usually involves a discussion between managers about the strategic choices facing the business and the likely outcomes. This can be a highly charged affair where personality clashes and pent-up antagonisms can surface. The result can be that the process degenerates into abusive argument and sets up deep chasms within the management team.

Lack of knowledge and skills

Another problem that can arise when setting up a marketing planning system is that the management team do not have the knowledge and skills to perform the tasks adequately.[37] Basic marketing knowledge about market segmentation, competitive advantage and the nature of strategic objectives may be lacking. Similarly skills in analysing competitive situations and defining core strategies may be inadequate.

How to handle marketing planning problems

Some of the problems revealed during the market planning process may be deep-seated managerial inadequacies rather than being intrinsic to the planning process itself. As such the attempt to establish the planning system may be seen as a benefit to the business by revealing their nature. However, various authors have proposed recommendations for minimizing the impact of these problems.[38,39]

1 *Senior management support*: top management must be committed to planning and be seen by middle management to give it total support. This should be ongoing support, not a short-term fad.

2 *Match the planning system to the culture of the business*: how the marketing planning process is managed should be consistent with the culture of the organization. For example, in some organizations the top-down/bottom-up balance will move towards top-down; in other less directive cultures the balance will move towards a more bottom-up planning style.

3 *The reward system*: this should reward the achievement of longer-term objectives rather than exclusively focus on short-term results.

4 *Depoliticize outcomes*: less emphasis should be placed on rewarding managers associated with build (growth) strategies. Recognition of the skills involved in defending share and harvesting products should be made. At General Electric managers are classified as growers, caretakers and undertakers and matched to products that are being built, defended or harvested in recognition of the fact that the skills involved differ according to the strategic objective. No stigma is attached to caretaking or undertaking; each is acknowledged as contributing to the success of the organization.

5 *Clear communication*: plans should be communicated to those charged with implementation.

6 *Training*: marketing personnel should be trained in the necessary marketing knowledge and skills to perform the planning job. Ideally the management team should attend the same training course so that they each share a common understanding of the concepts and tools involved and can communicate using the same terminology.

Summary

Marketing planning is the process by which businesses analyse the environment, decide upon courses of marketing action, and implement those decisions. It involves answering the questions where are we now, how did we get there, where are we heading, where would we like to be, how do we get there, and are we on course? In business these questions translate to the business mission, the marketing audit, a SWOT analysis, setting marketing objectives, deciding core strategy, marking marketing mix decisions, organization, implementation and control.

This framework provides a useful overview of marketing decision-making but it must be recognized that not all companies practise this neat, step-by-step marketing planning process. Often marketing planning is incremental in that

decision-making is problem focused: as solutions to problems arise, so strategy emerges. When a systematic approach to strategy development is implemented, organizational, political and cultural problems must be faced. Ways of limiting these problems include fostering senior management support, marketing the planning system to the culture of the organization, linking rewards to long-term achievement, depoliticizing outcomes, communicating clearly to implementers, and using training to provide planning skills.

Internet exercise

Mission statements

Sites to visit
http://www.shell.com
http://www.greenpeace.org

Exercise
On the Shell site, find the Shell General Business Principles and related documentation.

On the Greenpeace site, find the latest Annual report and look at the Executive Directors' Statement.

Compare and contrast:

✦   The clarity with which each organization's mission is stated.

✦   The different purposes of the two organizations.

What business is Greenpeace in?
What business is Shell in?

Note that for many organizations a mission statement goes under a different name.

Study questions

1   Is a company that forecasts future sales and develops a budget on the basis of these forecasts conducting marketing planning?

2   Explain how each stage of the marketing planning process links with the fundamental planning questions identified in Table 2.1.

3   Under what circumstances may *incremental* planning be preferable to *synoptic* marketing planning and vice versa?

4   Why is a clear business mission statement a help to marketing planners?

5   What is meant by core strategy? What role does it play in the process of marketing planning?

6   Distinguish between strategic thrust and strategic objectives.

References

1. Day, G. S. (1984) *Strategic Marketing Planning: The Pursuit of Competitive Advantage*, St Paul, MN: West, 41.

2. Weitz, B. A. and R. Wensley (1988) *Readings in Strategic Marketing*, New York: Dryden, 4.

3. Piercy, N. (1997) *Market-led Strategic Change: Transforming the Process of Going to Market*, Oxford: Butterworth-Heinemann.

4. Day (1984) op. cit., 48.

5. Ackoff, R. I. (1987). Mission statements, *Planning Review*, **15** (4), 30-2.

6. Hooley, G. J., A. J. Cox and A. Adams (1992) Our Five Year Mission: To Boldly Go Where No Man Has Been Before ... , *Journal of Marketing Management*, **8** (1), 35-48.

7. Abell, D. (1980) *Defining the Business: The Starting Point of Strategic Planning*, Englewood Cliffs, NJ: Prentice-Hall, ch. 3.

8. Levitt, T. (1960) Marketing Myopia, *Harvard Business Review*, July–August, 45-6.

9. Wilson, I. (1992) Realizing the Power of Strategic Vision, *Long Range Planning*, **25** (5), 18-28.

10. Campbell, A. and K. Tawadey (1990) *Mission and Business Philosophy: Winning Employee Commitment*, Oxford: Heinemann, ch. 1.

11. Business Portrait (1997) Shopkeeper with a Taste for Expansion, *The European*, 13-19 February, 28.

12. Mitchell, A. (1999) Home Shopping to Count Cost of Consumer Time, *Marketing Week*, 30 September, 34-5.

13. Hamel, G. and C. L. Prahalad (1989) Strategic Intent, *Harvard Business Review*, May–June, 63-76.

14. Klemm, M., S. Sanderson and G. Luffman (1991) Mission Statements: Selling Corporate Values to Employees, *Long Range Planning*, **24** (3), 73-8.

15. Cox, A. (1992) A Preliminary Study into the Use of Mission Statements in Marketing Strategy Development and Implementation, *Proceedings of the British Academy of Management Conference*, Bradford, September, 137-8.

16. Day, G. S. (1999) *Market Driven Strategy: Processes for Creating Value*, New York: Free Press, 16-17.

17. Piercy (1997) op. cit., 259.

18. McDonald, M. H. B. (1999) *Marketing Plans*, London: Butterworth-Heinemann, 2nd edn.

19. Jackson, T. (1999) How to Teach Old Dogs Valuable New Tricks, *Financial Times*, 26 May, 15.

20. Day (1999) op. cit., 9.

21. Porter, M. E. (1980) *Competitive Strategy: Techniques for Analysing Industries and Competitors*, New York: Free Press, ch. 2.

22. Phillips, L. W., D. R. Chang and R. D. Buzzell (1983) Product Quality, Cost Position and Business Performance: A Test of Some Key Hypotheses, *Journal of Marketing*, **47** (Spring), 26-43.

23. Drucker, P. F. (1993) *Management Tasks, Responsibilities, Practices*, New York: Harper and Row, 128.

24. Piercy, N. (1986) The Role and Function of the Chief Marketing Executive and the Marketing Department, *Journal of Marketing Management*, **1** (3), 265-90.

25. Leppard, J. W. and M. H. B. McDonald (1991) Marketing Planning and Corporate Culture: A Conceptual Framework which Examines Management Attitudes in the Context of Marketing Planning, *Journal of Marketing Management*, **7** (3), 213-36.

26. Greenley, G. E. (1986) *The Strategic and Operational Planning of Marketing*, Maidenhead: McGraw-Hill, 185-7.

27. Terpstra, V. and R. Sarathy (1991) *International Marketing*, Orlando, FL: Dryden, ch. 17.

28. Oktemgil, M. and G. Greenley (1997) Consequences of High and Low Adaptive Capability in UK Companies, *European Journal of Marketing*, **31** (7), 445-66.

29. Raimond, P. and C. Eden (1990) Making Strategy Work, *Long Range Planning*, **23** (5), 97-105.

30. Driver, J. C. (1990) Marketing Planning in Style, *Quarterly Review of Marketing*, **15** (4), 16-21.

31. Saker, J. and R. Speed (1992) Corporate Culture: Is It Really a Barrier to Marketing Planning?, *Journal of Marketing Management*, **8** (2), 177-82. For information on marketing and planning in small and medium-sized firms see Carson, D. (1990) Some Exploratory Models for Assessing Small Firms' Marketing Performance: A Qualitative Approach, *European Journal of Marketing*, **24** (11) 8-51 and Fuller, P. B. (1994) Assessing Marketing in Small and Medium-Sized Enterprises, *European Journal of Marketing*, **28** (12), 34-39.

32. O'Shaughnessy, J. (1995) *Competitive Marketing*, Boston, Mass: Allen and Unwin.

33. Greenley, G. (1987) An Exposition into Empirical Research into Marketing Planning, *Journal of Marketing Management*, **3** (1), 83-102.

34. Armstrong, J. S. (1982) The Value of Formal Planning for Strategic Decisions: Review of Empirical Research, *Strategic Management Journal*, **3** (3), 197-213.

35. McDonald, M. H. B. (1984) The Theory and Practice of Marketing Planning for Industrial Goods in International Markets, Cranfield Institute of Technology, PhD thesis.

36. Mintzberg, H. (1975) The Manager's Job: Folklore and Fact, *Harvard Business Review*, July–August, 49-61.

37. McDonald, M. H. B. (1989) The Barriers to Marketing Planning, *Journal of Marketing Management*, **5** (1), 1-18.

38. McDonald (1999) op. cit.

39. Abell, D. F. and J. S. Hammond (1979) *Strategic Market Planning*, Englewood Cliffs, NJ: Prentice-Hall.

Key terms

marketing planning the process by which businesses analyse the environment and their capabilities, decide upon courses of marketing action and implement those decisions

strategic business unit a business or company division serving a distinct group of customers and with a distinct set of competitors, usually strategically autonomous

business mission the organization's purpose, usually setting out its competitive domain, which distinguishes the business from others of its type

strategic intent a driven focused objective of winning such as encircle Caterpillar (Komatsu) or beat Xerox (Canon)

marketing audit a systematic examination of a business's marketing environment, objectives, strategies, and activities with a view to identifying key strategic issues, problem areas and opportunities

Macroenvironment a number of broader forces that affect not only the company but the other actors in the environment, e.g. social, political, technological and economic

customer analysis a survey of who the customers are, what choice criteria they use, how they rate competitive offerings and on what variables they can be segmented

distribution analysis an examination of movements in power bases, channel attractiveness, physical distribution and distribution behaviour

competitor analysis an examination of the nature of actual and competitor analysis and their objectives and strategies

strategic issue analysis an examination of the suitability of marketing objectives and segmentation bases in the light of changes in the marketplace

product portfolio the total range of products offered by the company cf. Product mix

marketing mix a framework for the tactical management of the customer relationship, including product, place, price, promotion (4Ps). In the case of services three other elements to be taken into account are: process, people and physical evidence.

marketing structures the marketing frameworks (organization, training and internal communications) upon which marketing activities are based

marketing systems sets of connected parts (information, planning and control) which support the marketing function

SWOT analysis a structured approach to evaluating the strategic position of a business by identifying its strengths, weaknesses, opportunities and threats

marketing objectives there are two types of marketing objectives—strategic thrust, which dictates which products should be sold in which markets, and strategic objectives, i.e. product-level objectives, such as build, hold, harvest and divest

strategic thrust the decision concerning which products to sell in which markets

strategic objectives product-level objectives relating to the decision to build, hold, harvest or divest products

core strategy the means of achieving marketing objectives, including target markets, competitor targets and competitive advantage

target market a segment which has been selected as a focus for the company's offering or communications

competitor targets the organizations against which a company chooses to compete directly

control the stage in the marketing planning process or cycle when the performance against plan is monitored so that corrective action, if necessary, can be taken

Case 3 Heron Engineering

John Toft was the newly appointed marketing director for the European division of Heron Engineering. Established in 1899 and based in Manchester, Heron was the global market leader in the industrial stacking and storage business. The European market alone was estimated to be worth around £275 million and Heron had generated some £100 million sales revenue and £24 million gross profits in it during the financial year to March 1999. However, the market had changed markedly in recent years and Toft's first responsibility was to review the overall marketing situation and if necessary to propose a new long-term marketing plan for the European region.

To help with his review, Toft had held a briefing meeting in February 2000 with his predecessor Peter Box who had retired the week before. Box had begun by explaining that Heron had divided the market geographically into the Western European ('WE') region and the Central and Eastern European ('CEE') region and that in each geography it served a low-technology storage products sector and a high-technology storage systems sector.

The low-technology sector consisted of customers for shelving brackets and simple storage units into which trays and small pallets could be placed by hand. These latter products were often used by supermarkets to stock and display bread and other items in-store. However, the vast majority of customers in this sector were in the manufacturing, wholesaling and distribution industries. The prime customer choice criterion in this sector in both WE and CEE was price while product availability was very important. Product functionality was also important to customers although minimum acceptable standards of this were met by all suppliers in the market.

The high-technology sector was made up of customers seeking to buy high-value sophisticated storage and materials handling systems. These consisted of advanced mechanical storage units, conveyor systems, overhead lifting and carrying technologies and so on for use in factories, airports, docks, warehouses and other large facilities. Customers in WE applied product functionality and systems customization as their prime supplier selection criteria. However, they also valued having close relationships with suppliers and the benefits these provide such as easy contact, empathy, trust, advice, training in systems usage and help in crises. In many CEE countries, customers faced difficulties in being able to pay for the high-cost sophisticated storage systems due to hard currency shortages and inaccessibility to international credit. Consequently, the main choice criteria among these customers were attractive financing as well as systems functionality. Customers also regarded price as important as well as customization and local contact with suppliers.

Approximately 65 per cent of Heron's 1999 European revenue had been generated in WE with the remainder in CEE. Around 65 per cent of the WE revenue was gained from sales of high-technology systems whereas some 65 per cent of CEE revenue was for sales of the low-technology products. There had been a marked inter-regional contrast in market growth rates and Heron's market share performance during the 1990s. In WE, market growth had been negligible and as competition had intensified Heron's shares had fallen from over 50 per cent in 1990 to around 40 per cent in 1999 in both the high-technology and low-technology sectors. Conversely, demand for storage technologies had grown strongly in CEE during the decade following the collapse of the former communist regimes in the region. Moreover, Heron had been among the first Western firms to enter the CEE market and had achieved approximately a 50 per cent market share in both technologies by 1995. After that time, however, Heron's sales volume had stabilized and as the market continued to grow the company's market shares had fallen to about 30 per cent in both the high- and low-technology sectors.

Peter Box explained to John Toft that he had been neither surprised nor alarmed by the changes in Heron's market shares in CEE. Numerous local producers of the low-technology products had emerged after 1992. These firms had achieved much lower costs and prices than Heron and it had to be expected that they would win some market share in this very price-sensitive market. Also, from 1995 several other WE companies had been offering high-technology systems in CEE and it had been inevitable that they would gain some success. Even so, Box had felt content that Heron remained the market leader in both technologies in CEE and was the only firm in that region offering the full range of high- and low-technology products.

Peter Box had expressed some concern about the reduction of Heron's market shares and profits in the mature WE market as this had always been the company's main business. However, he had also felt that the demise was understandable. He had admitted that Heron had been focusing most of its attention on achieving growth in CEE during the 1990s and had perhaps been slow to react to changing competitive conditions in WE. Throughout the decade, WE-based rivals had been attacking aggressively in the high-technology sector while rivals in CEE had been exporting low-technology products into WE at very low prices. Nevertheless, Box had contended that the division was in better shape at the end of the decade than at the beginning. Heron had become firmly established in CEE. Moreover, with the right strategy, the company would be able to re-establish its former position in WE.

In summarizing Heron's competitors, Peter Box had noted that whereas WE rivals were strong in high-technology systems they were weak in low-technology products. Conversely, CEE competitors were strong in the low-technology sectors but lacked the technological capability needed to produce the high-technology systems. Box had then opined that he did not anticipate any further shrinkage of Heron's market shares and that indeed, the share trends could easily be reversed. The low-technology competitors produced only crude simple products with far less functionality than Heron's range. The CEE rivals' low-cost situation did enable them to produce what he described as 'cheap and nasty' products which might be of interest to some customers and distributors. Nevertheless, although these firms were price-sensitive, Box was confident that Heron's global reputation, extensive and high quality product range and its own wide distribution network provided the necessary basis for a market share recovery exercise in both CEE and WE.

Box had been similarly optimistic about Heron's potential for rebuilding high technology market shares in both regions. The company's high-quality products offered more functionality and productivity than those of other WE firms. Allied to Heron's outstanding reputation and other competencies this provided a strong competitive base. Most of the WE rivals were more willing than Heron to customize their offerings to meet customer requirements. Further, they each had a wide network of sales offices throughout Europe which they had used in 'going to extraordinary lengths to buy their way into customers' favours' by forming local relationships with them. They had started to offer very generous financial terms, systems training and a host of other 'customer bribes to ingratiate themselves'. However, these were very costly activities, Box had noted, and Heron had been able to undercut its rivals' prices in the high technology sector in both geographic regions.

In line with industry convention, Heron used distributors for sales of low technology products in both WE and CEE. Distributors had been selected on the basis of being financially sound and having storage products experience, established customer contacts, stocking facilities and service capabilities. Heron offered slightly smaller distributor margins than its rivals. However, Heron endeavoured to keep distributors motivated by providing company information, product training, catalogues and advertising support in the English, German and French languages, two months' trade credit and other supports. However, many of the distributors were often difficult to communicate with and did not appear to push sales energetically.

All of the distributors were independent companies and all had exclusive rights to distribute Heron's products in their local areas. A problem was that many distributors had often sold products at prices above or below those stipulated by Heron. Also some of them had been violating their neighbours' exclusivity rights by attacking their territories. Further, many of Heron's distributors had started to carry competitor products and some others had switched their loyalties to rivals entirely. Due to this, local producers had collectively established wider market coverage than Heron in CEE although Heron had managed to retain the widest coverage in WE.

Heron handled its high technology business directly. For this purpose the company had established sales offices in Paris, Brussels, Frankfurt, Milan, Vienna, Warsaw and Moscow to build and maintain customer contacts. These offices were staffed by indigenous technological salespeople who provided customers with technical assistance and advice about storage systems design. Heron had three technically qualified key account managers based in Manchester to make sales calls throughout Europe and to assist the personnel in the regional sales offices as required. Heron's headquarters also accommodated an effective research and development department and a department responsible for tendering and financing.

Heron maintained a continuous product innovation policy to maintain its strong reputation for product functionality and quality. The company also utilized a cost-plus pricing method. Sales personnel were allowed some freedom to adjust prices to meet local demand and competitive conditions. However, company policy precluded acceptance of any orders for sales with profit margins less than 12 per cent above full average costs.

After his meeting with Peter Box, John Toft had felt very dispirited. Despite the optimism that had been displayed by his predecessor, Toft had wondered whether his division of the company was in dire trouble. He had also wondered about what, if anything, he could do to remedy the situation.

This case was prepared by David Shipley, Professor of Marketing, Trinity College, University of Dublin, Ireland. The name of the company, financial data, market characteristics and other matters have been disguised. Copyright © David Shipley 2000.

Questions

Propose a long-term marketing plan for Heron's high technology and low technology businesses in the two European regions.

Case 4 Weatherpruf Shoe Waxes

Peter Smith, sales director at Weatherpruf Shoe Waxes, was asked by the company chairman and sole owner, Austin Thomas, to prepare a forecast of expected sales during the coming year. The last few years had seen some dramatic changes in the market for shoe waxes, in particular the introduction by a major competitor of liquid polishes in plastic bottles with foam pad applicators. The whole market seemed in a state of flux and Mr Thomas was concerned that the company predict, and therefore be in a better position to meet, market demand.

Weatherpruf Shoe Waxes were manufacturers of high quality men's and women's solid shoe waxes marketed under the Weatherpruf brand name. The waxes were produced in a range of colours—black, light tan and dark tan—and sold in half-inch deep, two-inch diameter, resealable tins. The company has been in the market since the 1930s when it was started by Mortimer Thomas, father of the current chairman. Since its inception the company had built, without recourse to media advertising, an enviable reputation for high quality products that both protected (especially from water) and enhanced the appearance of the leather to which they were applied. The majority of sales were achieved through high street speciality shoe shops although the product was also available through multiple grocery stores.

Margins on solid shoe waxes were good. Accumulated experience of producing waxes had seen unit variable costs fall consistently to the current level of 15p. An average selling price to the retailers of 20p per unit gave Weatherpruf an annual gross contribution to selling expenses, overheads and profit of £5 million. Mr Thomas was well pleased.

The market and competition

The total market for shoe polish (both solid and waxes and liquids) had been static, in volume, for the past five years. Liquid polishes were, however, growing at about 20 per cent per year. The market currently stood at around 300 million per year with a total value of £100 million. Waxes accounted for two-thirds of the market by volume and half by value.

Weatherpruf was market leader in solid shoe waxes. Its market dominance of the 1950s (80 per cent by volume) had, however, been affected by a major competitor brand, Bloom. Bloom, launched three years previously and manufactured and marketed by Smart Shoe Co., now held approximately 30 per cent of the solid shoe wax market compared to 50 per cent held by Weatherpruf.

The remainder of the market was made up of smaller, speciality application waxes (e.g. 'Everest' for climbing boots). The success of Bloom was believed to lie in aggressive selling to gain distribution in grocery multiples, extensive advertising to create customer brand awareness and a wider range of colours in the waxes marketed. Smart Shoe had a declared aim of dominating the shoe polish market within five years.

Market developments

The major market development of recent years had been the introduction of liquid shoe polishes. These were not wax based but offered a quick, clean method of improving shoe appearance. With a built-in applicator (a sponge at the top of the plastic bottle) the liquid was easily spread on the shoe and left to dry to a glossy shine. This development was particularly welcomed by parents as it helped to make scuffed and worn children's shoes look respectable again. 'Scuffer', a product of Smart Shoe, had developed the liquid polish market and currently command approximately 70 per cent market share by volume. The only other competitor was 'Patent', manufactured and marketed by the Patent Leather Company (PLC). PLC also manufactured patent leather for shoes, handbags, briefcases, etc.

Weatherpruf estimated that unit costs for liquid shoe polishes (including the plastic bottle and applicator) were approximately twice those of solid waxes. They were sold into multiple grocery stores at around 40p per unit.

Uses of shoe polishes

Most shoe polishes were bought as household items during supermarket shopping trips. Around 80 per cent of sales were through the major grocery multiples. A trade survey conducted by an independent marketing research agency had identified three main uses of shoe polish.

Approximately one-third of all polish bought was used primarily to protect the shoes or boots to which it was applied. For this use solid waxes were considered far superior to liquid polishes as the wax filled the pores of the leather and stitch-holes, making the footwear more water resistant. Weatherpruf dominated this use on the basis of a high brand awareness built over a considerable period of time and a reputation for quality second to none. This use was not expected to show any growth in the foreseeable future.

A further one-third of purchases were primarily to enhance the appearance of adults shoes. For this application a good quality wax was preferred although 25 per cent of this market (predicted to rise to 30 per cent in the next year) and now accounted for by liquid polishes. A disturbing trend for solid wax manufacturers was the growth of sales of non-leather footwear. This footwear required less polishing; even when it was polished it was better accomplished by liquid polish rather than by waxing. This use was thought to be in long-term decline at an annual rate of about 15 per cent.

The remainder of purchases were made by parents wishing to improve the appearance of children's shoes, especially after rough treatment during play. For this purpose liquid polishes had achieved significant inroads accounting for three-quarters of sales. This use was growing at around 15 per cent per year.

The research report also revealed that the usage of solid waxes and liquids were different. On average a solid wax lasted for 50 per cent longer than an equivalent bottle of liquid polish.

This case was prepared by Graham Hooley, Professor of Marketing, Aston University. Company names, financial data and market characteristics have been disguised.

Questions

Peter Smith is not a marketing specialist, but he realizes that the preparation of merely a sales forecast is a woefully inadequate response to the recent worrying developments. He has hired you as a marketing consultant to develop an effective marketing plan for the company's salvation.

CHAPTER THREE

Understanding Consumer Behaviour

'You can be done with the past, but the past isn't done with you.'

PAUL THOMAS ANDERSON   (from the film *Magnolia*)

Learning Objectives   *This chapter explains:*

1   The dimensions of buyer behaviour

2   The role of the buying centre: who buys

3   The consumer decision-making process: how people buy

4   The marketing implications of the need recognition, information search, evaluation of alternatives, purchase and post-purchase evaluation stages

5   The differences in evaluation of high versus low involvement situations

6   The nature of choice criteria: what are used

7   The influences on consumer behaviour—the buying situation, personal and external influences—and their marketing implications

In Chapter 2 we saw that a fundamental marketing decision was the choice of target customer. Marketing-orientated companies make clear decisions about the type of customers to whom they wish to aim their product offerings. Thus an in-depth knowledge of customers is a prerequisite of successful marketing; it influences the choice of target market and the nature of the marketing mix developed to serve it. Indeed, understanding customers is the cornerstone upon which the marketing concept is built.

In this chapter we shall explore the nature of consumer behaviour and in Chapter 4 organization buyer behaviour will be analysed. We shall see that the frameworks and concepts used to understand each type of customer is similar although not identical. Furthermore we shall gain an understanding of the dimensions we need to consider in order to grasp the nuances of buyer behaviour and the influences on it.

Before going on to discuss the framework for understanding buyer behaviour let us consider consumer behaviour in a European context. Much debate has taken place recently about the emergence of the so-called *Euro-consumer*. Will the creation of closer ties within Europe strengthened by the development of the Single European Market bring about a convergence of tastes and preference? Marketing in Action 3.1 examines the arguments supporting and refuting the existence of the Euro-consumer.

What is certain is that European consumers are changing. While average incomes rise income distribution is more uneven in most nations, household size is gradually decreasing in all EU nations, more women have jobs outside the home, the consumption of services is rising at the expense of consumer durables and the demand for, and supply of, health, green (ecological), fun/luxury and convenience products is increasing. Examples of luxury or fun goods are 'gourmet', exotic and ethnic food especially in Denmark, the UK and Germany, expensive off-roaders and two-seater cars and other expensive brands such as Rolex, Cartier and Armani. Concern for the environment and European legislation has led to an increase in recyclable and reusable packaging, while concern for value for money and increasing retailer concentration has led to an increase in market share for private (own) label brands.[1]

The dimensions of buyer behaviour

Consumers are individuals who buy products or services for personal consumption. Organizational buying, on the other hand, focuses on the purchase of products and services for use in an organization's activities. Sometimes it is difficult to classify a product as being a consumer or organizational good. Cars, for example, sell to consumers for personal consumption and organizations for use in carrying out their activities (e.g. to provide transport for a sales executive). For both types of buyers, an understanding of customers can be geared only by answering the following questions (see Fig. 3.1).

✦ *Who* is important in the buying decision?
✦ *How* do they buy?
✦ *What* are their choice criteria?
✦ *Where* do they buy?
✦ *When* do they buy?

Answers to these questions can be provided by personal contact with customers and, increasingly, by the use of marketing research. Chapter 6 examines the role and techniques of marketing research. These questions define the five key dimensions of buyer behaviour.

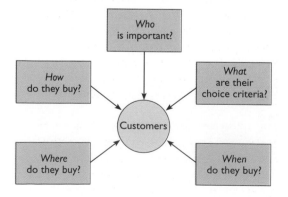

Figure 3.1 Understanding customers: the key questions

Buyer behaviour as it relates to consumers will now be examined. The structure of this analysis will be based upon the first three questions: who, how and what. These are often the most intractable aspects of buyer behaviour; certainly answering the questions where and when do customers buy is usually much more straight-forward.

Consumer behaviour

Who buys

Many consumer purchases are individual. When purchasing a Mars bar a person may make an impulse purchase upon seeing an array of

---

3.1   Marketing in Action

The Euro-consumer: Myth or Reality?

Will national markets in Europe retain their individuality or become like those of American states where there is a considerable convergence in product and service preferences? Many multinational advertising agencies believe that the creation of the Single European Market will presage the growth of the Euro-consumer. As barriers fall so consumer tastes will become similar, creating a massive pan-European market for consumer goods.

Those who support the pan-European argument put forward four reasons for its emergence. First, young Europeans appear to share similar tastes (e.g. pop music, clothing) and cultural values. Second, affluence is not determined by national boundaries. For example, the gold circle which extends for a 250 mile ring around Cologne contains many of Europe's wealthiest consumers and is multinational. Third, the advent of multinational communication systems (e.g. satellite television) and the growth in multilingual consumers means that pan-European advertising messages may be possible in the future. Fourth, the growth of global brands reflected in the merger activity within certain industries will promote the development of a pan-European culture. For example in the West European food and drinks industry there were over 400 mergers and acquisitions between 1988 and 1990.

The sceptics also have four powerful arguments. First, they point out the wide variety of tastes which exist between consumers in different countries (e.g. eating habits and tastes vary markedly between the UK, France and Germany) and within countries (e.g. the German beer market is dominated by powerful regional brewers who cater for diverse local tastes). The advent of the Single European Market, it is claimed, will do little to change these fundamental differences. Second, despite good intentions, many of the national differences in product standards, safety regulations, and distribution systems will remain post-1993. Third, linguistic differences (unlike the USA) will hamper pan-European communicational strategies despite satellite television. Fourth, entrenched national competitors will fight penetration of their markets by pan-European marketers.

These conflicting arguments suggest that the outcome is far from clear. The conclusion that most observers draw is that the degree of pan-European marketing is likely to differ between industries and markets. Where large-scale economies of scale combine with convergent tastes pan-European marketing is likely to thrive. The confectionery industry is a possible example. However, where strong national differences in taste persist, marketing is likely to remain fragmented in deference to the myth of the Euro-consumer.

confectionery at a newsagent's counter. However, decision-making can also be made by a group such as a household. In such a situation a number of individuals may interact to influence the purchase decision. Each person may assume a role in the decision-making process. Engel, Blackwell and Miniard describe five roles.[2] Each may be taken by parents, children or other members of the *buying centre*.

1 *Initiator*: the person who begins the process of considering a purchase. Information may be gathered by this person to help the decision.

2 *Influencer*: the person who attempts to persuade others in the group concerning the outcome of the decision. Influencers typically gather information and attempts to impose their choice criteria on the decision.

3 *Decider*: the individual with the power and/or financial authority to make the ultimate choice regarding which product to buy.

4 *Buyer*: the person who conducts the transaction. The buyer calls the supplier, visits the store, makes the payment and effects delivery.

5 *User*: the actual consumer/user of the product.

One person may assume multiple roles in the buying group. In a toy purchase, for example, a girl may be the *initiator*, and attempt to *influence* her parents, who are the *deciders*. The girl may be *influenced* by her sister to buy a different brand. The *buyer* may be one of the parents who visits the store to purchase the toy and brings it back to the home. Finally both children may be *users* of the toy. Although the purchase was for one person, in this example marketers have four opportunities—two children and two parents—to affect the outcome of the purchase decision. The importance of understanding the decision-making unit is shown in the advertisement for Lego.

Much of the research into the roles of household members has been carried out in the USA. Woodside and Mote, for example, found that roles differed according to product type with the woman's influence stronger for carpets and washing machines while the man's influence was stronger for television sets.[3] Also the respective roles may change as the purchasing process progresses. In general one or other partner will

tend to dominate the early stages, then joint decision-making tends to occur as the process moves towards final purchase. Joint decision-making is more common when the household consists of two income-earners.

As roles change within households so do purchasing activities. Men now make more than half of their family's purchase decisions in food categories such as cereals, food, and soft drinks.[4] Women, however, still purchase the majority of men's sweaters, socks and sports shirts in the USA.[5] Working-woman families spend more on eating out, and child care.[6] However, they do not spend more on time-saving appliances, convenience foods or spend less time on shopping when income and life cycle stage are held constant.[7] Working women are forming a growing market segment for cars. Teenagers also play an important role in an increasing range of products, including cars and household appliances, and may be seen as the household experts when considering high technology products such as video recorders and compact-disk players.[8]

Families often work hard to minimize the effects of disagreements.[9] Three ways of reducing disagreement appear to be used: the additional search for information, family discussion, and delegation of responsibility to the most knowledgeable family member. Five influence styles are used by partners when discussing family purchasers.[10] The most usual is the *low-level influence* where only infrequent attempts to influence their partners are made. When an attempt to influence is made it usually takes the form of *expert influence strategies* in which one spouse tries to convince the other of being more knowledgeable, perhaps by presenting detailed information. The second influence style is that of *subtle influence*. This not only involves the use of an expert influence strategy but also includes a *reward/referent strategy* based on a spouse's ability to reward the partner or to appeal to special feelings or closeness. Third, an *emotional influence* style combines reward/referent strategies with the use of emotion (crying, displays of anger, and silences). Finally a combination of all three influence strategies can be used either moderately (*combination influence*) or frequently (*heavy influence*).

The marketing implications of understanding who buys lie within the areas of marketing communications and segmentation. An identification of the roles played within the buying centre is a prerequisite for targeting persuasive communications. As the previous discussion has demonstrated, the person who actually uses or consumes the product may not be the most influential member of the buying centre, nor the decision-maker. Even when they do play the predominant role, communication to other members of the buying centre can make sense when their knowledge and opinions may act as persuasive forces during the decision-making process. The second implication is that the changing roles and influences within the family buying centre are providing new opportunities to creatively segment hitherto stable markets (e.g. cars).

How they buy

How consumers buy may be regarded as a decision-making process beginning with the recognition that a problem exists. For example, a personal computer may be bought to solve a perceived problem, e.g. slowness or inaccuracy in calculations. Problem solving may thus be considered a thoughtful reasoned action undertaken to bring about need satisfaction. In this example the need was fast and accurate calculations. Blackwell, Miniard and Engel define a series of steps a consumer may pass though before choosing a brand.[11] Figure 3.2 shows these stages which form the ***consumer decision-making process***.

Need recognition/problem awareness

In the calculator example *need recognition* is essentially *functional* and recognition may take place over a period of time. Other problems may occur as a result of routine depletion (e.g. petrol, food) or unpredictably (e.g. the breakdown of a television set or video recorder). In other situations consumer purchasing may be initiated by more *emotional* or *psychological* needs. For example, the purchase of Chanel perfume is likely to be motivated by status needs rather than any marginal functional superiority over other perfumes.

The degree to which the consumer intends to resolve the problem depends on two issues: the magnitude of the discrepancy between the desired and present situation, and the relative importance of the problem.[12] A problem may

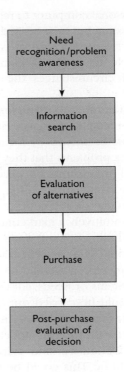

Figure 3.2 The consumer decision-making process.

Source: Blackwell, R. D., P.W. Miniard and J. F. Engel (2000) *Consumer Behaviour*, Orlando, FL: Dryden, 28

be perceived but if the difference between the *current and desired situation* is small then the consumer may not be sufficiently motivated to move to the next step in the decision-making process. For example a person may be considering upgrading their personal computer from a Pentium II to a Pentium III model. The Pentium III model may be viewed as desirable but if the individual considers the difference in benefits to be small then no further purchase activity may take place.

Conversely, a large discrepancy may be perceived but the person may not proceed to information search because the *relative importance* of the problem is small. A person may feel that a Pentium III has significant advantages over a Pentium II computer but that the relative importance of these advantages compared with other purchase needs (for example, the mortgage or a holiday) are small.

The existence of a need, however, may not activate the decision-making process in all cases. This is due to the existence of *need inhibitors*.[13] For example a small businessperson may feel the need for a personal computer to replace a manual accounting system but be inhibited from carrying out search activities because of concerns about not being able to master a computer and its cost. In such circumstances the need remains passive.

There are a number of marketing implications of the need recognition stage. First, marketing managers must be *aware of the needs* of consumers and the problems that they face. By being more attuned to customer's needs companies have the opportunity of creating a competitive advantage. This may be accomplished by intuition. For example, intuitively a marketing manager of a washing machine company may believe that consumers would value a silent machine. Alternatively marketing research could be used to assess customer problems or needs. For example, group discussions could be carried out among people who used washing machines to assess their dissatisfaction with current models, what problems they encountered and what their ideal machine would be. This could be followed by a large-scale survey to determine how representative the views of the group members were. The results of such research can have significant effects on product redesign. Second, marketers should be *aware of need inhibitors*. In the personal computer example fears of not being able to use a computer might suggest offering easy hands-on opportunities to use a computer. Apple Computers provided such opportunities through their 'Test-drive a Mac' dealer promotion when they launched the Macintosh.

Third, marketing managers should be aware that needs may arise because of *stimulation*. Their activities such as developing advertising campaigns and training salespeople to sell product benefits may act as cues to needs arousal. For example an advertisement displaying the features and benefits of a Pentium computer may stimulate customers to regard their lack of a computer, or the limitations of their current model, to be a problem that warrants action. As we have seen, activating problem recognition depends on the size of the discrepancy between the current and desired situation and the relative importance of the problem. The advertisement could therefore focus on the advantages of a Pentium III over a Pentium II to create awareness of a large discrepancy, and also stress the importance of owning a top-of-the-range model as a symbol of innovativeness and professionalism

(thereby increasing the relative importance of purchasing a computer relative to other products).

Not all consumer needs are readily apparent. Consumers often engage in exploratory consumer behaviour such as being early adopters of new products and retail outlets, taking risks in making product choices, recreational shopping and seeking variety in purchasing products. Such activities can satisfy the need for novel purchase experiences, offer a change of pace and relief from boredom, and satisfy a thirst for knowledge and the urge of curiosity.[14]

Information search

If problem recognition is sufficiently strong the second stage in the consumer decision-making process will begin. *Information search* involves the identification of alternative ways of problem solution. The search may be internal or external. *Internal search* involves a review of relevant information from memory. This review would include potential solutions, methods of comparing solutions, reference to personal experiences and marketing communications. If a satisfactory solution is not found then *external search* begins. This involves *personal sources* such as friends, the family, work colleagues and neighbours, and *commercial sources* such as advertisements, and salespeople. *Third party reports* such as *Which?* reports and product testing reports in newspapers and magazines may provide unbiased information, and *personal experiences* may be sought such as asking for demonstrations and viewing, touching or tasting the product.

The objective of information search is to build up the *awareness set*, that is the array of brands that may provide a solution to the problem. Using the computer example, an advertisement may not only stimulate search for more unbiased information regarding the advertised computer, but also stimulate external search for information about rival brands.

Information search by consumers is facilitated by the growth of Internet usage and companies which provide search facilities. e-Marketing 3.1 explores some consumer behaviour trends.

Evaluation of alternatives and the purchase

The first step in *evaluation* is to reduce the awareness set to a smaller set of brands for serious consideration. The awareness set of brands pass through a screening filter to produce an *evoked set*: those brands that the consumer seriously considers before making a purchase. In a sense, the evoked set is a short list of brands for careful evaluation. The screening process may use different choice criteria from those used when making the final choice, and the number of choice criteria used is often fewer.[15] One choice criteria used for screening may be price. Those Pentium III computers machines priced below a certain level may form the evoked set. Final choice may then depend on such choice criteria as reliability, storage capacity and physical size. The range of choice criteria used by consumers will be examined in more detail later in this chapter.

Although brands may be perceived as similar, this does not necessarily mean they will be equally preferred. This is because different product attributes (e.g. benefits, imagery) may be used by people when making similarity and preference judgements. For example two brands may be perceived as similar because they provide similar functional benefits and yet one may be preferred over the other because of distinctive imagery.[16]

A key determinant of the extent to which consumers evaluate a brand is their level of *involvement*. Involvement is the degree of perceived relevance and personal importance accompanying the brand choice.[17] When a purchase is highly involving, the consumer is more likely to carry out extensive evaluation. High involvement purchases are likely to include those incurring high expenditure or personal risk such as car or home buying. In contrast, low involvement situations are characterized by simple evaluations about purchases. Consumers use simple choice tactics to reduce time and effort rather than maximize the consequences of the purchase.[18] For example when purchasing baked beans or breakfast cereal consumers are likely to make quick choices rather than agonize over the decision.

This distinction between high and low involvement situations implies different evaluative

3.1   e-Marketing

On-line Consumer Search

In the off-line consumer world, comparing products or services was both time consuming and expensive. A clear advantage of the Internet is the capability of the technology to offer a wealth of information at the click of a button. What is becoming evident, however, is that as consumers gain experience of shopping in cyber world, they are very keen on being provided with vendor neutral distribution channels. For example, Sony's website which only offers Sony brand CDs is nowhere near as busy as their competitor CDsnow.com which offers a choice of 250 000 from five different major music labels.

The other emerging customer behaviour trend is the desire to be offered the facility for fast search through a diversity of product information and price offerings. In response to this trend for extensive information and supplier neutrality, the Internet is now seeing the emergence of a new business entity; the 'information intermediary'. Two of the earliest providers of this service proposition are Jungle and C2B Technologies. Both of these firms use databases that integrate information from dozens of on-line merchants and other information sources to identify the best possible deal available on specific products. By logging on to the Jungle or C2B site, consumers can gain access to this knowledge and thereby save themselves the hours that would be needed if they undertook their own search using a web browser.

Based on: Hamel and Sampler (1998)[19]

processes. For high involvement purchases the Fishbein and Ajzen theory of reasoned action[20] has proven robust in predicting purchase behaviour,[21] while in low involvement situations work by Ehrenberg and Goodhart has shown how simple evaluation and decision-making can be.[22] Each of these models will now be examined.

Fishbein and Ajzen model this model suggests that an attitude towards a brand is based upon a set of *beliefs* about the brand's attributes (e.g. value for money, durability). These are the perceived consequences resulting from buying the brand. Each attribute is weighted by how good or bad the consumer believes the attribute to be. Those attributes that are weighted highly will be that person's choice criteria and have a large influence in the formation of attitude. *Attitude* is the degree to which someone likes or dislikes the brand overall. The link between personal beliefs and attitudes is shown in Fig. 3.3a. However, evaluation of a brand is not limited to personal beliefs about the consequences of buying a brand. Outside influences also play a part. Individuals will thus evaluate the extent to which *important others* believe that they should or should not buy the brand. These beliefs may conflict with their personal beliefs. People may personally believe that buying a sports car may have positive consequences (providing fun driving, being more attractive to other people) but refrain from doing so if they believe that important others (e.g.

parents, boss) would disapprove of the purchase. This collection of *normative beliefs* forms an overall evaluation of the degree to which these outside influences approve or disapprove of the purchase (*subjective norms*). The link between normative beliefs and subjective norms is shown in Fig. 3.3b. This clearly is a *theory of reasoned action*. Consumers are highly involved in the purchase to the extent that they evaluate the consequences of the purchase *and* what others will think about it. Only after these considerations have taken place does purchase intention and the ultimate purchase result.

Ehrenberg and Goodhart model in low involvement situations the amount of information processing implicit in the earlier model may not be worth while or sensible. A typical low involvement situation is the *repeat purchase* of fast-moving consumer goods. The work of Ehrenberg and Goodhart suggests that a very simple process may explain purchase behaviour (see Fig. 3.3b). According to this model awareness precedes trial, which if satisfactory, leads to repeat purchase. This is an example of a behavioural model of consumer behaviour: the behaviour becomes *habitual* with little conscious thought or formation of attitudes preceding behaviour. The limited importance of the purchase simply does not warrant the reasoned evaluation of alternatives implied in the Fishbein and Ajzen model. The notion of low involvement suggests that awareness precedes

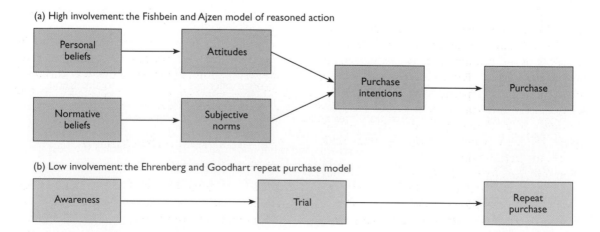

(a) High involvement: the Fishbein and Ajzen model of reasoned action

(b) Low involvement: the Ehrenberg and Goodhart repeat purchase model

Figure 3.3 Evaluation and purchase model

behaviour and behaviour precedes attitude. In this situation the consumer does not actively seek information but is a passive recipient. Furthermore since the decision is not inherently involving the consumer, it is likely to satisfice.[23] Consequently any of several brands that lie in the evoked set may be considered adequate.

Distinguishing between high and low involvement situations the distinction between these two purchasing situations is important because the variations in how consumers evaluate products and brands lead to contrasting marketing implications. The complex evaluation outlined in the *high involvement* situation suggests that marketing managers need to provide a good deal of information about the positive consequences of buying. Messages with *high information content* would enhance knowledge about the brand; because the consumer is actively seeking information high levels of repetition are not needed.[24] Print media may be appropriate in the high involvement case since they allow detailed and repeated scrutiny of information. Car advertisements often provide information about the comfort, reliability and performance of the model, and also appeal to status considerations. All of these appeals may influence the consumer's beliefs about the consequence of buying the model. However, persuasive communications should also focus on how the consumer views the influence of important others. This is an area which is underdeveloped in marketing and provides avenues for further development of communications for high involvement products.

The salesforce also has an important role to play in the high involvement situation by ensuring that the customer is aware of the important *attributes* of the product and correctly evaluates their consequences. For example, if the differential advantage of a particular model of a car is fuel economy the salesperson would raise fuel economy as a salient product attribute and explain the cost benefits of buying that model *vis-à-vis* the competition.

For *low involvement* situations, as we have seen, the evaluation of alternatives is much more rudimentary and attitude change is likely to follow purchase. In this case, attempting to gain *top-of-the-mind awareness* through advertising and providing positive *reinforcement* (e.g. through sales promotion) to gain trial may be more

important than providing masses of information about the consequences of buying the brand. Furthermore, as this is of little interest, the consumer is not actively seeking information but is a passive receiver. Consequently advertising messages should be *short* with a small number of key points but with *high repetition* to enhance learning.[25] Television may be the best medium since it allows passive reception to messages while the medium actively transmits it. Also, it is ideal for the transmission of short, highly repetitive messages. Much soap powder advertising follows this format.[26]

Marketers must be aware of the role of emotion in consumer evaluation of alternatives. A major source of high emotion is when a product is high in symbolic meaning. Consumers believe that the product helps them to construct and maintain their self-concept and sense of identity. Furthermore, ownership of the product will help them communicate the desired image to other people. In such cases, non-rational preferences may form and information search is confined to providing objective justification for an emotionally based decision. Studies have shown the effects of emotion on judgement to be less thought, less information seeking, less analytical reasoning and less attention to negative factors that might contradict the decision.[27] The illustration overleaf featuring Sony shows the distinction between emotions and objective justifications (rationalizations). Instead, consumers consult their feelings for information about a decision: 'How do I feel about it?' Consequently, many marketers attempt to create a feeling of warmth about their brands. The mere exposure to a brand name over time, and the use of humour in advertisements can create such feelings.

Impulse buying is another area that can be associated with emotions. Consumers have described a compelling feeling that was 'thrilling', 'wild', 'a tingling sensation', 'a surge of energy', and 'like turning up the volume'.[28]

Post-purchase evaluation of the decision

The art of effective marketing is to create customer satisfaction. In both high and low involvement situations this is true. Marketing managers want to create positive experiences from the purchase of their products or services. Nevertheless, it is common for customers to

The importance of emotion and the relationship between feelings and rationalizations is highlighted in this Sony ad

experience some post-purchase concerns, called **cognitive dissonance**. These arise because of the uncertainty of making the right decision. This is because the choice of one product often means the rejection of the attractive features of the alternatives.

Dissonance is likely to increase in four ways: with the *expense* of purchase, when the decision is *difficult* (e.g. many alternatives, many choice criteria, and each alternative offering benefits not available with the others), when the decision is *irrevocable*, and when the purchaser has a *tendency to experience anxiety*.[29] Thus it is often associated with high involvement purchases. Shortly after purchase, car buyers may attempt to reduce dissonance by looking at advertisements and brochures for their model, and seeking reassurance from owners of the same model. Rover buyers are more likely to look at Rover advertisements and avoid Renault or Ford ads. Clearly advertisements can act as positive reinforcers in such situations, and follow-up sales efforts can act similarly. Car dealers can reduce *buyer remorse* by contacting recent purchasers by letter to reinforce the wisdom of their decision and to confirm the quality of their after-sales service.

However, the outcome of post-purchase evaluation is dependent on many factors besides this kind of reassurance. The quality of the product or service is obviously a key determinant, and the role of the salesperson acting as a problem solver for the customer rather than simply pushing the highest profit margin product also can help create customer satisfaction, and thereby reduce cognitive dissonance.

Choice criteria

Choice criteria are the various attributes (and benefits) a consumer uses when evaluating products and services. They provide the grounds for deciding to purchase one brand or another. Different members of the buying centre may use different choice criteria. For example a child may use the criterion of self-image when choosing shoes whereas a parent may use price. The same criterion may be used differently. For example a child may want the most expensive video game while the parent may want a less expensive alternative. Choice criteria can change over time due to changes in income through the family life

Table 3.1   Choice criteria used when evaluating alternatives

Type of criteria	Examples
Technical	Reliability
	Durability
	Performance
	Style/looks
	Comfort
	Delivery
	Convenience
	Taste
Economic	Price
	Value for money
	Running costs
	Residual value
	Life cycle costs
Social	Status
	Social belonging
	Convention
	Fashion
Personal	Self-image
	Risk reduction
	Morals
	Emotions

cycle. As disposable income rises so price may no longer be a key criterion but is replaced by considerations of status or social belonging.

Table 3.1 lists four types of choice criteria and gives examples of each. *Technical criteria* are related to the performance of the product or service and include reliability, durability, comfort and convenience. *Economic criteria* concern the cost aspects of purchase and include price, running costs and residual values (e.g. a trade-in value of a car). The importance of price is reflected in the advertisement overleaf featuring the Internet company bigsave.com. *Social criteria* concern the impact that the purchase makes on the person's perceived relationships with other people, and the influence of social norms on the person. The purchase of a BMW car may be due to status considerations as much as any technical advantages over its rivals. Choosing a brand of trainer may be determined by the need for social belonging. Nike and Reebok recognize the need for their trainers to have 'street cred'. Social norms such as convention and fashion can also be important choice criteria with some

Price is an important choice criterion when buying brands. The Internet provides access to low prices over a wide range of product categories

brands being rejected as too unconventional (e.g. fluorescent spectacles) or out of fashion (e.g. Mackeson).

Personal criteria concern how the product or service relates to the individual psychologically. Self-image is our personal view of ourselves. Some people might view themselves as young, upwardly mobile, successful executives, and wish to buy products that reflect that conception. Audi ran an advertising campaign which suggested that Audi drivers 'arrived' more quickly than other drivers. This was an attempt to associate the product with upwardly mobile, successful people who might buy an Audi because it fitted their own self-image. Risk reduction can affect choice decisions since some people are risk averse and prefer to choose 'safe' brands. The IBM advertising campaign that used the slogan 'No one ever got the sack for buying IBM' reflected its importance. Moral criteria can also be employed. For example, brands may be rejected because they are manufactured by companies that have offended a person's moral code of behaviour.

Emotional criteria can be important in decision-making. The rejection of new formula Coca-Cola in 1985 despite product tests which showed it to be preferred on taste criteria to traditional Coca-Cola has been explained in part by emotional reactions to the withdrawal of an old well-loved brand.[30] Many purchase decisions are experiential in that they evoke feelings such as fun, pride, pleasure, boredom or sadness. Research by Elliot and Hamilton showed that a decision about out-of-home leisure activities such as going for a drink, a meal, to the cinema, a disco, or to play sport is affected by the desire to 'do something different for a change' and 'do what I'm in the mood to do', both of which reflect emotional criteria.[31] Concern about store design and ambience at stores such as Next, Principles, and Marks and Spencer reflect the importance of creating the right feeling or atmosphere when shopping for clothes. Saab ran a two-page advertising campaign that combined technical and economic appeals with an emotional one. The first page was headlined '21 Logical Reasons to Buy a SAAB'. The second page ran the headline 'One Emotional Reason'. The first page supported the headline with detailed body copy explaining the technical and economic rationale for purchase. The second page showed a Saab powering through a rain-drenched road.

Marketing managers need to understand the choice criteria which are being used by customers to evaluate their products and services. Such knowledge has implications for priorities in product design, and the appeals to use in advertising and personal selling.

Understanding consumers is undoubtedly being helped by the growth in e-commerce which facilitates the flow of information between consumers and companies. e-Marketing 3.2 discusses how a US bank uses this information stream to improve its service to customers.

Influences on consumer behaviour

As we saw when discussing the evaluation of alternatives, not all decisions follow the same decision-making process. Nor do all decisions involve the same buying centre or use identical choice criteria. The following is a discussion of the major influences on the process, buying centre and choice criteria in consumer behaviour. They are classified into three groups: the buying situation, personal influences, and social influences (see Fig. 3.4).

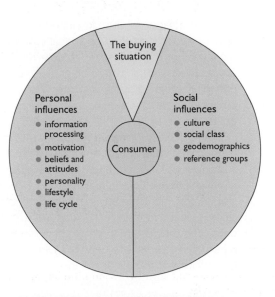

Figure 3.4 Influences on consumer purchasing behaviour

The buying situation

Three types of buying situations can be identified: extended problem solving, limited problem solving, and habitual problem solving.

Extended problem solving

Extended problem solving involves a high degree of information search, and close examination of alternative solutions using many choice criteria.[32] It is commonly seen in the purchase of cars, video and audio equipment, houses and expensive clothing where it is important to make the right choice. Information search and evaluation may focus not only on which brand/model to buy but also on where to make the purchase. The potential for cognitive dissonance is greatest in this buying situation.

Extended problem solving is usually associated with three conditions: the alternatives are differentiated and numerous; there is an adequate amount of time available for deliberation; and the purchase has a high degree of *involvement*.[33]

Figure 3.5 summarizes these relationships. High involvement means that the purchase is personally relevant and is seen as important with respect to basic motivations and needs.[34] Differentiation affects the extent of problem solving because more comparisons need to be made and uncertainty is higher. Problem solving is likely to be particularly extensive when all alternatives possess desirable features that others do not have. If alternatives are perceived as being similar then less time is required in assessment. Extended problem solving is inhibited by time pressure. If the decision has to be made quickly, by definition, the extent of problem-solving activity is curtailed. However, not all decisions follow extended problem solving even though the alternatives may be differentiated and there is no time pressure. The decision-maker must also feel a high degree of involvement in the choice. Involvement—how personally relevant and important the choice is to the decision-maker—varies from person to person. Research by Laurent and Kapferer has identified four factors that affect involvement:[35]

3.2 e-Marketing

Understanding the E-Commerce Customer

Once an organization has developed e-commerce links with their market, this will generate a vast flow of information about individual customer needs and buying behaviour. This knowledge about the customer can be analysed to determine how the firm throughout every stage of the purchase process, from initial customer enquiry through to the provision of post-purchase services, is providing value to each customer. The next stage is to begin to differentiate the firm from competition by mechanisms such as carefully targeted promotional offers or customized service delivery systems.

NationsBank in America has adopted customer value management to implement a customer-defined vision of an ideal interaction with the bank via a telephone banking service. The way in which customers use the automated voice response units when requesting services permits identification of which forms of information they would prefer to receive electronically rather than speaking to a real person. For those services where the customer requires human contact it is then possible to analyse what information they require from a bank representative and the guidance they need in optimizing their use of the bank's financial services portfolio. This database of customer behaviour is permitting the bank to begin to build customized automated and human response systems of the type which will improve the management of relationships with differing customer groups.

Based on: Thomson (1998)[36]

1 *Self-image*: involvement is likely to be high when the decision potentially affects one's self-image. Thus purchase of jewellery, cars and clothing invoke more involvement than choosing a brand of soap or margarine.

2 *Perceived risk*: involvement is likely to be high when the perceived risk of making a mistake is high. The risk of buying the wrong house is much higher than buying the wrong chewing gum, because the potential negative consequences of the wrong decision are higher. Risk usually increases with the price of the purchase.

3 *Social factors*: when social acceptance is dependent upon making a correct choice, involvement is likely to be high. The purchase of golf clubs may be highly involving because the correct decision may affect social standing among fellow golfers.

4 *Hedonic influences*: when the purchase is capable of providing a high degree of pleasure, involvement is usually high. The choice of restaurant when on holiday can be highly involving since the difference between making the right or wrong choice can severely affect the amount of pleasure associated with the experience.

Marketers can help in this buying situation by providing information-rich communications via advertising and the salesforce. Table 3.2 shows how the consumer decision-making process changes between high and low involvement purchases.

Salespeople should be trained to adopt a problem-solution approach to selling. This involves identifying customer needs and acting as an information provider to help the customer evaluate alternatives. This approach will be discussed in Chapter 12 on personal selling.

Limited problem solving

Many consumer purchases fall into the *limited problem-solving* category. The consumer has some experience with the product in question so that information search may be mainly internal through memory. However, a certain amount of external search and evaluation may take place (e.g. checking prices) before purchase is made. This situation provides marketers with some opportunity to affect purchase by stimulating the need to conduct search (e.g. advertising) and reducing the risk of brand switching (e.g. warranties).

Habitual problem solving

Habitual problem solving occurs when a consumer repeat buys the same product with little or no evaluation of alternatives. The consumer may recall the satisfaction gained by purchasing a brand, and automatically buy it again. Advertising may be effective in keeping the brand name in

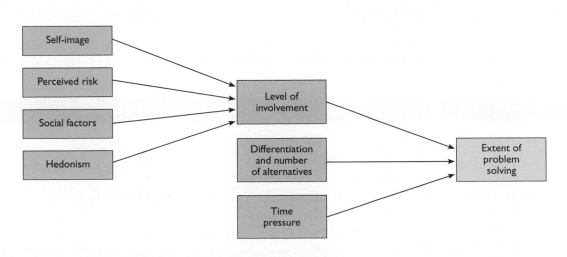

Figure 3.5 Determinants of the extent of problem solving

the consumer's mind and reinforcing already favourable attitudes towards it.

Personal influences

There are six personal influences on consumer behaviour: information processing, motivation, beliefs and attitudes, personality, lifestyle, and life cycle.

Information processing

Information processing refers to the process by which a stimulus is received, interpreted, stored in memory and later retrieved.[37] It is therefore the link between external influences including marketing activities and the consumer's decision-making process. Two key aspects of information processing are perception and learning.

Perception this is the complex process by which people select, organize and interpret sensory stimulation into a meaningful picture of the world.[38] Three processes may be used to sort out the masses of stimuli which could be perceived into a manageable amount. These are selective attention, selective distortion and selective retention. **Selective attention** is the process by which we screen out those stimuli that are not meaningful to us nor consistent with our experiences and beliefs. Upon entering a supermarket there are thousands of potential stimuli (brands, point-of-sale displays, prices, etc.) to which we could pay attention. To do so would be unrealistic in terms of time and effort. Consequently we are selective in attending to these messages. Selective attention has obvious impli-

cations for advertising considering that studies have shown that consumers consciously attend to only 5–25 per cent of the advertisements to which they are exposed.[39] A number of factors influence attention. We pay more attention to stimuli that contrast with their background than to stimuli that blend with it. The name Apple Computer is regarded as an attention-getting brand name because it contrasts with the technologically orientated names usually associated with computers. The size, colour and movement of a stimulus also affect attention. Position is also critical. Objects placed near the centre of the visual range are more likely to be noticed than those on the periphery. This is why there is intense competition to obtain eye-level positions in supermarkets. We are also more likely to notice those messages that relate to our needs (benefits sought)[40] and those that provide surprises (for example large price reductions).

Selective distortion occurs when consumers distort the information they receive according to their existing beliefs and attitudes. We may distort information that is not in accord with our existing views. Methods of doing this include thinking that we misheard the message, and discounting the message source. Consequently it is very important to present messages clearly without the possibility of ambiguity and to use a highly credible source. In a classic experiment a class of students was presented with a lecturer who was introduced as an expert in the area. To another comparable group of students the same lecturer was presented without such an introduction. The ratings of the same lecture were significantly higher in the former group. Another important implication of selective distortion is always to present evidence of a sales message whenever possible. This again reduces the scope for

Table 3.2 The consumer decision-making process and level of purchase involvement		
Stage	*Low involvement*	*High involvement*
Need recognition/problem awareness	Minor	Major, personally important
Information search	Limited search	Extensive search
Evaluation of alternatives and the purchase	Few alternatives evaluated on few choice criteria	Many alternatives evaluated on many choice criteria
Post-purchase evaluation of the decision	Limited evaluation	Extensive evaluation including media search

selective distortion of the message on the part of the recipient.

Distortion can occur because people interpret the same information differently. Interpretation is a process whereby messages are placed into existing categories of meaning. A cheaper price, for example, may be categorized not only as providing better value for money but also as implying lower quality. *Information framing* can affect interpretation. Framing refers to ways in which information is presented to people. Levin and Gaeth asked people to taste minced beef after telling half the sample that it was 70 per cent lean and the other half that it was 30 per cent fat.[41] Despite the fact that the two statements are equivalent the sample that had the information framed positively (70 per cent lean) recorded higher levels of taste satisfaction. Information framing has obvious implications for advertising and sales messages. The weight of evidence suggests that messages should be positively framed. Colour is another important influence on interpretation. Blue and green are viewed as cool and evoke feelings of security. Red and yellow are regarded as warm and cheerful. Black is seen as an indication of strength. By using the appropriate colour in pack design it is possible to affect the consumer's feelings about the product. The packaging of full-strength cigarettes is usually black. The complete branding concept may also be based on colour. For example, mobile phone company Orange has achieved success with the 'colour as brand' approach. The colour orange is distinctive in its sector and conveys the feelings of energy and warmth.[42] The illustrations overleaf show how Orange and the Ford Ka convey meaning using colour.

Selective retention refers to the fact that only a selection of messages may be retained in memory. We tend to remember messages that are in line with existing beliefs and attitudes. In another experiment twelve statements were given to a group of Labour and Conservative supporters. Six of the statements were favourable to Labour and six to the Conservatives. They were asked to remember the statements and to return after seven days. The result was that Labour supporters remembered the statements that were favourable to Labour and the Conservatives supporters remembered the pro-Conservative statements. Selective retention has a role to play in reducing cognitive dissonance: when reading reviews of a recently purchased car, positive messages are more likely to be remembered than negative ones.

Retailers understand how the senses affect perception. Marketing in Action 3.2 illustrates how they are used.

Learning   Learning is any change in the content or organization of long-term memory and is the result of information processing.[43] There are numerous ways in which learning can take place. These include *conditioning* and *cognitive learning*. *Classical conditioning* is the process of using an established relationship between a stimulus and response to cause the learning of the same response to a different stimulus. Thus in advertising, humour which is known to elicit a pleasant response may be used in the belief that these favourable feelings will be a condition to the product. The promotion of Labbatts lager on the body of racing cars generates the feeling of excitement for the brand by association. Similarly, the use of heavy metal music when advertising Irn-Bru, a soft drink, imbues the brand with youthfulness, and strength connotations.

Operant conditioning differs from classical conditioning by way of the role and timing of the reinforcement. In this case, reinforcement results from rewards: the more rewarding the response the stronger the likelihood of the purchase being repeated. Operant conditioning occurs as a result of product trial. The use of free samples is based upon the principles of operant conditioning. For example, free samples of a new shampoo are distributed to a large number of households. Because the use of the shampoo is costless it is used (desired response) and because it has desirable properties it is liked (reinforcement) and the likelihood of it being bought is increased. Thus the sequence of events is different between classical and operant conditioning. In the former, by association, liking precedes trial; in the latter, trial precedes liking. A series of rewards (reinforcements) may be used over time to encourage the repeat buying of the product. Thus the free sample may be accompanied with a coupon to buy the shampoo at a discount rate (reinforcement). On the pack may be another discount coupon to encourage repeat buying. Only after this purchase does the shampoo rely on its own intrinsic reward—product performance—to encourage purchase. This process is known as *shaping*. Repeat purchase behaviour will have been shaped by the application of repeated reinforcers so that the consumer will have learned that buying the shampoo is associated with pleasurable experiences.

Cognitive learning involves the learning of knowledge and development of beliefs and attitudes without direct reinforcement. *Rote learning* involves the learning of two or more concepts without conditioning. Having seen the headline 'Lemsip is for 'flu attacks' the consumer may remember that Lemsip is a remedy for 'flu attacks without the kinds of conditioning and reinforcement previously discussed. *Vicarious learning* involves learning from others without direct experience or reward. It is the promise of the reward which motivates. Thus we may learn the type of clothes that attract potential admirers by observing other people. In advertising, the 'admiring glance' can be used to signal approval of the type of clothing being worn. We imagine that the same may happen to us if we dress in a similar manner. *Reasoning* is a more complex form of cognitive learning and is usually associated with high-involvement situations. For example some advertising messages rely on the recipient to draw their own conclusions, through reasoning. An anti-Richard Nixon ad campaign in the USA used a photograph of Nixon under the tag-line 'Would You Buy a Used Car From This Man? to dissuade people from voting for him in the presidential election.

Whichever type of learning has taken place the result of the learning process is the creation of *product positioning*. The market objective is to create a clear and favourable position in the mind of the consumer.[44]

Motivation

An understanding of *motivation* lies in the relationship between needs, drives and goals.[45]

3.2   Marketing in Action

Customer Psychology and Retailing

How people perceive and respond to messages is vitally important to marketers. Retailers recognize that psychological devices can be used to influence consumer behaviour in this way. Aroma can provoke an emotional response, whether it is the smell of cakes baking or of disinfectant which is reminiscent of school. Luxury car manufacturers are believed to spray their cars and showrooms with essence of leather to convey the perception of luxury.

Lighting can also have a psychological impact. Red-toned lighting is used in areas of impulse purchases. For example one stationer uses red tones at the front of its stores for impulse buys such as pens and stationery. Blue tones are used at the back of the stores because they convey a feeling of relaxation in a situation where consumers are making decisions on large purchases such as computers.

Sound also needs to be managed. Research has shown that consumers regard quiet stores as intimidating. In such cases, retailers may consider the use of 'white noise': a dull hum like that of a refrigerator which is barely discernible but eliminates the awkwardness of silence.

The gestalt (the perceived whole) is also important in a retail environment. Sales of the components of a snack lunch—sandwiches, crisps, fruit and drinks, etc.—are believed to have increased by 30 per cent in Marks and Spencer's when standalone sandwich shops were introduced in their foodhalls because of the convenience of buying them in one place rather than wandering around trying to find them. This grouping of products together is called consumer preference layout and works for supermarkets as well. This is why fruit may be grouped together—fresh, tinned and dried—because consumers think in terms of fruit rather than tins.

Based on: Jones (1996)[46]

Marketers use colour to convey meaning in these Orange and Ford Ka advertisements

The basic process involves needs (deprivations) that set drives in motion (deprivations with direction) to accomplish goals (anything which alleviates a need and reduces a drive). Motives can be grouped into five categories as proposed by Maslow.[47]

Physiological the fundamentals of survival, e.g. hunger or thirst.

Safety protection from the unpredictable happening in life, e.g. accidents, ill health.

Belongingness and love striving to be accepted by those to whom we feel close and to be an important person to them.

Esteem and status striving to achieve a high standing relative to other people; a desire for prestige and a high reputation.

Self-actualization the desire for self-fulfilment in achieving what one is capable of for one's own sake, i.e. actualized in what one is potentially.

The motives that drive consumers are important to understand because they determine choice criteria. For example, a consumer who is driven by the esteem and status motive may use self-image as a key choice criterion when considering the purchase of a car, clothes, shoes, and other visible accessories.

Variety seeking is an important consumer motive. Consumers seek variety to satisfy their need to experiment with different brands, seek new experiences and to explore a product category. Usually, it can be explained by experiential or hedonistic motives rather than by utilitarian aspects of consumption.[48]

Beliefs and attitudes

A *belief* is a thought that a person holds about something. In a marketing context, it is a thought about a product or service on one or more choice criteria. Beliefs about a Volvo car might be that it is safe, reliable and high status. Marketing people are very interested in consumer beliefs because they are related to attitudes. In particular, misconceptions about products can be harmful to brand sales. Duracell batteries were believed by consumers to last three times as long as Ever Ready batteries but in continuous use they lasted over six times as long. This promoted Duracell to launch an advertising campaign to correct this misconception.

An *attitude* is an overall favourable or unfavourable evaluation of a product or service. The consequence of a set of beliefs may be a positive or negative attitude towards the product or service. As we have seen, beliefs and attitudes play an important part in the evaluation of alternatives in the consumer decision-making process. They may be developed as part of the information search activity and/or as a result of product use. As such they play an important role in product design (matching product attributes to beliefs and attitudes), persuasive communications (reinforcing existing positive beliefs and attitudes, correcting misconceptions, and establishing new beliefs, for example 'Radion kills odours') and pricing (matching price with customers' beliefs about what a 'good' product would cost).

Personality

Our everyday dealings with people tell us that people differ enormously in their personalities. *Personality* is the inner psychological characteristics of individuals that lead to consistent responses to their environment.[49] A person may tend to be warm–cold, dominant–subservient, introvert–extrovert, sociable–loner, adaptable–inflexible, competitive–cooperative, etc. If we find from marketing research that our product is being purchased by people with certain personality profile, then advertising could show people of the same type using the product.

The concept of personality is also relevant to brands. *Brand personality* is their characterization as perceived by consumers. Brands may be characterized as 'for young people' (Levi's), 'for winners' (Nike), or 'intelligent' (Guinness). This is a dimension over and above the physical (e.g. colour) or functional (e.g. taste) attributes of a brand. By creating a brand personality a marketer may create appeal to people who value that characterization. Research by Ackoff and Emsott into brand personalities of beers showed that most consumers preferred the brand of beer that matched their own personality.[50]

Lifestyle

Lifestyle patterns have attracted much attention from marketing research practitioners. *Lifestyle* refers to the pattern of living as expressed in a person's activities, interests and opinions. Lifestyle analysis (*psychographics*) groups consumers according to their beliefs, activities, values and demographic characteristics such as education and income. For example Research Bureau Ltd, a UK marketing research agency, investigated lifestyle patterns among married women and found eight distinct groups.[51]

The young sophisticates   extravagant, experimental, non-traditional; young, ABC1 social class, well-educated, affluent, owner-occupiers, full-time employed; interested in new products; sociable, cultural interests.

The home-centred   conservative, less quality conscious, demographically average, middle class, average income and education; lowest interest in new products; very home-centred; little entertaining.

Traditional working class   traditional, quality conscious, unexperimental in food, enjoy cooking; middle-aged, DE social group, less education, lower income, council house tenants; sociable; husband and wife share activities, like betting.

Middle-aged sophisticates   experimental, not traditional; middle aged, ABC1 social class, well-educated, affluent, owner-occupiers, full-time housewives, interested in new products; sociable with cultural interests.

Coronation Street housewives   quality conscious, conservative, traditional; DE social class, tend to live in Lancashire and Yorkshire TV areas, less educated, lower incomes, part-time employment; low level of interest in new products; not sociable.

The self-confident   self-confident, quality conscious, not extravagant; young, well-educated, owner-occupier, average income.

The homely   bargain seekers, not self-confident, houseproud, C1C2 social class, tend to live in Tyne Tees and Scotland TV areas; left school at an early age; part-time employed; average level of entertainment.

The penny-pinchers   self-confident, houseproud, traditional, not quality conscious; 25–34 years, C2DE social class, part-time employment, less education, average income; betting, saving, husband and wife share activities, sociable.

Lifestyle analysis has implications for marketing since lifestyles have been found to correlate with purchasing behaviour.[52] A company may choose to target a particular lifestyle group (e.g. the middle-aged sophisticates) with a product offering, and use advertising which is in line with the values and beliefs of this group. As information on readership/viewership habits of lifestyle groups becomes more widely known so media selection may be influenced by lifestyle research.

Changes in lifestyle can create new business opportunities for companies who monitor such changes and develop strategies that meet the new consumer needs that emerge. Marketing in Action 3.3 describes how Unilever has reacted to changes in consumer lifestyle.

Life cycle

Consumer behaviour may also depend on the stage that people have reached during their life. Of particular relevance is a person's *life cycle stage* (shown in Fig. 3.6) since disposable income and purchase requirements may vary according to life cycle stage. For example, young couples with no children may have high disposable income if both work and may be heavy purchasers of home furnishings, and appliances since they may be setting up home. When they have children disposable income may fall, particularly if they become a single income family and the purchase of baby and children related products increases. At the empty-nester stage disposable income may rise due to the absence of dependent children, low mortgage repayments and high personal income. This type of person may make a high potential target for financial services and holidays.

It is important to note that not all people follow the classic family life cycle stages. Figure 3.6 also shows alternative paths which may have consumer behaviour and market segmentation implications.

Social influences

There are four social influences on consumer behaviour: culture, social class, geodemographics, and reference groups.

Culture

Culture refers to the traditions, taboos, values and basic attitudes of the whole society within which an individual lives. It provides the framework within which individuals and their lifestyles develop. Cultural norms are the rules that govern behaviour, and are based upon values: beliefs about what attitudes and behaviour are desirable. Conformity to norms is created by reward giving (e.g. smiling) and sanctioning (e.g. criticism). Cultural values affect how business is conducted. In the UK people are expected to arrive on time for a business appointment; in Spain this norm is not so deeply held. In Arabian countries it is not unusual for a salesperson to conduct a sales presentation in the company of a competitor's salesperson. Culture also affects consumption behaviour. In France, for example, chocolate is sometimes eaten between slices of bread.

In a comparative study of materialism and life satisfaction in The Netherlands and the USA, Bamossy and Dawson found that the Dutch displayed higher levels of possessiveness than Americans but no overall differences in envy, generosity, or general materialism were found.[53] The 'possessiveness' of the Dutch is reflected in their reluctance to partake in second-hand markets: car-boot sales and flea markets, for example, are virtually nonexistent in The Netherlands. Another notable difference was that

lower income Americans were more envious than their Dutch counterparts. The higher level of social welfare spending in The Netherlands may have accounted for this result. The greatest difference, however, we found in the levels of life satisfaction with the Dutch being significantly more satisfied with life. Thus, even in countries that are very similar in economic development, cultural variations can be seen that have implications for consumption behaviour.

Some cultural boundaries are moving. In Europe, restaurants based upon Far Eastern foods have grown in number over the last 20 years while in the Far East there is greater acceptance of Western foods. Marketing in Action 3.4 discusses some of the changes happening in Hong Kong.

Social class

Social class has been regarded as an important determinant of consumer behaviour for many years. In the UK it is based upon occupation (often that of the *chief income earner*). This is one way in which respondents in marketing research surveys are categorized, and it is usual for advertising media (e.g. newspapers) to give

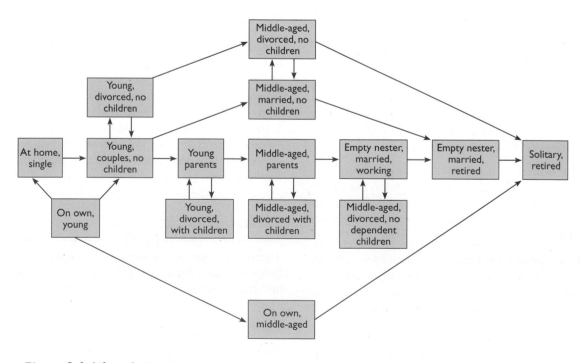

Figure 3.6 Life cycle stages

3.3   Marketing in Action

Unilever Moves into Services

Changes in work patterns and the growth of two income families have led to the emergence of cash-rich/time-poor consumers who are looking for convenience and are prepared to pay for someone else to do their home cleaning and washing and ironing of clothes. This marketing opportunity has not been missed by Unilever who manufactures cleaning products such as Jif and Persil. It estimates that the UK home-cleaning market is worth £1.3 billion and is growing.

Unilever's response has been to launch a new home-cleaning and laundry service called 'myhome'. Their target customers want more space and time to escape from the pressures of life but find household tasks an impediment. Myhome was tested in south-west London and rapidly achieved sales of £1.3 million a year to 1000 customers. A key communicational vehicle in keeping with its target market is its myhome.co.uk Internet site. Sales are handled through call centres.

To move from a business which manufactures cleaning products to one which provides fresh clean clothes ready to wear is a challenging task for Unilever. But by monitoring lifestyle changes the company has been able to seize a marketing opportunity that has the potential of providing sales and profit growth for the future.

Based on: Mitchell (2000);[54] Teanby (1999);[55] Willman (2000)[56]

3.4   Marketing in Action

Eating Out in Hong Kong

Hong Kong has always been famed for its high quality cuisine but the traditional Chinese restaurant is in decline. The arrival of Western-style burger, pizza and sandwich chains in Asia is mainly the cause. As the takings of Chinese restaurants have dropped so the sales through fast-food outlets has risen. Western food is proving very popular in the region with half of McDonald's 50 busiest restaurants being found in Asia. More upmarket operations such as Delifrance, a French bakery and coffee shop chain are also expanding across Asia.

The downside is that since 1990, 1000 out of Hong Kong's 5300 traditional Chinese restaurants have closed. Apart from changing consumer tastes, high labour and rental costs have forced up prices making fast-food outlets and street stalls more attractive. Some have moved upmarket by concentrating on their specialities such as the city's best egg-steamed crab, roast duck or shark's fin but even here competition is intense from hotels who are competing for events such as weddings and business banquets that previously were held in restaurants.

Based on: Anonymous (1996)[57]

readership figures broken down by social class groupings. Indeed one of the most widely used classification is based upon the National Readership Survey that was designed to measure readership of certain magazines and newspapers. Each occupation is placed in one of the six social classes shown in Table 3.3.

Recently, however, the use of social class to explain differences in consumer behaviour has been criticized. Certainly social class categories may not relate to differences in disposable income. It is perfectly possible for a household in the C2 or D category to have more disposable income than an AB household (after, say, mortgage and private education payments). Also within the C2 group (skilled manual workers) it has been found that some people spend a high proportion of their income on buying their own house, furniture, carpets and in-home entertainment, while others prefer to spend their money on more transitory pleasures such as drinking, smoking and playing bingo. Clearly social class fails to distinguish between these contrasting consumption patterns. Nevertheless, two important studies by the Market Research Society and by O'Brien and Ford have produced similar conclusions when measuring the discriminatory power of social class compared to other methods such as lifestyle, and life-stage analysis:[58,59]

1 Social class provides satisfactory power to discriminate between consumption patterns (e.g. owning a dishwasher, having central heating, privatization share ownership).

2 No alternative classification provides consistently better discriminatory power.

3 No one classification system works best across all product fields.

To which O'Brien and Ford added a fourth conclusion:

4 Sometimes other classifications discriminate better and often are just as powerful as social class.

The implication is that social class as a predictive measure of consumption differences is not dead but can usefully be supplemented by other measures such as life stage and lifestyle.

Geodemographics

An alternative method of classifying households is based upon their geographic location. This analysis—called **geodemographics**—is based upon population census data. Households are grouped into geographic clusters based upon such information as type of accommodation, car ownership, age, occupation, number and age of

Table 3.3	Social class		
Social grade	Social status	Occupation	Percentage in UK population (all adults over 15 years old)
A	Upper middle class	Higher managerial, administrative or professional	2.8
B	Middle class	Intermediate managerial, administrative or professional	18.8
C1	Lower middle class	Supervisory or clerical, and junior managerial, administrative or professional	27.5
C2	Skilled working class	Skilled manual workers	22.1
D	Working class	Semi-skilled or unskilled manual workers	17.6
E	Those at lowest level of subsistence	State pensioners or widows (no other earner), casual or lowest grade workers	11.4

Based upon grades of the chief income earner
Source: National Readership Survey, July 1998–June 1999

children and (since 1991) ethnic background. These clusters can be identified by means of their postcodes so that targeting households by mail is easy. There are a number of systems in use in the UK including PINPOINT and MOSAIC but the best known is ACORN (A Classification of Residential Neighbourhoods) which has identified eleven neighbourhood types. These are discussed in more detail in Chapter 7 on market segmentation and positioning, as they form an effective method of segmenting many markets including financial services and retailing. ACORN has proven to be a powerful discriminator between different life-styles, purchasing patterns and media exposure.[60]

Reference groups

The term **reference group** is used to indicate a group of people that influences an individual's attitude or behaviour. Where a product is conspicuous, for example clothing or cars, the brand or model chosen may have been strongly influenced by what buyers perceive as acceptable to their reference group. They may consist of the family, a group of friends or work colleagues. Some reference groups may be formal (e.g. members of a club or society) while others may be informal (friends with similar interests). Reference groups influence their members by the roles and norms expected of them. For example students may have to play several roles. To lecturers the role may be as a learner; to other students, the role may vary from peer to social companion. Depending on the role, various behaviours may be expected based upon group norms. To the extent that group norms influence values and attitudes, these reference groups may be seen as an important determinant of behaviour. Sometimes reference group norms can conflict as when reference to

the learning role suggests different patterns of behaviour from that of social companion. In consumption terms reference group influence can affect student purchasing of clothing, drink, social events and textbooks, for example. The more conspicuous the choice is to the reference group, the stronger is its influence.

An opinion leader is someone in a reference group to whom other members seek guidance on a particular topic. As such opinion leaders can exert enormous power on purchase decisions. As opinion leaders on the type of off-the-road, four-wheel-drive vehicle to buy, the British Royal Family act as significant opinion leaders. The sight of members of royalty driving Range Rovers on television and in newspapers and magazines is invaluable publicity indicating the right model to buy.

Summary

This chapter has examined three key dimensions of consumer buying behaviour: who are important in the buying decisions, how they buy, and what choice criteria they use. These dimensions are affected by three factors: the buying situation, personal influences and social influences.

Three types of buying situations are extended, limited and habitual problem solving. Six personal influences are information processing, motivation, beliefs and attitudes, personality, lifestyle, and life cycle. Social influences include culture, social class, geodemographics, and reference groups. Marketing managers need to be aware of these influences and their effects on consumer behaviour, and their implications for marketing decision-making.

Internet exercise

Consumer behaviour

Sites to visit
http://www.ncc.org.uk
http://www.consumer.gov.uk/

Exercise
What roles can private and public consumer bodies play in a modern economy?

Study questions

1   Choose a recent purchase that included not only yourself but also other people in making the decision. What role(s) did you play in the buying centre? What roles did these other people play and how did they influence your choice?

2   What decision-making process did you go through? At each stage—need recognition, information search, etc.—try to remember what you were thinking about and what activities took place.

3   What choice criteria did you use? Did they change between drawing up a short list and making the final choice?

4   Think of the last time you made an impulse purchase. What stimulated you to buy? Have you bought the brand again?

Why or why not? Did your thoughts and actions resemble those suggested by the Ehrenberg and Goodhart model?

5   Can you think of a brand that has used the principles of classical conditioning in its advertising?

6   Are there any brands that you buy (e.g. beer, perfume) that have personalities that match your own?

7   To what kind of lifestyle do you aspire? How does this affect the type of products (particularly visible ones) you buy now and in the future?

8   Are you influenced by any reference groups? How does this group influence what you buy?

References

1.   Leeflang, P. S. H. and W. F. van Raaij (1995) The Changing Consumer in the European Union: A Meta-Analysis, *International Journal of Research in Marketing*, **12**, 373–87.

2.   Blackwell R. D., P.W. Miniard and J. F. Engel (2000) *Consumer Behavior*, Orlando, FL: Dryden, 174.

3.   Woodside, A. G. and W. H. Mote (1979) Perceptions of Marital Roles in Consumer Processes for Six Products, in Beckwith *et al.* (eds) *American Marketing Association Educator Proceedings*, Chicago: American Marketing Association, 214–19.

4.   Donation, S. (1989) Study Boosts Men's Buying Role, *Advertising Age*, 4 December, 48.

5.   Anonymous (1990) Business Bulletin, *Wall Street Journal*, 17 May, A1.

6.   Weinberg, C. B. and R. S. Winer (1983) Working Wives and Major Family Expenditures: Replication and Extension, *Journal of Consumer Research*, **7** (September), 259–63.

7.   Bellante, D. and A. C. Foster (1984) Working Wives and Expenditure on Services, *Journal of Consumer Research*, **11** (September), 700–7.

8.   Swasey, A. (1990) Family Purse Strings Falls into Young Hands, *Wall Street Journal*, 2 February, B1.

9.   Moore-Shaw, E. S. and W. L. Wilkie (1988) Recent Developments in Research on Family Decisions, *Advances in Consumer Research*, **15**, 454–60.

10.   Spiro, R. L. (1983) Persuasion in Family Decision-Making, *Journal of Consumer Research*, **9** (March), 393–402.

11.   Blackwell, Miniard and Engel (1990) op. cit., 16–28.

12.   Hawkins, D. I., R. J. Best and K. A. Coney (1989) *Consumer Behaviour: Implications for Marketing Strategy*, Boston, Mass: Irwin, 536.

13.   O'Shaughnessey, J. (1987) *Why People Buy*, New York: Oxford University Press, 161.

14.   Baumgartner, H. and J.-Bem Steenkamp (1996) Exploratory Consumer Buying Behaviour: Conceptualisation and Measurement, *International Journal of Research in Marketing*, **13**, 121–37.

15.   Kuusela, H., M.T. Spence and A.J. Kanto (1998) Expertise Effects on Prechoice Decision Processes and Final Outcomes: A Protocol Analysis, *European Journal of Marketing*, **32** (5/6), 559–76.

16.   Creusen, M. E. H. and J. P. L. Schoormans (1997) The Nature of Differences between Similarity and Preference Judgements: A Replication and Extension, *International Journal of Research in Marketing*, **14**, 81–7.

17.   Blackwell, Miniard and Engel (1993) op. cit., 34.

18.   Elliott, R. and E. Hamilton (1991) Consumer Choice Tactics and Leisure Activities, *International Journal of Advertising*, **10**, 325–32.

19.   Hamel, G. and J. Sampler (1998) The E-Corporation, *Fortune*, 7 December, 80–9.

20.   Ajzen, I. and M. Fishbein (1980) *Understanding Attitudes and Predicting Social Behaviour*, Englewood Cliffs, NJ: Prentice-Hall.

21.   See e.g. Budd, R. J. and C. P. Spencer (1984) Predicting Undergraduates' Intentions to Drink, *Journal of Studies on Alcohol*, **45** (2), 179–83; Farley, J., D. Lehman and M. Ryan (1981) Generalizing from 'Imperfect' Replication, *Journal of Business*, **54** (4), 597–610; Shimp, T. and A. Kavas (1984) The Theory of Reasoned Action Applied to Coupon Usage, *Journal of Consumer Research*, **11**, 795–809.

22. Ehrenberg, A. S. C. and G. J. Goodhart (1980) *How Advertising Works*, J. Walter Thompson/MRCA.

23. Wright, P. L. (1974) The Choice of a Choice Strategy: Simplifying vs. Optimizing, Faculty Working Paper no. 163, Champaign, Ill: Department of Business Administration, University of Illinois.

24. Rothschild, M. L. (1978) Advertising Strategies for High and Low Involvement Situations, *American Marketing Association Educator's Proceedings*, Chicago: 150-62.

25. Rothschild (1978) op. cit.

26. For a discussion of the role of involvement in package labelling see Davies, M. A. P. and L. T. Wright (1994) The Importance of Labelling Examined in Food Marketing, *European Journal of Marketing*, **28** (2) 57-67.

27. Elliott, R. (1997) Understanding Buyers: Implications for Selling, in D. Jobber (ed.) *The CIM Handbook of Selling and Sales Strategy*, Oxford: Butterworth-Heinemann.

28. See Elliott, R. (1998) A Model of Emotion-Driven Choice, *Journal of Marketing Management*, **14**, 95-108; Rook, D. (1987) The Buying Impulse, *Journal of Consumer Research*, **14** (1), 89-99.

29. Hawkins, Best and Coney (1989) op. cit., 664-5.

30. Mowen, J. C. (1988) Beyond Consumer Decision Making, *Journal of Consumer Research*, **5** (1), 15-25.

31. Elliot and Hamilton (1991) op. cit.

32. Hawkins, Best and Coney (1989) op. cit., 30.

33. Engel, Blackwell and Miniard (1990) op. cit., 29.

34. Bettman, J. R. (1982) A Functional Analysis of the Role of Overall Evaluation of Alternatives and Choice Processes, in Mitchell, A. (ed.) *Advances in Consumer Research 8*, Ann Arbor, Mich: Association for Consumer Research, 87-93.

35. Laurent, G. and J. N. Kapferer (1985) Measuring Consumer Involvement Profiles, *Journal of Marketing Research*, **12** (February), 41-53.

36. Thomson, H. (1998) What do your customers really want? *Journal of Business Strategy*, 19 (4), 17-22.

37. Engel, Blackwell and Miniard (1990) op. cit., 363.

38. Williams, K. C. (1981) *Behavioural Aspects of Marketing*, London: Heinemann.

39. Hawkins, Best and Coney (1989) op. cit., 275.

40. Ratneshwar, S., L. Warlop, D. G. Mick and G. Seegar (1997) Benefit Salience and Consumers' Selective Attention to Product Features, *International Journal of Research in Marketing*, **14**, 245-9.

41. Levin, L. P. and G. J. Gaeth (1988) Framing of Attribute Information Before and After Consuming the Product, *Journal of Consumer Research*, **15** (December), 374-78.

42. Key, A. (2000) The Colour-Coded Secrets of Brands, *Marketing*, 6 January, 21.

43. Hawkins, Best and Coney (1989) op. cit., 317.

44. Ries, A. and J. Trout (1982) *Positioning: The Battle for your Mind*, New York: Warner.

45. Luthans, F. (1981) *Organisational Behaviour*, San Francisco: McGraw-Hill.

46. Jones, H. (1996) Psychological Warfare, *Marketing Week*, 2 February, 32-5.

47. Maslow, A. H. (1954) *Motivation and Personality*, New York: Harper and Row, 80-106.

48. Van Trijp, H. C. M., W. D. Hoyer and J. J. Inman (1996) Why Switch? Product Category-Level Explanations for True Variety-Seeking Behaviour, *Journal of Marketing Research*, **33**, August, 281-92.

49. Kassarjan, H. H. (1971) Personality and Consumer Behaiour: A Review, *Journal of Marketing Research*, November, 409-18.

50. Ackoff, R. L. and J. R. Emsott (1975) Advertising at Anheuser-Busch, Inc., *Sloan Management Review*, Spring, 1-15.

51. Lunn, T., S. Baldwin and J. Dickens (1982) Monitoring Consumer Lifestyles, *Admap*, November, 18-23.

52. O'Brien, S. and R. Ford (1988) Can We At Last Say Goodbye to Social Class? *Journal of the Market Research Society*, **30** (3), 289-332.

53. Bamossy, G. and S. Dawson (1991) A Comparison of the Culture of Consumption between Two Western Cultures: A Study of Materialism in the Netherlands and United States, *Proceedings of the European Marketing Academy Conference*, Dublin, May, 147-68.

54. Mitchell, A. (2000) Brands Must Become Total Solution Providers, *Marketing Week*, 27 April, 38-9.

55. Teanby, D. (1999) Changing Times in Retail, *Admap*, May, 21-4.

56. Willman, J. (2000) Myhome Offers to Clean Your Home, *Financial Times*, 13 March, I.

57. Anonymous (1996) Chinese Restaurants Under the Knife, *The Economist*, 16 November, 113.

58. Anonymous (1981) *An Evaluation of Social Grade Validity*, London: Market Research Society.

59. O'Brien and Ford (1988) op. cit., 309.

60. Baker, K., J. Germingham and C. Macdonald (1979) The Utility to Market Research of the Classification of Residential Neighbourhoods, *Market Research Society Conference*, Brighton: March, 206-17.

Key terms

buying centre   a group who are involved in the buying decision (also known as a decision-making unit)

consumer decision-making process   the stages a consumer goes through when buying something, namely, problem awareness, information search, evaluation of alternatives, purchase and post-purchase evaluation

information search   the identification of alternative ways of problem solving

awareness set   the set of brands that the consumer is aware may provide a solution to the problem

evoked set   the set of brands that the consumer seriously evaluates before making a purchase

beliefs   descriptive thoughts that a person holds about something

attitude   the degree to which a customer or prospect likes or dislikes a brand

cognitive dissonance   post-purchase concerns of a consumer arising from uncertainty as to whether a decision to purchase was the correct one

information processing   the process by which a stimulus is received, interpreted, stored in memory and later retrieved

choice criteria   the various attributes (and benefits) people use when evaluating products and services

perception   the process by which people select, organize and interpret sensory stimulation into a meaningful picture of the world

selective attention   the process by which people screen out those stimuli that are not meaningful to them nor consistent with their experiences and beliefs

selective distortion   the distortion of information received by people according to their existing beliefs and attitudes

information framing   the way in which information is presented to people

selective retention   the process by which people only retain a selection of messages in memory

classical conditioning   the process of using an established relationship between a stimulus and a response to cause the learning of the same response to a different stimulus

operant conditioning   the use of rewards to generate reinforcement of response

cognitive learning   the learning of knowledge and development of beliefs and attitudes without direct reinforcement

rote learning   the learning of two or more concepts without conditioning

vicarious learning   learning from others without direct experience or reward

reasoning   a more complex form of cognitive learning where conclusions are reached by connected thought

motivation   the process involving needs that set drives in motion to accomplish goals

personality   the inner psychological characteristics of individuals that lead to consistent responses to their environment

lifestyle   the pattern of living as expressed in a person's activities, interests and opinions

culture   the traditions, taboos, values, and basic attitudes of the whole society in which an individual lives

geodemographics   the process of grouping households into geographic clusters based upon such information as type of accommodation, occupation, number and age of children and ethnic background

reference group   a group of people that influences an individual's attitude or behaviour

Consumer Behaviour Exercise 1: Understanding Consumer Decision-Making

Choose one of the four types of product shown below and conduct a depth interview to try to understand how the product was bought, the choice criteria used to evaluate competing brands and who influenced the choice.

1 Motor car.

2 Breakfast cereal.

3 Foreign holiday.

4 Pair of jeans.

Locate someone who has recently bought one of these products and ask their consent to interview them. Prepare an interview schedule listing the topics you wish to cover. Below are a number of issues you may wish to include. These are guidelines only and presented in random order. Your task is to choose those topics you believe are important and structure the interview in a logical way recognizing that you need to be flexible enough to allow the interviewee scope to discuss issues that are important to her or him. Remember to talk their language, not jargon.

Guideline discussion areas

1 Information search—how much information was gathered, what sources were used?

2 What triggered the purchase?

3 How long did the decision-making process take? What were the stages?

4 Who forms the decision-making unit? What roles did they play?

5 What choice criteria did they use? Were different criteria used at different stages of the decision-making process? What were the respective roles of technical, economical, social and personal criteria?

6 How many alternatives were considered?

You may use a cassette recorder or notes to record responses. Prepare a report and a short presentation to communicate the main findings.

This exercise was prepared by David Jobber, Professor of Marketing , University of Bradford.

Consumer Behaviour Exercise 2:
The Symbolic Meaning of Brands

Branded consumer products are often purchased in large part for their symbolic meaning, that is, what they communicate about us to other people. Collect three advertisements that you think are focusing on the symbolic meaning of a product and identify how the ads are attempting to influence their target market. What do you see as the key advantages and disadvantages of using symbolic meaning as a branding strategy?

This exercise was prepared by Richard Elliott, Professor of Marketing and Consumer Research, University of Exeter.

CHAPTER FOUR

Understanding Organizational Buying Behaviour

'People are people at work or at play'

ANONYMOUS

Learning Objectives *This chapter explains:*

1   The characteristics of organizational buying

2   The dimensions of organizational buying

3   The nature and marketing implications of who buys, how organizations buy and the choice criteria used to evaluate products, services and suppliers

4   The influences on organizational buying behaviour—the buy class, product type and purchase importance—and their marketing implications

5   The developments in purchasing practice: just-in-time and centralized purchasing, reverse marketing and leasing

6   The nature of relationship marketing and how to build customer relationships

7   The development of buyer–seller partnerships

Organizational buying concerns the purchase of products and services for use in an organization's activities. There are three types of organizational markets. First, the *industrial market* concerns those companies that buy products and services to help them produce other goods and services. Industrial goods include raw materials, components and capital goods such as machinery. Second, the *reseller market* comprises organizations that buy products and services to resell. Mail order companies, retailers, and supermarkets are examples of resellers. Manufacturers of consumer goods such as toys, groceries and furniture require an understanding of the reseller market since, as we shall see with the marketing of Müller yoghurt in Chapter 8, success depends on persuading resellers to stock their products. Third, the *government market* consists of government agencies that buy products and services to help them carry out their activities. Purchases for local authorities and defence are examples.

An understanding of organizational buying behaviour in all of these markets is a prerequisite for marketing success. One of the fascinating aspects of marketing to organizations is that different players in the buying company may be evaluating suppliers' offerings along totally choice criteria. The key is to be able to satisfy these diverse requirements in a single offering. A product which gives engineers the performance characteristics they demand, production managers the delivery reliability they need, purchasing managers the value for money they seek and the shopfloor workers the ease of installation they desire is likely to be highly successful. This complexity of organizational buying makes marketing an extremely interesting task.

This chapter examines some characteristics of organizational buying and marketing before examining the three key elements of buying identified in Chapter 3: who buys, how they buy, and what choice criteria they use. For each element the marketing implications will be addressed. Finally, some recent developments in purchasing practice—just-in-time purchasing, materials, requirement planning, centralized purchasing and reverse marketing—will be discussed and the implications for marketing explored.

Characteristics of organizational buying

Nature and size of customers

Typically the number of customers in organizational markets will be small. The Pareto rule often applies with 80 per cent of output being sold to 20 per cent of customers who may number fewer than twelve. The reseller market is a case in point where Tesco, Sainsbury and Asda account for the dominant share of supermarket sales in the UK. Similarly in the industrial market component suppliers to the UK motor car industry sell to a small number of large car manufacturers: Ford, Vauxhall, Rover, Nissan, Toyota and Honda. Clearly the importance of one customer is paramount. If a component supplier loses the Ford account, or Kelloggs loses the Tesco account this would have a serious impact on sales (and careers). Because order sizes are large it becomes economic to sell directly from manufacturer to organizational customer, dispensing with the services of middlemen. Also, the importance of large customers makes it sensible to invest in close, long-term relationships with them. Dedicated sales and marketing teams are sometimes used to service large accounts.

Complexity of buying

Often, organizational purchases, notably those which involve large sums of money and which are new to the company, involve many people at different levels of the organization. The managing director, product engineers, production managers, purchasing managers and operatives may influence the decision of which expensive machine to purchase. The sales task may be to influence as many of these people as possible and may involve multilevel selling by means of a sales team, rather than an individual salesperson.[1]

Economic and technical choice criteria

Although organizational buyers, being people, are affected by emotional factors, such as like or dislike of a salesperson, organizational buying is often made on economic and technical criteria. This is because organizational buyers have to justify their decisions to other members of their organization.[2] Also the formalization of the buying function through the establishment of purchasing departments leads to the use of economic rather than emotional choice criteria. As purchasing becomes more sophisticated, economic criteria came to the fore with techniques such as life cycle cost and value-in-use analysis. British Rail, for example, calculates the life cycle costs including purchase price, running and maintenance costs when commissioning a new diesel locomotive.

Risks

Industrial markets are sometimes characterized by a contact being agreed before the product is made. Further, the product itself may be highly technical and the seller may be faced with unforeseen problems once work has started. Thus, Scott-Lithgow won an order to build an oil rig for British Petroleum, but the price proved uneconomic given the nature of the problems associated with its construction. In the government market, GEC won the contract to develop the Nimrod surveillance system for the Ministry of Defence, but technical problems caused the project to be terminated with much money being wasted. British Rail had technical problems with the commissioning of the Class 60 diesel locomotive built by Brush Traction although these were eventually resolved.

Buying to specific requirements

Because of the large sums of money involved organizational buyers sometimes draw up product specifications and ask suppliers to design their products to meet them. Services, too, are often conducted to specific customer requirements, marketing research and advertising services being examples. This is much less a feature of consumer marketing, where a product offering may be developed to meet a need of a market segment but, beyond that, meeting individual needs would prove uneconomic.

Reciprocal buying

Because an industrial buyers may be in a powerful negotiating position with a seller, it may be possible to demand concessions in return for placing an order. In some situations, buyers may demand that sellers buy some of their products in return for securing the order. For example, in negotiating to buy computers a company like Volvo might persuade a supplier to buy a fleet of Volvo company cars.

Derived demand

The demand for many organizational goods is derived from the demand for consumers goods. If the demand for compact disks increases, the demand for the raw materials and machinery used to make the disks will also expand. Clearly raw material and machinery suppliers would be wise to monitor consumer trends and buying characteristics as well as their immediate organizational customers. A further factor based upon the derived demand issue is the tendency for demand for some industrial goods and services to be more volatile than that for consumer goods and services. For example a small fall in demand for compact disks may mean the complete cessation of orders for the machinery to make them. Similarly a small increase in demand if manufacturers are working at full capacity may mean a massive increase in demand for machinery as investment to meet the extra demand is made. This is known as the *accelerator principle*.[3]

Negotiations

Because of the existence of professional buyers and sellers, and the size and complexity of organization buying, negotiation is often important. Thus supermarkets will negotiate with manufacturers about price since their buying power allows them to obtain discounts. Car manufacturers will negotiate attractive prices from tyre manufacturers such as Pirelli and Michelin since the replacement brand may be dependent upon the tyre fitted to the new car. The supplier's list price may be regarded as the starting-point for negotiation and the profit margin ultimatcly achieved will be heavily influenced by the negotiating skills of the seller. The implication is that sales and marketing personnel need to be conversant with negotiation skills and tactics. These will be discussed in Chapter 12 which covers personal selling.

The dimensions of organizational buying behaviour

As with consumer behaviour, marketing to organizations involves the understanding of who buys, how they buy, the choice criteria used, where and when they buy. As in Chapter 3 we shall examine the first three of these issues in detail.

Who buys

An important point to understand in organizational buying is that the buyer or purchasing officer is often not the only person who influences the decision, or who actually has the authority to make the ultimate decision. Rather, the decision is in the hands of a ***decision-making unit*** (DMU), or buying centre as it is sometimes called. This is not necessarily a fixed entity. Members of the DMU may change as the decision-making process continues. Thus a managing director may be involved in the decision that new equipment should be purchased, but not in the decision as to which manufacturer to buy it from. Six roles have been identified in the structure of the DMU:[4]

1 *Initiators*: those who begin the purchase process, e.g. maintenance contracts.

2 *Users*: those who actually use the product, e.g. welders.

3 *Deciders*: those who have authority to select the supplier/model, e.g. production managers.

4 *Influencers*: those who provide information and add decision criteria throughout the process, e.g. accountants.

5 *Buyers*: those who have authority to execute the contractual arrangements, e.g. purchasing.

6 *Gatekeepers*: those who control the flow of information, e.g. secretaries who may allow or prevent access to a DMU member, or a buyer whose agreement must be sought before a supplier can contact other members of the DMU.

For very important decisions the structure of the DMU will be complex, involving numerous people within the buying organization. The marketing task is to identify and reach the key members in order to convince them of the product's worth. Often communicating only to the purchasing officer will be insufficient, as this person may be only a minor influence on supplier choice. Relationship management (discussed later in this chapter) is of key importance in many organizational markets.

When the problem to be solved is highly technical, suppliers may work with engineers

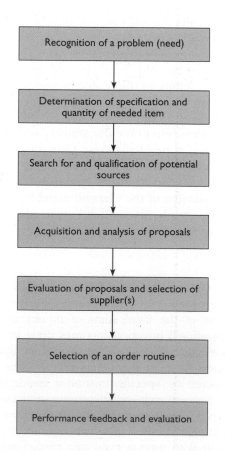

Figure 4.1 Buy phases: the organizational decision-making process

in the buying organization in order to solve problems and secure the order. An example where this approach was highly successful involved a small company who won a large order from a major car company owing to its ability to work with them in solving the technical problems associated with the development of an exhaust gas recirculation valve.[5] In this case, their policy was to work with company engineers and to keep the purchasing department out of the decision until the last possible moment, by which time only they were qualified to supply the part.

Often organizational purchases are made in committees where the salesperson will not be present. The salesperson's task is to identify a person from within the decision-making unit who is a positive advocate and champion of the supplier's product. This person (or 'coach') should be given all the information needed to win the arguments which may take place within the decision-making unit. For example, even though the advocate may be a technical person, he or she should be given financial information which may be necessary to justify buying the most technologically superior product.

Where DMU members are inaccessible to salespeople, advertising or direct mail may be used as an alternative. Also where users are an important influence and the product is relatively inexpensive and consumable, free samples may be effective in generating preference.

How they buy

Figure 4.1 describes the *decision-making process* for an organizational product.[6] The exact nature of the process will depend on the buying situation. In some situations some stages will be omitted; for example in a routine re-buy situation the purchasing officer is unlikely to pass through the third, fourth and fifth stages (search for suppliers and analysis and evaluation of their proposals). These stages will be bypassed, as the buyer, recognizing a need—perhaps shortage of stationery—routinely reorders from an existing supplier. In general, the more complex the decision and the more expensive the item, the more likely it is that each stage will be passed through and that the process will take more time.

Recognition of a problem (need)

Needs and problems may be recognized through either *internal or external factors*.[7] An example of an internal factor would be the realization of undercapacity leading to the decision to purchase plant or equipment. Thus, internal recognition leads to active behaviour (internal/active). Some problems which are recognized internally may not be acted upon. This condition may be termed internal/passive. A production manager may realize that there is a problem with a machine but, given more pressing problems, decide to put up with it. Other potential problems may not be recognized internally, and become problems only because of external cues. Production managers may be quite satisfied with the production process until they are made aware of another more efficient method. Clearly, these different problems have important implications for marketing and sales. The internal/passive condition implies that there is an opportunity for a salesperson, having identified the condition, to highlight the problem by careful analysis of cost inefficiencies and other symptoms, so that the problem is perceived to be more pressing and in need of solution (internal/active). The internal/active situation requires the supplier to demonstrate a differential advantage of its products over the competition. In this situation problem stimulation is unnecessary, but where internal recognition is absent, the marketer can provide the necessary external cues. A fork-lift truck sales representative might stimulate problem recognition by showing how the truck can save the customer money, due to lower maintenance costs, and lead to more efficient use of warehouse space through higher lifting capabilities. Advertising or direct mail could also be used to good effect.

Determination of specification and quantity of needed item

At this stage of the decision-making process the DMU will draw up a description of what is required. For example, it might decide that five lathes are required to meet certain specifications. The ability of marketers to influence the specification can give their company an advantage at later stages of the process. By persuading the buying company to specify features that only their product possesses, the sale may be virtually closed

Ireland.
A different place to meet.

What's

on

top of

the

Ireland agenda?

A great conference needs a great place to happen.
And things really happen in Ireland. Barely an hour by plane
and you'll find everything you dreamt of and a lot more besides.
Like golf or a chance to entertain guests at the races.
Food fit for a king. A zest for life and marvellous places
to live it. Between the Welcome and the Wrap-up speeches we
promise you a conference to remember. So before you forget,
put Ireland at the top of your list. For more information
about conference opportunities in Ireland call on

020 7518 0800
www.ireland.travel.co.uk

Ireland Travel create awareness and present the benefits of Ireland as a conference venue to business people at this stage. This is the process of setting up *lock-out criteria*.

Search for and qualification of potential sources

A great deal of variation in the degree of search takes place in industrial buying. Generally speaking, the cheaper and less important the item, and the more information the buyer possesses, the less search takes place. Marketers can use advertising to ensure that their brands are in the buyers' awareness set and are, therefore, considered when evaluating alternatives. The illustration opposite shows Ireland Travel creating awareness and selling their benefits of Ireland as a conference venue.

Acquisition and analysis of proposals

Having found a number of companies who, perhaps through their technical expertise and general reputation, are considered to be qualified to supply the product, proposals will be called and analysis of them undertaken.

Evaluation of proposals and selection of supplier(s)

Each proposal will be evaluated in the light of the choice criteria deemed to be more important to each DMU member. It is important to realize that various members may use different criteria when judging proposals. Although this may cause problems, the outcome of this procedure is the selection of a supplier or suppliers.

Selection of an order routine

Next the details of payment and delivery are drawn up. Usually this is conducted by the purchasing officer. In some buying decisions this stage is merged into the acquisition and evaluation stages when delivery is an important consideration in selecting a supplier.

Performance feedback and evaluation

This may be formal, where a purchasing department draws up an evaluation form for user departments to complete, or informal through everyday conversations.

The implications of all this are that sales and marketing strategy can affect a sale through influencing need recognition, through the design of product specifications and by clearly presenting the advantages of the product or service over competition in terms which are relevant to DMU members. By early involvement, a company can benefit through the process of *creeping commitment*, whereby the buying organization becomes increasingly committed to one supplier through its involvement in the process and the technical assistance it provides.

Choice criteria

This aspect of industrial buyer behaviour refers to the criteria used by members of the DMU to evaluate supplier proposals. These criteria are likely to be determined by the performance criteria used to evaluate the members themselves.[8] Thus purchasing managers who are judged by the extent to which they reduce purchase expenditure are likely to be more cost conscious than production engineers who are evaluated in terms of the technical efficiency of the production process they design.

As with consumers, organizational buying is characterized by *technical, economic, social (organizational) and personal criteria*. Key considerations may be, for plant and equipment, return on investment, while for materials and components parts they may be cost savings, together with delivery reliability, quality and technical assistance. Because of the high costs associated with production down-time, a key concern of many purchasing departments is the long-run development of the organization's supply system. Personal factors may also be important, particularly when suppliers' product offerings are essentially similar. In this situation the final decision may rest upon the relative liking for the supplier's salesperson. The Vodaphone advertisement overleaf illustrates the importance of economic criteria in organizational buying.

Customers' *choice criteria* can change in different regions of the world. For example, Xerox is generally known as a company that provides solutions for creating documents. In the West, when choosing a printer, a consumer considers the print quality and how easy the machine is to network and update. In Eastern Europe other choice criteria prevail. Networking and servicing

ahead ⊘ for business Group Saver is a unique tariff that lets you pool all the inclusive minutes of your company's Vodafone mobiles. By allowing you to share between 150 and 7,500 minutes across as many as 100 handsets, you can be sure everyone in your business has all the call-time they need. And because you only receive one bill, you won't waste time wading through endless paperwork. It's just one of the ways Vodafone's Ahead for Business programme is helping companies make the most of their mobiles. So sign up today, call Vodafone on 08080 808080 and let the world come to you.

vodafone
YOU ARE HERE

Vodafone recognise the importance of economic choice criteria in organizational buying

are not issues that are considered very much, rather value for money is the key. The consumer attitude is: 'I can buy a Xerox, or I can buy a Canon and a car'. The marketing task for Xerox is to reduce the consumer's price sensitivity by stressing its reliability, quality, after-sales service, wide range of suppliers and medium- to long-term value for money.[9]

What are the range of motives that key players in organizations use to compare supplier offerings? Economic considerations play a part because commercial firms have profit objectives and work within budgetary constraints. Emotional factors should not be ignored, however, as decisions are made by people who do not suddenly lose their personalities, personal likes and dislikes and prejudices simply because they are at work. Let us examine a number of important technical and economic motives (quality, price and life cycle costs, and continuity of supply) and then some organizational and personal factors (perceived risk, office politics, and personal liking/disliking).

Quality

The emergence of **total quality management** as a key aspect of organizational life reflects the important of quality in evaluating suppliers' products and services. Many buying organizations are unwilling to trade quality for price. In particular, buyers are looking for consistency of product or service quality so that end products (e.g. motor cars) are reliable, inspection costs are reduced and production processes run smoothly. They are installing just-in-time delivery systems which rely upon incoming supplies being quality guaranteed. Jaguar cars under Sir John Egan moved from a price-orientated purchasing system to one where quality was central and purchasing were instructed to pay more provided the price could be justified in terms of improved quality of components. Marketing in Action 4.1 describes the moves made by Nissan in the UK to build quality into its cars.

Price and life cycle costs

For materials and components of similar specification and quality, price becomes a key consideration. For standard items such as ball-bearings, price may be critical to making a sale given that a number of suppliers can meet delivery and specification requirements. However, it should not be forgotten that price is only one component of cost for many buying organizations. Increasingly buyers take into account **life cycle costs** which may include productivity savings, maintenance costs and residual values as well as initial purchase price when evaluating products. Marketers can use life cycle costs analysis to break into an account. By calculating life cycle costs with a buyer, new perceptions of value may be achieved.

Continuity of supply

Another major cost to a company is a disruption of a production run. Delays of this kind can mean costly machine down-time and even lost sales. Continuity of supply is, therefore, a prime consideration in many purchase situations. Companies which perform badly on this criteria lose out even if the price is competitive because a small percentage price edge does not compare with the costs of unreliable delivery. Supplier companies who can guarantee deliveries and realize their promises can achieve a significant differential advantage in the marketplace. Organizational customers are demanding close relationships with *accredited suppliers* who can guarantee reliable supply, perhaps on a just-in-time basis.

Perceived risk

Perceived risk can come in two forms: *functional risk* such as the uncertainty with respect to product or supplier performance, and *psychological risk* such as criticism from work colleagues.[10] This latter risk—fear of upsetting the boss, losing status, being ridiculed by others in the department, or, indeed, losing one's job—can play a determining role in purchase decisions. Buyers often reduce uncertainty by gathering information about competing suppliers, checking the opinions of important others in the buying company, buying only from familiar and/or reputable suppliers and by spreading risk through multiple sourcing.

Office politics

Political factions within the buying company may also influence the outcome of a purchase decision. Interdepartmental conflict may manifest itself in the formation of competing camps over the purchase of a product or service. Because department X favours supplier 1, department Y automatically favours supplier 2. The outcome has not only purchasing implications but also political implications for the departments and individuals concerned.

Personal liking/disliking

A buyer may personally like one salesperson more than another and this may influence supplier choice, particularly when competing products are very similar. Even when supplier selection is on the basis of competitive bidding it is known for purchasers to help salespeople they like to be competitive.[11] Obviously perception is important in all organizational purchases as how someone behaves depends upon the perception of the situation. One buyer may perceive a salesperson as being honest, truthful and likeable while another may not. As with consumer behaviour, three selective processes may be at work on buyers:

1 *Selective attention*: only certain information sources may be sought.

2 *Selective distortion*: information from those sources may be distorted.

3 *Selective retention*: only some information may be remembered.

In general, people tend to distort, avoid and forget messages that are substantially different to their existing beliefs and attitudes.

Implications

The implications of understanding the content of the decision are that first appeals may need to change when communicating to different DMU members: discussion with a production engineer may centre on the technical superiority of the product offering, while much more emphasis on cost factors may prove effective, when talking to the purchasing officer. Furthermore, the criteria

4.1 Marketing in Action

Building Quality and Flexibility at Nissan

Nissan's Sunderland plant in north-east England is Europe's most productive car factory. Labour content is not the most important factor in a car's cost these days: components can account for up to two-thirds of cost. Nissan have not followed the traditional European practice of forcing down parts supplier prices to uneconomic levels by threatening to move business to a competitor. Such practices may drive down short-term costs but do nothing for the financial viability of the supplier, its relationship with the buyer nor for the quality of the component (and therefore the car).

Instead, Nissan cooperate on design and development with component suppliers to force up quality. Rejected parts have fallen from 5000 per million in 1990 to just 150. By implementing quality standards that are among the strictest in the industry and identifying problems in its own production processes so that they can be engineered out, Nissan is striving for the fault-free car at the end of the production line and satisfied customers on the road.

Since Renault bought a 37 per cent stake in Nissan in 1999 making it the world's fourth largest car group, Nissan is experiencing rapid change as customer expectations drive the need for even higher quality and flexible production methods. Customers will no longer tolerate an attitude which says they can have any colour so long as it is black. Manufacturing methods have moved to greater automation, shorter production runs and more flexible shift systems, to provide the greater choice of models customers demand.

Based on: Lewin (1996);[12] Lorenz (1999);[13] Milner and Bannister (1999)[14]

used by buying organizations change over time as circumstances change. Price may be relatively unimportant to a company when trying to solve a highly visible technical problem, and the order will be placed with the supplier who provides the necessary technical assistance. Later, after the problem has been solved and other suppliers become qualified, price may be of crucial significance.

Influences on organizational buying behaviour

Figure 4.2 shows the three factors which influence who and how organizations buy and the choice criteria they use: the buy class, the product type, and the importance of purchase.[15]

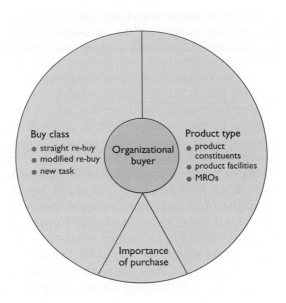

Figure 4.2 Influences on organizational purchasing behaviour

The buy class

Organizational purchases may be distinguished between a new task, a straight re-buy and a modified re-buy.[16] A *new task* occurs when the need for the product has not arisen previously so that there is little or no relevant experience in the company, and a great deal of information is required. A *straight re-buy* occurs where an organization buys previously purchased items from suppliers already judged acceptable. Routine purchasing procedures are set up to facilitate straight re-buys. The *modified re-buy* lies between the two extremes. A regular requirement for the type of product exists, and the buying alternatives are known, but sufficient change (e.g. a delivery problem) has occurred to require some alteration to the normal supply procedure.

The buy classes affect organizational buying in the following ways. First, the membership of the DMU changes. For a straight re-buy possibly only the purchasing officer is involved, whereas for a new buy senior management, engineers, production managers and purchasing officers may be involved. Modified re-buys often involve engineers, production managers and purchasing officers, but senior management, except when the purchase is critical to the company, is unlikely to be involved. Second, the decision-making process may be much longer as the buy class changes from a straight re-buy to a modified re-buy and to a new

task. Third, in terms of influencing DMU members, they are likely to be much more receptive for new task and modified re-buy situations than straight re-buys. In the latter case the purchasing manager has already solved the purchasing problem and has other problems to deal with. So why make it a problem again?

The first implication of this buy class analysis is that there are big gains to be made if a company can enter the new task at the start of the decision-making process. By providing information and helping with any technical problems which can arise, the company may be able to create goodwill and creeping commitment which secures the order when the final decision is made. The second implication is that since the decision process is likely to be long, and many people are involved in the new task, supplier companies need to invest heavily in sales personnel for a considerable period of time. Some firms employ missionary sales teams, comprising their best salespeople, to help secure big new-task orders.

Companies in straight re-buy situations must ensure that no change occurs when they are in the position of the supplier. Regular contact to ensure that the customer has no complaints may be necessary, and the buyer may be encouraged to use automatic reordering systems. For the out-supplier the task can be difficult unless poor service or some other factor has caused the buyer to become dissatisfied with the present supplier. The obvious objective of the out-supplier in this situation is to change the buy class from a straight re-buy to a modified re-buy. Price alone may not be enough since changing supplier represents a large personal risk to the purchasing officer. The new supplier's products might be less reliable, and delivery might be unpredictable. In order to reduce this risk, the company may offer delivery guarantees with penalty clauses and be very willing to accept a small (perhaps uneconomic) order at first in order to gain a foothold. Supplier acquisition of a total quality management standard such as EM29000, ISO9000 or BS5750 may also have the effect of reducing perceived buyer risk. Many straight re-buys are organized on a contract basis, and buyers may be more receptive to listening to non-suppliers prior to contract renewal.

Value analysis and life cycle cost calculations are other methods of moving purchases from a straight re-buy to a modified re-buy situation. *Value analysis*, which can be conducted by either supplier or buyer, is a method of cost reduction in which components are examined to see if they can be made more cheaply. The items are studied to identify unnecessary costs that do not add to the reliability or functionality of the product. By redesigning, standardizing or manufacturing by less expensive means, a supplier may be able to offer a product of comparable quality at lower cost. Simple redesigns like changing a curved edge to a straight one may have dramatic cost implications.[17] *Life cycle cost analysis* seeks to move the cost focus from the initial purchase price to the total cost of owning and using a product. There are three types of life cycle costs: purchase price, start-up costs, and post-purchase costs.[18] Start-up costs would include installation, lost production, and training costs. Post-purchase costs include operating (e.g. fuel, operator wages), maintenance, repair and inventory costs. Against these costs would be placed residual values (e.g. trade-in values of cars). Life cycle cost appeals can be powerful motivators. For example, if the out-supplier can convince the customer organization that its product has significantly lower post-purchase costs than the in-supplier despite a slightly higher purchase price, it may win the order. This is because it will be delivering a *higher economic value to the customer*. This can be a powerful competitive advantage and, at the same time, justify the premium price.

The product type

Products can be classified according to four types: materials, components, plant and equipment, and MROs (maintenance repair and operation):

1   Materials to be used in the production process, e.g. aluminium.

2   Components to be incorporated in the finished product, e.g. headlights.

3   Plant and equipment, e.g. bulldozer.

4   Products and services for maintenance repair and operation (MROs), e.g. spanners, welding equipment and lubricants.

This classification is based upon a customer perspective—how the product is used—and may be employed to identify differences in organizational buyer behaviour. First, the people who take part in the decision-making process tend to change according to product type. For example, senior management tend to get involved in the purchase of plant and equipment or, occasionally, when new materials are purchased if the change is of fundamental importance to company operations, e.g. if a move from aluminium to plastic is being considered. Rarely do they involve themselves in component or MRO supply. Similarly, design engineers tend to be involved in buying components and materials but not normally MRO and plant equipment. Second, the decision-making process tends to be slower and more complex as product type moves from:

> MRO → components → materials → plant and equipment

For MRO items, *blanket contracts* rather than periodic purchase orders are increasingly being used. The supplier agrees to resupply the buyer on agreed price terms over a period of time. Stock is held by the seller and orders are automatically printed out by the buyer's computer when stock falls below a minimum level. This has the advantage to the supplying company of effectively blocking the effort of the competitors for long periods of time.

Classification of suppliers' offerings by product type gives clues as to who is likely to be influenced in the purchase decision. The marketing task is then to confirm this in particular situations and attempts to reach those people involved. A company selling MROs is likely to be wasting effort attempting to communicate with design engineers, whereas attempts to reach operating management are likely to prove fruitful.

The importance of purchase

A purchase is likely to be perceived as being important to the buying organization when it involves large sums of money, when the cost of making the wrong decision, e.g. in production down-time is high and when there is considerable uncertainty about the outcome of alternative offerings. In such situations, many people at different organizational levels are likely to be involved in the decision and the process will be long, with extensive search and analysis of information. Thus extensive marketing effort is likely to be required, but great opportunities present themselves to sales teams who work with buying organizations to convince them that their offering has the best pay-off; this may involve acceptance trials, e.g. private diesel manufacturers supply railway companies with prototypes for testing, engineering support and testimonials from other users. Additionally, guarantees of delivery dates and after-sales service may be necessary when buyer uncertainty regarding these factors is high. An example of the time and effort which may be required to win very important purchases is the order secured by GEC to supply £250 million worth of equipment for China's largest nuclear power station. The contract was won after 6 years of negotiation, 33 GEC missions to China and 4000 person days of work.

Developments in purchasing practice

A number of trends have taken place within the purchasing function which have marketing implications for supplier firms. The advent of just-in-time purchasing and the increased tendency towards centralized purchasing, reverse marketing and leasing have all changed the nature of purchasing and altered the way in which suppliers compete.

Just-in-time purchasing

The just-in-time concept aims to minimize stocks by organizing a supply system which provides materials and components as they are required.[19] Stockholding costs are significantly reduced or eliminated and thus profits are increased. Furthermore, since the holding of stocks is a hedge against machine breakdowns, faulty parts and human error they may be seen as a cushion which acts as a disincentive to management to eliminate such inefficiencies.

A number of *just-in-time* (JIT) practices are also associated with improved quality. Suppliers are evaluated on their ability to provide high-quality products. The effect of this is that suppliers may place more emphasis on product quality. Buyers are encouraged to specify only essential product characteristics which means that suppliers have more discretion in product design and manufacturing methods. Also, the emphasis is on the supplier certifying quality which means that quality inspection at the buyer company is reduced and overall costs are minimized since quality control at source is more effective than further down the supply chain.

The total effects of JIT can be enormous. Purchasing inventory and inspection costs can be reduced, product design can be improved, delivery streamlined, production down-time reduced, and the quality of the finished item enhanced.

However, the implementation of JIT requires integration into both purchasing and production operations. Since the system requires the delivery of the exact amount of materials or components to the production line as they are required delivery schedules must be very reliable and suppliers must be prepared to make deliveries on a regular basis, perhaps even daily. Lead-times for ordering must be short and the number of defects be very low. An attraction for suppliers is that it is usual for long-term purchasing agreements to be drawn up. The marketing implications of the JIT concept is that to be competitive in many industrial markets, for example, motor cars, suppliers must be able to meet the requirements of this fast-growing system.

An example of a company that employs just-in-time is the Nissan car assembly plant at Sunderland in the UK. The importance of JIT to its operations has meant that the number of component suppliers in the north-east of England has increased from 3 when Nissan arrived in 1986 to 27 in 1992.[20] Nissan adopt what they term *synchronous supply*: parts are delivered only minutes before they are needed. For example, carpets are delivered by Sommer Allibert, a French supplier, from its nearby facility to the Nissan assembly line in sequence for fitting to the correct model. Only 42 minutes elapse between the carpet being ordered and fitted to the car. The stockholding of carpets for the Nissan Micra is now only 10 minutes. Just-in-time practices do carry risks, however, if labour stability cannot be guaranteed. Renault discovered this to their cost when a strike at their engine and gearbox plant caused their entire French and Belgian car production lines to close in only 10 days.

Centralized purchasing

Where several operating units within a company have common requirements and where there is an opportunity to strengthen a negotiating position by bulk buying, *centralized purchasing* is an attractive option. Centralization encourages purchasing specialists to concentrate their energies on a small group of products, thus enabling them to develop an extensive knowledge of cost factors and the operation of suppliers.[21] The move from local to centralized buying has important marketing implications. Localized buying tends to focus on short-term cost and profit considerations whereas centralized purchasing places more emphasis on long-term supply relationships. Outside influences, for example engineers, play a greater role in supplier choice in local purchasing organizations since less specialized buyers often lack the expertise and status to question the recommendations of technical people. The type of purchasing organization can therefore give clues to suppliers regarding the important people in the decision-making unit and their respective power positions.

Reverse marketing

The traditional view of marketing is that supplier firms will actively seek the requirements of customers and attempts to meet those needs better than the competition. This model places the initiative with the supplier. Purchasers could assume a passive dimension relying on their

Supplier sells by taking

Traditional marketing

Reverse marketing

Buyer takes initiative to persuade supplier to provide

Figure 4.3 Reverse marketing

suppliers' sensitivity to their needs, and technological capabilities to provide them with solutions to their problems. However, this trusting relationship is at odds with a new corporate purchasing situation that has developed during the 1980s and is gaining momentum. Purchasing is taking on a more proactive, aggressive stance in acquiring the products and services needed to compete. This process whereby the buyer attempts to persuade the supplier to provide exactly what the organization wants is called *reverse marketing*.[22] Zeneca, an international supplier of chemicals, uses reverse marketing very effectively to target suppliers with a customized list of requirements concerning delivery times, delivery success rates, and how often sales visits should occur. Figure 4.3 shows the difference between the traditional model and this new concept.

The essence of reverse marketing is that the purchaser takes the initiative in approaching new or existing suppliers and persuading them to meet their supply requirements. Marketing in Action 4.2 describes reverse marketing in action where it is used to acquire materials at lower cost and to develop a new technology for the manufacture of components. The implications of reverse marketing are that it may pose serious threats to non-cooperative in-suppliers but major opportunities to responsive in- and out-suppliers. The growth of reverse marketing presents two key benefits to suppliers who are willing to listen to the buyer's proposition and carefully consider its merits. First, it provides the opportunity to develop a stronger and longer-lasting relationship with the customer; and second, it may be a source of new product opportunities that may be developed to a broader customer base later on.

Leasing

A *lease* is a contract by which the owner of an asset (e.g. a car) grants the right to use the asset for a period of time to another party in exchange for payment of rent.[23] The benefits to the customer are that a leasing arrangement avoids the need to pay the cash purchase price of the product or service, is a hedge against fast product obsolescence, may have tax advantages, avoids the problem of equipment disposal and, with certain types of leasing contracts, avoids some maintenance costs. These benefits need to be weighed against the costs of *leasing* which may be higher than outright buying.

There are two main types of leases: financial (or full payment) leases and operating leases (sometimes called rental agreements). A *financial lease* is a longer-term arrangement that is fully amortized over the term of the contract. Lease payments, in total, usually exceed the purchase price of the item. The terms and conditions of the lease vary according to convention and competitive conditions. Sometimes the supplier will agree to pay maintenance costs over the leasing period. This is common when leasing photocopiers, for example. The lessee may also be given the option of buying the equipment at the end of the period. An *operating lease* is for a shorter period of time, is cancellable, and is not

4.2   Marketing in Action

Reverse Marketing in Action

Peter Brown, head of purchasing at Keestone Bakery, was concerned about continuous increases in flour costs, a major component in the cost of producing bread. Keestone used six flour suppliers but attempts to negotiate lower prices had failed. However, Brown heard that the managing director of Wheatex, a producer of soft wheat flour which was used for cake and biscuit manufacture, was eager to expand. The problem was that Wheatex would need financing to move to hard wheat flour, which is used in breakmaking. To secure this finance, assurances of large sales volumes were needed. Furthermore, Wheatex needed technical and quality assurance advice in this new area. Brown realized that Keestone could provide these and so held discussions with Wheatex with a view to a mutually beneficial outcome. The result was that Brown persuaded Wheatex to accept a 7 per cent below-market price in return for a contract to supply flour to Keestone Bakery. This use of reverse marketing resulted in the generation of a new supplier and the renegotiation of price with the existing six suppliers. Total cost savings approached £500 000.

The second example of reverse marketing involves the acquisition of technology. Bush Equipment was a supplier of components for packaging machines. The components were important in the packaging process as they precisely aligned the containers to be filled on the production line. Paul Jones, the managing director, believed that the components could be more efficiently produced by the application of computer technology. In so doing his company would gain a competitive advantage in the production of the components. After several unproductive attempts to interest suppliers, Jones joined forces with a German manufacturer which had already applied the technology he was considering in other fields, and a computer manufacturer with a track record in this area. The project took seven years to complete but resulted in Bush Equipment being supplied with a leading-edge product.

In both these cases the customers assumed the initiative in getting what they wanted from their suppliers. This process is called reverse marketing.

Based on: Blenkhorn and Banting (1991)[24]

completely amortized.[25] Operating leases are usually higher than financial lease rates since they are shorter term. When equipment is required intermittently this form of acquisition can be attractive because it avoids the need to let plant lie idle. Many types of equipment such as diggers, bulldozers and skips may be available on short-term hire, as may storage facilities.

Leasing may be advantageous to suppliers because it provides customer benefits that may differentiate product and service offerings. As such it may attract customers who otherwise may find the product unaffordable or uneconomic. The importance of leasing in such industries as cars, photocopying and data processing has led an increasing number of companies to employ leasing consultants to work with customers on leasing arrangements and benefits. A crucial marketing decision is the setting of leasing rates. These should be set with the following in mind:

1 The desired relative attractiveness of leasing v. buying (the supplier may wish to promote/discourage buying compared with leasing).

2 The net present value of lease payments v. outright purchase.

3 The tax advantages of leasing v. buying to the customer.

4 The rates being charged by competition.

5 The perceived advantages of spreading payments to customers.

6 Any other perceived customer benefits, e.g. maintenance and insurance costs being assumed by the supplier.

Relationship management

Four types of relationship have been identified.[26] The first two are market relationships between suppliers and customers. They make up the core of relationship marketing and are externally orientated. The first is classic market relationships concerning the supplier–customer, supplier–customer–competitor, and the physical distribution network. These types of relationships are discussed in this chapter and in Chapter 16. The second type is special market relationships such as the customer as a member of a loyalty programme and the interaction in the service encounter. They are examined in the Direct Marketing and Marketing Services chapters.

The third type of relationship is called mega-relationships and concerns the economy and society in general. Examples of such relationships are mega-marketing (lobbying, public opinion and political power), mega-alliances (the European Union which forms a stage for marketing) and social relationships (friendships and ethnic bonds). These issues are covered in the Consumer Behaviour and Marketing Environment chapters. Finally, nano-relationships concern the internal operations of an organization such as relationships between internal customers, internal markets, divisions and business areas inside organizations. Such relationships are discussed within the Managing Products (portfolio planning) and Marketing Implementation Organization and Control chapters.

Managing relationships is a key ingredient in successful organizational marketing. *Relationship marketing* concerns the shifting from activities of attracting customers to activities concerned with current customers and how to retain them. Customer retention is critical since small changes in retention rates have significant effects on future revenues.[27] At its core is the maintenance of relations between a company and its suppliers, channel intermediaries, the public and its customers. The key idea is to create customer loyalty so that a stable, mutually profitable and long-term relationship is developed.[28] The idea of relationship marketing implies at least two essential conditions. First, a relationship is a mutually rewarding connection between the parties so that they expect to obtain benefits from it. Second, the parties have a commitment to the relationship over time and are, therefore, willing to make adaptations to their own behaviour to maintain its continuity.[29] An absolutely central feature of relationship marketing is the role that trust plays in creating satisfaction between parties in the relationship. Building trust is a very effective way to increase satisfaction and develop long-term relationships.[30] The illustration opposite shows a business relationship built up by Siemens to create a competitive advantage.

The discussion of reverse marketing has given examples of buyers adopting a proactive stance in their dealings with suppliers, and has introduced the importance of buyer–seller relationships in marketing between organizations. The Industrial Marketing and Purchasing Group developed the *interaction approach* to explain the

JWT+H+F

SIEMENS

HAN FU:
"No money, no fish."

"Using the internet,
I can make deals all around
the globe."

"My business is fish.
And I have my finger on the pulse
of the world markets."

"E-commerce saves me from
spending money on overhead."

"I manage my business
online all over the world, so
success comes with
minimal effort."

Han Fu, fish broker from Hong Kong, can achieve his ambitious goals, because he has taken on a strong partner: Siemens. Together they redefined Han's traditional business and, with minimal cost and effort, created a tailor-made e-business solution that gives him a competitive advantage in the shark pool of global fish brokers. Han Fu needs neither warehouses for his perishable merchandise nor a truck fleet for deliveries because his e-commerce solution lets him easily coordinate all the logistics – from fishing fleet to client. With incredible efficiency, he has the world market converging at his finger tips with a global solution from Siemens including the latest in e-business and call center applications.

Siemens Convergence Advantage – Creating a Universe of One.

Come see the Siemens Convergence Advantage at www.siemens.com/ic

 **Information and
Communications**

Siemens builds relationships with companies around the world

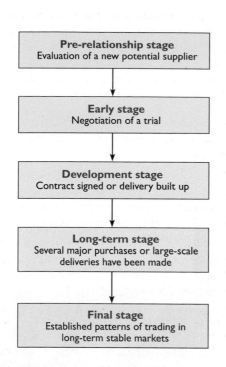

Figure 4.4 The development of buyer–seller relationships in industrial markets

complexity of buyer–seller relationships.[31] This approach views these relationships as taking place between two active parties. Thus reverse marketing is one manifestation of the interaction perspective. Both parties may be involved in adaptations to their own process or product technologies to accommodate each other, and changes in the activities of one party are unlikely without consideration of or consultation with the other party. In such circumstances a key objective of industrial markets will be to manage customer relationships. This means considering not only formal organizational arrangements such as the use of distributors, salespeople and sales subsidiaries but also the informal network consisting of the personal contacts and relationships between supplier and customer staff. Marks and Spencer's senior directors meet the boards of each of its major suppliers twice a year for frank discussions. When Marks and Spencer personnel visit a supplier it is referred to as a royal visit. Factories may be repainted, new uniforms issued and machinery cleaned: this reflects the exacting standards that the company demands from its suppliers and the power it wields in its relationship with them.[32]

The development of technology is facilitating the improvement of buyer–seller relationships. Developments in the use of the Internet to strengthen such relationships are gathering pace. e-Marketing 4.1 describes how the Cisco Corporation uses the Internet in its business-to-business marketing.

A key aspect of the work of the IMP group is an understanding of how relationships are established and developed over time. Ford[33] has modelled the development of buyer–seller relationships as a five-stage process (see Fig. 4.4).

Stage 1: The pre-relationship stage

Something has caused the customer to evaluate a potential new supplier. Perhaps a price rise or a decline in service standards of the current supplier has triggered the need to consider a change. The customer will be concerned about the perceived risk of change and the distance which is perceived to exist between itself and the potential supplier. Distance has five dimensions:

+ *Social distance*: the extent to which both the individuals and organizations in a relationship are unfamiliar with each other's ways of working.

+ *Cultural distance*: the degree to which the norms and values or working methods between two companies differ because of their separate national characteristics.

+ *Technological distance*: the differences between the two companies' product and process technologies.

+ *Time distance*: the time which must elapse between establishing contact or placing an order, and the actual transfer of the product or service involved.

+ *Geographical distance*: the physical distance between the two companies.

Stage 2: The early stage

At this stage potential suppliers are in contact with buyers to negotiate trial deliveries for frequently purchased supplies or components or to develop a specification for a capital good purchase. Much uncertainty will exist and the supplier will be working to reduce perceived risk of change. The reputation of the potential supplier is likely to be important and the lack of social relationships may mean a lack of trust on the part of both supplier and buyer. The supplier may believe that it is being used as a source of information and that the buyer has no intention of placing an order. The buyer may fear that the supplier is promising things which it cannot deliver in order to make a sale. Both companies will have little or no evidence on which to judge their partner's commitment to the relationship.

Stage 3: The development stage

This stage occurs as deliveries of frequently purchased products increase, or after contract signing for major capital purchases. The development stage is marked by increasing experience between the companies of the operations of each other's organizations, and greater knowledge of each other's norms and values. As this occurs, uncertainty and distance reduces. A key element in the evaluation of a supplier or customer at this stage of their relationship depends on perceptions of the degree of commitment to its development. Commitment can be shown by:

1 Reducing social distance through familiarization with each other's way of working.

2 Making formal adaptations which are contractually agreed methods of meeting the needs of the other company by incurring costs or by management involvement.

3 Making informal adaptations beyond the terms of the contract to cope with particular issues and problems that arise as the relationship develops.

This stage is characterized by an increasing level of business between the companies. Many of the difficulties experienced in the early stages of relationship are overcome through the processes at work in the development stage.

4.1   e-Marketing

Integrated Internet Business-to-Business Marketing at Cisco

One of the world leaders in developing integrated information exchange systems based around the Internet is the Cisco Corporation, an $8 billion manufacturer of network routers and switches. As a leading producer of the electronic components that provide the infrastructure underpinning the World Wide Web, it is understandable that the company has sought to exploit technology to improve the management of customer relationships. Features of their system include:

1 An on-line customer enquiry and order placement system which handles over 80 per cent of all orders received by the company.

2 A website that allows customers to configure and price their router and switch product orders on-line.

3 An on-line customer care service which permits the customer to identify a solution from Cisco's data warehouse of technical information and then to download relevant data or computer software. The firm estimates that this facility has saved $250 million per year in the cost of distributing software and an additional $75 million savings in the staffing of their customer care operation.

Based on: Pollack (1999)[34]

Stage 4: The long-term stage

By this stage both companies share mutual dependence on each other. It is reached after large-scale deliveries of continuously purchased products have occurred, or after several purchases of major capital products. Experience of the operations of each party and trust is high with the accompanying low levels of uncertainty and distance. The reduction in uncertainty can cause problems in that routine ways of dealing with the partner may cease to be questioned by this stage. This can happen even though these routines may no longer relate well to either party's needs. This is called *institutionalization*. For example, the seller may be providing greater product variety (and incurring higher production costs) than the buyer really needs. Since no one questions the arrangements, the inefficiencies continue. Institutionalized practices may make a supplier appear less responsive to a customer or exploit the customer by taking advantage of its lack of awareness of changes in market conditions (for example by not passing on cost savings) or by accepting annual price rises without question. Strong personal relationships will have developed between individuals in the two companies and mutual problem solving and informal adaptations will occur. In extreme cases, problems arising from 'side changing' can arise where individuals act in the interests of the other company and against their own on the strength of their personal allegiances.

Extensive formal adaptations resulting from successive contracts and agreements narrow the technological distance between the companies. Close integration of the operations of the companies are motivated by cost reductions and increased control of the other partner. For example, automatic reordering systems based on information technology may act as a barrier to the entry of other supplier companies.

Commitment to the relationship will have been shown by extensive adaptations which have occurred. However, the supplier has to be aware of two difficulties. First, the need to demonstrate commitment to a customer must be balanced by the danger of becoming too dependent on that customer. The supplier may feel the need to make the customer feel it is important yet does not wield too much power in the relationship. Second, there is a danger that the customer's perception of a supplier's commitment to the

relationship is lower than it actually is. This is because the peak of investment of resources has taken place before the long-term stage has been reached. And so, ironically, when a supplier is at its most committed to a long-term and important customer, it may appear less committed than during the development stage.

Stage 5: The final stage

This stage is reached in stable markets over long time periods. The institutionalization process begun during the long-term stage continues to the point where the conduct of business may be based upon industry codes of practice. These may stipulate the 'right way to do business' such as the avoidance of price cutting. Often attempts to break out of institutionalized patterns of trading will be met by sanctions from other trading partners.

This model of how buyer–seller relationships develop highlights some of the dangers that can occur during the process. Furthermore, suppliers can segment their customers according to the stage of development. Each stage requires differing actions based upon the differing requirements of customers. The market for a supplier can be seen as a network of relationships. Each must be assessed according to the opportunity it represents, the threats posed by competitive challenges, and the costs of developing the relationship. The marketing task is the establishment, development and maintenance of these relationships. They also need to be managed strategically. Decisions need to be made regarding the relative importance of a portfolio of relationships and resources allocated to each of them based upon their stage of development and likely return.

The reality of organizational marketing is that many suppliers and buying organizations have been conducting business between themselves for many years. For example Lucas has been supplying components to Rover (and its antecedents) for over 50 years. Marks and Spencer has trading relationships with suppliers that stretch back almost 100 years. Such long-term relationships can have significant advantages to both buyer and seller. Risk is reduced for buyers as they get to know people in the supplier organization and know who to contact when problems arise.

Communication is thus improved and joint problem solving and design management can take place. Sellers gain through closer knowledge of buyer requirements, and by gaining the trust of the buyer an effective barrier to entry for competing firms may be established. New product development can benefit from such close relationships. The development of machine-washable lambswool fabrics and easy-to-iron cotton shirts came about because of Marks and Spencer's close relationship with UK manufacturers.[35]

Closer relationships in organizational markets are inevitable as changing technology, shorter product life cycles and increased foreign competition places marketing and purchasing departments in key strategic roles. Buyers are increasingly treating trusted suppliers as *strategic partners*, sharing information and drawing on their expertise when developing cost-efficient, quality-based new products. The marketing implication is that successful organizational marketing is more than the traditional manipulation of the 4-Ps: product, price, promotion, and place. Its foundation rests upon the skilful handling of customer relationships. This had led some companies to appoint customer relationship managers to oversee the partnership and act in a communicational and coordinated role to ensure customer satisfaction. Still more companies have reorganized their salesforces to reflect the importance of managing key customer relationships effectively. This process is called key or national account management.

The term *national account* is generally used to refer to large and important customers who may have centralized purchasing departments that buy or coordinate buying for decentralized, geographically dispersed business units. Selling to such firms involves

1   Obtaining acceptance of the company's products at the buyer's headquarters.

2   Negotiating long-term supply contracts.

3   Maintaining favourable buyer–seller relationships at various levels in the buying organization.

4   Establishing first-class customer service.

This depth of selling activity frequently calls for the expertise of a range of personnel in the supplying company in addition to the salesperson. It is for this reason that many companies serving national accounts employ team selling.

Team selling involves the combined efforts of salespeople, product specialists, engineers, sales managers and even directors if the buyer's decision-making unit includes personnel of equivalent rank. Team selling provides a method of responding to the various commercial, technical and psychological requirements of large buying organizations.

Companies are increasingly structuring both external and internal staff on the basis of specific responsibility for accounts. Examples of such companies are those in the electronics industry, where internal desk staff are teamed up with outside staff around key customers. An in-depth understanding of the buyer's decision-making unit is developed by the salesperson being able to develop a relationship with a large number of individual decision-makers. In this way, marketing staff can be kept informed to customer requirements, enabling them to improve products, services and plan effective communications.

Where companies offer similar high levels of product quality, the quality of an ongoing relationship becomes a means of gaining a competitive advantage. Putting resources into the development and continuation of a relationship with customers is most appropriate where purchasers involve a high level of risk, where a stream of product and service benefits is produced and consumed over a period of time or where the costs associated with repeat purchase can be reduced by close relations.[36] The success of the German machine tool industry is attributable not only to excellent product quality but its capability and willingness to engage in long-term relationship building through first-rate after-sales service.[37]

How to build relationships

A key decision that marketers have to make is the degree of effort to put into *relationship building*.[38] Some organizations' customers may prefer more distant contact because they prefer to buy on price and do not perceive major benefits accruing to closer ties. A supplier who attempts a relationship-building programme may be wasting resources in this situation. However, in most situations there is some potential benefits from

4.3   Marketing in Action

Changes in Buyer–Seller Relationships

The ability to blend technology with customer requirements is an important success factor for many industrial companies but managing customer relationships is also critical. Increasingly, companies have been focusing on improving customer relationships as a method of differentiating themselves from competition. Texas Instruments in the UK, for example, have increased their contact with their customers from seeing the customer only when trying to sell a product, or only when something went wrong. They send teams of managers and engineers to talk to customers in order to improve service quality. Such dialogue led to an improvement in the way in which they supplied components to ICL, a UK-based computer manufacturer. Previously upon receipt of components from Texas Instruments, ICL staff had to open each package to confirm the contents listed on the packaging note, which could be anything up to 10000 items. Then the data had to be entered into a computer. The new system involves the use of bar-codes which are checked by hand-held bar-code readers. The data are thus directly fed into the computer, saving a great deal of time at ICL.

Many companies, including ICL, are introducing a system of *accredited vendor status* to suppliers who pass the buyer's test of supply worthiness. Toyota UK, for example, assess supplier capabilities on four criteria:

1   The attitude and capability of management.

2   The quality of manufacturing facilities and the level of investment in technology.

3   The system for quality control.

4   Capability in research and development.

The chosen suppliers are left in no doubt about the standards expected of them and the necessity to earn long-term relationships. To aid the relationship-building process Toyota UK have set up *technology help teams* to help suppliers understand what their requirements are and how to go about meeting them.

Peugeot and Renault run joint audits to maintain quality at component suppliers. Suppliers are graded according to their ability to conduct their own quality control. Suppliers are also expected to deliver more frequently to meet just-in-time control requirements in both groups' factories.

A trend in buyer–seller relationships is to reduce the number of suppliers so that closer relationships can be built. Rank Xerox, for example, reduced their number of suppliers from 5000 to 500 when they found that they used nine times more suppliers than Japanese rivals like Canon. Similarly, Nissan have reduced the number of suppliers from 1145 to 600. It buys only from firms which can supply on a global basis, be cost efficient and work closely with its engineers to develop new models.

Lean manufacturing has also meant changes in buyer–seller relationships. The maturing of the market for high tech products such as video recorders has meant that production and delivery processes can be stabilized with resultant cost savings. Sony UK, for example, replaced the practice of keeping a month's supply of stock with a 48-hour ordering system and reduced by two-thirds the time taken to assemble a video recorder. Lean production requires product cycles to be long to allow integration of production processes and coordination among components' suppliers but marketing benefits can accrue. Sony UK, for example, had problems in the past when a particular colour television set had sold out. With shorter production time and fast-parts supply, Sony can quickly change production to counter such occurrences.

Just-in-time manufacturing was once seen as a Japanese innovation that gave their country's car manufacturers a competitive edge. Now supplier parks—where component makers are grouped around car plants—are commonplace, reducing delivery costs and giving the geographical proximity that aids the building of buyer–seller relationships.

Based on: Griffiths (1991);[39] Johnson (1992);[40] Butler (1992);[41] Dawkins (1992);[42] Bannister (1999)[43] Milne and Bannister (1999)[44]

relationship development. Indeed as Marketing in Action 4.3 describes, there has been a movement towards the establishment of buyer–supplier partnerships and a concomitant reduction in the number of accredited suppliers.

Some features of close partnership relationships are that the parties adapt their processes and products to achieve a better match with each other, and share information and experiences which reduces insecurity and uncertainty. Sharing information and experiences demonstrates commitment leading to trust and a better atmosphere for future business.[45]

A key method of building relationships and goodwill is the provision of *customer services*. The supplier at zero or nominal cost to the customer gives the latter help in carrying out its operations. This help can take a number of forms.[46]

Technical support

This can take the form of research and development cooperation, before-sales or after-sales service, and providing training to the customer's staff. The supplier is thus enhancing the customer's know-how and productivity.

Expertise

Suppliers can provide expertise to their customers. Examples include the offer of design and engineering consultancies, and dual selling where the customer's salesforce is supplemented by the supplier. The customer benefits through acquiring extra skills at low cost.

Resource support

Suppliers can support the resource base of customers by extending credit facilities, giving low interest loans, agreeing to cooperative promotion and accepting reciprocal buying practices where the supplier agrees to buy goods from the customer. The net effect of all of these activities is a reduced financial burden for the customer.

Service levels

Suppliers can improve their relationships with customers by improving the level of service offered to them. This can involve providing more reliable delivery, fast or just-in-time delivery, setting up computerized reorder systems, offering fast, accurate quotes, and reducing defect levels. In so doing the customer gains by lower inventory costs, smoother production runs and lower warranty costs. By creating systems that link the customers to the supplier, for example, through recorder systems or just-in-time delivery, *switching costs* may be built making it more expensive to change supplier.[47]

Advances in technology are providing opportunities to improve service levels. e-marketing 4.2 describes how the use of electronic data interchange (EDI) and the Internet offer the potential to enhance service provision.

Risk reduction

This may involve free demonstrations, the offer of products for trial at zero or low cost to the customer, product and delivery guarantees, preventative maintenance contracts, swift complaint handling and proactive follow-ups. These activities are designed to provide customers with reassurance.

Summary

Eight characteristics of organizational buying have been identified. These are the nature and size of customers, complexity of buying, economic and technical choice criteria, risks, buying to specific requirements, reciprocal buying, derived demand, and negotiation.

Three key dimensions of organizational buying are who buys (the structure of the decision-making unit), how they buy (the decision-making process), and choice criteria (used to evaluate competing products and suppliers). Each of these dimensions is affected by three key influences: the buy class, the product type and the importance of purchase to the buying organization. This chapter explains how each of the dimensions is affected and the implications for sales and marketing management.

The advent of just-in-time purchasing and the growth in centralized purchasing, reverse marketing and leasing have all changed the nature of purchase and how suppliers compete.

4.2   e-Marketing

Enhancing Service Provision through the Use of Information Technology

Forms UK Ltd is a company which produces business forms and stationery for companies throughout the UK. Current annual turnover is £15 million and the firm employs 95 full-time staff. Since inception, the company has sought to exploit new technology to improve the management of their service provision process. Using an IBM AS400 linked to 250 terminals the company has already created the ability to offer both customers and suppliers an electronic data interchange (EDI) facility.

The EDI system means that customers can electronically communicate purchase orders. Forms Ltd is able to provide data on the current status of orders in progress and issue electronic invoices. The advent of the Internet permitted the firm to examine new ways of electronically enhancing the provision of services to customers. Their first move was for the design department to use the Internet to download graphic materials. This was followed by the establishment of a website containing basic information about the company (www.formsuk.com).

The firm recognized that the Internet offers great potential, but their perception is that their EDI system using leased lines, direct and dedicated fixed links and ISDN technology offers more security, speed and reliability than that which is available via the Internet. Hence the company's decision is to operate a concurrent technology development strategy of choosing between upgrading current systems and bringing in Internet applications when seeking new ways of further enhancing customer service.

Based on: Lymer et al. (1998)[48]

A major task of marketing management is to manage supplier–customer relationships. Buyers are increasingly treating trusted suppliers as strategic partners, and devoting dedicated sales teams to key accounts. By helping the customer through the provision of free or low cost services, suppliers can build goodwill, and foster close relationships with them.

Internet exercise

Business-to-business marketing

Sites to visit
http://www.dti.gov.uk/about/suppliers/foreword.htm
DTI Guide to Suppliers
http://gecmarc02.uuhost.uk.uu.net/gpi/sld001.htm
Marconi Global Purchasing Initiative
http://www.cisco.com

Exercises

1   Compare and contrast the organizational buying of the UK Department of Trade and Industry with that of Marconi

2   Review Cisco's site—what aspects of business marketing can you see here?

Study questions

1   What are the six roles that form the decision-making unit (DMU) for the purchase of an organizational purchase? What are the marketing implications of the DMU?

2   Why do the choice criteria used by different members of the DMU often change with the varying roles?

3   What are creeping commitment and lock-out criteria? Why are they important factors in the choice of a supplier?

4   Explain the difference between a straight re-buy, a modified re-buy and a new task purchasing situation. What implications do these concepts have for the marketing of industrial products?

5   Why is relationship management important in many supplier–customer interactions? How can suppliers build up close relationships with organizational customers?

6   Explain the meaning of reverse marketing. What implications does it have for suppliers?

References

1. Corey, E. R. (1991) *Industrial Marketing: Cases and Concepts*, Englewood Cliffs, NJ: Prentice-Hall.
2. Jobber, D. and G. Lancaster (2000) *Selling and Sales Management*, London: Pitman, 27.
3. Bishop, W. S., J. L. Graham and M. H. Jones (1984) Volatility of Derived Demand in Industrial Markets and its Management Implications, *Journal of Marketing*, fall, 95–103.
4. Webster, F. E. and Y. Wind (1972) *Organizational Buying Behaviour*, Englewood Cliffs, NJ: Prentice-Hall, 78–80. The sixth role of initiator was added by Bonoma, T. V. (1982) Major Sales: Who Really does the Buying, *Harvard Business Review*, May–June, 111–19.
5. Clinc, C. E. and B. P. Shapiro (1978) *Cumberland Metal Industries (A): Case Study*, Boston, Mass: Harvard Business School.
6. Robinson, P. J., C. W. Faris and Y. Wind (1967) *Industrial Buying and Creative Marketing*, Boston, Mass: Allyn and Bacon.
7. Jobber and Lancaster (2000) op. cit., 35.
8. Draper, A. (1994) Organisational Buyers as Workers: The Key to their Behaviour, *European Journal of Marketing*, **28** (11) 50–62.
9. Parker, D. (1996) The X Files, *Marketing Week*, 8 March, 73–4.
10. For a discussion of the components of risk see Stone, R. N. and K. Gronhaug (1993) Perceived Risk: Further Considerations for the Marketing Discipline, *European Journal of Marketing*, **27** (3) 39–50.
11. Jobber, D. (1994) What Makes Organisations Buy, in Hart, N. (ed.) *Effective Industrial Marketing*, London: Kogan Page, 100–18.
12. Lewin, T. (1996) Nissan Puts Quality First, *The European*, 25–31 July, 27.
13. Lorenz, A. (1999) Nissan's Showpiece Plant at Crossroads, *The Sunday Times*, 5 September, 8.
14. Milner, M. and N. Bannister (1999) Ghosn Steers Refit at Nissan, *The Guardian*, 19 October, 27.
15. Cardozo, R. N. (1980) Situational Segmentation of Industrial Markets, *European Journal of Marketing*, **14** (5/6), 264–76.
16. Robinson, Faris and Wind (1967) op. cit.
17. Lee, L. and D. W. Dobler (1977) *Purchasing and Materials Management: Text and Cases*, New York: McGraw-Hill, 265.
18. Forbis, J. L. and N. T. Mehta (1981) *Value-Based Strategies for Industrial Products, Business Horizons*, May–June, 32–42.
19. Hutt, M. D. and T. W Speh (1997) *Business Marketing Management*, New York: Dryden Press, 3rd edn, 40.
20. Done, K. (1992) 0 to 130,000 in 14 Weeks, *Financial Times*, 23 September, 11.
21. Briefly, E. G., R. W. Eccles and R. R. Reeder (1998) *Business Marketing*, Englewood Cliffs, NJ: Prentice-Hall, 105.
22. Blenkhorn, D. L. and P. M. Banting (1991) How Reverse Marketing Changes Buyer–Seller's Roles, *Industrial Maketing Management*, **20**, 185–91.
23. Anderson, F. and W. Lazer (1978) Industrial Lease Marketing, *Journal of Marketing*, **42** (January), 71–9.
24. Blenkhorn, D. L. and P. M. Banting (1991) How Reverse Marketing Changes Buyer–Seller's Roles, *Industrial Marketing Management*, **20**, 185–91.
25. Morris, M. H. (1988) *Industrial and Organisation Marketing*, Columbus, OH: Merrill, 323.
26. Gummerson, E. (1996) Relationship Marketing and Imaginary Organisations: A Synthesis, *European Journal of Marketing*, **30** (2) 33–44.
27. Andreassen, T. W. (1995) Small, High Cost Countries Strategy for Attracting MNC's Global Investments, *International Journal of Public Sector Management*, **8** (3), 110–18.
28. Ravald, A. and C. Gronroos (1996) The Value Concept and Relationship Marketing, *European Journal of Marketing*, **30** (2), 19–30.
29. Takala, T. and O. Uusitalo (1996) An Alternative View of Relationship Marketing: A Framework for Ethical Analysis, *European Journal of Marketing*, **30** (2), 45–60.
30. Geyskens, I., J.-B. E. M. Steenkamp and N. Kumar (1998) Generalizations About Trust in Marketing Channel Relationships Using Meta-Analysis, *International Journal of Research in Marketing*, **15**, 223–48; and Selnes, F. (1998) Antecedents and Consequences of Trust and Satisfaction in Buyer–Seller Relationships, *European Journal of Marketing* **32** (3/4), 305–22.
31. See e.g. Ford, D. (1980) The Development of Buyer–Seller Relationships in Industrial Markets, *European Journal of Marketing*, **14** (5/6), 339–53; Hakansson, H. (1982) *International Marketing and Purchasing of Industrial Goods: An Interaction Approach*, New York: Wiley; Turnbull, P. W. and M. T. Cunningham (1981) *International Marketing and Purchasing*, London: Macmillan; Turnbull, P. W. and J. P. Valla (1986) *Strategies for Industrial Marketing*, London: Croom-Helm.
32. Thornhill, J. and A. Rawsthorn (1992) Why Sparks are Flying, *Financial Times*, 8 January, 12.
33. Ford (1980) op. cit.
34. Pollack, B. (1999) The State of Internet Marketing, *Direct Marketing*, January, 18–22.
35. Thornhill and Rawsthorn (1992) op. cit.
36. See Lovelock, C. H. (1983) Classifying Services to Gain Strategic Marketing Insight, *Journal of Marketing*, **47**, Summer, 9–20 and Wray, B., A. Palmer and D. Bejou (1994) Using Neural Network Analysis to Evaluate Buyer–Seller Relationships, *European Journal of Marketing*, **28** (10), 32–48.
37. See Shaw, V. (1994) The Marketing Strategies of British and German Companies, *European Journal of Marketing*, **28** (7), 30–43 and Meissner, H. G. (1986) A Structural Comparison of Japanese and German Marketing Strategies, *Irish Marketing Review 1*, Spring, 21–31.
38. Jackson, B. B. (1985) Build Customer Relationships that Last, *Harvard Business Review*, Nov.–Dec., 120–5.
39. Griffiths, J. (1991) How Toyota Follows its Component Suppliers, *Financial Times*, 10 April, 18.
40. Johnson, M. (1992) Rank Xerox Seeks a Sharper Image, *Marketing*, 20 August, 16–17

41. Butler, S. (1992) Sony's Lean New Manufacturing Machine, *Financial Times*, 10 November, 10

42. Dawkins, W. (1992) The Road to Recovery, *Financial Times*, 3 June, 11.

43. Bannister, N. (1999) 21 000 Go in Nissan Rescue, *The Guardian*, 19 October, 22.

44. Milner, M. and N. Bannister (1999) Ghosn Steers Refit at Nissan, *The Guardian*, 19 October, 27.

45. Zineldin, M. (1998) Towards an Ecological Collaborative Relationship Management: A 'Co-operative Perspective', *European Journal of Marketing*, **32** (11/12), 1138–64.

46. Shipley, D. (1991) Key Customer Services, private papers.

47. Jackson (1985) op. cit., 127.

48. Lymer, A., A. Nayak, R.. Johnson, and B. Spaul, (1998) UK Business and the Information Highway, ACCA Occasional Research Paper No. 23, Association of Chartered Certified Accountants, London, 49–51.

Key terms

decision-making unit   a group of people within an organization who are involved in the buying decision (also known as the buying centre)

decision-making process   the stages which organizations and people pass through when purchasing a physical product or service

choice criteria   the various attributes (and benefits) people use when evaluating products and services

total quality management   the set of programmes designed to constantly improve the quality of physical products, services and processes

life cycle costs   all the components of costs associated with buying, owning and using a physical product or service

new task   refers to the first time purchase of a product or input by an organization

straight re-buy   refers to a purchase by an organization from a previously approved supplier of a previously purchased item

modified re-buy   where a regular requirement for the type of product exists and the buying

alternatives are known but sufficient (e.g. a delivery problem) has occurred to require some alteration to the normal supply procedure

value analysis   a method of cost reduction in which components are examined to see if they can be made more cheaply

JIT   the just-in-time (JIT) concept aims to minimise stocks by organizing a supply system which provides materials and components as they are required

reverse marketing   the process whereby the buyer attempts to persuade the supplier to provide exactly what the organization wants

relationship marketing   the process of creating, maintaining and enhancing strong relationships with customers and other stakeholders

interaction approach   an approach to buyer–seller relations which treats the relationships as taking place between two active parties

team selling   the use of the combined efforts of salespeople, product specialists, engineers, sales managers and even directors to sell products

Case 5 Winters Company

Mr J. Herbert, a trainee salesman with Winters Company Ltd, observed the following incident while spending part of his introductory tour of the company in the purchasing department.

Mr Jones, the purchasing officer of Winters, received a request from his company's R&D department to order 100 fluidic drives from the Gillis Company. The attached documentation indicated that the R&D department had recently had a lot of contact with representatives of Gillis; in fact, a price and delivery date had been quoted for this order by Gillis. In effect, Mr Jones was being asked only to rubber stamp the company's approval of an arrangement arrived between R&D and Gillis.

Mr Jones phoned the R&D department on the pretext that the information on the requisition was incomplete, but in fact he did so in order to establish whether or not the drives were, as he believed, standard ones also made by several other well-known companies. The information gained from R&D confirmed his opinion that the drives were standard items, but he also learned that a Gillis representative had given R&D a lot of help with technical problems associated with the installation of the drives, and that Mr Smith, head of R&D, therefore felt that Gillis was entitled to the order. However, instead of ordering the components from Gillis, Mr Jones asked three other companies, who also listed these drives in their catalogues, to quote price and delivery dates for a batch of 100.

At about this time, Mr Scott, the production manager of Winters, was discussing with Mr Jones the difficulties he was having in keeping production up to schedule because of late deliveries of some plastic components from a supplier whose products he considered were of above average quality. In the course of this discussion Mr Scott commented, 'The situation reminds me of the problem we had with Gillis Company about two years ago when they were about four weeks late'.

When the quotations from the three other companies arrived, Mr Jones assembled them and compared them with the Gillis figures (see Table C5.1). His assessment of the situation was that the order should go to the Richards Company. The fact that the total cost of the order would then be less than £5000, and thus within the limits which he was allowed to operate without higher authority, was an added incentive for him to make this choice as it saved him from having to prepare a special report to explain his decision.

Mr Herbert, who was kept fully informed of all the above developments by Mr Jones, wondered what this situation could teach him about the problems he might face when selling to industrial customers.

This case was prepared by David Jobber, Professor of Marketing, University of Bradford.

Table C.5.1   Competing quotations

Company	Price per unit (£)	Delivery (from date of order)
Gillis	51.00	2 months
Herman	49.50	3 months
Richards	48.00	10 weeks
Satilmatic	51.50	9 weeks

Questions

1 Identify the decision-making unit, the roles played and the choice criteria of each player.

2 Why did different decision-making unit players use different choice criteria when evaluating potential suppliers?

Case 6 Morris Services

Claire Morris, managing director of Morris Services, a small company providing cleaning services to industry, had reluctantly come to the conclusion that a personal computer was needed for her business. Her immediate problem was cash-flow monitoring; a year ago she had fallen into cash-flow difficulties because, for a variety of reasons, her short-term expenditures exceeded her receipts. Consequently she was looking for a computer that would store information on outgoings and receipts so that at the touch of a button she could monitor cash flow at any particular point in time. Also, she felt that a computer would be useful for her secretary, who was forever complaining of not having word-processing facilities.

She viewed her visit to a local computer outlet with trepidation, as she knew very little about computers. For support she invited along her secretary, Helen Berry, although she knew very little about computers too. They approached a salesperson seated behind a desk.

Claire: Good morning, I'm looking for a personal computer for my business.

Salesperson: I think we can help here. We have a wide range of computers as you can see. I have to go to the storeroom for a few minutes but here are some brochures. Have a look around and see if there is one that you like.

The salesperson hands over the brochure, and leaves Claire and Helen alone in the shop.

Helen: These look really complicated. Why are some bigger than others?

Claire: I don't know. Perhaps the bigger they are the more they can do. What worries me are all these buttons. I don't know what half of them mean.

After five minutes the salesperson returns.

Salesperson: Sorry about that but I had to sort out a delivery problem. Have you seen anything you like?

Claire: No. They all look alike to me.

Salesperson: Don't worry. You say you want a computer for work. I have just the one for you. If you come this way I would like to show it to you. (Claire and Helen follow.)

Salesperson: This incorporates the latest technology. This machine is based on the Intel 750 MHz Pentium III processor. It has 128 megabytes of SD RAM and a 10 Gb hard drive. It contains ATI's best selling Rage Pro AGP graphics card and the latest DVD-ROM drive. The machine comes with nine software applications to cover all business requirements.

Claire: I bet it is expensive. How much will it cost?

Salesperson: Not as much as you think. The price of this machine is £1000 which is good value given its high tech specification.

Claire: I have seen advertisements in newspapers for computers for a lot less than that.

Salesperson: Yes, but do they have graphic facilities and Pentium III Technology?

Claire: I have no idea but they looked fairly good to me.

Helen: It looks quite complicated to use.

Salesperson: No problem at all. My 10-year-old daughter uses one of these. But I've left the best until last: if you buy this month we are giving an extra 10 per cent discount reducing the price to only £900. What a bargain!

Claire: Actually my business is quite small. I only employ ten people. I do not think it is ready for a computer yet. Perhaps when we grow a little we'll be ready.

Anyway thanks for your time.

Claire and Helen retire to a nearby snack bar for coffee. They discuss their reactions to the sales encounter. Undismayed they decide to visit another computer shop to give themselves one last chance to buy a computer.

This case was prepared by David Jobber, Professor of Marketing, University of Bradford.

Questions

1   What choice criteria were important to Claire and Helen?

2   Did the salesperson understand what was important to the customers? If not, why not? Did the salesperson make any other mistakes? Why do you think the salesperson chose that particular computer model?

3   You are the salesperson in the second shop they are about to visit. Based upon your knowledge of buyer behaviour, plan how you would conduct the sales interview.

CHAPTER FIVE

The Marketing Environment

'Change is the only constant'

A. TOFFLER

Learning Objectives *This chapter explains:*

1   The nature of the marketing environment

2   The distinction between the microenvironment and the macroenvironment

3   The impact of economic, social, political and legal, physical, and technological forces on marketing decisions

4   Social responsibility and marketing ethics

5   How to conduct environmental scanning

6   How companies respond to environmental change

A marketing-orientated firm looks outward to the environment in which it operates adapting to take advantage of emerging opportunities, and to minimize potential threats. In this chapter we shall examine the marketing environment, and how to monitor it. In particular we shall look at some of the major forces acting on companies such as the economic, social, legal, physical and technological issues which affect corporate activities. Attention will be given to two recent developments that have implications for marketing management into the twenty-first century; the establishment of the Single European Market and the opportunities posed by the transition to market economics of Central and Eastern European countries such as Poland, Hungary, and the former USSR.

The ***marketing environment*** consists of the actors and forces that affect a company's capability to operate effectively in providing products and services to its customers. It is useful to classify these forces into the microenvironment and the macroenvironment (see Fig. 5.1). The ***microenvironment*** consists of the actors in the firm's immediate environment that affect its capabilities to operate effectively in its chosen markets. The key actors are suppliers, distributors, customers and competitors. The ***macroenvironment*** consists of a number of broader forces that affect not only the company but also the other actors in the microenvironment. These can be grouped under economic, social, legal, physical and technological forces. These shape the character of the opportunities and threats facing a company, and yet are largely uncontrollable.

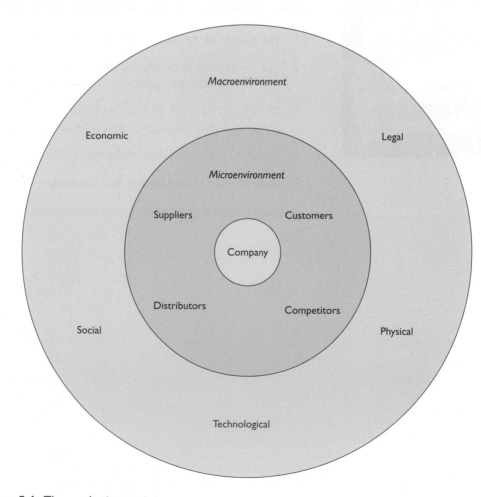

Figure 5.1 The marketing environment

Already we have examined the changes taking place between suppliers and their customers (Chapter 4) and the nature of the influences on customers (Chapters 3 and 4). Distribution and competitive factors will be examined in Chapters 16 and 17. Consequently this chapter will focus on the major macroeconomic forces that affect marketing decisions: economic, social, legal, physical and technological.

Economic forces

The *economic environment* can have a critical impact on the success of companies through its effect on supply and demand. Companies must choose those economic influences which are relevant to their business and monitor them. We shall examine three major economic influences on the marketing environment of companies: economic growth and unemployment, the development and implications of the Single European Market, and the economic changes that are accompanying the transition to market economies of Eastern bloc countries.

Economic growth and unemployment

The general state of a nation's and the world economy can have a profound effect on a company's prosperity. Economies tend to fluctuate according to the *business cycle*. The UK economy was depressed during the early 1980s with low annual growth rates but gathered momentum during the late 1980s only to be followed by a further spell of low growth and high unemployment during the early 1990s. The fortunes of many retail organizations such as Body Shop, Next and Sock Shop closely mirrored this economic pattern. A major marketing problem is predicting the next boom or slump. Investments made during periods of high growth can become massive cash drains if consumer spending suddenly falls. The problems facing Next in the early 1990s were partly caused by this trap.

The second, economic problem is the long-term slow-down in economic growth in Western economies.[1] No longer can companies rely on high levels of long-term growth in capitalist economies to provide opportunities for sales expansion. As stagnation replaces growth, production capacity exceeds demand. The early 1990s were characterized by world overcapacity in industries such as cars, computers and semi-conductors.

Low growth rates are reflected in high unemployment levels. Table 5.1 shows unemployment rates for 12 European countries.[2] Although levels fell in most countries during the late 1980s, unemployment levels were much higher than in the 1960s when 3–6 per cent was the norm.

Development of the Single European Market

The Single European Act 1986 provided the foundation for a free internal market in the European Union (EU). The intention was to create a massive deregulated market of 320 million consumers by abolishing barriers to the free flow of products, services, capital and people among the 12 member states. Clearly this development has the potential for creating opportunities and threats and the changes which it brings need to be closely monitored by marketers.

One objective was to improve economic performance by lowering the costs of operating throughout Europe. Barriers to competition are being reduced by removing physical, fiscal and technical barriers and by establishing a strict competition policy.

Physical barriers

The Single European Market will reduce the barriers that restrict the movement of products and people. Transportation in the EU has been over-burdened with regulations and excessive amounts of documentation. For example, a lorry travelling from Glasgow to Athens, a distance of 2368 miles, and crossing five national boundaries, including a sea crossing, would travel at an average of only eight miles per hour.[3] On average lorry drivers spent 30 per cent of their time at border crossings just waiting or filling in as many as 200 forms. The European Commission estimated that such delays increased overall prices by 2 per cent and cut EU firms' profits by 25 per cent. Although border controls cannot be eliminated completely, the introduction in 1988 of the Single Administrative Document enabled 70 pieces of paperwork to be replaced by a single form.[4]

Fiscal barriers

Although differences in tax rates—e.g. value-added tax (VAT)—still exist between member countries, the Single European Market has created greater freedom of capital movements. This means that financial markets are becoming more competitive and that investment in any EU country is easier.

Technical barriers

An objective of the Single European Market is to reduce the differences in technical standards, testing and certification procedures between countries that cause costly product modifications. To comply with national requirements a product like a car would have to be built in different versions (e.g. different windscreen standards between France and Germany, and special wiring requirements in the UK) that create inefficiencies and a lack of economies of scale. However, countries are still able to restrict entry to those products that do not meet their *essential requirements*. Products can be refused entry if they infringe national regulations on health, safety and environmental protection.

Competition policy

The Single European Market is bringing a continuation of the European Commission's stance on anticompetitive practices. In 1990 the Commission fined 23 European chemicals companies around £30 million for illicit price-fixing and production sharing in the low-density polyethylene and polyvinylchloride markets.[5] Governments are also subject to Commission control regarding the support of local industries; for example, Rover, Peugeot and Alfa Romeo have been ordered to repay state aid on the basis that it distorted competition.

Mergers and acquisitions that are judged to be anti-competitive can be scrutinized by the European Commission (EC). Regulations which came into force in 1990 removed the need for companies to gain approval from both domestic and European authorities, and laid out the criteria used to judge them. The EC's merger taskforce vetted the proposed take-over of Perrier by Nestlé. Their concern was that the deal would give Nestlé and BSN, France's largest food company, a duopoly of the French mineral water market. This was the first time that the EC had challenged a

---

Table 5.1   European Union unemployment rates (%)

	1995	1996	1997	1998	1999
Austria	3.9	4.4	4.4	4.5	3.7
Belgium	9.9	9.8	9.4	9.5	9.0
Denmark	7.2	6.9	5.6	5.2	5.2
Finland	16.3	15.4	12.7	11.4	10.2
France	11.7	12.4	12.3	11.8	11.3
Germany	8.2	8.9	9.9	9.4	8.7
Greece	9.2	9.6	9.8	10.7	n/a
Ireland	12.3	11.8	9.9	7.6	5.8
Italy	11.9	12.0	11.7	11.8	11.3
Luxembourg	2.9	3.3	2.7	2.7	2.3
Netherlands	6.9	6.3	5.2	4.0	3.3
Portugal	7.3	7.3	6.8	5.2	4.5
Spain	22.9	22.1	20.8	18.8	15.9
Sweden	9.2	10.0	9.9	8.3	7.2
UK	8.7	8.2	7.0	6.3	6.1

n/a Not available

Source: *Eurostat*; European Research

take-over on duopoly grounds and hence the important implications for the implementation of competition policy.[6] Although the merger was eventually approved, the EC forced Nestlé to sell a number of Perrier brands to ensure a *third force* would emerge in the French mineral market to compete with Nestlé and BSN.

It is important to recognize that the Single Market is a process which will unfold gradually over time and will vary by country, industry and company. Nevertheless the creation of the Single European Market has the potential of redefining the way that competition is waged. For example companies that could rely on a protected home market are having to rethink their marketing strategies. Fiat of Italy is just such a company and the impact that the Single Market is having on its operation is described in Marketing in Action 5.1.

Implications of the Single European Market

Although the full impact of the Single European Market is far from clear there are a number of likely implications: scale building, reorganization, pan-European marketing, foreign investment by Japanese companies, and foreign investment by US companies.

Scale building

The Single European Market creates an internal market of 320 million consumers compared with 220 million in the United States and 120 million in Japan.[7] This gives European industry an opportunity to organize on a scale big enough to compete with its main rivals in the USA and Japan. Many European high technology industries suffer from a fragmented structure, making it difficult to keep pace with research and development expenditures of foreign competitors. For example in 1990 there were eleven companies battling for the $8 billion European market for central-office telephone exchanges compared with only four in the USA.[8] In order to compete, European companies are forming *strategic alliances* (e.g. AT&T and Italtel) to reduce the effects of fragmentation. Other European companies who wish to become world leaders are building scale (e.g. Unilever, Electrolux, Nestlé, Lufthansa and Deutsche Bank).

The period before 1993 saw a wave of mergers and acquisitions. Nestlé acquired Rowntree, the British chocolate company, and Buitoni, the Italian food company. Pearson and Elsevier have joined forces in the publishing industry. Banco de Bilbao and Banco Vizcaya have combined to become the only Spanish bank to rank among the top 30 in Europe. In consumer electronics, Philips acquired Grundig, the German television producer, and France's Thompson bought Thorn EMI's British television manufacturing arm. Mergers are not confined to the EU, however, with countries of the European Free Trade Association (EFTA) also feeling the effects. For example Nokia of Finland has taken over a number of poor-performing consumer electronics companies in the EU, and consolidations in the Swedish paper industry have led to the establishment of producer groups like Stora Kopparbergs Bergslags and Svenska Cellulosa.

Reorganization

A second feature of the period preceding 1993 was the move towards new organization structures in anticipation of a unified Europe.[9] For example, Philips reorganized their consumer electronics business by replacing their 60-year-old structure of autonomous national subsidiaries—a Dutch Philips, a British Philips, etc.—with Europe-wide product-based businesses. Pilkington, Europe's second largest glass manufacturer, relocated their headquarters from St Helens in north-west England to Brussels and at the same time reduced their head office staff from 500 to 130.[10] BSN, the French food giant, has aggressively rationalized its production of yoghurt to one plant near Lyon that will supply the entire European market. Jacobs Suchard, the Swiss packaged-foods manufacturer, has consolidated production of individual brands to specific factories to gain economies of scale. Electrolux rationalized their production of white-goods, manufacturing all front-loading washing machines in Pordenone, Italy, all top loaders in Revin, France, and all microwave ovens in Luton, England.[11]

Pan-European Marketing

There is considerable debate about the extent to which the Single European Market will promote the realization of pan-European marketing. On the one hand, the increasing mobility of European

5.1 Marketing in Action

Fiat's Strategy in the Single European market

The Single European Market means freer competition in national markets. Old barriers to trade will gradually be broken down. A case in point is Fiat, Italy's car giant which hitherto had been cushioned from foreign competition in their home market by government protection. This took the form of grants, favourable tax laws and import restrictions. The result was a market share which reached over 60 per cent in the 1980s. With Europe's free market these barriers to trade are disappearing.

The sheltered home market meant that Fiat focused on the Italian market to the detriment of overseas performance. In 1988 Fiat vied with Volkswagen for European auto leadership. By 1992 market share had fallen from 15 to 12 per cent and Fiat had declined to fourth place. Traditionally Fiat were renowned for mass-produced small cars but underinvestment meant that the average age of their cars was too old and the quality of some of their models (e.g. the Tipo) did not match that of their rivals (e.g. the Volkswagen Golf and Renault 19). Furthermore, the trend to use common components meant that Fiat, and sister marques Lancia and Alfa Romeo, began to make cars that looked too similar.

Fiat's response to the Single European Market and its associated competitive effects has been an £18 billion investment programme. They have replaced virtually all of their model range between 1993 and 1996 as well as building new state-of-the-art factories in the south of Italy. The marketing task has been to change the image of Fiat cars from being anonymous, dull, with questionable reliability to being full of Italian brio, distinctive, and high quality. New computer-aided design techniques are being used to design cars that look different yet still share many common components, and they plan to revise their coupé and sports car tradition.

The impact of the Single European Market on Fiat has not solved all of its problems, however. In 1999 the owner of Fiat, Giovanni Agnelli, commented 'Too big for Italy maybe but too small for the world'. His solution was to recruit Paolo Fresco who worked for Jack Welch at General Electric. The essence of Mr Welch's successful strategy at General Electric was to make GE number one or two in all of its businesses. Already Fiat appears to be following a similar policy. The take-over by Fiat's farm machinery and construction-equipment subsidiary, New Holland, of Case looks a classic GE-style move. It will create a company that will rival John Deere for leadership on the farm side and Caterpillar and Komatsu on the construction side.

Two other deals seem to have similar motives. The purchase of Progressive Tools and Industries Co. which makes machinery to assemble car bodies turns Comau, Fiat's robotic and automation company into a global leader. Also the merger of Fiat and Renault's foundry divisions into a company two-thirds owned by Fiat makes it world leader in producing car parts made from cast iron, aluminium or magnesium. Meanwhile such businesses as pharmaceuticals and telecoms which have been underperforming have been sold or closed down.

Fiat also appears to be keen to follow a similar strategy for Fiat Auto. Fiat and General Motors have unveiled a cross-shareholding alliance which will see GM acquire a 20 per cent stake in Fiat Auto and Fiat a 5 per cent stake in the US group. The deal is designed to reduce the two car-makers' costs through a series of joint ventures in engine and power train production as well as general purchasing. It also provides an opportunity for Fiat to re-enter the US market through GM's distribution network. Alfa Romeo is expected to be the first marque to return.

Based on: Maddocks. (1993);[12] Anonymous (1999);[13] Anonymous (1999);[14] Betts and Tait (2000)[15]

consumers, the accelerating flow of information across borders, and the publicity surrounding 1992 itself promoted a pan-European marketing approach; on the other, the persistence of local tastes and preferences means that the elimination of formal trade barriers may not bring about the standardization of marketing strategies between countries. Standardization appears to depend on product type. In the case of many industrial goods, consumer durables (such as cameras, toasters, watches, radios) and clothing (Gucci shoes, Benetton sweaters, Levi jeans) standardization is well advanced. However, for fast-moving consumer goods such as food, standardization of products is more difficult to achieve because of local tastes. Even a global brand like McDonald's has to make concessions to national tastes. For example in Norway customers are offered a salmon sandwich invented to cater for Norwegian tastes and in Italy where the demand for fresh foods is strong there are salad bars, the only country in Europe where they operate this service.

Each element of the marketing mix may be affected by the changes accompanying the Single European Market.[16]

1 *Product*: as standards, testing and certification procedures harmonize, manufacturers should benefit by avoiding expensive product modifications and market entry delays (e.g. pharmaceuticals) due to different country-specific requirements. For example, Philips will no longer have to produce seven types of television set to cope with different national standards in Europe. Costs will be greatly reduced as prior to 1992, 40 per cent of their development effort went into designing for the various transmission systems, approval and safety requirements. As cross-border segmentation of markets develops, new Euro-brands may be launched targeted at newly identified pan-European consumer segments. Patenting of products may become even more important because of the larger potential market.

2 *Price*: the European Commission has estimated that the price of goods and services throughout the EU could decrease by as much as 8 per cent. Quelch and Buzzell argue that the downward pressure on prices will be caused by decreased costs, the opening up of public procurement contracts on broader competition, foreign investment that raises production capacity, more vigorous enforcement of anti-monopoly measures, and the general intensified competition resulting from the lowering of barriers post-1992.[17] The potential for parallel importing whereby goods sold in different countries at varying prices are exported from low to high price countries may also depress price levels. A countervailing force may be that as European consumers become wealthier, quality rather than price becomes the major strategic weapon for producers.

3 *Promotion*: despite the attraction of a common advertising campaign (with different voice-overs) directed at 320 million Europeans, variations in tastes, attitudes and perceptions restrict its application. Even Coca-Cola, the ultimate 'one sight, one sound, one sell' global brand modifies the advertising of its other drinks such as Fanta to national markets. A study of advertising standardization practices by Whitelock and Kalpaxoglou concluded that many fast-moving consumer goods do not lend themselves readily to standardization, except for products that are not culture bound, for example cosmetics.[18]

Differences in living standards mean that products need to be repositioned in different markets. The Renault 11, for example, was regarded as a good economical car in the UK, but a luxury car in Spain.[19] Also, a variation in business culture affect the behaviour of salespeople: the relaxed attitude to timekeeping for meetings in Spain contrasts sharply with German punctuality. Furthermore, difficulties in sales promotional regulations mean that premiums (gifts), given as promotional items with products, and money-off vouchers are not allowed in Denmark or West Germany, but are perfectly acceptable in the UK or France.

4 *Place*: Transportation in the EU should become much freer from bureaucratic delays and formalities after 1992. The effects will be to reduce journey times and lower distribution costs. Franchising is likely to increase as global companies link with local franchises combining buying and marketing

muscle with local know-how. European-wide competition between supermarkets is likely to increase. Already the German supermarket chain, Aldi, and Denmark's Netto have established a beachhead in the UK market.

In spite of these implications of the Single European Market some business people remain sceptical regarding its impact on their industries. Calori and Lawrence studied its strategic implications by interviewing managers in France, Germany, Britain, Italy, Spain, Denmark and The Netherlands.[20] The industries chosen in the study were cars, brewing, book publishing and retail banking. Their conclusion was that for those industries 'the perception of the Single European Market as a "non event" or secondary force in the dynamics of the market' prevailed.

This finding is in line with an earlier survey carried out by the journal *Marketing* into attitudes in the brewing industry, which found that

> despite the rhetoric about the free movement of goods, liquids remain extremely expensive to shift around in large quantities. It is better to make them locally, and despite the talk of a 'single' European market, the drinks industry will remain fragmented according to local preferences ... the chances of turning British bitter into a major export are low, the Italians are unlikely to drop grappa for scotch and the Greeks are unlikely to drop brandy and ouzo for gin.[21]

Foreign investment

The trade restrictions implicit in the creation of the Single European Market have encouraged foreign companies, notably from Japan and the USA to invest in EU countries. For example, major investments have been made by Japanese car manufacturers such as Nissan, Toyota and Honda (UK), Mitsubishi (The Netherlands) and Suzuki (Spain). These investments have added to the competitive rivalry within Europe.

Central and Eastern Europe

Besides the development of the Single European Market, another major economic change that has far-reaching marketing implications is the move from centrally planned to market-driven economies by Central and Eastern European countries. The most obvious implication is the opening up of vast potential markets. The population of Central and Eastern Europe including the former USSR—now the Confederation of Independent States (CIS)—is over 400 million, which is larger than the USA (220 million) and the EU (320 million). This opportunity needs to be tempered, of course, by the lower living standards, the low or negative economic growth rates and the political instability of some of these countries.

Nevertheless, with these Central and Eastern European countries accounting for around 15 per cent of world gross national product and wage rates that are much lower than in Spain, Portugal and Greece, it represents not only an important market but also a major low-cost manufacturing opportunity.[22] A perspective on the scale of the market opportunity is given by Xerox, who estimate that there were only 60 000 photocopiers in the former USSR in 1989; in a Western country with a population of the same size there would be 5 million.[23] The opportunity of gaining a low cost source of light bulbs to compete against Philips in Europe was a major factor in General Electric's 50 per cent stake in Tungsram, a Hungarian light bulb manufacturer.[24]

A major threat to EU-based companies may lie in the ability of Central and Eastern European metal producers to undercut them in price. For example, the CIS is a major world producer of uranium using fully depreciated equipment and without the requirement to pay shareholders. Furthermore, increased competition in the marketing of such commodities as coal, steel, titanium and aluminium may have profound effects on the price competitiveness of European and North American producers. The marketing of wine from Bulgaria, Hungary and Romania similarly poses a threat to producers in the traditional wine countries of France, Germany, Italy and Spain. In the UK the links with the Sainsbury and Tesco supermarkets provide a ready-made distribution chain for their wines.

A key marketing question is the relative attractiveness of the former Eastern bloc countries. The countries can be divided into two groups: Hungary, Poland and East Germany are adjusting more rapidly to a market economy than the Czech and Slovak Republics, Bulgaria, Romania, the former Yugoslavia and the Confederation of Independent States. Hungary has a history of

Western investment, Poland is experiencing a wave of new companies, and the former East Germany is benefiting from reunification with West Germany.

As with the EU, the market potential of the Eastern bloc (and its low wage structure) has proved attractive for foreign investment. Hungary has proved attractive to Ford, General Motors (GM), Suzuki and Volvo. Labour costs were, in 1992, £1.60 per hour, compared with £14–16 in Germany. Ford opened a car component plant, and GM a car and engine plant in 1992. Suzuki manufacture 50 000 cars per year and Volvo assemble the Lapplander all-terrain vehicles in Hungary. Renault have a presence in Romania where the cars are being assembled under licence using a combination of French and Romanian components.

Clearly the changes which are taking place in Eastern bloc countries are having a major effect on supply and demand conditions. For many companies monitoring the opportunities and threats that result may be a critical factor for long-term corporate survival.

Social forces

Four key *social forces* that have implications for marketing are the changes in the demographic profile of the population, cultural differences within and between nations, social responsibility and marketing ethics, and the influence of the consumer movement. Each will now be examined.

Demographic forces

Demographic forces concern changes in population. Three major forces are world population growth, the changing age distribution, and the rise in the number of two-income households.

World population growth

A report quoted in the *Guardian* showed that the population in developed economies is expected to be stable or shrinking whereas countries of Africa, India, Other Asia and Latin America are expected to account for over 90 per cent of the projected population increase during the twenty-

first century (see Fig. 5.2).[25] As these countries grow more youthful, the developed countries will experience an ageing population. In 2025, half the population of Europe will be over 45 years old. In 1998, world population reached 6 billion and for the next decade the world population is expected to grow by an average of 97 million per year.

The changing world-population distribution suggests that new markets outside of the developed economies may provide attractive opportunities although the extent to which this force progresses will depend upon a concomitant rise in income levels in the less developed world. The problem is that the major growth is predicted to be in countries that are already poor. Concern for their well-being is growing among people in the developed world. One response is the *social marketing* of family planning and birth control.[26]

Age distribution

A major demographic change that will continue to affect the demand for products and services is the rising proportion of people over the age of 45 in the EU and the decline in the younger age group. Figure 5.3 gives age distribution trends in the EU between 1995 and 2010. The fall in the 15–44-year-old group suggests a slow-down in sales of such products as records, denim jeans and housing. However, the rise in the over-45-year-olds creates substantial marketing opportunities because of their high level of per capita income. They have much lower commitments on mortgage repayments than younger people, tend to benefit from inheritance wealth, are healthier than ever before, and hold the highest proportion of building society funds in the UK. In France, for example, the average per capita disposable income for households headed by a retired person is now higher than the average for all households, and people over 60 who constitute 18 per cent of the population consume more than 22 per cent of the French gross domestic product.[27]

Although the retirement age of 60 for women and 65 for men in the UK is unlikely to fall, early retirement schemes and redundancies have meant that a high proportion of people below this age group are, in effect, retired; for example, over 30 per cent of men aged 55–64 have already left the labour market.[28] High disposable income coupled with increasing leisure time mean that the demand for holidays and recreational activities such as golf, fishing and walking should continue to increase. Also there should be increasing demand for medical products and services, housing designed for elderly couples and singles, and single-portion foods. It is conceivable that the current trend for high street clothing stores to target young and young-adult consumers will be replaced by shops catering for the tastes of the over-50s.[29] Understanding the needs of the over-45-year-olds presents a huge marketing opportunity so that products and services can be created that possess differential advantages valued by these people. In reality it is likely that there are a number of subgroups according to age band which will allow market segmentation to be used. The overall implication of these trends is that many consumer companies may need to reposition their product and service offerings to take account of the rise in *grey purchasing power*.

Two-income households

Over half the couples with dependent children in the UK are dual-earner families. This is very different from the time when women were supported to work in the home, and only men engaged in paid employment. The rise of two-income households among professional and middle-class households means that this market segment has high disposal income leading to reduced price sensitivity and the capacity to buy luxury furniture and clothing products (e.g. up-market furniture and clothing) and expensive services (c.g. forcign holidays, restaurant meals). Also the combination of high income and busy lives has seen a boom in connoisseur convenience foods. Marks and Spencer, in particular, has catered for this market very successfully. Demand for child and homecare facilities has also risen.

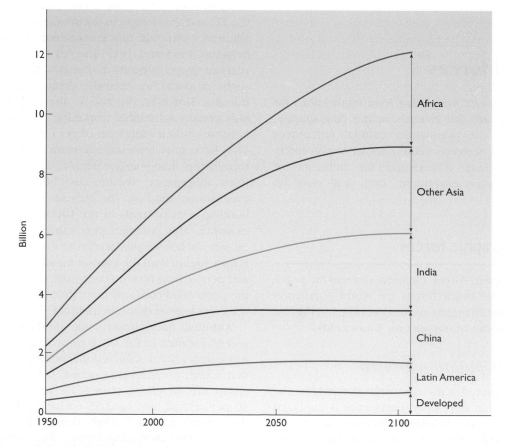

Figure 5.2 World population growth

Cultural forces

A number of distinctive subcultures in the UK provides a rich tapestry of lifestyles, and the creation of new markets. The Asian population, for example, has provided restaurants, and stores supplying food from that part of the world. This influence is now seen in supermarkets where Asian foods are readily available and multi-nationals such as Campbell Foods market 'Tastes of the World' products such as the premium-priced Indian Chicken Korma soup.

Within Europe, *cultural differences* have implications for the way in which business is conducted. Humour in business life is acceptable in the UK, Italy, Greece, The Netherlands and Spain but less commonplace in France and Germany. These facts of business life need to be recognized when interacting with European customers.

A study by Mole examined business culture in the European Union and the USA.[30] Management styles were analysed using two dimensions: type of leadership and organization. Figure 5.4 shows the position of each of the fourteen nations according to these two characteristics. Individual leadership (autocratic, directive) is to be found in Spain and France whereas organic leadership style (democratic, equalitarian) tends to be found in Italy and the Netherlands. Systematic organization (formal, mechanistic) is found in Germany, Denmark and The Netherlands while organic companies (informal, social) are more likely to exist in Spain, Portugal and Greece. The systematic nature of German business and its implications for

conducting business are explained in Marketing in Action 5.2.

Based upon the Mole survey, Wolfe describes business life in Italy, Spain and The Netherlands.[31] As Fig. 5.4 shows, Italian organizations tend to be informal with democratic leadership. Decisions are taken informally usually after considerable personal contact and discussion. Italian managers are flexible improvisers who have a temperamental aversion to forecasting and planning. Interpersonal contact with deciders and influencers in the decision-making unit (DMU) is crucial for suppliers. Finding the correct person to talk to is not easy since DMUs tend to be complex with authority vested in trusted individuals outside of the apparent organizational structure. Suppliers must demonstrate commitment to a common purpose with their Italian customers.

In Spain, on the other hand, business is typified by the family firm where the leadership style is autocratic and the organizational system is informal. Communications tend to be vertical with little real teamwork. Important purchasing decisions are likely to be passed to top management for final approval but good personal relations with middle management is vital to prevent them blocking approaches.

Leadership in The Netherlands is more democratic although organizational style tends to be systematic with rigorous management systems designed to involve multilevel consensus decision-making. Buying is, therefore, characterized by large DMUs and long decision-making processes as members attempt to reach

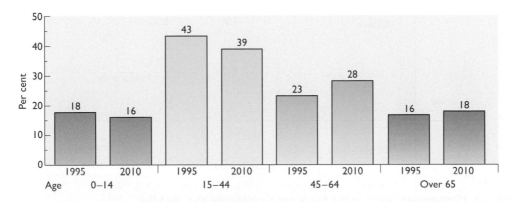

Figure 5.3 Changes in European Union population

agreements without conflict or one-sided outcomes.

Cultural differences between European consumers must also be appreciated. German preferences for locally brewed beer has proved a major barrier to entry for foreign brewers such as Guinness who have attempted to penetrate that market. The slower-than-expected take-off of the Euro-Disney complex near Paris was partly attributed to the French consumer's reluctance to accede to the US concept of spending a lot of money on a one-day trip to a single site. Once there the French person, being an individualist, 'hates being taken by the hand and led around'.[32]

Social responsibility and marketing ethics

Companies need to be aware that they have a responsibility to society which is beyond their legal responsibilities. *Social responsibility* refers to the ethical principle that a person or an organization should be accountable for how its acts might affect the physical environment and the general public. Concerns about the environment and public welfare are represented by pressure groups such as Greenpeace and ASH (Action on Smoking and Health).

Marketing managers need to recognize that organizations are part of a larger society and are accountable to that society for their actions. Such concerns led Perrier to recall 160 million bottles of water in 120 countries after traces of a toxic chemical was found in 13 bottles. The recall cost a total of £50 million even though there was no evidence that the level of the chemical found in the water was harmful to humans. Perrier acted because it believed the least doubt in the consumers' minds should be removed to maintain the image of the quality and purity of its

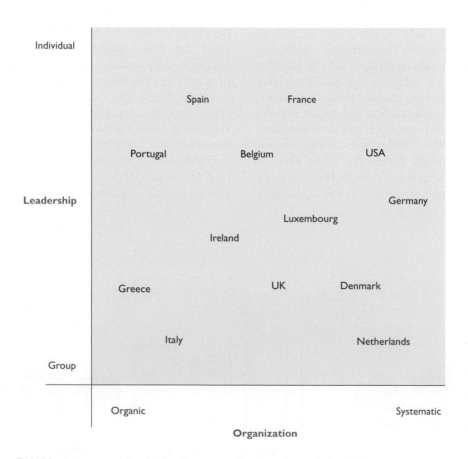

Figure 5.4 Management styles in the European Community and the USA.

Source: Mole, J. (1990) *Mind Your Manners*, London: Industrial Society

product. Companies are increasingly conscious of the need to communicate their socially resposible activities, as the illustration for Du Pont overleaf demostrates. The term 'green marketing' is used to describe marketing efforts to produce, promote, and reclaim environmentally sensitive products.[33]

Social responsibility is no longer an optional extra but is a key part of business strategy that comes under close scrutiny from pressure groups, private shareholders and institutional investors some of whom manage ethical investment funds. Companies are increasingly producing corporate social responsibility reports to communicate their activities to these key audiences. Marketing in Action 5.3 examines the practice of social reporting.

Companies are becoming more proactive in this acceptance of social responsibility through the practice of *cause-related marketing*. This is a commercial activity by which businesses and

5.2   Marketing in Action

Doing Business in Germany

Although national stereotypes can be misleading there do appear to be differences between how business is conducted in European countries. Two German employees of a British computer manufacturer Psion described important differences between the British and German modes of business:

> With German firms much emphasis is placed on bureaucracy and proper procedure. With British firms things are done in a much more off-the-cuff way which means that they can react more flexibly. It is possible to act on a client's requirements very rapidly. In Germany, particularly with big German companies, you have to go through a very long bureaucratic procedure.

> I think the Germans are very precise. The attitude is:
> 'I want this thing by 10.15 a.m. not at 10.16 a.m.' 'If you order something in the UK, you ask:
> 'When will it arrive?' You will be told: 'You'll have it next month.'

There tends to be something very serious-minded, even moral, in the German approach to business. The office hierarchy and formality is a way of life in German business and it has to be recognized by foreigners. For example, subordinates may not be willing to take even the smallest decision while their boss is away. The Germans place much store on personal contact and usually expect to meet business partners face-to-face. But one-to-one meetings are rare; senior executives usually bring along at least one departmental colleague. They can appear confident, almost arrogant. The correct approach is to be polite and discreet. Covering up uncertainty with humour, particularly at first meetings, is contrary to German norms.

The correct address is title and surname: Herr Schmidt or Frau Strauss. Dress is sober: dark suits and ties. Business entertainment outside working hours tends to be low key, although this is changing gradually. Business guests are rarely invited home or out for lavish meals. Lunch, however, is an important element in German business although it may well be in the company canteen.

Purchasing departments are often powerful and suppliers' salesforces are expected to negotiate with them. Attempts to bypass purchasing may cause ill-feeling. Trade fairs and advertising are often used to communicate with technical specialists such as engineers.

Based on: BBC2 Television (1993);[34] Forden (1988);[35] Welford and Prescott (1992);[36] Wolfe (1991)[37]

Companies like Du Pont promote their socially responsible activities

charities or causes form a partnership with each other to market an image, good or service for mutual benefit. As consumers increasingly demand greater accountability and responsibility from businesses so companies such as Procter and Gamble, Tesco, Cadbury, Schweppes, Barclays, Diageo and Lever Brothers have all incorporated major cause-related marketing programmes into their marketing activities. Marketing in Action 5.4 describes how Tesco have developed their cause-related marketing programme.

Cause-related marketing works well when the business and charity have a similar target audience. For example, Nambarrie Tea Company, a Northern Ireland winner of the annual Business in the Community award for excellence in cause-related marketing, chose to sponsor the breast cancer agency Action Cancer. The company and the charity targeted women aged 16–60. In a two-month period, Nambarrie released 100 000 specially designed packs promoting its sponsorship of Action Cancer and covered media costs for a TV advertising campaign. This generated income of over £200 000.[38]

5.3   Marketing in Action

Social Reporting

No longer are companies solely judged by financial success. The interest taken by such groups as environmental agencies, journalists, private and institutional investors, government bodies and employees in the social performance of companies means that the need for a well-presented social report has moved up the corporate agenda. Some companies employ consultants such as Pricewaterhouse Coopers or KPMG to conduct independent audits of their social performance. The audit often includes surveys of employees and other stakeholders and can throw up some surprising results as when a Body Shop survey showed 8 per cent of suppliers 'strongly disagreed' with the statement that they had never encountered unethical behaviour from Body Shop employees. This has resulted in the introduction of a code of conduct for its purchases.

Social audits normally take the form of printed reports but observers believe that this will be replaced by the Internet as the main communication medium. The EMI Group has already moved in this direction using a bi-media approach. A short printed summary report allows readers access to key points but also acts as a signpost for more detailed information on EMI's website. The advantages of the Internet are that it is easy to update, cost effective to distribute, searchable, swiftly produced and environmentally friendly.

Whatever the medium used there are a few key guidelines that can enhance the quality of a social report.

✦   Gain credibility by providing hard evidence, full facts and open disclosure.

✦   The hard evidence should be verified independently.

✦   Trust should be sought by honestly presenting both the good and the bad.

✦   Design should be uncluttered and reflecting the company personality and style.

✦   Presentation should not rely on dull facts—these need inspiration and character to engage and add credibility.

✦   Social reporting should be placed within the context of overall business strategy.

✦   An action plan should be presented and feedback encouraged and listened to.

Based on: Buxton (2000);[39] Slavin (2000)[40]

A set of cause-related marketing principles has been developed by Business in the Community:[41]

1 Integrity: behaving honestly and ethically.

2 Transparency: misleading information could cast doubt on the equity of the partnership.

3 Sincerity: consumers need to be convinced about the strength and depth of a cause-related marketing partnership.

4 Mutual respect: the partner and its values must be appreciated and respected.

5 Partnership: each partner needs to recognize the opportunities and threats that the relationship presents.

6 Mutual benefit: for the relationship to be sustainable both sides must benefit.

Cause-related marketing is often focused on consumers but social responsibility also concerns the environment. Six environmental issues will be discussed later in this chapter when examining physical forces on companies. These are the use of environmentally friendly ingredients in products, recyclable and non-wasteful packaging, protection of the ozone layer, animal testing of new products, pollution and energy conservation. We will now turn our attention to a related issue: marketing ethics.

Ethics are the moral principles and values that govern the actions and decisions of an individual or group.[42] They involve values about right and wrong conduct. There can be a distinction between the legality and ethicality of marketing decisions. Ethics concern personal moral principles and values, while laws reflect society's principles and standards that are enforceable in the courts.

Not all unethical practices are illegal. For example, it is not illegal to include genetically modified ingredients in products sold in supermarkets. However, some organizations such as Greenpeace believe it is unethical to sell GM

5.4 Marketing in Action

Cause-Related Marketing at Tesco

Corporate support for charities and causes can take the form of a straightforward donation with different organizations getting the money each year. However, companies that wish to pursue cause-related marketing need to form a very different relationship with their chosen voluntary organization. A key element is a long-term commitment to a charity or cause. An example is the Tesco Computers for Schools campaign which has been running since 1992. Tesco recognize the need to add value as reflected in its strapline 'Every little helps'. Tesco Computers for Schools is one such extra. Customers shop in Tesco supermarkets, collect vouchers, pass them on to schools and the schools then choose and receive computers and related equipment. Over £50 million-worth of information technology equipment for schools has been funded this way.

This campaign is an excellent example of how the fusion of corporate, marketing and cause-related objectives can prove to be both economically sustainable and enormously beneficial to all parties. Tesco's image and sales have improved and school children have benefited from the infusion of technology. Even today consumer interest is very high with voucher redemption for the scheme remaining at 65 per cent. Tesco views cause-related marketing as a core part of its marketing mix through its ability to grow customer loyalty, enhancing brand image, and providing added value as a differentiator. The process has to be managed well otherwise consumers will view corporate support as a cynical marketing ploy.

Based on: Adkins (1999);[43] Anderson. (1999)[44]

products when their effect on health has not been scientifically proven. Such concerns have led to supermarket chains such as Iceland and Sainsbury to remove GM foods from their shelves.

Ethical principles reflect the cultural values and norms of society. Norms guide what ought to be done in a particular situation. For example, being truthful is regarded as good. This societal norm may influence marketing behaviour. Hence, since it is good to be truthful, deceptive, untruthful advertising should be avoided. Often unethical behaviour may be clear-cut but, in other cases deciding what is ethical is highly debatable. Ethical dilemmas arise when two principles or values conflict. For example, Ben & Jerry, the US ice cream firm was a leading member of the Social Venture Network in San Francisco, a group who promote ethical standards in business. A consortium, Meadowbrook Lane Capital, was part of this group and was formed to raise enough capital to make Ben & Jerry's a private company again. However, their bid was lower than that made by the Anglo-Dutch food multinational Unilever NV. If Ben & Jerry stayed true to its ethical beliefs it would have accepted the Meadowbrook bid. On the other hand, if the company wished to do the best financially for shareholders it would accept the Unilever bid. It faced an ethical dilemma because one of its values and preferences inhibited the achievement of the other. Financial considerations won the day: the Unilever bid was accepted.[45]

Many ethical dilemmas derive from a conflict between profits and business actions. For example, by using child labour the costs of producing products is kept low and profit margins are raised. Nevertheless, this has not stopped companies such as Reebok from monitoring its overseas production of sporting goods to ensure that no child labour is used.

Because of the importance of marketing ethics many of the chapters in the book end with a discussion of ethical issues. For example, Managing Products finishes with an examination of product safety and planned obsolescence issues.

The consumer movement

The *consumer movement* is a collection of individuals, organizations and groups whose objective is to protect the rights of consumers. For example, the Consumers' Association in the UK campaigns for consumers and provides information about products often on a comparative basis allowing consumers to make more informed choices between products and services. This information is published in their magazine *Which?*.

Besides providing unbiased product testing and campaigning against unfair business practices, the consumer movement has been active in areas such as product quality and safety, and information accuracy. Notable successes have been the campaign for real ale, improvements in car safety, the stipulation that advertisements for credit facilities must display the true interest charges (annual percentage rate), and health warnings on cigarette packets and advertisements.

Consumer groups can influence production processes. For example, pressure from both environmental movements in Finland and Germany on UPM-Kymmene, Finland's largest company and Europe's biggest paper-making firm, ensures that replanting of new trees matches felling. German customers (which constitute its biggest market) such as Springer write clauses on forest sustainability and biodiversity in their contracts with paper companies.[46]

Marketing management should not consider the consumer movement a threat to business but an opportunity to create new product and service offerings to meet the needs of emerging market segments. For example, in the detergent market brands have been launched which are more environmentally friendly; this issue will be explored in more detail when we examine the physical environment later in this chapter.

Political and legal forces

Political and legal forces can influence marketing decisions by determining the rules by which business can be conducted. Close relationship with politicians are often cultivated by organizations both to monitor political moods and also to influence them. The cigarette industry, for example, has a vested interest in maintaining close ties with government to counter proposals from pressure groups such as ASH (Action on Smoking and Health) who demand that cigarette advertising is banned. Companies sometimes make sizeable contributions to the funds of political parties in an attempt to maintain favourable relationships.

The relationships between government and business organizations can have major implications not only for the respective parties, but also other companies. An example was the alleged corruption connected with a large order given to a Swedish firm Bofors by the Indian Defence Ministry. Not only were Bofors affected (they have since withdrawn from the market), but other Swedish firms in India (Ericsson, ABB and Uri Civil) faced serious problems because of the scandal.[47]

Political action, then, through legislation and less formal directives can have a profound influence on business conduct. As we saw in Chapter 4, the government and its agencies form a massive market for producers and services and so they can exert economic influence on company actions.

Governments can also influence the marketing environment by the stance they take on inward Investment. e-Marketing 5.1 illustrates the role the Irish government has taken in attracting new e-commerce operations.

National laws governing advertising across Europe mean that what is acceptable in one country is banned in another. For example, toys cannot be advertised in Greece, tobacco advertising is illegal in Scandinavia and Italy, alcohol advertising is banned on television in France and at sports grounds, and in Germany any advertisement believed to be in bad taste can be prohibited. This patchwork of national advertising regulations means that companies attempting to create a brand image across Europe often need to make substantial changes to advertising strategy on a national basis.

We shall now review some of the more important legal influences on marketing activities.

5.1   e-Marketing

Building E-Commerce Operations in Ireland

Ireland's is one of the most trade dependent economies in the world. Hence the Irish government takes a keen interest in creating infrastructures designed to attract a high level of inward investment by major multinational corporations. This has caused the government to take a very farsighted view in relation to attracting new e-commerce operations.

In the mid-1990s it recognized that successful e-commerce operations are critically dependent upon access to the latest telecommunications infrastructure. Thus in 1996 it created the Information Society Commission to address the issues associated with formulating and coordinating a national 'information age' strategy. This organization has defined a vision of the country needing to be flexible enough to respond to changing market needs through (a) the specification of a non-restrictive regulatory regime and (b) a number of areas of specific action.

One action has been to totally deregulate the telecommunications market. This has led to 45 different operators being licensed. A second action has been the passing of the Copyright Bill in 1999 which gives electronic signatures equal standing with paper-based signatures. A third action has been educational spending to increase the number of young people studying for degrees in information technology. The final action has been to invest in an awareness building campaign targeted at stimulating acceptance of e-commerce by consumers, businesses and Government agencies.

Based on: Anderson (1999)[48]

Monopolies and mergers

Control of monopolies in Europe was through Article 86 of the Treaty of Rome which was aimed at preventing the 'abuse' of a dominant market position. However, control was increased in 1990 when the EU introduced its first direct mechanism for dealing with mergers and take-overs: the Merger Regulation. This gave the Competition Directorate of the European Commission jurisdiction over 'concentrations with a European dimension'.

The Commission found against a joint bid for de Havilland, a Canadian aircraft producer, by two state-owned concerns. Aérospatiale of France and Alenia of Italy. The reason was that the acquisition would have given the enlarged group half of the world market and three-quarters of the EU market for commuter aircraft of 20–70 seats. In the Commission's view this constituted an unacceptable degree of concentration with the proposed group facing only limited competition from other EU manufacturers, such as British Aerospace and Fokker of The Netherlands, and from American and Japanese producers.[49] As noted earlier the Commission also intervened to force Nestlé to sell a number of Perrier brands to another company as a condition for allowing the acquisition.

European regulations are often supplemented by national bodies for example the Monopolies and Mergers Commission in the UK. This body has the authority to investigate monopolies and mergers that are thought to be anticompetitive.

Restrictive practices

In Europe, Article 85 of the Treaty of Rome was designed to ban practices 'preventing, restricting or distorting competition' except where these contribute to efficiency without inhibiting consumers' 'fair share of the resulting benefit' and without eliminating competition. A notable success for the Commission was the breaking of the plastics cartel involving Britain (ICI), France (Atochem), West Germany (BASF) and Italy (Montedison) among others. In addition to the work of the Commission, organizations such as the Bundeskartellamt in Germany and the Competition Council in France provide national protection against anticompetitive practices. Many countries in Europe supplement cross border regulations with their own national laws.

Codes of practice

In addition to laws, various industries have drawn up codes of practice to protect consumer interests, sometimes as a result of political pressure. The UK advertising industry, for example, has drawn up a self-regulatory Code of Advertising Standards and Practice designed to keep advertising 'legal, decent, honest and truthful'. Similarly the marketing research industry has drawn up a code of practice to protect people from unethical activities such as using marketing research as a pretext for selling.

Marketing management must be aware of the constraints on their activities made by the political and legal environment. They must assess the extent to which they feel the need to influence political decisions that may affect their operations, and the degree to which industry practice needs to be self-regulated in order to maintain high standards of customers satisfaction and service.

Physical forces

Whereas the consumer movement attempts to protect the rights of consumers, environmentalists attempt to protect the *physical environment* from the costs associated with producing and marketing products and services. They are concerned with the social costs of consumption not just the personal costs to the consumer. Six environmental issues are of particular concern. These are the use of environmentally friendly ingredients in products, recyclable and non-wasteful packaging, protection of the ozone layer, animal testing of new products, pollution, and energy conservation. Marketers need to be aware of the threats and opportunities associated with each of these issues.

Use of environmentally friendly ingredients

Environmentalists favour the use of biodegradable and natural ingredients when practicable. For example, Smith and Vandiver introduced in the UK the botanical range of skincare, soap and bath products based upon essential oils and herbs. This marked them both environmentally and animal friendly. In Germany Estée Lauder introduced the Origins skincare and cosmetics range of vegetable-based products containing no animal ingredients.[50] ICI, the UK chemical group, have developed Biopol which they claim is the first fully biodegradable commercial plastic. They state that its application include disposable nappies, rubbish bags, and paper plates and cups coated with a thin plastic film. Already it is being used in Germany to make bottles for Wella's Sanara shampoo, in the USA for Brocato International's Evanesce shampoo and in Japan for Ishizawa Kenkyujo's Earthic Alga shampoos and conditioners.[51]

Recyclable and non-wasteful packaging

Germany took the lead in the recycling of packaging when they introduced the Verpackvo, a law which allows shoppers to return packaging to retailers and retailers to pass it back to suppliers. In response suppliers promised to assume responsibility for the management of packaging waste. Over 400 companies have created a mechanism called the Dual System Deutschland (DSD). Consumers are asked to return glass bottles and waste paper to recycling bins and are also encouraged to separate other recyclable materials such as plastics, composite packaging and metals and place them in yellow bags and bins supplied by DSD. Collection is every month and that together with separation of the refuse is paid for by DSD and is eventually absorbed by the packaging manufacturers.[52]

In Austria, used batteries, PCs, refrigerators and other products containing potentially dangerous wastes have to be returned by consumers, gathered by retailers and become centrally recycled or treated. Household waste is sorted into materials to be recycled: biological waste and the non-reusable rest. Because Austrians are environmentally conscious, this has led to an over-supply of recycled material raising the price for waste disposal. As a result, consumers have put pressure on retailers and manufacturers to avoid overpackaging.[53] Recycling is also important in

Sweden where Swedish industry has established a special company to organize the collection and sorting of waste for recycling, and in Finland where 35 per cent of packaging is recycled.[54]

Cutting out waste in packaging not only is environmentally friendly but also makes commercial sense. Thus companies have introduced concentrated detergents, refill packs and removed the cardboard around some brands of toothpaste, for example. The savings can be substantial; in Germany Lever GmbH saved 15 per cent paper, carton and corrugated board, 30 per cent by introducing concentrated detergents, 20 per cent by using lightweight plastic bottles, and the introduction of refills for concentrated liquids reduced the weight of packaging materials by a half. Henkels has introduced special 22-gramme *light packs* which are polyethylene bottles that save 270 tons of plastic a year.[55] Environmental concern is being taken seriously by retailers in the UK. Sainsbury, for example, employs an environment affairs manager. Recyclability of products is also being promoted in advertisements; the Ford Mondeo is claimed to be 84 per cent recyclable, for example.[56]

Protection of the ozone layer

This issue has had a dramatic effect on the production of chlorofluorocarbons (CFCs) which are used in refrigerators and aerosols but are a major contributor to the breakdown of the ozone layer, allowing harmful radiation to pass through. The Montreal Protocol Conference in 1990 ruled that production of CFCs should be completely phased out by the year 2000.

Animal testing of new products

Many potential new products such as shampoos and cosmetics are first tested on animals before launch to reduce the risk that they will be harmful to humans. This has aroused much opposition. One of the major concepts underlying the initial success of Body Shop, the UK retailer, was that its products were not subject to animal testing. This is an example of Body Shop's ethical approach to business. This extends to its suppliers also. Other larger stores, responding to Body Shop's success, have introduced their own range of animal-friendly products.

Pollution

The manufacture, use and disposal of products can have a harmful effect on the quality of the physical environment. The production of chemicals which pollute the atmosphere, the use of nitrates as a fertilizer which pollutes rivers, and the disposal of by-products into the sea have caused considerable public concern. In recent years the introduction of lead-free petrol and catalytic converters has reduced the level of harmful exhaust emissions. Chemical companies have increased their levels of spending on the physical environment. In 1991 ICI spent 1.8 per cent and Bayer, the German chemical company, 8 per cent of sales on environmental protection.[57]

Eastern Europe countries such as East Germany, Poland and Czechoslovakia have poor pollution records. In Eastern Germany three of the worst industries were power generation, chemicals and metal processing. The use of high sulphur lignite for domestic and industrial power generation caused East Germany to have the worst air pollution in Europe through sulphur dioxide and dust emissions. The chemical complexes at Bitterfeld were infamous for polluting land, air and water, and high concentrations of arsenic, cadmium and zinc have been found in the ground near the Mansfield metal working area.[58] Although the situation is improving in Eastern Europe the process of environmental cleanup is hampered by out-dated production processes, heavily depreciated machinery and a lack of financial resources.

Denmark has introduced a series of anti-pollution measures including a charge on pesticides and a CFC tax. In The Netherlands higher taxes on pesticides, fertilizers and carbon monoxide emissions are proposed. Not all of the activity is simply cost raising, however. In the former West Germany one of the marketing benefits of its involvement in *green technology* has been a thriving export business in pollution-control equipment.

Consumer groups can exert enormous power on companies by influencing public opinion. For example, environmentalist protests convinced Shell to abandon its plans to dump its obsolete North Sea oil installation, Brent Spa, at sea. The company now plans to consult environmental groups about any sensitive projects it may be considering. The advertisement overleaf describes how the World Wide Fund for Nature acts as a pressure group to reduce carbon dioxide emissions.

Energy conservation

The finite nature of the world's energy resources has stimulated the drive to conserve energy. This is reflected in the demand for energy efficient housing and fuel efficient motor cars, for example. In Europe, Sweden has taken a lead in developing an energy policy based on domestic and renewable resources. The tax system penalizes the use of polluting energy sources like coal and oil while less polluting and domestic sources such as peat and woodchip receive favourable tax treatment. In addition nuclear power is to be phased out by 2010. More efficient use of energy and the development of energy efficient products (backed by an energy technology fund) will compensate for the shortfall in nuclear energy capacity.

Technological forces

Technology can have a substantial impact on people's lives and companies' fortunes. Technological breakthroughs have given us body scanners, robotics, camcorders, computers, and many other products that have contributed to the quality of life. Many technological breakthroughs change the rules of the competitive game. The launch of the calculator made slide-rules obsolete; the growth of television spelt the decline of the film industry; and the rise of the motor car and lorry has threatened rail transport.

Monitoring the *technological environment* may result in the spotting of opportunities and major investments into new technological areas. ICI, for example, invested heavily in the bio-technology area, and are the leaders in the market for the equipment used for genetic fingerprinting. Japanese companies are investing heavily in such areas as microelectronics, biotechnology, new materials and telecommunications. The key to successful technological investment is market potential, however, not technological sophistication for its own sake. The classic example of a high technology initiative driven by technologists rather than pulled by the market is Concorde.

It's a cool place to live. Let's keep it that way.

Increasing air pollution means our world is warming faster than at any time in the last 10,000 years, affecting the world's forests, oceans, atmosphere, animals and ourselves. WWF is urging governments and businesses to reduce the carbon dioxide emissions responsible for global warming.

Let's leave our children a living planet.
www.panda.org

WWF

The World Wide Fund for Nature lobbies governments and businesses to reduce pollution levels

Although technologically sophisticated, management knew before its launch that it never had any chance of being commercially viable. A major revolution is taking place with the rapid spread of digital technology. Marketing in Action 5.5 discusses some of the issues.

Technological change can also pose threats to companies which gradually find that they cannot compete effectively with their more advanced rivals. The technological gap between Europe and the USA and Japan has widened since the early 1980s. With the exception of a small number of areas such as computer-aided manufacturing, Europe trails the USA and Japan. This is despite the fact that Europe has an enviable record in science. Between 1940 and 1990, Europeans won 86

5.5   Marketing in Action
Going Digital

Digital technology, which uses microchips to manipulate and store 'bits' of data under the control of software is fuelling a boom in the semiconductor industry especially in Europe. Applications of the technology are widespread from hearing aids to television. For example, Oticon of Denmark has produced the world's first fully digital hearing aid. Weighing only four grammes it uses a software-controlled digital audio processor chip.

Major changes are taking place within the world of television as a result of digital technology. The most immediate change is a massive increase in the number of television channels. Consumer choice has rocketed. This is already happening in France and Italy where Telepiv has a digital station called DSTV which allows football fans to watch any live game being played on a pay-per-view basis. Video choice will also widen as numerous different digital channels are used to screen the same film at staggered start times. These are some of the reasons why major European pay-television companies such as Sky, Canal+ and Bertelsmann believe that people will pay the upfront cost of a decoder as well as programme charges.

Digital technology also opens up opportunities for terrestrial television stations. For example, the BBC has broadcast BBC1 and BBC2 in widescreen as well as launching a 24-hour news service and interactive channels. Competitors include Sky Digital and ONdigital.

Not only does digital technology affect consumer choice for programmes it also means that the television set can be used to shop, bank, gamble, play games, buy tickets and access the Internet. A question arises regarding digital television versus the Internet as the main source of home shopping. By 2000 Sky Digital, Cable 8 Wireless, NTL and Telewest had launched digital interactive home shopping services in the UK. Digital interactive TV allows viewers to access services through their television set. Purchasing products, making financial enquiries, booking holidays, playing games and sending e-mails can be done at the touch of a remote control button. French satellite broadcaster TPS which has been running interactive ads since 1998 claims that a massive 80 per cent of viewers who are aware of the interactive option on an ad use it. It seems that when it comes to making purchases and enquiring about products via their television sets many viewers are happy to engage. However, despite the potential, the use of digital interactive technology is still in its infancy and heavy marketing expenditures are likely to be needed to persuade consumers to interact with their television sets.

Based on: Fry (1996);[59] Johnson (1995);[60] Benady (2000);[61] Garside (2000);[62] Reynolds (2000)[63]

Nobel prizes in medicine, physics and chemistry, the USA won 143 and the Japanese 5. While expenditure on research and development is somewhat lower at a percentage of GDP (Europe 2 per cent, USA 2.8 per cent, Japan 2.9 per cent) the high technology gap is probably explained more in terms of American and Japanese firms being better at using the results of scientific research; the links between scientists and businesspeople are stronger.[64]

A major technological change which is affecting marketing is developments in information technology. The Internet is revolutionizing how companies conduct business. For example Dell, the computer firm, was one of the first businesses to implement e-commerce combining marketing and sales opportunities into one electronic experience. Dell is also using the Internet as a direct marketing tool. It has a database of addresses to which it sends e-mail, targeting only those people who have requested it. It can do this at a fraction of the price of a paper-based campaign because print and postage costs are eliminated. Sophisticated database software is also used to segment customers for its more traditional direct marketing campaigns. Clearly, technological advances can also create opportunities for companies to improve their marketing systems.[65]

Another technological area which is set to provide new product opportunities is developments in Wireless Application Protocol (WAP) technology. This allows access to the Internet from mobile phones. This is where the industry expects Internet access to really take off. By 2004 it is predicted that one-third of Europeans will regularly access the Internet via their mobile phone.[66]

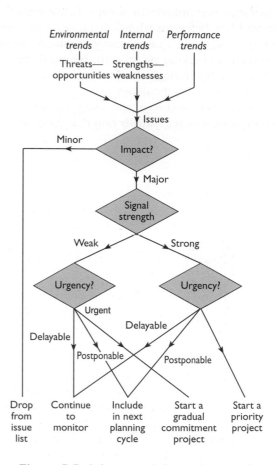

Figure 5.5 A framework for analysing and responding to environmental (strategic) issues.

Source: Ansoff, H. I. (1991) *Implementing Strategic Management*, Englewood Cliffs, NJ: Prentice-Hall, 396. Reproduced with permission

Environmental scanning

The process of monitoring and analysing the marketing environment of a company is called ***environmental scanning***. Two key decisions that management need to make are what to scan and how to organize the activity. Clearly in theory every event in the world has the potential to affect a company's operations but to establish a scanning system which covers every conceivable force would be unmanageable. The first task, then, is to define a feasible range of forces that require monitoring. These are the *potentially relevant environmental forces* that have the most likeli-

hood of affecting future business prospects. The second prerequisite for an effective scanning system is to design a system which provides a fast response to events that are only partially predictable and emerge as surprises, and grow very rapidly. This is essential because of the increasing turbulence of the marketing environment. Ansoff proposes that environmental scanning monitors the company's environment for signals of the development of *strategic issues* which can have an influence on company performance.[67]

Figure 5.5 provides the framework for corporate response which is dependent on an analysis of the perceived impact, signal strength and urgency of the strategic issue.

There are four approaches to the organization of environmental scanning:[68]

1   *Line management*: functional managers (e.g. sales, marketing, purchasing) can be required to conduct environmental scanning in addition to their existing duties. This approach can falter because of line management resistance to the imposition of additional duties, and their lack of specialist research and analytical skills required of scanners.

2   *Strategic planner*: environmental scanning is made part of the strategic planner's job. The drawback of this approach is that a head office planner may not have the depth of understanding of a business unit's operations to be able to do the job effectively.

3   *Separate organizational unit*: regular and *ad hoc* scanning is conducted by a separate organizational unit and is responsible for disseminating relevant information to managers. General Electrics use such a system with the unit's operations funded by the information recipients. The advantage is that there is a dedicated team concentrating their efforts on this important task. The disadvantage is that it is very costly and unlikely to be feasible except for large, profitable companies.

2   *Joint line/general management teams*: a temporary planning team consisting of line and general (corporate) management may be set up to identify trends and issues that may have an impact on the business. Alternatively an environmental trend or issue may have emerged which requires closer scrutiny. A joint team may be set up to study its implications.

The most appropriate organizational arrangement for scanning will depend on the unique circumstances facing a firm. A judgement needs to be made regarding the costs and benefits of each alternative. The size and profitability of the company and the perceived degree of environmental turbulence will be factors which impinge on this decision.

Brownlie suggests that a complete environmental scanning system would perform the following:[69]

1   Monitor trends, issues and events and study their implications.

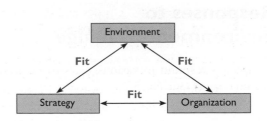

Figure 5.6 Strategic marketing fit

2   Develop forecasts, scenarios and issues analysis as input to strategic decision-making.

3   Provide a focal point for the interpretation, and analysis of environmental information identified by other people in the company.

4   Establish a library or database for environmental information.

5   Provide a group of internal experts on environmental affairs.

6   Disseminate information on the business environment through newsletters, reports and lectures.

7   Evaluate and revise the scanning system itself by applying new tools and procedures.

The benefits of formal environmental scanning were researched by Diffenbach, who found that practitioners believed that it provided the following:[70]

1   Better general awareness of and responsiveness to environmental changes.

2   Better strategic planning and decision-making.

3   Greater effectiveness in dealing with government.

4   Improved industry and market analysis.

5   Better foreign investment and international marketing.

6   Improved resource allocation and diversification decisions.

7   Superior energy planning.

Environmental scanning provides the essential informational input to create strategic fit between strategy, organization and the environment (see Fig. 5.6). Marketing strategy should reflect the environment even if it means a fundamental reorganization of operations.

Responses to environmental change

Companies respond in various ways to environmental change (see Fig. 5.7).

Ignorance

Because of poor environmental scanning companies may not realize that salient forces are affecting their future prospects. They therefore continue as normal, ignorant of the environmental issues that are threatening their existence, or opportunities that could be seized. No change is made.

Delay

The second response is to delay action once the force is understood. This can be caused by *bureaucratic decision processes* that stifle swift action. The slow response by the Swiss watch manufacturers to the introduction of digital watches was thought, in part, to be caused by the bureaucratic nature of their decision-making. *Marketing myopia* can slow response through management being product focused rather than customer focused. Management believe that there will always be a need for made-to-measure suits, for example, and delay responding to the growth in casual wear. A third source of delay is *technological myopia* where a company fails to respond to technological change. The example of Pollitt and Wigsell, a steam engine manufacturer, who were slow to respond to the emergence of electrical power, is an example of technological myopia. The fourth reason for delay is *psychological recoil* by managers who see change as a threat and thus defend the status quo. These are four powerful contributors to inertia.

Retrenchment

This response tackles efficiency problems but ignores effectiveness issues. As sales and profits decline, management cut costs; this leads to a period of higher profits but does nothing to stem declining sales. Costs (and capacity) are reduced

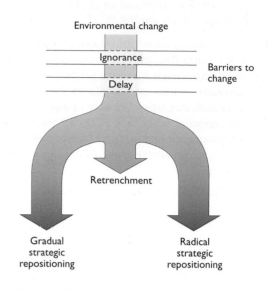

Figure 5.7 Responses to environmental change

once more but the fundamental strategic problems remain. Retrenchment policies only delay the inevitable.

Gradual strategic repositioning

This involves a gradual, planned and continuous adaptation to the changing marketing environment. Marks and Spencer are a company who have continually repositioned themselves in response to changing demographic and economic trends (connoisseur convenience foods, financial services, and European expansion, for example) in order to maintain a fit between the organization, its strategies, and the environment. If occasionally a strategic move fails (e.g. moving into North America) the organization can cope and survive because of earlier successful repositionings.

Radical strategic repositioning

When procrastination leads to a crisis companies may have to consider a radical shift in strategic positioning: the direction of the entire business is fundamentally changed. An example was Burtons, the UK clothing retailer, which moved out of made-to-measure suits and into casual wear. Another UK clothing retailer, Hepworths, was radically repositioned as Next, a more up-market outlet for women's wear targeted at 25–35-year-old working women. Radical strategic repositioning is much riskier than gradual repositioning because, if unsuccessful, the company is likely to fold.

This chapter has explored a number of major events that are occurring in the marketing environment and has discussed methods of scanning for these and other changes that may fundamentally reshape the fortunes of companies. Failure to respond to a changing environment would have the same effect on companies that lack of adaption had on animals: extinction.

Summary

The marketing environment can be divided into the microenvironment, which consists of suppliers, distributors, customers and competitors, and the macroenvironment, which can be grouped under economic, social, political and legal, physical, and technological forces. This chapter examines the marketing implications of each of these macroeconomic forces. In particular the likely effects of the Single European Market are examined.

Environmental scanning is the process of monitoring and analysing the marketing environment. It provides the essential informational input to create strategic fit between strategy, organization and the environment. Response to change can vary from no change through ignorance, delay, retrenchment, gradual repositioning to radical repositioning.

Internet exercise

Environmental change

Sites to visit
http://www.sonymusic.com
http://www.umusic.com/ Universal Music Group
http://www.bertelsmann.com/themes/music/music.cfm
http://www.bandreg.com/music.html The Band Register
http://www.getmusic.com
http://www.metallica.com/news/2000/napfaq.html
http://www.napster.com/metallica-notice.html

Exercise

1   Discuss the changes which are happening in the music industry owing to the development of technology.

2   What were the key issues in the Napster/Metallica lawsuit?

Study questions

1   Choose an organization (if you are in paid employment use your own organization) and identify the major forces in the environment that are likely to affect its prospects in the next five to ten years.

2   Assess the impact of the Single European Market on the prospects for a motor car manufacturer such as the Rover Group.

3   What are the major opportunities and threats to EU businesses arising from the move to market-driven economies of Eastern bloc countries?

4   Generate two lists of products and services. The first list will identify those products and services that are likely to be associated with falling demand as a result of changes in the age structure in Europe. The second list will consist of those that are likely to increase in demand. What are the marketing implications for their providers?

5   Discuss how you would approach the task of selling to German buyers.

6   Evaluate the marketing opportunities and threats posed by the growing importance of the socially conscious consumer.

References

1. Thurow, L. (1992) The Importance of Manufacturing in the United States, Keynote speech, British Academy of Management Conference, Bradford, September.

2. Eurostat (2000) Eurostatistics: Data for Short-Term Economics Analysis, Theme 1: General Statistics, Brussels.

3. Abell, J. N. (1990) Europe 1992: Promises and Prognostications, *Financial Executive*, 6 (1), 37–41.

4. Welford, R. and K. Prescott (1996) *European Business: An Issue-Based Approach*, London: Pitman, 8.

5. Friberg, E. G. (1989) 1992: Moves Europeans are Making, *Harvard Business Review*, May–June, 85–9.

6. Jonquières, G. de (1992) Brussels Plays the Duopoly Card, *Financial Times*, 29 June, 16.

7. Stone, N. (1989) The Globalization of Europe: An Interview with Wisse Dekker, *Harvard Business Review*, May–June, 90–5.

8. Friberg (1989) op. cit.

9. Drucker, P. K. (1988) Strategies for Survival in Europe in 1993, *McKinsey Quarterly*, autumn, 41–5.

10. Lorenz, C. (1992) Transparent Moves to European Unity, *Financial Times*, 24 July, 16.

11. Friberg (1989) op. cit.

12. Maddocks, T. (1993) Fiat's Fight, *The Money Programme*, BBC Television, 21 February.

13. Anonymous (1999) Fiat al Fresco, *The Economist*, 22 May, 112.

14. Anonymous (1999) Friendless Fiat, *The Economist*, 7 August, 62.

15. Betts, P. and N. Tait (2000) Fiat and GM Forge $2.4bn Alliance, *Financial Times*, 14 March, 25.

16. Guido, G. (1991) Implementing a Pan European Marketing Strategy, *Long Range Planning*, 24 (5), 23–33.

17. Quelch, J. A. and R. D. Buzzell (1989) Marketing Moves through EU Crossroads, *Sloan Management Review*, 31 (1), 63–74.

18. Whitelock, J. and E. Kalpaxoglou (1991) Standardized Advertising for the Single European Market? An Exploratory Study, *European Business Review*, 91 (3), 4–8.

19. Guido (1991) op. cit.

20. Calori, R. and P. Lawrence (1992) 1992: Diversity Still Remains: View of European Managers, *Long Range Planning*, 25 (2), 33–43.

21. Mitchell, A. (1989) Single Market Survey 2: Drinks, *Marketing*, 8 December, 21–2.

22. Quelch, J. A., E. Joachimsthaler and J. L. Nueno (1991) After the Wall: Marketing Guidelines for Eastern Europe, *Sloan Business Review*, winter, 82–93.

23. Lindsay, M. (1989) The Missing Photocopiers, *Financial Times*, 8 December, 19.

24. Quelch, Joachimsthaler and Nueno (1991) op. cit.

25. Brown, P. (1992) Rise of Women Key to Population Curb, *Guardian*, 30 April, 8.

26. Roberto, E. (1975) *Strategic Decision-Making in a Social Program: The Case of Family-Planning Diffusion*, Lexington, Mass: Lexington Books.

27. Haut Conseil de la Population et de la Famille (1989) *Vieillissement et Emploi, Vieillissement et Travail*, Paris: Documentation Française, 31.

28. Johnson, P. (1990) Our Ageing Population: The Implications for Business and Government, *Long Range Planning*, 23 (2), 55–62.

29. Johnson (1990) op. cit.

30. Mole, J. (1990) *Mind Your Manners*, London: Industrial Society.

31. Wolfe, A. (1991) The 'Eurobuyer': How European Businesses Buy, *Marketing Intelligence and Planning*, 9 (5), 9–15.

32. Writers, F. T. (1992) Queuing for Flawed Fantasy, *Financial Times*, 13/14 June, 5.

33. For a discussion of some green marketing issues see Pujari, D. and G. Wright (1999) Integrating Environmental Issues into Product Development: Understanding the Dimensions of Perceived Driving Forces and Stakeholders, *Journal of Euromarketing*, 7 (4), 43–63; Peattie, K. and A. Ringter (1994) Management and the Environment in the UK and

Germany: A Comparison, *European Management Journal*, **12** (2), 216-25.

34. BBC2 Television (1993) Germany means Business: The Frankfurt Contenders, 5 January.

35. Forden, J. (1988) Doing Business with the Germans, *Director*, July, 102-4.

36. Welford, R. and K. Prescott (1992) *European Business*, London: Pitman, 208,

37. Wolfe, A. (1991) The 'Eurobuyer': How European Business Buy, *Marketing Intelligence and Planning*, 9 (5), 9-15.

38. Anderson, P. (1999) Give and Take, *Marketing Week*, 26 August, 39-41.

39. Buxton, P. (2000) Companies with a Social Conscience, *Marketing*, 27 April, 33-4.

40. Slavin, T. (2000) Canny Companies Come Clean, *The Observer*, 27 June 1999, 16.

41. Anderson (1999) op. cit.

42. Berkowitz, E. N., R. A. Kerin, S. W. Hartley and W. Rudelius (2000) *Marketing*, Boston, MA: McGraw-Hill.

43. Adkins, S. (1999) The Wide Benefits of Backing a Good Cause, *Marketing*, 2 September, 20-1.

44. Anderson, P. (1999) Give and Take, *Marketing Week*, 26 August, 39-41.

45. Reed, C. (2000) Ethics Frozen Out in the Ben & Jerry Ice Cream War, *The Observer*, 13 February, 3; Anonymous (2000) Slippery Slops, *The Economist*, 15 April, 85.

46. Business Portrait (1997) Early Riser Reaches the Top, *The European*, 17-23 April, 32.

47. Hadjikhani, A. and H. Hakansson (1996) Political Actions in Business Networks: A Swedish Case, *International Journal of Research in Marketing*, **13**, 431-47.

48. Anderson, A. (1999) Study Finds European Business at Cross-roads of E-Commerce, www.ac.ac.com/showcase/ecommerce/ecom estudy98.html

49. Pass, C. and B. Lowes (1992) Maintaining Competitive Markets: UK and EU Merger Policy, *Management Decisions*, **30** (4), 44-51.

50. Mitchell, A. (1992) The Ripening of Green Toiletries, *Marketing*, 13 February, 12.

51. Cookson, C. (1992) It Grows on Trees, *Financial Times*, 12 August, 8.

52. See Schypek, J. (1992) Germany on Trial over Green Packaging, *Marketing*, 2 July, 14-16; and Thornhill, J.

(1992) The Hiccs Come Out of the Sticks, *Financial Times*, 5 February, 11.

53. Muhlbacker, H., M. Botschen and W. Beutelmeyer (1997) The Changing Consumer in Austria, *International Journal of Research in Marketing*, **14**, 309-20.

54. See Wilkstrom, S. R. (1997) The Changing Consumer in Sweden, *International Journal of Research in Marketing*, **14**, 261-75; Laaksonen, P., M. Laaksonen and K. Moller (1998) The Changing Consumer in Finland, *International Journal of Research in Marketing*, **15**, 169-80.

55. Schypek (1992) op. cit.

56. Samuel, J. (1993) Billion Pound World Beater?, *Guardian*, 30 January, 52.

57. Abrahams, P. (1992) Green Fashion Dulls Edge of German Chemical Industry, *Financial Times*, 1 July, 15.

58. Fisher, A. (1992) Counting the Cost of Cleaning Up, *Financial Times*, 12 February, 29.

59. Fry, A. (1996) TV in the Digital Age, *Marketing Week*, 28 November, 22-3.

60. Johnson, M. (1995) Europe Cashes in on the Chip Boom, *The European*, 21-27 September, 21.

61. Benady, D. (2000) TV Takes Over, *Marketing Week*, 13 April, 28-9.

62. Garside, J. (2000) Will Viewers Interact with TV Advertising?, *Marketing*, 16 March, 9.

63. Reynolds, E. (2000) Digital TV Puts DM into Sharper Focus, *Marketing*, 9 March, 5.

64. Anonymous (1993) Europe's Technology Policy: How Not to Catch Up, *Economist*, 9 January, 21-3.

65. Littlewood, F. (1999) Driven by Technology, *Marketing*, 11 March, 29.

66. Reed, M. (2000) Why the Future Will be Wireless, *Marketing*, 3 February, 22-3.

67. Ansoff, H. I. (1991) *Implementing Strategic Management*, Englewood Cliffs, NJ: Prentice-Hall.

68. Brownlie, D. (1999) Environmental Analysis, in Baker, M. J. (ed.) *The Marketing Book*, Butterworth-Heinemann, Oxford.

69. Brownlie (1999) op. cit.

70. Diffenbach, J. (1983) Corporate Environmental Analysis in Large US Corporations, *Long Range Planning*, **16** (3), 107-16.

Key terms

marketing environment   the actors and forces that affect a company's capability to operate effectively in providing products and services to its customers

microenvironment   the actors in the firm's immediate environment that affect its capability to operate effectively in its chosen markets, namely, suppliers, distributors, customers and competitors

macroenvironment   a number of broader forces that affect not only the company but the other actors in the environment, e.g. social, political, technological and economic

social responsibility   the ethical principle that a person or an organization should be accountable for how its acts might affect the physical environment and general public

cause-related marketing   the commercial activity by which businesses and charities or causes form a partnership with each other to market an image, good or service for mutual benefit

ethics   the moral principles and values that govern the actions and decisions of an individual or group

environmental scanning   the process of monitoring and analysing the marketing environment of a company

Case 7 Marks and Spencer

Background

Marks and Spencer, founded in Leeds market in 1884 had grown some 100+ years later to become a major international retailer. As reported in the 1999 Reports and Accounts, M&S operated stores in 718 locations across 34 countries. About 80 per cent of 1998–99 Sales (£8224 million) were made in the UK via 294 stores and a relatively small, but growing mail order business. A classification of UK stores is shown in Table C7.1.

Of the company's overseas outlets approximately 50 per cent were franchised to local partners. M&S operated stores outside of the UK in the USA, continental Europe (e.g. France, Spain, Germany and Luxembourg), the Republic of Ireland, the Middle and Far East particularly Hong Kong. In the USA the company owned the up-market preppy clothing retailer Brooks Brothers and the King's Supermarket Chain. The decision was announced during 1998–99, because of ongoing problems to withdraw from Canada.

All M&S's goods are manufactured to the company's specifications and are sold under the exclusive St Michael brand name. The company differentiates itself 'by serving the mass market with innovative, high quality goods and competitive prices'. It is best known for clothing (outer and underwear), food products, increasingly financial services, homewares and other general merchandise.

Annus horribilis

Throughout the 1980s and 1990s M&S showed steadily improving levels of sales and profitability. It is true that particular difficulties had been experienced in France and more generally Canada, but overall progress was achieved on a broad range of fields. This state of affairs came to a halt in 1999 sending a shock through both the retail trade and the financial community. As compared to 1998, sales in 1999 were stagnant at £8224 million while profit before tax halved from £1155 million to £546 million. The company share price collapsed also falling 50 per cent to the bracket £2.30–2.40.

In his review of the year's trading the company chairman, Sir Richard Greenbury, recognized 1999 as a major reversal to company fortunes drawing particular attention to flat sales in the peak trading Christmas period, the need for heavy price reductions to shift large quantities of fashion merchandise, a cyclical downturn in housewares, overseas economic turmoil (e.g. riots in Indonesia and currency problems in Thailand, Malaysia and Indonesia), adverse trading conditions in the Far East, together with the strength of the £ sterling and difficulties in the supply chain sourcing from relatively high-cost UK-based manufacturers.

When asking the almost polemical question 'what went wrong?' the company chief executive, Peter Salsbury, went on to say 'the answer is

Table C.7.1 UK store classification

UK store categories	No. of stores	000 ft²	%
Departmental, such as Bluewater or Newcastle, average size 101 000 ft²	44	4 435	37
Regional centres, such as Blackpool or Exeter, average size 54 000 ft²	62	3 323	28
High street, such as Southampton, average size 34 000 ft²	68	2 280	19
Small, such as Mill Hill, average size 34 000 ft²	120	1 922	16
Total	294	11 960	100

Figures as of 31 March 1999.

simple . . . we have not kept pace with the tremendous changes taking place in the retail market'.

Anecdotal evidence

To some extent the fall in the share price, dramatic though it was, was not as great as it might have been as the anticipated bad news had already been built into the share price as the stock market listened to press, analyst and trade comment suggesting all was not well. A broad spectrum of comments had been aired suggesting that M&S was not only increasingly becoming out of touch with its retail market but also, and more importantly, losing touch with both its more general macro- and micro-environment.

In no particular order the kinds of comment that were being voiced as possible explanations for M&S's demise included the following:

✦ The merchandise, especially ladies outerwear (e.g. trousers, skirts, suits, jackets and knitwear) was not of modern design and cut. Indeed, the offering was of staid fashion with little category breadth or depth. The colours too, it was often said, were dreary and monotonous.

✦ The attempt to satisfy in one store a broad array of age groups from say teenage daughter via mother and aunt to grandmother was proving difficult.

✦ Resistance, especially by the younger age group, to shop in a store selling M&S labelled merchandise. Clearly for such a group there were brand perception problems with ego-intensive fashion clothing items.

✦ A lack of flair, cut, style and colour for the older female age group. Famously, one 50-something female shareholder berated the board at the 1999 AGM. She explained she had visited a major M&S store to buy a series of items for her wardrobe prior to going on a summer holiday. Failing to find anything at M&S she had bought all her requirements from competitive outlets. She challenged the mainly male board to understand the physiological and psychological needs of the older woman!

✦ Problems of being out of stock of the more popular selling clothing items.

✦ The non-performance of the home delivery/shopping service even sometimes involving wedding lists. Customers were told items were out of stock, no longer available (although still listed in the home shopping catalogue) and that china patterns had been withdrawn meaning it was not possible to replace breakages.

✦ A refusal to accept credit cards. The company would only accept three forms of payment—cash/direct debit; cheque or the M&S Chargecard.

✦ Increasingly the company was offering poor value for money—full prices being combined with deteriorating quality, i.e. wear, wash and care. This comment was often made of lingerie, a product class in which M&S was once pre-eminent.

✦ High prices of food especially the convenience value-added items.

✦ Political and planning constraints on out-of-town shopping developments and the encouragement of the use of brown- as compared to green-field sites. Brown-field sites though often have significant preparation costs (clearance and possibly pollution) and more importantly are rarely in preferred locations.

✦ The emergence of shopping over the Internet. Some customers particularly seek out the opportunity of buying from the USA where branded clothing prices are regularly lower than in the UK.

✦ Aspiration purchasing of brand labels by affluent younger consumers/executives, e.g. Paul Smith; Hugo Boss, etc.

✦ Competition from specialist trendy niched retailers, often American, e.g. Gap, the Limited, Warehouse, Next and Bennetton.

✦ The success of specialist mail order operations, e.g. Lands End, Cotton Traders and James Meade.

✦ In the financial services sector concerns about charges for savings plans (PEPs (Personal Equity Plans) ISAs (Individual Savings Accounts) etc.) for management, entry and exit. As a result a number of companies and brokers are offering low cost options, e.g. Virgin, Legal and General, David Aaron.

✦ The increasing acceptance by consumers of discounters, e.g. What Everyone Wants, TM Hughes, Peacocks and Matalan.

✦ The practice of dressing down on Fridays.

✦ Problems of the stretchability of the St Michael brand value, e.g. to golf and sportswear.

✦ A general strengthening of M&S's mainstream competitors, e.g. in food: Tesco and J Sainsbury especially in value-added designer boutiqued convenience food; in clothing: a spectrum of competitors ranging from discounters to Harvey Nichols and niche operators.

✦ Recession in the Far East.

✦ The relative over reliance by M&S as compared to their main line clothing competitors on high-cost UK-based suppliers. Often the relationship with such suppliers stretched back 100+ years.

✦ An ageing UK population often with high disposable income, i.e. empty nest and no mortgage.

✦ The high cost of IT investment.

✦ General problems of product design and delivery in the supply chain.

✦ A general decline in the UK of the department store sector.

✦ The fact that a large number of stores in the M&S portfolio are located in cities/town centres where cars are discouraged and conveniently located, inexpensive parking scarce.

✦ The strength of the £ sterling working to the disadvantage of those UK retailers sourcing at home with markets in both the UK and overseas and to the advantage of those sourcing predominately overseas with markets particularly in the UK.

✦ General problems forecasting the next season's strong sellers in the fashion industry and purchasing flexibility to meet 'hot' selling items.

✦ Boardroom debate and argument as to the succession to Sir Richard Greenbury (Chairman throughout the 1990s).

This case was prepared by David Cook, Senior Lecturer in Marketing, University of Leeds.

Questions

1 As a marketing consultant you are asked to research and analyse M&S's macro- and micro-environment for the period 1995–99.

2 Research and identify M&S's unique strengths and weaknesses.

3 Summarize your analysis as a SWOT chart offering whatever advice to M&S that you consider appropriate.

Case 8 The Friendly Bank

John Wilson, Marketing manager of the Friendly Bank, a regional savings bank, was pondering a tricky problem. Marketing research had shown that many customers were dissatisfied with the service provided at the bank during peak demand periods. The major problem was queuing and congestion, causing a visit to the bank to be perceived as an unpleasant experience. A survey of lost customers revealed that 10 per cent had moved to another bank because of this problem.

Another problem had also arisen during this period. The financial experts at the bank had calculated that any account that had an average of £100 or less each month was unprofitable for the bank. The large majority of people who fell into this category used the bank as a receipt of their wages or salary, drew money from the bank regularly throughout the month, and received low incomes.

The solution appeared obvious. By raising the minimum average deposit to £150 the bank would retain its profitable customers, reduce queuing and congestion problems and thereby solve two problems simultaneously. However, John felt that this recommendation was almost too easy. He was unsure about unforeseen consequences that might reflect badly on the bank.

This case was prepared by David Jobber, Professor of Marketing, University of Bradford.

Questions

1 What other issues should be considered by John Wilson when deciding whether to recommend this course of action to the bank's board of directors?

2 Should the bank be expected to provide a subsidized banking service to low income customers?

3 What alternative strategies might the bank consider?

CHAPTER SIX

Marketing Research and Information Systems

'Knowledge is power'

MACHIAVELLI

Learning Objectives *This chapter explains:*

1   The nature and purpose of marketing information systems and the role of marketing research within such systems

2   The options facing a marketing manager who wants to gather marketing research information

3   The stages in the marketing research process

4   How to prepare a research brief and proposal

5   The nature and role of exploratory research

6   Survey design decisions: sampling, survey method, and questionnaire design issues

7   Analysis and interpretation of data

8   Report writing and presentation

9   The factors that affect the usage of marketing information systems and marketing research reports

10   Ethical issues in marketing research

What kinds of people buy my products? What do they value? Where do they buy? What kinds of new products would they like to see on the market? These and other related questions are the key to informed marketing decision-making. As we have seen, a prerequisite for the adoption of a marketing orientation is knowledge about customers and other aspects of the marketing environment that affect company operations. Managers obtain this information by informal and formal means. Casual discussions with customers at exhibitions or through sales calls can provide valuable informal information about their requirements, competitor activities and future happenings in the industry. Some companies, particularly those who have few customers, rely on this type of interaction gathering to keep abreast of market changes.

As the customer base grows, such methods may be inadequate to provide the necessary in-depth market knowledge to compete effectively. A more formal approach is needed to supply information systematically to managers. This chapter focuses this formal method of information provision. First, we shall describe the nature of a marketing information system and its relationship to marketing research. Then we look at the process of marketing research and its uses in more detail. Finally, we shall examine the influences on information system and marketing research use. Marketing information system design is important since the quality of a marketing information system has been shown to affect the effectiveness of decision-making.[1]

Marketing information systems

A *marketing information system* has been defined as:[2]

> A system in which marketing information is formally gathered, stored, analysed and distributed to managers in accord with their informational needs on a regular planned basis.

The system is built upon an understanding of the information needs of marketing management, and supplies that information when, where and how the manager requires it. Data are derived from the marketing environment and transferred into information that marketing managers can use in their decision-making. The difference between data and information is as follows:

+ **Data**: the most basic form of knowledge, e.g. the brand of butter sold to a particular customer in a certain town; this statistic is of little worth in itself but may become meaningful when combined with other data.

+ **Information**: combinations of data that provide decision-relevant knowledge, e.g. the brand preferences of customers in a certain age category in a particular geographic region.

An insight into the nature of marketing information systems (MkIS) is given in Fig. 6.1. The MkIS comprises four elements: internal continuous data, internal *ad-hoc* data, environmental scanning, and marketing research.

Internal continuous data

Companies possess an enormous amount of marketing and financial data that may never be used for marketing decision-making unless organized by means of an MkIS. One advantage of setting up an MkIS is the conversion of financial data into a form usable by marketing management. Traditionally, profitability figures have been calculated for accounting and financial reporting purposes. This has led to two problems. First, the figures may be too aggregated (e.g. profitability by division (SBU)) to be of much use for marketing decisions at a product level, and, second, arbitrary allocations of marketing expenditures to products may obscure their real profitability.

The setting up of an MkIS may stimulate the provision of information that marketing managers can use, e.g. profitability of a particular product, customer or distribution channel, or even the profitability of a particular product to an individual customer.

Another application of the MkIS concept to internal continuous data is within the area of salesforce management. As part of the sales management function, many salesforces are monitored by means of recording sales achieved, number of calls made, size of orders, number of new accounts opened, etc. This can be recorded in total or broken down by product or customer/customer type. The establishment of an MkIS where these data are stored and analysed over time can provide information on salesforce effectiveness. For example, a fall-off in performance of a salesperson can quickly be identified and remedial action taken.

Internal *ad-hoc* data

Company data can also be used for a specific (*ad-hoc*) purpose. For example, management may look at how sales have reacted to a price increase or a change in advertising copy. Although this could be part of a continuous monitoring programme, specific one-off analyses are inevitably required from time-to-time. Capturing the data on the MkIS allows specific analyses to be conducted when needed.

Environmental scanning

The environmental scanning procedures discussed in Chapter 5 also form part of the MkIS. Although often amorphous in nature, environmental analysis, whereby the economic, social, legal, technological and physical forces are monitored, should be considered part of the MkIS.

These are the forces that shape the context within which suppliers, the company, distributors and the competition do business. As such, environmental scanning provides an early warning system for the forces which may impact a company's products and markets in the future.[3] In this way, scanning enables an organization to act upon rather than react to opportunities and threats. The focus is on the longer-term perspective allowing a company to be in the position to plan ahead. It is a major input into such strategic decisions as which future products to develop and market to enter, and the formulation of competitive strategy (e.g. to attack or defend against competition).

Marketing research

Whereas environmental scanning focuses on the longer term, **marketing research** considers the more immediate situation. It is primarily concerned with the provision of information about markets and the reaction of these various product, price, distribution and promotion actions.[4] As such it is a key part of the MkIS because it make a major contribution to marketing mix planning. It is used by a wide range of industrial and commercial sectors in Europe as Fig. 6.2 shows.

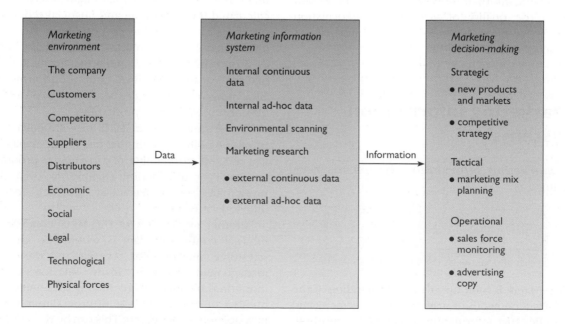

Figure 6.1 A marketing information system

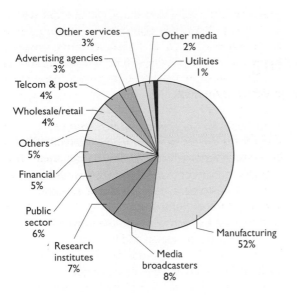

Figure 6.2 Sources of market research turnover in Europe by type of client.

Source: ESOMAR Annual Study on the Market Research Industry 1998. Copyright © 2000 by ESOMAR, Amsterdam, The Netherlands. All rights reserved. No part of this publication may be reproduced or transmitted without prior written permission of ESOMAR. Permission for using this material has been granted by ESOMAR. For further information please visit the ESOMAR website: www.esomar.nl

Two types of marketing research can be distinguished: external continuous data and external *ad-hoc* data. This does mean that internal data are never used by marketing researchers, but usually the emphasis is on external data sources. *External continuous data sources* include television audience monitoring and consumer panels where household purchases are recorded over time. Loyalty cards are also a source of continuous data providing information on customer purchasing patterns and responses to promotions. The growth of e-commerce has led to new forms of continuous data collection, for example the measurement of visits to websites. E-Marketing 6.1 describes how companies use this information for marketing activities. *External ad-hoc data* are often gathered by means of surveys into specific marketing issues including usage and attitude studies, advertising and product testing, and corporate image research. The rest of this chapter will examine the process of marketing research and the factors that affect the use of research information.

Importance of marketing research

The importance of marketing research was highlighted in a study of the factors that were significant in the selection of an industrial goods supplier.[5] The company as part of its marketing audit (see Chapter 2) wanted to know what were the main considerations its customers took into account when deciding to do business with themselves or their competitors. Before conducting marketing research, they asked their marketing staff. They said that the main two factors were price and product quality; next the sales staff were asked the same question and their response was that customers mainly considered company reputation and quick response to customer needs (see Table 6.1). When marketing research was carried out, however, the results were very different. Their customers explained that to them the key issues were technical support services and prompt delivery.

Clearly the viewpoints within and outside the company were at odds with each other. The lesson is that it is dangerous to rely solely on the internal views of managers. Only when this company really understood what their customers wanted could they put into action marketing initiatives which improved technical and delivery services. The result was higher customer satisfaction which led to increased sales and profits.

Marketing research is used by political parties as well as commercial organizations. In the 1996 presidential election, the winner Bill Clinton was reported to be awash with marketing research findings.[6] The pollsters told him to be a father figure with a powerful red tie and suggested how he should spend his holidays. 'Can I golf?' asked Clinton sarcastically, 'Maybe if I wear a baseball cap?' 'No sir', came the reply, 'Go rafting'.

The value of marketing research information is reflected in a European market size of over 4000 million ECU. Figure 6.3 shows how the European market is divided between countries.[7] The importance of marketing research means that data must be accurate, otherwise wrong decisions are likely. Unfortunately, a number of problems has arisen in recent times which means that great care is needed to ensure valid survey findings. Marketing in Action 6.1 (page 159) discusses the issues.

6.1 e-Marketing

Providing Information through Website Analysis

A fundamental principle in effective management of markets is to undertake research to gain an in-depth understanding of customer buying behaviour. Until the advent of e-commerce linking the supplier in real time directly with the customer, market research required intermittent studies using techniques such as mail surveys or telephone interviewing. For those companies who are now using e-commerce to build closer, faster response links with their customers, they are in the enviable position of being able to acquire concurrently new data on customer behaviour.

The e-commerce marketer is provided with a wealth of data by each visitor to the company's website. One can measure which areas of the site are most frequently visited and how long each customer spends seeking out information. This data can then be linked with additional knowledge generated about which products are purchased, payment method used and the nature of questions asked of staff in the firm's tele-sales operation. This very detailed understanding of every customer can be exploited to create customer profiles that permit more effective targeting of future promotional campaigns.

Government Computer Sales Inc., based in Issaquah, Washington, DC, sells software programs and computer products to 3400 government customers across six different states. By using their on-line data, the company has built customer profiles that have assisted in developing targeted marketing campaigns that have doubled the number of software programs and computer products purchased by each customer.

Based on: Anonymous (1999)[8]

Table 6.1 Factors in the selection of a manufacturer

Factor	Users	Salespeople	Marketing
Reputation	5	(1)	4
Credit	9	11	9
Sales reps	8	5	7
Technical support services	(1)	3	6
Literature	11	10	11
Prompt delivery	(2)	4	5
Quick response to customer need	3	(2)	3
Price	6	6	(1)
Personal relationships	10	7	8
Complete product line	7	9	10
Product quality	4	8	(2)

Source: Kotler, P., W. McGregor and W. Rodgers (1977) The Marketing Audit Comes of Age, *Sloan Management Review*, winter, 30. Reprinted with permission. Copyright © 1977 by the Sloan Management Review Association. All rights reserved

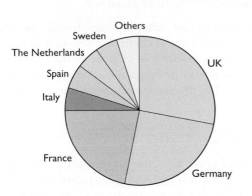

Figure 6.3 European Union market research markets 1998 (total is 4525 million EURO, an increase of 10 per cent over 1997).

Source: ESOMAR Annual Study on the Market Research Industry 1998. Copyright © 2000 by ESOMAR, Amsterdam, The Netherlands. All rights reserved. No part of this publication may be reproduced or transmitted without prior written permission of ESOMAR. Permission for using this material has been granted by ESOMAR. For further information please visit the ESOMAR website: www.esomar.nl

Approaches to conducting marketing research

Depending on the situation facing a company, particularly the resources allocated to marketing research, there are four ways of carrying out marketing research.

Do it yourself—personally

Where a company has marketing staff but a low or nonexistent marketing research budget the only option may be for marketing staff to carry out the marketing research task themselves. This is particularly feasible when the study is small scale, perhaps involving data gathering from libraries. Where sample sizes are small, for example in some industrial marketing research studies involving interviews with a small number of organizational customers, this option may also be feasible. Training in research techniques may be necessary. Fortunately there are many good courses available from professional organizations such as the Market Research Society.

Do it yourself—using a marketing research department

By hiring a marketing research executive, a company would benefit from professional specialist skills. It could be possible for the executive to design, implement and present marketing research surveys to marketing management. If the outside services of a marketing research agency are used, the executive would act as the link between the company and agency.

Do it yourself—using a fieldwork agency

Where the design of the study can be done in-company but interviewing by internal staff is not possible, the fieldwork could be conducted by a marketing research agency. These organizations provide a wide range of services which include fieldwork services; indeed, some specialize in fieldwork only. One possibility would be for the survey design, questionnaire design and analysis of results to be done in-company but the administration of the questionnaire to be handled by fieldwork staff employed by the marketing research agency.

Use the full services of a marketing research agency

Where resources permit, a company (client) could use the full range of skills offered by marketing research agencies. The company would brief the agency about their marketing research requirements and the agency would do the rest. A complete service would mean that the agency would:

1 Prepare a research proposal stating the survey design and costs.

2 Conduct exploratory research.

3 Design the questionnaire.

4 Select the sample.

5 Choose the survey method (telephone, postal or face-to-face).

6   Conduct the interviewing.

7   Analyse and interpret the results.

8   Prepare a report.

9   Make a presentation.

Table 6.2 shows the top world and European marketing research agencies.[9]

Types of marketing research

A major discussion is between *ad-hoc* and *continuous research*.

Ad-hoc research

An *ad-hoc study* focuses on a specific marketing problem and collects data at one point in time from one sample of respondents. Examples of *ad-hoc* studies are usage and attitude surveys, product and concept tests, advertising development and evaluation studies, corporate image surveys, and customer satisfaction surveys. *Ad-hoc* surveys are either custom-designed or omnibus studies.

Custom-designed studies

Custom-designed studies are based on the specific needs of the client. The research design is based on the research brief given to the marketing research agency or internal marketing researcher. Because they are tailor-made, such surveys can be expensive.

Omnibus studies

The alternative is to use an *omnibus survey* in which space is bought on questionnaires for face-to-face or telephone interviews. The interview may cover many topics as the questionnaire space is bought by a number of clients who benefit from cost sharing. Usually the type of information sought is relatively simple (e.g. awareness levels and ownership data). Often the survey will be based on demographically balanced samples of 1000–2000 adults. However, more specialist surveys covering the markets for children, young adults, mothers and babies, the 'grey' market and motorists exist.

Continuous research

Continuous studies interview the same sample of people repeatedly. Major types of continuous

---

Table 6.2   Top World and European Union marketing research agencies

World		European Union	
Agency	*Research revenue (US$)*		*Research revenue (US$)*
AC Nielsen Corp	1425	AC Nielsen Corp	460
IMS Health Inc	1084	IMS Health INC	387
The Kantar Group	675	TN Sofres plc	379
TN Sofres plc	549	The Kantar Group	376
Information Resources Inc	511	GfK AG	262
NFO Worldwide	424	NFO Worldwide Inc	178
Nielsen Media Research	402	IPSOS Group SA	151
GfK Group AG	353	United Information Group	111
IPSOS Group SA	226	Information Resources Inc	98
Westat Inc	205	Sample Institut GmbH & Co KG	43

Source: ESOMAR Annual Study on the Market Research Industry 1998. Copyright © 2000 by ESOMAR, Amsterdam, The Netherlands. All rights reserved. No part of this publication may be reproduced or transmitted without prior written permission of ESOMAR. Permission for using this material has been granted by ESOMAR. For further information please visit the ESOMAR website: www.esomar.nl

research are consumer panels, retail audits and television viewership panels.

Consumer panels

Consumer panels are formed by recruiting large numbers of households which provide information on their purchases over time. For example, a grocery panel would record the brands, pack sizes, prices and stores used for a wide range of supermarket brands. By using the same households over a period of time, measures of brand loyalty and switching can be achieved together

with a demographic profile of the type of person who buys particular brands.

Retail audits

Retail audits are a second type of continuous research. By gaining the cooperation of retail outlets (e.g. supermarkets) sales of brands can be measured by means of laser scans of bar-codes on packaging which are read at the checkout. Although brand loyalty and switching cannot be measured, retail audits can provide accurate assessment of sales achieved by store. A major

6.1   Marketing in Action

Validity in Marketing Research

In most advanced economies there are few manufacturers, advertising agencies, government departments, public bodies, universities and service providers who do not integrate research into their decision-making processes. Yet despite its widespread acceptance, marketing researchers are concerned about three trends.

First, some members of the public actually enjoy taking part in research surveys and group discussions (focus groups). The paid interviewers know who they are and some may be tempted to return to them again and again leading to biased results. So concerned is the industry that the Association of Qualitative Research Practitioners has introduced measures to protect the validity of focus group members. In the future focus group participants will have to provide proof of their identity each time they attend a group and will be warned that they could face criminal prosecution for deception if they deliberately mislead researchers. Second, other people are fed up with marketing research and refuse to take part. In Britain over 15 million interviews are conducted and 100 million questionnaires are mailed every year. The result is lower response rates. For example the National Readership Survey achieves just over 60 per cent after eight calls. In 1954 when it began 85 per cent was reached after only six calls on respondents. So concerned are marketing researchers in Europe that they are considering following the USA and making it standard practice to pay respondents.

Finally, as respondents become more accustomed to research they have begun to play games with market researchers. They understand the process and consciously manipulate their responses. For example, many know that questions about an acceptable price for a new brand will influence its launch price and so respond with low figures. It takes only a small percentage of such respondents to invalidate findings. So important is this problem that at a recent Association of Market Survey Organizations conference several of the key papers addressed the issue of the increasingly uncertain relationship between market researchers and the public.

Based on: Fletcher (1997);[10] Cook (1999);[11] Hemsley (1999)[12]

provider of retail audit data is the AC Nielsen Corp.

Television viewership panels

Television viewership panels measure audience sizes minute by minute. Commercial breaks can be allocated *ratings points* (the proportion of the target audience watching) which are the currency by which television advertising is bought and judged. In the UK the system is controlled by the Broadcasters' Audience Research Board (BARB) and run by AGB and RSMB. AGB handles the measurement process and uses *peoplemeters* that record whether the set is on/off, which channel is being watched, and by means of a hand-console, who is watching.

The breakdown between expenditure on *ad-hoc* and continuous research in Europe is given in Fig. 6.4.

Stages in the marketing research process

Although an *ad-hoc* marketing research study will vary to fit the requirements and resources of different clients, Fig. 6.5 provides a description of a typical marketing research process. Each of these stages will now be discussed.

Initial contact

The start of the process is usually the realization that a marketing problem (e.g. a new product development or advertising decision) requires information to help its solution. Marketing management may contact internal marketing research staff or an outside agency. Let us assume that the research requires the assistance of a marketing research agency. A meeting will be arranged to discuss the nature of the problem and the client's research needs. If the client and its markets are new to the agency, some rudimentary exploratory research (e.g. a quick library search for information about the client and its markets) may be conducted prior to the meeting.

Research brief

At the meeting, the client will explain the marketing problem and outline the research

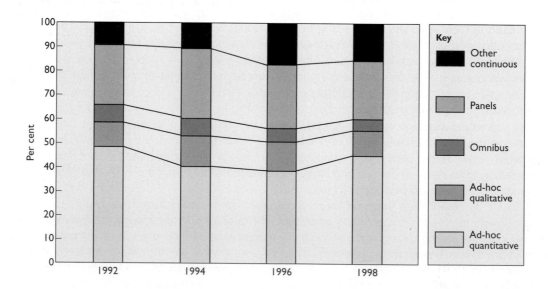

Figure 6.4 European expenditures on ad-hoc and continuous research.

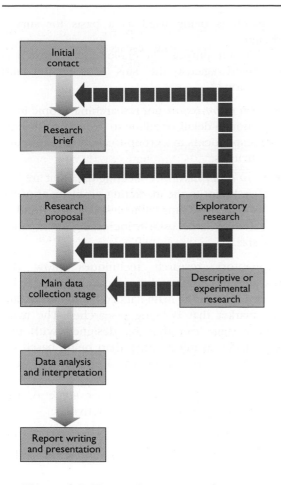

Figure 6.5 The marketing research process

4   *The timetable*: when is the information required?

The client should produce a specific written ***research brief***.This may be given to the research agency prior to the meeting and perhaps modified as a result of it, but without fail should be in the hands of the agency before it produces its *research proposal*.The research brief should state the client's requirements and should be in written form so that misunderstandings are minimized. In the event of a dispute later in the process, the research brief (and proposal) form the benchmarks against which it can be settled.

Commissioning good research is similar to buying any other product or service. If marketing management can agree on why the research is needed, what it will be used for, when it is needed, and how much they are willing to pay for it, they are likely to make a good buy.

Four suggestions for buying good research are the following:

1   Clearly define terms: if market share information is required the term 'market' should clearly be defined.The car manufacturer TVR have a very small share of the car market but a much higher share of the specialist, exclusive segment in which it markets.

2   Beware of researchers who bend research problems so that they can use their favourite technique.They may be specialists in a particular research gathering method (e.g. group discussion) or statistical technique (e.g. factor or cluster analysis) and look for ways of using them no matter what research problem they face.This can lead to irrelevant information and unnecessary expense.

3   Do not be put off by researchers who ask what appear to be naive questions, particularly if the researcher is new to the client's industry.

4   Brief two or three agencies: the extra time involved is usually rewarded by the benefits of more than one viewpoint on the research problem and design, and a keener quote.

objectives. The marketing problem might be to attract new customers to a product group, and the research objectives would be to identify groups of customers (market segments) who might have a use for the product and the characteristics of the product that appeals to them most.[13]

Other information that should be provided for the research agency includes the following.[14]

1   *Background information*: the product's history and the competitive situation.

2   *Sources of information*: the client may have a list of industries that might be potential users of the product.This helps the researchers to define the scope of the research.

3   *The scale of the project*: is the client looking for a 'cheap and cheerful' job or a major study? This has implications for the research design and survey costs.

Research proposal

The ***research proposal*** defines what the marketing research agency promises to do for its client, and how much it will cost. Like the research brief, the proposal should be written to avoid misunderstandings. A client should expect the following to be included:

1 *A statement of objectives*: to demonstrate an understanding of the client's marketing and research problems.

2 *What will be done*: an unambiguous description of the research design including the survey method, the type of sample, the sample size, and how the fieldwork will be controlled.

3 *Timetable*: if and when, a report will be produced.

4 *Costs*: how much the research will cost and what specifically is/is not being included in those costs.

When assessing proposals a client might usefully check the following points:

1 *Beware of vagueness*: if the proposal is vague assume that the report is also likely to be vague. If the agency does not state what is going to be done, why, who is doing it and when, assume that they are not clear in their own minds about these important issues.

2 *Beware of jargon*: there is no excuse for jargon-ridden proposals. Marketing research terminology can be explained in non-expert language, so it is the responsibility of the agency to make the proposal understandable to the client.

3 *Beware of omissions*: assume that anything not specified will not be provided. For example, if no mention of a presentation is made in the proposal, assume it will not take place. If in doubt ask the agency.

Exploratory research

Exploratory research involves the preliminary exploration of a research area prior to the main qualitative data collection stage. It usually occurs between acceptance of the research proposal and the main data collection stage but can also take place prior to the client–agency briefing meeting (as we have seen) and before submission of the research proposal, as an aid to its construction. The discussion which follows assumes that the proposal has been accepted and that exploratory research is being used as a basis for survey design.

A major purpose of exploratory research is to guard against the sins of omission and admission.[15]

✦ *Sin of omission*: not researching a topic in enough detail, or failing to provide sufficient respondents in a group to allow meaningful analysis.

✦ *Sin of admission*: collecting data that are irrelevant to the marketing problem, or using too many groups for analysis purposes and thereby unnecessarily increasing the sample size.

Exploratory research techniques allow the research to understand the people who are to be interviewed in the main data collection stage, and the market that is being researched. The main survey stage can thus be designed with this knowledge in mind rather than being based on the researcher's ill-informed prejudices and guesswork.

A project may involve all or some of the following exploratory research activities:

1 Secondary research

2 Qualitative research: group discussions and depth interviews

3 Consultation with experts

4 Observation.

Secondary research

Secondary research is so-called because the data come to the researcher 'second-hand'; other people have compiled the data. When the researcher actively collects new data, for example by interviewing respondents, this is called primary research.

Secondary data can be found by examination of internal records, and reports of research previously carried out for the company. External sources include government and European Commission statistics, publishers of reports and directories on markets, countries and industries, trade associations, banks, newspapers, magazines and journals. The development of compact disk read-only memory (CD-ROM) facilities on personal computers means that secondary information searches on newspapers and journals can be quickly and simply accomplished. By typing in the appropriate keywords the computer searches the relevant publications and can provide a printout of the article. The European Community is well blessed with secondary sources of data and Marketing in Action 6.2 lists some of the major sources of marketing information classified by research questions.

Secondary research should be carried out before primary research. Without the former, an expensive primary research survey might be commissioned to provide information that is already available from secondary sources. Furthermore, directories such as *Kompass* can be invaluable when selecting a sample in an industrial marketing research project.

Qualitative research

The main forms of **qualitative research** are group discussions and depth interviews. Qualitative research aims to establish customers' attitudes, values, behaviour and beliefs.

Group discussions   sometimes called *focus groups*, these involve unstructured or semi-structured discussions between a *moderator* or group leader, who is often a psychologist, and a group of consumers. The moderator has a list of areas to cover within the topic but allows the group considerable freedom to discuss the issues which are important to them. The topic might be coffee drinking, do-it-yourself car mechanics, or holiday pursuits. By arranging groups of 6–12 people to discuss their beliefs, attitudes, motivation, behaviour and preferences a good deal of knowledge is gained about the consumer. This can be helpful when designing questionnaires which can be designed to focus on what is important to the respondent (as opposed to the researcher) and worded in the language that the respondent uses and understands.

The traditional focus group takes place face to face but the rise of the Internet has led to the practice of on-line focus groups. The Internet offers 'communities of interests' which can take the form of chat rooms or websites dedicated to specific interests or issues. They are useful forums for conducting focus groups or at least identifying suitable participants. Questions can be posed to participants who are not under time pressure to respond. This can lead to richer insights since they can think deeply about questions put to them on-line. Another advantage is that they

can comprise people located all over the world at minimal cost. Furthermore, technological developments mean it is possible for clients to communicate secretly on-line with the moderator while the focus group is in session. The client can ask the moderator certain questions as a result of hearing earlier responses. Clearly, a disadvantage of on-line focus groups compared with the traditional form is that the body language and interaction between focus group members is missing.[16]

Depth interviews   these involve the interviewing of consumers individually for perhaps one or two hours about a topic. The aims are broadly similar to a group discussion but are used when the presence of other people could inhibit honest answers and viewpoints, when the topic requires individual treatment as when discussing an individual's decision-making process, and where the organization of a group is not feasible; for example, it might prove impossible to arrange for six busy purchasing managers to come together for a group discussion.

Care has to be taken when interpreting the results of qualitative research in that the findings are usually based on small sample sizes, and the more interesting or surprising viewpoints may be disproportionately reported. This is particularly significant when qualitative research is not followed by a quantitative study.

Qualitative research accounts for 10 per cent of all European expenditure on marketing research, of which 60 per cent is spent on group discussions, 30 per cent on depth interviews and 10 per cent on other qualitative techniques. Because of its ability to provide in-depth understanding it is of growing importance within the field of consumer research.[17]

With the interest in European markets growing, more use of qualitative research techniques is being made across national boundaries. This brings its own problems, which are discussed in Marketing in Action 6.3.

Consultation with experts

Qualitative research is based upon discussions and interviews with actual and potential buyers of a brand or service. However, consultation with experts involves interviewing people who may not form part of the target market but who, nevertheless, can provide important marketing-related

6.2   Marketing in Action

Sources of European Marketing Information

Is there a survey of the industry?

Marketsearch: International Directory of Published Market Research; Keynote Reports
Size of market, economic trends, prospects and company performance.
Market Research: A Guide to British Library Holdings
Lists titles of reports arranged by industries. Some items are available on Inter-Library loan; others may be seen at the British Library in London.

How large is the market?

European Marketing Data and Statistics
European Marketing Pocket Book
International Marketing Data and Statistics
Business Monitor series is the principal source for detailed product information (Government publications). Other statistics sources include:
Monthly Digest of Statistics
CEO Bulletin
A–Z of UK Marketing Data

Who are the competitors?

Dun's Europa
Europe's 15 000 Largest Companies
Extel's European Companies Services
Major Companies of the USA
Principal International Businesses
Kompass (most European countries have their own edition)
Key British Enterprises
Quarterly Review BWD Rensburg
Sell's Directory of Products and Services
For more detailed company information consult:
Extel's British Companies Services
Companies' Annual Reports Collection
Fame CD-ROM
Asia's 7500 Largest Companies

What are the trends?

Possible sources to consider:
The Book of European Forecasts
Marketing in Europe
European Trends
Consumer Europe
Family Expenditure Survey

Social Trends
Retail Business
Mintel Market Intelligence

EU statistical and information sources

Eurostat is a series of publications which provide a detailed picture of the EU. They can be obtained by visiting European Documentation Centres (often in university libraries) in all EU countries. Themes include general statistics, economy and finance, and population/social conditions. *European Access* is a bulletin on issues, policies, activities and events concerning EU member states. *Marketing and Research Today* is a journal which examines social, political, economic and business issues relating to western, Central and Eastern Europe.
European Report is a twice-weekly news publication from Brussels on industrial, economic and political issues.

Abstracts and indexes

Business Periodicals Index
ANBAR Marketing and Distribution Abstracts
Research Index

Guides to sources

A great variety of published information sources exists. The following source guides may help you in your search:

Marketing information

Guide to European Marketing Information
Compendium of Marketing Information Sources
Croner's A–Z of Business Information Sources
McCarthy Cards: a card service on which are reproduced extracts from the press covering companies and industries and it produces a useful guide to its sources:
UK and Europe Market Information: Basic Sources

Statistics

Guide to Official Statistics
Sources of Unofficial UK Statistics

Sources: The author thanks Jenny Finder and Maggie Fleming of the University of Bradford Management Centre Library for help in compiling this list

insights. Many industries have their experts in universities, financial institutions and the press who may be willing to share their knowledge. They can provide invaluable background information and can be useful for predicting future trends and developments.

Observation

Observation can also help in exploratory research when the product field is unfamiliar. Watching people buy wine in a supermarket or paint in a do-it-yourself store may be useful background

Group discussions (focus groups) allow companies to understand the beliefs, motivations and behaviour of consumers

knowledge when planning a survey in these markets, for example.

The objective of exploratory research, then, is not to collect quantitative data and form conclusions but to get better acquainted with the market and its customers. This allows the researcher to base the quantitative survey on *informed assumptions* rather than guesswork.

The main data collection stage

Following careful exploratory research, the design of the main data collection procedures will be made. Two alternative approaches are descriptive and experimental research.

Assuming the main data collection stage requires interviewing, the research design will be based upon the following questions:

✦ Who and how many people to interview: the sampling process?

✦ How to interview them: the survey method?

✦ What questions to ask: questionnaire design?

These research approaches and methods will now be examined.

Descriptive research

Survey research may be undertaken to describe customers' beliefs, attitudes, preferences, behaviour, etc. For example, a survey into advertising effectiveness might measure awareness of the brand, recall of the advertisement, and knowledge about its content.

Experimental research

The aim of experimental research is to establish cause and effect. *Experimental research* involves the setting up of control procedures to isolate the impact of a factor (e.g. a money-off sales promotion) on a dependent variable (e.g. sales). The key to successful experimental design is the elimination of other explanations of changes in the dependent variable. One way of doing this is to use random sampling. For example, the sales promotion might be applied in a random selection of stores with the remaining stores selling the brand without the money-off

offer. Statistical significance testing can be used to test whether differences in sales are likely to be caused by the sales promotion, or are simply random variations. The effects of other influences on sales are assumed to impact randomly on both the sales promotion and the no promotion alternatives.

The sampling process

Figure 6.6 outlines the *sampling process*. It begins by *defining the population*, that is the group which forms the subject of study in a

6.3   Marketing in Action

Pan-European Qualitative Research

The time when a qualitative study involved nothing more than four group discussions in two towns in one country is fast disappearing. Increasingly, marketing research agencies are being asked to arrange discussion groups in centres such as Milan, Paris, Madrid and London.

Coordinating such pan-European research bring its own problems. Typically the agency will brief overseas associate companies. Each uses its own local moderator who conducts the research, analyses the results and sends it to the coordinating agency. Each foreign report is then combined and an international report written for the client.

One problem is that qualitative research is viewed differently in various countries. In France, it is often used to generate new questions and ideas; in the UK, it is common for it to be used to answer questions without qualitative followup; in Germany, it is usual for it to have a quantitative backup. The reality is that many local agencies are reluctant to change the way they operate in response to a brief from an overseas agency. The result is not only inconsistency but also coordination problems.

Another problem is inconsistencies in the quality of the researchers in various countries. In Central and Eastern Europe difficulties have arisen because researchers were not used to marketing surveys where the results were supposed to have commercial applications. Their experience was limited to opinion polling and sociological surveys. Extensive training by marketing researchers from EU countries has helped to reduce this difficulty.

One way of coping with the problems of inconsistency is to use the agency's own bilingual research staff. However, the gain in consistency may be outweighed by the loss of cultural understanding and sensitivity to important nuances.

Large multinational agencies who have experience of working together have an advantage. They can plan the survey centrally while using foreign nationals in overseas offices to conduct the interviewing. An example is Research International with around 40 offices worldwide. It benefits from years of sharing information on methodologies and techniques between its international, multilingual staff.

Based on: Thomas (1992)[18]

particular survey. The survey objective will be to provide results that are representative of this group. Sampling planners, for example, must ask questions like: do we interview all people over the age of 18 or restrict the population to those aged 18–60? Do we interview purchasing managers in all textile companies or only those that employ more than 200 people?

Once the population is defined the next step is to search for a *sampling frame*, that is a list or other record of the chosen population from which a sample can be selected. Examples include a register of electors, or the *Kompass* directory of companies. The result determines whether a random or non-random sample can be chosen. A random sample requires an accurate sampling frame; without one the researcher is restricted to non-random methods.

Three major *sampling methods* are simple random sampling, stratified random sampling, and quota sampling. It is also important to determine *sample size*.

Simple random sampling   each individual (or company) in the sampling frame is given a number, and numbers are drawn at random (by chance) until the sample is complete. The sample is random because everyone on the list has an equal chance of selection.

Stratified random sampling   the population is broken down into groups (e.g. by company size or industry) and a random sample is drawn (as above) for each group. This ensures that each group is represented in the sample.

Quota sampling   a sampling frame does not exist but the percentage of the population that falls in various groupings (e.g. gender, social class, age) is known. The sample is constructed by asking interviewers to select individuals on the basis of these percentages, e.g. roughly 50:50 females to males. This is a non-random method since not everyone has an equal chance of selection but it is much less expensive than random methods when the population is widely dispersed.

Sample size   this is a further key consideration when attempting to generate a representative sample. Clearly, the larger the sample size the more likely that the sample will represent the population. Statistical theory allows the calcu-

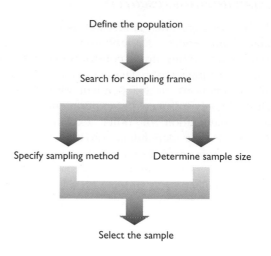

Figure 6.6 The sampling process

lation of sampling error, i.e. the error caused by not interviewing everyone in the population, for various sample sizes. In practice, the number of people interviewed is based on a balance between sampling error and cost considerations. Fortunately sample sizes of around 1000 (or fewer) can provide measurements that have tolerable error levels when representing populations counted in their millions.

The survey method

There are four options when choosing a *survey method*: face-to-face interviews, telephone interviews, mail surveys or Internet surveys. Each method has its own strengths and limitations; Table 6.3 gives an overview of these.

Face-to-face interviews   a major advantage of face-to-face interviews is that response rates are generally higher than for telephone interviews or mail surveys.[19] Seemingly the personal element in the contact makes refusal less likely. This is an important factor when considering how representative the sample is of the population and when using experimental designs. Testing the effectiveness of a stimulus would normally be conducted by face-to-face interview rather than a mail survey where high non-response rates and the lack of control over who completes the questionnaire would invalidate the results.

Face-to-face interviews are more versatile than

telephone and mail surveys. The use of many open-ended questions on a mail survey would lower response rates,[20] and time restrictions for a telephone interview limit their use. Probing is easier with face-to-face interviews. Two types of probes are *clarifying probes* (e.g. 'Can you explain what you mean by . . . ?') which help the interviewer understand exactly what the interviewee is saying, and *exploratory probes* which stimulate the interviewee to give a full answer (e.g. 'Are there any other reasons why . . . ?'). A certain degree of probing can be achieved with a telephone interview but time pressure and the less personalized situation will inevitably limit its use. Visual aids (e.g. a drawing of a new product concept) can be used where clearly they cannot with a telephone interview.

However, face-to-face interviews have their drawbacks. They are more expensive than telephone and mail questionnaires. Telephone and mail surveys are cheaper because the cost of contacting respondents is much less expensive, unless the population is very concentrated: face-to-face interviewing of students on a business studies course would be relatively inexpensive. The presence of an interviewer can cause bias (e.g. socially desirable answers) and lead to the misreporting of sensitive information. For example, O'Dell found that only 17 per cent of respondents admitted borrowing money from a bank in a face-to-face interview compared to 42 per cent in a comparable mail survey.[21]

Telephone interviews   in some ways these are a half-way house between face-to-face and mail surveys. They generally have a higher response rate than mail questionnaires but lower than face-to-face interviews; their cost is usually less than face-to-face but higher than for mail surveys; and they allow a degree of flexibility when interviewing. However, the use of visual aids is not possible and there are limits to the number of questions that can be asked before respondents either terminate the interview or give quick (invalid) answers to speed up the process. The use of computer-aided telephone interviewing (CATI) is growing. Centrally located interviewers read questions from a computer monitor and input answers via the keyboard. *Routing* through the questionnaire is computer-controlled helping the process of interviewing.

Mail surveys   given a reasonable response rate, mail survey research normally is the least expensive of the previous three options. A low research budget combined with a widely dispersed population may mean that there is no alternative to the mail survey. However, the major problem is the potential of low response rates and the accompanying danger of an unrepresentative sample. Much research has focused on ways of improving response rates to mail surveys and Table 6.4 gives a summary of the results.[22]

Mail questionnaires must be fully structured and so there is no opportunity to probe. Control

Table 6.3 A comparison of face-to-face, telephone and mail surveys				
	Face-to-face	*Telephone*	*Mail*	*Internet*
Questionnaire				
Use of open-ended questions	High	Medium	Low	Low
Ability to probe	High	Medium	Low	Low
Use of visual aids	High	Poor	High	High
Sensitive questions	Medium	Low	High	Low
Resources				
Cost	High	Medium	Low	Low
Sampling				
Widely dispersed populations	Low	Medium	High	High
Response rates	High	Medium	Low	Low
Experimental control	High	Medium	Low	Low
Interviewing				
Control of who completes questionnaire	High	High	Low	Low/High
Interviewer bias	Possible	Possible	Low	Low

over who completes the questionnaire is low; for example a marketing manager may pass the questionnaire to a subordinate for completion. However, visual aids can be supplied with the questionnaire and because of self-completion, interviewer bias is low although there may still be a source effect (e.g. whether the questionnaire was sent from a commercial or non-commercial source).

Internet surveys the Internet is a new medium for conducting survey research. The questionnaire is administered usually by e-mail or signalling its presence on a website by registering key words or using banner advertising on search engines such as Yahoo! or Excite to drive people to the questionnaire. e-Marketing 6.2 describes how the Internet has been used in marketing research.

The major advantage of the Internet as a marketing research vehicle is its low cost since printing and postal costs are eliminated, making it even cheaper than mail surveys. In other ways its characteristics are similar to mail surveys: the use of open-ended questions is limited (as they will reduce response rates) and its impersonal nature limits the ability to probe. Visual aids can be supplied with the questionnaire and response rates are likely to be lower than face-to-face and telephone interviews. Experimental control is low since there is not complete control over who responds to the questionnaire but interviewer bias is likely to be lower than for face-to-face and telephone interviews because of the impersonal administration of the questionnaire. A strength of the Internet survey is its ability to cover global populations at low cost although sampling problems can arise because of the skewed nature of Internet users. These tend to be from the younger and more affluent groups in society. For surveys requiring a cross-sectional sample this can be severely restricting.

When response is by e-mail the identity of the respondent will automatically be sent to the

6.2 e-Marketing

Using the Internet as a Survey Method

The Internet has advantages and disadvantages like any other survey method. It is often used because of its low cost and its ability to reach specific audiences. British Airways posted a questionnaire on its website exclusively used by the airline's Executive Club members with 9000 people responding within nine months.

Reuters has also been active in on-line research. A questionnaire was put on its website researching the potential demand for a new online news service for Irish expatriates. Traffic was driven to it by the registration of key words on search engines. For example, anyone searching for 'Irish News' would have been offered a link to the questionnaire site. The commercial think-tank, Future Foundation, used banner advertising on search engines Yahoo! and Excite to drive people to a questionnaire which yielded 826 respondents.

A problem when using e-mail to survey populations is the absence of accurate lists. Even when lists can be found researchers need to treat very carefully as 'spamming'—sending junk mail—is seen as very offensive by most e-mail users.

Nevertheless, the medium can offer tangible advantages over other survey methods particularly when surveying those groups who are accustomed to spending time on-line, most notably buyers of high-tech products.

Based on: Gray (1999);[23] Kleinman (1998)[24]

survey company. This lack of anonymity may restrict the respondent's willingness to answer sensitive questions honestly. However, for e-mail surveys, control over who completes the questionnaire is fairly high but for Internet surveys which invite anyone to complete the questionnaire using registration or banner advertising with search engines control is low.

European expenditure on *ad-hoc* quantitative research is shown in Fig. 6.7.

Questionnaire design

Three conditions are necessary to get a true response to a question. First, respondents must *understand* the question; second, respondents

---

Table 6.4   Methods of improving mail survey response rates

Activity	Effect on response rate
Prior notification by mail	Increase in consumer research but not for commercial populations
Prior notification by telephone	Increased response rate
Monetary and non-monetary incentives	Increased response rate
Type of postage	Higher response rates for stamped return envelopes
Personalization	The effect varies: it cannot be assumed that personalization always increases response
Granting anonymity to respondents	Higher response rate when issue is sensitive
Questionnaire length	Only a slight reduction in response rate as questionnaire lengthens
Coloured questionnaire	No effect on response rate
Deadline	No effect on response rate
Types of questions	Closed-ended questions get higher response than open-ended
Follow-ups	Follow-up telephone calls and mailings increase response rates

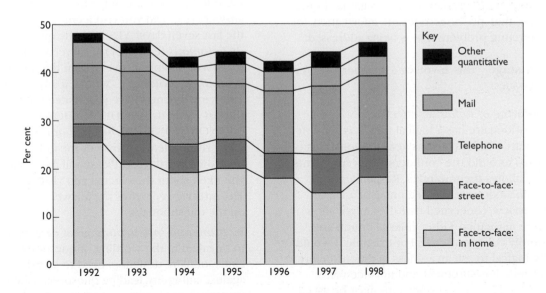

Figure 6.7 Ad-hoc quantitative expenditure, European averages (%).

must be *able to provide* the information; and third, they must be *willing to provide* it. Researchers must remember these conditions when designing questionnaires. Questions need to be phrased in the language that the respondent understands. This can prove problematical with some types of respondents, however. A psychological survey of footballers called upon club managers to pass on questionnaires to their players.[25] One manager replied 'Please feel free to send your questionnaires to me. I shall be happy to distribute them to the two or three players who can read or write, and have an attention span of longer than two minutes.'

Equally, researchers must not ask about issues that respondents cannot remember or are outside their experience. For example, it would be invalid to ask about attitudes towards a brand of which the respondent is not aware. Finally, researchers need to consider the best way to elicit sensitive or personal information. As we have already seen, the willingness to provide such information depends on the survey method employed.

Figure 6.8 shows the three stages in the development of *the questionnaire*: planning, design and pilot.

Planning stage this involves the types of decisions discussed so far in this chapter. It provides a firm foundation for designing a questionnaire that provides relevant information for the marketing problem that is being addressed.

Design stage this involves a number of inter-related issues:

1 *Ordering of topics*: an effective questionnaire has a logical flow. It is sensible to start with easy-to-answer questions. This helps to build the confidence of respondents and allows them to relax. Respondents are often anxious at the beginning of an interview, concerned that they might show their ignorance. Other rules-of-thumb are simply common sense. For example it would be logical to ask awareness questions before attitude measurement and not vice versa. Unaided awareness questions must be asked before aided ones. Classificatory questions that ask for personal information such as age and occupation are usually asked last.

2 *Types of questions*: *closed-ended questions* specify the range of answers that will be

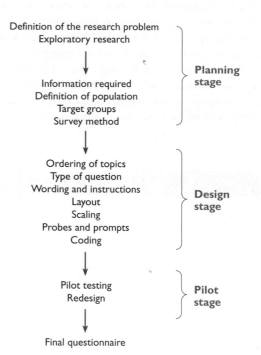

Figure 6.8 Stages in the development of a questionnaire

recorded. If there are only two possible answers (e.g. 'Did you visit a cinema within the last seven days?' YES/NO) the question is *dichotomous* (either/or). If there are more than two possible answers, then the question is *multiple choice* (e.g. 'Which, if any, of the following cinemas have you visited within the last seven days?' ODEON, SHOWCASE, CANNON, NONE). *Open-ended questions* allow respondents to answer the question in their own words (e.g. 'Please tell me what you liked about the cinema you visited?'). The interviewer writes the answer in a space on the questionnaire.

3 *Wording and instructions*: great care needs to be taken in the wording of questions. Questionnaire designers need to guard against ambiguity, leading questions, asking two-questions-in-one, and using unfamiliar words. Table 6.5 gives some examples of poorly worded questions and suggests remedies. Instructions should be printed in capital letters or underlined so that they are easily distinguished from questions.

4   *Layout*: the questionnaire should not appear cluttered. If possible, answers and codes should each form a column so that they are easy to identify. In mail questionnaires, it is a mistake to squeeze too many questions on one page so that the questionnaire length (in pages) is shortened. Response is more likely to be lower if the questionnaire appears heavy than if its page length is extended.[26]

5   *Scaling*: careful exploratory research may allow attitudes and beliefs to be measured by means of scales. Respondents are given lists of statements (e.g. 'My company's marketing information system allows me to make better decisions') followed by a choice of five positions on a scale ranging from 'strongly agree' to 'strongly disagree'. Exploratory research identifies statements, and a structured questionnaire is used to provide quantification.

6   *Probes and prompts*: probes seek to explore or clarify what a respondent has said. Following a question about awareness of brand names, the *exploratory probe* 'Any others?' would seek to identify further names. Sometimes respondents use vague words or phrases like 'I like going on holiday because it is nice'. A *clarifying probe* such as, 'In what way is it nice?' would seek a more meaningful response. *Prompts*, on the other hand, aid responses to a question. For example, in an aided recall question a list of brand names would be provided for the respondent.

7   *Coding*: by using closed questions the interviewer merely has to ring the code number next to the respondent's choice of answer. In computer-assisted telephone interviewing and with the increasing use of laptop computers for face-to-face interviewing, the appropriate code number can be directly keyed into computer memory. Such questionnaires are *pre-coded* making the process of interviewing and data analysis much simpler. Open-ended questions, however, require the interviewer to write down the answer verbatim. This necessitates *post-coding* whereby answers are categorized after the interview. This can be a time-consuming and laborious task.

Pilot stage   once the preliminary questionnaire has been designed it should be piloted with a representative subsample, to test for faults. Piloting is not the same as exploratory research. Exploratory research helps to decide upon the research design; piloting tests the questionnaire design and helps to estimate costs. Face-to-face piloting where respondents are asked to answer questions and comment on any problems concerning a questionnaire read out by an interviewer is preferable to impersonal piloting where the questionnaire is given to respondents for self-completion and they are asked to write down any problems found.[27] Once the pilot work proves satisfactory the final questionnaire can be administered to the chosen sample.

Table 6.5 Poorly worded questions	
Question	*Problem and solution*
What type of wine do you prefer?	'Type' is ambiguous: respondents could say 'French', 'red', 'claret' depending on their interpretation. Showing the respondent a list and asking 'from this list …' would avoid the problem
Do you think that prices are cheaper at Asda than at Aldi?	Leading question favouring Asda: a better question would be 'Do you think that prices at Asda are higher, lower or about the same as at Aldi?' Names should be reversed for half the sample
Which is more powerful and kind to your hands: Ariel or Bold?	Two questions in one: Ariel may be more powerful but Bold may be kinder to the hands. Ask the two questions separately
Do you find it paradoxical that X lasts longer and yet is cheaper than Y?	Unfamiliar word: a study has shown that less than a quarter of the population understand such words as paradoxical, chronological or facility. Test understanding before use

Data analysis and interpretation

Quantitative analysis of questionnaire data will invariably be carried out by computer. Basic marketing analyses can be carried out using such software analysis packages as SNAP or MARQUIS on a personal computer. More sophisticated analyses can be conducted using a package such as SPSS-PC.

Basic analysis may be at the descriptive level (e.g. means, standard deviations and frequency tables) or on a comparative basis (e.g. cross tabulations and t-tests). More sophisticated analysis may search for relationships (e.g. regression analysis), group respondents (e.g. cluster analysis) or establish cause and effect (e.g. analysis of variance techniques used on experimental data). Computer-aided analysis of marketing research data is not limited to quantitative data. Marketing in Action 6.4 describes how the analysis of vast volumes of qualitative data can be aided by the use of a software package called NUD.IST.

The growth in data captured through direct marketing activity and loyalty cards has led to the need to analyse this data so that meaningful purchasing information and trends can be observed. The analysis of this data is called 'data mining' and e-Marketing 6.3 discusses developments in this field.

Great care is required when interpreting marketing research results. One common failing is to infer cause and effect when only association has been established. For example, establishing a relationship that sales rise when advertising levels increase does not necessarily mean that raising advertising expenditure will lead to an increase in sales. Other marketing variables, e.g. salesforce effect, may have increased at the same time as the increase in advertising, or the advertising budget may have been dependent on sales levels. Either explanation would invalidate the claim that advertising causes sales to rise.

A second cautionary note concerns the interpretation of means and percentages. Given that a sample has been taken, any mean or percentage is an estimate subject to *sampling error*, that is the error in an estimate due to taking a sample rather than interviewing the entire population. A market research survey that estimates that 50 per cent of males but only 45 per cent of females smoke does not necessarily suggest that smoking is more prevalent among males. Given the sampling error associated with each estimate, the true conclusion might be that there is no difference between males and females. Statistical hypothesis testing allows sample differences to be evaluated in the light of sampling error to establish whether they are likely to be real

6.4   Marketing in Action

Qualitative Research and NUD.IST

For many years the power of the computer has been brought to bear on the quantitative analysis of data. More recently, however, software packages such as NUD.IST harness the computer's potential to analyse voluminous and complex qualitative data. Data can be filed, accessed and organized in more sophisticated ways than manual analysis. For example, text can be organized by category such as single men, married men and married men with children. The computer could be requested to perform a search like 'produce a list of quotations relating to the code "safety features in cars" as described by married men'. This can aid interpretation of data by drawing together the relevant quotations for close scrutiny, making analysis quicker, easier and more sophisticated than ever before.

Based on: Dembkowski and Hanmer-Lloyd (1995)[28]

differences (statistically significant) or likely to be a result of taking a sample (rather than interviewing the entire population).

Report writing and presentation

Crouch suggests that the key elements in a research report are as follows:[29]

1   Title page.
2   List of contents.
3   Preface: outline of agreed brief, statement of objectives, scope and methods of research.
4   Summary of conclusions and recommendations.
5   Previous related research: how previous research has had a bearing on this research.
6   Research method.
7   Research findings.
8   Conclusions.
9   Appendices.

Sections 1–4 provide a concise description of the nature and outcomes of the research for busy managers. Sections 5–9 provide the level of detail necessary if any particular issue (e.g. the basis of a finding, or the analytical technique used) needs checking. The report should be written in the language which the reader will understand. Jargon should be avoided.

Software packages such as Powerpoint or Freelance considerably ease the production of pie charts, histograms, graphs, etc., for use in the report or the presentational purposes, e.g. the production of acetates for overhead projection.

6.3   e-Marketing
Data Mining

The increasing use of information technology to capture data about customer purchase behaviour has, in recent years, provided companies with mountains of new data. Consider, for example, the data that is held by just one supermarket through the analysis of the loyalty cards which they issue to their customers. Clearly, such information has the potential to be a rich source of new knowledge. This only becomes a valid objective, however, if ways can be found to 'mine' these veins of knowledge.

This problem has attracted the attention of a number of software companies. The outcome has been the development of a new generation of data-mining tools from companies such as AbTech, Data Mining Technologies, Future Analytics, Information Discovery, NeoVista and Ultragem. Their tools permit the conversion of data 'warehoused' within the firm into predictive information on:

✦   Classifying data into meaningful entities for determining interactions between market variables

✦   Modelling explicit relationships between datasets

✦   Clustering data into understandable market categories or segments

✦   Determining deviations that may be indicative of new trends in customer behaviour.

The result is that those companies which have adopted data-mining systems have a much more detailed understanding of customer behaviour. This knowledge can be used for cross-product selling, making offers to enhance customer loyalty and identifying new ways of further improving the quality of customer services.

Based on: Baker (1998)[30]

The emergence of inexpensive colour printers means that colour graphics can be used.

The use of marketing information systems and marketing research

A key issue is an understanding of the factors which affect the use of marketing information systems and marketing research. Systems and marketing research reports that remain unused are valueless in decision-making. So what factors are likely to bring about increased usage?

Two studies of MkIS have examined the factors which affect usage. Systems are used more when:

✦ The system is sophisticated and confers prestige to its users.

✦ Other departments view the system as a threat.

✦ There is pressure from top management to use the system.

✦ Users are more involved in automation.

The system takes more of the marketing executive's time when:

✦ It provides information indiscriminately.

✦ It provides less assistance.

✦ It is changed without consultation.

These results have implications for the design of MkIS. Sophisticated systems should be designed which provide information on a selective basis (for example, by means of a direct, interactive capability).[31] Senior management should conspicuously support use of the system. These recommendations are in line with Ackoff's view that a prime task of an information system is to eliminate irrelevant information by tailoring information flows to individual manager's needs.[32] It also supports the prescription of Piercy and Evans that the system should be seen to have top management support.[33]

Research into the use of market research has shown that use is higher if:[34]

✦ Results conform to the client's prior beliefs.

✦ The research is technically competent.

✦ The presentation of results are clear.

✦ The findings are politically acceptable.

✦ The status quo is not challenged.

These findings suggest that marketing researchers need to appreciate not only the technical aspects of research and the need for clarity in report presentation but also the political dimension of information provision: it is unlikely that marketing research reports will be used in decision-making if the results threaten the status quo or are likely to have adverse political repercussions. As Machiavelli said, 'Knowledge is power'. The sad fact is that perfectly valid and useful information may be ignored in decision-making for reasons that are outside the technical competence of the research.

This chapter has examined the nature and role of marketing information systems and marketing research. We have seen that there are clearly prescribed procedures and techniques for gathering information to aid marketing decision-making. Its importance is reflected in a large and growing European market for marketing research services. As the barriers to cross-national competition fall there is likely to be a growth in multi-country research studies and a need for agencies to provide efficient means of gathering such data.

Ethical issues in marketing research

The intention of marketing research is to benefit both the sponsoring company and its consumers. The company learns about the needs and buyer behaviour of consumers with the objective of better satisfying their needs. Despite these good intentions there are four ethical concerns about marketing research. These are intrusions on privacy, the misuse of marketing research findings, competitive information gathering, and the use of marketing research surveys as a guise for selling.

Intrusions on privacy

While many consumers recognize the positive role marketing research plays in the provision of goods and services, some resent the intrusive nature of some marketing research surveys. Most consumer surveys ask for classificatory data such as age, occupation and income. While most surveys ask respondents to indicate an age and income band rather than request specifics, some people feel this is an intrusion on privacy. Other people object to receiving unsolicited telephone calls or mail surveys, and dislike being stopped in the street to be asked to complete a face-to-face survey. As the use of the Internet as a marketing research tool grows, ethical issues regarding the unsolicited receipt of e-mail questionnaires may arise. The rights of individuals to privacy is incorporated in the guidelines of many research associations. For example, a code of conduct of the European Society for Opinion and Marketing Research (ESOMAR) states that 'no information which could be used to identify informants, either directly or indirectly, shall be revealed other than to research personnel within the researchers' own organization who require this knowledge for the administration and checking of interviews and data processing'.[35] Under no circumstances should the information from a survey combined with the address/telephone number of the respondent be supplied to a salesperson.

Misuse of marketing research findings

Where the findings of marketing research are to be used in an advertising campaign or as part of a sales pitch there can be a temptation to bias the results in favour of the desired outcome. Respondents could be chosen who are more likely to give a favourable response. For example, a study comparing a domestic versus foreign brand of car could be biased by only choosing people who owned domestic-made cars. Another source of bias is by using leading questions. For example, 'In a world that is becoming increasingly environmentally aware, would you prefer more or less recyclable packaging?'

Another potential source of bias in the use of marketing research findings is where the client explicitly or implicitly communicates to the researcher the preferred research result. For example, a product champion for a new product may have a vested interest in the product being launched. For it to be ditched at the later stages

of the new product development process may represent a political defeat for the product champion who may have spent the last six months pushing it through a series of internal committees. In such circumstances, there is the potential for the most favoured outcome to be communicated to the research agency. Where the product champion is influential in the choice of agency, the latter may recognize that giving bad news to the client may sour their relationship and jeopardize future business. While most marketing researchers accept the need for objective studies where there is room for more than one interpretation or study findings, for example, the temptation to present the more favourable representation could be overpowering.

Competitive information gathering

The modern marketing concept stresses the need to understand both customers and competitors in order to build a competitive advantage. However, the methods which may be required to gather competitor intelligence can raise ethical questions. Questionable practices include using student projects to gather information without the student revealing the sponsor of the research, pretending to be a potential supplier who is conducting a telephone survey to understand the market, posing as a potential customer at an exhibition, bribing a competitor's employee to pass on proprietary information and covert surveillance such as through the use of hidden cameras. Thankfully, competitive information gathering does not exclusively depend on those methods since much useful information can be gathered by reading trade journals and newspapers, searching the Internet, analysing databases, and acquiring financial statements.

Selling under the guise of marketing research

This practice, commonly known as 'sugging' is a real danger to the reputation of marketing research. Despite the fact that it is not usually practised by bona fide marketing research agencies but unscrupulous selling companies who use marketing research as a means of gaining compliance to their requests to ask people questions, it is the marketing research industry which suffers from its aftermath. Usually, the questions begin innocently enough but move towards the real purpose of the exercise. Often this is to qualify prospects and ask whether they would be interested in buying the product or have a salesperson call. In Europe, ESOMAR encourages research agencies to adopt codes of practice to prevent the practice, and national bodies such as the Market Research Society in the UK draw up strict guidelines. However, the problem remains that the organizations who practice sugging are unlikely to be members of those bodies. the ultimate deterrent is the realization on the part of 'suggers' that the method is no longer effective.

Summary

Marketing research is a key element in a marketing information system (MkIS). It is mainly concerned with information about markets and the reaction of these to product, price, distribution and promotion decisions. Data can be gathered from secondary (e.g. directories, reports) or primary (e.g. surveys) sources. Secondary data may be found internally within companies (e.g. sales trends). Marketing research agencies provide a wide range of services to their client companies including drawing up research proposals, designing studies and questionnaires, analysing data and report writing. Four ethical issues are intrusions on privacy, the misuse of marketing research findings, competitive information gathering, and the use of marketing research surveys as a guise for selling.

Internet exercise

Code of ethics

Sites to visit
http://www.esomar.nl

Exercise
Discuss the Marketing Research Code of Ethics adopted by ESOMAR. What issues and challenges does it raise for marketers?

Study questions

1 What are the essential differences between a marketing information system and marketing research?

2 What are secondary and primary data? Why should secondary data be collected before primary data?

3 What is the difference between a research brief and proposal? What advice would you give a marketing research agency when making a research proposal?

4 Mail surveys should be used only as a last resort. Do you agree?

5 Discuss the problems of conducting a multi-country market research survey in the EU. How can these problems be minimized?

6 Why are marketing research reports more likely to be used if they conform to the prior beliefs of the client? Does this raise any ethical questions regarding the interpretation and presentation of findings?

7 What are the strengths and limitations of using the Internet as a data collection instrument?

References

1. Van Bruggen, A., A. Smidts and B. Wierenga (1996) The Impact of the Quality of a Marketing Decision Support System: An Experimental Study, *International Journal of Research in Marketing*, **13**, 331-43.

2. Jobber, D. and C. Rainbow (1977) A Study of the Development and Implementation of Marketing Information Systems in British Industry, *Journal of the Marketing Research Society*, **19** (3), 104-11.

3. Jain, S. C. (1981) *Marketing Planning and Strategy*, South Western Publishing.

4. Moutinho, L. and M. Evans (1992) *Applied Marketing Research*, Colorado Springs, CO: Wokingham: Addison-Wesley, 5.

5. Kotler, P., W. Gregor and W. Rodgers (1977) The Marketing Audit Comes of Age, *Sloan Management Review*, winter, 25-42.

6. Fletcher, W. (1997) Why Researchers are so Jittery, *Financial Times*, 3 March, 16.

7. ESOMAR Annual Study on the Marketing Research Industry (1998). Published by ESOMAR (2000), Amsterdam, The Netherlands.

8. Anonymous (1999) The Information Gold Mine, *Business Week*, 26 July, 10-17.

9. ESOMAR Annual Study 1998, op. cit.

10. Fletcher, W. (1997) Why Researchers are so Jittery, *Financial Times*, 3 March, 16.

11. Cook, R. (1999) Focus Groups Have to Evolve if they are to Survive, *Campaign*, 9 July, 14.

12. Hemsley, S. (1999) Paid Informers, *Marketing Week*, 19 August, 45-7.

13. Crouch, S. and M. Housden (1999) *Marketing Research for Managers*, Oxford: Butterworth-Heinemann, 253.

14. Crouch and Housden (1999) op. cit., 260.

15. Wright, L. T., and M. Crimp (2000) *The Marketing Research Process*, London: Prentice-Hall, 16.

16. Gray, R. (1999) Tracking the Online Audience, *Marketing*, 18 February, 41-3.

17. Goulding, C. (1999) Consumer Research, Interpretive Paradigms and Methodological Ambiguities, *European Journal of Marketing*, **33** (9/10), 859-73.

18. Thomas, H. (1992) Abroad Research Base, *Marketing*, 30 July.

19. Yu, J. and H. Cooper (1983) A Quantitative Review of Research Design Effects on Response Rates to Questionnaires, *Journal of Marketing Research*, **20** February, 156-64.

20. Falthzik, A. and S. J. Carroll (1971) Rate of Return for Close v Open-ended Questions in a Mail Survey of Industrial Organisations, *Psychological Reports*, **29**, 1121-2.

21. O'Dell, W. F. (1962) Personal Interviews or Mail Panels, *Journal of Marketing*, **26**, 34-9.

22. See Kanuk, L. and C. Berenson (1975) Mail Surveys and Response Rates: A Literature Review, *Journal of Marketing Research*, **12** (November), 440-53; Jobber, D. (1986) Improving Response Rates to Industrial Mail Surveys, *Industrial Marketing Management*, **15**, 183-95; Jobber, D. and D. O'Reilly (1998) Industrial Mail Surveys: A Methodological Update, *Industrial Marketing Management*, **27**, 95-107.

23. Gray, R. (1999) Tracking the Online Audience, *Marketing*, 18 February, 41-3.

24. Kleinman, P. (1998) a Survey of the Survey Trade, *Admap*, February, 11-12.

25. Price, R. (1992) Soccer Diary, *Guardian*, 19 December, 16.

26. Jobber, D. (1985) Questionnaire Design and Mail Survey Response Rates, *European Research*, **13** (3), 124-9.

27. Reynolds, N. and A. Diamantopoulos (1998) The Effect of Pretest Method on Error Detection Rates: Experimental Evidence, *European Journal of Marketing*, **32** (5/6), 480-98.

28. Dembkowski, S. and S. Hanmer-Lloyd (1995) Computer Applications—A New Road to Qualitative Data Analysis, *European Journal of Marketing*, **29** (11), 50-62.

29. Crouch (1992) op. cit.

30. Baker, K. (1998) Mine Over Matter, *Journal of Business Strategy*, **19** (4), 22-7.

31. Jobber, D. and M. Watts (1986) Behavioural Aspects of Marketing Information Systems, *Omega*, **14** (1), 69-79; Wierenga, B. and P. A. M. Oude Ophis (1997) Marketing Decision Support Systems: Adoption, Use and Satisfaction, *International Journal of Research in Marketing*, **14**, 275-90.

32. Ackoff, R. L. (1967) Management Misinformation Systems, *Management Science*, **14** (4) 147-56.

33. Piercy, N. and M. Evans (1983) Managing *Marketing Information*, Beckenham: Croom Helm.

34. See Deshpande, R. and S. Jeffries (1981) Attitude Affecting the Use of Marketing Research in Decision-Making: An Empirical Investigation, in *Educators' Conference Proceedings*, Chicago: American Marketing Association, 1-4; Lee, H., F. Acito and R. L. Day (1987) Evaluation and Use of Marketing Research by Decision Makers: A Behavioural Simulation, *Journal of Marketing Research*, **14** (May); 187-96.

35. Schlegelmilch, B. (1998) *Marketing Ethics: An International Perspective*, London: International Thomson Business Press.

Key terms

marketing information system a system in which marketing information is formally gathered, stored, analysed, and distributed to managers in accord with their informational needs on a regular, planned basis

data the most basic form of knowledge, the result of observations

information Combinations of data which provide decision-relevant knowledge

marketing research the gathering of data and information on the market

ad-boc research a research project which focuses on a specific problem collecting data at one point in time with one sample of respondents

continuous research repeated interviewing of the same sample of people

omnibus survey a regular survey usually operated by a market research specialist company which asks questions of respondents

consumer panel household consumers which provide information on their purchases over time

retail audit a type of continuous research tracking the sales of products through retail outlets

research brief written document stating the client's requirements

research proposal a document defining what the marketing research agency promises to do for its client and how much it will cost

exploratory research the preliminary exploration of a research area prior to the main data collection stage

secondary research data which has already been collected by another researcher for another pupose

qualitative research exploratory research which aims to understand consumers' attitudes, values, behaviour and beliefs

focus group a group normally of 6–8 consumers brought together for a discussion focusing on an aspect of a company's marketing

depth interviews the interviewing of consumers individually for perhaps one or two hours with the aim of understanding their attitudes, values, behaviour and/or beliefs

descriptive research research undertaken to describe customer's beliefs attitudes, preferences, behaviour

experimental research research undertaken in order to establish cause and effect

sampling process a term used in research to denote the selection of a sub-set of the total population in order to interview them

Case 9 WP Forty

WP Forty is a lubricant used throughout virtually all sectors of industry and by private consumers. It is a spray lubricant used to free up mechanisms that have become jammed. The company has recently successfully completed a market research study among *consumers* who buy the product from hardware stores for general use within the home and on their cars, boats, and so on. But the company is now about to embark on a study of the purchase of WP Forty in the industrial sector. It is important that the study covers all sectors of industry and commerce given WP Forty's widespread use.

Task: As research director at Industrial & Business Products Research, prepare a detailed research proposal outlining how you would construct a study that would provide feedback from a representative sample of national businesses on attitudes towards, and usage of, WP Forty. The aim of the survey is to assess to what extent WP Forty is continuing to meet the needs and requirements of its existing customers. Although it is unlikely that the core lubrication itself will change, consideration is being given to changing the dispenser (to make WP Forty easier to use in different applications) and the size and shape of the different containers. There are also concerns within W P Forty Ltd about whether the product should be branded differently now that the UK-based company has been taken over by the Munich-based industrial grease giant Sammers Inc. There is uncertainty about whether stressing W P Forty's worldwide international connections will strengthen the brand, or whether it will simply confuse the national customer. Your proposal should also address the critical question of how to identify the most appropriate person within the organization to discuss these matters with. You should also include precise recommendations on the data collection method you would propose to gather this information, providing a clear rationale for your choice.

This case was prepared by David Smith, Chief Examiner for the Market Research Society, UK. Copyright © 1997 MRS.

Case 10 Harveys Stores

Harveys is a family-owned departmental store located in a European city with a population of 300 000, though the surrounding urban area comprises over 3 million people in a 25-mile diameter. There are two branches, a city centre shop and a much smaller suburban outlet. The company was formed in 1854 and is still owned by the founding family.

Though there are other shops with the same kind of product range, all national chains, these are not seen as direct competitors by the board. Rather, a regional chain, Partridges, with five branches is seen as the key competitor. This conclusion is based on both companies sharing the values of high quality and good service, appealing to the AB socio-economic groups.

Just over a year ago, a young graduate was appointed as a management trainee. Flo Rohr has a degree in marketing and after a year on the management training programme, has assumed responsibility as marketing manager. As the company had no previous experience of formal marketing information systems, Flo suggested a market research department be formed. She appointed a market research assistant, Benny George, who has recently completed his first project.

Benny described this project to Flo as an image study, explaining that this would help in the positioning of the store *vis-à-vis* the competition. This sounded attractive to Flo, given the increasing competition in the high street together with the development of two large shopping malls within 25 miles of the city.

Benny used Harveys and Partridges as the comparison for the study. He decided to use a series of semantic differential scales to compare the images of these stores. Having read the company annual report and strategic plan, Benny knew the image that Harveys wanted to convey and who it wanted as its customer profile. Benny used this information and his knowledge about the store's image gathered from the management team, to compile the items for the scale. He used six-point scales for each item.

To find a sampling frame, Benny used local census data to identify housing areas with a median income higher than the area average. He then used a systematic random sample to select 2000 names from these areas from the current

Table C.10.1 Image study results—Harveys and Partridges

Scale items		Mean scores[1]	
Positive	*Negative*	*Harveys*	*Partridges*
High quality	Low quality	2.26	2.63[2]
Fast service	Slow service	4.56	4.03[2]
Dependable	Undependable	1.96	2.05
Friendly	Unfriendly	3.17	2.16[2]
Attentive staff	Unconcerned staff	3.97	3.93
Well displayed	Cluttered	1.23	3.26[2]
Clean	Scruffy	1.33	1.47
Helpful assistants	Unhelpful assistants	3.61	3.02[2]
Easy-to-find items	Hard to find	2.83	2.87
Modern	Old fashioned	1.86	2.32[2]
Pleasant	Unpleasant	2.15	1.91
Large selection	Limited selection	2.41	2.96[2]
Reliable	Unreliable	1.93	1.97
Easy parking	Difficult to park	3.84	3.92

[1] Low scores indicate agreement with the item on the left in the table.

[2] A difference between these two means of this size or greater would only occur less than one in ten times by chance.

telephone directory. The questionnaire was sent to each of those contacts. It presented two sets of the semantic differential scales—one for Harveys and one for Partridges. It also included questions about shopping frequency at both stores and a reply-paid envelope was enclosed; 120 were returned undeliverable. After two weeks 243 usable replies were received. Benny was happy with this sample size and so calculated the summary reactions of respondents. The images of the two firms were found to be as shown in Table C10.1.

This case was prepared by Gillian Wright, Professor of Strategic Management, John Moores University, Liverpool.

Questions

1   How would you have specified and planned this project?

2   Evaluate the choice of the scale items used.

3   Evaluate the sampling procedure and suggest alternatives.

4   What inferences and conclusions would you draw from these results?

5   What other analyses would be useful?

CHAPTER SEVEN

Marketing Segmentation and Positioning

'Pan Am takes good care of you.
Marks and Spencer loves you.
Securicor cares ...
At Amstrad: "We want your money"'

ALAN SUGAR

Learning Objectives *This chapter explains:*

1 The concepts of market segmentation and target marketing and their use in developing marketing strategy

2 The methods of segmenting consumer and organizational markets

3 The factors that can be used to evaluate market segments

4 Four target market strategies: undifferentiated, differentiated, focused and customized marketing

5 The concept of positioning and the keys to successful positioning

6 Positioning and repositioning strategies

Very few products or services can satisfy all customers in a market. Not all customers want or are prepared to pay for the same things. For example, airlines such as British Airways, KLM and SAS recognize that business and pleasure travellers are different in terms of their price sensitivity and level of service required. In the watch market, the type of person who buys a Swatch is very different from the type of person who buys a Rolex: their reasons for purchase are different (fashion v. status) and the type of watch they want is different in terms of appearance and materials. Therefore to implement the marketing concept and successfully satisfy customer needs, different product and service offerings must be made to the diverse customer groups that typically comprise a market.

The technique that is used by marketers to get a hold on the diverse nature of markets is called *market segmentation*. Market segmentation is defined as:

> The identification of individuals or organizations with similar characteristics that have significant implications for the determination of marketing strategy.

Market segmentation, then, consists of dividing a diverse market into a number of smaller, more similar submarkets. The objective is to identify groups of customers with similar requirements so that they can be served effectively while being of a sufficient size for the product or service to be supplied efficiently. Usually, particularly in consumer markets, it is not possible to create a marketing mix that satisfies every individual's particular requirements exactly. Market segmentation, by grouping together customers with *similar* needs, provides a commercially viable method of serving these customers. It is therefore at the heart of strategic marketing since it forms the basis by which marketers understand their markets and develop strategies for serving their chosen customers better than the competition

Why bother?

Why go to the trouble of segmenting markets? What are the gains to be made? Figure 7.1 identifies four benefits, which we will shall now discuss.

Target market selection

Market segmentation provides the basis for the *selection of target markets*. A *target market* is a chosen segment of market which a company has decided to serve. As customers in the target market segment have similar characteristics, a single marketing mix strategy can be developed to match those requirements. Creative segmentation may result in the identification of new segments that have not been served adequately hitherto and may form attractive target markets to attack. For example, the success of Carphone Warehouse which supplies mobile phones was originally based on the founder Charles Dunstone's realization that a key market segment, the self-employed such as builders, plumbers and roofers, were not being catered for. The main suppliers were targeting large corporate clients. His vision was to be the first to allow customers to visit a shop and see what mobile phones were available. His staff were trained to help customers decide which combination of rental and call charges best met their needs.[1] Later in this chapter we shall explore methods of segmenting markets so that new insight may be gained.

Tailored marketing mix

Market segmentation allows the grouping of customers based upon similarities (e.g. benefits sought) that are important when designing marketing strategies. Consequently this allows marketers to understand in-depth the requirements of a segment and *tailor a marketing mix package* that meets their needs. This is a fundamental step in the implementation of the marketing concept: segmentation promotes the notion of customer satisfaction by viewing markets as diverse sets of needs which must be understood and met by suppliers.

Differentiation

Market segmentation allows the development of *differential marketing strategies*. By breaking a market into its constituent subsegments a company may differentiate its offerings between segments (if it chooses to target more than one segment), and within each segment it can differentiate its offering from the competition. By creating a differential advantage over the competition a company is giving the customer a reason to buy from them rather than the competition.

Opportunities and threats

Market segmentation is useful when attempting to spot *opportunities and threats*. Markets are rarely static. As customers become more affluent, seek new experiences and develop new values, new segments emerge. The company that first spots a new underserved market segment and meets its needs better than the competition can find itself on a sales and profit growth trajectory. The success of Next, a UK clothing retailer, was founded on its identification of a new market segment: working women who wanted smart fashionable clothing at affordable prices. Similarly the neglect of a market segment can pose a threat if competition use it as a gateway to market entry. The Japanese manufacturers exploited British companies' disinterest in the low-powered motor cycle segment, and the reluctance of US motor car producers to make small cars allowed Japanese companies to form a beachhead from which they swiftly achieved market-wide penetration. The lesson is that market segments may need to be targeted by established competitors even though in short-term commercial terms they do not appear attractive if there is a threat that they might be used by new entrants to establish a foothold in the market.

The process of market segmentation and target marketing

The selection of a target market or markets is a three-step process as shown in Fig. 7.2. First, the requirements and characteristics of the individuals and/or organizations that comprise the market are understood. Marketing research has an important role to play here. Second, customers are grouped according to these requirements and characteristics into segments that have implications for developing marketing strategies. Note that a given market can be segmented in various ways depending on the choice of criteria at this

stage. For example, the market for motor cars could be broken down according to type of buyer (individual or organizational), by major benefit sought in a car (e.g. functionality or status) or by family size (empty nester v. family with children). The choice of the most appropriate basis for segmenting a market is a creative act. There are no rules which lay down how a market should be segmented. Using a new criterion, or using a combination of well-known criteria in a novel way may give fresh insights into a market. Marketing personnel should be alert to the necessity of visualizing markets from fresh perspectives. In this way they may locate attractive, under-exploited market segments, and be the first to serve their needs.

Finally, one or more market segments are chosen for targeting. A marketing mix is developed, founded on a deep understanding of what the target market customers value. The aim is to design a mix which is distinctive from that which the competition are offering. This theme of creating a *differential advantage* will be discussed in more detail when we examine how to position a product in the marketplace.

Segmenting consumer markets

As we have noted, markets can be segmented in many ways. Segmentation variables are the criteria that are used for dividing a market into segments. When examining criteria, the marketer is trying to identify good predictors of differences in buyer behaviour. There is an array of options and no single, prescribed way of segmenting a market.[2] Here, we shall examine the possible ways of segmenting consumer markets; in the next section we shall look at segmentation of organizational markets.

There are three broad groups of consumer segmentation criteria: *behavioural*, *psychographic* and *profile* variables. Since the purpose of segmentation is to identify differences in behaviour that have implications for marketing decisions, *behavioural variables* such as benefits sought from the product and buying patterns may be considered the ultimate bases for segmentation. Psychographic variables are used when researchers believe that purchasing behaviour is correlated with the personality or lifestyle of consumers: consumers with different personalities or lifestyles have varying product or service preferences and may respond differently to marketing mix offerings. Having found these differences, the marketer needs to describe the people who exhibit them and this is where profile variables such as socio-economic group or

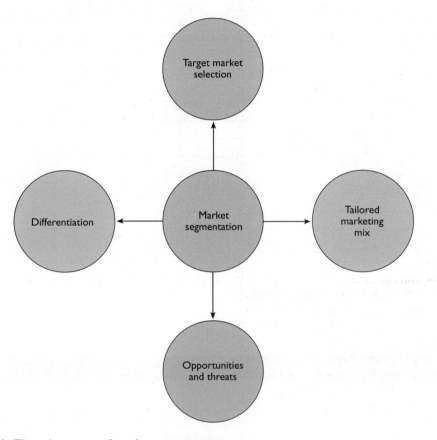

Figure 7.1 The advantages of market segmentation

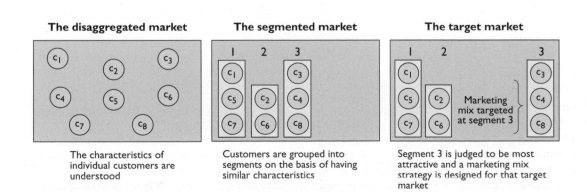

Figure 7.2 The process of market segmentation and target marketing

geographic location are valuable.[3] For example, a marketer may see whether there are groups of people who value low calories in soft drinks and then attempt to profile them in terms of their age, socio-economic groupings, etc.

In practice, however, segmentation may not follow this logical sequence. Often profile variables will be identified first and then the segments so described will be examined to see if they show different behavioural responses. For example, differing age or income groups may be examined to see if they show different attitudes and requirements towards cars. Figure 7.3 shows the major segmentation variables used in consumer markets and Table 7.1 describes each of these variables in greater detail.

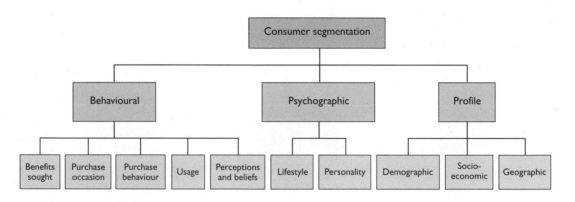

Figure 7.3 Segmenting consumer markets

Table 7.1	Consumer segmentation methods

Variable	Examples
Behavioural	
Benefits sought	Convenience, status, performance
Purchase occasion	Self-buy, gift
Purchase behaviour	Solus buying, brand switching, innovators
Usage	Heavy, light
Perceptions and beliefs	Favourable, unfavourable
Psychographic	
Lifestyle	Trendsetters, conservatives, sophisticates
Personality	Extroverts, introverts, aggressive, submissive
Profile	
Age	Under 12, 12–18, 19–25, 26–35, 36–49, 50–64, 65+
Gender	Female, male
Life cycle	Young single, young couples, young parents, middle-aged empty nesters, retired
Social class	Upper middle, middle, skilled working, unwaged
Terminal education age	16, 18, 21 years
Income	Income breakdown according to study objectives and income levels per country
Geographic	North v. South, urban v. rural, country
Geodemographic	Upwardly mobile young families living in larger owner-occupied houses, older people living in small houses, European regions based on language, income, age profile and location

Behavioural segmentation

The key behavioural bases for segmenting consumer markets are benefits sought, purchase occasion, purchase behaviour, usage, and perceptions and beliefs. Each will now be discussed.

Benefits sought

This segmentation criterion can be applied when people in a market seek different benefits from a product. For example, the fruit drink market could be segmented by benefits sought. Table 7.2 shows such a breakdown with examples of the brands targeting each segment. ***Benefit segmentation*** provides an understanding of why people buy in a market and can aid the identification of opportunities. For example, a UK segmentation study of the yellow fats (butter and margarine) market provided the basis for choosing a target market segment for Krona margarine. Prior to its launch people were trading down from more expensive brands of butter because of an economic recession. This created a segment who wanted a butter taste at a lower price and were buying own-label butter because none of the margarine brands on the market met that primary benefit. This presented a marketing opportunity for Van den Burgh's who had developed Krona as a butter substitute and had first launched it in Australia. They targeted the butter taste lower price segment with appeals such as 'The margarine that raised questions in an Australian parliament . . . so successful did this margarine become, that people were taking it off lorries at supermarkets to be certain of buying . . . for the rumour was that it wasn't margarine at all. Its taste was that good.' Within three months of its launch, Krona had achieved 10 per cent share of the yellow fats market.[4]

Table 7.2 Benefit segmentation in the fruit drink market

Benefits sought	Products favoured
Extra energy	Robinson's Barley water
Vitamins	Ribena
Natural	Pure orange juice
Low calories	'Diet' squash
Low cost	Supermarket own label

Based upon psychological research across Europe, Sampson has shown how the benefits sought from a car can predict car and motor accessory/consumables buying:[5]

1 *Pleasure seekers*: driving is all about pleasure (freedom, enjoyment and well-being).

2 *Image seekers*: driving is all about self-image. The car provides feelings of power, prestige, status and self-enhancement. Driving is important too, but secondary.

2 *Functionality seekers*: driving is only a means of getting from A to B. They enjoy the convenience afforded by the car rather than the act of driving.

Benefit segmentation is a fundamental method of segmentation because the objective of marketing is to provide customers with benefits which they value. Knowing the various benefits which people value is therefore a basic prerequisite of understanding markets. Benefit segmentation provides the framework of classifying individuals based upon this knowledge. Profile analyses can then be performed to identify the type of people (e.g. by age, gender, socio-economic groupings) in each benefit segment so that targeting can take place.

Purchase occasion

Customers can be distinguished according to the occasions when they purchase a product. For example, a product (e.g. tyres) or service (e.g. plumbing) may be purchased as a result of an emergency or as a routine unpressurized buy. Price sensitivity, for example, is likely to be much lower in the former case than the latter. Some products (e.g. electric shavers) may be bought as gifts or as self-purchases. These differing occasions can have implications for marketing mix and targeting decisions. If it is found that the gift market is concentrated at Christmas, advertising budgets will be concentrated in the pre-Christmas period. Package design may differ for the gift v. personal buy segment also. Some brands, such as Black Magic chocolates, are targeted at the gift segment of the confectionery market.

Often special occasions such as Easter and Christmas are associated with higher prices. For example, the prices of chocolate Easter eggs fall dramatically after Easter Sunday. Also marketers have to be aware that the price of a gift can be too low to make it acceptable as a present. Gift occasions, then, pose very interesting marketing problems and opportunities.

Purchase behaviour

Differences in purchase behaviour can be based on the time of purchase relative to the launch of the product or on patterns of purchase. When a new product is launched a key task is to identify the *innovator segment* of the market. These people (or organizations) may have distinct characteristics which allow communication to be specifically targeted at them (e.g. young, middle class). Innovators are more likely to be willing to buy the product soon after launch. Other segments of the market may need more time to assess the benefits and delay purchase until after the innovators have taken the early risks of purchase. Marketing in Action 7.1 describes how innovativeness can be used as a key segmentation variable.

The degree of *brand loyalty* in a market may also be a useful basis for segmenting customers. Solus buyers are totally brand loyal, buying only one brand in the product group. For example, a person might buy Ariel Automatic washing powder invariably. Most customers brand switch,

however. Some may have a tendency to buy Ariel Automatic but also buy two or three other brands; others might show no loyalty to any individual brand but switch brands on the basis of special offers (e.g. money-off) or because they are variety seekers who look to buy a different brand each time. By profiling the characteristics of each group a company can target each segment accordingly. By knowing the type of person (e.g. by age, socio-economic group, media habits) who is brand loyal a company can channel persuasive communications to defend this segment. By knowing the characteristics and shopping habits of the offer seekers, sales promotions can be correctly targeted.

In the consumer durable market, brand loyalty can be used as a segment variable to good purpose. For example, Volkswagen has divided its customers into first-time buyers, replacement buyers (model-loyal replacers and company-loyal replacers) and switch replacers. These segments are used to measure performance and market trends, and for forecasting purposes.[6]

A recent trend in retailing has been to bio-graphics. This is the linking of actual purchase behaviour to individuals. The growth in loyalty schemes in supermarkets has provided the

7.1 Marketing in Action

Innovators as a Key Market Segment

Segmenting markets on the basis of 'innovativeness' can be a powerful process, particularly for the launch of new products or the radical repositioning of existing products. The skill is to identify the 'innovator' segment of the market as this is likely to be the consumer's most responsive to the new product when it is first launched. An example is the highly successful launch of Boddingtons draught beer. To build the credentials of the brand, Campaign for Real Ale members and beer connoisseurs were initially targeted to gain acceptance first among those most difficult to impress. Only when credentials had been established was the brand gradually moved to a wider target audience.

A second beer brand to follow this process was Fuller's brand London Pride. Research showed the London pride's innovator segment was fans of rugby union who tend to be accomplished real beer drinkers. Fuller's placed ads around BSkyB rugby broadcasts creating a very limited but highly concentrated campaign. Fuller's were able to reach real beer innovators directly, cost-effectively and nationally. This helped Fuller's to increase sales by 18 per cent in a declining market.

Based on: Carter (1998)[7]

mechanism for gathering this information. Customers are given cards that are swiped through an electronic machine at the checkout so that points can be accumulated towards discounts and vouchers. The more loyal the shopper, the higher the number of points gained. The super-market also benefits by knowing what a named individual purchases and where. Such biographic data can be used to segment and target customers very precisely. For example, it would be easy to identify a group of customers who were 'ground coffee' purchasers and target them through direct mail. Analysis of the data allows the supermarkets to stock products in each of their stores more relevant to their customers' age, lifestyle and expenditure.

Usage

Customers can also be segmented on the basis of heavy users, light users and non-users of a product category. The profiling of heavy users allows this group to receive most marketing attention (particularly promotion efforts) on the assump-tion that creating brand loyalty among these people will pay heavy dividends. Sometimes the 80:20 rule applies where about 80 per cent of a product's sales come from 20 per cent of its customers. Beer is a market where this rule often applies.[8] However, attacking the heavy user seg-ment can have drawbacks if all of the competition are following this strategy. Analysing the light (and non-user) category may provide insights that permit the development of appeals that are not being mimicked by the competition. The identity of heavy, light and non-user categories and their accompanying profiles for many consumer goods can be accomplished by using survey information provided by the Target Group Index. This is a large-scale annual survey of buying and media habits in the UK.

Segmenting by use highlights an important issue in market segmentation. Some observers of markets have noted that an individual may buy product offerings that appear to appeal to different people in the market.[10] For example, the same person may buy shredded wheat and corn-flakes, cheap wine and chateau-bottled wine, and an economy-class and business-class air ticket. These critics argue that markets are not made up of segments with different requirements because buyers of one brand buy other brands as well. However, the fact that an individual may purchase two completely different product offerings does not in itself imply the absence of meaningful segments.[9] The purchases may reflect different use occasions, purchases for different family members or for variety. For example, the purchase of shredded wheat and cornflakes may reflect variety-seeking behaviour or purchases for different family members. Cheap wine may be bought as a family drink and chateau-bottled wine for a dinner party with friends. Finally, someone may purchase an economy-class air ticket when going on holiday and a business-class ticket when on a business trip. Both the wine and air-ticket examples reflect purchasing behaviour that is dependent on use occasion.

The key issue to remember is that market segmentation concerns the grouping of individ-uals or organizations with similar characteristics that have implications for the determination of marketing strategy. The fact that an individual may have differing requirements at different points in time (e.g. use occasions) does not mean that segmentation is not warranted. For example, it is still worthwhile targeting businesspeople through the media they read to sell business-class tickets and charging a higher price; and the leisure traveller through different media with a lower price to sell economy flights. The fact that there will be some overlap on an individual basis does not deny the sense in formulating a different marketing strategy for each of the two segments.

Perceptions, beliefs and values

The final behavioural base for segmenting consumer markets is by studying perceptions, beliefs and values. This is classified as a behaviour variable because perceptions, beliefs and values are often strongly linked to behaviour. Consumers are grouped by identifying these people who view the products in a market in a similar way (perceptual segmentation) and have similar beliefs (belief segmentation). These kinds of segmentation analyses provide an understanding of how groups of customers view the market-place. To the extent that their perceptions and beliefs are different, opportunities to target specific groups more effectively may arise.

Values-based segmentation is based on the principles and standards that people use to judge what is important in life. Values are relatively consistent and underpin behaviour. Values form the basis of attitudes and lifestyles which in turn manifest as behaviour. One research company has developed seven value groups: self-explorers, experimentalists, conspicuous consumers, belongers, social resisters, survivors and the aimless.[11] Marketers have recognized the importance of identifying the values that trigger purchase for many years but now it is possible to link value groups to profiling systems that make targeting feasible (see the later section on 'combining segmentation variables').

Psychographic segmentation

Psychographic segmentation involves grouping people according to their lifestyle and personality characteristics.

Lifestyle

This form of segmentation attempts to group people according to their way of living as reflected in their activities, interests and opinions. As we saw in Chapter 3, marketing researchers attempt to identify groups of people with similar patterns of living. The question which arises with lifestyle segmentation is the extent to which general lifestyle patterns are predictive of purchasing behaviour in specific markets.[12] Nevertheless, *lifestyle segmentation* has proven popular among advertising agencies who have attempted to relate brands (e.g. Martini) to a particular lifestyle (e.g. aspirational). The advertisement for Claritas on the opposite page shows the usefulness of lifestyle data for segmentation and targeting purposes.

Personality

The idea that brand choice may be related to personality is intuitively appealing. Indeed, as we saw in Chapter 3, there is a relationship between the brand personality of beers and the personality of the buyer.[13] However, the usefulness of personality as a segmentation variable is likely to depend on the product category. Buyer and brand personalities are likely to match where brand choice is a direct manifestation of personal values but for most fast-moving consumer goods (e.g. detergents, tea, cereals), the reality is that people buy a repertoire of brands.[14] Personality (and lifestyle) segmentation is more likely to work when brand choice is a reflection of self-expression; the brand becomes a *badge* which makes public an aspect of personality: 'I choose this brand to say this about me and this is how I would like you to see me.' It is not surprising, then, that successful personality segmentation has been found in the areas of cosmetics, alcoholic drinks and cigarettes.[15]

Profile segmentation

Profile segmentation variables allow consumer groups to be classified in such a way that they can be reached by the communications media (e.g. advertising, direct mail). Even if behaviour and/or phychographic segmentation have successfully distinguished between buyer preferences, there is often a need to analyse the resulting segments in terms of profile variables such as age and socio-economic group to communicate to them. The reason is that readership and viewership profiles of newspapers, magazines and television programmes tend to be expressed in that way.

We shall now examine a number of demographic, socio-economic and geographic segmentation variables.

Demographic variables

The demographic variables we shall look at are age, gender, and life cycle.

Age age has been used to segment many consumer markets.[16] For example, children receive their own television programmes; cereals, computer games, and confectionery are other examples of markets where products are formulated with children in mind. The sweeter tooth of children is reflected in sugared cereal brands targeted at children (e.g. Kellogg's Frosties). Lego, the Danish construction toy manufacturer, segments the children's market by age. In broad terms, Duplo targets the up-to-6-year-olds, the Lego ranges aims at the 5–12-year-olds and the Technic range caters for the 8–16 age group. Age is also an important segmentation variable in services. The holiday market is heavily age segmented with offerings targeted at the Under 30s and the Over 60s segments for example. This reflects the differing requirements of these age groups when on holiday. As noted in Chapter 3, age distribution changes within the European Union are having profound effects on the attractiveness of various age segments.

Is lack of real data limiting your marketing vision?

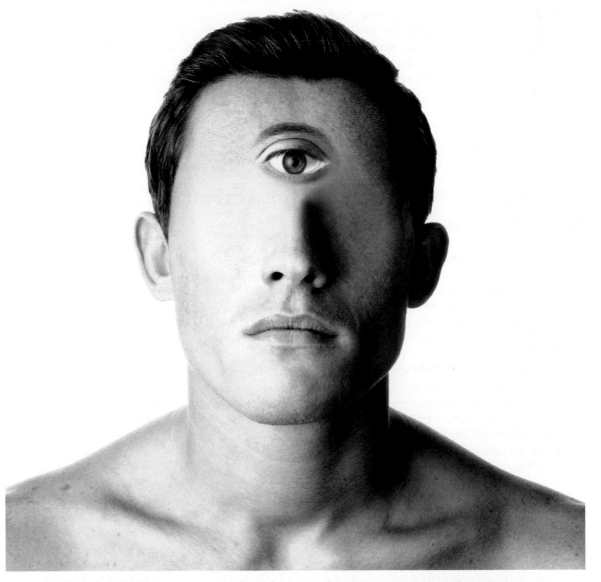

If so, look no further than Lifestyle Universe from Claritas.

Every single household in the UK has come under our gaze.

With over 380 variables available for selection, it's built from the UK's largest source of lifestyle information.

No other company can match this.

Lifestyle Universe makes the nationwide targeting of your most profitable prospects and customers more precise than ever.

And as each variable provides a definitive answer rather than just a score, it is easier to understand and work with.

Lifestyle Universe can also be tagged onto your existing database to boost its power in carrying out analysis and segmentation to drive cross-selling, up-selling, NPD, customer retention and loyalty building programmes.

What's more, it provides you with a clearer view of your market to enhance media planning, territory planning and defining catchment areas of high potential.

To find out more about Lifestyle Universe call Claritas on **020 8213 5500 or visit www.claritas.co.uk.**

For national coverage, it's as close as you can get to 20/20 vision.

Claritas. Adding intellect to information.

Lifestyle data helps to segment and target markets

Many companies covet the youth segment who are major purchasers of items such as clothing, consumer electronics, drinks, personal care products and magazines. Marketing in Action 7.2 explores some of the issues relating to understanding this key market segment.

Gender differing tastes and customs between men and women are reflected in specialist products aimed at these market segments. Magazines, clothing, hairdressing and cosmetics are product categories that have used segmentation based on gender. More recently the car market has segmented by gender: the Corsa range of cars from General Motors in Europe is specifically targeted at women.

Life cycle the classic family life cycle stages have been shown in Chapter 3. To briefly recap, disposal income and purchase requirements may vary according to life cycle stage (e.g. young single v. married with two children). Consumer durable purchases may be dependent on life cycle stage with young couples without children

7.2 Marketing in Action

Understanding the Youth Market

Today's young people have experienced very different technologies to their parents. Whereas older people may be described as the television generation, the current crop of young people have grown up with VCRs, cable, satellite and digital choices. They will have learnt from an early age how to use computers, the Internet and games consoles. But they are not just observers of the media explosion, they are learning how to control that media. They are growing up wise to marketing and media messages. For example, research into men's style magazines shows that boys use them almost as cultural catalogues.

The importance of the youth market has promoted the growth of research into their behaviour and attitudes. This has shown that stereotypical viewpoints can be misleading. For example, the notion that young people spend hours on the Internet is misguided. As one young person said 'I used to think that the Internet was really cool. I really pestered my Mum to get me a computer but people don't really think it is cool now. I'd much rather be out playing football or computer games, but not on my computer, they are better on PlayStation.'

Research into the youth market does not always take the form of standard questionnaire or focus group approaches. In order to understand their customers, the marketing executives for Unilever's Lynx (known as Axe outside the UK) deodorant for males, and Impulse body spray for females hang out once a month in the coolest clubs and check out the hottest bands. The company has formed a 'youth board' to get closer to the consumers for whom the two products are part of teenage rites of passage. Made up of brand and marketing managers, advertising executives and PR people, it operates through all-day immersion events away from head office. A day's programme might include examining in detail youth brands such as Sony's PlayStation or the energy drink Red Bull to see how they promote themselves through channels such as the Internet or dance clubs. One outcome was the realization that advertising executions needed to be changed very frequently. They observed that PlayStation had 19 different advertising executions in one year because Sony knew young people get bored quickly. Their response was to raise the number of Lynx executions from 3 to 10 a year.

Based on: Considine (1999);[17] Green (1999);[18] Willman (1999)[19]

being a prime target market for furnishings and appliances as they set up home. The use of life cycle analysis may give better precision in segmenting markets than age because family responsibilities and the presence of children may have a greater bearing on what people buy than age. The consumption pattern of a single 28-year-old is likely to be very different from that of a married 28-year-old with three children.

Socio-economic variables

Socio-economic variables include social class, terminal education age and income. As we saw in Chapter 6, there has been progress in developing a socio-economic status scale that can be applied across Europe. One use of such a scale would be to enable Europe-wide segmentation on socio-economic variables to be attempted. Here we shall look at social class as a predictor of buyer behaviour.

Social class   social class is measured in varying ways across Europe; in the UK occupation is used, whereas in other European centres a combination of variables is used. Like the demographic variables previously discussed, social class has the advantage of being fairly easy to measure and is used for media readership and viewership profiles. The extent to which social class is a predictor of buyer behaviour, however, has been open to question. Clearly many people who hold similar occupations have very dissimilar lifestyles, values and purchasing patterns. Nevertheless, social class has proven useful in discriminating between owning a dishwasher, having central heating, and privatization share ownership for example and therefore should not be discounted as a segmentation variable.[20]

Geographic variables

The final set of segmentation variables are based on geographic differences. A marketer can use pure geographic segmentation or a hybrid of geographic and demographic variables called geodemographics.

Geographic   this segmentation method is useful where there are geographic locational differences in consumption patterns and preferences. For example, in the UK beer drinkers in the north of England prefer a frothy head on their beer, whereas in the south local taste dictates that beer should not have a head. In Germany, local tastes for beer are reflected in numerous local brewers. In Europe, differences between countries may form geographic segments. For example, variations in food preferences may form the basis of geographic segments: France, Spain and Italy are oil-based cooking markets while Germany and the UK are margarine and butter orientated.[21] Differences in national advertising expectations may also form geographic segments for communicational purposes. Germans expect much factual information in their advertisements to the extent that would bore French or British audiences. France, with its more relaxed attitudes to nudity, broadcasts commercials that would be banned in the UK. In the highly competitive Asian car market both Honda and Toyota have launched their first 'Asia Specific' cars, designed and marketed solely for Asian consumers.

Geodemographic   in countries which produce population census data the potential for classifying consumers on the combined basis of location and certain demographic (and socio-economic) information exists. Households are classified into groups according to a wide range of factors depending on what is asked on census returns. In the UK variables such as household size, number of cars, occupation, family size and ethnic background are used to group small geographic areas (known as enumeration districts) into segments that share similar characteristics. A number of research companies (e.g. Pinpoint, CNN) provide such analyses but the best known is that produced by CACI Market Analysis and is known as ACORN (A Classification of Residential Neighbourhoods). The main groups and their characteristics are shown in Table 7.3.

Such information has been used to select recipients of direct mail campaigns, to identify the best locations for stores and to find the best poster sites. This is possible because consumers in each group can be identified by means of their postcodes. Another area where census data are employed is in buying advertising spots on television. Agencies depend upon information from viewership panels who record their viewing habits so that advertisers have an insight into who watches what. In the UK, census analyses performed by Pinpoint are combined with viewership data via the postcodes of panelists.[22]

This means that advertisers who wish to reach a particular geodemographic group can discover the type of programme they prefer to watch and buy television spots accordingly.

A major strength of geodemographics is to link buyer behaviour to customer groups. Buying habits can be determined by large-scale syndicated surveys (for example, the Target Group Index and MORI Financial Services) or from panel data (for example, the grocery and toiletries markets are covered by Superpanel from AGB). By geocoding respondents, those ACORN groups most likely to purchase a product or brand can be determined. This can be useful for branch location since many service providers use a country-wide branch network and need to match the market segments to which they most appeal to the type of customer in their catchment area. Merchandise mix decisions of retailers can also be affected by customer profile data. Media selections can be made more precise by linking buying habits to geodemographic data.[23]

Geodemographic data can also be used to assess how well the catchment area profile of a retail outlet matches its target market and to understand what factors influence the performance of the outlets. Marketing in Action 7.3 describes how MOSAIC, a geodemographic system similar to ACORN, was used in this way.

Combining segmentation variables

We have seen that there are a wide range of variables that can be used to segment consumer markets. Often a combination of variables will be used to identify groups of consumers that respond in the same way to marketing mix strategies. For example, Research Services Ltd, a UK marketing research company, has developed SAGACITY, a market segmentation scheme based on a combination of life cycle, occupation and income. Twelve distinct consumer groupings are formed with differing aspirations and behaviour patterns.

Research companies are also combining lifestyle and values-based segmentation schemes with geodemographic data. For example, CACI's Census Lifestyle system classifies segments using lifestyle and geodemographic data. Also, CCN have produced Consumer Surveys which combines

---

Table 7.3　The ACORN targeting classification

Categories	% in population	Groups	% in population
A Thriving	20	1. Wealthy achievers, suburban areas	15
		2. Affluent greys, rural communities	2
		3. Prosperous pensioners, retirement areas	3
B Expanding	12	4. Affluent executives, family areas	4
		5. Well-off workers, family areas	8
C Rising	7	6. Affluent urbanites, town and city areas	2
		7. Prosperous professionals, metropolitan areas	2
		8. Better-off executives, inner city areas	3
D Settling	24	9. Comfortable middle-agers, mature home-owning areas	13
		10. Skilled workers, home-owning areas	11
E Aspiring	14	11. New home owners, mature communities	10
		12. White collar workers, better-off multi-ethnic areas	4
F Striving	23	13. Older people, less prosperous areas	4
		14. Council estate residents, better-off homes	12
		15. Council estate residents, high unemployment	3
		16. Council estate residents, greatest hardship	3
		17. People in multi-ethnic, low income areas	2

Source: © CACI Limited (Data source BMRB and OPCS/GRO(S)). © Crown Copyright All rights reserved. ACORN is a registered trademark of CACI Limited. Reproduced with permission.

social value groups with geodemographic data. In both cases the link to geodemographic data, which contains household address information, means that targeting of people with similar lifestyles or values is feasible.

Flexibility and creativity are the hallmarks of effective segmentation analyses; for example, one study of Europeans used a combination of demographic, psychographic and socio-economic variables to identify these segments that appeared to be ready for a pan-European marketing approach.[24] Segment 1 comprised young people across Europe who have more unified tastes in music, sports and cultural activities than was the case in previous generations. Trendsetters (intelligent pleasure seekers longing for a rich and full life) and social climbers formed the second segment. The third segment was Europe's businesspeople totalling over 6 million people (mostly male) who regularly travel abroad and have a taste for luxury goods.

An example of a study which used a combination of variables to segment a market is given in e-Marketing 7.1. Variables such as age, socio-economic group, gender and lifestyle were used to segment users of the Internet.

Segmenting organizational markets

While the consumer goods marketer is interested in grouping individuals into marketing-relevant segments, the business-to-business marketer profiles organizations and organizational buyers. The organizational market can be segmented on several factors broadly classified into two major categories, macrosegmentation and microsegmentation.[25]

Macrosegmentation focuses on the characteristics of the buying organization such as size, industry and geographic location. **Microsegmentation** requires a more detailed level of market knowledge as it concerns the characteristics of

---

7.3   Marketing in Action
Using MOSAIC to Analyse Retail Outlet Performance

Camerons Brewery has 170 public houses in North and East Yorkshire. In an age where public houses are operating in an increasingly competitive environment, the company needed a way of analysing pub performance and determining how the population in each catchment influenced sales revenue.

The company contracted with Experian, an information solutions company, who used their MOSAIC database to analyse the socio-demographic mix of each pub catchment area to determine whether this matched Camerons' target customer specification. This analysis also assessed pub performance in relation to factors such as turnover, return on assets and profit per square foot.

MOSAIC is capable of separating every household in Britain into 52 different lifestyle segments. These include segments such as 'clever capitalists', 'corporate careerists', 'stylish singles' and 'gentrified villagers'. The software permitted evaluation of relationships between elements within catchment areas that had particularly good performing outlets. Camerons were then able to subdivide their pubs into three performance bands—good, average and below average. This has assisted the company to concentrate on implementing actions to help poor performing pubs, plan a future investment strategy and develop a brand marketing campaign.

Based on: Enterprise Report (1999)[26]

decision-making within each macrosegment based on such factors as choice criteria, decision-making unit structure, decision-making process, buy class, purchasing organization and organizational innovativeness. Often organizational markets are first grouped on a macrosegment basis and then finer subsegments are identified through microsegmentation.[27]

Figure 7.4 shows how this two-stage process works. The choice of the appropriate macrosegmentation and microsegmentation criteria is based upon the marketer's evaluation of which criteria are most useful in predicting buyer behaviour differences that have implications for developing marketing strategies. Figure 7.5 shows the criteria that can be used.

Macrosegmentation

The key macrosegmentation criteria of organizational size, industry and geographic location are now discussed.

Organizational size

The size of buying organizations may be used to segment markets. Large organizations differ from

7.1   e-Marketing

Segmenting the Web Audience

As the importance of the Internet grows so the understanding of the audience of users becomes imperative. A study of the research and consulting company, Netpoll, has produced profiles of Internet users. Based upon such criteria as age, socio-economic group, gender and lifestyle, the analysis has highlighted a number of segments some of which are now described.

✦ *The gameboy*: aged 15 he accesses the Internet mainly at home. He is into playing on-line games. He thinks he is net-savvy and pretty hip. Other interests include football.

✦ *The cyberlad*: aged 23 he uses the Internet at work and home. He is a bit of a Jack-the-Lad and thinks that he is an expert at all things to do with the Internet. He spends a lot of time on-line searching for smut and e-mailing it to his mates. Interests include sex and sport.

✦ *The net sophisticate*: aged 28 this person straddles the border between cool and nerd. Could be a gee-whizz executive, or unemployed and living with his mother. He is really into the Internet and believes that he knows more about it than anyone.

✦ *The cybersec*: aged 31 this person works as a PA to the boss of a small company. She only accesses the Internet at the office and is not really into computers. She started to use the Internet to do research for her boss and to make travel arrangements but more recently has started to explore on her own.

✦ *The hit 'n' runner*: aged 38 he or she is a successful professional or a high-flying marketing executive. Internet access is at work and it is not seen as a form of entertainment. They are very impatient if the web is slow or they cannot find what they want. They bank on-line and use the net to manage their investment portfolio and to research holidays.

✦ *The infojunky*: aged 40, married with two children he or she might be a middle-ranking civil servant or a partner in a small firm of solicitors. Likes feeling of being in control and in touch through the Internet. Perhaps wrongly, feels that time spent on-line is a big benefit to their job.

Based on: Lord (1999)[28]

medium and small organizations in having greater order potential, more formalized buying and management processes, increased specialization of function, and special needs (e.g. quantity discounts). The result is that they may form important target market segments and require tailored marketing mix strategies. For example, the salesforce may need to be organized on a key account basis (see Chapter 12) where a dedicated sales team are used to service important industrial accounts. List pricing of products and services may need to take into account the inevitable demand for volume discounts from large pur-

chasers, and the sales force team will need to be well versed in the art of negotiation.

Industry

Another common macrosegmentation variable is industry sector, sometimes identified by using Standard Industrial Classification (SIC) codes. Different industries may have unique requirements from products. For example, computer suppliers can market their products to various sectors such as banking, manufacturing, health care, and education, each of which has unique

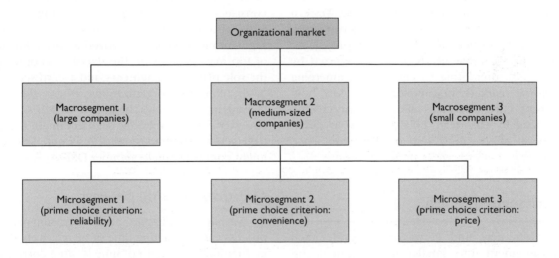

Figure 7.4 Macrosegmentation and microsegmentation of organizational markets

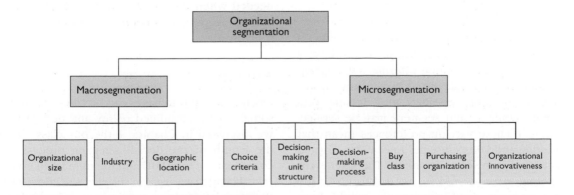

Figure 7.5 Segmenting organizational markets

needs in terms of software programs, servicing price and purchasing practice. By understanding each industry's needs in depth, a more effective marketing mix can be designed. In some instances further segmentation may be required. For example, the education sector may be further divided into primary, secondary and further education as their product and service requirements may differ.

Geographic location

Regional variations in purchasing practice and needs may imply the use of geographic location as a basis for differentiating marketing strategies. The purchasing practices and expectations of companies in Central and Eastern Europe are likely to differ markedly from those in Western Europe. Their more bureaucratic structures may imply a fundamentally different approach to doing business that needs to be recognized by companies attempting to enter these emerging industrial markets. In Chapter 5, we saw how different cultural factors affect the purchasing practices in European countries. These differences, in effect, imply regional segments since marketing needs to reflect these variations.

Microsegmentation

Marketers may find it useful to divide each macrosegment into smaller microsegments on the basis of the buyer's choice criteria, decision-making unit structure, decision-making process, buy class, purchasing organization, and organizational innovativeness.

Choice criteria

This factor segments the organizational market on the basis of the key choice criteria used by buyers when evaluating supplier offering. One group of customers may rate price as the key choice criterion, another segment may favour productivity, while a third segment may be service-orientated. These varying preferences mean that marketing and sales strategies need to be adapted to cater for each segment's needs. Three different marketing mixes would be needed to cover the three segments, and salespeople would have to stress different benefits when talking to customers in each segment. Variations in key choice criteria can be powerful predictors of buyer behaviour. For example, Moriarty found differences in choice criteria in the computer market.[29] One segment used software support and breadth of product line as key criteria and bought IBM equipment. Another segment was more concerned with price and the willingness of suppliers to negotiate lower prices; these buyers favoured non-IBM machines.

Decision-making unit structure

Another way of segmenting organizational markets is based on decision-making unit (DMU) composition: members of the DMU and its size may vary between buying organizations. As discussed in Chapter 4, the decision-making unit consists of all these people in a buying organization who have an effect on supplier choice. One segment might be characterized by the influence of top management on the decision; another by the role played by engineers; and a third segment might comprise organizations where the purchasing manager plays the key role. DMU size can also vary considerably: one segment might feature large, complex units, while a second segment might comprise single member DMUs.

Decision-making process

As we saw in Chapter 4, the decision-making process can take a long time or be relatively short in duration. The length of time is often correlated with DMU composition. Long processes are associated with large DMUs. Where the decision time is long high levels of marketing expenditure may be needed with considerable effort being placed on personal selling. Much less effort is needed when the buy process is relatively short and where, perhaps, only the purchasing manager is involved.

Buy class

Organizational purchases can be categorized into straight re-buy, modified re-buy and new task. As we discussed in Chapter 4, the buy class affects the length of the decision-making process, the complexity of the DMU and the number of choice criteria which are used in supplier selection. It can therefore be used as a predictor of different forms of buyer behaviour, and hence is useful as a segmentation variable.

Purchasing organization

Decentralized versus centralized purchasing is another microsegmentation variable because of its influence on the purchase decision.[30] Centralized purchasing is associated with purchasing specialists who become experts in buying a range of products. Specialization means that they become more familiar with cost factors and the strengths and weaknesses of suppliers than decentralized generalists. Furthermore, the opportunity for volume buying means that their power base to demand price concessions from suppliers is enhanced. They have also been found to have greater power within the DMU *vis-à-vis* technical people, like engineers, than decentralized buyers who often lack the specialist expertise and status to challenge their preferences. For their reasons purchasing organization provides a good base for distinguishing between buyer behaviour and can have implications for marketing activities. For example, the centralized purchasing segment could be served by a national account salesforce whereas the decentralized purchasing segment might be covered by territory representatives.

Organizational innovativeness

A key segmentation variable when launching new products is the degree of innovativeness of potential buyers. In Chapter 9 we shall discuss some general characteristics of innovator firms but marketers need to identify the specific characteristics of the innovator segment since these are the companies that should be targeted first when new products are launched. Follower firms may be willing to buy the product but only after the innovators have approved it. Although categorized here as a microsegmentation variable it should be borne in mind that organizational size (a macrosegmentation variable) may be a predictor of innovativeness also.

Table 7.4 summarizes the methods of segmenting organizational markets and provides examples of how each variable can be used to form segments.

Target marketing

Market segmentation is a means to an end: *target marketing*. This is the choice of specific segments to serve and is a key element in marketing strategy. A firm needs to evaluate the segments and decide which ones to serve. For example, CNN targets its news programmes to what are known as 'influentials'. This is why CNN has globally focused so much of its distribution effort into gaining access to hotel rooms. Business people know that wherever they are in the world they can see international news on CNN in their hotel. Its sports programming is also targeted with plenty of coverage of up-market sports such as golf and tennis. We shall first examine how to evaluate market segments, and then how to make a balanced choice about which ones to serve.

Table 7.4 Organizational segmentation methods

Variable	Examples
Macrosegmentation	
Organizational size	Large, medium, small
Industry	Engineering, textiles, banking
Geographic location	Local, national, European, global
Microsegmentation	
Choice criteria	Value in use, delivery, price, status
Decision-making unit structure	Complex, simple
Decision-making process	Long, short
Buy class	Straight re-buy, modified re-buy, new task
Purchasing organization	Centralized, decentralized
Organizational innovativeness	Innovator, follower, laggard

Evaluating market segments

When evaluating market segments, the company should examine two broad issues: market attractiveness and the company's capability of competing in the segment. *Market attractiveness* can be assessed by looking at market factors, competitive factors, and political, social and environmental factors.[31]

Market factors

Segment size generally large-sized segments are more attractive than small ones since sales potential is greater, and the chance of achieving economies of scale is improved. However, large segments are often highly competitive since other companies are realizing their attraction, too. Furthermore, smaller companies may not have the resources to compete in large segments, and so may find smaller segments more attractive.

Segment growth rate growing segments are usually regarded as more attractive than stagnant or declining segments as new business opportunities will be greater. However, growth markets are often associated with heavy competition (e.g. the personal computer market during the late 1980s). Therefore an analysis of growth rate should always be accompanied by an examination of the state of competition.

Price sensitivity in segments where customers are price sensitive there is a danger of profit margins being eroded by price competition. Low price sensitive segments are usually more attractive since margins can be maintained. Competition may be based more on quality and other non-price factors.

Bargaining power of customers both end and intermediate customers (e.g. distributors) can reduce the attraction of a market segment if they can exert high bargaining pressure on suppliers. The result is usually a reduction in profit margins as customers (e.g. supermarket chains) negotiate lower prices in return for placing large orders.

Bargaining power of suppliers a company must assess not only the negotiating muscle of its customers but also its potential suppliers in the new segment. Where supply is in the hands of a few dominant companies the segment will be less attractive than when served by a large number of competing suppliers.

Barriers to market segment entry for companies considering entering a new segment there may be substantial entry barriers that reduce its attractiveness. Barriers can take the form of high marketing expenditures necessary to compete, patents, or high switching costs for customers. However, if a company judges that it can afford or overcome barriers to entry, their existence may raise segment attractiveness if the company judges that the barriers will deter new rivals from entering.

Barriers to market segment exit a segment may be regarded less attractive if there are high barriers to exit. Exit barriers may take the form of specialized production facilities that cannot be easily liquidated, or agreements to provide spare parts to customers. Their presence may make exit extremely expensive and therefore segment entry more risky.

Competitive factors

Nature of competition segments that are characterized by strong aggressive competition are less attractive than where competition is weak. The weakness of European and North American car manufacturers made the Japanese entry into seemingly highly competitive (in terms of number of manufacturers) market segments relatively easy. The quality of the competition is far more significant than the number of companies operating in a market segment.

New entrants a segment may seem superficially attractive because of the lack of current competition but care must be taken to assess the dynamics of the market. A judgement must be made regarding the likelihood of new entrants, possibly with new technology which might change the rules of the competitive game.

Competitive differentiation segments will be more attractive if there is a real probability of creating a differentiated offering that customers value. This judgement is dependent on identifying unserved customer requirements, and capability of the company to meet them.

Political, social and environmental factors

Political issues   political forces can open up new market segments (e.g. the deregulation of telecommunications in the UK paved the way for Mercury to enter the organizational segment of the telecommunications market). Alternatively the attraction of entering new geographic segments may be reduced if political instability exists or is forecast.

Social trends   changes in society need to be assessed to measure their likely impact on the market segment. Changes in society can give rise to latent market segments, underserved by current products and services. Big gains can be made by first entrants, as Next discovered in fashion retailing.

Environmental issues   the trend towards more environmentally friendly products has affected market attractiveness both positively and negatively. The Body Shop took the opportunity afforded by the movement against animal testing of cosmetics and toiletries; conversely the market for CFCs has declined in the face of scientific evidence linking their emission and depletion of the ozone layer.

Capability

Against the market attractiveness factors must be placed on the firm's *capability to serve the market segment*. The market segment may be attractive but outside the resources of the company. Capability may be assessed by analysing exploitable marketing assets, cost advantages, technological edge, and managerial capabilities and commitment.

Exploitable marketing assets   does the market segment allow the firm to exploit its current marketing strengths? For example, is segment entry consonant with the image of its brands, or does it provide distribution synergies? However, where new segment entry is inconsistent with image a new brand name may be created. For example, Toyota developed the Lexus model name when entering the upper middle executive car segment.

Cost advantages   companies who can exploit cheaper material, labour or technological cost advantages to achieve a low cost position compared to the competition may be in a strong position particularly if the segment is price sensitive.

Technological edge   strength may also be derived by superior technology which is the source of differential advantage in the market segment. Patent protection (e.g. in pharmaceuticals) can form the basis of a strong defensible position leading to high profitability. For some companies, segment entry may be deferred if they do not possess resources to invest in technological leadership.

Managerial capabilities and commitment   a segment may look attractive but a realistic assessment of managerial capabilities and skills may lead to rejection of entry. The technical and judgemental skills of management may be insufficient to compete against strong competitors. Furthermore, the segment needs to be assessed from the viewpoint of managerial objectives. Successful marketing depends on implementation. Without the commitment of management, segment entry will fail on the altar of neglect.

Target marketing strategies

The purpose of evaluating market segments is to choose one or more segments to enter. Target market selection is the choice of which and how many market segments in which to compete. There are four generic target marketing strategies from which to choose; undifferentiated marketing, differentiated marketing, focused marketing, and customized marketing (see Fig. 7.6). Each option will now be examined.

Undifferentiated marketing

Occasionally, a market analysis will show no strong differences in customer characteristics that have implications for marketing strategy. Alternatively the cost in developing a separate market mix for separate segments may outweigh the potential gains of meeting customer needs more exactly. Under these circumstances a company may decide to develop a single marketing mix for the whole market. This absence of segmentation is called **undifferentiated marketing**. Unfortunately this strategy can occur by default. For example, companies who lack a marketing orientation may practise undifferentiated marketing through lack of customer knowledge. Furthermore, undifferentiated marketing is more convenient for managers since they have to develop only a single product. Finding out that customers have diverse needs that can be met only by products with different characteristics means that managers have to go to the trouble and expense of developing new products, designing new promotional campaigns, training the salesforce to sell the new products, and developing new distribution channels. Moving into new segments also means that salespeople have to start prospecting for new customers. This is not such a pleasant activity as calling on existing customers who are well known and liked.

The process of market segmentation, then, is normally the motivator to move such companies from practising undifferentiated marketing to one of the next three target marketing strategies.

Differentiated marketing

When market segmentation reveals several potential targets, specific marketing mixes can be developed to appeal to all or some of the segments. This is called **differentiated marketing**. For example, Walters and Knee showed how differentiated marketing was applied by the Burton Group.[32] Segmentation of the fashion market revealed distinct customer groups to which a specific marketing mix (including shop name, style of clothing, décor and ambience of the shop) was developed, for example the style market (Principles) and young women's market (Dorothy Perkins), the larger women's market (Evans) and the family market (Debenhams). A differentiated target marketing strategy exploits the differences between marketing segments by designing a specific marketing mix for each segment. The identification of distinct pan-European market segment discussed earlier in this chapter suggests the possibility of differentiated marketing being used to serve them. Specific marketing mixes would be developed to target cross-border segments of consumers and organizations, thereby reaping high profits through customer satisfaction and economies of scale.

One potential disadvantage of a differentiated compared to a undifferentiated marketing strategy is the loss of cost economies. However, the use of flexible manufacturing systems can minimize such problems.

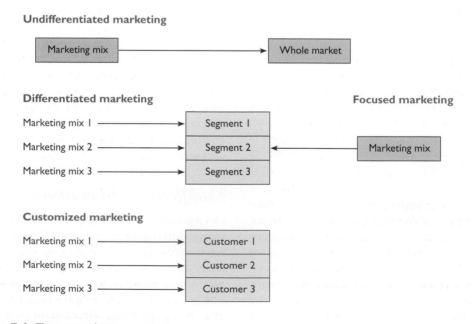

Figure 7.6 Target marketing strategies

Focused marketing

The identification of several segments in a market does not imply that a company should serve all of them. Some may be unattractive or be out of line with business strengths. Perhaps the most sensible route would be to serve just one of the market segments. When a company develops a single marketing mix aimed at one target market (*niche*) it is practising *focused marketing*. This strategy is particularly appropriate for companies with limited resources. Small companies may stretch their resources too far by competing in more than one segment. Focused marketing allows research and development expenditure to be concentrated on meeting the needs of one set of customers, and managerial activities can be devoted to understanding and catering for their needs. Large organizations may not be interested in serving the needs of this one segment, or their energies may be so dissipated across the whole market that they pay insufficient attention to their requirements. The exclusive high-performance car manufacturer TVR is an example of a successful focused marketer. One danger that such niche marketers face is attracting competition from larger organizations in the industry. In the UK, for example, Sock Shop and Tie Rack grew very quickly during the 1980s and were conspicuously successful. The reaction from larger stores such as Marks and Spencer was to jazz up their range of socks and ties to key into this niche segment.[33]

Another example of focused marketing is given by Bang & Olufsen, the Danish audio electronics firm. They target upmarket consumers who value self-development, pleasure and open-mindedness with stylish music systems. Anders Kwitsen, its chief executive describes its positioning as 'high quality but we are not Rolls-Royce; more BMW'. Focused targeting and cost control mean that B & O defy the conventional wisdom that a small manufacturer could not make profits marketing consumer electronics in Denmark.[34]

Another form of focused marketing is to target a particular age group. For example, Saga target the over 50s. Originally a specialist holiday company, they have broadened the range of products marketed to this age group to include financial services such as an award-winning share-dealing service.[35]

One form of focused marketing is to concentrate efforts on the relatively small percentage of customers that account for a disproportionately large share of sales of a product (the heavy buyer). For example, in some markets 20 per cent of customers account for 80 per cent of sales. Some companies aim at such a segment because it is so superficially attractive. Unfortunately they may be committing the *majority fallacy*.[36] The majority fallacy is the name given to the blind pursuit of the largest, most easily identified market segment. It is a fallacy because that segment is the one that everyone in the past has recognized as the best segment and therefore attracts the most intensive competition. The result is likely to be high marketing expenditures, price cutting and low profitability. A more sensible strategy may be to target a small, seemingly less attractive segment rather than choose the same customers that everyone else is after.

Customized marketing

In some markets the requirements of individual customers are unique and their purchasing power sufficient to make designing a separate marketing mix for each customer viable. Segmentation at this disaggregated level leads to the use of *customized marketing*. Many service providers such as advertising and marketing research agencies, architects, and solicitors vary their offerings on a customer-to-customer basis. They will discuss face-to-face with each customer their requirements and tailor their services accordingly. Customized marketing is also found within organizational markets because of the high value of orders and special needs of customers. Locomotive manufacturers will design and build products upon specifications given to them by individual rail transport providers. Customized marketing is often associated with close relationships between supplier and customer in these circumstances because the value of the order justifies large marketing and sales efforts being focused on each buyer.

Positioning

So far our discussion has taken us through market segmentation and on to target market selection. The next step in developing an effective marketing strategy is to clearly position a product or service offering in the marketplace. Figure 7.7

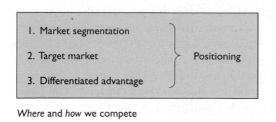

Where and how we compete

Figure 7.7 Key tasks in positioning

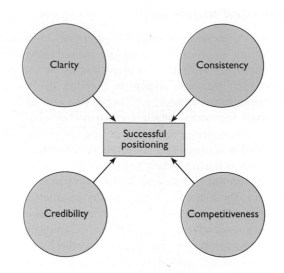

Figure 7.8 Keys to successful positioning

summarizes the key tasks involved, and shows where *positioning* fits into the process.

Positioning is the choice of:

✦ *Target market*: *where* we want to compete.

✦ *Differential advantage*: *how* we wish to compete.

The objective is to create and maintain a distinctive place in the market for a company and/or its products. The advertisement opposite shows the positioning of Magnum ice cream.

Target market selection, then, has accomplished part of the positioning job already. But to compete successfully in a target market involves providing the customer with a differential advantage. This involves giving the target customer something better than what the competition are offering. Creating a differential advantage will be discussed in detail in Chapter 17. Briefly, it involves using the marketing mix to create something special for the customer. Product differentiation may result from added features which give customers benefits that rivals cannot match. Promotional differentiation may stem from unique, valued images created by advertising, or superior service provided by salespeople. Distribution differentiation may arise through making the buy situation more convenient for customers. Finally, price differentiation may involve giving superior value for money through lower prices.

A landmark book by Ries and Trout suggested that marketers are involved in a battle for the minds of target customers.[37] Successful positioning is often associated with products and services possessing favourable connotations in the minds of customers. For example McDonald's is associated with cleanliness, consistency of product, fast service and value for money. These add up to a differential advantage in the minds of its target customers whether they be in London, Amsterdam or Moscow. Such positioning is hard won and relies on four factors as shown in Fig. 7.8. There are four keys to successful positioning:

1 *Clarity*: the positioning idea must be clear in terms of both target market and differential advantage. Complicated positioning statements are unlikely to be remembered. Simple messages such as 'BMW, The Ultimate Driving Machine', 'A Mars A Day Helps You Work Rest and Play' and 'Good Food Costs Less at Sainsbury's' are clear and memorable.

2 *Consistency*: people are bombarded with messages daily. To break through this noise a consistent message is required. Confusion will arise if this year we position on 'quality of service', then next year we change it to 'superior product performance'.

3 *Credibility*: the differential advantage that is chosen must be credible in the minds of the target customer. Attempting to position roll-your-own cigarette tobacco as an up-market exclusive product failed because of the lack of credibility. Similarly the attempt to position Lada as an exciting, sporty car by showing it charging through dirt tracks in Africa in advertisements failed because of the lack of consonance between image and reality.

4 *Competitiveness*: the differential advantage should have a competitive edge. It should

Positioning the Magnum brand using the sensual properties of ice cream

offer something of value to the customer which the competition is failing to supply. For example, the success of the Apple Macintosh computer in the educational segment was based on the differential advantage of easy-to-use software programs, a benefit that was highly valued in this segment. Because of different system architecture, IBM was unable to match the Macintosh on this feature.

Marketing in Action 7.4 describes how the four brands of imported premium lagers—Budweiser, Grolsch, Holsten Pils and Beck's—have used positioning to achieve market domination. In their market segment, both image and product quality are vital ingredients in the race to be the brand to be seen with.

Perceptual mapping

A useful tool for determining the position of a brand in the marketplace is the *perceptual map*. This is a visual representation of consumer perceptions of the brand and its competitors using attributes (dimensions) that are important to consumers. The key steps in developing a perceptual map are:

1   Identify a set of competing brands.

2   Identify important attributes that consumers use when choosing between brands using qualitative research (e.g. group discussions).

3   Conduct quantitative marketing research where consumers score each brand on all key attributes.

4   Plot brands on a two-dimensional map(s).

7.4   Marketing in Action

Positioning in the Imported Premium Bottled Lager Market

Since the growth years of the early 1990s the premium bottled lager market has stagnated due to the rise of draught equivalents in pubs and bars. The dominant brands are Budweiser from the USA, Grolsch from The Netherlands, and Holsten Pils and Beck's from Germany. Together these four brands account for over 80 per cent of the imported premium bottled lager market. The key to success is clear positioning through advertising and packaging.

Budweiser emphasizes its long US heritage and supports its positioning with humour, for example, the 'frogs and lizards' campaign. Grolsch gains distinctiveness with its swing-top embossed bottle. Its ads stress the heritage of the lager and the fact that the beer brews for three times longer than most lagers resulting in its distinctive taste. Holsten Pils stresses the integrity of the drink which is free from additives 'pure, clean and unsullied' and employs humour in the form of familiar characters from the TV comedy programme *The Fast Show*. Beck's promotion features a series of natural images such as fields of hops, galloping horses and rain washing a woman's face. The brand also sponsored a Channel 4 drama series in 1999. Channel 4 attracts a young audience in line with Beck's target market.

Positioning in this segment is critical for brand legitimacy. The aim is to make Budweiser, Grolsch, Holsten Pils and Beck's the brands to be seen with. To do this two factors are vital: first, a fashionable and stylish image and, second, a track record of product quality (emphasized in the brand's promotion) that sustains its attraction after the novelty has worn off.

Based on: Anonymous (1999);[38] Anonymous (1999);[39] Buxton (1998);[40] Luhan (1998);[41] Michalczyk (2000);[42] Rogers (1999)[43]

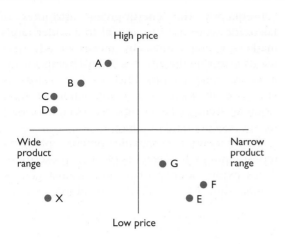

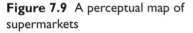

Figure 7.9 A perceptual map of supermarkets

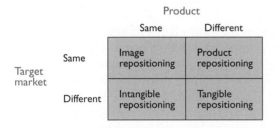

Figure 7.10 Repositioning strategies

Figure 7.9 shows a perceptual map for seven supermarket chains. Qualitative marketing research has shown that consumers evaluate supermarkets on two key dimensions of price and the width of product range. Quantitative marketing research is then carried out using scales that measure consumers' perception of each supermarket on price and width of product range. Average scores are then plotted on a perceptual map.

The results show that the supermarkets are grouped into two clusters: the high price, wide product range group and the low price, narrow price range group. These are indicative of two market segments and show that supermarkets C and D are close rivals as measured by consumers' perceptions and have very distinct perceptual positions in the marketplace compared with E, F

and G. Perceptual maps are useful in considering strategic moves. For example, an opportunity may exist to create a differential advantage based upon a combination of wide product range and low prices (as shown by the theoretical position at X).

Perceptual maps can also be valuable in identifying the strengths and weaknesses of brands as perceived by consumers. Such findings can be very revealing to managers whose own perceptions may be very different from those of consumers. Consumers can also be asked to score their ideal position on each of the attributes so that actual and ideal positions can be compared.

Repositioning

Occasionally a product or service will need to be repositioned because of changing customer tastes or poor sales performance. **_Repositioning_** involves changing the target markets, the differential advantage or both. A useful framework for analysing repositioning options is given in Fig. 7.10. Using product differentiation and target market as the key variables, four generic repositioning strategies are shown.

Image repositioning

The first option is to keep product and target market the same but to change the image of the product. In markets where products act as a form of self-expression, the product may be acceptable in functional terms but fail because it lacks the required image. Marketing in Action 7.5 describes the repositioning of the Nike and Adidas brands to create the _street cred_ image needed in the sports shoe market.

Product repositioning

With this strategy the product is modified to make it more acceptable to its present target market. For example, in 1992 Allied Breweries rejigged the formulation and can size of its Castlemaine XXXX lager brand to improve its appeal. Castlemaine's alcohol content was raised from 3.7 to 3.9 per cent in pubs and 4 per cent in supermarkets; its can size was also increased from 440 ml to 500 ml. An example of product repositioning in services is the rebranding of Talk Radio, a generalist speech-based radio station, as talkSPORT. The target market of 25–44-year-old males remains the same but the product changes to focus on sport.[44]

Intangible repositioning

This strategy involves targeting a different market segment with the same product. Lucozade, a carbonated drink, was initially targeted by Beecham's Foods at ill children. Marketing research found that mothers were drinking it as a midday pick-me-up and the brand was consequently repositioned to aim at this new segment.

Subsequently the energy-giving attributes of Lucozade were used to appeal to a wider target market—young adults—by means of advertisements featuring the athletes Daley Thompson and more recently Linford Christie. The history of Lucozade shows how a combination of repositioning strategies over time has been necessary for successful brand building.

Pharmaceutical companies practise intangible repositioning when patents on their prescription drugs expire. Rather than fight against generic competition by price cutting in the prescription

7.5   Marketing in Action

Repositioning at Nike and Adidas

The European sports shoe market is characterized by intense rivalry between Adidas, Nike and Reebok. Adidas's supremacy in Europe was successfully challenged by Nike through highly creative ads underscored by Nike's corporate line 'Just Do It'. Adidas, by contrast, was perceived as reliable but dull. Adidas successfully repositioned itself as having the necessary 'street cred' by signing up famous sports personalities to equate the brand with success. This was a tactic used by Nike for many years, who reinvented trainers and sportswear as a rebellious statement. Teenagers saw Eric Cantona, Charles Barclay, Michael Jordan and Ian Wright wearing Nike and believed that through buying a pair of trainers they, too, could be seen to have 'attitude'.

Part of Adidas's repositioning strategy was to sponsor stars such as David Beckham, Tim Henman and Prince Naseem while Reebok countered with Ryan Giggs, Pat Rafter and Dennis Bergkamp. All of this activity helped to imbibe the brands' personalities with credibility and success among its target audiences, but by the turn of the century new approaches were needed to freshen up the appeal of these brands.

Nike's response was to move the brand towards local-level sporting events in cities across Europe. In the UK this involved the introduction of 'Park Football' an ad campaign and website celebrating the joy and diversity of the grass-roots game. There was a belief that Nike had overdone it in the ad and sponsorship stakes and needed to refresh its brand personality. This is not to say that high-profile sponsorship and big event advertising will disappear but the balance between large-scale global and locally-based promotions has changed. Adidas has also emphasized its grass-roots commitment to tennis and athletics. Its marketing team puts in time at local athletics events, sports clinics and running and tennis clubs. It has also begun to use humour in its advertising to make the brand image more colourful for the youth market.

Brands such as Nike and Adidas have been highly successful across the globe but they recognize that they need to keep reinventing themselves to keep pace with changing youth demand.

Based on: Darby (2000);[45] Darby (1999);[46] McLuhan (1999);[47] Rogers (1999)[48]

7.6   Marketing in Action

Product and Tangible Repositioning at Mercedes-Benz

Mercedes-Benz, the Stuttgart-based company, built their success on building rugged, high quality, prestige saloon cars. For many years their dedication to engineering excellence placed them in a strong position to compete on the world stage.

During the early 1990s, however, Japanese luxury cars—notably the Lexus (Toyota) and the Acura (Honda)—have significantly penetrated their market segment. Part of the problem was the Mercedes culture of engineering perfection at any price, an expensive quality control system which saw one-third of their workforce's time being spent correcting faults made during manufacturing and a slow product replacement process. While Mercedes could charge ultra-premium prices, profitability could still be achieved, but the Japanese companies changed the rules of the game. Their strategy was to achieve high quality differentiation at low cost (lean manufacture, tight cost controls, short product development times, etc.) and it worked: in 1992 the Lexus outsold Mercedes in the vital US market by one-third.

Mercedes responded by attempting product repositioning. For their current market segment, they have introduced a product development process based on target costing. Rather than continuing to use a lavishly generous cost-plus system, Mercedes now employ a much tighter target product cost based on competitive market prices for their components. The aim is to reposition their products so that they are no longer over-engineered and, therefore, are more price-competitive. New models such as the Mercedes-Benz C-Class launched in 2000 and S-Class launched in 1999 have benefited from these changes.

Their accompanying move is to use tangible repositioning to make their product range more attractive to a new breed of customer. Mercedes are broadening its range to fill new market niches. The new Smart car is a joint venture with Switzerland's SMH group, makers of the famous Swatch range of watches. This is a two-seater city car targeting the young urban segment, providing an affordable first rung on the ladder of Mercedes ownership. Next comes the A-class series which is 7 cm shorter than a Ford Fiesta yet is more roomy because the engine is mounted under the floor. The sports car sector is attacked with the SLK roadster and Mercedes has entered the growing 'people carrier' multi-purpose segment with the V-class model. Finally, Mercedes has entered the all-activity vehicle sector with its M-class model which challenges Range Rover and Jeep. In line with its focus on cost control many of these vehicles will be manufactured outside high cost Germany in new plants in such countries as Brazil, the USA, France and China. Although the A-class and Smart cars had early problems, the launches of the SLK roadster, which takes a healthy 34 per cent share of the luxury 2-seater roadster market in Western Europe, 37 per cent in Germany, 13 per cent in the US and 47 per cent in Brazil, and the M-class all-activity vehicle have been successful.

Implementing two repositioning strategies concurrently is a risky manoeuvre but the problems besetting Mercedes have made these moves necessary.

Based on: Pearman (1993);[49] Anonymous (1993);[50] Lorenz (1993);[51] Lewin (1996);[52] Simonian (1996);[53] Anonymous (2000);[54] Anonymous (1999);[55] Haasen (1999);[56] Krebs (1999)[57]

segment they often switch to the over-the-counter (OTC) sector where they can fight by investing in brand equity. Market leaders benefit by being able to claim 'the product most often prescribed by doctors'. An example is Tagamet, SmithKline Beecham's indigestion drug which by switching to the OTC sector was able to transfer to the new segment the value which the consumer associated with the brand name developed through doctors' prescriptions.[58]

Tangible repositioning

When both product and target market are changed a company is practising tangible repositioning. For example, a company may decide to move up- or down-market by introducing a new range of products to meet the needs of the new target customers. Marketing in Action 7.6 shows how Mercedes-Benz found it necessary to use tangible and product repositioning in the face of Japanese competition. Tangible repositioning took the form of developing new products (e.g. a city car) to appeal to new target customers. Product repositioning was also required in their current market segments to bring down the cost of development and manufacture in the face of lower priced rivals such as Toyota's Lexus.

Summary

This chapter has explored the key strategic issues of market segmentation and positioning. Market segmentation is the foundation upon which a positioning strategy is developed. Positioning entails the choice of target market and differential advantage. The keys to successful positioning are clarity, consistency, credibility and competitiveness. When circumstances dictate a change in market position, marketers have a choice of four options: image, product, intangible and tangible repositioning. Repositioning may be necessary as market opportunities and threats develop. It is the process by which companies attune their product offerings to the changing requirements of customers and the competitive advances occurring in the marketplace.

Internet exercise

Product differentiation and market segmentation

Sites to visit
1
http://www.gap.com/onlinestore/gap/
http://www.bananarepublic.com/home.htm

Exercise
In what ways does The Gap use different products to reach different segments? How would you describe the different segments this organization is targeting?

2
http://www.unilever.com/
http://www.nestle.com/in_your_life/index.htmlhttp://www.pg.com/

Exercise
What are the key issues for organizations with large brand/product portfolios?

Study questions

1 What are the advantages of market segmentation? Can you see any advantages of mass marketing, i.e. treating a market as homogeneous and marketing to the whole market with one marketing mix?

2 Choose a market that you are familiar with and use benefit segmentation to identify market segments. What are the likely profiles of the resulting segments?

3 In what kind of markets is psychographic segmentation likely to prove useful? Why?

4 How might segmentation be of use when marketing in Europe?

5 One way of segmenting organizational markets is to begin with macrosegmentation variables and then develop subsegments using micro segmentation criteria. Does this seem sensible to you? Are there any circumstances where the process should be reversed?

6 Why is *buy class* a potentially useful method of segmenting organizational markets? (Use both this chapter and Chapter 4 when answering the question.)

7 What is the majority fallacy? Why should it be taken into account when evaluating market segments?

8 What is the difference between positioning and repositioning? Choose three products and services that describe how they are positioned in the marketplace, i.e. what is their target market and differential advantage?

References

1. Steiner, R. (1999) How Mobile Phones Came to the Masses, *The Sunday Times*, 31 October, 6.
2. Wind, Y. (1978) Issues and Advances in Segmentation Research, *Journal of Marketing Research*, August, 317–37.
3. Van Raaij, W. F. and T. M. M. Verhallen (1994) Domain-specific Market segmentation, *European Journal of Marketing*, 28 (10), 49–66.
4. Benson, S. (1981) How Advertising Helped Make Krona Brand Leader, in Broadbent, S. (ed.) *Advertising Works*, Eastbourne: Holt, Reinhart and Winston.
5. Sampson, P. (1992) People are People the World Over: The Case for Psychological Market Segmentation, *Marketing and Research Today*, November, 236–44.
6. Hooley, G. J., J. Saunders and N. Piercy (1998) *Marketing Strategy and Competitive Positioning: The Key to Market Success*, Hemel Hempstead: Prentice-Hall, 148.
7. Carter, J. (1998) Why Settle for 'Early Adopters', *Admap*, March, 41–4.
8. Cook, V. J. Jr. and W. A. Mindak (1984) A Search for Constants: The 'Heavy-User' Revisited!, *Journal of Consumer Marketing*, 1 (4), 79–81.
9. Ehrenberg, A. S. C. and G. J. Goodhardt (1978) *Market Segmentation*, New York: J. Walter Thompson.
10. O'Shaughnessy, J. (1995) *Competitive Marketing: A Strategic Approach*, London: Routledge.
11. Reed, D. (1995) Knowledge is Power, *Marketing Week*, 9 December, 46–7.
12. Sampson (1992) op. cit.
13. Ackoft, R. L. and J. R. Emsott (1975) Advertising at Anheuser-Busch Inc, *Sloan Management Review*, spring, 1–15.
14. Lannon, J. (1991) Developing Brand Strategies across Borders, *Marketing and Research Today*, August, 160–8.
15. Young, S. (1972) The Dynamics of Measuring Unchange, in Haley, R. I. (ed.) *Attitude Research in Transition*, Chicago: American Marketing Association, 61–82.
16. Tynan, A. C. and J. Drayton (1987) Market Segmentation, *Journal of Marketing Management*, 2 (3), 301–35.
17. Considine, P. (1999) The Young Ones, *Campaign*, 17 September, 31.
18. Green, H. (1999) New Generation, New Media, *Campaign*, 17 September, 34.
19. Willman, J. (1999) Elida Returns to its Youth to Find Secrets of Success, *Financial Times*, 5 November, 16.
20. O'Brien, S. and R. Ford (1988) Can We at Last Say Goodbye to Social Class?, *Journal of the Market Research Society*, 30 (3), 289–332.
21. Kossoff, J. (1988) Europe: Up for Sale, *New Statesman and Society*, 7 October, 43–4.
22. Garrett, A. (1992) Stats, Lies and Stereotypes, *Observer*, 13 December, 26.
23. Mitchell, V.-W. and P. J. McGoldrick (1994) The Role of Geodemographics in Segmenting and Targeting Consumer Markets: A Delphi Study, *European Journal of Marketing*, 28 (5), 54–72.
24. Kossoff (1988) op. cit.
25. See Wind, Y. and R. N. Cardozo (1974) Industrial Market Segmentation, *Industrial Marketing Management*, 3, 153–66; R. E. Plank (1985) A Critical Review of Industrial Market Segmentation, *Industrial Marketing Management*, 14, 79–91.
26. Enterprise Report (1999) The Enterprise Network, *The Sunday Times*, 19 September, 7.
27. Wind and Cardozo (1974) op. cit.
28. Lord, R. (1999) The Web Audience, *Campaign Report*, 28 May, 10–11.

29.   Moriarty, R.T. (1983) *Industrial Buying Behaviour*, Lexington, Mass: Lexington Books.

30.   Corey, R. (1978) *The Organisational Context of Industrial Buying Behaviour*, Cambridge, Mass: Marketing Science Institute, 6–12.

31.   See Abell, D. F. and J. S. Hammond (1979) *Strategic Market Planning: Problems and Analytical Approaches*, Hemel Hempstead: Prentice-Hall; Day, G. S. (1986) *Analysis for Strategic Market Decisions*, New York: West; Hooley, Saunders and Piercy (1998) op. cit.

32.   Walters, D. and D. Knee (1989) Competitive Strategies in Retailing, *Long Range Planning*, **22** (6), 74–84.

33.   Laurance, B. (1990) It was Niche Work if You Could Get It, *Guardian*, 10 February, 12.

34.   Richards, H. (1996) Discord Amid the High Notes, *The European*, 16–22 May, 23.

35.   Anonymous (2000) Saga, Dealing in Satisfaction, *The Observer*, 19 March, 29.

36.   Zikmund, W. G. and M. D'Amico (1999) *Marketing*, St Paul, MN: West, 249.

37.   Ries, A. and J. Trout (1982) *Positioning: The Battle for your Mind*, New York: Warner.

38.   Anonymous (1999) Playing Games with Grolsch, *Marketing*, 8 April, 25.

39.   Anonymous (1999) Beck's Renews C4 Sponsor Deal After Spring Pull Out, *Marketing*, 15 July, 5.

40.   Buxton, P. (1998) Bass Seeks New Market in £8m Grolsch Relaunch, *Marketing Week*, 3 December, 6.

41.   Luhan, R. (1998) Holsten Buys into TV Humour, *Marketing*, 10 September, 22.

42.   Michalczyk, I. (2000) Bass Redesigns Beers Prior to Sell-Off, *Marketing*, 13 April, 4.

43.   Rogers, D. (1999) Beck's Returns to TV After Five Years, *Marketing*, 10 June, 5.

44.   Brech, P. (2000) MacKenzie Plans Sports Revolution, *Marketing*, 20 January, 9.

45.   Darby, I. (2000) Adidas Adds Humour to Global Push, *Marketing*, 10 February, 5.

46.   Darby, I. (1999) Can Adidas Go the Distance, *Marketing*, 28 January, 18.

47.   McLuhan, R. (1999) Nike Ads Focus on Products to Fight Sportswear Decline, *Marketing*, 22 April, 29.

48.   Rogers, D. (1999) How Nike's Brand is Bouncing Back, *Marketing*, 21 October, 18.

49.   Pearman, H. (1993) A Bad Case of the Benz, *Sunday Times*, 7 February, section 8, 13.

50.   Anonymous (1993) New Mercedes, *Financial Times*, 28 January, 21.

51.   Lorenz, C. (1993) Mercedes Sees the Writing on the Wall, *Financial Times*, 5 February, 16.

52.   Lewin, T. (1996) A-Class Year for Mercedes, *The European*, 26 December 1996–1 January 1997, 26.

53.   Simonian, M. (1996) Car Trip into the Unknown, *Financial Times*, 9 August, 13.

54.   Anonymous (2000) C-Class Gets Fresh New Look, *Ward's Auto World*, April, 26.

55.   Anonymous (1999) Business: Crunch Time, *The Economist*, 25 September, 73–4.

56.   Haasen, A. (1999) M-class: The Making of a New Daimler-Benz, *Organisational Dynamics*, Spring, 74–8.

57.   Krebs, M. (1999) Mercedes S-class: Lots of Luxury, Lots of Great New Gadgets, *Medical Economics*, 12 July, 172–81.

58.   Platford, R. (1997) Fast Track to Approval, *Financial Times*, 24 April, 27.

Key terms

market segmentation   the process of identifying individuals or organizations with similar characteristics that have significant implications for the determination of marketing strategy

differential marketing strategies   market coverage strategies where a company decides to target several market segments and develops separate marketing mixes for each

benefit segmentation   the grouping of people based upon the different benefits they seek from a product

psychographic segmentation   the grouping people according to their lifestyle and personality characteristics

lifestyle segmentation   the grouping of people according to their pattern of living as expressed in their activities, interests and opinions

profile segmentation   the grouping of people in terms of profile variables such as age and socio-economic group so that marketers can communicate to them

macrosegmentation   the segmentation of organizational markets by size, industry and location

microsegmentation   segmentation according to choice criteria, DMU structure, decision-making process, buy class, purchasing structure and organizational innovativeness

target marketing   selecting a segment as a focus for the company's offering or communications

undifferentiated marketing   a market coverage strategy where a company decides to ignore market segment differences and develops a single marketing mix for the whole market

differentiated marketing   a market coverage strategy where a company decides to target several market segments and develops separate marketing mixes for each

focused marketing   a market coverage strategy where a company decides to target one market segment with a single marketing mix

customized marketing   the market coverage strategy where a company decides to target individual customers and develops separate marketing mixes for each

positioning   the choice of target market (where the company wishes to compete) and differential advantage (how the company wishes to compete)

repositioning   Changing the target market or differential advantage or both

Case 11 Repositioning Budweiser

Budweiser in the USA

Anheuser-Busch is the biggest brewer not only in America but also globally. Its 14 brands account for approximately 45 per cent of the total US beer market which translated into a 9 per cent share of the total world beer sales.[1] AB's flagship brand, *Budweiser* is the number one selling brand in the US, with 21.8 per cent market share. In addition, *Bud Light* is the best-selling light beer in America and claims an 8.2 per cent share of the total beer market. Brand extensions such as *Bud Dry* and *Bud Light Dry* account for an additional 5 per cent or so of the US market.[2]

Anheuser-Busch produced 88.5 million barrels (104 million hectolitres) of beer in 1994.[3] This was almost four times the volume of AB's closest competitor, Heineken. But while Anheuser-Busch clearly dominated its home market, the US beer market was quickly becoming saturated. This was not good news for AB, which still has 95 per cent of its sales in America.

Within the US market, Budweiser had a dominant 44 per cent share of the US market in 1994. The brand had, however, declined over a period of five years because of recession, higher taxes and a price war in California. Budweiser was not alone in facing more competitive market conditions. Rival brands Coors and Miller High Life faced a dramatic loss of brand share over the same period. Anheuser-Busch's Bob Lachky commented: 'We are not overly concerned at Bud's leakage . . . The "family" is up 4 per cent and flagship brands Budweiser and Bud Light are outperforming competitors'.[4]

Still, Anheuser-Busch's move from long-standing agency D'Arcy, Masius, Benton and Bowles (DMB&B) to DDB Needham suggested that there was concern that the brand image needed refreshing. Some commentators were suggesting that the Budweiser brand positioning was no longer appropriate to its target market.

Figure C11.1 The *Budweiser* classic brown bottle

The Budweiser brand

The core US market for Anheuser-Busch's *Budweiser* are 18 to 24-year-old blue-collar males. There is strong association between the brand and its American origins. Brand analysts describe Budweiser as the 'safe back-up buy for hosts uncertain what guests will want'. This positioning as the brand for everybody, however, may run counter to the needs and wants of the target market it describes as its core.

Budweiser seemed to have become a victim of its own success—a brand that had grown so strong that it was institutionalized, established, difficult to move. There is strong identification with the classic brown bottle and busy label (see Fig. C11.1). Says AB: 'Our customers say, whatever you do, don't change that.'

However, so great is the tradition surrounding Budweiser, that it may be viewed by today's youngsters as 'Dad's beer'.[5]

[1] Anheuser-Busch Annual Report, 1994.
[2] Tenowitz, Ira (1994) Bud Tops Turnaround of Premium-Priced Beers, *Advertising Age*, 28 September, 13.
[3] Anheuser-Busch Annual Report, 1994.
[4] *Ibid*.

[5] Gibson, R. and M. Charlier (1994) Corporate Focus: Fresher Bud Image Requires Light Touch, *Wall Street Journal*, 25 November, 1.

Researchers into the beer market suggest that its ongoing success depends on a continual inflow of drinkers in their early 20s. If the younger age group associate Budweiser with their parents' generation, then it may be less attractive to them.

The US beer market

In the early 1990s, the US beer market had undergone significant upheaval. For 10 years, the size of the market had been relatively static, with a small decline in the total market in 1992 and 1993. At the same time, established beer brands were under attack from all sides. Imports had risen significantly and comprised almost 5 per cent of the market. The regional and microbrewing segment of the market had become a significant force, claiming 4.6 per cent of the market in 1994.[6] In addition, niche products like ice beer, dry beer and red beer, and a host of new non-alcoholic beverages were all growing at the expense of large, established beer brands. Sales of Budweiser actually declined 16 per cent in volume terms from 1991 to 1993, from 50 million barrels to 42 million barrels. At the same time, However, sales of *Bud Light* rose 49 per cent from 10.6 million barrels to 15.8 million barrels.[7,8]

Anheuser-Busch employed several strategies to deal with this competitive situation in its domestic market. First, it pursued new, innovative products. This led to the launch of its own ice beer and dry beer products. However, innovation in the brewing industry can only go so far. AB therefore began to acquire equity stakes in microbreweries and regional breweries to tap into the surge in consumer interest for these beers. Finally, and most importantly, AB has begun to focus intensively on new markets abroad.[9]

AB's international marketing strategy

Anheuser-Busch first launched itself seriously on to the international scene in 1981, with the formation of its international division. In the period from 1981–94, international sales climbed from a paltry 900 000 barrels to 4.5 million barrels in 1994.[10] This growth in sales was achieved through a combination of exporting, licensing and contracting-out production of AB's beer. While AB sold some *Michelob* and *Busch* brands of beer abroad, *Budweiser* remains its primary international brand. Interestingly, while domestically *Budweiser* is positioned as a mainstream, and to some extent working man's beer, internationally *Budweiser* is positioned as a premium product with a premium price attached.

Figure C11.2 shows AB's growth in international sales from 1981–94. While AB initially concentrated on developing a foothold in established beer markets like Canada and Europe, it now sees greater profits in equity stakes and acquisitions in developing markets.[11] This has led AB to aggressively pursue partnerships in China, other Asian markets, and in Latin America. In the early 1990s, AB concluded an 80 per cent stake in a joint venture with Kirin brewery in Japan, an 80 per cent interest in a joint venture with the Zhongde brewery in Wuhan China, a 5 per cent stake in the Chinese Tsingtso Brewery and a partnership with a brewery in India, to name only a few of its international deals.[12]

AB's activities in Europe

While AB has focused on the fast growing beer markets of the developing world, it did not put Europe on the back burner. Figure C11.3 shows AB's European sales of the *Budweiser* and *Michelob* brands in 1993.

Despite significant sales volumes in Europe, Anheuser-Busch's marketing is seriously constrained by the trademark dispute with Budvar (see Appendix 1). AB can sell under the *Busweiser* name in Cyprus, Denmark, Finland, Iceland, Ireland, Malta, Sweden and the UK, having won law suits against Budvar in these countries.

However, AB is restricted to using the *Bud* name in Belgium, France, Greece, Italy, Luxembourg, the Netherlands, Portugal, Spain and Switzerland, the Canary Islands and Gibraltar due to the trademark

[6] *Ibid.*

[7] Lubove, S. (1995) Get 'em before they get you', *Forbes*, 31 July, 93.

[8] 1 barrel = 1.18 hectolitres.

[9] Anheuser-Busch, 1993 and 1994 Annual Reports.

[10] Anheuser-Busch Public Relations Materials, July 1995.

[11] Anheuser-Busch Annual Report, 1994.

[12] Anheuser-Busch Public Relations Materials, July 1995.

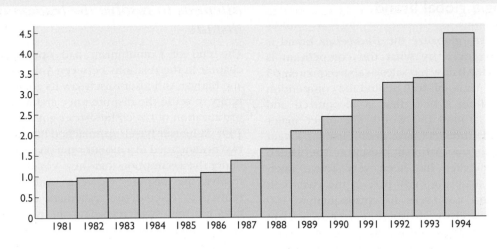

Figure C11.2 Anheuser-Busch international sales 1981–94 (in million barrels).

International sales include export, contract- and license-brewing volume. *Source*: Anheuser-Busch public relations material

Region	Country	1993 AB brand volume (hl)
British Isles	UK, Ireland	70 000
Scandinavia	Finland, Sweden	56 000
Continental wine countries	Spain, Canaries & Gibraltar	43 000
	France	15 000
	Italy	13 500
	Greece	11 000
	Switzerland	9 600
Continental beer countries	Germany (Michelob only)	4 500
	Netherlands	4 500
	Belgium	1 400

Source: Anheuser-Busch Annual Report 1994

Figure C.11.3 AB sales in Europe in 1993 (Budweiser and Michelob brands)

dispute. Currently AB cannot sell under the name *Budweiser* or *Bud* in Germany, Austria, or Norway. Moreover, they are technically prevented from entering the newly-opened beer markets of Central and Eastern Europe. AB recently began selling as *Bud* in Russia, but Budvar considers this an infringement of its trademark and is likely to sue AB if the dispute goes unresolved. Fig. C11.4 shows the different brand names and the similarity in identity and positioning adopted for these by Budweiser.

Figure C11.4 The brand names and similarity in positioning by Budweiser

Building a global brand

AB's drive to globalize the *Budweiser* brand is partly influenced by what the competition is doing. While AB now has sales in approximately 65 countries,[13] it is still well behind the competition in establishing a beer that is recognized and consumed around the world. The other major international brewers have been busy far longer building an international presence. The Dutch brewer Heineken has been very active internationally since the early part of the twentieth century and now sells in approximately 160 countries. Similarly, Carlsberg, currently sells in over 140 countries, and has 80 per cent of sales outside its home market of Denmark.[14] Guinness also has successfully been building a global presence in the past decade.

While industry analyses once thought that the brewing industry would remain dominated by regional and national brewing companies, Carlsberg, Heineken and Guinness have proven that beer has global branding potential. Resolution of the trademark dispute with Budvar is crucial for Anheuser-Busch's effort to build a global beer brand out of *Budweiser*. Without unrestricted access to the European market, AB will not be able to utilize a unified branding strategy, and will not be able to freely pursue new opportunities for *Budweiser*.

While AB initially concentrated on developing a foothold in established beer markets such as Canada and Europe, AB now sees greater profits in equity stakes and acquisitions in developing markets.[15] This has led AB to aggressively pursue partnerships in China, other Asian markets, and in Latin America. In the past five years, AB has concluded an 80 per cent stake in a joint venture with Kirin brewery in Japan, an 80 per cent interest in a joint venture with the Zhongde brewery in Wuhan China, a 5 per cent stake in the Chinese Tsingtso Brewery and a partnership with a brewery in India, to name only a few of its international deals.[16]

Attempts to resolve the trademark dispute

The end of Communism had opened a new chapter in the relations between Anheuser-Busch and Budvar. Anheuser-Busch saw its golden opportunity to settle the dispute once and for all when privatization of Czech industries got underway in 1991. Anheuser-Busch approached Budvar, and the two firms agreed to a moratorium on legal actions, under the assumption that they would attempt to resolve the dispute. However, Anheuser-Busch refused to discuss the trademark dispute until talks got underway regarding the purchase of a stake in Budvar. This was the ideal opportunity to end the dispute forever.

Stephen J. Burrows, vice president of Anheuser-Busch International was quoted as implying that AB would employ a carrot-and-stick approach with Budvar. He suggested that if AB could invest in Budvar, resolution of the dispute could be quick and painless, but that if Budvar were sold to another party, settling the dispute might be far more difficult.[17] In early 1993, AB suggested a 'strategic alliance', which would ensure co-existence in the world market between Budvar's and AB's *Budweiser* brands. AB's proposal included providing Budvar access to Anheuser-Busch's formidable marketing and distribution network and gave guarantees of continuous investment in the Budejovice brewery. AB also promised that they would not tamper with Budvar's taste, production process or ingredients. The only changes which would be necessary, according to AB were 'appropriate name and label modifications to avoid confusion whenever necessary'.[18]

Full scale public relations campaign

Anheuser-Busch' recognized that their proposal would be greeted with suspicion by the Czech public. In early 1993, AB started a massive public relations campaign explaining why they wanted to buy a stake in Budvar. AB took out full page advertisements in several national daily news-

---

[13] Anheuser-Busch Public Relations Materials, July 1995.

[14] Guttman, R. J. (1995) Danish Business Goes Global, *Europe*, 10.

[15] Anheuser-Busch Annual Report, 1994.

[16] Anheuser-Busch Public Relations Materials, July 1995.

[17] Guyon, J. (1993) Row Over Budweiser Brand Name Highlights the Value of Brands', *Wall Street Journal Europe*, 16 September, page unknown.

[18] Newton, J. S. (1993) Stalking Budvar, Disregarding Heritage, *Prognosis*, 14–27 May, 11.

papers discussing their intentions and giving promises to maintain the distinctive quality of the beer and the centuries-old brewing traditions.

AB also spent over one million dollars to build the 'St Louis Cultural Centre' in Ceske Budejovice. The centre offers English language classes and a library, and sponsors events. Some residents of Ceske Budejovice believe the centre serves as a thinly veiled public relations arm for AB in Budvar's hometown, and the centre has been compared to a Trojan horse.[19] Despite its extensive public relations campaign, the Czech government made it clear that AB would need to follow the normal procedures of the Czech privatization process, and would not receive special treatment. AB would need to put in its bid along with any other interested party when, and if, the government decided that a stake in Budvar should be sold to a foreign investor.

Back to the negotiating table

The government's indecision over the Budvar privatization situation endured until July 1995, when the prime minister suddenly announced publicly that privatization would definitely not proceed until the trademark dispute with AB was resolved. Anheuser-Busch had little choice but to agree to meet Budvar for a fresh attempt at negotiations to resolve the trademark dispute.

Anheuser-Busch's final offer included a 10-year agreement to purchase Czech hops worth $76 million and a down payment of $20 million on the future purchase of shares in Budvar by Anheuser-Busch. But Budvar general manager, Jiri Bocek, was concerned that the final offer 'would [leave] his company playing second fiddle to US Budweiser in European markets ... Mr Bocek said the offer was unacceptable to Budvar and the government. "I believe the decision was rational and based on pragmatic considerations. Budvar is capable of developing itself without becoming a vassal of Anheuser-Busch." '[20]

Budvar's uncertain future was hindering other privatizations. Bass of the UK, Denmark's Carlsberg and Anheuser-Busch were bidding for a

minority stake in Jihoceske Pivovary (South Bohemian Breweries), a regional Czech brewery. As there was a simultaneous plan to merge SBB with Budvar, this plan was suspended by the Czech government until the outcome of the SBB privatization was clear: 'If SBB selected Anheuser-Busch, any merger with Budvar would be abandoned.'[21] Finally, in September 1996, Anheuser-Busch pulled out of the talks when the Czech government finally decided to privatize Budvar, but indicated that it would remain in domestic hands.[22]

Anheuser-Busch recently won court rulings allowing it to use the Budweiser name in Spain, and the Bud name in Norway. It has had nine wins in European countries—five in the past year—and has 27 underway.[23] Anheuser-Busch believes that it has achieved 'undisputed access' to Europe, with sales of 2.2 hectolitres of beer, an increase of 25 per cent.

However, each legal battle involves both time and expense and hinders its expansion strategy. Anheuser-Busch recently pulled out of a $145 million Vietnamese brewing joint venture because Budvar registered the name there in 1960.

Repositioning the Budweiser brand

The trademark dispute notwithstanding, AB has a number of positioning issues to consider for its brand. First, in the USA, AB's brand positioning seemed more appropriate to an age group older than that described as AB's target market. Second, the positioning of *Budweiser* in the USA and other international markets differed from mass market to premium respectively. This would appear to have a number of consequences for designing an appropriate marketing strategy. Finally, a number of obstacles stood in the path of AB's stated intent to develop a global beer brand.

[19] Newton, J. S. (1993) Stalking Budvar, Disregarding Heritage, *Prognosis*, 14–27 May, 11.
[20] Boland, V. (1996) Companies and Finance: International: Budvar Takes Lid Off US Rival's Offer', *Financial Times*, 20 December.
[21] Boland, V. (1996) International Company News: Brewing Bid Battle May Affect Budvar', *Financial Times*, 5 March.
[22] Boland, V. (1996) Back Page—First Section: Anheuser-Busch Pulls Out of Budweiser Name Talks, *Financial Times*, 23 September.
[23] Boland, V. and R. Oram (1996) Companies and Finance: Europe: US Brewer Leaves Budvar Fighting for Identity: Czech Group Faces Marketing Challenge after Collapse of Brand Right Talks with Anheuser-Busch, *Financial Times*, 1 November.

Questions

1 What challenges did the established Budweiser brand face in repositioning itself for a more youthful market?

2 What are the implications for Budweiser's international marketing strategy of its different positioning in the US and other international markets?

3 What are the advantages and disadvantages for AB of creating a global beer brand rather than pursuing a local or regionally adapted branding strategy?

Appendix C11.1

Background to the trademark dispute

Use of the *Budweiser* name in connection with beer dates back to as early as 1531. In that year, the German king Ferdinand whose royal court was in the town of Ceske Budejovice (then called Budweis) gave the city the right to brew beer for his court. This beer was identified as *Budweiser*, literally meaning beer 'from the town of Budweis'. *Budweis* beer became known as the 'Beer of Kings' due to its link with Ferdinand's court.[24]

Several centuries later, in the mid-1860s, a German immigrant named Adolphus Busch established a small brewery in St Louis, USA, called the Bavarian Brewery. In 1876, in searching for a name for a new beer which would appeal to the many German immigrants living in and around St Louis, Busch appropriated the name *Budweiser* from the beer long-produced in the Bohemian town of Budweis. Busch also borrowed upon the old slogan of the *Budweiser* beer, 'Beer of Kings', but inverted it, called American *Budweiser* the 'King of Beers'.[25] In 1879 Busch's brewery merged with another brewery and changed its name to Anheuser-Busch.

Two decades later, in 1895, a group of Czech investors founded Budejovicky Budvar (also called Budweiser Budvar) and also laid claim to the name *Budweiser*. The Czechs cited the historical precedent for using the name, dating back to the early sixteenth century. Moreover, they claimed the right to the name as it properly identified the origin of their beer.

1911 Agreement

As Budvar and Anheuser-Busch grew, it was inevitable that they would eventually run into conflict over use of the *Budweiser* name. By the early twentieth century, the two breweries were warring over the right to the name. In 1911, the two breweries came together and signed an agreement which they hoped would end the dispute. The agreement recognized AB's right to the name *Budweiser*, as it was a registered trademark of AB in the United States. However, the agreement also acknowledged Budvar's legal right to the *Budweiser* name. AB was thus given the right to *Budweiser* in the US and all other non-European countries. AB could use the *Budweiser* name in any way it chose, however, it had to stop using the word 'original' in combination with their product, in order to avoid giving the impression to the consumer that their product was the first beer to be known as *Budweiser*.

In exchange, Budvar was given the exclusive right to use the *Budweiser* name in the European market. In addition, recognizing that *Budweiser* was the name which identified the origin of their product, Budvar could still market its beer as *Budweiser* in *any* country of the world, including the US.[26]

Over the next several decades, Anheuser-Busch grew from a provincial brewery, to the largest brewery in the world. Perhaps predictably, AB began to chafe under the 1911 agreement, which

---

[24] Masek, I. (1993) Jiri Bocek: Anheuser-Busch je Pouze Jednim ze Zajemcu! *Magazin Uspech*, September, 19.

[25] *Ibid.*, 19.

[26] Original mutual restraint agreement between Budvar and Anheuser-Busch, 19 August 1911.

allowed Budvar to sell as *Budweiser* in AB's home market.

1939 agreement

By the late 1930s, Budvar was selling significant quantities of Czech *Budweiser* in the USA. Anheuser-Busch clearly felt that Budvar was over-stepping its bounds in AB's home market.

AB charged that the US public associated the *Budweiser* and *Bud* names with AB products. Since Budvar was exporting its beer to the US under the name *Budweiser*, Budvar was confusing the customer, and unfairly using the brand name that AB had built.[27]

Anheuser-Busch went to Budvar with an agreement which blocked Budvar's access to the North American market. In the settlement proposed by AB, Budvar agreed to surrender all rights to the *Budweiser*, *Budweis* and *Bud* names, and all other named containing 'Bud', in all territories north of Panama, as well as all US colonies and territories. In addition, Budvar could not market other beer brands in these market using the words 'manu-factured in Budweis'. Instead, they had to use the words 'manufactured in Ceske Budejovice'. In return, Anheuser-Busch agreed to pay $50 000 to Budvar and $15 000 to Budvar's American distributor, provided Budvar's *Budweiser* was removed from the North American markets within six months.[28]

Although the agreement seemed rather slanted against Budvar, AB managed to convince Budvar to sign it. The conditions under which Budvar agreed to sign the agreement are not altogether clear, but what is known is that the agreement was signed several days before the Nazis invaded what remained of Czechoslovakia in 1939. The Czechs later claimed that the 1939 agreement was signed under duress and declared it invalid.

AB's attempt to buy rights to Budweiser

The period after 1939 saw the start of World War II and then the imposition of communism in Czechoslovakia. During this time, Budvar's exports went primarily to Western Europe and Budvar was not in any position to threaten AB. Therefore, the two restraint agreements between Budvar and AB endured until 1970.

That year, Anheuser-Busch was striving for further international expansion. However, the terms of the restraint agreements effectively locked them out of the countries of Western Europe, some of the most attractive beer markets in the world at that time. Attempting to settle the trademark dispute once and for all, Anheuser-Busch offered the communist Czechoslovak government $1 million for the European rights to the *Budweiser* trademark.[29]

Perhaps Anheuser-Busch under-estimated the degree of national pride Czechs held in their small but internationally known brewer. Perhaps the ideology at the time, which viewed Americans as 'capitalist imperialists', predominated in the Czechs' decision. Whatever the motivation, the offer by Anheuser-Busch to purchase the rights to the *Budweiser* name in Europe was categorically refused.

Legal battles

After failing to buy the right to the *Budweiser* name in Europe, Anheuser-Busch attempted an attack from a different angle. AB launched legal challenges to Budvar's right to the *Budweiser* name in 15 countries throughout Europe.[30] In 1984, AB won a decisive victory in its battle to enter the European market when a UK court judged that AB's *Budweiser* should be allowed to co-exist with Budvar's *Budweiser* brand. The court ruled that the co-existence should be reinforced by the two firms using their respective names in different ways.[31] In Finland and Sweden, Anheuser-Busch also succeeded in legal battles, and were able to market *Budweiser*. However, in France, Italy, Portugal, and a number of other markets, AB's legal offensives failed. In these markets, however, AB was able to sell its beer under the name '*Bud*'.

[27] Original mutual restraint agreement between Budvar and Anheuser-Busch, 7 March 1939.
[28] 1939 mutual restraint agreement.
[29] Masek, I. (1993) Jiri Bocck: Anheuser Busch je Pouze Jednim ze Zajemcu! *Magazin Uspech*, September, 19.
[30] *Ibid.*, 20.
[31] Gever, F., trademark attorney. Conflict between appellation of origin and trademark, preliminary answers, June 1995.

The appellation of origin issue

AB's legal defeat in the 1980s in a number of European countries was ultimately the result of the development of a new concept in intellectual property called the 'appellation of origin'. An appellation of origin is a name which serves to identify the geographic origin of a product. If registered, the appellation of origin cannot be used by a producer from outside that town or region. The names Champagne, Cognac and Bordeaux are three of the best known names which are protected appellations of origin. Over the past several decades, the appellation of origin has emerged as a strongly protected element of intellectual property in many European countries, as well as in a group of non-European countries which have signed on to a special multilateral convention on intellectual property called the Lisbon Agreement.[32]

Budvar had registered and uses a number of appellations of origin. Most importantly, '*Budweiser*' is a registered appellation of origin, designating Budvar's beer as a product of Budweis. For the European countries which recognized the appellation of origin, it was an infringement of Budvar's rights for Anheuser-Busch to use the name *Budweiser*.

In 1989, the end of communist rule of Czechoslovakia, and the formation of the independent Czech republic seemed finally to offer potential for a solution to the ongoing dispute. In need of capital, to increase production capacity and for international expansion, Budvar seemed a likely privatization prospect. Anheuser-Busch saw investment in the company as a final solution to gaining rights to the brand in Europe.

---

[32] A very prominent legal case involving appellations of origin concerned the champagne-makers of the Champagne region of France. French champagne-makers were able to force producers from outside the Champagne region to cease calling their product 'Champagne', as this word had been a registered appellation of origin and served to identify the origin of the product. Producers outside the Champagne region must now call their product 'sparkling wine'.

Case 12 Automatic Vehicle Location: Civilian Uses for Military Skills

A technological demonstration

In the last few days of July 1990, Saddam Hussein's Iraqi army invaded Kuwait, claiming that Kuwait in reality was part of Iraq. Despite United Nations' resolutions, shuttle diplomacy, threats and international pressure, the Iraqi army refused to return to Iraqi soil. As a result, an allied fighting force, with contributions *inter alia* from the USA, UK, Egypt and Saudi Arabia was assembled in the Middle East under the American General 'Storming Norman' Schwarzkopf. The military strategy was to use air power to soften up the enemy before the commencement of the land battle. The resultant TV pictures of smart bombs dropping precisely down chimneys and guided weapons 'being driven down streets to turn right at the traffic lights' before accurately hitting specific targets in developed urban landscapes were transmitted nightly around the world. The satellite system that allowed such pinpoint bombing and gunnery is now being applied to civilian and commercial uses.

Civilian extension

The generic name for the technology initially deployed by the military and increasingly being applied to civilian uses is GIS (geographic information system) or GPS (global positioning system). The essential purpose of the extension of GIS/GPS to civilian use is to precisely fix geographically the location of any given vehicle either as an individual unit or as part of a larger fleet. Vehicle navigation/location issues have traditionally been tackled in two, not necessarily mutually exclusive, ways.

1 The vehicle driver and/or passenger can use a map. However, maps, especially of large areas, can be cumbersome to use and in moving vehicles, especially at night, difficult to read. Even if a map is readable, the navigator still has the problem of trying to locate a precise position on the map.

2 Where a large fleet of vehicles is involved, the use of one or more dedicated radio channels becomes economic and effective. A controller can locate the vehicle positions and direction of travel on a master map. Such an approach, though, requires regular updating.

However, using 1990s technology, vehicle location can be solved automatically using publicly available satellite systems, on board navigation devices, electronic map representation and two-way (driver control) communication. Hence, the total system is sometimes called AVL (automatic vehicle location). Fleet management based on these principles of mapping, communications and position location allows for the more effective use of resources whether the fleet involved is comprised of delivery vehicles, taxis, ambulances, police cars, buses, trains or company cars, etc.

VT Limited

Vehicle Track started trading in 1994. Turnover by 1996 was £15 million. The number of employees varied because of the use of part time and temporary staff recruited to write software packages to meet particular contract requirements but on average was no more than 50. The company was not surprisingly technologically driven and sales orientated.

Success to date had been as a result of responding to enquiries and chasing contracts. There was no formal marketing function and although the company prepared a document called a 'marketing strategy and plan' it contained little marketing analysis. At best it was a sales plan.

The flow of enquiries and potential opportunities was increasingly proving to be more than the company could cope with. Indeed, it was becoming recognized that help would be required to prioritize opportunities and formally prepare a marketing strategy to guide future developments.

The configuration of the AVL system is shown diagrammatically in Fig. C12.1. Using this system, vehicle location is determined by a calculation process using navigation data obtained from three sources:

- ✦ Signals from a number of international very low frequency (VLF) transmitting stations.

- ✦ Position data derived from global position satellites.

- ✦ Direction and speed data taken from in-vehicle dead reckoning sensors.

Particular features of the system include:

- ✦ Use of publicly funded international navigation systems established for the safe progress of ships and aircraft. Such systems are freely available worldwide and guaranteed into the twenty-first century.

- ✦ Lack of reliance on either privately owned transmitting stations or locally funded street/motorway hardware.

- ✦ The ability to operate on dedicated data channels within existing communication set ups. This can be particularly useful in large fleet situations operating with high load factors.

- ✦ 100 per cent control from base station.

- ✦ The capability of interfacing with any existing mobile ratio system.

- ✦ A high level of location accuracy viz 50 metres.

- ✦ Unlimited, geographic area coverage and fleet-size application.

As a result of the application of such an AVL system, a controller at the base station will be aware of any vehicle's call sign, position, status, direction and speed. In addition, the system allows two-way direct communication, initiated by either party between the base station and the mobile unit.

Customer groups

The company possessed no reliable data as to the likely size of the market for AVL but it is argued that there were three main types of customers, viz:

- ✦ *Freight carriers*: better control of cargoes with improved security for both drivers and goods. End customers can be given real time progress reports on deliveries. Public transport systems, especially buses, can be regarded as 'freight' carriers.

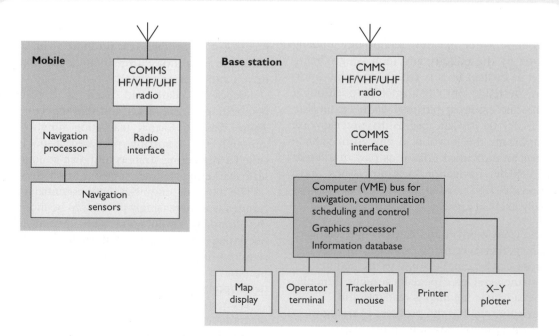

Figure C12.1 The configuration of the AVL system

✦ *Incident motivated fleets*: Service engineers, taxis, couriers, etc. can be directed more efficiently for improved productivity, better utilization of vehicles and reductions in non-revenue mileage. This improves customer relations through faster response times and on-line progress reports.

✦ *Emergency services*: Command, control and resource management systems are optimized. The clear presentation of a changing situation, as it happens, means that Operations Rooms can concentrate on their prime task of incident control. Voice channels are cleared of position reports, improving tactical command. Response times improve and dead mileage reduces. Emergency services include the three main '999' public services of police, fire and ambulance, but additionally subscription motor vehicle breakdown services, e.g. the AA or RAC.

An analysis of the possible fit of user benefits by market segment is shown below:

	Freight	*Incident*	*Emergency*
Automatic vehicle location identification	x	x	x
Optimum usage of vehicle fleet	x	x	x
Reduced operating costs	x	x	x
Faster vehicle response times		x	x
Continual vehicle monitoring	x		x
Greater vehicle security and crew safety	x	x	x
History of vehicle movements			x
More voice channel space for other messages		x	x
Reliable accuracy in built-up areas and mountainous terrain	x	x	x

This case was prepared by David Cook, Senior Lecturer in Marketing, University of Leeds.

Questions

As a marketing consultant at start up:

1   How would you recommend that AVL segment their market?

2   In the light of your segmentation advice, outline a proposed marketing plan.

PART TWO

Marketing Mix Decisions

CHAPTER EIGHT

Managing Products

'...a rose
By any other name would smell as sweet'

SHAKESPEARE   *Romeo and Juliet*

'Or would it'

ANONYMOUS

Learning Objectives   *This chapter explains:*

1 The concept of a product, brand, product line and product mix

2 The difference between manufacturer and own-label brands

3 The difference between a core and augmented product (the brand)

4 Brand building issues

5 The arguments for and against global and pan-European branding

6 The strategic options that can be used to build global and pan-European brands

7 The differences between family, individual and combined brand names and the characteristics of an effective brand name

8 The concepts of brand extension and stretching, their uses and limitations

9 The issues involved with the product life cycle concept, its uses and its limitations

10 The uses and limitations of product portfolio evaluation models as a means of managing groups of products

11 The four product growth strategies

12 Ethical issues in managing products

The core element in the marketing mix is the company's product because this provides the functional requirements sought by customers. For example, a watch that does not tell the time or a car that does not start in the morning will rapidly be rejected by consumers. Marketing managers develop their products into brands which help to create a unique position (see Chapter 7) in the minds of customers. Brand superiority leads to high sales, the ability to charge price premiums and the power to resist distributor power. Firms attempt to retain their current customers through brand loyalty. Loyal customers are typically less price sensitive, and the presence of a loyal customer base provides the firm with valuable time to respond to competitive actions.[1] The management of products and brands is therefore a key factor in marketing success.

This chapter will explore the nature of products and brands, and examine ways of building successful brands. We shall discuss the product life cycle and how this concept can be used to plan marketing strategies. Finally, we shall look at portfolio analysis which provides a framework for managing groups of products and brands. The essential task of developing new products and brands is dealt with in Chapter 9.

Products and brands

A *product* is anything which is capable of satisfying customer needs. In everyday speech we often distinguish between products and services, with products being tangible (e.g. a car) and services mainly intangible (e.g. a medical examination). However, when we look at what the customer is buying, it is essentially a service whether the means is tangible or intangible. For example, a car provides the service of transportation; the medical examination provides the service of a health check. Consequently, it is logical to include services within the definition of the product. Hence, there are *physical products* such as a watch, car or gas turbine, or *service products* such as medical services, insurance or banking. All of these products satisfy customer needs, for example a gas turbine provides a power and insurance reduces financial risk. The principles discussed in this chapter apply equally to physical and service products. However, because there are special considerations associated with service products (e.g. intangibility) and as services industries (e.g. fast-food restaurants, tourism and public sector) form an important and growing sector within the EU, Chapter 20 is dedicated to examining services marketing in detail.

Branding is the process by which companies distinguish their product offerings from the competition. By developing a distinctive name, packaging and design, a *brand* is created. Some brands are supported by logos, for example the Nike SWOOSH and the prancing horse of Ferrari. By developing an individual identity, branding permits customers to develop associations with the brand (e.g. prestige, economy) and eases the purchase decision.[2] The marketing task is to ensure that they are positive and in line with the chosen positioning objectives (see Chapter 7). Branding affects perceptions since it is well known that in blind product testing consumers often fail to distinguish between brands in each product category: hence the questioning of Shakespeare's famous statement at the start of this chapter.

A key function of brands is quality certification. Brand reputation has considerable value particularly where consumers find it difficult to judge quality for themselves such as with fragrances and drinks. In these markets strong brands command large price premiums such as Chanel perfume or Holsten Pils lager: it is worth more than a functionally equivalent product. Chanel No. 5 is a brand because of this; Euston station in London is not because the brand name does not confer added value. Its worth is the same if it were called something else.[3]

The product line and product mix

Brands are not often developed in isolation. They normally fall within a company's product line and mix. A *product line* is a group of brands that are closely related in terms of their functions and the benefits they provide (e.g. Dell's range of personal computers or Philips Consumer Electronics line of television sets). The *depth* of the product line depends upon the pattern of customer requirements (e.g. the member of segments to be found in the market), the product depth being offered by competitors, and company resources. For example, although customers may require wide product variations a small company may decide to focus on a narrow product line serving only sub-segments of the market.

A *product mix* is the total set of brands marketed in a company. It is the sum of the product lines offered. Thus, the *width* of the product mix can be gauged by the number of product lines that an organization offers. Philips, for example, offer a wide product mix comprising the brands found within their product lines of television, audio equipment, video recorder, camcorders, etc. Other companies have a much narrower product mix comprising just one product line such as TVR, who produce high-performance cars.

Managing brands and product lines are key elements of product strategy. First, we shall examine the major decisions involved in managing brands namely the type of brand to market (manufacturer v. own label), how to build brands, brand name strategies, brand extension and stretching, and the brand acquisition decision. Then we shall look at how to manage brands and product lines over time using the product life cycle concept. Finally, managing brand and product line portfolios will be discussed.

Brand types

The two alternatives regarding brand type are manufacturer and own-label brands. *Manufacturer brands* are created by producers and bear their own chosen brand name. The responsibility for marketing the brand lies in the hands of the producer. Examples include Kellogg's Cornflakes, Gillette Sensor razors and Ariel washing powder. The value of the brand lies with the producer and by building major brands producers can gain distribution and customer loyalty.

A fundamental distinction that needs to be made is between category, brands and variants (see Fig. 8.1). A category (or product field) is divided into brands which in turn may be divided into variants based on flavour, formulation or other feature.[4] For example, Heinz Tomato Soup is the tomato variant of the Heinz brand of the category 'soup'.

Own-label brands (sometimes called distributor brands) are created and owned by distributors. Sometimes the entire product mix of

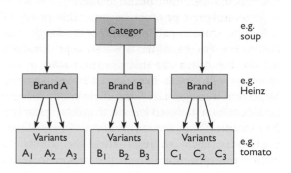

Figure 8.1 Categories, brands and variants

a distributor may be own label (e.g. Marks and Spencer's brand name St Michael) or only part of the mix may be own label as in the case with many supermarket chains. Own-label branding, if associated with tight quality control of suppliers, can provide consistent high value for customers, and be a source of retail power as suppliers vie to fill excess productive capacity with manufacturing products for own-label branding. The power of low price supermarket own-label brands has focused many producers of manufacturers' brands to introduce so-called *fighter brands* (i.e. their own low price alternative).

A major decision that producers have to face is whether to agree to supply own-label products for distributors. The danger is that should customers find out they may believe that there is no difference between the manufacturer brand and its own-label equivalent. This has led some companies such as Kellogg's to refuse to supply own-label products. For other producers supplying own-label goods may be a means of filling excess capacity and generating extra income from the high sales volumes contracted with distributors.

The growth in own labels, however, has not led to the demise of major brands. Some have proven remarkably resilient to own-label attack as Marketing in Action 8.1 explains.

Brand building

Successful brand building can reap benefits in terms of premium prices, achieving distribution more readily, and sustaining a high and stable sales and profits through brand loyalty.[5] This feeds through in terms of profitability. A major study of the factors that lead to high profitability (the Profit Impact of Marketing Strategy project) shows that return on investment is related to a brand's share of the market: bigger brands yield higher returns than smaller brands.[6] These findings are supported by research into return on investment for US food brands. The category leader's average return was 18 per cent, number 2 achieved 6 per cent, number 3 returned 1 per cent, while number 4 position was associated with a −6 per cent average return on investment.[7]

Brand building is not solely the province of fast-moving consumer goods. All sectors of business can benefit from investing in brands. e-Marketing 8.1 discusses the benefits of brand building in high-technology markets.

A brand is created by augmenting a core product with distinctive values that distinguish it from the competition. To understand the notion of **brand values** we first need to understand the difference between features and benefits. A *feature* is an aspect of a brand that may or may not confer a customer benefit. For example, adding fluoride (feature) to a toothpaste confers the customer *benefits* of added protection against tooth decay and decreased dental charges. Not all features necessarily confer benefits: a cigarette lighter (feature) in a car confers no benefit to non-smokers, for example. The advertisement for Eurostar overleaf shows how the benefit of 'convenience' is promoted.

Core benefits derive from the *core product* (see Fig. 8.2). Toothpaste, for example, cleans teeth and therefore protects against tooth decay. But all toothpastes achieve that. Branding allows marketers to create added values that distinguish one brand from another. Successful brands are those which create a set of brand values that are superior to other rival brands. So brand building involves a deep understanding of both the functional (e.g. ease of use) and emotional (e.g. confidence) values that customers use when choosing between brands, and the ability to combine them in a unique way to create an *augmented product* that customers prefer. This unique, augmented product is what marketers call

8.1   Marketing in Action

The Power of Branding: The Baked Bean War

Even in the face of own-label branding, leaders have shown how they can maintain their customer franchise. One advantage they have is that the supermarkets recognize the need to stock the leading two manufacturer brands in each product category. But some have had to weather intense price competition as own-label brands have slashed their prices.

In early 1995, Heinz was market leader of the UK baked beans market with 45 per cent share. It charged 33p for a can of beans compared with 25p for a standard own-label brand and 16p for budget own-label lines. By 1996 the budget line price had dropped to 9p and then 3p. Heinz could have been severely hit by the price war that left it charging 10 times more than its cheapest competition.

Heinz' response was to research its customers. They told the company that Heinz beans were still good value for money. This convinced Heinz that far from entering into price competition it should keep prices high—if anything put them up! The result was that in the year to June 1996, Heinz volume share declined by a mere 7 per cent while its value share increased by 2 per cent.

Many years of investment in brand building through advertising, quality and consistency had reaped its reward. These brand values were sufficiently strong to maintain customer loyalty in the face of intense own-label attack.

Based on: Abraham (1996)[8]

the *brand*. The success of the Swatch brand was founded on the recognition that watches could be marketed as fashion items to younger age groups. By using colour and design, Swatch successfully augmented a basic product—a watch—to create appeal for their target market. Unsuccessful brands provide no added values over the competition; they possess no differential advantage and, therefore, no reason for customers to purchase them rather than a competitive brand.

Managing brands involves the constant search for ways of achieving the full brand potential. To do so usually means the creation of major global brands. Leading brands such as Coca-Cola, Microsoft, IBM, General Electric and Ford have achieved this as Table 8.1 shows.

How are successful brands built? A combination of some or all of seven factors can be important.[9] These are shown in Fig. 8.3 and described below.

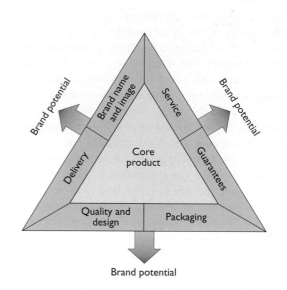

Figure 8.2 Creating a brand

8.1   e-Marketing

Brand Building in High-Technology Markets

There is a tendency of managers in high-tech markets to believe it is only the performance of their products versus competition that influences market destinies. These individuals often feel that there is little point in expending funds on building a brand identity for their product. They perceive spending money to build brands is only relevant in markets such as coffee or detergents where technically there is only marginal performance variation between the products being offered for sale.

Such a mind-set can be dangerous. Perhaps if Netscape had invested in building a strong brand name in the browser market, Microsoft would not have had such an easy time entering this market sector. Powerful brands make promises that are enduring and this is a powerful source of competitive advantage. It is no doubt the case that as IBM has moved to rebuild a damaged market position its strength of brand recognition in the business-to-business market has proved to be an extremely valuable asset. For example, its Server Group realized it could no longer succeed by just 'selling boxes'. It therefore pursued new partners to develop a wide array of software applications, technical features and support services. Having evolved this very different portfolio, its rapid market share is clearly influenced by its ability to exploit the IBM brand in promotional campaigns directed at large corporate customers.

Based on: Goldstine and Light (1999)[10]

Eurostar promotes the benefit of greater convenience compared to airlines

Quality

Building quality into the core product is vital: a major reason for brand failure is the inability to get the basics right. Marketing a computer that overheats, a car that refuses to start, and a garden fork that breaks is courting disaster. The core product must achieve the basic functional requirements expected of it. A major study of factors that affect success has shown statistically that higher quality brands achieve greater market share and higher profitability than their inferior rivals.[11] Total quality management techniques (see Chapter 4) are increasingly being employed to raise quality standards. Product quality improvements have been shown to be mainly driven by market pull (changing customer tastes and expectations), organizational push (changed in the technical potential and resources of a company) and competitor actions.[12]

Positioning

Creating a unique position in the market-place involves the careful choice of target market and establishing a clear differential advantage in the minds of those people. This can be achieved through brand names and image, service, design, guarantees, packaging, and delivery. In today's highly competitive global marketplace, unique positioning will normally rely on combinations of these factors. For example, the success of BMW is founded on a quality, well-designed product, targeted at distinct customer segments, and supported by a carefully-nurtured exclusive brand name and image. Viewing markets in novel ways can create unique positioning concepts. For example, Swatch was built on the realization that watches could be marketed as fashion items to younger age groups. The award-winning advertisement for Diet Tango overleaf shows how radical thinking is sometimes necessary for building brand positions in the market place. Diet Tango's positioning demanded that the project team took Tango to the diet sector rather than the other way round. This led to the idea of Tango, the disruptive diet drink. The advertisements appeared across television, radio and poster. There was also a promotional CD. The caption explains the thinking behind the execution.

An analytical framework that can be used to dissect the current position of a brand in the marketplace and form the basis of a new brand positioning strategy is given in Fig. 8.4. The strength of a brand's position in the marketplace is built upon six elements: brand domain, brand heritage, brand values, brand assets, brand personality and brand reflection. The first element, brand domain, corresponds to the choice of target market (where the brand competes); the other five elements provide avenues for creating a clear differential advantage with these target consumers. Each will now be explained.

1   *Brand domain*: the brand's target market, i.e. where it competes in the marketplace.

	Brand name	Brand value (£m)[b]	Brand strength score[a]
Table 8.1	**The world's leading brands**		
1	Coca-Cola	52 403	82
2	Microsoft	35 408	80
3	IBM	27 363	75
4	General Electric	20 939	71
5	Ford	20 748	72
6	Disney	20 172	79
7	Intel	18 763	74
8	McDonald's	16 394	78
9	AT&T	15 113	70
10	Marlboro	13 155	74

[a] The brand strength score was based on factors such as leadership, market stability, and geographic coverage.
[b] Brand value was based on brand strength score, financial forecasts, analysts' reports, and revenue and profit figures.
Source: Interbrand, 1999.

2   *Brand heritage*: the background to the brand and its culture. How it has achieved success (and failure) over its life.

3   *Brand value*: the core values and characteristics of the brand.

4   *Brand assets*: what makes the brand distinctive from other competing brands such as symbols, features, images and relationships.

5   *Brand personality*: the character of the brand described in terms of other entities such as people, animals or objects.

6   *Brand reflection*: how the brand relates to self-identity; how the customer perceives him/herself as a result of buying/using the brand.

By analysing each element brand managers can form an accurate portrait of how brands are positioned in the marketplace. From there thought can be given to whether and how the brand can be repositioned to improve performance.

Repositioning

As markets change and opportunities arise, repositioning may be needed to build brands from their initial base. Lucozade was first built as a brand providing energy to children who were ill. When market research found that mothers were drinking Lucozade as a midday pick-me-up it was repositioned accordingly. More recently it has been repositioned using the athletes Daley Thompson and Linford Christie as a mass market energy drink. Johnson's baby lotion brand was also built through repositioning when it was found that women were using it themselves. In the popular music industry Elvis Presley and Cliff Richard maintained their success by repositioning themselves from rock and roll artists to middle-of-the-road singers as their target audience matured.

Well-blended communications

Brand positioning is based upon customer perception. To create a clear position in the minds of a target audience requires considerable thought

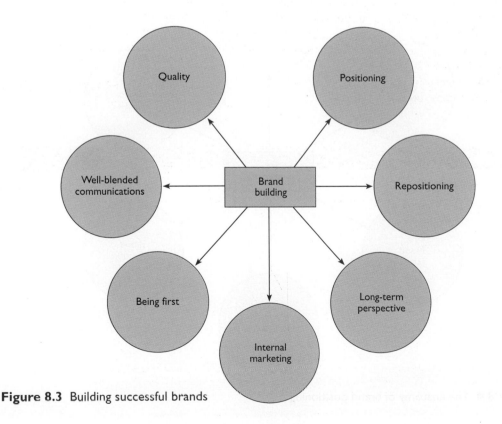

Figure 8.3 Building successful brands

and effort regarding advertising, selling and other promotional activities. Awareness needs to be built, the brand personality projected and favourable attitudes reinforced. Advertising is often the major communication medium for many classic leaders, such as:[13]

✦ Esso: the tiger (grace and power).

✦ Andrex: the puppy (soft and durable).

✦ Persil: mother love (metaphor for taking care of clothes).

✦ Mr Kipling: the voice (metaphor for traditional craftsmanship).

These themes need to be reinforced by sales-people, public relations, and sales promotional campaigns.

Marketers can make their brands more notice-able through attractive display or package design, and also through generating customer familiarity with brand names, brand logos and a brand's visual appearance. A well-blended communi-

cations strategy is necessary to achieve these objectives.[14]

Being first

Research has shown that pioneer brands are more likely to be successful than follower brands.[15] Being first gives a brand the opportunity to create a clear position in the minds of target customers before the competition enters the market. It also gives the pioneer the opportunity to build customer and distributor loyalty. Nevertheless, being first into a market with a unique marketing proposition does not guarantee success; it requires sustained marketing effort, and the strength to withstand competitor attacks. Being first into a niche market, as achieved by the Body Shop, Tie Rack and Sock Shop, usually guarantees short-term profits but the acid test arrives when competitors (sometimes with greater resources) enter with similar products.

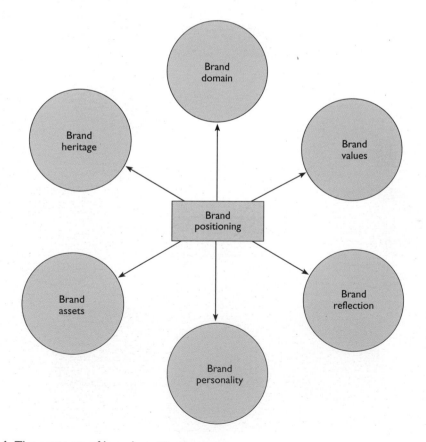

Figure 8.4 The anatomy of brand positioning

The observation that people drink diet drinks when they have been bad was put through the Britvic planning machine and 'Tangoized'. It became 'We will make people bad so they have to buy diet drinks, in particular Diet Tango'

www.hp.com/go/printers

Only reality looks more real.

You can't avoid the sparks. They're almost real.
It's because they were printed using the most advanced inkjet printing process
available. Hewlett-Packard's revolutionary PhotoREt precision technology.

Not only can it blend up to 29 drops of ink on every microscopic dot but this can be done at high speed.
So no matter how much of a rush you're in you'll always have outstanding photographic images.
Nothing else does it better. Except of course reality itself.

The HP PhotoSmart and DeskJet printers.

invent

Brands require substantial, sustained investment to improve their position in the marketplace

Being first into a market can also bring the potential advantages of technological leadership, cost advantages through the experience curve effect, the acquisition and control of scarce resources and the creation of switching costs to later entrants (for example, the costs of switching from one computer system to another may be considerable).[16] Late entry can be costly: one study showed that a delay of one year in launching the Sierra after GM's Cavalier cost Ford $1 billion in lost profits over five years.[17]

Companies are, therefore, speeding up their new product development processes even if that means being over budget.[18] A McKinsey and Co. study showed that being 50 per cent over NPD budget and on time can lead to a 4 per cent reduction in profits. However, being on budget and six months late to launch can lead to a 33 per cent reduction in profits.[19]

Being first does not necessarily mean pioneering the technology. Bigger returns may come to those who are first to enter the mass market. For example, America's Ampex pioneered video recorder technology in the mid-1950s but their machines sold for $50 000. It made little effort to cut costs and expand its market. It was left to Sony, JVC and Matsushita who had the vision to see the potential for mass-market sales. They embarked on a research and development programme to make a video recorder that could be sold for $500—a goal that took them 20 years to achieve.[20]

Long-term perspective

Brand building is a long-term activity. There are many demands on people's attention. Consequently generating awareness, communicating brand values and building customer loyalty usually takes many years. Management must be prepared to provide a consistently high level of brand investment to establish and maintain the position of a brand in the marketplace. Unfortunately it can be tempting to cut back on expenditure in the short term. Cutting the advertising spend by £0.5 million immediately cuts costs and increases profits. Conversely, for a well-established brand, sales are unlikely to fall substantially in the short term because of the effects of past advertising. The result is higher short-term profits. This may be an attractive proposition for brand managers who are often in charge of a brand for less than two years. One way of overcoming this

danger is to measure brand manager (and brand) performance by measuring brand equity in terms of awareness levels, brand associations, intentions to buy, etc. and being vigilant in resisting short-term actions that may harm it. To underline the importance of consistent brand investment Sir Adrian Cadbury (then chairman of Cadbury's Schweppes) wrote:

> For brands to endure they have to be maintained properly and imaginatively. Brands are extremely valuable properties and, like other forms of property, they need to be kept in good repair, renewed from time to time and defended against squatters.[21]

The Hewlett Packard advertisement opposite illustrates how this company invests to create technologically superior brands.

Internal marketing

Many brands are corporate in the sense that the marketing focus is on building the company brand.[22] This is particularly the case in services with banks, supermarkets, insurance companies, airlines and restaurant chains attempting to build awareness and loyalty to the services they offer. A key feature in the success of such efforts is *internal marketing*, that is training and communicating with internal staff. Training of staff is crucial because service companies rely on face-to-face contact between service providers (e.g. waiter) and service user (e.g. diner). Also, brand strategies must be communicated to staff so that they understand the company ethos upon which the company brand is built. Investment in staff training is required to achieve the service levels required for the brand strategy. Top service companies like McDonald's, Sainsbury and British Airways place training as a central element in their company brand building plans.

Marketing in Action 8.2 shows how Grand Metropolitan has gone about the brand building process with Häagen-Dazs ice cream and illustrates some of the key aspects of how to build a successful brand.

Managers also need to be aware of the importance of the corporate brand as represented by its *corporate identity*. There are differing views regarding the meaning of corporate identity. First, it has been viewed as synonymous with organizational nomenclature, logos, company housestyle and visual identity—the graphic design paradigm. The second view equated corporate identity with integrated communications so that the corporation could communicate effectively and consistently to its stakeholders (shareholders, customers, suppliers, distributors and employees). Finally, corporate identity was associated with a multidisciplinary approach that acknowledges the importance of behaviour, communications and symbolism (the corporate identity mix).

Corporate identity articulates the corporate ethos, aims, values and presents a sense of individuality that can help to differentiate the organization from its competitors. A key ingredient is visual cohesion necessary to ensure that all corporate communications are consistent with each other and result in an image in line with the organization's defining ethos and character. The

objective is to establish a favourable reputation with an organization's stakeholders which it is hoped will be translated by them into a greater likelihood of purchasing the organization's goods and services, to work for or to invest in the organization.[23]

From the stakeholders' point of view, corporate identity is what they perceive, feel and think about their organization. It is a collective understanding of the organization's distinctive values and characteristics.[24]

An example of the successful use of corporate identity building is Arcadis, an infrastructural engineering company with its headquarters in The Netherlands but with operations all over the world. A strong corporate identity was particularly important to give a sense of unity to a company that has grown largely through acquisition. The

8.2 Marketing in Action

Brand Building: The Case of Häagen-Dazs

Häagen-Dazs, the up-market ice cream, was launched as an adult confection in advertisements which often used scantily clad young men and women. The ads oozed sexuality, associating the eating of the brand with a 'dedication to pleasure'. The advertising copy ran 'We find the fresh eggs in Häagen-Dazs provide delicate flavour, BODY and TEXTURE'. In another the copy stated:

to ensure our Belgium chocolates
LOSE
none of their smoothness, we strictly
CONTROL
their temperature and humidity

The launch established Häagen-Dazs as the new product of the year (1991) in the UK and as a successful premium-priced brand in Europe. How did Grand Metropolitan, who were responsible for building the brand, do it? A combination of factors played their part.

Marketing research revealed that the sensual pleasure of eating ice cream was sometimes the prelude to sex:

— Targeting marketing: affluent, fun-loving, young adults
— Product: high quality, use of fresh eggs
— Brand name: invented to sound European (it also sells in the USA)
— Brand image: associates ice cream with sexuality
— Price: premium to support positioning concept.

The result was a brand that was skilfully positioned to a distinct target group that valued the powerful image projected in its high-profile advertising campaign.

company believes that its identity which brings with it a set of specific values has produced benefits both with internal staff and external customers.[25] An example of a corporate identity move that proved less successful was BA's tail-fin painting. Originally, all BA tail fins were the colour of the Union Jack symbolizing its British heritage. In an attempt at global repositioning, most of these were repainted using the colours of the national emblem of many overseas countries. The move allegedly backfired as passengers, especially businesspeople, disliked the multifarious tail-fin designs.[26]

Global and pan-European branding

Global branding is the achievement of brand penetration worldwide. Levitt is a champion of global branding, arguing that intensified competition and technological developments will force companies to operate globally, ignoring superficial national differences.[27] A *global village* is emerging where consumers seek reliable quality products at a low price and the marketing task to offer the same products and services in the same way, thereby achieving enormous global economies of scale. His position is that the new commercial reality is the emergence of global markets for standardized products and services on a previously unimagined scale. The engine behind this trend is the twin forces of customer convergence of tastes and needs, and the prospect of global efficiencies in production, procurement, marketing and research and development. Japanese companies have been successful in achieving these kind of economies to produce high quality, competitively priced global brands (e.g. Toyota, Sony, Nikon and Fuji).

In Europe, the promise of pan-European branding has caused leading manufacturers to seek to extend their market coverage and to build their portfolio of brands. Nestlé have widened their brand portfolio by the acquisition of such companies as Rowntree (confectionery) and Buitoni-Perugina (pasta and chocolate), and have formed a joint venture (Cereal Partners) with the US giant General Mills to challenge Kellogg's in the European breakfast cereal market. Mars have replaced their Treets and Bonitos brands with M & M's and changed the name of their third

largest UK brand—Marathon—to the Snickers name that is used in the rest of Europe.

The counterargument to global branding is that it is the exception rather than the rule. It has undoubtedly occurred with high tech, rapid roll-out products such as audio equipment, cameras, video recorders and camcorders. Furthermore, some global successes such as Coca-Cola, BMW, Gucci and McDonald's can be noted but national varieties in taste and consumption patterns will ensure that such achievements in the future will be limited. For example, the fact that the French eat four time more yoghurt than the British and the British buy eight times more chocolate than the Italians reflects the kinds of national differences that will affect the marketing strategies of manufacturers.[28] Indeed, many so-called global brands are not standardized, claim the 'local' marketers. For example, Coca-Cola in Scandinavia tastes different from that in Greece.

The last example gives a clue to answering the dilemma facing companies which are considering building global brands. The question is not whether brands can be built on a global scale (clearly they can) but which parts of the brand can be standardized and which must be varied across countries. A useful way of looking at this decision is to separate out the elements that comprise the brand as shown in Fig. 8.5. Can brand name and image, advertising, service, guarantees, packaging, quality and design, and delivery be standardized or not?

Gillette's global success with their Sensor razor was based on a highly standardized approach: the product, brand name, the message 'The Best a Man Can Get', advertising visuals and packaging were standardized; only the voice-overs in the advertisement were changed to cater for 26 languages across Europe, the USA and Japan.

Lever Brothers found that for detergent products brand image and packaging could be standardized but the brand name, communications execution and brand formulation needed to vary across countries.[29] For example, their fabric conditioner used a cuddly teddy bear across countries but was named differently in Germany (Kuschelweich), France (Cajoline), Italy (Coccolini), Spain (Mimosin), USA (Snuggle) and Japan (Fa-Fa). Brand image and packaging were the same but the name and formulation (fragrance, phosphate levels and additives) differed between countries.

In other circumstances, the brand form and

additions may remain the same (or very similar) across countries but the brand communications may need to be modified. For example, a BMW car may be positioned as having an exclusive image but what Dutch and Italian car buyers consider are the qualities that amount to exclusiveness are very different.[30] Consequently differing advertising appeals would be needed to communicate the concept of exclusiveness in these countries.

Much activity has taken place over recent years to achieve global and pan-European brand positions. There are three major ways of doing this:[31]

1   *Geographic extension*: taking present brands into the geographic markets.

2   *Brand acquisition*: purchasing brands.

3   *Brand alliance*: joint venture or partnerships to market brands in national or cross-national markets.

Managers need to evaluate the strengths and weaknesses of each option and Fig. 8.6 summarizes these using speed of market penetration, control of operations, and the level of investment required as criteria. Brand acquisition give the fastest method of developing global brands. For example, Unilever's 1989 acquisition of Fabergé, Elizabeth Arden and Calvin Klein immediately made them a major player in fragrances, cosmetics and skincare. Brand alliance usually gives moderate speed. For example, the use of the Nestlé name for the Cereal Partners (General Mills and Nestlé) alliance's breakfast cereal in Europe should help retailer and consumer acceptance. Geographic extension is likely to be the slowest unless the company is already a major global player with massive resources, as brand building from scratch is a time-consuming process.

However, geographic extension provides a high degree of control since companies can choose which brands to globalize and plan their global extensions. Brand acquisition gives a moderate degree of control although many may prove hard to integrate with in-house brands. Brand alliance fosters the lowest degree of control as strategy and resource allocation will need to be negotiated with the partner.

Finally, brand acquisitions are likely to incur the highest level of investment. For example, Nestlé paid £2.5 billion for Rowntree, a figure that was over five time net asset value. Geographic extension is likely to be more expensive than brand

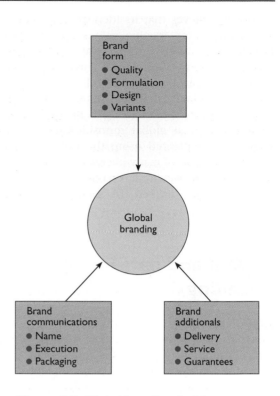

Figure 8.5 Global branding decisions

alliance since in the latter case costs are shared, and one partner may benefit from the expertise and distribution capabilities of the other. For example, in the Cereal Partners' alliance, General Mills gained access to Nestlé's expertise and distribution system in Europe. Although the specifics of each situation need to be carefully analysed, Fig. 8.6 provides a framework for assessing the strategic alternatives when developing global and pan-European brands.

Brand name strategies and choices

Another key decision area is the choice of brand name. Three brand name strategies can be identified: family, individual and combination.

Family brand names

A *family brand name* is used for all products (e.g. Philips, Campbell's, Heinz, Del Monte). The goodwill attached to the family brand name benefits all brands, and the use of the name in advertising helps the promotion of all of the brands carrying the family name. The risk is that if one of the brands receives unfavourable publicity or is unsuccessful the reputation of the whole range of brands can be tarnished. This is also called umbrella branding. An example is the advertisement for Nescafé coffee overleaf. Some companies create umbrella brands for part of their brand portfolios to give coherence to their range of products. For example, Cadbury created the umbrella brand of Cadburyland for its range of children's chocolate confectionery.[32]

Individual brand names

An *individual brand name* does not identify a brand with a particular company (e.g. Procter and Gamble do not use the company name on their brands such as Ariel, Fairy Liquid, Daz and Pampers). This may be necessary when it is believed that each brand requires a separate, unrelated identity. In some instances, the use of a family brand name when moving into a new market segment may harm the image of the new product line. An example was the decision to use the Levi family brand name on a new product line—Levi's Tailored Classics—despite marketing research information which showed that target

customers associated the name 'Levis' with casual clothes which was incompatible with the smart suits they were launching. This mistake was not repeated by Toyota, who abandoned its family brand name when it launched its up-market executive car which was simply called the Lexus.

Nevertheless, the lack of company association can prove risky. For example, Sainsbury's, a UK supermarket chain, launched a successful own-label detergent, Novon, after extensive research found that since consumers did not care whether Ariel, Daz or Persil was made by Proctor and Gamble or Lever Brothers, why should they worry that Novon was 'made by' Sainsbury's.

Combination brand names

A *combination of family and individual brand names* capitalizes on the reputation of the company while allowing the individual brands to be distinguished and identified (e.g. Kellogg's All Bran, Rover 400, Microsoft Windows).

Criteria for choosing brand names

The choice of brand name should be carefully thought out since names convey images. For example, Renault chose the brand name Safrane

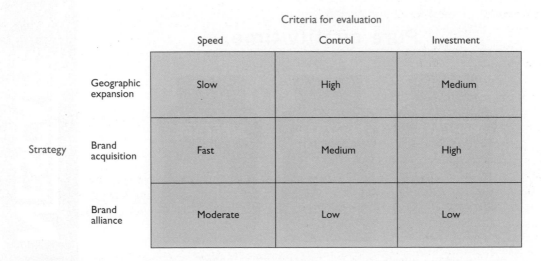

Figure 8.6 Developing global and pan-European brands.

Source: Barwise, P. and T. Robertson (1992) Brand Portfolios, *European Management Journal*, 10 (3), 279. Copyright © 1992 with kind permission from Elsevier Science Ltd, The Boulevard, Langford Lane, Kidlington, OX5 1GB, UK

Umbrella branding under the Nescafé brand name. Their three sub-brands provide different features to appeal to various coffee drinking tastes

Table 8.2   Brand name considerations

A good brand name should:

1 Evoke positive associations
2 Be easy to pronounce and remember
3 Suggest product benefits
4 Be distinctive
5 Use numerals when emphasizing technology
6 Not infringe an existing registered brand name

Table 8.3   Brand name categories

People: Cadbury, Mars, Heinz

Places: National Westminster, Halifax Building Society

Descriptive: I Can't Believe It's Not Butter, The Body Shop, Going Places

Abstract: Kit Kat, Kodak, Prozac

Evocative: Egg, Orange, Fuse

Brand extensions: Dove Deodorant, Virgin Direct, Playtex Affinity

Foreign meanings: Lego (from 'play well' in Danish), Thermos (meaning 'heat' in Greek)

Adapted from Miller, R. (1999) Science Joins Art in Brand Naming, Marketing, 27 May, 31–2.

for one of their executive saloons because research showed that the brand name conveyed the image of luxury, exotica, high technology and style. The brand name Pepsi Max was chosen for Pepsi's diet cola targeted at men as it conveyed a masculine image in a product category that was associated with women. So one criterion for deciding upon a good brand name is that it evokes *positive associations*. When the Rover Group discovered that one of their brand names 'Austin' had negative connotations (e.g. unreliability) they dropped it from their Montego product range.

A second criterion is that the brand name should be easy to *pronounce and remember*. Short names such as Esso, Shell, Daz, Ariel, Novon and Mini fall into this category. There are exceptions to this general rule as is the case of Häagen-Dazs which was designed to sound European in the USA where it was first launched. A brand name may suggest *product benefits* such as Right Guard (deodorant), Alpine Glade (air and fabric freshener), Head and Shoulders (anti-dandruff shampoo), Compaq (portable computer) or express what the brand is offering in a *distinctive way* such as Toys 'Я' Us. Technological products may benefit from numerical brand naming (e.g. BMW 300, Lotus 1-2-3, Porsche 911). This also overcomes the need to change brand names when marketing in different countries.

Specialist companies have established themselves as brand name consultants. Market research is used to test associations, memorability, pronunciation and preferences. One such consultancy is Mastername, who has an international team of name creation specialists, linguists, and legal experts. Legal advice is important so that a brand name *does not infringe an existing brand name*. Table 8.2 summarizes the issues that are important when choosing a brand name.

A considerable amount of research goes into choosing a brand name. One successful financial services brand in the UK is Egg, a savings account launched by Prudential. Marketing in Action 8.3 describes the work that went into its selection. Brand names can be categorized, as in Table 8.3.

Brand extension and stretching

The goodwill that is associated with a brand name adds tangible value to a company through the higher sales and profits that result. This higher financial value is called *brand equity*. Brand names with high brand equity are candidates to be used on other new brands since their presence has the potential of enhancing their attractiveness. A *brand extension* is the use of an established brand name on a new brand within the same broad market. For example, the Anadin brand name has been extended to related brands: Anadin Extra, Maximum Strength, Soluble, Paracetamol, and Ibuprophen. The Lucozade brand has undergone a very successful brand extension with the introduction of Lucozade Sport, with isotonic properties that rehydrate more quickly than other drinks and replace minerals lost through perspiration. Unilever have successfully expanded their Dove soap brand into deodorants, shower gel, liquid soap and bodywash.[33] *Brand stretching* is when an established brand name is used for brands in unrelated markets such as the use of the Yamaha motor cycle brand name on hi-fi equipment, skis and pianos. The Tommy Hilfiger brand has also been extended from clothing to fragrances, footwear and home furnishings.[34] Table 8.4 gives some examples of brand extensions and stretching.

Some companies have used brand extensions and stretching very successfully. Richard Branson's Virgin company is a classic example. Beginning in 1970 as Virgin Records the company grew through Virgin Music (music publishing), Megastores (music retailing), Radio, Vodka, Cola, Atlantic Airways (long-haul routes), Express (short-haul routes), Rail, Direct (direct marketing of financial services) and One (one-stop banking). Others have been less successful such as Levi's move into suits, the Penguin ice-cream bar and Timotei facial-care products.

Brand extension is an important marketing tactic. A study by Neilson showed that brand extensions account for approximately 40 per cent of new grocery launches.[35] Two key advantages of brand extension in releasing new products are that it reduces risk and is less costly than alternative launch strategies.[36] Both distributors and consumers may perceive less risk if the new brand comes with an established brand name. Distributors may be reassured about the saleability of the new brand and therefore be more willing to stock it. Consumers appear to attribute the quality associations they have of the original brand to the new one.[37] An established name enhances consumer interest and willingness to try the new brand.[38] Consumer attitudes towards brand extensions are more favourable when the perceived quality of the parent brand is high.[39]

Launch costs can also be reduced by using brand extension. Since the established brand name is already well known, the task of building awareness of the new brand is eased. Consequently, advertising, selling and promotional costs are reduced. Furthermore, there is the likelihood of achieving advertising economies of scale since

8.3 Marketing in Action

Naming Egg

Egg, the financial services brand launched by Prudential reached its five-year target of savers in just six months. It has closed its offerings to new telephone customers and is now focusing on its Internet services. Competitive interest rates are a major factor in its attraction, but the name has clearly captured the imagination of the consumer.

The work on the name began by briefing a corporate naming agency. Prudential wanted something genuinely new and distinctive. They wanted to challenge the idiom of the marketplace where many corporate names were names of people or places such as Barclays or Halifax.

Consumer research was used beginning by testing of 'marker' names which were not serious contenders but types of names which made clear the limits that consumers would accept. The research showed that the name could be radical but consumers would not accept frivolity. The second stage was to work on a range of names from straight descriptive to the more adventurous. At the final stage, the options included 360° suggesting all of the consumer's financial services taken care of, Oxygen suggesting a breath of fresh air (but also slightly colder than Egg and rather scientific) and ID suggesting identity and individuality.

The name had to convey the notion of having a relationship with the customer, be contemporary and be reassuring. The name Egg was chosen because it is a reassuring word with cosy, warm connotations.

Based on: Miller (1999)[40]

advertisements for the original brand and its extensions reinforce each other.[41]

However, these arguments can be taken too far. Brand extensions that offer no functional, psychological or price advantage over rival brands often fail.[42] Consumers shop around and brand extensions that fail to meet expectations will be rejected. There is also the danger that marketing management underfunds the launch believing that the spin-off effects from the original brand name will compensate. This can lead to low awareness and trial. *Cannibalization*, which refers to a situation where the new brand gains sales at the expense of the established brand, can also occur. Anadin Extra, for example, could cannibalize the sales of the original Anadin brand. Further, brand extension has been criticized as leading to a managerial focus on minor modifications, packaging changes and advertising rather than the development of real innovations.[43] There is also the danger that bad publicity for one brand affects the reputation of other brands under the same name. An example was a problem of sudden, sharp acceleration of the Audi 5000, which affected sales of both the Audi 4000 and the Audi Quattro even though they did not suffer from the problem.[44] A related problem is the danger of the new brand failing or generating connotations that damage the reputation of the core brand. Both of these risks were faced by Guinness, whose core brand is stout, when they launched their canned beer under the Guinness brand name, and Mars when they extended the Mars brand name into ice cream.

A major test of any brand extension opportunity is to ask if the new brand concept is compatible with the values inherent in the core brand. Mention has already been made of the failure to extend the Levi brand name to suits in the USA partly as a result of consumers refusing to accept the casual, denim image of Levi as being suitable for smart, exclusive clothing. Brand extensions, therefore, are not viable when a new brand is being developed for a target customer who hold different values and aspirations from those in the original market segment. When this occurs the use of the brand extension tactic would detract from the new brand. The answer is to develop a separate brand name as did Toyota with the Lexus, and Seiko with their Pulsar brand name developed for the lower priced mass market for watches.

Finally, management need to guard against the loss of credibility if a brand name is extended too far. This is particularly relevant when brand stretching. The use of the Pierre Cardin name for such disparate product as clothing, toiletries, and cosmetics had diluted the brand name's credibility.[45]

Brand extensions are likely to be successful if they make sense to the consumer. If the values and aspirations of the new target segment(s) match those of the original segment, and the qualities of the brand name are likewise highly prized then success is likely. The prime example is Marks and Spencer, who successfully extended their brand name, St Michael, from clothing to food based upon their core values of quality and reliability.

Table 8.4 Brand extension and stretching	
Brand extension	*Brand stretching*
Anadin brand name used for Anadin Extra, Maximum Strength, Soluble, Paracetamol and Ibuprophen	Cadbury (confectionery) launched Cadbury's Cream Liqueur
Guinness launched Guinness draught beer in a can	Yamaha (motor cycles) brand name used on hi-fi, skis, pianos and summerhouses
Unilever used Persil brand name for washing-up liquid	Pierre Cardin (clothing) brand name used on toiletries, cosmetics, etc.
United Distillers used Johnnie Walker brand name for liqueur	Bic (disposable pens) brand name used on lighters, razors, perfumes and women's tights
Unilever used Dove brand name for deodorants, shower gel, liquid soap and bodywash	Tommy Hilfiger brand name used on fragrances, footwear and home furnishings

Managing product lines and brands over time: the product life cycle

No matter how wide the product mix, both product lines and individual brands need to be managed over time. A useful tool for conceptualizing the changes that may take place during the time that a product is on the market is called the *product life cycle*. It is quite flexible and can be applied to both brands and product lines.[46] For simplicity, in the rest of this chapter brands and product lines will be referred to as products. We shall now describe the *product life cycle*, before discussing its uses and limitations.

The classic product life cycle has four stages (see Fig. 8.7): introduction, growth, maturity, and decline.

Introduction

When first introduced on to the market a product's sales growth is typically low and losses are incurred because of heavy development and promotional costs. Companies will be monitoring the speed of product adoption and if disappointing may terminate the product at this stage.

Growth

This stage is characterized by a period of faster sales and profit growth. Sales growth is fuelled by rapid market acceptance and, for many products, repeat purchasing. Profits may begin to decline towards the latter stages of growth as new rivals enter the market attracted by twin magnets of fast sales growth and high profit potential. The personal computer market is an example of this during the 1980s when the sales growth was mirrored by a vast increase in competitors. The end of the growth period is often associated with *competitive shake-out* whereby weaker suppliers cease production. How to survive a shakeout is discussed in Marketing in Action 8.4.

Maturity

Eventually sales peak and flatten as saturation occurs, hastening competitive shake-out. The survivors battle for market share by product improvements, advertising and sales promotional offers, dealer discount and price cutting; the result is strain on profit margins particularly for follower brands. The need for effective brand building is acutely recognized during maturity as brand leaders are in the strongest position to resist the pressure on profit margins.[47]

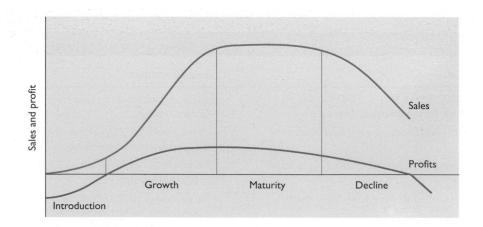

Figure 8.7 The product life cycle

Decline

Sales and profits fall during the decline stages as new technology or changes in consumer tastes work to reduce demand for the product. Suppliers may decide to cease production completely or reduce product depth. Promotional and product development budgets may be slashed and marginal distributors dropped as suppliers seek to maintain (or increase) profit margins.

Uses of the product life cycle

The product life cycle (PLC) concept is useful for product management in several ways.

Product termination

First, the PLC emphasizes the fact that nothing lasts forever. There is a danger that management may fall in love with certain products. Maybe a company was founded on the success of a particular product; perhaps the product champion of a past success is now the chief executive. Under such circumstances there can be emotional ties with the product that can transcend normal commercial considerations. The PLC underlines the fact that companies have to face the fact that products need to be terminated and new products developed to replace them. Without this sequence a company may find itself with a group of products all in the decline stage of their PLC.

Growth projections

The second use of the PLC concept is to warn against the dangers of assuming growth will continue forever. Swept along by growing order books, management can fall into the trap of believing that the heady days of rising sales and profits will continue forever. The PLC reminds managers that growth will end, and suggests the need for caution when planning investment in new production facilities.

Marketing objectives and strategies over the PLC

The PLC emphasizes the need to review marketing objectives and strategies as products pass through the various stages. Changes in market and competitive conditions between the PLC stages suggests that marketing strategies should be adapted to meet them. Table 8.5 shows a set of stylized marketing responses to each stage. Note that these are broad generalizations rather than exact prescriptions but they do serve to emphasize the need to review marketing objectives and strategies in the light of environmental change.

Table 8.5 Marketing objectives and stategies over the product life cycle

	Introduction	Growth	Maturity	Decline
Strategic marketing objective	Build	Build	Hold	Harvest/manage for cash
Strategic focus	Expand market	Penetration	Protect share	Productivity
Brand objective	Product awareness/ trial	Brand preference	Brand loyalty	Brand exploitation
Products	Basic	Differentiated	Differentiated	Rationalized
Promotion	Creating awareness/ trial	Creating awareness/trial/ repeat purchase	Maintaining awareness/repeat purchase	Cut/eliminated
Price	High	Lower	Lowest	Rising
Distribution	Patchy	Wider	Intensive	Selective

Introduction

The strategic marketing objective is to build sales by expanding the market for the product. The brand objective will be to create product (as well as brand) awareness so that customers will become familiar with generic product benefits.

The marketing task facing pioneer video recorder producers was to gain awareness of the general benefits of the video recorder (e.g. convenient viewing through time-switching, viewing programmes that are broadcast when out of the house) so that the market for video recorders in general would expand. The product is likely to

8.4   Marketing in Action

Surviving a Shakeout

The change from booming growth to a static mature industry can prove traumatic for many companies. The growth phase may have been associated with entrepreneurial drive backed by a strong vision such as that of Michael Dell who founded Dell Computers in 1984. With maturity comes the need to put a premium on operational efficiency, a greater sensitivity to customer needs and increased responsiveness to competitor threats. For strong, well-positioned companies the looming shakeout provides an opportunity to stabilize the industry and gain market power. For such *adaptive survivors*, there is a need to face three key issues.

✦   Leadership and management style: survival necessitates the recruitment of talented managers who have experience in large organizations and understand the systematic approach needed to manage a large company. Such a move by Dell Computers changed the orientation from 'growth, growth, growth' to 'liquidity, profitability and growth'.

✦   Resources: much energy is required to critically evaluate options so that resources are allocated to the most attractive opportunities and resources withdrawn from past mistakes. For example, Dell Computers invested to increase global sales while withdrawing from retail stores and dropping its failing line of notebook computers.

✦   Controls: information systems need to be installed to identify such problems as excessive costs, bulging inventories and failures to meet promises to customers.

Smaller, also-ran companies are particularly vulnerable during a shake-out. They need to choose a *buffer strategy* to provide some protection during the crisis.

✦   Market niching: niches can serve as buffer zones when competitive pressures are not too strong and growth is possible. Managers need to accept a shrinking of aspirations and pruning of operations. Segments where the major companies are underperforming (perhaps because small segment size does not warrant heavy investment) are prime targets.

✦   Strategic alliances: small companies can buffer themselves by forming alliances to pool resources, access expensive assets and increase negotiating power.

If neither of these strategies is viable, then the also-ran company will need to face the decision to sell the company. An early sale may make sense if a buyer can be found who still has an optimistic view of the future. However, patience can be a virtue if the company can survive until prospective buyers have weathered the storm and have gained confidence in their new strategies.

Based on: Day (1997)[48]

be fairly basic with emphasis on reliability and functionality rather than special features to appeal to different customer groups. Promotion will support the brand objectives by gaining awareness for the brand and product type, and stimulating trial. Advertising has been found to be more effective in the beginning of the life of a product than in later stages.[49] Typically price will be high because of the heavy development costs and the low level of competition. Distribution will be patchy as some dealers are wary of stocking the new product until it has proved to be successful in the marketplace.

Growth

The strategic marketing objective during the growth phase is to build sales and market share. The strategic focus will be to penetrate the market by building brand preference. To accomplish this task the product will be redesigned to create differentiation and promotion will stress the functional and/or psychological benefits that accrue from the differentiation. Awareness and trial are still important but promotion will begin to focus on repeat purchasers. As development costs are defrayed and competition increases, prices will fall. Rising consumer demand and increased salesforce effort will widen distribution.

Maturity

As sales peak and stabilize the strategic marketing objective will be to hold on to profits and sales by protecting market share rather than embarking on costly competitive challenges. Since sales gains can only be at the expense of competition, strong challenges are likely to be resisted and lead to costly promotional or price wars. Brand objectives now focus on maintaining brand loyalty, and promotion will defend the brand stimulating repeat purchase by maintaining brand awareness and values. For all but the brand leader, competition may erode prices and profit margins, while distribution will peak in line with sales.

Decline

Falling sales may tempt some companies to raise prices and slash marketing expenditures in an effort to bolster profit margins. The strategic focus, therefore, will be on improving marketing productivity rather than holding or building sales. The brand loyalty that has built up over the years will in effect be exploited to create profits that can be channelled elsewhere in the company (e.g. new products). Product development will cease, the product line depth reduced to the bare minimum of brands and promotional expenditure cut, possibly to zero. Distribution costs will be analysed with a view to selecting only the most profitable outlets. Product elimination is likely as non-viable sales levels are encountered. Many product elimination decisions are based upon intuition and judgement rather than formalized analysis.[50]

Product planning

The PLC emphasizes the need for *product planning*. We have already discussed the need to replace old products with new. The PLC also stresses the need to analyse the balance of products that a company markets from the point of view of the PLC stages. A company with all of its products in the mature stage may be generating profits today but as they enter the decline stage, profits may fall and the company become unprofitable. A nicely balanced product array would see the company marketing some products in the mature stage of the PLC, a number of the growth stage, with the prospect of new product launches in the near future. The growth products would replace the mature products as the latter enter decline, and the new product successes would eventually become the growth products of the future. The PLC is, then, a stimulus to thinking about products as an interrelated set of profit-bearing assets that need to be managed as a group. We shall return to this theme when discussing product portfolio analysis later in this chapter.

Dangers of overpowering

The PLC concept highlights the dangers of over-powering. A company that introduces a new-to-the-world product may find itself in a very powerful position early in its product life cycle. Assuming that the new product confers unique benefits to customers there is an opportunity to charge a very high price during this period of monopoly supply. However, unless the product is patent protected this strategy can turn sour when competition enters during the growth phase (as predicted by the PLC concept). This situation arose for a small components manufacturer who was the first to solve the technical problems associated with developing a seal in an exhaust recirculation valve used to reduce pollution in car emissions. The company took advantage of its monopoly supply position to charge very high prices to Ford. The strategy rebounded when competition entered and Ford discovered that they had been overcharged.[51] Had the small manufacturer been aware of the predictions of the PLC concept they may have anticipated competitive entry during the growth phase, and charged a lower pricing during introduction and early growth. This would have enabled them to begin a relationship-building exercise with Ford, possibly leading to greater returns in the long run.

Limitations of the product life cycle

The product life cycle is an aid to thinking about marketing decisions but it needs to be handled with care. Management needs to be aware of the limitations of the PLC so that they are not misled by its prescriptions.

Fads and classics

Not all products follow the classic S-shaped curve. The sales of some products 'rise like a rocket then fall like the stick'. This is normal for *fad* products such as skateboards which saw phenomenal sales growth followed by a rapid sales collapse as the youth market moved on to another craze.

Other products (and brands) appear to defy entering the decline stage. For example, classic confectionery products and brands such as Mars bars, Cadbury's Milk Tray and Toblerone have survived for decades in the mature stage of the PLC. Nevertheless research has shown that the classic S-shaped curve does apply to a wide range of products including grocery food products, pharmaceuticals, and cigarettes.[52]

Marketing effects

The PLC is the result of marketing activities not the cause. One school of thought argues that the PLC is not a God-given fact of life—unlike living organisms—but is simply a pattern of sales that reflects marketing activity.[53] Clearly, sales of a product may flatten or fall simply because it has not received enough marketing attention, insufficient product redesign, or promotional support. Using the PLC, argue the critics, may lead to inappropriate action (e.g. harvesting or dropping the product) when the correct response should be increased marketing support (e.g. product replacement, positioning reinforcement, or repositioning).

Unpredictability

The duration of the PLC stages is unpredictable. The PLC outlines the four stages that a product passes through without defining their duration. Clearly this limits its use as a forecasting tool since it is not possible to predict when maturity or decline will begin. The exception to this problem is when it is possible to identify a comparator product that serves as a template for predicting the length of each stage. Two sources of comparator products exist: first, countries where the same product has already been on the market for some time, and second, similar products are in the mature or decline stages of their life cycle but which are thought to resemble the new product in terms of consumer acceptance. In practice, the use of comparator products is fraught with problems. For example, the economic and social conditions of countries may be so different that simplistic exploitation of the PLC from one country to another may be invalid; the use of similar products may prove inaccurate predictions in the face of ever-shortening product life cycles.

Misleading objective and strategy prescriptions

The stylized marketing objectives and strategy prescriptions may be misleading. Even if a product could be accurately classified as being in a PLC stage, and sales are not simply a result of marketing activities, the critics argue that the stylized marketing objectives and strategy prescriptions can be misleading. For example, there can be circumstances where the appropriate marketing objective in the growth stage is to harvest (e.g. in the face of intense competition), in the mature stage to build (e.g. when a distinct, defensive differential advantage can be developed), and in the decline stage to build (e.g. when there is an opportunity to dominate). An example of the later strategy is the UK cinema market. Cinemas were clearly in the decline stage of their product life cycle with attendances falling over a period of many years as other evening leisure pursuits gained ground (e.g. restaurants, sports halls, television). The response of cinema owners was to rationalize (close cinema) and reduce investment in those that survived to a minimum: a classic harvesting approach. However, one company saw this scenario as a marketing opportunity. Showcase Cinemas were launched during the 1980s offering a choice of around twelve films in the modern purpose-built cinemas (with their own car park) near large conurbations. The result was an upturn in cinema attendance (and profits) as customers valued the experience of visiting the convenient upgraded facilities and wide choice of films much more than the old cinema concept. Thus the classic PLC prescription of harvesting in the decline stage was revealed by a company who was willing to invest in order to reposition cinemas as an attractive means of evening entertainment.

A summary of the usefulness of the product life cycle concept

Like many marketing tools, the product life cycle should not be viewed as a panacea to marketing thinking and decision-making but as an aid to managerial judgement. By emphasizing the changes that are likely to occur as a product is marketed over time, the concept is a valuable stimulus to strategic thinking. Yet as a prescriptive tool it is blunt. Marketing management must monitor the real-life changes that are happening in the marketplace before setting precise objectives and strategies.

Managing brand and product line portfolios

So far in this chapter we have treated the management of products as separate, distinct entities.

However, many companies are multi-product serving multi-markets and segments. Some of these product will be strong, others weak. Some will require investment to finance their growth, others will generate more cash than they need. Somehow companies must decide how to distribute their limited resources among the competing needs of products so as to achieve the best performance for the company as a whole. Specifically within a product line, management need to decide which brands to invest in, hold, or withdraw support. Similarly within the product mix, decisions regarding which product lines to build, hold or withdraw support need to be taken.

Clearly, these are strategic decisions since they shape where and with what brands/product lines a company competes and how its resources should be deployed. Furthermore these decisions are complex because many factors (e.g. current and future sales and profit potential, cash flow) can affect the outcome. The process of managing groups of brands and product lines is called *portfolio planning*.

Key decisions regarding portfolio planning involve decisions regarding the choice of which brands/product lines to build, hold, harvest or divest. Marketing in Action 8.5 discusses Unilever's approach to portfolio planning.

In order to get to grips with the complexities of decision-making two methods have received wide publicity. These are the Boston Consulting Group Growth-Share Matrix and the General Electric Market Attractiveness—Competitive Position portfolio evaluation models. Like the product life cycle these are very flexible tools and can be used at both the brand and product line levels. Indeed, corporate planners can also use them when making resource allocation decisions at the strategic business unit level.

Boston Consulting Group Growth-Share Matrix

A leading management consultancy, the Boston Consulting Group, developed the well-known BCG Growth-Share Matrix (see Fig. 8.8). The matrix allows portfolios of products to be depicted on a 2 × 2 box, the axes of which are based on market growth rate and relative market share. The following discussion will be based on an analysis at the product line level.

Market growth rate forms the vertical axis and indicates the annual growth rate of the market in which each product line operates. In Fig. 8.8 it is shown as 0–15 per cent although a different range could be used depending on economic conditions, for example. In this example the dividing line between high and low growth rates is considered to be 7 per cent. Market growth rate is used as a proxy for market attractiveness.

Relative market share is shown on the horizontal axis and refers to the market share of each product relative to its largest competitor. It acts as a proxy for competitive strength. The division between high and low market share is 1. Above this figure a product line has a market share greater than its largest competitor. For example, if our product had a market share of 40 per cent and our largest competitor's share was 30 per cent this would be indicated as 1.33 on the horizontal axis. Below 1 we have a share less than the largest competitor. For example, if our share was 20 per

cent and the largest competitor had a share of 40 per cent our score would be 0.5.

The Boston Consulting Group argued that cash flow is dependent on the box in which a product falls. Note that cash flow is not the same as profitability. Profits add to cash flow but heavy investment in such assets as plant, equipment and marketing capital can mean that a company can make profits and yet have a negative cash flow.

Stars are likely to be profitable because they are market leaders but require substantial investment to finance growth (e.g. new production facilities) and to meet competitive challenges. Overall cash flow is therefore likely to be roughly in balance. *Problem children* are products in high growth markets which causes a drain on cash flow but these are low share products. Consequently they are unlikely to be profitable. Overall, then, they are big cash users. *Cash cows* are market leaders in mature (low growth) markets. High market share leads to high profitability and low

8.5 Marketing in Action
Portfolio Planning at Unilever

Intense retail pressure and the need to create major global brands were two of the driving forces behind a massive portfolio planning analysis conducted by Unilever. In a classic portfolio exercise, Unilever decided to axe 1200 or 75 per cent of its 1600 consumer brands and concentrate its marketing muscle behind 400 high-growth brands. All brands that are not among the top two sellers in their market segment will be dropped either immediately or over a period of time. Buyers will be sought for those that are to be divested immediately; the rest will be harvested (milked) and the cash generated ploughed into support for the big brands. This will mean £450 million of extra marketing expenditure put behind such global brands as Calvin Klein fragrances, Magnum ice cream, Dove soap and Lipton tea. Local successes such as Persil washing powder and Colman's mustard in the UK will also be supported heavily. The objective is to generate 6–8 per cent volume growth per year from its 400 star brands.

A major outcome of the portfolio analysis was the revelation that only a quarter of Unilever's brands provided 90 per cent of its turnover and that disposing of the other three-quarters would lead to a more efficient supply chain and reduced costs of £1 billion over three years. Brands scheduled to be harvested or divested include Timotei shampoo, Brut deodorant, Radion washing powder, Harmony hairspray, Pear's soap and Jif lemons.

Based on: Doward and Islam (1999);[54] Finch (1999);[55] Macalister (2000);[56] Whitfield. (2000)[57]

market growth means that investment in new production facilities is minimal. This leads to a large positive cash flow. *Dogs* also operate in low growth markets but have low market share. Except for some products near the dividing line between cash cows and dogs (sometimes called *cash dogs*) most dogs produce low or negative cash flows. Relating to their position to the product life cycle, they are the also-rans in mature or declining markets.

What are the strategic implications of the BCG analysis? It can be used for setting strategic objectives and for maintaining a balanced product portfolio.

Guidelines for setting strategic objectives

Having plotted the position of each product on the matrix, a company can begin to think about setting the appropriate strategic objective for each line. As you may recall from Chapter 2 there are four possible *strategic objectives*: build, hold, harvest and divest. Figure 8.9 shows how each relates to the star, problem children, cash cow and dog categories. However, it should be emphasized that the BCG matrix provides guidelines for strategic thinking and should not be seen as a replacement for managerial judgement.

Stars   these are the market leaders in high growth markets. They are already successful and the prospects for further growth are good. As we

have seen when discussing brand building, market leaders tend to have the highest profitability so the appropriate strategic objective is to build sales and/or market share. Resources should be invested to maintain/increase the leadership position. Competitive challenges should be repelled. These are the cash cows of the future and need to be protected.

Problem children   as we have seen these are cash drains because they have low profitability and need investment to keep up with the market growth. They are called problem children because management has to consider whether it is sensible to continue the required investment. The company faces a fundamental choice: to increase investment (*build*) to attempt to turn the problem child into a star, or to withdraw support by either *harvesting* (raising price while lowering marketing expenditure) or *divesting* (dropping or selling it). In a few cases a third option may be viable: to find a small market segment (*niche*) where dominance can be achieved. Unilever, for example, identified its speciality chemicals business as a problem child. It realized that it had to invest heavily or exit. Its decision was to sell and invest the billions raised in predicted future winners such as personal care, dental products and fragrances.[58]

Cash cows   the high profitability and low investment associated with high market share in low growth markets mean that cash cows should

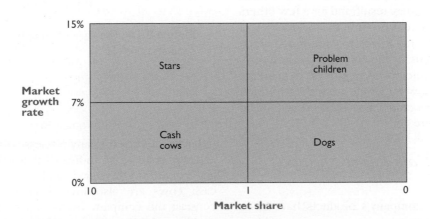

Figure 8.8   The Boston Consulting Group Growth-Share Matrix

Stars *Build* sales and/or market share Invest to maintain/increase leadership position Repel competitive challenges	**Problem children** *Build* selectively Focus on defendable niche where dominance can be achieved *Harvest* or *divest* the rest
Cash cows *Hold* sales and/or market share Defend position Use excess cash to support stars, selected problem children and new product development	**Dogs** *Harvest* or *Divest* or Focus on defendable niche

Figure 8.9 Strategic objectives and the Boston Box

be defended. Consequently the appropriate strategic objective is to *hold* sales and market share. The excess cash that is generated should be used to fund stars, problem children that are being built, and research and development for new products.

Dogs dogs are weak products that compete in low growth markets. They are the also-rans that have failed to achieve market dominance during the growth phase and are floundering in maturity. For those products that achieve second or third position in the marketplace (cash dogs) a small positive cash flow may result, and for a few others it may be possible to reposition the product into a defendable *niche* (as Rover has attempted since the late 1980s). But for the bulk of dogs the appropriate strategic objective is to *harvest* to generate a positive cash flow for a time, or to *divest*, which allows resources and managerial time to be focused elsewhere.

Maintaining a balanced product portfolio

Once all of the company's products have been plotted it is easy to see how many stars, problem children, cash cows, and dogs are in the portfolio. Figure 8.10 shows a product portfolio that is

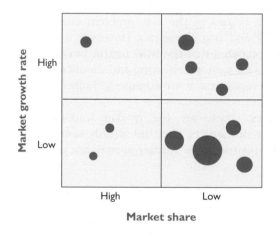

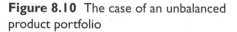

Figure 8.10 The case of an unbalanced product portfolio

unbalanced. The company possesses only one star and the small circle indicates that sales revenue generated from the star is small. Similarly the two cash cows are also low revenue earners. In contrast the company owns four dogs and four problem children. The portfolio is unbalanced because there are too many problem children and dogs and not enough stars and cash cows. What many companies in this situation do is to spread what little surplus cash is available equally between the products in the growth markets.[59] To do so would leave each with barely enough money to maintain market share leading to a vicious circle of decline.

The BCG remedy would be to conduct a detailed competitive assessment of the four problem children and select one or two for investment. The rest should be harvested (and the cash channelled to those that are being built) or divested. The aim is to build the existing star (which will be the cash cow of the future) and to build market share of the chosen problem children so that they attain star status.

The dogs also need to be analysed. One of them (large circle) is a large revenue earner which despite low profits may be making a substantial contribution to overheads. Another product (on the left) appears to be in the cash dog situation. But for the other two the most sensible strategic objective may be to harvest or divest.

Criticisms of the BCG Growth-Share Matrix

The simplicity, ease of use and importance of the issues tackled by the BCG Matrix saw its adoption by a host of North American and European companies who wanted to get a handle on the complexities of strategic resource allocation. But the tool has also attracted a litany of criticism.[60] The following draws together many of the points raised by the critics:

1 The assumption that cash flow will be determined by a product's position on the matrix is weak. For example, some stars will show a healthy positive cash flow (e.g. IBM PCs during the growth phase of the PC market) as will some dogs in markets where competitive activity is low.

2 The preoccupation of focusing on market share and market growth rates distracts managerial attention from the fundamental principle in marketing: attaining a sustainable competitive advantage.

3 Treating market growth rate as a proxy for market attractiveness, and market share as an indicator of competitive strength is over-simplistic. There are many other factors that have to be taken into account when measuring market attractiveness (e.g. market

size, strengths and weaknesses of competitors) and competitive strengths (e.g. exploitable marketing assets, potential cost advantages) besides market growth rates and market share.

4 Since the position of a product on the matrix depends upon market share, it can lead to an unhealthy preoccupation with market share gain. In some circumstances this objective makes sense (see brand building) but when competitive retaliation is likely the costs of share building may outweigh the gains.

5 The matrix ignores interdependencies between products. For example, a dog may need to be marketed because it complements a star or a cash cow. For example, the dog may be a spare part for star or cash cow. Alternatively customers and distributors may value dealing with a company that supplies a full-product line. For these reasons dropping products because they fall into a particular box may be naive.

6 The classic BCG Matrix prescription is to build stars because they will become the cash cows of the future. However, some products have a very short product life cycle in which case the appropriate strategy should be to maximize profits and cash flow while in the car category (e.g. fashion goods).

7 Marketing objectives and strategy are heavily dependent on an assessment of what competitors are likely to do. How will they react if we lower or raise prices when implementing a build or harvest strategy, for example? This is not considered in the matrix.

8 The matrix assumes that products are self-funding. For example, selected problem children are built by using cash generated by cash cows. But this ignores capital markets which may mean that a wider range of projects can be undertaken so long as they have positive net present values of their future cash flows.

9 The matrix is vague regarding the definition of market. Should we take the whole market (e.g. for confectionery) or just the market segment that we operate in (e.g. expensive

boxed chocolates). The matrix is also vague when defining the dividing line between high and low growth markets. A chemical company which tends to generate in lower growth markets might use 3 per cent, whereas a leisure goods company whose markets on average experience much higher rates of growth might use 10 per cent. Also over what period do we define market growth? These issues question the theoretical soundness of the underlying concepts, and allow managers to manipulate the figures so that their products fall in the right boxes.

10 The matrix was based upon cash flow but perhaps profitability (e.g. return on investment) is a better criterion for allocating resources.

11 The matrix lacks precision in identifying which problem children to build, harvest or drop.

General Electric Market Attractiveness–Competitive Position model

As we have already noted the BCG Matrix enjoyed tremendous success as management grappled with the complex issue of strategic resource allocation. Stimulated by this success and some of the weaknesses of the model (particularly the oversimplistic criticism) McKinsey and Co developed a more wide-ranging Market Attractiveness–Competitive Position (MA-CP) model in conjunction with General Electric in the USA.

Market attractiveness criteria

Instead of market growth alone a range of market attractiveness criteria were used, such as:

1 Market size
2 Market growth rate
3 Strength of competition
4 Profit potential
5 Social, political and legal factors

Competitive strength criteria

Similarly, instead of using only market share as a measure of competitive strength a number of

factors were used, such as:

1 Market share
2 Potential to develop a differential advantage
3 Opportunities to develop cost advantages
4 Reputation
5 Distribution capabilities

Weighting the criteria

Management was allowed to decide which criteria were applicable for their products. This gave the MA-CP model flexibility. Having decided the criteria, management would then agree upon a weighting system for each set of criteria, with those factors which were more important having a higher weighting. For example, management might decide upon the following weights (which sum to 1.0):

Market attractiveness

Market size	0.15
Market growth rate	0.20
Strength of competition	0.30
Profit potential	0.30
Social, political and legal factors	0.05
	1.00

Competitive strengths

Market share	0.20
Differential advantage	0.40
Cost advantages	0.05
Reputation	0.10
Distribution capabilities	0.25
	1.00

Each market attractiveness factor is then scored out of 10 (from 1 meaning unattractive to 10 meaning very attractive) to reflect how each product rates on that factor. Similarly each competitive strength factor is scored out of 10 (from 1 meaning very weak to 10 meaning very strong). Each score is multiplied by the factor weight and summed to obtain overall market attractiveness and competitive strength scores for each product. These can then be plotted on the MA-CP Matrix.

Setting strategic objectives

The matrix is shown in Fig. 8.11. Like the BCG Matrix the recommendations for setting strategic objectives are dependent on the products posi-

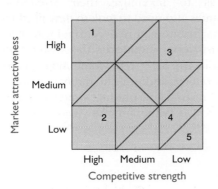

Figure 8.11 The General Electric Market Attractiveness–Competitive Position Model

tion on the grid. Five zones are shown in Fig. 8.11. The strategic objectives associated with each zone are as follows.[61]

Zone 1   build—manage for sales and market share growth as the market is attractive and competitive strengths are high (equivalent to star products).

Zone 2   hold—manage for profits consistent with maintaining market share as the market is not particularly attractive but competitive strengths are high (equivalent to cash cows).

Zone 3   build/hold/harvest—this is the question mark zone. Where competitors are weak or passive, a build strategy will be used. In the face of strong competitors a hold strategy may be appropriate, or harvesting where commitment to the product/market is lower. (Similar to problem children.)

Zone 4   harvest—manage for cash as both market attractiveness and competitive strengths are fairly low.

Zone 5   divest—improve short-term cash yield by dropping or selling the product (equivalent to dog products).

Criticisms of the GE portfolio model

The proponents of the GE portfolio model argue that the analysis is much richer than BCG analysis due to more factors being taken into account, and

flexible. Critics argue that it is harder to use than the BCG Matrix since it requires managerial agreement on which factors to use, their weightings, and scoring. Furthermore, its flexibility provides a lot of opportunity for managerial bias to enter the analysis whereby product managers argue for factors and weightings that show their products in a good light (zone 1). This last point suggests that the analysis should be conducted at a managerial level higher than that being assessed. For example, decisions as to which product lines to be built, held, etc., should be taken as the strategic business unit level, and allocations of resources to brands should be taken at the group product manager level.

The contribution of product portfolio planning

Despite the limitations of the BCG and the GE portfolio evaluation models both have made a contribution to the practice and portfolio planning. We shall now discuss the contribution and suggest how the models can usefully be incorporated into product strategy.

Different products and different roles

The models emphasize the important strategic point that *different products should have different roles* in the product portfolio. Hedley points out that some companies believe that all product lines and brands should be treated equally, that is set the same profit requirements.[62] The portfolio planning models stress that this should not necessarily be the case, and may be harmful in many situations. For example to ask for a 20 per cent return on investment (ROI) for a star may result in under-investment in an attempt to meet the profit requirement. On the other hand 20 per cent ROI for a cash cow or a harvested product may be too low. The implication is that products should be set profitability objectives in line with the strategic objective decisions.

Different reward systems and types of managers

By stressing the need to set different strategic objectives for different products, the models by implication support the notion that *different reward systems and types of managers* should be linked to them. For example managers of products being built should be marketing-led, and rewarded for improving sales and market share. Conversely, managers of harvested (and to some extent cash cow) products should be more cost-orientated, and rewarded by profit and cash flow achievement (see Fig. 8.12).

Aid to managerial judgement

Managers may find it useful to plot their products on both the BCG and GE portfolio grids as an initial step in pulling together the complex issues involved in product portfolio planning. This can help them get a handle on the situation and issues to be resolved. The models can then act as an *aid to managerial judgement* without in any way supplementing that judgement. Managers should feel free to bring into the discussion any other factors that they feel are not adequately covered by the models. The models can therefore be seen as an aid to strategic thinking in multi-product, multi-market companies.

Product strategies for growth

The emphasis on product portfolio analysis is managing an *existing* set of products in such a way as to maximize their strengths. But companies also need to look to new products and markets for future growth. A useful way of looking at growth opportunities is the Ansoff Matrix as shown in Fig. 8.13.[63] By combining present and new products, and present and new markets into a 2 × 2 matrix, four product strategies for growth are revealed. Although the Ansoff Matrix does

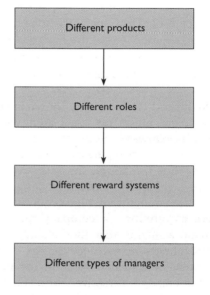

Figure 8.12 Implications of portfolio planning

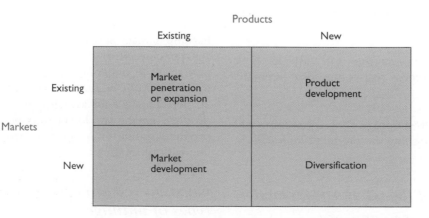

Figure 8.13 Product growth strategies: the Ansoff Matrix

not prescribe when each strategy should be employed, it is a useful framework for thinking about the ways in which growth can be achieved through product strategy.

Figure 8.14 shows how the Ansoff Matrix can be used to implement a growth strategy.

Market penetration the most basic method of gaining penetration in existing markets with current products is by *winning competitor's customers*. This may be achieved by more effective use of promotion or distribution, or by cutting prices. Another way of gaining market penetration is to *buy competitors*. This achieves an immediate increase in market share and sales volume. To protect the penetration already gained in a market a business may consider methods of *discouraging competitive entry*. *Barriers* can be created by cost advantages (lower labour costs, access to raw materials, economies of scale), highly differentiated products, high switching costs (the costs of changing from existing supplier to a new supplier for example), and displaying aggressive tendencies to retaliate.

Market expansion a company may attempt to expand a market that they already serve by *converting non-users to users* of their product. This can be an attractive option in new markets when non-users form a sizeable segment and may be willing to try the product given suitable inducements. Thus when Carnation entered the powdered coffee whitening market with Coffeemate, a key success factor was their ability to persuade hitherto non-users of powdered

whiteners to switch from milk. Lapsed users can also be targeted. Kelloggs have targeted lapsed breakfast cereal users (fathers) who rediscover the pleasure of eating cornflakes when feeding their children. Market expansion can also be achieved by *increasing usage rate*. Colman's attempted to increase the use of mustard by showing new combinations of mustard and food. Kelloggs have also tried to increase the usage (eating) rate of their cornflakes by promoting eating in the evening as well as at breakfast.

Product development the product development option involves the development of new products for existing markets.[64] One variant is to *extend existing product lines* to give current customers greater choice. When new features are added (with an accompanying price rise) trading up may occur with customers buying the enhanced value product upon repurchase. *Product replacement* activities involve the replacement of old brands/models with new ones. This is common in the car market and often involves an upgrading of the old model with a new (more expensive) replacement. A final option is the replacement of an old product with a fundamentally different one often based on technology change. The business thus replaces an old product with an *innovation* (although both may be marketed side-by-side for a time). The development of the compact disk (CD) is an example.

Market development this entails the promotion of *new uses of existing products to new*

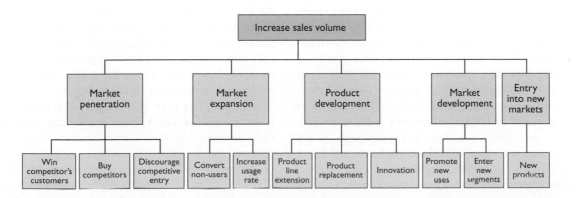

Figure 8.14 Strategic options for increasing sales volume

customers or the marketing of *existing products (and their current uses) to new **market segments**.* The promotion of new uses accounted for the growth in sales of nylon, which was first marketed as a replacement for silk in parachutes but expanded into shirts, carpets, tyres, etc. Market development through entering new segments could involve the search for overseas opportunities. Andy Thornton Ltd, an interior design business, successfully increased sales by entering Scandinavia and Germany, two geographic segments which provided new expansion opportunities for their services.

Entry into new markets   this option concerns the development of *new product* for *new markets*. This is the most risky option especially when the entry strategy is not based upon the **core competences** of the business. However, it can be the most rewarding also exemplified by Honda's move from motor cycles to cars (based on their core competence in engines) and Sony's move into 8mm camcorders (based on their core competences in miniaturization and video technology).[65]

Ethical issues concerning products

There are three major issues regarding ethical issues with products: product safety, planned obsolescence and deceptive packaging.

Product safety

A major concern about product safety has been the issue of the safety of genetically modified products. Vociferous pressure groups such as Greenpeace have spoken out about the dangers of genetic modification. This process allows scientists to manipulate the genetic code of plants to create new characteristics never seen in nature. They are able to isolate any one gene in an organism and insert it into a completely unrelated species. For example, scientists can inject a gene from a bacterium into a grape to make it resistant to viruses; they can engineer maize to make it drought resistant or potatoes that resist pests. People are sharply divided as to whether this can

be safe. Although plant breeders for thousands of years have been tampering with the genes of plants through traditional cross-pollination of plants of the same species, genetic modification goes one step further as it allows scientists to cross the species barrier. This, the critics claim, is fundamentally unnatural. Furthermore, they state, no scientist can be sure that all of this genetic manipulation can be safe. Such concerns, and the attendant publicity have led to one of the pioneers of genetic modification, Monsanto, to back away from further development of genetically modified foods and supermarket chains to ban such produce from their shelves. Supporters state that many new products are introduced with a certain degree of risk being acceptable. For example, a new pharmaceutical product may harm a tiny percentage of users but the utilitarianist principle of 'the greatest good for the greatest number' would support its launch.

It is the reality of modern-day business that new products such as cars, pharmaceuticals and foods undergo extensive safety testing before launch. Anything less would violate the consumer's 'right to safety'.

Planned obsolescence

Many products are not designed to last a long time. From the producers' point of view this is sensible as it creates a repeat purchase situation. Hence, cars rot, clothes wear out and fashion items are replaced by the latest styles. Consumers accept that nothing lasts forever, but the issue concerns what is an acceptable length of time before replacement is necessary. One driving force is competition. To quell the Japanese invasion, car manufacturers such as Ford and Volkswagen have made the body shells of their cars much more rot resistant than before. Furthermore, it has to be recognized that many consumers welcome the chance to buy new clothes, new appliances with the latest features and the latest model of car. Critics argue that planned obsolescence reduces consumers' 'right to choose' since some consumers may be quite content to drive an old car so long as its body shell was free from rust and the car functions well. As we have noted, the forces of competition may act to deter the excesses of planned obsolescence.

Deceptive packaging

This can occur when a product appears in an oversized package to create the impression that the consumer is buying more than is the case. This is known as 'slack' packaging[66] and has the potential to deceive when the packaging is opaque. Products such as soap powders and breakfast cereals have the potential to suffer from 'slack' packaging. A second area where packaging may be deceptive is through misleading labelling. This may take the form of the sin of omission. For example, the failure of a package to state that the product contains genetically modified soya beans. This relates to the consumer's 'right to be informed', and can include the stating of ingredients (including flavouring colourants), nutritional contents and country of origin on labels. Nevertheless, labelling can be misleading. For example, in the UK country of origin is only the last country where the product was 'significantly changed'. So oil pressed from Greek olives in France can be labelled 'French' and foreign imports that are packed in the UK can be labelled 'produce of the UK'. Consumers should be wary of loose terminology. For example, smoked bacon may well have received its 'smoked flavour' from a synthetic liquid solution, 'farm fresh eggs' are likely to be undatemarked eggs of indeterminate age laid by battery hens, and 'farmhouse cheese' may not come from farmhouses but from industrial factories.[67]

Summary

We have explored in this chapter the difference between a product and a brand. A product is anything that is capable of satisfying customer needs. Brands create individual identities by developing a distinctive name, packaging and design. A product line is a group of brands that are closely related in terms of their functions and benefits. A product mix is the total set of brands marketed by a company. Manufacturer brands are created by producers, whereas own-brand labels are created by distributors (although they may be manufactured by producers). Branding permits the augmenting of core products to create differentiation, and extra value to customers.

This chapter has also explored the way in which marketing personnel develop products into brands. In particular we have examined brand building and extension strategies and identified seven key methods of brand building: quality, positioning, repositioning, well-blended communications, being first, taking a long-term perspective and internal marketing. The move to global and pan-European branding and the arguments both for and against the likelihood of these trends becoming dominant have been presented. The conclusion was that the fundamental question was not whether global and pan-European branding will occur but the decision as to which parts of the brand can be standardized and which must be varied between customer groups.

Our discussion of brand strategies and choices looked at the decision to use individual family brand names and the characteristics of good brand names. The product life cycle was used to stress the need to modify strategy over the lifetime of brands and product lines. Its uses and limitations were discussed. Next, we examined management of product portfolios, the uses and criticisms levelled at the Boston Consulting Group-Share Matrix and the General Electric Market Attractiveness–Competitive Position Model were discussed. Finally, we looked at the four growth options: market penetration, product development, market development and diversification.

Three ethical issues concerning products were discussed, namely product safety, planned obsolescence and deceptive pakaging.

Internet exercise

Brand positioning

Sites to visit
http://www.lotuscars.co.uk/
http://www.skoda.co.uk/

Exercise
Using the anatomy of brand-positioning framework, compare and contrast Lotus and Skoda.

Study questions

1 Why do companies develop core products into brands?

2 Suppose you were the marketing director of a medium-sized bank. How would you tackle the job of building the company brand?

3 Think of five brand names. To what extent do they meet the criteria of good brand naming as laid out in Table 8.3? Do any of the names legitimately break these guidelines?

4 Do you think that there will be a large increase in the number of pan-European brands over the next ten years or not? Justify your answer.

5 What are the strategic options for pan-European brand building? What are the advantages and disadvantages of each option?

6 The product life cycle is more likely to mislead marketing management than provide useful insights. Discuss.

7 Evaluate the usefulness of the BCG Matrix. Do you believe that it has a role to play in portfolio planning?

8 What is the difference between product and market development in the Ansoff matrix? Give examples of each form of product growth strategy.

9 Discuss the major ethical concerns relating to products.

References

1. DeKimpe, M. C., J.-B. E. M. Steenkamp, M. Mellens and P. Vanden Abeele (1997) Decline and Variability in Brand Loyalty, *International Journal of Research in Marketing*, **14**, 405–20.
2. Chernatony, L. de (1991) Formulating Brand Strategy, *European Management Journal*, **9** (2), 194–200.
3. Kay, J. (1996) What's in a Name?, *Financial Times*, 6 December, 12.
4. East, R. (1995) *Consumer Behaviour*, Hemel Hempstead: Prentice-Hall Europe.
5. Ehrenberg, A. S. C., G. J. Goodhardt and T. P. Barwise (1990) Double Jeopardy Revisited, *Journal of Marketing*, **54** (July), 82–91.
6. Buzzell, R. and B. Gale (1987) *The PIMS Principles*, London: Collier Macmillan.
7. Reyner, M. (1996) Is Advertising the Answer?, *Admap*, September, 23–6.
8. Abraham, B. (1996) Own Label's Outer Limits, *Marketing*, 21 November, 24–5.
9. See S. King (1991) Brand Building in the 1990s, *Journal of Marketing Management*, **7** (1), 3–14; and P. Doyle (1989) Building Successful Brands: The Strategic Options, *Journal of Marketing Management*, **5** (1), 77–95.
10. Goldstine, J. and L. Light (1999) What High-tech Managers Need to Know About Brands, *Harvard Business Review*, July–August, 85–97.
11. Buzzell and Gale (1987) op. cit.
12. Lemmink, J. and H. Kaspar (1994) Competitive Reactions to Product Quality Improvements in Industrial Markets, *European Journal of Marketing*, **28** (12), 50–68.
13. King (1991) op. cit.
14. Pieters, R. and L. Warlop (1999) Visual Attention during Brand Choice: The Impact of Time Pressure and Task Motivation, *International Journal of Research in Marketing*, **16**, 1–16.

15. For example Urban, G. L.,T. Carter, S. Gaskin and Z. Mucha (1986) Market Share Rewards to Pioneering Brands:An Empirical Analysis and Strategic Implications, *Management Science*, **32** (June), 645-59, showed that for frequently purchased consumer goods the second firm in the market could expect only 71 per cent of the market share of the pioneer and the third only 58 per cent of the pioneer's share. Also Lambkin, M. (1992) Pioneering New Markets:A Comparison of Market Share Winners and Losers, *International Journal of Research in Marketing*, **9** (1), 5-22, found that the pioneers which invest heavily from the start in building large production scale, in securing wide distribution and in promoting their products achieve the strongest competitive position and earn the highest long-term returns.

16. Leibernan, M. B. and D. B. Montgomery (1988) First Mover Advantage, *Strategic Management Journal*, **9**, 41-56.

17. Nayak, P. R. (1991) *Managing Rapid Technological Development*, London:A. D. Little.

18. Oakley, P. (1996) High-tech NPD Success through Faster Overseas Launch, *European Journal of Marketing*, **30** (8), 75-81

19. Reinertsen, R. G. (1983) Whodunit? The Search for the New Product Killers, *Electronic Business*, 9 July, 62-6.

20. Tellis, G. and P. Golder (1995) First to Market, First to Fail? Real Causes of Enduring Market Leadership, *Sloan Management Review*, **37** (2), 65-76.

21. Cadbury,A. (1988) *Annual Report of Cadbury Schweppes*, Bournville.

22. King (1991) op. cit.

23. Riel, C. B. M. and J. M.T. Balmer (1997) Corporate Identity:The Concept, its Measurement and Management, *European Journal of Marketing*, **31** (5/6), 340-55.

24. Hatch, M. J. and M. Schultz (1997) Relations between Organisational Culture, Identity and Image, *European Journal of Marketing*, **31** (5/6), 356-65.

25. Gander, P. (2000) Image Bank, *Marketing Week*, 16 March, 43-4.

26. Martin, M. and I. Heath (1999) BA Redesign was Global Failure, *Marketing*, 2 December, 21.

27. Levitt,T. (1983) The Globalisation of Marketing, *Harvard Business Review*, May-June, 92-102.

28. Barwise, P. and T. Robertson (1992) Brand Portfolios, *European Management Journal*, **10** (3), 277-85.

29. Halliburton, C. and R. Hünerberg (1993) Pan-European Marketing-Myth or Reality, *Proceedings of the European Marketing Academy Conference*, Barcelona, May, 490-518.

30. Kern, H., H. Wagner and R. Hassis (1990) European Aspects of a Global Brand:The BMW Case, *Marketing and Research Today*, February, 47-57.

31. Barwise and Robertson (1992) op. cit.

32. Wilkinson,A. (1999) Trebor Slims Down for Leaner Branding, *Marketing Week*, 26 August, 20.

33. Pandya, N. (1999) Soft Selling Soap Brings Hard Profit, *The Guardian*, 2 October, 28.

34. Beale, C. (1999) Tommy Hilfiger Kicks Off £8m Media Review, *Campaign*, 15 October, 5.

35. Sullivan, M. W. (1990) Measuring Image Spillovers in Umbrella-branded Products, *Journal of Business*, July, 309-29.

36. Sharp, B. M. (1990) The Marketing Value of Brand Extension, *Marketing Intelligence and Planning*, **9** (7), 9-13.

37. Aaker, D.A. and K. L. Keller (1990) Consumer Evaluation of Brand Extensions, *Journal of Marketing*, **54** (January), 27-41.

38. Aaker, D.A. (1990) Brand Extensions:The Good, the Bad and the Ugly, *Sloan Management Review*, Summer, 47-56.

39. Bottomley, P.A. and J. R. Doyle (1996) The Formation of Attitudes towards Brand Extensions:Testing and Generalising Aaker and Keller's Model, *International Journal of Research in Marketing*, **13**, 365-77.

40. Miller, R. (1999) Science Joins Art in Brand Naming, *Marketing*, 27 May, 31-2.

41. Roberts, C. J. and G. M. McDonald (1989) Alternative Naming Strategies: Family versus Individual Brand Names, *Management Decision*, **27**, (6), 31-7.

42. Saunders, J. (1990) Brands and Valuations, *International Journal of Advertising*, **9**, 95-110.

44. Bennett, R. C. and R. G. Cooper (1981) The Misuse of the Marketing Concept:An American Tragedy, *Business Horizons*, Nov.-Dec., 51-61.

44. Sharp (1990) op. cit.

45. Aaker (1990) op. cit.

46. Polli, R. and V. Cook (1969) Validity of the Product Life Cycle, *Journal of Business*, October, 385-400.

47. Doyle (1989) op. cit.

48. Day, G. (1997) Strategies for Surviving a Shakeout, *Harvard Business Review*, March-April, 92-104.

49. Vakratsas, D. and T.Ambler (1999) How Advertising Works:What Do We Really Know? *Journal of Marketing*, **63**, January, 26-43.

50. See Greenley, G. E. and B. L. Barus (1994) A Corporative Study of Product Launch and Elimination Decisions in UK and US Companies, *European Journal of Marketing*, **28** (2) 5-29; Hart, S. J. (1989) Product Deletion and Effects of Strategy, *European Journal of Marketing*, **23** (10), 6-17 and Avlonitis, G. J. (1987) Linking Different Types of Product Elimination Decisions to their Performance Outcome, *International Journal of Research in Marketing*, **4** (1), 43-57.

51. Cline, C. E. and B. P. Shapiro (1979) *Cumberland Metal Industries (A): Case Study*, Cambridge, Mass: Harvard Business School.

52. Polli and Cook (1969) op. cit.

53. Dhalia, N. K. and S. Yuspeh (1976) Forget the Product Life Cycle Concept, *Harvard Business Review*, Jan.-Feb., 102-12.

54. Doward, J. and F. Islam (1999) Household Names Face Axe as Unilever Slims Down, *The Observer*, 26 September, 3.

55. Finch, J. (1999) Unilever Washes Hands of 1200 Brands, *The Guardian*, 22 September, 25.

56. Macalister,T. (2000) 25 000 Unilever Jobs Go in Cull of Brands, *The Guardian*, 23 February, 27.

57. Whitfield, P. (2000) Unilever A-Brands to Get £1bn Boost, *Marketing*, 24 February, 1.

58. Brierley, D. (1997) Spring-Cleaning a Statistical Wonderland, *The European*, 20-26 February, 28.

59. Hedley, B. (1977) Boston Consulting Group Approach to the Business Portfolio, *Long Range Planning*, February, 9-15.

60. See e.g. Day, G. S. and R. Wensley (1983) Marketing Theory with a Strategic Orientation, *Journal of Marketing*, fall, 79–89; Haspslagh, P. (1982) Portfolio Planning: Uses and Limits, *Harvard Business Review*, Jan.–Feb., 58–73; and Wensley, R. (1981) Strategic Marketing: Betas, Boxes and Basics, *Journal of Marketing*, Summer, 173–83.

61. Hofer, C. and D. Schendel (1978) *Strategy Formulation: Analytical Concepts*, St Paul, MN: West.

62. Hedley (1977) op. cit.

63. Ansoff, H. L. (1957) Strategies for Diversification, *Harvard Business Review*, Sept.–Oct., 114.

64. Ansoff, I. (1957) Strategies for Diversification, *Harvard Business Review*, Sept.–Oct., 113–24.

65. Prahalad, C. K. and G. Hamel (1990) The Core Competence of the Corporation, *Harvard Business Review*, May–June, 79–91.

66. Smith, N. C. (1995) Marketing Strategies for the Ethics Era, *Sloan Management Review*, Summer, 85–97. See also T. W. Dunfee, N. C. Smith and W. T. Ross Jr (1999) Social Contracts and Marketing Ethics, *Journal of Marketing*, **63** (July), 14–32.

67. Young, R. (1999) First Read the Label, Then Add a Pinch of Salt, *The Times*, 30 November, 2–4.

Key terms

product   a good or service offered or performed by an organization or individual which is capable of satisfying customer needs

brand   a distinctive product offering created by the use of a name, symbol, design, packaging, or some combination of these intended to differentiate it from its competitors

product line   a group of brands which are closely related in terms of the functions and benefits they provide

product mix   the total set of products marketed by the company

manufacturer brands   brands which are created by producers and bear their chosen brand name

own-label brands   brands created and owned by distributors or retailers

fighter brands   low-cost manufacturers' brands introduced to combat own-label brands

brand values   the core values and characteristics of a brand

brand domain   the brand's target market

brand heritage   the background to the brand and its culture

brand assets   the distinctive features of a brand

brand personality   the character of a brand described in terms of other entities such as people, animals and objects

brand reflection   the relationship of the brand to self-identity

internal marketing   the training, motivating and communicating with service to cause them to work effectively in providing customer satisfaction. More recently the term has been expanded to include marketing to all staff with the aim of achieving the acceptance of marketing ideas and plans

corporate identity   the ethos, aims and values of an organization, presenting a sense of its individuality which helps to differentiate it from its competitors

global branding   achievement of brand penetration worldwide

family brand name   a brand name used for all products in a range

individual brand name   a brand name which does not identify a brand with a particular company

brand equity   the good will associated with a brand name which adds tangible value to a company through the resulting higher sales and profits

brand extension   the use of an established brand name on a new brand within the same broad market

brand stretching   the use of an established brand name for brands in unrelated markets

product life cycle   a four-stage cycle in the life of a product illustrated as a curve representing the demand, the four stages being introduction, growth, maturity and decline

portfolio planning   managing groups of brands and product lines

strategic objectives   product level objectives relating to the decision to build, hold, harvest, or divest products

market penetration   to continue to sell an existing product in an existing market

market expansion   the attempt to increase the size of a market by converting non-users to users of the product and by increasing usage rates

product development   increasing sales by improving present products or developing new products for current markets

market development   to take current products and sell them in new markets

entry into new markets (diversification)   the entry into new markets by new products

Case 13 Levi Jeans

In a conference room at the global headquarters of Levi Strauss & Company in San Francisco, Robert Holloway, the new vice-president of marketing, addressed Levi's new brand management team. 'What kids want is to be acceptable to their peers. They're looking to make an impact with potential partners as well and therefore they want to look right. Part of looking right is wearing what's cool.'

The problem facing Levi Strauss was that jeans were increasingly regarded as 'uncool'. In 1996, the company reported record one-year sales of $7.1 billion and a profit of more than $1 billion. By the end of 1999, sales had fallen to $5.1 billion and they barely broke even on profits despite closing 30 of their 51 factories and laying off about 15 000 people or 40 per cent of their workers.

The root causes go back as far as 1992 when rap music emerged as a cultural phenomenon and baggy trousers were its generational signature. Unfortunately Levi's failed to connect with young customers. While competitors such as Gap, Diesel, Wrangler and Pepe stole market share Levi's market share shrank from 31 to 14 per cent. The problem was complacency; for years Levi's had been cool—the kind of cool that seems as if it will never end.

Levi Strauss, a Jewish immigrant from Bavaria, began selling waist overalls from his San Francisco store in 1873 as a utilitarian tool of daily life to farmers, ranchers, miners and factory workers. In the 1950s and 1960s, however, they became associated with teenage rebellion and counter culture. Marlon Brando, Elvis Presley and Bob Dylan were all photographed wearing Levi's. Based on the proposition 'genuine, original, authentic, real' sales grew tenfold during the late 1960s and early 1970s but it was not until the mid-1980s that the company aggressively use television advertising to launch its 501 Blues campaign. Sales and profits began a continuous 12-year rise. The engine room for this growth was one product, its 501 five-pocket jean brand that represented social acceptance and yet a kind of individuality and rebelliousness among its wearers.

But nothing lasts forever. One survey repeated that the proportion of US teenage males who considered Levi's to be a 'cool' brand plummeted from 21 per cent to 7 per cent between 1994 and 1998. This was reflected in the comment made by a 16-year-old male who commented that his peers preferred loose brands with non-tapered legs, like the ultra-baggy JNCO jeans. 'But JNCO is more last year. Now it's more Polo, Hilfiger and Boss.' When asked about Levi's he replied: 'If I buy Levi's, it's like I bought Wranglers and people think I'm cheap, but it's still expensive!' Another 15-year-old female stated that her friends will not wear anything from Levi's: 'It doesn't make styles we want. Levi's styles are too tight and for the older generation, like middle-aged people.' She prefers baggy pants from JNCO and Kikwear.

While Levi's remained impervious to the cultural changes in the jeans market, other newer brands have emerged. One major contributor, Gap, began in 1969 ironically as a retail chain selling Levi's exclusively. By staying responsive to consumer changes, the company saw a 40 per cent rise in sales during 1998. Two others, Diesel and Pepe, have stolen Levi's rebellious attitude making Levi jeans less distinctive in the minds of consumers.

By 2000, traditional styles of jeans (Levi's heartland) made up only 20 per cent of sales, down from more than 50 per cent in 1996. To make matters worse there are forecast to be a fall of over five million 15–25-year-olds between 1994 and 2003 in Europe reducing the size of Levi's key target market.

New strategies for the new millennium

The continued segmentation and fragmentation of the UK jeans market has led Levi's to organize its marketing around three customer groups: urban opinion-formers; extreme sports; and regular girls and guys. Each will handle its own new product development, have its own brand managers and marketing team. The core market will remain the 15–25 age group.

In a major attempt to turnaround this grim situation, Levi Strauss have developed new marketing strategies. A new range of non-denim jeans branded 'Sta-Prest' was launched in 1999 backed up by a major TV advertising campaign starring a furry animal called Flat Eric. This campaign has been well received by its youth audience.

In 2000, Levi launched Engineered Jeans, an aggressive modern range billed as a 'reinvention' of the five-pocked style to replace the old 501 brand. Described as the 'twisted original' the new jeans featured side seams that follow the line of the leg, and a curved bottom hem that is slightly shorter at the back to keep it from dragging on the ground. The jeans also have a larger watch pocket to hold items like a pager. Under its youth-orientated Silver Tap brand, Levi's is introducing the Mobile Zip-Off Pant with legs that unzip to create shorts and the loose Ripcord Pant which rolls up. Levi's is also extending its successful Docker brand to a business-casual line called Dockers Recode using stretch fabrics that appeal to older consumers who passed through their teens wearing Levi's blue jeans.

Levi Strauss are also innovating on the retail front. In 1999 the company opened their first unbranded store Cinch! in London with plans to open other stores with the same format but different names around European capitals. Cinch! will target customers which it calls 'cultural connoisseurs', fashionable less mainstream customers. It stocks the new Levi's up-market Red collection and Vintage Clothing and Collectable ranges rather than the mainstream Red Tab or Sta-Prest products. There is no Levi's branding on the store fascia and garments are hung on the walls. Non-Levi's products including Casio watches; Japanese magazines and art books are also stocked. There is a 'chill-out' television room. Cultural connoisseurs like to 'discover' brands for themselves and appreciate an intimate retail experience.

Levi Strauss have also altered their approach to massified promotion. They believe that a 'massified' image is a hindrance to being accepted among young consumers. They studied how rave promoters publicized their parties using flyers, 'wild posting' on construction sites and lamp-posts, pavement markings, and e-mail. They are exploring how such 'viral communications' could be used to infiltrate youth culture. The idea is to introduce the Levi's brand name into the target consumers' clubs, concert venues, websites and fanzines in order for the kids to discover the company's tag for themselves. Levi's are spending massive sums sponsoring and supporting musicians, bands, and concerts in order to communicate with today's youth who are now so smart about media campaigns that the best strategy—as with the 'Flat Eric' campaign—is to try to prod them gently towards the idea that Levi's is again the 'cool' brand. As the president of their advertising agency says: 'If you go into their environment where they are hanging out, and you speak to them in a way that's appropriate, then the buzz created from that is spread, and that's an incredibly powerful way to impact the market-place.'

Based on: Day, J. (1999) Levi's Plans New Stores, *Marketing Week*, 2 September, 7; Espan, H. (1999) Coming Apart at the Seams, *The Observer*, Review, 28 March, 1–2; Lee, J. (1999) 'Can Levi's Ever Be Cool Again?', *Marketing*, 15 April, 28–9; Lee, L. (2000) 'Can Levi's Ever Be Cool Again?', *Business Week*, 13 March, 144–8.

This case was prepared by David Jobber, Professor of Marketing, University of Bradford.

Questions

1 Using the anatomy of brand positioning framework analyse the Levi's brand in 1996 and 1999. Why has the positioning of the brand changed?

2 Do you believe that the Levi's brand positioning is retrievable? Should Levi's relaunch using a different brand name?

3 Assess the steps taken by Levi Strauss to restore Levi's as a successful brand?

Case 14 Müller Dairy UK: Cornering the Yoghurt Market

Introduction

In April 1998, Ken Wood stood before members of the Marketing Society to make a speech as the managing director of Müller Dairy (UK), a post only he had held. He was there to outline the secrets of Müller's amazing success over the past ten years, not only in entering but capturing and transforming the UK yoghurt market. Speaking in a tone that reassured everyone in the audience that they too could have done it, if only they had the chance, he wooed them with the mantra that has been the company's consistent strategy throughout his time as MD: *Genuine innovation, excellence of quality and strong marketing support*.

This is the story of Müller's route to market leadership in the UK. By looking back at what has happened in the yoghurt and chilled pot dessert markets over the past ten years, a clear story of how Müller achieved this marketing success emerges.

Still waters don't always run deep

It was in 1986 that Theo Müller, the owner of Müller (a wholly owned subsidiary of Molkerie Alois Müller GmbH & Co) decided it was time to tackle the UK market with products that were highly successful in his home market of Germany.

At that time, the UK market offered yoghurts with a 2.8 per cent fat content in 125 gram pots most of which were sold in multi-packs. Market trends were all in one direction: smaller pots, lower fat content and the reduction of E numbers which were no longer considered politically correct. In effect, this meant that manufacturers like Eden Vale, with their leading Ski brand, were busy taking everything out of their yoghurts: they hadn't delivered anything radically new to the market for five years.

To Theo Müller, the UK market was an irresistible opportunity to pursue with his own very different products. In comparison to Germany, he considered the product offer taste-less and was not surprised to learn that the population ate only a third of the amount of yoghurts eaten by Germans. The only question in his mind was how to make it happen. Rumours about joint venture negotiations surfaced and soon faded when Ken Wood resigned from his post at Eden Vale to head-up the UK company for Müller. Müller Dairy UK became a one-man company which consisted of Ken Wood!

As it turned out, he proved to be a good choice (see Exhibit C14.1). Commentators reported his business philosophy of 'meticulous opportunism and hard graft' was to stand him in good stead as he inched his way into the retailers' chilled cabinets with single split-pots of Müller Fruit Corner and Müller Crunch Corner. These luxury yoghurts came in 175 gram pots with 5 per cent fat, E-numbers and preservatives, at a time when the low fat segment was by far the manufacturer's favourite and E-numbers were considered the kiss of death! Everything about them was different from anything else on offer in the UK, including the price which was pitched at a premium.

> When I think about Müller's arrival in the UK, I see parallels with a book on disruption theory by Jean Marie Drew. The book explains that within all organizations there are conventions which shape standard approaches to business and get in the way of free thinking. Disruption theory is about shattering these conventions, unleashing creativity in order to forge a radical new vision of a product or a service. It is about spearheading change rather than reacting to it. And I think that is what Müller did just over ten years ago albeit subconsciously. Metaphorically speaking, we threw a huge rock into a still pool.
>
> Ken Wood

Distribution, distribution, distribution

Ken Wood continued his speech by explaining that the market research conducted prior to entry was very small scale. Only 200 people had been asked to participate in qualitative research on brand positioning and eight focus groups had helped develop brand names. However, this did not mean that he discounted the value of market research:

To be fair to my friends and respected colleagues in the MRS (Market Research Society), I think our entry to the UK market was very low risk. In fact, I can remember thinking that the main thing at risk at the time was my job. From the outset we had three clear objectives: distribution, distribution, distribution. Our view was that where there is a chiller, there is an opportunity, and this still holds true today!'

Key to this aim was getting hold of accurate market intelligence about their relative sales from the chilled cabinet. An example stuck in his memory of having an account that they thought was distributing their product to 150 stores. It later turned out to be just 40 stores and each cabinet had been very poorly merchandised. This resulted in some apparently horrendous rate of sales for Müller and, on this basis, they were destocked by the store.

Exhibit C14.1 Profile of Ken Wood—Müller's MD

Once you cut through the 'good bloke', 'nice guy' stuff, the one thing all his colleagues say is that Wood is very bright.

Summary biography

1969 Wednesday College of Commerce, HND Business Studies, specializing in personnel management

1973 GKN trainee assistant personnel manager

1973 Heinz sales promotion assistant marketing intelligence office, head market researcher

1976 Eden Vale product manager, senior marketing manager, marketing director

1986 Müller UK managing director

Despite an asinine careers officer pushing personnel, the student Wood gravitated towards the long-haired layabouts doing marketing. He ditched his personnel sandwich course sponsors after three months and set off for pastures FMCG-er as a sales promotion assistant at Heinz.

Networker extraordinaire, he got into marketing and research through a mate in the department and was just as quick to seize the change of promotion: 'One day, I heard the head researcher saying "I've had enough of this, I'm resigning." I popped into the manager's office after him, said "I understand there's a vacancy." I got the job'.

But product manager was the true holy grail, finally offered to him by Express Dairies—younger than he would have made it at Heinz. 'There was a pecking order. You could have six product managers lined up and always tell the Ski product manager because he was standing proudest and tallest'.

Wood soon zipped through Ski on his way to the prize job, marketing director. He's pretty scathing about the attitude to innovation at Express. The disastrous Eden Vale Snack Pack, a precursor to the twin pot with muesli and yoghurt, is a typical example. 'The idea was great but it was a lousy product. We did it on a shoestring. Consumers aren't stupid; they appreciate quality'.

(Excerpt from *Marketing* 23.6.94)

Table C14.1 Manufacturers' shares of the UK yoghurt market, 1995 and 1997

	1995 £m	% market share	1997 £m	% market share	% change 1995–97
Müller	125.5	24.0	157.0	27.1	+25.1
Eden Vale	56.5	10.8	70.7	12.2	+25.1
St Ivel	40.3	7.7	62.6	10.8	+54.2
Onken	6.8	1.3	12.8	2.2	+88.2
Danone	4.2	0.8	8.1	1.4	+92.9
Other brands	49.1	9.4	48.4	8.3	−1.4
Own label	240.6	46.0	220.4	38.0	−8.4
Total	523.0		580.0		+10.9

Source: Mintel

The solution for Wood was to recruit his own sales support team, a move which helped him check and influence distribution on a store-by-store basis. The same team were used to conduct in-store demonstrations and tastings. Having his own people on-the-ground enabled Wood to assess stock levels nationally across key store groups, a practice which he continues today, albeit in a slightly more sophisticated manner.

> Early on, it was crucial that everyone knew and understood our products. So we delivered sets of chilled samples and sales report literature, directly and painstakingly to each store manager to make them aware of the product proposition.
>
> Another crucial factor in gaining distribution was the test market that we carried out in the Border TV region, which gave us data on the sales performance of our products. It meant that we could give retailers real data about real consumers parting with cash in a really competitive shopping environment. The test market launch was very successful. Throughout, local TV adverts were supported with in-store tastings and promotional activity.

The national roll-out was to commence shortly after the test market using the same marketing strategy.

Strong marketing support

> Almost a decade before the phrase 'efficient consumer response'[1] was commonplace, we could pre-determine that sales accruing from Müller yoghurts would be largely incremental to the category. This was because the yoghurt and its format, appealed to people who previously had not been interested in yoghurt. Distribution apart, we would not have been able to achieve what we achieved in the early days without the willingness of the parent company to make a huge investment in terms of brand support. In fact, the company put an exceptional investment behind advertising.

The first TV commercials featured Larry Hagman. Because of the popularity of Dallas at that time, awareness grew dramatically, but by far the most important commercials for Müller in creating brand awareness were those which featured Joanna Lumley in the five-year period to 1995 (see Fig. C14.1). The account director at Müller's creative agency at that time said:

> We chose Joanna because the communication about the product needed to be sophisticated and have a sense of humour. The typical Müller consumer in the UK is a housewife with children. However, the yoghurts and desserts are particularly favoured by men. Although they are typically less frequent purchasers of yoghurt than women, they represent a significant group.

The advertising campaign and Müller's marketing strategy were very successful. In 1993, Müller was voted FMCG Brand of the Year at the ITV awards for marketing. But after five years of continuous growth and advertising excellence, Wood decided it was time for a change. In 1996, Naomi Campbell appeared in a new commercial for Müller which worked extremely well, but not in the way Wood had anticipated. The media interpreted the introduction of Campbell as being ageist; it just so happened that Naomi was half Joanna's age. News broke on a Thursday and by the same weekend, there was enough media speculation to cause Wood some anxiety:

> Dozens of articles appeared, and I was even personally invited to join the set of Kilroy, God forbid, to discuss the subject! Ironically over the course of the next few days my reaction changed from horror to astonishment as we saw Müller Fruit Corner sales rocket and consumer awareness grow to about 80 per cent prompted recall. The adage is that all publicity is good publicity but, believe me, sometimes it can be a tough way to increase awareness.

Wood described the Müller advertising strategy as product-led, designed to create a corporate character which was known in the industry as Müllerness. The essence of this was quality, innovation and value for money. In 1997, Lumley was bought back to launch Müller's latest innovation—the Candy Corner range. Wood hailed it as their best advertising so far.

---

[1] Efficient Consumer Response (ECR) is the food industry's equivalent of the Just-in-Time (JIT) concept employed in other industries. It was first introduced as a concept in the US in 1993 and necessitates manufacturers and retailers working closely together to introduce greater efficiency and cost savings into the supply chain.

During its history, Müller has invested more in advertising than any of its UK competitors (see Table C14.2). Wood has consistently repeated his intention to continue to dominate the advertising spend tables, seeing it as the market leader's responsibility to stimulate interest in the category and to grow the market through the execution of highly creative commercials.

However, not all of his marketing support initiatives have been a success. His preoccupation with capturing the male consumer backfired on him in 1993 when he decided to sponsor Aston Villa football club. The sponsorship deal cost £1 million over two years and was, by Wood's own admission, a disaster.

Lowest cost, highest price

From the outset, there was a clear intent to manufacture at low cost. To achieve this, the company built a state-of-the-art dairy in Market Drayton (Shropshire) early in 1991. Later, a sophisticated high bay warehousing and distribution facility was added which became fully operational in May 1998 (see Appendix C14.1). By this time, the company had invested £50 million in assets in the UK.

Building the scale volume to feed Market Drayton (and reap economies of scale to keep costs low) was achieved by creating awareness and consumer preference through aggressive marketing activity, but without compromising on retail prices which were set at a premium.

> Pressure on pricing is a big issue in the category, but we have decided not to get into this

Table C14.2 Media spend on yoghurt—top five brands 1993–97

	£m spend 1993–97	% of total spend
Müller fruit corner	9.0	19.1
Müllerlight	7.3	15.5
Müller Crunch Corner	1.4	3.0
Müller Breakfast Bio	1.2	2.6
Other Müller	3.5	7.4
Total Müller	22.4	47.7
St Ivel Shape	6.0	12.8
St Ivel Prize	0.3	0.6
Total St Ivel	6.3	13.4
Eden Vale Ski	5.4	11.5
Eden Vale Munch Bunch	2.4	5.1
Total Eden Vale	7.8	16.6
Others	10.5	22.3
Total spend	47.0	100.0

Source: AC Nielsen—MEAL/Mintel

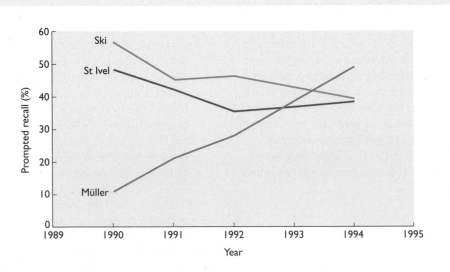

Figure C14.1 Consumer awareness – Müller, 1990–94

Source: Adwatch

downward spiral. We don't see long-term cheap offers as an endorsement of brand values. We are single-minded in our dedication to the brand and for that reason we are not involved in own-label supply.

With a low-cost manufacturing operation and a high retail price, Müller was able to offer retailers an attractive margin proposition (see Fig. C14.2). This extra 'win' for retailers encouraged them to give Müller more space in the chiller which improved Müller's exposure to consumers and their position relative to the competition. The outcome of this marketing strategy was to push products to higher points in their life cycles relatively quickly, establishing lines before copy-cat manufacturers could have a chance to react. By the time competitors had reacted, Müller was often able to beat the newcomer on superior quality delivered at lower cost. Wood knew that innovation was critical to staying ahead.

Innovation

Our strategy of innovation means that, providing we continue to come out with fresh and exciting ideas, without looking over our shoulders, there is a tendency for our competitors just to copy. As the late Sir James Goldsmith commented, if you see the bandwagon it is already too late. We have genuinely innovated, both in terms of packaging and products, while others have really been a variation around a theme. We know that it is genuine innovation that counts . . .'

The Fruit Corner range (strawberry, peidmont cherry and orchard fruit) and Crunch Corner (crunchy muesli and cereal, nuts and raisins) were chosen to make Müller's entry into the UK market. They were soon joined in 1993 by Müllerlight, a 0.1 per cent fat product for those health-conscious families more interested in cholesterol than indulgence. Over the next three years, the fast pace of innovation continued with the introductions of:

✦ Müllerice—a creamy rice dessert with a fruit corner

✦ Müller Thick and Creamy

✦ Müller Breakfast Bio—the first single-serve breakfast yoghurt with added cereal grains and vitamins

✦ Müller flavoured fromage frais—targeted at adults in a sector traditionally geared toward children

✦ Crumble Corner—a creamy yoghurt layered over fruit pieces with a separate helping of crumble

✦ Kids Corner—the first children's yoghurt product, followed by Jelly Invaders.

The split-pot packing idea was introduced to the German market in 1980, carrying rice and fruit sauce in separate compartments. The concept was first transferred to yoghurt in 1984. With their long experience of the product and a typically German passion for quality, Wood was confident that Müller would redefine the quality and style of the UK yoghurt market by setting new gold standards when these packs were introduced in 1987.

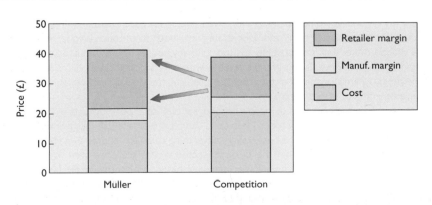

Figure C14.2 Trade margins on Müller and competitive products

Speaking at the Marketing Society Conference, He said:

> It has been argued that the last stage of fitting the product to the market is fitting the market to the product. In our case, over the last ten years we have radically changed the profile of the total market. In effect, the yoghurt market now reflects the Müller proposition.

By then, Müller had grown to become the eighth largest UK grocery brand and was market leader, with a 27 per cent share of the yoghurt market. Annual turnover was £240 million, equivalent to some 700 million pots of yoghurt, fromage frais and chilled desserts and the company employed over 700 people, the majority of whom worked at the production site in Market Drayton.

Independent market research (Table C14.1) confirmed the now-accepted view that Müller Fruit and Crunch corner products had stimulated substantial growth in the Yoghurt market during the 1990s by single-mindedly pursuing their belief in luxury products which were commonplace in Germany.

By 1996, Müller had 14 lines in the chilled dessert and yoghurt market (summary in Appendix C14.2 and Appendix C14.3 for details of the current Müller website).

The competition really had remarkably little effect on Müller as the new product development (NPD) programme was implemented. In 1994, *The Grocer* reported, 'The introduction of 36 look-alikes, branded and own-label, in the split-pot yoghurt sector has not affected market leader Müller. In fact, it has helped it become the UK's fastest growing grocery brand.'

By 1998, the momentum appeared to be continuing at an unrelenting pace (see Exhibit C14.2).

From niche to mass market

Ken Wood was coming to the end of his speech to the Marketing Society audience. He went on to assert that Müller, having started as a niche product at the rather untrendy end of the yoghurt market, was now well and truly a mass market phenomenon. He paid tribute to the enthusiasm of the retail trade for his market offerings and restated that success was due to ubiquitous distribution, great product quality at a very

---

Exhibit C14.2 Yoghurts and pot desserts

The UK yoghurt market reached £531m in 1997, with chilled desserts valued at £257m. . . . Brand leader is Müller which makes three of the top selling yoghurts.

Müller is the major brand in the yoghurt market, where its share stands at 27.3%. Managing director Ken Wood attributes this to the impetus of new product development. 'As one of the key innovators in the market we understand that new product development is vitally important, bringing excitement to the market and helping to attract consumers to the fixture.'

But isn't there a danger of the sector becoming overcrowded? Wood is well aware of the pitfalls: 'Too many introductions can mean products are perceived as short lived. The finite space available in the chiller cabinet means a new product must offer true innovation,' he says. 'Our strategy has been to produce unique, market leading products which break new ground, rather than 'me toos'. He says the company targets 10% of annual volume to come from new product innovation, which he believes is an optimum level to ensure its products have built-in longevity.

Looking at the most dynamic segments of the market, Müllerlight, the virtually fat free brand, is growing at around 41% year-on-year, amounting to sales of £47m.

In the vibrant children's segment, the company introduced two split pot yoghurts—Yogz Crunchz and Yogz Budblasterz—aimed at 12-year-olds, last October. Despite its short time on-shelf, the Yogz brand has pushed Müller's sector share to 15%. It has been backed by a heavyweight advertising campaign and its own web site.

He also sees enormous potential within the desserts sector where Müllerice grew by 22% last year. A key development will be Candy Corner, launched a year ago, and based on internationally famous desserts such as Mississippi Mud Pies and Raspberry Pavlova. 'It's an interesting concept because it blurs the boundaries between yoghurts and desserts, offering unusual ingredients and taste combinations not usually found in yoghurts' adds Wood.

Source: The Grocer, 1998

acceptable price which had resulted in massive consumer repeat purchase. He concluded his speech:

> Our strategy of innovation, quality and consumer support has remained the same although the size of our operations has changed dramatically. And whilst the retail environment has become much more complex and consumer media more fragmented, we have benefited from increased analytical information. Everybody in this room is faced with any number of critical questions on a daily basis. Should our brand be advertised when promoted or not? Is our advertising working? Are we advertising too much, are we advertising enough? How does advertising one product affect sales of another? How should we balance money spent on advertising versus promotion spend? And what's the relationship between price, promotion and volume sales?
>
> We have been helped in understanding some of these fundamental issues thanks to a new sales and media tracking initiative. This isn't the Holy Grail, but it is a very powerful marketing tool. It has, for example, enabled us to measure the impact that advertising one brand has on another, and has therefore helped us to plan our media buying strategies with much greater clarity.
>
> While our systems are second to none and we subscribe to the importance of marketing metrics, we still believe at Müller that intuition and creativity have incredibly strong roles to play. Without creative zeal and entrepreneurial spirit we are lost. Innovation remains central to our marketing strategy.
>
> Our latest launch is a new range of twinpot luxury flavoured ice creams which have a separate helping of either sauces or crunchy topping [see Appendix C14.4]. We have cornered the yoghurt market and we look forward to cornering another market, albeit in a rather modest way ...
>
> People often ask how we determine our NPD programme. Ultimately it is the consumer who must decide if a product works. As a company we have to be sufficiently in tune with our consumers to know if we have fulfilled the success criteria for a new launch. I believe that our marketing team delivers the promise that Müller products will always be different. We have to believe that our new products are winners.

Questions

1   What do you think are the critical success factors behind the Müller brand?

2   The company is committed to 10 per cent of annual volume coming from new product innovation. If you were responsible for developing these new products at Müller, what would be your recommendations to Ken Wood and how would you prioritise them?

3   If Ken Wood were to leave Müller Dairy UK, would the equity of the Müller brand be significantly affected? Give your reasons.

Appendix C14.1

Müller's dairy and warehousing facilities at Market Drayton

Müller claim that their modern manufacturing facilities deliver highest quality at lowest cost. Their low cost-base is driven by large volumes and highly efficient production operations. New warehouse and distribution facilities were added in 1998 which enabled Müller to make speedier delivery of its products to retailers' chiller cabinets.

Appendix C14.2

Product innovation by market segment

An up-to-date list of all Müller products can be found on their website : www.muller.co.uk. The dedicated kids site can be found at: www.yogz.com (see Appendix C14.3).

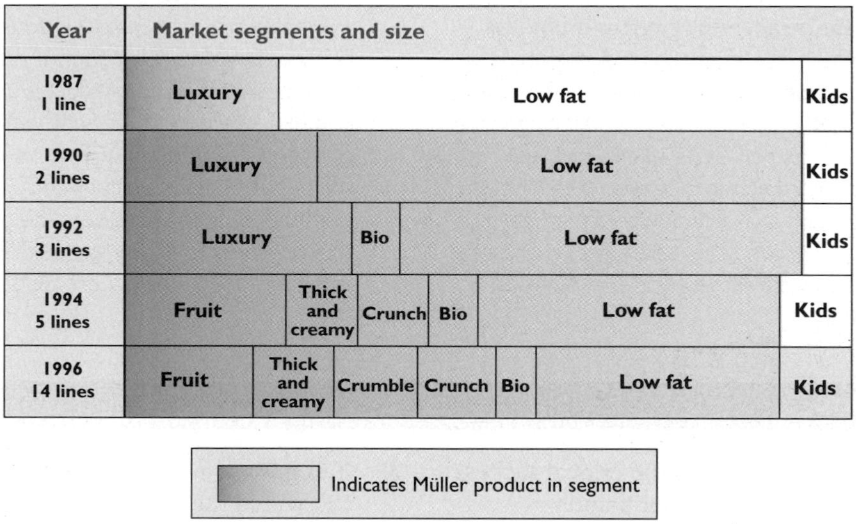

Year	Market segments and size						
1987 1 line	Luxury		Low fat				Kids
1990 2 lines	Luxury		Low fat				Kids
1992 3 lines	Luxury		Bio	Low fat			Kids
1994 5 lines	Fruit	Thick and creamy	Crunch	Bio	Low fat		Kids
1996 14 lines	Fruit	Thick and creamy	Crumble	Crunch	Bio	Low fat	Kids

Indicates Müller product in segment

Figure C14.3 Product innovation by market segment

Appendix C14.3

Müller websites

http://www.muller.co.uk/

http://www.yogz.com/

Appendix C14.4

Müller luxury ice-cream advertisement

This case was prepared by Julie Verity, Lecturer in Strategy, and Simon Knox, Professor of Brand Marketing, Cranfield University, School of Management, as a basis for class discussion rather than to illustrate effective or ineffective handling of an administrative situation. Copyright 1999 © Cranfield School of Management. All rights reserved.

CHAPTER NINE

Developing New Products

'I met R&D people who never left the lab ... and who were so snobbish about the salesforce that they wouldn't know a customer if they tripped over one. I saw financial controllers whose projections sounded exciting but who didn't have a clue about how to make a company grow with new products'

DON FREY   *Learning the Ropes: My Life as a Product Champion*

Learning Objectives *This chapter explains:*

1 The different types of new products that can be launched

2 How to create and nurture an innovation culture

3 The organizational options applying to new product development

4 Methods of reducing time to market

5 How marketing and R&D staff can work effectively together

6 The stages in the new product development process

7 How to stimulate the corporate imagination

8 The six key principles of managing product teams

9 The diffusion of innovation categories and their marketing implications

10 The key ingredients in commercializing technology quickly and effectively

The life-blood of corporate success is bringing new products to the marketplace. Changing customer tastes, technological advances and competitive pressures mean that companies cannot afford to rely on past product success. Instead they have to develop new product development programmes and nurture an innovation climate to lay the foundation for new product success. The 3M company, for example, place a heavy reliance on new product introduction. Each of its divisions is expected to achieve a quarter of its revenue from products that have been on the market for less than six years.

The reality of new product development is that it is a risky activity: most new products fail. But as we shall see, new product development should not be judged in terms of the percentage of failures. To do so could stifle the innovation spirit. The acid test is the number of successes. Failure has to be tolerated; it is endemic in the whole process of developing new products.

To fully understand new product development we need to distinguish between invention and innovation. *Invention* is the discovery of new ideas and methods. *Innovation* occurs when an invention is commercialized by bringing it to market. Not all countries that are good at invention have the capability to innovate successfully. For example, the UK has an excellent record of invention. Among major UK inventions and discoveries are the steam engine, the steamboat, the locomotive, the steam turbine, the electric heater, the hydraulic press, cement, the telegraph, the stethoscope, rubber tyres, the bicycle, television, the computer, the radio valve, radar, celluloid, the Hovercraft and the jet engine. In terms of innovation, however, the British fall far short of the Japanese, who have the ability to successfully market products by constantly seeking to improve and develop, a process called Kaisan.[1] The classic example is the Sony Walkman, which was not an invention in the sense that it was fundamentally new; rather its success (over 75 million have been sold worldwide) was based on the innovation marketing of existing technologies.

Scandinavian countries have many businesses built on a local invention. For example, Tetra Pak was founded by a person who conceived of 'pouring milk into a paper bag'. Lego bricks have revolutionized toys and Gambro invented a machine that can take the place of kidneys.[2] In all these cases, the key was not just the invention but the capability to innovate by bringing the product successfully to market.[2]

A key point to remember is that the focus of innovation should be providing new solutions which better meet customer needs. Innovative solutions often do not require major break-throughs in technology. For example, Marks and Spencer leapfrogged the competition in men's suits by being the first to sell jackets and trousers separately so that customers could get a better fit. Direct Line became the leader in car insurance by removing the need for brokers through its tele-marketing operation. Body Shop's success was based upon the modern woman's concern for the environment, and Dell became the most profitable computer company by becoming the first to market computers directly to its customers.[3]

In this chapter we shall ask the question 'What is a new product?' and we shall examine three key issues in new product development, namely organization, developing an innovation culture, and the new product development process. Then we shall examine the strategies involved in product replacement, the most common form of new product development. Finally, we shall look at the consumer adoption process, which is how people learn about new products, try them, and adopt or reject them. Throughout this chapter reference will be made to research that highlights the success factors in new product development.

What is a new product?

Some new products are so fundamentally different from products that already exist that they reshape markets and competition. For example, the pocket calculator created a new market and make obsolete the slide-rule. At the other extreme a shampoo which is different from existing products only by means of its brand name, fragrance, packaging and colour is also a new product. In fact four brand categories of new product exist.[4]

1 *Product replacements*: these account for about 45 per cent of all new product launches and include revisions and improvements to existing products (e.g. the Ford Mondeo replacing the Sierra),

repositioning (existing products such as Lucozade being targeted at new market segments) and cost reductions (existing products being reformulated or redesigned to cost less to produce).

2   *Additions to existing lines*: these account for about 25 per cent of new product launches and take the form of new products that add to a company's existing product lines. This produces greater product depth. An example is the launch by Weetabix of a brand extension, Fruitibix, to compete with the numerous nut-fruit-cereal product combinations that have been gaining market share. In the Netherlands, Mona introduced a breakfast drink called 'Goedemorgan' (Good Morning) to defend its marketing position against the successful introduction of Honig's 'Wake Up!' Additions can have more offensive objectives as was the case when Mentadent added a mouthwash to their toothpaste line, which moved the brand into a new product category to expand overall sales of the brand.[5]

3   *New product lines*: these total around 20 per cent of new product launches, and represent a move into a new market. For example, in Europe Mars has launched a number of ice cream brands which is a new product line for this company. This strategy widens a company's product mix.

4   *New-to-the-world products*: these total around 10 per cent of new product launches, and create entirely new markets. For example, the fax machine, the video recorder and camcorder have created new markets because of the highly valued customer benefits they provide.

Clearly the degree of risk and reward varies according to new product category. New-to-the-world products normally carry the highest risk since it is often very difficult to predict consumer reaction. Often market research will be unreliable in predicting demand as people do not really understand the full benefits of the product until it is on the market and they get the chance to experience them. Furthermore, it may take time for the products to be accepted. For example, the Sony Walkman was initially rejected by marketing research since the concept of being seen in a public place wearing ear-phones was alien to most people. After launch, however, this behaviour was gradually accepted by younger-aged groups who valued the benefit of listening to music when on a train, bus, walking down the street, etc. At the other extreme, adding a brand variation to an existing product line lacks significant risk but is also unlikely to proffer significant returns.

Effective new product development is based upon creating and nurturing an innovative culture, organizing effectively for new product development, and managing the new product development process. We shall now examine these three issues.

Creating and nurturing an innovative culture

The foundation for successful new product development is the creation of a corporate culture that promotes and rewards innovation. Figure 9.1 shows the kinds of attitudes and actions that can foster an innovation culture. People in organizations observe those actions that are likely to lead to success and punishment. The surest way to kill innovative spirit is to conspicuously punish those people who are prepared to create and champion new product ideas through to communication when things go wrong, and to reward those people who are content to manage the status quo. Such actions will breed the attitude: 'Why should I take the risk of failing when by carrying on as before I will probably be rewarded?' Research has shown that companies that have supportive opportunities to rewards and risk, and have a tolerant attitude towards failure, are more likely to innovate successfully.[6] This was recognized as early as 1941 in 3M when the former president William McKnight said: 'Management that is destructively critical when mistakes are made kills initiative, and it is essential that we have people with initiative if we are able to continue to grow'.[7]

An innovation culture can also be nurtured by senior management visibly supporting new product development in general, and high profile projects in particular.[8] British Rail's attempt to develop the ill-fated Advanced Passenger Train, which involved new technology, was hampered by the lack of this kind of support. Consequently individual managers took a subjective view on whether they were for or against the project. Beside sending clear messages about the role and importance of new product development, senior management should reinforce their words by allowing time off from their usual duties to people who wish to develop their own ideas, make available funds and resources for projects and make themselves accessible when difficult decisions need to be taken.[9]

A company which displays its commitment to innovation is 3M. It invests around 7 per cent of its global sales of around £10 billion in research and development and places a high value on staff input. This is formalized by allowing staff to spend 15 per cent of their work time on their own projects. By motivating staff to dedicate time to new product development, 3M generates 30 per cent of sales from products that are less than four years old.[10]

Finally, management at all levels should resist the temptation of automatic 'nay saying'. Whenever a new idea is suggested the tendency of the listener is to think of the negatives. For example, suppose you were listening to the first-ever proposal that someone at Marks and Spencer made concerning a move into food retailing. Your response might have been: 'We know nothing about that business', 'The supermarkets have got the economies of scale', 'If we succeed they will undercut us with price' and 'Our customers associate us with clothing; it could undermine our core business'. All of these perfectly natural responses serve only to demotivate the proposer. The correct response is to resist expressing such doubts. Instead encourage the proposer to take the idea further, to research and develop it. There will come a time to scrutinize the proposal but only after the proposer has received an initial encouraging response. Stifling new ideas at conception serves only to demotivate the proposer from trying again.

Marketing in Action 9.1 describes how Unilever is attempting to change its innovative culture through organizational change.

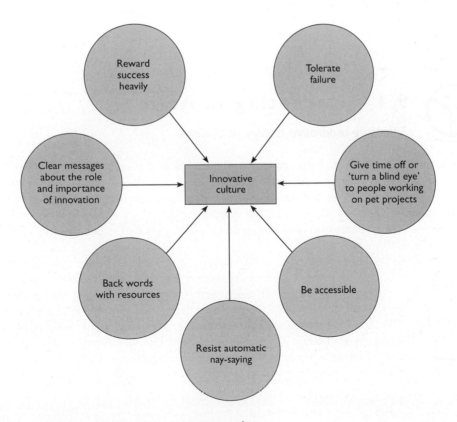

Figure 9.1 Creating and nurturing an innovative culture

Organizing effectively for new product development

The second building block of successful innovation is an appropriate organization structure. Most companies use one or a combination of the following methods: project teams, product and brand managers, and new product departments and new product committees.

Project teams

Project teams involve the bringing together of staff from such areas as R&D, engineering, manufacturing, finance and market to work on a new product development project. Specialized skills are combined to form an effective team to develop the new product concept. This organization form is in line with Kanter's belief that to compete in today's global marketplace, companies must move from rigid functional organizational structures to highly integrated ones.[11] People are assigned to the venture team as a major undertaking and the team is linked directly to top management to avoid having to communicate and get approval from several layers of management before progressing a course of action. This form of organization was used by IBM to successfully develop their first personal computer.

Such teams are sometimes called *skunkworks* when they are put together in a location physically separate from other employees to work on a project free from bureaucratic intrusion. The team is headed by a production champion (perhaps the person who first conceived of the idea) who coordinates activities and communicates with senior management. Members of the venture team may continue to manage the product after commercialization. This form of organization is often used in high technology companies such as Sony, Honda and 3M. Its advantages include the fostering of a group identity and common purpose, fast decision-making, and the lowering of bureaucratic barriers.

An organizational change that has reduced

9.1   Marketing in Action

Releasing Innovative Energy at Unilever

Unilever, the Anglo–Dutch multinational is changing. Shaken by the embarrassment caused by the withdrawal of Persil Power (also known as Omo Power or Skip Power) shortly after launch amid claims that it damaged clothes, and conscious of its sluggish profit growth, it is turning to innovation in products and marketing to revitalize the company. Much of its energy will be focused on emerging markets. Joint chairman Niall FitzGerald believes that half of its business may come from such markets in 10 years' time.

This focus on new markets has had a major effect on research and development. Previously, a small number of big development centres created products for mature markets (e.g. washing powders and deodorants) some of which were then marketed in emerging markets. Recently, however, a network of more than 50 R&D centres have been set up around the world to cater for regional needs. The Latin American region, for example, is now producing high levels of innovation and some new products are flowing into mature markets. Within six months of Unilever Thailand having a success with Organics shampoos the range was in production in Europe. By decentralizing its centres for innovation Unilever is releasing energy to fuel its drive for new product success.

Based on: Oram (1996);[12] Brierley (1997)[13]

product development cycle time is the bringing together of design and manufacturing engineers to work as a team. Traditionally, design engineers would work on product design and then the blueprint would be passed on to production engineers. By working together each group can understand the problems of the other and effectively reduce the time it takes to develop a new product. The process—*simultaneous engineering*—was pioneered in Japan but is being adopted by European companies. For example, Ford of Europe bring together design and production engineers, purchasing engineers, finance and quality control specialists and support staff to work as teams to develop future Ford cars in long-term collaboration with component suppliers.[14] Fast-moving consumer goods companies also recognize the need to cut time to market. Procter and Gamble have announced that they are reducing new product development times from four years to eighteen months. Once

more the old linear path of development is rejected in favour of project teams consisting of brand and marketing managers, external design, advertising and research agency staff to develop simultaneously the brand and launch strategies.[15] The use of computer-aided technology is also helping this process as e-Marketing 9.1 demonstrates.

Product and brand managers

Product and brand management entails the assignment of product managers to product lines (or groups of brands within a product line) and/or brand managers to individual brands. These managers are then responsible for their success and have the task of coordinating functional areas (e.g. production, sales, advertising and marketing research). They are also often responsible for new product development including the creation of

9.1   e-Marketing
On-Line Product Development

The modern computer has made an immeasurable impact on accelerating time-to-market. Designers can now use computer-aided-design (CAD) systems to develop and evaluate virtual reality prototypes. By linking these systems to computer-aided-manufacturing (CAM) systems, engineers can often assess the feasibility of manufacturing a new product idea prior to construction of a new product line. Furthermore, if the manufacturer is willing to overcome reservations about project confidentiality, the firm can provide suppliers with real time data links, thereby permitting these latter organizations to remain totally informed about all the new product projects as they progress from idea through to manufacture of early prototypes.

Boeing Corporation, for example, adopted a philosophy of linking customers and suppliers into their internal data systems to optimize the development of their next generation of wide-body jet—the 777. The company used a three-dimensional CAD system to design the aircraft and shared the output from the system with their subcontractors. Customers such as British Airways and United Airlines also participated in the on-line design process by being permitted to engage in debates over the implications of alternative cabin layouts suited to their specific operating needs. During prototype construction, subcontractors located anywhere in the world could gain access to the Boeing CAM system to obtain project progress up-dates and/or to gain immediate real-time approval for specification changes when experience of actual manufacturing processes revealed a need to alter component specifications.

Based on: Chaston (1999)[16]

new product ideas, improving existing products and brand extensions. They may be supported by a team of assistant brand managers and a dedicated marketing researcher. In some companies a new product development manager may help product and brand managers in the task of generating and testing new product concepts. This form of organization is common in the grocery, toiletries and drinks industries.

New product departments and committees

The review of new product projects is normally in the hands of high-ranking functional managers who listen to progress reports and decide whether further funds should be assigned to the project. They also may be charged with deciding new product strategies and priorities. No matter whether the underlying structure is venture team, product and brand management or new product department, a new products committee often oversees the process and services to give projects a high corporate profile through the stature of its membership.

Importance of teamwork

Whichever method (or combination of methods) is used, effective cross-functional teamwork is crucial for success.[17] In particular, as the quotation by Frey at the beginning of this chapter implies, there has to be effective communication and teamwork between R&D and marketing.[18] Although all functional relationships are important during new product development, the cultural difference between R&D and marketing are potentially the most harmful and difficult to resolve. The challenge is to prevent technical people developing only things that interest them professionally, and to get them to understand the realities of the marketplace.

Role of marketing directors

A study of Gupta and Wileman asked marketing directors of technology-based companies what they believed they could do to improve their relationship with R&D and achieve greater integration of effort.[19] There were six major suggestions made by the marketing directors.

Encourage teamwork   marketing should work with R&D to establish clear, mutually agreed project priorities to reduce the chance of pet projects. Marketing, R&D and senior management should hold regular joint project review meetings.

Improve the provision of marketing information to R&D   one of the major causes of R&D rejecting input from marketing was the lack of quality and timely information. Many marketing directors admitted that they could do a better job of providing such information to R&D. They also believed that the use of information would be enhanced if R&D personnel were made part of the marketing research team so that the questions on their minds could be incorporated into studies. They also felt that such a move would improve the credibility and trust between marketing and R&D.

Take R&D people out of the lab   marketing should encourage R&D to be more customer aware by inviting them to attend trade shows, take part in customer visits and prepare customer materials.

Develop informal relationships with R&D   they noted that there were often important personality and value differences between the two groups that can cause conflict as well as being a stimulus to creativity. More effort could be made to break down these barriers by greater socializing, going to lunch together, and sitting with each other at seminars and presentations.

Learn about technology   the marketing directors believed that improving their *technological savvy* would help them communicate more effectively with R&D people, understand various product design trade-offs and comprehend the capabilities and limits of technology to create competitive advantages and provide solutions to customer problems.

Formalize the product development process   they noted that marketing people were often preoccupied with present products to the neglect of new products, and that the new product development process was far too unstructured. They advocated a more formal process including formal new project initiation, status reports and review procedures, and a formal requirement that involvement in the process was an important part of marketing personnel's jobs.

Role of senior management

The study also focused on marketing directors' opinions of what senior management could do to help improve the marketing/R&D relationship. We have already noted when discussing how to create an innovative culture the crucial role that senior management play in creating the conditions for a thriving new product programme. Marketing directors mentioned six major ways in which senior management could play a part in fostering better relations.

Make organizational design changes   senior management should locate marketing and R&D near to each other to encourage communication and the development of informal relationships. They should clarify the roles of marketing and R&D in developing new products and reduce the number of approvals required for small changes in a project which would give both R&D and marketing greater authority and responsibility.

Show a personal interest in new product development   organizational design changes should be backed up by more overt commitment and interest in innovation through early involvement in the product development process, attending product planning and review meetings and helping to coordinate product development plans.

Provide strategic directions   many marketing directors felt that senior management could provide more strategic vision regarding new product/market priorities. They also needed to be more long term with their strategic thinking.

Encourage teamwork   senior management should encourage or even demand teamwork between marketing and R&D. Specifically they should require joint R&D/marketing discussions, joint planning and budgeting, joint marketing research and joint reporting to them.

Increase resources   some marketing directors pointed to the need to increase resources to foster product development activities. The alternative

was to reduce the number of projects. Resources should also be provided for seminars, workshops and training programmes for R&D and marketing people. The objective of these programmes would be to develop a better understanding of the roles, constraints and pressures of each group.

Understand marketing's importance   marketing directors complained of senior management's lack of understanding of marketing's role in new product development and the value of marketing in general. They felt that senior management should insist that marketing becomes involved with R&D in product development much earlier in the process so that the needs of customers are more prominent.

This research has provided valuable insights into how companies should manage the marketing/ R&D relationship. It is important that companies organize themselves effectively since cross-functional teamwork and communication has proven to be a significant predictor of successful innovation in a number of studies.[20]

Managing the new product development process

There are three inescapable facts about *new product development*: it is expensive, risky, and time consuming. For example, Gillette spent an excess of £100 million over more than ten years developing its Sensor razor brand. The new product concept was to develop a non-disposable shaver that would use new technology to produce a shaver that would follow the contours of a man's face giving an excellent shave (through two spring-mounted platinum-hardened chromium blades) with fewer cuts. This made commercial sense since shaving *systems* are more profitable than disposable razors and allow more opportunity for creating a differential advantage. Had the brand failed, Gillette's position in the shaving market could have been irreparably damaged.

Managing the process of new product development is an important factor in reducing cost, time and risk. Studies have shown that having a formal process with review points, clear new product goals and a strong marketing orientation underlying the process lead to greater success whether the product be a physical good or a service.[21]

An eight-step new product development process to provide these characteristics is shown in Fig. 9.2 and consists of setting new product strategy, idea generation, screening, concept testing, business analysis, product development, market testing, and commercialization. Although the reality of new product development may resemble organizational chaos, the discipline imposed by the activities carried out at each stage leads to a greater likelihood of developing a product that not only works, but also confers customer benefits. We should note, however, that new products pass through each stage at varying speeds: some may dwell at a stage for a long period while others may pass through very quickly.[22]

New product strategy

As we have already seen, marketing directors value strategic guidance from senior management about their vision and priorities for new product development. By providing clear guidelines about which product/markets the company is interested in serving, senior management can provide a focus for the areas in which idea generation should take place. Also by outlining their objectives (e.g. market share gain, profitability, technological leadership) for new products they can provide indicators for the screening criteria that should be used to evaluate those ideas. An example of a company with a clearly developed new product strategy is Mars, which developed ice cream products capitalizing on the brand equity of their confectionery brand names such as Twix, Mars and Milky Way.

Idea generation

One of the benefits of developing an innovative corporate culture is that it kindles the imagination. The objective is to motivate the search for ideas so that salespeople, engineers, top management, marketers and other employees are alert to new opportunities. Interestingly, questioning Nobel Prize Winners about the time and circumstances when they had the important germ of an idea that led to great scientific discovery

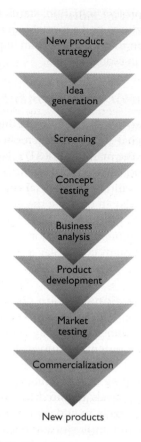

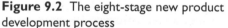

Figure 9.2 The eight-stage new product development process

revealed that it can occur at the most unexpected time; just before going to sleep, upon wakening in the morning, and at church were some of the occasions mentioned. The common factor seems to be a period of quite contemplation uninterrupted by the bustle of everyday life and work.

Successful new product ideas are not necessarily based on technological innovation. Often they are based on novel applications of existing technology (e.g. velcro poppers on disposable nappies) or new visions of markets (e.g. Levi Strauss's vision of repositioning jeans which originally were used as working clothes into fashion statements through their 501 brand).

The sources of *new product ideas* can be internal to the company: scientists, engineers, marketers, salespeople and designers, for example. Some companies use *brainstorming* as a technique to stimulate the creation of ideas and use financial incentives to persuade people to put forward ideas they have had. The 3M Post-It adhesive-backed notepaper was a successful product that was thought of by an employee who initially saw the product as a means of preventing paper falling from his hymn book as he marked the hymns that were being sung. Because of the innovative culture within 3M, he bothered to think of commercial applications and acted as a *product champion* within the company to see the project through a commercialization and global success. In a survey of Dutch industrial goods, over 60 per cent of companies claimed to use brainstorming to generate new product ideas.[23]

Hamel and Prahalad argue that global competitive battles will be won by those companies who have the *corporate imagination* to build and dominate fundamentally new markets.[24] Introducing such products as speech-activated appliances, artificial bones, and automatic language translators would effectively create new and largely uncontested competitive space.

Often fundamentally new product/markets are created by small businesses that are willing to invent new business models or radically redesign existing models. e-Marketing 9.2 discusses these issues within the context of information technology and provides some ways for large companies to break out of the tendency towards incremental innovations.

Sources of new product ideas can also be external to the company. Examining competitors' products may provide clues to product improvements. Competitors' new product plans can be gleaned by training the salesforce to ask distributors about new activities. Distributors can also be a source of new product ideas directly since they deal with customers, and have an interest in selling improved products.

A major source of good ideas is customers themselves. Their needs may not be satisfied with existing products and they may be genuinely interested in providing ideas that lead to product improvement. In organizational markets keeping in close contact with customers who are innovators and market leaders in their own marketplaces are likely to be a fruitful source of new product ideas.[25] These *lead customers* are likely to recognize required improvements ahead of other customers as they have advanced needs and are likely to face problems before other product users. Marketing research can play a role in

providing feedback when the product line is familiar to customers. For example, the original idea for Hewlett-Packard's successful launch of their Desk-Jet printer came from marketing research which revealed that personal computer users would value a relatively slow-speed printer that approached the quality of a laser printer but sold at less than half the price.[26] Marketing research also uncovered a need for a flexible ceiling covering that prevented cracks in the ceiling reappearing after they had been painted. This new product idea was developed into Polycell's Evenceil, which was a rapid success. However, for radically new products customers may be unable to articulate their requirements and so conventional marketing research may be ineffective as a source of ideas. In this situation, as can be seen in E-Marketing 9.2, companies need to be proactive in their search for new markets rather than relying on customer suggestions.[27]

New product development agencies have been set up to help companies source and test new product ideas. For example, McVities, the biscuit manufacturer, approached a UK agency, Redwood Associates, with the brief of identifying a new product concept that when commercialized would use an idle production line, which dictated biscuit size, shape and ingredients. Redwoods suggested a caramel-flavoured coating for the biscuit and after test marketing the new brand —'Gold'—it was successfully launched in 1988.[28]

Screening

Having developed new product ideas they need to be screened to evaluate their commercial worth. Some companies use formal checklists to help them judge whether the product idea should be rejected or accepted for further evaluation. This ensures that no important criterion is overlooked. Criteria may be used which measure the attractiveness of the market for the proposed product, the fit between the product and company objectives and the capability of the company to produce and market the product. Texas Instruments focused on financial and market-based criteria when *screening* new semiconductor products. To pass their screen a new product idea had to have the potential to sustain a 15 per cent compound sales growth rate, give

9.2 e-Marketing

Creating Radical Innovation

One of the power houses of new ideas in the world's e-commerce industry is the huge number of new firms based in Silicon Valley, California. These 'minnows of business' are frequently challenging the long-established giants in market sectors as diverse as retailing, insurance, book selling and the broadcast media. The reason for their success is that unlike large corporations, who tend to focus on incremental ideas built upon an existing brand franchise (e.g. Diet Coke from Coca-Cola; Persil detergent tablets from Unilever), these small upstarts in Silicon Valley are often prepared to invent completely new business models (e.g. downloading music from the Internet instead of visiting a retail store) or radically redesign existing models (e.g. Dell selling customized computers via a website).

Silicon Valley's success is due to the fact that large, established corporations usually adopt a disciplined, top-down approach to approving ideas and realizing funds to support R&D. This approach clearly ensures top management never loses control over its employees. But at the same time, this attitude communicates a corporate desire for incremental business performance improvement; not a willingness to risk moving the organization into a totally new, radically different range of business activities. Over time, however, even Silicon Valley entrepreneurs can develop conservative habits orientated towards building upon existing expertise and avoiding major risks.

An example is Sun Microsystems who founded the workstation sector of the computer industry. Having achieved market leadership offering workstations which sold for up to $40 000, one of the founders, Andy Bechtolschiem, suggested using a radical new approach to build a $10 000 product. Sun was not willing to fund the idea because it did not follow their favoured strategy of incremental improvements to existing products. Andy left the company and used his own money to fund the prototype. When Sun saw the elegance of his solution, they invited him back to the firm and together launched the extremely successful SPARC workstation.

Avoiding an incremental approach to new product development involves a sharpening of the corporate imagination to become more alive to new market opportunities. Four factors can help this development.

Escaping the tyranny of served markets Looking outside markets that are currently served can be assisted by defining core competencies and looking at product/markets that lie between existing business units. For example, Motorola's core competencies in wireless technology led them to look beyond current product/markets (e.g. mobile phones) towards global positioning satellite receivers. Looking for white space between business units led Kodak to envisage a market for storing and viewing photographs.

Searching for innovative product concepts This can be aided by viewing markets as a set of customer needs and product functionalities. This has led to adding an important function to an existing product (e.g. Yamaha's electronic piano), creating a new way to deliver an existing function (e.g. electronic notepad), or creating a new functionality (e.g. fax machine).

Weakening traditional price-performance assumptions Traditional price-performance assumptions should be questioned. For example, it was Sony and JVC who questioned the price tag of £25 000 on early video recorders. They gave their engineers the freedom and the technology to design a video recorder that cost less than £500.

Leading customers A problem with developing truly innovative products is that customers rarely ask for them. Successful innovating companies lead customers by imagining unarticulated needs rather than simply following them. They gain insights into incipient needs by talking in-depth to and observing closely a market's most sophisticated and demanding customers. For example, Yamaha set up a facility in London where Europe's most talented musicians could experiment with state-of-the-art musical hardware. The objective was not only to understand the customer but also to convey to the customer what might be possible technologically.

Based on: Hamel (1999);[29] Hamel and Prahaled (1991)[30]

25 per cent return on assets, and be of a unique design that lowered costs or gave a performance advantage. Other companies may use a less systematic approach, preferring more flexible open discussion among members of the new product development committee to gauge likely success.

Concept testing

Once the product idea has been accepted as worthy for further investigation, it can be framed into a specific concept for testing with potential customers. In many instances the basic product idea will be expanded into several product concepts, each of which can be compared by testing with target customers. For example, a study into the acceptability of a new service—a proposed audit of software development procedures that would lead to the award of a quality assurance certificate—was expressed in eight service concepts depending on which parts of the development procedure would be audited (e.g. understanding customer needs, documentation, bench-marking, etc.). Each concept was evaluated by potential buyers of the software to gauge which were the most important aspects of software development that should be audited.[31] *Concept testing* thus allows the views of customers to enter the new product development process at an early stage.

Group discussion can also be used to develop and test product concepts. For example, a major financial services company decided that they should launch an interest-bearing transaction account (product idea) because their major competition had done so.[32] Group discussions were carried out to develop the product idea into a specific product concept (a chequebook feature was rejected in favour of a cash card) with a defined target market (the under 25s). This concept was then developed further using group discussions to refine the product features (a telephone banking service was added) and to select the lifestyle image that should be used to position the new product.

The concept may be described verbally or pictorially so that the major features are understood. Potential customers can then state whether they perceive any benefits accruing from the features. A questionnaire is used to ascertain such queries as the extent of liking/disliking what is liked/disliked, the kind of person/organization that might buy the product, how/where/when/how often would the product be used, price acceptability, and how likely they would be to buy the product.

Often the last question (buying intentions) is a key factor in judging whether any of the concepts are worth pursuing further. In the grocery and toiletries industries, for example, companies (and their marketing research agencies) often use *action standards* (e.g. more than 70 per cent of respondents must say they intend to buy) based on past experience to judge new product concepts. Concept testing allows a relatively inexpensive judgement to be made by customers before embarking on a costly product development programme. Although not foolproof, obvious non-starters can be eliminated early on in the process.

Business analysis

Based upon the results of the concept test and considerable managerial judgement, estimates of sales, costs and profits will be made. This is the **business analysis** stage. In order to produce sensible figures a *marketing analysis* will need to be undertaken. This will identify the target market, its size, and projected product acceptance over a number of years. Consideration will be given to various prices and the implications for sales revenue (and profits) discussed. By setting a tentative price this analysis will provide sales revenue estimates.

Costs will also need to be estimated. If the new product is similar to existing products (e.g. a brand extension) is should be fairly easy to produce accurate cost estimates. For radical product concepts costings may be nothing more than informal guesstimates.

Break-even analysis, where the quantity needed to be sold to cover costs is calculated, may be used to establish whether the project is financially feasible. *Sensitivity analysis* in which variations from given assumptions about price, cost and customer acceptance, for example, are checked to see how they impact on sales revenue and profits, can also prove useful at this stage. Optimistic, most likely and pessimistic scenarios can be drawn up to estimate the degree of risk attached to the project.

If the product concept appears commercially feasible this process will result in marketing and product development budgets being established based on what appears to be necessary to gain customer awareness and trial, and the work required to turn the concept into a marketable product.

Product development

At this stage the new product concept is developed into a physical product. As we have seen, the trend is to move from a situation where this is the sole responsibility of the R&D and/or engineering department. Multi-disciplinary project teams are established with the task of bringing the product to the marketplace. A study by Wheelwright and Clark lays out six key principles for the effective management of such teams:[33]

1 *Mission*: senior management must agree to clear mission through a project charter which lays out broad objectives.

2 *Organization*: appointment of a heavyweight project leader and a core team consisting of one member from each primary function in the company. Core members should not occupy a similar position on another team.

3 *Project plan*: creation by the project leader and core team of a contract book which includes a work plan, resource requirements, and objectives against which it is willing to be evaluated.

4 *Project leadership*: heavyweight leaders not only lead, manage and evaluate other members of the core team, but also act as product champion. They spend time talking to project contributors inside and outside the company, as well as customers and distributors so that the team keeps in touch with the market.

5 *Responsibilities*: all core members share responsibility for the overall success of the project as well as their own functional responsibilities.

6 *Executive sponsorship*: an executive sponsor in senior management is required to act as a channel for communication with top management and to act as coach and mentor for the project and its leader.

The aim is to integrate the skills of designers, engineers, production, finance and marketing specialists so that product development is quicker, less costly and results in a high quality product that delights customers. For example the practice of simultaneous engineering means that designers and production engineers work together rather than passing the project from one development to another once the first department's work is finished. Costs are controlled by a method called target costing. Target costs are worked out on the basis of target prices in the marketplace, and given as engineering/design and production targets.

Cutting time to market by reducing the length of the product development stage is a key marketing factor in many industries. Allied to simultaneous engineering, companies are using *computer-aided design and manufacturing equipment and software (Cadcam)* to cut time and improve quality. In particular, the use of 3D solid modelling, which completely defines an object in three dimensions on a computer screen and has the ability to compute masses, is very effective in shortening the product development stage.[34]

There are two reasons why product development is being accelerated. First, markets such as personal computers, video cameras and cars change so fast that to be slow means running the risk of being out of date before the product is launched. Second, cutting time to market can lead to competitive advantage. This may be short-lived but is still valuable while it lasts. For example, Rolls-Royce gained an 18-month window of opportunity by cutting lead times on its successful Trent 800 aero-engine.[35]

Marketing has an important role to play in the product development stage. R&D and engineering may focus on the functional aspects of the product whereas seemingly trivial factors may have an important bearing on customer choice. For example, the foam which appears when washing up liquid is added to water has no functional value: a washing-up liquid could be produced which cleans just as effectively but does not produce the bubbles. However, the customer sees the foam as a visual cue indicating the power of the washing-up liquid. Therefore, to market a brand which did not produce them would be suicidal. Marketing needs to keep the project team aware of such psychological factors when developing the new product. They need to understand and communicate the important attributes that customers are looking for in the product.

In the grocery market, marketing will usually brief R&D staff on the product concept, and the latter will be charged with the job of turning the concept into reality. For example, Yoplait, the French market leader in fruit yoghurts, found by marketing research that a yoghurt concept based upon the following attributes could be a winner.

✦ Top of the range dessert.

✦ Position on a health–leisure scale at the far end of the pleasure range: the ultimate taste sensation.

✦ A fruit yoghurt that is extremely thick and creamy.

This was the brief given to the Yoplait research and development team who had the task of coming up with recipes for the new yoghurt and the best way of manufacturing it. Their job was to experiment with different cream/fruit combinations to produce the right product—one that matched the product concept—and to do it quickly. Time to market was crucial in this fast-moving industry. To help them, Yoplait employed a panel of expert tasters to try out the new recipes and evaluate them in terms of texture, sweetness, acidity, colour, smell, consistency and size of the fruit.

Product testing focuses on the functional aspects of the product and on consumer acceptance. Functional tests are carried out in the laboratory and out in the field to check such aspects as safety, performance, and shelf-life. For example, a car's braking system must be efficient, a jet engine must be capable of generating a certain level of thrust, and a food package must be capable of keeping its contents fresh.

Besides conforming to these basic functional standards, products need to be tested with consumers to check acceptability in use. For consumer goods this often takes the form of in-house product placement. *Paired companion tests* are used when the new product is used alongside a rival so that respondents have a bench-mark against which to judge the new offerings. Alternatively two (or more) new product variants may be tested alongside one another. A questionnaire is administered at the end of the test which gathers overall preference information as well as comparisons on specific attributes. For example, two soups might be compared on taste, colour, smell and richness. In *monadic placement tests* only the new product is given to users for trial. Although no specific rival is used in the test, in practice, users may make comparisons with previously bought products, market leaders, or competitive products that are quickly making an impact on the market. For example, Qualcast placed its Concorde electric cylinder lawn-mower in a monadic test with potential buyers, and asked questions about its cutting ability, ease of use, reliability, and the user's intention to buy. Users indicated that the lawn-mower performed efficiently but the intention to buy question revealed that very few would buy the machine. When asked why, most said that they preferred the more trendy Flymo hover-mower. This marketing research information led Qualcast to promote the Concorde with the hard-hitting 'It's A Lot Less Bovver than a Hover' advertising campaign. Clearly product placement tests can have communication implications also.

Another way of providing customer input into development is through *product clinics*. For example, prototype cars and trucks are regularly researched by inviting prospective drivers to such clinics where they can sit in the vehicle, comment on its design, comfort and proposed features. For example, an idea to provide a hook for a woman's handbag in the Ford Mondeo was firmly rejected when researched in this way, and the feature discarded.

Experts can also be used when product testing. For example, the former World Champion racing driver Jackie Stewart was used in the development work leading to the launch of the Ford Mondeo. Although there is a danger that expert views may be unrepresentative of the target market, it was found with the Mondeo that Stewart's opinion carried the necessary political clout to force changes in the design of the car that may not have been made without his input.

Information technology is assisting the product development process by allowing various combinations of product features to be displayed on a laptop so that customer preferences can be identified. e-Marketing 9.3 discusses how this works in practice.

In organizational markets, products may be placed with customers free of charge or at below cost to check out the performance characteristics. Parkinson contrasted the attitudes of West German machine tool manufacturers with their less successful British competitors towards product development.[36] The West German companies sought partnerships with customers and developed and tested prototypes jointly with them. British attitudes were vastly different: marketing research was seen as a way of delaying product development, and customers were rarely involved for fear that they would stop buying existing products.

Market testing

So far in the development process, potential customers have been asked if they intend to buy the product but have never been placed in the position of having to pay for it. *Market testing*

9.3 e-Marketing

The Impact of Information Technology on Product Testing

Computer Assisted Personal Interviewing has been in use for many years, enabling interviewers to key answers to questions directly into a computer. Within the area of product testing, it has allowed researchers greater flexibility than can be achieved with mock-up boards and other traditional methods. A recent innovation by Harris Research incorporates the latest technology in a multimedia software tool.

The tool is particularly useful in designing new prototypes helping researchers to measure preferences among target consumers. For example, for a new mobile phone, various combinations of size, colour, screen display, keyboard layout and special facilities can be shown to respondents via a laptop enabling them to construct their ideal product. The software also produces market share estimates based on combinations of format, prices and special features. One of the advantages of this system is that in an age when time-to-market is crucial the research can be conducted very speedily.

. The software has been used by Guinness to identify optimum packaging designs and Ericsson to analyse the impact of price changes in the market for mobile phone accessories.

Based on: McLuhan (1999)[37]

takes measurement of customer acceptance one crucial step further than product testing by forcing consumers to vote with their money. The basic idea is to launch the new product in a limited way so that consumer response in the marketplace can be assessed. There are two major methods: the simulated market test and test marketing.

The *simulated market test* can take a number of forms but the principle is to set up a realistic market situation in which a sample of consumers choose to buy goods from a range provided by the organizing company, usually a marketing research company. For example, a sample of consumers may be recruited to buy their groceries from a mobile supermarket which visits them once a week. They are provided with a magazine in which advertisements and sales promotions for the new product can appear. This method allows measurement of key success indicators such as *penetration* (the proportion of consumers who buy the new product at least once) and *repeat purchase* (the rate at which purchasers buy again) to be made. If penetration is high but repeat purchase low, buyers can be asked why they rejected the product after trial. Simulated market tests are therefore useful as a preliminary to a test marketing by spotting problems, such as in packaging and product formulation that can be rectified before test market launch. They can also be useful in eliminating new products that perform so badly compared to competition in the marketplace that test marketing is not justified.

Test marketing involves the launch of the new product in one or a few geographical areas chosen to be representative of its intended market. Towns or television areas are chosen in which the new product is sold into distribution outlets so that performance can be gauged face-to-face with rival products. Test marketing is the acid test of new product development since the product is being promoted as it would in national launch and consumers are being asked to choose it against competitor products as they would if the new product went national. It is a more realistic test than the simulated market test and therefore gives more accurate sales penetration and repeat purchasing estimates. By projecting test marketing results to the full market an assessment of the new product's likely success can be gauged.

Test marketing does have a number of potential problems. Test towns and areas may not be representative of the national market and thus sales projections may be inaccurate. Competitors may invalidate the test market by giving distributors incentives to stock their product, thereby denying the new product shelf-space. Also test markets need to be long enough to measure the repeat purchase rate for the product since this is a crucial indicator of success for many products (e.g. groceries and toiletries). This can mean a delay in national launch stretching to many months or even years. In the meantime, more aggressive competitors can launch a rival product nationally and therefore gain market pioneer advantages. A final practical problem is gaining the cooperation of distributors. In some instances supermarket chains refuse to take part in test marketing activities or charge a hefty fee for the service.

The advantages of test marketing are that the information it provides facilitates the *Go/No Go* national launch decision, and the effectiveness of the marketing mix elements—price, product formulation/packaging, promotion and distribution—can be checked for effectiveness. Sometimes a number of test areas are used with different marketing mix combinations to predict the most successful launch strategy. Its purpose therefore is to reduce the risk of a costly and embarrassing national launch mistake.

Although commonly associated with fast-moving consumer goods, service companies use test marketing to check new service offerings. Indeed when they control the supply chain, as is the case with banks and restaurants, they are in an ideal situation to do so. Companies selling to organizations can also benefit from test marketing when there products have short repeat purchase periods (e.g. adhesives and abrasives). For very expensive equipment, however, test marketing is usually impractical, although as we have seen product development with lead users is to be recommended.

On a global scale many international companies roll-out products (e.g. cars and consumer electronics) from one country to another. In so doing they are gaining some of the benefits of test marketing in that lessons learned early on can be applied to later launches.

Commercialization

In this section we shall examine four issues: a general approach to developing a commercialization strategy for a new product, specific options for product replacement strategies, success factors when commercializing technology and reacting to competitors' new product introductions.

Developing a commercialization strategy for a new product

An effective commercialization strategy relies upon marketing management making clear choices regarding the target market (where it wishes to compete), and the development of a marketing strategy that provides a differential advantage (how it wishes to compete). These two factors define the new product positioning strategy as discussed in Chapter 7.

A useful starting-point for choosing a target market is an understanding of the **diffusion of innovation process**.[38] This explains how a new product spreads throughout a market over time. Particularly important is the notion that not all people or organizations who comprise the market will be in the same state of readiness to buy the new product when it is launched. In other words, different actors in the market will have varying degrees of innovativeness, that is their willingness to try something new. Figure 9.3 shows the *diffusion of innovation* curve which categorizes people or organizations according to how soon they are willing to adopt the innovation.

The curve shows that those actors (*innovators* and *early adopters*) who were willing to buy the new product soon after launch are likely to form a minor part of the total number of actors who eventually will be willing to buy it. As the new product is accepted and approved by these customers and the decision to buy the new product therefore becomes less risky, so the bulk of the market comprising the *early and late majority* begin to try the product themselves. Finally after the product has gained full market acceptance, a group suitably described as the *laggards* adopt the product. By the time laggards have begun buying the product, innovators and early adopters have probably moved on to something new.

The diffusion of innovation categories have a crucial role to play in the choice of target market. The key is to understand the characteristics of the innovator and early adopter categories and target them at launch. Simply thinking about the kinds of people or organizations who are more likely to buy the new product early after launch may suffice. If not, marketing research can help. To stimulate the thinking process, Rogers suggests various broad characteristics for each category.[39]

Innovators these are often venturesome and like to be different; they are willing to take a chance with an untried product. In consumer

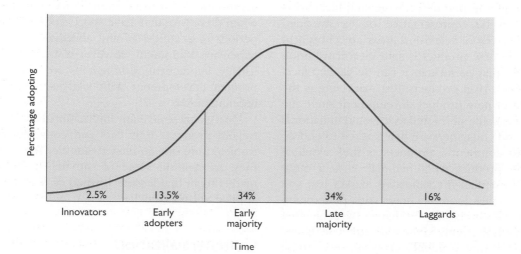

Figure 9.3 Diffusion of an innovation

markets they tend to be younger, better educated, more confident and more financially affluent, and consequently can afford to take a chance on buying something new. In organizational markets, they tend to be larger and more profitable companies if the innovation is costly and have more progressive, better educated management. They may themselves have a good track record in bringing out new products and may have been the first to adopt innovations in the past. As such they may be easy to identify.

Early adopters these are not quite so venture-some; they need the comfort of knowing someone else has taken the early risk. But they soon follow their lead. They still tend to have similar characteristics to the innovator group since they need affluence and self-confidence to buy a product that has not yet gained market acceptance. They, together with the innovators, can be seen as *opinion leaders* who strongly influence other people's views on the product. As such they have a major bearing on the success of the product. One way of looking at the early adopters is that they filter the products accepted by the innovator group and popularize them leading to acceptance by the majority of buyers in the market.[40]

Early and late majorities these form the bulk of the customers in the market. The early majority are usually deliberate and cautious in their approach to buying products. They like to see products prove themselves on the market before they are willing to part cash for them. The late majority are even more cautious, and possibly sceptical of new product. They are willing to adopt only after the majority of people or organizations have tried the products. Social pressure may be the driving force moving them to purchase.

Laggards these are tradition-bound. The innovation needs to be perceived almost as a traditional product before they consider buying it. In consumer markets they are often older and less well-educated members of the population.

These categories, then, can provide the basis of segmenting the market for an innovation product (see Chapter 7) and target market selection.[41] Note that the diffusion curve can be linked to the product life cycle which was discussed in Chapter 8. At introduction, innovators buy the product

followed by early adopters as the product enters the growth phase. Growth is fuelled by the early and late majority, and stable sales during the maturity phase may be due to repurchases of these groups. Laggards may enter the market during late maturity or even decline. Thus promotion designed to stimulate trial may need to be modified as the nature of new buyers changes over time.

The second key decision at commercialization is the choice of marketing strategy to establish a differential advantage. Understanding the requirements of customers (in particular the innovator and early adopter groups) is crucial to this process and should have taken place earlier in the new product development process. The design of the marketing mix will depend on this understanding and the rate of adoption be affected by such decisions. For example, advertising, promotion and sales efforts can generate awareness and reduce the customer's search costs, sales promotional incentives can encourage trial, and educating users in product benefits and applications have been found to speed the adoption process.[42]

As we have seen, the characteristics of customers affect the rate of adoption of an innovation and marketing's job is to identify and target these with a high willingness to adopt upon launch. Also the characteristics of the product being launched also affects the diffusion rate and has marketing strategy implications. First, its *differential advantage* compared to existing products affects the speed of adoption. The more added customer benefits a product gives to a customer the more customers will be willing to buy. The high differential advantage of a fax machine over sending telegrams (e.g. convenience) or letters (e.g. speed) meant fast adoption. Note that benefits may be offset by costs. For example, the diffusion of Europe's first HDTV set was hampered by its price of £3500.

Second, the innovation's *compatibility* with people's values, experiences, lifestyles and behaviours. The congruence between personal computers and the lifestyle of many middle-class people helped their diffusion. Conversely, the initial incongruence between the values and experiences of young people and walking in the street wearing ear-phones was a major hurdle that Sony had to face when marketing the Walkman. Promotion showing opinion leaders using the Walkman was important here. Also the fact that compact-disk players could not play vinyl records slowed their adoption initially as people were reluctant to replace their record players with equipment that would make their existing stock of records unplayable.

A third factor affecting diffusion rate is the innovation's *complexity*. Products which are difficult to understand or use may take longer to be adopted. For example, Apple launched their Macintosh computer backed by the proposition that existing computers were too complex to gain widespread adoption. By making their model more user friendly they hoped to gain fast adoption among the large segment of the population who were repelled by the complexity of using computers.

Fourth, an innovation's *divisibility* also affects its speed of diffusion. Divisibility refers to the degree to which the product can be tried on a limited basis. Inexpensive products can be tried without risk of heavy financial loss. One of the tasks of marketing is to devise launch strategies that allow low cost, risk free trial of more expensive innovations. For example, Apple devised the 'Test Drive a Mac' scheme whereby people could try out a Macintosh at a dealer before purchase.

The final product characteristic that affects the rate of diffusion of an innovation is its *communicability*. Adoption is likely to be faster if the

benefits and applications of the innovation can be readily observed or described to target customers. If product benefits are long term or difficult to quantify then diffusion may be longer. For example, Rover's attempt to produce more reliable cars took time to communicate as buyers' acceptance of this claim depended upon the long-term experience of driving their cars. In services industries, marketing innovations like providing more staff to improve the quality of service are hard to quantify in financial terms (i.e. extra revenue generated) and therefore have a low adoption rate by the management of some companies. The marketing implications are that marketing management must not assume that what is obvious to them will be clear to customers. They need to devise a communications strategy that allows potential customers to become aware of the innovation, and understand and be convinced of its benefits.

Product replacement strategies

As we found at the start of this chapter product replacement is the most common form of new product introduction. A study of the marketing strategies used to position *product replacements* in the marketplace found eight approaches based upon a combination of product change, and other marketing modifications (i.e. marketing mix and

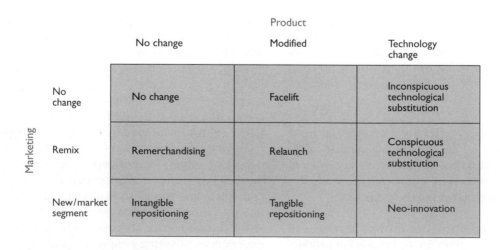

Figure 9.4 Product replacement strategies

Source: Saunders, J. and D. Jobber (1994) Strategies for product launch and deletion, in Saunders, J. (ed.) *The Marketing Initiative*, Hemel Hempstead: Prentice-Hall, 227

target market changes).[43] Figure 9.4 shows the eight replacement strategies used by companies.

Facelift minor product change with little or no change to the rest of the marketing mix or target market. Cars often undergo facelifts midway through their life cycle by undergoing minor styling alterations for example. Japanese companies constantly facelift current electronic products such as video recorders and camcorders by changing product features, a process known as *product churning*.

Inconspicuous technological substitution a major technological change with little or no alteration of the other elements of the marketing mix. The technological change is not brought to the consumer's attention. For example, brand loyalty to instant mashed potatoes was retained through major technological process and product changes (powder to granules to flakes) with little attempt to highlight these changes through advertising.

Remerchandising a modification of name, promotion, price, packaging and/or distribution while maintaining the basic product. For example, an unsuccessful men's deodorant was successfully remerchandised by repackaging, heavier advertising, a higher price and new brand name 'Brut'.

Relaunch both the product and other marketing mix elements are changed. Relaunches are common in the car industry when every four to five years a model is replaced with an upgraded version. The replacement of the Ford Sierra with the Mondeo is an example.

Conspicuous technological substitution a major technological change is accompanied by heavy promotional (and other mix changes) to stimulate awareness and trial. The replacement of the IBM PC by the IBM PS/2 is an example.

Intangible repositioning the basic product is retained but other mix elements and target customers change. Lucozade is an example of a product which kept its original formulation but was targeted at different customer segments over time.

Tangible repositioning both the product and target market change. In the UK Kendalls—a down-market women's accessories chain—was repositioned as Next, a more up-market women's clothing store.

Neo-innovation a fundamental technology change accompanied by target market and mix changes. For example, Compaq became a market leader in computers for a time by replacing its down-market inexpensive IBM PC compatible machines with up-market premium-priced computers based on the 286 chip.

Companies, therefore, face an array of replacement options with varying degrees of risk. Figure 9.4 categorizes these options and provides an aid to strategic thinking when considering how to replace products in the marketplace.

Commercializing technology

Superior commercialization of technology has, and will continue to be, a key success factor in many industries. Some companies such as Canon, Sony, and Philips already have the capability to bring sophisticated high tech products to market faster than other companies who treat the commercialization process in a less disciplined manner. Consistently beating the competition has been found to rest on four capabilities: being faster to market, supplying a wider range of markets, executing a larger number of product launches, and using a wider breadth of technologies.[44] Marketing in Action 9.2 discusses how Canon have successfully commercialized technology.

Many major market innovations appear in practice to be technologically driven: a technology seeking a market application rather than a market opportunity seeking a technology.[45] Marketing's input in such situations is to provide the insight as to how the technology may provide customer benefits within a prescribed target market. For example X-ray brain scanner was developed from a system used to X-ray metal. It was marketing insight that led to its application in medical diagnosis. As we have already discussed, traditional marketing research techniques have only a limited role to play when using technology to create new markets: people find difficulty articulating their views on subjects that are unfamiliar, and acceptance may come only over time (the diffusion of innovation). Indeed the price which the customer will be asked to pay is usually unclear during the early stage of technological development. A combination of these factors may have been responsible for the first-ever forecast for computers that predicted worldwide sales of ten units. The advertisement for Kodak opposite illustrates how the commercialization of technology can lead to a competitive advantage.

The marketing of technological innovations, therefore, calls for a blend of technology and marketing. The basic marketing question 'What potential benefits over existing products is this product likely to provide?' needs to be constantly asked during product development. Furthermore the lessons from the diffusion of innovation curve need to be remembered:

1 The innovator/early adopter segments need to be identified and targeted initially.

2 Initial sales are likely to be low: these groups are relatively small.

3 Patience is required as the diffusion of an innovation takes time as people/organizations originally resistant to it, learn of its benefits and begin to adopt it.

4 The target group and message will need to be modified over time as new categories of customer enter the market.

9.2 Marketing in Action

Commercializing Technology at Canon

An organization which continues to exploit internal competencies to vision and exploit the future is the Japanese corporation Canon. Created 60 years ago, the firm's first core competence was in the area of optics because the firm spent the first 30 years of their life making cameras. In 1962 the decision was made to enter the office equipment market. As Xerox Corporation held patents on photocopying technology and would not grant licences, Canon drew upon both existing and newly acquired competencies to develop new photocopying technology which did not infringe Xerox patents. Launched in 1970, their first product the NP-1100 had a number of entrepreneurial features including the first ever toner cartridge which removed the need for service calls.

Having become world leader in photocopying machines, the firm then applied existing and some newly acquired competencies to enter the desktop printer market. Their rationale for entering this new market was based on a simple but highly relevant vision; namely photocopiers would eventually become obsolete because, as computer costs decline, increasingly people would send information via e-mail which would be downloaded to an adjacent printer. Although Hewlett-Packard beat Canon in terms of launching the first low-cost ink-jet printer (as reflected by HP currently holding a 52 per cent share versus Canon's 22 per cent share of world markets), Canon have continued to sustain their vision concerning opportunities in electronic printing. Currently they are concentrating on two areas of opportunity. The first is in applying ink-jet technology for printing directly on to fabrics. They are now the market leaders in supplying massive printing machines to the clothing and textile industry. The second, and potentially even larger opportunity, was to create a digital camera which can be linked to a printer without the need for the intervention of a computer. Consequently consumers can now produce their own photographs without having to own a computer or buy film for their camera. This latest vision clearly links together Canon's competencies across the areas of optics, cameras, digital data transmission, print reproduction and specialist inks and undoubtedly will permit the organization to sustain their strategy of acting entrepreneurially to develop and expand their increasingly extensive line of innovative products.

Based on: Desmond (1998)[46]

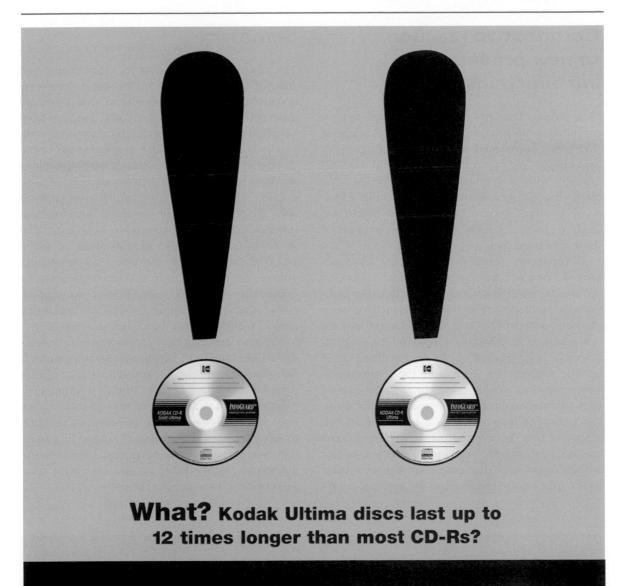

What? Kodak Ultima discs last up to 12 times longer than most CD-Rs?

CD-Rs are supposed to be durable. But some are more durable than others. Most CD-Rs are made with silver. Silver, however, can degrade – putting your data at risk. Gold is far more stable. So Kodak has developed Kodak CD-R Ultima, using a **unique silver+gold alloy**, which lasts up to 6 times longer than silver-only discs. For the most demanding users, there's professional-quality Kodak CD-R Gold Ultima, made with a layer of 100% gold for up to 12 times longer life. So if you want to keep your data safe, remember it lasts longer with Kodak.

Up to 6x longer life

Up to 12x longer life

Nothing lasts like Kodak.

Kodak

For more information call: 0870 243 0270 or visit our website at: www.kodak.com/go/cdr
© Eastman Kodak Company 2000. Kodak is a trademark of the Eastman Kodak Company.

Available from: TEMPO **Dixons** **JESSOPS** **PC WORLD** and other good stores.

Companies like Kodak invest in new technology to develop new products that possess competitive advantages

Competitive reaction to new product introductions

New product launches may be in response to new product entries by competitors. Research suggests that when confronted with a new product entry by a competitor, incumbent firms should respond quickly with a limited set of marketing mix elements. Managers should rapidly decide which ones (product, promotion, price and place) are likely to have the most impact and concentrate their efforts on them.[47]

Competitors' reaction times to the introduction of a new product have been found to depend on four factors.[48] First, response is faster in high-growth markets. Given the importance of such markets, competitors will feel the need to take fast action in response to a new entrant. Second, response is dependent on the market shares held by the introducing firm and its competitors. Response time is slower when the introducing firm has higher market share and faster for those competitors who have higher market share. Third, response time is faster in markets characterized by frequent product changes. Finally, it is not surprising to find that response time is related to the time needed to develop the new product.

Summary

This chapter has looked at the importance and role of new products in bringing long-term corporate success. We have seen that there are different types of new products ranging from variation of existing products to new-to-the-world products that reflect major technological break-throughs. Effective new product development of any kind relies upon the creation of an innovative culture, appropriate organizational arrangements and an efficient new product development process. Each of these issues has been examined in depth including the identification of seven ways of creating and nurturing an innovation culture, developing close relationships between marketing and R&D, cutting time to market, stimulating the corporate imagination, managing project teams and commercializing technology.

We have seen that new product development is a rewarding but risky venture: most new products fail. But without them competitive and market dynamics will eventually erode a company's position in the marketplace. New product development activity should not be seen as a reaction to faltering sales and profits. It should be placed high on the agenda of corporate priorities and a proactive stance taken on the search for commercializable new product ideas.

Internet exercise

A new product

Sites to visit
http://www.cocacola.co.uk
http://www.pepsi.co.uk/
http://www.tango.co.uk/
http://www.ribena.co.uk/home.html
http://www.irn-bru.co.uk/
http://www.lucozade.co.uk/

Exercise
Develop a new soft drink and discuss how you would position it in the marketplace.

Study questions

1   Try to think of an unsatisfied need that you feel could be solved by the introduction of a new product. How would you set about testing your idea to examine its commercial potential?

2   The Sinclair C5 was soon withdrawn from market in the UK. The three-wheeled vehicle was designed to provide electric-powdered transport over short distances. If you can remember the vehicle try to think of reasons why the product was a failure. Video recorders and fax machines have been huge successes. Why?

3   Why is it difficult for a service company such as a bank to develop new products that have lasting success?

4   You are the marketing manager for a fast-food restaurant chain. A colleague returns from France with an idea for a new dish that she thinks will be a winner. How would you go about evaluating the idea?

5   What are the advantages and disadvantages of test marketing? In what circumstances should you be reluctant to use test marketing?

6   Your company has developed a new range of spicy flavoured soups. They are intended to compete against the market leader in curry-flavoured soups. How would you conduct product tests for your new line?

7   What are the particular problems associated with commercializing technology? What are the key factors for success?

8   Discuss how marketing and R&D can form effective teams to develop new products.

References

1.   Pearson, D. (1993) Invent, Innovate and Improve, *Marketing*, 8 April, 15.

2.   Richard, H. (1996) Why Competitiveness is a Dirty Word in Scandinavia, *The European*, 6–12 June, 24.

3.   Doyle, P. (1997) From the Top, *The Guardian*, 2 August, 17.

4.   Booz, Allen and Hamilton (1982) *New Product Management for the 1980's*, New York: Booz, Allen and Hamilton Inc.

5.   Hultink, E., A. Griffin, H. S. J. Robben and S. Hart (1998) In Search of Generic Launch Strategies for New Products, *International Journal of Research in Marketing*, **15**, 269–85.

6.   See Gupta, A. K. and D. Wileman (1990) Improving R&D/Marketing Relations: R&D Perspective, *R&D Management*, **20** (4), 277–90; Koshler, R. (1991) Produkt—Innovationasmanagement als Erfolgsfaktor, in Mueller-Boehling, D. *et al.* (eds) *Innovations—und Technologiemanagement*, Stuttgart: C. E. Poeschel Verlagi; Shrivastava, P. and W. E. Souder (1987) The Strategic Management of Technological Innovation: A Review and a Model, *Journal of Management Studies*, **24** (1), 24–41.

7.   Aceland, H. (1999) Harnessing Internal Innovation, *Marketing*, 22 July, 27–8.

8.   See Booz, Allen and Hamilton (1982) op. cit.; Maidique, M.A. and B. J. Zirger (1984) A Study of Success and Failure in Product Innovation: The Case of the US Electronics Industry, *IEEE Transactions in Engineering Management*, **EM-31** (November), 192–203.

9.   See Bergen, S.A., R. Miyajima and C. P. McLaughlin (1988) The R&D/Production Interface in Four Developed Countries, *R&D Management*, **18** (3), 201–16; Hegarty, W. H. and R. C. Hoffman (1990) Product/Market Innovations: A Study of Top Management Involvement among Four Cultures, *Journal of Product Innovation Management*, 7, 186–99; Cooper, R. G. (1979) The Dimensions of Industrial New Product Success and Failure, *Journal of Marketing*, **43** (summer), 93–103; Johne, A. and P. Snelson (1988) Auditing Product Innovation Activities in Manufacturing Firms, *R&D Management*, **18** (3), 227–33.

10. Aceland, H. (1999) Harnessing Internal Innovation, *Marketing*, 22 July, 27–8.

11. Kanter, R. M. (1983) *The Change Masters*, New York: Simon and Schuster.

12. Oram, R. (1996) New Recipes for Growth, *Financial Times*, 11 September, 2.

13. Brierley, D. (1997) Spring-Cleaning a Statistical Wonderland, *The European*, 20–26 February, 28.

14. Done, K. (1992) From Design Studio to New Car Showroom, *Financial Times*, 11 May, 10.

15. Buxton, P. (2000) Time to Market is NPD's Top Priority, *Marketing*, 30 March, 35-6.

16. Chaston, I. (1999) *New Marketing Strategies*, London: Sage.

17. See Hise, R. T., L. O'Neal, A. Parasuraman and J. U. NcNeal (1990) Marketing/R&D Interaction in New Product Development: Implications for New Product Success Rates, *Journal of Product Innovation Management*, 7, 142-55; Johne and Snelson (1988) op. cit.; Walsh, W. J. (1990) Get the Whole Organisation Behind New Product Development, *Research in Technological Management*, Nov.-Dec., 32-6.

18. Frey, D. (1991) Learning the Ropes: My Life as a Product Champion, *Harvard Business Review*, Sept.-Oct., 46-56.

18. Gupta, A. K. and D. Wileman (1991) Improving R&D/Marketing Relations in Technology-based Companies: Marketing's Perspective, *Journal of Marketing Management*, 7 (1), 25-46.

20. See Dwyer, L. M. (1990) Factors Affecting the Proficient Management of Product Innovation, *International Journal of Technological Management*, 5 (6), 721-30; Gupta and Wileman (1990) op. cit; and Adler, P. S., H. E. Riggs and S. C. Wheelright (1989) Product Development Know-How, *Sloan Management Review*, 4, 7-17.

21. Brentani, U. de (1991) Success Factors in Developing New Business Services, *European Journal of Marketing*, 15 (2), 33-59; and Johne, A. and C. Storey (1998) New Source Development: A Review of the Literature and Annotated Bibliography, *European Journal of Marketing*, 32 (3/4), 184-251.

22. Cooper, R. G. and E. J. Kleinschmidt (1986) An Investigation into the New Product Process: Steps, Deficiencies and Impact, *Journal of Product Innovation Management*, June, 71-85.

23. Nijssen, E. J. and K. F. M. Lieshout (1995) Awareness, Use and Effectiveness of Models and Methods for New Product Development, *European Journal of Marketing*, 29 (10), 27-44.

24. Hamel, G. and C. K. Prahalad (1991) Corporate Imagination and Expeditionary Marketing, *Harvard Business Review*, July-August, 81-92.

25. Parkinson, S. T. (1982) The Role of the User in Successful New Product Development, *R&D Management*, 12, 123-31.

26. Nevens, T. M., G. L. Summe, and B. Uttal (1990) Commercializing Technology: What the Best Companies Do, *Harvard Business Review*, May-June, 154-63.

27. Johne, A. (1992) Don't Let your Customers Lead You Astray in Developing New Products, *European Management Journal*, 10 (1), 80-4.

28. Weston, C. (1992) Brand New Ideas to Help Adopt to a Fast-Changing Marketplace, *Guardian*, 2 June, 12.

29. Hamel, G. (1999) Bringing Silicon Valley Inside, *Harvard Business Review*, September-October, 71-84.

30. Hamel, G. and C. K. Prahaled (1991) Corporate Imagination and Expeditionary Marketing, *Harvard Business Review*, July-August, 81-92.

31. Jobber, D., J. Saunders, G. Hooley, B. Gilding and J. Hatton-Smooker (1989) Assessing the Value of a Quality Assurance Certificate for Software: An Exploratory Investigation, *MIS Quarterly*, March, 19-31.

32. Edgett, S. and S. Jones (1991) New Product Development in the Financial Services Industry: A Case Study, *Journal of Marketing Management*, 7 (3), 271-84.

33. Wheelwright, S. and K. Clark (1992) *Revolutionizing Product Development*, New York: Free Press.

34. Baxter, A. (1992) Shifting to High Gear, *Financial Times*, 14 May, 15.

35. Pullin, J. (1997) Time is Money on the Way to Market, *The Guardian*, 5 April, 99.

36. Parkinson (1982) op. cit.

37. McLuhan, R. (1999) Careful Research Continues to Pay, *Marketing*, 15 April, 31-2.

38. Rogers, E. M. (1983) *Diffusion of Innovations*, New York: Free Press.

39. Rogers (1983) op. cit.

40. Zinkmund, W. G. and M. D'Amico (1999) *Marketing*, St Paul, MN: West.

41. Easingwood, C. and C. Beard (1989) High Technology Launch Strategies in the UK, Industrial *Marketing Management*, 18, 125-38.

42. See Mahajan, V., E. Muller and R. Kerin (1987) Introduction Strategy for New Product with Positive and Negative Word-of-Mouth, *Management Science*, 30, 1389-404; Robertson, T. S. and H. Gatignon (1986) Competitive Effects on Technology Diffusion, *Journal of Marketing*, 50 (July), 1-12; and Tzokas, N. and M. Saren (1992) Innovation Diffusion: The Emerging Role of Suppliers Versus the Traditional Dominance of Buyers, *Journal of Marketing Management*, 8 (1), 69-80.

43. Saunders, J. and D. Jobber (1994) Product Replacement Strategies: Occurrence and Concurrence, *Journal of Product Innovation Management* (November).

44. Nevens, Summe and Uttal (1990) op. cit.

45. Brown, R. (1991) Managing the 'S' Curves of Innovation, *Journal of Marketing Management*, 7 (2), 189-202.

46. Desmond, E. W. (1998) Can Canon Keep Clicking? *Fortune Magazine*, 2 February, 58-64.

47. Gatignon, H., T. S. Robertson and A. J. Fein (1997) 'Incumbent Defence Strategies Against New Product Entry, *International Journal of Research in Marketing*, 14, 163-76.

48. Bowman, D. and H. Gatignon (1995) Determinants of Competitor Response Time to a New Product Introduction, *Journal of Marketing Research*, 33, February, 42-53.

Key terms

invention   the discovery of new methods and ideas

innovation   the commercialization of an invention by bringing it to market

project teams   the bringing together of staff from such areas as R&D, engineering, manufacturing, finance, and marketing to work on a project such as new-product development

simultaneous engineering   the involvement of manufacturing and product development engineers in the same development team in an effort to reduce development time

brainstorming   the technique where a group of people generate ideas without initial evaluation. Only when the list of ideas is complete is each idea then evaluated

concept testing   testing new product ideas with potential customers

business analysis   a review of the projected sales, costs and profits for a new product to establish whether these factors satisfy company objectives

market testing   the limited launch of a new product to test sales potential

test marketing   the launch of a new product in one or a few geographic areas chosen to be representative of the intended market

diffusion of innovation process   the process by which a new product spreads throughout a market over time

product churning   a continuous spiral of new product introductions

Case 15 Swatch: Coping with Market Changes

Introduction

In the spring of 1998, members of the management team at Swatch were reflecting on the success of their product and the challenges ahead. Developed 15 years previously, the Swatch watch had revolutionized the Swiss watch industry and, in doing this, had exceeded the most optimistic expectations both of its creator, Nicholas Hayek, and Ernst Thomke, the technological brain behind it.

What was seen initially by many to be a funny plastic watch, had been launched during the climax of the onslaught on the Swiss watch industry by Japanese and Hong Kong competitors. It was a meticulously planned response to the Far Eastern companies who had almost eliminated the Swiss presence in the high volume and relatively low price market segments that made up more than 80 per cent of unit sales worldwide.[1] Hayek had succeeded in creating an entirely new market segment, appealing to the hitherto largely unserved teenage market and people who were young at heart. The concept proved so successful that the brand sole more than 200 million units within the next decade and established a strong presence in all major markets. However, in 1998, Hayek and his team had reason to be thoughtful about the further development of their brand. The changing watch market, changes in style and fashion, and strong competition had all conspired to put Swatch under pressure.

The situation in 1998

The company

In 1988, Swatch was a global brand with subsidiaries or agencies in more than 70 countries. The global marketing strategy had resulted in very high levels of brand awareness, clear positioning, a universally appealing product range, a well-formulated global pricing strategy, and a worldwide promotional strategy. The company's success was due largely to their first product, the Standard.

However, between 1990–94 Standard sales had remained relatively stable and had only increased by 30 per cent since 1986. Despite more than 70 different models per season, and a high variety of limited editions, the novelty of Swatch appeared to have faded as it moved into the mature phase of the life cycle (see Fig. C15.1).

For this reason, Swatch had introduced numerous new product lines including chrono, Automatic, Scuba, Pop, MusiCall, The Beep, Aquachrono, Pop-up, and most recently Irony, Access, and the SwatchSkin (see Table C15.1). At the same time, the company also began a programme of diversification into textiles, clothing, and, initially with Volkswagen but subsequently with Mercedes-Benz, the Smart car. (It should be noted that in November 1998, Swatch and Mercedes-Benz announced the withdrawal of Mercedes from the joint venture.)

Some of the new models such as Chrono, Scuba and Irony had proved to be very successful. Others, however, such as MusiCall and Pop Swatch were, on the face of it at least, less successful. The Standard had therefore maintained its position as the most popular Swatch product, even though sales declined slightly between 1993 and 1994. Overall, therefore, Swatch had managed to extend their life cycle through the launch of new products, even though the majority of the new lines failed to play more than a marginal role (see Fig. C15.2).

Further analysis of sales figures revealed another worrying factor to Hayek's management team: the extension of Swatch's life cycle had been largely supported by two new lines, Chrono and Scuba. None of the other new lines had been nearly as successful and none had been able to repeat the performance of the Standard. However, the team's expectations of Irony were high, as the watch was more in line with the growing trend for metal watches.

The customer base

A detailed analysis of customers showed the team that lifestyles in their traditional European

[1] Swatch's past is extensively discussed in three other case studies: Jeannet, J.P., S.W. Nye and B. Priovolos (1985) The Swatch project, IMEDE, Lausanne; Pinson, C. and H.C. Kimball (1987) I've got a Swatch, INSEAD-Cedep, Fontainebleau; Joachimsthaler, E. (1993) The Swatch Story, IESE, University of Navarra, Barcelona-Madrid. These case studies discuss the factors that led to its development, the initial marketing strategy and the early years after its launch.

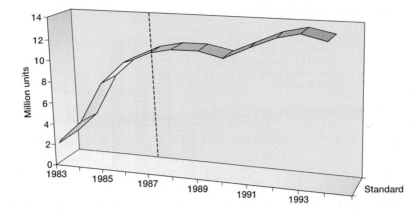

Figure C15.1 Standard production between 1983 and 1994

Table C15.1   The Swatch product line in 1998

Product line	Features
Pop Swatch	Large flexible cotton wristband to fit over clothes
Chrono	Stopwatch for sprinters with intermediate and finishing times
Scuba	Diver's watch with rotary ring, electroluminescent dial face and waterproof to 200 m
Automatic	Mechanical watch
Stop Swatch	Stopwatch where the two hands can be reset to the 12 mark and no additional hands or displays are needed
MusiCall	Alarm clock that plays a melody composed by Jean Michel Jarre and other musicians
Solar	Powered by sunlight
The Beep	The world's first pager integrated into a wristwatch
Irony	Metal watch targeted at more conservative customers
Access	An internal microchip giving access to ski lifts
Swatch Skin	The world's thinnest plastic watch with a diameter of 3.9 mm; feels like a second 'Skin'

markets had changed. Due to the long and severe recession of the late 1980s and early 1990s, customers had become more price conscious. At the same time, attitudes towards materials had also changed. The plastic throw away mentality of the buoyant early to mid-1980s had been replaced by a new trend towards more solid, longer lasting products, a trend that had been led by a growing environmental awareness among customers that rebelled against the excessive use of plastic in favour of the more easily recycled glass.

The other constraint to Swatch's future growth was proving to be a series of far-reaching demographic changes. Research[2] demonstrated to the

team that the typical Swatch customer age group (between 15 and 29 years) would decline heavily over the next decade. The significance of this is illustrated by the way in which in 1993 Swatch had more than 80 million potential customers in the European Union. Market projections showed that by 2008 this market segment will have declined to 65 million consumers, a decrease of more than 20 per cent (see Tables C15.2 and C15.3).

These problems were, in turn, being compounded by the way in which the market was becoming ever more competitive, with a greater number of companies competing for the decreasing number of customers. The team also realized that the market was demanding more durable, solid and upmarket watches than 10

[2] *Source*: Euromonitor (1997) *European Marketing Data and Statistics*, 32nd edn, London, 124.

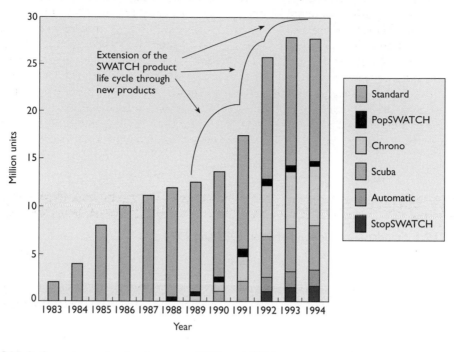

Figure C15.2 Swatch production between 1983 and 1994.

Source: Adapted from Miller, A. (1997) Nur an der Burse tickt die SMH nicht richtig, *CASH*, **32**, (8), August, 5

years earlier. But, most importantly, the watch's fashionable character made it vulnerable to changes in fashion and raised the fundamental question of whether the brand still had its novelty, unique appeal and symbolic character.

The competition

Competition in Swatch's market segment had increased considerably throughout the late 1980s and into the 1990s (see Fig. C15.3). When Swatch was launched in 1983, it created a completely new market. However, other companies quickly followed and launched their own brands that appealed to the newly created 'teeny segment'. Many of these companies copied Swatch's designs, positioning and price strategy. Although this made life difficult for the company, Swatch's clear branding, marketing creativity and aggression ensured that it was consistently far more successful than its rivals. This was illustrated by the fact that the company had sold its 200 millionth Swatch back in 1996. The market was, however, changing and other companies were

becoming more innovative and successful. The trend away from plastic towards more robust metal sports watches was, for example, posing a serious threat. The launch of Irony had acknowledged this change, but at the beginning of 1998 the management team was being forced to consider whether the company had fully appreciated the nature and significance of the changing market.

Swatch's leading competitor today is The Timex Corporation. In 1997 their market share in America, Swatch's major export market, was 11 per cent compared with Swatch's share of 1–2 per cent.[3] The majority of their sales are generated in Swatch's traditional market segments. By contrast with Swatch's strategy in which all watches have the Swatch logo, Timex watches are marketed under several leading names, including Indiglo, Benetton, Timberland, Joe Boxer, Burwood and Guess. All are marketed as fashion accessories, but are positioned slightly differently in order to cover a wider market. The differentiated market-

[3] *Source*: Euromonitor (1996) *European Marketing Data and Statistics*, London, 54.

ing strategy ranges from economic plastic watches (Benetton) to more upmarket metal watches with leather straps (Timberland). Timex's DataLink was developed in conjunction with Microsoft and allows comprehensive databases to be downloaded straight from a computer.

Guess is Swatch's second strongest competitor in the US, with sales of 5.5 million units, and a turnover of US$75 million. Launched in 1984, the Guess strategy might loosely be labelled as a Swatch strategy in reverse in that the Guess brand was established in 1981 by a French group marketing clothes and leather products. Having established the brand in that sector, the watch collection was then launched. By contrast Swatch established the watch brand first, and then tried to diversity into textiles and apparel. Today, Guess is part of the Timex Group.

Another strong competitor in Swatch's segment is Fossil. This American brand, produced in

Table C15.2   The typical demographic Swatch customer group in 1993 (000s)

Age group	0–4 years	5–9 years	10–14 years	15–19 years	20–24 years	25–29 years	30–34 years	35–39 years
Belgium	621	592	618	618	713	791	804	760
Denmark	318	274	291	348	374	424	379	372
France	3738	3803	3917	3938	4341	4335	4323	4269
Germany (E)	1063	1129	1010	981	1230	1392	1261	1232
Germany (W)	4441	4421	4380	4161	5809	7166	6736	5912
Greece	518	595	716	714	768	812	766	712
Ireland	266	305	350	321	290	247	248	245
Italy	2809	2846	3193	4025	4525	4827	4339	3884
Luxembourg	26	23	22	21	27	34	34	32
Netherlands	972	913	906	955	1247	1308	1277	1183
Portugal	551	589	720	843	794	734	703	666
Spain	2054	2241	2800	3254	3270	3289	3038	2642
UK	3898	3692	3538	3648	4463	4795	4331	3830
Total	21273	21421	22461	**23826**	**27851**	**30153**	28239	25739

Table C15.3   The typical demographic Swatch customer group in 2008 (000s)

Age group	0–4 years	5–9 years	10–14 years	15–19 years	20–24 years	25–29 years	30–34 years	35–39 years
Belgium	–	–	–	621	591	618	618	713
Denmark	–	–	–	318	274	291	348	374
France	–	–	–	3738	3803	3917	3938	4341
Germany (E)	–	–	–	1063	1129	1010	981	1230
Germany (W)	–	–	–	4441	4421	4380	4161	5809
Greece	–	–	–	518	595	716	714	768
Ireland	–	–	–	266	305	350	321	290
Italy	–	–	–	2809	2846	3193	4025	4525
Luxembourg	–	–	–	26	23	22	21	27
Netherlands	–	–	–	972	913	906	955	1247
Portugal	–	–	–	551	589	720	843	794
Spain	–	–	–	2054	2241	2800	3254	3270
UK	–	–	–	3898	3692	3538	3648	4463
Total	–	–	–	**21273**	**21421**	**22461**	23826	27851

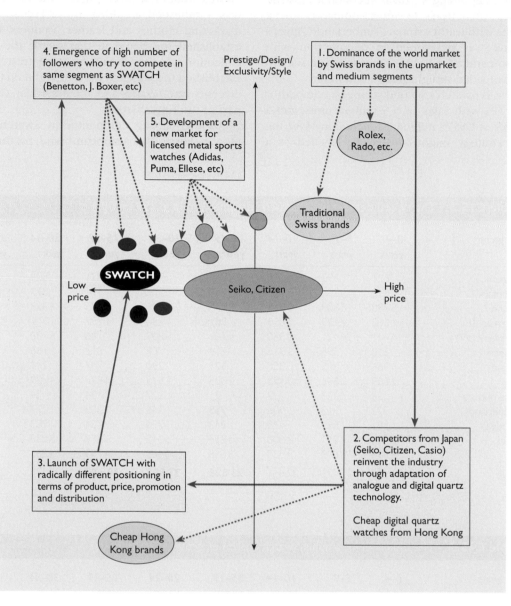

Figure C15.3 The development of the world watch market

Hong Kong, has copied the Swatch marketing strategy, but has positioned the brand slightly further upmarket than Swatch. According to Fossil manager Tim Hale, 'The company does exactly the same as the Swiss [Swatch], just in a different [metal] segment.[4] The annual collection of metal watches is designed in the style of the 1950s, and is supplied in aluminium boxes. This is designed to emphasize the watch's solidity, robustness and greater "value for money" than Swatch's plastic product and packaging.' Having established themselves in the United States, Fossil began expanding into Europe. Within four years, sales soared from $50 million to more than $200 million. Fossil's growth is highlighted in Fig. C15.4

A further competitive threat was posed by

[4] Willmanns, B. (1997) Das jüngste Fossil der Zeitgeschichte, *Facts*, **25**, 67.

Casio who, when the market for digital quartz watches started declining, introduced analogue quartz watches. These are offered in the same price segment as Swatch and typically feature additional digital features that cannot be provided by conventional analogue quartz watches. Examples of these include elaborate sports watches that can be used not just as stop watches, but also to measure blood pressure, spent calories and for storing up to 100 different lap times.

Together, these competitors had begun squeezing Swatch in a number of its traditional sectors; this is illustrated in the market map in Fig. C15.5.

The way ahead

Given the nature of these changes within its markets, it was obvious to Swatch's management team that the company was faced with a number of major challenges. Critics were beginning to say Swatch had not really adapted to the new market conditions. If the company ignored these developments, its future would be under serious threat. So what alternatives did they have? In the watch market, there appeared to be a number of possibilities. They could fight to retain their current position, reposition the brand by moving upmarket through extensions of the metal Irony line, or begin licensing prestigious fashion brands such as the Calvin Klein that the parent company

SMH was running. Alternatively, they could build upon the core competencies of ETA, a subsidiary, to expand in the economical digital segment and compete with companies like Casio. They might also think about developing a new market in the high-technology segment where the Beep and Access were positioned. More dramatically, they might even think about letting Swatch fade out and concentrate instead of reinventing the industry with a completely new product and brand as Hayek had done 15 years previously. A major consideration in all of this was the scope that existed for capitalizing upon possible synergies with SMH's other successful brands such as Tissot, Rado and Omega. At the same time, they needed to think about whether they should continue their activities in other industries like telecommunications or automobiles. At the heart of all of this was the question of what the company's *real* core competencies and organizational capabilities were that would help to defeat the competition once again.

This case was prepared by Professor Colin Gilligan, Professor of Marketing at Sheffield Business School and Franz Weisbrod, Regional Export Manager, CompAir Rucklufttechnik GmbH. It is intended to be used as a basis for class discussion rather than to illustrate either effective or ineffective handling of an administrative situation. Copyright © 1998 Colin Gilligan and Franz Weisbrod.

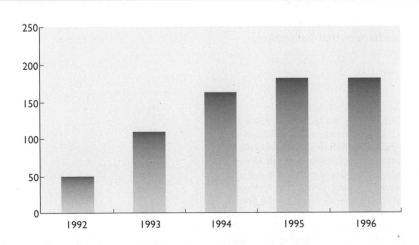

Figure C15.4 Turnover of Fossil between 1992 and 1996 in ($million).

Source: Willmanns, B. (1997) Das jüngste Fossil der Zeitgeschichte, *Facts,* **25**, 67.

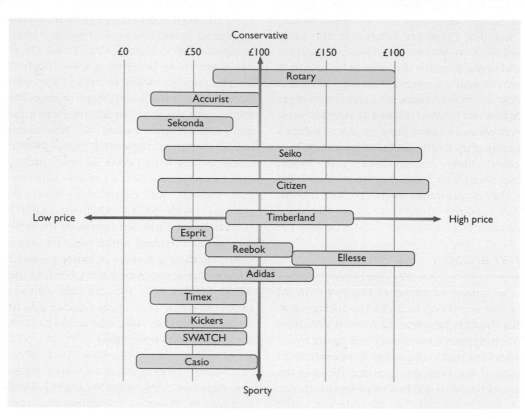

Figure C15.5 Product positioning of Swatch in comparison to other major brands in the low/medium price segment[5]

[5] This research was conducted by the authors in major UK catalogue shops (Argos, Index), retail chains (Goldsmiths, H. Samuel) and a major mail order company (Littlewoods) in August 1997. A very similar pattern emerged when German companies were researched. This survey included major mail order companies (Neckermann, Quelle, Wenz), as well as major retail chains (Christ and Gold Meister). Note: Several brands that are promoted in the UK are not marketed in Germany (Accurist, Rotary, Sekonda), but have been included in the map to demonstrate the high level of competition in the lower/medium segment.

Questions

1 Review the market and how it has developed.

2 What are the changes that have taken place?

3 What should Swatch do next?

Case 16 Philips' Aqua Wave

Philips Electronics Inc. is a large Dutch multi-national with shares on the Amsterdam, New York and London stock exchanges. In 1994, Philips had 253 000 employees and an annual turnover of 61.0 billion Dutch guilders (NLG). Due to a reorganization, total profits were 2.1 billion NLG over the same time period. Philips Electronics Inc. consists of eight product divisions: Lighting, Sound and Vision, Components, Semiconductors, Communication Systems, Medical Systems, Industrial Electronics, and Domestic Appliances and Personal Care (DAP). This case is situated in the DAP division.

Each division within Philips is responsible for its own worldwide policy. While each division's head office is situated in The Netherlands, production takes place all over the world (e.g. The Netherlands, Mexico, Singapore and China). The company has over 60 National Sales Organizations (NSOs) in all major countries. In several other countries, sales agents represent the company and take care of the sales of the product lines.

Philips Domestic Appliances and Personal Care (DAP)

Philips DAP has been a separate division since 1992. This division focuses on the production and sales of electrical products for personal care and household convenience. DAP's head office or Corporate Centre is located in Groningen, The Netherlands. This division employs 8500 people of which 3000 work in The Netherlands.

Philips DAP consists of two 'business groups': 'Domestic Appliances' and 'Personal Care'. The business group 'Domestic Appliances' develops and markets food preparation equipment and home comfort products such as vacuum cleaners, flat irons, air-treatment equipment, beverage systems and tabletop cooking equipment. The business group 'Personal Care' develops and markets personal care appliances. This group consists of the following 'article groups':

+ Shaving and cutting (e.g. the Philishave);
+ Haircare, fitness and suncare (HFS); and
+ Dental care.

Production centres of Philips DAP are located, for instance, in The Netherlands (Drachten and Hoogeveen), the UK (Hastings), Austria (Klagenfurt), Brazil (São Paulo), Mexico (Mexico City), Japan (Tokyo) and Singapore. These facilities produce for local markets as well as for export markets. Apart from producing its own products, Philips DAP also orders products from third parties.

The product group haircare

The article groups are subdivided in 'product groups'. Managers within the product groups are responsible for the worldwide policy of the product category (i.e. product life-cycle management), new product development, and long-term planning. Haircare is one of the product groups of the 'Personal Care' department. This group develops and markets electrical haircare products for consumers all over the world. Production centres are located in Singapore and China.

Product types

There are three major product types in the haircare market:

1 *Pistol dryers*: Standard hairdryers representing around 65 per cent of the world market. This major group consists of several subgroups (for example, dryers with diffusers and semiprofessional dryers). Diffusers are used to create volume in the hair, to enhance the drying of curls, or just to dry the hair more gently;

2 *Airstylers*: These products are used to create curls and waves, or for styling purposes. Airstylers are offered in various versions with all kinds of attachments. They use warm air to dry and style the hair. Their shape is most often cylindrical. Airstylers represent around 20 per cent of the world market; and

3 *Curlers*: Curlers are cylindrical curling tongs, brushes and heated rollers. They use heat for styling purposes. A new product category in the heated roller subsegment are rollers which use steam. The curlers segment

represents about 15 per cent of the world market (mainly in the UK and USA).

General market characteristics (not only Philips)

The haircare total market size is about 120 million pieces with a total value of about 3.1 billion Dutch guilders (NLG). The USA is the largest market (29 per cent), both in volume (40 million pieces) and value (920 million NLG). The Western European market has a value of about 575 million NLG (19 per cent) and the Asia Pacific market 760 million NLG (25 per cent). The rest of the world accounts for 27 per cent of the total market.

The Haircare group belongs to the top five world players in the electrical haircare market. The main competitors in the European, US and Asia/Pacific markets are depicted in Table C16.1. Apart from these major players there are many small players each with a worldwide market share below 2 per cent. Overall, the market is fragmented with the top five players having a combined worldwide market share between 25 and 30 per cent.

The world market has remained stable in the last five years (1990–95). While the haircare markets in Europe and the USA have declined somewhat (5–10 per cent depending on the country), growth has taken place in emerging markets like China, India and Eastern Europe. Overall, the haircare market can be characterized by the following key terms: highly competitive, trade controlled and low brand loyalty. The haircare market offers little technical innovation, but many concept innovations (i.e. new features). An introduced innovative concept, however, is quickly copied by competitors within a year or less.

Dutch market

The total Dutch market volume amounts to 900 000 pieces with an average retail price of NLG 44.00. See Table C16.2 for a more complete view of the developments in Philips volume and turnover in the World and Dutch markets.

Four major competitors operate in the Dutch market: Philips, Carmen, Babyliss and Braun. Other brands account for about 10 per cent of the market. Developments in the market shares of the major players in The Netherlands are provided in Table C16.3.

All four major brands offer a full range of haircare products on the market (i.e. dryers, airstylers and curlers). The major innovations in the last years have been in the field of the diffusers.

Table C16.1   Major competitors in Europe, USA, and Asia/Pacific

Companies (brands)	Europe	USA	Asia/Pacific
Braun	✔	✔	✔
Matsushita (National)			✔
Conair (Conair, Revlon, Babyliss)	✔	✔	✔
Helen of Troy (Vidal Sassoon)		✔	✔
Carmen	✔		
Philips	✔		✔

Table C16.2   Philips turnover and volume in world and Dutch markets (1990 = 100)

	1990	1991	1992	1993	1994	1995
Volume world	100	94	99	98	106	116
Turnover world	100	95	90	82	92	102
Volume Holland	100	73	61	59	56	55
Turnover Holland	100	85	69	64	56	58

The new product

The Dutch NSO of Philips has been confronted with a loss of turnover and declining market shares in the last five years. In 1995, Philips updated and modified its haircare product range considerably in order to regain its lost position. Among these new products were, for example, the Discovery 1200 travel, the Compact 1000, the Style Control 1650 autosensor with diffuser, the Silence 1000, the Salon Select 1600 with diffuser, and the Styler-Air Deluxe. As part of this programme the launch of Philips Aqua Wave (a steam roller set) was planned for 1996. This product was a new concept for the Dutch market and an innovation in the haircare market.

Philips' Aqua Wave

For a few years there has been a growing interest in the heated roller segment of the haircare market. The largest setment is in the USA where it represents 10 per cent of the volume and 15 per cent of the total value. Although this segment is small in Europe and in Asia/Pacific, Philips Haircare want to operate in the heated roller segment because presence in this segment:

✦ helps to establish Philips as a haircare specialist;

✦ provides an opportunity for Philips to develop this segment in countries where this segment hardly exists; and

✦ provides an opportunity to strengthen Philips' haircare image where this segment is more developed.

Description of the Aqua Wave

The Aqua Wave is a Velcro steam roller which is in line with the latest trends in haircare: volume, care and non-damaging to the hair. The principle works as follows: first, rollers with a foam layer are put on a steam outlet to absorb the steam, then the rollers are rolled into dry hair and then removed when the hair is dry. Philips claims that with the Aqua Wave the same hairstyles can be created as with traditional heated roller sets but much quicker and with better results.

The Aqua Wave comes with 1 and 1½ inch rollers that are suitable for volume and wave in short to half-length hair. The rollers have a Velcro finishing so that they can be positioned in the hair without using clips (i.e. caresse rollers). These rollers have become more and more popular with consumers because they can be bought at almost every drugstore and they can be used in wet as well as dry hair. The main advantages of these rollers are that they are very light and that they stick to the hair. In addition, they are heat resistant, washable and safe to use with hair-styling lotions.

The combination of Velcro and Steam was new to the market. According to Philips, the main key benefits of the product are:

✦ gentle method to create volume, waves or curls;

✦ combination of moisture and heat gives longlasting results;

✦ Velcro rollers are comfortable to use;

✦ no clips needed;

✦ heat up very quick; and

✦ easy to use.

Table C16.3   Sales of haircare equipment

Hair care total	Market share (units)			Market share (guilders)			Selling price (guilders)		
	Jan '93	Jan '95		Jan '93	Jan '95		Jan '93	Jan '95	
Philips	16%	20%	+25%	15%	18%	+16%	46.7	40.5	−13%
Braun	25%	27%	+7%	29%	34%	+17%	56.0	57.0	+2%
Carmen	33%	25%	−24%	34%	25%	−27%	49.0	44.2	−10%
Babyliss	18%	19%	+7%	16%	17%	+12%	42.2	41.2	−3%
Others	8%	9%	+12%	6%	6%	−5%	34.3	27.1	−21%
Total	100%	100%	−3%	100%	100%	−10%	48.0	44.8	−7%

Developments in the market shares of the major players in the curling segment are provided in Table C16.4.

Competing solutions

Since last year, two solutions similar to the Aqua Wave were introduced in the UK and France: the Steam Setter from Remington, and the Steam Curl from Babyliss. Three years ago, a similar product was introduced in the USA: the Caruso Steamsetter. Of course, traditional rollersets are also substitutes. At the time of launch only one direct competitor was present on the Dutch market. This was the Remington Steam Setter which was priced at 90 Dutch guilders. Remington was not a very well known brand name and sales were disappointing.

Team assignment

Your team has been hired by the product manager of the Dutch NSO to advise him on the launch of the Aqua Wave in the Dutch market. The budget which you are allowed to spend on the launch is NLG 200000 (see Table C16.5 for some indications of advertising costs). The main objective of the launch plan is, according to this product manager, to create '*a hype in the market with limited budgets*'. In the proposal, your team should address all major launch and marketing mix tasks including:

✦ Commercialization objectives.
✦ Launch timing.
✦ Segmentation, targeting and positioning.
✦ Forecasting.
✦ Industry and competitor analysis.
✦ Pricing strategy and tactics.
✦ Choice of the distribution channels (see Table C16.6).
✦ Push versus pull promotion.
✦ Allocation of the launch budget.
✦ Marketing communications (including customer, dealer and salesforce promotion).

Table C16.4 Sales of curling equipment

Curlers	Market share (units)			Market share (guilders)			Selling price (guilders)		
	Jan '93	Jan '95		Jan '93	Jan '95		Jan '93	Jan '95	
Philips	19%	25%	+33%	14%	22%	+53%	30.3	35.7	13%
Braun	26%	17%	−32%	25%	18%	−31%	40.6	42.0	4%
Carmen	38%	36%	−4%	47%	43%	−9%	50.6	49.0	−3%
Babyliss	13%	16%	+18%	12%	16%	+31%	36.8	41.8	14%
Others	4%	5%	+24%	1%	2%	+55%	10.9	13.8	27%
Total	100%	100%	−11%	100%	100%	−10%	40.7	41.5	2%

Table C16.5 Indication of advertising costs

	Costs (in Dutch guilders)
Radio (20 seconds)	200–2000 (depending on channel and time)
TV (30 seconds, excluding production costs)	10000 (depending on channel and time)
Magazine (one page)	15000
Trade show (all expenses included)	10000/day

Prices are indications

Table C16.6   Distribution of haircare equipment (in percentages)

	Dec–Jan ('95)	Feb–Mar	Apr–May	June–Jul	Aug–Sep	Oct–Nov	Dec–Jan ('96)
Volume							
Department Stores	31	35	32	33	38	40	38
Household Appliances	10	9	10	10	8	10	9
Electrical Appliances	36	31	30	36	32	28	30
Independents	23	25	29	21	22	23	22
Turnover							
Department Stores	31	32	30	32	36	36	36
Household Appliances	9	8	10	9	8	9	8
Electrical Appliances	34	31	28	34	31	28	31
Independents	27	29	33	26	26	27	25

This case was prepared by Erik Jan Hultink, Delft University of Technology, Delft, The Netherlands.

CHAPTER TEN

Pricing Strategy

'Everything is worth what its purchasers will pay for it'

SYRUS

'There are two fools in every market.
One charges too little; the other charges too much'

RUSSIAN PROVERB

Learning Objectives *This chapter explains:*

1 The economist's approach to price determination

2 The differences between full cost and direct cost pricing

3 An understanding of going-rate pricing and competitive bidding

4 The advantages of marketing-orientated pricing over cost-orientated and competitor-orientated pricing methods

5 The factors which affect price setting when using a marketing-orientated approach

6 When and how to initiate price increases and cuts

7 When and when not to follow competitor-initiated price increases and cuts; when to follow quickly and when to follow slowly

8 Ethical issues in pricing

Price is the odd-one-out of the marketing mix, because it is the revenue earner. The price of a product is what the company gets back in return for all the effort that is put into manufacturing and marketing the product. The other three elements of the marketing mix—product, promotion, and place—are costs. Therefore, no matter how good the product, how creative the promotion or how efficient the distribution, unless price covers costs the company will make a loss. It is therefore essential that managers understand how to set prices, because both undercharging (lost margin) and overcharging (lost sales) can have dramatic effects on profitability.

One of the key factors that marketing managers need to remember is that price is one element of the marketing mix. Price should not be set in isolation; it should be blended with product promotion, and place to form a coherent mix that provides superior customer value. The sales of many products, particularly those that are a form of self-expression such as drinks, cars, perfume and clothing, could suffer from prices that are too low. As we shall see, price is an important part of positioning strategy since it often sends quality cues to customers.

Understanding how to set prices is an important aspect of marketing decision making not least because of changes in the competitive arena which many believe will act to drive down prices in many countries. Since price is a major determinant of profitability, developing a coherent pricing strategy assumes major significance. Marketing in Action 10.1 discusses the major forces that are predicted to drive down prices.

Many people's introduction to the issue of pricing is a course in economics. We will now very briefly consider some of the ideas discussed by economists when considering price.

Economists' approach to pricing

Although a full discussion of the approach taken by economists to pricing is beyond the scope of this chapter the following gives a flavour of some of the important concepts relating to price. The discussion will focus on demand since this is of fundamental importance in pricing. Economists

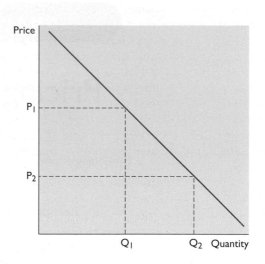

Figure 10.1 The demand curve

talk of the *demand curve* to conceptualize the relationship between the quantity demanded and different price levels. Figure 10.1 shows a typical demand curve. At a price of P_1, demand is Q_1. As price drops so demand rises. Thus at P_2 demand increases to Q_2. For some products a given fall in price leads to a large increase in demand. The demand for such products is said to be price elastic. For other products a given fall in price leads to only a small increase in demand. The demand for these products is described as price inelastic. Clearly it is useful to know price elasticity of demand. When faced with elastic demand marketers know that a price drop may stimulate much greater demand for their products. Conversely, when faced with inelastic demand, marketers know that a price drop will not increase demand appreciably. An obvious practical problem facing marketers who wish to use demand curve analysis is plotting demand curves accurately. There is no one demand curve that relates price to demand in real life. Each demand curve is based on a set of assumptions regarding other factors such as advertising expenditure, salesforce effectiveness, distribution intensity and the price of competing products which also affect demand. For the purposes of Fig. 10.1, these have been held constant at a particular level so that one unique curve can be plotted. A second problem regarding the demand curve relates to the estimation of the position of the curve even when other influences are held constant. Some companies conduct experiments to estimate likely demand at various price levels. However, it is not always feasible to do so since they may rely on the cooperation of retailers who may refuse or demand unrealistically high fees. Second, it is very difficult to implement a fully controlled field experiment. Where different regions of the country are involved differences in income levels, variations in local tastes and preferences, and differences in level of competitor activities may confound the results. The reality is that while the demand curve is a useful conceptual tool for thinking about pricing issues, in practice its application is limited. In truth traditional economic theory was not developed as a management tool but as an explanation of market behaviour. Managers therefore turn to other methods of setting prices and it is these methods that we shall discuss in this chapter.

Shapiro and Jackson identified three methods used by managers to set prices (see Fig. 10.2).[1] The first reflects a strong internal orientation and is based upon costs. The second is to use competitor-orientated pricing where the major emphasis is on competitor activities. The final approach is called marketing-orientated pricing as it focuses on the value that customers place on a product in the marketplace and its marketing strategy. In this chapter we shall examine each of these approaches and draw out their strengths and limitations. We shall also discuss how to initiate and respond to price changes.

Cost-orientated pricing

Companies often use cost-orientated methods when setting prices.[2] Two methods are normally used: full cost pricing and direct (or marginal) cost pricing.

Full cost pricing

Full cost pricing can best be explained by using a simple example (see Table 10.1). Imagine that you are given the task of pricing a new product (a widget) and the cost figures given in Table 10.1 apply. Direct costs such as labour and materials work out at £2 per unit. As output increases, more people and materials will be needed and so total costs increase. Fixed costs (or overheads) per year are calculated at £200 000. These costs (such as office and manufacturing facilities) do not change as output increases. They have to be paid

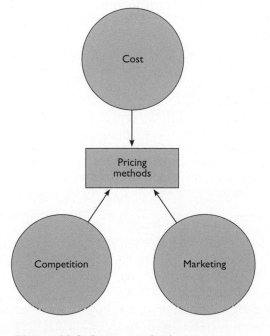

Figure 10.2 Pricing methods

Table 10.1	Full cost pricing
Year 1	
Direct costs (per unit)	= £2
Fixed costs	= £200 000
Expected sales	= 100 000
Cost per unit	
Direct costs	= £2
Fixed costs (200 000 ÷ 100 000)	= £2
Full costs	= £4
Mark-up (10%)	= £0.40p
Price (cost plus mark-up)	= £4.40p
Year 2	
Expected sales	= 50 000
Cost per unit	
Direct costs	= £2
Fixed costs (200 000 ÷ 50 000)	= £4
Full costs	= £6
Mark-up (10%)	= £0.60p
Price (cost plus mark-up)	= £6.60p

10.1 Marketing in Action

Price Drivers in the Twenty-first Century

Many commentators believe that changes in technology, competitive pressures and consumers' attitudes mean that prices are likely to fall relative to earnings. One item of information supports this view: for the first time in its 16-year history the Confederation of British Industry recorded no increase in retail prices during a three-month period in 1999. So what are the drivers that check the upward movement in prices?

First, technology is having a major impact on prices. This takes two forms: the emergence of the Internet and technological advances that drive down cost of manufacture. The Internet means that price-discounting new entrants can gain access to global markets at low cost. It also means that the cost of bargain hunting falls. Before the Internet, bargain hunters often needed to spend time and money searching retail outlets for the best offers. Now with the Internet search activity is quick and convenient. The other force is technology-driven price reductions. For example, the prices of video recorders, camcorders and mobile phones have fallen dramatically over recent years as advancing technology and economies of scale have driven down costs.

The second force impacting prices is internationalization. As companies globalize so competition intensifies, driving down prices. No longer can local producers rely on a protected home market to maintain high prices. The lowering of trade barriers, for example, through the creation of the Single European Market, is speeding this process. Consumers are becoming more international in outlook and are prepared to cross borders to seek bargains such as cheaper alcoholic drinks and cars. Companies are becoming more international in their sourcing policies. For example, Marks and Spencer, which once boasted that the majority of its clothing was sourced in the UK, is increasingly looking abroad for suppliers. Parallel importing is also practised where a retailer sources goods in one country (where prices are low) and sells them in their own country (where prices are higher) at a low price, thus undercutting prices at the manufacturer's traditional outlets.

The third pressure is supply-side induced. The growth in price-discounters such as easyJet and Go (airlines), Matalan (clothing), Aldi, Netto and Lidl (grocery) and the emergence of Wal-Mart (grocers and do-it-yourself products) in Europe is transforming the competitive landscape. The concept of everyday low prices is based on companies committed to driving down costs within their supply chain and passing some of the savings back to the consumer. Their reward is higher market share and greater economies of scale.

Finally, prices are being checked by the increasing price sensitivity of consumers. The rise in popularity of own-label products is evidence of this fact. Perhaps driven by some of the factors previously discussed such as the ease of making price comparisons via the Internet and the emergence of price-discounters, many consumers are questioning the wisdom of paying top prices for products.

All of these issues have implications for marketers. As Marketing in Action 8.1 showed, Heinz could resist the emergence of ultra-low-priced baked beans through its strong brand. The pressure on prices means that brand building is even more important to differentiate from low-priced alternatives. The second implication stems from the fact that price pressure will not hit all markets uniformly. A task of marketing strategists is to predict where its impact will be greatest and to look for markets where downward pressure is relatively weak. It is the latter markets that hold the greater attraction and may well be found in services where the impact of global competition is often less than that for manufactured goods.

Based on: Cook (1999);[3] Mitchell (1999);[4] Mitchell (1999);[5] Rodgers (1999)[6]

for whether 1 widget or 200 000 widgets are produced.

Having calculated the relevant costs, the next step is to estimate how many widgets we are likely to sell. We believe that we produce a good quality widget and therefore sales should be 100 000 in the first year. Therefore total (full) cost per unit is £4 and using the company's traditional 10 per cent mark-up a price of £4.40 is set.

In order to appreciate the problem of using full cost pricing, let us assume that the sales estimate of 100 000 is not reached by the end of the year. Because of poor economic conditions or as a result of setting the price too high, only 50 000 units are sold. The company believes that this level of sales is likely to be achieved next year. What happens to price? Table 10.1 gives the answer: it is raised because cost per unit goes up. This is because fixed costs (£200 000) are divided by a small expected sales volume (50 000). The result is a price rise in response to poor sales figures. This is clearly nonsense and yet can happen if full cost pricing is followed blindly. A major UK engineering company priced one of its main product lines in this way, and suffered a downward spiral of sales as prices were raised each year with disastrous consequences.

The first problem with full cost pricing, then, is that it leads to an increase in price as sales fall. Second, the procedure is illogical because a sales estimate is made *before* a price is set. Third, it focuses on internal costs rather than customers' willingness to pay. Finally, there may be a technical problem in allocating overheads in multi-product firms.[7]

However, inasmuch as the method forces managers to calculate costs, it does give an indication of the minimum price necessary to make a profit. Once direct and fixed costs have been measured *break-even analysis* can be used to estimate the sales volume needed to balance revenue and costs at different price levels. There-

fore the procedure of calculating full costs is useful when other pricing methods are used since full costs may act as a constraint. If they cannot be covered then it may not be worthwhile launching the product.

Direct cost pricing

In certain circumstances, companies may use *direct* (or marginal) *cost pricing*. This involves the calculation of only those costs which are likely to rise as output increases. In the example shown in Table 10.1 direct cost per unit is £2. As output increases so total costs will increase by £2 per unit. Like full cost pricing, direct cost pricing includes a mark-up (in this case 10 per cent) giving a price of £2.20.

The obvious problem is that this price does not cover full costs and so the company would be making a loss selling a product at this low price. However, there are situations where selling at a price above direct costs but below full cost makes sense. Suppose a company is operating at below capacity and the sales director receives a call from a buyer who is willing to place an order for 50 000 widgets but will pay only £2.20 per unit. If in management's judgement to refuse the order will mean machinery lying idle, a strong case for accepting the order can be made since the 0.20p per unit (£10 000) over direct costs is making a contribution to fixed costs that would not be made if the order was turned down. The decision is not without risk, however. The danger is that customers who are paying a higher price become aware of the £2.20 price, and demand a similar deal.

Direct cost pricing is useful for services marketing, for example where seats in aircraft or rooms in hotels cannot be stored; if they are unused at any time the revenue is lost. In such situations, pricing to cover direct costs plus a contribution to overheads is sensible. Like the previous example the risk is that customers who have paid the higher price find out and complain.

Direct costs, then, indicate the lowest price at which it is sensible to take business if the alternative is to let machinery (or seats or rooms) lie idle. Also, direct cost pricing does not suffer from the 'price up as demand down' problem that was found with full cost pricing, as it does not take account of fixed costs in the price calculation. Finally, it avoids the problem of allocating overhead charges found with full cost pricing for the same reason. However, when business is buoyant it gives no indication of the correct price because it does not take into account customers' willingness to pay. Nor can it be used in the long term as at some point fixed costs must be covered to make a profit. Nevertheless, as a short-term expedient or tactical device, direct cost pricing does have a role to play in reducing the impact of excess capacity.

Competitor-orientated pricing

A second approach to pricing is to focus on competitors rather than costs when setting prices. This can take two forms: *going-rate pricing* and *competitive bidding*.

Going-rate pricing

In situations where there is no product differentiation, for example a certain grade of coffee bean, a producer may have to take the going-rate for the product. This accords most directly to the economist's notion of perfect competition. To the marketing manager it is anathema. A fundamental marketing principle is the creation of a differential advantage which enables companies to build monopoly positions around their products. This allows a degree of price discretion dependent upon how much customers value the differential advantage. Even for what appear to be commodity markets, creative thinking can lead to the formation of a differential advantage upon which a premium price can be built. A case in point was Austin-Trumans, a steel stockholder, who stocked the same kind of basic steels held by many other stockholders. Faced with a commodity product, Austin-Trumans attempted to differentiate on delivery. They guaranteed that they would deliver on time or pay back 10 per cent of the price to the buyer. So important was delivery to buyers (and so unreliable were many of Austin-Truman's rivals) that they were willing to pay a 5 per cent price premium for this guarantee. The result was that Austin-Trumans were consistently the most profitable company in their sector for a number of years. This example shows how companies can use the creation of a differential advantage to move away from going-rate pricing.

Competitive bidding

Many contracts are won or lost on the basis of competitive bidding. The most usual process is the drawing up of detailed specifications for a product and putting the contract out for tender. Potential suppliers quote a price which is confidential to themselves and the buyer (sealed bids). All other things being equal, the buyer will select the supplier which quotes the lowest price. A major focus for suppliers, therefore, is the likely bid prices of competitors.

Statistical models have been developed by management scientists to add a little science to the art of competitive bidding.[8] Most use the concept of *expected profit* where:

Expected profit = Profit × Probability of winning

It is clearly a notional figure based upon actual profit (bid price – costs) and the probability of the bid price being successful. Table 10.2 gives a simple example of how such a competitive

Table 10.2 Competitive bidding using the expected profit criterion

Bid price (£)	Profit	Probability	Expected
2000	0	0.99	0
2100	100	0.90	90
2200	200	0.80	160*
2300	300	0.40	120
2400	400	0.20	80
2500	500	0.10	50

*Based on the expected profit criterion
Recommended bid price is £2200

bidding model might be used. Based on past experience the bidder believes that the successful bid will fall in the range of £2000–£2500. As price is increased so profits will rise (full costs = £2000) and the probability of winning will fall. The bidder uses past experience to estimate a probability of each price level being successful. In this example the probability ranges from 0.10 to 0.99. By multiplying profit and probability an expected profit figure is calculated for each bid price. Expected profit peaks at £160 which corresponds to a bid price of £2200. Consequently this is the price at which the bid will be made.

Unfortunately this simple model suffers from a number of limitations. First, it may be difficult if not impossible for managers to express their views on the likelihood of a price being successful in precise statistical probability terms. Note that if the probability of the £2200 bid was recorded as 0.70 rather than 0.80 and likewise the £2300 bid was recorded as 0.50 rather than 0.40 the recommended bid price would move from £2200 (expected profit = £140) to £2300 (expected profit = £150). Clearly the outcome of the analysis can be dependent on small changes in the probability figures. Second, use of the expected profit criterion is limited to situations where the bidder can play the percentage game over the medium to long term. In circumstances where companies are desperate to win an order, taking to trade-off profit for an improved chance of winning. In the extreme case of a company fighting for survival, a more sensible bid strategy might be to price at below full cost (£2000) and simply make a contribution to fixed costs as we discussed under direct cost pricing.

Clearly the use of competitive bidding models is restricted in practice. However, successful bidding depends on having an efficient competitor information system. One Scandinavian ball-bearing manufacturer which relied heavily on effective bid pricing installed a system which was dependent on salespeople feeding into its computer-based information system details of past successful and unsuccessful bids. The salespeople were trained to elicit successful bid prices from buyers, and then to enter them into a customer database which recorded order specifications, quantities, and the successful bid price.

Because not all buyers were reliable when giving their salespeople information (sometimes it was in their interest to quote a lower successful bid price than actually occurred), competitor successful bid prices were graded as category A (totally reliable: the salesperson had seen documentation supporting the bid price or it came from a totally trustworthy source), category B (probably reliable: no documentary evidence but the source was normally reliable) and category C (slightly dubious: the source may be reporting a lower than actual price to persuade us to bid very low next time). Although not as scientific as the competitive bidding model, this system built up over time is a very effective database which salespeople could use as a starting-point when they were next asked to bid by a customer.

Marketing-orientated pricing

Marketing-orientated pricing is more difficult than cost-orientated or competitor-orientated pricing because it takes a much wider range of factors into account. In all, ten factors need to be considered when adopting a marketing-orientated approach: these are shown in Fig. 10.3.

Marketing strategy

The price of a product should be set in line with *marketing strategy*. The danger is that price is viewed in isolation (as with full cost pricing) with no reference to other marketing decisions such as positioning, strategic objectives, promotion, distribution and product benefits. The result is an inconsistent mess which makes no sense in the marketplace and causes customer confusion.

The way around this problem is to recognize that the pricing decision is dependent on other earlier decisions in the marketing planning process (see Chapter 2). For new products, price will depend upon positioning strategy, and for existing products price will be affected by strategic objectives. First, we shall examine the setting of prices for new products. Second, we shall consider the pricing of existing products.

Pricing new products

In this section we shall explore the way in which positioning strategy affects price, launch strategies based upon skimming and penetration pricing, and the factors which affect the decision to charge a high or low price.

Positioning strategy a key decision that marketing management faces when launching new products is *positioning strategy*. This in turn will have a major influence on price. As we discussed in Chapter 7, product positioning involves the choice of target market and the creation of a differential advantage. Each of these factors can have an enormous impact on price.

When strategy is being set for a new product, marketing management is often faced with an array of potential target markets. In each, the product's differential advantage (value) may differ. For example, when calculators were commercially developed for the first time three distinct segments existed: S1 (engineers and scientists who placed a high value on calculators because their jobs involved a lot of complex calculations), S2 (accountants and bankers who also placed a high value on a calculator because of the nature of their jobs, although not as high as S1), and S3 (the general public who were the largest segment but placed a much lower value on the benefits of calculation).[9]

Clearly the choice of target market had a massive impact on the price that could be charged. If engineers/scientists were targeted, a high price could be set reflecting the large differential advantage of the calculator to them. For accountants/bankers, the price would have to be slightly lower, and for the general public a much lower price would be needed. In the event, the S1 segment was chosen and price set high (around

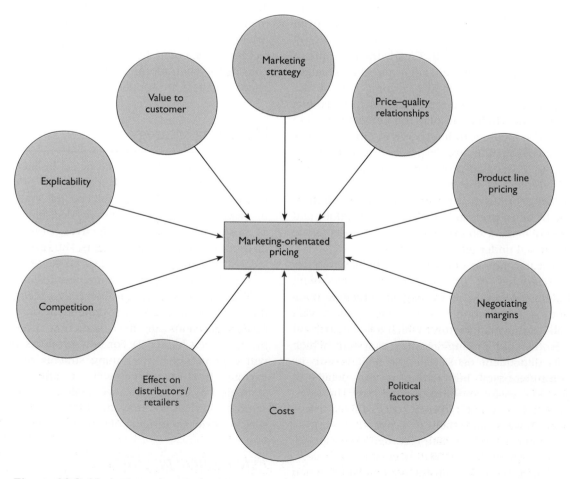

Figure 10.3 Marketing-orientated pricing

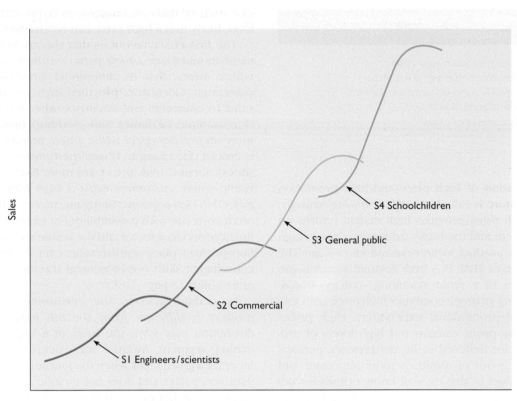

Figure 10.4 Adoption of innovations by segments: calculators

£250). Over time, price was reduced to draw into the market segments S2 and S3 (and a further segment S4 when examination regulations were changed to allow schoolchildren to use calculators). The development of the market for calculators based upon targeting increasingly price sensitive market segments is shown in Fig. 10.4.

Two implications follow from this discussion. First, for new products, marketing management must decide upon target market and the value that people in that segment place on the product (the extent of its differential advantage): only then can a market-based price be set which reflects that value. Second, where multiple segments appear attractive, modified versions of the product should be designed, and priced differently, not according to differences in costs, but in line with the respective values that each target market places on the product.

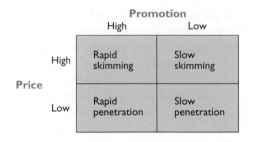

Figure 10.5 New product launch strategies

Launch strategies price should also be blended with other elements of the marketing mix. Figure 10.5 shows four marketing strategies based upon combinations of price and promotion. Similar matrices could also be developed for product and distribution, but for illustrative purposes promotion will be used here. A

Table 10.3   Characteristics of high price market segments

1   Product provides high value
2   Customers have high ability to pay
3   Consumer and bill payer are different
4   Lack of competition
5   High pressure to buy

combination of high price and high promotion expenditure is called a *rapid skimming strategy*. The high price provides high margin returns on investment and the heavy promotion creates high levels of product awareness and knowledge. The launches of IBM PCs and Polaroid cameras are examples of a rapid skimming strategy. A *slow skimming strategy* combines high price with low levels of promotional expenditure. High prices mean big profit margins but high levels of promotion are believed to be unnecessary, perhaps because word of mouth is more important and the product is already well known (Rolls-Royce) or because heavy promotion is thought to be incompatible with product image as with *cult* products. A company that uses a skimming pricing policy effectively is Bosch, the German car components supplier; it has applied an extremely profitable skimming strategy, supported by patents, to its launch of fuel injection and antilock brake systems.[10] Companies which combine low prices with heavy promotional expenditure are practising a *rapid penetration strategy*. The aim is to gain market share rapidly, perhaps at the expense of a rapid skimmer. For example, Amstrad successfully attacked IBM in the personal computer market by adopting a rapid penetration strategy. Finally, a *slow penetration strategy* combines a low price with low promotional expenditure. Own-label brands use this strategy: promotion is not necessary to gain distribution and low promotional expenditure helps to maintain high profit margins for these brands. This price/promotion framework is useful in thinking about marketing strategies at launch.

A major question remains, however: when is it sensible to use a *high price (skimming) strategy* and when should a *low price (penetration) strategy* be used? To answer this question we need to understand the characteristics of market segments that can bear a high price. These characteristics are shown in Table 10.3. The more

that each of these characteristics is present, the more likely that a high price can be charged.[11]

The first characteristic is that the market segment should place a *high value on the product*, which means that its differential advantage is substantial. Calculators provided high functional value to engineers and scientists, other products (for example perfumes and clothing) may rely more on *psychological value* where brand image is crucial (for example Chanel perfume or Gucci shoes). Second, high prices are more likely to be viable where *customers have a high ability to pay*. *Cash rich segments* in organizational markets often correlate with profitability. For example, the financial services sector and the textile industry in Europe may place similar values on marketing consultancy skills but in general the former has more ability to pay.

In certain markets the *consumer of the product is different from the bill payer*. This distinction may form the basis of a high price market segment. Airlines, for example, charge more for a given flight when the journey is for less than seven days and does not include a Saturday night. This is because that type of air traveller is more likely to be a businessperson, whereas the more price sensitive leisure travellers who pay for themselves and tend to stay at least a week can travel at a lower fare. Rail travel is also often segmented by price sensitivity. Early morning long-distance trips are more expensive than midday journeys since the former are usually made by business people.

The fourth characteristic of high price segments is *lack of competition* among supplying companies. The extreme case is a monopoly where customers have only one supplier from which to buy. When customers have no, or very little choice of supply, power to determine price is largely in the hands of suppliers. This means that high prices can be charged if suppliers so wish.

The final situation where customers are likely to be less price sensitive is where there is *high pressure to buy*. For example, in an emergency situation where a vital part is required to repair a machine which is needed to fulfil a major order, the customer may be willing to pay a high price if a supplier can guarantee quick delivery. The task of the marketing manager is to evaluate the chosen target market for a new product using the checklist provided by Table 10.3. It is unlikely that all five conditions will apply and so judgement is

Table 10.4 Conditions for charging low prices

1 Only feasible alternative
2 Market presence *or* domination
3 Experience curve effect
4 Make money later
5 Make money elsewhere
6 Barrier to entry
7 Predation

still required. But the more that these characteristics are found in the target market, the higher the chances that a high price can be charged.

Table 10.4 lists the conditions when a *low price (penetration) strategy* should be used. The first situation is when an analysis of the market segment using the previous checklist reveals that a low price is the *only feasible alternative*. For example, a product which has no differential advantage launched on to a market where customers are not cash rich, pay for themselves, have little pressure to buy, and have many suppliers to choose from has no basis for charging a price premium. At best it could take the going-rate price but more likely would be launched using a penetration (low price) strategy, otherwise there would be no incentive for customers to switch from their usual brand. Often markets contain a segment of price-sensitive consumers. These can be targeted with low priced brands as the advertisement for the VW Polo overleaf shows.

There are, however, more positive reasons for using a low price strategy. First, a company may wish to gain *market presence or domination* by aggressively pricing its products. A recent example of using price to gain market presence is the Proton car which in the UK achieved a 2 per cent market share within five years of launch by drastically undercutting the competition on price. In 1992 in a depressed market sales rose by 40 per cent. Penetration pricing for market presence is sometimes followed by price increase once market share has reached a satisfactory level. Mercedes followed this strategy in the US car market by pricing close to the market average in 1967 but had moved to over double the market average price by 1982.[12] The Lexus, Toyota's new luxury model, appears to be following a similar strategy. Ratners, a jewellery chain (now renamed Cignet), achieved market domination using price

as the major competitive weapon although indiscreet comments by its chairman regarding the quality of its merchandise dampened sales.

Low prices may also be charged to increase output and so bring down costs through the *experience curve effect*. Research has shown that for many products costs decline by around 20 per cent when production doubles.[13] Cost economies are achieved by learning how to produce the product more effectively through better production process, and improvements in skill levels. Economies of scale through, for example, the use of more cost effective machines at higher output levels also act to lower costs as production rises. Marketing costs per unit of output also may fall as production rises. For example, an advertising expenditure of £1 million represents 1 per cent of revenue when sales are £100 million but rises to 10 per cent of revenue when sales are only £10 million. Therefore a company may choose to price aggressively to become the largest producer and therefore, if the experience curve holds, the lowest cost supplier. Texas Instruments used a penetration pricing strategy for its semi-conductors for this reason. By becoming the lowest cost supplier it had the option of driving out competition by pricing at cost (to match their price, competition would have to price at below their costs) or price above costs and gain the largest profit margin in the industry.

Fourth, a low price strategy can make sense when the objective is to *make money later*. Two circumstances can provoke this action. First, the sale of the basic product may be followed by profitable after-sales service and/or spare parts. For example, the sale of an aero engine at cost may be worthwhile if substantial profits can be made on the later sale of spare parts. Second, the price sensitivity of customers may change over time: initially customers may be price sensitive implying the need for a low price, but as circumstances change they may become much less sensitive to price. For example, a publisher of management journals based their pricing strategy on this change. A key customer group were librarians who, faced by budget constraints, were price sensitive to new journals. Consequently they were priced low to encourage adoption. Once established in the library their use by students and staff meant that there would be considerable resistance to them being delisted. The strategy, therefore, was to keep price low until target penetration was achieved. Then

VW targets price sensitive car buyers

price was raised consistently above inflation in response to the fall in price sensitivity.

Marketers also charge low prices to *make money elsewhere*. For example, retailers often use loss leaders that are advertised in an attempt to attract customers into their stores and to create a low-cost image. Manufacturers selling a range of products to organizations may accept low prices on some goods in order to be perceived by customers as a full-range supplier. In both cases, sales of other higher priced and more profitable products benefit.

Low prices can also act as a *barrier to entry*. A company may weigh the longer-term benefits of deterring competition by accepting low margins to be greater than the short-term advantages of a high price, high margin strategy which may attract rivals into its market.

Finally, low prices may be charged in an attempt to put other companies out of business. British Airways and TWA were accused of *predatory pricing* against Laker Airlines on its Atlantic routes.

An alternative strategy to charging permanently low prices is to run sales promotions (e.g. temporary price cuts or bulk-buy offers). Retailers and manufacturers are increasingly considering the relative merits of these approaches. Marketing in Action 10.2 considers the issues.

Pricing existing products

The pricing of existing products should also be set within the context of strategy. Specifically, the *strategic objective* for each product will have a major bearing on pricing strategy. As with new products, price should not be set in isolation, but should be consistent with strategic objectives. Four strategic objectives are relevant to pricing: build, hold, harvest and reposition.

Build objective   for price sensitive markets, a build objective for a product implies a *price lower than competition*. If the competition raise their prices we would be slow to match them. For price insensitive markets, the best pricing strategy becomes less clear cut. Price in these circumstances will be dependent on the overall positioning strategy thought appropriate for the product.

Hold objective   where the strategic objective is to hold sales and/or market share, the appropriate

pricing strategy is to *maintain or match price* relative to the competition. This has implications for price changes: if competition reduce prices then our prices would match this price fall.

Harvest objective   a harvest objective implies the maintenance or raising of profit margins even though sales and/or market share are falling. The implication for pricing strategy would be to set *premium prices*. For products that are being harvested, there would be much greater reluctance to match price cuts than for products that were being built or held. On the other hand, price increases would be swiftly matched.

Reposition objective   changing market circumstances and product fortunes may necessitate the repositioning of an existing product. This may involve a *price change*, the direction and magnitude of which will be dependent on the new positioning strategy for the production. As we discussed under product replacement strategies (Chapter 9), Brut's repositioning involved new packaging and an increase in price.

The above examples show how developing clear strategic objectives helps the setting of price and clarifies appropriate reaction to competitive price changes. Price setting, then, is much more sophisticated than simply asking 'How much can I get for this product?' The process starts by asking more fundamental questions like 'How is this product going to be positioned in the marketplace?' and 'What is the appropriate strategic objective for this product?'. Only after these questions are answered can price be sensibly determined.

Value to the customer

A second marketing consideration when setting prices is estimating a product's value to the customer. Already when discussing marketing strategy its importance has been outlined: price should be accurately keyed to the value to the customer. In brief, the more value that a product gives compared to the competition, the higher the price that can be charged. In this section we shall explore a number of ways of estimating value to the customer. This is critical because of the close relationship between value and price. Four methods of estimating value will now be discussed: the buy-response method, trade-off

10.2   Marketing in Action

Everyday Low Prices Versus Sales Promotions

A debate is raging over whether the everyday low pricing (permanent low prices) strategies used by such firms as Proctor & Gamble, Sainsbury and Esso are as effective as the sales promotions employed by their rivals. In an attempt to throw light on this issue a study by A.C. Nielson in the UK examined consumer attitudes to price and promotions for supermarket goods. The result was a segmentation scheme that allows retailers and manufacturers to tailor their approach to the customer profile of individual stores. The study has identified five behavioural types:

Branded everyday low price seekers   (19 per cent of all households) these consumers work on tight budgets and are prepared to shop around for the lowest prices on their favoured brand. However, they are not tempted by money-off promotions or bulk-buy offers on other brands. They tend to be old-fashioned and demographically downmarket. Their key motivation is everyday low prices.

Low price fixture ferrets   (23 per cent) these tend to be young families with an income earner. With children in tow, they want fast shopping. Working on a tight budget, they use coupons, store loyalty schemes, price reductions and free items to keep costs down but not bulk buys because of the high initial outlay. They tend to switch brands and 20 per cent of their purchases are related to promotional offers.

Promotion junkies   (18 per cent) they have very low brand and store loyalty, high awareness of prices and brag about the bargains they get. Their most appealing promotions are aggressive price cuts, quantity deals and multibuys. They buy 30 per cent more on offer than the average consumer despite the fact they are better off than most. They will weigh up the relative attraction of different offers but, while value is important, the main motivating factor is the presence of the promotion itself.

Stockpilers   (21 per cent) this group is affluent and shows high brand and store loyalty. They are motivated by multipacks and bulk offers but tend not to switch brands for the sake of a promotion. They are partially responsible for the boost in sales during the promotional period but also the trough afterwards as they use up the bulk purchases.

Promotionally oblivious   (18 per cent) these people are indifferent to sales promotions and low prices. They are creatures of habit and where promotions are taken up they tend to be for 'soft' promotions such as coupons, free gifts or sendaways rather than more aggressive price reductions. They are attractive to retailers and manufacturers as they require very little additional incentive to buy.

The task for retailers is to understand the proportion of each category that shops at individual stores. For example, if a store was dominated by branded everyday low price seekers, pricing strategy would be set accordingly. For another store, which tended to attract promotion junkies, a greater emphasis on sales promotions would be warranted.

Based on: Mille (1997);[14] Killgren and Cook (1999)[15]

analysis, experimentation, and economic value to the customer analysis.

The buy-response method

The **buy-response method** estimates directly the value that customers place on a product by asking them if they would be willing to buy it at varying price levels.[16] The proportion of people who would be willing to buy the product is plotted against price to produce a buy-response curve (see Fig. 10.6). As the figure shows, the curve is usually bell-shaped indicating prices which are too high and too low (indicating poor quality).

The methodology is as follows:

1　Up to ten prices are chosen within the range usual for the product field.

2　Respondents are shown the product and asked 'Would you buy X at . . . ?' The price first quoted will be near the average for the product field and the other prices stated at random.

3　The percentage of respondents indicating that they would buy is calculated for each price and plotted to form the buy-response curve.

The curve shows the prices at which willingness to buy drops sharply and thus gives an indication of the acceptable price range for the product (in Fig. 10.6 this would be between 23p and 25p).

Although simple to administer and analyse, the buy-response method suffers from one severe drawback. The methodology focuses the respondent's attention on price, which may induce an unrealistically high price-consciousness.[17] In reality, customers weigh price against product features and the benefits they give. The next technique—trade-off analysis—overcomes this problem.

Trade-off analysis

Trade-off analysis (otherwise known as conjoint analysis) measures the trade-off between price and other product features so that their effects on product preference can be established.[18] Respondents are not asked direct questions about price, instead product profiles consisting of product features and price are described and respondents are asked to name

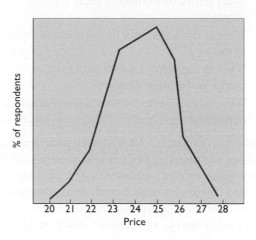

Figure 10.6 The buy-response curve.

Source: A. Gabor (1977) *Price as a quality indicator in pricing: principles and practices,* London: Heinemann

their preferred profile. From their answers the effect of price and other product features can be measured using a computer model. The following gives a brief description of the procedure.

The first step is to identify the most important product features (*attributes*) and benefits that are expected to be gained as a result of buying the product. Product profiles are then built using these attributes (including price) and respondents are asked to choose which product they would buy from pairs of product profiles. Statistical analysis allows the computation of *preference contributions* that permit the preference for attributes to be compared. For example, if the analysis was for an industrial product, trade-off analysis might show that increasing delivery time from one week to one day is worth a price increase of 5 per cent. In addition the relative importance of each of the product attributes including price can be calculated. By translating these results into market share and profit figures for the proposed new product the optimal price can be found.

This technique has been used to price a wide range of industrial and consumer products and services and can be used to answer such questions as:[19]

1　What is the value of a product feature including improving service levels in price terms?

2 What happens to market share if price changes?

3 What is the value of a brand name in terms of price?

4 What is the effect on our market share of competitive price changes?

5 How do these effects vary across European countries?

Marketing in Action 10.3 shows how trade-off analysis was used to price a new German car. By developing product profiles based on four key product attributes—the brand, maximum speed, petrol consumption, and price—and interviewing target customers, an optimal price could be set.

Experimentation

A limitation of trade-off analysis is that respondents are not asked to back up their preferences with cash expenditure. Consequently there can be a doubt that what they say they prefer may not be reflected in actual purchase when they are asked to part with money. *Experimental pricing research* attempts to overcome this drawback by placing a product on sale at different locations with varying prices.

The major alternatives are to use a controlled store experiment or test marketing. In a *controlled store experiment* a number of stores are paid to vary the price levels of the product under test. Suppose 100 supermarkets are being used to test two price levels of a brand of coffee; 50 stores would be chosen at random (perhaps after controlling for region and size) and allocated the lower price, the rest would use the higher price. By comparing sales levels and profit contributions between the two groups of stores the most profitable price would be established. A variant of this procedure would test price differences between the test brand and major rival brands. For example, in half the stores a price differential of 2p may be compared with 4p. In practice considerable sums need to be paid to supermarkets to obtain approval to run such tests, and the implementation of the price levels needs to be carefully monitored to ensure that the stores do sell at the specified prices.

Test marketing can be used to compare the effectiveness of varying prices so long as more than one area is chosen. For example, the same product could be sold in two areas using an identical promotional campaign but with different prices between areas. A more sophisticated design could measure the four combinations of high/low price and high/low promotional expenditure if four areas were chosen. Obviously, the areas would need to be matched (or differences allowed for) in terms of target customer profile so that the result would be comparable. The test needs to be long enough so that trial and repeat purchase at each price can be measured. This is likely to be between 6 and 12 months for products whose purchase cycle lasts more than a few weeks.

A potential problem of using test marketing to measure price effects is competitor activity designed to invalidate the test results. For example, competitors could run special promotions in the test areas to make sales levels atypical if they discovered the purpose and location of the test marketing activities. Alternatively they may decide not to react at all. If they know that a pricing experiment is taking place and that syndicated consumer panel data are being used to measure the results they may simply monitor the results since competitors will be receiving the same data as the testing company.[20] By estimating how successful each price has been, they are in a good position to know how to react when a price is set nationally.

Economic value to the customer analysis

Experimentation is more usual when pricing consumer products. However, industrial markets have a powerful tool at their disposal when setting the price of their products: **economic value to the customer (EVC)** analysis. Many organizational purchases are motivated by economic value considerations since reducing costs and increasing revenue are prime objectives of many companies. If a company can produce an offering that has a high EVC, it can set a high price and yet still offer superior value compared to the competition. A high EVC may be because the product generates more revenue for the buyer than competition or because its operating costs (such as maintenance, operation or start-up costs) are lower over its lifetime. EVC analysis is usually particularly revealing when applied to products whose purchase price represents a small proportion of the lifetime costs to the customer.[21]

10.3   Marketing in Action

Pricing a German Car Using Trade-Off Analysis

A German car company used conjoint measurement to set the price for its new Tiger model (name disguised). The managers involved in the decision raised questions like the following: What is the 'price value' of our brand? How much is the customer willing to pay for a higher maximum speed? (There is no speed limit in Germany.) How does petrol consumption relate to price acceptance?

The managers proceeded in the following steps. First, they determined that the most relevant product attributes were brand, maximum speed, petrol consumption, and price.

Second, they chose characteristics for each attribute. They would test three brands: one German, one Japanese, and their own; three maximum speeds: 200, 220, and 240 kilometres per hour; three levels of petrol consumption: 12, 14, and 16 litres per 100 kilometres; and three prices: DM 50 000, 60 000, and 70 000.

Third, they designed a questionnaire and collected data. The attributes and characteristics yielded eighty-one possible product profiles, but the company needed only nine profiles to answer their questions. Researchers developed the nine profiles and presented them to target group respondents in pairs, as shown below. Respondents, interviewed by computer, indicated whether they would buy A or B. Thirty-two such comparisons were presented.

Attribute	Profile A	Profile B
Brand	Tiger	Japanese
Maximum speed	200	240
Petrol consumption	12	16
Price	50 000	70 000

From the data, the company calculated preference contributions, numerical values that allow the preference for attributes to be compared. Preference contributions allow you to discover that, say, increasing car speed by 20 kilometres per hour generates the same increase in preference for the car as would decreasing the price by DM 10 000. Adding up the preference contributions results in an overall preference index.

The greater the difference between the lowest and the highest *preference contribution* within one attribute (that is, the greater the disparity between preference for, say, the most popular brand and the least popular brand), the more important is this attribute. These differences can be translated into percentage importance weights that add up to 100 per cent. In this case:

Brand	35%
Maximum speed	30%
Price	20%
Petrol consumption	15%

Thus customers in this target group were very interested in brand and maximum speed but less sensitive to price and petrol consumption.

Taking the known attribute levels for the Tiger model, the managers could calculate market shares and profits for alternative prices. They found that the optimal price was at the upper end of the price range; they set it slightly below DM 70 000.

Based on: Simon (1992)[22]

Figure 10.7 illustrates the calculation of EVC and how it can be used in price setting. A reference product is chosen (often the market leader) with which to compare costs. In the example the market leader is selling a machine tool for £50 000. However this is only part of a customer's life cycle costs. In addition £30 000 start-up costs (installation, lost production, and operator training) and £120 000 post-purchase costs (operator, power, and maintenance) are incurred. The total life cycle costs are, therefore, £200 000.

Our new machine tool (product X) has a different customer cost profile. Technological advances have reduced start-up costs to £20 000 and post-purchase costs to £100 000. Therefore total costs are reduced by £30 000 and the EVC which our new product offers is £80 000 (£200 000 − £120 000). Thus the EVC figure is the amount which a customer would have to pay to make the total life cycle costs of the new and reference products the same. If the new machine

tool was priced at £80 000 this would be the case. Below this price there would be an economic incentive for customers to buy the new machine tool.

EVC analysis is clearly a powerful tool for price setting since it establishes the upper economic limit for price. Management then has to use judgement regarding how much incentive to give the customer to buy the new product and how much of a price premium to charge. A price of £60 000 would give customers a £20 000 lifetime cost saving incentive while establishing a £10 000 price premium over the reference product. In general, the more entrenched the market leader, the more loyal its customer base, and the less well known the newcomer, the higher the cost saving incentive needs to be.

In the second example shown in Fig. 10.7 the new machine tool (product Y) does not affect costs but raises the customer's revenues. For example, faster operation may result in more output, or greater precision may enhance product

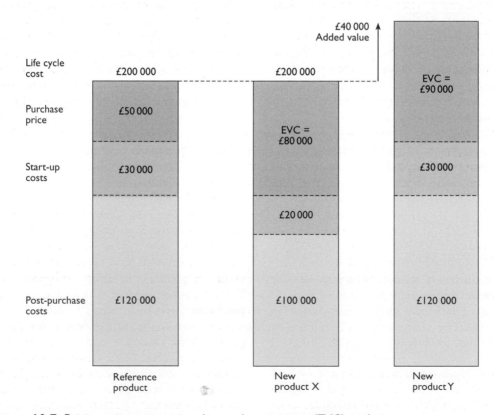

Figure 10.7 Pricing using economic value to the customer (EVC) analysis

quality leading to higher prices. This product is estimated to give £40 000 extra profit contribution over the reference product because of higher revenues. Its EVC is, therefore, £90 000 indicating the highest price the customer should be willing to pay. Once more marketing management has to decide how much incentive to give to customers and how much price premium to charge.

EVC analysis can be useful in target market selection since different customers may have varying EVC levels. A decision may be made to target that market segment which has the highest EVC figure since for these customers the product has the greatest differential advantage. The implementation of EVC-based pricing strategy relies on a well-trained salesforce who are capable of explaining sophisticated economic value calculations to customers and field-based evidence that the estimates of cost savings and revenue increases will occur in practice.

Price–quality relationships

A third consideration when adopting a marketing-orientated approach to pricing is the relationship between price and perceived quality. Many people use price as an indicator of quality. This is particularly the case for products where objective measurement of quality is not possible such as drinks and perfume. But the effect is also to be found with consumer durables and industrial products. A study of price and quality perceptions of cars, for example, found that higher priced cars were perceived to possess (unjustified) high quality.[23] Also sales of a branded agricultural fertilizer rose after the price was raised above its generic competitors despite the fact that it was the same compound. Interviews with farmers revealed that they believed the fertilizer to improve crop yield compared with rival products. Clearly price had influenced quality perceptions.

Product line pricing

Marketing-orientated companies also need to take account of where the price of a new product fits into its existing product line. For example, when Ford developed the Orion they had to carefully price-position the model range within their existing product line of Fiesta, Escort, Sierra and Granada.

Some companies prefer to extend their product lines rather than reduce the price of existing brands in the face of price competition. They launch cut-price *fighter brands* to compete with the low-price rivals. This has the advantage of maintaining the image and profit margins of existing brands.

By producing a range of brands at different price points, companies can cover the varying price sensitivities of customers and encourage them to trade-up to the more expensive, higher margin brands.

Explicability

The capability of salespeople to explain a high price to customers may constrain price flexibility. In markets where customers demand economic justification of prices, the inability to produce cost and/or revenue arguments may mean that high prices cannot be set. In other circumstances the customer may reject a price that does not seem to reflect the cost of producing the product. For example, sales of an industrial chemical compound that repaired grooves in drive-shafts suffered because many customers believed that the price of £500 did not reflect the cost of producing the compound. Only when the salesforce explained that the premium price was needed to cover high research and development expenditure did customers accept that the price was not exploitative.

Competition

Competition factors are important determinants of price. At the very least competitive prices should be taken into account; yet it is a fact of commercial life that many companies do not know what the competition is charging for their products.

Care has to be taken when defining competition. When asked to name competitors, many marketing managers list companies who supply technically similar products. For example, a paint manufacturer will name other paint manufacturers. However, as Fig. 10.8 illustrates, this is only one layer of competition. A second layer consists of dissimilar products solving the same problem in a similar way. Polyurethane varnish manufacturers would fall into this category. A third level of competition would come from products solving the problem (or eliminating it) in a dissimilar way. Since window frames are often painted, PVC double glazing manufacturers would form competition at this level.

This analysis is not simply academic as the effects of price changes can be misleading without realizing these three layers of competition. For example, if all paint manufacturers raised their prices simultaneously they might believe that overall sales would not be dramatically affected if they mistakenly defined competition as technically similar products. The reality is, however, that such price collusion would make polyurethane varnish and, over a longer period, PVC double glazing more attractive to customers. The implication is that companies must take into account all three levels of competition when setting and changing prices.

In Europe a potential competitive threat is the development of *parallel importing* which is the practice of importing goods from low-priced markets into high-priced ones by distributors. This produces the novel effect of a brand competing with itself (on price). The impact of parallel importing on prices is analysed in Marketing in Action 10.4.

Negotiating margins

In some markets customers expect a price reduction. Price paid is therefore very different from list prices. In the car market, for example, customers expect to pay less than the asking price in return for a cash sale. For organizational customers Marn

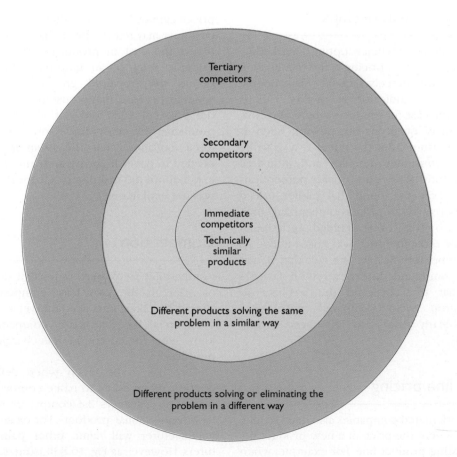

Figure 10.8 Layers of competition

and Rosiello describe the difference between list price and realized or transaction price as the **price waterfall**.[24] The difference can be accounted for by order-size discounts, competitive discounts (a discretionary discount negotiated before the order is taken), a fast payment discount, an annual volume bonus and promotional allowances.

Managing this price waterfall is a key element in achieving a satisfactory transaction price. Marketing-orientated companies recognize that such discounting may be a fact of commercial life and build in *negotiating margins* that allow prices to fall from list price levels but still permit profitable transaction prices to be achieved.

Effect on distributors/retailers

When products are sold through intermediaries such as distributors or retailers, the list price to the customer must reflect the margins required by them. As we saw with Müller yoghurt, a major factor in gaining distribution in a mature market was the fact that its high price allowed attractive profit margins for the supermarket chains. Conversely, the implementation of a penetration pricing strategy may be hampered if distributors refuse to stock the product because the profit per unit sold is less than competitive products.

10.4   Marketing in Action

Parallel Importing and Pricing

Parallel importing involves distributors such as retailers buying products in one country (where prices are low) and selling them in another (where prices are higher) at a low price. For example, a pharmaceutical company might sell its drugs in a developing country at a low price only to discover that these discounted drugs are exported to another country where they are in direct competition with the same product sold for higher prices by the same firm.

Not surprisingly manufacturers have a lot to lose by this activity. First, it lowers average selling prices and therefore reduces profit margins. Second, manufacturers lose control over where and to whom their products are sold. This can damage brand image (compounded by the price drop) as the product range is sold in retail outlets that are incompatible with the brand's position in the marketplace. Finally, the relationship between manufacturers and their traditional distributors can be damaged as the latter see their sales decline in favour of their price-cutting rivals.

An important ruling on parallel importing by the European Court of Justice found in favour of Silhouette, an upmarket Austrian sunglass manufacturer who sold 21 000 pairs of an older model to a Bulgarian company on the understanding that they would be sold only in Bulgaria or the former Soviet Union. However, the sunglasses were soon back in Austria being sold at the discount chain Hartlaver at a low price. The Court ruled that Silhouette should have the right to choose its distributor.

The implications are wide-ranging with Levi Strauss UK describing the ruling as 'most helpful' but Tesco, the UK supermarket which uses global sourcing for some of its non-food products, argued that the ruling would help to create a European price cartel which would work against consumer interests through higher prices.

Based on: Anonymous (1998);[25] Cateora et al. (2000);[26] Welford and Prescott (1996)[27]

The implication is that pricing strategy is dependent on understanding not only the ultimate customer but also the needs of the distributors and retailers who form the link between them and the manufacturer. If their needs cannot be accommodated product launch may not be viable, or a different distribution system (for example, direct selling) required.

Political factors

High prices can be a contentious public issue which may invoke government intervention. In recent years, public opprobrium has focused on the price of compact disks and children's computer games. Where price is out-of-line with manufacturing costs, political pressure may act to force down prices. The European Commission and national bodies such as the Monopolies Commission (now known as the Competition Commission) have been active in discouraging anticompetitive practices such as price-fixing. Indeed the establishment of the Single European Market was a result of the desire to raise competitive pressures and thereby reduce prices throughout the European Union.

Companies need to take great care that their pricing strategies are not seen to be against the public interest. Exploitation of a monopoly position may bring short-term profits but incur the backlash of a public inquiry into pricing practices.

Costs

The final consideration that should be borne in mind when setting prices is costs. This may seem a contradiction of an outward-looking marketing-orientated approach but in reality costs do enter the pricing equation. The secret is to consider costs alongside all of the other considerations discussed under marketing-orientated price setting rather than in isolation. In this way costs act as a constraint: if the market will not bear the full cost of producing and marketing the product it should not be launched.

What should be avoided is the blind reference to costs when setting prices. Simply because one product costs less to make than another does not imply its price should be less. Two examples from the car industry illustrate this point. Because the

Fiat Tipo is manufactured in a more modern plant than the Fiat Uno it costs less to produce; it is priced higher than the Uno, however, because it is a larger car conferring more customer benefits. Similarly the Rover 400 costs less to manufacture than the Rover 200. Marketing research has shown, however, that because the Rover 400 is a bigger car with a larger boot customers expect to pay more for that model. Rover price the two models in line with customer expectations, not costs.

Initiating price changes

Our discussion of pricing strategy so far has looked at the factors which affect pricing strategy. By taking into account the ten marketing-orientated factors, managers can judge the correct level at which to set prices. But in a highly competitive world, pricing is dynamic: managers need to know when and how to raise or lower prices, and whether or not to react to competitors' price moves. First, we shall discuss initiating price changes before analysing how to react to competitors' price changes.

Three key issues associated with initiating price changes are the *circumstances* that may lead a company to raise or lower prices, the *tactics* that can be used, and *estimating competitor reaction*. Table 10.5 illustrates the major points relevant to each of these considerations.

Circumstances

A price increase may be justified as a result of marketing research (for example trade-off analysis or experimentation) which reveals that customers place a higher *value* on the product than is reflected in its price. *Rising costs* and hence reduced profit margins may also stimulate price rises. Another factor that leads to price increases is *excess demand*. A company that cannot supply the demand created by its customers may choose to raise prices in an effort to balance demand and supply. This can be an attractive option as profit margins are automatically widened. The final circumstance when companies may decide to raise prices is when embarking on a *harvest objective*. Prices are raised to increase margins even though sales may fall.

Correspondingly, price cuts may be provoked by the discovery that price is high compared to the *value* that customers place on the product, *falling costs* (and the desire to bring down costs further through the experience curve effect), and where there is *excess supply* leading to excess capacity. A further circumstance which may lead to price falls is the adoption of a *build objective*. When customers are thought to be price sensitive, price cutting may be used to build sales and market share. A damper on this tactic would be when a *price war* might be provoked, as happened when Reemtsma Cigarettenfabriken cut the price of its West brand from DM 3.80 to DM 3.30 in West Germany.[28] This was the first price-cutting move of this severity since the 1940s and led to competitor retaliation that saw the collapse of cigarette prices and margins.

The final circumstance that might lead to price cuts is the desire to *pre-empt competitive entry* into a market. Proactive price cuts—before the new competitor enters—is painful to implement because it incurs short-term profit sacrifices but immediately reduces the attractiveness of the market to the potential entrant and reduces the risk of customer annoyance if prices are reduced only after competitive entry.[29] This was the tactic used in 1984 by Cummins Engines, who slashed the prices of their small diesels by 30 per cent to prevent the entry of Japanese companies in their market.[30]

Tactics

Price increases and cuts can be implemented in many ways. The most direct is the *price jump or fall* that increases or decreases the price by the full amount at one go. A price jump avoids prolonging the pain of a price increase over a long period but may raise the visibility of the price increase to customers. Using *staged price increases* might make the price rise more palatable but runs the risk of being charged with 'always rising your prices'. A *one-stage price fall* can have a high impact dramatic effect that can be heavily promoted but also has an immediate impact on profit margins. *Staged price reductions* have a less dramatic effect but may be used when a price cut is believed to be necessary but the amount necessary to stimulate sales is unclear. Small cuts may be initiated as a learning process which proceeds until the desired effect on sales is achieved.

Price can also be raised by using escalator clauses. The contracts for some organizational purchases are drawn up before the product is made. Constructing the product, for example a new defence system or motorway, may take a number of years. An escalator clause in the contract allows the supply to stipulate price increases in line with a specified index, for example increases in industry wage rates, or the cost of living.

Table 10.5 Initiating price changes		
	Increases	*Cuts*
Circumstances	Value greater than price Rising costs Excess demand Harvest objective	Value less than price Excess supply Build objective Price war unlikely Pre-empt competitive entry
Tactics	Price jump Staged price increases Escalator clauses Price unbundling Lower discounts	Price fall Staged price reductions Fighter brands Price bundling Higher discounts
Estimating competitor reaction	Strategic objectives Self-interest Competitive situation Past experience	

Price unbundling is another tactic that effectively raises prices. Many product offerings actually consist of a set of products to which an overall price is set (for example computer hardware and software). Price unbundling allows each element in the offering to be separately priced in such a way that the total price is raised. A variant on this process is charging for services that previously were included in the product's price. For example, manufacturers of mainframe computers have the option of unbundling installation and training services and charging for them separately.

A final tactic is to maintain the list price but *lower discounts* to customers. In periods of heavy demand for new cars, dealers lower the cash discount given to customers, for example. Quantity discounts can also be manipulated to raise the transaction price to customers. The percentage discount per quantity can be lowered, or the quantity that qualifies for a particular percentage discount can be raised.

Companies that are contemplating a price cut have three options besides a direct price fall. A company defending a premium-priced brand that is under attack from a cut-price competitor may choose to maintain its price while introducing a *fighter brand*. The established brand keeps its premium-price position while the fighter brand competes with the rival for price sensitive customers. Where a number of products and services that tend to be bought together are separately priced, *price bundling* can be used to effectively lower price. For example, televisions can be offered with 'free three-year repair warranties' or cars offered with 'free labour at first service'. Finally, *discount terms* can be made more attractive by increasing the percentage or lowering the qualifying levels.

Estimating competitor reaction

A key factor in the price change decision is the extent of competitor reaction. A price rise that no competitor follows may turn customers away while a price cut that is met by the competition may reduce industry profitability. Four factors affect the extent of competitor reaction: their strategic objectives, what is in their self-interest, the competitive situation at the time of the price change, and past experience.

Companies should try to gauge their *com-petitor's strategic objectives* for their products. By observing pricing and promotional behaviour, talking to distributors and even hiring their personnel, estimates of whether competitor products are being built, held or harvested can be made. This is crucial information: their response to our price increase or cut will depend upon it. They are more likely to follow our price increase if their strategic objective is to hold or harvest. If they are intent on building market share, they are more likely to resist following our price increase. Conversely they are more likely to follow our price cuts if they are building or holding and more likely to ignore our price cuts if they are harvesting.

Self-interest is also important when estimating competitor reactions. Managers initiating price changes should try to place themselves in the position of their competitors. What reaction is in their best interests? This may depend on the circumstances of the price change. For example, if price is raised in response to a general rise in cost inflation, competition are more likely to follow than if price is raised because of the implementation of a harvest objective. Price may also depend upon the *competitive situation*. For example, if competition has excess capacity a price cut is more likely to be matched than if this is not the case. Similarly, a price rise is more likely to be followed if competition is faced with excess demand.

Competitor reaction can also be judged by looking at their reactions to previous price changes. While *past experience* is not always a reliable guide it may provide insights into the way in which competition view price changes and the likely responses they might take.

There is no doubt that the entry of new competitors into a mature market can radically alter price structures. e-Marketing 10.1 describes how the entry of Microsoft into the encyclopaedia market fundamentally changed price levels through competitor response and counter response.

Reacting to competitors' price changes

When competitors initiate price changes, companies need to analyse their appropriate reactions. Three issues are relevant here: when to follow, what to ignore, and the tactics if the price change is to be followed. Table 10.6 summarizes the main considerations.

When to follow

Competitive price increases are more likely to be followed when they are due to general *rising cost* levels, or industry-wide *excess demand*. In these circumstances the initial pressure to raise prices is the same on all parties. Following a price rise is also more likely when customers are relatively *price insensitive* which means that the follower will not gain much advantage by resisting the price increase. Where *brand image is consistent* with high prices a company is more likely to follow a competitor's price rise as to do so would be consistent with the brand's positioning strategy. Finally, a price rise is more likely to be followed when a company is pursuing a *harvest or hold objective* because in both cases the emphasis is more on profit margin than sales/market share gain.

Price cuts are likely to be followed when they are stimulated by general *falling costs* or *excess supply*. Falling costs allow all companies to cut prices while maintaining margins, and excess supply means that a company is unlikely to allow a rival to make sales gains at their expense. Price cuts will also be followed in *price sensitive markets* since allowing one company to cut price without retaliation would mean large sales gains for the price cutter. The image of the company can also affect reaction to price cuts. Some companies

 ## 10.1   e-Marketing

Price Wars in the Information Market

A fundamental characteristic of information products is that once the investment in producing the first item has been made, ongoing production costs are minimal. The concept has been known in the book industry for centuries. The first copy of a new book is expensive but subsequent units can be printed for very little additional expenditure.

This aspect of information products can result in price wars where the winner is usually the firm who moves first and is prepared to be the most aggressive. Until the 1990s, *Encyclopaedia Britannica* was regarded as the classic reference work selling for a premium price of well over $1000 per copy. Then in 1992, Microsoft entered the market by buying the rights to the Funk & Wagnall encyclopaedia. They created a CDROM-based product known as *Encarta* which they marketed at $49.95.

Britannica tried to react by offering an online product to libraries at a cost of $2000 for a multi-user site licence. But the firm continued to lose share to *Encarta*, so next they offered an online subscription product at a fee of $200 per year. This was followed in 1996 by a CD version for $200, still significantly higher priced than *Encarta*. Jacob Safra, a Swiss entrepreneur purchased the Britannica company in late 1996, disbanded the salesforce network and experimented with direct marketing. Both *Britannica* and *Encarta* became available in computer stores at very similar prices.

The latest twist in the price battle is that both products can be obtained free of charge. *Encarta* can be obtained within a bundle of extras which are given away 'free' with some PC purchases. The *Encyclopaedia Britannica* is available free on the Internet. Britannica.com. hopes that by giving away for free its core product it will attract enough site visits to become a major advertising site.

Based on: Shapiro and Varian (1999);[31] Mitchell (1999)[32]

position themselves as low price manufacturers or retail outlets. In such circumstances they would be less likely to allow a price reduction by a competitor to go unchallenged for to do so would be *incompatible with their brand image*. Finally, price cuts are likely to be followed when the company has a *build or hold strategic objective*. In such circumstances an aggressive price move by a competitor would be followed to prevent sales/market share loss. In the case of a build objective, response may be more dramatic with a price fall exceeding the initial competitive move.

When to ignore

The circumstances associated with companies not reacting to a competitive price move are in most cases simply the opposite of the above. Price increases are likely to be ignored when *costs are stable or falling*, which means that there are no cost pressures forcing a general price rise. In the situation of *excess supply* companies may view a price rise as making the initiator less competitive and therefore allow the price to take place unchallenged, particularly when customers are *price sensitive*. Companies occupying low-price positions may regard a price rise in response to a price increase from a rival to be *incompatible with their brand image*. Finally, companies pursuing a *build objective* may allow a competitor's price rise to go unmatched in order to gain sales and market share.

Price cuts are likely to be ignored in conditions of *rising costs*, *excess demand* and when servicing *price insensitive customers*. Premium price positioners may be reluctant to follow competitor's price cuts for to do so would be *incompatible with brand image*. Lastly, price cuts may be resisted by companies using a *harvest objective*.

Tactics

When a company decides to follow a price change it can do so quickly or slowly. A *quick price reaction* is likely when there is an urgent need to *improve profit margins*. Here the competitor's price increase will be welcomed as an opportunity to achieve this objective.

Conversely, a *slow reaction* may be desirable when an *image of being the customer's friend* is being sought. The first company to announce a price increase is often seen as the high-price supplier. Some companies have mastered the art of playing the low cost supplier by never initiating price increases and following competitors' increases slowly.[33] The key to this tactic is timing the response: too quickly and customers do not notice; too long and profit is foregone. The optimum period can be found only by experience but during it salespeople should be told to stress to customers that the company is doing everything it can to hold prices as long as possible.

Table 10.6 Reacting to competitors' price changes		
	Increases	*Cuts*
When to follow	Rising costs	Falling costs
	Excess demand	Excess supply
	Price insensitive customers	Price sensitive customers
	Price rise compatible with brand image	Price fall compatible with brand image
	Harvest or hold objective	Build or hold objective
When to ignore	Stable or falling costs	Rising costs
	Excess supply	Excess demand
	Price sensitive customers	Price insensitive customers
	Price rise incompatible with brand image	Price fall incompatible with brand image
	Build objective	Harvest objective
Tactics		
Quick response	Margin improvement urgent	Offset competitive threat
Slow response	Gains to be made by being customer's friend	High customer loyalty

A *quick response* to a competitor's price fall will happen to ward off a *competitive threat*. In the face of undesirable sales/market share erosion, fast action is needed to nullify potential competitor gains. However, reaction will be slow when a company has a *loyal customer base* willing to accept higher prices for a period so long as they can rely on price parity over the longer term.

Ethical issues in pricing

Key issues regarding ethical issues in pricing are price fixing, predatory pricing, deceptive pricing, price discrimination and product dumping.

Price fixing

One of the driving forces towards lower prices is competition. Therefore, it can be in the interests of producers to agree among themselves not to compete on price. This is the act of collusion and is banned in many countries and regions including the EU. Article 83 of the Treaty of Rome is designed to ban practices preventing, restricting or distorting competition except where these contribute to efficiency without inhibiting consumers' fair share of the benefit. Groups of companies who collude are said to be acting as a cartel and these are by no means easy to uncover. One of the European Commission's most famous success stories is the uncovering of the illicit cartel among 23 of Europe's top chemical companies from the UK, France, Germany, Belgium, Italy, Spain, the Netherlands, Finland, Norway and Austria. Through collusion they were able to sustain levels of profitability for low-density polyethylene and PVC in the face of severe over-capacity. Quotas were set to limit companies' attempts to gain market share through price competition and prices were fixed to harmonize the differences between countries to discourage customers from shopping around for the cheapest deals.[34] Opponents of price fixing claim that it is unethical because it restrains the consumer's freedom of choice and interferes with each firm's interest in offering high-quality products at the best price. Proponents argue that under harsh economic conditions price fixing is necessary to ensure a fair profit for the industry and to avoid price wars that might lead to bankruptcies and unemployment.

Predatory pricing

This refers to the situation where a firm cuts its prices with the aim of driving out the competition. The firm is content to incur losses with the intent that high profits will be generated through higher prices once the competition is eliminated. As we have seen, British Airways and TWA were accused of this practice to eliminate Laker Airlines from their Atlantic routes. More recently easyJet have accused British Airways of predatory pricing through their no-frills subsidiary Go. EasyJet claim that the low prices charged by Go are being subsidized by the profits made by British Airways' other operations.

Deceptive pricing

This occurs when consumers are misled by price deals offered by companies. Two examples are misleading price comparisons and 'bait and switch'. Misleading price comparisons occur when a store sets artificially high prices for a short time so that much lower 'sale' prices can be claimed later. The purpose is to deceive the customer into believing they are being offered bargains. Some countries, such as the UK and Germany, have laws which state the minimum period over which the regular price should be charged before it can be used as a reference price in a sale. Bait and switch is the practice of advertising a very low price on a product (the bait) to attract customers to a retail outlet. Once in the store the salesperson persuades the customer to buy a higher priced product (the switch). The customer may be told that the lower priced product is no longer in stock or that it is of inferior quality.

Price discrimination

This occurs when a supplier offers a better price for the same product to a buyer resulting in an unfair competitive advantage. Price discrimination can be justified when the costs of supplying different customers varies, where the price differences reflect differences in the level of competition and where different volumes are purchased. Price discrimination can take place at a regional level. For example, according to the European Commission UK car prices were 35 per cent higher than elsewhere in Europe before tax.[35] This led to some buyers travelling to mainland Europe to buy new cars and to some dealers planning to import cars for private buyers.[36]

Product dumping

This involves the export of products at much lower prices than charged in the domestic market, sometimes below the cost of production. Products are 'dumped' for a variety of reasons. First, unsold stocks may be exported at a low price rather than risk lowering prices in the home market. Second, products may be manufactured for sale overseas at low prices to fill otherwise unused production capacity. Finally, products which are regarded as unsafe at home may be dumped in countries which do not have such stringent safety rules. For example, the US Consumer Product Safety Commission ruled that three-wheel cycles were dangerous. Many companies responded by selling their inventories at low prices in other countries.[37]

Summary

Price is a major element in developing an effective marketing strategy because it is the only component of the marketing mix that directly generates revenue: all the others are costs. It is also the marketing mix variable that can be changed most quickly. However, competitors can react equally fast. Consequently relying on aggressive pricing without a cost advantage can be a dangerous strategy.

Price setting can be cost-orientated, competitor-orientated or marketing-orientated. Cost-orientated and competitor-orientated methods have severe drawbacks and so pricing should be based on marketing-orientated considerations. These are marketing strategy, value to the customer, price-quality relationships, product line pricing, explicability, competition, negotiating margins, effect on distributors and retailers, political factors, and costs.

Marketing-orientated pricing is both an art and a science. Techniques such as trade-off analysis, economic value to the customer analysis, and experimentation can give estimates of customer value but there is still a great deal of management judgement that has to enter the equation. It is much more difficult to practise because of its complexity than cost-based methods but the pay-off is high sales revenue and profits.

Pricing dynamics examines the important issues affecting the initiation of price changes and reactions to competitor price moves. In the competitive marketplace when and how to initiate price changes and follow competitor price initiatives are important problems. This chapter has examined the factors which impinge on these decisions.

Five ethical issues have been discussed: price fixing, predatory pricing, deceptive pricing, price discrimination, and product dumping.

Internet exercise

Different prices for different usage (mobile phones)

Sites to visit
http://www.vodafone.co.uk
http://www.cellnet.co.uk

Exercise
Examine the tariffs currently on offer from each site. What conclusions can you draw about how each company is segmenting the market? Is there any evidence that the companies are targeting individual segments with particular emphasis? Which site gives the clearer pricing information?

Study questions

1   Accountants are always interested in profit margins; sales managers want low prices to help push sales; and marketing managers are interested in high prices to establish premium positions in the marketplace. To what extent do you agree with this statement in relation to the setting of prices?

2   You are the marketing manager of a company that is about to launch the first voice-activated language translator. The owner talks into the device, the machine electronically translates into the relevant language and speaks to the listener. What factors should you take into consideration when pricing this product?

3   Why is value to the customer a more logical approach to setting prices than cost of production? What role can costs play in the setting of prices?

4   Discuss the advantages and disadvantages of experimentation in assessing customers' willingness to pay.

5   What is economic value to the customer analysis? Under what conditions can it play an important role in price setting?

6   Under intense cost inflationary pressure you are considering a price increase. What other considerations would you take before initiating the price rise?

7   You are the marketing manager of a premium priced industrial chemical. A competitor has launched a cut-price alternative that possesses 90 per cent of the effectiveness of your product. If you do not react you estimate that you will lose 30 per cent of sales. What are your strategic pricing options? What would you do?

8   The only reason that companies set low prices is that their products are undifferentiated. Discuss.

9   By far the most criticized ethical issue is the practice of price fixing. Discuss.

References

1.   Shapiro, B. P. and B. B. Jackson (1978) Industrial Pricing to Meet Customer Needs, *Harvard Business Review*, Nov.–Dec., 119–27.

2.   See Shipley, D. (1981) Pricing Objectives in British Manufacturing Industry, *Journal of Industrial Economics*, **29** (June), 429–43; Jobber, D. and G. J. Hooley (1987) Pricing Behaviour in the UK Manufacturing and Service Industries, *Managerial and Decision Economics*, **8**, 167–71.

3.   Cook, R. (1999) Does Price Advertising Kill Brands, *Campaign*, 16 April, 19.

4.   Mitchell, A. (1999) Technology Breaks Chain Linking Price with Value, *Marketing Week*, 11 November, 54–5.

5.   Mitchell, A. (1999) Lure of Discounters Will Raise Price Awareness, *Marketing Week*, 9 December, 9.

6.   Rodgers, D. (1999) How Many Brands Can Fly the Budget Skies, *Marketing*, 16 September, 15.

7.   Christopher, M. (1982) Value-in-Use Pricing, *European Journal of Marketing*, **16** (5), 35–46.

8.   Edelman, F. (1965) Art and Science of Competitive Bidding, *Harvard Business Review*, July–August, 53–66.

9.   Brown, R. (1991) The S-Curves of Innovation, *Journal of Marketing Management*, **7** (2), 189–202.

10.   Simon, H. (1992) Pricing Opportunities—And How to Exploit Them, *Sloan Management Review*, winter, 55–65.

11.   Jobber, D. and D. Shipley (1998) Marketing-Orientated Pricing Strategies, *Journal of General Management*, **23** (4), 19–34.

12.   Simon (1992) op. cit.

13.   Abell, D. F. and J. S. Hammond (1979) *Strategic Marketing Planning*, Englewood Cliffs, NJ: Prentice-Hall.

14.   Miller, R. (1997) Does Everyone Have a Price? *Marketing*, 24 April, 30–3.

15.   Killgren, L. and C. Cook (1999) Multibuy Push May Backfire, *Marketing Week*, 16 September, 44–5.

16.   Gabor, A. (1977) *Price as a Quality Indicator in Pricing: Principles and Practices*, London: Heinemann.

17.   Simon, H. and E. Kucher (1992) The European Pricing Time Bomb: And How to Cope with It, *European Management Journal*, **10** (2), 136–45.

18.   Kucher, E. and H. Simon (1987) Durchbruch bei der Preisentscheidung: Conjoint-Measurement, eine neue Technik zur Gewinnoptimierung, *Harvard Manager*, **3**, 36–60.

19.   Cattin, P. and D. R. Wittink (1989) Commercial Use of Conjoint Analysis: An Update, *Journal of Marketing*, July, 91–6.

20.   Moutinho, L. and M. Evans (1992) *Applied Marketing Research*, Wokingham: Addison-Wesley, 161.

21. Forbis, J. L. and N. T. Mehta (1979) Economic Value to the Customer, McKinsey Staff Paper, Chicago: McKinsey and Co. Inc., February, 1–10.

22. Simon, H. (1992) Pricing Opportunities and How to Exploit Them, *Sloan Management Review*, winter, 62. Copyright © 1992 by the Sloan Management Review Association. Reproduced with permission. All rights reserved.

23. Erickson, G. M. and J. K. Johansson (1985) The Role of Price in Multi-Attribute Product-Evaluations, *Journal of Consumer Research*, September, 195–9.

24. Marn, M. V. and R. L. Rosiello (1992) Managing Price, Gaining Profit, *Harvard Business Review*, Sept.–Oct., 84–94.

25. Anonymous (1998) Grey Market Ruling Delights Brand Owners, *Financial Times*, 17 July, 8.

26. Cateora, P. R., J. L. Graham and P. N. Ghauri (2000) *International Marketing*, London: McGraw-Hill.

27. Welford, R. and K. Prescott (1996) *European Business: An Issue-Based Approach*, London: Pitman.

28. Simon (1992) op. cit.

29. Simon (1992) op. cit.

30. Schacht, H. (1988) Leading a Company through Change, *Harvard Business School Seminar*, 11 November.

31. Shapiro, C. and H. R. Varian (1999) *Information Rules*, Boston, MA: Harvard Business School Press, 19–20.

32. Mitchell, A. (1999) Technology Breaks Chain Linking Price with Volume, *Marketing Week*, 11 November, 54.

33. Ross, E. B. (1984) Making Money with Proactive Pricing, *Harvard Business Review*, Nov.–Dec., 145–55.

34. Welford, R. and K. Prescott (1996) *European Business*, London: Pitman Publishing.

35. Mitchell, A. (2000) Why Car Trade is Stalling Over New Pricing Policy, *Marketing Week*, 17 February, 40–1.

36. Griffiths, J. (2000) Dealers Draw up Plan to Import Cheap New Cars, *Financial Times*, 19 January, 1.

37. Schlegelmilch, B. (1998) *Marketing Ethics: An International Perspective*, London: International Thomson Business Press.

Key terms

full cost pricing   pricing so as to include all costs and based on certain sales volume assumptions

direct cost pricing   the calculation of only those costs which are likely to rise as output increases

going-rate pricing   pricing at the rate generally applicable in the market, focusing on competitors offerings rather than on company costs

competitive bidding   drawing up detailed specifications for a product and putting the contract out for tender

market-oriented pricing   an approach to pricing which takes a range of marketing factors into account when setting prices

positioning   the choice of target market (where the company wishes to compete) and differential advantage (how the company wishes to compete)

buy-response method   a study of the value customers place on a product by asking them if they would be willing to buy it at varying price levels

trade-off analysis   a measure of the trade-off customers make between price and other product features so that their effects on product preference can be established

economic value to the customer (EVC)   the amount a customer would have to pay to make the total life cycle costs of a new and a reference product the same

fighter brands   low-cost manufacturers' brands introduced to combat own-label brands

parallel importing   when importers buy products from distributors in one country and sell them in another to distributors who are not part of the manufacturer's normal distribution; caused by big price differences for the same product between different countries

price waterfall   the difference between list price and realized or transaction price

price unbundling   pricing each element in the offering so that the price of the total product package is raised

Case 17 Hansen Bathrooms (A)

Hansen Bathrooms is a producer of baths, washbasins, toilets and bidets. The company has been in the bathroom market for over 50 years and while sales have never been spectacular the company has managed to withstand the impact of several economic recessions by prudent cash flow management. Experts in the industry describe Hansen as a traditional, reliable producer that tends to follow market trends rather than lead.

As a response to changing times Hansen recruited a 30-year-old marketing director Rob Vincent and a 25-year-old assistant Susan Clements. Rob's responsibilities include suggestions for new bathroom designs, advertising and promotion and formulating pricing strategies, although the final decisions (except for day-to-day issues) are taken by the board of directors, which is headed by Karl Hansen, the son of the founder of the company.

Rob Vincent and Susan Clements have been in post for nearly two years and, at times, have found the work frustrating because of the board's tendency towards conservatism. However, an exciting development rekindled their enthusiasm. A technologist at the company had developed a special coating that could be applied to all bathroom items (baths, toilets, washbasins and tiles). The coating contained an agent that dispersed the usual grime and grease that accumulated in baths and washbasins, etc. Susan Clements commissioned a market research study that showed that people cleaned their bathroom fittings on average once every two weeks and it was one of the most unpopular household chores. The new coating made this unnecessary. Product trials with a prototype bathroom incorporating the new coating showed that cleaning could easily be extended to once every three months. Respondents in the test were delighted with the

reduction in workload. Hansen sought and obtained a patent on the new coating.

Rob felt sure that the board would approve the launch of a new bathroom range using the new coating and was pondering what price to charge. As a starting-point Rob set about using Hansen's tried and tested pricing formula. This produced the following calculations:

Per bathroom (washbasin, toilet and bath)

	£
Direct materials	40
Direct labour	40
Total direct cost	80
Fixed cost (150% of direct labour)	60
Total cost	140
Profit mark-up (20% of total cost)	28
Basic price to retailers (BPR)	168
Allowance for promotional costs (10% of BPR)	17
Allowance for retailer discounts (20% of BPR)	34
List price to retailers (LPR)	219
Retailer profit mark-up (100% of LPR)	219
Recommended price to consumers	438

Rob felt very pleased. The price to consumers of £438 was very competitive with the price of other bathroom suppliers (for example the main two competitors charged £450 and £465). After the usual 25 per cent consumer discount this would mean the Hansen bathroom would sell for £328 compared to £337 and £348 for its main rivals. 'I wish all my marketing decisions were this easy', thought Rob. However, before making a final decision he thought he ought to consult Susan.

This case was prepared by David Jobber, Professor of Marketing, University of Bradford.

Questions

1 If you were Susan, would you agree or disagree with Rob Vincent's proposal?

2 What other factors should be taken into account?

3 What alternative strategies exist, if any?

Case 18 Computron Inc., 1994

In January 1994, Mr Thomas Zimmermann, manager of the East European Sales Division of Computron Inc., was preparing his bid to sell a 1000X computer to Slavisky & Cie., Poland's largest chemical company. The decision facing him was deciding how to determine the appropriate price for this computer. If Mr Zimmermann were to follow Computron's standard pricing policy of adding a 33⅓ per cent mark-up to factory costs—and then including transportation costs and import duty, the bid he would submit would amount to US$155 600. Mr Zimmermann was afraid that a bid of this magnitude would not be low enough to win the contract for Computron.

Four other computer manufacturers had been invited by Slavisky to submit bids for the contract. Mr Zimmermann had received information from what he considered to be a 'reliable trade source', indicating that at least one of these four competitors was planning to name a price around $109 000. Computron's usual price of $155 600 would be $46 600—i.e. 43 per cent—higher than the competitor's price. In conversations with Slavisky's vice-president of purchasing, Mr Zimmermann had been led to believe that Computron's chances of winning the contract depended on its bid being no more than 20 per cent higher than that of the lowest competitor. As Slavisky was Computron's most important Polish customer, Mr Zimmermann was particularly concerned about this contract and was wondering what strategy to use in pricing his bid. The deadline for submitting bids was 1 February 1994.

Background on Computron and its products

Computron Inc. was a US firm which had, in the summer of 1988, opened a sales office in Vienna, Austria, with Mr Zimmermann as its manager. The company's main product, both in Western and Eastern Europe, was the 1000X computer.

Though it could be considered a general purpose computer, the Computron 1000X—which sold in the medium price range—was designed primarily for solving specific engineering problems. Ordinarily, it found its basic applications in chemical companies, public utilities, and areas of nuclear engineering. In these fields, it was typically used to solve problems of chemical process control, and design and control of power plants and nuclear reactor stations.

During the first six months after its opening, the Austrian sales office did only about $550 000 worth of business. In 1993, however, sales increased sharply, to reach a total for the year of $2 500 000. Computron's total world-wide sales for that same year were roughly $22 000 000. Of the Eastern European countries, Poland constituted one of Computron's most important markets, having contributed $600 000—or 24 per cent—of the Eastern European sales total in 1993. Hungary and the Czech Republic were likewise important markets, having contributed 22 per cent and 18 per cent, respectively, to the 1993 total. The remaining 36 per cent of sales was spread over the rest of Europe.

The Computron computers sold to European customers were manufactured and assembled in Austria, then shipped to Eastern Europe for installation. Because of their external manufacture, these computers were subject to an import duty. The amount of this tariff varied from country to country. The Polish tariff on computers of the type sold by Computron was 17½ per cent of the imported sales price.

Prompted primarily by a desire to reduce this import duty, Computron was constructing a plant near Warsaw, Poland. This plant, which would serve all the Eastern European Common Market, was scheduled for opening on 15 March 1994. Initially, it was to be used only for the assembly of 1000X computers. Assembly in Poland would lower the import duty from 17½ per cent to 15 per cent. Ultimately, the company planned to use the plant for the fabrication of component parts as well.

The new plant was to occupy 10 000 square feet and would employ 20–30 people in the first year. The initial yearly overhead for this plant was expected to be approximately $150 000. As of January 1994, the Eastern European sales office still had no contracts for the new plant to work on, although it was anticipated that training the employees and assembling/installing a pilot model 1000X computer in the new plant could keep the plant busy for two or three months after it opened. Mr Zimmermann was somewhat concerned about the possible risk that the new plant might have to sit idle after these first two or three months unless Computron could win the present Slavisky contract.

Company pricing policy

Computron had always concentrated on being the quality 'preferred' company in its segment of the process control computer industry. The company prided itself on manufacturing what it considered to be the best all-around computer of its kind in terms of precision, dependability, flexibility, and ease of operation.

Computron did not try to sell the 1000X on the basis of price. The price charged by Computron was very often higher than that being charged for competing equipment. In spite of this fact, the superior quality of Computron's computers had, to date, enabled the company to compete successfully both in Western and Eastern Europe.

The Austrian price for the 1000X computer was normally figured as follows:

Austria 'cost'	(Includes factory cost and factory overhead)
plus	
Mark-up of 33⅓% on 'cost'	(To cover profit, research, research and development allowances, and selling expenses)
Transportation and installation costs plus	
Importation duty	
Total Eastern European price	

Prices calculated by the above method tended to vary slightly because of the country-to-country difference in tariffs and the difference in components between specific computers. (Depending on the specific application in question, the components of the 1000X varied slightly so that each machine was somewhat different from the rest.) In the case of the present Slavisky application, Mr Zimmermann had calculated that the 'normal' price for the 1000X computer would be $155 600. (Table C18.1 shows these calculations.)

The 33⅓% mark-up on cost used by the company was designed to provide a before-tax profit margin of 15 per cent, a research and development allowance of 10 per cent, and a selling and administrative expense allowance of 8 per cent. The stated policy of top management was clearly against cutting this mark-up in order to obtain sales.

Management felt that the practice of cutting prices 'not only reduced profits, but also reflected unfavourably on the company's quality image.' Mr Zimmermann knew that Computron's president was especially eager not to cut prices at this particular moment, as Computron's overall profit before taxes had been only 6 per cent of sales in 1993 (compared to 17 per cent in 1992). Consequently, the president had stated that he not only wanted to try to maintain the 33⅓ per cent mark-up on cost, he was in fact eager to raise it.

In spite of Computron's policy of maintaining prices, Mr Zimmermann was aware of a few isolated instances when the mark-up on cost had been dropped to around 25 per cent in order to obtain important orders in the UK. He was, for example, aware of one instance in France when the mark-up had been cut to 20 per cent. In the Eastern European markets, however, Computron

Table C18.1   Estimated price for the 1000X computer for the Slavisky experimental pilot plant based on 'usual' calculations

Factory cost	$96 000
33⅓% mark-up on cost	32 000
Austrian list price	128 000
Import duty (15% of Austrian list price)	19 200
Transportation and installation	8 400
Total 'usual' price	$155 600

had never yet deviated from the policy of maintaining a $33\frac{1}{3}$ per cent mark-up on cost.

The customer

Slavisky and Cie. was one of the largest manufacturers and processors of basic chemicals and chemical products in Poland. It operated a number of chemical plants located throughout the country. To date, it had purchased three digital computer systems, all from Computron. The three systems had been bought during 1993 and had represented $500 000 worth of business for Computron. Thus, Slavisky was Computron's largest customer and had alone constituted over 80 per cent of Computron's 1993 sales to Poland.

Mr Zimmermann felt that the primary reason Slavisky had purchased Computron computer systems in the past was because of their proven reputation for flexibility, accuracy, and overall high quality. So far, Slavisky officials seemed very pleased with the performance of their Computron computers.

Looking ahead, Mr Zimmermann felt that Slavisky would continue to represent more potential future business than any other single Polish customer. He estimated that, during the next year or two, Slavisky would have a need for another $500 000 worth of digital computer equipment.

The computer currently being bid on was to be used for training the operators of a new chemical plant. The training programme would last approximately four to five years. At the end of the programme, the computer would either be scrapped or converted for other uses. The calculations which the computer would need to perform were highly specialized and would therefore not require much machine flexibility. In the specifications which had been published with the invitation to bid, Slavisky management had stated that their primary interest in selecting a computer would be dependability and a reasonable price. Machine flexibility and pinpoint accuracy were listed as being of very minor importance, since the machine would mostly be used for training purposes rather than design work.

Competition

In the Polish market, approximately nine companies were competing with Computron in the sale of medium-priced computers designed to perform scientific and engineering work. Four companies accounted for 80 per cent of industry-wide sales in 1993. (Table C18.2 shows a breakdown of sales for these companies over one year.) Mr Zimmermann was primarily concerned about the competition offered by the following companies:

Ruhr Machinenfabrik AG

This very aggressive Austrian company was trying hard to expand its share of the market in Poland. Ruhr sold a medium quality general purpose machine at a price which was roughly $22\frac{1}{2}$ per cent lower than Computron charged for its 1000X computer. Of this price differential, $17\frac{1}{2}$ per cent was because there was no import duty on the Ruhr machine, which was entirely manufactured in Poland. Though, to date, Ruhr had sold only general purpose computers, reliable trade sources indicated that the company was currently developing a special computer in an effort to win the Slavisky bid. The price that Ruhr intended for this special purpose computer was reported to be around $109 000.

Table C18.2 Market share for companies selling medium-priced computers to the Polish market

	Estimated sales volume	
Computron Inc.	$600 000	30.0%
Ruhr Machinenfabrik AG	400 000	20.0%
Elektronische Datenverarbeitungsanlagen AG	250 000	12.5%
Digitex	350 000	17.5%
Six other companies (combined)	400 000	20.0%
Total	$2 000 000	100.0%

Elektronische Datenverarbeitungsanlagen AG

This German company had recently developed a general purpose computer that was comparable in quality to Computron's 1000X. Mr Zimmermann felt that Elektronische Datenverarbeitungsanlagen presented a real long-range threat to Computron's position in the industry. In order to gain a foothold in the industry, the company had sold its first computer 'almost at cost'. Since that time, however, it had undersold Computron only by an amount equal to the import duty on Computron's computers.

Digitex

This local firm had complete manufacturing facilities in Poland which could produce a wide line of computer equipment. The quality of the Digitex computer that competed with the Computron 1000X was only fair. Digitex often engaged in price-cutting tactics; in fact, the price of its computer had sometimes been even 50 per cent lower than what Computron charged for its 1000X. Despite this difference, Computron had usually been able to compete successfully against Digitex because of the technical superiority of the 1000X.

Mr Zimmermann was not overly concerned about the remaining competitors, as he did not consider them to be significant in Computron's segment of the computer industry.

The Polish market for medium-priced computers

The total estimated Polish market for medium-priced computers of the type manufactured by Computron was currently around $2 000 000 per year. Mr Zimmermann thought that this market could be expected to increase at an annual rate of about 25 per cent for the next several years. For 1994, he was already aware of confirmed specific new business worth about $650 000 (broken down as follows):

Slavisky & Cie	
Warsaw plant	US$150 000
Pruszkow plant	125 000
Gdansk plant	75 000
Central Power Commission	220 000
Polish Autowerk	80 000
Total	US$659 000

This business was in addition to the computer for Slavisky's new experimental pilot plant. None of the business already confirmed was expected to materialize until late spring or early summer.

Deadline for bids

In light of these various facts and considerations, Mr Zimmermann was wondering what price to place on the bid for the Slavisky contract. The deadline for submitting bids to Slavisky was 1 February 1994. Since this date was less than two weeks away, he knew he would have to reach a decision sometime within the next few days.

This case was originally prepared by Professor Ralph Z. Sorenson and revised by Dominique Turpin, IMD, Lausanne, Switzerland.

CHAPTER ELEVEN

Advertising

'The codfish lays ten thousand eggs,
The homely hen lays one,
The codfish never cackles
To tell you what she's done.

And so we scorn the codfish,
While the humble hen we prize,
Which only goes to show you
That it pays to advertise'

ANONYMOUS

Learning Objectives *This chapter explains:*

1   The role of advertising in the promotional mix

2   The factors that affect the choice of the promotional mix

3   The key characteristics of the four major promotional tools

4   The communication process

5   The differences between the strong and weak theories of how advertising works

6   How to develop advertising strategy: target audience analysis, objective setting, budgeting, message and media decisions and advertising evaluation

7   How campaigns are organized including advertising agency selection and payment systems

8   Ethical issues in advertising

To many people advertising epitomizes marketing: it is what they believe marketing to be. Readers of this book will recognize the fallacy in this: marketing concerns much broader issues than simply how to advertise. Nevertheless, advertising is an important element in the *promotional mix*. Five major components of the promotional mix are advertising, personal selling, direct marketing, sales promotion, and publicity:

✦ *Advertising*: any paid form of non-personal communication of ideas or products in the prime media, i.e. television, the press, posters, cinema and radio.

✦ *Personal selling*: oral communication with prospective purchasers with the intention of making a sale.

✦ *Direct marketing*: the distribution of products, information and promotional benefits to target consumers through interactive communication in a way which allows response to be measured.

✦ *Internet and on-line marketing*: the distribution of products, information, and promotional benefits to consumers and businesses through electronic media.

✦ *Sales promotion*: incentives to consumers or the trade that are designed to stimulate purchase.

✦ *Publicity*: the communication of a product or business by placing information about it in the media without paying for the time or space directly.

In addition to these key promotional tools the marketer can use exhibitions and sponsorship, to communicate with target audiences. These, together with sales promotion and publicity, will be discussed in Chapter 15.

A key marketing decision is the choice of the promotional blend needed to communicate to the target audience. Each of the five major promotional tools has its own strengths and limitations and these are summarized in Table 11.1. Marketers will carefully weigh these factors against promotional objectives to decide how much resources to channel into each tool. Usually five considerations will have a major impact on the choice of the promotional mix:

1 *Resource availability and the cost of promotional tools*: to conduct a national advertising campaign may require several million pounds. If resources are not available, cheaper tools such as sales promotions or publicity may have to be used.

2 *Market size and concentration*: if a market is small and concentrated then personal selling may be feasible, but for mass markets that are geographically dispersed selling to the ultimate customer would not be cost effective. In such circumstances advertising or direct marketing may be the correct choice.

3 *Customer information needs*: if a complex technical argument is required, personal selling may be preferred. If all that is required is the appropriate brand image, advertising may be more sensible.

4 *Product characteristics*: because of the above arguments, industrial goods companies tend to spend more on personal selling than advertising, whereas consumer goods companies tend to do the reverse.

5 *Push versus pull strategies*: a push strategy involves an attempt to sell into channel intermediaries (e.g. retailers) and is dependent on personal selling and trade promotions. A pull strategy bypasses intermediaries to communicate to consumers directly. The resultant consumer demand persuades intermediaries to stock the product. Advertising and consumer promotions are more likely to be used.

Two points need to be stressed. First, marketing communications is not the exclusive province of the promotional mix. All of the marketing mix communicates to target customers. The product itself communicates quality; price may be used by consumers as an indicator of quality, and the choice of distribution channel will affect customer exposure to the product. Second, effective communication is not a one-way producer to consumer flow. Producers need to understand the needs and motivation of their target audience before they can talk to them in a meaningful way. For example, marketing research may be used to understand large consumer segments before designing an advertising campaign, and salespeople may ask questions of buyers to unfold their particular circumstances, problems and needs before making a sales presentation.

Advertising decisions should not be taken in isolation. marketers need to consider the complete communication package with advertising forming one element of the whole. There is a need to blend the components of the promotional mix so that a clear and consistent message is received by target audiences. This has led to the development of an integrated marketing communications which will now be examined.

Integrated marketing communications

An organizational problem which many companies face is that the various components of the promotional mix are the responsibility of different departments or agencies. Advertising is controlled by the advertising department in conjunction with an advertising agency. Personal selling strategies are decided by sales management. Publicity is the province of the publicity department and their agency. Other functions are in charge of direct marketing, Internet and on-line marketing and sales promotions. The danger is that the messages sent to consumers becomes blurred at best and conflicting at worst. For example, advertising messages which convey prestige may be discredited by heavy discounting by the sales team, or frequent use of money-off sales promotions. Logos and typefaces used in advertising may differ from those used in direct mail campaigns.

As the array of communications media expands so the need to coordinate the messages and their execution rises. This has led to the adoption of *integrated marketing communications* by an increasing number of companies. Integrated marketing communications is the concept that companies coordinate their marketing communications tools to deliver a clear, consistent, credible and competitive message about the organization and its products. The objective is to position products and organizations clearly and distinctively in the marketplace. As we discussed in Chapter 7, successful positioning is associated with products possessing favourable connotations in the minds of consumers. Integrated marketing communications facilitates the process by which this is achieved by sending out consistent messages through all of the components of the promotional mix so that they reinforce one another. For example, it means that website visuals are consistent with the images portrayed in advertising and that the messages conveyed in a direct marketing campaign are in line with those developed by the public relations department.

Achieving this consistency can be difficult because of office politics. Some advertising creatives are unwilling to be shackled by an overall branding theme which is inconsistent with their latest 'big idea' for a television commercial. Others may feel threatened when an integrated marketing communications campaign calls for a shift in expenditure from advertising to direct or Internet marketing. However, to be successful these impediments need to be overcome by the appointment of a high-ranking communications officer to oversee the company's communications activities. Perhaps using the title 'marketing communications director' this person is responsible for deciding the extent to which each of the components of the promotional mix will be used based on communication objectives and the role that each can play in their achievement.

Integrated marketing communications can lead to improved consistency and clearer positioning of companies and their brands in the minds of consumers. One company which benefited from this approach was American Express which found that the messages, images and styles of presentation between its advertising and direct marketing vehicles were inconsistent. Using an integrated marketing communications approach, the team worked to produce the consistency required to achieve a clear position among its target audience.

Having placed advertising in its context within the promotional mix, Fig. 11.1 shows the advertising expenditure of 14 European countries to show the context in which advertising is practised. The rest of this chapter will examine the communication process, how advertising works, developing advertising strategies, and the selection and work of advertising agencies.

The communication process

A simple model of the *communication process* is shown in Fig. 11.2. The *source* (or communicator) *encodes* a message by translating the idea to be communicated into a symbol consisting of words, pictures and numbers. Some advertisements attempt to encode a message using the minimum of words. The Marlboro cowboy is a good example. The message is *transmitted* through media such as television or posters which are selected for their ability to reach the desired target audience in the desired way. Communication requirements may affect the choice of media. For example, if the encoded message requires the product to be demonstrated, television and cinema may be preferred to posters and the press. *Noise*, which is distractions and distortions during the communication process, may prevent transmission to some of the target audience. A television advertisement may not reach a member of the household because of conversation or the telephone ringing. Similarly a press advertisement may not be noticed because of the competing attention of editorial.

When a *receiver* sees or hears the message it is *decoded*. This is the process by which the receiver interprets the symbols transmitted by the source.

Table 11.1   Key characteristics of five key promotional mix tools

Advertising
- ✦ Good for awareness building because it can reach a wide audience quickly
- ✦ Repetition means that a brand positioning concept can be effectively communicated. TV is particularly strong
- ✦ Can be used to aid the sales effort: legitimize a company and its products
- ✦ Impersonal: lacks flexibility and questions cannot be answered
- ✦ Limited capability to close the sale

Personal selling
- ✦ Interactive: questions can be answered and objectives overcome
- ✦ Adaptable: presentations can be changed depending on customer needs
- ✦ Complex arguments can be developed
- ✦ Relationships can be built because of its personal nature
- ✦ Provides the opportunity to close the sale
- ✦ Sales calls are costly

Direct marketing
- ✦ Individual targeting of consumers most likely to respond to an appeal
- ✦ Communication can be personalized
- ✦ Short-term effectiveness can easily be measured
- ✦ A continuous relationship through periodic contact can be built
- ✦ Activities are less visible to competitors
- ✦ Response rates are often low
- ✦ Poorly targeted direct marketing activities cause consumer annoyance

Internet and Online marketing
- ✦ Global reach at relatively low cost
- ✦ The number of site visits can be measured
- ✦ A dialogue between companies and their customers and suppliers can be established
- ✦ Catalogues and prices can be changed quickly and cheaply
- ✦ Convenient form of searching for and buying products
- ✦ Avoids the necessity of negotiating and arguing with salespeople

Sales promotion
- ✦ Incentives provide a quick boost to sales
- ✦ Effects may be only short term
- ✦ Excessive use of some incentives (e.g. money off) may worsen brand image

Publicity
- ✦ Highly credible as message comes from a third party
- ✦ Higher readership than advertisements in trade and technical publications
- ✦ Lose control: a press release may or may not be used and its content distorted

The aim is for the receiver's decoding to coincide with the source's encoding process. The receiver thus interprets the message in the way intended by the source. A Marlboro advertisement may aim to associate the brand name with masculinity. If this is the way the message is decoded then the communications objective has been achieved. However, a non-smoker may interpret the advertisement in an entirely different way, rejecting the association and replacing it with risks to health. Messages that rely on words more than pictures can also be decoded differently. For example, a message such as 'the most advanced washing machine in the world' may be accepted by some receivers but rejected by others. Communicators

need to understand their targets before encoding messages so that they are credible. Otherwise the response may be disbelief and rejection. In a personal selling situation, *feedback* from buyer to salesperson may be immediate as when objections are raised, or a sale is concluded. For other types of promotion such as advertising and sales promotion, feedback may rely on marketing research to estimate reactions to commercials, and increases in sales due to incentives.

An important point to recognize in the communication process is the sophistication of receivers. It is just as important to understand what people do with communication (e.g. advertising) as what communication does to

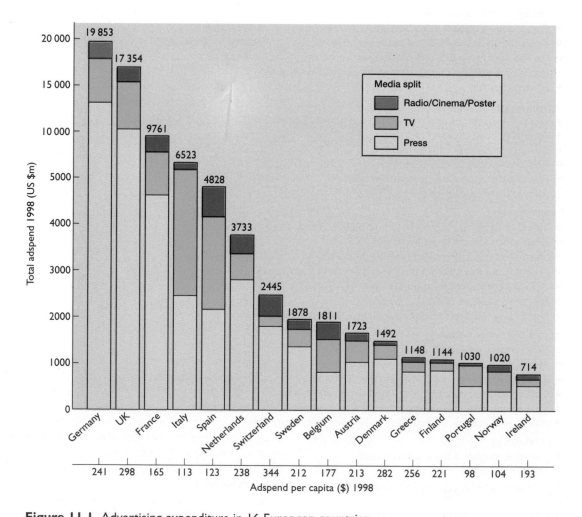

Figure 11.1 Advertising expenditure in 16 European countries.

Adapted from Advertising Expenditure by Country and Medium, *European Marketing Pocket Book 2000*, Henley-on-Thames: NTC Publications

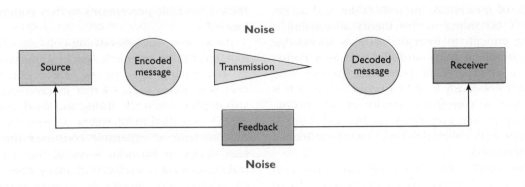

Figure 11.2 The communication process

them. Uses and gratifications theory suggests that the mass media constitute a resource on which audiences draw to satisfy various needs. Its assumptions are (i) the audience is active and much mass media use is need directed; (ii) the initiative in linking need satisfaction with media choice lies mainly with the individual; (iii) the media compete with other sources of need satisfaction; and (iv) the gratifications sought from the media include diversion and entertainment as well as information.[1]

Research suggests that people use advertising for at least seven kinds of satisfaction, namely product information, entertainment, risk reduction, added value, past purchase reassurance, vicarious experience and involvement.[2] Vicarious experience is the opportunity to experience situations or lifestyles to which an individual would not otherwise have access. Involvement refers to the pleasure of participation in the puzzles or jokes contained in some advertisements. Research among a group of young adults aged 18–24 added other uses of advertising including escapism, ego enhancement (demonstrating their intelligence by understanding the advertisement) and checking out the opposite sex.[3]

Strong and weak theories of how advertising works

For many years there has been considerable debate about how advertising works. The con-

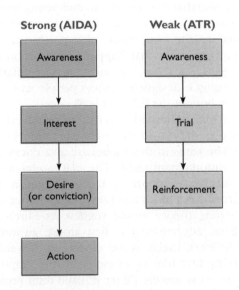

Figure 11.3 Strong and weak theories of how advertising works

sensus is that there can be no single all-embracing theory that explains how all advertising works because it has varied tasks.[4] For example, advertising that attempts to make an instant sale by incorporating a return coupon which can be used to order a produce is very different from corporate image advertising that is designed to reinforce attitudes.

The competing views on how advertising works have been termed the ***strong*** and ***weak theories of advertising***.[5] The strong theory has its base in the USA and is shown on the left-hand side of Fig. 11.3. A person passes through the stages of awareness, interest, desire and action (AIDA). According to this theory, advertising is strong enough to increase people's knowledge and change people's attitudes and as a consequence is capable of persuading people who had not previously bought a brand to buy it. It is therefore a conversion theory of advertising: non-buyers are converted to become buyers. Advertising is assumed to be a powerful influence on consumers.

This model has been criticized on two grounds.[6] First, for many types of products there is little evidence that consumers experience a strong desire before action (buying the brand). For example, in inexpensive product fields a brand may be bought on a trial basis without any strong conviction that it is superior to competing brands. Second, the model is criticized because it is limited to the conversion of a non-buyer to a buyer. It ignores what happens after action (i.e. first purchase). Yet in most mature markets advertising is designed to affect people who have already bought the brand at least once.

The major alternative to the strong advertising theory is shown on the right-hand side of Fig. 11.3. The steps in this model are awareness, trial and reinforcement (ATR). The ATR model, which has received support in Europe, suggests that advertising is a much less powerful influence than the strong theory would suggest. As Ehrenberg explains, 'advertising can first arouse awareness and interest, nudge some customers towards a doubting first trial purchase (with the emphasis on trial, as in "maybe I'll try it") and then provide some reassurance and reinforcement after that first purchase. I see no need for any strong AIDA-like Desire or Conviction before the first purchase is made.'[7] His work in fast-moving consumer goods markets has shown that loyalty to one brand is rare. Most consumers buy a repertoire of brands. The proportions of total purchases represented by the different brands show little variation over time, and new brands join the repertoire only in exceptional circumstances. A major objective of advertising in such circumstances is to defend brands. It does not work to increase sales by bringing new buyers to the brand advertised. Its main function is to retain existing buyers, and sometimes to increase the frequency with which they buy the brand.[8] Therefore, the target is existing buyers who presumably are fairly well disposed to the brand (otherwise they would not buy it), and advertising is designed to reinforce these favourable perceptions so they continue to buy it.[9]

As we saw when discussing consumer behaviour, level of involvement has an important role in determining how people make purchasing decisions. Jones suggests that involvement may also explain when the strong and weak theories apply.[10] For high involvement decisions such as the purchase of expensive consumer durables, male order, or financial services, the decision-making process is studied with many alternatives considered and information search extensive. Advertising, therefore, is more likely to follow the strong theory either by creating a strong desire to purchase (as with mail order) or by convincing people that they should find our more about the brand (for example, by visiting a showroom). Since the purchase is expensive it is likely that a strong desire (or conviction) is required before purchase takes place.

However, for low involvement purchase decisions (such as low cost packaged goods) people are less likely to thoroughly consider a wide range of brands before purchase and it is here that the weak theory of advertising almost certainly applies. Advertising is mainly intended to keep consumers doing what they already do by providing reassurance and reinforcement. Advertising repetition will be important to maintain awareness and to keep the brand on the consumer's repertoire of brands from which individual purchases will be chosen.

Developing advertising strategy

The starting-point for developing advertising strategy is a clear definition of *marketing strategy*. Advertising is one element of the marketing mix and decisions regarding advertising expenditure should not be taken in isolation. In particular a product's competitive positioning needs to be taken into account: what is the target market and what differential advantage does the product possess? Target market definition allows the ***target audience*** to be identified in broad terms (e.g. 25–45-year-old men, or purchasing officers in the chemical industry) and recognition of the product's differential advantage point to the features and benefits of the product that should

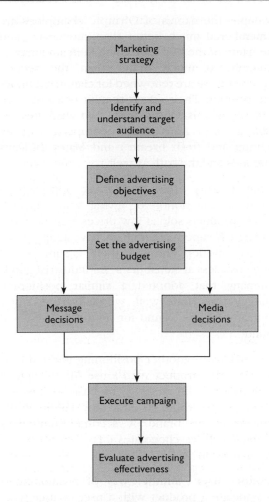

Figure 11.4 Developing advertising strategy

needs to be understood. Buyer motives and choice criteria need to be analysed. Choice criteria are those factors which buyers use to evaluate competing products. Advertising in organizational markets is particularly interesting since different members of the decision-making unit may use different choice criteria to evaluate a given product. For example, a purchasing manager may use cost-related criteria whereas an engineer may place more emphasis on technical criteria. This understanding is vital: it has fundamental implications for message and media decisions. Where costs allow, two different advertisements may be needed with one stressing cost benefits using media read by purchasing managers, and another focusing on technical issues in media read by engineers.

Define advertising objectives

Ultimately advertising is used to stimulate sales and increase profits, but of more operational value is a clear understanding of its *communication objectives*. Advertising can create awareness, stimulate trial, position products in consumers' minds', correct misconceptions, remind and reinforce, and provide support for the salesforce. Each objective will now be discussed.

Create awareness

Advertising can create awareness of a company, a brand, an event, and a solution to solve a problem. Creating company awareness helps to legitimize a company, its products and representatives to its customers. Instead of customers saying 'I've never heard of them', their response might be 'They are quite well known, aren't they?' In this way advertising may improve the acceptance of products and salespeople. Brand awareness is an obvious precondition of purchase and can be achieved through advertising. For example, when Amstrad launched their first portable computer they ran press advertisements creating awareness of the brand, its price and features.

Advertising can also be used to create awareness of an event. For example, Comet, an electrical retailer, ran an advertisement with the copy 'Comet Sale Now On'. Finally, advertising can be used to make the target audience aware of a solution to a problem. For example, Hewlett-Packard used the following headline in a press

be stressed in its advertising. Figure 11.4 shows the major decisions that need to be taken when developing advertising strategy. Each decision will now be addressed.

Identify and understand target audience

The target audience is the group of people at which the advertisement is aimed. In consumer markets, it may be defined in terms of socio-economic group, age, gender, location, buying frequency (e.g. heavy v. light buyers) and/or lifestyle. In organizational markets, it may be defined in terms of role (e.g. purchasing manager, managing director) and industry type.

Once the target audience has been identified it

advertisement: 'Why can't somebody make a computer that'll get our orders in and out the same day?' 'Somebody does.' The advertisement then explained how Hewlett-Packard did this and contained a coupon for further information. This form of advertising is also used by Xerox. The problem is described, followed by an explanation of how Xerox provides the solution, as shown in the advertisement opposite.

Stimulate trial

The sale of some products suffer because of lack of trial. Perhaps marketing research has shown that, once consumers try the product, acceptance is high but for some reason only a small proportion of the target group have tried it. In such circumstances advertising that focuses on trial may be sensible. For example, the Irish whiskey brand Jameson ran advertisements which claimed 'You'll never know until you've tried it. Jameson, the spirit of Ireland'. Similarly, Saab are encouraging trial (a test drive) of their diesel range, as the advertisement overleaf shows.

Position products in consumers' minds

Advertising copy and visuals have a major role to play in positioning brands in the minds of the target audience.[11] Creative positioning involves the development or reinforcement of an image, or set of associations for a brand. There are seven ways in which this objective can be achieved:[12]

Product characteristics and customer benefits this is a common positioning strategy. For example, BMW use performance with respect to handling and engineering competence as attributes summed up in the statement 'The Ultimate Driving Machine'. Remy Martin advertisements imbue the brandy with status connections. Other examples are Murphy's Irish stout ('Like Murphy's, I'm not bitter'), Stella Artois ('Reassuringly expensive'), Volkswagen ('If only everything in life was as reliable as a Volkswagen'), Galaxy ('Why have cotton when you can have silk?'), and Kellogg's All Bran ('The great fibre provider').

A powerful attribute for positioning purposes is being number one. This is because people tend to remember objects that are number one but may easily forget number two positions. For example, the names of Olympic champions are remembered much better than runners-up, and the name of the highest mountain in a country is remembered much better than the second highest. Canon are renowned for claiming number one position. Their advertisement overleaf is an example of this. Occasionally two attributes are used as with Aqua Fresh toothpaste ('Cavity fighting and fresh breath') and Matey ('Cleans your kids and the bath as well').

Price quality this positioning approach is based on the notion of giving value through quality products sold at low prices. Sainsbury, the leading UK supermarket chain, have adopted this market position through their tag-line 'Good food costs less at Sainsbury's'. An industrial goods company that adopted a similar positioning strategy was Honeywell, who advertised their control valves as 'Pound for pound the best—all round'.

Product use another positioning method is to associate the product with a use. An example is 'Lemsip is for 'flu attacks'. The basic idea is that when people think of 'flu, they automatically remember the brand. A second example is Cadbury's Roses chocolates ('The chocolates to say "thank you" ').

Product user another way of positioning is to associate a product with a user or user type. Personalities may be used such as Andre Agassi (Nike), Linford Christie (Lucozade) and Tim Henman (Adidas). Positioning against user type has been successfully achieved by Audi (upwardly mobile socially) and Guinness (intelligent, individualist). The advertisement overleaf shows how Suzuki positions its 4x4 soft top in terms of user type.

Product class some products can benefit by positioning themselves within a product class. For example, Red Mountain coffee positioned itself within the ground coffee class with the tag-line 'Ground coffee taste without the grind' and a margarine called 'I Can't Believe It's Not Butter' was positioned within the butter class by virtue of its name and advertising.

Symbols the use of symbols to position brands in the marketplace has been achieved by Michelin (Michelin Man), McDonald's (golden arches) and Apple (a multicoloured apple logo). The use of symbols is particularly effective when the symbol

ANCIENT DILEMMA

NO ONE HEAD IS BIG ENOUGH

TO HOLD ALL THE KNOWLEDGE

A BUSINESS NEEDS

TO KNOW.

XEROX SOLUTIONS

MAKE IT SIMPLER TO FIND,

CAPTURE AND SHARE THE

KNOWLEDGE IN YOUR COMPANY.

NOW ALL YOUR HEADS CAN

WORK TOGETHER.

KEEP THE CONVERSATION GOING.

SHARE THE KNOWLEDGE.

0800 787 787
www.xerox-emea.com
Quote Ref. 2149

XEROX®, The Document Company®, the digital X®.
Keep the Conversation Going. Share the Knowledge.
and any product names mentioned are trademarks of
XEROX CORPORATION. Some calls may be monitored
for training purposes.

DIGITAL
THE DOCUMENT COMPANY
XEROX

Problem-solution advertising by Xerox

Saab vs.
the Puritans

It is sinful to seek any form of pleasure. Overt joy is to be avoided. Do not drive a Saab 9-3 Convertible. Is this how the Puritans would instruct today? Would they shun the 9-3's turbocharged engine for fear of enjoying the 194ft.-lb. of torque? Surely the Saab's aircraft inspired cockpit would be too much for them to take. In fact, just looking at the car's sleek shape could be considered lustful. Be careful modern-day Puritans. Who knows what this car could lead to. Call 0800 626 556 or visit our website to request a 24 hour test drive.

www.saab.co.uk

THE SAAB 9-3 CONVERTIBLE RANGE STARTS FROM £24,945 ON THE ROAD (INCLUDING DELIVERY, PLATES, VAT, RFL AND NEW VEHICLE FIRST REGISTRATION FEE).

Advertisements can be used to encourage trial, as this Saab advertisement describes

London   Paris   Milan   Silicon Valley

Introducing the gorgeous DIGITAL IXUS, the world's smallest and lightest optical zoom digital camera. Its beauty, however, is more than skin deep. This 2.1 mega-pixel camera features a 35-70mm 2 x zoom lens and a USB interface, all encased in a classic IXUS body. That makes it perfect for the catwalks of Europe and the desktops of America. The DIGITAL IXUS can be yours for around £600. Canon also offers IXUS Advanced Photo System cameras, which cost from £60 to £250. Visit www.digital-ixus.com

READY TO WEAR, ANYWHERE.

DIGITAL IXUS

Canon

Imaging across networks

Strap shown is available separately from Canon's IXUS collection. LCD screen image simulated for clarity of reproduction. As of 8th May 2000.

The Canon Digital Ixus claims the No. 1 position as the world's smallest and lightest optical zoom digital camera reflects a quality desired in the brand as with the Andrex puppy (softness).

Competition positioning against well-entrenched competitors can be effective since their image in the marketplace can be used as a reference point. For example, Subaru positioned against Volvo by claiming 'Volvo has built a reputation for surviving accidents. Subaru has built a reputation for avoiding them', based on ABS for better braking and four-wheel drive for better traction. The airline Delta positioned against British Airways' tag-line 'The world's favourite airline' by running the counter-campaign 'We don't want to be the world's favourite airline—we just want to be yours'.

Correct misconceptions

A fourth objective of advertising can be to correct misconceptions which consumers hold against brands. For example, McCain's, the market leader in the UK for oven chips, ran a successful advertising campaign claiming that oven chips contained 40 per cent less fat than home cooked chips. However, marketing research showed that consumers still believed that their oven chips contained 30 per cent fat. A new campaign was designed to correct this misconception by stating that they contained only 5 per cent fat.

Remind and reinforce

Once a clear position in the minds of the target audience has been established, the objective of advertising may be to remind consumers of the brand's existence, and to reinforce its image. For many leading brands in mature markets such as Coca-Cola and Mars bars the objective of their advertising is to maintain top-of-the-mind awareness, and favourable associations. Given their strong market position, a major advertising task is to defend against competitive inroads, thus maintaining high sales, market share and profits.

Provide support for the salesforce

Advertising can provide invaluable support for the salesforce by identifying warm prospects and communicating with otherwise unreachable members of a decision-making unit. Some industrial advertising contains return coupons which potential customers can send to the advertiser indicating a degree of interest in the product. The

Suzuki positions its Jimny 4x4 soft top by user type: consumers who wish to express their individuality by the type of car they drive

identification of such warm prospects can enable the salesforce to use their time more efficiently by attempting to call upon them rather than spend time cold calling on potential customers who may or may not have an interest in the product.

Given the size and complexity of many organizational decision-making units a salesperson cannot be expected to call upon every member. One estimate is that out of ten decision-making unit members salespeople manage to talk to three or four on average. Advertising can be used to reach some of the others, for example, the numerous (secretaries) or the inaccessible (managing directors).

Set the advertising budget

The achievement of communication objectives will depend upon how much is spent on advertising. Four methods of *setting budgets* are the percentage of sales, affordability, matching competition, and the objective and task methods.

Percentage of sales

This method bases advertising expenditure on a specified percentage of current or expected sales revenue. The percentage may be based on company or industry tradition. The method is easy to apply and may discourage costly advertising wars if all competitors keep to their traditional percentage. However, the method encourages a decline in advertising expenditure when sales decline, a move which may encourage a further downward spiral of sales. Furthermore, it ignores market opportunities which may suggest the need to spend more (or less) on advertising. For example, an opportunity to build market share may suggest raising advertising expenditure, and conversely a decision to harvest a product would suggest reducing expenditure. Finally, the method fails to provide a means of determining the correct percentage to use.

Affordability

This method bases advertising expenditure on what executive judgement regards as an amount which can be afforded. While affordability needs to be taken into account when considering any corporate expenditure, its use as the sole criterion for budget setting neglects the communication

objectives that are relevant for a company's products and the market opportunities that may exist to grow sales and profits.

Matching competition

Some companies set their advertising budgets based upon matching expenditure, or using a similar percentage of sales figure as their major competitor. Matching expenditure assumes that competition have arrived at the correct level of expenditure, and ignores market opportunities and communication objectives. Using a similar percentage of sales ratio similarly lacks strategic vision and can be justified only if it can be shown to prevent costly advertising wars.

Objective and task

This method has the virtue of being logical since the advertising budget depends upon communication objectives and the costs of the tasks required to achieve them, and was the most popular method in all five European countries. If the objective was to increase awareness of a brand name from 30 per cent to 40 per cent, the costs of developing the necessary campaign, and using appropriate media (e.g. television, posters) would be made. The total costs would represent the advertising budget. In practice, however, the level of effort required to achieve the specified awareness increase may be difficult to estimate. Nevertheless, the method does encourage management to think about objectives, media exposure levels and the resulting costs.

In practice, the advertising budgeting decision is a highly political process.[13] Finance may argue for monetary caution whereas marketing personnel, who view advertising as a method of long-term brand building, are more likely to support higher advertising spend. The outcome of the debate may depend as much on the political realities within the company as on adherence to any particular budgetary method.

Some companies, notably in food, toiletries and the car industry, spend huge amounts on advertising. For example, in one year alone Procter and Gamble spent over £8 million encouraging consumers to switch from squash to Sunny Delight, the orange drink which became the most successful grocery product launch of the 1990s.[14] A list of the top five advertisers in ten European countries is given in Table 11.2. Procter and

Gamble appear in six of the ten countries featured.

Message decisions

Before a message can be decided, a clear understanding of the *advertising platform* should be made. The advertising platform is the foundation on which advertising messages are built. It is the basic selling proposition used in the advertisement (e.g. reliability or convenience). The platform should:

✦ Be important to the target audience.

✦ Communicate competitive advantages.

This is why an understanding of the motives and choice criteria of the target audience is essential for effective advertising. Without this knowledge a campaign could be built upon an advertising platform that is irrelevant to its audience.

An *advertising message* translates the platform into words, symbols and illustrations which are attractive and meaningful to the target audience. In the 1980s IBM realized that many customers bought their computers because of the reassurance they felt with dealing with a well-known supplier. They used this knowledge to develop an advertising campaign based upon the advertising platform of reassurance/low risk. This platform was translated into the advertising message 'No one ever got the sack for buying IBM'.

Table 11.2 Top five advertisers in ten European countries

Belgium
Procter & Gamble
Unilever
Etat Belge
Danone Group
Philip Morris Group

Finland
Sonera (Telecoms)
Valio (Food)
Nokia Mobile Phones
Radiolinja (GSM Services)
Toyota Auto

Germany
Procter & Gamble
Ferrero
Deutsche Telecom
Opel
Effem

Norway
Lilleborg
Møller Harald
Norsk Tipping
Hennes & Mauritz
Time Norsk Meierier

Sweden
ICA
Telia
Procter & Gamble
Volvo
Föreningssparbanken

Denmark
FDB
Thorn EMI
Tele Danmark
Dansk Supermarked
Carlsberg

France
Vivendi
L'Oréal
PSA Group
France Telecom
Nestlé

The Netherlands
Procter & Gamble
KPN Telecom
Lever Fabergé
Van Den Bergh
Laurus Helmond

Spain
Telephonica Servicios Moviles
El Corte Ingles
Procter & Gamble Espana
Telephonica de Espana
Fasa Renault

UK
Procter & Gamble
British Telecom
Vauxhall
Renault
Kellogg's

Source: European Marketing Pocket Book, 2000 edition, Henley-on-Thames: NTC Publications.

Using the right message is important. John Caples, a top direct response copyrighter, once wrote:[15]

> I have seen one ad actually sell not twice as much, not three times as much but 19 times as much as another. Both ads occupied the same space. Both were run in the same publication. Both had photographic illustrations. Both had carefully written copy. The difference was that one used the *right* appeal and the other used the *wrong* appeal.

David Ogilvy, an extremely successful advertising practitioner, has suggested that press advertisements should follow a number of guidelines:[16]

1 The message appeal (benefit) should be important to the target audience.

2 The appeal should be specific; evidence to support it should be provided.

3 The message should be couched in the customers' language, not the language of the advertiser.

4 The advertisement should have a headline which might
   (a) promise a benefit
   (b) deliver news
   (c) offer a service
   (d) tell a significant story
   (e) identify a problem
   (f) quote a satisfied customer.

5 If body copy (additional copy supporting and flowing from the headline) is to be used:
   (a) long copy is acceptable if it is relevant to the need of the target audience
   (b) long paragraphs and sentences should be avoided
   (c) the copy should be broken up using plenty of white space to avoid it looking heavy to read
   (d) if the advertiser is after enquiries, use a coupon *and* put the company address and telephone number at the end of the body copy. This is particularly important for industrial advertisements when more than one member of the decision-making unit (perhaps from different departments) may wish to send off for further details. With the address and telephone number appearing outside of the coupon, the second enquirer has the relevant information with which to

contact the advertiser even if the coupon has already been used.

Most people who read a press advertisement read the headline but not the body copy. Because of this some advertisers suggest that the company or brand name should appear in the headline otherwise the reader may not know the source of the advertisement. For example, the headlines 'Good food costs less at Sainsbury's' and 'United Colours of Benetton' score highly because in one sentence they link a customer benefit or attribute with the name of the company. Even if no more copy is read the advertiser has got one message across by means of a strong headline.

Television messages also need to be built on a strong advertising platform. Because television commercials are usually 30 seconds or less duration, most communicate only one major selling appeal—sometimes called the *single-minded proposition*— which is the single most motivating and differentiating thing that can be said about the brand.[17]

Television advertising often uses one of three creative approaches.[18] First, the *benefits* approach where the advertisement suggests a reason for the customer to buy (customer benefit). An example is the Red Mountain advertisement 'Ground coffee taste without the grind'. The second approach is more subtle: no overt benefit is mentioned. Instead the intention is to *involve* the viewer. An example of involvement advertising is the commercial for Heinz Spaghetti in which a young couple's son tells them that the tomato on his plate is the sun, the triangles of toast are the mountains, and the Heinz Spaghetti is the sea. When the father enters into the game and asks 'So that's the boat then', the boy responds witheringly 'No, it's a sausage'. The third type of creative approach attempts to register the brand as significant in the market, and is called *salience advertising*. The assumption is that advertising which stands out as being different will cause the brand to stand out as different. Two examples are the surreal advertising for the Benson and Hedges cigarette campaign, and the Toshiba 'Tosh' campaign. In the latter case the significance of Toshiba as a brand was supported by more conventional benefit advertising (e.g. 'Stronger components to last longer').

Television advertising is often used to build a brand personality. The **brand personality** is the message that the advertisement seeks to convey.

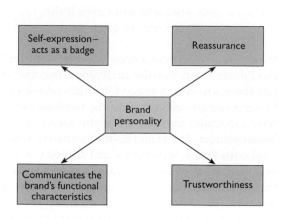

Figure 11.5 How brand personality is used by consumers

Lannon suggests that people use brand personalities in different ways.[19] Figure 11.5 shows that brand personality acts as a form of self-expression, reassurance, a communicator of the brand's function and an indicator of trustworthiness. The value of the brand personality to consumers will differ by product category and this will depend on what they use brand imagery for. In *self-expressive* product categories such as perfumes, cigarettes, alcoholic drinks and clothing, brands act as *badges* for making public an aspect of personality ('I choose this brand [e.g. Holsten Pils bottled lager] to say this about myself').

Brand personality can also act as *reassurance*. For example, the personality of After Eight Mints is sophistication and upper classness which does not necessarily correspond to the type of people who buy this mass market brand. What the imagery is doing is providing reassurance that the brand is socially acceptable. Martini advertising also provides this kind of reassurance.

A third use of brand personality is to *communicate the functional characteristics* of the brand. Timotei shampoo advertising is an emotional representation of its functional characteristics: natural, herbal, gentle, pure. Finally, personalities of brands such as Persil and Andrex act to signal *trustworthiness*, a benefit valued by many consumers in their product categories.

Advertisers neglect at their peril the role of *emotion* in consumer decision-making. When choice depends upon symbolic meaning helping to define a person's self-concept and sense of identity and communicate it to other people,

decision-making may be largely emotion-driven. Consumers consult their feelings about the decision. For example, a car buyer may ask 'How do I feel about being seen in that car?' If the answer is positive, information search may be confined to providing an objective justification of the choice (for example, the car's reliability, fuel economy, etc.). Television advertising is often used to convey the desired emotional response and the print media to supply objective information. Brands such as Nike with its 'just do it' attitude, Virgin for its 'us against them' approach and Benetton with its controversial advertising campaigns including a black stallion mounting a white mare and portraits of American prisoners on death row have all tried to plug into consumers' emotions.[20] In low involvement situations, such as with the choice of drinks and convenience foods, humour is sometimes used to create a feeling of warmth about a brand and even regular exposure to a brand name over time can generate the desired feeling of warmth.[21]

Media decisions

There used to be a joke among media people that the client's attitude to their part in advertising was 'Ten minutes to go before lunch. Just enough time to discuss media'.[22] As media costs have risen and brands become more sharply targeted this attitude has disappeared.

Two key media decisions are the choice of media class (for example, television versus the press) and media vehicle (e.g. a particular newspaper or magazine). Both these decisions will now be examined.

The media class decision

Table 11.3 lists the major ***media class*** options (the media mix). The media planner faces the choice of using television, the press, cinema, posters, radio or some combination of media classes. Five considerations will be taken into account. First, *creative factors* may have a major bearing on the decision. The key question that needs to be addressed is 'Does the medium allow the communication objectives to be realized?' For example, if the objective is to position the brand as having a high-status aspirational personality, television would be better than posters. However, if the communication objective is to remind the target audience of a brand's existence a poster campaign may suffice. Each medium possesses its own set of creative qualities and limitations, described below.

Television advertisers can demonstrate the product in action. For example, a lawn-mower can be shown to cut grass efficiently, or the ease of application of a paint can be demonstrated. The capability of television to combine colour, movement and sound (unlike the press, posters and radio) means that it is often used when brand image building is required. It is easier to create an atmosphere using television than other media that lack its versatility. Advertisements can be repeated over a short time period but it is a transitory medium (unless the commercial is video recorded) so that consumers cannot refer back to the advertisement once it has been broadcast (unlike the press).

Digital television technology means that signals can be compressed allowing more to be sent to the viewer. The result is the escalation of the number of channels that can be received. The extra 'bandwidth' created by digital technology is likely to reduce costs enabling small players to broadcast to small target audiences such as small geographical areas and special interest groups (e.g. shoppers). Also digital technology will allow the development of interactive services promoting the potential for home shopping.[23] During an advertisement, viewers will be able to click on an icon leading them to an interactive shopping area, the equivalent to an Internet site.[24] Marketing in Action 11.1 examines how pan-European media owners are responding.

Press factual information can be presented in a press advertisement (e.g. specific features of a

---

Table 11.3 Media class options

1 Television
2 Press
   National newspapers
   Regional newspapers
   Trade and technical
   Magazines
3 Posters
4 Cinema
5 Radio

---

compact disk system) and the readers are in control of how long they take to absorb the information. Allied to this advantage is the possibility of re-examination of the advertisement at a later date. But it lacks movement and sound, and advertisements in newspapers and magazines compete with editorial for the reader's attention.

Posters simplicity is required in the creative work associated with posters because many people (for example, car drivers) will have the opportunity only to glance at a poster. Like the press it is visual only, and is often used as a support medium (backing a television or press campaign) because of its creative limitations. It is believed to be effective for reminder advertising. Carlsberg have used posters effectively using the headline 'Carlsberg—Probably the best lager in the world', showing the necessity for simplicity. Often poster advertising sites are sold as a package targeting specific audiences. For example, targeting supermarket shoppers can be realized by buying a retail package where advertisers can buy space on panels in supermarket stores; if businesspeople are the target it is possible to buy a package of sites at major airports.[25] The poster advertisement for Guinness overleaf indicates the advantages of simplicity.

Cinema advertisement can benefit from colour, movement and sound, and exposure is high due to the captive nature of the audience. Repetition may be difficult to achieve given the fact that people visit cinemas intermittently, but the nature of the audience is predictable, usually between 15 and 25 years of age.

Radio creatively limited to sound and thus may be better suited to communicating factual information (for example, a special price reduction) than attempting to create a brand image. The nature of the audience changes during the day (for example, motorists during rush hours) and so a measure of targeting is possible. Production costs are relatively low. The arrival of digital radio is likely to begin in cars as car manufacturers install digital radios into new models on the production line. Radio listening may rise with the growth of the Internet as people listen to the radio while surfing and because radio listening through web browsers is fast becoming a reality.[26]

The second consideration when making the media class decisions is the *size of the advertising budget*. Some media are naturally more expensive than others. For example, £250 000 may be sufficient for a national poster campaign but woefully inadequate for television. Advertisements with less than £1 million to spend on a national campaign may decide that television advertising is not feasible.

Third, the relative *cost per opportunity to see* is also relevant to the decision: the target audience may be reached much more cheaply using one medium rather than another. However, the calculation of opportunity to see differs according to media class, making comparisons difficult. For cxamplc, in the UK, an opportunity to see for the press is defined as 'read or looked at any issue of the publication for at least two minutes', whereas for posters it is 'traffic past site'.

A fourth consideration is *competitive activity*. Two conflicting philosophies are to compete in the same medium, and to dominate an alternative medium. The decision to compete in the same medium may be taken because of a belief that the medium chosen by the major competition is the most effective, and that to ignore it would be to hand the competition a massive communication advantage. Domination of an alternative medium may be sensible for third or fourth players in a product market who cannot match the advertising budgets of the big two competitors. Supposing the major players were using

11.1 Marketing in Action
Pan-European Media Developments

Many pan-European media owners including MTV are taking advantage of the application of digital technology to television broadcasting to customize their services for local tastes. Pan-European channels recognize that much of their competitition is local and therefore they need to tailor their output to local tastes. For example, MTV has four European services: UK, pan-northern, central and southern. The musical emphasis changes accordingly: UK and pan-northern focus on Britpop and indie music, the central German service emphasizes techno and dance music and the Italian-focused southern channel plays more Europop. Other broadcasters have also concluded that a single service across all of Europe is not viable. Eurosport, for example, provides 16 separate language tracks across Europe and has launched a customized UK network on digital. CNNI also runs a Spanish-language news channel and a German-language morning news service from Berlin.

Advertisers wishing to hit specific pan-European target segments are benefiting from an expanding number of channels and print media from which to choose. Business people can be reached through EBN, CNBC, CNNI, *Newsweek*, *Financial Times* and *Business Week*, 16–24-year-olds via MTV, 16–34-year-olds through NBC Europe, TNT and Eurosport, men aged 16–44 by Eurosport, children via Cartoon Network, and women aged 16–44 by NBC, Eurosport and *Reader's Digest*.

Audience measurement is improving. For example, Eurosport has around 70 per cent of its audience people-metered. Advertisers need to take care when selecting advertising spots as the audience for a tennis match (more women) is very different to that for Indy Car (more men).

As digital technology is applied, so the number of channels will grow. These extra channels will allow 'near-video-on-demand' which transmits films on several channels starting at different times, 'multiplexing' which broadcasts the same programmes in a different order on several channels, and 'pay-per-view' where viewers are charged for each programme they watch.

Based on: Shelton (1997);[27] Anonymous (1995);[28] Fry (1999)[29]

An award-winning advertisement from Guinness showing how a simple but striking visual can convey the right poster message

television, the third or fourth competitor might choose the press or posters where it could dominate achieving higher impact than if it followed competition into television.

Finally, for many consumer-good producers, *the views of the retail trade* (for example, supermarket buyers) may influence the choice of media class. Advertising expenditure is often used by salespeople to convince the retail trade to increase shelf space of existing brands, and to stock new brands. Since distribution is a key success factor in these markets the views of retailers will be important. For example, if it is known that supermarkets favour television advertising in a certain product market, the selling impact on the trade of £1 million spent on television may be viewed as greater than the equivalent spend of 50:50 between television and the press.

Sometimes a combination of media classes is used in an advertising campaign to take advantage of their relative strengths and weaknesses. For example, a new car launch might use television to gain awareness and project the desired image, with the press being used to supply more technical information. Later, posters may be used as a support medium to remind and reinforce earlier messages.

The media vehicle decision

The **media vehicle** decision concerns the choice of the particular newspaper, magazine, television spot, poster site, etc. Although creative considerations still play a part *cost per thousand calculations* are more dominant. This requires readership and viewership figures. In the UK readership figures are produced by the National Readership survey based upon 28 000 interviews per year. Viewership is measured by the Broadcasters' Audience Research Board (BARB) which produces weekly reports based on a panel of 3000 households equipped with metered television sets. Traffic past poster sites is measured by Outdoor Site Classification and Audience Research (OSCAR) which classifies 130 000 sites according to visibility, competition (one or more posters per site), angle of vision, height above ground, illumination and weekly traffic past site. Cinema audiences are monitored by Cinema and Video Industry Audience Research (CAVIAR) and radio audiences are measured by Radio Joint Audience Research (RAJAR). Table 11.4 shows how a viewer or reader is measured in terms of opportunity to see.

Media buying is a specialized skill and many thousands of pounds can be saved off rate card prices by powerful media buyers. Media buying is accomplished through one of three methods: full service agencies, media specialists, and media buying clubs. Full service agencies provide a full range of advertising services for their clients including media buying. Independent media specialists grew in the early 1990s as clients favoured their focused expertise and negotiating muscle. Media buying clubs were formed by full service agencies joining forces to pool buying power. However, the current trend is back to full service agencies, but with one major difference: today the buying is done by separate profit-making subsidiaries. With very few exceptions, all the world's top media buying operations are now owned by global advertising companies

---

Table 11.4 Definition of an opportunity to see (OTS)

Television
Presence in room with set switched on at turn of clock minute to relevant channel, providing presence in room with set on is for at least 15 consecutive seconds

Press
Read or looked at any issue (for at least two minutes) within the publication period (for example for weeklies within the last seven days)

Posters
Traffic past site (including pedestrians)

Cinema
Actual cinema admissions

such as Omnicom, WPP, Saatchi and Saatchi and Cordiant.[30]

The media planner's job has been made more complicated but also more interesting by the technological developments and changing competitive arena within broadcasting. e-Marketing 11.1 discusses some of the changes and how they affect the media planner's job.

Execute campaign

Once the advertisements have been produced and the media selected, they are sent to the relevant media for publication or transmission. A key organizational issue is to ensure that the right advertisements reach the right media at the right time. Each media vehicle has its own deadlines after which publication or transmission may not be possible.

Evaluate advertising effectiveness

Three key questions in *advertising research* are what, when and how to evaluate advertising. What should be measured depends on whatever the advertising is trying to achieve. As we have already seen, advertising objectives include gaining awareness, trial, positioning, correcting misconceptions,

---

11.1   e-Marketing

Media Planning in a Technological World

For 30 years until the mid-1980s, the mass media landscape was very stable with terrestrial television allowing brands to reach a high proportion of the market using a relatively simple media schedule. In the UK, ITV permitted the advertiser to reach 90 per cent of the population with relative ease. The first crack in this solid structure was caused by the arrival of the satellite and cable television channels. Over the next 10 years, ITV's share of audience declined from 44 per cent to 38 per cent. As this trend developed, media planners in advertising agencies had to learn to adopt new approaches in planning which accommodated the expanded diversity of viewing opportunities now available to the general public.

The next media planners' headache was the arrival of the Internet, with consumers switching to this new medium to acquire product information and make on-line purchases. Media planners were forced to acquire rapidly an understanding of how websites work, the behaviour of the consumer as they 'click through cyberspace' and how the purchase of banner headlines on high visitor-level sites can be used to reinforce brand awareness. Then along came digital television which offers the consumer yet again, a major expansion in their range of viewing choices. Additionally digital television will also attract new consumers into the world of Internet shopping. Then to further complicate the scene, new players are entering the broadcast market. For example, Microsoft and British Telecom are experimenting with web TV products.

All of these trends will increase the uncertainty of how best to manage the scheduling of mass marketing promotional campaigns in the future. Media channels will proliferate and the fragmentation of customer viewing groups will vastly complicate the lives of the media planners. Industry experts are divided on the eventual outcome of all these changes. Nevertheless, no matter what happens, media planners will have to learn how to optimize their clients' advertising budgets in the rapidly disappearing world where one single channel delivered 90 per cent of a country's viewing population.

Based on: Abrahams (1998)[31]

reminding, and providing support for the salesforce (for example, by identifying warm prospects). By setting targets for each objective, advertising research can assess whether objectives have been achieved. For example, a campaign might have the objective of increasing awareness from 10 to 20 per cent, or of raising beliefs that the product is the 'best value brand on the market' from 15 to 25 per cent of the target consumers.

If advertising objectives are couched in sales or market share terms, advertising research would monitor the sales or market share effects of advertising. Finally, if trade objectives are important, distribution and stock levels of wholesalers and/or retailers and perhaps their awareness and attitudes should be measured.

Measurement can take place before, during and after campaign execution. *Pre-testing* takes place before the campaign is run and is part of the creative process. In television advertising, *rough* advertisements are created and tested with target consumers. This is usually done with a *focus group* who are shown perhaps three alternative commercials and asked to discuss their likes, dislikes and understanding for each one.[32] Stills from the proposed commercial are shown on a television screen with a voice-over. This provides an inexpensive but realistic portrayal of what the commercial will be like if it is shot. The results provide important input from target consumers themselves rather than solely relying on advertising agency views. Voice-overs that are disliked, misunderstanding, and lack of credibility of messages are examples of problems that can be identified at the pre-testing stage and, therefore, rectified before the cost of shooting a commercial is incurred. Such research is not without its critics, however. They suggest that the impact of a commercial that is repeated many times cannot be captured in a two-hour group discussion. They point to the highly successful Heineken campaign 'Refreshes the parts that other beers cannot reach' which was rejected by target consumers in pre-test.[33]

Press advertisements can be pre-tested using the *folder techniques*.[34] Suppose that two advertisements are being compared, two folders are prepared containing a number of advertisements with which the test advertisements will have to compete for attention. The test advertisements are placed in the same position in each folder. Two matched samples of around 50–100 target consumers are each given one of the folders and

asked to go through it. Respondents are then asked to state which advertisements they have noticed (*unaided recall*). They are then shown a list of the advertised brands and asked such questions as which one was most liked, which was least liked, and which they intend-to-buy. Attention is gradually focused on the test advertisement and respondents are asked to recall its content.

Once the campaign has run, *post-testing* can be used to assess its effectiveness. Sometimes formal post-testing is ignored through laziness, fear, or lack of funds. However, checking how well an advertising campaign has performed can provide the information necessary to plan future campaigns. In the UK, image/attitude, statistical analysis of sales data and usage surveys (usage rates, changes in usage) were the most popular TV post-testing techniques.[35] The top three measures used in post-test television advertising research mirror the most popular techniques: image/attitude change, actual sales, and usage. Image/attitude change was believed to be a sensitive measure that was a good predictor of behavioural change. Some of those agencies favouring the actual sales measure argued that, despite difficulties in establishing cause and effect, sales change was the ultimate objective of advertising and therefore was the only meaningful measure. Recall was also popular (63 per cent used it regularly). Despite the evidence suggesting that recall may not be a valid measure of advertising effectiveness, those favouring recall gave reasons varying from the sweeping 'It usually means good advertising if good recall is present' to the pragmatic 'Because it shows the advertisement is seen and remembered, it is very reassuring to the client'.

Many of the measures used to evaluate television advertising can also be used for press advertisements. For example, spontaneous recall of a brand name could be measured before and after a press campaign. In addition, readers of a periodical in which the advertisement appeared could be asked to recall which advertisements they saw and, if the test advertisement is recalled, its content. In addition, press advertisements that incorporate coupons to promote enquiries or actual sales can be evaluated by totalling the number of enquirers, or value of sales generated.

The key to evaluating advertising is to consult with the target audience, not rely on industry awards as a measure of effectiveness. These can give very different results. For example, a Norwegian charity won an award for an advertising campaign on which it spent NKr3 million (£300 000) only to find that it attracted only NKr1.7 million (£170 000) of donations.

Organizing for campaign development

An advertiser has four options when organizing for campaign development. First, small companies may develop the advertising *in cooperation* with people from the media. For example, advertising copy may be written by someone from the company but the artwork and final layout of the advertisement may be done by the newspaper or magazine. Alternatively, commercial radio stations provide facilities for commercials to be produced. Second, the advertising function may be conducted in-house by creating an *advertising department* staffed with copy writers, media buyers and production personnel. This form of organization locates total control of the advertising function within the company, but since media buying is on behalf of only one company, buying power is low.

Third, because of the specialist skills that are required for developing an advertising campaign, many advertisers opt to work with an *advertising agency*. Larger agencies offer a full service comprising creative, media planning and buying, planning and strategy development, market research and production. Figure 11.6 shows a typical structure of a large advertising agency. Key figures in the development of a campaign are account directors and executives who liaise with client companies and coordinate the work of the other departments on behalf of their clients. Because agencies work for many clients they have a wide range of experience, and can provide an objective outsider's view of what is required, and how problems can be solved. Table 11.5 lists the top ten European agencies (by income) in 1998.

A fourth alternative is to use in-house staff (or their full service agency) for some advertising functions but to use *specialist agencies* for others. Their attraction, in part, stems from the large volume of business that each specialist controls. This means that they have enormous buying power when negotiating media prices. Alternatively, an advertiser could employ the services of a *creative hot shop* to supplement their own or their full service agency's skills. Saatchi and Saatchi began life as a creative hot shop before developing into a full service agency.

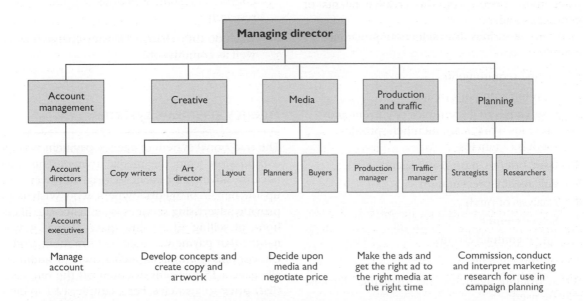

Figure 11.6 The structure of a large advertising agency

Table 11.5	The top ten European advertising agencies

Agency	Income ($m)
1 Publicis	727
2 Young and Rubicam	645
3 Euro RSCG	640
4 McCann-Erickson	638
5 BBDO Europe	628
6 DDB International	513
7 Ogilvy and Mather	512
8 Grey International	497
9 J Walter Thompson Europe	435
10 TBWA Worldwide	422

Source: Top European Agency Networks, *Campaign Report*, 9 July 1999.

Agency selection

As with buying any product, agency selection begins by clearly defining requirements. For example, a do-it-yourself or furniture chain may place most emphasis on media selection and buying capabilities so that the lowest cost per thousand can be achieved for their relatively straightforward black and white product information advertisements.[36] On the other hand, a company marketing drinks or perfume may place more priority on the creative talents of prospective agencies.

White describes the selection procedure as follows:[37]

1 Define requirements.
2 Develop a pool list of agencies.
3 Credentials (e.g. examples of current and previous work, team members; profiles) pitch by agencies.
4 Issue brief to short-listed agencies.
5 Full agency presentation.
6 Analysis of pitch.
7 Select winner.
8 Agree contract details.
9 Announce winner.

When briefing agencies the following checklist may be used:

1 *Product history*: e.g. sales, market share, trends, price, past campaigns, competition.

2 *Product features and benefits*: the product's competitive advantages and disadvantages.

3 *Objectives*: the product's marketing and communication objectives.

4 *Target audience*: who they are, their motives and choice criteria.

5 *Timetable*: when the agency presentation is required, when the campaign is planned to commence.

6 *Budget*: how much money is available, which may affect choice of media.

Analysis of the agency presentation will depend on six key questions:

1 How good is their creative/media/research work?

2 Does the agency have people who you think you can work with?

3 Does your account appear to be important to them?

4 What is their background: who are their clients, how long have they worked with them, is their client list growing or contracting, have they worked in your field before and if so why did they lose the account?

5 Are they a full service agency or do they contract out some functions (e.g. media, research)?

6 What do they charge? Do they charge fees as well as commission?

Agency payment systems

The traditional system of agency payment was by *commission* from the media owners. This was because advertising agencies originally were set up on behalf of media owners who wished to provide advertising services to enhance the likelihood of selling advertising space. Hence, it was natural that payment should be from them. Under the commission system, media owners traditionally gave a 15 per cent discount off the rate card (list) price to agencies. For example, a £1 million television advertising campaign would result in a charge to the agency of £1 million minus 15 per cent (£850 000). The agency invoiced the client at the full rate card price (£1 million). The agency commission therefore totalled £150 000.

Large advertisers have the power to demand some of the 15 per cent in the form of a rebate. For example, Unilever announced that it was allowing its advertising agencies 13 per cent commission.[38] Given its worldwide advertising expenditure of £1.5 billion it could probably have demanded a lower figure (possibly 11 per cent) but the company chose not to exercise all of its muscle since it believed that low commission rates ultimately meant poor quality advertising.

The second method of paying agencies is by *fee*. For smaller clients, commission alone may not be sufficient to cover agency costs. Also some larger clients are advocating fees rather than commission on the basis that this removes a possible source of agency bias towards media that pay commission rather than a medium like direct mail for which no commission is payable.

The third method of remuneration is through *payment by results*. This involves measuring the effectiveness of the advertising campaign using marketing research and basing payment on how well communication objectives have been achieved. For example, payment might be based on how awareness levels have increased, brand image improved or intentions-to-buy risen. Another area where payment by results has been used is media buying. For example, if the normal cost per thousand to reach men in the age range 30–40 is £4.50, and the agency achieves a 10 per cent saving, this might be split 8 per cent to the client and 2 per cent to the agency.[39] Procter and Gamble use payment-by-results as the method to pay their advertising agencies which include Saatchi and Saatchi, Leo Burnett, Grey Advertising and D'Arcy Masius Benton & Bowles. Remuneration is tied to global brand sales so aligning their income more closely with the success (or otherwise) of their advertising.[40]

Ethical issues in advertising

Because it is so visible most people have a view on the value of advertising. Certainly advertising has its critics (and its supporters). Their views will be discussed within the following areas: misleading advertising, advertising's influence on society's values and advertising to children.

Misleading advertising

This can take the form of exaggerated claims and concealed facts. For example, it would be unethical to claim that a car achieved 50 miles to the gallon when in reality it was only 30 miles. Nevertheless, most countries accept a certain amount of puffery, recognizing that consumers are intelligent and interpret the claims in such a way that they are not deceptive. In the UK, the advertising slogan 'Carlsberg—Probably the Best Lager in the World' is acceptable because of this. However, in Europe advertisers should be aware that a European directive on misleading advertising states that the burden of proof lies with the advertiser should the claims be challenged. Advertising can also deceive by omitting important facts from the message. Such concealed facts may give a misleading impression to the audience. For example, an advertisement that promotes a food product as 'healthy' because it contains added vitamins might be considered misleading if it failed to point out its high sugar and fat content. Many industrialized countries have their own codes of practice that protect the consumer from deceptive advertising. For example, in the UK the Advertising Standards Authority administers the British Code of Advertising Practice. It insists that advertising should be 'legal, decent, honest and truthful'.

Advertising's influence on society's values

Critics argue that advertising images have a profound effect on society. They claim that it promotes materialism, and takes advantage of human frailties. Advertising is accused of stressing the importance of material possessions such as the ownership of an expensive car or the latest in consumer electronics. Critics argue that this promotes the wrong values in society. A related criticism is that advertising takes advantage of human frailties such as the need to belong and the desire for status. It promotes the idea that people should be judged on what they possess rather than who they are. For example, advertisements for some cars use status symbol appeals rather than their functional characteristics. Supporters of advertising counter by arguing that these are not human frailties but basic psychological characteristics. They point out that the acquisition of status symbols occurs in societies that are not exposed to advertising messages such as some African tribes where status is derived from the number of cows a person owns.

Advertising to children

Advertising to children is a controversial issue. Critics argue that children are especially susceptible to persuasion and that they therefore need special protection from advertising. Others counter by claiming that the children of today are remarkably 'streetwise' and can look after themselves. They are also protected by parents who can counteract advertising influence to some extent. Many European countries have regulations which control advertising to children. For example, in Germany advertising specific types of toys is banned and in the UK alcohol advertising is controlled.[41] An example of self-regulation at work was the dropping of an advertisement for a soft drink which featured a gang of ginger-haired middle-aged men taunting a fat youth. The advertisement was withdrawn after numerous complaints were received contending that it encouraged bullying in schools.[42]

Summary

Advertising is a highly visible component of marketing but it is only one element of the promotional mix. Also included in the promotional mix are personal selling, sales promotion, publicity, exhibitions, sponsorship, and direct marketing. Advertising decisions need to be be made in the light of a product's overall marketing strategy rather than in isolation.

Advertising may work in different ways depending on the particular situation. Two alternative views on how advertising works—the so-called strong and weak theories of advertising—are explained and contrasted. The strong theory is more likely to apply when advertising high involvement products such as expensive consumer durables, and financial services, whereas the weak theory is more applicable to low involvement products such as supermarket brands.

Advertising strategy involves an analysis of the target audience, setting objectives, budgeting decisions, message and media decisions and evaluating advertising effectiveness. We examined the key issues associated with each of these factors.

Advertisers can organize for campaign development in one of four ways: by themselves using facilities and help from the media, by setting up a full-service advertising department, by using a full-service advertising agency, and by using in-house staff (or a full-service agency) for some functions, and specialist agencies for creative or media work. Agency selection should begin by clearly defining requirements, providing a well-delivered brief, working with a structured selection procedure with well-thought-out selection criteria. Part of the selection process will involve the choice of remuneration method. Three methods of payment —commission, fee, and payment by results—are discussed.

Important ethical issues in advertising are misleading advertising, advertising influence on society's values, and advertising to children.

Internet exercise

Advertising regulation

Sites to visit
http://www.asa.org.uk
http://www.itc.org.uk/

Exercise
Discuss the key provisions of advertising regulation in different media.

Study questions

1 Compare the situations where advertising and personal selling are more likely to feature strongly in the promotional mix.

2 Describe the strong and weak theories of how advertising works. Which theory is more likely to apply to the purchase of a car, and the purchase of a soap powder?

3 Within an advertising context, what is 'positioning in the mind of the consumer'? Using examples, discuss the alternative positioning options available to an advertiser.

4 Advertising has no place in the industrial marketing communications mix. Discuss.

5 Media class decisions should always be based on creative considerations, while media vehicle decisions should solely be determined by cost per thousand calculations. Do you agree?

6 Discuss the contention that advertising should be based on the skills of the creative team, not the statistics of the research department.

7 Describe the structure of a large advertising agency. Why should an advertiser prefer to use an advertising agency rather than set up a full-service internal advertising department?

8 Discuss the advantages and limitations of developing pan-European advertising campaigns.

9 As a highly visible communication tool advertising has its share of critics. What are their key concerns? How far do you agree or disagree with their arguments?

References

1. Katz, E., M. Gurevitch and H. Haas (1973) On the Use of the Mass Media for Important Things, *American Sociological Review*, **38**, 164–81.

2. Crosier, K. (1983) Towards a Praxiology of Advertising, *International Journal of Advertising*, **2**, 215–32.

3. O'Donohoe, S. (1994) Advertising Uses and Gratifications, *European Journal of Marketing*, **28**, 8/9, 52–75.

4. Wright, L.T. and M. Crimp (2000) *The Marketing Research Process*, London: Prentice-Hall, 180.

5. Jones, J. P. (1991) Over-promise and Under-delivery, *Marketing and Research Today*, November, 195–203.

6. Ehrenberg, A. S. C. (1992) Comments on How Advertising Works, *Marketing and Research Today*, August, 167–9.

7. Ehrenberg (1992) op. cit.

8. Jones (1991) op. cit.

9. Dall'Olmo Riley, F., A. S. C. Ehrenberg, S. B. Castleberry, T. P. Barwise and N. R. Barnard (1997) The Variability of Attitudinal Repeat-Rates, *International Journal of Research in Marketing*, **14**, 437–50.

10. Jones (1991) op. cit.

11. Ries, A. and J. Trout (1981) *Positioning: The Battle for your Mind*, New York: McGraw-Hill.

12. Aaker, D. A., R. Batra and J. G. Myers (1992) *Advertising Management*, New York: Prentice-Hall.

13. Piercy, N. (1987) The Marketing Budgeting Process: Marketing Management Implications, *Journal of Marketing*, **51** (4), 45–59.

14. Finch, J. (2000) P&G Brings Delight to the Ad Business, *The Guardian*, 2 March, 29.

15. Ogilvy, D. (1983) *Ogilvy on Advertising*, London: Pan, 70–102.

16. Ogilvy (1983) op. cit.

17. Saatchi and Saatchi Compton (1985) Preparing the Advertising Brief, 9.

18. Hall, M. (1992) Using Advertising Frameworks: Different Research Models for Different Campaigns, *Admap*, March, 17–21.

19. Lannon, J. (1991) Developing Brand Strategies across Borders, *Marketing and Research Today*, August, 160–7.

20. Tomkins, R. (1999) Images with the Power to Shock, *Financial Times*, 18 February, 10.

21. Elliott, R. (1997) Understanding Buyer Behaviour: Implications for Selling, in D. Jobber (ed.) *The CIM Handbook of Selling and Sales Strategy*, Oxford: Butterworth-Heinemann.

22. Syedain, H. (1992) Taking the Expert Approach to Media, *Marketing*, 4 June, 20–21.

23. Campaign Report (1997) Global Review of Digital TV, *Campaign*, 30 May, 8–10.

24. See Furber, R. (2000) Early Start, *Marketing Week*, 9 March, 65–6; Reed, D. (2000) Rapid Response, *Marketing Week*, 25 May, 63–5.

25. Tomkins, R. (1999) Reaching New Heights of Success, *Financial Times*, 28 May, 16.

26. Croft, M. (1999) Listeners Keep Radio On Air, *Marketing Week*, 8 July, 30–1.

27. Shelton, E. (1997) Tailoring TV, *Marketing*, 17 July, 23–7.

28. Anonymous (1995) The Battle for Europe's Telly Addicts, *The European*, 22 April, 81–2.

29. Fry, A. (1999) Euro TV Builds on Decade's Growth, *Marketing*, 13 May, 43–4.

30. See Fletcher, W. (1999) Independents May Have Had Their Day, *Financial Times*, 27 August, 15; and Anonymous (2000) Star Turn, *The Economist*, 11 March, 91.

31. Abrahams, B. (1998) The Only Certainty is Uncertainty, *Marketing*, 23 April, 22–4.

32. Jobber, D. and A. Kilbride (1986) How Major Agencies Evaluate TV Advertising in Britain, *International Journal of Advertising*, **5**, 187–95.

33. Bell, E. (1992) Lies, Damned Lies and Research, *Observer*, 28 June, 46.

34. Wright and Crimp (2000) op. cit.

35. Jobber and Kilbride (1986) op. cit.

36. Smith, P. R. (1993) *Marketing Communications: An Integrated Approach*, London: Kogan Page, 116.

37. Smith (1993) op. cit.

38. Mead, G. (1992) Why the Customer is Always Right, *Financial Times*, 8 October, 17.

39. Smith (1993) op. cit.

40. See Tomkins, R. (1999) Getting a Bigger Bang for the Advertising Buck, *Financial Times*, 24 September, 17; and Waters, R. (1999) P&G Ties Advertising Agency Fees to Sales, *Marketing Week*, 16 September, 1.

41. Schlegelmilch, B. (1998) *Marketing Ethics: An International Perspective*, London: International Thomson Business Press.

42. Anonymous (2000) IPA Chief Denies Tango Ad Own Goal, *Marketing Week*, 9 March, 12.

Key terms

advertising   any paid form of non-personal communication of ideas or products in the prime media, i.e. television, the press, posters, cinema and radio, the internet and direct marketing

personal selling   oral communication with prospective purchasers with the intention of making a sale

direct marketing   (1) acquiring and retaining customers without the use of an intermediary; (2) the distribution of products, information and promotional benefits to target consumers through interactive communication in a way which allows response to be measured

integrated marketing communications the concept that companies co-ordinate their marketing communications tools to deliver a clear, consistent, credible, and competitive message about the organization and its products

sales promotion   incentives to customers or the trade that are designed to stimulate purchase

publicity   the communication of a product or business by placing information about it in the media without paying for time or space directly

internet and on-line marketing   the distribution of products, information and promotional benefits to consumers through electronic media

strong theory of advertising   the notion that advertising can change people's attitudes sufficiently to persuade people who have not previously bought a brand to buy it. Desire and conviction precede purchase

weak theory of advertising   the notion that advertising can first arouse awareness and interest, nudge some consumers towards a doubting first trial purchase and then provide some reassurance and reinforcement. Desire and conviction do not precede purchase

target audience   the group of people at which an advertisement or message is aimed

advertising platform   the aspect of the seller's product that is most persuasive and relevant to the target consumer

advertising message   the use of words, symbols and illustrations to communicate to a target audience using prime media

media class decision   the choice of prime media, i.e. the press, cinema, television, posters, radio, or some combination of these

media vehicle decision   the choice of the particular newspaper, magazine, television spot, poster site, etc.

advertising agency   an organization which specializes in providing services such as media selection, creative work, production and campaign planning to clients

Case 19 DHL Keeps Your Promises

Founded in California in 1969 by Adrian Dalsey, Larry Hillblom and Robert Lynn, DHL was the first international express-delivery business. Currently, DHL delivers time-sensitive packages and business documents across five continents. The worldwide express industry has shown the fastest growth ever during the 1990s. In 1982, the total worldwide express market was worth only $0.5 billion. By the end of the decade, it had grown to $4.5 billion with a growing rate of 4.5 per cent per annum. The industry has expanded from an air express market in an emergency document service to become an integrated logistic partner where distribution is seen as a major business tool and a key contributor to competitive advantage. Therefore, companies like DHL have to form an integral part of their customers' distribution strategy. In order to take up this challenge, DHL has recently formulated a new marketing strategy.

Marketing objectives

DHL aims to set the industry standards through exemplary levels of customer care with tailor-made programmes and services designed around customers' business needs. DHL's objective is to remain the market leader and to be recognized as the industry bench-mark for excellence in consistent customer responsiveness, the latest pick-ups and equipment, the earliest possible deliveries, the fastest transit times and the best access to shipment information. In order to achieve these objectives, DHL is working on a new marketing strategy based on market segmentation and target-market segments, focusing on building even stronger relations with current users as well as creating bonds with new ones. In this attempt, DHL concentrates on penetration and awareness. That is, DHL wants to penetrate the market in order to increase its market share and make users aware of its services and strengths, as compared to competitors, when buying distribution services.

Market segmentation and target markets

DHL is moving into market segmentation in order to be better able to divide the market into distinct groups of buyers with different needs and characteristics of behaviour, such as reasons for buying and the scale of purchases. These groups require separate products, services and marketing mixes. DHL distinguishes three market segments:

✦ Standard customers (occasional users).

✦ Knowledgeable customers (informed users).

✦ Super-user customers (heavy users, day-to-day basis).

These market segments are further evaluated, looking at the value and growth of different industries. High-value industries according to DHL are:

✦ Bank and finance sector.

✦ Pharmaceutical industry.

✦ High-tech and computer industry.

✦ Telecommunication industry.

DHL focuses on continuously developing new products and services to create profit margins for its customers, such as timed delivery and Sunday delivery. Some industries, such as the textile

Table C19.1	Image of DHL and its competitors		
DHL	**UPS**	**FedEx**	**TNT**
✦ Young	✦ Military machine	✦ High quality	✦ Rough cowboys
✦ Dynamic	✦ Big	✦ Not much local	✦ Capable
✦ Trendy	✦ Efficient		
✦ Arrogant			

industry, require certain types of packaging, aircraft space and containers. In addition, this requires further investment for DHL and also further growth in some local markets. For instance, a delivery for the textile industry from Italy to the USA requires, in addition, a delivery from the USA to Europe in order to bring the aircraft and containers back again. To bring return on the investment, DHL has to become stronger in the States before entering this subsegment and investing in essential equipment.

Positioning

Because of DHL's intention to follow a more focused market segmentation approach, it would like to be perceived by customers as a friendly, approachable and helpful company that has a strong functional performance and is proactive in the sense that if the customer has a problem, DHL delivers creative solutions. However, according to the results of a recent market research in five European countries (UK, Italy, The Netherlands, France, Germany) during the period October 1998–February 1999, people currently associate other characteristics with DHL, as shown in case Table C19.1.

DHL, as well as its main competitors, has mainly been using a service differentiation by stressing speedy and reliable delivery. Keeping in mind the position that it is going for, it will try to position itself further on product and services differentiation to create the strong functional performance association. This type of differentiation is reflected in the variety of products offered by the company. However, to achieve a perception of being friendly, approachable, helpful, and proactive it will also stress a personnel differentiation. It already acknowledges that 'our success is ultimately due to our people. Their attitude, commitment and obsession with excellence are regularly acknowledged among the best of the best'.

Marketing mix

DHL is a typical example of the 'think global, act local' philosophy. Although it operates globally, marketing mixes are designed locally. A general description of the main instruments of the marketing mix looks as follows. It offers express logistic solutions and international services for documents, small packages and heavier shipment. Shipment modes consist of air, road and Internet. In view of DHL's 'Global Service Commitment' which stands for the anticipation and following of customers' growth, it will respond by developing logistic solutions to help the customer whenever the latter's business is becoming more global. To this end, a range of new products and services were developed, such as export assistance, insurance services, flexible billing, help desks for key account customers and weekend collections and deliveries.

DHL's price is comparable to its main competitors, but it is higher than small local firms, situating itself in the medium- to high-price segment. Because of local conditions (labour and system costs, for example) prices differ between countries. This implies that the price of a shipment from Madrid to Stockholm will not be the same as the same shipment from Stockholm to Madrid. Through the Web, electronic data interchange, PC applications and touch-tone phones the customer is connected directly to DHL and can receive instant service, information and track the status of deliveries.

Marketing communication

The objective of DHL's communication is to create customer value. Customer value is not only the benefit of fast and reliable service gained by using the company, but it is also about making the customer feel more important by using DHL. Target groups consist of a wide range of users and decision-makers going from secretaries to shipment and export managers. Examples of messages that have been used by DHL are 'We Keep Your Promises', 'Trust is never a matter of luck', 'The strongest partnership work hand in hand', 'Nothing moves without them', and 'I don't work with amateurs'. Key aspects that are stressed are speed, reliability, trust and passion. Reliability is also stressed in competitors' messages. FedEx, for example, has used the baseline 'The World On Time', UPS has conveyed the message 'Consider it done', while TNT has come up with 'We take it personally'. In the future, DHL wants to stress more the elements of speed, fun and humour in its ads. In this vane, a campaign has already been launched in Belgium using jungle animals such as tigers together with the well known baseline 'We keep your promises'.

The communication mix consists of several tools. Advertising has been extensively used in several media. For example, ads in local newspapers, distribution and logistic magazines, and in the national press were used to create awareness. Furthermore, billboards have been used, as well as ads on buses and in the metro to reach decision makers who use public transport. Radio advertisements had the objective to reach the post-room clerks. Since they usually have the radio on, timing is chosen towards the end of the day when all mail and express deliveries are about to be sent believing that this will influence the decision. Besides advertising, DHL sponsors secretarial shows, world express conferences and sailing tournaments. Public relations are used as well. In Germany, for example, it launched, together with a top German dance aerobics firm, a fitness and back exercise programme for employees and customers, called 'Work well with DHL'. Furthermore, DHL obtained media coverage aiding and supporting crisis areas and countries in need, such as Bosnia. Personal selling also forms part of its communication mix. Local station managers, key account managers and local sales staff are used to create close and familiar long-term relationships with customers and to approach decision-makers to build preferences.

Results

How far has previous marketing actions brought DHL up to now? It has been doing very well in the past. It employs more than 60 000 employees, operates in 227 countries and has almost 3000 operating stations around the world (Table C19.2.). The latter means a greater worldwide coverage than Coca Cola and McDonald's.

DHL carries 200 parcels every 60 seconds,

Table C19.2	Worldwide activities of DHL		
Region	Number of countries	Number of stations	Number of employees
Europe/Africa	118	1 470	28 762
Asia/Pacific	40	793	14 134
Middle East	11	96	1 582
The Americas	58	595	16 008
Totals	227	2 954	60 486

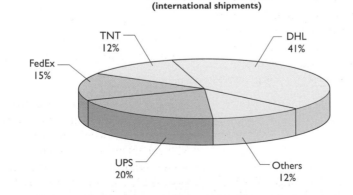

Worldwide market share
(international shipments)

TNT 12%
DHL 41%
FedEx 15%
UPS 20%
Others 12%

Figure C19.1 Worldwide market shares of express shipments

which makes more than 100 million documents and packages a year and currently is the global market leader in international air express (Fig. C19.1). However, DHL is mainly operating with shipments up to 250 kg. If heavier weight were to be included, TNT would have the largest share. Also, market share looks different if specific regions are considered. For instance, FedEx followed by UPS are market leaders in the USA. The future will show whether DHL's new marketing strategy can retain its leadership and create the desired image and position in the customer's mind.

This case was prepared by Patrick de Pelsmacker, M. Geuens and J. van den Berg, University of Antwerp.

Questions

1 What type of marketing management philosophy does DHL adhere to?

2 How would you define DHL's mission statement?

3 Develop a SWOT analysis for DHL.

4 In view of DHL's target groups, do you think stressing fun and humour in its messages is a good idea? Would you advise DHL to use the same message for its different target groups?

5 In view of DHL's new marketing strategy and marketing objectives, do you think the current communication mix needs to be adapted? If so, in what way?

Case 20 Blue Lagoon

Market background

The world's very first chocolate bar was produced in the USA at the turn of the century. To mark the entry into the new millennium a large US company has been looking for a way to enter the British confectionery market and gain a foothold from which to begin to tackle the European market. It has produced a brand of after-dinner mint called 'Blue Lagoon' with which they intend to launch into that sector.

The origins of the after-dinner mint market lie in the 1960s when After Eight mints were first launched by Rowntree. The wafer thin mints in their distinctive dark green box were positioned as having the kind of cachet associated with the very smartest dinner parties, and effectively invented the whole sector. Having captured this very posh reputation the brand was in fact sold in great volume, thereby assuring its place as a successful mass-market product which could afford to be advertised on television. The advertising campaign has always very much reinforced the image of After Eights as the ultimate way to finish a sophisticated dinner party.

The after-dinner mint market was valued at £14 million in 1996, which represented a slight decline of minus 5 per cent on the previous year. It is the view of the company launching Blue Lagoon that the market has been neglected in terms of advertising and promotional support, and that this represents a great opportunity for it to enter the arena and take the limelight.

The market is currently divided among the brands shown in Table C20.1.

Distribution is dominated by the major multiples (supermarkets) although new forms of outlet have been growing such as service stations as shown in Table C20.2.

The product

Blue Lagoon is so called because of the blue colour of the mint inside the classic dark US chocolate. The texture of the hard chocolate contrasts in an interesting way with the soft minty centre. The delicious taste has been described as totally absorbing—tingling around the mouth before leaving it feeling smooth and fresh. Each mint is oval in shape and individually wrapped in electric blue coloured foil. The packaging consists of an oval shaped box containing 24 mints and the design has been executed to give a very high quality feel. The words Blue Lagoon are written in gold against an electric blue background.

The consumer

Purchasers of after-dinner mints are female biased (on average 70 per cent being purchased by women), older (i.e. bought by over 40s) and mass market. The historical heartland of this sector had always been upmarket and younger (25–35) but there is evidence that as the bulk of consumers grew older new younger consumers were not coming in to replace them. In addition, traditional consumers are purchasing far fewer boxes than they used to and the 'specialness' of the purchase has been eroded. There are hints of this in reference to 'eating them while I do the hoovering/ironing' and having them available for the whole family to nibble in front of the TV. A significant number of consumers have lapsed

Table C20.1 Brand market share

	Brand share	% change year on year of sales
After Eight	34%	−13%
Twilight	18%	+10%
Own label	13%	+24%
Bendicks	6%	+9%
Elizabeth Shaw	5%	−26%
Others	5%	−19%

Table C20.2 Share of sales by outlet

Multiple grocers	51%
Independent grocers	10%
Multiple newsagents	18%
Independent newsagents	14%
Co-ops	3%
Service stations	4%

from using after-dinner mints completely and in preference buy Belgian chocolates.

All after-dinner mints are bought to share, rather than as a present or for self-consumption. Thus the most popular occasion for usage is after a dinner party (17 per cent) or after dinner (12 per cent). If they are given as a gift this tends to be when going to a dinner party as a guest and at Christmas time. Unlike other boxed chocolates they do not tend to be associated either with romance or saying 'thank you'.

After Eight mints have the most powerful and developed brand imagery. Initially there are strong associations with the elegance and sophistication of swish dinner parties. Rolls-Royce, smoking jackets, twin set and pearls and Penelope Keith. However, on further probing consumers admit that the brand is more like your next-door neighbour and Wendy Craig. The product itself is felt to be very delicate and sensual with its wafer thin slices and individual envelopes.

Bendicks has posh connotations as well with strong associations with Range Rovers and the landed gentry. A brand you could imagine the Queen might eat.

Elizabeth Shaw was also regarded as special and tended to be most favoured as a gift to take to dinner parties. Consumers found it more difficult to personify the brand.

Own label were generally seen as more everyday and less special with little to choose between the retail outlets.

Marketing objective

The company want to launch the brand with a target of achieving brand leadership within four years. Blue Lagoon will be priced at a 10 per cent price premium over the other brands and will focus their distribution push through supermarkets, flower shops and off-licences.

The task

Devise an advertising strategy which includes answers to the following questions

1 What are the advertising objectives?

2 Who are the people the advertising must affect/reach?

3 What message should be used and what evidence can be used to support the message?

4 What do we want people to think/feel after seing the advertisements?

5 What should the style of the advertising be?

6 Where should the advertising appear (i.e. TV, newspapers, magazines, posters, radio, etc.).

This case has been prepared by Jan Gooding, BLUE-dOOR. © IPC.

BLUE LAGOON
CHOCOLATE MINTS

New Blue Lagoon.
24 individually wrapped
chocolates with a blue
mint filling

CHAPTER TWELVE

Personal Selling and Sales Management

'Everyone lives by selling something'

ROBERT LOUIS STEVENSON

Learning Objectives *This chapter explains:*

1 Environmental and managerial forces affecting sales

2 The different types of selling jobs

3 Sales responsibilities

4 How to prepare for selling

5 The stages in the selling process

6 The tasks of sales management

7 How to design a salesforce

8 How to manage a salesforce

9 Key account management

10 Ethical issues in personal selling and sales management

Personal selling is the marketing task involving face-to-face contact with a customer. Unlike advertising, promotion, sponsorship and other forms of non-personal communication, personal selling permits a direct interaction between buyer and seller. This two-way communication means that the seller can identify the specific needs and problems of the buyer and tailor the sales presentation in the light of this knowledge. The particular concerns of the buyer can also be dealt with on a one-to-one basis.

This flexibility comes only at a cost. The cost of a car, travel expenses and sales office overheads can mean that the total annual bill for a field salesperson is often twice the level of salary. In industrial marketing over 70 per cent of the marketing budget is usually spent on the salesforce. This is because of the technical nature of the products being sold, and the need to maintain close personal relationships between the selling and buying organizations. A survey by McGraw-Hill in 1990 revealed the costs of a sales visit in EU countries. These ranged from a high of $1439 in Denmark to a low of $128 in Ireland. The UK figure was $304. Given that a sale takes six visits, the cost of a sale in Denmark was estimated to be $8634; in the UK it was $1824 and in Ireland it amounted to $768.

However, the nature of the personal selling function is changing. Organizations are reducing the size of their salesforces in the face of greater buyer concentration, moves towards centralized buying, and recognition of the high costs of maintaining a field sales team. The concentration of buying power into fewer hands has also fuelled the move towards relationship management often through key account selling. This involves the use of dedicated sales teams who service the accounts of major buyers. As the commercial director of HP Foods said, 'Twenty years ago we had between 70 and 100 salespeople. The change in the retail environment from small retailers to central warehouses and supermarkets has meant a big change in the way we communicate with our customers. Instead of sending salespeople out on the road, we now collect a large proportion of our sales by telephone or computer. We have replaced the traditional salesforce with 12 business development executives who each have a small number of accounts dealing with customers at both national and regional levels.'[1] Selling and sales management are experiencing a period of rapid change.

The next section explores the major forces at work.

Environmental and managerial forces affecting sales

A number of major behavioural and managerial forces are influencing how selling and sales management is and will be carried out.[2] These are listed in Table 12.1.

Behavioural forces

Just as customers adapt to their changing environment so the sales function has to adapt to these forces which are: (i) rising customer expectations,

---

Table 12.1   Forces influencing selling and sales management practices

Behavioural forces
   Rising customer expectations
   Customer avoidance of buyer–seller negotiations
   Expanding power of major buyers
   Globalization of markets
   Fragmentation of markets

Technical forces
   Sales force automation
   ✦ Laptop computers and software
   ✦ Electronic data interchange
   ✦ Desktop videoconferencing
   Virtual sales offices
   Electronic sales channels
   ✦ Internet
   ✦ Television home shopping

Managerial forces
   Direct marketing
   ✦ Direct mail
   ✦ Telemarketing
   ✦ Computer salespeople
   Blending of sales and marketing
   ✦ Intranets
   Qualifications for salespeople and sales managers

Adapted from Anderson, R. (1996) Personal Selling and Sales Management in the New Millennium, *Journal of Personal Selling and Sales Management*, **16** (4), 17–32.

(ii) customer avoidance of buyer–seller negotiations, (iii) the expanding power of major buyers, (iv) globalization of markets and (v) fragmentation of markets.

Rising customer expectations

As consumers experience higher standards of product quality and service so their expectations are fuelled to expect even higher levels in the future. This process may be accelerated by experiences abroad, and new entrants to industries (possibly from abroad) that set new standards of excellence. As the executive of the customer satisfaction research firm J. D. Power explained: 'What makes customer satisfaction so difficult to achieve is that you constantly raise the bar and extend the finish line. You never stop. As your customers get better treatment, they demand better treatment.' The implication for salespeople is that they must accept that both consumer and organizational buyer expectations for product quality, customer service and value will continue to rise, and that they must respond to this challenge by advocating and implementing continuous improvements in quality standards.

Customer avoidance of buyer–seller negotiations

Studies have shown that the purchase of a car is the most anxiety-provoking and least satisfying experience in retail buying.[3] Some car salespeople are trained in the art of negotiation supported by high-pressure sales tactics. Consequently, customers have taken to viewing the purchase as an ordeal to be tolerated rather than a pleasurable occasion to be savoured. In response, some car companies have moved to a fixed price, no pressure and full-book value for the trade-in approach. This was used for the successful launch of the Saturn by General Motors in the USA and is the philosophy behind the marketing of Daewoo cars in the UK.

Expanding power of major buyers

The growing dominance of major players in many sectors (notably retailing) is having a profound influence on selling and sales management. Their enormous purchasing power means that they are able to demand and get special services including special customer status (key account management), just-in-time inventory control, category management and joint funding of promotions. Future success for salespeople will be dependent on their capabilities to respond to the increasing demands of major customers.

Globalization of markets

As domestic markets saturate, companies are expanding abroad to achieve sales and profit growth. Large companies such as Coca-Cola, Colgate-Palmolive and Avon Products now earn the largest proportion of their revenues in foreign markets. The challenges include the correct balance between expatriate and host country sales personnel, adapting to different cultures, lifestyles and languages, competing against world-class brands, and building global relationships with huge customers based in many countries. For example, 3M has a variety of global strategic accounts from industrial high tech (Motorola, Hewlett-Packard, IBM, Texas Instruments) to original equipment manufacturers in electronics, appliances, automotive, electrical, aerospace, furniture, consumer products and health care.[4] A major challenge for such a transnational corporation is the coordination of global sales teams which sell to the Nortels, Samsungs, Siemens, or P&Gs of this world, where the customer may be located in over twenty countries and require special terms of sale, technical support, pricing and customization of products. This complexity means that strategic account managers require both enhanced teamwork and coordination skills to ensure that customers receive top quality service.

Fragmentation of markets

Driven by differences in income levels, lifestyles, personalities, experiences and race, markets are fragmenting to form market segments. This means that markets are likely to become smaller with an increasing range of brands marketed to cater for the diverse requirements (both functional and psychological) of customers. Marketing and sales managers need to be adept at identifying changes in consumer tastes and developing strategies that satisfy an increasingly varied and multicultural society.

Technological forces

Three major forces are at play: (i) salesforce automation, (ii) virtual sales offices and (iii) electronic sales channels.

Salesforce automation

Salesforce automation includes laptop and palm-top computers, mobile phone, fax machines, e-mail and sophisticated sales-orientated software which aid such tasks as journey and account planning, recruitment and selection and evaluation of sales personnel. In addition, electronic data interchange (EDI) provides computer links between manufacturers and resellers (retailers, wholesalers and distributors) allowing the exchange of information. For example, purchase orders, invoices, price quotes, delivery dates, reports and promotional information can be exchanged. Technological innovations have also made possible desktop videoconferencing, enabling sales meetings, training and customer interaction to take place without the need for people to leave their offices.

Virtual sales office

Improved technology has also encouraged the creation of virtual offices allowing sales personnel to keep in contact with head office, customers and co-workers. The virtual office may be the home or even a car. This can mean large cost and time savings, and enhanced job satisfaction for sales personnel who are spared some of the many traffic jams that are a part of the life of a field salesperson.

Electronic sales channels

The fastest growing electronic sales channel is undoubtedly the Internet. However, another emerging channel is worthy of mention as it will reduce the need for field salesforces. This is television home shopping where viewers watch cable television presenters promote anything from jewellery to consumer electronics and order by telephone. In effect, the presenter is the salesperson.

Managerial forces

Managers are responding to the changes in the environment by developing new strategies to enhance effectiveness. These include: (i) employing direct marketing techniques, (ii) improving the blend between sales and marketing, and (iii) encouraging salespeople to gain professional qualifications.

Direct marketing techniques

The increasing role of direct marketing is reflected in the growth of direct mail and telemarketing activities. However, a third emerging change is the use of computer stations in US retail outlets to replace traditional salespeople. Although in Europe the use of computer-assisted sales in car showrooms has begun with Daewoo's employment of kiosks where customers can gather product and price information, the process has moved a stage further in the USA where several Ford dealerships have installed computer stations which fully replace salespeople. Customers can compare features of competitive models, calculate running costs, compute monthly payments, and use the computer to write up the order and telephone it to the factory, without the intervention of a salesperson.

Blending sales and marketing

Although the development of effective relationships between sales and marketing personnel is recognized by all, often in practice blending the two functions into an effective whole is hampered by, among other things, poor communication. The establishment of intranets, which are similar to the Internet except that they are proprietary company networks that link employees, suppliers and customers through their PCs, can improve links and improve information exchange. Intranets are used for such diverse functions as e-mail, team projects and desktop publishing. Clearly, their use can enhance the effectiveness of a field salesforce that requires fast access to rapidly changing information such as product specifications, competitor news and price updates, and allows the sharing of information between sales and marketing.

Professional qualifications

Finally, sales management is responding to the new challenges by recognizing the importance of professional qualifications. In the UK, this has led to the formation of a new professional body, the Institute of Professional Sales. This body is charged with enhancing the profile of the sales function, promoting best practice, and developing education and training programmes to improve salespeople and sales managers' professionalism, skills and competencies.

Next, we shall examine the different types of sellers, the major responsibilities of salespeople and the process and techniques of personal selling. We shall then explore the tasks of the sales manager including the setting of objectives and strategy, determining salesforce size and organization, and how to recruit, train, motivate and evaluate salespeople.

Types of selling

The diverse nature of the buying situation inevitably means that there are many types of selling jobs: selling varies according to the nature of the selling task. Figure 12.1 shows that a fundamental distinction is between order-takers, order-creators, and order-getters. Order-takers respond to already committed customers; order-creators do not directly receive orders as they talk to specifiers rather than buyers; order-getters attempt to persuade customers to place an order directly.

There are three types of order-takers: inside order-takers, delivery salespeople and outside order-takers. Order-creators are termed missionary salespeople. Order-getters are either front-line salespeople consisting of new business, organizational or consumer salespeople, or sales support salespeople who can be either technical support salespeople or merchandisers.[5] Both types of order-getters are in situations where a direct sale can be made. Each type of selling job will now be discussed.

Order-takers

Inside order-takers

The typical inside order-taker is the retail sales assistant. The customer has full freedom to choose products without the presence of a salesperson. The sales assistant's task is purely transactional: receiving payment and passing over the goods. Another form of inside order-taker is the telemarketing sales team who support field sales by taking customers' orders over the telephone.

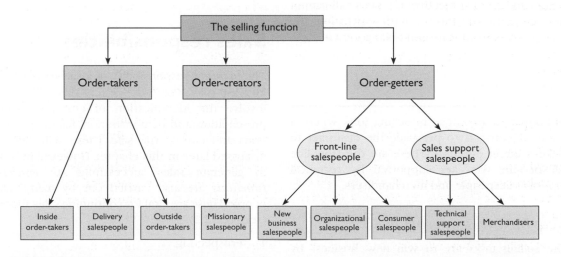

Figure 12.1 Types of selling

Delivery salespeople

The salesperson's task is primarily concerned with delivering the product. In the UK, milk, newspapers and magazines are delivered to the door. There is little attempt to persuade the household to increase the milk order or number of newspapers taken: changes in order size are customer-driven. Winning and losing orders will be heavily dependent on the reliability of delivery.

Outside order-takers

Unlike inside order-takers, these salespeople visit the customer but also primarily respond to customer requests rather than actively seek to persuade. Unlike delivery salespeople, outside order-takers do not deliver. Outside order-takers are a dying breed being replaced by the more cost-efficient telemarketing teams.

Order-creators

Missionary salespeople

In some industries, notably pharmaceuticals, the sales task is not to close the sale but to persuade the customer to specify the seller's products. For example, medical representatives calling on doctors cannot make a direct sale since the doctor does not buy drugs but prescribes (specifies) them for patients. Similarly in the building industry, architects act as specifiers rather than buyers and so the objective of a sales call cannot be to close the sale. Instead in these situations the selling task is to educate and build goodwill.

Order-getters

Order-getters are those in selling jobs where a major objective is to persuade the customer to make a direct purchase. These are the front-line salespeople, who are supported by technical support salespeople and merchandisers.

New business salespeople

The selling tasks are to win new business by identifying and selling to prospects (people or organizations who have not previously bought from the salesperson's company).

Organizational salespeople

The salespeople have the job of maintaining close long-term relationships with organizational customers. The selling job may involve team selling where mainstream salespeople are supported by product and financial specialists.

Consumer salespeople

This type of selling task involves selling to individuals physical products and services such as double glazing, encyclopaedias, cars, insurance and personal pension plans.

Technical support salespeople

Where a product is highly technical and negotiations complex, a salesperson may be supported by product and financial specialists who can provide the detailed technical information required of customers. This may be on-going as part of a key account team or as a temporary basis with the specialists being called into the selling situation when required.

Merchandisers

These provide sales support in retail and wholesale selling. Orders may be negotiated nationally at head office but sales to individual outlets are supported by merchandisers who give advice on display, implement sales promotions, check stock levels, and maintain contact with store managers.

Sales responsibilities

The *primary* responsibility of a salesperson is to increase sales. For order-getters this will usually involve the identification of customer needs, presentation and demonstration, handling objections and closing the sale. These skills will be discussed later in this chapter. However, in order to generate sales successfully, *six enabling functions* are also carried out by many salespeople. These are vital for continuing sales success (see Fig. 12.2):

1 Prospecting.
2 Maintaining customer records and information feedback.
3 Providing service.

4   Handling complaints.

5   Self-management.

6   Relationship management.

Prospecting

Prospecting is the searching for and calling upon potential customers. A problem sometimes associated with salespeople who have worked for the same company for many years is that they rely on established customers rather than actively seeking new business. They work in their *comfort zone* calling upon old contacts rather than searching out and selling to new customers. Prospects can be identified from several sources.

Existing customers

Satisfied customers should be asked if they know of anyone who may be interested in the lines of products being sold. This is common practice in insurance and industrial selling but can be used in other industries also. Having obtained the name of a prospect the salesperson should then ask if the customer's name can be used as an example of a satisfied customer. This is called *reference selling*.

Trade directories

Trade directories such as *Kompass* or *Dun and Bradstreet's Key British Enterprises* can be used to provide names of prospects. These directories give names, addresses, telephone numbers, size of firm and types of products made or distributed.

Enquiries

Enquiries can be stimulated by advertising, direct mail or exhibitions. The enquiry should be dealt

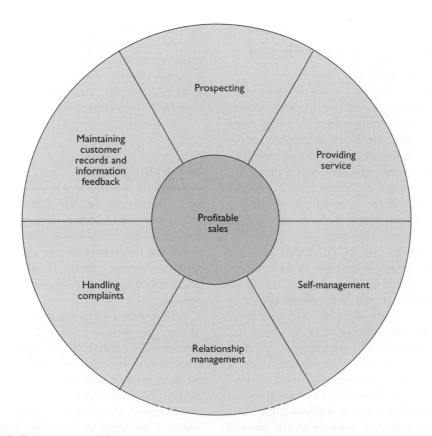

Figure 12.2 Sales responsibilities

with promptly and checked to establish its seriousness and worth. This process of checking leads to establish their potential is called *qualifying*.

The press

It is worth while checking the press for advertisements and articles that can give clues to potential sources of new business. Advertisements may reveal expansion plans that may suggest potential business and articles may reveal new product developments that may have new business implications.

Cold canvassing

This involves calling on prospects who may or may not have a need for the salesperson's product. *Cool canvassing* is a variant of this method where only certain groups are called upon. For example, only companies over a certain size may be judged viable prospects.

Maintaining customer records and information feedback

Customer record-keeping is an important activity for all repeat-call salespeople. For industrial salespeople record cards can be an invaluable source of information on the decision-making unit: who are the important people to see, when they have been seen and what are their choice criteria. Before each visit the record card can be used to check for important details that can be used by the salesperson in the sales plan.

Salespeople should also be encouraged to send customer and market information to head office. Test market activity by competition, news of imminent product launches, rumours of policy changes on the part of trade and industrial customers and competitors, and feedback on company achievement regarding product performance, delivery and after-sales service are just some of the kinds of information which may be useful to management.[6] One method of encouraging feedback of information from salespeople is to reward them not only on the basis of sales but also according to the amount of relevant information they feedback to the company.[7]

Providing service

Salespeople can build goodwill by providing service to their customers. Since they meet many customers each year, they become familiar with solutions to common problems. For example, advice on improving productivity or cutting costs may provide tangible customer benefits.

Salespeople may also be called upon to provide after-sales service to customers. Sales engineers may be required to give advice on the operation of a newly acquired machine or provide assistance in the event of a breakdown. Sometimes they may be able to solve the problem themselves, while in other cases they will call in technical specialists to deal with the problem.

Handling complaints

Dissatisfied customers tell on average six other people about their cause for complaint. Dealing with complaints quickly and efficiently is therefore a key aspect of selling. The ability of the salesperson to empathize with the customer and react sympathetically can create considerable goodwill. Instead of telling six people of their dissatisfaction, the complainants will say how well they have been treated.

Self-management

One area that may be delegated to the salesperson is *journey routing*. Many salespeople believe that the most efficient routing plan involves driving out to the furthest customer and then zigzagging back to home base. However, adopting a round-trip approach will usually result in lower mileage.

Call frequencies may also be the responsibility of the salesperson. If so, it is sensible to grade customers according to potential. For example, a grade A customer may be called upon every two weeks, a grade B customer every four weeks, and grade C customers once every two months. One problem with allowing the salesperson discretion over call planning is that they may over-call on established, friendly customers even though they do not have much growth potential.

Relationship management

Many selling situations are not one-off situation-specific encounters but long term. This is particularly true in organizational markets where supplier and trade, governmental or industrial customers work together to create, develop and maintain a network within which both parties thrive.[8] It is within such relationships that the core of marketing activity is found. The management of the relationships with key customers is a major responsibility of salespeople reflected in the fact that although the number of salespeople overall is falling, the number of key account managers is growing.[9]

Relationship management has already been discussed in Chapter 4. The objective is to build goodwill that is reciprocated by placing orders. To recap, this can be achieved by providing exceptional customer service through:

✦ Technical support.

✦ Expertise.

✦ Resource support.

✦ Improving service levels.

✦ Lowering perceived risk.

In addition, salespeople should develop *trust* through high frequency of contact, ensuring that promises are kept, and reacting quickly and effectively to problems.

Clearly the tasks of salespeople are onerous. Developments in information and telecommunications technology have eased some of the burdens but have created new pressures. Some of the issues are discussed in e-Marketing 12.1.

Personal selling skills

Many people's perception of a salesperson is of a slick fast-talking confidence trickster devoted to forcing unwanted products on innocent customers. Personal experience will tell the reader that this is unrealistic in a world of educated consumers and professional buyers. Success in selling comes from implementing the marketing concept when face-to-face with customers, not denying it at the very point when the seller and buyer come into contact. The sales interview offers an unparalleled opportunity to identify individual customer needs and match

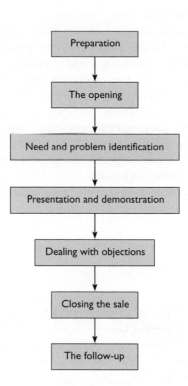

Figure 12.3 The selling process

behaviour to the specific customer that is encountered.[10]

Research has shown that far from using high-pressure selling tactics, success is associated with:[11]

1   Asking questions.

2   Providing product information, making comparisons, and offering evidence to support claims.

3   Acknowledging the viewpoint of the customer.

4   Agreeing with the customer's perceptions.

5   Supporting the customer.

6   Releasing tension.

All of these findings are in accord with the marketing concept.

In order to develop personal selling skills it is useful to distinguish six phases of the selling process (see Fig. 12.3). Each will now be discussed.

Preparation

Preparation before a sales visit can reap dividends by enhancing confidence and performance when face-to-face with the customer. Some situations cannot be prepared for: the unexpected question or unusual objection, for example. But many customers face similar situations and certain questions and objections will be raised repeatedly. Preparation can help the salesperson respond to those recurring situations.

Salespeople will benefit from gaining knowl-edge of their own products, competitors' prod-ucts, sales presentation planning, setting call objectives, and understanding buyer behaviour.

Product knowledge

Product knowledge means understanding both product features and the customer benefits that they confer. Understanding product features alone is not enough to convince customers to buy because they buy products for the benefits that the features provide, not the features in them-

12.1   e-Marketing
Technology and the Salesperson's Job

Technological developments in information and telecommunications technology have revolution-ized the way salespeople operate. Advances include:

✦ Remote access through portable PCs/laptops/palmtops to branch office or headquarters' computer systems for up-to-the-minute information or order status, prices availability and competitive data. Sales orders and queries can be sent to the sales office and catalogues held on the computer.

✦ Electronic mail and faxes to speed communications, facilitate links with hard-to-reach people and hold messages sent by other people.

✦ Word processing, spreadsheet and presentation software for customizing sales letters, automating call reports, preparing quotations and proposals, generating sales forecasts, and preparing text and graphics for presentations.

✦ Time management software for journey planning and the automatic updating of call reports.

✦ Contact management systems that hold information on prospects, customers, sales and competitors to facilitate call planning and execution.

✦ Mobile phones to ease communication to and from salespeople and the reduction of wasted travelling time.

✦ Telemarketing software to improve inbound and outbound call productivity.

✦ Personal digital assistants that are starting to provide an easy form of data transportation, allowing salesforces to access information on consumer populations and local territories.

The resulting improvements in productivity do not mean that the job of the salesperson is easier, however. The time savings mean that there is more time for other duties and greater access to and from the salesperson means that customers and sales management expect faster response times.

Based on: Croft (1995);[12] Wendell and Hempeck (1987);[13] Reed (1999)[14]

selves. Salespeople need to ask themselves what are the benefits that a certain feature provides for customers. For example, a computer mouse (product feature) provides a more convenient way of issuing commands (customer benefit) than using the keyboard. The way to turn features into benefits is to view products from the customer's angle. A by-product of this is the realization that some features may provide no customer benefit whatsoever.

Competitors' products

Knowledge of competitors' products allows their strengths to be offset against their weaknesses. For example, if a buyer claims that a competitor's product has a cost advantage, this may be offset against the superior productivity advantage of the salesperson's product. Similarly, inaccuracies in a buyer's claims can be countered. Finally, competitive knowledge allows the salespeople to stress the differential advantage of their products compared to the competition.

Sales presentation planning

Preparation here builds confidence, raises the chances that important benefits are not forgotten, allows visual aids and demonstrations to be built into the presentation, and permits the anticipation of objections and the preparation of convincing counterarguments. Although preparation is vital there should be room left for flexibility in approach since customers have different needs. The salesperson has to be aware that the features and benefits that should be stressed with one customer may have much less emphasis placed on them for another.

Setting call objectives

The key to setting call objectives is to phrase them in terms of what the salesperson wants the customer to do rather than what the salesperson should do. For example:

✦ For the customer to define what his or her needs are.

✦ For the customer to visit a showroom.

✦ For the customer to try the product, e.g. drive a car.

✦ For the customer to be convinced of the cost saving of our product compared with the competition.

This is because the success of the sales interview is customer-dependent. The end is to convince the customer; what the salesperson does is simply a means to that end.

Understanding buyer behaviour

Thought should also be given to understanding *buyer behaviour*. Questions should be asked: Who are the likely key people to talk to? What are their probable choice criteria? Are there any gate-keepers preventing access to some people who need to be circumvented? What are the likely opportunities and threats that may arise in the selling situation? All of the answers to these questions need to be verified when in the actual selling situation but prior consideration can help salespeople to be clear in their own minds about the important issues.

The opening

Initial impressions often affect later perceptions, and so it is important for salespeople to consider how to create a favourable initial response from customers. The following factors can positively shape first impressions:

1 Be business-like in appearance and behaviour.

2 Be friendly but not over-familiar.

3 Be attentive to detail such as holding a briefcase in the hand which is not used for handshaking.

4 Observe common courtesies like waiting to be asked to sit down.

5 Ask if it is convenient to see you. This signals an appreciation of their needs (they may be too busy to be seen). It automatically creates a favourable impression on which to develop the sales call but also a long-term relationship because the salesperson has earned the right to proceed to the next stage in selling: need and problem identification.

6 Do not take the sales interview for granted: thank the customer for spending time with you and stress that you believe that it will be worthwhile.

WITH FIXED PRICES AND
NO HAGGLING, IT COULDN'T
BE EASIER SHOPPING
FOR A NEW DAEWOO.

Why can't buying a car be as problem free as going to a supermarket? Well, when you buy a Daewoo, it is. That's because buying a

 **DAEWOO**

Daewoo has always been (and always will be) a hassle free experience. How do we manage this? Well, our showrooms welcome families, and we only employ non commissioned Customer Advisers who are there to help you, not haggle over prices. And our fixed pricing policy with no hidden costs means that the price you see on a Daewoo is exactly the price you pay. And as well as launching three new car ranges, the 3, 4 and 5 door Lanos, the Nubira Saloon and Estate and the Leganza Saloon, we also include as standard: 1) 3 year/60,000 mile free servicing including labour and parts 2) 3 year/60,000 mile comprehensive warranty 3) 3 year Daewoo Total AA cover 4) 6 years anti-corrosion warranty 5) Free courtesy car 6) Delivery, number plates, 12 months road tax and a full tank of fuel 7) Dual airbags 8) Power steering 9) Engine immobiliser 10) Metallic paint. So when you see how hassle free it is to buy a Daewoo, combined with the fact that our fixed prices range from £8,795 to £14,995, the only difficult decision you'll have to make is which car you like best. Tricky isn't it? For more information call 0800 666 222.

Hassle free car buying? That'll be the Daewoo.

A new type of selling from Daewoo: no more pushy salespeople; instead customer advisors who are there to help not haggle over prices

Need and problem identification

People buy products because they have problems that give rise to needs. For example, machine unreliability (problem) causes the need to replace it with a new one (purchase). Therefore the first task is to identify the needs and problems of each customer. Only by doing so can the salesperson connect with each customer's situation. Having done so, the salesperson can select the product that best fits the customer's need and sell the appropriate benefits. It is benefits that link customer needs to product features as in:

Customer need → Benefit ← Product feature

In the previous example it would be essential to convince the customer that the salesperson's machine possessed features that guaranteed machine reliability. Knowledge of competitors' products would allow salespeople to show how their machine possessed features that gave added reliability. In this way salespeople are in an ideal situation to convince customers of a product's differential advantage. Whenever possible factual evidence of product superiority should be shown to customers. This is much more convincing than mere claims by the salesperson.

Effective needs and problem identification requires the development of questioning and listening skills. The problem is that people are more used to making statements than asking questions. Therefore the art of asking sensible questions that produce a clear understanding of the customer's situation requires training and considerable experience. The hallmark of inexperienced salespeople is that they do all the talking; successful salespeople know how to get the customer to do most of the talking. In that way they gain the information necessary to make a sale.

Presentation and demonstration

The presentation and demonstration provides the opportunity for the salesperson to convince customers that the salesperson can supply the solution to their problem. It should focus on **customer benefits** rather than **product features**. These can be linked by using the following phrases:

✦ Which means that.

✦ Which results in.

✦ Which enables you to.

For example, the machine salesperson might say that the machine possesses proven technology (product feature) which means that the reliability of the machine (customer benefit) can be relied upon. Evidence should then be supplied to support this sales argument. Perhaps scientific tests have proved the reliability of the machine (these should be shown to the customer), satisfied customers' testimonials could be produced or a visit to a satisfied customer could be arranged.

The salesperson should continue asking questions during the presentation to ensure that the customer has understood what the salesperson has said and to check that what the salesperson has mentioned really is of importance to the customer. This can be achieved by asking: 'Is that the kind of thing you are looking for?'

Demonstrations allow the customer to see the product in operation. As such some of the claims made for the product by the salesperson can be verified. Demonstrations allow the customer to be involved in the selling process through participation. They can, therefore, be instrumental in reducing the *perceived risk* of a purchase and move the customer towards purchase.

Dealing with objections

It is unusual for salespeople to close a sale without the need to overcome objections. Although objections can cause problems they should not be regarded negatively since they highlight the issues that are important to the buyer.

The secret of *dealing with objections* is to handle both the substantive and emotional aspects. The substantive part is to do with the objection itself. If the customer objects to the product's price the salesperson needs to use convincing arguments to show that the price is not too high. But it is a fact of human personality that the argument that is supported by the greater weight of evidence does not always win since people resent being proven wrong. Therefore, salespeople need to recognize the emotional aspects of objection handling. Under no circumstances should the buyer lose face or be antagonized during this process. Two ways of minimizing this risk are to listen to the objection without interruption and to employ the agree and counter technique.

Listen and do not interrupt

Experienced salespeople know that the impression given to buyers by salespeople who interrupt buyers when they are raising an objection is that the salesperson believes that:

✦ The objection is obviously wrong.

✦ It is trivial.

✦ It is not worth the salesperson's time to let the buyer finish.

Interruption denies buyers the kind of respect they are entitled to receive and may lead to a mis-understanding of the real substance behind the objection.

The correct approach is to listen carefully, attentively and respectfully. The buyer will appreciate the fact that the salesperson is taking the problem seriously and the salesperson will gain through having a clear and full understanding of what the problem really is.

Agree and counter

The salesperson agrees with the buyers' view-point before putting forward an alternative point of view. The objective is to create a climate of agreement rather than conflict, and shows that the salesperson respects the buyer's opinion, thus avoiding loss of face. For example:

> *Buyer*: The problem with your bulldozer is that it costs more than the competition.
> *Salesperson*: You are right, the initial cost is a little higher, but I should like to show you how the full lifetime costs of the bulldozer are much lower than the competition.

Closing the sale

Inexperienced salespeople sometimes think that an effective presentation followed by convincing objection handling should mean that the buyer will ask for the product without the seller needing to close the sale. This does occasionally happen but more often it is necessary for the salesperson to take the initiative. This is because many buyers still feel doubts in their minds which may cause them to wish to delay the decision to purchase.

But if the customer puts off buying, the decision may be made when a competitor's salesperson is present, resulting in a lost sale.

Buying signals

The key to closing a sale is to look for **buying signals**. These are statements by buyers that indicate that they are interested in buying, for example:

That looks fine.
I like that one.
When could the product be delivered?
I think that product meets my requirements.

These all indicate a very positive intention to buy without actually asking for the order. They provide excellent opportunities for the salesperson to ask the buyer to make a decision without appearing pushy.

Closing techniques

A variety of *closing techniques* can be used.

Simply ask for the order a direct question such as 'Would you like that one?' may be all that is needed.

Summarize and then ask for the order with this approach the salesperson reminds the buyer of the main points of the sales discussion in a manner which implies that the time for decision-making has arrived and that buying is the natural next step:

> Well, Ms Jones, we have agreed that the ZX4 model best meets your requirements of low noise and high productivity at an economical price. Would you like to place an order for this machine?

Concession close by keeping a concession back to use in the close, a salesperson may convince an indecisive buyer to place an order:

> I am in a position to offer an extra 10 per cent discount on price if you are willing to place an order now.

Action agreement in some situations it is inappropriate to try to close the sale. To do so would annoy the buyer because the sale is not in the hands of one person but a decision-making unit. Many organizational purchasing decisions are of this kind, and the decision may be made in committee without any salesperson being present. Alternatively, the salesperson may be talking to a specifier (such as a doctor or architect) who does not buy directly. In such circumstances, the close may be substituted by an *action agreement*: instead of closing the sale the salesperson attempts to achieve an action agreement with the customer. For example, in the selling of prescription drugs, either the salesperson or the doctor agree to do something before the next meeting. The salesperson might agree to bring details of a new drug, or attempt to get agreement from the doctor to read a leaflet on a drug before the next meeting. This technique has the effect of maintaining the relationship between the parties and can be used as the starting-point of the discussion when they next meet.

The follow-up

Once the order is placed there could be a temptation for the salesperson to move on to other customers, neglecting the follow-up visit. However, this can be a great mistake since most companies rely on repeat business. If problems arise, customers have every right to believe that the salesperson was interested only in the order, and not their complete satisfaction. By checking that there are no problems with delivery, installation, product use and training (where applicable), the follow-up can show that the salesperson really cares about the customer.

The follow-up can also be used to provide reassurance that the purchase was the right thing to do. As we discussed when analysing consumer behaviour, people often feel tense after deciding to buy an expensive product. Doubts can materialize about the wisdom of spending so much money, or whether the product best meets their needs. This anxiety, known as *cognitive dissonance*, can be minimized by the salesperson reassuring the customer about the purchase during the follow-up phase.

The salespeople operating in overseas markets need to be aware of the cultural nuances that shape business relationships. For example, in the West a deadline is acceptable whereas in many Middle Eastern cultures, it would be taken as an insult. Marketing in Action 12.1 discusses some of the cultural issues that affect business dealings with Chinese people.

Sales management

In many respects the functions of the sales manager are similar to those of other managers. Sales managers, like their production, marketing, and finance counterparts, need to recruit, train, motivate and evaluate their staff. However, there are several peculiarities of the job which make effective sales management difficult and the job considerably demanding.

Problems of sales management

Geographic separation

The geographic separation between sales managers and their field salesforce create problems of motivation, communication and control.

Repeated rejections

Salespeople may suffer repeated rejections when trying to close sales. This may cause attrition of the salesperson's enthusiasm, attitudes and skills. A major role for the sales managers is to provide support and renew motivation in these adverse circumstances.

Salesperson's personality v. the realities of the job

Most people who go into sales are outgoing and gregarious. These are desirable characteristics for people who are selling to customers. However, the reality of the job is that typically only 30 per cent of a salesperson's time is spent face-to-face with customers, with travelling (50 per cent) and administration (20 per cent) contributing the rest.[15] This means that over half of salespeople's time is spent by themselves, which can cause frustration in people who like the company of others.

Oversimplification of the task

Some sales managers cope with the difficulties of management by oversimplifying the task. They take the attitude that they are interested only in results. It is their job to reward those who meet sales targets, and severely punish those who fail. Such an attitude ignores the contribution that

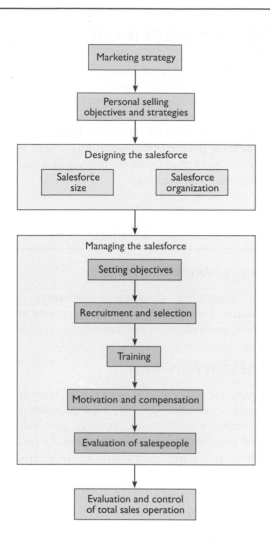

Marketing strategy

↓

Personal selling
objectives and strategies

↓

Designing the salesforce

Salesforce
size

Salesforce
organization

↓

Managing the salesforce

Setting objectives

↓

Recruitment and selection

↓

Training

↓

Motivation and compensation

↓

Evaluation of salespeople

↓

Evaluation and control
of total sales operation

Figure 12.4 Marketing strategy and the management of the salesforce

sales management can make to the successful achievement of objectives. Figure 12.4 shows the functions of a sales manager and the relationship between marketing strategy and the personal selling function.

Marketing strategy

As with all parts of the marketing mix, the personal selling function is not a stand-alone element but one that must be considered in the light of overall marketing strategy. At the product level, two major marketing considerations are the choice of target market and the creation of a

differential advantage. Both of these decisions impact personal selling.

Target market choice

The definition of target market has clear implications for sales management because of its relationship to *target accounts*. Once the target market has been defined (e.g. organizations in a particular industry over a certain size) sales management can translate that specification into individual accounts to target. Salesforce resources can, therefore, be deployed to maximum effect.

Differential advantage

The creation of a differential advantage is the starting-point of successful marketing strategy but this needs to be communicated to the salesforce and embedded in a sales plan which ensures that the salesforce is able to articulate it convincingly to customers.

Two common dangers

First, the salesforce undermines the differential advantage by repeatedly giving in to customer demands for price concessions. Second, the features that underlie the differential advantage are communicated but the customer benefits are neglected. Customer benefits need to be communicated in terms which are meaningful to customers. This means, for example, that advantages such as higher productivity may require translation into cash savings or higher revenue for financially minded customers.

Four strategic objectives

Marketing strategy also affects the personal selling function through strategic objectives. Each objective—build, hold, harvest, and divest—has implications for *sales objectives* and strategy; these are outlined in Table 12.2. Linking business or product area strategic objectives with functional area strategies is essential for the efficient allocation of resources, and effective implementation in the marketplace.[16]

Personal selling objectives and strategies

As we have seen, selling objectives and strategies are derived from marketing strategy decisions, and should be consistent with other elements of the marketing mix. Indeed marketing strategy will determine if there is a need for a salesforce at all, or whether the selling role can be better accomplished using some other medium such as direct mail. Objectives define what the selling function is expected to achieve. Objectives are typically defined in terms of:

I   Sales volume (e.g. 5 per cent growth in sales volume).

12.1   Marketing in Action
Personal Selling and the Chinese Culture

Cultural factors mean that salespeople need to understand and respect the values of overseas customers and alter their approach accordingly. Visiting salespeople are often invited to long banquets when selling to Chinese people. They usually begin in late morning or early evening. Some Chinese hosts regard visitors as having enjoyed themselves if they become a little intoxicated.

In China, negotiations often last longer than in many Western countries. Arriving late for a business appointment is regarded as acceptable behaviour. In Hong Kong, however, this would result in the visitor 'losing face', an extremely serious issue in Chinese culture. Visiting salespeople should avoid creating a situation where a Chinese person might 'lose face' by finding themselves in an embarrassing situation (e.g. by displaying lack of knowledge or understanding). Chinese people like to gather as much information as possible before revealing their thoughts to avoid losing face or displaying ignorance. Business relations should be built on the basis of harmony and friendship.

Displaying arrogance and the showing of extreme confidence are not admired. Instead, salespeople should make modest, reasoned, down-to-earth points. They should avoid trying to win arguments with customers who may suffer 'loss of face' and react negatively.

Western salespeople also need to understand the importance of *Guanxi* networks which provide access to influencers who can make things happen. *Guanxi* is a set of personal relationships/connections on which an individual can draw to secure resources or advantage when doing business. For foreigners, it means having as part of their *Guanxi* network, an influential person in an organization or government position. Developing such a network may involve performing favours and the giving of gifts. For example, a businessperson may participate in a public ceremonial function or a professor could send books to a Chinese university. The 'giving of face' is also important. This is done by giving respect, courtesy and praise to other people. The status and reputation of Chinese negotiators should always be recognized, and aggressive behaviour avoided.

Many salespeople make the mistake of using 'self-reference' criteria when selling abroad. They assume that the values and behavioural norms that apply in their own country are equally applicable abroad. To avoid this failing, they need training in the special skills required to sell to people of different cultures.

Based on: Bradley. (1991);[17] Jeannet and Hennessey (1995);[18] Buttery and Leung (1998);[19] Arias (1998);[20] Cateora et al. (2000)[21]

2 Market share (e.g. 1 per cent increase in market share).

3 Profitability (e.g. maintenance of gross profit margin).

4 Service levels (e.g. 20 per cent increase in number of customers regarding salesperson assistance 'good or better' in annual customer survey).

5 Salesforce costs (e.g. 5 per cent reduction in expenses).

Salesforce strategy defines how those objectives will be achieved. The following may be considered:

I Call rates

2 Percentage of calls on existing versus potential accounts.

3 Discount policy (the extent to which reductions from list prices is allowed).

4 Percentage of resources
(a) targeted at new v. existing products
(b) targeted at selling v. providing after-sales service
(c) targeted at field selling v. telemarketing
(d) targeted at different types of customers (e.g. high v. low potential).

5 Improving customer and market feedback from the salesforce.

6 Improving customer relationships.

Once sales managers have a clear idea of what they hope to achieve, and how best to set about accomplishing these objectives, they can make sensible decisions regarding salesforce design.

Designing the salesforce

Two critical design decisions are determining salesforce size and salesforce organization.

Salesforce size

The most practical method for deciding the number of salespeople is called the *workload approach*. It is based on the calculation of the total annual calls required per year divided by the average calls per year that can be expected from one salesperson.[22] The procedure follows seven steps:

I Customers are grouped into categories according to the value of goods bought and their potential for the future.

2 The call frequency (number of calls per year to an account) is assessed for each category of customer.

3 The total required workload per year is calculated by multiplying the call frequency by the number of customers in each category and then summing for all categories.

Table 12.2 Marketing strategy and sales management

Strategic marketing objective	Sales objective	Sales strategy
Build	Build sales volume	High call rates on existing accounts
	Increase distribution	High focus during call
	Provide high service levels	Call on new accounts (prospecting)
Hold	Maintain sales volume	Continue present call rates on current accounts
	Maintain distribution	Medium focus during call
	Maintain service levels	Call on new outlets when they appear
Harvest	Reduce selling costs	Call only on profitable accounts
	Target profitable accounts	Consider telemarketing or dropping the rest
	Reduce service costs and inventories	No prospecting
Divest	Clear inventory quickly	Quantity discounts to targeted accounts

Source: Adapted from Strahle, W. and R. L. Spiro (1986) Linking Market Share Strategies to Salesforce Objectives, Activities and Compensation Policies, *Journal of Personal Selling and Sales Management*, August, 11–18.

4 The average number of calls that can be expected per salesperson per week is estimated.

5 The number of working weeks per year is calculated.

6 The average number of calls a salesperson can make per year is calculated by multiplying (4) and (5).

7 The number of salespeople required is determined by dividing the total annual calls required by the average number of calls one salesperson can make per year.

The formula is:

$$\text{Number of salespeople} = \text{Number of customers}$$
$$\times \text{call frequency} \div \text{Average weekly call rate}$$
$$\times \text{number of working weeks per year}$$

An example of how the workload approach can be used is now given. Steps (1), (2) and (3) are summarized thus:

Customer group	No of accounts		Call frequency		
A (Over £500 000 per year)	20	×	12	=	240
B (£250 000–£500 000 per year)	100	×	9	=	900
C (£100 000–£249 000 per year)	300	×	6	=	1800
D (Less than £100 000 per year)	500	×	3	=	1500
Total annual workload				=	4440

Step (4) gives:
Average number of calls per week
per salesperson   =   20

Step (5) gives:
Number of weeks   =   52
Less:
Holidays   4
Illness   1
Conferences/meetings   3
Training   1   =   9
Number of working weeks   =   43

Step (6) gives:
Average number of calls per salesperson
per year   = 43 × 20
                                                        =   860

Step (7) gives
$$\text{Salesforce size} = \frac{4440}{860} = 6 \text{ salespeople}$$

When prospecting forms an important part of the selling job, a separate category (or categories) can be formed with their own call rates to give an estimation of the workload required to cover prospecting. This is then added to the workload estimate based on current accounts to give a total workload figure.

Salesforce organization

There are three basic forms of *salesforce organization*: geographic, product, and customer-based structures. The strengths and weakness of each will now be discussed.

Geographic the sales area is broken down into territories based on workload and potential, and a salesperson is assigned to each one to sell all of the product range. This provides a simple, unambiguous definition of each salesperson's sales territory, and proximity to customers encourages the development of personal relationships. It is also a more cost efficient method of organization than product or customer-based systems. However, when products are technically different and sell in a number of diverse markets, it may be unreasonable to expect a salesperson to be knowledgeable about all products and their applications. Under such circumstances a company is likely to move to a product or customer-based structure.

Product product specialization is effective where a company has a diverse product range selling to different customers (or at least different people within a given organization). However, if the products sell essentially to the same customers, problems of route duplication (and consequently higher travel costs) and multiple calls on the same customer can arise. When applicable, product specialization allows each salesperson to be well informed about a product line, its applications and customer benefits.

Customer-based salesforces can be organized along market segment, account size, or new versus existing accounts lines. First, computer firms have traditionally organized their salesforce on the basis of industry served (e.g. banking, retailing and manufacturing) in recognition of their varying needs, problems and potential applications. Specialization by these *market segments* allows salespeople to gain in-depth knowledge of customers and to be able to monitor trends in the industry that may affect demand for their products. In some industries, the applications knowledge of market-based salespeople has led them to be known as *fraternity brothers* by their customers.[23]

Second, an increasing trend in many industries is towards **key account management**, which reflects the increasing concentration of buying power into fewer but larger customers. These are serviced by a key account salesforce comprising senior salespeople who develop close personal relationships with customers, can handle sophisticated sales arguments, and are skilled at the art of negotiation. A number of advantages are claimed for a key account structure:

1 *Close working relationships with the customer*: the salesperson knows who makes what decisions and who influences the various players involved in the decision. Technical specialists from the selling organization can call on technical people (e.g. engineers) in the buying organization, and salespeople can call upon administrators, buyers and financial people armed with the commercial arguments for buying.

2 *Improved communication and coordination*: the customer knows that a dedicated salesperson or sales team exists so that it is clear who to contact when a problem arises.

3 *Better follow-up on sales and service*: the extra resources devoted to the key account mean that there is more time to follow-up and provide service after a major sale has been made.

4 *More in-depth penetration of the DMU*: there is more time to cultivate relationships within the key account. Salespeople can *pull* the buying decision through the organization from the users, deciders and influencers to the buyer, rather than the more difficult task of pushing it through the buyer into the organization, as is done with more traditional sales approaches.

5 *Higher sales*: most companies who have adopted key account selling claim that sales have risen as a result.

6 *The provision of an opportunity for advancement for career salespeople*: a tiered salesforce system with key (or national) account selling at the top provides promotional opportunities for salespeople who wish to advance within the salesforce rather than enter a traditional sales management position.

The development and management of a key account can be understood as a process that takes place over time between buyers and sellers. The key account management (KAM) relational development model plots the typical progression of a buyer–seller relationship based upon the nature of the customer relationship (transactional–collaborative) and the level of involvement with customers (simple–complex).[24] Figure 12.5 shows five stages: Pre-KAM, Early-KAM, Mid-KAM, Partnership-KAM and Synergistic-KAM. A sixth stage (Uncoupling-KAM) represents the breakdown of the relationship which can happen at any point during the process.

Pre-KAM this describes preparation for KAM or 'prospecting'. The task is to identify those with the potential for moving towards key account status and to avoid wasting investment on those accounts that lack potential. Pre-KAM selling strategies involve making products available while attempting to gather information about customers so that their key account potential can be assessed. Where an account is thought to have potential but breaking into the account is proving difficult patience and persistence is required. A breakthrough may result from the 'in' supplier doing something wrong, for example refusing to quote for a low-profit-order or failing to repair equipment promptly.

Early KAM this involves the exploration of opportunities for closer collaboration by identifying the motives, culture and concerns of the customer. The selling company needs to convince the customer of the benefits of being a 'preferred supplier'. It will seek to understand the customer's decision-making unit and processes, and the problems and opportunities that relate to the value adding activities. Product adaptations may be made to fit customer needs better. An objective of the sales effort will be to build trust based on consistent performance and open communications.

Most communication is channelled through one salesperson (key account manager) and a single contact at the buying organization. This makes for a fragile relationship, particularly as it is likely that the seller is one of many supplying the account. The customer will be monitoring the supplier's performance to assess competence and to identify any problems that might arise. The account manager will be seeking to create a more attractive offering, establish credibility and deepen personal relationships.

Mid-KAM by now trust has been established and the supplier is one of a small number of preferred sources of the product. The number and range of contacts increases. These may include social events which help to deepen relationships across the two organizations. The account review process carried out at the selling organization will tend to move upwards to involve senior management because of the importance of the customer and the level of resource allocation. Since the account is not yet exclusive, the activities of competitors will require constant monitoring.

Partnership KAM at this stage the buying organization regards the supplier as an important strategic resource. The level of trust will be sufficient for both parties to be willing to share sensitive information. The focus of activities moves to joint problem solving, collaborative product development and mutual training of the other firm's staff.

The buying company is now channelling nearly all of its business in the relevant product group(s) to the one supplier. The arrangement is formalized in a partnership agreement of at least three years' duration. Performance will be monitored and contacts between departments of the two organizations are extensive. The buying organization will expect guaranteed continuity of supply, excellent service and top-quality products. A key task of the account manager is to reinforce the high levels of trust to form a barrier against potential competitors.

Synergistic-KAM this is the ultimate stage of the relational development model. Buyer and seller see one another, not as two separate organizations, but as part of a larger entity. Top management commitment manifests itself in joint board meetings. Joint business planning, research and development and marketing research take place. Costing systems become transparent, unnecessary costs are removed, and process improvements are mutually achieved. For example, a logistics company together with one of its retail key accounts has six cross-boundary

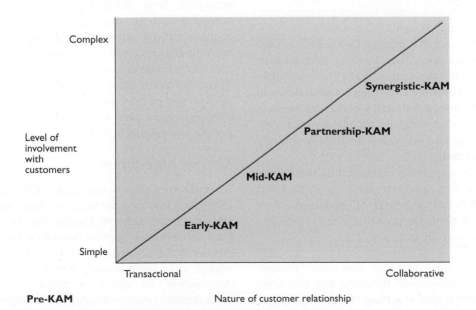

Figure 12.5 Key account relational development model

teams working on process improvements at any one time.[25]

Uncoupling-KAM this is when transactions and interaction cease. The causes of uncoupling need to be understood so that it can be avoided. Breakdowns are more often attributable to changes in key personnel and relationship problems than price conflicts. The danger of uncoupling is particularly acute in early-KAM when the single point of contact prevails. If, for example, the key account manager leaves to be replaced by someone who in the buyer's eyes is less skilled, or there is a personality clash, the relationship may end.

A second cause of uncoupling is a breach of trust. For example, the breaking of a promise over a delivery deadline, product improvement or equipment repair can weaken or kill a business relationship. The key to handling such problems is to reduce the impact of surprise. The supplier should let the buying organization know immediately a problem becomes known. It should also show humility when discussing the problem with a customer.

Companies, also, uncouple through neglect. Long-term relationships can foster complacency and customers can perceive themselves as being taken for granted. Cultural mismatches can occur, for example, when the customer stresses price whereas the supplier focuses on life cycle costs. Difficulties can also occur between bureaucratic and entrepreneurial styles of management.

Product or service quality problems can also provoke uncoupling. Any kind of performance problem, or the perception that rivals now offer superior performance can trigger a breakdown in relations. 'In' suppliers must build entry barriers by ensuring that product quality is constantly improved and any problems dealt with speedily and professionally.

Not all uncoupling is instigated by the buying company. A key account may be derated or terminated because of loss of market share or the onset of financial problems that impair the attractiveness of the account.

Some companies adapt a *three-tier system*, with senior salespeople handling key accounts, sales representatives selling to medium-sized accounts, and a telemarketing team dealing with small accounts. Telemarketing is a systematic programme placing outbound sales calls to customers and prospects, and receiving orders and enquiries from them. It is discussed in some detail in Chapter 13.

A third way of organizing along customer lines is by *new versus existing accounts*. One sales team focuses on the skills of prospecting while the other team services existing customers. This recognizes the differing skills involved, and the possible neglect of opening new accounts by salespeople who may view their time as being more profitable spent with existing customers.

In practice a combination of structures may be used to gain the economies of the geographic form with the specialization inherent in the product or customer-based systems. For example, a company using a two-product line structure may divide the country into geographically based territories with two salespeople operating in each one.

As marketing and sales become more international, companies have to address the problem of organizing the salesforce across national borders.[26] This is particularly important in Europe as cross-border activity intensifies. Marketing in Action 12.2 discusses some of the organizational issues of international selling based upon the experiences of multinational enterprises.

Managing the salesforce

Besides deciding personal selling objectives and strategies, and designing the salesforce, the company has to manage the salesforce. This requires setting specific salesperson objectives, recruitment and selection, training, motivation and compensation, and evaluation of salespeople. These activities have been shown to improve salesperson performance indicating the key role sales managers play as facilitators helping salespeople to perform better.[27]

Setting objectives

In order to achieve aggregate sales objectives, individual salespeople need to have their own sales targets to achieve. Usually targets are set in sales terms (sales quotas) but increasingly profit targets are being used, reflecting the need to guard against sales being bought cheaply by excessive discounting. To gain commitment to targets consultation with individual salespeople is recommended but in the final analysis it is the sales manager's responsibility to set targets. Payment may be linked to their achievement.

Sales management may also wish to set input objectives such as the proportion of time spent developing new accounts, and the time spent introducing new products. They may also specify the number of calls expected per day, and the precise customers who should be called upon.

Recruitment and selection

The importance of recruiting high-calibre salespeople cannot be overestimated. A study into salesforce practice asked sales managers the following question: 'If you were to put your most

---

12.2   Marketing in Action
International Selling and Salesforce Organization

The increasing internationalization of companies means that sales management have the task of organizing overseas salesforces. Often multinational corporations start with international divisions but as their product lines expand or as they enter new markets, problems with communications and coordination of product and country strategies lead to the choice of either geographic or product-based structures.

As companies grow, a product-based organization becomes unwieldy as it becomes stretched over more markets leading to problems of coordination and control. Similarly geographic structures lose their effectiveness as product lines are added. The result is a move to a matrix structure. For example in the mid-1980s Philips, the Dutch electronics company, had a 5-tier structure comprising 14 product divisions, a global product service organization (reporting to product and country managers), a management-board (overseeing all operations) and at a geographic level, regional bureaux to coordinate major geographic operating units.

What factors affect the choice of international organizational structure? Industry habits have an important effect. Many multinational organizations take proven domestic structures into overseas markets. Only when growth makes simple (e.g. geographic or product) structures unwieldy do they move to more specialized forms (e.g. product × customer, or geographic × product). Taking proven structures overseas has its advantages; for example, the product structure that high tech companies often favour allow overseas subsidiaries to compete on technology, while the geographic structure used by consumer goods companies allows the fine-tuning of sales and marketing strategies to local conditions.

Independent salesforces are used to supplement internal salespeople in geographically large markets such as Australia, Brazil and Canada, and in geographically and culturally diverse markets like Indonesia and the Philippines. Large and geographically diverse markets make the use of company salesforces uneconomic in outlying areas, and cultural diversity means that it is sensible to recruit locally based independent salesforces with the necessary social and language skills, and religious backgrounds.

Common language is also a factor in organizing across borders. For example, the French language makes shared salesforces sensible over France and southern Belgium, while Flemish-speaking northern Belgium is often combined with The Netherlands to form a geographically based sales organization. Also small market sizes of individual countries make geographical sales liaison practical in Scandinavia, where the combined populations of Denmark, Sweden, Finland and Norway are only 22 million people.

Based on: Hill and Still (1990)[28]

successful salesperson into the territory of one of your average salespeople, and made no other changes, what increases in sales would you expect after, say, two years?'[29] The most commonly stated increases was 16–20 per cent, and one-fifth of all sales managers said they would expect an increase of over 30 per cent. Clearly the quality of salespeople that sales managers recruit has a substantial effect on performance.

When recruiting salespeople a commonly held assumption is that money is the most valued attraction. This has been challenged by a study by Galbraith, Kiely and Watkins, which examined the features of the job that were of more interest and value to salespeople.[30] Their findings showed that working methods and independence were more important then earnings as the key attraction to a selling career and that independence was also the most highly valued aspect of doing the selling job. The implication of this study is that sales managers need to discover the reasons why people want to become salespeople in their industry so that they can develop recruitment strategies that reflect those desires.

The recruitment and selection process follows five stages:

1　Preparation of the job description and personnel specification.

2　Identification of sources of recruitment and methods of communication.

3　Design of the application form and preparation of a short list.

4　The interview.

5　Use of supplementary selection aids.

Preparation of the job description and personnel specification a job description will normally include the job title, duties and responsibilities to whom the salesperson will report, the technical requirements (e.g. product knowledge), geographic area to be covered, and the degree of autonomy given to the salesperson.

This job description acts as a blueprint for the personnel specification which details the type of person the company is seeking. For example, the technical aspects of the job may require a salesperson with an engineering degree or to have worked in a particular industry. The personnel specification will also determine the qualities sought in the recruit.

Based on extensive research, Mayer and Greenberg reduced the number of qualities believed to be important for effective selling to empathy and ego drive.[31] *Empathy* is the ability to feel as the buyer feels: to be able to understand customer problems and needs. *Ego drive* is the need to make a sale in a personal way not merely for money. These qualities can be measured using a psychological test, such as the Minnesota Multiphasic Personality Inventory.

Identification of sources of recruitment and methods of communication sources of recruitment include company personnel, recruitment agencies, education, competitors, other industries, and unemployed people. Advertising is the most common method of communication, with national and local press the most often used media. Recruiters should not attempt to squeeze copy into the smallest possible space since size of advertisement is correlated with impact. The advertisement should contain a headline which attracts the attention of possible applicants.

Design of the application form and preparation of a short list the design of the application form should allow the sales manager to check if the applicant is qualified in the light of the personnel specification. It thus provides a common basis for drawing up a short list of candidates, provides a foundation for the interview, and is a reference point at the post-interview decision-making stage.

The interview most companies employ a screening interview and a selection interview. The overall objective of the interview is to form a clear and valid impression of the strengths and weaknesses of each candidate in terms of the personnel specification. The following criteria may be used:

✦　Physical requirements (e.g. speech, appearance).

✦　Attainments (e.g. educational attainment, previous sales success).

✦　Qualities (e.g. drive, ability to communicate).

✦　Disposition (e.g. maturity, sense of responsibility).

✦　Interests (e.g. any interests that may have a positive impact on building customer relationships).

The interview should start with a few easy-to-answer questions that allow the candidate to talk freely and relax. Interviewers should be courteous and appear interested in what the candidate says. Open questions (e.g. 'Can you tell me about your experiences selling cosmetics?') should be used during the interview to encourage candidates to express themselves. Probes can be used to prompt further discussion or explanation. For example, the candidate might say 'The one-week introductory sales training course was a waste of my time', to which the interview might respond 'That's interesting, why was that?'. At the end of the interview the candidate should be told when the decision will be made and how it will be communicated.

Use of supplementary selection aids some companies use *psychological tests* as an aid to candidate selection although their use has been criticized on the grounds that many measure personality traits or interests that do not predict sales success. Consequently, before the use of such tests validation is necessary to show that test scores are likely to correlate with sales success. A test that may be useful in selecting car salespeople may be useless when filling a vacancy for an aero-engine sales job.

Another selection aid is the use of *role-playing* in order to gauge the potential of applicants. Obviously previous sales experience has to be allowed for, and the limitations of the exercise need to be recognized. At best role-playing may be useful in estimating potential in making short-term sales, but is unlikely to provide a reliable guide when the emphasis is on building long-term relationships with customers.

Training

Many sales managers believe that their salespeople can best train themselves by doing the job. This approach ignores the benefits of a training programme which provides a frame of reference in which learning can take place. *Training* should include not only product knowledge but also skills development. Success at selling comes when the skills are performed automatically without consciously thinking about them, just as a tennis player or footballer succeeds.

A training programme should include knowledge about the company (its objectives, strategies and organization), its products (features and benefits), its competitors and their products,

selling procedures and techniques, work organization including report preparation, and relationship management. Salespeople need to be trained in the management of long-term customer relationships as well as context specific selling skills.[32]

Lectures, films, role-playing and case studies can be used in a classroom situation to give knowledge and understanding and to develop competencies. These should be followed up with in-the-field training where skills can be practised face-to-face with customers. Sales managers and trainers should provide feedback to encourage on-the-job learning. In particular the sales manager needs to:

1 Analyse each salesperson's performance.

2 Identify strengths and weaknesses.

3 Communicate strengths.

4 Gain agreement that a weakness exists.

5 Train the salesperson in how to overcome the weakness.

6 Monitor progress.

Sales managers themselves need training in the considerable range of skills that they require including analytical, teaching, motivational, and communicational skills, and the ability to organize and plan. Some of the skills are not essential to be able to sell (e.g. teaching and motivating others): hence, the old adage that the best salespeople do not always make the best sales managers.

Motivation and compensation

Effective *motivation* is based on a deep understanding of salespeople as individuals, their personalities and value systems. In one sense, sales managers do not motivate salespeople; they provide the enabling conditions in which salespeople motivate themselves. Motivation can be understood through the relationship between needs, drives and goals. Luthans stated that, 'the basic process involves needs (deprivations) which set drives in motion (deprivations with direction) to accomplish goals (anything which alleviates a need and reduces a drive)'.[33] For example, the need for more money may result in a drive to work harder in order to receive increased pay.

Motivation has been the subject of much research over many years. Maslow, Herzberg,

Vroom, Adams, and Likert among others have produced theories which have implications for the motivation of salespeople.[34] Some of their important findings are summarized here:

1 Once a need is satisfied it no longer motivates.

2 Different people have different needs and values.

3 Increasing the level of responsibility/job enrichment, giving recognition of achievement, and providing monetary incentives work to increase motivation for some people.

4 People tend to be motivated if they believe that effort will bring results, results will be rewarded and the rewards are valued.

5 Elimination of disincentives (such as injustices or unfair treatment) raises motivational levels.

6 There is a relationship between the performance goals of sales managers and those of the salespeople they lead.

The implication of these findings are that sales managers should:

1 Get to know what each salesperson values and what each one is striving for (unrealized needs).

2 Be willing to increase the responsibility given to salespeople in mundane jobs.

3 Realize that training can improve motivation as well as capabilities by strengthening the link between effort and performance.

4 Provide targets that are believed to be attainable yet provide a challenge to salespeople.

5 Link rewards to the performance they want improved.

6 Recognize that rewards can be both financial and non-financial (e.g. praise).

Churchill, Ford and Walker developed a salesforce motivation model that integrated the work of the motivational theorists, in particular Vroom and Herzberg.[35] This model is shown in Fig. 12.6, and suggests that there is a cycle of motivation. The higher the salesperson's motivation, the greater the effort resulting in higher performance. Better performance leads to greater rewards and job

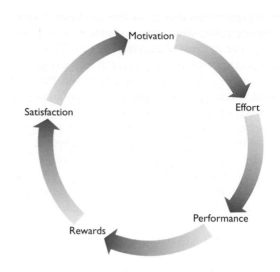

Figure 12.6 The cycle of motivation.
Source: adapted from Churchill Jr, G. A., N. M. Ford and O. C. Walker Jr (1985) *Sales Force Management: Planning, Implementation and Control*, Homewood, Ala: Irwin

satisfaction. The cycle is completed through higher satisfaction causing still more motivation.

The implications for sales managers are that they should:

1 Convince salespeople that they will sell more by working harder or by being trained to work smarter (e.g. more efficient call planning, developing selling skills).

2 Convince salespeople that the rewards for better performance are worth the extra effort. This implies that the sales manager should give rewards that are valued, and attempt to sell the worth of those rewards to the salesforce. For example, a sales manager might build up the worth of a holiday prize by stating what a good time he or she personally had when there.

Motivation can be affected by the type of compensation plan used by a company. However, as revealed by the research of the motivational theorists, not all people are equally motivated by money. Darmon revealed that there are five types of salespeople, defined by their goal structure.[36]

1 *Creatures of habit*: these salespeople try to maintain their standard of living by earning a predetermined amount of money.

2   *Satisfiers*: these salespeople perform at a level just sufficient to keep their jobs.

3   *Trade-offers*: these salespeople allocate their time based upon a personally determined ratio between work and leisure that is not influenced by the prospect of higher earnings.

4   *Goal-orientated*: these salespeople prefer recognition as achievers by their peers and superiors and tend to be sales-quota orientated with money mainly serving as recognition of achievement.

5   *Money-orientated*: these salespeople aim to maximize their earnings. Family relationships, leisure and even health may be sacrificed in the pursuit of money.

Consequently sales managers must categorize their salespeople before deciding their motivational and compensation plan. For example, if a salesforce consists of creatures of habit, satisfiers and trade-offers, increasing commission opportunities is unlikely to be successful. However, where most of the salesforce are goal-orientated or money-orientated, improving commission opportunities is likely to be effective in raising motivation and performance.

Compensation plans are not only determined by motivational considerations. The nature of the selling task which may determine if the payment of commission is feasible is another major factor. We shall now examine three types of compensation: fixed salary, commission only and salary plus commission/bonus.

Fixed salary   because payment is not directly tied to sales, salespeople paid by fixed salary are more willing to carry out tasks which do not result in short-term sales such as providing technical backup, completing information feedback reports and prospecting than those paid by commission only. A fixed salary also provides the income security that many salespeople value although the direct incentive to earn more money by increasing sales is lost. Also the system may lead to perceived injustices if higher performing salespeople are not being paid more than their low achieving colleagues.

Commission only   the lack of a fixed element to income provides a strong incentive to sell, perhaps too strong at times leading to overbearing salespeople desperate to close the sale. Other disadvantages are an unwillingness to take time off from direct selling tasks to attend training courses, or fill in reports, and a tendency for there to be high turnover of staff in jobs where commission only is the norm, for example in insurance selling.

Salary plus commission/bonus   this hybrid system provides some incentive to sell with an element of security. Usually salary makes up about 70 per cent of income. This system is attractive to ambitious salespeople who wish to combine a base level of income with the opportunity to earn more by greater effort and ability. For those reasons it is the most commonly used method of payment.[37] Bonuses are usually paid on the achievement of some task such as achieving a sales target or opening a certain number of new accounts.

For many companies their market is the world which means that they are faced with motivating international salesforces. Marketing in Action 12.3 discusses some of the problems and their solutions.

Evaluation of salespeople

Salesforce evaluation provides the information necessary to check if targets are being achieved and provides the raw information to guide training and motivation. By identifying the strengths and weakness of individual salespeople, training can be focused on the areas in need of development, and incentives can be aimed at weak spots such as poor prospecting performance.

Often performance will be compared to standards of performance such as sales or profit quotas although other comparisons such as salesperson-to-salesperson or current-to-past sales are also used. Two types of performance measures are used based on quantitative and qualitative criteria.

Quantitative measures of performance   salespeople can be assessed on input, output, and hybrid criteria. Output criteria include:

+   Sales revenue.
+   Profits generated.
+   Gross profit margin.
+   Sales per active account.
+   Number of new accounts opened.

Input criteria include:

✦ Number of calls.

✦ Calls per active account.

✦ Calls on new accounts (prospects).

✦ Number of prospects visited.

Hybrid criteria are formed by combining output and input criteria, for example:

✦ Sales revenue per call.

✦ Profit per call.

✦ Prospecting success ratio = Number of new accounts opened ÷ Number of prospects visited.

These quantitative measures can be compared against target figures to identify strengths and weaknesses. Many of the measures are diagnostic, pointing to reasons why a target is not being reached. For example, a poor call rate might be a cause of low sales achievement. Some results will merit further investigation. For example, a low prospecting success ratio would suggest an examination of why new accounts are not being opened despite a high number of prospects visited.

Qualitative measures of performance whereas quantitative criteria will be measured with hard figures, qualitative measures rely on soft data. They are intrinsically more subjective and include assessment of:

✦ Sales skills, e.g. questioning, making presentations.

✦ Customer relationships, e.g. how much confidence do customers have in the salesperson, is rapport good?

✦ Product knowledge, e.g. how well informed is the salesperson regarding company and competitor products?

✦ Self-management, e.g. how well are calls prepared, routes organized?

✦ Cooperation and attitudes, e.g. to what extent does the salesperson show initiative, follow instructions?

12.3 Marketing in Action

Motivating an International Salesforce

Sales managers should not assume that a motivation and compensation system which works well in their home country will work in overseas markets: the values and expectations of their foreign-based salespeople need to be understood. For example, in Europe financial incentives are often used to motivate salespeople but in Japan and the Middle East commission is rarely used. Instead non-financial factors such as increased responsibility or higher job security are more common. An understanding of local customs is essential. In Japan, for example, salary increases are based on seniority. Political factors can also determine the level of fringe benefits provided for employees.

Care needs to be taken over salaries paid to an overseas salesforce when it consists of a mixture of expatriates and local salespeople. Because a salary increase often accompanies an expatriate's overseas move, they may be paid more than local recruits. If this becomes common knowledge, the motivation of locally recruited salespeople may decline.

A common complaint among international salespeople is that their head office does not understand them. They often feel alone or deserted. Their motivation can be boosted through the setting of realistic sales targets, giving them full support and improving communication.

Based on: Cundif and Hilger (1988);[38] Hill et al. (1991);[39] Cateora et al. (2000)[40]

The use of quantitative and qualitative measures is interrelated. For example, a poor sales per call ratio will mean a close qualitative assessment of sales skills, customer relationships and product knowledge.

A final form of qualitative assessment does not focus on the salesperson directly but the likelihood of *winning or losing an order*. Particularly for major sales, a sales manager needs to be able to assess the chances of an order being successfully concluded in time to rectify the situation if things seem to be going astray. Unfortunately, asking salespeople directly will rarely result in an accurate answer. This is not because they are trying to deceive but because they may be deluding themselves. The answer is to ask a series of who, when, where, why and how questions to probe deeper into the situation. It also means working out acceptable and unacceptable responses. Table 12.3 provides an illustration of how such questions could be employed in connection with a major computer sale.

The losing answers are thin and unconvincing. The salesperson may be convinced that the sale will be achieved but the answers show that it is unlikely. The winning answers are much more assured and credible. The sales manager can be confident that there is no need to take action.

However, with the losing answer the sales manager will need to act and the response will depend on how important the sale and the salesperson are to the company. If they both have high potential the sales manager should work with the salesperson. He or she should be counselled so that they know why they are being helped and what they will learn from the experience. The aim is to conclude the sale, and convince the salesperson that their personal development will be enhanced by the experience.

If the salesperson has high potential but not the sale, only a counselling session is needed. Care should be taken not to offend the salesperson's ego. When only the sale has high potential, the alternatives are not so pleasant. Perhaps the salesperson could be moved to a more suitable post. When neither the salesperson nor the sale has potential, the only question to ask is whether the salesperson is redeployed before or after the sale is lost.

Evaluation and control of total sales operation

Evaluation of the total personal selling function is necessary to assess its overall contribution to

---

Table 12.3   Winning and losing major orders

Question	Poor (losing answer)	Good (winning answer)
Who will authorize the purchase?	The director of MIS	The director of MIS but it requires an executive director's authorization, and we've talked it over with this person.
When will they buy?	Right away. They love the new model.	Before the peak processing load at the year end.
Where will they be when the decision is made: in the office alone, in their boss's office, in a meeting?	What difference does that make? I think they have already decided.	At a board meeting. But don't worry, the in-supplier has no one on their board and we have two good customers on it.
Why will they buy from us? Why not their usual supplier?	They and I go way back. They love our new model.	The next upgrade from the in-supplier is a big price increase, and ours fits right between their models. They are quite unhappy with the in-supplier about that.
How will the purchase be funded?	They've lost of money, haven't they?	The payback period on reduced costs will be about 14 months and we've a leasing company willing to take part of the deal.

marketing strategy. The results of this assessment may lead to more cost efficient means of servicing accounts being introduced (e.g. direct mail or telemarketing), the realization that the selling function is under resourced, or the conclusion that the traditional form of sales organization is in need of reform. One company who suspected that its salesforce had become complacent moved every salesperson to a different territory. Despite having to forge new customer relationships, sales increased by a quarter in the following year.

Ethical issues in personal selling and sales management

Four ethical issues which salespeople may have to face are deception, the hard sell, bribery and reciprocal buying.

Deception

A dilemma which sooner or later faces most salespeople is the choice of telling the customer the whole truth and risk losing the sale, or misleading the customer to clinch the sale. The deception may take the form of exaggeration, lying or withholding important information that significantly reduces the appeal of the product. Such actions should be avoided by influencing salespersons' behaviour by training, by sales management encouraging ethical behaviour by their own actions and words, and by establishing codes of conduct for their salespeople. Nevertheless, from time to time evidence of malpractice in selling reaches the media. For example, in the UK it was alleged that some financial services salespeople mis-sold pensions by exaggerating the expected returns. The scandal cost the companies involved millions of pounds in compensation.[41]

The hard sell

Personal selling is also criticized for employing high-pressure sales tactics to close a sale. Some car dealerships have been deemed unethical by using hard-sell tactics to pressure customers into making a fast decision on a complicated purchase which may involve expensive credit facilities.

Such tactics encouraged Daewoo to approach the task of selling cars in a fundamentally different way as we have seen earlier in this chapter.

Bribery

This is the act of giving payment, gifts or other inducements to secure a sale. Bribes are considered unethical because they violate the principle of fairness in commercial negotiations. A major problem is that in some countries bribes are an accepted part of business life: to compete bribes are necessary. When an organization succumbs it is usually castigated in its home country if the bribe becomes public knowledge. Yet without the bribe it may have been operating at a major commercial disadvantage. Companies need to decide whether they are going to market in countries where bribes are commonplace. Taking an ethical stance may cause difficulties in the short term but in the long run the positive publicity that can follow may be of greater benefit.

Reciprocal buying

Another practice that might be considered unethical is reciprocal buying. This is where a customer only agrees to buy from a supplier if that supplier agrees to purchase something from the buying organization. This may be considered to be unfair to other competing suppliers who may not agree to such an arrangement or may not be in a position to buy from the customer. Supporters of reciprocal buying argue that it is reasonable for a customer to extract the best terms of agreement from a supplier: if this means reaching agreement to sell to the supplier then so be it. Indeed, countertrade where goods may be included as part of the payment for supplies has been a feature of international selling for many years and can benefit poorer countries and companies which can not afford to pay in cash.

Summary

The personal selling function has to adapt to the challenges of the new competitive order. This means not only being skilled in the traditional techniques of questioning, making presentations and demonstrations, handling objections and closing but also being adept at building long-term relationships. Goodwill can be created by providing exceptional service and relationships cemented by building trust.

Sales management involves the determination of objectives and strategy, salesforce design, and the management of the salesforce. It covers a much wider range of issues than the traditional view of the sales manager as someone who simply provides a well-deserved kick up the pants to underperforming salespeople. Sales managers need to be skilled in market analysis, strategy formulation, organization, recruitment, training, motivation and evaluation. It requires a formidable range of abilities, and considerable energy. But the function is vital as for many companies, selling is where marketing comes face-to-face with the customer. It should, therefore, be integrated with marketing strategy, and salesperson's messages should be consistent with that strategy.

Four ethical issues were discussed: deception, the hard sell, bribery, and reciprocal buying.

Internet exercise

Customer and competitor review

Sites to visit
http://www.mintel.co.uk

Exercise
What information is available on consumers and competitors in a consumer market of your choice?

Study questions

1 Select a car with which you are familiar. Identify its features and translate them into customer benefits.

2 Imagine you are face-to-face with a customer for that car. Write down five objections to purchase and prepare convincing responses to those objections.

3 You are the new sales manager of a company selling abrasives to the motor trade. Your salesforce are paid by fixed salary, and you believe them to be suffering from motivational problems. Discuss how you would handle this problem.

4 Because of its inherent efficiency the only sensible method of organizing a salesforce is by geographically-defined territories. Discuss.

5 Quantitative methods of salesforce organization are superior to qualitative methods because they rely on hard numbers. Evaluate this statement.

6 A company wishes to strengthen its relationships with key customers. How might it approach this task?

7 The key to sales success lies in closing the sale. Discuss.

8 How practical is the workload approach to deciding salesforce size?

9 What are the key stages in the key account relational development model? What implications do they have for marketing to organizational customers?

10 From your own personal experiences do you consider salespeople to be unethical? Can you remember any sales encounters when you have been subject to unethical behaviour?

References

1. Rines, S. (1995) Forcing Change, *Marketing Week*, 1 March, 10-13.
2. See Anderson, R. E. (1996) Personal Selling and Sales Management in the New Millennium, *Journal of Personal Selling and Sales Management*, **16** (4), 17-52; Magrath, A. J. (1997) A Comment on 'Personal Selling and Sales Management in the New Millennium', *Journal of Personal Selling and Sales Management*, **17** (1), 45-7.
3. Anonymous (1996) Revolution in the Showroom, *Business Week*, 19 February, 70-6.
4. Magrath (1997) op. cit.
5. This classification of selling types is supported by the research of McMurry, R. N. (1961) The Mystique of Super-Salesmanship, *Harvard Business Review*, **26** (March–April), 114-32; McMurry, R. N. and J. S. Arnold (1968) *How to Build a Dynamic Sales Organisation*, New York: McGraw-Hill; Montcrief, W. C. (1986) Selling Activity and Sales Position Taxonomies for Industrial Salesforces, *Journal of Marketing Research*, **23** (3), 261-70.
6. Jobber, D. and G. Lancaster (2000) *Selling and Sales Management*, London: Pitman.
7. Wickstrom, S. (1996) The Customer as Co-producer, *European Journal of Marketing*, **30** (4), 6-19.
8. Gummesson, E. (1987) The New Marketing: Developing Long Term Interactive Relationships, *Long Range Planning*, **20**, 10-20.
9. Abberton Associates (1991) *Balancing the Sales Force Equation: The Changing Role of the Sales Organisation in the 1990's*, Thame: CPM Field Marketing Ltd.
10. Weitz, B. A. (1981) Effectiveness in Sales Interactions: A Contingency Framework, *Journal of Marketing*, **45**, 85-103.
11. Schuster, C. P. and J. E. Danes (1986) Asking Questions: Some Characteristics of Successful Sales Encounters, *Journal of Personal Selling and Sales Management*, May, 17-27.
12. Croft, M. (1995) Homing in on the Mobile, *Marketing Week*, 10 November, 45-50.
13. Wendell, A. and D. Hempeck (1987) Sales Force Automation - Here and Now, *Journal of Personal Selling and Sales Management*, **7** (3), 11-16.
14. Reed, D. (1999) Field Force, *Marketing Week*, 23 September, 55-7.
15. McDonald, M. H. B. (1999) *Marketing Plans*, London: Heinemann.
16. Strahle, W. and R. L. Spiro (1986) Linking Market Share Strategies to Salesforce Objectives, Activities and Compensation Policies, *Journal of Personal Selling and Sales Management*, August, 11-18.
17. Bradley, F. (1991) *International Marketing Strategy*, London: Prentice-Hall.
18. Jeannet, J. P. and H. D. Hennessey (1995) *Global Marketing Strategies*, Boston: Houghton-Mifflin.
19. Buttery, E. A. and T. K. P. Leung (1998) The Difference between Chinese and Western Negotiations, *European Journal of Marketing*, **32** (3/4), 374-89.
20. Arias, J. T. G. (1998) A Relationship Marketing Approach to Guanxi, *European Journal of Marketing*, **32** (1/2), 145-56.
21. Cateora, P. R., J. L. Graham and P. N. Ghauri (2000) *International Marketing*, London: McGraw-Hill.
22. Talley, W. J. (1961) How to Design Sales Territories, *Journal of Marketing*, **25** (3), 16-28.
23. Magrath, A. J. (1989) To Specialise or Not to Specialise?, *Sales and Marketing Management*, **14** (7), 62-8.
24. Millman, T. and K. Wilson (1995) From Key Account Selling to Key Account Management, *Journal of Marketing Practice*, **1** (1), 9-21.
25. McDonald, M. and B. Rogers (1998) *Key Account Management*, Oxford: Butterworth-Heinemann.
26. Hill, J. S. and R. R. Still (1990) Organizing the Overseas Sales Force: How Multinationals Do It, *Journal of Personal Selling and Sales Management*, **10** (Spring), 57-66.
27. Piercy, N., D. W. Cravens and N. A. Morgan (1998) Salesforce Performance and Behaviour Based Management Processes in Business-to-Business Sales Organisations, *European Journal of Marketing*, 32 (1/2), 79-100.
28. Hill, J. S. and R. R. Still (1990) Organizing the Overseas Sales Force: How Multinationals Do It, *Journal of Personal Selling and Sales Management*, **10**, spring, 57-66.
29. P.A. Consultants (1979) *Sales Force Practice Today: A Basis for Improving Performance*, Cookham: Institute of Marketing.
30. Galbraith, A. J., Kiely and T. Watkins (1991) Sales Force Management: Issues for the 1990's, *Proceedings of the Marketing Education Group Conference*, Cardiff, July, 425-45.
31. Mayer, M. and G. Greenberg (1964) What Makes a Good Salesman, *Harvard Business Review*, **42** (July–August), 119-25.
32. Wilson, K. (1993) Managing the Industrial Sales Force in the 1990's, *Journal of Marketing Management*, **9** (2), 123-40.
33. Luthans, F. (1981) *Organizational Behaviour*, New York: McGraw-Hill.
34. See Maslow, A. H. (1954) *Motivation and Personality*, New York: Harper and Row; Herzberg, F. (1966) *Work and the Nature of Man*, Cleveland: W Collins; Vroom, V. H. (1964) *Work and Motivation*, New York: Wiley; Adams, J. S. (1965) Inequity in Social Exchange, in Berkowitz, L. (ed.) *Advances in Experimental Social Psychology*, 2, New York: Academic Press; Likert, R. (1961) *New Patterns of Sales Management*, New York: McGraw-Hill.
35. Churchill Jr, G. A., N. M. Ford and O. C. Walker, Jr (1985) *Sales Force Management: Planning, Implementation and Control*, Homewood, Ala: Irwin.
36. Darmon, R. Y. (1974) Salesmen's Response to Financial Initiatives: An Empirical Study, *Journal of Marketing Research*, November, 418-26.
37. See Avlonitis, G., C. Manolis and K. Boyle (1985) Sales Management Practices in the UK Manufacturing

Industry, *Journal of Sales Management*, **2** (2), 6–16; Shipley, D. and D. Jobber (1991) Sales Force Motivation, Compensation and Evaluation, *The Services Industries Journal*, **11** (2), 154–70.

38.   Cundiff, E. and M.T. Hilger (1988) *Marketing in the International Environment*, Englewood Cliffs, NJ: Prentice-Hall.

39.   Hill, J. S., R. R. Still and U. O. Boya (1991) Managing the International Sales Force, *International Marketing Review*, **8** (1), 19–31.

40.   Cateora, P. R., J. L. Graham and P. H. Ghauri (2000) *International Marketing*, London: McGraw-Hill.

41.   Mackintosh, J. (1999) Pensions Mis-selling Cost May Rise by £1bn, *Financial Times*, 18/19 December, 2.

Key terms

prospecting   searching for and calling upon potential customers

product features   the characteristics of a product that may or may not convey a customer benefit

customer benefits   those things that a customer values in a product. Customer benefits derive from product features

buying signals   statements by a buyer which indicates she is interested in buying

target accounts   organizations or individuals whose custom the company wishes to obtain

key account management   an approach to selling which focuses resources on major customers and uses a team selling approach

empathy   to be able to feel as the buyer feels, to be able to understand customer problems and needs

ego drive   the need to make a sale in a personal way, not merely for money

salesforce motivation   the motivation of salespeople by the process involving needs that set encouraging drives in motion to accomplish goals

salesforce evaluation   the measurement of salesperson performance so that strengths and weaknesses can be identified

Case 21 Glaztex

Glaztex plc was a UK-based supplier of bottling plant used in production lines to transport and fill bottles. Two years ago it opened an overseas sales office targeting Scandinavia, Germany, France and the Benelux countries. It estimated that there were over 1000 organizations in those countries that had bottling facilities, and that a major sales push in northern Europe was therefore warranted. Sales so far had been disappointing with only three units having been sold. Expectations had been much higher than this, given the advantages of its product over that produced by its competitors.

Technological breakthroughs at Glaztex meant that its bottling lines had a 10 per cent speed advantage over the nearest competition with equal filling accuracy. A major problem with competitor products was unreliability. Downtime due to a line breakdown was extremely costly to bottlers. Tests by Glaztex engineers at its research and development establishment in the UK had shown its system to be the most reliable on the market. Glaztex's marketing strategy was based around high quality, high price competitive positioning. It believed that the superior performance of its product justified a 10 per cent price premium over its major competitors who were all priced at around £1 million for a standard production line. Salespeople were told to stress the higher speed and enhanced reliability when talking to customers. The sales organization in northern Europe consisted of a sales manager with four salespeople assigned to Scandinavia, Germany, France and the Benelux countries, respectively. A technical specialist was also available when required. When a sales call required specialist technical assistance, a salesperson would contact the sales office to arrange for the technical specialist to visit the prospect, usually together with the salesperson.

Typically, four groups of people inside buying organizations were involved in the purchase of bottling equipment, namely the production manager, the production engineer, the purchasing officer and, where large sums of money were involved (over £1½ million), the technical director. Production managers were mainly interested in smooth production flows and cost savings. Production engineers were charged with drawing up specifications for new equipment, and in large firms, they were usually asked to draw up state-of-the-art specifications. The purchasing officers, who were often quite powerful, were interested in the financial aspects of any purchase, and technical directors, while interested in technical issues, also appreciated the prestige associated with having state-of-the-art technology.

John Goodman was the sales executive covering France. While in the sales office in Paris, he received a call from Dr Leblanc, the technical director of Commercial SA, a large Marseille-based bottling company who bottled under licence a number of major soft drink brands. They had a reputation for technical excellence and innovation. Goodman made an appointment to see Dr Leblanc on 7 March. He was looking forward to making his first visit to this company. The following extracts are taken from his record of his sales calls.

7 March
Called on Dr Leblanc who told me that Commercial SA had decided to purchase a new bottling line as a result of expansion, and asked for details of what we could provide. I described our system and gave him our sales literature. He told me that three of our competitors had already discussed their system with him. As I was leaving, he suggested that I might like to talk to M. Artois, their production engineer to check specifications.

8 March
Visited M. Artois who showed me the specifications that he had drawn up. I was delighted to see that our specifications easily exceeded them but was concerned that his specifications seemed to match those of one of our competitors, Hofstead Gm., almost exactly. I showed M. Artois some of our technical manuals. He did not seem impressed.

11 March
Visited Dr Leblanc who appeared very pleased to see me. He asked me to give him three reasons why they should buy from us. I told him that our system was more technologically advanced than the competition, was more reliable and had a faster bottling speed. He asked me if I was sure it was the most technologically advanced. I said that there was no doubt about it. He suggested I contact M. Bernard the purchasing manager. I

made an appointment to see him in two days' time.

13 March

Called on M. Bernard. I discussed the technical features of the system with him. He asked me about price. I told him I would get back to him on that.

15 March

Visited Dr Leblanc who said a decision was being made within a month. I repeated our operational advantages and he asked me about price. I told him I would give him a quote as soon as possible.

20 March

Saw M. Bernard. I told him our price was £1.1 million. He replied that a major competitor had quoted less than £1 million. I replied that the greater reliability and bottling speed meant that our higher price was more than justified. He remained unimpressed.

21 March

Had a meeting with Mike Bull my sales manager to discuss tactics. I told him that there were problems. He suggested that all purchasing managers liked to believe they were saving their company money. He told me to reduce my price by £50 000 to satisfy M. Bernard's ego.

25 March

Told M. Bernard of our new quotation. He said he still did not understand why we could not match the competition on price. I repeated our technical advantages over the competition and told him that our 10 per cent faster speed and higher reliability had been proven by our research and development engineers.

30 March

Visited Dr Leblanc who said a meeting had been arranged for 13 April to make the final decision but that our price of £1.05 million was too high for the likes of M. Bernard.

4 April

Hastily arranged a meeting with Mike Bull to discuss the situation. Told him about Dr Leblanc's concern that M. Bernard thought our price was too high. He said that £1 million was as low as we could go.

5 April

Took our final offer to M. Bernard. He said he would let me know as soon as a decision was made. He stressed that the decision was not his alone; several other people were involved.

16 April

Received a letter from M. Bernard stating that the order had been placed with Hofstead Gm. He thanked me for the work I had put into the bid made by Glaztex.

This case was prepared by Professor David Jobber, Professor of Marketing, University of Bradford.

Questions

Analyse the reasons for the failure to win the order and discuss the lessons to be learnt for key account management.

Case 22 Selling Exercise

You are the salesperson in the electrical department of a small store. For the past few minutes a man has been looking at the range of torches you have for sale. He comes up to you and says, 'I'm looking for a good torch'.

You take the interview from this point. You have a display of six torches (A–F) with features as described in Table C22.1.

This case was prepared by Robert Edwards, Zeneca.

Table C22.1 Six torches

Torch	Cost (excl. batteries)	Batteries	Light rays	Duration of light on new batteries	Construction material	Size/weight (incl. batteries)
A	£12	2 × 6V £1.50 each	Beam/spread by focus	10 hrs	Metal/plastic	20 cm 1½ kg
B	£4	2 × 1½V 70p each	Beam	2½ hrs	Plastic	16 cm 1 kg
C	£2	2 × 1½V 70p each	Beam	2 hrs	Plastic	12 cm ¾ kg
D	£2.50	2 × 1½V 70p each	Spread	2 hrs	Plastic	10 cm ½ kg
E	£2.00	2 × pencil 35p each	Weak spread	2 hrs	Plastic	12 cm ¼ kg
F	£1.70	1 × pencil 35p each	Weak beam	1¼ hrs	Plastic	8 cm ⅕ kg

Torch	Colours	brightness	Other features	
A	Various	8w ½w red bulb	Supplied with a 10-foot lead to plug into car cigarette lighter. Has a red bulb in opposite end to use as car light in emergencies. Made in UK.	
B	Red/white	3w	Complete with hanging hook and push button flasher. Made in Far East	
C	Red/white	2w	Complete with bicycle bracket and turn switch. Made in France	
D	Various	1½w	Neat and convenient shape. Hand held. Made in Far East	
E	Yellow/red	1½w	Neat and small. Made in Hong Kong	
F	Red	½w	Made in Far East	

CHAPTER THIRTEEN

Direct Marketing

'There is nothing more exciting than getting a favourable response by mail'

ROBERT STONE

Learning Objectives *This chapter explains:*

1 The meaning of direct marketing

2 The reasons for the growth in direct marketing activity

3 The nature and uses of database marketing

4 How to manage a direct marketing campaign

5 The media used in direct marketing

6 Ethical issues in direct marketing

n recent years, direct marketing has established itself as a major component of the promotional mix. Whereas mass advertising reaches a wide spectrum of people, some of whom may not be in the target audience and may only buy at some later unspecified date, direct marketing uses media which can more precisely target consumers and request an immediate direct response. Although the origins of direct marketing lie in direct mail and mail-order catalogues, today direct marketers use a wide range of media including telemarketing, direct response advertising, the Internet and on-line computer shopping to interact with people. No longer is direct marketing synonymous with 'junk mail' but has grown to be an integral part of the relationship marketing concept where companies attempt to establish ongoing direct and profitable relationships with customers. Expenditure on direct marketing in Europe has grown in recent years. Expenditure by country is given in Fig. 13.1.

In this chapter, we will examine the types of media, including the potential of the new interactive electronic communications systems, which direct marketers use to reach their targets. The chapter will explore the issues relating to database management and the use of direct marketing in Europe. The management of a direct marketing campaign will be analysed including the need for integrated communications, setting objectives, targeting, achieving customer retention and creating action plans. Finally, a number of ethical issues will be discussed.

First, however, we begin by describing what direct marketing is and the reasons for its growing popularity among marketers.

Defining direct marketing

Direct marketing attempts to acquire and retain customers by contacting them without the use of an intermediary. Unlike many other forms of

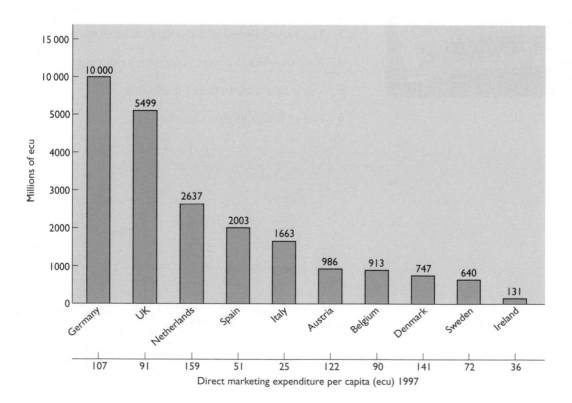

Figure 13.1 Expenditure on direct marketing in Europe.

Adapted from Direct Marketing Expenditure and Direct Marketing Expenditure Per Capita, *European Marketing Pocket Book 2000*, Henley-on-Thames: NTC Publications

communication, it usually requires an immediate response which means that the effectiveness of most direct marketing campaigns can be assessed quantitatively.

A definition of ***direct marketing*** is:

The distribution of products, information and promotional benefits to target consumers through interactive communication in a way that allows response to be measured.

Direct marketing campaigns are not necessarily short-term response driven activities. More and more companies are using direct marketing to develop ongoing direct relationships with customers. Some marketers believe that the cost of attracting a new customer is five times that of retaining existing customers. Direct marketing activity can be one tool in the armoury of marketers in their attempt to keep current customers satisfied and spending money. Once a customer has been acquired, there is the opportunity to sell that customer other products marketed by the company. Direct Line, a UK insurance company became market leader in motor insurance by bypassing the insurance broker to reach the consumer directly through direct response television advertisements using a free-phone number and financial appeals to encourage car drivers to contact them. Once sold on motor insurance, their trained telesales people offer substantial discounts on other insurance products including buildings and contents insurance. In this way, Direct Line have built a major business through using a combination of direct marketing methods.

Direct marketing covers a wide array of methods including:

✦ Direct mail.

✦ Telemarketing (both inbound and outbound).

✦ Direct response advertising (coupon response or 'phone now').

✦ Catalogue marketing.

✦ Electronic media (Internet, e-mail, interactive cable TV).

✦ Inserts (leaflets in magazines).

✦ Door-to-door leafleting.

The first four of these direct marketing channels will be analysed later in the chapter when discussing media selection for a campaign. Electronic media will be discussed in Chapter 14,

'Internet and On-Line Marketing'. A survey of large consumer goods companies across Europe by the International Direct Marketing Network measured the use of these techniques (excluding catalogue marketing and on-line channels).[1] It was found that 84 per cent of companies used some form of direct marketing but there was wide variation between countries. For example, 40 per cent used outbound telemarketing in Germany whereas none did in France. Overall, direct mail was the most commonly used technique (52 per cent) followed by coupon advertisements in the press (41 per cent). Telemarketing was not widely employed, although its use is more often associated with business-to-business marketing.

Another European study of consumer and business-to-business direct marketing by Ogilvy and Mather Direct found that the split was 65:35 of all activity across Europe.[2] However, there were national differences. For example, in the Netherlands business-to-business direct marketing accounted for 60 per cent. In all countries, targeted direct mail to a custom-built database was seen as highly effective in business-to-business marketing, as was out-bound tele-marketing (usually in conjunction with direct mail). In-bound telemarketing was considered essential for business customers. Advertising in the national press was rated highly in the UK, Denmark and Germany. Business magazines and inserts scored highest in The Netherlands and Sweden.

Much of this activity is carried out within national boundaries. The number of consumer direct marketers who run large-scale pan-European campaigns are few. These include American Express, Yves Rocher, Polaroid and Mattel. Business-to-business direct marketing activity is more international with companies such as Rank Xerox, IBM and Hewlett-Packard treating Europe as a single market for many years.

Direct marketing activity including direct mail, telemarketing and telephone banking is regulated by a European Commission Directive that came into force at the end of 1994. Its main provisions were that suppliers cannot insist upon pre-payments; consumers must be told the identity of the supplier, the price, quality of the product and any transport changes, the payment and delivery methods, and the period over which the solicitation remains valid; orders must be met within 30 days unless otherwise indicated; a cooling-off period of 30 days is mandatory and cold calling by telephone, fax or electronic mail is restricted unless the receiver has given prior consent.

As with all marketing communications, direct marketing campaigns should be integrated both within themselves and with other communication tools such as advertising, publicity and personal selling. Uncoordinated communication leads to blurred brand images, low impact and customer confusion.

Growth in direct marketing activity

Like other communication areas such as sales promotion, direct marketing activities over the last 10 years have grown. Smith outlines five factors that have fuelled this rise:[3]

1 *Market and media fragmentation*
   The trend towards market fragmentation has limited the capability of mass marketing techniques to reach market segments with highly individualized needs. As markets segment the importance of direct marketing media to target distinct consumer groups with personalized appeals will grow. One growing segment is women in paid employment who have less time to shop. Direct marketing can satisfy their need for speed and convenience through shopping by telephone or mail using a credit card as a mechanism for payment. Also, specialist interest groups (e.g. bird watchers or personal computer enthusiasts) can be reached directly and efficiently by direct mail and by inserts in direct response advertising in specialist magazines.

   The growth of specialist media (media fragmentation) has meant that direct response advertising is more effective since market niches can be tightly targeted. The range of specialist magazines in bookshops these days and the emergence of specialist TV channels such as MTV mean that it is easier to reach a closely defined target segment.

2 *Developments in technology*
   The rise in accessibility of computer technology and the increasing sophistication of software allowing the generation of personalized letters and telephone scripts

has eased the task of direct marketers. Large databases holding detailed information on individuals can be stored, updated and analysed to enhance targeting. Automated telephone systems make it possible to handle dozens of calls simultaneously, reducing the risk of losing potential customers. Furthermore, developments in technology in telephone, cable and satellite television and the Internet have triggered the rise in home-based electronic shopping.

3 *The list explosion*
   The increased supply of lists and their diversity (e.g. 25 000 Rolls-Royce owners, 20 000 women executives, 100 000 house improvers or 800 brand managers in fast-moving consumer goods and service companies) has provided the raw data for direct marketing activities. List brokers act as an intermediary in the supply of lists of names and addresses from list owners (often either companies who have built lists through transactions with their customers, or organizations that have compiled lists specifically for the purpose of renting them). List brokers thus aid the process of finding a suitable list for targeting purposes. Lists are rented usually on a one-time use basis. To protect the supplier against multiple use by the client, 'seeds' are planted on the list. These are usually employees of the list broking firm who will receive the mailing so that any multiple mailings from a once-only list will easily be identified.

4 *Sophisticated analytical techniques*
   By using geodemographic analysis, households can be classified into a neighbourhood type. For example, 'modern private housing, young families' or 'private flats, single people'. These, in turn, can be cross-referenced with product usage, media usage and lifestyle statements to create market segments that can be targeted by direct mail (geodemographic information contains the postcode for households).

5 *Co-ordinated marketing systems*
   The high costs of personal selling have led an increasing number of companies to take advantage of direct marketing techniques such as direct response advertising and telemarketing to make salesforces more cost-effective. For example, a coupon response

advertisement or direct mail may generate leads that can be screened by outbound telemarketing. Or in-bound telemarketing can provide the mechanism for accommodating enquiries stimulated by other direct marketing activities.

Database marketing

At the heart of much direct marketing activity is the marketing database since direct marketing depends on customer information for its effectiveness. A marketing database is an electronic filing cabinet containing a list of names, addresses, telephone numbers, lifestyle and transactional data. Information such as the types of purchase, frequency of purchase, purchase value and responsiveness to promotional offers may be held.

Database marketing is defined as:[4]

An interactive approach to marketing which uses individually addressable marketing media and channels (such as mail, telephone and the sales-force) to:

(i)   provide information to a target audience
(ii) stimulate demand
(iii) stay close to customers by recording and storing an electronic database memory of customers, prospects and all communication and transactional data.

Some key characteristics of database marketing are that, first, it allows direct communication with customers through a variety of media including direct mail, telemarketing and direct response advertising. Second, it usually requires the customer to respond in a way that allows the company to take action (such as contact by telephone, sending out literature or arranging sales visits). Third, it must be possible to trace the response back to the original communication.[5]

The computer provides the capability of storing and analysing large quantities of data from diverse sources and present information in a convenient, accessible and useful format.[6] The creation of a database relies on the collection of information on customers which can be sourced from:

◆   Company records.
◆   Responses to sales promotions.

◆   Warranty and guarantee cards.
◆   Offering samples that require the consumer to give name, address, telephone number, etc.
◆   Enquiries.
◆   Exchanging data with other companies.
◆   Salesforce records.
◆   Application forms (e.g. to join a credit or loyalty scheme).
◆   Complaints.
◆   Responses to previous direct marketing activities.
◆   Organized events (e.g. wine tastings).

Collecting information is easiest for companies that have direct contact with their customers such as those in financial services or retailing. However, even for those where the sales contact is indirect building a database is often possible. For example, Seagrams, the drinks company built up a European database through telephone and written enquiries from consumers, sales promotional returns, tastings in store, visits to company premises, exhibitions and promotions that encourage consumers to name like-minded friends or colleagues.[7]

Figure 13.2 shows typical information that is recorded on a database. This is:[8]

1   *Customer and prospect information*
    This provides the basic data required to access customers and prospects (e.g. name, address, telephone number) and contains their general behavioural characteristics (e.g. psychographic and behavioural data). For organizational markets, information on key decision-makers and influencers and the choice criteria they use would also be stored.

2   *Transactional information*
    Past transactions are a key indicator of likely future transactions. Transactional data must be sufficiently detailed to allow FRAC (Frequency, Recency, Amount and Category) information to be extracted for each customer. *Frequency* refers to how often a customer buys. Both the average frequency and the trend (is the customer tending to buy more or less frequently?) is of use to the direct marketer. *Recency* measures when the customer last bought. If customers are

waiting longer before they rebuy (i.e. recency is increasing) the reasons for this (e.g. less attractive offers or service problems) need to be explored. *Amount* measures how much a customer has bought and is usually recorded in value terms. Analysis of this data may reveal that 20 per cent of customers are accounting for 80 per cent of the value of transactions. Finally, *category* defines the type of product being bought. Cross-analysing category data with type of customer (e.g. geodemographics or lifestyle data) can reveal the customer profile most likely to buy a particular product. Also, promotions can be targeted at those individuals known to be interested in buying from a particular product category.

3 *Promotional information*
This covers information on what promotional campaigns have been run, who has responded to them and what the overall results were in terms of contacts, sales and profits. The database will contain information on which customers were targeted and the media and contact strategy employed.

4 *Product information*
This information would include which products have been promoted, who responded, when and from where.

5 *Geodemographic information*
Information about the geographic areas of customers and prospects and the social, lifestyle or business category they belong to would be stored. By including postcodes in the address of customers and employing the services of an agency which conducts geodemographic analysis (such as ACORN) a customer profile would be built up. Direct mail could then be targeted at people with similar geodemographic profiles.

An example of the type of data held on a marketing database for a business-to-business company is give in Table 13.1. Both hard (quantitative) and soft (qualitative) data will be held as a basis for direct marketing, salesforce activities and marketing planning applications.

How might a marketing database be used? One application is to target those people who are more likely to respond to a direct marketing campaign. For example, a special offer on garden tools from a mail-order company could be targeted at those people who have purchased gardening products in the past. Another example would be a car dealer who, by holding a database of customers' names and addresses and dates of car purchase, could use direct mail to promote service offers and new model launches. Telemarketing campaigns can be similarly targeted.

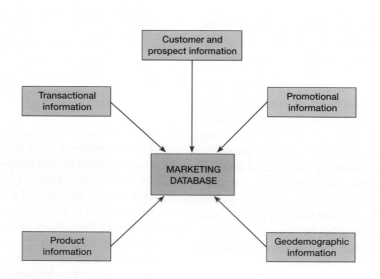

Figure 13.2 A marketing database

Database marketing can be used strategically to improve customer retention with long-term programmes established to maximize customer lifetime value. This issue will be discussed further when we examine customer retention strategies. Many retailers have created loyalty schemes where customers apply for a card which entitles them to discounts but also enables the retailer to record and store transactional data (e.g. which products are bought, their frequency, value, etc.) on an individual basis. Marketing in Action 13.1 shows how a database could be used by a retailer.

The main applications of database marketing are:

1 *Direct mail*: a database can be used to select customers for mailings.

2 *Telemarketing*: a database can store telephone numbers so that customers and prospects can be contacted. Also when customers contact the company by telephone, relevant information can be stored, including when the next contact should be made.

3 *Distributor management systems*: a database can be the foundation upon which information is provided to distributors and their performance monitored.

4 *Loyalty marketing*: highly loyal customers can be selected from the database for special treatment as a reward for their loyalty.

5 *Target marketing*: other groups of individuals or businesses can be targeted as a result of analysing the database. For example, buyer behaviour information stored by supermarkets can be used to target special promotions to individuals who are likely to be receptive to them. For example, a consumer promotion for wine could be sent to wine drinkers exclusively.

6 *Campaign planning*: using the database as a foundation for sending consistent and co-ordinated campaigns and messages to individuals and market segments.

7 *Marketing evaluation*: by recording responses to marketing mix inputs (e.g. price promotions, advertising messages and product offers) it is possible to assess how effective different approaches are to varying individuals and market segments.

Managing a direct marketing campaign

As we shall see, the marketing database is an essential element in creating and managing a

Table 13.1 A major account information system		
	Hard	*Soft*
General	Addresses, telephone, facsimile and telex numbers, e-mail addresses	Decision-making unit members
	Customer products sold and markets served (size and growth rates)	Choice criteria
		Perceptions and attitudes
	Sales volume and revenue	Buying process
	Profits	Assessment of relationships
	Capital employed	Problems and threats
	Operating ratios (e.g. return on capital employed, profit margin)	Opportunities
		Suppliers' strengths and weaknesses
		Competitors' strengths and weaknesses
		Environmental changes affecting account now and in the future
Specific	Suppliers' sales to account by product	
	Suppliers' price levels and profitability by product	
	Details of discounts and allowances	
	Competitors' products, price levels and sales	
	Contract expiry dates	

direct marketing campaign. However, it is not the starting point for campaign development. As with all promotional campaigns, direct marketing should be fully integrated with all marketing mix elements to provide a coherent *marketing strategy*. Direct marketers need to understand how the product is being *positioned* in the marketplace that means that its target market and differential advantage must be recognized.

It is crucial that messages sent out as part of a direct marketing campaign do not conflict with those communicated by other channels such as advertising or the salesforce. The integrating mechanism is a clear definition of marketing strategy. Figure 13.3 shows the steps in the management of a direct marketing campaign. Each will now be discussed.

Identify and understand target audience

David Ogilvy, the famous advertising guru, once wrote: 'Never sell to a stranger'. The needs and purchasing behaviour of the **target audience** must be understood from the start.

The target audience is the group of people at which the direct marketing campaign is aimed. The usual ways of segmenting consumer and organizational markets described in Chapter 7 can

---

13.1 Marketing in Action

Using a Marketing Database in Retailing

The potential for using marketing databases is enormous allowing integrated planning of marketing communications. Suppose a retailer wanted to increase sales and profits using a database, how might this happen? First, the retailer analyses its database to find distinct groups of customers for whom the retailer has the potential to offer superior value. The identification of these target market segments allows tailored products, services and communications to be aimed at them.

Purchasing patterns of individuals are established by means of a loyalty card programme. The scheme's main objective is to improve customer loyalty by rewarding varying shopping behaviours differently. The scheme allows customers to be tracked by frequency of visits, expenditure per visit and expenditure per product category. Retailers can gain an understanding of the types of products that are purchased together. For example, Boots, the UK retailer, uses its Advantage Card loyalty scheme to conduct these kinds of analyses. One useful finding is that there is a link between buying films and photoframes and the purchase of new baby products. Because they are organized along product category lines it never occurred to them to create a special offer linked to picture frames for the baby products buyer, yet these are the kinds of products new parents are likely to want.

Integrated marketing communications is possible using the marketing database as the system tracks what marketing communications (e.g. direct mail, promotions) customers are exposed to and measures the cost-effectiveness of each activity via electronic point of sale data and loyalty cards.

The retailer's customers are classified into market segments based on their potential, their degree of loyalty and whether they are predominantly price or promotionally sensitive. A different marketing strategy is devised for each group. For example, to trade up high potential, promotionally sensitive, low loyalty shoppers who do their main shopping elsewhere, high value manufacturers' coupons for main shopping products are mailed every two months until the consumer is traded up to a different group.

Based on: Patron (1996);[9] Wilson (1999)[10]

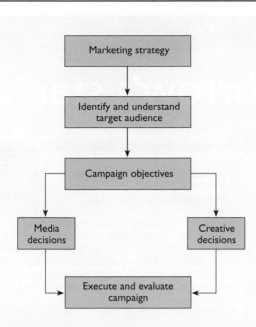

Figure 13.3 Managing a direct marketing campaign

be applied. Companies like Experian (see illustration overleaf) provide segmentation breakdowns, such as by lifestyle, that can be used for targeting. However, a particularly useful method of segmentation for direct marketing purposes is as follows:

1 *Competitors' customers*: all people who buy the types of product our company produces but from our competitors.

2 *Prospects*: people who have not bought from our company before but qualify as potential purchasers (e.g. our customers are large companies, therefore other large companies should be targeted).

3 *Enquirers*: people who have contacted the organization and shown interest in one or more products but, as yet, have not bought.

4 *Lapsed customers*: people who have purchased in the past but appear to have ceased buying.

5 *Referrals*: people who have been recommended to the organization as potential customers.

6 *Existing customers*: people who are continuing to buy.

Note how an analysis of existing customers can

help in identifying prospects. By identifying criteria that describe our customers (e.g. age, location, size of firm) the marketing database can be used to identify other people who may be receptive to a direct marketing campaign.

Having defined the group(s) that are to be targeted, a list is required which may be obtainable from an in-house database or through an external broker. However, direct marketers need to be aware of possible problems when buying externally. People may have moved address, job or died; duplication of addresses occurs, job titles may be inaccurate, and standard industrial classifications of companies may not accurately describe the type of business the organization is engaged in.

Understanding buying behaviour of the chosen target groups is important. In particular, understanding the choice criteria of the targeted individuals helps in message development. For example, if a key choice criterion of people buying from competitors rather than our company is technical reputation, we can stress (with evidence) our technical competences when targeting competitors' customers.

Campaign objectives

Campaign objectives can be expressed in financial (for example sales, profits and return on investment), in marketing (for example to acquire or retain customers, or to generate enquiries) and/or in communication terms (for example to create awareness or change beliefs). The first set of objectives is self-apparent and the third set is discussed in Chapter 11. Here we shall focus on acquisition and retention objectives.

Achieving acquisition objectives may be less cost-effective than comparable retention objectives as it is significantly more expensive to retain an existing customer than attract a new one. Furthermore, maintaining customer loyalty has the additional benefit that loyal customers not only repeat purchase but advocate products to their friends, pay less attention to competitive brands and often buy product line extensions.[11] Nevertheless, in order to grow and offset lost customers, direct marketing campaigns aimed at attracting new customers are inevitable. When measuring the attractiveness of a potential customer, the concept of *lifetime value* is important. This measures the profits that can be expected

Tomorrow's star?

Tomorrow he may be exactly the prospective customer you're looking for. In a world that's changing daily, you need a consumer information source that can keep up, one that can spotlight the latest prospects.

The star you need is Canvasse - the complete source of the UK's 44 million adults and regularly updated through millions of completed consumer questionnaires.

With Canvasse, specific lifestyle variables mean individual consumers can be carefully targeted, and lead to purchase information guarantees prospects who are in the market for your products now.

Add to that Experian's unique Canvasse lifestyle contacts models and you have a single source for your direct marketing that's larger than 'lifestyle' alone.

But Canvasse isn't just about getting new customers, it's about getting the right customers; responders who you want as customers, who'll be loyal, and who'll provide the best bottom-line impact.

If you'd like to know more about Canvasse, the last word in targeting accuracy, call (020) 7664 1222 or e-mail us at: prospect.targeting@experian.com

Experian is an information solutions company. We use the power of information to help our clients target prospective customers, manage existing customer relationships and identify opportunites for profitable growth.

experian

Experian segmentation analysis can form the basis for direct marketing campaigns

from customers over their expected life with a company. Banks know, for example, that gaining student accounts has very high lifetime values since switching between banks is unusual. This means that the allowable marketing cost per acquisition (or how much can a company afford to spend to acquire a new customer) can be quite high. If the calculation was based on potential profits while a student the figure would be much lower. The establishment of a marketing database can over time provide valuable information on buying patterns that aids the calculation of lifetime value.

Where a marketing database does not hold information on prospects and where external lists are either unavailable or unreliable, another option is 'member-get-member' programmes. Existing members (e.g. of motoring organizations) or customers (e.g. of an insurance company) are incentivized to recruit new people to join or buy from the organization. For example, the Royal Society for the Protection of Birds launched a 'Recruit a Friend and Help Yourself to a Free Pocket Organiser' campaign targeted at young ornithologists. New members were offered free gifts as an incentive to join.

Once acquired, the objective is to retain the business of the customer. This is because keeping customers has a direct impact on profitability. A study conducted by Price Waterhouse showed that a 2 per cent increase in customer retention has the same profit impact as a 10 per cent reduction in overhead costs.[12] Customer loyalty programmes have blossomed as a result with direct marketing playing a key role. Retention programmes are aimed at maximizing a customer's lifetime value to the company. Maintaining a long-term relationship with a customer provides the opportunity to up-sell, cross-sell and renew business. Up-selling involves the promotion of higher value products, for example a more expensive car. Cross-selling entails the switching of customers to other product categories as when a music club promotes a book collection. Renewal involves the timing of communication to existing customers when they are about to repurchase. For example, car dealers often send direct mail promotional material two years after the purchase of a car, since many people change cars after that period.

Often the achievement of retention objectives depends upon the identification of a company's best customers defined in terms of current and potential profitability. FRAC data (discussed earlier in this chapter) which measures purchasing behaviour in terms of Frequency (how often), Recency (how recent), Amount (of what volume and value) and Category (what product type) forms the basis of this analysis. The identity and profile of high value customers are then drawn up. Profiling enables the identification of similar types of individuals or organizations for the achievement of acquisition programmes. Major international airlines have developed frequent flyers schemes along these lines. Their best customers (often business travellers) are identified by analysis of their database and rewarded for their loyalty. By collecting and analysing data the airlines identify and profile their frequent flyers, learn how best to develop a relationship with them, and attempt to acquire new customers with similar profiles. Databases can therefore be used to segment customers so that the most attractive groups can be targeted with a tailored direct marketing campaign.

The importance of customer retention has prompted many supermarkets to develop store loyalty cards that are swiped through a machine at the checkout. The loyalty card contains customer information such as the name and address of the individual and so purchasing data such as expenditure per visit, the range of products purchased, the brands purchased, when and how often the customer shops and which branch was used can be linked to individuals. This means that supermarkets such as Tesco and Sainsbury in the UK know what sort of products and services to offer in different stores and to different customers. One proponent of loyalty schemes claimed: 'Profiling based on spend, frequency and product gives more information about a customer than knowing where someone lives or what their salary is. We won't need demographic information any more.'[13]

Direct mail can be used to send targeted promotional offers to people who are known to purchase from a particular product category. For example, a special offer for an Australian red wine could be sent to people who are known to drink red wine. Tesco's Clubcard scheme began in 1995 and has been widely regarded as successful. Customers accumulate points that are electronically added onto the card when swiped at the checkout. Effectively points mean money-off future purchases at the checkout (plus other promotional offers). Thus the more money a customer spends the greater the points and the higher the discounts on future purchases. This process, it is claimed, generates higher rates of repeat buying and loyalty benefiting the store, as well as providing in-depth purchasing data.

Despite their growth in such industries as petrol retailing, airlines, supermarkets and hotels, loyalty schemes have attracted their critics. Loyalty schemes may simply raise the cost of doing business and, if competitors respond with 'me-toos', the final outcome may be no more than minor tactical advantages.[14] The costs are usually very high when technology, software, staff training, administration, communications and the costs of the rewards are taken into account. Shell, for example, are reported to have spent £20 million on hardware and software alone to support their smart card which allows drivers to collect points when purchasing petrol.[15] The danger is that loyalty schemes cost too much when price has become more important in the competitive arena.[16] A second criticism is that the proliferation of loyalty schemes is teaching consumers promiscuity. Evidence from a MORI poll found that 25 per cent of loyalty card holders are ready to switch to a rival scheme if it has better benefits.[19] Far from seeing a loyalty scheme as a reason to stay with a retailer, consumers may be using such schemes as criteria for switching. Third, the basis of loyalty schemes, rewarding loyal customers is questioned. A company that has a band of loyal customers is presumably already doing something right. Rather than giving them discounts why not do more of that (e.g. wide product range, better service). Even if loyal customers spend a little more, do the extra revenues justify the extra costs? Nevertheless, loyalty schemes are seen by many companies as an essential element in doing business. What needs to be questioned by marketing managers is whether exceptional loyalty can be expected from such schemes, what are the true costs and whether focusing on a select group of customers (as with frequent flyer schemes) leads to the neglect of others.

Media decisions

Direct marketers have a large number of media which they can use to reach customers and prospects. Each of the major media will now be examined.

Direct mail

Direct mail is material sent through the postal service to the recipient's home or business address with the purpose of promoting a product and/or maintaining an ongoing relationship. Direct mail at its best allows close targeting of individuals in a way not possible using mass advertising media. For example, Heinz employs direct mail to target its customers and prospects. Since it markets 360 products, above-the-line advertising for all of them is impossible. By creating a database based on responses to promotions, lifestyle questionnaires and rented lists, Heinz built a file of 4.6 million households. Each one now receives the four-times-a-year 'At Home' mailpack which has been further segmented to reflect loyalty and frequency of purchase. Product and nutritional information is combined with coupons to achieve product trials.[20] An example of a direct mail leaflet is shown in the illustration promoting the Gold Mastercard.

A key factor in the effectiveness of a direct mail campaign is the quality of the mailing list. Mailing lists are variable in quality. For example, in one year in the UK, 100 million items were sent back marked 'return to sender'.[17] List houses supply lists on a rental or purchase basis. Since lists go out of date quickly, it is usually preferable to rent. *Consumer lists* may be compiled from subscriptions to magazines, catalogues, membership or organizations, etc. Alternatively, consumer lifestyle lists are compiled from questionnaires. The electoral roll can also be useful when combined with geodemographic analysis. For example, if a company wished to target households living in modern private housing with young families, the electoral roll can be used to provide names and addresses of people living in such areas. One problem with consumer lists is people moving house and dying. Specialized data-suppression services such as the 'gone away suppression file' offered by the REaD Group can reduce the difficulty. It claims to identify over 94 per cent of all home movements and over 80 per cent of deceased people.[18] *Business-to-business lists* may be bought from directory producers such as the *Kompass* or *Key British Enterprises* directories, from trade magazine subscription lists (e.g. *Chemicals* or *Purchasing Managers' Gazette*) or from exhibition lists (e.g. Which Computer Show). Perhaps the most productive mailing list is that of a company's own customers: the *house list*. This is because of the existing relationship that a company enjoys with its own customers. Also of use would be names of past buyers who have become inactive, enquirers and those who have been referred or recommended by present customers of the company. It is not uncommon for a house list to be far more productive than an outside compiled list.[21] Customer behaviour such as the products purchased, recency, frequency and expenditure can also be stored on the database.

The management of direct mail involves asking five questions:[22]

1 *Who:* who is target market? Who are we trying to influence?

2 *What:* what response is required? A sale, an enquiry?

3 *Why:* why should they buy or make an enquiry? Is it because our product is faster, cheaper, etc?

4 *Where:* where can they be reached? Can we obtain their home or working address?

5 *When:* when is the best time to reach them? Often this is weekends for consumers, and Tuesday, Wednesday or Thursday for businesspeople (Monday can be dominated by planning meetings and on Friday they may be busy clearing their desk for the weekend).

Other management issues include the organization for addressing and filling the envelopes; *mailing houses* provide these services, and for large mailings the postal service needs to be notified so that the mailing can be scheduled.

Direct mail allows *specific targeting to named individuals*. For example, by hiring lists of subscribers to gardening catalogues a manufacturer of gardening equipment could target a specific group of people who would be more likely to be interested in a promotional offer than the public in general. *Elaborate personalization* is possible and the results directly measurable. Since the objective of direct mail is immediate—usually a sale or an enquiry—success can easily be *measured*. Some organizations such as Reader's Digest spend money researching alternative creative approaches before embarking on a large-scale mailing. Such factors as type of promotional offer, headlines, visuals and copy can be varied in a systematic manner and by using code numbers

on reply coupons, response can be tied to the associated creative approach.

The effectiveness of direct mail relies heavily on the quality of the list. Poor lists raise costs and can contribute to the criticism of *junk mail* since recipients are not interested in the contents of the mailing. *Initial costs* can be much higher than advertising in cost per thousand people reached and response can be low (an average response rate of 2 per cent is often quoted). Added to these costs is the expense of setting up a database. In these terms direct mail should be viewed as a medium to long-term tool for generating repeat business from a carefully targeted customer group. An important concept is the *lifetime value of a customer* which is the profit made on a customer's purchase over the customer's lifetime.

The UK direct mail industry is regarded as one of the most professional, with a reputation for quickly adopting new mailing techniques. Figure 13.4 shows the volume of direct mail in eleven European countries.

In Central and Eastern Europe consumer and business reaction to direct mail is almost always positive. It is seen as something new, interesting and important. Practical, factual appeals work best. For example, the benefit may refer to a family's health or a company's access to capital. The major problem of direct mail in this region is the poor quality of the mailing lists.[23]

In EU countries, direct marketers need to be aware that the national laws governing the collection and storage of personal information can be very different. Advice should be sought on the nature of individual national laws. Marketing in Action 13.2 discusses some of the variations in national laws covering data protection and collection.

Telemarketing

Telemarketing is a marketing communication system where trained specialists use telecommunications and information technologies to conduct marketing and sales activities.

Inbound telemarketing occurs when a prospect contacts the company by telephone, whereas outbound telemarketing involves the company calling the prospect. Developments in IT have affected both forms. For example, Quick Address is a package that enables telemarketing people handling inbound calls to quickly identify the address and account details of the caller with the minimum amount of typing time and also ensure it is accurate. The caller is asked for their name and postcode (either for the household or company). From this the correct address will appear on the computer screen. If the caller wishes to purchase (using a credit card, for example) over the telephone, the tedium of giving (and spelling) their address to allow postage is removed. This has gained penetration in such areas as selling football or theatre tickets. Even more sophisticated developments in telecommunications technology allow the caller to be identified even before the agent has answered the call. The caller's telephone number is relayed into the customer database and outlet details appear on the agent's screen before the call is picked up. This service (called *integrated telephony*) has gained penetration in the customer service area.

An integrated telemarketing package would, in response to an incoming call, bring up the customer's file on the computer screen, record the order, check stocks, and provide field sales-

people with updated inventory information and estimated delivery times.

A more controversial technological development is the use of interactive voice response (IVR) where the caller talks to a machine rather than a person. IVR is beneficial when the nature of calls is specific such as a brochure request. It can also be used to cover busy periods including the period following a direct response television advertisement. When the majority of callers want the same basic information, IVR permits this to be provided quickly and accurately. It is sometimes used in conjunction with a personalized service when a caller requires it. The main disadvantage of the approach is some callers may dislike dealing with a machine and prefer to talk to a person. Also some queries may not be covered by the automated service.[24]

Computerization can also enhance productivity in outbound telemarketing. Large databases can store information that can easily be accessed by telemarketing agents. Call lists can be automati-

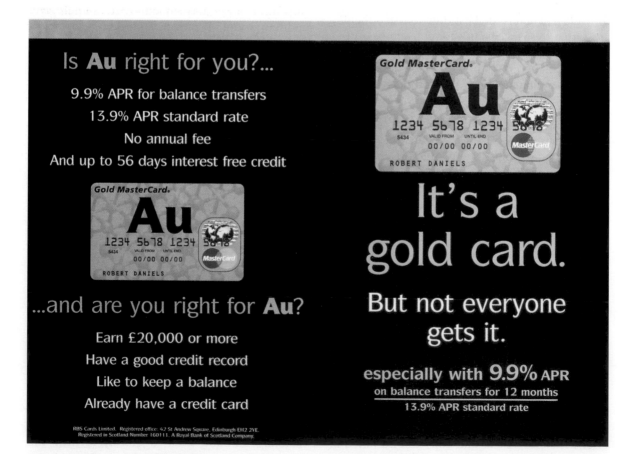

A direct mail leaflet promoting the Gold MasterCard. Low cost credit targeted at low risk, higher income earners

cally allocated to agents. Scripts can be created and stored on the computer so that operators have ready and convenient access to them on screen. Orders can be automatically processed and follow-up actions (such as call-back in one month or send literature) can be recorded and stored. In addition, productivity can be raised by autodiallers.

A major technological advance is predictive dialling which makes multiple outbound calls from a call centre. Calls are only delivered to agents when the customer answers, therefore cutting out wasted calls to answer machines, engaged signals, fax machines and unanswered calls. It is claimed to dramatically improve call centre efficiency by providing agents with a constant flow of calls. However, agents get no time to psych themselves up for the call (they are alerted by a bleep and the relevant details appear on a screen). Call centre staff have to work extremely intensively.[25]

Telemarketing automation also allows simple keystroke retrieval of critical information such as customer history, product information or schedules. If the prospect or customer is busy, automated systems can reschedule a callback and allow the operator to recall the contact on screen at a later date simply by pressing a single key.

Versatility of telemarketing

It can be used in a number of roles, and it is this versatility that has seen telemarketing activities grow in recent years. Its major roles are as follows:

Direct selling   When the sales potential of a customer does not justify a face-to-face call from a salesperson, telemarketing can be used to service the account. The telephone call may simply take the form of an enquiry about a reordering possibility, and as such does not require complex sales arguments that need face-to-face interaction. Alternatively, an inbound telephone call may be the means of placing an order in response to a direct mail, or television advertising campaign. For example, freefone facilities are often used for order placing in conjunction with advertising of record collections on television.

Supporting the salesforce   Customers may find contacting the field salesforce difficult given the nature of their job. A telemarketing operation

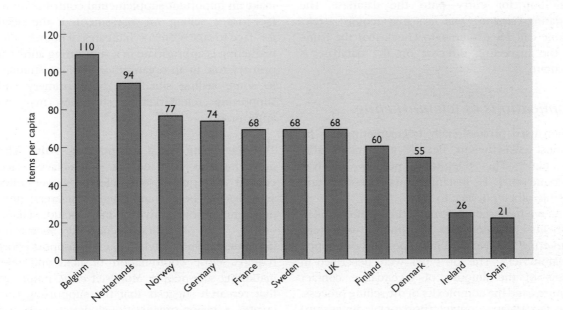

Figure 13.4 Volume of direct mail in Europe.
Adapted from Advertising Expenditure by Country and Medium, *European Marketing Pocket Book 2000*, Henley-on-Thames: NTC Publications

can provide a communications link to the salesforce, and an enquiry or order handling function. In this way customers know that there is someone at the supplier company who they can easily contact if they have a problem, enquiry or wish to place an order.

Generating and screening leads An outbound telemarketing team can be used to establish contact with prospective customers, and attempt to arrange a salesforce visit. Alternatively, it can be used to screen leads that have been generated by direct mail or coupon response to advertising. People who have requested further information can be contacted by telephone to ascertain their potential (qualifying a lead) and, if qualified, to try to arrange a salesforce visit.

Marketing database building and updating A secondary source of information such as a directory can provide a list of companies that partially qualify them for inclusion in a marketing database. However, the telephone may be required to check that they fulfil other conditions. For example, one criterion may be that they are textile companies. A directory such as *Kompass* may be used to identify them; however, a telephone call may be necessary to check that they have a marketing department, which may be a second condition for entry onto the database. The updating (*cleaning*) of lists may require a telephone call, for example, to check that the name of the marketing director on the database is accurate.

Applications of telemarketing

When used professionally telemarketing can be a most cost-efficient, flexible and accountable medium.[26] The telephone permits two-way dialogue that is instantaneous, personal and flexible, albeit not face to face.

As we have seen, telemarketing is often linked to field selling activities. The link between telemarketing and five field job types was developed by Moncrief.[27] The job types were described in terms of the amount of face-to-face contact required and the complexity of the selling process. The face-to-face contact (horizontal dimension) of Fig. 13.5 is particularly useful to illustrate the possible roles of telemarketing in selling strategy.

The missionary seller (making new initial customer contact) and the order-taker job types

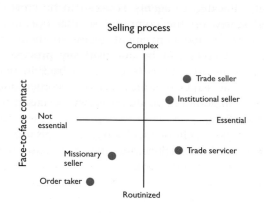

Figure 13.5 Sales job types.

Source: Moncrief, W. C., S. H. Shipp, C. W. Lamb and D. W. Cravens (1989) Examining the Roles of Telemarketing in Selling Strategy, *Journal of Personal Selling and Sales Management*, 9 (3), 2. Reproduced with permission

offer potential opportunities of using telemarketers as the organization's primary salesforce. The role of telemarketing in the institutional seller, trade servicer and trade seller job categories is to supplement field-selling efforts. The more routinized the selling process (vertical dimension of Fig. 13.5), the more likely telemarketing can make an important supplemental contribution to face-to-face selling. An assessment of the need for face-to-face contact indicates whether telemarketing is appropriate in a supporting and/or a primary role in an organization's selling strategy. In some selling situations, both primary and supporting telemarketing strategies may be appropriate.

Telemarketing as a supporting role The need for this role occurs when face-to-face contact is required, but selected buyer–seller activities can be accomplished by telemarketing personnel. These activities may include taking orders and handling reorders. Successful implementation of a telemarketing support effort requires close coordination of field and telemarketing salespeople. Moncrief *et al.* point out that research suggests that the supporting role creates a major organizational design task and resistance from field personnel will be likely to occur.[28] A carefully formulated plan is essential to assure co-operation of the telemarketing and the field salesforce. When face-to-face interaction is needed, telemarketing plays a secondary role in selling strategy.

Primary role Telemarketing can provide a complete sales and customer support effort for selling situations in which face-to-face contact is not required. Conditions suggest using telemarketing in a primary role include a routinized selling process, low cash value of purchases, a large and widely dispersed customer base, and non-technical products. Regardless of other considerations, a significant factor in deciding not to use face-to-face contact lies in the cost of field sales calls and the margins available to cover these costs.

Combination role Some companies have adopted selling strategies that utilize telemarketing in both supporting and primary roles. Organizations which may benefit from this strategy are ones with large and widely dispersed customer bases whose purchasers range from very small accounts to very large accounts. The accounts signed to the primary telemarketing functions are those that cannot economically be served on a face-to-face basis. Telemarketers often have primary responsibility for smaller customers and provide backup services for other customers when face-to-face salespeople are not available.

No role Importantly, certain selling situations are not appropriate for any type of telemarketing support. Conditions that may require face-to-face customer contact by a field salesperson greatly reduce or eliminate telemarketing's value, for example where the selling process complexity, contact requirements and importance of the purchase demand face-to-face contact.

13.2 Marketing in Action

European Direct Mail and the Law

Anyone attempting to compile a *database for mailing lists* on a pan-European basis needs to be aware of the differing national laws covering data protection and collection. For example, in the UK, The Netherlands and France, organizations holding personal data have to be registered whereas in Denmark and Germany this is not required. In Denmark, The Netherlands and Germany, personal data can be held only with the knowledge of the subject whereas in the UK and France no such restrictions apply.

The laws regarding *list broking* (for sale or rent) are very strict in Germany, which restricts the number of publicly available lists to fewer than 500. In the UK list broking is more widespread but requires the notification of the people on the list. In The Netherlands and France no such notification is required, only that the list broker is registered.

Clearly, before data collection and storage of personal information is begun, advice concerning the national laws of each target country should be sought. Also the European Commission directive on data protection should be consulted.

European Commission legislation covering direct mail could have a dramatic effect on its use. Restrictive laws can kill it off. It is no coincidence that Belgium and Portugal, the only two countries in Europe with laws against asking for prepayments for products, have very small direct marketing industries. Also the strict data protection laws in Germany have reduced the number of lists from 2500 to 250 today. With the stakes so high intense lobbying has taken place to convince the European Parliament that restrictive legislation is unnecessary.

Based on: Guide 26 (1993);[29] Short (1996)[30]

Guidelines for telemarketing

An eight-step guide to telephone selling has been published by the Bell Telephone System of America:[31]

1 Identify yourself and your company.

2 Establish rapport: this should come naturally since you have already researched your potential clients and their business.

3 Make an interesting comment (e.g. to do with cost savings or a special offer).

4 Deliver your sales message: emphasize benefits over features (e.g. your production people will like it because it helps to overcome downtime through waiting for the material to set).

5 Overcome objections: be skilled at objection-handling techniques.

6 Close the sale: when appropriate do not be afraid to ask for the order (e.g. 'Would you like to place an order now?) or fulfil another sales objective (e.g. 'Can I send you a sample?').

7 Action agreement: arrange for a sales call or the next telephone call.

8 Express your thanks.

Advantages of telemarketing

There are a number of reasons why telemarketing has grown in recent years. First, it has lower costs per contact than a face-to-face salesperson visit. Second, it is less time consuming than personal visits. Third, the growth in telephone ownership has increased access to households, and the use of toll-free lines (800 or 0800 numbers) has reduced the cost of responding by telephone. Next, the increasing sophistication of new telecommunications technology has encouraged companies to employ telemarketing techniques. For example, digital networks allow the seamless transfer of calls between organizations. The software company Microsoft and its telemarketing agency can smoothly transfer calls between their respective offices. If the caller then asks for complex technical information it can be transferred back to the relevant Microsoft department.[32] Finally, despite the reduced costs, compared to a personal visit, the telephone retains the advantage of two-way communication.

Disadvantages of telemarketing

It is not a panacea since it suffers from a number of disadvantages. First, telemarketing lacks the visual impact of a personal visit and it is not possible to assess the mood or reactions of the buyer through observing body language, especially facial expressions. It is easier for a customer to react negatively over the telephone and the number of rejections can be high. Telephone selling can be considered intrusive and some people may object to receiving unsolicited telephone calls. Finally, although cost per contact is cheaper than a personal sales call, it is more expensive than direct mail or media advertising. Labour costs can be high although computerized answering can cut the cost of receiving incoming calls.

A threat to the continuing growth of telemarketing is the growth of the Internet. e-Marketing 13.1 discusses some of the issues.

Direct response advertising

Direct response advertising appears in the prime media such as television, newspapers and magazines but differs from standard advertising as it is designed to elicit a direct response such as an order enquiry or a request for a visit. Often a Freefone telephone number is included in the advertisement or for the print media a coupon response is used. This mechanism combines the ability of broadcast media to reach large sections of the population with direct marketing techniques which allow a swift response on behalf of both prospect and company. The acceptability and accessibility of a Freefone number was proven during the launch of Daewoo cars in the UK. All Daewoo advertising and literature contained its Freefone number when its cars were launched in April 1995. Daewoo hoped that the campaign would attract about 3500 enquiries in the first month following launch. The actual response was over 43 000 rising to over 190 000 four months after launch for a previously unknown product. Direct response advertising had played its part in the successful introduction of a car brand in a new overseas market.[33]

Most telephone numbers are just tacked on the end of an advertisement. There are a few examples where the telephone number or call for action has been incorporated into the creative treatment. The most notable are the creative use of numbers such as 40 40 40 by the leisure group Forte and 28 28 20 (mimicking the sound of a tawny owl) by the insurance company Guardian Royal Exchange which has as its emblem an owl.

Direct response television (or teleshopping as it is sometimes called) has experienced fast growth. It is an industry worth £3 billion globally and comes in many formats. The most basic is the standard advertisement with telephone number. 60-, 90- or 120-second advertisements are sometimes used to provide the necessary information to persuade viewers to use the Freefone number for ordering. Other variants are the 25-minute product demonstration (generally referred to as infomercials) and live home shopping programmes broadcast by companies such as QVC.

A popular misconception regarding direct response television (DRTV) is that it is suitable only for products such as music compilations and cut-price jewellery. In Europe, a wide range of products are marketed (such as leisure and fitness products, car and household goods, books and beauty care products) through pan-European satellite channels such as Eurosport, Super Channel and NBC. Quantum International, the European market leader in this field, has adopted a strategy of marketing products not yet available through other outlets. As with other media DRTV has to adapt to local cultural variations. For example, in the UK the credit card is an accepted method of payment while in Germany there is a reluctance to do so. This means that Quantum's UK operation is based on payments by credit card, while cash is used in its Germany counterpart.[34]

Four circumstances increase the likelihood of DRTV application and success:

1   Goods that benefit from demonstration or a service which needs to be explained.

13.1   e-Marketing

Telemarketing Versus the Web

One of the key driving forces behind the growth of telemarketing has been the reduction in costs allowing expensive salespeople and retail outlets to be replaced with cheaper telephone-based services. Huge call centres where perhaps a hundred people operate telephones making and receiving calls have emerged. Now that same logic is being applied to the replacement of call centres with websites. Customers communicating with companies via e-mail can drastically cut the volume of telephone traffic, and companies are eager to encourage such a change. One industry observer estimates that at the moment it costs a bank about 65p per transaction in an outlet, 32p per telephone transaction and 2.5p per Internet transaction.

A company that is encouraging Internet bookings is easyJet. Following a cheap flights promotion easyJet were taking about six e-mail bookings per second. Banking is moving in this direction, too, with Egg offering new accounts only to Internet customers.

These trends have been closely monitored by telemarketing bureaux. Their response has been to open 'web-enabled' call centres which offer a full package of telephone, e-mail, fax, Internet access and interactive digital television facilities. An example of a telemarketing bureau doing just that is 7C, which has invested in web-enabled customer contact centres allowing agents to deal with customers in a fully integrated multimedia environment. Their clients include Virgin and Dun & Bradstreet.

Based on: Booth (1999);[35] Curtis (1999);[36] Jones and Nicholson (1999);[37] Reed (1999)[38]

2   A product that has mass consumer appeal (although specialist products could be placed on a single-interest channel).

3   A good DRTV promotion must make good television to attract and maintain the interest of the audience.

4   Supporting DRTV with an efficient telemarketing operation to handle the response generated by the advertisement.

The last of these four influences is discussed in more detail in Marketing in Action 13.3.

Catalogue marketing

Catalogue marketing is the sale of products through catalogues distributed to agents and customers, usually by mail or at stores if the catalogue marketer is a store owner. Catalogue marketing is popular in Europe with such organizations as Otto Versand and Quelle Schikedanz (Germany), GUS and Next Directory (UK) and Trois Suisse and La Redoute (France). Many of them operate in a number of countries such as La Redoute which has operations in France, Belgium, Norway, Spain and Portugal, and Trois Suisse which operates in France, The Netherlands, Belgium, Austria, Germany, Italy, Spain, Portugal and the UK. Catalogue marketing is popular in Austria because legislation restricts retail opening hours.[39]

A common form of catalogue marketing is mail order where catalogues are distributed and, traditionally, orders received by mail. This form of

13.3   Marketing in Action

Telemarketing Support for Direct Response Television

The most usual method of responding to direct response television advertising is through the telephone. This means big business for telemarketing call centres as a recent survey showed that 25 per cent of all TV advertisements in the UK carry a telephone number, and the number is growing. This means that good communication between advertisers and telemarketing call centres is vital to cope with the number of calls generated by an advertisement. Unfortunately, the problem of estimating demand and, therefore, having enough operators to handle demand has not been solved.

The result is that one in three calls are being lost. The response of most bureaux has been to introduce automated back-up. When all operators are engaged, an electronic answering service take details and follow-up calls or mailings can then be made. Although not ideal, the alternative of having more operators can prove expensive since 90 per cent of DRTV calls arrive very shortly after exposure to the advertisement.

The best way to estimate operator demand is to test before a full roll-out. Either off-peak airtime or a campaign limited to a few television regions can be used as a learning device. This is especially needed when the advertiser is new to DRTV. The telemarketing bureaux needs to be fully briefed regarding the timing of the advertising slots so that their operators can be ready to respond to calls.

Research has shown that some days and times of day are better than others. Using the number 100 to represent an 'average' response, ads shown between midnight and 6 a.m. score 110, those between noon and 2 p.m. on weekdays score 230. The score drops to 86 between 4 p.m. and 6 p.m. and collapses to 38 between 10 p.m. and midnight. Weekdays are better than weekends with Tuesday scoring 139 while Saturday has the lowest score with only 54.

Based on: Rines, (1995);[40] Anderson. (1999) [41]

marketing suffered from an old-fashioned down-market image and was based on an agency system where agents passed around the catalogue among friends and relatives, collecting and sending orders to the mail-order company in return for commission. Delivery was slow (up to 28 days) and the range of merchandise usually targeted at lower status social groups who valued the credit facility of weekly payment. Some enterprising companies, notably Next and Trois Suisse, saw catalogue marketing as an opportunity to reach a new target market: busy, affluent, middle-class people who valued the convenience of choosing products at home.

The Next Directory story is an example of how store retailers can use catalogue marketing to reach a wider range of customers. Laura Ashley, Habitat and Marks and Spencer are other examples, some of which charge for their catalogues. Some retailers, notably Argos in the UK, based their entire operation on the catalogue. A wide range of products including household goods, cameras, jewellery, toys, mobile phones, furniture and gardening equipment are sold through their catalogue. A customer can select at home, visit a catalogue shop where only a restricted selection of goods are on display and purchase products instantly. Argos' success is based on low prices and an efficient service and inventory system that controls costs and ensures a low out-of-stock situation.

When used effectively, catalogue marketing to consumers provides a convenient way of selecting products at home that allows discussion between family members in a relaxed atmosphere away from crowded shops and streets. Often credit facilities are available. For remote rural locations it provides a valuable service obviating the necessity to travel long distances to town shopping centres. For catalogue marketers, the expense of high street locations is removed and there is the opportunity to display a wider range of products than could feasibly be achieved in a shop. Distribution can be centralized, lowering costs. Nevertheless, catalogues are expensive to produce (hence the need for some retailers to charge for them) and they require regular updating, particularly when selling fashion items. They do not allow goods to be tried (e.g. a vacuum cleaner) or tried on (e.g. clothing) before purchase. Although products can be seen in the catalogue, variations in colour printing can mean that the curtains or suite that are delivered do not

have exactly the same colour tones as those appearing on the printed page.

Catalogue marketers have taken full advantage of the potential of database marketing to segment their customers, record purchasing behaviour (types of products bought, when, sizes, etc.) and monitor creditworthiness. Some develop 'scoring systems' to enable them to predict the chances of payment defaults, high merchandise return ratios and low ordering rates, based on an individual's location and personal characteristics.[42]

Catalogues are also important in business-to-business markets. They provide an invaluable aid to the salesperson when calling on customers and when in their hands are a perpetual sales aid, acting as a reference book allowing them to select and order at their convenience (often by telephone). A new development in this area is the creation of CD-ROM based catalogues.

Business-to-business catalogues often contain an enormous amount of information such as product specifications and prices. Once in the hands of customers and prospects, direct mail and telemarketing campaigns can be used to persuade them to consult their catalogues. It is hardly surprising, then, that for any supplier of a wide range of products such as component and office supply companies the catalogue remains a key marketing tool.

Integrated media campaigns

In an earlier chapter on advertising, the need for *integrated marketing communications* has been stressed. Communications strategy must be consistent with, and reinforce, other elements of the marketing mix (product, place and price). Within the promotional mix (advertising, personal selling, direct marketing, sales promotion and publicity) the same consistency and reinforcement should apply. Following this logic, messages sent out using various direct marketing media should also form a coherent whole. For example, information disseminated through the Internet should be consistent with that sent out via a direct mail campaign.

In practice direct marketing does not always use multiple contacts or multiple media. A marketer wishing to attract delegates to a conference might use a single-medium, single-stage campaign, that is one direct mailing to the target audience. A campaign designed to retain customers (e.g. subscribers to a charity or magazine) might

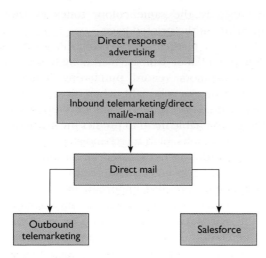

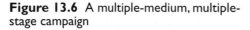

Figure 13.6 A multiple-medium, multiple-stage campaign

use a single-medium, multiple-campaign. Three direct mail letters might be sent to encourage renewal. However, direct marketers have the opportunity to use a combination of media in sequence to achieve their objectives. This is termed a multiple-medium, multiple-stage campaign.

A business-to-business company marketing a new adhesive might place a direct response advertisement in trade magazines to stimulate trial and orders. A response coupon, Freefone telephone number and e-mail address would be provided and prospects invited to choose their most convenient method of contact. An inbound telemarketing team would be trained to receive calls and take either orders or requests for samples for trial. Another team would deal with mail and e-mail correspondence. An outbound telemarketing team would follow up prospects judged to be of small and medium potential and the salesforce targeted at large potential customers and prospects. The sequence would be as shown in Fig. 13.6.

In this way, the company has identified prospects, generated an initial sales response, created interest in the new product, begun a dialogue with customers and prospects and, where necessary, arranged demonstrations. Each medium has been used to its best advantage and salesforce time and effort targeted at prospects and customers who have both the interest and potential to justify a sales call.

Creative decisions

Most direct marketing campaigns have different objectives from those of advertising, Whereas advertising usually attempts to create awareness and position the image of a brand in prospects' minds, the aim of most direct marketing is to make a sale. It is more orientated to immediate action than advertising. Recipients of direct marketing messages (particularly through direct mail) need to see a clear benefit in responding. For example, Direct Line's success in the motor insurance business was built on a clear customer benefit—substantial cost savings from insuring with them rather than the traditional insurance company—using direct response advertising and a highly efficient telemarketing team. Positioning Direct Line as a telemarketing-based motor insurer was achieved through advertising featuring a red telephone supported on wheels. Their *creative strategy* was consistent with the objectives and message of the campaign.

A *creative brief* will include the following elements (see Fig. 13.7):

✦ *Communication objectives*: what is the campaign hoping to achieve? Common objectives for direct marketing are sales volume and value, number of orders or enquiries and cost-effectiveness. These will be outlined in more detail when discussing campaign evaluation.

✦ *Product benefits (and weaknesses)*: the product features will be identified and their associated customer benefits. Features can be linked to benefits by the phrases 'which results in' or 'which means that'. Key sources of competitive advantage will be spotlighted which means that a thorough analysis of competitor products' strengths and weaknesses will have to be made.

✦ *Target market analysis*: target customers and prospects will be profiled and/or identified individually and their needs and purchasing behaviour analysed. It is essential that creative people understand the type of people they are communicating with since messages to be effective must be important to the target audience, not simply the 'pet' ideas of the creatives.

✦ *Development of the offer*: the offer should be valued by the target audience (pretesting offers through group discussions and/or

Figure 13.7 Creative decisions

small-scale tests can measure the attractiveness of alternative offers). Some offers are price related. For example, an offer for a Capital One Visa credit card announced 'Lowest Rate in the UK for Credit Card Purchases 7.9% APR Variable and No Annual Fee'. This message was emblazoned on the envelope and letter and was supported by financial data showing cost savings compared to the competition. Other offers may take the form of free gifts. Monthly magazines often offer three free copies for a year's subscription. Another example is Legal and General Direct, a financial services company who offered a free pen to all those who asked for a home insurance quote and a free telephone/radio alarm clock to those who took up insurance with them.

✦ *Communication of the message*: as seen in the previous example the offer or key message can be communicated on the envelope as well as the internal contents. Supporting evidence should be provided wherever possible. Several enclosures in a

direct mail slot can be included each with a different objective but each should have one clear single-minded purpose. Recipients must be told clearly how to respond. Research has shown that including a Freefone number as well as the usual freepost envelope can increase response by 50–125 per cent.[43] Today's direct marketers also have the option of including e-mail addresses as well. Letters should be personalized and the tone of the communication carefully thought out. Should a razz-ma-tazz high pressure sell or a gentler more subtle approach be used? Pretesting various approaches can give invaluable information on this issue. Scripts are often used in telemarketing to communicate messages. When combined with powerful software and information technology (as discussed earlier under telemarketing) they can provide an efficient way of communicating with customers and prospects.

✦ *Action plan*: decisions regarding when the campaign should be run, how often and suggestions regarding the most appropriate media to use to communicate the message and achieve the campaign's objectives must be made. For telemarketing campaigns, estimates of the number of operators required and when need to be produced.

Execute and evaluate the campaign

Execution of the campaign may be in-house or through the use of a specialist agency.

Direct marketing activity usually has clearly defined short-term objectives against which performance can be measured. Some of the most frequently used measurements are:

✦ Response rate (the proportion of contacts responding).

✦ Total sales (volume and value).

✦ Number of contacts purchasing.

✦ Sales rate (percentage of contacts purchasing).

✦ Number of enquiries.

✦ Enquiry rate.

✦ Cost per contact.

✦ Cost per enquiry.

✦ Cost per sale.

✦ Conversion rate from enquiry to sale.

✦ Average order value.

✦ Renewal rate.

✦ Repeat purchase rate.

Direct marketers should bear in mind the longer-term effects of their activities. A campaign may seemingly be unprofitable in the short term but when renewals and repeat purchases are taken into account the long-term value of the campaign may be highly positive.

Ethical issues in direct marketing

The use of direct marketing has raised a number of consumer concerns relating to *ethics*:

✦ *The quantity of poorly targeted direct mail*: although designed to foster close targeting of consumers, some direct mail is of little reference to the recipient. The double glazing promotion received by a household that already has double glazing, or the direct mail shot promoting bathroom suites arriving at a new house are clear sources of irritation. Much worse is the distress caused to widows and widowers by mail that continues to arrive for their deceased partner.

✦ *The timing and intrusive nature of telemarketing calls*: consumers also complain of the annoyance by unsolicited telephone calls pressuring them to buy products at inconvenient times (e.g. in the middle of bathing the baby).

✦ *The content of direct mail envelopes*: most direct mail enclosures are harmless but attempts to be novel and different have led some direct marketers to include devices that have been considered offensive or dangerous. One campaign targeted at marketing managers enclosed a bullet as an attention-getting measure. The response of some recipients was that someone somewhere had them in their sights! The complaints flowed in resulting in a severe reprimand for the culprit. Bullets, scissors and devices that make ticking sounds are all evidence that some direct marketers have paid insufficient attention to the potentially annoying and harmful effects of their actions.

✦ *Invasion of privacy*: many consumers fear that every time they subscribe to a club, society or magazine, apply for a credit card or buy anything by telephone or direct mail, their names, addresses and other information will be entered onto a database that will guarantee a flood of mail from the supplier. Furthermore, where country legislation does not restrict it, their names will be sold, without their knowledge, to other direct marketing organizations who are free to send further unsolicited mail.

The direct marketing industry is well aware of these public concerns and is responding, and companies are getting much more sophisticated with targeting. For example, Barclays, a UK bank, has moved into direct marketing for personal loans. A few years ago all current account customers could have received a direct mail shot. Now an in-house team prepares a target list using software that analyses its customer database. Only 9 per cent of current account customers are chosen as suitable recipients based on an analysis of an array of characteristics.

A second method of reducing public concern is to provide the opportunity for people who do not wish to receive direct mail or unsolicited telephone calls to enter onto a suppression file.[44] This is a list of names, addresses and telephone numbers that direct marketers should check against their own lists and remove any names appearing on it. In the UK two suppression lists exist: the Mailing Preference Service and the Telephone Preference Service with 320 000 and 75 000 people registered, respectively. A major factor in getting these instruments accepted by the direct marketing industry was the threat of EC directives. If the industry did not regulate itself, the fear was that Europe would impose restrictive legislation for it.

Summary

Direct marketing is the distribution of products, information and promotional benefits to target consumers through interactive communication in a way that allows response to be measured. It includes direct mail, telemarketing, direct response advertising, catalogue marketing, electronic media (e.g. the Internet), inserts in print media and door-to-door leafleting.

The growth in direct marketing activity has been driven by market and media fragmentation, developments in technology, the list explosion, sophisticated analytical techniques and coordinated marketing systems.

A marketing database is an electronic filing cabinet containing a list of names, addresses, telephones, lifestyle and transactional data. Database marketing is an interactive approach to marketing that uses individually addressable marketing media and channels to provide information, stimulate demand and staying close to the customer. Uses are to identify people who are more likely to respond to a direct mail or telemarketing campaign, to provide the basis for a long-term customer retention programme, to provide information and evaluate distributors, to select loyal customers for special treatment, to coordinate campaigns so that individuals receive consistent messages and to evaluate marketing mix inputs.

Managing a direct marketing campaign involves identifying and understanding the target audience, campaign objectives, making media and creative decisions, and executing and evaluating the campaign. Potential targets are competitors' customers, prospects, enquirers, lapsed customers, referrals and existing customers. Key objectives are the acquisition and retention of customers. Media decisions should take into account the benefits of integrated direct marketing campaigns. Creative decisions should be expressed in a brief which includes a statement of communication objectives, product benefits and weaknesses, target market analysis, development of the offer, communication of the message and an action plan. Execution may be in-house or through the use of a specialist agency. Short-term evaluation is through measures such as total sales, sales rate, number of enquiries, cost per sale and renewal rate. Longer-term evaluation is through repeat purchasing rates and the long-term value of customers generated by a given campaign.

The advantages of direct mail are that it allows close targeting of named individuals, elaborate personalization is possible and response can be measured. It depends upon access to accurate lists and initial costs can be much higher than advertising. Poor targeting can lead to the criticism of junk mail. Telemarketing also allows close targeting, two-way dialogue, lower costs than face-to-face salesperson visits and is less time consuming. However, it lacks the visual impact of a personal visit, body language cannot be assessed, some people object to receiving unsolicited telephone calls and, on a per contact basis, it is more expensive than direct mail or media advertising.

Direct response advertising can reach large sections of the population and allow a swift response by both message receiver and sender. Direct response advertising campaigns are invariably linked to direct mail and/or telemarketing response mechanisms. Niche markets can sometimes be reached through specialist magazines and television channels. Catalogue marketing has become increasingly sophisticated in recent years. The trend has been to target specific market niches. It provides consumers with a convenient way of selecting products away from crowded shops and streets, and for rural areas it removes the necessity to travel long distances to shop. However, catalogues do not allow goods to be tried before purchase. In business-to-business markets they aid the salesperson's job when talking to customers and act as a perpetual sales aid when in the hands of customers. Responses to catalogues can be fed into a database marketing system to segment customers, record purchasing behaviour and monitor creditworthiness. Catalogue marketing can lower distribution costs although catalogues are expensive to produce and require regular updating.

The major advantages of direct marketing come when integrated marketing communication campaigns are developed. The strengths of each media can be used to maximize overall impact.

Ethical issues concerning direct marketing are the quantity of poorly targeted direct mail, the timing and intrusive nature of telemarketing calls, the content of direct mail envelopes, and the invasion of privacy. Both the direct mail and telemarketing industries are taking steps to overcome these problems.

Internet exercise

Cutting out the middleman

Sites to visit
http://www.directline.com
http://www.dell.com

Exercise
Each of these companies made significant amounts of money by cutting out the middleman and going direct to the consumer. Contrast the different markets in which they operate and discuss the ways in which they are offering customer benefits.

Study questions

1 Compare the strengths and weaknesses of direct mail and telemarketing.

2 What are the key differences between direct marketing and media advertising?

3 Define direct marketing. What are the seven forms of direct marketing? Give an example of how at least three of them can be integrated into a marketing communications campaign.

4 What is database marketing? Explain the types of information that are recorded on a data-base.

5 What are the stages of managing a direct marketing campaign? Why is the concept of lifetime value of a customer important when designing a campaign?

6 What are the advantages and disadvantages of loyalty schemes? Why are many companies employing such schemes?

7 What benefits does catalogue marketing provide consumers and companies? Give the traditional catalogue marketing approach with its modern equivalent.

8 Discuss the major concerns relating to ethics in direct marketing.

References

1. North, B. (1995) Consumer Companies Take Direct Stance, *Marketing*, 20 May, 24–5.
2. Guide 26 (1993) International Direct Marketing, *Marketing*, 22 April, 23–6.
3. Smith, P. R. (1993) *Marketing Communications: An Integrated Approach*, London: Kogan Page.
4. Stone, M., D. Davies and A. Bond (1995) *Direct Hit: Direct Marketing with a Winning Edge*, London: Pitman.
5. Fletcher, K., C. Wheeler and J. Wright (1990) The Role and Status of UK Database Marketing, *Quarterly Review of Marketing*, Autumn, 7–14.
6. Linton, I. (1995) *Database Marketing: Know What Your Customer Wants*, London: Pitman.
7. Nancarrow, C., L. T. Wright and J. Page (1997) Seagram Europe and Africa: The Development of a Consumer Database Marketing Capability, *Proceedings of the Academy of Marketing*, July, Manchester, 1119–30.
8. Stone, Davies and Bond (1995) op. cit.
9. Patron, M. (1996) The Future of Marketing Databases, *Admap*, October, 21–23.
10. Wilson, R. (1999) Discerning Habits, *Marketing Week*, 1 July, 45–8.
11. Stone, Davies and Bond (1995) op. cit.
12. Murphy, J. (1997) The Art of Satisfaction, *Financial Times*, 23 April, 14.
13. A quotation by G. Harrison in Rines, S. (1995) Blind Data, *Marketing*, 17 November, 26–7.
14. Dowling, G. R. and M. Uncles (1997) Do Loyalty Programs Really Work? *Sloan Management Review*, **38** (4), 71–82.

15. Burnside, A. (1995) A Never Ending Search for the New, *Marketing*, 25 May, 31–5.
16. East, R. and W. Lomax (1999) Loyalty Value, *Marketing Week*, 2 December, 51–5.
17. Michell, A. (1995) Preaching the Loyalty Message, *Marketing Week*, 1 December, 26–7.
18. Reed, D. (1996) Direct Fight, *Marketing Week*, 1 November, 45–7.
19. Murphy, C. (1999) Addressing the Data Issue, *Marketing*, 28 January, 31.
20. Clegg, A. (2000) Hit Or Miss, *Marketing Week*, 13 January, 45–9.
21. Baier, M. (1985) *Elements of Direct Marketing*, New York: McGraw-Hill, 184.
22. Bird, D. (1994) *Commonsense Direct Marketing*, London: Kogan Page, 180.
23. Guide 26 (1993) op. cit.
24. Miller, R. (1999) Phone Apparatus, *Campaign*, 18 June, 35–6.
25. Miller (1999) op. cit.
26. McHatton, N. R. J. (1988) *Total Telemarketing*, New York: Wiley, 269.
27. Moncrief, W. C. (1986) Selling Activity and Sales Position Taxonomies for Industrial Sales Forces, *Journal of Marketing Research*, **23** (2), 261–70.
28. Moncrief, W. C., S. H. Shipp, C. W. Lamb and D. W. Cravens (1989) Examining the Roles of Telemarketing in Selling Strategy, *Journal of Personal Selling and Sales Management*, **9** (3), 1–20.
29. Guide 26 (1993) International Direct Marketing, *Marketing*, 22 April, 24.
30. Short, D. (1996) Lobbying Keeps the Legislators in Line, *The European*, 4–10 April, 13.
31. Jobber, D. and G. Lancaster (2000) *Selling and Sales Management*, London: Pitman, 192–3.
32. Stevens, M. (1993) A Telephony Revolution, *Marketing*, 16 September, 38.
33. Starkey, M. (1997) Telemarketing in D. Jobber (ed.) *The CIM Handbook of Selling and Sales Strategy*, Oxford: Butterworth-Heinemann, 130.
34. Carman, D. (1996) Audiences Dial 'S' for Shopping, *The European*, 4–10 April, 13.
35. Booth, E. (1999) Will the Web Replace the Phone? *Marketing*, 4 February, 25–6.
36. Curtis, J. (1999) Call Centres Must Adapt Their Ways, *Marketing*, 2 December, 33–4.
37. Jones, S. and M. Nicholson (1999) Digital Revolution May Sound the Death Knell for Call Centres, *Financial Times*, 20 September, 14.
38. Reed, D. (1999) Back-up Call, *Marketing Week*, 18 November, 45–7.
39. Mühlbacher, H., M. Botshen and W. Beutelmeyer (1997) The Changing Consumer in Austria, *International Journal of Research in Marketing*, **14**, 309–19.
40. Rines, S. (1995) Call or Nothing, *Marketing Week*, 27 October, 45–60.
41. Anderson, P. (1999) Break Time, *Marketing Week*, 23 September, 45–9.
42. Stone, Davies and Bond (1995) op. cit.
43. Roman, E. (1995) *The Cutting Edge Strategy for Synchronizing Advertising, Direct Mail, Telemarketing and Field Sales*, Lincolnwood IL: NTC Business Books.
44. Croft, M. (1996) Clean-up Operation, *Marketing Week*, 8 March, 61–4.

Key terms

direct marketing   (1) acquiring and retaining customers without the use of an intermediary; (2) the distribution of products, information and promotional benefits to target consumers through interactive communication in a way which allows response to be measured

database marketing   an interactive approach to marketing which uses individually addressable marketing media and channels to provide information to a target audience, stimulate demand and stay close to customers

target audience   the group of people at which a direct marketing campaign is aimed

campaign objectives   goals set by an organization in terms of e.g. sales, profits, customers won or retained or awareness creation

direct mail   material sent through the postal service to the recipient's house or business address promoting a product and/or maintaining an ongoing relationship

telemarketing   a marketing communications system whereby trained specialists use telecommunications and information technologies to conduct marketing and sales activities

direct response advertising   the use of the prime advertising media such as television, newspapers and magazines to elicit an order, enquiry or a request for a visit

catalogue marketing   the sale of products through catalogues distributed to agents and customers, usually by mail or at stores

Case 23 Seagram Europe and Africa

The Seagram Company is a large and diversified drinks and entertainment group. Best known for its beverages worldwide, the company has a global portfolio of around 150 brands in as many countries. Seagram is one of the world's global leaders in the production and marketing of distilled spirits, wines, fruit juices, coolers, beers and mixers, with healthy annual increases in sales. By January 1996 it had gross revenues of more than $6.6 billion. Its committed involvement in the entertainment market came with the acquisition of an 80 per cent interest in Universal (formerly MCA Inc) in the USA in 1995. Universal produces and distributes motion picture, television and home video products, recorded music, books, operates theme parks and retail stores. Seagram ranks as Canada's second largest company with a market capitalization value of US$13 731.4 million (*Financial Times*, 24 January 1997, p. 35).

This case study focuses on Seagram Europe & Africa (SE&A), a major division of the Seagram Company and the issues concerning an increase in its direct marketing activities to be supported by the building of a relevant customer database. The leading SE&A brands and their competitors in the product categories are shown in Table C23.1. Each regional marketing team works with the relevant global brand manager for each brand.

Seagram Europe and Africa (SE&A) is concerned with the positioning and sales of its premium brands, especially those which are in or approaching the mature stages of their product life cycles. Changes in the marketing environment necessitated the review of methods used to communicate with and to motivate consumers.

Consumers in Europe are more adventurous in their tastes and increasingly willing to experiment. Markets are becoming more fragmented as consumers seek ways of expressing their individualism and satisfying their personal preferences. Fragmented markets can mean lower sales targets with inevitably smaller marketing expenditures to support brands. Consequently both product and brand loyalties are threatened.

In the North West European countries such as the UK, Eire, Germany, France and Scandinavia, saturation in mature markets and increased competition has made it difficult to sustain the sales of leading brands. In the South European countries, for example in the Mediterranean, demand is also slowing in markets which are approaching maturity. However, with the introduction of liberalization of their market economies, growth opportunities are present in East Europe—the Baltic States, Ukraine, Romania, Poland, Russia, Hungary and the Czech Republic. Increasing global competition and volatility of consumer demands require efficiency gains and a stronger consumer focus. The search for efficiencies means that marketing expenditure is more closely scrutinized across all divisions in Seagram with questions asked about the role and effectiveness of all communication and promotion methods.

Direct marketing to 'get closer to consumers'

Direct marketing has been used only occasionally by Seagram in Europe and by its SE&A division.

Table C23.1	Product categories and competing brands	
Product category	*SE&A*	*Competitors' brands*
Deluxe whisky	Chivas Regal	Johnny Walker, Black Label, Dimple
Malt whisky	The Glenlivet	Glenfiddich, Glenmorangie, Macallan
Cognac	Martell	Courvoisier, Hennessy, Remy Martin
Vodka	Absolut	Stolichnaya, Smirnoff
Champagne	Mumm	Moet & Chandon, Veuve Clicquot
Port/sherry	Sandeman	Cockburn, Taylors, Grahams
Fruit juice	Tropicana	Varies across Europe

The major communications methods used by SE&A are advertising, sponsorship, public relations, in-store display, consumer and trade promotions. Rising advertising costs and wastage have led the SE&A management to examine other forms of the communications mix, including direct marketing, with the objective of 'getting closer to consumers'. Television, poster and press media inflation across much of Europe has out-stripped retail price indices (RPI). In real terms the rising cost of reaching target audiences, as measured in cost per thousand, has prompted SE&A's management to evaluate its traditional communications methods. Sponsorship of the Grand National for its Martell brand or the Admiral's Cup for its Mumm brand in 1996 has been of value, but a major limitation is finding suitable sponsorship opportunities for SE&A.

Storing and manipulating large amounts of data efficiently is an affordable option due to decreasing computer hardware and software costs in the last two decades. So there can be greater sophistication in using direct marketing by more efficiently targeting consumers from databases most likely to respond to SE&A campaigns. Personalized direct mail using data-base information about consumers, such as their individual names, reference to personal circum-stances and preferences is a more involving method than advertising, since opening an envelope and reading a letter invites the customer to participate in the activity. While direct mail is less personal than telemarketing and personal selling, it is financially more viable. Its effective-ness is easier to measure than other major forms of marketing communications. SE&A could deliver a number of services to consumers, for example through newsletters, suggestion booklets, food and drinks guides. Questionnaire surveys could canvas customers' opinions and requirements, serving also to convey the fact that Seagram is genuinely interested in them.

Experience in direct marketing

The US division, the House of Seagram (HoS), has developed expertise in the direct marketing of premium brands. The principles of good practice in the USA could be disseminated within the organization and adapted for European markets and cultures. In the UK, SE&A's direct marketing consultant, Ogilvy & Mather Data Consult has

demonstrated in a market research experiment that combining direct mail and direct response advertising can be more cost effective than advertising alone.

Moreover, the creation of its own direct marketing consumer database for marketing communications might possibly lead to a stronger negotiating position for Seagram in its dealings with the major multiple stores in Europe. Retailers' own-label brands are an added source of competition and price promotions are regularly introduced by retail chains with consequent pressures on SE&A's profit margins. Retailers provide valuable services which consumers want, such as variety, information, personal service, occasional tastings and convenience.

Issues in building a consumer database for direct marketing purposes

How can an in-house database of prospective consumers be built? Names and addresses of current and potential customers are needed, but it can be problematic to identify individuals who purchase from retail and 'on-licence' premises. The buying cycle by retailers of bottles of whisky, cognac, champagne, etc., is a long one and conse-quently results of a field pretest might not be meaningful unless many months or even a year is monitored. The need in the long term is to measure the pay-off in consumer acquisition and the building of consumer loyalty in direct marketing activities. Consultations with Ogilvy & Mather Data Consult in the UK and the US HoS's direct marketing team concluded that building a database could be a feasible option using direct marketing and indirect methods:

✦ *Direct marketing*—sales promotions incentives for member-get-member schemes, telephone enquires and sales promotions held at company premises, conferences and exhibitions;

✦ *Indirect methods*—incorporating narrow targeting applying usage & attitude (U&A) studies, postcode data which identifies prime neighbourhood prospective types— geodemographic analysis and lifestyle profiling. U&A studies of whisky and cognac consumption have been used for more than a decade by the company's 'Chivas and Glenlivet Group' to monitor and evaluate consumer trends in Europe.

SE&A could build a computerized database which would make it possible to address each consumer as a microsegment in his or her own right. One important consideration is at what point the costs of building both the direct marketing campaigns and a computerized consumer database to support them break even. Cost-effectiveness is based upon the cost/benefit analysis of communications and promotions (creative production, mail-outs and prizes, etc.), the resultant pay-offs (increases in trial and loyalty) and the creation of the database (data inputs and updates, analysis and evaluation). These efforts would also lead to additional market research information as a spin-off, though this was not a criterion used in the decision about creating the database.

A database has the potential advantage over a subsample of a U&A study of including large numbers of users for analysis and profiling. For example a U&A study on the Scotch market might include 40 people for The Glenlivet whisky while the database can be used to target thousands of actual and potential consumers, though care in validation needs to be taken. To maintain consistency, all marketing research projects and database forms could use the same classification questions and breakdowns, for example, age: 16–24/25–34).

The management of a database within an European operation also has to be taken into account. Decisions have to be made about either having one centralized database or allowing managers in each country to build their own databases (software and hardware applications), staffing requirements (recruitment of skills to run their databases) and monitoring of quality standards. Besides the set-up costs, a centralized system poses difficulties. European affiliates already had various formats with differences in types of data stored and there were different country regulations controlling the divulging of consumer data which were problematic for the transfer of files on individual consumers.

However, a centralized database has some advantages. There would be cost savings in operating only one centralized database in the long term. The best expertise to manage one database can be bought in. The ease and speed of international comparisons with standardization of data collection can be facilitated.

There is already a precedence in marketing research that international research design should aim for the collection of comparable information across borders while allowing for specific local needs. 'Think globally, act locally' has been part of the company's international advertising and marketing research history, for example, in advertising, which has allowed for cultural differences in its implementation.

This principle could be used for the concerted effort in developing a database-driven direct marketing activity. Countries involved would agree the types of key data to be collected and the methods for collection in as similar a format as possible permitting centralization with valid inter-country comparisons quickly and easily.

Since the goal is to increase the numbers of consumers and the retention of their loyalty, the long-term perspective, rather than that of short-term gains, has to be taken. In this the experience of previous HoS direct marketing campaigns in the USA is taken into account. It may be more efficient for SE&A to operate its direct marketing as a multinational region rather than to have managers in every country building their own campaigns.

SE&A concludes that the likely size of the database could be cost-effective both in absolute terms and relative to other marketing communications methods. To add to its knowledge about database marketing and the expertise needed in the sophisticated statistical analyses to support the effectiveness of its direct marketing activity, SE&A has appointed 'a manager with European responsibility' for such an operation and who can also work with a Seagram dedicated consultant from Ogilvy & Mather Data Consult.

This case was prepared by Len Tiu Wright, Professor of Marketing, De Montfort University, Leicester; Clive Nancarrow, University of the West of England, Bristol; and Julie Page, Seagram Company.

Questions

1   Discuss whether SE&A's deliberations on direct marketing are appropriate given the changes in the marketing environment.

2   Compare and evaluate the feasibility of direct marketing with the various marketing communication methods for SE&A's leading brands.

3   Assess how the benefits of a database-driven direct marketing activity can help Seagram maintain its competitiveness in its mature and growth markets in European countries.

Case 24 Houstons

Houstons Ltd is a wholly owned subsidiary of County Hotels Ltd, a three-star national chain of 42 hotels catering primarily for business people and week-end bargain-seekers. Turnover in 1993 was £390 million. The registered head office is in London where it also has a central reservation system as well as its senior management team, including marketing.

In 1991, in order to diversify and spread risks, County Hotels began to test-market a new restaurant brand, Houstons, at five locations in Surrey. The restaurants were based on a US model located in Kansas, Missouri, which management had encountered on a visit to the USA in 1990.

The concept, American at heart, was, however, adapted to middle-class English tastes. Each of the 100-seater restaurants was furbished to a high standard, with brass, mirrors and soft leather seats and high-settle benches. An island bar dominated the centre of each restaurant and around it was created a range of ambiances to suit different customer groups' requirements. For instance, each high-street entrance led into a light, open area favoured by people seeking a down-to-earth, brisk, social environment, whereas the much more dimly-lit area behind the island bar, with its high-back leather settles and table lamps, attracted a more discrete clientele. Around the bar, would be found those seeking a quick drink or light meal and those simply wishing to be seen.

Food was high quality, simply cooked ribs, burgers, steaks, fish, omelettes, salads, vegetables and fries. Drinks were highly varied, featuring unusual North American beers, cocktails and obscure continental wines and liqueurs.

The combination of quality food and drink in a modern, stylish environment, supported by a highly friendly and efficient service, positioned Houstons in a unique market niche with no direct competition. None of the rash of US theme restaurants—T.G.I. Fridays, Old Orleans, etc. —really captured the essence of Houstons' recession-conscious chic: the formula was sufficiently flexible and subtle to distance Houstons from the brash, 'we will entertain you, American style, whether you like it or not' newcomers increasingly popping up in British high streets. The opening hours and flexibility of menus more closely resembled a good French brasserie. The positioning strategy was supported by prices which indicated quality without any of the pain that went with quality in the heady days of the mid-1980s.

The test-market

From April 1991 to April 1993 five Surrey locations provided the basis for a market test of the Houstons concept: Richmond-upon-Thames, Weybridge, Guildford, Farnham and Camberley. Opening at 11.00 a.m. and closing at 11.00 p.m., the five restaurants averaged 60 per cent capacity on a 58-minute average seat occupancy and returned a gross margin of 70 per cent on a 1992–93 turnover of just over £12 million. The average spend per customer was £12. Allowing for fixed overheads, the net profit before tax was £0.5 million.

The 15 per cent return on capital employed was sufficient to justify management's initial decision to go ahead with the project. As a result an expansion programme was drawn up in the summer of 1993 which, by January 1994, had established 25 more restaurants in locations throughout England and Wales (see Table C24.1).

The marketing strategy

The test market had achieved its initial objectives with a total advertising and promotion (A&P) spend of only £200 000—all of which, had been allocated to local media advertising and promotion—to create awareness, encourage trial and lead to positive word-of-mouth recommendations.

To some extent this has indeed happened: although the results were patchy, and little post-launch advertising was done, targets had been met. However, both Claire Phillips, Houston's marketing manager, and David Wallace, County's Group marketing director were conscious that more could have been done, indeed needed to be done, to build loyalty to Houstons. Some very simple analysis of research questionnaires left on tables showed that the level of repeat visits was disappointingly low. Questionnaire comments particularly focused on the service, which wasn't quite up to comparable US standards, and the lack of alternatives to traditional dishes. Vegetarians

Table C24.1   Houstons UK Ltd—new locations

Brighton
Birmingham (2)
Bristol
Cardiff
Derby
Halifax
Ipswich
London (5)
Liverpool (2)
Manchester (2)
Newcastle
Oxford
Plymouth
Portsmouth
Southampton
Swansea
Wigan
Wallasey

Note: All these locations have 100-seat restaurants furbished and equipped to the same levels as the test market sites. They are all prime high-street sites in central and busy suburban locations where there is plenty of competition and highly developed commercial and transport infrastructures.

were particularly disappointed by the lack of choice on the menu; and there were several requests for ethnic alternatives. In the second year of the test market these, and other, issues were addressed by Phillips and Wallace. In particular:

✦ Target markets were more closely defined, not simply in terms of basic demographics and psychographics, but also in terms of benefits sought and usage patterns. As a result, within both business and consumer segments were identified potential clusters segmentable by time, payment methods, sales mix, frequency and monetary value.

✦ Product benefits were more closely identified and communicated. Increasing emphasis was placed upon the multisensory experience of a visit to Houstons—the visual excitement of the decor, the oral experience of the food and the social and emotional elements in the total package.

✦ Differential pricing was introduced with discounts on published prices for different time segments, categories of customer and

customer loyalty. In addition a £9.95 'price fix' menu was introduced at lunchtime with limited choice, a guarantee of a seat within 10 minutes of arrival and promise of a turnaround within 45 minutes. Similarly, evening 'special occasion' menus were introduced offering a wider range of dishes, exotic specials and additional services. The average price of such packages was in the £25–30 per head range.

✦ Service problems were addressed by more exacting recruitment criteria for front and back-room staff and by product, service and sales training courses at regular intervals.

✦ More effort was paid to customer retention through sales promotions encouraging customers to return, e.g. vouchers, coupons and discounts.

These measures had undoubtedly improved the effectiveness of the marketing spend which had risen by the end of the year to an annual equivalent of £300 000. But both Phillips and Wallace knew that more needed to be done in 1995 and recessionary times. At a meeting of the two early in January 1994 agreement on the marketing objectives for the first three years, 1995–98, of the newly formed, wholly owned subsidiary—Houstons Ltd.—were thrashed out.

Marketing objectives 1995–98

✦ To generate pre-tax profits in year one of £2.5 million with a year-on-year increase to 1996 of 10 per cent.

✦ To raise the average spend per customer visit to £18 in 1997 at 1993 prices.

Both Phillips and Wallace felt that these were tough, but achievable targets, given the strengths of the Houstons operation, notably:

✦ Stronger financial and technical support from the parent company, County Hotels.

✦ Access to County Hotels' central reservation system and database.

✦ Opportunities to use County's marketing programme for 'piggy-backing'.

✦ A well-tested concept that had clearly worked in Surrey.

✦ Capable, well-trained staff.

- ✦ A commitment to service quality.
- ✦ Highly experienced, talented marketers in Phillips and Wallace.

However, both recognized the weaknesses and problems facing them:

- ✦ *Inadequate customer knowledge*. Beyond the intelligence provided by the table questionnaires and the information derived from the promotional campaigns, management knew little about its customers. In particular, no effort had yet been made to begin the process of building a genuine marketing database.

- ✦ *Locational problems*. Not all the test market sites had performed equally well. For instance, the Richmond restaurant had been particularly successful both during the week and at weekends, with an average capacity ratio of 68 per cent and a per capita spend of £16. Elsewhere, occupancy levels had been closer to 57 per cent with per capita spend around £10. But there were still local variations. For instance, the Guildford restaurant did well in the evenings, profiting from its proximity to the Yvonne Arnaud Theatre, but lunch-time trade was relatively poor. The others had good lunch-time trade, with quieter evenings.

- ✦ *Increasing competition*, both on price and offers, with the risk of trading down.

- ✦ *Continuing economic recession*, with no immediate prospect of a revival in consumer confidence and spending.

Marketing objectives—1995

The shorter term objectives for 1995 were less clearly formulated at the January meeting. There had been differences of opinion between Phillips and Wallace. The latter, his eyes permanently fixed on end-of-year results, stressed the importance of improving turnover and cash flow while tightly controlling costs, including marketing expenditure. But Phillips pointed out that the longer term objectives could only be met by investing now in more effective marketing. In particular, she argued for an immediate review of information systems with a view to quickly establishing a marketing database.

But Wallace was doubtful about the value of a database, insisting instead that such money would work more effectively if spent on more national advertising. No agreement was therefore reached at their meeting. Instead, Wallace asked Phillips to prepare a draft marketing plan for 1995 to be discussed at a meeting provisionally arranged for 3 March 1994, less than two months hence. The plan, Wallace asserted, should focus on the objectives and the strategy for 1995, and should provide a rigorous financial justification for the proposed strategies, particularly if he was to get it past the Board of County Hotels.

The day following their meeting, Claire Phillips received the following memo confirming the task ahead.

Memorandum

From: David Wallace (Group Marketing Director)
To: Claire Phillips (Houstons UK Marketing Manager)
Date: 15 January 1994
Subject: The 1995 Marketing Plan, Houstons Ltd.

Our meeting yesterday led to agreement on the long-term marketing objectives for Houstons. But we still have a lot of work to do to agree both the 1995 objectives and the appropriate strategies to achieve those objectives.

Would you therefore draft a provisional plan for 1995 to reach me one week before our scheduled meeting on 3 March. I feel that your plan should meet the following criteria in particular:

- ✦ your recommendations for 1995 should be consistent with our longer term objectives.

- ✦ focus on the strategic issues (we can thrash out the operational details at a later meeting).

- ✦ explain how you feel your ideas about a marketing database will fit in to current marketing activity. In particular why and how would a marketing database work?

- ✦ indicate an outline budget (bearing in mind your remarks yesterday about customer acquisition costs, retention costs and life-time values—which, frankly, I didn't fully understand!—I'd particularly like to see how your budgetary proposals take account of these ideas).

I appreciate that this is asking a lot of you in the time, Claire, but I feel we must get the basic strategic thinking done by March. We can then concentrate on the media plan, etc.

To make your task manageable—and my job of reading your plan equally manageable!—please limit yourself to a 4000 word report.

David Wallace

This case was prepared by Melanie Howard, The Future Foundation, and Ian Smith, The Institute of Direct Marketing.

CHAPTER FOURTEEN

Internet and On-line Marketing

The minute you start to do business on the web, you now have to think about your competition as global, your readers as global, your suppliers as global, and your partners as global.

THOMAS FRIEDMAN, KILLING GOLIATH.COM

Learning Objectives *This chapter explains:*

1 On-line marketing growth rates

2 Alternative uses for the Internet ranging from delivering information through to offering a complete on-line purchase facility

3 Benefits the Internet offers to customers and companies

4 How to apply the fundamental rules of marketing to the world of on-line marketing

5 Organizational competencies for on-line success

6 How to achieve competitive advantage on-line

7 The design of an e-commerce marketing mix

Introduction

The *Internet* is a global web of over 50 000 computer networks which permit instant global communication. Each of these computers is called a server which maintains an address book covering every other server which is linked to the Internet. To access the Internet, users need to connect to a server. Many of these servers are owned by communications companies (often known as Internet Service Providers—ISPs) such as CompuServe or America OnLine. A glossary of Internet terms is provided in Table 14.1.

The *World Wide Web* has revolutionized the Internet by breaking up written materials with graphics and allowing colour and sound to be used. It is a collection of millions of computer files that can be accessed via the Internet. The original users of the Internet were academics, research scientists and students. Over recent years, however, this situation has changed dramatically as commercial organizations have moved to incorporate the World Wide Web into their promotional campaigns and by offering the facility of on-line purchasing. In short, the Internet and the World Wide Web are changing the ways consumers and businesses communicate as the Philips advertisement overleaf illustrates. One of the original obstacles facing early users of the Internet was how to find the information being sought rapidly. The solution to this problem was the creation of portals such as Yahoo! and Alta Vista which provide search engines to locate the *websites* containing the information sought by the user. This has led to an explosion in consumer and business-to-business use as Fig. 14.1 illustrates.

The scale of potential influence of the Internet is dramatically illustrated by a research project commissioned by the American corporation Cisco Systems and undertaken by the University of Texas.[1] The researchers concluded that during 1999 within just the US economy, the Internet generates an annual revenue of $332 billion and supports almost 1 400 000 jobs. These figures are made even more dramatic if one realizes that these US Internet-based revenues cause this

---

Table 14.1   A glossary of common Internet and e-commerce terms

Ad view: the number of times an on-line advertisement is seen by a site visitor

Browser: computer software such as Netscape or Internet Explorer that can guide the user around the Internet

Chatroom: a site that allows visitors to communicate with each other about a topic of common interest to them

Click-through: the number of times a site visitor 'clicks' onto an Internet page

Domain name: this is the address which most Internet sites have that performs the role of being the telephone number for individuals wishing to reach them

E-commerce: electronic (or 'e-') commerce is the description applied to a wide range of technologies to streamline business interactions. Examples of these technologies include the Internet, electronic data interchange (EDI), e-mail, electronic payment systems, advanced telephone systems, hand-held digital appliances, interactive televisions, self-service kiosks and smart cards

EDI (or electronic data interchange): this is a pre-Internet technology which was developed to permit organizations to use linked computers to rapidly exchange information

Extranet: a website where access is restricted to approved users

Firewall: computer software that protects the customer's on-line purchase transaction from being accessed by others

Hit: a single request from a browser to an Internet server

Home page: a website's welcome page providing details of site contents and guidance about using the site

Intranet: a website which operates inside an organization and does not offer access to any users external to the organization

Internet Service Provider: companies such as Dixons Freeserve and AOL who offer users access to the Internet. ISP software can be obtained over the Internet, from computer disks or CDROMs supplied by the ISP

Portal: a website that serves as an 'entry point' to the World Wide Web. Portals usually offer guidance on using the Internet and 'search engines' that permit keyword searches

TCP/IP: the language protocol which enables different machines using different operating languages to communicate with each other

Website: a www file that contains text, pictures and/or sound

sector by itself to be one of the top 20 economies in the world, ranked almost equal to the entire GDP of Switzerland. Another observation which can be drawn from these data is that, although the World Wide Web was only launched in the mid-1990s, in terms of total market size, the Internet is already rivalling well-established sectors such as energy, cars and telecommunications.

Another source of evidence of the apparent potential of the Internet and e-commerce was demonstrated by a study undertaken by the Boston Consulting Group.[2] They concluded that by the end of 1999, revenues to US retailers marketing goods on-line would exceed $36 billion and, furthermore, during the next 12 months their projected growth rate for this sector of retailing was 145 per cent. Interestingly this research demonstrated that it is not the pure Internet outlets like Amazon.com who are enjoying the real benefits of the Internet. This is because 62 per cent of all revenues are earned by traditional retailers who have added a website to their existing shop-based operations. One reason for this situation is that it is much cheaper for a multi-channel retailer to attract web customers than the costs facing the pure on-line only only operations (i.e. $22 per customer for the former versus $42 for the latter).

The remainder of this chapter explores the range of on-line marketing activities, the forms of e-commerce, the context of on-line marketing, the benefits of on-line marketing to consumers and businesses, how to assess the competencies needed for on-line success, the competitive advantages of on-line marketing and the design of an e-commerce marketing mix.

More than just a website

Although in the popular press, emphasis tends to be given to the World Wide Web, it is critical for organizations to recognize that exploiting this new technology goes way beyond just putting a brochure on-line. Essentially what is happening on a global basis is that technologies such as tele-communications, satellite broadcasting, digital television and IT are on a convergence path through which the world is being offered a more flexible, more rapid and extremely low-cost way of exchanging information. Hence when discussing this new technology, it is safer not to restrict any assessment of opportunity to the role of the Internet. Instead the debate should be expanded to cover all aspects of information interchange. This is increasingly being recognized by organizations who are moving to exploit the huge diversity of opportunities now offered by on-line marketing. It should also be recognized that before the advent of the World Wide Web organizations had been conducting business electronically for decades. For example, many large firms have been using a technology known as **_electronic data interchange_** (EDI) to manage

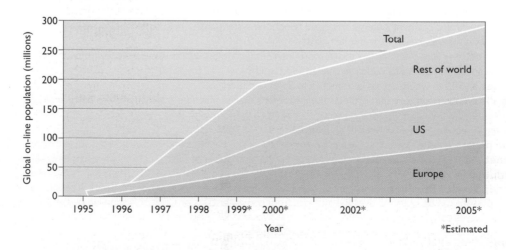

Figure 14.1 Growth of the global on-line populations.

Source: Financial Times Survey: Information Technology, 7 April 2000

Technology is changing the way we communicate as this advertisement for Philips illustrates

their relationships with both suppliers and customers.

Marketers should extend their thinking beyond the Internet to encompass all of the platforms which permit a firm to do business electronically.[3] **E-commerce** involves applying a wide range of technologies to streamline business interactions. Examples of these technologies include the Internet, EDI, e-mail, electronic payment systems, advanced telephone systems, hand-held digital appliances, interactive televisions, self-service kiosks and smart cards. e-Marketing 14.1 discusses how Wal-Mart have used e-commerce to gain competitive advantage.

Once a company decides to embrace e-commerce as a path through which to exploit new, entrepreneurial opportunities, then an immediate outcome is that the organization's knowledge platform becomes much more closely linked with other knowledge sources elsewhere within the market system such as suppliers and customers. The reason why this occurs is that once buyers and sellers become electronically linked, the volumes of data interchange dramati-

cally increase as trading activities begin to occur in real-time. The outcome is the emergence of very dynamic, rapid responses by both customer and supplier to changing circumstances within their market system.

The degree to which e-commerce is likely to change the way organizations operate in the future is effectively illustrated by Arthur Anderson's 1999 research project on e-commerce trends in Europe.[4] From this study the consulting firm have proposed the following 'five basic truths':

1 *Vertical disintegration*
   In the past, firms have sought to be self reliant by maximizing their ownership of aspects of their role within their supply chain (e.g. IT departments, logistics fleets and warehouses). The speed with which information and decisions can now be made using e-commerce means that in many cases costs can be saved and flexibility of response enhanced by collaborating with outsiders.

14.1 e-Marketing

Early Entry into E-Commerce

In 1980 Wal-Mart was a small niche retailer based in the southern states of the USA, yet within 10 years the company became the largest and most profitable retailer in the world. The fundamental competence driving this success was its early entry into exploiting Information Technology to develop its 'cross-docking' technique of inventory management. This is a computer-based just-in-time system which keeps inventory on the move through the value chain. Goods are continuously delivered to its warehouses, almost instantaneously picked for reshipment, repacked and forwarded to stores. The result is that Wal-Mart can run 85 per cent of goods through its own warehouse system and purchase full truckloads from suppliers to the extent that it achieves a 3 per cent inventory handling cost advantage that supports the funding of everyday low prices.

The system took years to evolve and is based around investing in the latest available technology. The company, for example, developed a satellite-based EDI system using a private satcom system that sends daily point-of-sale data to 4000 suppliers. The firm also worked with Procter & Gamble to develop their 'Efficient Consumer Response', an integrated, computer-based system which provides the bench-mark against the firm's entire supply chain operations. Finally, in order to ensure employees have access to critical information, store and aisle managers are provided with detailed information of customer buying patterns and a video link to permit stores to share success stories.

2 *The vale of intangibles*

In the past firms measured success by the value of their physical assets such as land and buildings. Although the financial markets have always recognized that intangibles such as company reputation and brand names had value, analysts have tended to use the fixed assets in the balance sheet to value firms. In a rapidly changing world, however, physical assets can be a barrier to rapidly restructuring a firm and/or adopting a different, more flexible response to emerging new market opportunities. As a result there is growing support that the real value of the firm in the next millennium will be based on the knowledge resources and technological skills contained within the organization.

3 *Increasing returns*

In traditional manufacturing industries to expand the business usually requires additional investment to build new production capacity. The world of knowledge follows a very different path. For, as demonstrated by the world of computer software, once the initial investment in product development has been made, ongoing costs to support market expansion are almost zero. All you have to do is take some money out of petty cash, and copy some more CD-ROMs from your master disk.

4 *Perfect information*

Economists often talk about their theory of perfect information in which price equilibrium is rapidly achieved because both customers and suppliers have total knowledge of market conditions. Through on-line services that offer price comparisons and on-line auctions, the world of perfect information may now have almost arrived. The outcome will be that suppliers will find it increasingly difficult to retain control over market prices because increasingly this power will move into the hands of the customer.

5 *Instant supply chains*

The ability to link all aspects of business, from ordering materials through to automatically shipping goods to customers, means that the e-commerce supply chain is one where actions will not be delayed because employees are slow to pass information to each other. Those firms, however, that fail to create integrated electronic communication channels and undertake some actions off-line (e.g. manually checking customer credit before accepting an order) will soon find they are being overtaken by competitors who have realized the necessity of offering instant response to the customer.

Forms of e-commerce

The extent of e-commerce is borne out by the fact that all possible combinations of exchange between consumers and business organizations take place (see Fig. 14.2). Business-to-business exchanges take place through the use of EDI interchanges and companies such as Cisco have transferred nearly all of their purchases to the Internet. This is probably the largest form of e-commerce at present.

The most apparent form of e-commerce is from business-to-consumer with established retailers such as Tesco setting up home shopping facilities, and relatively newcomers such as Amazon building a book-selling operation via the Internet. As consumers become accustomed to trading electronically this form of e-commerce is forecast to escalate.

E-commerce from consumer to business is less common but demonstrates the versatility of the Internet. An example is the facility provided by Priceline.com whereby would-be passengers bid for airline tickets leaving the airlines to decide whether or not to accept these offers.[5]

The Internet also permits consumers to trade with other consumers via auctions (consumer-to-consumer). Would-be sellers can offer products

	From **business**	From **consumer**
To **business**	B2B Cisco	C2B Priceline
To **consumer**	B2C Amazon	C2C eBay

Figure 14.2 Forms of e-commerce

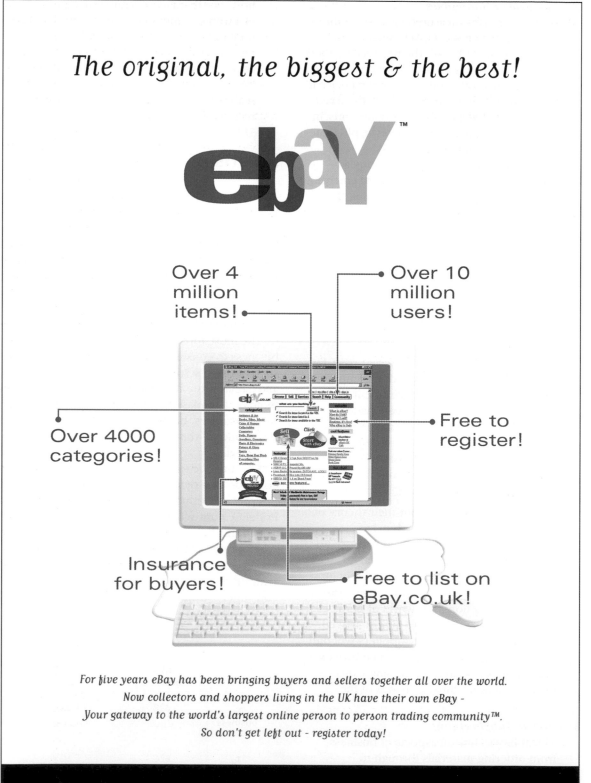

Companies like eBay provide new services for consumers over the Internet

through such sites as eBay or QXL to potential customers. The advertisement for eBay opposite shows the services it provides buyers and sellers.

Putting on-line marketing into context

When managers are first confronted by the Internet, it is not unusual for them to be overwhelmed by both the apparent complexity of the technology and the diversity of alternative pathways through which a firm can enter the world of on-line marketing. O'Connor and Galvin[6] have proposed that e-commerce can take place on four levels; namely:

1 *Publishing* electronic information. This is essentially a one-way process (e.g. putting annual reports and press releases on a company website).

2 *Interaction* where there is active involvement of the user (e.g. customers can contact the Dell website to obtain responses to technical questions).

3 *Transaction* through which the user can purchase goods and services on-line (e.g. the facility offered by the leader in electronic book retailing Amazon.com).

4 *Integration* where participants integrate their computer systems to build stronger trading relationships with each other (e.g. Mobil Oil's extranet that provides global data and automated transaction services to 300 distributors).

Another approach to classifying different forms of e-commerce is shown in Fig. 14.3. This diagram proposes that there are two dimensions of application available to an organization. One is the role of on-line marketing in the provision of information to customers such as price, product availability and delivery terms. The other dimension is the role of on-line marketing in the management of the purchase transaction.

As proposed in Fig. 14.3, the degree to which an organization uses on-line marketing to deliver information and/or support transactions can be classified as high or low. This taxonomy then yields four choices. The organization can opt to have low involvement in both information provision and transaction management. For example, many of the fast moving consumer goods (f.m.c.g.) companies have created somewhat static websites to communicate a limited degree of additional information about their products. Alternatively the organization can restrict the use of the Internet to supporting transactions, but exploit the technology as a major element in the process of communicating with customers. This approach has been taken by a number of firms in the computing industry who have established free on-line magazines.

A third alternative is to use on-line marketing to assist transactions but concurrently only offer a limited amount of on-line information. Typically this scenario will be found in industries where the information provided to customers is extremely complex but the product or service simple to distribute electronically. A number of computer software houses have taken this approach where the primary customer contact point is dialogue with the supplier's technical salesforce. Having determined the appropriateness of the software, the customer then orders on-line and in some cases also takes delivery via an electronic channel. The last option is high involvement in both provision of information and support of the purchase transaction. Examples of the last scenario are provided by on-line retailers such as Amazon.com and eToys.com who only exist in cyberspace because they have no retail outlets that can be visited by their customers.

For the firm only just beginning to evolve an on-line marketing strategy, visiting sites like Dell or American Airlines can be somewhat depressing because clearly a massive investment will need to be made before one can ever aspire to match

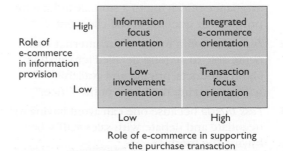

Figure 14.3 shows: High / Role of e-commerce in information provision / Low dimension with quadrants: Information focus orientation, Integrated e-commerce orientation, Low involvement orientation, Transaction focus orientation. Horizontal axis: Low to High — Role of e-commerce in supporting the purchase transaction

Figure 14.3 An e-commerce alternative orientation matrix

these 'e-commerce excellent' organizations. The first, and possibly most critical, point to make, however, is that the organization should not throw away all the experience and marketing knowledge which it has acquired during its operation over the years. The good news is that as we begin to observe on-line marketing in operation, virtually all of the established guidelines about good marketing practice apparently still apply. These have been described as the 'Interactive Rules of the Road'; namely:[7]

1   Technology is merely a facilitator for a marketing strategy that focuses upon customer benefits.

2   The marketer must strive to balance the company's marketing objectives against the customer's needs and preferences.

3   Each technology-based programme should provide multiple benefits to the customer.

The benefits of the Internet and e-commerce

As with all forms of marketing, on-line marketing should be customer-orientated.[8] Organizations should pose the questions of (i) does the Internet change the target or scope of the market, (ii) does the Internet help satisfy customer needs and (iii) will customers use the Internet over the long term? One way of examining these issues is for the organization to examine which of the following benefits can be offered to consumers from involvement in e-commerce:

1   *Convenience* in terms of being able to provide access 24 hours a day, 365 days a year. Furthermore the customer can permit avoidance of driving to a store, searching for products or queuing at the checkout.

2   *Information* in terms of the Internet user being able to acquire detailed information about products, pricing and availability without leaving the home or the office.

3   *Less hassle* because one can avoid having to negotiate and debate with sales staff when buying the product.

4   *Multimedia* which, through exploitation of the latest technology, customers can use to gain a better understanding of their needs by, for example, examining 3-D displays of

car interiors or selecting the best fabric design for a piece of furniture.

5   *New products and services* in areas such as on-line financial services and the ability to mix together audio, music and visual materials to customize the entertainment goods being purchased.

6   *Lower prices* because it is possible to search for the lowest price available for brands. The advertisement for jungle.com opposite describes how this company allows consumers to surf the Internet for the best price.

The Internet also offers the following benefits to companies; namely:

1   *Lower costs* through actions such as replacing retail outlets with an on-line shopping mall or saving on paper by converting a sales catalogue into an electronic form.

2   *Improved distribution* because once information-based products such as magazines or software are made available on-line the company can achieve global distribution without having to invest in obtaining placements in traditional outlets.

3   *Reduced personal selling costs* because the role of the salesperson as a provider of one-to-one information can be replaced with an interactive website.

4   *Relationship building* because, via a website, the firm can acquire data on customers' purchase behaviour that can be used to develop higher levels of customer service.

5   *Customized promotion* because, unlike traditional media such as television or print advertising, the firm can develop communications materials on the website designed to meet the needs of small, specific groups of customers.

6   *Rapid market response* because, having recognized the need to respond to changing market situations (e.g. reaction to a price change by competitors) at virtually the click of a button, the company can rapidly distribute new information to customers via the Internet.

7   *New market opportunities* because e-commerce permits firms, whether they are

large or small, to offer their products or services to any market in the world.

8   *Marketing research* because e-mail surveys provide a low cost method of questioning large samples although the representativeness of the sample needs to be considered as does the acquisition of e-mail lists and the potential resentment that unsolicited e-mail questionnaires can cause. The Internet also provides a rich source of secondary information through websites.

The Internet is a key vehicle for forcing down prices

Thus, having reviewed these potential benefits, the organization is then at the stage where it can begin to determine an entry point into e-commerce. Most organizations will soon realize that the Internet is a technological tool, the use of which will evolve and change as the organization gains experience of trading in cyberspace. McGovern presented this evolving view in terms of 'e-commerce life cycles' in his analysis of how logistics and transportation services providers have implemented their e-commerce strategies.[9] Initially many firms used the technology to provide general information about their firm on a website. This was followed by using on-line marketing as a vehicle to permit customers to access information for tracking their goods throughout each phase of the shipment process. The next evolutionary stage is typically that of offering on-line customized rate quotes. More recently this has been followed by the leading firms permitting customers to use an on-line marketing platform to initiate every phase of the shipment process from order placement through to post-delivery resolution of service delivery problems. e-Marketing 14.2 provides an example of how on-line strategy may evolve.

Assessing on-line competence

For the marketer, on-line marketing primarily offers both a new promotional medium and an alternative channel through which to consummate the product purchase and delivery process. In view of this situation it seems reasonable to propose that success in cyberspace markets will be influenced by the degree to which a firm can develop unique capabilities in the area of exploiting superior technical knowledge and internal organizational routines as the basis for supporting competitive advantage. This perspective leads to the conclusion that on-line marketing provides an important example of how the 'resource-based' view of the firm will provide the basis for determining whether a firm will achieve market success.[10]

Although on-line marketing exhibits some unique technological features, the processes which it supports are not new to the world of marketing. A web page, for example, offers promotional information using the same format as a magazine or a newspaper. The key difference is

14.2 e-Marketing

Evolving an On-line Strategy

A useful example of evolving e-commerce applications is given by PrePRESS Solutions Inc., a $50 million player in the $2.3 billion industry of image-setting manufacturers. When in the late 1980s pre-press publishing capabilities began to migrate to less expensive computer platforms (from minicomputers to desktop systems), PrePRESS augmented its direct salesforce with a catalogue business catering to new buyers looking for lower cost computer hardware and software. When fax-on-demand began to appear in the market, the company adopted this technology to communicate lengthy technical specifications to its customers. Then in April 1995 PrePRESS opened its first commercial website which took the innovative step of carrying both sector and company specific information. Contained within an ever-evolving site are features such as an on-screen newspaper updated daily, the Cafe Moire chat site, a Convention Centre covering major trade shows in the industry, a free reference library, the PrePRESS on-line Superstore and a Print Shop where users can download tips and tools for improving their pre-press processes.

Based on: Cross and Smith (1995)[11]

that the former has the facility to provide much more information and the user if they so desire, can undertake interactive searches for more data. Many websites go beyond communicating a promotional message by also offering the additional feature of permitting the customer to place an order. Here again, processes associated with this activity of product identification, provision of delivery information and payment using a credit card are the same procedures that the customer will have already encountered when ordering goods through direct marketing. By drawing upon the resource-based view of the firm it seems reasonable to propose that successful implementation of an on-line marketing plan will be critically dependent upon the firm having appropriate competencies for managing strategy, finance management and operations. These are shown in Fig. 14.4.

Strategic competence

The long-term survival of all organizations is critically dependent upon their ability to both identify new market trends and to determine how the internal capabilities of the organization can be used to exploit emerging opportunities. In the case of on-line marketing Ghosh has proposed that the following four distinct strategic marketing opportunities exist:[12]

1 Establishing a direct link with customers (or others with whom the firm has an important relationship) to complete transactions or exchange trade information more easily (e.g. Staples, the office superstore chain, selling supplies on-line to large corporate customers).

2 Utilizing the technology to bypass others within a value chain (e.g. on-line retailers such as the bookstore Amazon.com).

3 Developing and delivering new products and services (e.g. the on-line share trading system developed by Charles Schwab in the USA).

4 Becoming a dominant player in the electronic channel of a specific industry by creating and setting new business rules (e.g. Dell Computers' dominance in the electronic direct selling of computers to large corporate customers).

Financial competence

To be successful it is critical that the organization has the financial resources required to fund the level of investment which is needed to support any new marketing strategy. To those lacking in Internet trading experience, initial examination would tend to indicate that creation of a website is an extremely low-cost proposition. All that seems to be needed is to register a domain name

Figure 14.4 Assessing on-line competences

and to then use low-cost software from suppliers such as Microsoft to construct the organization's web pages. This observation is correct if the marketer merely wants to use the Internet to launch a static brochure into cyberspace. Unfortunately, if the website is also required to attract visitors and generate sales, a much larger scale investment will be required to (i) establish the hardware/software systems that can provide instant response to the diversity of demands which will be placed on the site by potential customers, (ii) create the capability to up-date the site on almost a daily basis in order to sustain customer interest and (iii) ensure integration of the firm's internal information management systems such that customers receive a seamless service from the point of initial enquiry through to final delivery of purchase products.[13]

Moreover, once the firm has made the investment to establish an effective Internet operation, there still remains the problem of sustaining visits to the site by both new and existing customers. Merely being able to appear high on the list of sites identified by a customer using a search engine such as Yahoo! or Alta Vista is not sufficient. For most marketing propositions, the only way to generate a high level of site visitors is to continually invest in building customer awareness through expending funds on traditional promotional vehicles such as advertising, public relations and sales promotions.[14]

Innovation

To prosper and grow all organizations need to continually engage in finding new ways of improving their products and process technologies. Unfortunately for the e-marketer, at the 'click of a button' your competitors can rapidly gain an in-depth understanding of your operation. As graphically illustrated by the war which has broken out between Amazon.com and new market entries from the traditional retail book trade such as Barnes & Noble and W. H. Smiths, having analysed a firm's web operation, a very likely response is that competitors will offer similar services and use heavy promotional spending and/or deep price cuts to steal your customers. Thus, to prosper and grow in cyberspace the e-marketer will need to continually engage in finding new ways of improving e-commerce products and process technologies.

Workforce

In most on-line markets, because all firms understand the nature of customer needs and internal operations utilize very similar computer technologies, it is often extremely difficult to achieve a long-term sustainable advantage over competition. Two variables which are clearly critical influencers of customer satisfaction are (i) the speed and accuracy of service delivery and (ii) sustaining the technical reliability of all on-line systems. The importance of these variables does mean that the e-marketer will need to ensure that the human resource management (HRM) practices within their organization are focused on continually investing in upgrading employee skills in order that all staff are capable of fulfilling their job roles to a standard that exceeds that which is achieved by competition. Furthermore, the e-marketer should seek to understand what causes certain employees to consistently achieve high performance standards within the organization and then determine how effective management of these factors can contribute to sustaining a market lead over competition.

Appropriate HRM practices for achieving optimal workforce performance of back-office staff will usually be based around the same principles that are to be found in any type of organization. At the moment, the greatest HRM problem facing the e-commerce industry is the recruitment, retention and ongoing skills development of the technical staff responsible for the development and operation of e-commerce systems. Even in Silicon Valley, California, the greatest constraint facing firms wishing to gain competitive advantage in their Internet operations is the availability of computer staff with knowledge of the latest advances in network systems operations, telecommunications and programming.[15]

Quality

Correction-based quality is founded on what is now considered to be an outmoded concept; namely waiting until something goes wrong and then initiating remedial work to correct the fault. By moving to prevention quality, the organization develops processes that minimize the occurrence of the mistakes that have been causing the defects to occur.[16] One outcome of the efforts by the large multinational firms to improve service quality is that customers now have much higher expectations of their suppliers and, furthermore, are willing to proactively seek out alternative suppliers.

In relation to the management of quality, on-line marketing can be treated as a service business. As with any service business, customer loyalty is critically dependent upon the actions of the supplier being able to totally fulfil the expectations of the customer. The critical variables influencing whether the customer perceives that expectations are being met include reliability, tangibles, responsiveness, assurance and empathy.[17]

In many service encounters, the customer is forced to accept some degree of supplier failing and continue to patronize the same service source because the supplier is the most conveniently placed (e.g. the businessperson who frequents a somewhat poor hotel because it is located next to a customer's office; the consumer who uses a local store because the nearest supermarket is some miles away). It is important, however, that the on-line marketer recognizes that the 'loyalty due to convenience' scenario will rarely apply to customers purchasing in cyberspace. For example, if the website visited fails to fulfil expectations, then at the click of a button the potential customer can instantaneously travel to a new location offering a higher level of service quality.[18] Amazon is a good example of how service quality can be achieved on-line as e-Marketing 14.3 discusses.

Productivity

Productivity is usually measured in terms of level of value-added activities per employee and/or per number of hours worked. By increasing productivity in terms of value-added/employee or per hours of labour input, the firm can expect to enjoy an increase in profitability.[19] Given the major influence of productivity on organizational performance, it is very clear that this is an area of internal competence that will have significant influence on any marketing plan. In relation to on-line marketing, possibly the two most important elements of the productivity equation are customer interface productivity and logistics productivity. In the case of customer interface productivity, this can usually be improved by ensuring that through investment in the latest computer technologies, virtually all aspects of customer need from product enquiry through to ordering can occur without any human intervention by supplier employees. Additionally, however, where human support is needed, this must be delivered by highly trained support staff aided with the latest on-line customer assistance tools in order to sustain the productivity of the interface. Then once an order is placed, employee productivity of back-office staff involved in order processing, order assembly and product delivery must be of the highest level. e-Marketing 14.4 shows how high levels of productivity are achieved by the Dell Corporation.

14.3   e-Marketing

On-line Service

Possibly one of the most effective examples of what can be achieved in terms of service quality is provided by the on-line bookstore Amazon.com. Gaining access to the site is extremely fast, the user is presented with search engines, book reviews, a 'shopping trolley' for purchases, a purchase decision review screen summarizing the cost of items in the trolley and a wide variety of delivery alternatives. Then once the order is placed, Amazon.com automatically confirm the order by e-mail, permit on-line checking of delivery status on-line and some weeks after the purchase, based upon the books purchased by the customer, e-mail suggestions of other titles which may be of interest.

Information systems

For those firms which decide the Internet can provide the primary channel through which to attract new customers and retain the loyalty of existing customers, poorly integrated information systems are not an acceptable option. Success can only occur if all data flows are integrated, and to stay ahead of the competition continuous investment must be made in further upgrading and enhancing the company information systems. Hence information management competence is clearly critical if a firm is seeking to base its brand differentiation on the Internet around offering on-line services superior to those delivered by the competition. e-Marketing 14.5 discusses the role of information systems at Marshall Industries.

Competitive on-line advantage and strategy

Marketers have long accepted that success demands identification of some form of *competitive advantage* capable of distinguishing the organizations from other firms operating in the same market sector. The unique characteristics of the Internet offer some opportunities to establish new forms of competitive advantage. These include lower costs and prices, instant response, improved service quality, greater product variety and product customization. The secret of the success of most e-commerce operations is that they have exploited one or more of these characteristics as a strategy through which to deliver a purchase proposition superior to that available from their off-line competitors. The advertisement for CompuServe overleaf shows how it is creating a competitive advantage through superior service quality to its on-line customers.

Lower costs and prices

In relation to the issue of lower costs, the Internet permits suppliers to make contact with customers without using an intermediary. The savings generated by the removal of the intermediary from the transaction can be passed onto the customer in the form of lower prices. An example of this form of competitive advantage is provided by the UK airline easyJet. This firm established some years ago and is now the country's leading 'no-frills'/low-price airline. Similar to operators in the USA, the company uses smaller regional airports and limits the scale of ground and in-flight services offered to customers. The advent of the Internet has permitted the company to create an automated, on-line flight enquiry, booking service and ticket assurance system. Since opening this facility, total flight bookings have risen dramatically, and it is

14.4 e-Marketing

E-Commerce Productivity

An excellent example of e-commerce productivity is provided by Dell Corporation, the world's largest computer direct marketing operation. Customers visiting the Dell website are provided not just with an effective ordering system, but in addition a multitude of tools for answering technical questions and for configuring their own personalized computer design. If customers hit a problem, by the click of a button they will be put in telephone contact with a highly trained Dell service employee who can offer an appropriate solution. Once an order is placed, the Dell automated procurement, manufacturing and distribution system then ensures that logistics productivity is at a standard that is the envy of their competition.

expected that in the near future the system will overtake the existing tele-sales operation in terms of servicing customer transaction needs.

The real-time interactive information exchange capability of the Internet provides a potential competitive advantage in those market sectors where the customer wishes to minimize the time taken to plan and implement a purchase. One market sector where this scenario applies is the travel industry. Many people would prefer to avoid the time it takes to visit a railway station or travel agent when planning their trip or purchasing tickets. In the case of rail travel in the UK, the website www.thetrainline.com offers an on-line timetable from which to select the most convenient travel time and having reached this

decision, the customer can immediately purchase tickets which are then mailed to their home. A similar facility in the case of airline travel is available at the UK website www.lastminute. com.

Improved service quality

In most service markets it is almost impossible to offer a product proposition which is very different from the competition. As a result one of the few ways of gaining a competitive advantage is through being able to deliver a superior level of customer service. A key influencer of service quality is the speed of information interchange

14.5   e-Marketing

On-line Information Systems

Marshall Industries is the fourth largest distributor of electronic components and production supplies in the USA. The company distributes 125 000 products manufactured by over 100 suppliers through 38 distribution branches in North America and Europe. In 1994 the firm began to implement their on-line marketing strategy of becoming a superior knowledge provider by creating an on-line browser that provided customers with a 24-hour, automated, order fulfilment process system. This system was complemented by an EDI automatic replenishment channel for large customers plus a fax and telephone-based order entry system. The following year, the company launched an object-relational database which provides customers with a dynamic picture of the products which Marshall Industries can supply. Behind the system is a database containing information on almost 200 000 parts, over 100 000 data sheets and a real-time inventory system. The site allows the customer to order parts and request samples. To assist customers track the progress of their orders, Marshall has linked their system with that of their logistics partner, United Parcels.

The system offers an extensive range of additional knowledge provision services. RealAudio broadcasts news about the electronics industry. Visitors can also talk to Marshall engineers on-line 24 hours of the day to obtain assistance in the selection of products, troubleshooting problems and product design. The NetSeminar element of the system links together customers and suppliers to assist in the design of new products. It also offers after-sales training on new technologies. From a studio in El Monte, the firm broadcasts product information in real-time video and audio streams. Viewers and listeners can post questions to the presenters of these programmes using a GlobalChat system.

Based on: Young et al. (1997)[20]

Got to get some information. Got to get it fast. OK. Go to the net, log on... eventually. OK, find search engine thingy, and type in "Retail Trends", and off it goes. Press "Print" without thinking. Ooops. Place is disappearing under mountain of paper, because stupid thing has found 314,000 pages. THREE HUNDRED AND FOURTEEN THOUSAND PAGES!! What's the use of that? Needles. Haystacks. Arrrgh. And still haven't

got the information I need.

We all know where the Internet goes wrong. You want to find something specific, and back comes a billion bits of information. Not with CompuServe.

With our Infofast service, you brief professional researchers and they do the searching, and – more importantly – the sifting and analysis, for you. It's just like having your own private research company with their own sources.

And yet this is just one small part of the CompuServe story. Our online Travel Agent does everything a high street one does, only without the queuing.

For people who just don't have enough time, the myriad of time saving features on CompuServe is like the answer to a prayer.

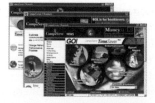

CompuServe.

FIND YOURSELF SOME TIME. CALL 0800 923 0100

CompuServe differentiates itself in the marketplace to gain competitive advantage between the supplier and the customer. Clearly, therefore, the information interchange capability of the Internet offers some interesting opportunities to be perceived as superior to other firms in the same market. For many years, Federal Express has been a global leader in the application of IT to provide a superior level of customized delivery services to major corporate customers. The firm has enhanced its original customer-service software system COSMOS by providing major clients with terminals and software which use the Internet to take them into the Federal logistics management system. In effect Federal Express now offers customers the ability to create a state-of-the-art distribution system without having to make any investment in self-development of shipping expertise inside their own firms (www.fedex.com).

Greater product variety

The average high street retail shop is physically restricted in terms of the amount of space which is available to display goods. Hence its customers, who may have already faced the inconvenience of having to travel to the retailer's location, may encounter the frustration of finding that the shop does not carry the item which they wish to purchase. On-line retailers do not face the same space restrictions of their 'bricks and mortar' competitors. As a result, they can use their website to offer a much greater variety of goods to potential customers. Possibly one of the best-known examples of a firm which exploited this source of competitive advantage is the on-line bookseller Amazon.com.

Product customization

Over the last 20 years, many manufacturers have come to realize that adoption of just-in-time (JIT) production can offer the potential to customize products to meet the needs of individual customers. For example, Dell, the computer giant, exploited JIT to assist it to build a product to meet the specific needs of each customer. One obstacle which exists in implementation of a product customization strategy, however, is the volume of information interchange that may be required between the customer and supplier during the design, selection and pricing phases of the

purchase transaction. The arrival of the Internet has removed this obstacle because, having created a website, the supplier is in a position to offer the customer an almost infinite amount of information. Dell's existing extensive experience of computer direct marketing permitted them to be a 'first mover' in exploiting the Internet as part of its strategy to offer customized products. Customers who visit the Dell website are offered assistance in selecting the type of technology most suited to their needs. These data provide the inputs to an on-line help system which guides the customer through the process of evolving the most appropriate specification from a range of choices. Once a final selection is made, the customer receives an instant quote on both the price of their purchase and the date upon which it will be delivered.

A key factor influencing the ability of firms to exploit the Internet as part of a product customization strategy has been the increasing availability of lower cost computer hardware and very affordable, powerful software tools. This has had the effect of rapidly driving down the cost of analysing the huge amounts of data that are generated by customers visiting websites. This trend has sparked off a new concept in market research which is known as '***data warehousing***' or 'data mining'. Baker and Baker have proposed that this new approach should be based upon exploiting information provided by customers to:

> Classify customers into distinct groups based upon their purchase behaviour.
> Model relationships between possible variables such as age, income, location to determine which of these influence purchase decisions.
> Cluster data into finite clusters that define specific customer types.
> Use this knowledge to tailor products and other aspects of the marketing mix such as promotional message or price to meet the specific needs of individual customers.[21]

Customers' use of the Internet in both business-to-business and consumer goods markets means that e-commerce firms can use data warehousing to gain in-depth insights into the behaviour of their customers. As a result, mass customization has become a practical reality for firms that in the past were positioned as mass marketers. The reason for this situation is that when customers start surfing the Internet they are asked to provide detailed information to potential suppliers. One can link together information on what pages they visit, data provided to questions asked as they register to be considered as customers, their e-mail address and data from their credit card. In commenting on this new world, Jeffrey Bezos, the founder of Amazon.com, has used the analogy that the e-commerce retailer can behave like the small-town shopkeeper of yesteryear because large firms can also now develop a deep understanding of everybody who comes into the on-line store. Armed with such in-depth knowledge, like the shopkeeper in a village store, the large retailer can personalize service to suit the specific needs of every individual customer across a widely dispersed geographic domain.

As with the mass customization opportunities available to large firms, the Internet also permits small firms to become involved in the practice of one-to-one marketing. The outcome is that niche marketers now find it feasible to operate as 'micro-nichers', customizing products to meet individual customer needs. Acumin, for example, is a web-based vitamin company that blends vitamins, herbs and minerals according to the specific instruction of the customer. New York's CDucTIVE offers customers the facility of designing their own CDs on-line containing their favourite mix of music tracks.

Selecting an e-commerce marketing mix

Selecting an *e-commerce marketing mix* will usually involve applying established marketing management principles as the basis for defining how electronic technologies are to be integrated into a firm's existing operations. In many organizations, e-commerce marketing mix proposals will be based around enhancing existing off-line activities by utilizing the Internet to provide new sources of information, customer–supplier interaction and/or alternative purchase transaction channels.

In view of this situation, it seems logical to propose that the selection of an e-commerce marketing mix will involve processes similar to those utilized in conventional, off-line marketing planning activities. The areas which need to be examined are illustrated in Fig. 14.5.

Marketing audit and SWOT analysis

Within the marketing audit there should be coverage of the strategic situation facing the organization. This will be based on a description of e-market size, e-market growth trends, e-customer benefit requirements, utilization of the marketing mix to satisfy e-customer needs, e-commerce activity of key competitors and the potential influence of changes in any of the variables which constitute the core and macro-environmental elements of the e-market system. This review should include analysis of whether the firm is merely going to service end user market needs or will concurrently seek to integrate e-commerce systems with those of key suppliers.

The internal e-capabilities of the organization are reviewed within the context of whether they represent strengths or weaknesses which might influence future performance. One of the key issues will be that of whether staff have appropriate e-commerce operational skills, whether new staff will need to be recruited or aspects of the project outsourced to specialist e-commerce service providers. Another issue is the degree to which existing databases can be integrated into a new e-commerce system on either a real-time or batch processing basis.

E-market circumstances are assessed in relation to whether these represent opportunities or threats. Consideration will need to be given to whether the move is proactive or a reactive response to initiatives already implemented by competition. Other issues to be examined include (i) the degree to which existing markets will be served through e-commerce and (ii) whether e-commerce will be used to support entry into new markets. Combining the external and internal market analysis will permit execution of the SWOT analysis. The SWOT, when linked with the situation review, will provide the basis for defining which key issues will need to be managed in order to develop an effective e-commerce plan for the future.

Marketing objectives and strategy

The degree to which e-commerce marketing objectives will be defined can vary tremendously. Some organizations will merely restrict aims to increasing the effectiveness of their promotional activities. Others may specify overall forecasted e-sales and desired e-market share targets. Some organizations may extend this statement by breaking the market into specific e-market target segments, detailed aims for e-sales, e-expenditure and e-profits for each product and/or e-market sector. The e-marketing core strategy will define how, by positioning the company in a specific way, stated marketing objectives will be achieved.

E-commerce marketing mix

Marketing mix considerations will need to be extended to cover how each element within the e-commerce mix (product, price, promotion and distribution) will be utilized to support the specified strategy.

Product and pricing

This will be necessary to determine whether the e-commerce offering provides an opportunity for product enhancement. Such opportunities include improving customer service, and broadening the product line. As far as pricing is concerned, thought must be given to whether off-line and on-line prices will be different and the potential implications of any price variance for existing off-line customers. When the move to e-commerce involves new distribution costs consideration should be given to delivery charges.

For example, Tesco impose a delivery charge for their home shopping service.

Promotion

Given the important role of the Internet in making information available to customers, the first issue to be addressed when considering promotional mix decisions is the design of a company's website. Some large companies will decide this is an activity over which they wish to retain absolute control. In this situation the firm will hire a team of employees to manage the website creation process. Other large firms may decide that it will be faster and more effective to contract the design process to an external supplier such as a major consulting firm, a 'blue chip' computer company such as IBM or an Internet specialist such as the organization Agency.com. Although the latter approach of hiring specialist advisers will reduce the time to evolve and execute an e-commerce strategy, it is an expensive solution where the client can expect to pay as much as £10–15 million before the project is completed.

For smaller firms there is also a range of options for the creation of a website. One approach is to use a website authoring package. One of the more expensive, but highly popular authoring software packages, is Drumbeat 2000 produced by Macromedia (www.macromedia.com). This product, as well as containing a plethora of design options, also has features such as a shopping-cart function,

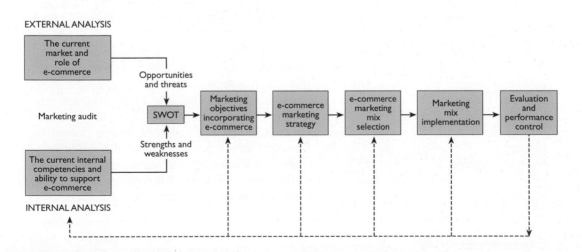

Figure 14.5 The e-commerce marketing mix selection

secure credit card transactions and an integrated database system. One major advantage of this package is that all programming can be done visually which means the user does not have to have extensive prior experience in Internet programming languages.

For those firms which do not feel able to operate their own Internet operation, the alternative is to join an existing website which acts as host for a number of organizations. These hosting services usually provide a host of basic website templates to suit different types of business. The firm is provided with software by the hosting service which permits them to customize a template to develop their own visual identity. An example of a hosting service is mindspring.com (www.mindspring.com). The company provides software for a firm to build a product catalogue and storefront which is then featured on the mindspring site. A similar service is available from www.stumpworld.com. This company offers an on-line shopping mall facility. The cost of being featured on the site is a monthly fee plus the payment of a 15 per cent commission on sales.

The scale of an e-commerce promotional plan will be strongly influenced by the degree to which a company already has a strong off-line market presence. Thus, for example, when Tesco, the largest UK supermarket chain, began to offer an on-line grocery purchasing service, the launch promotional campaign was quite simple. As the company already has strong brand recognition in the market, the main aim of their promotional activity was to register awareness for their website address. This was achieved by using traditional channels such as some television advertising, mail shots to Tesco loyalty card holders and in-store merchandising displays. e-Marketing 14.6 describes how the Internet is used to advertise services.

Promotional planning for an e-commerce start-up is more difficult because the company has the dual task of (i) communicating the benefits of using the firm's on-line facilities and (ii) registering awareness for their website

14.6 e-Marketing

Using the Internet to Promote Services

One of the critical aspects for an organization establishing an Internet presence is to find a way of attracting customers to the site. Part of the solution is to communicate the service using traditional promotional media such as television and magazine advertising. The advertisement for Planet Kids opposite is an example of this. The other alternative is to use the Internet itself as a media channel.

In the USA, the financial services sector is extremely keen to achieve wide communication of their on-line product portfolios. The leading on-line browser services can offer companies access to millions of customers who are surfing the net. Firms such as America Online (AOL) fully recognize that their knowledge of Internet visitors has massive commercial value and have exploited this by selling advertising space on their sites. In 1998, E*trade, a leading on-line share brokerage firm, agreed to pay $12.5 million per year to be displayed on AOL's personal finance channel. In November of the same year, Bank One, the fifth-largest bank in America, paid what is said to be a fee in the region of $125 million to Excite in return for exclusive rights to market its products and services on the Excite home page at www.excite.com. This action followed on from earlier announcements that the bank had agreed to a $90 million advertising commitment with Microsoft's MSN website.

Based on: Hennington (1999)[22]

Internet companies still use traditional media (in this case newspapers) to communicate to consumers

address. Although there appears to be little solid data on the scale of the required promotional spending required for a successful e-commerce launch, the Boston Consulting Group have estimated that in the consumer goods markets, the expenditure will have to at least double that required to build website awareness for a company which already has a well-established off-line operation. Evidence is now growing that it is this need for massive promotional expenditure which represents the largest aspect of risk in the launch of a new e-commerce business. A tragic example of the scale of risk is the attempt by the UK firm boo.com to launch a global on-line sports clothing business. Well over £75 million was invested in the creation and launch of the new business. Unfortunately revenue inflows from sales were much lower than expected and the outcome was that in May 2000, boo.com went into receivership and were taken over by fashion-mall.com.

Distribution

The advent of e-commerce is causing many firms to reassess their approach to utilizing distribution systems to acquire and sustain competitive advantage. One approach to determining an optimal mix decision when selecting an e-commerce distribution channel is to assume that there are two critical dimensions influencing the decision: whether to retain control or delegate responsibility for transaction management and logistics management.

An example of an e-commerce market where the supplier tends to manage all aspects of the distribution management function is the financial services sector. On-line banks usually wish to retain absolute control over both the transaction and delivery processes. The alternative of the e-commerce transaction being delegated, but delivery responsibility retained, can be found in the airline industry. Many of the airlines use on-line service providers such as www.cheap-flights.co.uk to act as retailers of their unsold seat capacity.

Possibly the most frequently encountered e-commerce distribution model is that of retaining control over transactions and delegation of distribution. It is the standard model that is in use among most on-line tangible goods retailers. These organizations, having successfully sold a product to a website visitor, will use the global distribution capabilities of organizations such as FedEx or UPS to manage all aspects of distribution logistics.

In the majority of off-line consumer goods markets, the commonest distribution model is to delegate both transaction and logistics processes (e.g. major brands such as Coca-Cola being marketed via supermarket chains). This can be contrasted with the on-line world where absolute delegation of all processes is a somewhat rarer event. The reason for this situation is that many firms, having decided that e-commerce offers an opportunity for revising distribution management practices, perceive cyberspace as a way to regain control over transactions by cutting out intermediaries and selling direct to their end-user customers. This process, in which traditional intermediaries may be squeezed out of channels, is usually referred to as 'disintermediation'. Hence for those firms engaged in assessing e-commerce distribution aspects of their marketing mix, there is the need to recognize that the technology has the following implications:

1 Distance ceases to be a cost influencer because on-line delivery of information is substantially the same no matter what the destination of the delivery.

2 Business location becomes an irrelevance because the e-commerce corporation can be based anywhere in the world.

3 The technology permits continuous trading, 24 hours a day, 365 days a year.

A characteristic of off-line distribution channels is the difficulty that smaller firms face in persuading intermediaries (e.g. supermarket chains) to stock their goods. This scenario is less applicable in the world of e-commerce. Firms of any size face a relatively easy task in establishing an on-line presence. Market coverage can then be extended by developing trading alliances based upon offering to pay commission to other on-line traders who attract new customers to the company's website. This ease of entry variable will reduce the occurrence of firms' marketing effort being frustrated because they are unable to gain the support of intermediaries in traditional distribution channels. Eventually e-commerce may lead to a major increase in the total number of firms offering goods and services across world markets. As this occurs, markets will become more efficient, many products will be perceived as commodities with the consequent outcome that average prices will decline.

Marketing mix implementation

Once all the issues associated with the e-commerce marketing mix selection have been resolved, these variables will provide the basis for specifying the technological infrastructure that will be needed to support the planned e-commerce operation. In some cases the firm will decide to manage all of these matters in-house but in other cases the firm may outsource a major proportion of their e-commerce operations to specialist subcontractors.

An action plan is needed in order that all employees can be provided with detailed descriptions of all actions to be taken to manage the e-marketing mix. This plan will include timings and definition of which specific individual(s)/department(s) are responsible for managing the marketing mix. Financial forecasts provide a detailed breakdown of e-revenue, cost of e-goods, all e-expenditures and resultant e-profits.

Evaluation and performance control

Evaluation and control systems need to be created which permit management to rapidly identify variance of actual performance versus forecast for all aspects of the marketing mix. Management also will require mechanisms that generate diagnostic guidance on the cause of any variance. To achieve this aim, the control system should focus on measurement of key variables within the plan such as targeted e-market share, e-customer attitudes, awareness objectives for e-promotion, e-market distribution targets by product and expected versus actual behaviour of competition.

This section has discussed the key issues in planning an on-line presence. As markets change even established players such as Reuters need to consider their on-line strategy as e-marketing 14.7 explains.

Ethical issues in Internet and on-line marketing

The growth of internet and on-line marketing has had many beneficial effects such as increasing customer choice and convenience, and allowing smaller companies access to global markets. However, there are concerns about intrusions on privacy and social exclusion.

Intrusions on privacy

Some Internet users are very wary about on-line shopping because of the information provided about them by cookies. These are tiny computer files that a marketer can download onto the computer of on-line shoppers who visit the marketer's website to record their visits. Cookies serve many useful functions. They remember users' password so that they do not have to log on each time they revisit a site; they remember users' preferences so they can be provided with the right pages or data; and they remember the contents of consumers' shopping baskets from one visit to the next. However, because they can provide a record of users' movements around the web, cookies can give very detailed pictures of people's interests and circumstances.[23] For example, cookies contain information provided by visitors such as product preferences, personal data and financial information, including credit card numbers.[24] From a marketer's point of view, cookies allow customized and personalized content for on-line shoppers. However, most Internet users probably do not know this information is being collected and would object if they knew. (Incidentally, on-line users can check if their drive contains cookies by opening any file named 'cookies'.) Some people fear that companies will use this information to build psychographic profiles that enable them to influence a customer's behaviour. Others simply object that information about them is being held without their express permission. Although users are identified by a code number rather than a name and address (and therefore do not violate the EU data protection objective), the fear is that direct marketing databases will be combined with information on on-line shopping behaviour to create a vast new way of peering into people's private lives.

Social exclusion

Another ethical consideration is the fear that the Internet excludes the poorest members of society from partaking of the benefits of on-line shopping since they cannot accord a computer and the associated charges.[25] For example, Prudential, the financial services company, has faced strong criticism for the way Egg, its high-interest savings bank, cut itself off from mainstream customers by offering Internet-only access, thereby creating a system that ensures it attracts only its wealthiest customers. Some utility companies, also, may be discriminating against low-income groups by offering cut-price energy only over the Internet.[26] However, as computer prices fall and more and more service providers offer free access and low telephone charges, this situation may improve.

14.7   e-Marketing

Planning an On-line Presence at Reuters

Founded 150 years ago, Reuters has spent most of its life as a news agency. Twenty years ago the company moved into the financial services market supplying information to over 60 000 companies around the world. The company has retained a major market share of the $6 billion financial information market (Anon, 2000). One emerging problem is that the big brokerage houses are under pressure as their profit margins fall in the face of competition from on-line brokers. Another, possibly even greater, threat is that the Internet is opening up new channels of information. In the past sellers of real-time information such as the New York Stock Exchange needed to go through an intermediary such as Reuters to reach the final buyers of information. Now information suppliers can use low-cost, e-commerce systems to communicate directly with end-user markets.

One possible solution for Reuters, in the face of potential Internet disintermediation, is to move from being a wholesaler to becoming a retailer of information. In the past the company sold information to hundreds of thousands of customers using dedicated telephone lines. The Internet offers the potential to sell to millions of potential users. Reuters.com could become a financial portal to a whole range of retail investors. Concurrently, however, the company will need to invest almost $500 million in converging its proprietary data distribution system into an operation which is compatible with Internet communication protocols. however, one risk facing Reuters is that by moving into the retail information business, this may cannibalize revenues generated from the existing wholesale financial market information system.

The company plans to continue operating the very successful news agency business. In fact the Internet has opened up a new market of supplying a news service to over 900 websites around the world. In America sales to this customer group are now higher than revenues from supplying information to newspapers. Similar to the financial information market, Reuters is planning to move from wholesaler to retailer of news. Here again, however, the company may face a sales cannibalization scenario.

At the moment Reuters has possibly one of the most extensive news-gathering operations in the world. In addition, unlike most Internet information retailers, the company does not just collect data. The company reports, analyses, offers real-time price information and operates in 23 languages. Clearly, however, as the Internet will obsolete the company's proprietary information distribution system, evolving a plan based upon sustaining a new, long-term competitive advantage will be no easy task.

Based on: Anonymous (2000)[27]

Summary

The concept of on-line marketing is a much larger concept than merely establishing a website. It encompasses all aspects of utilizing advances in electronic communications as a basis for linking the company more closely with customers. The on-line marketer is offered a variety of choices from just providing a web page containing product information through to offering the customer the facility of remaining in cyberspace throughout the implementation of all aspects of the purchase transaction process. Although the Internet is changing a number of facets of the market process, it is now becoming clear that the fundamental theories upon which the marketing concept is based apply whether a firm is seeking to serve the customer either on or off-line. It is critical that the firm makes a careful assessment of strategic, financial and operational competencies when determining whether the organization has the capability to implement an effective on-line marketing plan. Market success will also be strongly influenced by selecting an appropriate on-line competitive advantage. Having determined the nature of the competitive advantage, the firm needs to select an e-commerce marketing mix. It is suggested this selection can only be undertaken after the firm has completed a marketing audit and SWOT analysis, defined objectives and specified an e-commerce strategy. Marketers need to be aware of ethical issues in Internet and on-line marketing, such as intrusions on privacy and social exclusion.

Internet exercise

What makes a good website?

Sites to visit
Here is a full list of the web-sites covered in these Internet Exercises. Visit a few and see which aspects work well for you and which do not.

Exercise No.	Companies/Brands	URLs
1	Virgin	http://www.virgin.co.uk
		http:www//gucci.com
		http://www.ikea.com
		http://www.starbucks.com/
2	Shell	http://www.shell.com www.shell.com
	Greenpeace	http://www.greenpeace.org
3	National Consumer Council	http://www.ncc.org.uk
	UK Government	http://www.consumer.gov.uk/
4	DTI	http://www.dti.gov.uk/about/suppliers/foreword.htm
	GEC Marconi	http://gecmarc02.uuhost.uk.uu.net/gpi/
	Cisco	http://www,cisco.com
5	Sony	http://www.sonymusic.com
	Universal	http://www.umusic.com/Universal Music Group
	Bertelsmann	http://www.bertelsmann.com/themes/music/music.cfm
	The Band register	http://www.bandreg.com/music.html
		The Band Register
	GetMusic	http://www.getmusic.com
	Metallica	http://www.metallica.com/news/2000/napfaq.html
	Napster	http://www.napster.com/metallica-notice.htm
6	ESOMAR	http://www.esomar.nl

7	Gap	http://www.gap.com/onlinestore/gap/
	Banana republic	http://www.bananarepublic.com/home.htm
	Unilever	http://www.unilever.com/
	Nestle	http://www.nestle.com/in_your_life/index.html
	P & G	http://www.pg.com/
8	Lotus	http://www.lotuscars.co.uk/
	Skoda	http://www.lotuscars.co.uk/
9	Coca-Cola	http://www.thecoca-colacompany.com/
	Pepsi	http://www.pepsi.co.uk/
	Tango	http://www.tango.co.uk/
	Ribena	html http://www.ribena.co.uk/home.html
	Irn-Bru	http://www.irn-bru.co.uk/
	Lucozade	http://www.lucozade.co.uk/
10	Vodafone	http://www.vodafone.com
	BTCellnet	http://www.btcellnet.co.uk
11	ASA	http://www.asa.org.uk/
	ITC	http://www.itc.org.uk/
12	Mintel	http://www.mintel.co.uk
13	Directline	http://www.directline.com
	Dell	http://www.dell.co.uk
14	Virgin	http://www.virgin.co.uk/news/news.jsp
15	Iceland	http://www.iceland-shop.co.uk/
	Tesco	http://www.tescodirect.com
	Sainsbury's	http://www.sainsburys.co.uk
16	Nike	http://www.nike.com
	Reebok	http://www.reebok.com
	Adidas	http://www.adidas.com
17	Waterstones	http://www.waterstones.co.uk
	Borders	http://www.borders.com
	Bertelsmann	http://www.bertelsmann.de
	WH Smith	http://www.whsmith.co.uk
	Amazon	http://www.amazon.com
18	Marriott	http://www.marriott.com/
		http://www.careers.marriott.com/extras.asp
	Novotel/Accor	http://www.accor.com
19	EasyJet	http://www.easyjet.com
20	Coca-Cola	http://www.thecoca-colacompany.com/

Study questions

1 Marketing on the Internet is a growing business. Why is this so? What are the barriers to its more rapid expansion?

2 Discuss the ways that the operations of organizations are likely to change as a result of the development of e-commerce.

3 What are the benefits of the Internet and e-commerce to customers and organizations? Are there any potential disadvantages and pitfalls of marketing on the Internet?

4 Discuss the key competences necessary to successfully implement an on-line marketing plan.

5 Discuss the unique characteristics that the Internet offers which can be used as a basis for competitive advantage.

6 How can the marketing mix be extended and utilized to support an e-marketing strategy?

7 Discuss the key ethical issues relating to the Internet and on-line marketing.

References

1. Internet Indicators (1999) The Internet Economy Indicators, http://www.internetindicators.com/features.html, 22 June, 1–5.
2. Boston Consulting Group (1999) Online Retailing to Reach $36 Billion, www.bcg.com/features/shop/main_shop.html.
3. Seybold, P. B. and R.T. Marshak (1998) *Customer.com: How to Create a Profitable Business Strategy for the Internet and Beyond*, New York: Random House.
4. Anderson, A. (1999) Study Finds European Business at Crossroads of E-Commerce, www.ac.ac.com/showcase/ecommerce/ecom_estudy98.html.
5. Anonymous (2000) Define and Sell, *The Economist: A Survey of E-Commerce*, 26 February, 6–7.
6. O'Connor, J. and E. Galvin (1998) *Creating Value Through E-Commerce*, London: Financial Times/Pearson Education.
7. Cross, R. and J. Smith (1995) Internet Marketing that Works for Customers, *Direct Marketing*, **58** (4), 22–5.
8. Eckmann (1996)
9. McGovern, J. M. (1998) Logistics on the Internet, *Transportation & Distribution*, 39 (7), 68–72.
10. See Hitt, M. A. and R. D. Ireland (1985) Corporate Distinctive Competence, Strategy, Industry and Performance, *Strategic Management Journal*, **6**, 273–93 and Mahoney, J.T. and J. R. Pandian (1992) The Resource-Based View within the Conversation of Strategic Management, *Strategic Management Journal*, **13**, 363–80.
11. Cross, R. and J. Smith (1995) Internet Marketing That Works for Customers, *Direct Marketing*, **58** (4), 22–5.
12. Ghosh (1998)
13. Seybold and Marshak (1998) op. cit.
14. Chaston, I. (1999) *Entrepreneurial Marketing*, London, MacMillan Business and Garvin, D.A. (1987) Competing on the 8 Dimensions of Quality, *Harvard Business Review*, November–December, 101–9.
15. Anon. (1999) Barriers in E-Commerce, *Today Newspaper*, New York, 6 August, 8–9.
16. Schonberger, R. J. (1990) *Building a Chain of Customers: Linking Business Functions to Create the World Class Company*, London: Hutchinson.
17. Parasuraman, A., V. A. Zeithmal and L. L. Berry (1988) A Conceptual Model of Service Quality and its Implications for Future Research, *Journal of Marketing*, **48**, Fall, 34–45.
18. Shapiro, C. and H. R. Varian (1999) *Information Rules*, Harvard, MA: Harvard Business School Press.
19. Hornell, E. (1992) *Improving Productivity for Competitive Advantage: Lessons from the Best in the World*, London: Pitman.
20. Young, K. M., O. A. El Sawy, A. Malhotra and S. Gosain (1997) The Relentless Pursuit of 'Free Perfect Now': IT Enabled Value Innovation at Marshall Industries. 1997 SIM International Papers Aware Competition. http://www.simnet.ord/public/programs/capital/97paper1.html.
21. Baker, S. and K. Baker (1998) Mine Over Matter, *Journal of Business Strategy*, **19** (4), 22–7.
22. Hennington, M. (1999) Bank Marketing, January–February, 12–14.
23. Tomkins, R. (2000) Cookies Leave a Nasty Taste, *Financial Times*, 3 March, 16.
24. Berkowitz, E. N., R. A. Kerin, S. W. Hartley and W. Rudelius (2000) *Marketing*, Boston, MA: Irwin McGraw-Hill.
25. Cowe, R. (2000) Dark Side of the Web, *The Guardian*, 24 February, 7.
26. Benady, D. (2000) Class War, *Marketing Week*, 27 January, 28–31.
27. Anonymous (2000) Reuters, *The Economist*, 12 February, 67–71

Key terms

Internet   a vast global computer network that permits instant global communication such as the gathering and sharing of information and the ability of users to communicate with each other

World wide web   a collection of computer files that can be accessed via the Internet allowing documents containing text, images, sound and video to be used

website   a www file that contains text, pictures and/or sound

e-commerce   the use of technologies such as the Internet, electronic data interchange, e-mail and electronic payment systems to streamline business transactions

See also Table 14.1 above.

electronic data interchange   a pre-Internet technology which was developed to permit organizations to use linked computers to exchange information rapidly

data warehousing (or mining)   the storage and analysis of customer data gathered from their visits to websites for classificatory and modelling purposes so that products, promotions and price can be tailored to the specific needs of individual customers

e-commerce marketing mix   the extension of the traditional marketing mix to include the opportunities afforded by the new electronic media such as the intranet

Case 25 Netiva Corporation: Trouble in Techieland

In June 1997, Gary Steele was recruited as the chief executive officer to manage Netiva Corporation, a Silicon Valley, California, company. The company was founded by a group of 'techies' who realized that the then relatively new computer language offered significant opportunities to build and operate very powerful website databases. These techies approached a number of large corporations offering to develop Internet systems software and once these systems were operational, to provide ongoing maintenance services. This plan assumed that customers would want a variety of systems and that for each installed system the client would pay a multiple licence fee because each software application would be run on a number of work stations.

Five months after joining Netiva, Steele started to recognize some disturbing signs about software contracts which had been signed. It was taking a very long period to successfully negotiate each contract. Furthermore, because the sales staff knew their colleagues in product development were enthusiastic about using every new advance in software, each contract tended to be a 'one-off' design task. This means that the company's software developers were being forced to spend an excessive amount of time on each contract. Additionally, for most contracts the customers did not want multiple applications of the software tools and hence few multiple licensing fees were being signed.

By April 1988, Steele concluded that Netiva was doomed if it continued to operate in this way because operating costs were greatly in excess of revenues being generated. After reviewing the problem, he saw drastic measures were needed so he decided to lay off 40 per cent of the staff. His next step was to try to determine where a viable market might exist for the development of Internet software. By talking to customers, he found that their real need was the desire for technology that could streamline and automate aspects of the e-commerce operations without the hassle of endlessly installing new software systems.

By the summer of 1998, Steele was confident enough to rehire engineers and software designers to develop a new product to be marketed to consulting firms. The product, called ServicePort, is a business communications system for use by employees who tend to be out of the office but need a convenient way of interchanging data while based in remote locations and making purchases of various products or services. Using a web browser, consultants can share client reports, schedule meetings, make travel reservations, purchase computing equipment on-line from a range of different suppliers and get press releases about their client firms. The system can be installed and operational within 10 days (cf. Netiva's earlier systems which took 30+ days to install). The new product provides two revenue streams. One from charging the customer a subscription fee per month per user and another from a commission on all clients' on-line purchases.

This case was prepared by Ian Chaston, Principal Lecturer in Marketing, University of Plymouth.

Questions

1 What was the original orientation exhibited by the company founders?

2 What was the outcome of this orientation?

3 How did Gary Steele change the strategic plan for the business and why did this greatly increase the probability for long-term survival of the business?

Source: Warner, M. (1999) Nightmare on Net Street, Fortune, 6 September, 285–8.

Case 26 Pane Window Systems Ltd

Pane Window Systems Ltd manufactures the component materials used by UK companies who fabricate and install new and replacement windows. The industry originally used aluminium as the standard material for window frames. The first significant technological advance was the introduction of 'double glazed' frames containing two pieces of glass which, by creating a thermal barrier, offers superior heat conservation properties. Approximately 50 per cent of industry unit volume comes from sales in the domestic housing market, with the balance of sales split between industrial products (windows, shop fronts, office buildings, etc.) and the public sector (e.g. local government and housing association dwellings).

Important trends in the domestic market were the introduction of low-cost, plastic (or uPVC) frames and, for performance-orientated end-users, the introduction of 'composite frames' made by coating aluminium with polyvinyl compounds. The industrial market mainly still considers that aluminium is the best material for meeting their specification for durability and variability of shape.

Pane supplies (i) bar lengths of all four product types (i.e. aluminium, thermal break aluminium, uPVC and composites) to customers who wish to fabricate windows and (ii) window frame kits to customers who wish to install frames without any involvement in fabrication.

From the first day of the company being created, the founders recognized that because Pane was too small to capture the economies of scale available to its larger, national competitors, they recognized that the firm would be unable to compete on the basis of low price. Consequently they consistently operated on a market positioning of offering (i) high-quality products, (ii) exceptional customer service and (iii) a free technical advisory service for customers confronted with a difficult or unusual window replacement contract. This strategic orientation has resulted in the firm developing strong downstream relationships with window fabricators and installers who make their purchase decision on the basis of factors such as product quality, JIT deliveries and provision of technical support to assist the resolution of any very significant technical problems which may be encountered during either the pre- or post-purchase phase. Although limited industry data prevents an accurate assessment or market share, Pane is believed to be a market leader in the supply of premium quality, advanced design, bar lengths and kit form products.

Over the years, the company has invested in new technologies to sustain quality and further enhance its speed of response in order fulfilment. It was one of the first replacement window firms in the UK to invest in a computer integrated design/computer integrated manufacturing system (CAD/CAM). Although the intended use for this system was to optimize the organization's manufacturing productivity, it soon found that the system was useful when negotiating an order with customers needing 'one-off' designs to overcome complex installation problems.

Three years ago, the firm's problem-solving reputation led it to be approached by architects and larger building firms involved in complex renovation contracts such as the refurbishment of older hotels and office buildings. Pane had for some years been producing a range of conservatories for domestic homes. When one of its new architect customers who was working on the renovation of a 150-year-old hotel became aware of Pane's involvement in this product area, he asked if it would be possible for the firm to develop a massive customized conservatory, reminiscent of the orangeries which had been popular in the Victorian era. By using its CAD/CAM system Pane was able to develop, manufacture and deliver the components for the conservatory in eight weeks.

Currently the firm uses a salesforce to call on major customers. These meetings are strategic in nature, focusing upon customers' future needs and how Pane can assist in the resolution of complex problems. Customers are supplied with a detailed catalogue listing Pane's product line. Price lists which accompany this catalogue are up-dated on an 'as needed' basis. If a customer has a specific design need or installation problem, they contact Pane's technical department by mail, telephone or fax. Orders are placed with the sales-service department, again using mail, telephone or fax. This department also acts as a contact point advising customers on the status of product shipment and delivery dates. At the moment one obstacle facing the firm is that various computer systems are used within the firm (e.g. an accounting system, a sales management order entry system, a computer-based manufacturing scheduling system and a CAD/CAM system) and there is only limited capability for automated data interchange between these various systems.

The increasingly competitive nature of the replacement industry has been putting pressure on Pane's net profits over the last two or three years. Hence, in a strategic planning exercise, the issues of factors such as market size, intensity of competition, orientation towards cooperation by customers, manufacturing costs, modernity of production assets and workforce skills were utilized to develop the Directional Policy matrix shown in Fig. C26.1. As can be seen from the matrix, the firm has some products which fall

in the phased withdrawal/resource withdrawal categories, a core thermal break business, an area for competence enhancement, a market expansion opportunity and the need for new product investment to retain leadership in the composite materials market.

The directors recognize that there are few opportunities for introducing new products into the industry or cost-reduction benefits to be gained from purchasing new production equipment. Their decision, therefore, is to seek new ways of enhancing customer service and they feel that a move into e-commerce would greatly assist them deliver this new strategy.

This case was prepared by Ian Chaston, Principal Lecturer in Marketing, University of Plymouth.

MARKET ATTRACTIVENESS

	Low	Average	High
Low	**Immediate Withdrawal** No relevant product	**Phased Withdrawal** No relevant product	**One-off Upgrade** No relevant product
Average	**Phased Withdrawal** Aluminium products supplied to price sensitive customers in industrial markets	**Sustain Position** Thermal break products in both industrial and domestic markets	**Capability Enhancement** Improve product and service quality of UPVC products in both markets
High	**Resource Withdrawal** Aluminium products supplied to small fabricators/installers in domestic market	**Market Expansion** Enter market for fabrication of large customised specification conservatories for domestic and industrial markets	**Leadership Retention** Invest in new product development for composite products

(COMPANY COMPETENCE — vertical axis label)

Figure C26.1 The Pane Windows Directional Policy Matrix

Questions

Develop a plan which advises Pane Window Systems Ltd on how the firm can utilize the various technologies which constitute e-commerce to further enhance its capability to offer outstanding customer service.

Sources; Chaston, I. (1999) *New Marketing Strategies*, London: Sage and Chaston, I. (2000) *Entrepreneurial Marketing*, London: Macmillan.

CHAPTER FIFTEEN

Other Promotional Mix Methods

'Advertising brings the horse to water, sales promotion makes it drink'

JULIAN CUMMINS

'Don't tell my mother I'm in public relations, she thinks I play a piano in a brothel'

JACQUES SEQUELA

Learning Objectives *This chapter explains:*

1 The growth in sales promotion

2 The major sales promotion types

3 The objectives and evaluation of sales promotion

4 The objectives and targets of public relations

5 The key tasks and characteristics of publicity

6 The guidelines to use when writing a news release

7 The objectives and methods of sponsorship

8 How to select and evaluate a potential sponsored event or programme

9 The objectives, conduct and evaluation of exhibitions

10 Ethical issues in sales promotion and public relations

In Chapters 11, 12, 13 and 14 we examined the role and use of advertising, personal selling, direct marketing and Internet marketing in the promotional mix. This chapter provides an analysis of other methods of promoting products: *sales promotion, public relations and publicity, sponsorship, and exhibitions.* Traditionally, these were regarded as playing a secondary role compared to advertising and personal selling. In recent years, though, one common factor links them: they are all growth areas in the promotional mix, and marketing people need to know how to manage them effectively. Each method needs to be used as part of a consistent communication programme so that all elements of the promotional mix support and reinforce one another. The message needs to be consistent with the product's positioning strategy.

Sales promotion

As we saw in Chapter 11, sales promotions are incentives to consumers or the trade that are designed to stimulate purchase. Examples include money off and free gifts (consumer promotions) and discounts and salesforce competitions (trade promotions). Incentives to in-company sales people are sometimes included within the definition of sales promotion but these have been dealt with in Chapter 12—personal selling and sales management—and consequently will not be discussed in this chapter.

A vast amount of money is spent on sales promotion. Peattie and Peattie explain the growth in sales promotion as follows:[1]

1 *Increased impulse purchasing*: the retail response to greater consumer impulse purchasing is to demand more sales promotions from manufacturers.

2 *Sales promotions are becoming respectable*: through the use of promotions by market leaders and the increasing professionalism of the sales promotion agencies.

3 *The rising cost of advertising and advertising clutter*: these factors erode advertising's cost effectiveness.

4 *Shortening time horizons*: the attraction of the fast sales boost of a sales promotion is raised by greater rivalry and shortening product life cycles.

5 *Competitor activities*: in some markets, sales promotions are used so often that all competitors are forced to follow suit.[2]

6 *Measurability*: measuring the sales impact of sales promotions is easier than for advertising since its effect is more direct and, usually, short term. The growing use of electronic point-of-sale (EPOS) scanner information makes measurement easier.

This growth in overall expenditure on sales promotion is mirrored in the trend towards joint promotions between two or more companies. Marketing in Action 15.1 discusses the benefits and dangers of adopting this approach to sales promotion.

The effects of sales promotion

Sales promotion is often used to provide a short, sharp shock to sales. In this sense it may be regarded as a short-term tactical device. Figure 15.1 shows a typical sales pattern. The sales promotion boosts sales during the promotion period because of the incentive effect. This is followed by a small fall in sales to below normal level because some consumers will have stocked up on the product during the promotion. The long-term sales effect of the promotion could be positive, neutral or negative. If the promotion has attracted new buyers who find that they like the brand, repeat purchases from them may give rise to a positive long-term effect.[3] Alternatively, if the promotion (e.g. money off) has devalued the brand in the eyes of consumers, the effect may be negative.[4] Where the promotion has caused consumers to buy the brand only because of its incentive value with no effect on underlying preferences, the long-term effect may be neutral.[5] An international study of leading grocery brands has shown that the most likely long-term effect of a price promotion for an existing brand is neutral. Such promotions tend to attract existing buyers of the brand during the promotional period rather than new buyers.[6]

Some sales promotions may have a more strategic focus, however. Smith describes how Pears, the premium-priced transparent soap, is supported by an annual 'Miss Pears' competition.[7] The competition attracts 20 000 entries each year and the photograph of the winning child is featured on the Pears soap cartons. The objective of the promotion is to enhance Pears's caring family image.

Major sales promotion types

Sales promotion can be directed at the consumer or the trade (see Fig. 15.2). Major consumer sales promotion types are money off, bonus packs, premiums, free samples, coupons, prize promotions and loyalty cards. A sizeable proportion of sales promotions are directed at the trade, including price discounts, free goods, competitions, and allowances.

Money off

Money-off promotions provide a direct value to the customer, and therefore an unambiguous incentive to purchase. They have a proven track record of stimulating short-term sales increases. However, price reductions can easily be matched by the competition and if used frequently can devalue brand image. Consumer response may be 'If the brand is that good why do they need to keep reducing the price?'

Bonus packs

These give *added value* by giving consumers extra quantity at no additional cost. ***Bonus packs*** are often used in the drinks, confectionery and detergent markets. For example, cans of lager may

be sold on the basis of '12½% extra free!'. Because the price is not lowered this form of promotion runs less risk of devaluing brand image. Extra value is given by raising quantity rather than cutting price. With some product groups it encourages buyers to consume more. For example, a Mars bar will be eaten, or a can of lager drunk, whether there is extra quantity or not. The illustrations show the use of bonus pack promotions for Lucozade and Bacardi Breezer.

Premiums

Premiums are any merchandise offered for free or at low cost as an incentive to purchase a brand. There are three major forms: free in-or-on-pack gifts, free in-the-mail offers, and self-liquidating offers.

Free in-or-on-pack gifts   gifts may be given away free with brands. For example, Twiglets, a snack food, was promoted by enclosing a small can of Appletize, a fizzy apple drink, in its pack; PG Tips, a brand of tea, used a plastic dinosaur attached to the outside of the package to promote sales. A free in-pack promotion for Nestlé's Shreddies designed to appeal to children, and an on-pack promotion for Nestlé's Fruitful are shown over the next few pages. Occasionally the gift is a free sample of one brand that is banded to another brand (*banded pack offer*). The free sample may be a new variety or flavour which benefits by getting trial. In other cases the brands are linked,

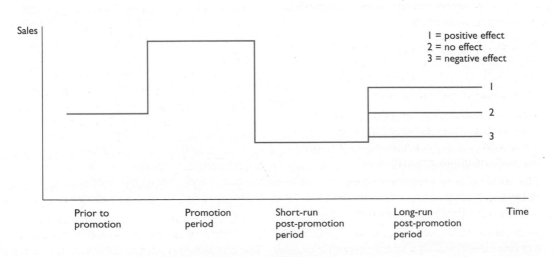

Figure 15.1 The effect of a sales promotion on sales

as when Nestlé promoted its Cappuccino brand by offering a free Kit Kat to eat while drinking the coffee, and Cadbury ran a similar promotion with a packet of Cadbury's Chocolate Chip Cookies attached to their Cadbury's Chocolate Break, a milk chocolate drink. The illustration over the page shows an advertisement promoting Carling Black Label by a catalogue and free draw.

When two or more items are banded together the promotion is called a multibuy and can involve a number of items of the same brand being offered together. Multibuys are a very popular form of promotion. They are frequently used to protect market share by encouraging consumers to stock up on a particular brand when two or more items of the same brand are packaged together. However, unlike price reductions, they do not encourage trial because

15.1 Marketing in Action

The Growing Use of Joint Promotions

Commercial partnerships are an increasing part of the promotional landscape. Joint promotions can make budgets stretch further, bring new resources and skills to a project and provide a powerful incentive to buy. Problems can occur, however. Brand identity differences, company culture clashes, budgetary arguments and conflicting objectives can make implementation difficult.

Putting together a joint promotion requires both partners to be clear about what they want to achieve from the alliance and to communicate their needs and objectives to each other. Trust is also a vital ingredient since a brand's reputation can be harmed if the other party mismanages its activities. For example, the prestige of a brand may depend on the second party dispatching a voucher on time or ensuring that a prize is of the quality promised. Above all the joint promotion must make sense to the consumer and this frequently requires prior testing through focus groups. Finally, joint promotions make most sense when each brand is targeting the same market segment without being in competition with each other.

A major joint promotion was the Fostralia 2000 promotion which Fosters claim was Europe's biggest ever beer promotion. It ran in 50 000 pubs, clubs and supermarkets across 13 European countries. Fosters worked in partnership with such companies as Virgin Radio and Cathay Pacific, the merchandise brand Rip Curl, the travel agents Ausbound and ProTravel, and the lads' magazine FHM. The main objective of the promotion was to reinforce Fosters' image as an Australian brand, bringing to life the Australian 'no worries' way of living. The prizes for the 354 winners were ringside seats overlooking Sydney's millennium firework display plus 10 days on the Gold Coast. The mechanics of the promotion involved a scratchcard device on special cans and bottles. In addition drinkers could participate via competitions on national and local radio. The through-the-line approach built a massive presence. Consumers could hear Chris Tarrant talking about the competition on the radio and then see the promotion featured in a supermarket and pub.

A second example of a joint promotion featured skincare company Elida Fabergé and designer clothes label Timberland for a co-promotion centred on Vaseline Intensive Care. The promotion featured a competition with the first prize being a trip for two to the USA and £2000 to spend at a Timberland store. The competition strapline 'Win yourself a second skin, when you let us take care of you first' pulled together the synergy between the two brands that, in different ways, protect the skin. It took eight months to agree the details of the campaign and approve the point-of-sale material for the Timberland stores.

Based on: Hemsley(1999);[8] Miller (2000)[9]

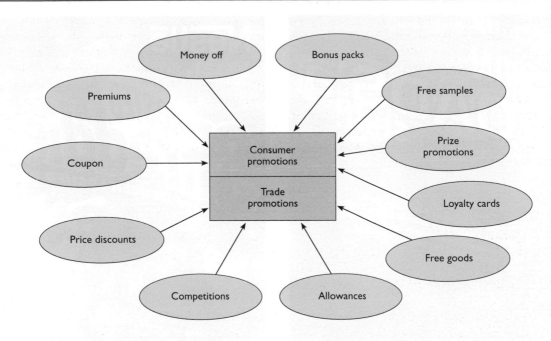

Figure 15.2 Consumer and trade promotions

Lucozade energy drink featuring a bonus offer

Extra value is provided by this bonus pack of Bacardi Breezer

Carling Black Label

Nestlé Shreddies: a free in-pack gift to appeal to children

consumers do not bulk buy a brand they have not tried before. When multibuys take the form of two different brands, range trial can be generated. For example, a manufacturer of a branded coffee launching a new brand of tea could band the two brands together, thus leveraging the strength of the coffee brand to gain trial of the new tea brand.[10]

Free in-the-mail offers this promotion involves the collection of packet tops or labels which are sent in the mail as proof of purchase to claim a free gift or money voucher. Kellogg's Ricicles is promoted by such an offer (see opposite). Gifts can be quite valuable because redemption rates can be very low (less than 10 per cent redemption is not unusual). This is because of *slippage*: consumers collect labels with a view to mailing but never collect the requisite number.

Self-liquidating offers these are similar to free-in-the-mail offers except that consumers are asked to pay a sum of money to cover costs of the merchandise plus administration and postage charges. The consumer benefits by getting the

goods at below normal cost because the manufacturer passes on the advantage of bulk buying and prices at cost. The manufacturer benefits by the self-funding nature of the promotion, although there is the danger of being left with surplus stocks of the merchandise. A self-liquidating offer used to promote the weetabix Bananabix brand is shown overleaf.

Free samples

Free samples of a brand may be delivered to the home or given out in a store. The idea is that having tried the sample a proportion of consumers will begin to buy it. For new brands or brand extensions (for example, a new shampoo or fabric conditioner) this form of promotion is an effective, if expensive, way of gaining consumer trial. However, sampling may be ineffective if the brand has nothing extra to offer the consumer. For existing brands which have a low trial but high purchasing rate sampling may be effective. As it would appear that many of those who try the brand like it and buy it again, raising the trial rate

Nestlé Fruitful uses a free on-pack gift to promote the brand

Kellogg's Ricicles: the use of a free-in-the-mail Lego offer. Repeat purchase is encouraged by the need to send three tokens. The offer also allows the collection of marketing research information

through free samples could have a beneficial long-term effect.

Coupons

There are three ways of couponing. *Coupons* can be delivered to the house, appear in magazines or newspapers, or appear on packs. *Home couponing*, after home sampling, is the best way to achieve trial for new brands.[9] *Magazine or newspaper couponing* is much cheaper than home delivery and can be used to stimulate trial but redemption rates are much lower at around 5 per cent on average. The purpose of *on-pack couponing* is to encourage initial and repeat purchase of the same brand, or trial of a different brand. A brand carries an on-pack coupon redeemable against the consumer's next purchase usually for the same brand. Redemption rate is high, averaging around 40 per cent.[12] The coupon can offer a higher face value than the equivalent cost of a money-off pack since the effect of the coupon is on both initial and repeat sales. However, it is usually less effective in raising initial

sales than money off because there is no immediate saving and its appeal is almost exclusively to existing consumers.[13]

Prize promotions

There are three main types of *prize promotions*: competitions, draws, and games. Unlike other promotions the cost can be established in advance and does not depend on the number of participants. *Competitions* require participants to exercise a certain degree of skill and judgement. For example, a competition to win free cinema seats might require entrants to name five films based upon stills from each. Entry is usually dependent on at least one purchase. Compared to premiums and money off, competitions offer a less immediate incentive to buy and one that requires time and effort on the part of entrants. However, they can attract attention and interest

A self-liquidating offer used to promote the Weetabix Bananabix brand

A multipack of Perrier water featuring a prize competition

in a brand. The illustration shows the use of a competition to promote a multipack of Perrier water. *Draws* make no demands on skill or judgement: the result depends on chance. For example, a supermarket may run an out-of-the-hat draw where customers fill in their name and address on an entry card and on a certain day a draw is made. Another example of a draw is when direct mail recipients are asked to return a card on which there is a set of numbers. These are then compared against a set of winning numbers.

An example of a *game promotion* is where a newspaper encloses a series of bingo cards and customers are told that over a period of time sets of bingo numbers will be published. If these numbers form a line or full house on a bingo card a prize is won. Such a game encourages repeat purchase of the newspaper.

The national laws governing sales promotions in European vary tremendously. Table 15.1 provides an indication of what can and cannot be done in 20 European countries. It must be

emphasized that it is a rough guide only. Local legal advice should be taken before implementing a sales promotion. Nevertheless it does show the great differences that exist. The UK, Ireland, Spain, Portugal, Greece, Russia and the Czech Republic have fairly relaxed laws about what can be done. Germany, Luxembourg, Austria, Norway, Switzerland and Sweden are much more restrictive. For example, in Sweden free mail-ins, free draws, and money-off next purchase promotions, and in Norway self-liquidating offers, free draws, money-off vouchers and money-off next purchase, are not allowed.

Price discounts

The trade may be offered (or demand) *discounts* in return for purchase. The concentration of buying into fewer trade outlets has placed increasing power with these organizations. This power is often translated into discounts from manufacturers. The discount may be part of a joint promotion whereby the retailer agrees to devote extra shelf space, buy larger quantities, engage in a joint competition, and/or allow in-store demonstrations.

Free goods

An alternative to a price discount is to offer more merchandise at the same price. For example, the *Baker's Dozen* technique involves offering 13 items (or cases) for the price of 12.

Competitions

This involves a manufacturer offering financial inducements or prizes to distributors' salesforces in return for achieving sales targets for their products. Alternatively a prize may be given to the salesforce with the best sales figures.

Allowances

A manufacturer may offer an *allowance* (a sum of money) in return for retailers providing promotional facilities in store (*display allowance*). For example, allowance would be needed to persuade a supermarket to display cards on its

---

Table 15.1   Guidelines to sales promotion regulations in Europe

	UK	Ireland	Spain	Germany	France	Denmark	Belgium	The Netherlands	Portugal	Italy	Greece	Luxembourg	Austria	Finland	Norway	Sweden	Switzerland	Russia	Hungary	Czech Republic
On-pack price reductions	Y	Y	Y	Y	Y	Y	Y	Y	Y	Y	Y	Y	Y	Y	Y	Y	Y	Y	Y	Y
Banded offers	Y	Y	Y	C	Y	C	C	Y	Y	Y	Y	N	C	C	C	C	N	Y	Y	Y
In-pack premiums	Y	Y	Y	C	C	C	C	C	Y	Y	Y	N	C	Y	C	C	N	Y	Y	Y
Multiple-purchase offers	Y	Y	Y	C	Y	C	C	Y	Y	Y	Y	N	C	C	C	C	N	C	Y	Y
Extra product	Y	Y	Y	C	Y	C	C	C	Y	Y	Y	Y	C	Y	Y	C	C	Y	Y	Y
Free product	Y	Y	Y	Y	Y	Y	C	Y	Y	Y	Y	Y	Y	Y	Y	Y	Y	Y	Y	Y
Reusable/ alternative use pack	Y	Y	Y	Y	Y	Y	Y	Y	Y	Y	Y	Y	Y	C	Y	Y	Y	Y	Y	Y
Free mail-ins	Y	Y	Y	N	Y	C	C	Y	Y	Y	Y	C	N	Y	C	N	N	Y	Y	Y
With-purchase premiums	Y	Y	Y	C	Y	C	C	C	Y	Y	Y	N	C	Y	C	C	N	Y	Y	Y
Cross-product offers	Y	Y	Y	N	Y	C	N	C	Y	Y	Y	N	C	C	C	C	N	Y	Y	Y
Collector devices	Y	Y	Y	N	C	C	C	C	Y	Y	Y	N	N	C	N	N	N	Y	Y	Y
Competitions	Y	Y	Y	C	C	C	Y	C	Y	Y	Y	C	C	C	Y	Y	Y	Y	Y	Y
Self-liquidating premiums	Y	Y	Y	Y	Y	Y	Y	C	Y	Y	Y	N	Y	Y	N	Y	N	Y	Y	Y
Free draws	Y	Y	Y	N	Y	N	N	N	Y	Y	Y	N	N	Y	N	N	N	Y	C	Y
Share-outs	Y	Y	Y	N	C	N	N	N	Y	C	Y	N	N	C	C	N	N	Y	Y	Y
Sweepstake/ lottery	C	C	C	C	C	N	C	C	C	C	C	C	N	C	Y	N	N	N	Y	C
Money-off vouchers	Y	Y	Y	N	Y	C	Y	Y	Y	Y	C	Y	C	C	C	N	C	N	Y	Y
Money-off next purchase	Y	Y	Y	N	Y	N	Y	Y	Y	C	Y	N	N	C	N	N	N	Y	Y	Y
Cash backs	Y	Y	Y	C	Y	Y	Y	Y	Y	N	Y	N	C	C	C	Y	N	Y	Y	Y
In-store demos	Y	Y	Y	Y	Y	Y	Y	Y	Y	Y	Y	Y	Y	Y	Y	Y	Y	Y	C	Y

Y permitted
N Not permitted
C May be permitted with certain conditions
Note: This guide should be used only as a first indication of promotional opportunities. Local legal advice should be taken before implementing any activities
Source: IMP Europe, London. Reproduced with permission

shelves indicating that a brand was being sold at a special low price. An *advertising allowance* would be paid by a manufacturer to a retailer for featuring its brands in the retailer's advertising.

Loyalty cards

A major development in retailing is the offering of *loyalty cards* to customers who gain points every time they spend money at an outlet. Points can be swapped for money-off vouchers for purchases at the store or bargain offers on other purchases such as cinema tickets. The intention is to attract customers back to the outlet but the retailer gains other advantages. The card contains information on the customer including his or her name and address and when it is swiped through the checkout machine detailed information on purchases is recorded. This means that the purchasing behaviour of individual customers is known to the retailer who can then use this information to, among other things, target tailored direct mail promotions and those who are likely to be responsive since it is known they purchase within a product category (e.g. wine) or buy certain types of product within a category (e.g. herbal tea).

Sales promotion objectives

The most basic objective of any sales promotion is to provide extra value that encourages purchase. When targeted at consumers the intention is to stimulate **consumer pull**; when the trade is targeted **distribution push** is the objective. Specific sales promotion objectives are now discussed.

Fast sales boost

As we saw when discussing the effects of sales promotion, the usual response is for sales volume to increase. Short-term sales increases may be required for a number of reasons including the need to reduce inventories or meet budgets prior to the end of the financial year, moving stocks of an old model prior to a replacement, and to increase stockholding by consumers and distributors in advance of the launch of a competitor's product.[14] Promotions that give large immediate benefits such as money off or

bonus packs have bigger effects on sales volume than more distant promotions such as competitions or self-liquidators. What needs to be realized, however, is that sales promotion should not be used as a means of patching up more fundamental inadequacies such as inferior product performance, or poor positioning.

A sales promotion that went seriously wrong was Hoover's attempt to boost sales of its washing machines, vacuum cleaners, refrigerators and tumble driers by offering two free US flight tickets for every Hoover product purchased over £100. The company was the target of much bad publicity as buyers discovered that the offer was wreathed in difficult conditions (found in the promotion's small print) and complained bitterly to Hoover and the media. In an attempt to limit the danger done to its reputation, the company announced that it would honour its offer to its customers, at an estimated cost of £20 million.

Encourage trial

Sales promotions can be highly successful by encouraging trial. If these new buyers like the brand the long-term effect of the promotion may be positive. Home sampling and home couponing are particularly effective methods of inducing trial. Promotions which simply give more product (e.g. bonus packs) are likely to be less successful since consumers will not place much value on the extra quantity until they have decided they like it.

Encourage repeat purchase

Certain promotions by their nature encourage repeat purchase of a brand over a period of time. Any other which requires the collection of packet tops or labels (e.g. free mail-ins and promotions such as bingo games) attempt to raise repeat purchase during the promotional period. Loyalty cards are designed to offer consumers an incentive to repeat purchase at a store.

Stimulate purchase of larger packs

Promotions that are specifically linked to larger pack sizes may persuade consumers to switch from the less economical smaller packs. For example, in the UK Unilever ran a highly successful promotion linked to their jumbo-sized Persil detergent packs offering free rail vouchers.

Gain distribution and shelf space

Trade promotions are designed to gain distribution and shelf space. These are major promotional objectives since there is a strong relationship between sales and these two factors. Discounts, free gifts and joint promotions are methods used to encourage distributors to stock brands. Also consumer promotions that provide sizeable extra value may also persuade distributors to stock or give extra shelf space.

Evaluating sales promotion

There are two types of research which can be used to evaluate sales promotions: *pre-testing research* is used to select from a number of alternative promotional concepts the most effective in achieving objectives; *post-testing research* is carried out to assess whether promotional objectives have been achieved or not.

Pre-testing research

Three-major pre-testing methods are group discussions, hall tests and experimentation. **Group discussions** may be used with target consumers to test ideas and concepts. They can provide insights into the kinds of promotions that might be valued by them and allow assessment of several promotional ideas so that some can be tested further and others discounted. Group discussions should be used as a preliminary rather than a conclusive tool.

Hall tests involve bringing a sample of target consumers to a room that has been hired, usually in a town or city location so that alternative promotional ideas can be tested. For example, a bonus pack, a free gift v. a free in-the-mail offer might be tested. The promotions are ranked on the basis of their incentive value. No more than eight alternatives should be tested and the promotions should be of a similar cost to the company.[15] Usually a sample of 100 to 150 is sufficient to separate the winners from the losers.

Experimentation closes the gap between what people say they value and what they actually value by measuring actual purchase behaviour in the marketplace. Usually two panels of stores are used to compare two promotional alternatives, or one promotion against no promotion (control). The two groups of stores must be chosen in such a way that they are comparable (a matched sample) so that the difference in sales is due to the two promotions rather than differences in the stores themselves. Experimentation may be used in a less sophisticated way where one or a small number of stores is used simply as a final check on promotional response before launching the promotion nationally. For service companies the process may be even easier. Leaflets are produced to communicate the offer and are distributed to a sample of target consumers.[16] Group discussions and hall tests can be used prior to an experiment to narrow the promotional alternatives to a manageable few.

Post-testing research

After the sales promotion has been implemented the effects must be carefully monitored. Care should be taken to check sales both during *and* after the promotion so that post-promotional sales dips can be taken into account (a *lagged effect*). In certain situations a sales fall can precede a promotion (a *lead effect*). If consumers believe a promotion to be imminent they may hold back purchases until it takes place. Alternatively, if a retail sales promotion of consumer durables (e.g. gas fires, refrigerators, televisions) is accompanied by higher commission rates for salespeople, they may delay sales until the promotional period.[17] If a lead effect is possible, sales prior to the promotion should also be monitored.

Ex-factory sales figures are usually an unreliable guide to consumer off-take at the retail level. Consequently consumer panels and retail audits (see Chapter 5) are usually employed to measure sales effects. **Consumer panel data** also reveal the types of people who responded to the sales promotion. For example, they would indicate whether any increase in sales was due to heavy buyers stocking up, or new buyers trying the brand for the first time. **Retail audit data** could be used to establish whether the promotion was associated with retail outlets increasing their stock levels, and rise in the number of outlets handling the brand as well as measuring sales effects.

An attempt may also be made to assess the long-term impact of a sales promotion. However, in money promotion-prone markets such as food, drink and toiletries, the pace of promotional activity means that it is impossible to disentangle the long-term effects of one promotion from another.

Public relations and publicity

A company is dependent on many groups if it is to be successful. The marketing concept focuses on customers and distributors but the needs and interests of other groups are also important, such as employees, shareholders, the local community, the media, government and pressure groups. *Public relations* is concerned with all of these groups and may be defined as:

> The management of communications and relationships to establish goodwill and mutual understanding between an organization and its public.

Public relations is therefore more wide ranging than marketing, which focuses on markets, distribution channels and customers. By communicating to other groups, public relations creates an environment in which it is easier to conduct marketing.[18] These publics are shown in Fig. 15.3.

Public relations activities include publicity, corporate advertising, seminars, publications, lobbying and charitable donations. It can accomplish many objectives:[19]

1 *Prestige and reputation*: it can foster prestige and reputation which can help companies to sell products, attract and keep good employees, and promote favourable community and government relations.

2 *Promotion of products*: the desire to buy a product can be helped by the unobtrusive things that people read and see in the press, radio and television. Awareness and interest in products and companies can be generated.

3 *Dealing with issues and opportunities*: the ability to handle social and environmental issues to the mutual benefit of all parties involved.

4 *Goodwill of customers*: ensuring that customers are presented with useful information, are treated well and have their complaints dealt with fairly and speedily.

5 *Goodwill of employees*: promoting the sense of identification and satisfaction of employees with their company. Activities such as internal newsletters, recreation activities and awards for service and achievement can be used.

6 *Overcoming misconceptions*: managing misconceptions about a company so that unfounded opinions do not damage its operations.

7 *Goodwill of suppliers and distributors*: building a reputation as a good customer

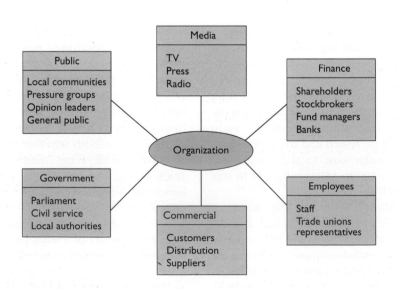

Figure 15.3 An organization and its publics

(for suppliers) and a reliable supplier (for distributors).

8 *Goodwill of government*: influencing the opinions of public officials and politicians so that they feel that the company operates in the public interest.

9 *Dealing with unfavourable publicity*: responding quickly, accurately and effectively to negative publicity such as an oil spill or an air disaster.

10 *Attracting and keeping good employees*: creating and maintaining respectability in the eyes of the public so that the best personnel are attracted to work for the company.

A study by Kitchen and Proctor showed that public relations is a growth area in the UK.[20] The three major reasons for this were recognition by marketing teams of the power and value of public relations, increased advertising costs leading to an exploration of more cost effective communication routes, and improved understanding of public relations' role.

Its growing importance is reflected in a move to establish pan-European public relations programmes. Marketing in Action 15.2 discusses how to organize a pan-European operation and the new communications technologies (video news releases, video conferences, satellite conferencing and video magazines) that are transforming international public relations.

Publicity

A major element of public relations is *publicity*. It can be defined as the communication about a product or organization by the placing of news about it in the media without paying for the time or space directly.

Three key tasks of a publicity department are:[21]

1 Responding to requests from the media. Although a passive service function, it requires well-organized information, and prompt response to media requests.

2 Supplying the media with information on events and occurrences relevant to the organization. This requires general internal communication channels and knowledge of the media.

3 Stimulating the media to carry the information and viewpoint of the organization. This requires creative development of ideas, developing close relationships with media people and understanding their needs and motivations.

Characteristics of publicity

Information dissemination may be through news releases, news conferences, interviews, feature articles, photocalls and public speaking (at conferences and seminars for example). No matter which way is used to carry the information, publicity has five important characteristics.

The message has high credibility the message has higher credibility than advertising because it appears to the reader to have been written independently (by a media person) rather than by an advertiser. Because of the high credibility it can be argued that it is more persuasive than a similar message used in an advertisement.

No direct media costs   since space or time in the media is not bought there is no direct media cost. However, this is not to say that it is cost free. Someone has to write the news release, take part in the interview or organize the news conference. This may be organized internally by a press officer or publicity department or externally by a public relations agency.

Lose control of publication   unlike advertising, there is no guarantee that the news item will be published. This decision is taken out of the control of the organization and into the hands of an editor. A key factor in this decision is whether the item is judged to be newsworthy. The item must be *distinctive* in the sense of having *news value*. For example, an organization that is the first to launch a voice-activated personal computer would receive massive publicity; the second company to do so would barely get any. The topic of the news item must also be judged to be of *interest* to publications' readers. Table 15.2 lists a number of potentially newsworthy topics.

Lose control of content   there is no way of ensuring that the viewpoint expressed by the news supplier is reflected in the published article.

15.2   Marketing in Action

Developments in European Public Relations

Two major alternatives for setting up an effective public relations (PR) programme across Europe exist. First, a client could select a PR consultancy that has a presence in each of the targeted markets. This approach combines coordination with local knowledge of language, customs and media. Second, a client company could appoint different consultancies in each country. The disadvantage of this method is the time-consuming tasks of coordination and briefings. The advantages of the first approach have led most sizeable public relations agencies to either set up their own offices throughout Europe or establish networks and working partnerships between agencies in different European countries. A lead agency acts as the interface with the client and coordinates the work of the network of agencies. An example of this is the appointment of Ogilvy Public Relations by IBM to manage its 28-strong European PR agency network. Ogilvy's UK office hires local agencies to form bespoke networks for the information technology company. A dedicated team trawl Europe for 'best of breed' PR agencies to work mainly on IBM's massive e-business marketing campaign. Once a part of the network, Ogilvy pays them, dictates strategy and has the power to fire them.

Public relations work across Europe is being transformed by the development of new communications technology. Four new media technologies are now described.

Video news releases

Coverage of a public relations event is edited to 3–4 minutes and sent to television news departments around the world via cassette, vision circuits or by satellite. No commentary is added and the releases can be edited and voice-overs included as news departments see fit. TV is very choosy about which stories it will use. The brand must play only a supporting role in the story as overtly promotional messages are rejected almost always. Birth control pill manufacturer Schering obtained an audience of nearly six million through a VNR on its sponsorship of an exhibition on fertility control.

Video conferencing

This is two-way communication of both words and pictures via telephone lines. The process can be used to manage pan-European sales and marketing conferences.

Satellite conferencing

This can be used to transmit a message from one location to many sites around Europe. It is gaining popularity for pan-European product launches, press conferences and conventions.

Video magazines

This medium can be used for disseminating a corporate message to customers and employees. Compared with print magazines it is more personal and can create a sense of involvement for remote subsidiaries.

Based on: Cobb (1993);[22] Guide 28 (1993);[23] Cobb (1997);[24] Goddard (1999)[25]

Table 15.2   Potentially newsworthy topics

Being or doing something first

Marketing issues
    New products
    Research breakthroughs: future new products
    Large orders/contracts
    Sponsorships
    Price changes
    Service changes
    New logos
    Export success

Production issues
    Productivity achievements
    Employment changes
    Capital investments

Financial issues
    Financial statements
    Acquisitions
    Sales/profit achievements

Personal issues
    Training awards
    Winners of company contests
    Promotions/new appointments
    Success stories
    Visits by famous people
    Reports of interviews

General issues
    Conferences/seminars/exhibitions
    Anniversaries of significant events

For example, a news release pointing to an increase in capital expenditure on pollution but negatively (for example, the increase being inadequate) in another.

Lose control of timing   an advertising campaign can be coordinated to achieve maximum impact. The timing of the publication of news items, however, cannot be controlled. For example, a news item publicizing a forthcoming conference to encourage attendance could appear in a publication after the event has taken place or, at least, too late to have any practical effect on attendance.

Writing news releases

Perhaps the most popular method of disseminating information to the media is through the news release. By following a few simple guide-lines, the writer can produce news releases that please editors and therefore stand a greater chance of being used.[26]

The headline   make the headline factual and avoid the use of flamboyant, flowery language that might irritate editors. The headline should briefly introduce the story, e.g. 'A New Alliance to be Formed between Virgin and Delta Airlines'.

Opening paragraph   this should be a brief summary of the whole release. If this is the only part of the news release that is published the writer will have succeeded in getting across the essential message.

Organizing the copy   the less important messages should be placed towards the end of the new release. The lower the paragraph the more chance of being cut by an editor.

Copy content   like headlines, copy should be factual not fanciful. An example of bad copy would be 'We are proud to announce that Virgin Airlines, the world's most innovative airline, will fly an exciting new route to Singapore'. Instead, this should read 'A new route to Singapore will be flown by Virgin Airlines'. Whenever possible statements should be backed up by facts. For example, a statement claiming 'fuel economy' for a car should be supported by figures.

Length   new releases should be as short as possible. Most are written on one page, some are merely one paragraph. The viewpoint that long releases should be sent to editors so that they can cut out the parts they do not want is a fallacy. Editors' self-interest is that their job should be made as easy as possible; the less work they have to do amending copy the greater the chances of publication.

Layout   the release should contain short paragraphs with plenty of *white space* to make it appear easy to read. There should be good sized margins on both sides and the copy should be double-spaced so that amendments and printing instructions can be inserted by the editor. When a story runs to a second or third page, 'more' should be typed in the bottom right-hand corner and succeeding pages numbered with the headline repeated in the top left-hand corner.

Publicity can be a powerful tool for creating awareness and strengthening the reputation of organizations. For example, it was the inherent newsworthiness of Anita Roddick's Body Shop business with its emphasis on environmental and animal friendly products that provided media coverage, not advertisements. The trick is to motivate everyone in an organization to look for newsworthy stories and events, not simply to rely on the publicity department to initiate them.

Public relations and publicity should be part of an integrated communications strategy so that they reinforce the messages consumers receive from other communication vehicles. Marketing in Action 15.3 discusses some important issues.

Sponsorship

Sponsorship has been defined by Sleight as:[27]

> A business relationship between a provider of funds, resources or services and an individual, event or organization which offers in return some rights and association that may be used for commercial advantage.

Potential sponsors have a wide range of entities and activities from which to choose including sports, arts, community activities, teams, tournaments, individual personalities or events, competitions, fairs and shows. Sports sponsorship is by far the most popular sponsorship medium as it

15.3 Marketing in Action

Integrated Public Relations

The development of integrated communications agencies all too often meant offering advertising, direct marketing and sales promotion. Public relations was usually not included being seen as little more than the sending out of press releases. Yet there have been examples of public relations playing a strategic role in an integrated communications campaign. For example, Unilever faced restrictions on the health claims it could use when advertising Flora margarine. The solution was to lead with a public relations campaign reporting medical research that found that polyunsaturated fats were relatively good for health. This was supported by an advertising campaign that focused on the message that Flora was 'rich in polyunsaturates'.

There are three methods of establishing integrated communications. The first is for clients to bring all their specialist agencies around a table and insist upon an integrated approach. Another is to use a large international agency that can offer a complete package such as the Young and Rubicam group which owns the PR agency Burson-Marsteller. Finally, clients can choose a single integrated agency that includes public relations in its offering. One practical problem is that no matter which option is chosen, the different agencies or sections within agencies may fight for a bigger share of the communications budget. Even using one agency does not prevent this since each section may operate as a separate profit centre. A problem from the client side is that it may give the strategic thinking role to those representing advertising. The other communication areas are then asked to fall in line, even if it is very difficult to translate the advertising message into public relations, sales promotion or a direct marketing campaign.

The role of the client in achieving integrated public relations is vital. Unless the client provides strong leadership, clear objectives and develops a cooperative culture, the various parties will fight each other for credit, resources and importance.

Based on: Gofton (1996);[28] Flack (1999)[29]

offers high visibility through extensive television press coverage, the ability to attract a broad cross-section of the community and to service specific niches, and the capacity to break down cultural barriers.[30]

Companies should be clear about the reasons they are spending money on sponsorship. The five principal objectives of sponsorship are gaining publicity, creating entertainment opportunities, fostering favourable brand and company associations, improving community relations, and creating promotional opportunities.

Gaining publicity

Sponsorship provides ample opportunities to create publicity in the news media. Worldwide events such as major golf, football and tennis tournaments supply the platform for global media coverage. Sponsorship of such events can provide brand exposure to millions of people. Some events such as athletics have mass audience appeal while others such as golf have a more up-market profile. Dunhill's sponsorship of major golf tournaments allows the brand name to be exposed to their more up-market customer segment.

The publicity opportunities of sponsorship can produce major *awareness* shifts. For example, Canon's sponsorship of football in the UK raised awareness of the brand name from 40 per cent to 85 per cent among males, awareness of the name of an insurance company sponsoring a national cricket competition increased from 2–16 per cent and Texaco's prompted recall improved from 18–60 per cent because of motor racing sponsorship.[31]

Sponsorship can also be used to position brands in the marketplace. For example, Procter & Gamble spend the entire marketing budget for their shampoo Wash & Go totalling £6 million on sponsoring the English Premier League. The intention is to position it as a sports brand with the strapline 'A simply great supporter of football' among its target market of young, active males.[32]

Creating entertainment opportunities

A major objective of much sponsorship is to create entertainment opportunities for customers and the trade. Sponsorship of music, the performing arts and sports events can be particularly effective. For example, BMW supported classical concerts in stately homes in the UK to provide dealers with customer entertainment opportunities.[33] The Tetley Bitter sponsorship deal with the England Cricket Team provided not only wide publicity but also important opportunities to invite key customers to watch the Test Matches. Often sports personalities are invited to join the sponsors' guests. Attendance at sponsored events can also be used to reward successful employees.

Fostering favourable brand and company associations

The third objective of sponsorship is to create favourable associations for a brand and company. For example, sponsorship of athletics by Smith Kline Beecham for its Lucozade Sport brand reinforces its market position and its energy associations. Dunhill's golf sponsorship is consistent with its up-market positioning and Stella Artois's tennis sponsorship had a major impact in establishing the brand in the premium lager market segment. Marlboro's motor racing sponsorship and Budweiser's sponsorship of the television programme showing American football reinforce their masculine images.

Both the sponsor and sponsored activity become involved in a relationship with a transfer of values from the activity to the sponsor. The audience, finding the sponsor's name, logo and other symbols threaded through the event, learn to associate sponsor and activity with one another. The task facing the sponsor is to ensure its presence is clearly associated with the activity and transfer the activity values onto the brand. Support promotions and mainstream advertising can help in this respect.[25] Figure 15.4 shows some broad values conferred on the sponsor from five sponsorship categories.

Improving community relations

Sponsorship of schools, for example, by providing low cost personal computers, and supporting community programmes can foster a socially responsible, caring reputation for a company. A survey in the Republic of Ireland found that

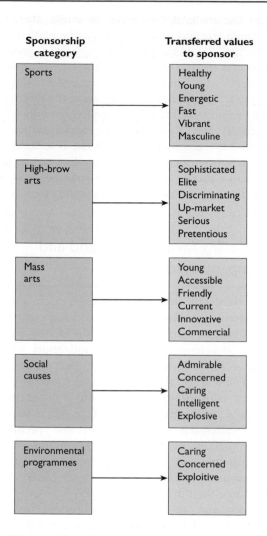

Sponsorship category	Transferred values to sponsor
Sports	Healthy Young Energetic Fast Vibrant Masculine
High-brow arts	Sophisticated Elite Discriminating Up-market Serious Pretentious
Mass arts	Young Accessible Friendly Current Innovative Commercial
Social causes	Admirable Concerned Caring Intelligent Explosive
Environmental programmes	Caring Concerned Exploitive

Figure 15.4 Values transfered from sponsorship categories.

Based on: Meenaghan, T. and D. Shipley (1999) Media Effect in Commercial Sponsorship, *European Journal of Marketing,* **33** (3/4), 432. They point out that these are composite views. Values may depend on a specific activity or event, for example football versus tennis

developing community relations was the most usual sponsorship objective for both industrial and consumer companies.[34]

Creating promotional opportunities

Sponsored events provide an ideal opportunity to promote company brands. Sweat shirts, bags,

pens, etc., carrying the company logo at the name of the event can be sold to a captive audience. Where the brand can be consumed during the event (e.g. Stella Artois at a tennis tournament) it provides an opportunity for customers to sample the brand perhaps for the first time.

Sponsorship can also improve the effectiveness of other promotional vehicles. For example, responses to the direct marketing materials issued by the Visa credit card organization and featuring its sponsorship of the Olympic Games were 17 per cent higher than for a control group to whom the sponsorship images were not transmitted.[35]

Expenditure on sponsorship

Sponsorship has experienced major growth in the 1990s. Six factors account for this growth:[36]

1 Restrictive government policies on tobacco and alcohol advertising.
2 Escalating costs of media advertising.
3 Increased leisure activities and sporting events.
4 The proven record of sponsorship.
5 Greater media coverage of sponsored events.
6 The reduced efficiencies of traditional media advertising (e.g. clutter and zapping between television programmes).

Although most money is spent on *event sponsorship* such as a sports or arts event, of increasing importance is *broadcast sponsorship* where a television or radio programme is the focus. Both forms of sponsorship are of growing importance. Marketing in Action 15.4 discusses how to get the most from a sponsorship deal.

Broadcast sponsorship of programmes can extend into the sharing of production costs. This is attractive to broadcasters, who face increasing costs of programming, and sponsors, who gain a greater degree of influence in negotiations with broadcasters, an opportunity to benefit from cheaper advertising, and having the rights to exploit the programme, its characters and actors for promotional purposes. In Europe, composite programmes like Unilever's game show *Wheel of*

Fortune, which can be customized for each market, already achieves some success.[37]

Accompanying the growth of event sponsorship has been the phenomenon of **ambush marketing**. Originally this term referred to activities of companies who tried to associate themselves with an event (e.g. the Olympics) without paying any fee to the event owner. The activity is legal so long as no attempt is made to use an event symbol, logo or mascot. More recently the term has been broadened to include a range of activities such as sponsoring the television coverage of a major event, sponsoring national teams and the support of individual sportspeople.

Selection and evaluation of an event or programme to sponsor

Selection

Selection of an event or programme to sponsor should be undertaken by answering a series of questions.

Communications objectives what are we trying to achieve? Are we looking for awareness or image, improvement in community relations or entertainment opportunities? Does the personality of the event match the desired brand image?

15.4   Marketing in Action

Exploiting Sponsorship Deals

Both event and broadcast sponsorship are growing in popularity with companies keen to exploit the marketing opportunities that links with television and sporting events provide. Major global companies like Sony with their PlayStation (Euro 2000) and Nike (Sydney Olympics) have sought official sponsor status. But if all a sponsor does is badge an event it gets media exposure and brand association with the event but is still failing to fully exploit its asset. Sports sponsorship provides a theme around which clients can build a wide-ranging marketing programme. For example, Pringles and Cereal Partners World-wide, two sponsors of Euro 2000, offered tickets to matches through competitions thus driving up sales. Sainsbury's, the UK supermarket chain, sponsored Team England at France '98 and acquired licensing rights to support their investment. This was backed up with a massive in-store presence including soccer coins, posters, shirts, and mugs. There is no doubt that sales rose during the event.

Broadcast sponsorship also requires through-the-line support to take full advantage of its opportunities. Sega's sponsorship of MTV's The Lick is supported by off-air monthly regional parties to promote its Dreamcast console. The on-screen associations with DJ Trevor Nelson and with MTV gives Dreamcast awareness and credibility. Further activity off-air allows the brand to integrate itself into the 16–34-year-old lifestyle. The parties are supported by extensive local PR and cross-promotions with HMV. They allow people to try out the Dreamcast consoles. The programme and brand are linked by the design of an integrated logo, and joint web activity allows Dreamcast owners to interact regularly on-line, many of whom check out the latest Lick details on the site. By developing a fully integrated TV sponsorship package, Sega have created awareness and credibility, and built lasting relationships with their customers.

Based on: Armitage (2000);[38] Fry (2000)[39]

Target market who are we trying to reach? Is it the trade or final customers? How does the profile of our customer base match the likely audience of the sponsored event or programme?

Risk what are the associated risks? What are the chances that the event or programme might attract adverse publicity (e.g. football hooliganism tainting the image of the sport and, by implication, the sponsor)? To what extent would termination of the sponsorship contract attract bad publicity (e.g. mean the closing of a theatre)?

Promotional opportunities what are the potential sales promotion and publicity opportunities?

Past record if the event or programme has been sponsored before.what were the results? Why did the previous sponsor withdraw?

Cost does the sponsorship opportunity represent value for money?

Evaluation

This process should lead to a clear idea of why an event or programme is being sponsored. Understanding *sponsorship objectives* is the first step in evaluating its success. As we have seen, Canon used football sponsorship to improve awareness levels and market research was carried out as a monitor. Sponsorship of a school by providing personal computers would be monitored by measuring coverage in local newspapers, radio stations and possibly television.

For major sponsorship deals, evaluation is likely to be more formal and involve measurement of *media coverage and name mentions/sightings* using a specialist monitoring agency. For example, Volvo's £2 million sponsorship of tennis resulted in 1.4 billion impressions (number of mentions or sightings × audience size) which they calculated was worth £12 million in media advertising.[40]

Meenaghan[41] recommends the following evaluation procedure designed to measure the effects of the exposure:

1 Determination of the company's brand's present position in terms of pre-sponsorship awareness and image with the target audience, and the setting of objectives.

2 Tracking to detect movements in customer awareness and attitudes towards the company/brand.

3 Post-sponsorship comparison of performance levels against initial objectives.

However, a survey into the evaluation of football sponsorship found that while two-thirds of companies evaluated their sponsorship activities few went beyond the basic measurement of media coverage.[42]

Exhibitions

Exhibitions are unique in that of all the promotional tools available they are the only one that brings buyers, sellers and the competitors together in a commercial setting. In Europe, the Cologne trade exhibitions bring together 28 000 exhibitors from 100 countries with 1.8 million buyers from 150 countries.[43] Overall, the number of exhibitions, exhibitors and visitors is growing. Nevertheless, the perceived value of exhibitions is debatable. The following comments illustrate the wide variation of opinion:

> While all elements within the communication program are vital, perhaps only the exhibition will involve all disciplines, and will present the greatest opportunity to present Gould as a total company.[44]

> Exhibitions are usually a form of mass hysteria. It is a foregone conclusion that they are very expensive. Even though there may be thousands of visitors, there are also thousands of exhibits. The retention factor is very debatable … every time we exhibit at a trade show, our conclusion is 'never again'.[45]

Despite these differing views, exhibitions appear to be an important part of the industrial promotion mix. One study into the relative importance of promotional media place exhibitions as a source of information in the industrial buying process second only to personal selling, and ahead of direct mail and print advertising.[46]

Their importance is mirrored in the expansion of the number of exhibitions taking place in Europe despite the fact that the difficulty in evaluating their success means that they are often the first to suffer when a marketing budget needs to be cut.[47] Besides the usual major industry exhibitions such as motor shows more specialized lifestyle exhibitions are emerging targeting niche markets. For example, the Cosmo Show featuring cosmetics targets young women and attracts over 55 000 visitors. The 1999 event was the launch pad for Olay Colour (formerly Oil of Ulay) to reveal its new identity and for the launch of Cussons new moisturizer Aqua Source.[48]

Exhibition objectives

Exhibitions can achieve a number of objectives including:

1 An opportunity to reach an audience with a distinct interest in the market and the products on display.
2 Create awareness and develop relationships with new prospects.
3 Strengthen existing customer relationships.
4 Provide product demonstrations.
5 Determine and stimulate needs of customers.
6 Gather competitive intelligence.
7 Introduce a new product.
8 Recruit dealers or distributors.
9 Maintain/improve company image.

10 Deal with service and other customer problems.
11 Generate a mailing list.
12 Make a sale.

Bonoma has organized many of these objectives into a matrix depending on whether the objective concerns current or potential customers, and selling versus non-selling objectives (Fig. 15.5).[49] Research into why companies exhibit at trade shows found that the major reasons were:[50]

1 To generate leads/enquiries.
2 To introduce a new product or service.
3 Because competitors are exhibiting.
4 To recruit dealers or distributors.

Whatever objectives are set they should be clear and measurable. This enables the exhibitor to identify the real opportunities presented by the event and allows the degree of success of the exhibition to be evaluated.[51]

In no other medium will advertising, publicity, sales promotion, product demonstration, sales staff, key management, present customers and prospects join together in a live event that offers the opportunity to impress key audience perceptions of the company, its operations and products.[52]

	Selling objectives	Non-selling objectives
Current customers	Maintain relationship Transmit benefits Remedy service problems Stimulate extra sales	Maintain image Demonstrate products Gather competitive intelligence Widen exposure
Potential customers (prospects)	Contact prospects Determine needs Transmit benefits Commit to follow-up or sale	Contact prospects Foster image building Demonstrate products Gather competitive intelligence

Figure 15.5 Exhibition objectives.

Source: adapted from Bonoma, T.V. (1985) Get More out of your Trade Shows, in Gumpbert, D. E. (ed.), *The Marketing Renaissance*, New York: Wiley. Copyright © 1985 John Wiley & Sons Inc. Reprinted by permission

Planning for an exhibition

Success at an exhibition involves considerable pre-event planning. Clear objectives should be set, selection criteria for evaluating exhibition attendance determined and design and promotional strategies decided. Pre-show promotion to attract visitors to the stand include direct mail, telephoning, a personal sales call before the event and an advertisement in the trade or technical press.

A high degree of professionalism is required by the staff who attend the exhibition stand. The characteristics of a good exhibitor have been found to be:[53]

1 Exhibiting a wider range of products, particularly large items that cannot be demonstrated on a sales call.

2 Staff always in attendance at the stand: visitors should never hear that 'the person who covers that product is not here right now'.

3 Well-informed staff.

4 Informative literature available.

5 Seating area or office provided on the stand.

6 Refreshments provided.

Evaluating an exhibition

Post-show evaluation will examine performance against objectives. This is a learning exercise which will help to judge whether the objectives were realistic, how valuable the exhibition appears to be and how well the company was represented.

Quantitative measures include:

1 The number of visitors to the stand.

2 The number of key influencers/decision-makers who visited the stand.

3 How many leads/enquiries were generated.

4 The cost per lead/enquiry.

5 The number and value of orders.

6 The cost per order.

7 The number of new distributorships opened/likely to be opened.

Other more subjective, qualitative criteria include:

1 The worth of competitive intelligence.

2 Interest generated in the new products.

3 The cultivation of new/existing relationships.

4 The value of customer query and complaint handling.

5 The promotion of brand values.

Sales and marketing may not always agree on the key evaluation criteria to use. For example, sales may judge the exhibition on the number of leads while marketing may prefer to judge the show on the longer-term issue of the promotion of brand values.[54]

Finally, since a major objective of many exhibitors is to stimulate leads and enquiries, mechanisms must be in place to ensure that these are followed up promptly. Furthermore, the leads generated at an exhibition can be used to build a marketing database for future direct mail campaigns.[55]

Ethical issues in sales promotion and public relations

Ethical concerns regarding sales promotion and public relations include the use of trade inducements, malredemption of coupons and the use of third-party endorsements.

Use of trade inducements

Retailers sometimes accept inducements from manufacturers to encourage their salespeople to push the manufacturers' products. This often takes the form of bonus payments to salespeople. The result is that there is an incentive for salespeople to pay special attention to those product lines which are linked to such bonuses when talking to customers. Customers may, therefore, be subjected to pressure to buy products which do not best meet their needs.

Malredemption of coupons

This ethical issue concerns the behaviour of customers in supermarkets who attempt to redeem reduced price coupons without buying the associated product. When faced with a large shopping trolley of goods it is easy for super-market checkout attendants to accept coupons without verification. The key to stopping this practice is thorough training of supermarket employees so that they always check coupons against goods purchased.

Third-party endorsements

An ethical question is related to the use of third-party endorsements to publicise a product. The person gives a written, verbal and/or visual recommendation for the product. A well-known, well-respected person is usually chosen but given that payment often accompanies the endorsement the question arises as to its credibility. Supporters of endorsements argue that consumers know that endorsers are usually paid and are capable of making their own judgements regarding their credence.

Summary

This chapter has explored five promotional mix methods: sales promotion, public relations and publicity, direct marketing, sponsorship, and exhibitions. All of these methods have one thing in common: they are all of increasing importance in the promotional mix with expenditures rising. Sales promotions are usually intended to give a short-term boost to sales. Care must be exercised to ensure that their effect does not conflict with long-term brand building strategies. Publicity is an important aspect of public relations which seeks to create and maintain good relationships between the company and its various publics. Publicity is sometimes referred to as free adver-tising but often there are real costs as the function needs to be managed, either internally or by an outside agency.

Direct marketing covers such communication devices as direct mail, telemarketing, direct response advertising, magazine inserts, door-to-door leafleting and mail order catalogues. It seeks to elicit a direct response (e.g. an order or enquiry) from consumers. For much direct marketing activity an accurate marketing database is essential so that target consumers can be reached efficiently. Telemarketing has many func-tions including direct selling, generating and screening leads, supporting the salesforce and database building and updating.

Sponsorship can be used to gain publicity, create entertainment opportunities, foster favour-able brand and company associations, improve community relations and create promotional opportunities. Two key methods are event and broadcast sponsorship. Unlike all other pro-motional methods, exhibitions bring together in one building buyers, sellers and competitors. Care must be taken in selecting the most appropriate exhibitions to support. However, if managed well, exhibiting can provide an opportunity to reach an audience with a distinct interest in the market and the products on display.

Three key ethical issues were examined: use of trade inducements, malredemption of coupons, and third-party endorsements.

Internet exercise

Publicity

Sites to visit
http://www.virgin.co.uk/news/news.jsp

Exercise
Review the news stories on Virgin's website. What conclusions would you draw about the organization's management of publicity?

Study questions

1 When you next visit a supermarket examine three sales promotions. What type of promotion are they? What are their likely objectives?

2 Why would it be wrong to measure the sales effect of a promotion only during the promotional period? What are the likely long-term effects of a promotion?

3 Distinguish between public relations and publicity. Is it true that publicity can be regarded as free advertising?

4 There is no such thing as bad publicity. Discuss.

5 The major reason for event sponsorship is to indulge senior management in their favourite pastime. Discuss.

6 Exhibitions are less effective than personal selling and more costly than direct mail so why use them?

References

1. Peattie, K. and S. Peattie (1993) Sales Promotion: Playing to Win?, *Journal of Marketing Management*, **9**, 255-69.
2. Lal, R. (1990) Manufacturer Trade Deals and Retail Price Promotion, *Journal of Marketing Research*, **27** (6), 428-44.
3. Rothschild, M. L. and W. C. Gaidis (1981) Behavioural Learning Theory: Its Relevance to Marketing and Promotions, *Journal of Marketing*, **45**, (spring) 70-8.
4. Tuck, R. T. J. and W. G. B. Harvey (1972) Do Promotions Undermine the Brand?, *Admap*, January, 30-3.
5. Brown, R. G. (1974) Sales Response to Promotions and Advertising, *Journal of Advertising Research*, **14** (4), 33-9.
6. Ehrenberg, A. S. C., K. Hammond and G. J. Goodhardt (1994) The After-Effects of Price-Related Consumer Promotions, *Journal of Advertising Research*, **34** (4), 1-10.
7. Smith, P. R. (1993) *Marketing Communications: An Integrated Approach*, London: Kogan Page, 240-3.
8. Hemsley, S. (1999) Joint Statement, *Marketing Week*, 21 October, 45-8.
9. Miller, R. (2000) Making the Most of Brand Alliances, *Marketing*, 3 February, 25-6.
10. Killigran, L. and R. Cook (1999) Multibuy Push May Backfire, *Marketing Week*, 16 September, 44-5.
11. Davidson, J. H. (1998) *Offensive Marketing*, Harmondsworth: Penguin, 249-71.
12. Cummins, J. (1989) *Sales Promotion*, London: Kogan Page, 79.
13. Davidson (1987) op. cit.
14. Cummins (1989) op. cit.
15. Collins, M. (1986) Research on 'Below the Line' Expenditure, in Worcester, R. and J. Downham (eds) *Consumer Market Research Handbook*, Amsterdam: North Holland, 537-50.
16. Cummins (1989) op. cit.
17. Doyle, P. and J. Saunders (1985) The Lead Effect of Marketing Decisions, *Journal of Marketing Research*, **22** (1), 54-65.
18. White, J. (1991) *How to Understand and Manage Public Relations*, London: Business Books.
19. Lesly, P. (1991) *The Handbook of Public Relations and Communications*, Maidenhead: McGraw-Hill, 13-19.
20. Kitchen, P. J. and T. Proctor (1991) The Increasing Importance of Public Relations in Fast Moving Consumer Goods Firms, *Journal of Marketing Management*, **7** (4), 357-70.
21. Lesly (1991) op. cit.
22. Cobb, R. (1993) Follow the PR Leader, *Marketing*, 29 April, 29.
23. Guide 28 (1993) International Public Relations, *Marketing*, 1 July, 21-24.
24. Cobb, R. (1997) Small Screen Big Prospects, *Marketing*, 27 February, 6-9.
25. Goddard, L. (1999) Building PR Teams to Conquer Europe, *Marketing*, 24 June, 34.
26. Jefkins, F. (1985) Timing and Handling of Material, in Howard, W. (ed.) *The Practice of Public Relations*, Oxford: Heinemann, 86-104.
27. Sleight, S. (1989) *Sponsorship: What It Is and How to Use It*, Maidenhead: McGraw-Hill, 4.
28. Gofton, K. (1996) Integrating the Delivery, *Marketing*, 31 October, Special Supplement on Choosing and Using Public Relations, 8-10.
29. Flack, J. (1999) Public Speaking, *Marketing Week*, 4 November, 51-2.
30. Bennett, R. (1999) Sports Sponsorship, Spectator Recall and False Consensus, *European Journal of Marketing*, **33** (3/4), 291-313.
31. Mintel (1991) *Sponsorship, Special Report*, London: Mintel International Group Ltd.
32. McKelvey, C. (1999) TV Washout, *Marketing Week*, 2 December, 27-9.
33. Meenaghan, T. and D. Shipley, Media Effects in Commercial Sponsorship, *European Journal of Marketing*, **33** (3/4), 328-47.
34. Haywood, R. (1984) *All About PR*, Maidenhead: McGraw-Hill, 186.

35. Crowley, M. G. (1991) Prioritising the Sponsorship Audience, *European Journal of Marketing*, **25** (11), 11-21.

36. Miles, L. (1995) Sporting Chancers, *Marketing Director International*, **6** (2), 50-2.

37. Meenaghan, T. (1991) Sponsorship: Legitimising the Medium, *European Journal of Marketing*, **25** (11), 5-10.

38. Armitage, B. (2000) TV Sponsorship is not Enough to Boost Brands, *Marketing Week*, 13 April, 14.

39. Fry, A. (2000) Why Sponsors are Great Fans of Sport, *Marketing*, 30 March, 41-2.

40. Mould (1992) op. cit.

41. Smith (1993) op. cit.

42. Meenaghan, T. (1991) The Role of Sponsorship in the Marketing Communications Mix, *International Journal of Advertising*, **10**, 35-47.

43. Thwaites, D. (1995) Professional Football Sponsorship—Profitable or Profligate?, *International Journal of Advertising*, **14**, 149-64.

44. O'Hara, B., F. Palumbo and P. Herbig (1993) Industrial Trade Shows Abroad, *Industrial Marketing Management*, **22**, 233-7.

45. Couretas, J. (1984) Trade Shows and the Strategic Mainstream, *Business Marketing*, **69**, 64-70.

46. Anonymous (1979) Trade Shows are Usually a Form of Mass Hysteria, *Industrial Marketing*, **64** (4), 6-10.

47. Parasuraman, A. (1981) The Relative Importance of Industrial Promotional Tools, *Industrial Marketing Management*, **10**, 277-81.

48. Zappaterra, Y. (1999) Proving Your Worth, *Marketing*, 25 February, 35-6.

49. McLuhan, R. (1999) Hitting the Target at Lifestyle Events, *Marketing Week*, 20 May, 27-8.

50. Bonoma, T. V. (1985) Get More Out of your Trade Shows, in Gumpert, D. E. (ed.) *The Marketing Renaissance*, New York: Wiley.

51. Trade Show Bureau (1983) *The Exhibitor: Their Trade Show Practices*, Research Report no. 19, East Orleans, Mass: Trade Show Bureau.

52. Russell, I. (1999) Driving Force, *Marketing Week*, 7 October, 69-73.

53. Couretas (1984) op. cit.

54. Lancaster, G. and H. Baron (1977) Exhibiting for Profit, *Industrial Management*, November, 24-7.

55. Blaskey, J. (1999) Proving Your Worth, *Marketing*, 25 February, 35-6.

Key terms

money-off promotions   sales promotions that discount the normal price

bonus pack   giving a customer extra quantity at no additional cost

premiums   any merchandise offered free or at low cost as an incentive to purchase

consumer pull   the targeting of consumers with communications (e.g. promotions) designed to create demand that will pull the product into the distribution chain

distribution push   the targeting of channel intermediaries with communications (e.g. promotions) to push the product into the distribution chain

group discussion   a group usually of 6-8 consumers brought together for a discussion focusing on an aspect of a company's marketing

Hall tests   bringing a sample of target consumers to a room that has been hired so that alternative marketing ideas (e.g. promotions) can be tested

experimentation   the application of stimuli (e.g. two price levels) to different matched groups under controlled conditions for the purpose of measuring their effect on a variable (e.g. sales)

consumer panel data   a type of continuous research where information is provided by household consumers on their purchases over time

retail audit data   a type of continuous research tracking the sales of products through retail outlets

public relations   the management of communications and relationships to establish goodwill and mutual understanding between an organization and its public

publicity   communication about a product or organization by placing news about it in the media without paying for the time or space directly

sponsorship   A business relationship between a provider of funds, resources or services and an individual, event, or organization which offers in return some rights and association that may be used for commercial advantage

event sponsorship   sponsorship of a sporting or other event

broadcast sponsorship   a form of sponsorship where a television or radio programme is the focus

ambush marketing   originally referred to activities of companies who try to associate themselves with an event (e.g. the Olympics) without paying any fee to the event owner; now meaning the sponsoring of the television coverage of a major event, national teams and the support of individual sportspeople

exhibition   an event which brings buyers and sellers together in a commercial setting

Case 27 New Sponsorship: Launching the Lincoln

Sponsorship, in its early years, was really about getting exposure for brands. Big companies would sponsor big sporting events (for big money) in exchange for having the brand logo on boards at the sides of the ground, or displayed on racing cars, or otherwise put where the TV cameras were likely to pick it up. Most of the integration of the communications campaigns was actually carried out by using expensive advertising and on-pack announcements: 'sponsors of . . .' announcements which cost the brand owner millions to produce. For example, Endsleigh Insurance paid £1 million a year to sponsor the football league, but apart from its exposure there was little capitalization on the sponsorship.

The second phase of sponsorship thinking was to use the sponsorship to link to the brand—to sponsor events which were relevant to the brand in some way. Marketers realized that sponsorship could add qualitatively to the brand as well as build awareness. In other words the currently evolving third stage goes back to basics: the sponsorship starts with the consumers rather than with the brands. Lesa Ukman, president of the IEG corporate research consultancy, says 'In an environment where what a company stands for is as important as what it sells, sponsorship is not an optional activity, but core to brand and business building. What companies should be buying now is not the right to claim they are a sponsor, but rather the right to create experiential overlays for customers.'

The lesson has not been lost on the Ford Motor Company, owners of the Lincoln–Mercury luxury car brand. In 1996, sales of Lincoln–Mercury cars were at an all-time low of 141 476 cars—a 40 per cent drop over only six years. Lincoln's new marketing manager, Jim Rogers, realized that the situation required drastic action—not least because research showed that the average age of the Lincoln customer was 57 years. Clearly the lifetime value of these customers was likely to be low, as they were rapidly heading towards old age and would be unlikely to be driving for very much longer. Elderly people also change their cars less frequently: given that the Lincolns were in the luxury class, and therefore had a longer life-span

than cheap models, it seemed entirely possible that most of Lincoln's existing customers would never buy another car.

Clearly Rogers did not want to lose the existing customers, but at the same time he needed to establish a presence in a younger market— preferably the affluent 35–49-year-olds who were turning to BMW and Lexus. This meant that the company needed to launch new brands, and to launch them in a novel way.

Rogers began by moving production from Michigan to California, and introducing a new model—the Lincoln Navigator. This stopped the rot temporarily, but he was well aware that this could not become a permanent solution. 'Changing the product was not enough', he said. 'We needed to change what the brand stood for on an emotional basis. After all, nobody needs to pay $40–50 000 for a car.'

Rogers committed $90 million to the most integrated car campaign ever undertaken: the campaign centred around yet another new model, the Lincoln LS. The central linking feature of the campaign was a three-year sponsorship deal with the innovative Cirque du Soleil, a Montreal-based circus group which has no animal acts, but does have spectacular, exciting and by no means traditional performances by its human members. Rogers knew that the target audience has little knowledge of the Lincoln marque, so his first move was to generate a database of targets to whom the company could deliver its message.

The initial result of this was a mini-tour of three of the Cirque du Soleil acts to eight major cities, ahead of the Lincoln-sponsored main tour of the entire circus. The mini-tour pulled in hundreds of potential buyers who were able to see the car in a casual and intimate environment, but more important the presence of the Cirque du Soleil encouraged these people to recommend the circus to their friends and acquaintances. This meant that, when the full circus came to town, the audience was packed with people who were in the right age and income bracket to represent potential Lincoln customers. In this way Rogers was able to attract target-audience members who would otherwise have been inaccessible.

Rogers realized the importance of creating a

communications link between the circus and the car. 'We created two different displays', he said. 'One a kinetic water display designed by the Cirque set designer, Stephane Roy, and the other an interactive display to demonstrate the car, but not to sell it.'

Dealerships in each town coordinated their activities with the main campaign, giving away tickets for test-drives and organizing fund-raising events for local charities and art events. Many even devised and funded their own schemes, linked to the overall theme. Young and Rubicam were commissioned to run an innovative national TV and press campaign, but were instructed to use non-traditional approaches to reach the target audience.

Ford's approach to the LS launch had more in common with launches of luxury spirits and fashionable clothing: using this approach to launch a high-ticket luxury car was innovative in

itself. What marked out the campaign as being truly innovative was its use of a close partnership between the sponsor and the recipient to create a completely new series of events in which the 'car was the star'.

And the results of all this effort? By August 1999, Lincoln had sold all the LS Sedans they could make—30 000 cars in all, representing some $1.4 billion of gross revenue. More importantly, the company was able to tap into a target market with a known propensity to buy cars, buying a new car on average every two years or so: coupled with the firm's relationship approach to those customers, the potential long-term stream of revenue from the target group is likely to be worth tens of billions of dollars—a worthwhile return for a mere $90 million.

This case was prepared by Jim Blythe, Senior Lecturer in Marketing, University of Glamorgan.

Questions

1   Why would Lincoln aim for the 35–49 age group rather than a younger target audience?

2   Why might Rogers have chosen the Cirque du Soleil rather than sponsoring a more car-orientated event such as motor sports?

3   Apart from the sponsorship money, how might Cirque du Soleil have benefited from the partnership?

4   Having generated a good mailing list, and commissioned Young and Rubicam, why might Rogers have decided not to simply mailshot those individuals with information about the car?

5   Rogers created a display which demonstrated the car but did not sell it— why *not* sell it?

Case 28 Kuala Lumpur 1998: The XVI Commonwealth Games

The increasing expense of hosting major international sporting events has led organizing committees to seek both financial and material assistance from the corporate sector through the provision of a range of sponsorship opportunities. For example, Malaysia won the bid to host the 1998 Commonwealth Games; the first time in its history that the event will be held in Asia. The government of Malaysia and the country's Olympic Council set up SUKOM NINETY EIGHT BERHAD as the organizing committee for the Games. An initial launching fund of RM10 million (approximately £2.5 million) was made available to SUKOM on the understanding that the remaining budget would be raised from the private sector, both nationally and internationally.

In addition to the usual individual sports such as athletics, boxing and weightlifting the Kuala Lumpur 98 Games included team sports such as cricket, hockey and rugby. In all 14 sports were accommodated and 68 nations took part. Through a combination of network and satellite broadcasts an estimated audience of 500 million viewers was reached spread across 80 countries. The transmission covered over 1000 television hours. Approximately 6000 athletes and officials attended the event together with 2500 print media and photo journalists and 2000 domestic/international broadcasters. In the region of 60 000 foreign spectators attended in addition to the millions from within Malaysia. The Games clearly provided a great opportunity for both domestic and international companies to promote their goods and services through a variety of sponsorship opportunities. SUKOM has identified various classifications of sponsor which include:

+ Partners programme.
+ Official Sponsors package.
+ Licensee.
+ Official Suppliers package.
+ Proud Supporters.
+ Friend of SUKOM.

Many internationally known companies have recognized the marketing opportunities which exist and became associated with the Games. For example Carlsberg, Kodak and Siemens were Official Sponsors while Nestlé and Unilever were Official Suppliers. The package available to an Official Supplier is illustrated in Table C28.1.

Ambush marketing

Accompanying the growth of event sponsorship has been the phenomenon of ambush marketing (sometimes referred to as guerrilla or parasite marketing) by which a company (invariably a competitor) seeks to reduce the effectiveness of the sponsor's activity and enhance its own position. Many examples of this practice are cited in the literature although the following cases illustrate the point.

+ In 1988 American Express discontinued its Olympic sponsorship at which point Visa became the official credit card sponsor. American Express subsequently launched an advertising campaign featuring former Olympic stars. Visa's response was to advertise that American Express cards were not accepted at the Games. American Express then stated that it was possible to purchase items with their card and there was no need to have a 'visa' to enjoy the Games.

    The battle continued in 1992 when American Express purchased advertising space on room key tags at the Hotel Princess Sophia in Barcelona. This was the official accommodation of members of the International Olympic Committee. Visa was the official credit card of the Games.

+ Billboards showing the Nike name and 'swoosh' logo were erected on a building specifically constructed by Nike close to Atlanta's Olympic Park. Reebok was the official sponsor in the sports goods category.

+ Federal Express promoted its sponsorship of the United States men's basketball dream team although UPS was the official overnight mail sponsor of the Olympics.

Research at major sporting events such as the Olympic Games and World Cup Soccer suggests that being recognized as a sponsor bestows significant benefits on a company. For example, they are more inclined to be perceived as leaders in their field, dedicated to excellence, modern and innovative, and providers of high quality products. The propensity to purchase their products also increases. Ambush marketers may therefore dilute these perceptions of the major sponsor while acquiring some of the benefits for themselves.

The success of ambush marketing may be viewed in relation to the extent to which the public is confused regarding the names of event sponsors. For example during the 1990 Soccer World Cup only 2 of the 10 official worldwide sponsors, which included household names such as Coca-Cola and Mars, achieved greater recognition (more people citing them as a sponsor) than National Power which merely sponsored some of the broadcasting. Likewise at the 1992 Olympic Games non-sponsors such as Federal Express and Sears outperformed Express Mail

---

Table C28.1   Official supplier rights and benefits

Exclusive product category rights

✦   Only one Official Supplier within a given category will be permitted to associate with the Games.

Designation

✦   Freedom to use the expression 'Official Supplier of (product)' and use the SUKOM logo.

Special logo rights

✦   SUKOM will seek ways of associating the supplier's logo with SUKOM's logo to enhance public appreciation of the relationship between the two organizations.

Ticketing

✦   Complimentary tickets for each day of the Games.

✦   Preferential access to additional tickets.

✦   Some priority in seat selection.

Advertising and promotions

✦   SUKOM will promote the Official Supplier's involvement through advertising media releases, brochures, newsletters, etc.

✦   Receipt of regular copies of SUKOM's official reports, bulletins and other publications.

Access to television airtime

✦   SUKOM will negotiate with the purchasers of broadcast rights to allow Official Suppliers the first opportunity to buy commercial airtime.

Access to the games' licensed publications

✦   Some priority in securing advertising space.

Exclusive premium lines

✦   SUKOM Licensees will produce items suitable for use as premiums. Official Suppliers will have access to the lines at wholesale prices.

Corporate hospitality village

✦   Opportunity to purchase space.

Preferred supplier status

✦   Possible sales opportunities where SUKOM requirements exceed the total contributed by the Official Supplier.

✦   Other sponsors are recommended to use Official Suppliers.

✦   Concessionaires at SUKOM—controlled venues are precluded from offering and displaying products which compete with the products of an Official Supplier.

and J. C. Penney the official sponsors of the same categories.

As the cost of major sports events continues to rise perhaps it is not surprising that companies will attempt to maximize their opportunities for affiliation at minimal expense. However if the companies who are investing significant sums in the sponsorship of sporting events (and Coca-Cola is reputed to have paid $42 million to become associated with the 1996 Olympic pro-gramme) feel that ambush strategies are reducing their promotional effectiveness, this could have significant implications for the continued corporate funding of major sporting events. Given the heavy dependency on this source of funding it could even bring into question the future of the events themselves.

This case study was prepared by Dr Des Thwaites, Leeds University Business School.

Questions

1   Is ambush marketing immoral or a legitimate commercial practice?

2   Imagine you are a category sponsor at the Commonwealth Games:
    (a) What safeguards would you expect SUKOM to put in place on your behalf?
    (b) What would you do to protect your own investment?

3   Imagine you are a leading player in a particular category and that a major competitor has become the official sponsor of the Games. What ambush strategies would you employ?

CHAPTER SIXTEEN

Distribution

'Uphill slow, downhill fast
Cargo first, safety last'

US TRUCKING MOTTO CIRCA 1950

Learning Objectives *This chapter explains:*

1 The functions and types of channels of distribution

2 How to determine channel strategy

3 The three components of channel strategy: channel selection, intensity and integration

4 The factors affecting channel management

5 The five key channel management issues: member selection, motivation, training, evaluation and conflict management

6 The cost–customer service trade-off in physical distribution

7 The components of a physical distribution system, customer service, order processing, inventory control, warehousing, transportation and materials handling

8 How to improve customer service standards in physical distribution

9 Ethical issues in distribution

Producing products that customers want, pricing them correctly and developing well-designed promotional plans are necessary but not sufficient conditions for customer satisfaction. The final part of the jigsaw is distribution, the *place* element of the marketing mix. Products need to be available in adequate quantities, in convenient locations and at times when customers want to buy them. In this chapter we shall examine the functions and types of distribution channels, the key decisions that determine channel strategy, how to manage channels and issues relating to the physical flow of goods through distribution channels (physical distribution management).

Producers need to consider not only the needs of their ultimate customer but also the requirement of *channel intermediaries*, those organizations who facilitate the distribution of products to customers. For example, success for Müller yoghurt in the UK was dependent on convincing a powerful retailer group (Tesco) to stock the brand. The high margins that the brand supported was a key influence in Tesco's decision. Without retailer support Müller would have found it uneconomic to supply consumers with their brand. Clearly, establishing a supply chain that is efficient and meets customers' needs is vital to marketing success. This supply chain is termed a *channel of distribution*, which is the means by which products are moved from producer to the ultimate customer. Gaining distribution outlets does not come easily. Advertising to channel intermediaries is sometimes used to promote the benefits of stocking a brand, as with the advertisement for Dove Nourishing Body Wash (opposite), which appeared in *The Grocer*.

The choice of the most effective channel of distribution is an important aspect of marketing strategy. The development of supermarkets effectively shortened the distribution channel between producer and consumer by eliminating the wholesaler. Prior to their introduction the typical distribution channel for products like food, drink, tobacco and toiletries was producer to wholesaler to retailer. The wholesaler would buy in bulk from the producer and sell smaller quantities to the retailer (typically a small grocery shop). By building up buying power supermarkets could shorten this chain by buying direct from producers. This meant lower costs to the supermarket chain, and lower prices to the consumer. The competitive effect was to drastically reduce the numbers of small grocers and wholesalers in this market. By being more efficient and better meeting customers' needs supermarkets had created a competitive advantage for themselves.

More recently the growing use of the Internet as a promotional and distribution channel is having a major impact on the way companies including supermarkets distribute their goods and services. e-Marketing 16.1 discusses the changes that are occurring as a result of this trend.

Next, we shall explore the functions of channel intermediaries and then examine the different types of channels that manufacturers can use to supply their products to customers.

Functions of channel intermediaries

The most basic question to ask when deciding channel strategy is whether to sell directly to the ultimate customer, or to use channel intermediaries such as retailers and/or wholesalers. To answer this question we need to understand the functions of channel intermediaries, that is, what benefits might producers derive from their use. Their functions are to reconcile the needs of producers and customers, to improve efficiency by reducing the number of transactions or creating bulk, to improve accessibility by lowering location and time gaps between producers and consumers, and to provide specialist services to customers. Each of these functions is now examined in more detail.

Reconciling the needs of producers and consumers

Manufacturers typically produce a large quantity of a limited range of goods, whereas consumers usually want only a limited quantity of a wide range of goods.[1] The role of channel intermediaries is to reconcile these conflicting situations. For example, a manufacturer of tables sells to retailers that each buy from a range of manufacturers of furniture and furnishings. The manufacturer can gain economies of scale by producing large quantities of tables and each retailer provides a wide assortment of products offering their customers considerable choice under one roof.

EF
ELIDA FABERGÉ
LONDON

New!
Dove
Nourishing
Body Wash.

Help yourself to well fed skin.

Whilst other shower products merely moisturise, new Dove Nourishing Body Wash with its dual-chamber formulation goes deeper – to actively feed and restore the skin with nutrients and Vitamin E, leaving it incredibly soft, with a radiant glow.

Dove Nourishing Body Wash is pioneering a new level of pampering that really justifies its premium price, offering you a real profit building opportunity.

With a massive Dove master brand investment of £20 million, new Dove Nourishing Body Wash will benefit from specific support on TV and in the Press including a 2 million sampling campaign.

ORDER NOW! Help yourself to well fed profits!

Dove
NOURISHING
Body Wash

Advertising to Retailers: Elida Fabergé understand the importance of good distribution

A related function of channel intermediaries is *breaking bulk*. A wholesaler may buy large quantities from a manufacturer (perhaps a container load) and then sell smaller quantities (such as by the case) to retailers. Alternatively large retailers such as supermarkets buy large quantities from producers, and break bulk by splitting the order between outlets. In this way, producers can produce large quantities while consumers are offered limited quantities at the point of purchase.

Improving efficiency

Channel intermediaries can improve distribution efficiency by *reducing the number of trans-*

16.1   e-Marketing
The Impact of the Internet on Distribution

One of the most obvious signs that e-commerce has taken off is the sight of new automated warehouses and thousands of vans delivering little packets to households, that is the distribution end of the Internet revolution. Although placing an order over the Internet may be simple, it is distribution that is causing most problems, for example at peak periods as Toys 'Я' Us and Wal-Mart found when they could not guarantee delivery of website orders by Christmas. The trend now is to outsource website distribution. For example, Wal-Mart, which possesses the most highly praised distribution system in the world when supplying its stores, was unable to cope with individual orders delivered to households. In the US, it has had to outsource its website distribution to two rivals: Fingerhut and Books-a-million. Etoys also outsource to Fingerhut.

The major beneficiary of this trend is UPS which claims to distribute two-thirds of all goods ordered on-line in the USA, and has developed a sophisticated website-based tracking service that allows consumers to check exactly where their order is at any time of the day or night.

Regarding picking and packing the tendency is to keep it in-house since a contractor working for many web merchants cannot give all of them top priority at periods of peak demand. Many e-suppliers have followed Amazon's example and built giant automated warehouses to carry out these tasks.

Distribution is also key to the success of the new on-line grocery business. Companies like Peapod.com in the USA and Tesco in the UK have begun an on-line shopping service. One of the big problems is cost. Instead of customers turning up at the store, picking their goods, packing them and then taking them home, retailers have to do it all and still charge a low price.

Another problem is delivering when the shopper is at home. Some US-based firms are guaranteeing delivery times, the most ambitious of which is Webvan which is guaranteeing delivery of groceries within a 30-minute window.

For other types of products distribution direct via the Internet is possible. Much computer software is now digitally downloaded by the user. Music and films are likely to be the next business to go down this route. In 1999, a new release from Public Enemy became the first commercial piece of music to be distributed over the Internet before appearing in the record shops.

The difficulty and expense of distribution are important determinants of which categories of goods and services will be sold over the Internet. Services which do not require physical distribution such as those provided by airlines, travel companies, banks and credit card companies are likely to be major winners in the Internet technology boom. Goods which can be easily and cheaply posted such as books and CDs are also early winners.

Based on: Anonymous (2000);[2] Read (1999);[3] Rushe (1999);[4] Sugar (1999)[5]

actions and *creating bulk for transportation*. Figure 16.1 shows how the number of transactions between three producers and three customers is reduced by using one intermediary. Direct distribution to customers results in nine transactions whereas the use of an intermediary cuts the number of transactions to six. Distribution (and selling) costs and effort, therefore, are reduced.

Small producers can benefit by selling to intermediaries who then combine a large number of small purchases into bulk for transportation. Without the intermediary it may prove too costly for each small producer to meet transportation costs to the consumer. Agricultural products such as coffee, vegetables and fruit which are grown by small producers sometimes benefit by this arrangement.

Improving accessibility

Two major divides that need to be bridged between producers and consumers are the location and time gaps. The *location gap* derives

from the geographic separation of producers from the customers they serve. Many of the cars produced in the UK by Nissan and Toyota are exported to Europe. Car dealers in Europe provide customer access to these cars in the form of display and test drive facilities, and the opportunity to purchase locally rather than deal direct with the producer thousands of miles away.

The *time gap* results from discrepancies between when a manufacturer wants to produce goods and when consumers wish to buy. For example, manufacturers of car spare parts may wish to produce Monday to Friday but consumers may wish to purchase throughout the week and especially on Saturday and Sunday. By opening at the weekend, car accessory outlets bridge the time gap between production and consumption.

Providing specialist services

Channel intermediaries can perform specialist customer services that manufacturers may feel ill-equipped to provide themselves. Distributors may

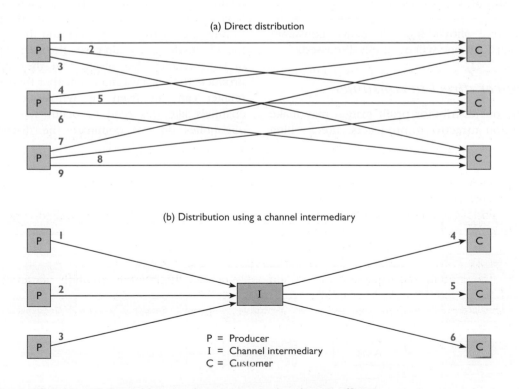

Figure 16.1 How a channel intermediary increases distribution efficiency

have long-standing expertise in such areas as selling, servicing and installation to customers. Producers may feel that these functions are better handled by channel intermediaries so that they can specialize in other aspects of manufacturing and marketing activity.

Types of distribution channels

All products whether they be consumer goods, industrial goods or services require a channel of distribution. Industrial channels tend to be shorter than consumer channels because of the small number of ultimate customers, the greater geographic concentration of industrial customers, and the greater complexity of the products which require close producer-customer liaison. Service channels also tend to be short because of the intangibility of services and the need for personal contact between the service provider and consumer.

Consumer channels

Figure 16.2 shows four alternative consumer channels. Each one will be briefly discussed.

Producer direct to consumer

Cutting out distributor profit margin may make this option attractive to producers. Direct selling

between producer and consumer has been a feature of the marketing of Avon Cosmetics and Tupperware plastic containers. As we discussed in Chapter 13, direct marketing is of growing importance in Europe and includes the use of direct mail, telephone selling and direct response advertising.

Producer to retailer to consumer

The growth in retailer size has meant that it becomes economic for producers to supply retailers directly rather than through wholesalers. Consumers then have the convenience of viewing and/or testing the product at the retail outlet. Supermarket chains exercise considerable power over manufacturers because of their enormous buying capabilities.

Producer to wholesaler to retailer to consumer

For small retailers (e.g. small grocery or furniture shops) with limited order quantities, the use of wholesalers makes economic sense. Wholesalers can buy in bulk from producers, and sell smaller quantities to numerous retailers. The danger is that large retailers in the same market have the power to buy directly from producers and thus cut out the wholesaler. In certain cases, the buying power of large retailers has meant that they can sell products to their customers cheaper than a small retailer can buy from the wholesaler. Longer channels like this tend to occur where retail oligopolies do not dominate the distribution

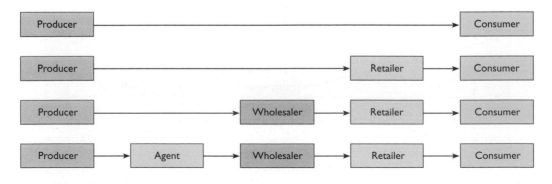

Figure 16.2 Distribution channels for consumer goods

system. In Europe long channels involving wholesalers are common in France and Italy. In France, for example, the distribution of vehicle spare parts is dominated by small independent wholesalers.[6]

Producer to agent to wholesaler to retailer to consumer

This long channel is sometimes used by companies entering foreign markets. They may delegate the task of selling the product to an agent (who does not take title to the goods). The agent contacts wholesalers (or retailers) and receives commission on sales. Overseas sales of books are sometimes generated in this way.

Some companies use multiple channels to distribute their products. Grocery products, for example, use both producer to wholesaler to retailer (small grocers), and producer to retailer (supermarkets). In Japan distribution channels to consumers tend to be long and complex, with close relationships between channel members, a fact that has acted as a barrier to entry for foreign companies. An example of the complexity of Japanese distribution channels for cosmetics is given in Fig. 16.3.[7]

Industrial channels

Common industrial distribution channels are illustrated in Fig. 16.4. Usually a maximum of one-channel intermediary is used.

Producer to industrial customer

Supplying industrial customers directly is common for expensive industrial products such as gas turbines, diesel locomotives, and aero-engines. There needs to be close liaison between supplier and customer to solve technical problems, and the size of the order makes direct selling and distribution economic.

Producer to agent to industrial customer

Instead of selling to industrial customers using their own salesforce, an industrial goods company could employ the services of an agent who may sell a range of goods from several suppliers (on a commission basis). This spreads selling costs and may be attractive to companies without the reserves to set up their own sales operation. The

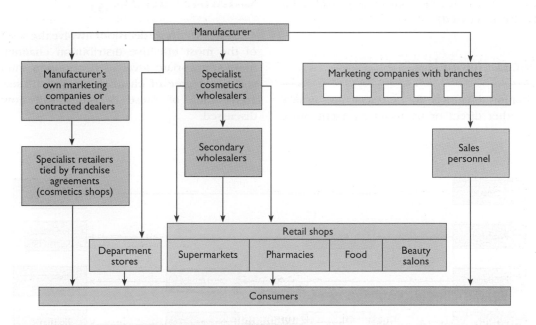

Figure 16.3 Distribution channels for cosmetics in Japan.
Source: Kearney, A. T. (1991) Trade and Investment in Japan: The Current Environment, A Study for the American Chamber of Commerce in Japan

disadvantage is that there is little control over the agent, who is unlikely to devote the same amount of time selling on products compared with a dedicated sales team.

Producer to distributor to industrial customer

For less expensive, more frequently bought industrial products, distributors are used. These may have both internal and field sales staff.[8] Internal staff deal with customer-generated enquiries and order placing, order follow-up (often using the telephone) and checking inventory levels. Outside sales staff are more proactive: their practical responsibilities are to find new customers, get products specified, distribute catalogues and gather market information. The advantage to customers of using distributors is that they can buy small quantities locally.

Producer to agent to distributor to industrial customer

Where industrial customers prefer to call upon distributors the agent's job will require selling into these intermediaries. The reason why a producer may employ an agent rather than a dedicated salesforce is usually cost based (as previously discussed).

Services channels

Distribution channels for services are usually short, either direct or by using an agent. Since stocks are not held, the role of the wholesaler, retailer or industrial distributor does not apply. Figure 16.5 shows the two alternatives whether they be to consumer or industrial customers.

Service provider to consumer or industrial customer

The close personal relationships between service providers and customers often mean that service supply is direct. Examples include health care, office cleaning, accountancy, marketing research and law.

Service provider to agent to consumer or industrial customer

A channel intermediary for a service company usually takes the form of an agent. Agents are used when the service provider is geographically distant from customers, and where it is not economical for the provider to establish their own local sales team. Examples include insurance, travel, secretarial and theatrical agents.

Channel strategy

Channel strategy decisions involve the selection of the most effective distribution channel, the most appropriate level of distribution intensity and the degree of channel integration (see Fig. 16.6). Each of these decisions will now be discussed.

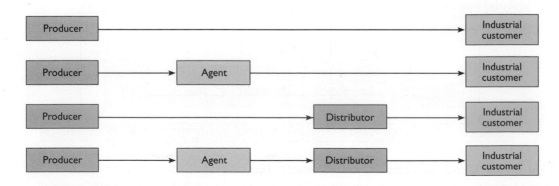

Figure 16.4 Distribution channels for industrial goods

Channel selection

Why does Procter and Gamble sell its brands through supermarkets rather than selling direct'? Why does Brush sell its diesel and electrical locomotives direct to train operating companies rather than using a distributor? The answers are to be found by examining the following factors which influence *channel selection*. These influences can be grouped under market, producer, product, and competitive factors.

Market factors

An important market factor is buyer behaviour: buyer expectations may dictate that the product be sold in a certain way. Buyers may prefer to buy locally and in a particular type of shop. Failure to match these expectations can have catastrophic consequences as when Levi Strauss attempted to sell a new range of clothing (suits) in department stores, even though marketing research had shown that their target customers preferred to buy suits from independent outlets. The result was

that the new range (called Tailored Classics) was withdrawn from the marketplace.

Buyer needs regarding product information, installation and technical assistance also have to be considered. A judgement needs to be made about whether the producer or channel intermediary can best meet these needs in terms of expertise, commitment and cost. For example, products that require facilities for local servicing, such as cars, often use intermediaries to carry out the task. Where the service requirement does not involve large capital investment the producer may carry out the service. For example, suppliers of burglar alarms employ their staff to conduct annual inspection and servicing.

The willingness of channel intermediaries to market a product is also a market-based factor which influences channel decisions. Direct distribution may be the only option if distributors refuse to handle the product. For industrial products this may mean the recruitment of salespeople, and for consumer products direct mail may be employed to communicate to and supply customers. The profit margins demanded by

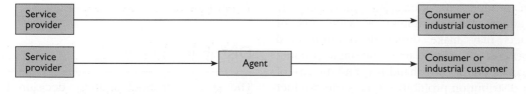

Figure 16.5 Distribution channels for services

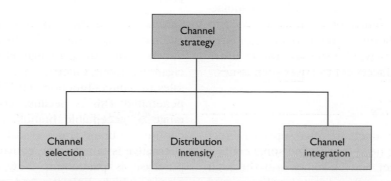

Figure 16.6 Channel strategy

wholesalers and retailers and the commission rates expected by sales agents also affect their attractiveness as channel intermediaries. These costs need to be assessed in comparison with those of a salesforce.

The location and geographical concentration of customers also affects channel selection. The more local and clustered the customer base, the more likely direct distribution is feasible. Direct distribution is also more prevalent when buyers are few in number, and buy large quantities. A large number of small customers may mean that using channel intermediaries is the only economical way of reaching them (hence supermarkets).

Producer factors

A constraint on the channel decision is when the producer lacks adequate resources to perform the functions of the channel. Producers may lack the financial and managerial resources to take on channel operations. Lack of financial resources may mean that a salesforce cannot be recruited and sales agents and/or distributors are used instead. Producers may feel that they do not possess the customer-based skills to distribute their products and prefer to rely on intermediaries instead.

The product mix offered by a producer may also affect channel strategy. A wide mix of products may make direct distribution (and selling) cost effective. Narrow or single product companies, on the other hand, may find the cost of direct distribution prohibitive unless the product is extremely expensive.

The final product influence is the desired degree of control of channel operations. The use of independent channel intermediaries reduces producer control. For example, by distributing their products through supermarkets, manufacturers lose total control of the price charged to consumers. Furthermore, there is no guarantee that new products will be stocked. Direct distribution gives producers control over such issues.

Product factors

Large complex products are often supplied direct to customers. The need for close personal contact between producer and customer, and the high prices charged mean that direct distribution and selling is both necessary and feasible. Perishable products such as frozen food, meat and bread require relatively short channels to supply the customer with fresh stock. Finally, bulky or difficult to handle products may require direct distribution because distributors may refuse to carry them if storage or display problems arise.[9]

Competitive factors

If competition control traditional channels of distribution, for example, through franchise or exclusive dealing arrangements, an innovative approach to distribution may be required. Two alternatives are to recruit a salesforce to sell direct or to set up a producer-owned distribution network (see vertical marketing channels discussed later in this chapter). Producers should not accept that the channels of distribution used by competitors are the only ways to reach target customers. Direct marketing provides opportunities to supply products in new ways. Increasingly, traditional channels of distribution for personal computers through high-street retailers are being circumvented by direct marketers who use direct response advertising to reach buyers. The emergence of the more computer-aware and experienced buyer, and the higher reliability of these products as the market reaches maturity has meant that a local source of supply (and advice) is less important.

Distribution intensity

The second channel strategy decision is the choice of *distribution intensity*. The three broad options are intensive, selective, and exclusive distribution.

Intensive distribution

Intensive distribution aims to provide saturation coverage of the market by using all available outlets. With many mass market products such as cigarettes, foods, toiletries, beer and newspapers, sales are a direct function of the number of outlets penetrated. This is because consumers have a range of acceptable brands from which they choose. If a brand is not available in an outlet an alternative is bought. The convenience aspect of purchase is paramount. New outlets may be sought which hitherto had not stocked the products such as the sale of confectionery and grocery items at petrol stations.

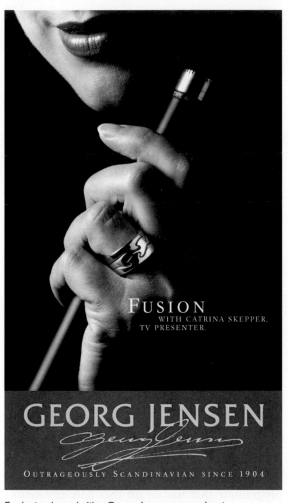

FUSION
WITH CATRINA SKEPPER.
TV PRESENTER.

GEORG JENSEN

OUTRAGEOUSLY SCANDINAVIAN SINCE 1904

Exclusive brands like Georg Jensen use selective
distribution channels which match their up-market image

Selective distribution

Market coverage may also be achieved through
selective distribution in which a producer uses
a limited number of outlets in a geographical
area to sell its products. The advantages to the
producer are the opportunity to select only
the best outlets to focus its efforts to build close
working relationships and to train distributor staff
on fewer outlets than with intensive distribution,
and, if selling and distribution is direct, to reduce
costs. Up-market aspirational brands like Georg
Jensen (see advertisement) are often sold in carefully selected outlets. Retail outlets and industrial
distributors like this arrangement since it reduces
competition. Selective distribution is more likely
to be used when buyers are willing to shop
around when choosing products. This means that
it is not necessary for a company to have its
products available in all outlets. Products such as
audio and video equipment, cameras, personal
computers and cosmetics may be sold in this way.

Problems can arise when a retailer demands
distribution rights but is refused by producers.
This happened in the case of Superdrug, a UK
discount store chain, that requested the right to
sell expensive perfume but was denied by manufacturers. They claimed that the store did not have
the right ambience for the sale of luxury products.
Superdrug maintained that its application was
refused because the chain wanted to sell
perfumes for less than their recommended prices.
A Monopolies and Mergers Commission investigation supported current practice. European rules
allow perfume companies to confine distribution
to retailers who measure up in terms of décor and
staff training. Manufacturers are not permitted to
refuse distribution rights on the grounds that the
retailer will sell for less than the list price.[10]

Exclusive distribution

This is an extreme form of selective distribution in
which only one wholesaler, retailer or industrial
distributor is used in a geographic area. Cars are
often sold on this basis with only one dealer
operating in each town or city. This reduces a
purchaser's power to negotiate prices for the
same model between dealers since to buy in a
neighbouring town may be inconvenient when
servicing or repairs are required. It also allows
very close cooperation between producer and
retailer over servicing, pricing and promotion.
The right to **exclusive distribution** may be
demanded by distributors as a condition for
stocking a manufacturer's product line. Similarly,
producers may wish for exclusive dealing where
the distributor agrees not to stock competing lines.

Exclusive dealing can reduce competition in
ways that may be considered contrary to the
consumers' interests. The European Court of
Justice rejected an appeal by Unilever over the
issue of exclusive outlets in Germany. By
supplying freezer cabinets Unilever maintained
exclusivity by refusing to allow other competing
ice creams into its cabinets. The Court's ruling
may affect ice cream distribution in other
European countries including the UK.[11] Also,
Coca-Cola, Schweppes Beverages and Britvic's
exclusive ties with the leisure trade such as sports
clubs was broken up by the Office of Fair Trading,
making competitive entry easier.[12]

However, the European Court rejected an appeal by the French Leclerc supermarket group over the issue of the selective distribution system used by Yves Saint Laurent perfumes. The judges found that the use of selective distribution for luxury cosmetic products increased competition and that it was in the consumer's and manufacturer's interest to preserve the image of such luxury products.

Channel integration

Channel integration can range from conventional marketing channels comprising an independent producer and channel intermediaries, through a franchise operation to channel ownership by a producer. Producers need to consider the strengths and weaknesses of each system when setting channel strategy.

Conventional marketing channels

The independence of channel intermediaries means that the producer has little or no control over them. Arrangements such as exclusive dealing may provide a degree of control but separation of ownership means that each party will look after their own interest. Conventional marketing channels are characterized by hard bargaining and occasionally conflict. For example, a retailer may believe that cutting the price of a brand is necessary to move stock, even though the producer objects because of brand image considerations.

However, separation of ownership means that each party can specialize in the function in which it has strengths: manufacturers produce, intermediaries distribute. Care needs to be taken by manufacturers to stay in touch with customers and not abdicate this responsibility to retailers.

A manufacturer who dominates a market through its size and strong brands may exercise considerable power over intermediaries even though they are independent. This power may result in an *administered vertical marketing system* where the manufacturer can command considerable cooperation from wholesalers and retailers. Major brand builders such as Procter and Gamble and Lever Brother had traditionally held great leverage over distribution but recently power has moved towards large dominant supermarket chains through their purchasing and

market power. Marks and Spencer are a clear example of a retailer controlling an administered vertical marketing system. Through their dominant market position they are capable of exerting considerable authority over their suppliers.

Franchising

A *franchise* is a legal contract in which a producer and channel intermediaries agree each member's rights and obligations. Usually, the intermediary receives marketing, managerial, technical and financial services in return for a fee. Franchise organizations such as McDonald's, Benetton, Hertz, The Body Shop and Avis combine the strengths of a large sophisticated marketing-oriented organization with the energy and motivation of a locally owned outlet. Franchising is also commonplace in the car industry where dealers agree exclusive deals with manufacturers in return for marketing and financial backing. Although a franchise operation gives a degree of producer control there are still areas of potential conflict. For example, the producer may be dissatisfied with the standards of service provided by the outlet, or the franchisee may believe that the franchising organization provides inadequate promotional support. Goal conflict can also arise. For example, some McDonald's franchisees are displeased with the company's rapid expansion programme that has meant that new restaurants have opened within a mile of existing outlets. This has led to complaints about lower profits and falling franchise resale values.[13] A franchise agreement provides a *contractual vertical marketing system* through the formal coordination and integration of marketing and distribution activities. Some franchises exert a considerable degree of control over marketing operations. A case in point is Benetton, which is discussed in Marketing in Action 16.1 which also discusses The Body Shop's franchise operation.

Three economic explanations of why a producer might choose franchising as a means of distribution have been proposed. Franchising may be a means of overcoming resource constraints, as an efficient system to overcome producer-distributor management problems and as a way of gaining knowledge of new markets.[14] Franchising allows the producer to overcome internal resource constraints by providing access to the franchisee's resources. For example, if the producer has limited financial resources, access to additional

16.1   Marketing in Action

Benetton and The Body Shop: International Forces in Franchising

During the early 1990s Benetton, the Italian clothing company, gained much publicity through its controversial advertising campaign which included an HIV-positive sufferer on his deathbed surrounded by his family, a bloody newborn baby, a nun and priest kissing, and an oil-soaked bird. In marketing terms, though, the company is better known for its successful franchise operations.

A Benetton franchisee pays a one-off lump sum—so-called *key money*—with no ongoing fee payments. In return, the franchisee benefits from Benetton's brand name—synonymous with fashion and colour—and exclusive rights to distribution within a given geographic area.

Benetton exercise considerable control over the franchise operation, choosing the location of the outlet, determining retail prices, store layout and colour blocking of the clothes. Some control is also taken over stocking; some product ranges have to be bought by the franchisee. Once purchased they cannot be returned to Benetton. Instead, twice yearly sales periods in January and August provide an opportunity to off-load surplus stock. Even here Benetton head office exert influence on prices allowing 10–15 per cent mark down on selected current lines, and up to 50 per cent on previous season's stock. Sales periods are important to a Benetton franchisee with up to 40 per cent of revenue being generated then.

This arrangement gives Benetton considerable flexibility: if things go wrong Benetton is sheltered from most of the financial implications. In the USA, 300 shops closed but the company was protected as it did not own any of them. The overall picture, though, is one of aggressive expansion with over 7000 outlets in 1993.

Flexibility is also maintained on the manufacturing front: 80 per cent of the manufacturing is done by 600 subcontractors in north-west Italy. Benetton concentrates on design and dyeing. Most garments arrive in white and are dyed after Benetton's fashion experts have decided the season's colours. Subcontracting protects the company from down-turns in demand as it has few overheads and can easily cut production by placing fewer orders with its suppliers. Also, the competition to be a Benetton supplier means that the company has great negotiating power over its subcontractors.

The Body Shop, the retailer of environmentally friendly personal care products, operates franchising agreements in 45 countries. Necessity was the driving force in the early days as its owners Anita and Gordon Roddick had neither the capital nor the commercial track record to attract bank funding for expansion from their UK base. A key criterion for becoming a Body Shop franchise is a keen concern for the environment and animal welfare issues as well as business aptitude.

The Body Shop ethos is maintained by methods such as videos dispatched to franchisees on the latest group issues and campaigns. They also receive a detailed franchising agreement and manual which describes their responsibilities for upholding the company's style and image, display of products, and the proportion of non-Body Shop products that can be sold. Although franchising has not always been a success (as in the USA), its strengths have allowed the group to grow into an international force in retailing without borrowing. Nevertheless, even companies like Body Shop which was founded on a novel idea need to move with the times. This has led to recent moves to introduce loyalty cards in an attempt to get closer to customers, and to outsource manufacturing to provide the flexibility to turn ideas into products more quickly.

Based on: Vignali et al. (1993);[15] Mohabir-Collins and Connor (1993);[16] Chapman (1996);[17] Smith (1999)[18]

finance may come from the franchisee. The second explanation of franchising relates to the problems of managing geographically dispersed operations. In such situations, producers may value the notion of the owner-manager who has a vested interest in the success of the business. Although some control may still be necessary, the franchisee benefits directly from increases in sales and profits and so has a financial incentive to manage the business well. Finally, franchising may be a way for a producer to access the local knowledge of the franchisee. Franchising may therefore be attractive when a producer is expanding into new markets and where potential franchisees have access to information that is important in penetrating such markets.

Franchising can occur at four levels of the distribution chain:

Manufacturer and retailer the car industry is dominated by this arrangement. The manufacturer gains retail outlets for its cars and repair facilities without the capital outlay required with ownership.

Manufacturer and wholesaler this is commonly used in the soft drinks industry. Manufacturers such as Schweppes, Coca Cola and Pepsi Cola grant wholesalers the right to make up and bottle their concentrate in line with their instructions, and to distribute the products within a defined geographic area.

Wholesaler and retailer this is not as common as other franchising arrangements but is found with car products and hardware stores. It allows wholesalers to secure distribution of their product to consumers.

Retailer and retailer an often used method which frequently has its roots in a successful retailing operation seeking to expand geographically by means of a franchise operation, often with great success. Examples include McDonald's, Benetton, Pizza Hut and Kentucky Fried Chicken.

Channel ownership

Total control over distributor activities comes with channel ownership. This establishes a ***corporate vertical marketing system***. By purchasing retail outlets, producers control their purchasing, production and marketing activities. In particular, control over purchasing means a captive outlet for the manufacturer's products. For example, the purchase of Pizza Hut and Kentucky Fried Chicken by Pepsi Cola has tied these outlets to the company's soft drinks brands.

The advantages of control have to be weighed against the high price of acquisition and the danger that the move into retailing will spread managerial activities too widely. Nevertheless corporate vertical marketing systems have successfully operated for many years in the oil industry where companies such as Shell, Texaco and BP own not only considerable numbers of petrol stations but also the means of production.

Channel management

Once the key channel strategy decisions have been made, effective implementation is required. Specifically a number of channel management issues must be addressed (see Fig. 16.7). These are the selection, motivation, training, and evaluation of channel members, and managing conflict between producers and channel members.

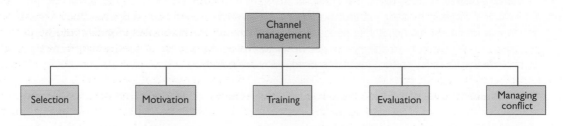

Figure 16.7 Channel management

Selection

For some producers (notably small companies) the distribution problem is not so much channel selection as channel acceptance. Their problem is to convince key channel intermediaries (especially retailers) to stock their products. However, let us assume that we have a certain amount of discretion in choosing specific channel members to distribute our product. Selection then involves identifying candidates and developing *selection criteria.*

Identifying sources

Sources for identifying candidates include trade sources, reseller enquiries, customers of distributors, and the field salesforce.[19] *Trade sources* include trade associations, exhibitions and trade publications. Talking to trade associations can supply names of prospective distributors. Other trade publications may be published commercially and names of possible distributors may be compiled. Exhibitions provide a useful means of meeting and talking to possible distributors. Sometimes channel members may be proactive in contacting a producer to express an interest in handling their products. Such *reseller enquiries* show that the possible distributor is enthusiastic about the possibility of a link. *Customers of distributors* are a useful source since they can comment on their merits and limitations. Finally, if a producer already has a *field salesforce* calling on intermediaries, salespeople are in a good position to seek out possible new distributors in their own territory.

The use of target country-based distributors is a common method of foreign market entry in Europe. A study of the sources of identifying overseas distribution found that the five most common methods were personal visits to search the market, the national trade board, customer and colleagues' recommendations, and trade fairs.[20]

Developing selection criteria

Common selection criteria include market product and customer knowledge, market coverage, quality and size of the salesforce (if applicable), reputation among customers, financial standing, the extent to which competitive and complementary products are carried, managerial competence

and hunger for success, and the degree of enthusiasm for handling the producer's lines. In practice selection may be complex because large, well-established distributors may carry many competing lines and lack enthusiasm for more lines. Smaller distributors, on the other hand, may be less financially secure and have a smaller salesforce but be more enthusiastic and hungry for success. Top selection criteria of overseas distributors were market knowledge, enthusiasm for the contract, hunger for success, customer knowledge and the fact that the distributor does not carry competitors' products.

Motivation

Once selected, channel members need to be motivated to agree to act as a distributor, and allocate adequate commitment and resources to the producer's lines. The key to effective motivation is to understand the needs and problems of distributors since needs and motivators are linked. For example, a distributor who values financial incentives may respond more readily to high commission than one who is more concerned with having an exclusive territory. Possible motivators include *financial rewards, territorial exclusivity, providing resource support* (e.g. sales training, field sales assistance, provision of marketing research information, advertising and promotion support, financial assistance and management training) and *developing strong work relationships* (e.g. joint planning, assurance of long-term commitment, appreciation of effort and success, frequent interchange of views and arranging distributor conferences).

In short, management of independent distributors is best conducted in the context of informal *partnerships.*[21] Producers should seek to develop strong relationships with their distributors based on a recognition of their performance and integrated planning and operations. For example, jointly determined sales targets could be used to motivate and evaluate salespeople who might receive a bonus upon achievement. A key element in fostering a spirit of partnership is to provide assurances of a long-term business relationship with the distributor (given satisfactory performance). This is particularly important in managing overseas distributors as many fear that they will be replaced by the producer's own salesforce once the market has been developed. The effort to develop partnerships appears to be worthwhile: a study of Canadian exporters and their British distributors found that success was related to partnership factors like joint decision-making and close and frequent contact with distributors.[22]

The most popular methods cited by export managers and directors to motivate their overseas distributors were territorial exclusivity, provision of up-to-date product and company information, regular personal contact, appreciation of effort and understanding of the distributors' problems, attractive financial incentives, and provision of salespeople to support the distributors' sales-force.[23] Given overseas distributors' fears that they may be replaced, it was disappointing to note that only 40 per cent of these exporters provided assurances of a long-term business commitment to their distributors as a major motivator.

Mutual commitment between channel members is central to successful relationship marketing. Two types of commitment are affective commitment that expresses the extent to which channel members like to maintain their relationship with their partners and calculative commitment where channel members need to maintain a relationship. Commitment is highly dependent on the interdependence and trust between the parties.[24]

Training

The need to train channel members obviously depends on their internal competences. Large market supermarket chains, for example, may regard an invitation by a manufacturer to provide marketing training as an insult. However, many smaller distributors have been found to be weak on sales management, marketing, financial management, stock control, and personnel management and may welcome producer initiatives on training.[25] From the producer's perspective training can provide the necessary technical knowledge about a supplier company and its products, and help to build a spirit of partnership and commitment.

However, the training of overseas distributors by British exporters appears to be the exception rather than the norm.[26] When it is provided it usually takes the form of product and company knowledge. Nevertheless when such knowledge

is given it can help to build strong personal relationships and give distributors the confidence to sell those products. Marketing in Action 16.2 describes how Ford, Vauxhall and Naim Audio educate and train their dealers.

Evaluation

The evaluation of channel members has an important bearing on distributor retention, training and motivation decisions. Evaluation provides the information necessary to decide which channel members to retain and which to drop. Shortfalls in distributor skills and competences may be identified through evaluation, and appropriate training programmes organized by producers. Where a lack of motivation is recognized as a problem, producers can implement plans designed to deal with the root causes of demotivation (e.g. financial incentives and/or fostering a partnership approach to business).[27]

It needs to be understood, however, that the scope and frequency of evaluation may be limited where power lies with the channel member. If producers have relatively little power because they are more dependent on channel members for distribution than channel members are on individual producers for supply, in-depth evaluation and remedial action will be restricted. Channel members may be reluctant to spend time providing the producers with comprehensive information on which to base evaluation. Remedial action may be limited to tentative suggestions when products do suspect there is room for improvement.

Where manufacturer power is high through having strong brands, and many distributors from which to choose, evaluation may be more frequent and wider in scope. Channel members are more likely to comply with the manufacturer's demands for performance information and agree for their sales and marketing efforts to be monitored by the manufacturer.

Evaluation criteria include sales volume and value, profitability, level of stocks, quality and position of display, new accounts opened, selling and marketing capabilities, quality of service provided to customers, market information feedback, ability and willingness to keep commitments, attitudes, and personal capability.

Although the evaluation of overseas distributors and agents is more difficult than their domestic counterparts, two studies have shown that over 90 per cent of producers do carry out evaluation, usually at least once a year.[28] For distributors, sales-related criteria were most widely applied, with sales volume, sales value and creating new business three of the top four most commonly applied measures. Channel inputs were also widely used with provision of market feedback, customer services, selling/marketing inputs and keeping commitments cited frequently. Given the importance of distributors in marketing to Europe, it is important that such evaluation takes place. However, a somewhat disappointing finding was that, with the exception of value of sales, less than half of the exporters used *mutually agreed objectives* to evaluate performance. Such a method is consistent with the partnership approach to channel management, and provides clarity and commitment to objectives since both parties have contributed to their setting. The most common method was to *compare against past performance* which requires great care to ensure that account is taken of changes in the competitive environment over time.

Managing conflict

When producers and channel members are independent, inevitably conflict occurs from time to time. The intensity of conflict can range from occasional, minor disagreements that are quickly forgotten, to major disputes that fuel continuous bitter relationships.[29]

16.2   Marketing in Action
Educating and Training Distributors

In the face of tough competition Ford presents a modern progressive image to car buyers through advertising. This message needs to be understood and reinforced by its dealer network so the customer receives consistent communication. To achieve this Ford flew senior dealers to Berlin from across Europe to attend a branded internal communication programme—Project Aurora. The idea was not only to launch both the Focus and Cougar models to the dealers in front of the motoring press, but also to give them a clearer understanding of what the Ford brand stands for. Vauxhall (General Motors) also flew 16 000 dealers from all over the world to Morocco for three days to achieve similar objectives at the launch of the Astra. Vauxhall recognized the major education job it needed to undertake so that its dealers understood exactly what was required of them.

Companies in other businesses also recognize the key role distributors play in the marketing of their products. One such company is Naim Audio, manufacturer of high-quality audio equipment. It believes that a key to success is the training of dealers to give them sufficient product knowledge (including how to assemble the systems) to be confident about selling its products. Dealers need to be confident about answering customers' questions. The training includes a factory tour where dealers can see how the products are built, what goes into the equipment, how to connect the units in an audio system, how to get the best sound and how to display the equipment in the shop. No sales training is given as Naim believes their dealers are already competent at that.

Naim believes that giving dealers the confidence to talk about and recommend its products gives it a big competitive advantage. As its Swedish distributor commented: 'If the salesperson feels confident and secure, the customer will feel confident and secure'.

Based on: Barratt (1998);[30] BBC1 Television (1993)[31]

Sources of channel conflict

The major sources of *channel conflict* are differences in goals, differences in views on the desired product lines carried by channel members, multiple distribution channels, and inadequacies in performance.

Differences in goals most resellers attempt to maximize their own profit. This can be accomplished by improving profit margin, reducing inventory levels, increasing sales, lowering expenses and receiving greater allowances from suppliers. In contrast, producers might benefit from lower margins, greater channel inventories, higher promotional expenses, and fewer allowances given to channel members. These inherent conflicts of interest mean that there are many potential areas of disagreement between producers and their channel members.

Differences in desired product lines resellers who grow by adding product lines may be regarded as disloyal by their original suppliers. For example, W. H. Smith a UK retailer, originally specialized in books, magazines and newspapers but has grown by adding new product lines such as computer disks, videotape and software supplies. This can cause resentment among its primary suppliers who perceive the reseller as devoting too much effort to selling secondary lines. Alternatively, retailers may decide to specialize by reducing their product range. For example, in Europe there has been a growth in the number of speciality shops selling, for example, athletics footware. A sports outlet that decides to narrow its product range will wish to increase the assortment of the specialized items that make it distinct. This can cause conflict with its original suppliers of these product lines since the addition of competitors' brands makes the retailer appear disloyal.[32]

Multiple distribution channels in trying to achieve market coverage a producer may use multiple distribution channels. For example, a producer may decide to sell directly to key accounts because their size warrants a key account salesforce, and use channel intermediaries to give wide market coverage. Conflict can arise when a channel member is denied access to a lucrative order from a key account because it is being serviced directly by the producer. Disagreements can also occur when the producer owns retail outlets that compete with independent retailers who also sell the producer's brands. For example, Clarks, a footwear manufacturer, owns a chain of outlets that compete with other shoe outlets that sell Clarks's shoes.[33]

Inadequacies in performance an obvious source of conflict is when parties in the supply chain do not perform to expectations. For example, a channel member may underperform in terms of sales, level of inventory carried, customer service, standards of display and salesperson effectiveness. Producers may give poor delivery, inadequate promotional support, low profit margins, poor quality goods and incomplete shipments. These can all be potential areas of conflict.

Avoiding and resolving conflict

How can producers and channel members avoid and resolve conflict? There are several ways of managing conflict.

Developing a partnership approach this calls for frequent interaction between producer and resellers to develop a spirit of mutual understanding and cooperation. Producers can help channel members with training, financial help and promotional support. Distributors, in term, may agree to mutually agreed sales targets and provide extra sales resources. The objective is to build confidence in the manufacturer's products and relationships based on trust. When conflicts arise there is more chance they will be resolved in a spirit of cooperation. Organizing staff exchange programmes can be useful in allowing each party to understand the problems and tensions of the other rather than animosity.

Training in conflict handling staff who handle disputes need to be trained in negotiation and communication skills. They need to be able to handle high pressure conflict situations without resorting to emotion and *blaming behaviour*. Instead, they should be able to handle such situations calmly and be able to handle concession analysis, in particular the identification of *win-win situations*. These are situations where both the producer and reseller benefit from an agreement.

Market partitioning to reduce or eliminate conflict from multiple distribution channels, producers can try to partition markets on some logical basis such as customer size or type. This can work if channel members accept the basis for the partitioning. Alternatively, different channels can be supplied with different product lines. For example, Hallmark sells its premium greetings cards under its Hallmark brand name to up-market department stores, and its standard cards under the Ambassador name to discount retailers.[34]

Improving performance many conflicts occur because of genuine reasons. For example, poor delivery by manufacturers or inadequate sales effort by distributors can provoke frustration and anger. Rather than attempt to placate the aggrieved partner, the most effective solution is to improve performance so that the source of conflict disappears. This is the most effective way of dealing with such problems.

Channel ownership an effective but expensive way of resolving conflicting goals is to buy the other party. Since producer and channel member is under common ownership the common objective is to maximize joint profits. Conflicts can still occur but the dominant partner is in a position to resolve them quickly. Some producers in Europe have integrated with channel intermediaries successfully. For example, over 40 per cent of household furniture is sold through producer-owned retail outlets in Italy.[35]

Coercion In some situations, conflict resolution may be dependent on coercion: one party forces compliance through the use of force. For example, producers can threaten to withdraw supply, deliver late or withdraw financial support; channel members, on the other hand, can threaten to delist the manufacturer's products, promote competitive products and develop own-label brands. In Europe, the increasing concentration of retailing into groups of very large groups has meant that the balance of power has moved away from manufacturers. The development of own-label brands has further strengthened the retailers' position while giving them the double advantage of a high profit margin (because their purchase price is low) and a low price to the customer.

Physical distribution

In the first part of this chapter we examined channel strategy and management decisions which concern the choice of the correct outlets to provide product availability to customers in a cost effective manner. Physical distribution decisions focus on the efficient movement of goods from producer to intermediaries and the consumer. Clearly channel and physical distribution decisions are interrelated although channel decisions tend to be made earlier. *Physical distribution* is defined as a *set of activities concerned with the physical flows of materials, components and finished goods from producer to channel intermediaries and consumers.*

The aim is to provide intermediaries and customers with the right products, in the right quantities, in the right locations, at the right time. Physical distribution activities have been a subject of managerial attention for some time because of the potential for cost savings and improving customer service levels. Cost savings can be achieved by reducing inventory levels, using cheaper forms of transport and shipping in bulk rather than small quantities. Customer service levels can be improved by fast and reliable delivery including just-in-time delivery, holding high inventory levels so that customers have a wide choice and the chances of stock-outs are reduced, fast order processing, and ensuring products arrive in the right quantities and quality.

Physical distribution management concerns the balance between cost reduction and meeting customer service requirements. Trade-offs are often necessary. For example, low inventory and slow, cheaper transportation methods reduce costs but lower customer service levels and satisfaction. Determining this balance is a key marketing decision as physical distribution can be a source of competitive advantage. A useful approach is to analyse the market in terms of customer service needs and price sensitivity. The result may be the discovery of two segments:

✦ *Segment 1*: low service needs, high price sensitivity.

✦ *Segment 2*: high service needs, low price sensitivity.

Unipart were the first to exploit segment 2 in the do-it-yourself car repair and servicing market.

They gave excellent customer service ('The answer's yes. Now what's the question?') but charged a high price. This analysis, therefore, defined the market segment to target and the appropriate marketing mix. Alternatively, both segments could be targeted with different marketing mixes. In industrial markets, large companies may possess their own service facilities while smaller firms require producer or distributor service as part of the product offering and are willing to pay a higher price. For example, Norsk Kjem, a Norwegian chemical company, discovered that the market for one of their product lines—wetting agents used in many processes to promote the retention and even distribution of liquids—was segmented in this way.[36] Small firms had less technical expertise and lower price sensitivity and they ordered smaller quantities than larger companies. This meant that Norsk Kjem required different physical distribution (including service levels) and price structures for the two market segments.

Not only are there trade-offs between physical distribution costs and customer service levels, but also there are possible conflicts between elements of the physical distribution system itself. For example, an inventory manager may favour low stocks to reduce costs, but if this leads to stock-outs this may raise costs elsewhere: the freight manager may have to accept higher costs resulting from fast freight deliveries. Low cost containers may lower packaging costs but raise the cost of goods damaged in transit. This fact and the need to coordinate order processing, inventory and transportation decisions mean that physical distribution needs to be managed as a *system* with a manager overseeing the whole process. A key role that the physical distribution manager would perform would be to reconcile the conflicts inherent in the system so that total costs are minimized subject to required customer service levels.

The physical distribution system

A system is a set of connected parts managed in such a way that overall objectives are achieved. The physical distribution system contains the following parts (see Fig. 16.8):

1 *Customer service*: what level of customer service should be provided?

2 *Order processing*: how should the orders be handled?

3 *Inventory control*: how much inventory should be held?

4 *Warehousing*: where should the inventory be located? How many warehouses should be used?

5 *Transportation*: how will the products be transported?

6 *Materials handling*: how will the products be handled during transportation?

Each of these decisions will now be explored.

Customer service

Customer service standards need to be set. For example, a customer service standard might be that 90 per cent of orders are delivered within 48 hours of receipt and 100 per cent are delivered within 72 hours. Higher customer service stan-

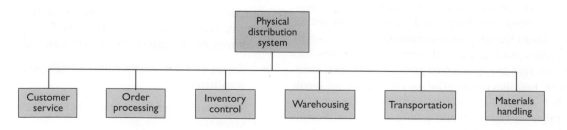

Figure 16.8 Components of the physical distribution system

dards normally mean higher costs as inventory levels need to be higher. Since inventory ties up working capital, the higher the inventory level the higher the working capital charge. The physical distribution manager needs to be aware of the costs of fulfilling various customer service standards (e.g. 80, 90 and 100 per cent of orders delivered within 48 hours) and the extra customer satisfaction which results from raising standards.

In some cases customers value consistency in delivery time rather than speed. For example, a customer service standard of guaranteed delivery within five working days may be valued more than 60 per cent within two, 80 per cent within five and 100 per cent within seven days. Since the latter standard requires delivery at 60 per cent within two days it may require higher inventory levels than the former. Therefore by understanding customer requirements it may be possible to increase satisfaction while lowering costs.

Customer service standards should be given considerable attention for they may be the differentiating factor between suppliers: they may be used as a key customer choice criterion. Methods of improving customer service standards in physical distribution are shown in Table 16.1. By examining ways of improving product availability and order cycle time, and raising information levels and flexibility, considerable goodwill and customer loyalty can be created.

The Internet is providing the means of improving customer service for some distribution companies. For example, if a customer of Federal Express wants to track a package over the Internet, it simply types 'Fedex' and the package number. On the computer screen will appear where it is, who signed for it and what time it was delivered. Also, since the customer no longer needs to call Federal Express, it is saving Fedex $10 million a year.[37]

Order processing

Reducing time between a customer placing an order and receiving the goods may be achieved through careful analysis of the components that make up order processing time. A computer link between salesperson and the order department may be effective. Electronic data interchange can also speed order processing time by checking the customer's credit rating, and whether the goods are in stock, issuing an order to the warehouse, invoicing the customer and updating the inventory records. Marketing in Action 16.3 discusses some European developments.

Many *order-processing systems* are inefficient because of unnecessary delays. Basic questions can spot areas for improvements, such as what happens when a sales representative receives an order? What happens when it is received in the order department? How long does it take to check inventory? What are the methods for checking inventory? Advances in on-line technology are providing ways for companies to improve their

Table 16.1 Methods of improving customer service standards in physical distribution

Improve product availability
    Raise in-stock levels
    Improve accuracy of deliveries

Improve order cycle time
    Shorten time between order and delivery
    Improve consistency between order and delivery time

Raise information levels
    Improve salesperson information on inventory
    Raise information levels on order status
    Be proactive in notifying customer of delays

Raise flexibility
    Develop contingency plans for urgent orders
    Ensure fast reaction time to unforeseen problems (e.g. stolen goods, damage in transit)

16.3   Marketing in Action

Distribution Trends and Problems in Europe

The ability to compete successfully in the Single European Market depends on the efficient distribution of products across national borders. Many companies have looked to a reduction in the number of warehouses in Europe to achieve cost efficiency. A regional approach, or even one central warehouse to service all European markets, has replaced a national structure. Vast warehouses have been built especially in the Benelux countries to service the distribution needs of multinationals across Europe. Companies such as Unilever, Sony, Honda, Kawasaki, Hewlett-Packard and Nike have opened massive storage centres to compress the chain between supplier, manufacturer, retailer and customer. The advantages of locating in the Benelux countries are their location near affluent industrialized centres, excellent road and rail links, a commercially minded multilingual workforce and some of the quickest customs procedures in Europe. Southern Finland has also seen the emergence of warehouses packed with clothes, electronic goods and foodstuffs that are destined for Russian markets.

However, the assumption that centralized warehousing is the best form of distribution has been challenged. To work well it relies on standardization of product formulation and packaging. Unfortunately, national differences in taste and language, for example, the idea that the product label could have as many as five languages, have not been found to be acceptable. Manufacturers are still having to produce different versions for each national market. Another problem is growing road congestion, lowering manufacturers' capability to provide fast delivery from a single centralized warehouse.

Where a manufacturer has several plants around Europe it makes no distributional sense to send goods to a central warehouse only to transport them back to retailers located near their plants. Whirlpool, who are expanding into Europe with the takeover of the Philips domestic appliance business, keep their goods moving in one direction by means of 16 regional warehouses.

SKF, the Swedish ball bearings group, are moving away from the one-central-warehouse-for-all-customers philosophy. Originally they intended to service all customers from one warehouse in Belgium. Instead, SKF supply large automotive customers directly from their factories in Europe, and use the warehouse for deliveries to dealers. One of the key lessons from the experiences of major companies in Europe is not to blindly chase economies of scale through centralized warehousing if it means losing flexibility to serve the customer adequately.

Another distribution trend in Europe is the development of electronic data interchange (EDI) especially in the retail sector. EDI links between suppliers and customers allow purchase orders, delivery notices, invoices and remittance advices to be electronically transmitted. The advantages are a reduction in paperwork and shorter lead times (as purchase orders are automatically linked to sales). Sales data are gathered periodically by a computer program at the customer end, automatically put into a standard EDI message and sent to a supplier's computer where it can be passed to accounting, warehouse and stock control systems. European companies who have implemented EDI systems include Fiat, Albert Heijn (a Dutch retailer) and Ciba-Geigy (pharmaceuticals).

Based on: Baxter (1993);[38] Gibson (1996);[39] Kavanagh (1996)[40]

ordering systems for customers as e-Marketing 16.2 describes.

Inventory control

Inventory levels can be a source of conflict between finance and marketing management. Since inventory represents costs, financial managers seek stock minimization; marketing management, acutely aware of the customer problems caused by stock-outs, want large inventories. In reality a balance has to be found, particularly as inventory cost rises at an increasing rate as customer service standards nears 100 per cent. This means that to always have in stock every conceivable item that a customer might order would normally be prohibitively expensive for companies marketing many items. One solution to this problem is to separate items into those that are in demand and those which are slower moving. This is sometimes called the 80 : 20 rule since for many companies 80 per cent of sales are achieved by 20 per cent of products. A high

customer service standard is then set for the high demand 20 per cent (e.g. in stock 95 per cent of the time) but a much lower standard used for those in less demand (e.g. in stock 70 per cent of the time).

Two related *inventory decisions* are knowing when and how much to order so that stocks are replenished. As inventory for an item falls, a point is reached when new stock is required. Unless a stock-out is tolerated the *order point* will be before inventory reaches zero. This is because there will be a *lead time* between ordering and receiving inventory. The *just-in-time inventory system* (discussed in Chapter 4) is designed to reduce lead time so that the order point (the stock level at which reordering takes place), and overall inventory levels for production items, are low. The key to the just-in-time system is the maintenance of a fast and reliable lead time so that deliveries of supplies arrive shortly before they are needed.

The order point depends on three factors: the viability of the order lead time, fluctuation in customer demand, and the customer service standard. The more variable the lead time between

16.2   e-Marketing

On-line Distribution Services

DB Cargo is the freight division of the German Railways (Deutsche Bahn AG). The organization focuses upon the provision of distribution services to major industrial firms in Germany. The company has already sought to exploit technology as a mechanism for enhancing customer service. As early as 1985, DB Cargo provided its largest customers with an electronic data interchange (EDI) system for managing order-entry activities.

In the mid-1990s, however, the company recognized that the Internet offered a system through which to upgrade service to large customers and concurrently offer a cost-effective order-entry system to its more numerous medium-sized customers. After completion of pilot testing, the new Internet system came on-line in May 1998. One major advantage of the new system is that customers only need a PC in order to use the system. The system allows any size of customer to enter orders, order empty rail cars and be provided with information on goods in transit. This means that customers are able to optimize their rail-based freight distribution services. The added advantage to DB Cargo is that the data from the Internet system can be used to generate knowledge that can contribute to maximizing the use of available carrying capacity.

Based on: Anderson (1999)[41]

ordering and receiving stocks, and the greater the fluctuation in customer demand, the higher the order point. This is because of the uncertainty caused by the variability leading to the need for **safety or buffer stocks** in case lead times are unpredictably long or customer demand unusually high. The higher the customer service standard, the higher will be the need for safety stocks, and hence the higher the order point. A simple inventory control system is shown in Fig. 16.9.

How much to order depends on the cost of holding stock and order-processing costs. Orders can be small and frequent, or large and infrequent. Small, frequent orders raise order-processing costs but reduce inventory carrying costs; large, infrequent orders raise inventory costs but lower order-processing expenditure. Therefore a trade-off between the two costs is required to achieve an **economic order quantity** (EOQ), the point at which total costs are lowest. Its calculation is shown diagrammatically in Fig. 16.10. Numerically it can be calculated as follows:

$$EOQ = \sqrt{\frac{2DO}{IC}}$$

where

D = annual demand in units
O = cost of placing an order
I = annual inventory cost as % of the cost of one unit
C = cost of one unit of the product.

As an example let us assume that:

Annual demand = 4000 units
Cost of placing an order = £4
Per unit annual inventory cost = 20p or 10% of the unit cost (£2)
Cost of one unit = £2

$$EOQ = \sqrt{\frac{2 \times 4000 \times 4}{0.10 \times 2}} = \frac{32\,000}{0.20}$$

$$= \sqrt{160000} = 400 \text{ units per order.}$$

Therefore the most economic order size, taking into account inventory and order processing costs, is 400 units.

Suppliers can build strong relationships with their customers through automated inventory restocking systems as e-Marketing 16.3 describes.

Warehousing

Warehousing involves all the activities required in the storing of goods between the time they are produced and the time they are transported to the customer. These activities include breaking bulk, making up product assortments for delivery to customers, storage and loading. *Storage warehouses* hold goods for moderate or long time periods whereas *distribution centres* operate as central locations for the fast movement of goods. Retailing organizations use regional distribution centres where suppliers bring products in bulk. These shipments are broken down into loads that are then quickly transported to retail outlets. Distribution centres are usually highly automated with computer-controlled machinery facilitating the movement of goods. A computer reads orders and controls fork-lift trucks that gather goods and move them to loading bays.

Warehousing strategy involves the determination of the location and the number of warehouses to be used. At the one extreme is one large central warehouse to serve the entire market; at the other is a number of smaller warehouses that are based near to local markets. In Europe, the removal of trade barriers between countries of the EU has reduced transportation time and costs. This change, together with distribution focus being on regional rather than national markets, has fuelled the trend towards fewer, larger warehouses where economies of scale can reduce costs. Marketing in Action 16.3 discusses this trend and its accompanying problems. As with most physical distribution decisions, the optimum number and location of warehouses is a balance between customer service and cost considerations. Usually the more locally based warehouses a company uses, the better the customer service but the higher the cost.

Transportation

Customer service ultimately depends on the ability of the physical distribution system to transport products on time and without damage. Timely delivery is even more important with the group use of the just-in-time system. Therefore the choice of *transportation mode* is vital to successfully implementing marketing strategy.

The five major transport methods are rail, road,

air, water and pipelines. Each has its strengths and limitations.

Rail

Railways are efficient at transporting large, bulky freight on land over large distances. Rail is often used to transport coal, chemicals, oil, aggregates and nuclear flasks. A problem is lack of flexibility. For many companies the use of rail would mean transport by lorry to and from a rail depot. Furthermore for small quantities the use of rail may prove uneconomic. In the UK British Rail withdrew their Speedlink service in which

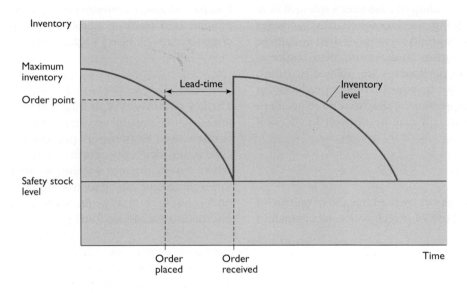

Figure 16.9 Inventory control

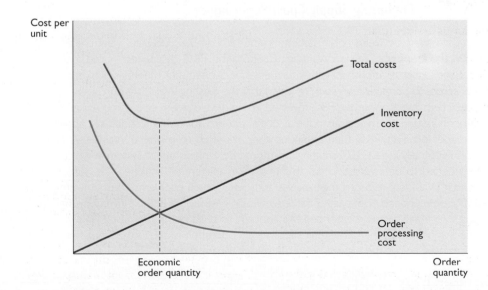

Figure 16.10 Determining the economic order quantity

container loads of various goods from different producers were combined into one rail load. However, the building of the Channel Tunnel between Britain and mainland Europe has given a boost to rail transport. British Rail and SNCF have built freight terminals to encourage rail transport across the Channel.

Rail is environmentally friendlier than road and is ideally suited to freight when it moves 400 kilometres or more in large regular quantities from supplier's siding to customer's siding. Where there is no siding, the journey usually is costlier than road and more likely to incur theft or damage to goods in transit. Furthermore, distributors of foodstuffs and perishables are obliged by health authorities to transport their products at controlled temperatures. They may be reluctant to rely on freight as it may be difficult to access if delayed.

Road

Motorized transport by road has the advantage of flexibility because of direct access to companies and warehouses. This means that lorries can transport goods from supplier to receiver without unloading en route. Furthermore, speed is likely to increase and costs fall in Europe as a result of the Single European Market. With cross-border restrictions removed—drivers spent an average of 30 per cent of their time waiting or filling in forms at border crossings prior to 1993—road transport in Europe is likely to grow.[42] However, the growth of road transport in Europe, and particularly the UK, has received considerable criticism because of increased traffic congestion and the damage done to roads by heavy juggernauts.

Air

The key advantages of air freight are its speed and long-distance capabilities. Its speed means that it is often used to transport perishable goods and emergency deliveries. Furthermore, in a period when companies are seeking to reduce inventories, air freight can be used to supply inventories under just-in-time systems. With the growth in international trade, air freight is predicted to be a

16.3 e-Marketing

Enhancing Supply Chain Performance

Following discussions between Lou Pritchett, Procter & Gamble's US vice president of Sales, and Sam Walton, the founder of the US Wal-Mart Corporation, P&G clearly recognized that there was a need to build closer relationships with intermediaries. Subsequent meetings between executives at all levels across the organization soon revealed that the existing Wal-Mart purchasing system was creating very high inventory levels. P&G invested in the development of a computerized inventory replenishment system to model an optimal order pattern for Wal-Mart. Initially applied to the Pampers diaper product, P&G then extended their research to examine Wal-Mart's warehouse system. This eventually led to P&G creating an automated replenishment system in which Wal-Mart no longer needed to be involved in day-to-day stock management activities. The outcome of this project is that Wal-Mart reduced their excess and out-of-stock problems, P&G's on-time delivery reached 99.6 per cent and both parties made significant cost savings in their inventory management operations. Wal-Mart has now extended this concept to build computer-based links with all their key suppliers and this automation of their supply-chain operation is one of the fundamental reasons why the firm now enjoys the highest net profit margin of any national US retail operation.

Based on: Wiersema (1997)[43]

growth activity. Its major disadvantages are high cost and the need to transport goods by road to and from air terminals.

In 1996 the European Air Shippers' Council published a set of recommendations to air carriers regarding guaranteed delivery and lead times. Although freight can account for up to 20 per cent of an airline's revenues, it is often treated unfairly in terms of investment. The report recommends that carriers focus their attention on providing better service to supply-chain managers.

Water

Water transportation is slow but inexpensive. Inland transportation is usually associated with bulky, low value, non-perishable goods such as coal, ore, grain, steel and petroleum. Ocean-going ships carry a wider range of products. When the cost benefits of international sea transportation outweigh the speed advantage of air freight, water shipments may be chosen. A large proportion of long-haul deliveries between Europe and the Pacific Rim is by sea transport. As with air freight, water transport normally needs road transportation of goods to and from docks.

Pipeline

Pipelines are a dependable and low maintenance form of transportation for liquids and gases. However, their construction is expensive and time consuming. They are usually associated with natural gas, water and crude petroleum. Ownership is in the hands of the companies that use them.

Materials handling

Materials handling involves the activities related to the moving of products in the producer's plant, warehouses and transportation depots. Modern storage facilities tend to be one storey, allowing a high level of automation. In some cases robots are used to conduct materials handling tasks. Lowering the human element in locating inventory and assembling orders has reduced error and increased the speed of these operations.

Two key developments in materials handling are unit handling and containerization. *Unit handling* achieves efficiency by combining multiple packages onto pallets that can be moved by fork-lift trucks. *Containerization* involves the combining of many quantities of goods (e.g. car components) into a single large container. Once sealed they can easily be transferred from one form of transport to another. For example, a container could be loaded onto a lorry and taken to a rail freight terminal to form part of a train load of containers destined for the docks. There the container can easily by transferred to a ship for transportation to a destination thousands of miles away. Since individual items are not handled, damage in transit is reduced.

An important element in materials handling is the quality of packaging. It is necessary to evaluate not only the appearance and cost of packaging, but also the ability to repackage into larger quantities for transportation. Packages must be sturdy enough to withstand the rigours of physical distribution such as harsh handling and stacking.

Ethical issues in distribution

Five key ethical issues in distribution are the use of slotting allowances, grey markets, exclusive dealing, restrictions on supply and fair dealing.

Slotting allowances

The power shift from manufacturers to retailers in the packaged consumer goods industry has meant that slotting allowances are often demanded to take products. A slotting allowance is a fee paid to a retailer in exchange for agreement to place a product on the retailer's shelves. Critics argue that they represent an abuse of power and work against small manufacturers who cannot afford to pay the fee. Retailers argue that they are simply charging rent for a valuable scarce commodity: shelf space.[44]

Grey markets

These occur when a product is sold through an unauthorized distribution channel. When this occurs in international marketing the practice is called parallel importing. Usually a distributor buys goods in one country (where prices are low) and sells them in another (where prices are high) at below the going market price. This causes anger among members of the authorized distribution channel who see their prices being undercut. Furthermore, the products may well be sold in down-market outlets that discredit the image of the product which has been built up by high advertising expenditures. Nevertheless, supporters of grey markets argue that it encourages price competition, increases consumer choice, and promotes the lowering of price differentials between countries.

Exclusive dealing

This is a restrictive arrangement whereby a manufacturer prohibits distributors that market its products from selling the products of competing suppliers. The act may restrict competition and restrict the entry of new competitors and products into a market. It may be found where a large supplier can exercise power over weaker distributors. The supplier may be genuinely concerned that anything less than an exclusive agreement will mean that insufficient effort will be made to sell its products by a distributor and that unless such an agreement is reached it may be uneconomic to supply the distributor.

Restrictions in supply

A concern of small suppliers is that the power of large manufacturers and retailers will mean that they are squeezed out of the supply chain. In the UK, farmers and small grocery suppliers have joined forces to demand better treatment from large supermarket chains who are forging exclusive deals with major manufacturers. They claim the problem is made worse by the growth of category management where retailers appoint 'category captains' from its suppliers who act to improve the standing of the whole product category such as breakfast cereals or confectionery. The small suppliers believe this forces them out of the category altogether as category captains look after their own interests. They would like to see a system similar to that in France where about 10 per cent of shelf space is by law given to small suppliers.[45]

Fair-trading

One problem of free market forces is that when small commodity producers are faced with large powerful buyers the result can be very low prices. This can bring severe economic hardship to the producers who may be situated in third world countries. In the face of a collapse in world coffee prices a fair trading brand, Cafédirect®, was launched. The company was founded on three principles: to influence positively producers' income security, to act as an example and catalyst for change and to improve consumer understanding of fair trade values. It pays suppliers a minimum price for coffee beans pegged above market fluctuations and provides tailor-made business support and development programmes. There are now more than 50 fair trade products on sale in the UK including Ridgways tea and Divine chocolate, and sales are rising.[46]

Summary

Distribution concerns the selection and management of channels and the management of the physical flow of the product to the consumer. Channel decisions can be broken down into strategic issues—selection of channels, the determination of distribution intensity and the degree of integration with producer (e.g. independent, franchise or producer owned)—and management decisions, which concern the selection of individual channel members, their training, motivation and evaluation, and the management of conflict. Management of the physical flow of goods is through a physical distribution system. A key decision is the level of customer service to be provided as higher levels of service normally are more expensive (e.g. higher inventory). A physical distribution system consists of customer service, order processing, inventory control, warehousing, transportation and materials handling. Each of these requires careful analysis and decision-making so that the goods reach the consumer at the right time and place and without damage.

Ethical issues in distribution are slotting allowances, grey markets, exclusive dealing, restrictions in supply, and fair trading.

Internet exercise

Distribution

Sites to visit
http://www.iceland.co.uk
http://www.tescodirect.com
http://www.sainsburys.co.uk

Exercise
Compare and contrast the direct delivery services offered by the grocery multiples.

Study questions

1 What is the difference between channel decisions and physical distribution management? In what ways are they linked?

2 Of what value are channels of distribution? What functions do they perform?

3 The best way of distributing an industrial product is direct from manufacturer to customer. Discuss.

4 Why is channel selection an important decision? What factors influence choice?

5 What is meant by the partnership approach to managing distributors? What can manufacturers do to help build partnerships?

6 Describe situations which can lead to conflict between channel members. What can be done to avoid and resolve conflict?

7 Why is there usually a trade-off between customer service and physical distribution costs? What can be done to improve customer service standards in physical distribution?

8 A distributor wishes to estimate the economic order quantity for a spare part. Annual demand is 5000 units, the cost of placing an order is £5, and the cost of one spare part is £4. The per unit annual inventory cost is 50p. Calculate the economic order quantity.

9 Unlike advertising, the area of distribution is free from ethical concerns. Discuss.

References

1. Stern, L.W. and El-Ansany (1995) *Marketing Channels,* Englewood Cliffs, NJ: Prentice-Hall, 6.

2. Anonymous (2000) Distribution Dilemmas, E-Commerce Survey, *The Economist*, 26 February, 23–8.

3. Read, M. (1999) Online Sales Go Uptempo, *Marketing*, 7 January, 23–4.

4. Rushe, D. (1999) UK Leads European Net Shopping Book, *Marketing Week*, 27 June, 10.

5. Sugar, A. (1999) Net Implosion, *Sunday Times*, 21 February, 5.

6. Dudley, J.W. (1990) *1992 Strategies for the Single Market,* London: Kogan Page, 327.

7. Kearney, A.T. (1991) *Trade Investment in Japan: The Current Environment,* A Study for the American Chamber of Commerce in Japan, June, 16.

8. Narus, J.A. and J. C. Anderson (1986) Industrial Distributor Selling: The Roles of Outside and Inside Sales, *Industrial Marketing Management*, **15**, 55–62.

9. Rosenbloom, B. (1987) *Marketing Channels: A Management View,* Hinsdale, Ill: Dryden, 160.

10. Laurance, B. (1993) MMC in Bad Odour Over Superdrug Ruling, *Guardian*, 12 November, 18.

11. Anonymous (1993) EC Rejects Unilever Appeal on Cabinets, *Marketing*, 25 February, 6.

12. Meller, P. (1992) Isostar Enters the Lucozade League, *Marketing*, 2 July, 9.

13. Helmore, E. (1997) Restaurant Kings or Just Silly Burgers, *The Observer*, 8 June, 5.

14. Hopkinson, G. C. and S. Hogarth Scott (1999) Franchise Relationship Quality: Microeconomic Explanations, *European Journal of Marketing*, **33** (9/10), 827–43.

15. Vignali, C., R. A. Schmidt and B. J. Davies (1993) The Benetton Experience, *International Journal of Retail and Distribution Management*, **21** (3), 53–9.

16. Mohabir-Collins, S. and S. Connor (1993) The Benetton Affair: Unethical Behaviour or Competitive Advantage?, *Proceedings of the Marketing Education Group Conference*, Loughborough, 701.

17. Chapman, P. (1996) Keeping Body Shop and Soul Together, *The European*, 4–10 July, 36.

18. Smith, A. (1999) Body Shop Group to Restructure, *Financial Times*, 27 January, 1.

19. Rosenbloom (1987) op. cit.

20. Shipley, D. D., D. Cook and E. Barnett (1989) Recruitment, Motivation, Training and Evaluation of Overseas Distributors, *European Journal of Marketing*, **23** (2), 79–93.

21. Shipley, Cook and Barnett (1989) op. cit.

22. Rosson, P. and I. Ford (1982) Manufacturer: Overseas Distributor Relations and Export Performance, *Journal of International Business Studies*, 13 (fall), 57–72.

23. Shipley, Cook and Barnett (1989) op. cit.

24. Kumar, N., L. K. Scheer and J-Bem Steenkamp (1995) The Effects of Perceived Interdependence on Dealer Attitudes, *Journal of Marketing Research*, **32** (August) 248–56.

25. See Shipley, D. D. and S. Prinja (1988) The Services and Supplier Choice Influences of Industrial Distributors, *Service Industries Journal* 8 (2), 176–87; Webster, F. E. (1976) The Role of the Industrial Distributor in Marketing Strategy, *Journal of Marketing*, **40**, 10–16.

26. Shipley, Cook and Barnett (1989) op. cit.

27. See Pegram, R. (1965) *Selecting and Evaluating Distributors*, New York: National Industrial Conference Board, 109–25; Shipley, Cook and Barnett (1989) op. cit.

28. Philpot, N. (1975) Managing the Export Function: Policies and Practice in Small and Medium Companies, *Management Survey Report no 16*, British Institute of Management; Shipley, Cook and Barnett (1989) op. cit.

29. Magrath, A. J. and K. G. Hardy (1989) A Strategic Paradigm for Predicting Manufacturer–Reseller Conflict, *European Journal of Marketing*, **23** (2), 94–108.

30. Barratt, L. (1998) Ford Educates the Dealers, *Marketing*, 13 August, 13.

31. BBC1 Television (1993) *Winning With Europe* Series.

32. Magrath and Hardy (1989) op. cit.

33. Magrath and Hardy (1989) op. cit.

34. Hardy, K. G. and A. J. Magrath (1988) Ten Ways for Manufacturers to Improve Distribution Management, *Business Horizons*, Nov.–Dec., 68.

35. Magrath and Hardy (1989) op. cit.

36. Hardy, K. G. (1985) Norsk Kjem A/S Case Study, University of Western Ontario, Canada.

37. Barksdale, J. (1996) Microsoft Would Like to Squash Me Like a Bug, *Financial Times*, Special Report on IT, 2 October, 2.

38. Baxter, A. (1993) Delivering the Goods, *Financial Times*, 18 January, 8.

39. Gibson, M. (1996) Hubs See Birth of New Bread of Warehouse, *The European*, 12–18 September, 32.

40. Kavanagh, J. (1996) Electronic Partnership with Supermarket Suppliers, *Financial Times*, Special Supplement on IT, 2 October, 6.

41. Anderson, A. (1999) Study Finds European Business at Cross-roads of E-Commerce, www.ac.ac.com/showcase/ecommerce/ecom_estudy98.html.

42. Samiee, S. (1990) Strategic Considerations of the EC 1992 Plan for Small Exporters, *Business Horizons*, March–April, 48–56.

43. Wiersema, F. (1997) *Customer Intimacy*, London: HarperCollins./

44. Schlegelmilch, B. (1998) *Marketing Ethics: An International Perspective*, London: International Thomson Business Press.

45. McCawley, I. (2000) Small Suppliers Seek Broader Shelf Access, *Marketing Week*, 17 February, 20.

46. Carter, M. (1999) Commercial Taste for an Ethical Brew, *Financial Times*, 22 October, 17.

Key terms

channel intermediaries   organizations which facilitate the distribution of products to customers

channel of distribution   the means by which products are moved from the producer to the ultimate consumer

channel strategy   the selection of the most effective distribution channel, the most appropriate level of distribution intensity and the degree of channel integration

intensive distribution   the aim is to provide saturation coverage of the market by using all available outlets

selective distribution   the use of a limited number of outlets in a geographical area to sell products of a supplier

exclusive distribution   an extreme form of selective distribution where only one wholesaler, retailer or industrial distributor is used in a geographical area to sell products of a supplier

channel integration   the way in which the players in the channel are linked together

administered vertical marketing system   a channel situation where a manufacturer who dominates a market through its size and strong brands may exercise considerable power over intermediaries even though they are independent

franchise   a legal contract in which a producer and channel intermediaries agree each other's rights and obligations. Usually the intermediary receives marketing, managerial, technical, and financial services in return for a fee

contractual vertical marketing system   a franchise arrangement (e.g. a franchise) tying producers and resellers together

corporate vertical marketing system   a channel situation where an organization gains control of distribution through ownership

safety (buffer) stocks   stocks or inventory held to cover against uncertainty about re-supply lead-times

economic order quantity   the quantity of stock to be ordered where total costs are at the lowest

Case 29 Mitsubishi Electric Ireland Ltd: Managing Changes in the Distribution Channel

'Cola Wars: It's the Real Thing'. As he relaxed over a cup of coffee one morning, Fergus Madigan was drawn to this headline in the business section of a Sunday newspaper. The editorial went on to describe how the traditional big brands seemed to be under attack and not even such bastions as Coca-Cola and Kellogg's Corn Flakes seemed to be safe. The world of marketing it appeared was being turned on its head and the correspondent wondered if it would ever be the same again. Marlboro Friday, diaper Tuesday and cola Thursday. These rumblings of the stock markets illustrated that attacks on big brands by new competitors were having a serious impact on the share prices of consumer goods giants such as Philip Morris, Proctor & Gamble and Coca-Cola. Aside from nimble competitors such as the Virgin Group, the central point of attack appeared to be from major distributors, who due to their increasing power, were able to launch their own brands to compete with the traditional manufacturer's brand. It seemed to reflect what many commentators had been forecasting which was that there would continue to be a powershift from manufacturers to retailers in the marketing channel.

The article struck a chord with Fergus Madigan, managing director of Mitsubishi Electric Ireland Ltd (MEIR) who had overseen the strong growth of Mitsubishi products on the Irish market. His company had always subscribed to the importance of brand building and now had a brand name which was both well known and associated with high quality, technologically advanced products. But he had noticed the home entertainment business in Ireland was undergoing a fundamental transformation. Not least among the changes was the emergence of a powerful group of discount chains following similar patterns in the USA and other developed nations. These chains seemed to have the capability to threaten consumer electronics firms in the same way that some food retailers were challenging the leading food and drinks companies. As he reflected on the plight of some of the world's biggest brand names Fergus Madigan's thoughts began to turn to the implications these trends were likely to have for the home entertainment business in Ireland.

The home entertainment industry

The home entertainment business had grown dramatically throughout the developed world since the end of the Second World War and appeared to be on the crest of another revolution. Home entertainment comprised a range of audio products (radio, stereo, compact and mini discs and compact cassettes), video products (VCR, TV, cable, satellite and camcorders) and interactive products such as computer games and 'smart boxes'. The market for TVs and VCRs had reached saturation point in many developed countries. Competition for market share became intense and leading firms in the industry such as Sanyo and Philips had suffered losses (see Table C29.1). Other firms responded by developing multiple extensions of their basic product lines. For example, in 1994, Sony went as far as launching a water resistant television designed specifically for use in bathrooms.

The home entertainment industry was on the verge of a technological revolution. For example, the television has been a relatively stable product, remaining essentially the same since its introduction in the 1930s. Analogue signals, transmitted by cable or antenna were converted by the set into electrons and sprayed onto the picture tube. Since standards for broadcast TV were set in the 1950s, the only major change had been the addition of colour capability (CTV). However, a worldwide race to introduce a new form of high definition television (HDTV) appeared to have been won by the USA. In February 1994, the USA announced a new digital HDTV standard formulated by a 'Grand Alliance' of high-tech companies, including the two biggest European TV manufacturers, Philips and Thomson GE/RCA. Europe's own HDTV analogue standard development (HD-MAC) had been abandoned in 1993 and the US digital version was perceived to be superior to the Japanese analogue HDTV, though the latter persisted with developing their own standard.

The implications of digital transmission, however, extended well beyond HDTV applications. Digital technology, whereby any form of information (text, graphics, sound, video images) can be coded as a series of binary digits, had several advantages over analogue technology. First, the coded information could be reproduced more accurately than through analogue transmission, with the result that colours and patterns were crisper and clearer. Secondly, digital signals could be compressed allowing for various kinds of information to travel on the same channel which opened up possibilities for interactive multimedia. Finally, digitalization ended the necessity for real-time transmission, in other words, an hour's worth of programming could be delivered in seconds. Digital compact cassettes for video, digital stereo sound and digital satellite transmission were some of the innovations being developed in Europe.

A variety of firms not traditionally considered part of the home entertainment industry were likely to have a significant impact on its future.

Computer manufacturers such as Sega, Sun Microsystems and IBM were working on 'smart boxes' which facilitated interactive television. Matsushita, Philips and Sony were partners with General Magic, a software consortium while Microsoft and Intel also formed an alliance in the race to develop interactive TV. One of the possibilities provided by interactive television was the concept of 'movies on demand' which threatened to obliterate the traditional video rental industry. At the same time a number of telecommunications companies had invested in cable firms in order to develop strong market positions with regard to digital technology opportunities.

The home entertainment industry in Ireland

Ireland, in line with most other economies in the Western world, had a well-developed market of home entertainment products. In 1994, 98 per cent of Irish households had at least one television

Table C29.1   Market shares for TVs and VCRs in leading markets

	Television		VCR	
USA (1990)				
	Thomson GE/RCA	21	Matsushita	21
	Philips (US)	13	Thomson GE/RCA	15
	Zenith	12	Philips	9
	Sony	7	Emerson	9
	Matsushita	6	Sharp	7
	Sanyo/Fisher	5	JVC	5
Japan (1991)				
	Matsushita	22.5	Matsushita	28.6
	Toshiba	14.5	Victor Co. (Japan)	16.7
	Sharp	14.5	Mitsubishi	15.3
	Hitachi	10.5	Toshiba	12
	Sony	10.5	Sharp	8.7
Europe (1992)				
	Philips	13.4		
	Grundig	9.7		
	Sony	8.8		
	Telefunken	4.1		
	Sanyo	2.8		
	Samsung	2.7		
	Matsushita	2.5		
	Toshiba	2.4		
	Sharp	2.4		
	Hitachi	2.2		

set and 96 per cent of these were colour sets. Ownership of VCRs had grown to almost 60 per cent of all households (see Fig. C29.1 for ownership levels of TV and VCR products).

Ownership of TVs and VCRs was higher in urban households than in either urban apartments or rural households. Differences in ownership were less dramatic across age groups though the highest proportion of VCR owners are in the 18–35 age group. The average life of a television set was 5–7 years. Recent research indicated that some 25 per cent of the Irish market had purchased their main TV in the past three years indicating a strong replacement demand. This demand was particularly pronounced in the younger age groups and in urban segments (see Table C29.2).

Some notable trends had emerged in terms of product features and the pricing of TVs and VCRs. In terms of screen size, demand was strongest for large-screen TVs (greater than 27 inches) and for small-screen TVs (14–15 inches) reflecting

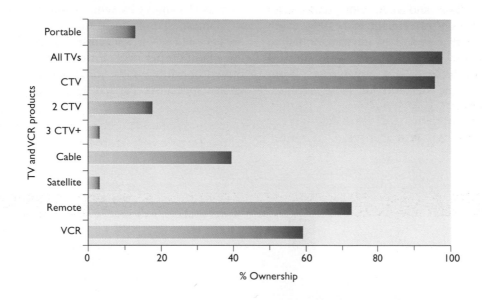

Figure C29.1 Ownership of TV and VCR products, 1994

Table C29.2   The Irish TV/VCR market

	Purchasing patterns		
	Average TV sets/household	*% ownership of VCRs*	*% acquiring main TV in last 3 years*
Age group			
18–25	1.5	24%	26%
26–49	1.6	20%	27%
50–59	1.4	25%	21%
60+	1.2	13%	20%
Household type			
Urban house	1.7	25%	30%
Urban apartment	1.0	22%	11%
Rural house	1.3	18%	20%

purchases of small second or third TVs as well as an upgrading of the main household TV. Demand for TVs with features such as Nicam stereo and Teletext was also growing with the latter rising to 27 pecent in 1994. With regard to VCRs, however, the demand for extra features such as Video Plus, long-play action and Nicam stereo had been less brisk with the majority of products sold being less sophisticated, two head systems with standard play action and mono sound. These patterns suggested that the Irish market was lagging other countries where there was a growing trend towards 'home theatre systems' encompassing large-screen TVs, a Dolby surround sound system, a laser disc player and VCR, with greater user control. In terms of pricing, the early 1990s were characterized by a period of stagnant or falling prices. However, 1994 had seen some upward movement reflecting the emergence from recession and the demand for more sophisti-

cated products in line with trends in Europe generally.

Distribution

Distribution was managed almost exclusively through direct contact with retailers. Wholesalers, while they were present in Ireland, accounted for only three per cent of total TV/VCR sales. Electrical goods retailers in Ireland could broadly be categorized as brown goods specialists, white goods specialists or combination dealers (general electric shops, department stores) (see Table C29.3). Brown goods were audio-visual products such as TVs and VCRs, while white goods refered to domestic appliances such as refrigerators, cookers and so on. Specialist dealers were those for whom 60 per cent of their sales were either brown or white goods. Some one-third of white goods specialists carried home entertainment

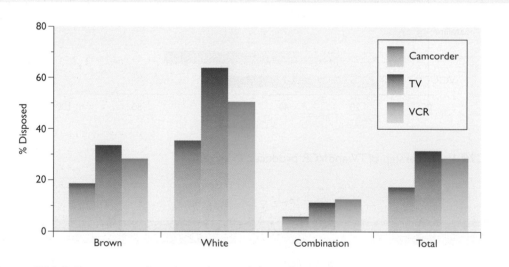

Figure C29.2 Percentage of products disposed through rental

Table C29.3	Dealer size by type	
Shop type	Small (Turnover <IR£250 000)	Large (Turnover >IR£250 000)
Brown	47%	53%
White	33%	67%
Combination dealer	50%	50%

products. These shops were expected to broaden their product range with an average of six per cent each year expected to begin stocking brown goods. The total market for brown goods in Ireland was estimated to be IR£140 million in 1994.

The rental market in Ireland had been declining in line with trends throughout Europe. Between 1990 and 1991, rental of TVs declined by three per cent while that of VCRs fell by a substantial 11 per cent. The rental market was an important one for white goods specialists accounting for some 50 per cent of all TVs/VCRs disposed in contrast with only 20 per cent for brown goods specialists (see Fig. C29.2). Repair services were also an important source of revenue in the industry accounting for on average about 10 per cent of sales. 92 per cent of brown goods specialists and 76 per cent of combination dealers provided repair services. However, this source of revenue was threatened by an increasing propensity among manufacturers to service their own products.

Each of the major manufacturers had varying degrees of success in their penetration of the alternative channels in Ireland. In the distribution of TVs and VCRs, Panasonic and Sony relied heavily on brown goods specialists, Sharp relied on white goods specialists, while Philips had secured high levels of penetration in both white

goods outlets and combination dealers. Mitsubishi had also successfully developed a dual distribution channel with strong coverage of both brown goods and combination dealers (see Fig. C29.3).

In 1989, Ireland had some 522 independent dealers (higher per capita than any other EC country) accounting for 84 per cent of total turnover. However, since then the number of electrical outlets in Ireland had declined at a rate of 10–15 per cent per year and the market was becoming increasingly concentrated. Large discounters had several advantages which made them a serious threat to the independent retailer. They carried a wide range of products in every segment of the TV/VCR market and could avail of economies of scale in buying operations that allowed them to retail these products at highly competitive prices. They were concentrated primarily in large urban areas but offered nationwide sales and service through telephone ordering and free delivery. Finally, in their suburban locations, these discounters maintained longer opening hours and could easily facilitate Sunday shopping. Equally, the independent dealers were at a competitive disadvantage *vis-à-vis* the Electricity Supply Board (ESB), the state electricity company. Its network of some 100 shops offered customers a unique form of

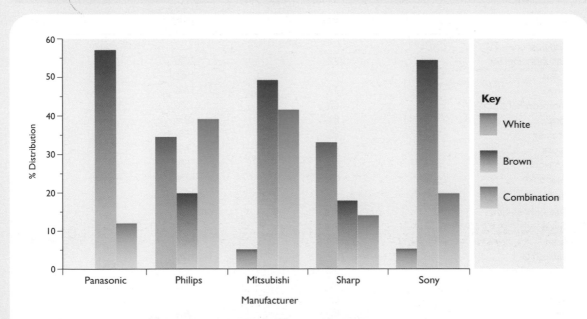

Figure C29.3 Percentage of CTV brand distribution by channel

financing whereby instalment payments were attached to utility bills.

Concentration of the market reflected international patterns where for example, in the USA, consumer electronic superstores offered zero percentage financing, extended warranties and toll-free service. The growth of such superstores in Europe was assisted by new regulations which allowed parallel importing of consumer electronics products. This increased the feasibility of distributors deciding to service the complete European market from a single base, taking the concept of scale and volume to a new level. A distributor in the UK, Argos, was pursuing this strategy by operating with very low overheads and devoting minimum resources to sales staff and merchandising. Careful use of information technology afforded these kinds of firms the opportunity to telemarket their products on a pan-European basis.

The relationships which manufacturers maintained with these different groups of dealers varied significantly. Small independent shops employed a strategy of carrying a limited range of brands which were tailored carefully to their local markets. Manufacturers with strong brands negotiated arrangements with independent dealers whereby certain products (which a dealer felt were necessary for success) would only be supplied if certain other products were bought as well. However, the position of the manufacturer was somewhat weaker with regard to the discount chains as the latter's volume of sales put them in a stronger bargaining position.

Mitsubishi Electric Ireland

Mitsubishi Electric Ireland (MEIR) was opened in 1981 as the Dublin branch office of Mitsubishi Electric UK. The initial staff consisted of a managing director, two salesmen, an accountant, secretary, engineer and a warehouse logistics specialist. Together this group generated sales of IR£1 million in the first year of operations. By 1982, turnover had grown to IR£4.5 million and a mere four years after opening, MEIR had become a market leader in sales of TVs and VCRs, a position which it has retained (see Table C29.4). As the company grew it reduced its dependence on TVs and VCRs. In 1984, the company set up an OEM unit to meet the demand coming from the computer industry for disk drives, monitors and

Table C29.4 Manufacturers' share of TV and VCR—Ireland			
Manufacturer	*1991*	*1992*	*1993*
Market share—TV			
Mitsubishi Electric	22%	20%	22%
Philips	17%	19%	19%
Sanyo	14%	16%	14%
Thomson/Ferguson	6%	5%	8%
Sony	8%	8%	7%
Grundig	8%	6%	7%
Salora	6%	6%	6%
Panasonic	8%	5%	5%
Blaupunkt	0%	1%	5%
Market share—VCR			
Mitsubishi Electric	24%	26%	28%
Philips	15%	19%	17%
Sanyo	12%	11%	14%
Matsushita	14%	10%	10%
Thomson/Ferguson	5%	6%	8%
JVC	8%	6%	7%
Salora	8%	7%	5%
Sony	8%	6%	5%
Grundig	6%	4%	3%

circuit protection products. In 1985, an industrial unit was established to meet the needs of industrial customers for energy saving motor components such as programmable logic controllers and inverters. In recent years a variety of other products have been added, including security products, air conditioning, facsimile and cellular phone ranges. TVs and VCRs now account for less than 50 per cent of MEIR's annual turnover.

MEIR was one of the 106 subsidiaries and affiliates of the Mitsubishi Electric Corporation located in over 90 countries. The corporation operated a dual reporting system so MEIR reported to both its head office in the UK as well as the corporate office in Tokyo. Other than this reporting obligation, MEIR operated autonomously in Ireland, which allowed it to be flexible in response to changing conditions. However, its scope was restricted by its dependence on its Japanese parent as a source of supply for new products. In keeping with its Japanese ethos, MEIR placed a great deal of emphasis on gaining long-term market share rather than on achieving short-term profitability. Indeed, it has become highly regarded within the corporation as it was the only branch which had achieved the number one market share position in its local market and its

branding capability was regarded as a significant strength. Its unofficial but well-articulated vision, spearheaded by the managing director and embraced by MEIR management and staff, was quite simply to be the best: best in terms of customer satisfaction, best in terms of distribution management, best in terms of perceived brand value and best in terms of market share. This was reflected in the company's three-tier strategy which was to maintain a good distribution network, to maintain a strong brand and to carefully position its product line. Its primary objective was to grow sales annually by 10 per cent through to 1997. Given the saturation in the TV and VCR markets this meant a need to focus attention on the importance of new products.

Company structure

The structure of the organization is illustrated in Fig. C29.4. It had three distinct business units to deal with each of its key constituents, namely, the consumer market, the industrial market and the OEM market. Each operated to pre-set budgets and were evaluated in terms of gross margin. Overhead and indirect costs were allocated according to company objectives and a considerable amount of cross-subsidization took place between the

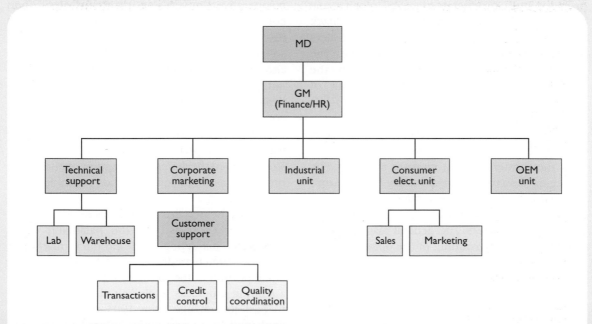

Figure C29.4 Company structure of Mitsubishi Electric Ireland (MEIR)

units. The strategies of each were co-ordinated with overall company goals.

In addition to the three operating units, the company had separate corporate marketing and technical support units. Corporate marketing had responsibility for servicing the other operating units as well as the customer support process. This process tracked every order from entry to dispatch and was designed to reflect the company's fanatical approach to customer service. Incoming customer calls were fed into an exchange. From there, they were automatically routed to the first free line in the customer support group. Orders were taken and once the necessary price and credit checks were made, the relevant operating unit was contacted to arrange delivery within 48 hours. Customer complaints were logged and forwarded to the relevant department for handling. One consequence of this system was that all incoming calls were treated with equal priority irrespective of whether the caller was a small retailer or a major OEM customer. Equally, it did not allow for any specialization within the customer support group and the system tended to come under pressure at the peak times such as November and December each year.

The technical support and quality control function consisted of the warehouse, inventory control and a technical laboratory. The laboratory provided both product testing and repair capabilities as well as customer and product feedback to MEIR through questionnaires which dealers filled out when repair work was done. The manager of this group monitored both the physical movement of goods in and out of the warehouse and company adherence to ISO quality standards.

Corporate responsibility was shared between the managing director and the general manager with the former holding ultimate authority. The managing director was responsible for the firm's external activities, primarily sales and marketing as well as sitting on a number of committees in the UK headquarters. The general manager oversaw the day-to-day running of the operation with responsibility for the finance/accounting function and human resource management.

Marketing strategy

The central plank of the company's marketing strategy had been the development of a strong brand image. MEIR's dedication to the concept of branding was the guiding principle in all its promotion from its simplest press coverage to its most extensive advertising campaigns. As a result, MEIR had been able to command a premium position in the marketplace which in turn allowed it to maximize its margins and profit potential.

The company devoted five per cent of its sales to brand development. This budget was based on sales forecasts rather than sales revenues, thus ensuring that brand support was not reduced during 'bad years'. Brand development took place at both the corporate and product levels. At the corporate level, the focus was on developing an image of the Mitsubishi name that was associated with a large, technologically advanced manufacturer of quality products. It also sought to demonstrate that it was a community-orientated company by including leading sports personalities such as Ronnie Delaney, an Olympic gold medalist and Ronnie Whelan, an Irish soccer international in its advertising. The company name was promoted through participation in community events as well as through the standard advertising media such as national newspapers and billboards.

At the product level, promotion centred on particular products which reflected state-of-the-art technology. This was achieved through co-operative advertising with dealers and consumer promotions such as rebates and discounts based on purchases made. Co-operative advertising was designed to incentivize dealers and proved particularly beneficial to small independent retailers who often lacked sophisticated promotion capability. The aim of consumer promotions aside from simply selling products was to promote their particular features. By emphasizing specific attributes, MEIR strengthened the general perception of Mitsubishi products as high quality and technologically advanced.

One of the perpetual problem's for MEIR, given its budget confines, was the balancing of its corporate marketing and product marketing activities which traditionally had been given an equal portion of the promotion budget. However, a shifting emphasis is illustrated in Table C29.5. In part the change from 1993 to 1994 can be explained by opportunities offered by Ireland's qualification for the 1994 Soccer World Cup. MEIR had a contract with the manager of the Irish team,

Jack Charlton, who was engaged primarily in their corporate promotions and to a lesser extent in trade marketing such as visits to top performing dealers. This promotion had been very effective in generating direct business during the World Cup when MEIR offered large-screen TVs to pub owners at a discount in a joint-promotion with Guinness Ireland.

Research conducted by MEIR indicated that it had been very successful in its brand-building efforts in Ireland. In terms of awareness and pitted against some well-established rivals, recognition of the Mitsubishi name which had initially been difficult for Irish consumers to pronounce had grown as high as 87 per cent in just 13 years. In terms of quality, Mitsubishi products were perceived by the consumer to be the highest by a wide margin and it was also the brand that most consumers automatically associated with Nicam stereo sound televisions which was arguably the single biggest advance in television technology since the advent of colour. However, the company recognized that this brand franchise faced a new challenge in the future due to the growing concentration of the distribution channel.

Channel management: a new competitive challenge

The nucleus of MEIR's dealer base could be traced back to the managing director and the relationships he had developed before forming the company. It targeted dealers that it had identified as being the strongest in local areas in the country for a projected portfolio of 100 in total. Rather than sell Mitsubishi products through unsuitable dealers, the company took a long-term view and began the process of developing both its product and company image. It created an atmosphere of exclusivity whereby only the most successful dealers in an area were given the opportunity to sell Mitsubishi products. Thus, a 'club' atmosphere was developed which created dealer demand for the product. This was reinforced by a strong package of dealer benefits which further developed the relationship. The package consisted of incentives, training, advertising support and marketing expertise intended to both reward the dealers and make them more competitive.

MEIR had five classes of dealers ranked on the basis of annual turnover. Class AA were the biggest consisting of accounts with an annual turnover of IR£200 000. Class A accounts had a turnover of between IR£100 000 and IR£199 000, Class B a turnover of IR£60 000 to IR£99 000, Class C a turnover of IR£20 000 to IR£59 000 and Class D a turnover of less than IR£19 000 (see Table C29.6). In 1993, the 48 dealers in the top three classes accounted for 90 per cent of total revenue while the 68 dealers in classes C and D accounted for the remaining 10 per cent. In terms of profit contribution, the pattern was somewhat different. Because of their competitive pricing patterns, sales through larger dealers typically resulted in smaller profit margins to MEIR. This profit pattern

Table C29.5   Changing brand strategy emphasis 1993–94

Promotion component	1993 (%)	1994 (%)
Corporate branding	30	65
Cooperative advertising	50	25
Consumer promotions	20	10

Table C29.6   Revenue contribution by class

Class	Revenue contribution over time (%)				
	1993	1992	1991	1990	1989
Class AA	68.23	58.09	49.26	55.0	50.0
Class A	10.10	12.05	13.64	19.0	24.0
Class B	11.72	13.08	14.93	12.0	13.0
Class C	7.67	10.38	11.72	9.0	4.0
Class D	2.29	5.80	10.44	2.0	4.0

was also influenced by the fact that support for dealers declined with their importance. For example, though Class D dealers were characterized by low turnover, they were also the least expensive to manage, not receiving any support from MEIR and paying for products on a cash-on-delivery basis.

Over the five-year period since 1989 there had been some significant movement within the dealer classes. In all cases there was a familiar pattern where some dealers move up or down between the categories to be replaced by others moving in the opposite direction. Class AA accounts consisted of discount chains, large independents and department stores. Most new AAs were previously in the A class though a major discount chain, Power city, started as an AA account. 55 per cent of AA accounts in 1993 had been in this class for more than five years. There had been a significant overall drop in Class A dealers which had fallen from 23 to 10 since 1989. A small number developed into AA accounts with the majority falling back to B, C and D levels. Of the 10 A accounts in 1993, 70 per cent had been in this category for at least five years.

The B class had traditionally provided the biggest margins to MEIR. The number of B accounts rose in 1993 though the profit contribution of this group remained relatively stable suggesting that the average B account was becoming smaller. Movements in the C class were greater than in any of the other classes. 28 per cent of accounts had been in this class for at least four years, while only three per cent had been there for more than five years. Similarly, the number of D accounts had grown by over 200 per cent since 1989. The revenue contribution of this group had declined significantly since 1991, implying that the average account had become smaller (see Table C29.7).

The growth in the lower classes indicated that either previously strong dealers were unable to fully adapt to the increasingly competitive environment or that they had been promoting other brands at the expense of the Mitsubishi brand. In either case, it indicated that a large proportion of MEIR's dealer portfolio had been decreasing their level of business with MEIR.

Managing the distribution channel

Conscious of the trends taking place in the market, the managing director decided to conduct an audit of the distribution channel. Sales patterns were analysed and discussions were held with channel members to solicit their views. From this research the following strategic alternatives appeared to be available to the company.

Reduce the number of channel members

The analysis of distribution revealed that a very high proportion of dealers provided little in the way of revenues and profits to the company. Nineteen class AA dealers contributed almost 70 per cent of revenue while 68 class C and D dealers combined contributed less than 10 per cent. MEIR could decide to remove these two classes from its portfolio and concentrate solely on the larger players enabling them to provide a better service to this strengthening group.

Provide a level playing field

Discussions with the company's dealers yielded evidence of some dissatisfaction with recent trends. The marketplace had become increasingly competitive, margins were eroding and many

---

Table C29.7 Number of dealers per class (1989–93)

Class	1993	1992	1991	1990	1989
Class AA	19	17	13	19	18
Class A	10	19	26	20	23
Class B	19	11	13	21	23
Class C	29	35	30	27	12
Class D	39	33	31	28	19

dealers felt that brown good specialists had very little future in the industry. With specific reference to MEIR, there was some dissatisfaction too as many dealers felt that the notion of the exclusive 'club' of which they once felt part seemed to have disappeared. MEIR now had some 116 dealers nationwide, but more significantly, there was a feeling that not all dealers were being treated equally. MEIR had always pursued the traditional Japanese practice of negotiating individually and privately with each dealer. The result of this was that there was little uniformity of business terms among dealers, to the extent that an aggressive B account dealer could gain better terms than a larger A account dealer. At the bottom end of the scale, the smaller independent brown goods specialist was being forced to operate on a cash-on-delivery basis while at the same time large discount chains were able to avail of exclusive promotions. Exclusive promotions like these, it was felt, eroded the premium image of the brand. At the same time, they created disquiet among dealers who felt hamstrung in their efforts to compete with the discount chains and became much more sensitive to marginal differences in the terms being offered. They proposed that all dealers be allowed to begin at the same starting point which would enable them to compete more effectively with the larger discount chains thus stalling the latter's growing power in the market-place.

The idea of a level playing field left MEIR with two options. One, it could seek to level the playing field for all its dealers by instituting a policy of recommended resale prices and national consumer promotions which would be advertised in the national media. This could be backed by a standard approach to cooperative advertising or all cooperative advertising could cease with the money saved moving to consumer promotions. Alternatively, MEIR could seek to reinstitute the notion of a club or clubs by tailoring sales terms to each class ensuring that members of the same class were given the same terms.

Work closely with dealers

Market research in the industry demonstrated that the dealers' salespeople were an important player in the consumer buying decision. It revealed that the salesperson rated higher than brand awareness, promotion and brand loyalty in influencing purchasing decisions. This was accentuated by a low level of brand loyalty in the industry despite high levels of brand recognition. For example, while awareness of the Mitsubishi name was as high as 87 per cent its market share of televisions in 1993 was 22 per cent. This implies that its ratio of brand loyalty to brand awareness was approximately one-quarter. Salespeople had the ability to convince customers to switch brands by highlighting particular features of the product and actively demonstrating these during a customer's visit to the shop. Inevitably, the brand a salesperson was likely to promote was going to be influenced by how he or she was motivated to promote the brand.

Trade promotions in the industry, such as free trips were typically aimed at store owners and not the sales staff. This again presented MEIR with two possible approaches. It could focus on directly incentivizing salespeople in its dealerships. This would involve replacing the current package of free trips with a system that directly links points earned by the sales staff with the number of MEIR products sold. The points accumulated could directly relate to the cumulative value of each of the products sold, with top margin items earning more points. These accumulated points could then be exchanged for holiday trips arranged by MEIR in a fashion similar to the frequent flyer programmes adopted by airlines. Alternatively, it could introduce a comprehensive package of sales training for the salespeople. The objective of this approach would be to create salesperson loyalty and to better equip them, in terms of technical knowledge and selling skills, to promote and sell MEIR products. Such training seminars would have the advantage of allowing MEIR staff to make direct contact with dealer salespeople, presenting a vehicle for transmitting its way of doing business as well as mechanisms for collecting market information and for training sales people in the proper use of Mitsubishi products and promotional material.

Increase its level of direct business

Its very successful direct promotion with Guinness Ireland and Irish pub owners during the 1994 Soccer World Cup had demonstrated to MEIR the potential available in direct sales. This joint promotion benefited all the parties concerned. MEIR was able to take advantage of the demand at the time for large-screen televisions and to significantly increase its volume of sales of this high value product. Guinness Ireland was able to enhance its relationships with the publicans by providing zero-per cent financing for the purchases. MEIR dealers then delivered and installed these presold products for the publican though at a somewhat reduced margins for themselves. Generally, an increasing proportion of MEIR's revenue had been coming from this kind of direct business.

Thinking ahead to next Monday's monthly review of operations, Fergus Madigan pondered on the choices available to the company. He wondered which approach or combinations of approaches might be most effective in the long term but as well he wanted to be sure that there were not any additional options that, as yet, he had failed to consider.

This case was prepared by John Fahy, Professor of Marketing, University of Limerick, Ireland.

Case 30 Cafédirect®:
The Building of a Unique Coffee Brand

Some of the 4000 Peruvian coffee producers that Luzmila Loayza visits can only be reached by donkey, even though most agents in this part of the world seldom bother to go further than the coffee processing plant. But then Ms Loayza is unusual, she buys coffee from small producers for an organization that processes, packages and sells it under the brand name 'Cafédirect' in order to give a fair return to small growers. According to Oxfam, these growers normally receive only about 10 p for a standard 8 oz pack of ground coffee selling in a supermarket for around £1.30. Over 80 per cent of the world's coffee is still grown on small plots farmed by families who depend for their livelihood on one of the world's most unstable commodity markets. Although news of 'frost in Brazil' may bring a *frisson* of excitement to informed supermarket shoppers, since it offers them a chance to 'win' by stocking up with coffee before price increases reach the supermarket shelves, for the growers the unpredictable rise and fall in market prices can be catastrophic.

For almost 50 years coffee production was controlled by quotas imposed through the operation of the International Coffee Agreement, a mechanism that effectively stabilized prices. When in 1989 the agreement collapsed, the price of green beans fell so low due to uncontrolled coffee production that marginal producers were unable to even cover their costs (Fig. C30.1, years 1990–93). There was no point in them harvesting an unsaleable crop, so farms were neglected and families could not afford sufficient food, school books or medical treatment. With no resources to tide them over, survival frequently meant giving up the farm and moving to the city to scratch a living among the urban poor, putting intolerable strains on the economic and welfare infrastructures of the countries concerned. Others drifted in desperation to the illegal coca fields in order to support their families.

A unique organization is born

Charities, such as Oxfam, had long been buying coffee from small producers, having it processed and selling it through their own outlets up and down the country. Since distribution through charity shops could only reach a very small market, the reality was that such 'campaign'[1] quality coffee was for the relatively few stalwart supporters who were prepared to make sacrifices in product quality and shopping convenience for a good cause. However, the collapse of the International Coffee Agreement and the problems caused by the consequent price fluctuations was the inspiration for some radical thinking.

In mid-1990, representatives of four organizations met to plan a new enterprise that would produce and market a brand of coffee that could compete successfully on supermarket shelves alongside the biggest brands in the business. Cafédirect, the company that emerged, has four partners (Oxfam, Twin Trading, Equal Exchange and Traidcraft), each with representation on the Board. It has no full-time employees, no production units and no distribution facilities. Sales became the responsibility of one person working four days a week, and brand management activities were undertaken by Media Natura, an agency that specializes in working for environmental and charitable organizations. The mission of the Cafédirect enterprise was to pass more of the proceeds back to the coffee farmers; instead of 10 p they would get 40 p for every 8 oz pack of Cafédirect coffee sold. A further objective agreed by the partners was to stabilize the fluctuations in the price of coffee beans. A crucial aspect of this was contracting to pay growers a guaranteed $1.26 per lb to cover basic production costs and wages, regardless of how low the market price drops.[2] With the security offered by a Cafédirect contract farmers could make plans for the future, obtain loans, improve their production methods and provide more security and welfare for their

---

[1] 'Campaign' coffees have a poor reputation for flavour, quality and availability. For some time associated with support from the Sandanistas in Nicaragua, it is imported, processed and sold through charity outlets to the more dedicated charity supporters.

[2] Later, in 1994, the market price for green coffee beans briefly exceeded $1.26 per lb. Cafédirect responded to this by changing the contract so that coffee growers were paid the market price plus 10 per cent, with a minimum floor price of $1.26 per lb.

families. Despite suggestions made by the big coffee processing companies that fair trade merely leads to overproduction and lower prices, experience has shown that few farmers risk planting new coffee trees since they take three years to bear fruit, and conditions in the international coffee market are too uncertain to make the investment viable. Instead, many farmers have sought to diversify into other products, such as honey, black-eyed beans, lemon grass or cocoa.

In developing the Cafédirect brand, the group was planning to take on the giants of the industry, such as Kraft General Foods, Paulig and Lavazza. What is more, it planned to do it with higher raw material costs, limited funds and none of the scale economies and marketing expertise enjoyed by its rivals.

It knew that it could not depend upon the fair trade message alone to convince buyers. In order to compete, it would have to deliver real value to the consumers and meet the needs of the supermarket buyers. It planned to do this by creating a vertically integrated network, linking small farmers, the coffee processor, supermarkets and consumers (Fig. C30.2).

Each of the four partners has relevant expertise to contribute in building the value chain of the brand. The long experience of Twin Trading in advising small-scale producers how to meet customer specifications and export requirements would be invaluable in ensuring quality and consistency of supply. The *raison d'être* of Equal Exchange is to market foodstuffs from small-scale Third World producers. Finally, Oxfam and

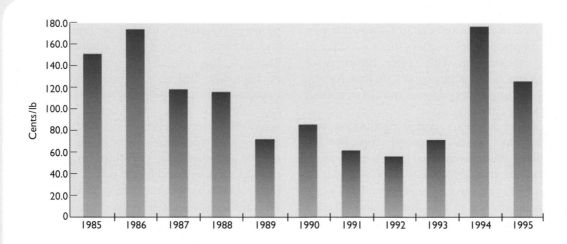

Figure C30.1 Market price of green coffee beans, Brazil

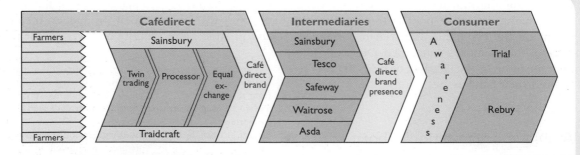

Figure C30.2 Cafédirect brand value chain

Traidcraft would bring their knowledge gained from their own retail experience, as well as their wealth of social, cultural and political intelligence from their contracts in countries all around the world, and their PR expertise in raising awareness of issues with the support of their many activists.

Identifying consumer value

It is a fundamental tenet of consumer marketing that corporate objectives are achieved by satisfying consumer needs more effectively than your competitors. Since Cafédirect had no marketing management, the task of planning how to provide this superior value fell to Bruce McKinnon of Media Natura, the advertising agency which was working for Cafédirect on a retainer basis. Media Natura was set up by the advertising industry to counter the image of greed which permeated the 1980s. Although industry funding has since dried up, the agency continues to offer an inexpensive service to charities, with the support of voluntary workers.

Bruce knew that in order to identify consumer perceptions of what constitutes superior brand value, he would need a thorough understanding of changing needs, economics and the coffee buying process. Ideally, the value proposition presented by the brand should be unique and not easy to emulate. Most food purchases are still made by women, so the potential coffee buyers were likely to be female aged 20–45 years (it was thought to be more difficult to change the behaviour of older buyers), in social groups A, B and C1 (having the disposable income needed for discretionary spending). In order to identify the target consumers more accurately, Bruce commissioned a market research study using standard questions from the Target Group Index omnibus research questionnaire.[3]

[3] Target Group Index is a service provided by the British Market Research Bureau, a commercial agency which offers omnibus research. This is operated through a standard questionnaire covering a wide range of consumer products, which TGI send out to its database of 24 000 respondents at regular intervals. Clients can commission studies by either subscribing to standard questions, or by adding specific questions to their own, at extra cost. Cafédirect could not afford to add its own questions. Nevertheless, using standard questions it was able to gather valuable market data, from a large sample, at very low cost.

The study served to identify three groups of consumer: Selfish, Ethical and Semi-ethical. The Selfish category were considered unlikely to be interested in the plight of Third World farmers at all, so they were excluded. Ethical consumers, on the other hand, were already committed, and so were quite likely to buy 'campaign' quality coffee from charity shops anyway. Semi-ethicals, the chosen target group, were found to be brand oriented, aware of fair trade issues, but largely uninformed.

The strategy for positioning the Cafédirect brand now became much clearer to Bruce. The brand values offered would have to reflect both functional and non-functional benefits: feeling good about supporting Third World coffee farmers without the usual hassle and without sacrificing flavour or convenience, at a price that was acceptable to this target market.

Building consumer value

Market research showed that the main motives behind buying ground coffee were pleasure and discernment. This meant using high quality arabica beans, that were processed under strict quality control schedules, then roasted to perfection, ground and packaged to retain the flavour. The main responsibility for ensuring product quality fell to Twin Trading. Using its many years of experience, it was able to help the coffee growers' co-operatives to meet the demanding European customer requirements, and advise them on export practices. For instance, imports of processed coffee into the European Union attract a customs tariff, whereas green coffee beans do not. Twin Trading therefore advised that the green coffee should be imported into Britain. They hired a consultant 'cupper' to determine just the right quality and roast to suit British palates, and negotiated a contract with a processor in Kent to roast, grind and package the coffee under tight quality controls. Through Twin Trading (who liaise closely with the processor), Cafédirect retains control of quality from the farm to the supermarket, unlike its international rivals who buy green coffee beans on the open market.

The market research also showed that consumers suffered some uncertainties about choosing and making ground coffee. This led them to seek the reassurance of a familiar brand which meant, in turn, that if the Cafédirect brand was to succeed, it would have to combine the fair trade appeal with a strong brand identity. Although the technical aspects of getting the flavour and quality right were within Cafédirect team's capabilities, building a brand and getting shelf space in major supermarkets was really breaking new ground. Nevertheless, these were the minimum requirements; the 'hygiene factors' that have to be met merely in order to compete but which do not bestow any additional competitive advantage.

Establishing the superior value needed to acquire this competitive edge, which would then justify a premium price to cover Cafédirect's high raw material cost and diseconomies of scale, essentially had to be achieved through the fair trade message and a pack design that denoted quality and conveyed fair trade symbolism.

The promotional campaign to launch the brand

One reason for entering the ground coffee sector was because it was thought to be much less competitive than the instant sector and the brands less well established. Furthermore, since research had indicated that people are sometimes confused and usually uncertain when buying ground coffee, the introduction of Cafédirect may just give them the reason to choose one coffee brand over another. However, to achieve this, Cafédirect needed to inform its potential customers of the product's unique offering and to build up the brand. Recognizing the need to invest in one thing, finding the capital to do it is another; resources were very limited at Cafédirect!

The choice of promotional techniques available for this purpose was further limited by the nature of the value being offered to consumers. Although sales promotion may be relatively inexpensive, and perhaps even self liquidating, special offers, coupons and contests were felt to conflict with Cafédirect's brand values. Money-off tactics left consumers wondering who was losing out.

Despite these constraints, by mid-1991 the Cafédirect team felt that its brand proposition was now sufficiently strong to make inroads in the ground coffee sector; the decision was taken to launch within a year and detailed launch plans were worked out. Prior to the launch date, stalls at the Good Food Show and the Global Partnership

Table C30.1 *Post hoc* research results, Cafédirect poster advertising campaign*

	Cafédirect	Norm
Recognition	36%	36%
Liking	74%	53%
Clarity	48%	n/a
Purchase incentive	43%	31%
Premium price acceptance	82%	n/a

*Sample frame: Travellers on the relevant railway routes.
Source: RSL Poster Advertising Research

Exhibition were used to raise awareness of fair trade issues. Early samples of Cafédirect coffee were served free to railway passengers and leaflets distributed by Oxfam staff who answered passengers' questions about fair traded products.

At the product launch, the main thrust of the promotional drive was an advertising campaign with the strapline 'Fair trade, excellent coffee', which appeared on 1000 Ad Rail poster sites on InterCity and some local routes. One such advert featured a young child in its mother's arms with the message: 'You get excellent coffee. They get vaccines.' Another version featuring two older children proclaimed 'You discover excellent coffee. They discover school.' Advertising agencies usually strive for a single definitive proposition, but Cafédirect had two important messages to communicate: the 'help the world' appeal and to be balanced with 'without sacrificing taste and quality'. Since the audience were defined as Semi-ethicals, they had to be told what the problem was *and* reassured about the product quality. A similar problem had been faced by Café Hag several years earlier when they had to explain the health hazards associated with caffeine intake before they could put across the benefits of decaffeinated coffee.

Posters were chosen as the launch advertising medium because the volume and breadth they offer can create the impression of a big advertising spend. In reality, promotional funds were so limited that the 'campaign' consisted of only a few different executions. *Post hoc* advertising research indicated that the campaign had been successful, despite its lack of scale (Table C30.1).

Consumers responded well to the advertisements in terms of their propensity to purchase at a price premium, but they still had to be induced to take the product off the supermarket shelf. For that, a good pack design was critically important. Fortunately, a key part of Media Natura's service was cheap (and sometimes free) access to excellent creative people. Those given the task of designing the Cafédirect pack thought that most coffee packs had a 1970s' look, which gave Cafédirect the opportunity to appear fresh and up-to-date by comparison. Colour was found to be an important discriminator; the final design was predominantly dark blue and gold because the combination suggested quality and was empathetic towards the values of the ground coffee consumer.

A picture may speak a thousand words, but research showed that consumers would not recognize a coffee tree or green coffee beans so these were avoided, as was the depiction of a mug, which implied poor quality. The research also showed that as people are uncertain about ground coffee (what sort to buy and how to make it), they tend to become quite involved in the purchase. Consequently, many people do read the information on ground coffee packs with some care, unlike the labels on other products. So, if consumers could be persuaded to pick up the Cafédirect pack, they were likely to take in the fair trade message mentioned briefly on the front, and in more detail on the back (Fig. C30.3).

Supporting this fair trade message is the logo of the Fair Trade Foundation which appears down the front and across the top of the pack. Cafédirect was one of the first products to be awarded this Fairtrade mark which is considered essential supporting evidence in providing consumers with the necessary reassurance to make a preferential brand selection.

Building supermarket distribution

No matter how well presented or how good the product actually is, it simply will not sell if it's not readily available to consumers. Although both Traidcraft and Oxfam have their own shops, these distribution channels are not able to reach a mass market. It was essential that Cafédirect competed for shelf space in the major supermarkets. But shelf space is also crucial to the success of the big players and, since there is limited availability, a gain by Cafédirect is a loss to companies such as Paulig and Kraft General Foods. This was the job of

the Cafédirect sales director, Lorna Young, who agreed to work four days a week on the account through Equal Exchange, her employer. The challenges facing Lorna were enormous, and her resources were minimal in comparison to those deployed by the account teams of her international rivals.

The first question Lorna Young had to address was, which supermarket chain would be most receptive to stocking yet another brand of coffee—particularly one with very little resources for advertising to 'pull through' sales.

The next question was, which supermarket chain would be the most accessible?

On the face of it, the Co-op supermarket seemed like a good choice since its current promotional platform emphasized the ethical nature of the whole organization, which it was able to reinforce through the historical roots of the Co-operative movement. The unique appeal of Cafédirect would complement this positioning very well. However, it emerged that the Co-op's response was coloured by plans to launch its own range of fairly traded products. Furthermore, younger, ABC1 consumers crucial to success, do not do much shopping at Co-op supermarkets, so the target group could not easily be accessed through Co-op outlets.

The supermarket group eventually selected for the 1992 product launch was Safeway. Not only does Safeway have the right consumer profile, built through an association with ethical consumerism over a number of years, it also has a reputation for supporting organic food and fair trade initiatives.

The choice of Safeway as the point of market entry had other advantages too. In Scotland, where the store group planned to test market Cafédirect, it has one single distribution depot. Furthermore, the beverages buyer was sympathetic to Cafédirect's cause and was willing to give help and guidance on matters such as delivery scheduling, tailgate heights and the division of responsibilities between supermarket and supplier. As Equal Exchange is also based in Scotland, Lorna Young was able to build relationships with Safeway managers on a day-to-day basis from her Edinburgh head office. These relationships were to prove invaluable to the success of the launch.

By the middle of 1996, the brand was stocked by all major British supermarkets and had achieved a national market share of 3.1 per cent

(Table C30.2). This was a remarkable achievement in a market that is traditionally image-led and which usually requires multi-million pound advertising expenditure as the cost of maintaining market share. Although the big three maintain an attitude of indifference, the management keep a very close watch on their monthly market share movement.

As it turned out, Lorna Young was not entirely alone in her quest for shop distribution. In the early days of the Cafédirect launch, Oxfam and Twin Trading activists called on supermarket managers to alert them to the issues and opportunities of fair trade products. The Fairtrade Foundation circulated hundreds of thousands of postcards to consumers so that they too could

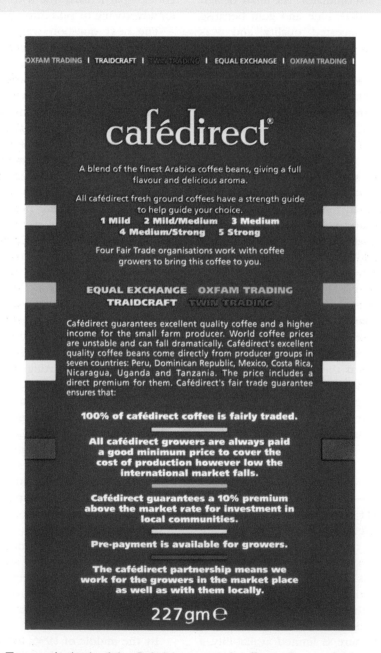

Figure C30.3 Text on the back of the Cafédirect ground coffee pack.

Table C30.2 Manufacturers' value share of the ground coffee market 1996

Manufacturer	Value share
Kraft General Foods	14%
Sara Lee	14%
Paulig (inc. Lyons Tetley*)	13%
Lavazza	7%
Cafédirect	3%
Other brands	5%
Own label	44%
Total	100%

*Paulig acquired Allied Lyon's ground coffee business in March 1994.
Source: IRI Infoscan, 12 months to May 1996

give them to supermarket managers with the message to stock fair trade products. After years of complaints about checkout queues filling the supermarket's postbags, suddenly failure to support Cafédirect became the top complaint.

Other retail marketers were all too aware of this shift in consumer values and were working with their buyers to search out suitable products. Cafédirect was considered to be in the vanguard of the fair trade movement, and ethically beyond reproach. Furthermore, it is no secret that many supermarkets like working with small suppliers because the imbalance of power means that they can get firms such as Cafédirect to 'do it their way'. Publicly, supermarket buyers give three reasons for listing Cafédirect. First, if it is not on the shelves it may just reflect badly on the store chain. Secondly, and more positively, it is seen to be the right thing to do and they hope that it will help to build consumer loyalty. Thirdly, with supermarket listings now multiplying, the brand is selling well. The latter is, of course, the real acid test.

Launch postscript

British supermarkets are giving the product a fair chance, the rest is really up to consumers and their willingness to repeat purchase the brand on a regular basis. Perhaps they will be prepared to do this. Research commissioned by the Co-operative movement indicates that, 'Consumers are willing to penalise retailers and brands which fail to meet their ethical standards and to reward those that do . . . one in three consumers reported that they had boycotted a shop or brand in the past. Six out of ten are ready to do so now.'

However, now that Cafédirect is supplying most of the supermarkets, the buyer–seller relationship has changed and the call of the more strident activists to 'protest march down to your supermarket' has become counterproductive.

It is time for the Cafédirect team to reassess their marketing strategy and to build closer relationships across their entire network.

This case was prepared by Simon Knox, Professor of Brand Management, Cranfield School of Management.

Questions

Cafédirect has formed a vertically integrated network to link Third World coffee producers into the markets of Western Europe.

1   What are the features that this network needs in order to implement relationship marketing practices?

2   Identify the main relationships in the Cafédirect network and their relative strength and importance. Show these relative positions on the relationship map opposite.

3   Use your analysis to determine which are the priority relationships for Cafédirect. How can these relationships be further developed to build on the success of the launch?

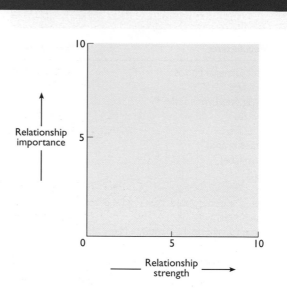

Competition and Marketing

CHAPTER SEVENTEEN

Analysing Competitors and Creating a Competitive Advantage

'The race is not always to the swift,
nor the battle to the strong, but that is the way to bet'

DAMON RUNYON

Learning Objectives *This chapter explains:*

1 The determinants of industry attractiveness

2 How to analyse competitors

3 The difference between differentiation and cost leadership strategies

4 The sources of competitive advantage

5 The value chain

6 How to create and maintain a differential advantage

7 How to create and maintain a cost leadership position

Satisfying customers is a central tenet of the marketing concept, but it is not enough to guarantee success. The real question is whether a firm can satisfy customers better than the competition. For example, many car manufacturers market cars that give customer satisfaction in terms of appearance, reliability and performance. They meet the basic requirements necessary to compete. Customer choice, however, will depend on creating a little more value than the competition. This extra value is brought about by establishing a competitive advantage, a topic that will be examined later in this chapter.

Since corporate performance depends upon both customer satisfaction and being able to create greater value than the competition, firms need to understand their competitors as well as their customers. By understanding competitors, a firm can better predict their reaction to any marketing initiative that the firm might make, and exploit any weaknesses that they might possess. Competitor analysis is thus crucial to the successful implementation of marketing strategy. The discussion will begin by examining competitive industry structure: rivalry between firms does not take place within a vacuum. For example, the threat of new competitors and the bargaining power of buyers can greatly influence the attractiveness of an industry and the profitability of each competitor.

Analysing competitive industry structure

An *industry* is a group of firms that market products which are close substitutes for each other. In common parlance we refer to the car, oil or computer industry, indicating that the definition of an industry is normally product-based. It is a fact of life that some industries are more profitable than others. For example, the car, steel, coal and textile industries have had poor profitability records for many years, whereas the book publishing, television broadcasting, pharmaceuticals and soft drinks industries have enjoyed high long-run profits. Not all of this difference can be explained by the fact that one industry provides better customer satisfaction than another. There are other determinants of industry attractiveness and long-run profitability that shape the rules of competition. These are the threat of entry of new competitors, the threat of substitutes, the bargaining power of buyers and of suppliers, and the rivalry between the existing competitors.[1] Where these forces are intense, below average industry performance can be expected; where these forces are mild, superior performance is common. Their influence is shown diagrammatically in Fig. 17.1, which is known as the Porter model of competitive industry structure. Each of the five forces is in turn comprised of a number of elements that together combine to determine the strength of each force, and its effect on the degree of competition. Each force is now discussed.

Threat of new entrants

New entrants can raise the level of competition in an industry thereby reducing its attractiveness. For example, in Denmark the largest banks, Den Danske Bank and Unibank, have been hit by new foreign entrants such as Sweden's SE-Banken and Norway's Finax.[2] The threat of new entrants depends on the barriers to entry. High entry barriers exist in some industries (e.g. pharmaceuticals) whereas other industries are much easier to enter (e.g. restaurants). Key *entry barriers* include:

+ Economies of scale.

+ Capital requirements.

+ Switching costs.

+ Access to distribution.

+ Expected retaliation.

To present competitors, industry attractiveness can be increased by raising entry barriers. High promotional and R&D expenditures and clearly communicated retaliatory actions to entry are some methods of raising barriers. Some managerial actions can unwittingly lower barriers. For example, new product designs that dramatically lower manufacturing costs can make entry by newcomers easier.

Bargaining power of suppliers

The cost of raw materials and components can have a major bearing on a firm's profitability. The higher the bargaining power of suppliers, the higher are these costs. The bargaining power of suppliers will be high when:

1 There are many buyers and few dominant suppliers.

2 There are differentiated highly valued products.

3 Suppliers threaten to integrate forward into the industry.

4 Buyers do not threaten to integrate backward into supply.

5 The industry is not a key customer group to the suppliers.

A firm can reduce the bargaining power of suppliers by seeking new sources of supply, threatening to integrate backward into supply, and designing standardized components so

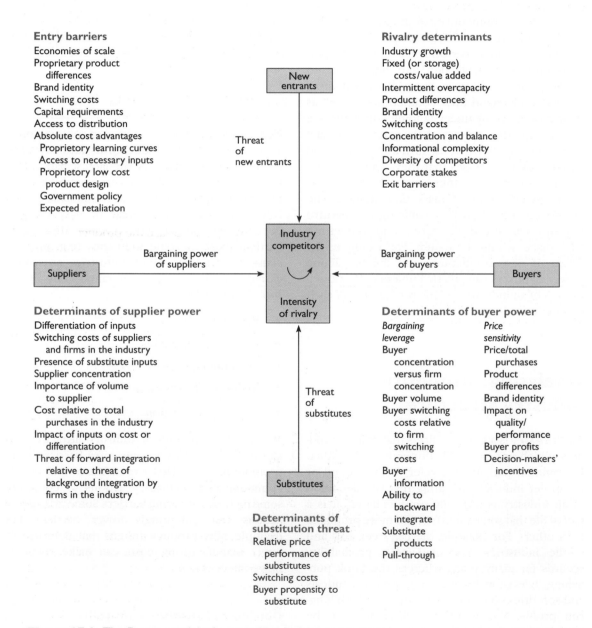

Entry barriers
Economies of scale
Proprietary product
  differences
Brand identity
Switching costs
Capital requirements
Access to distribution
Absolute cost advantages
  Proprietory learning curves
  Access to necessary inputs
  Proprietory low cost
    product design
  Government policy
  Expected retaliation

Rivalry determinants
Industry growth
Fixed (or storage)
  costs/value added
Intermittent overcapacity
Product differences
Brand identity
Switching costs
Concentration and balance
Informational complexity
Diversity of competitors
Corporate stakes
Exit barriers

Threat
of
new entrants

New entrants

Industry competitors

Intensity
of rivalry

Bargaining power
of suppliers

Bargaining power
of buyers

Suppliers

Buyers

Determinants of supplier power
Differentiation of inputs
Switching costs of suppliers
  and firms in the industry
Presence of substitute inputs
Supplier concentration
Importance of volume
  to supplier
Cost relative to total
  purchases in the industry
Impact of inputs on cost or
  differentiation
Threat of forward integration
  relative to threat of
  background integration by
  firms in the industry

Determinants of buyer power

*Bargaining
leverage*
Buyer
  concentration
  versus firm
  concentration
Buyer volume
Buyer switching
  costs relative
  to firm
  switching
  costs
Buyer
  information
Ability to
  backward
  integrate
Substitute
  products
Pull-through

*Price
sensitivity*
Price/total
  purchases
Product
  differences
Brand identity
Impact on
  quality/
  performance
Buyer profits
Decision-makers'
  incentives

Threat
of
substitutes

Substitutes

**Determinants of
substitution threat**
Relative price
  performance of
  substitutes
Switching costs
Buyer propensity to
  substitute

Figure 17.1 The Porter model of competitive Industry structure.

Source: adapted from Porter, M. E. (1980) *Competitive Strategy,* New York: Free Press, 4. Reprinted with permission of the Free Press, an imprint of Simon and Schuster. Copyright © 1980 by Free Press

that many suppliers are capable of producing them.

Bargaining power of buyers

The concentration of European retailing has raised their bargaining power relative to manufacturers. Benetton's use of many suppliers has increased its bargaining power. The bargaining power of buyers is greater when:

1   There are few dominant buyers and many sellers.

2   Products are standardized.

3   Buyers threaten to integrate backward into the industry.

4   Suppliers do not threaten to integrate forward into the buyer's industry.

5   The industry is not a key supplying group for buyers.

Firms in the industry can attempt to lower buyer power by increasing the number of buyers they sell to, threatening to integrate forward into the buyer's industry and producing highly valued, differentiated products. In supermarket retailing, the brand leader normally achieves the highest profitability partially because being number one means that supermarkets need to stock the brand, thereby reducing buyer power in price negotiations.

Threat of substitutes

The presence of substitute products can lower industry attractiveness and profitability because they put a constraint on price levels. For example, tea and coffee are fairly close substitutes in most European countries. Raising the price of coffee, therefore, would make tea more attractive. The threat of substitute products depends on:

1   Buyers' willingness to substitute.

2   The relative price and performance of substitutes.

3   The costs of switching to substitutes.

The threat of substitute products can be lowered by building up switching costs which may be psychological, for example, by creating strong distinctive brand personalities, and maintaining a price differential commensurate with perceived customer values.

Industry competitors

The intensity of rivalry between competitors in an industry will depend on:

1   *Structure of competition*: more intense rivalry when there are a large number of small competitors or a few equally balanced competitors; less rivalry when a clear leader (at least 50 per cent larger than the second) exists with a large cost advantage.

2   *Structure of costs*: high fixed costs encourage price cutting to fill capacity.

3   *Degree of differentiation*: commodity products encourage rivalry while highly differentiated products which are hard to copy are associated with less intense rivalry.

4   *Switching costs*: when switching costs are high because the product is specialized, the customer has invested a lot of resources in learning how to use the product or has made tailor-made investments that are worthless with other products and suppliers, rivalry is reduced.

5   *Strategic objectives*: when competitors are pursuing build strategies, competition is likely to be more intense than when playing hold or harvesting strategies.

6   *Exit barriers*: when barriers to leaving an industry are high due to such factors as lack of opportunities elsewhere, high vertical integration, emotional barriers or the high cost of closing down plant, rivalry will be more intense than when exit barriers are low.

Firms need to be careful not to spoil a situation of competitive stability. They need to balance their own position against the well-being of the industry as a whole. For example, an intense price or promotional war may gain a few percentage points in market share but lead to an overall fall in long-run industry profitability as competitors respond to these moves. It is sometimes better to protect industry structure than follow short-term self-interest.

A major threat to favourable industry structure is the use of a no frills, low price strategy by a minor player seeking positional advantage. For example, the launch of generic products in the pharmaceutical and cigarette industries has lowered overall profitability.

Despite meeting customers' needs with high quality, good value products, firms can compete away the rewards. An intensive competitive environment means that the value created by firms in satisfying customer needs is given away to buyers through lower prices, dissipated through costly marketing battles (e.g. advertising wars) or passed on to powerful suppliers through higher prices for raw materials and components.

In Europe the competitive structure of industries was fundamentally changed by the introduction of the Single European Market. The lifting of barriers to trade between countries has radically altered industry structure by affecting its underlying determinants. For example, the threat of new entrants, and the growth in buyer/supplier power through acquisition or merger are fundamentally changing the competitive climate of many industries.

Competitor analysis

The analysis of how industry structure affects long-run profitability has shown the need to understand and monitor competitors. Their actions can spoil an otherwise attractive industry, their weaknesses can be a target for exploitation, and their response to a firm's marketing initiatives can have a major impact on their success. Competitive information can be obtained from marketing research surveys, recruiting competitors' employees (sometimes interviewing them is sufficient), secondary sources (e.g. trade magazines, newspaper articles), distributors, stripping down competitors' products and gathering competitors' sales literature.

Competitor analysis seeks to answer five key questions.

1 Who are our competitors?

2 What are their strengths and weaknesses?

3 What are their strategic objectives and thrust?

4 What are their strategies?

5 What are their response patterns?

These issues are summarized in Fig. 17.2. Each question will now be examined.

Who are our competitors?

The danger when identifying competitors is that competitive myopia prevails. This malady reflects in a narrow definition of competition resulting in too restricted a view of which companies are in competition. Only those companies who are producing technically similar products are considered to be the competition (e.g. paint companies). This ignores companies purchasing substitute products that perform a similar function (e.g. polyurethane varnish firms) and those that solve the problem or eliminate it in a dissimilar way (e.g. PVC double glazing companies). The actions of all of these types of competitors can affect the performance of our firm and therefore need to be monitored. Their responses also need to be assessed as they will determine the outcome of any competitive move that our firm may wish to make. For example, we need to ask how likely it would be that polyurethane varnish companies would follow any price move we might wish to make.

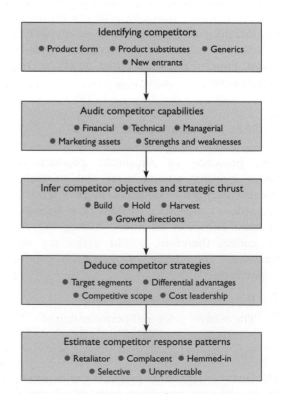

Figure 17.2 Competitor analysis

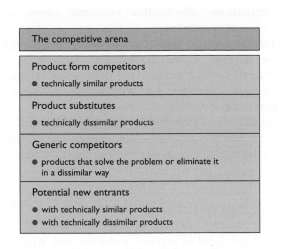

Figure 17.3 Competitor identification

Beyond these current competitors the environment needs to be scanned for potential entrants into the industry. These can take two forms: entrants with technically similar products and those invading the market with substitutes. Companies with similar core competences to present incumbents may pose a threat of entering with technically similar products. For example, Xerox's skills in office automation provided the springboard to enter (unsuccessfully) the computer market. The source of companies entering with substitute products may be more difficult to locate, however. A technological breakthrough may transform an industry by rendering the old product obsolete as when the calculator replaced the slide-rule, or when the car replaced the horse-drawn buggy. In such instances it is difficult to locate the source of the substitute product well in advance. Figure 17.3 illustrates this competitive arena.

What are their strengths and weaknesses?

Having identified our competitors the next stage is to complete a **competitor audit** in order to assess their relative strengths and weaknesses. A precise understanding of competitor strengths and weaknesses is an important prerequisite of developing competitor strategy. In particular it locates areas of competitive vulnerability. Military strategy suggests that success is most often

achieved when strength is concentrated against the enemy's greatest weakness.[3] This analogy holds true for business, as the success of Japanese companies in the car and motor cycle industries bears testimony.

The process of assessing competitors' strengths and weaknesses may take place as part of a marketing audit (see Chapter 2). As much internal, market and customer information as is practicable should be gathered. For example, financial data concerning profitability, profit margins, sales and investment levels, market data relating to price levels, market share and distribution channels used, and customer data concerning awareness of brand names, and perceptions of brand and company image, product and service quality, and selling ability may be relevant.

Not all of this information will be accessible, and some may not be relevant. Management needs to decide the extent to which each element of information is worth pursuing. For example, a decision is required regarding how much expenditure is to be allocated to measuring customer awareness and perceptions through marketing research.

This process of data gathering needs to be managed so that information is available to compare our company with its chief competitors on the *key factors for success* in the industry. A three-stage process can then be used, as follows.

Identify key factors for success in the industry

These should be restricted to about six to eight factors otherwise the analysis becomes too diffuse.[4] Their identification is a matter of managerial judgement. Their source may be functional (such as financial strength or flexible production) or generic (for example, the ability to respond quickly to customer needs, innovativeness, or the capability to provide other sales service). Since these factors are critical for success they should be used to compare our company with its competitors.

Rate our company and competitors on each key success factor using a rating scale

Each company is given a score on each success factor using a rating device. This may be a scale ranging from 1 (very poor) to 5 (very good). This results in a set of company capability profiles. An example is given in Fig. 17.4. Our company is rated alongside two competitors on six key success factors. Compared with our company, competitor 1 is relatively strong regarding technical assistance to customers and access to international distribution channels, but relatively weak on product quality. Competitor 2 is relatively strong on international distribution channels but relatively weak on innovativeness, financial strength and having a well-qualified workforce.

Consider the implications for competitive strategy

The competitive profile analysis is then used to identify possible competitive strategies. This analysis would suggest that our company should consider taking steps to improve technical assistance to customers to match or exceed competitor 1's capability on this factor. At the moment, our company enjoys a differential advantage over competitor 1 on product quality. Our strength in innovativeness should be used to maintain this differential advantage and competitor 1's moves to improve product quality should be carefully monitored.

Competitor 2 is weaker overall than competitor 1 and our company. However, it has considerable strengths in having access to

international distribution channels. Given our company's weakness in this area a strategic alliance with or take-over of competitor 2 might be sensible if our company's objective is to expand internationally. Our company's financial strength and their financial weakness suggests that a take-over might be feasible.

What are their strategic objectives and thrust?

The third part of competitor analysis is to infer their *strategic objectives*. Companies may decide to build, hold or harvest products and strategic business units (SBUs). To briefly recap, a build objective is concerned with increasing sales and/or market share, a hold objective suggests maintaining sales and/or market share, and a harvest objective is followed when the emphasis is on maximizing short-term cash flow through slashing expenditure and raising prices whenever possible. It is useful to know what strategic objectives are being pursued by competitors because their response pattern may depend upon objectives. Looking at this topic from a product perspective, if we are considering building market share of our product by cutting price, a competitor who is also building is almost certain to follow; one who is content to hold sales and market share is also likely to respond but a

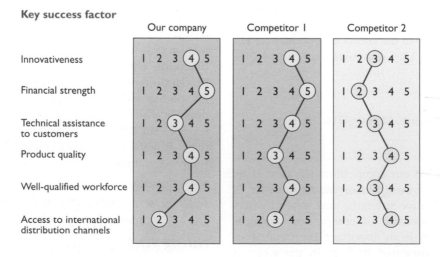

Figure 17.4 Company capability profiles

company following a harvest objective for its product is much less likely to reduce price because it is more concerned with profit margin than unit sales.

Conversely, if we are considering a price rise, a competitor pursuing a build strategy is not likely to follow; the price of a product subject to a hold objective is now likely to rise in line with our increase; and a company using a harvest objective will almost certainly take the opportunity to raise its product's price, maybe by more than our increase.

Knowing competitors' strategic objectives is also useful in predicting their likely strategies. For example, a build objective is likely to be accompanied with aggressive price and promotional moves, a hold objective with competitive stability, and a harvest objective with cost-orientated rather than marketing-orientated strategies.

Strategic thrust refers to the future areas of expansion that a company might contemplate. Broadly, a company can expand by penetrating existing markets more effectively with current products, launching new products in existing markets or by growing in new markets with existing or new products. Knowing the strategic thrust of competitors can help our strategic decision-making. For example, knowing that our competitors are considering expansion in North America but not Europe will make expansion into Europe a more attractive strategic option for our company.

What are their strategies?

At the product level, competitor analysis will attempt to deduce positioning strategy. This involves assessing a competitor product's target market and differential advantage. The marketing mix strategies (e.g. price levels, media used for promotion, and distribution channels) may indicate target market, and marketing research into customer perceptions can be used to assess relative differential advantages.

Companies and products need to be continuously monitored for changes in positioning strategy. For example, Volvo's traditional positioning strategy based on safety has been modified to give more emphasis to performance.

Strategies can also be defined in terms of competitive scope. For example, are competitors attempting to service the whole market, a few segments of a particular niche? If a niche player, is it likely that they will be content to stay in that segment or use it as a beachhead to move into other segments in the future? Japanese companies are renowned for their use of small niche markets as springboards for market segment expansion (e.g. the small car segments in the USA and Europe).

Competitors may be playing the cost leadership game, focusing on cost reducing measures rather than expensive product development and promotional strategies. Cost leadership will be discussed in more detail later in this chapter. If competitors are following this strategy it is more likely that they will be focusing research and development expenditure on process rather than product development in a bid to reduce manufacturing costs.

What are their response patterns?

A key consideration in making a strategic or tactical move is the likely response of competitors. As we have discussed, understanding competitor objectives and strategies are helpful in predicting competitor reactions. Indeed a major objective of competitor analysis is to be able to predict competitor response to market and competitive changes. Their past behaviour is also a guide to what they might do. Market leaders often try to control competitor response by retaliatory action. These are called *retaliatory* competitors because they can be relied on to respond aggressively to competitive challenges. Len Hardy, ex-chairman of Lever Brothers, explained the role of a retaliation as follows:

> A leader must enforce market discipline, must be ruthless in dealing with any competitive challenge. If you make a price move and a competitor undercuts it, then he should be shown that this action has been noticed and will be punished. If he is not punished he will repeat the move—and soon your leadership will be eroded.[5]

Thus by punishing competitor moves, market leaders can condition competitors to behave in predicted ways, for example, by not taking advantage of a price rise by the leader.

It is not only market leaders who retaliate aggressively. Where management are known to be assertive, and our move is likely to have a large impact on their performance, a strong response is usual.

The history, traditions and managerial personalities of competitors also have an influence on competitive response. Some markets are characterized by years of competitive stability with little serious strategic challenges to any of the incumbents. This can breed *complacency* with predictably slow reaction times to new challenges. For example, innovation that offers superior customer value may be dismissed as a fad, not worthy of serious attention.

Another situation where competitors are unlikely to respond is where their previous strategies have restricted their scope for retaliation. An example of such a *hemmed-in competitor* was a major manufacturer of car number plates which were sold to car dealerships. A new company was started by an ex-employee who focused on one geographical area, supplying the same quality product but with extra discount. The national supplier could not respond since to give discount in this region would have meant granting the discount nationwide.

A fourth type of competitor may respond *selectively*. Because of tradition or beliefs about the relative effectiveness of marketing instruments a competitor may respond to some competitive moves but not others. For example, extra sales promotion expenditures may be matched but advertising increases (within certain boundaries) may be ignored. Another reason for selective response is the varying degree of visibility of marketing actions. For example giving extra price discounts may be highly visible, but providing distributors with extra support (e.g. training, sales literature, loans) may be less discernible.

A final type of competitor is totally *unpredictable* in its response pattern. Sometimes there is a response; at other times there is no response. Some moves are countered aggressively; with others reaction is weak. No factors adequately explain these differences; they appear to be at the whim of management.

Some companies employ role-playing to assess competitor reactions: their most knowledgeable managers act out the roles of key competitors to aid prediction of their response to a proposed marketing initiative.[6] Interestingly, research has shown that managers tend to over-react more frequently than they under-react to competitors' marketing activities.[7]

Competitive advantage

The key to superior performance is to gain and hold a competitive advantage. Firms can gain a competitive advantage through *differentiation* of their product offering which provides superior customer value or by managing for *lowest delivered cost*. Evidence for this proposition was provided by Hall, who examined the competitive strategies pursued by the two leading firms (in terms of return on investment) in eight mature industries characterized by slow growth and intense competition.[8] In each industry the two leading firms offered either high product differentiation or the lowest delivered cost. In most cases, an industry's return on investment leader opted for one of the strategies, while the second-placed firm pursued the other.

Competitive strategies

These two means of competitive advantage when combined with the **competitive scope** of activities (broad v. narrow) result in four generic strategies: differentiation, cost leadership, differentiation focus, and cost focus. The differentiation and cost leadership strategies seek competitive advantage in a broad range of market or industry segments whereas differentiation focus and cost focus strategies are confined to a narrow segment.[9]

Differentiation

Differentiation strategy involves the selection of one or more choice criteria that are used by many buyers in an industry. The firm then uniquely positions itself to meet these criteria. Differentiation strategies are usually associated with a premium price, and higher than average costs for the industry as the extra value to customers (e.g. higher performance) often raises costs. The aim is to differentiate in a way that leads to a price premium in excess of the cost of differentiating. Differentiation gives customers a reason to prefer one product over another and thus is central to strategic marketing thinking. The advertisement opposite shows

www.dyson.com   08705 275104

Dyson's patented technology

The strongest constant suction

No other cleaner has this.   Or this.

Want a machine that starts with strong suction and doesn't lose it as you clean? There's still only one.

Dyson create a competitive advantage through differentiation how the Dyson cleaner is differentiated from the competition.

Cost leadership

This strategy involves the achievement of the lowest cost position in an industry. Many segments in the industry are served and great importance is placed on minimizing costs on all fronts. So long as the price achievable for its products is around the industry average, cost leadership should result in superior performance. Thus cost leaders often market standard products that are believed to be acceptable to customers. Heinz and United Biscuits are believed to be cost leaders in their industries. They market acceptable products at reasonable prices which means that their low costs result in above-average profits. Some cost leaders need to discount prices in order to achieve high sales levels. The aim here is to achieve superior performance by ensuring that the cost advantage over competitions is not offset by the price discount. No-frills supermarket discounters like Costco, Kwik Save, Aldi and Netto fall into this category.

Differentiation focus

With this strategy a firm aims to differentiate within one or a small number of target market segments. The special needs of the segment mean that there is an opportunity to differentiate the product offering from competitors who may be targeting a broader group of customers. For example, some small speciality chemical companies thrive on taking orders that are too small or specialized to be of interest to their larger competitors. Differentiation focuses must be clear that the needs of their target group differ from the broader market (otherwise there will be no basis for differentiation) and that existing competitors are underperforming.

Cost focus

With this strategy a firm seeks a cost advantage with one or a small number of target market segments. By dedicating itself to the segment the cost focuser can seek economies that may be ignored or missed by broadly targeted competitors. In some instances, competition, by trying to achieve wide market acceptance, may be over-performing (for example by providing unwanted services) to one segment of customers. By providing a basic product offering, a cost advantage will be gained that may exceed the price discount necessary to sell it.

Choosing a competitive strategy

The essence of corporate success, then, is to choose a generic strategy and pursue it with gusto. Below average performance is associated with failure to achieve any of these generic strategies. The result is no competitive advantage: a *stuck-in-the-middle position* that results in lower performance than the cost leaders, differentiators or focusers in any market segment. An example of a company that made the mistake of moving to a stuck-in-the-middle position was General Motors with their Oldsmobile car. The original car (the Oldsmobile Rocket V8) was highly differentiated with a 6 litre V8 engine, which was virtually indestructible, very fast, and highly reliable. In order to cut costs this engine was replaced by the same engine that went into the 5 litre Chevrolet V8. This had less power and was less reliable. The result was catastrophic: sales plummeted.

Firms need to understand the generic basis for their success and resist the temptation to blur its strategy by making inconsistent moves. For example, a no-frills cost leader or focuser should beware of the pitfalls of moving to a higher cost base (perhaps by adding on expensive services). A focus strategy involves limiting sales volume. Once domination of the target segment has been achieved there may be a temptation to move into other segments in order to achieve growth with the same competitive advantage. This can be a mistake if the new segments do not value the firm's competitive advantage in the same way.

In most situations differentiation and cost leadership strategies are incompatible: differentiation is achieved through higher costs. However, there are circumstances when both can be achieved simultaneously. For example, a differentiation strategy may lead to market share domination which lowers costs through economies of scale and learning effects. Or a highly differentiated firm pioneers a major process innovation that significantly reduces manufacturing costs leading to a cost leadership position. When differentiation and cost leadership coincide, performance is exceptional since a premium price can be charged for a low cost product.

Sources of competitive advantage

In order to create a differentiated or lowest cost position, a firm needs to understand the nature and location of the potential *sources of competitive advantage*. The nature of these sources are the superior skills and resources of a firm. Management benefit by analysing the superior skills and resources that are or could contribute to competitive advantage (i.e. differentiation or lowest cost position). Their location can be aided by value chain analysis. A *value chain* is the discrete activities that a firm carries out in order to perform its business.

Superior skills

Superior skills are the distinctive capabilities of key personnel that set them apart from the personnel of competing firms.[10] The benefit of superior skills is the resulting ability to perform functions more effectively than other firms. For example, superior selling skills may result in closer relationships with customers than competing firms achieve. Compaq Computers built strong relationships with corporate retailers by offering attractive margins and exclusive franchises.[11] Superior quality assurance skills can result in higher and more consistent product quality.

Superior resources

Superior resources are the tangible requirements for advantage that enable a firm to exercise its skills. Superior resources include:

1   The number of sales people in a market.
2   Expenditure on advertising and sales promotion.
3   Distribution coverage (the number of retailers who stock the product).
4   Expenditure on R&D.
5   Scale of and type of production facilities.
6   Financial resources.
7   Brand equity.
8   Knowledge.

Core competences

The distinctive nature of these skills and resources sum to a company's *core competences*. For example, a core competence of Sony is in miniaturization. Building on this capability, Sony launched the first minidisk digital Walkman in Europe during 1993. Minidisk technology allows the recording from conventional compact disks in high-quality digital stereo on to a disk one-third of the size of standard CDs. These can then be played in the Walkman in the same way as compact cassettes. By creating a superior sound quality in a convenient format, Sony have used their core competence to create a competitive advantage.

Value chain

A useful method for locating superior skills and resources is the value chain.[12] All firms consist of a set of activities that are conducted to design, manufacture, market, distribute and service its products. The value chain categorizes these into primary and support activities (see Fig. 17.5). This enables the sources of costs and differentiation to be understood and located.

Primary activities include in-bound physical distribution (e.g. materials handling, warehousing, inventory control), operations (e.g. manufacturing, packaging), out-bound physical distribution (e.g. delivery, order processing), marketing (e.g. advertising, selling, channel management) and service (e.g. installation, repair, customer training).

Support activities are found within all of these primary activities and consist of purchased inputs, technology, human resource management, and the firm's infrastructure. These are not defined within a given primary activity because they can be found in all of them. Purchasing can take place within each primary activity, not just in the purchasing department; technology is relevant to all primary activities, as is human resource management; and the firm's infrastructure which consists of general management, planning, finance, accounting and quality management, supports the entire value chain.

By examining each value creating activity, management can look for the skills and resources that may form the basis for low cost or differentiated positions. To the extent that skills and resources exceed or could be developed to exceed) competition, they form the key sources of competitive advantage. Not only should the skills and resources within value creating activities be examined but also the *linkages* between them should be examined. For example, greater coordination between operations and in-bound physical distribution may give rise to reduced costs through lower inventory levels.

Value chain analysis can extend to the value chains of suppliers, and customers. For example, just-in-time supply could lower inventory costs; providing salesforce support to distributors could foster closer relations. Thus, by looking at the linkages between a firm's value chain and those of suppliers and customers, improvements in performance can result that can lower costs or contribute to the creation of a differentiated position.

Overall, the contribution of the value chain is in providing a framework for understanding the nature and location of the skills and resources that provide the basis for competitive advantage. Furthermore, the value chain provides the framework for cost analysis. Assigning operating costs and assets to value activities is the starting point of cost analysis so that improvement can be made, and cost advantages defended. For example, if a firm discovers that its cost advantage is based on superior production facilities, it should be vigilant in upgrading those facilities to maintain its position against competitors. Similarly by understanding the sources of differentiation a company can build on these sources, and defend against competitive attack. For example, if differentiation is based upon skills in product design, then management knows that sufficient investment in maintaining design superiority is required to maintain the firm's differentiated position. Also, the identification of specific sources of advantage

can lead to their exploitation in new markets where customers place a similar high value on the resultant outcome. For example, Marks and Spencer's skills in clothing retailing were successfully extended to provide differentiation in food retailing.

Creating a differential advantage

Although skills and resources are the sources of competitive advantage, they are translated into a *differential advantage* only when the customer perceives that the firm is providing value above that of the competition.[13] The creation of a differential advantage, then, comes with the marrying of skills and resources with the key attributes (choice criteria) that customers are looking for in a product offering. However, it should be recognized that the distinguishing competing attributes in a market are not always the most important ones. For example, if customers were asked to rank safety, punctuality and on-board service in importance when flying, safety would undoubtedly be ranked at the top. Nevertheless, when choosing an airline, safety would rank low because most airlines are assumed to be safe. This is why airlines look to less important ways of differentiating their offerings (e.g. by giving superior on-board service).

A differential advantage can be created with

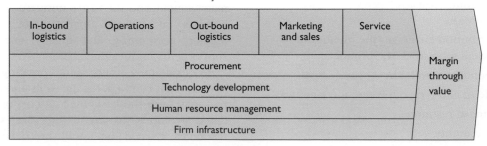

Figure 17.5 The value chain.

Source: Porter, M. E. (1985) *Competitive Advantage*, New York: Free Press, 37. Reprinted with the permission of The Free Press, an imprint of Simon and Schuster. Copyright © 1985 by Michael E. Porter

any aspect of the marketing mix. Product, distribution, promotion, and price are all capable of creating added customer value (see Fig. 17.6). The key to whether improving an aspect of marketing is worth while is to know if the potential benefit provides value to the customer. Table 17.1 lists ways of creating differential advantages and their potential impact on customer value.

Product

Product performance can be enhanced by such devices as raising speed, comfort and safety levels, capacity and ease of use, or improving taste or smell. For example, raising the speed of operation of a CT scanner can lower the cost of treating hospital patients. Improving comfort levels (e.g. of a car), taste (e.g. of food), or smell (e.g. of

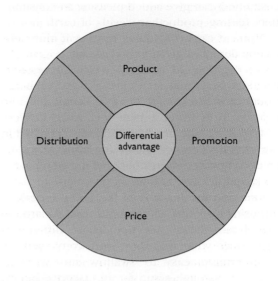

Figure 17.6 Creating a differential advantage

Table 17.1	Creating a differential advantage using the marketing mix	
Marketing mix	*Differential advantage*	*Value to the customer*
Product	Performance	Lower costs; higher revenue; safety; pleasure; status
	Durability	Longer life; lower costs
	Reliability	Lower maintenance and production costs; higher revenue; fewer problems
	Style	Good looks; status
	Upgradability	Lower costs; prestige
	Technical assistance	Better quality products; closer supplier–buyer relationships
	Installation	Fewer problems
Distribution	Location	Convenience; lower costs
	Quick/reliable delivery	Lower costs; fewer problems
	Distributor support	More effective selling/marketing; close buyer–seller relationships
	Delivery guarantees	Peace of mind
	Computerized reordering	Less work; lower costs
Promotion	Creative/more advertising	Superior brand personality
	Creative/more sales promotion	Direct added value
	Co-operative promotions	Lower costs
	Well-trained salesforce	Superior problem-solving
	Dual Selling	Sales assistance; higher sales
	Fast, accurate quotes	Lower costs; fewer problems
	Free demonstrations	Lower risk of purchase
	Free or low cost trial	Lower risk of purchase
	Fast complaint handling	Fewer problems; lower costs
Price	Lower price	Lower cost of purchase
	Credit facilities	Lower costs; better cash flow
	Low interest loans	Lower costs; better cash flow
	Higher price	Price-quality match

cosmetics) can give added pleasure to consumption. Raising productivity levels of earth-moving equipment can bring higher revenue if more jobs can be done in a given period of time.

An example of a brand which successfully gained a performance advantage was Beecham's Coughcaps. The brand brought cough relief in capsule form using a high tech drug delivery system. It was the first truly innovative product in the over-the-counter sector for many years. Its chief competitors were cough syrups, which were sticky, unpleasant tasting, inconvenient to carry around and use (each dose had to be measured out using a spoon), and brought relief for around four hours. Beecham's Coughcaps' differential advantages were that they were convenient to carry around, easy to swallow and were as effective as cough syrup for an extended period of about eight hours. The *durability* of product has a bearing on costs since greater durability means a longer operating life. Improving product *reliability* (i.e. lowering malfunctions or defects) can lower maintenance and production costs, raise revenues through lower downtime, and reduce the hassle of using the product. Product *styling* can also give customer value through the improved looks that good style brings. This can confer status to the buyer and allow the supplier to charge premium prices, as with Bang & Olufsen hi-fi equipment. Marketing in Action 17.1 discusses how style can be used as a differentiator. The capacity to *upgrade* a product (to take advantage of technological advances) or to meet changing needs (e.g. extra storage space in a computer) can lower costs, and confer prestige by maintaining state-of-the-art features. The advertisement for the iMac computer (overleaf) illustrates how style and practicality can be used to create a differential advantage for the iMac.

Products can be augmented by the provision of *guarantees* that give customers peace of mind and lower costs should the product need repair; by giving *technical assistance* to customers so that they provide better quality products. Both parties benefit from closer relationships and by providing product *installation*, which means that customers do not incur problems in properly installing a complex piece of equipment.

Differentiating commodity products requires considerable marketing creativity. Marketing in Action 17.2 describes how Marks and Spencer go about the task of differentiating their brussels sprouts from those sold by their competitors.

Distribution

Wide distribution coverage and/or careful selection of distributor *locations* can provide convenient purchasing for customers. *Quick and/ or reliable delivery* can lower buyer costs by reducing production down-time and lowering inventory levels. Reliable delivery, in particular, reduces the frustration of waiting for late delivery. Providing distributors with *support* in the form of training and financial help can bring about more effective selling and marketing, and bring both parties the advantage of closer relationships. Working with organizational customers to introduce *computerized reordering* systems can lower their costs, reduce their workload and increase their costs of switching to other suppliers.

Promotion

A differential advantage can be created by the *creative use of advertising*. For example, Heineken was differentiated by the use of humour and the tag-line 'Heineken refreshes the parts other beers cannot reach' at a time when many other lagers were promoted by showing groups of men in public houses enjoying a drink together. *Spending more on advertising* can also aid differentiation by creating a stronger brand personality than competitive brands. Similarly, using *more creative sales promotional methods* or simply *spending more on sales incentives* can give direct added value to customers. By engaging in *cooperative promotions* with distributors, producers can lower their costs and build goodwill.

The salesforce can also be a means of creating a differential advantage. Particularly when products are similar, a *well-trained salesforce* can provide superior problem-solving skills for their customers. Part of the success of IBM in penetrating the mainframe computer market in the early 1980s was due to their well-trained salesforce, who acted as problem solvers and information consultants for their customers. *Dual selling* whereby a producer provides salesforce assistance to distributors can lower the latter's costs and increase sales. For example, a chemical company might supply product specialists who support a distributor's salesforce by providing technical expertise when required. Sales responsiveness in the form of *fast, accurate quotes* can lower customer costs by making transactions more efficient, and reduce the hassle associated with ordering supplies. Furthermore, *free demonstrations* and *free (or low cost)* trial arrangements can reduce the risk of purchase for customers. Finally, *superior complaint handling* procedures can lower customer costs by speeding up the process, and reduce the inconvenience that can accompany it.

Price

Using *low price* as a means of gaining differential advantage can fail unless the firm enjoys a cost advantage, and has the resources to fight a price war. For example, Laker Airways challenged British Airways in transatlantic flights on the basis of lower price but lost the battle when British Airways cut their prices to compete. Without a cost advantage and with less resources, Laker Airways could not survive the retaliation. Less obvious means of lowering the effective price to the customer is to offer *credit facilities* or *low interest loans*. Both serve to lower the cost of purchase and improve cash flow for customers. Finally, a *high price* can be used as part of a premium positioning strategy to support brand image. Where a brand has distinct product, promotional or distributional advantages, a

17.1   Marketing in Action

Using Style to Differentiate Products

Two companies who have successfully used style to differentiate their products from the competition are Bang & Olufsen and Apple Computers. Bang & Olufsen have long been regarded as the style leaders in audio and television equipment and Apple created a stir in the computer world with the launch of iMac.

Bang & Olufsen has built a worldwide reputation for quality and a fanatically loyal customer base. Its sleek, tastefully discrete designs and high standards of production have earned it an elite status in the market. For decades, these have formed the basis of its advertising and marketing strategy. The company recognizes that style needs to be displayed distinctively in retail outlets. This has led to the creation of 'concept shops' where subtle images are projected onto walls and products are displayed in free-standing areas constructed from translucent walls. Their view is that you cannot sell Bang & Olufsen equipment when it is sandwiched between a washing machine and a shelf of videos. The concept shop gives the right look to make the most of the products.

Although not the market leader overall, Apple's iMac leads the competition in the design and publishing and education segments. It also sells well in the consumer market: over 30 per cent of iMac buyers are first-time home computer owners. A key point of differentiation is its looks. As John, chief executive at Apple, explains: 'If you look at it, our industry has done a pretty poor job of listening to its customers in the consumer market. The industry sold big, ugly beige load boxes that took up desks and everything else. The customers were saying "My God, I don't know how to connect all these cables;", "My God this thing is too noisy", "My God this doesn't fit on my desk", and "My God I have to hide it when visitors come over". The result was the colourful, curvaceous all-in-one iMac (see illustration). No consumer could mistake the distinctive design of the new model. The result was that over 2 million units have been sold and Apple's market share in the US has risen to a respectable 11 per cent.

Based on: McIntosh (1999);[14] Pickford (1999)[15]

17.2 Marketing in Action

Differentiating a Commodity Product

Marks and Spencer are UK retailers renowned for their ability to differentiate the products that they sell on quality. Their food retailing arm can command premium prices because customers value the special quality of the merchandise. Even in the case of the humble brussels sprout picked from the same Fenland field as sprouts destined for their supermarket competitors like Asda and Morrisons, Marks and Spencer achieve a differentiated product. How do they do it?

First, M&S prefer their sprouts to be hand picked to avoid the bruising that can sometimes occur with machine picking. Second, the sprouts are machine graded by size: M&S insist upon the smallest. Third, they are washed, except that M&S are not happy with just washing: they go through a jacuzzi to emerge glistening. Finally they are packed not in nets as with the competition but in polythene bags so that their pristine condition can be fully appreciated.

This attention to detail—putting the customer first, not convenience—adds up to superior value for the customer. The product is a little bit special, and it looks a little bit better too. The result is the virtuous circle of superior customer value, higher prices and good profit performance.

Based on: McNay (1992)[16]

Take the scenic route to the internet.

In the case of an iMac, it's also the fastest. You can be cruising the internet in ten minutes out of the box. Ready to select your favourite scenic route? Just call 0870 241 0212. ◆ Think different.

Style and practicality combine to create a differential advantage for iMac

premium price provides consistency within the marketing mix.

This analysis of how the marketing mix can be used to develop a differential advantage has focused on how each action can be translated into value to the customer. It must be remembered, however, that for a differential advantage to be realized a firm needs to provide not only customer value but also value that is superior to that offered by the competition. If all firms provide distributor support in equal measures, for example, distributors may gain value, but no differential advantage will have been achieved.

Fast reaction times

In addition to using the marketing mix to create a differential advantage many companies are recognizing the need to create *fast reaction times* to changes in marketing trends. For example, Benetton have installed state-of-the-art communications, manufacturing and distribution technology to give them flexibility and fast reaction time. Using advanced telecommunications, the company receives sales information from around the world 24 hours a day, every day of the year. They boast that if everyone decided to wear nothing but hats tomorrow, they would be ready to produce 50 million hats within a week.[17]

Sustaining a differential advantage

When searching for ways of achieving a differential advantage management should pay close attention to factors that cannot be easily copied by competition. The aim is to achieve a *sustainable differential advantage*. Competing on low price can often be copied by competition meaning that any advantage is short-lived. Means of achieving a longer term advantage include:

1 Patent-protected products.
2 Strong brand personality.
3 Close relationships with customers.
4 High service levels achieved by well-trained personnel.
5 Innovative product upgrading.
6 Creating high entry barriers (e.g. R&D or promotional expenditures)..

Eroding a differential advantage

However, many advantages are contestable. For example, IBM's stronghold in personal computers was undermined by cheaper-period clones. Three mechanisms are at work which can erode a differential advantage.[18]

1 Technological and environment changes that create opportunities for competitors by eroding the protective barriers (e.g. long-standing television companies are being challenged by satellite television).
2 Competitors learn how to initiate the sources of the differential advantage (e.g. competitors engage in a training programme to improve service capabilities).
3 Complacency leads to lack of protection of the differential advantage.

Creating cost leadership

Creating a cost leadership position requires an understanding of the factors that affect costs. Porter has identified ten major *cost drivers* that determine the behaviour of costs in the value chain (see Fig. 17.7).[19]

Economies of scale

Scale economies can arise from the use of more efficient methods of production at higher volumes. For example, United Biscuits benefit from more efficient machinery that can produce biscuits more cheaply than that used by Fox's Biscuits, who operate at much lower volume. Scale economies also arise from the less than proportional increase in overhead as production volume increases. For example, a factory with twice the floor area of another factory is less than twice the price to build. A third scale economy results from the capacity to spread the cost of R&D and promotion over a greater sales volume. However, economies of scale do not proceed indefinitely. At some point diseconomies of scale are likely to arise as size gives rise to overcomplexity and, possibly, personnel difficulties.

Learning

Costs can also fall through the effects of learning. For example, people learn how to assemble more quickly, pack more efficiently, design products that are easier to manufacture, layout warehouses more effectively, cut driving time and reduce inventories. The effects of learning on costs was seen in the manufacture of fighter planes for the Second World War. The time to produce each plane fell over time as learning took place. The combined effect of economies of scale and learning as cumulative output increases has been termed the ***experience curve***. The Boston Consulting Group have estimated that costs reduced on average by approximately 15–20 per cent each time cumulative output doubled. This suggests that firms with greater market share will have a cost advantage through the experience curve effect, assuming all companies are operating on the same curve. However, a move towards a new manufacturing technology can lower the experience curve for adopting companies allowing them to leap-frog more traditional firms and thereby gain a cost advantage even though cumulative output may be lower.

Capacity utilization

Since fixed costs must be paid whether a plant is manufacturing at full or zero capacity, under-utilization incurs costs. The effect is to push up the cost per unit for production. The impact of capacity utilization on profitability was established by the PIMS (Profit Impact of Marketing Strategy) studies which have shown a positive association between utilization and return on investment.[20] Changes in capacity utilization can also raise costs (e.g. through the extra costs of hiring and laying off workers). Careful production planning is required for seasonal products such as ice cream and fireworks to smooth output.

Linkages

These describe how the cost of activities are affected by how other activities are performed. For example, improving quality assurance activities can reduce after-sales service costs. In the car industry the reduction in the number of faults on a new car reduces warrantee costs. The activities of suppliers and distributors also link

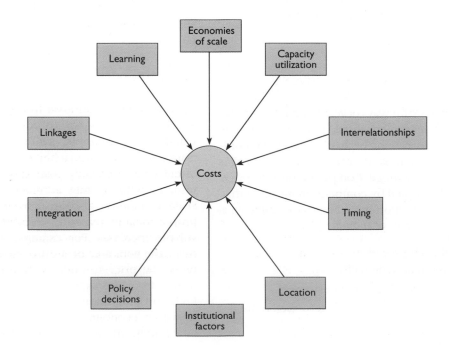

Figure 17.7 Cost drivers

to affect the costs of a firm. For example, the introduction of a just-in-time delivery system by a supplier reduces inventory costs of the firm. Distributors can influence a firm's physical distribution costs through their warehouse location decision. To exploit such linkages, though, the firm may need considerable bargaining power. In some instances it can pay a firm to increase distributor margins or pay a fee in order to exploit linkages. For example, Seiko paid their US jewellers a fee for accepting their watches for repair and sending them to Seiko: this meant that Seiko did not need local services facilities and their overall costs fell.[21]

Interrelationships

Sharing costs with other business units is another potential cost driver. Sharing the costs of R&D, transportation, marketing and purchasing lower costs. Know-how, also, can be shared to reduce costs by improving the efficiency of an activity.

Integration

Both integration and de-integration can affect costs. For example, owning the means of physical distribution rather than using outside contracts could lower costs. Ownership may allow a producer to avoid suppliers or customers with sizeable bargaining power. De-integration can lower costs and raise flexibility. For example, by using many small clothing suppliers, Benetton are in a powerful position to keep costs low, and also maintain a high degree of production flexibility.

Timing

Both first movers and late entrants have potential opportunities for lowering costs. First movers in a market can gain cost advantages: it is usually cheaper to establish a brand name in the minds of customers if there is no competition. Also, they have prime access to cheap or high-quality raw materials, and locations. However, late entrants to a market have the opportunity to buy the latest technology, and avoid high market development costs.

Policy decisions

Firms have a wide range of discretionary policy decisions that affect costs. Product width, level of service, channel decisions (e.g. small number of larger dealers v. large number of small dealers), salesforce decisions (e.g. in-company salesforce v. sales agents) and wage levels are some of the decisions that have a direct impact on costs. Care must be taken not to reduce costs on activities that have a major bearing on customer value. For example, moving from a company-employed salesforce to sales agents may not only cut costs but also destroy supplier–customer relationships.

Location

The location of plant and warehouses affects costs through different wage, physical distribution and energy costs. Amstrad, for example, manufacture their consumer electronics products in the Far East to take advantage of low wage costs. Locating near customers can lower out-bound distributional costs, and near suppliers reduces in-bound distributional costs.

Institutional factors

These include government regulations, tariffs and local content rules. For example, regulations regarding the maximum size of lorries affects distribution costs.

Firms employing a cost leadership strategy will be vigilant in pruning costs. This analysis of cost drivers provides a framework for searching out new avenues for cost reduction. In European retailing the entry of cost leaders in the form of no-frills, bulk purchase warehouse clubs is predicted to have a major impact on food and consumer durable purchase. Furthermore, by converting their cost advantage (and lower margins) into low prices they are creating a differential advantage over their more expensive rivals.

Summary

This chapter has explored the key issues in analysing competitors and creating a competitive advantage. Firms need to understand their competitors because corporate success results from providing more value to customers than the competition. Industry structure is the framework within which companies compete. Five forces determine the attractiveness of an industry: the threat of new entrants, the bargaining power of suppliers, the bargaining power of buyers, the presence of substitute products and the intensity of the rivalry between firms in the industry. Firms need to manage these factors so that industry structure is favourable.

Competitor analysis focuses on competitor identification, an audit of competitor capabilities, their objectives and strategies and prediction of response patterns. The aim is to provide a basis for creating a competitive advantage, anticipating their future actions, and estimating how they will react to future actions our company may take.

Creating and sustaining a competitive advantage can be achieved by offering superior value through a differential advantage, or managing for cost leadership. Differentiation can be created through managing the marketing mix; cost leadership through control of cost drivers. Companies also need to determine their competitive scope: a wide industry perspective or a narrow segment focus. These give rise to four generic strategies: industry-wide differentiation, cost leadership, differentiation focus and cost focus. Companies need to avoid a stuck-in-the-middle orientation where neither differentiation nor cost leadership is achieved.

The sources of competitive advantage are the skills and resources of the company. Analysing these factors can lead to the definition of the company's core competences. These are the skills and resources at which the company excels and can be used to develop new products and markets. Specific location of superior skills and resources can be aided by value chain analysis. A value chain is the set of activities that are conducted to design, manufacture, market, distribute and service a company's products. Analysis of these activities can lead to the location of actual and potential differentiated and lowest cost positions.

Internet exercise

Competitor analysis

Sites to visit
http://www.nike.com
http://www.reebok.com
http://www.adidas.com

Exercise
Compare and contrast the competitive advantages and disadvantages of these three sportswear companies.

Study questions

1 Using Porter's five forces framework discuss why profitability in the European textile industry is lower than that in book publishing.

2 For any product of your choice identify competition using the four layer approach discussed in this chapter.

3 Why is competitor analysis essential in today's turbulent environment? How far is it possible to predict competitor response to marketing actions?

4 Distinguish between differentiation and cost leadership strategies. Is it possible to achieve both positions simultaneously?

5   Discuss with examples ways of achieving a differential advantage.

6   How can value chain analysis lead to superior corporate performance?

7   Using examples, discuss the impact of the Single European Market on competitive structure.

8   What are cost drivers? Should marketing management be concerned with them, or is their significance solely the prerogative of the accountant?

References

1.   Porter, M. E. (1980) *Competitive Strategy: Techniques for Analysing Industries and Competitors,* New York: Free Press.
2.   Graham, G. (1997) Competition is Getting Tougher, *Financial Times*, Special Report on Danish Banking, 9 April, 2.
3.   Von Clausewitz, C. (1908) *On War,* London: Routledge and Kegan Paul.
4.   Macdonald, M. (1999) *Marketing Plans*, Oxford: Butterworth-Heinemann.
5.   Dudley, J. W. (1990) *1992: Strategies for the Single Market*, London: Kogan Page.
6.   Ross, E. B. (1984) Making Money with Proactive Pricing, *Harvard Business Review*, **62** (Nov.-Dec.), 145-55.
7.   Leeflang, P. H. S. and D. R. Wittink (1996) Competitive Reaction versus Consumer Response: Do Managers Over-react? *International Journal of Research in Marketing*, **13**, 103-19.
8.   Hall, W. K. (1980) Survival Strategies in a Hostile Environment, *Harvard Business Review*, **58** (Sept.-Oct.), 75-85.
9.   Porter (1980) op. cit.
10. Day, G. S. and R. Wensley (1988) Assessing Advantage: A Framework for Diagnosing Competitive Superiority, *Journal of Marketing*, **52** (April), 1-20.
11. Day, G. S. (1999) *Market Driven Strategy: Processes for Creating Value*, New York: Free Press.
12. Porter, M. E. (1985) *Competitive Advantage*, New York: Free Press.
13. For methods of calculating value in organizational markets see Anderson, J. C. and J. A. Narus (1998) Business marketing: Understand What Customers Value, *Harvard Business Review*, November-December, 53-65.
14. McIntosh, N. (1999) No Sleeping on the Jobs, *The Guardian*, 23 September, 8-9.
15. Pickford, J. (1999) Sounds Like a Better Vision, *Financial Times*, 1 December, 1514.
16. McNay, M. (1992) Brussels Directives, *The Guardian*, 19 December, 21.
17. Bruce, L. (1987) The Bright New Worlds of Benetton, International Management, November, 24-35.
18. Day (1990) op. cit.
19. Porter (1985) op. cit.
20. Buzzell, R. D. and B. T. Gale (1987) *The PIMS Principles*, New York: Free Press.
21. Porter (1985) op. cit.

Key terms

industry   a group of companies that market products which are close substitutes for each other

entry barriers   barriers which act to prevent new firms from entering a market, e.g. the high level of investment required

competitor audit   a precise analysis of competitor strengths and weaknesses, objectives and strategies

competitive scope   the breadth of a company's competitive challenge, e.g. broad or narrow

differentiation strategy   the selection of one or more customer choice criteria and positioning the offering accordingly to achieve superior customer value

competitive advantage   the attempt to achieve superior performance through differentiation to provide superior customer value or by managing to acheive lowest delivered cost

value chain   the set of the firm's activities that are conducted to design, manufacture, market and distribute and service its products

core competencies   the principal distinctive capabilities possessed by a company—what it is really good at.

differential advantage   a clear performance differential over competition on factors that are important to target customers

experience curve   the combined effect of economies of scale and learning as cumulative output increases

Case 31 Wal-Mart Buys Asda

In the Spring of 1999, the shareholders of Kingfisher, the UK retailer, were smiling. They had just seen their share price rocket from around £5 to over £9 in less than a year on the news that Kingfisher were to take over Asda, the UK supermarket chain. Geoffrey Mulcahy, who heads Kingfisher, saw the move as another step towards his ambition of being a 'world-class retailer' where efficiencies of buying merchandise in massive quantities, managing large stores and achieving lower prices and higher sales turnover would reap further benefits for shareholders, employees and customers alike.

Mulcahy, the normally taciturn former Harvard MBA (he even calls his 40 foot boat 'No Comment') had turned around the ailing Woolworth's chain by selling off their city sites to release cash that could be used for investment. He discovered that Woolworth's owned a small do-it-yourself chain called B&Q. By building large retail 'sheds' backed up by service provided by ex-plumbers, electricians, etc., an advertising campaign based on the strap-line 'Don't just do it, B&Q it', and low prices, the chain became a success story of the 1990s, beating off me-too rivals such as Do It All, Sainsbury's Homebase and US invaders such as Texas. By adding the electrical goods retailer, Comet and the health and beauty products chain, Superdrug, Kingfisher was on the road to fulfilling Mulcahy's dream; taking over Asda was the next step. Sadly, his vision was to be shattered by Wal-Mart, the US predator that wanted to expand its European presence that had already begun by the acquisition of the German warehouse chain Wertkauf.

Mulcahy was well aware that Wal-Mart was lurking in the wings, but all the talk was that the US retailer was cool about entering the UK market where retail competition was intense and planning restrictions made the likelihood of opening the kind of vast 'Supercentres' that it operates in the US unlikely. All that changed one June Monday morning when he received a 7.00 a.m. telephone call from Archie Norman, Asda's chief executive, to say that he had 'a bit of a problem'. The 'problem' was that Asda had agreed a deal with Wal-Mart.

Wal-Mart USA

Enter any Wal-Mart store in the US and consumers are struck by the sheer scale of the operation. These are stores of over 200 000 square feet into which seven UK superstores could be accommodated. Next, come the 'greeters', who welcome customers into the stores, give them their card in case they need help and put a smiley sticker on them. Then come the prices where, for example, a cotton T-shirt that would sell for around $15 in a UK department store, sells for $1 in Wal-Mart. The choice of products in wide ranging, from clothes through groceries and pharmaceuticals to electrical goods. Stores are well organized with the right goods always available, kept neat and clean in appearance and helpfully displayed.

At the heart of the Wal-Mart operation is its systems and information technology. One thousand information technologists run a 24 terabyte database. Its information collection, which comprises up to 65 million transactions (by item, time, price and store), drives most aspects of its business. Within 90 minutes of an item being sold, Wal Mart's distribution centres are organizing its replacement. Distribution is facilitated by state-of-the-art delivery tracking systems. So effective is the system that when a flu epidemic hit the US, Wal-Mart followed its spread by monitoring flu remedy sales in its stores. It then predicted its movement from east to west so that Wal-Mart stores were adequately stocked in time for the rise in demand.

Wal-Mart also uses real-time information systems to let consumers decide what appears in its stores. The Internet is used to inform suppliers what was sold the day before. In this way, it only buys what sells.

Its relationship with its suppliers is unusual in that they are only paid when an item is sold in its stores. Not only does this help cash flow, it also ensures that the interests of manufacturer and Wal-Mart coincide. Instead of the traditional system where once the retailer had purchased stock it was essentially the retailer's problem to sell it, if the product does not sell it hurts the manufacturer's cash flow more than Wal-Mart's. Consequently, at a stroke, the supplier's and retailer's interests are focused on the same measures and rewards. There is no incentive for the supplier to try to sell Wal-Mart under-producing brands since they will suffer in the same way as the retailer if they fail to sell in the store.

Its success is reflected in its ability to out-perform its rivals (sales are four times greater than its nearest competitor, KMart). Recent plans include returning to the high street with smaller stores to compete with 'Mom and Pop' local grocers. It is not without its critics, who claim that its success has driven high street stores out of business, leaving derelict, boarded-up downtown streets. Christened 'Sprawl-Mart' by its critics, it has been accused of being anti-union, and for causing the demise of 'Mom and Pop' stores.

Wal-Mart staff are called 'associates' and are encouraged to tell top management what they believe is wrong with their stores. They are offered share options and are encouraged to put the customer first.

Wal-Mart's overseas operations

Since 1992 Wal-Mart has moved into eight countries and trounced the competition. In Canada and Mexico it is already the market leader in discount retailing. In Canada it bought Woolco in 1994, quickly added outlets, and by 1997 became market leader with 45 per cent of the discount store market, a remarkable achievement. In countries such as China and Argentina it has been surprisingly successful and achieved inter-national sales of $12 billion in 1998.

In that year it entered Europe with the buying of Germany's Wertkauf warehouse chain, quickly followed by the acquisition of 74 Interspar hyper-markets. It immediately closed stores, then reopened them with price cuts on 1100 items, making them 10 per cent below competitors'

prices. The Germans' eye for bargains has meant that it has rapidly gained market share.

Wal-Mart's entry into the UK market is the next step in its move into the European market. Asda was a natural target since it shared its 'everyday low prices' culture. It is mainly a grocery super-market but also sells clothing. Its information technology systems have badly lagged behind its UK supermarket competitors and it has acted as 'consumer champion'; by selling cosmetics and over-the-counter pharmaceuticals for cheaper prices than traditional outlets. It has also bought branded products such as jeans from abroad to sell at low prices in its stores. Wal-Mart is intending to continue to use the Asda store name rather than rebranding with the Wal-Mart name. Most of Asda's stores are located in the north of the UK.

Commentators believe that the Wal-Mart–Asda partnership will send shock waves through the UK retailing sector, but others believe that it will be a tougher marketplace to compete in than those it has entered so far. Not all early signs are good, with two top Asda executives leaving within a year of the take-over.

Based on: Alexander, G. (1999) Wal-Mart Weighs Up Plan to Invade UK, *The Sunday Times*, 7 February, 7; Bummer, A. (1999) Uncle Sam Invades, *The Guardian*, G2, 15 June, 2–3; Farrelly, P. (1999) The Wonder of Woolies Takes on the World, *The Observer*, 25 April, 7; Hamilton, K. (1999) Wal-Smart, *The Sunday Times*, 20 June, 5; Laurance, B. (1999) How America Shoplifted Asda, *The Observer*, 20 June, 5; Merrilees, B. and D. Miller (1999) Defensive Segmentation Against a Market Spoiler Rival, *Proceedings of the Academy of Marketing Conference*, Stirling, July, 1–10; Mitchell, A. (1999) Wal-Mart Arrival Heralds Change for UK Marketers, *Marketing Week*, 24 June, 42–3; Voyle, S. (2000) Wal-Mart Expands Asda in Drive for Market Share, *Financial Times*, 10 January, 21.

This case was prepared by David Jobber, Professor of Marketing, University of Bradford.

Questions

1 What are Wal-Mart's sources of competitive advantage? How do these sources manifest themselves in creating competitive advantage for Wal-Mart customers?

2 Does Wal-Mart's acquisition of Asda make competitive sense?

3 What impact is Wal-Mart's entry into the UK likely to have on the retail sector and consumers?

Case 32 Netto: Expanding a Niche Market

Over the past six years Netto has become an increasingly visible and recognizable highstreet name with its distinctive black logo against a yellow background.

With a constantly changing range of products that covers nearly 90 per cent of the daily needs of customers, a highly competitive pricing stance and a distinctive, no frills store layout, the company has experienced considerable growth throughout its four prime markets—Denmark (240 stores), the UK (118 stores), Germany (121 stores) and Poland (15 stores).

The company, is part of a bigger retail group, Dansk Supermarked A/S which is the second largest Danish high street retailer. Dansk Supermarked currently trades under five different retail formats—Netto (a limited range discounter (LRD)), Fotex (a supermarket chain), Bilka (a successful chain of hypermarkets), Toj & Sko (a discount clothing and footwear chain) and A–Z (a variety stores chain).

Early years

The first Netto store opened in Copenhagen in 1981. The idea was piloted by Fotex and Bilka as a response to Aldi's entry from Germany into the Danish market. By 1983, Netto had opened some 20 stores in Denmark and subsequently took over 32 stores from its Danish rival, the Fakta Group. The move effectively consolidated its position in Sealand, the biggest of the Danish islands, and provided the basis for the organization's expansion into the west of the country. By 1990, Netto had become a nationwide food discounter with 100 stores located in Sealand, Fyn and Jutland.

With an annual growth of 15–25 outlets, Netto is currently the discount market leader in Denmark, with some 1.1 million customers each week, just over a fifth of the country's population.

The concept

We have made discount decent

(J. Rix—managing director of Netto Foodstores UK from 1994 to 1997)

The Netto concept is based on a self-service discount format with a store layout designed to promote quick and easy access to the merchandise. The company is a limited range discounter (LRD), offering about 900 items of 'standard and spot lines'. By comparison, a conventional supermarket such as Safeway, Sainsbury or Tesco offers a product range of 25 000 or more product lines. Netto sells groceries, fish, meat, fresh vegetables, organic products, beverages, a range of frozen and canned food and ready prepared dishes. The range consists of mainly tertiary brands (non-branded products—NBPs) at prices which are typically 15–20 per cent below those of well-known branded products. Currently the company has extended the share of the branded products to 25–30 per cent introducing them mainly as spot lines (once-only offers).

The unique features of the Netto offer stem from the flexibility of their range which includes 'once-only offers'—products that are often only in the store for a week and then replaced by other lines. It is this limited range of fast-selling products that allows Netto to buy goods at a low price and maintain a competitive retail price at a low profit margin. By having a narrow range coupled with low operating expenses and efficient working practices, economies of scale can be more easily achieved.

Currently spread over four European markets, Netto adheres to simple organizational structure. Its positioning as a discounter is different from that of supermarkets, sharing the view of one of the owners of the group, Herman Salling, that 'You are either a supermarket or a discounter, don't try to be both' (see Fig. C32.1).

Exporting the concept

By 1989, Netto had consolidated its position in Denmark and started looking at the possibility of exporting the concept. It looked at a number of markets including France, Spain, Germany and the UK, with a view to blending its retail concept with local retail practices. Two markets were finally chosen, Germany and the UK. The chairman of the company, Mads Krage and his senior mangers John Rix and Henrik Gundelach were all involved in assessing the possible areas and the viability of the sites for the initial start up of its German operation. The choice was finally made to expand into the eastern part of Germany by means of a joint venture with Spar AG of Germany. Netto Germany was registered on 13 July 1990 and on 13 September the same year, shortly after the fall of the Berlin Wall, the company opened its first outlet in Anklam in the northern part of the former DDR. By the end of the year another 11 stores had been opened. The eastern part of Germany proved to be an ideal market for the Netto concept, with price-sensitive customers who were used to discounting, and with positive attitudes towards everything coming from Denmark. In commenting on this, Mads Krage said, 'Our partners and customers appreciated our Danish culture. Even our TV comedy characters, Egon Olsen & Gang, were widely known and liked. This atmosphere of friendliness and mutual trust helped us a lot in building good relationships with customers and suppliers.'

Netto Germany operated initially in the north—most of the new Bundeslander—Mecklenburg, Vorpommern, Brandenburg, Sachsen-Anhalt, and Berlin—home to some 10 million Germans and subsequently expanded further to the south-eastern part of Germany.

The UK food retailing scene

By the end of the 1980s, the UK retail industry had become highly concentrated. Three categories of retailers had emerged—the national chains of supermarkets such as J. Sainsbury and Tesco, the regional multiples such as Wm Morrison and the discounters such as Kwik Save. The national supermarket sector was the largest and dominated by the 'Big Three' (J. Sainsbury, Tesco and Argyll-Safeway). Two other players, Asda and Gateway, though commanding substantial shares of the market, had at that time financial problems and were losing the superstores' battle.

Among the regional multiples were players such as Wm Morrison and Wm Low who occupied a mid-market position. Both were growing fast but were considerably smaller than the 'Big Three'. The third part of the market—the discount sector was at this time underdeveloped and to a large extent ignored by the major multiples, dominated by Kwik Save and Lo-Cost.

The UK grocery market was considerably different from that of other EC countries. The major supermarkets were universally pursuing strategies of quality, high levels of customer service, premium pricing and an extended product range. Trying to maximize their sales, they were leading a move to out-of-town locations and reducing the number of their high street and suburban sites, something which led to a niche developing for the discount concept 'of low price and no frills shopping for everyday items'.

For the big European discounters such as Aldi and Netto, the UK market presented attractive

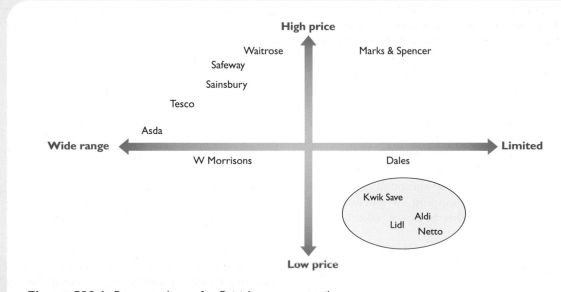

Figure C32.1 Perceptual map for British grocery retailers

opportunities for growth. In the late 1980s and early 1990s, UK retailers were enjoying what were perhaps the highest retail profit margins in Europe of between 6 per cent and 8 per cent. These profit margins were due largely to more favourable cost structures, with lower employment costs than in Continental Europe while the costs of land and leases on prime sites were growing, they still were lower compared to Denmark and Germany. Continental discounters therefore recognized the potential to earn 1–2 per cent more than in their domestic markets. These attractions of the UK market were, in turn, heightened by the more liberal planning regulations procedures and a less protected property market.

Although at this time the UK food retailing market seemed to be less affected by the recession than its continental counterparts, excess capacity in the industry and rising operating costs, coupled with reduced consumer confidence had resulted in sluggish sales. An increased consumer emphasis upon price, induced by the recession, stimulated the growth of the discount end of the market which, by 1992, was worth around £4 billion. Recognizing this the major foreign discount operators such as Aldi, Netto, Ed and Lidl began to move in.

By the mid-1990s, a new structure of grocery retailing had established itself in the UK operating a variety of discount formats alongside the conventional supermarkets. These discount formats fall in four main categories: limited range discounters (LRD), such as Aldi, Netto, Ed and Shoprite carrying up to 1000 lines; discount supermarkets such as Kwik Save, and Lo-Cost with a wider range of up to 4000 lines; the extended range discounters (ERD), such as Dales of Asda and Food Giant of Gateway; and the warehouse clubs Costco, and Price Club.

Although Kwik Save dominated the sector, the LRDs' growth was gaining momentum. Their success in Continental Europe was partly due to the established 'cross over' purchasing pattern, where higher income families would cross over from supermarkets to use discounters for their essential everyday shopping, a phenomenon which in the mid-1990s began to take hold in the UK.

Major players in the discount sector

Kwik Save is currently the UK's leading food discounter and the sixth largest grocery retailer

with a 6.5 per cent (1996) share of the grocery market. The company which was set up in 1959 under the name of Value Foods, acquired plc status in 1970 and was renamed the Kwik Save Discount Group. The chain currently operates from 861 (1996) stores and carries a product range up to 4000 lines with a high proportion of branded products. Although its format was successful in the late 1970s and 1980s, the company began facing a major challenge in the mid-1990s both from the Big Three supermarkets and the new limited range discounters. The effect of this was that while its sales and market share remained static, the company was faced in 1996, with a 28 per cent slump in profits and pressures to reconsider its positioning. Kwik Save responded by a move upmarket and gradually increased the share of the premium brands and own label in its product range. However, the company's problems were compounded by the UK entry and growth of the three major discount retailers Aldi, Lidl and Netto.

Aldi, the largest of the German discounters, entered the UK market in April 1990. With an estimated 2600 stores in Germany, the company operates in six European countries as well as in the USA. Being a private company that is 90 per cent controlled by the co-founders Carl and Theo Albreht, Aldi is characterized by a high degree of secrecy in its operations and financial deals. By mid-1994, Aldi was already trading in the UK from over 100 stores most of which were based in the North and the Midlands. However, despite or perhaps because of its fast growth in the UK the company continues to experience problems of profitability.

Lidl, another German-based retailer entered the UK in November 1994 simultaneously opening 10 stores and with plans to build a 200 strong operation. However, in 1996 its expansion appeared to be running out of momentum and in early 1997 Lidl sold some of its stores to Netto.

Netto Foodstores UK

The growth of Netto

In December 1990, Netto opened its first store in Leeds. The company chose the north of England as its start-up base for a number of reasons including its proximity to areas with a high concentration of population; relatively low prices of property;

the opportunities for easier expansion both south and northwards and the shopping habits and price sensitivity of the population in these areas which benefited the start of a discount operation.

By the end of 1992, the company had 31 stores. Its expansion continued at a similar rate in the years to follow. In 1993, the chain was 50 strong reaching a turnover of nearly £150 million.

In 1995, Netto took over 13 stores in the south-east from the French discounter Ed owned by Erteco UK, a subsidiary of Carrefour, and in this way developed a foothold in the lucrative south. Subsequently the company has increased its presence along the M4 corridor and in London. The company is one of the fastest growing food chains in Britain currently running 118 stores across the country (1997). Since 1991 its turnover has grown by 19-fold, exceeding £275 million.

In establishing itself, Netto has adapted its culture to the local retail market and, where possible, operates a 'Buy British' policy. The company's approach was summed up by John Rix, the managing director, as 'Here we are a British company and alongside with our retail activities we wish to grow as a neighbourhood retailer contributing to revitalize in many of our locations the spirit of the local store around which smaller traders will benefit'.

Netto Foodstores UK strategy

Vision and culture

Operating successfully in four international markets, each of them with very distinctive characteristics confirms Netto's ability to adapt. Perhaps the only standardized feature of its expansion has been the distinctive corporate culture characterized by strong patterns of informal vertical and horizontal communication, and a free flow and access to information. In commenting on this John Rix suggests that: 'In our competitive business, we have no other choice but to listen and be flexible and responsive to the market. That is embodied in our culture. For example, we encourage our shop employees to come up with ideas for 'new spot or clearing lines'. Every single member of staff can call into a buyer and say I do not think that is a good idea, why don't you do something else. We recently introduced a £1000 tax free prize for those

employees who give us a hint about a new location for a store. Perhaps there is one near where they live.'

This philosophy has been reinforced by the chairman, Mads Krage: 'Perhaps an underlying factor for our success is our ability to build teams that believe in and contribute to our winning culture and our ability to adapt ourselves to the local needs of customers.'

Structure

The organization's structure is a direct reflection of the Netto culture. The company operates with a simple structure with just two management levels. Level one is the head office team. The country managing director has the ultimate responsibility for the operation. In the case of the UK, the small head office at South Elmsall consists of a buying department, a marketing department, a property management and site acquisition department, finance, a management team which coordinates the activities of district managers, and a central distribution warehouse with capacity to accommodate 150 stores.

District and store managers are the next level. The thinking behind such a flat structure is straightforward and designed to facilitate communication, transmit changes in the market situation in the quickest possible way, and encourage entrepreneurship. In discussing this, John Rix says, 'It is very important that everything we do at the head office or at the warehouse is based on the needs of our stores so that the operation runs smoothly.'

Staff

Staff within the stores are recruited locally. The company places great emphasis on staff training. There are no job demarcations within the store and employees are trained in every aspect of the store's operation, from checkouts, filling shelves to cleaning and unloading deliveries. Store managers are no exception to that and are expected to be on the shop floor for 95 per cent of the time, to lead by example and create a positive team spirit. Each store employs approximately 20–25 people. For an organization of the size of Netto, the corporate headquarters are small, with limited staff and with 'no frills, open plan' office layout. Paperwork is kept to a minimum within the company.

Distribution centre

The distribution centre at South Elmsall is an important part of the trading operation. It has 225 000 sq ft storage area and the capacity to serve 150 stores. It does not operate a racking system, and is geared to a high turnover of stock, working to a just-in-time system of stock management. With the exception of milk, everything in the early days was delivered to the stores from the distribution centre at South Elmsall in order to reduce the wastage of time for multiple deliveries at the stores. However, the distance of the southern stores from South Elmsall led to a low utilization of vehicles and made the supply costly. Because of this, after the take-over of Ed stores, the company set up an additional depot in Reading, 25 miles west of London, to service the southern stores.

All of the distribution and delivery is subcontracted to haulage companies which are paid at a pallet rate, and the subcontractors are required to carry the Netto's logo.

Location decisions and store design

Netto UK stores are located either in the high street or in neighbourhood retail parks and shopping malls. Of the 900 products, 80 per cent are core lines and the rest variable product offers. The outlets have an average sales area of 8000 to 10 000 sq ft and most of the new generation UK stores offer car parking facilities. A considerable number of Netto continental stores are smaller, located in the central parts of the city and provide no car park facilities.

The UK store format is determined by a number of factors with experience having shown that customers prefer larger stores with greater space allocated to the different products together with good access, convenient location and free car parks; all of these are now seen by Netto as crucial factors for the customer store choice.

The larger sales areas also provide for the possibility of bringing in concessions such as a bakery, a newsagent, or a butcher. These increase the pulling power of the store and complement the limited range of the retailer. This pulling power has, in turn been increased in some areas with Netto stores being located next to Iceland where both retailers benefit from complementing each other's product ranges.

The choice of retail location goes through a number of stages. The property management department pinpoints areas with potential for store development and evaluates the available sites on the criteria of accessibility, neighbourhood classification, traffic, visibility, size of the site, nearby competition and the quality of their sites. With almost 500 stores in four markets, the potential store performance is forecasted on the basis of analogue comparison with similar store formats at similar locations. Assessment of competition is an important element in the store location process. It is a single decision for every new store.

Merchandising

While in all four markets the company is consistent in using its distinctive corporate logo and colours and in order to standardize the stores layout, its merchandising policy is adapted to meet local needs.

In the UK, for example, Netto operates a 'Buy British' policy, sourcing where possible the majority of products from local suppliers. Consumer tastes and buying habits are of prime importance in Netto buying policy. The UK range therefore has greater number of pallet lines and sells more tinned products compared with Denmark, Germany or Poland. Product depth is also determined by the consumer demand. In Germany, for example the company stocks a greater variety of beers and soft drinks while in Denmark the returnable glass beverage bottles require additional facilities and storage place.

Every Netto store has to carry the full product range. Recently, the company introduced regional variations to match the specific demand of the northern and southern customers. These adaptations are, however, limited within 20–30 products.

With the success of the operation came the growing temptation for increasing the range. The company, however, is committed to its strategy of a limited range discounter and updates its product offer on 'one in one out basis'. Criteria for product selection are the product's sales potential, quality and price. In order to attract brand loyal customers, Netto deliberately offers a limited range of leading brands such as Kellogg's, although they account for only around 25–30 per cent of the range. The rest belongs to a mix of competitively priced own-label and 'no-name' products.

The share of OB from the generated sales is approximately 25–30 per cent. OB create store loyalty. In which product group we shall offer an OB is a single decision based on our UK experience. In this case our international experience is not applicable, e.g. in Germany we offer a range of OB lagers which wouldn't sell that well in this country.

(J. Rix)

Concessions

In order to maximize its product offer and cost efficiency, Netto looks for opportunities for cooperating with other retailers. One example of this is the way in which in the neighbourhood shopping precincts, the company congregates with other retailers in order to increase the cumulative attraction of the location. Another way in which this is done is by increasing the number of concessions in Netto stores; these improve the efficiency of the selling space, extend the range of the retailer and improve the store traffic.

Pricing strategy

Pricing is a central part of Netto marketing strategy. It underpins its discount philosophy of providing the lowest price for a range of essential products. The success of the concept in Denmark and Germany was due primary to the fact that discounters managed to convince shoppers to buy the everyday essentials at a lowest price from them and then cross the road and do the rest of their shopping in the supermarkets: 'We compete on the basis of lowest price and high quality, our strategy is to be the cheapest but not cheaper' (J. Rix).

Communications mix

Netto's communication is geared in two directions: to promote the image and improve the appeal of discounting among C1, C2 socio-economic groups, and to reinforce the company stance as a neighbourhood retailer.

In Denmark the group is nationwide and employs a considerable amount of TV advertising. In the UK the use of TV as a medium is limited to a few conurbations, while the bulk of advertising is through the local press and radio stations. The company also attracts positive publicity through sponsorship and its participation in neighbour-hood initiatives. The company intensively uses in-store promotion to increase store loyalty and convey the idea that shopping in Netto is fun.

Competition

The company views competition on two levels: industry and regional level. On an industry level Netto competes directly with discounters such as Kwik Save, Aldi and Lidl. An essential part of this competition is the ability of the retailer to project a differentiated image and secure prime locations for its stores. On an area level Netto responds to local competition from the nearest store which in some cases could be Asda, Wm Morrison, or Tesco.

So far the major supermarkets have resisted direct price competition and continue to put the emphasis of their promotion on value for money and customer service. However, some of them restructure their operations on a price oriented basis. An illustration of this was the announcement by Asda of its 'Asda Price' as the group returned to its original values. Asda is also currently testing a discount format-Dales-aiming to increase its share in the discount market. At the same time, Tesco is offering a comprehensive generic range (value lines) priced to compete with the LRDs. Both Asda and Tesco are also running loyalty schemes aimed at strengthening its customer base and reducing the cross-store shopping.

The future

Since 1991 Netto has increased it sales by a factor of 19 from £14.6 million to £275.7 million and considerably improved its profitability. The company is now among the fastest growing retailers and has managed to become a household name in many areas of the country. An increasing variety of customers pass through the doors of Netto every day. The question is, of course, whether the discount concept will work in a period of economic recovery as well as it worked in recession. This remains to be seen. Shoppers are increasingly attracted by convenience and improved customer service. The big supermarket chains are constantly extending their range of offered services with some of them diversifying into areas previously untapped by retailers, such as retail banking, and considering new retail formats to respond to the growing consumer confidence. Will market price continue to be a main factor for consumer choice in the years to come? The future of Netto will obviously depend on its ability adequately to respond to the latest changes in the UK retail scene and maintain its entrepreneurial culture unaffected by the growth of the organization.

Postscript

Since the Netto case study was written in 1997, the British retail grocery market has undergone a series of major changes. Amongst the most prominent of these are:

+ Wal-Mart's entry to the UK by the takeover of Asda.

+ Kwik Save's merger in 1998 with Somerfield.

+ Tesco's strengthening of its position as the UK's leading retailer.

+ The continued growth of the market share of packaged groceries of the four major grocery multiples (Tesco, Sainsbury's, Asda and Safeway) to 70.1 per cent in 1999.

+ The ever faster move by the big supermarket chains, but particularly Tesco, into areas such as retail banking, brown goods, computers, mobile phones and cars.

+ The development of shopping via the Internet.

+ Loyalty cards as an increasingly common part of the retail mix. However, in 1999, Safeway, having seen its margins squeezed at the top end by the strategies being pursued by Sainsbury and Tesco, and at the bottom end by the discount retailers, withdrew its card and began to focus more firmly upon a price/value offer.

+ Links between the grocery retailers and petrol stations, with Tesco, Safeway, Somerfield and Budgens all developing a forecourt presence.

Faced with changes such as these, and with Asda and Tesco locked in a battle to prove themselves the UK's best value food retailer, Netto, in common with most of the other discount food retailers, saw its rate of market share growth slow. However, the success of the Netto strategy was reflected in the company reporting its first UK profit in 1998 (£7.4 million on sales of £326 million, against a lost of £746 000 in 1997 and £1.9 million in 1996). In 1999, sales reached £353 million, with reported pretax profits of £10.3 million. Margins were, however, slim: 1.6 per cent compared with Wm. Morrison's 6.5 per cent, Sainsbury's 6.1 per cent, Tesco's 5.8 per cent, Asda's 5.3 per cent, Somerfield's 4.0 per cent and Aldi's 2.3 per cent (*source*: *Retail Week*, 24 March 2000).

So what next?

Although Netto's move into the UK can be seen to have been generally successful, the future for the LRGDs (Limited Range Grocery Discounters) is seen by many analysts to be precarious. With a market that is becoming ever more competitive and a customer base that is ever more demanding, the continued success of a discount retailer such as Netto is heavily dependent upon clear strategic thinking and differentiation. With the company having struggled to make profits in the early years, losses were reduced in 1997, but sales volume growth then began to slow. This suggests that once the company stopped trying to buy market share and to increase margins instead, there was a trade-off with sales.

Although in a number of ways the strategy pursued has been seen to be clever and the findings of Mintel's Price Survey of budget own brands in 1998 indicated that Netto was the cheapest of the 12 retailers surveyed, the real issue for the management team revolves around the question of what they should do—or might do—next. Recently, the company has begun to place greater emphasis upon own-label products in an attempt to boost the image of the quality of its product range. At the same time, it has continued to broaden its operating base by strengthening its position in the south of England. However, when comparisons are made between the UK and continental European discount retailing scenes, an interesting picture emerges. The 'hard discounting' of a limited product range has, for example, proved to be phenomenally successful in Germany, with Aldi, the market leader in this sector, having a turnover in 1999 in its home market alone of some £12 billion. By contrast, its performance in the UK has always lagged behind, something which has led a number of commentators to suggest that there may well be a cultural difference between the shopping habits of the British and their northern European counterparts. George Wallace, the chief executive of Management Horizons, puts it simply: 'In Germany, cheap equals value. You always hear the word *billig* (cheap) being used and it means value. In the UK low prices are not necessarily equated with value and are more often associated with poor quality.' For companies such as Aldi and Netto it is this sort of issue that ultimately is likely to prove their biggest constraint. With the major grocery retailers such as Tesco and Safeway pushing price ever more aggressively, the challenge for Netto will be whether they can get away from the 'low price equals cheap' position to the 'low price equals value' position that would have the effect of attracting a greater number of the higher spending customers from social groups A and B.

This case was prepared by Latchezar Hristov, Senior Lecturer in Marketing and Professor Colin Gilligan, Sheffield Hallam University. The case was made possible by the cooperation of Netto. The authors wish to thank John Rix, managing director of Netto Foodstores Ltd, from 1994 to 1997 and his staff for the help that they provided in preparing this case study.

Questions

1   Identify the key elements of the marketing strategy pursued by Netto since its entry to the UK. How would you characterize the strategy?

2   Pricing is a central part of Netto's marketing strategy. What are the dangers of adopting such a strongly focused approach?

3   With the grocery market becoming ever more competitive and a greater number of organizations fighting for a share of the low-priced sector, how might Netto retain its competitive advantage? What problems might the organization face in doing this?

CHAPTER EIGHTEEN

Competitive Marketing Strategy

'The easiest victories are in those places where there is no enemy'

ANONYMOUS ARMY GENERAL

Learning Objectives *This chapter explains:*

1   The nature of competitive behaviour

2   How military analogies can be applied to competitive marketing strategy

3   The attractive conditions and strategic focus necessary to achieve the following objectives:
   + Build
   + Hold
   + Niche
   + Harvest
   + Divest

4   The nature of frontal, flanking, encirclement, bypass and guerrilla attacks

5   The nature of position, flanking, pre-emptive, counteroffensive and mobile defences and strategic withdrawal

n many markets, competition is the driving force of change. Without competition companies satisfice: they provide satisfactory levels of service but fail to excel. Where there is a conflict between improving customer satisfaction and costs, the latter often takes priority since customers have little choice and cost cutting produces tangible results. Competition, then, is good for the customer as it means that companies have to try harder or lose their customer base. A case in point is the impact of the Eurotunnel on cross-Channel ferry operators. As Barrett commented:[1]

> One thing is certain: Eurotunnel's plans have galvanised the ferry operators and the Dover Harbour Board into making long-overdue changes to their operating procedures. P&O European Ferries announced this month that from next spring [1993] it will operate a cross-Channel service every 45 minutes. Check-in time will also be cut from 30 minutes to 20 minutes.
>
> Dover Harbour Board has met the challenge by drastically streamlining the loading and unloading process. Last month, for the first time, I drove off the ferry at Dover and went straight out of the terminal without stopping—just the briefest pause to wave the passports at the immigration officer.

When developing marketing strategy, companies need to be aware of their own strengths and weaknesses, customer needs, and the competition. This three-pronged approach to strategy development has been termed the strategic triangle and is shown in Fig. 18.1. This framework recognizes that to be successful it is no longer sufficient to be good at satisfying customers' needs: companies need to be better than the competition. In Chapter 17 we discussed various ways of creating

and sustaining a competitive advantage. In this chapter we shall explore the development of marketing strategies in the face of competitive activity and challenges. First, we shall look at alternative modes of competitive behaviour and then, drawing on military analogy, examine when and how to achieve strategic marketing objectives.

Competitive behaviour

Rivalry between firms does not always lead to conflict and aggressive marketing battles. *Competitive behaviour* can take five forms: conflict, competition, coexistence, cooperation and collusion.[2] Competitive behaviour in the EU is likely to change as the impact of the Single Market takes effect. Marketing in Action 18.1 discusses some of the likely repercussions.

Conflict

Conflict is characterized by aggressive competition where the objective is to drive competitors out of the marketplace. British Airways and TWA's successful battle with Laker Airlines is an example of competitive conflict where the financial muscle of the established airlines brought down their price-cutting competitor. More recently British Airways' unsuccessful attempt to discredit Virgin Atlantic by its so-called 'dirty tricks' campaign is another manifestation of conflict.

Competition

The objective of competition is not to eliminate competitors from the marketplace but to perform better than them. This may take the form of trying to achieve faster sales and/or profit growth, larger size or higher market share. Competitive behaviour recognizes the limits of aggression. Competitor reaction will be an important consideration when setting strategy. Players will avoid spoiling the underlying industry structure which is an important influence on overall profit ability. For example, price wars will be avoided if competitors believe that their long-term effect will be to reduce industry profitability.

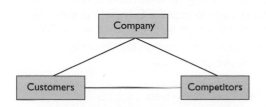

Figure 18.1 The strategic triangle

Coexistence

Three types of coexistence can occur. First, coexistence may arise because firms do not recognize their competitors owing to difficulties in defining market boundaries. For example, a manufacturer of fountain pens may ignore competition from jewellery companies since its definition may be product-based rather than market-centred (i.e. the gift market). Second, firms may not recognize other companies who they believe are operating in a separate market segment. For example, Waterman is likely to ignore the actions of Bic pens as they are operating in different market segments. Third, firms may choose to acknowledge the territories of their competitors (for example, geography, brand personality, market segment or product technology) in order to avoid harmful head-to-head competition.

18.1   Marketing in Action

Competitive Behaviour in the Single European Market

The lowering of trade barriers and the increased focus on cross-border competition in the Single Market are likely to have a bearing on competitive behaviour. There is likely to be a period of conflict as stronger competitors drive out their weaker rivals. Price competition in the face of over-capacity may bring the demise of less efficient, undifferentiated firms. This process is consistent with Europe's aim of becoming more competitive on the global stage.

Increased rivalry from foreign players will intensify competition in national markets. Already there has been an influx of American and Japanese companies setting up production capabilities within the Single Market and the pulling down of barriers between countries of the EU has meant easier access to markets. A particular feature of the more competitive environment is the opportunity for foreign companies to bid for government contracts.

The level of coexistence within national markets will probably fall as new entrants compete with indigenous competitors. The new competition is less likely to recognize the territories of national competitors; instead geographic, brand personality, market segment and product technology intrusion will lower the level of peaceful coexistence in the marketplace.

Cooperation between European companies has taken place long before the advent of the Single Market (for example, the joint development of the Airbus range of aircraft by French, German, UK, Spanish and Belgian manufacturers). However, the concept of a united Europe probably explains part of the growth of strategic alliances in this region. Since 1984 the number of strategic alliances in Europe has grown substantially, notably in electronics, car and aerospace industries, with R&D and production activities being most often involved.

The European Commission has taken an active role in trying to eliminate collusion among European companies. This has continued as part of the strategy to improve European competitiveness worldwide. Their action and the intervention of national anti-cartel bodies such as the Office of Fair Trading in the UK, the Competition Council in France and the German Bundeskartellamt will continue to deter European firms from entering into collusive agreements.

Based on: Bronde and Pritzl (1992);[3] Welford and Prescott (1996);[4] Easton and Araujo (1986)[5]

Cooperation

This involves the pooling of skills and resources of two or more firms to overcome problems and take advantage of new opportunities. A growing trend is towards **strategic alliances** where firms join together through a joint venture, licensing agreement, or joint research and development contract to build a long-term competitive advantage. In today's global market place where size is a key source of advantage, cooperation is a major type of competitive behaviour.

Collusion

The final form of competitive behaviour is collusion whereby firms come to some arrangement that inhibits competition in a market. For example, 23 top European chemical companies in the aftermath of the 1970 oil crisis agreed sales quotas to restrict market share gain through aggressive price cutting. Prices were fixed in order to discourage customers from shopping around to find the cheapest deal.[6] Collusion is more likely where there are a small number of suppliers in each national market, the price of the product is a small proportion of buyer costs, where cross-national trade is restricted by tariff barriers or prohibitive transportation costs, and where buyers are able to pass on high prices to their customers.

Developing competitive marketing strategies

The work of such writers as Ries and Trout and Kotler and Singh has drawn attention to the relationship between military and marketing warfare.[7,8] Their work has stressed the need to develop strategies that were more than customer based. They placed the emphasis on attacking and defending against the competition and used military analogies to guide strategic thinking. They saw competition as the enemy and thus recognized the relevance of the principles of military warfare as put forward by such writers as Sun Tzu and von Clausewitz to business.[9,10] As von Clausewitz wrote:

> Military warfare is a clash between major interests that is resolved by bloodshed—that is

the only way in which it differs from other conflicts. Rather than comparing it to an art we could more accurately compare it to commerce, which is also a conflict of human interests and activities.

Indeed, military terms have been used in business and marketing for many years. Terms such as *launching a campaign, achieving a break-through, company division* and *strategic business unit* are common in business language. Frequently sales and service personnel are referred to as *field forces*.[11]

The context in which we shall explore the development of competitive marketing strategy is the achievement of *strategic marketing objectives*. Four of these objectives have already been discussed—to *build, hold, harvest* and *divest*—to which a fifth objective—to *niche*—is added. The discussion of each objective will focus on the *attractive conditions* which favour its adoption, and the **strategic focus**, which comprises the strategies that can be employed to achieve the objective.*

Build objectives

Attractive conditions

A *build objective* is suitable in *growth markets*. Because overall market sales are growing, all players can achieve higher sales even if the market share of one competitor is falling. This is in marked contrast to mature (no growth) markets where an increase in sales of one player has to be at the expense of the competition (zero sum game).

Some writers point out that if competitors' expectations are high in a growth market (for example because they know that the market is growing) they may retaliate if those expectations are not met.[12] While this is true, their reaction is not likely to be as strong or protracted as in a no growth situation. For example, if expectations have led to an expansion of plant capacity which

---

* The format of this part of Chapter 18 is similar to that of 'Offensive and Defensive Marketing Strategies' in *Competitive Positioning* by John Saunders and Graham Hooley (London: Prentice-Hall). This is because the approach was developed by the author and Graham Hooley when they worked together at the University of Bradford Management Centre.

is not fully utilized because of competitor activity, the situation is not as serious as when over-capacity exists in a no growth market. In the former case, market growth will help fill capacity without recourse to aggressive retaliatory action, whereas, in the latter, capacity utilization will improve only at the expense of competition.

A build objective also makes sense in growth markets because new users are being attracted to the product. Since these new users have not an established brand or supplier loyalty it is logical to invest resources into attracting them to our product offering. Provided the product meets their expectations, trial during the growth phase can lead to the building of goodwill and loyalty as the market matures. A company which has pursued a build objective in growth markets is Cisco Systems as e-Marketing 18.1 explains.

A build objective is also attractive in mature (no growth) markets where there are *exploitable*

18.1   e-Marketing

Building at Cisco

A company which has successfully pursued a build objective is Cisco Systems. For 15 years the firm has doubled in size every year resulting in a company that by 2000 had 29 000 employees, revenue of $12 billion and profits of $3 billion per year. By 2004 Cisco's chief executive John Chambers set himself the ambitious goal of $50 billion in sales revenue. These objectives are possible because of Cisco's enviable position in growth markets.

Cisco make vital equipment for global communications. The backbone of their product line are 'routers' which are high-powered computers that direct traffic around the Internet and corporate intranets. On them, data such as e-mail or web pages are sent around in small packages with an address label. Routers inspect the label and work out the best path for a package to take, and to pass it to the next router. Its expertise in this growth market is such that it supplies 80 per cent of Internet routers.

Cisco is also building through diversification and acquisition. This has been driven by John Chambers, Cisco's chief executive since 1991, whose strategy is to track convergence in the data and telecommunications equipment markets. This has led to moves into other networking hardware such as expensive switches for telephone networks. Cisco's customers not only include large multinationals but also telephone network operators like Telia in Sweden and 'new telcos' like MCIWorld.com and Qwest.

Cisco's acquisition spree is innovative in two ways. First, many of its acquisitions are companies that it helped start-up. In this way it is acquiring the core competences (advanced technology) necessary to compete in highly volatile markets. Second, it has turned acquisitions—notoriously risky particularly in high-tech industries—into a business process. An acquisitions group of 60 people screen companies to see if they are culturally compatible and have the necessary potential. Cisco then works hard to retain staff in the acquired companies as these are their most valuable asset. They are quickly integrated, provided with new opportunities and much freedom.

One of the key ingredients in John Chambers' strategy is customer focus. He was even late for his first board meeting as chief executive because he was helping a customer solve a problem. Every evening he listens to taped telephone conversations with corporate clients. He even bought a company because a major company wanted Cisco to sell the technology it produced.

Based on: Anonymous (2000);[13] Taylor (2000)[14]

competitive weaknesses. For example, Japanese car producers exploited US and European car manufacturers' weaknesses in reliability and build quality; Travelworld, a UK travel agency, exploited their competitors' weakness in providing customer service to would-be holidaymakers; Rowntree Macintosh exploited a weakness in Cadbury's Dairy Milk chocolate bar that had been reduced in thickness to maintain its price as the cost of sugar rose. Group discussion research discovered that chocolate bar buyers were dissatisfied with the thinness of the Cadbury product. Rowntree Macintosh responded with the successful launch of the Yorkie bar, a thicker product positioned on a 'chunkiness' platform. Exploitable competitive weaknesses allow the creation of a differential advantage.

A third attractive condition for building sales and market share is when the company has *exploitable corporate strengths.* For example, Casio built on their core competence in micro-electronics to move from calculators to watches. Marks and Spencer exploited their strength as a reliable, trustworthy retailer to launch a low risk, medium return range of unit trusts. As one financial analyst commented, 'M&S unit trusts will never be in the top ten, but they will never be in the bottom ten either!'

When taking on a market leader, an attractive, indeed a necessary, condition is *adequate corporate resources.* The financial muscle that usually accompanies market leadership and the importance of the situation mean that forceful retaliation can be expected. We have already given the example of Laker Airlines failing to have the financial capability of winning a price war against British Airways and TWA.

Finally, a build objective is attractive when *experience curve effects* are believed to be strong. Some experience curve effects (the combined impact of economies of scale and learning on costs) are related to cumulative output, by building sales faster than the competition, a company can achieve the position of cost leader as United Biscuits have done in the UK.

Strategic focus

A build objective can be achieved in four ways: through market expansion, winning market share from the competition, by merger or acquisition, and by forming strategic alliances.

Market expansion

This is brought about by creating new users or uses, or by increasing frequency of purchase. *New users* may be found by expanding internationally, as Marks and Spencer have done in Europe, or by moving to larger target markets, as with Lucozade which initially was targeted at ill children but now has mass market appeal. *New uses* can be promoted, as when Johnson's Baby Lotion was found to be used by women as a facial cleanser. The technique of brand extension can be used in new use situations. The umbrella based 'Flash' has been extended from a bath cleaner to floors and cookers in this way. *Increasing frequency of use* may rely upon persuasive communications, for example, by persuading people to clean their teeth twice a day rather than only once. Kelloggs attempted to increase the frequency of consumption of their Corn Flakes brand by suggesting that it can be eaten as a snack during the day and at night rather than solely at breakfast time, a move that ran the risk of blurring its distinct brand image.

Winning market share

If a market cannot be expanded, a build strategy implies gaining marketing success at the expense of the competition. In these circumstances the principles of offensive warfare sometimes apply. These are to consider the strength of the leader's position, to find a weakness in the leader's strength and attack at that point. A classic example of these principles being applied in a political context was the 1988 US presidential election. In July 1988 the challenger Michael Dukakis was 17 percentage points ahead of George Bush in the opinion polls. By October 1988 when the election was held, Bush won by 17 percentage points. How did Bush do it? The answer was that Bush identified a weakness in Dukakis's position and attacked remorselessly at that point:

> The post-mortem has already begun. The consensus is that Dukakis allowed Bush to 'define' him, to paint him as a dangerous un-American left-winger before he could present himself to the voters on his own terms.[15]

Clearly in politics the concepts of positioning and competitive strategy apply just as forcefully as in product marketing.

In business, companies seek to win market share through product, distribution, promotional innovation and penetration pricing. Kotler and Singh have identified five competitor confrontation strategies (see Fig. 18.2) designed to win sales and market share.[16]

Frontal attack   this involves the challenger taking on the defender head-on. If the defender is a market leader the success of a head-on challenge is likely to depend upon four factors.[17] First, the challenger should have a clear and sustainable *competitive advantage*. If the advantage is based on cost leadership this will support a low price strategy to fight the market leader. A distinct differential advantage provides the basis for superior customer value. Sustainability is necessary to delay the leader's capability to respond.

Second, the challenger should achieve *proximity in other activities*. In the earth-moving market, John Deere took on Caterpillar with a machine that gave buyers productivity gains; they

failed due to their inability to match Caterpillar in after-sales service.

Third, success is more likely if there is some *restriction on the leader's ability to retaliate*. Restrictions include patent protection, pride, technological lead times and the costs of retaliation. Where a differential advantage or cost leadership position is supported by *patent protection,* imitation by the market leader will be very difficult. *Pride* may hamper retaliation; the market leader refused to imitate because to do so would admit that the challenger had outsmarted the leader. Where the challenge is based upon a technological innovation it may take the leader *time to put in place the new technology*. John Deere's challenge to Caterpillar was based on a hydrostatic drive that would take Caterpillar two to three years to install in their machines. Furthermore, retaliation may be difficult for the market leader because of the *costs* involved. In Chapter 17 we discussed the difficulty of a car number plate market leader marketing the discounts given by a regional competitor as to do so would mean

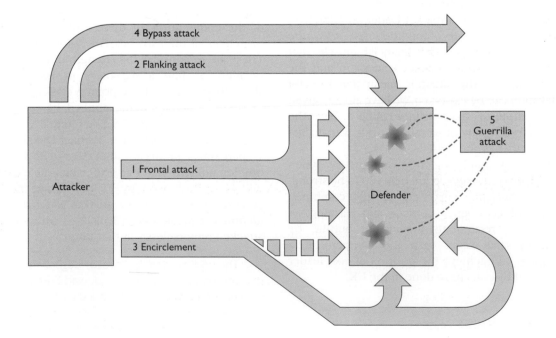

Figure 18.2 Attack strategies.

Source: Kotler, P. and R. Singh (1981) Marketing Warfare in the 1980s, *Journal of Business Strategy*, winter, 30–41. Reprinted with permission of Faulkner and Gray.

giving discounts nationally. The risk of damaging brand image and lowering profit margins may also deter market leaders from responding to price challenges.

Finally, the challenger needs adequate resources to withstand the battle that will take place should the leader retaliate. After studying thirty battles, General von Clausewitz observed that only two had been won by a side with inferior manpower. Napoleon supported the principle of superior force when he said, 'God is on the side of the big battalions'.[18]

In emerging markets, the resources of early challengers can play a vital role in attacking the market pioneer. Marketing in Action 18.2 discusses how Microsoft attacked Netscape in the early market development of the Internet Web browser market.

An example of a challenge to a market leader that succeeded because most of these conditions were met was IBM's attack on Apple, the market leader in the personal computer market.[19] Initially slow into the segment, IBM developed a computer that possessed a competitive advantage over Apple based on a 16-bit processor that was faster and more powerful than Apple's 8-bit machine. IBM also persuaded software houses to develop a wide range of software that would run only on their machines. Buyers would therefore have a wider choice of software from which to choose if they bought an IBM rather than an Apple computer (a major differential advantage). IBM also managed to achieve proximity to Apple in other activities, particularly in terms of reliability and after-sales service.

Apple refused to follow IBM's route regarding software, preferring to remain distinctive (perhaps pride was a factor here). Instead they retaliated by launching the MacIntosh based on an *ease of use* differential advantage. IBM, therefore, still held the software edge.

IBM's massive resources based upon their mainframe computer cash cows enabled them to launch a powerful promotional campaign aimed at the business market. IBM's ability to create a differential advantage, their ability initially to match Apple on other activities, Apple's inability to generate as wide a range of software as IBM, and IBM's superior resources were the platform which led to IBM overtaking Apple as market leader. Furthermore, IBM's inability to sustain their differential advantage with software as IBM clones entered the market with cheaper prices has been a major factor in their recent downturn in sales and profits.[20]

As Table 18.1 illustrates, many markets are characterized by head-to-head competition between the major protagonists. It is not only companies who compete head-to-head: countries do so also. For example, Malaysia and Singapore are rivals since both countries want to be the region's financial centre, both want to be its air and sea transport hub and each is competing to attract direct investment from leaders in information technology.[21]

Flanking attack this involves attacking unguarded or weakly guarded ground. In marketing terms it means attacking geographical areas or market segments where the defender is

Table 18.1 Major marketing head-to-heads	
Companies	*Competitive area*
Nike v. Reebok	Footwear
Sega v. Sony	Computer games
Ever Ready v. Duracell	Batteries
Coca-Cola v. Pepsi	Soft drinks
McDonald's v. Burger King	Fast food restaurants
GEC-Alsthom v. Asea Brown Boveri	Power engineering
Unilever v. Procter and Gamble	Fast moving consumer goods
Unilever v. Mars	Ice cream
Motorola v. Nokia	Mobile telephones
IBM v. Fujitsu	Computers
Microsoft v. Netscape	Internet Web-browsers

18.2 Marketing in Action

The Browser Wars

When Marc Andreeson launched the first commercial Web browser in 1995 his newly floated company Netscape was valued at $2.7 billion. Its value was based on the potential that its pioneer Navigator browser software made it easy to access the World Wide Web. Not that the software, itself, was profitable; it could not be since it was given away free to computer users. Profits were made by charging companies who run websites for its Netscape 'server' software. The server is the platform for providing online services to web users. The strategy was so successful that by 1996 Netscape had claimed 85 per cent market share, and the value of the company had risen to $6 billion.

The future looked anything but rosy, however. A strong rival by the name of Microsoft was set to challenge Netscape's dominance. The company marketed its own package but this was inferior to the market leader and Microsoft were regarded as being at least one year behind Netscape's technology. To catch up, Bill Gates, the boss at Microsoft, threw hundreds of millions of dollars and 2000 of his best programmers at the problem. The result was the launch of Internet Explorer 3.0 which matched its rival's performance. Meanwhile, financial economics meant that Netscape had begun to charge users $49 for its Navigator software. Microsoft's financial muscle meant that it would supply its browser software free of charge and that its domination of the PC software meant that Internet Explorer would be supplied as part of the Windows 95 package to 46 million users in 1997.

By the time Internet Explorer 4.0 (IE4) was launched in late 1997, Microsoft held 36 per cent market share in the USA and 47 per cent of the UK browser market. One of the main features of IE4 is the introduction of 'push technology' which enables users to receive several streams of automatically updated information on their screens. This has major appeal to media owners such as Pearson (who own the *Financial Times*) since it means that live news can flow on to users' screens automatically, rather than having websites that have to be visited.

A major twist in the 'browser wars' story took place in 1999 when Microsoft faced an anti-trust lawsuit by the US Government. Microsoft was accused of exploiting its monopoly power in order to reduce competition. The US Justice Department claimed that the practice of integrating its Internet Explorer software with its Windows operating system acted to shut out its main competitor Netscape Navigator. The department wanted Microsoft to stop making PC manufacturers use its browser software as a condition of being allowed to install Windows on their machines. Microsoft also faced accusations of applying pressure on America On-Line to prevent the promotion of the Netscape browser on its platform. By 1999 Microsoft market share had risen to 64 per cent with Netscape's share falling to 36 per cent. Netscape, unable to survive alone, was sold to America On-Line in that year. A legal ruling was made in 2000 with Microsoft being found guilty of violating sections of the Anti-trust Act, bringing the threat of Microsoft being split up a distinct possibility.

Based on: Barksdale (1996);[22] Garrett (1997);[23] Alexander (1999);[24] Alexander (1999);[25] Marsh (1998);[26] Anonymous (2000)[27]

Future-proof.

That's the Seiko Perpetual Calendar watch.

It will adjust the date automatically for the next 100 years.

Even leap years.

And it's travel-proof.

It stays accurate to within an amazing 20 seconds a year,

even when you adjust it for different time zones

and Winter/Summer Time.

It has an extra hour hand that shows you another time zone

simultaneously. And it's water resistant to 100 metres.

What more proof do you need?

SEIKO

www.seiko.co.uk   Tel: 01628 410344

IF YOU'RE GOING TO CREATE ELECTRICITY, USE IT.

Wear the watch that's electrically charged

every time you move your body.

The Seiko Kinetic Arctura.

No need to change a battery.

Quartz accuracy. Revolutionary.

SEIKO
KINETIC

www.seiko.co.uk   Tel: 01628 410344

Seiko produce hundreds of watches to cater for diverse customer tastes. Here are two technologically advanced watches targeting young women and men

poorly represented. For example, in the USA as major supermarket chains moved out of town, the 7–11 chain prospered by opening stores that provided the convenience of local availability and longer opening hours. The attack by Japanese companies on the European and US car markets was a flanking attack—the small car segment—from which they have expanded into other segments including sports cars. The success of Next, a retail clothing chain, was based on spotting an underserved, emerging market segment: working women aged 25–40 who were finding difficulty in buying stylish clothes at reasonable prices.

Another successful example of a flanking attack was Digital Equipment Company's move into minicomputers, a market segment that was inadequately served by IBM. More recently Mars attacked Unilever's Wall's ice cream subsidiary in Europe by launching a range of premium brands such as their ice cream Mars bar in 1988 and a series of ice cream versions of their chocolate brands such as Snickers, Galaxy and Bounty. This flanking attack was regarded by Unilever in the early 1990s as a major threat to their ice cream business. Their response was to launch a range of premium brands themselves, including Magnum and Gino Ginelli, and to defend vigorously their *shop exclusivity deals*, which prevent competitors from selling their products in shops which sell Wall's ice cream, and *freezer exclusivity*, which prohibits competitors from placing their ice cream in Unilever supplied freezer cabinets.

The advantage of a flanking attack is that it does not provoke the same kind of response as a head-on confrontation. Since the defender is not challenged in its main market segments, there is more chance that it will ignore the challenger's initial successes. If the defender dallies too long, the flank segment can be used as a beachhead from which to attack the defender in its major markets, as Japanese companies have repeatedly done.

Encirclement attack   this involves attacking the defender from all sides. Every market segment is hit with every combination of product features to completely encircle the defender. An example is Seiko, who produce over 2000 designs of watches for the market worldwide. They cover everything the customer might want in terms of fashion and features. The two advertisements here target young men and women. A variant on this approach is to cut off supplies to the defender. This could be achieved by the acquisition of major supply companies.

Bypass attack this circumvents the defender's position, as the German army did in 1940 when it bypassed the Maginot Line, built by the French to protect themselves from invasion.

In business, a bypass attack changes the rules of the game, usually through technological leap-frogging as Casio did when bypassing Swiss analogue watches with digital technology. A bypass attack can also be accomplished through diversification. An attacker can bypass a defender by seeking growth in new markets with new products, as Marks and Spencer have done with their move into financial services.

Guerrilla attack this hurts the defender by pin-pricks rather than blows. Just as the French Resistance used guerrilla tactics against the German forces in the Second World War, not to defeat the enemy but to weaken it, so in business the underdog can make life uncomfortable for its stronger rivals. Unpredictable price discounts, sales promotions or heavy advertising in a few television regions are some of the tactics that attackers can use to cause problems for the defender.

Guerrilla tactics may be the only feasible option for a small company facing a larger competitor. Such tactics allow the small company to make its presence felt without the dangers of a full frontal attack. By being unpredictable, guerrilla activity is difficult to defend against. Nevertheless, such tactics run the risk of incurring the wrath of the defender who may choose to retaliate with a full frontal attack if sufficiently provoked.

Merger or acquisition

A third approach to achieving a build objective is to merge with or acquire competitors. By joining forces costly marketing battles are avoided, and purchasing, production, financial, marketing and R&D synergies may be gained. Further, a merger can give the scale of operation that may be required to operate as an international force in the marketplace. Mergers are not without their risks not least when they involve parties from different countries. Differences in culture, language, business practices, and the problems associated

with restructuring may cause terminal strains. Two European examples of merger failure are Dunlop and Pirelli (rubber) and Hoechst and Hoogovens (steel). Indeed, a study by McKinsey management consultants into the success or failure of 319 mergers and acquisitions claimed that about half had been successful in terms of post acquisition return on equity and assets, and whether or not they exceeded the acquiror's cost of capital.[28]

In marketing terms, mergers and acquisitions give an immediate sales boost, and when the players operate in the same market an increase in market share. However, companies considering merger have to be very careful that the benefits exceed the costs as Marketing in Action 18.3 illustrates.

Forming strategic alliances

A final option for companies seeking to build is the strategic alliance. The aim is to create a long-term competitive advantage for the partners, often on a global scale. The partners typically collaborate by means of a joint venture (a jointly owned company), licensing agreements, long-term purchasing and supply arrangements, or joint R&D programmes. Strategic alliances maintain a degree of flexibility not apparent with a merger or acquisition. The advertisement overleaf illustrates the strategic alliance between AT&T and BT.

A major motivation for strategic alliances is the sharing of product development costs, and risks. For example, the cost of developing and creating manufacturing facilities for a new car targeted at world markets exceeds £2 billion and developing a new drug can cost over £25 million. Sharing these costs may be the only serviceable economic option for a medium-sized manufacturer in either of these industries.

Marketing benefits, also, can accrue. For example, access to new markets and distribution channels can be achieved, time to market reduced, product gaps filled and product lines widened.[29] It was to take advantage of marketing opportunities in financial services that Tesco partners a bank and Virgin an insurance company. Furthermore, a strategic alliance can be the initial stage to a merger or acquisition allowing each party to assess their abilities to work together effectively. Marketing in Action 18.4 describes how three strategic alliances have been used successfully to build sales, market share and profits.

18.3   Marketing in Action

Counting the Cost of Mergers and Acquisitions

Mergers and acquisitions remain a popular tool for growing businesses. Lured by the potential benefits of complementary businesses that allow the merger partners to increase sales revenues, and the cost savings that can be made, a large number of companies are following this route to strategic development including:

Ford–Volvo
Vodafone Airtouch–Mannesmann
Renault–Nissan
Glaxo Wellcome–SmithKline Beecham
Ford–Kwikfit
Wal-Mart–Asda
America Online–Time Warner
Carrefour–Promodès.

But studies have shown that 65 per cent of mergers fail to benefit shareholders. There are several reasons for this. One is poor implementation. A key issue is the blending of two different corporate cultures. It is not so much a problem of open warfare but a situation where the culture of the two partners do not meld quickly enough to take advantage of new opportunities. Meanwhile the marketplace has moved on. A second issue is that often too little time is spent before a merger thinking about whether the two organizations really are compatible and what the possible negative consequences might be. A classic case is PepsiCo's acquisition of major fast-food operators KFC, Pizza Hut and Taco Bell.

The marriage of a soft drinks manufacturer and fast-food seemed highly sensible. The offers were complementary: cola and fast-food is like bees and honey. Pepsi were guaranteed distribution in a high-growth market in a way which automatically excluded Coca Cola from key outlets. There were also numerous opportunities for joint promotional initiatives. What was underestimated were the problems. Becoming partners with KFC meant that rival fast food outlets such as McDonald's rejected Pepsi in favour of Coca-Cola. So what appeared to be a route to expansion actually tethered Pepsi leaving Coke a free rein.

The Pepsi link also constrained their fast-food outlets particularly in countries where Pepsi was a poor also-ran to Coke. In these markets, their fast-food outlets wanted to give the customers what they wanted (Coke) but could not do so because of their ownership. The result was conflict, not synergy.

A third issue with mergers is deciding who is in charge. Mergers of equals can be dangerous because it is not always clear who is the boss. This can lead to indecision while more nimble competitors move ahead.

Two key questions that companies need to ask themselves are: (i) what advantages will the merger or acquisition bring that competitors will find difficult to match and (ii) would the premium that is usually paid to the shareholders of the acquired company be better spent elsewhere, for example on improved customer service

Based on: Mitchell (2000);[30] Shapinker (2000)[31]

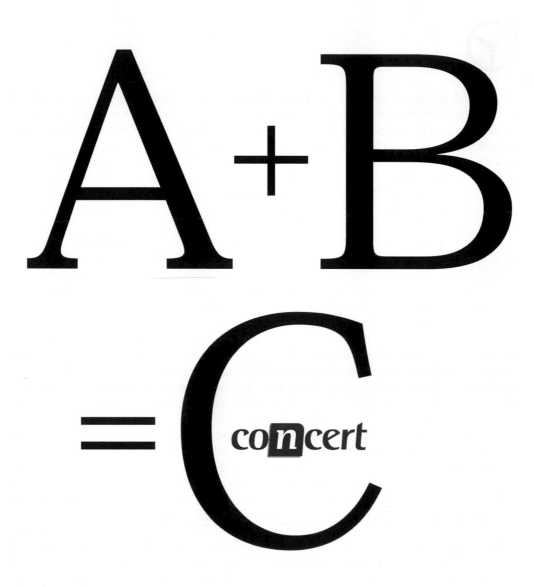

Simplicity^n

Announcing the creation of a new company that will provide simpler solutions to the complexities of global communications. Concert. A new joint venture that harnesses the resources of AT&T and BT to make connectivity work like never before. Whether you're a start-up Internet service provider, an established multinational or a global carrier, Concert offers the expertise to make sense of communications technology today, and the power to deliver your dreams tomorrow.
When communications are as simple as ABC, the possibilities are endless^n

Global communications simplified to the nth degree.

www.concert.com

AT&T and BT form a strategic alliance to compete in the global communications market

18.4   Marketing in Action

Building Through Strategic Alliances

Europe has encountered a wave of strategic alliances creating a *borderless world* where firms adopt to a changing environment by constantly changing shape. Instead of going-it-alone they form partnerships with their rivals for mutual benefit. Nowhere was the joining of arch-rivals for dual gain more striking than the alliance between Glaxo, the UK pharmaceutical company, and Hoffman-La Roche of Switzerland to market Zantac, a drug for treating stomach ulcers. Rather than building a large sales and distribution network to cover all US hospitals, Glaxo gave Hoffman-La Roche the rights to all US sales through their established distribution network. Similar deals were stuck with Sankyo (Japan), Merck (Germany) and Fournier (France). The result was that Zantac became the most successful pharmaceutical product of all time.

A second spectacular success for the strategic alliance was JVC's attempt to establish VHS as the global standard for video recording. Faced with a powerful rival—Sony's Betamax format that possessed superior picture quality—JVC formed a myriad of alliances with consumer electronics firms around the world. VHS was licensed to Japanese video recorder manufacturers, joint ventures were formed with Thorn-EMI-Ferguson (UK) and Telefunken (Germany) and JVC supplied RCA-branded video recorders for the US market.

A third success story was the alliance between German, French, UK, Belgian and Spanish aircraft manufacturers to compete with the US market leaders Boeing and McDonnell Douglas for civil transportation aircraft. The objectives of the European alliance was to gain the development and production expertise for civil aircraft for the twenty-first century, and to share the enormous R&D costs of a new aircraft. The result was that Airbus Industries developed and built a full range of civil aircraft, pushing McDonnell Douglas into third place in the industry.

These three examples show how the strategic alliance can be used to build sales, market share and profits. This is not to say that it is a panacea for growth. Cultural problems and differing managerial styles can cause the demise of an alliance. For example, the ill-fated alliance between the Metal Box Company (UK) and Carnaud (France) in packaging was plagued with these kinds of problems. Eurotunnel, too, suffered from the differences between the British and French way of doing business. For example, while British managers attended meetings to make decisions, the French went to find out what the boss had decided to do.

Nevertheless, the advantages of strategic alliances as a basis for growth are leading to a flurry of activity within the mobile computing sector. The big prize is leadership in the market for Internet access through mobile phones. These devices enable users to retrieve and answer their e-mail, surf the Internet or buy goods and services anywhere rather than being limited to PC access. This requires the combining of handheld cellular and Internet technologies leading to an alliance between Microsoft and BT, the formation of the Symbian alliance between Psion, the UK computer company, and Ericsson, Nokia and Motorola, the world's top three mobile-phone manufacturers, and an alliance between Siemens and Yahoo!

Based on: Bronder and Pritzl (1992);[32] Lorenz (1992);[33] Lorenz (1993);[34] Ohmae[35] Alexander (1999);[36] Cane (2000)[37]

Table 18.2	Some key European strategic alliances

Companies	Competitive area
Electrolux–AEG	Household appliances
Maersk–P&O	Shipping services to Middle East
Rolls-Royce–Pratt & Whitney	Aero-engines
GEC–Alsthom	Power engineering
Hoechst–Mitsubishi	Disperse dyes
Lufthansa–United Airlines	Airlines
Nestlé–Baxter Healthcare	Clinical nutrition
Nestlé–General Mills	Ready to eat breakfast cereals
Nestlé–Coca-Cola	Ready to drink tea and coffee
Unilever–PepsiCo	Develop and distribute tea-based products in USA
Unilever–BSN	Develop and market products combining ice cream and yoghurt
Glaxo–Roche	Pharmaceuticals
Ford–GM	Cars
Seagram–Bertelsmann	Sell disks on-line
Microsoft–BT	Internet and corporate data communications services
Psion–Ericsson–Nokia–Motorola	Computer and telecommunications products

A key factor in benefiting from strategic alliances is the desire and ability to learn from the alliance partner. Japanese companies have excelled at this, while European and US companies have traditionally lagged. The risk is that the alliance leaks technological and core capabilities to the partner thereby giving away important competitive information. This one-way transfer of skills should be avoided by building barriers to capability seepage: core competences should be protected at all costs. This is easier when a company has few alliances, when only a limited part of the organization is involved, and when the relationships built up in the alliance are stable.[38]

The number of strategic alliances in Europe has grown since 1984, particularly in electronics, car, aerospace and food industries.[39] For example, Philips has formed alliances with SGS Thomson (semi-conductors), Grundig (video equipment, cordless telephones), Motorola (semi-conductors), Kodak (Photo-CD) and Matsushita (intelligent audio-visual products).[40] Table 18.2 lists some of the other major alliances involving European firms.

A summary of the key attractive conditions and strategic focuses for build objectives is given in Table 18.3.

Table 18.3	Build objectives

Attractive conditions
Growth markets
Exploitable competitive weaknesses
Exploitable corporate strengths
Adequate corporate resources

Strategic focus
Market expansion
✦ New users
✦ New uses
✦ Increasing frequency of use
Winning market share
✦ Product innovation
✦ Distribution innovation
✦ Promotional innovation
✦ Penetration pricing
✦ Competitor confrontation
Merger or acquisition
Forming strategic alliances

Hold objectives

Hold objectives involve defending a company's current position against would-be attackers. The principles of defensive warfare are, therefore, relevant. Perhaps the principle that has the most relevance in business is the recognition that strong competitive moves should always be blocked. Earlier when discussing attack strategies, we saw how George Bush successfully applied a principle of offensive warfare by identifying a weakness in his opponent and concentrating a major attack at that point. It was Dukakis's failure to implement this principle of defensive warfare that compounded his problems. He recognized that Bush's attack should have been immediately countered:

> There was a poignant moment last week when a young boy told him [Dukakis] he would be playing his part in a school mock election. What advice did he have? 'Respond to the attacks immediately', said Dukakis, grinning.[41]

The lesson was not lost on Bill Clinton during his successful challenge to George Bush in the 1992 presidential election. His strategists established a 24-hour response capability to any Bush attack. As predicted, Bush attempted to position Clinton as a man of high taxes. Clinton was accused in a television advertisement of increasing taxes if elected. The advertisement featured the kinds of people who would suffer with the amount of extra tax they would have to pay. Within 24 hours Clinton ran his own advertisement quoting the *Washington Post* as stating that the Republican ad was misleading. This fast response capability was believed by the Democrats to be a major factor in Clinton's ability to maintain his opinion poll lead, and emerge the victor in the election. In the UK the Labour Party studied the electoral tactics of the Clinton administration and many, such as the fast response capability, were implemented in their successful challenge to the Conservative government in 1997.

We shall now analyse the conditions that make a hold objective attractive and the strategic focus necessary to achieve the objective.

Attractive conditions

The classic situation where a hold objective makes strategic sense is a *market leader in a mature or declining market*. This is the standard cash cow position discussed as part of the Boston Consulting Group market share/market growth rate analysis. By holding on to market leadership, a product should generate positive cash flows which can be used elsewhere in the company to build other products and invest in new product development. Holding on to market leadership

per se makes sense because brand leaders enjoy the marketing benefits of bargaining power with distribution outlets, and brand image (the number one position) as well as enjoying experience curve effects that reduce costs. Furthermore, in a declining market, maintaining market leadership may result in becoming a virtual monopolist as weaker competitors withdraw.

A second situation where holding is suitable is in *growth markets when the costs of attempting to build sales and market share outweigh the benefits*. This may be the case in the face of aggressive rivals who will respond strongly if attacked. In such circumstances it may be prudent to be content with the status quo, and avoid actions that are likely to provoke the competition.

Strategic focus

A hold objective may be achieved by monitoring the competition or by confronting the competition.

Monitoring the competition

In a market that is characterized by competitive stability the required focus is simply to *monitor the competition*. Perhaps everyone is playing the 'good competitor' game, content with what they have, and no one is willing to destabilize industry structure. Monitoring is necessary to check that there are no significant changes in competitor behaviour but beyond that no change in strategy is required.

Confronting the competition

In circumstances where rivalry is more pronounced, strategic action may be required to defend sales and market share from aggressive challenges. The principles of defensive warfare provide a framework for identifying strategic alternatives that can be used in this situation. Figure 18.3 illustrates six methods of defence derived from military strategy.[42]

Position defence this involves building a fortification around one's existing territory as the French did with their Maginot Line. Unfortunately this static defence strategy was unsuccessful because the Germans simply went around it. In marketing, the analogy is to build a fortification around existing products. It reflects a philosophy that the company has good products; all that is needed is to price them competitively and promote them effectively. This is more likely to work if the products have differential advantages that are not easily copied, for example through patent protection. Also marketing assets like brand names and reputation may provide a strong defence against aggressors but it can be a dangerous strategy. For example, Ever Ready's refusal to develop an alkaline battery in the face of an aggressive challenge to their market leadership by Duracell was an example of a position defence. Instead they stuck with their zinc-carbon product that had a shorter life than its alkaline rival, and invested £2 million in promotion. Only after Hanson acquired the company did Ever Ready develop their own alkaline battery. By 1991 the alkaline segment accounted for 58 per cent of the battery market by value.[43]

Land Rover and Range Rover provide another instance of an unsuccessful position defence. Based on a belief of their invincibility, they conducted very little new product development. This created the opportunity for Subaru to introduce their cheaper, 'fun' four-wheel-drive vehicles. Only belatedly did Land Rover respond by developing the successful Discovery model.

Flanking defence this is characterized by the defence of a hitherto unprotected market segment. The danger is that if the segment is left unprotected, it will provide a beachhead for new entrants to gain experience in the market, and attack the main market later. This means that it can make sense for a defender to compete in a segment that in pure short-term profitability terms looks unattractive if it helps to avoid or slow down competitive inroads. A further problem is that the defence of the segment may be half-hearted as it is not central to the main business. An example is General Motors and Ford's weak attempts to build a small car to compete with Volkswagen and the Japanese companies. The products—the Vega and Pinto—suffered from poor build quality and unreliability and proved ineffective in defending the exposed flank.

Failure to defend an emerging market segment can have catastrophic consequences. For example, Distillers, who were dominant in the market for blended Scotch Whisky with their Johnny Walker, Dewars and White Horse brands, ignored the growing malt whisky and white spirit segments. This preoccupation with the declining blended whisky segment resulted in disappointing performance and a successful take-over by Guinness in 1986.

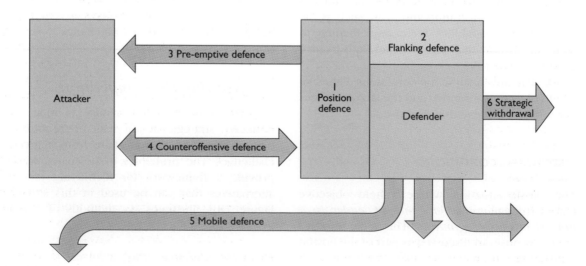

Figure 18.3 Defence strategies.

Source: Kotler, P. and R. Singh (1981) Marketing Warfare in the 1980s, *Journal of Business Strategy*, winter, 30–41. Reprinted with permission of Faulkner and Gray.

Pre-emptive defence this follows the philosophy that the best form of defence is to attack first. This may involve continuous innovation and new product development, a situation characteristic of the camcorder market. Japanese manufacturers are caught up in a continuous spiral of product introductions (known as *product churning*). Failure to maintain this rate of change would soon lead to product obsolescence and market share collapse.

A pre-emptive defence may also be used to dissuade a would-be attacker. For example, ICI, the market leader in the UK chemical fertilizer market, feared that Norsk Hydro's purchase of Fisons, the number two in the market, would bring a strong offensive from the Norwegian company. ICI's strategy was to launch a pre-emptive defence by severely cutting the price of their fertilizer brands, thereby reducing profitability which made future plant expansion less attractive to Norsk Hydro. These actions succeeded in discouraging Norsk Hydro from increasing capacity in the UK.[44]

Counteroffensive defence a defender can choose from three options when considering a counteroffensive defence. It can embark upon a head-on counterattack, hit the attacker's cash cow, or encircle the attacker.

With a *head-on counterattack* a defender matches or exceeds what the attacker has done. This may involve heavy price cutting or promotion expenditure, for example. This can be a costly operation but may be justified to deter a persistent attacker. Alternatively, the counterattack may be based on innovation, as when Apple counterattacked IBM's challenge in the personal computer market by launching the successful Macintosh.

Hitting the attacker's cash cow strikes at the attacker's resource supply-line. For example, when Xerox attacked IBM in the mainframe computer market, IBM counterattacked by striking at Xerox's cash cow (the medium-range photocopier) with a limited range of low-priced copiers plus leasing arrangements that were particularly attractive to Xerox's target market (smaller businesses). The result was that Xerox sold their computer business to Honeywell, and concentrated on defending copiers.[45]

The third strategic option is to *encircle the attacker*. This strategy was successfully employed by Heublein when their Smirnoff vodka brand

was attacked by the cheaper Wolfsmidt brand in the USA. Their response was to maintain the price of Smirnoff while launching two new brands, one at the same price as Wolfsmidt and one at a lower price. This manoeuvre successfully defended Heublein's position as market leader in the vodka market.

Mobile defence when a company's major market is under threat a mobile defence may make strategic sense. The two options are diversification and market broadening. A classic example of a company using *diversification* as a form of mobile defence was Imperial Tobacco, who responded to the health threat to their cigarette business by diversifying into food and leisure markets. *Market broadening* involves broadening the business definition, as film companies like Warner Brothers did in the face of declining cinema audiences. By defining their business as entertainment providers rather than film makers, they successfully moved into television, gambling and theme parks.

Strategic withdrawal a strategic withdrawal, or contraction defence, requires a company to define its strengths and weaknesses, and then to hold on to its strengths while divesting its weaknesses. This results in the company concentrating on its core business. At a business unit level this strategy was successfully carried out by Tube Investments (latterly TI) which sold their consumer divisions (e.g. Creda, Raleigh) to concentrate on supplying engineering products to industrial markets. Nokia, also practised strategic withdrawal moving initially from a paper, rubber goods and cables group into computers, consumer electronics and telecoms and then, very successfully, concentrating on mobile telecoms (mainly mobile telephones and telecoms infrastructure). Along with Motorola and Ericsson, Nokia dominate the mobile handset market. At the product level, Woolworth rationalized their product lines to specialize on strong areas such as do-it-yourself products, gardening items and confectionery, and ceased selling food and white goods (e.g. refrigerators) in their stores.

A strategic withdrawal allows a company to focus on its core competences and is often required when diversification has resulted in too wide a spread of activities away from what it does really well. Peters and Waterman termed this focus on core skills and competences *sticking to your knitting*.[46]

Table 18.4 summarizes the key points for hold objectives.

Niche objectives

A company may decide to pursue a market *niche objective* by pursuing a small market segment or even a segment within a segment. In doing so it may avoid competition with companies which are serving the major market segments. However, niche-orientated companies, if successful, run the risk that larger competitors are attracted into the segment. For example, the success of Sock Shop, a niche provider of stylish men's socks, stimulated large department stores such as Marks and Spencer to launch their own competitive ranges.

Attractive conditions

Nicheing may be the only feasible objective for companies with a *small budget* and where *strong competitors are dominating the main segments*. As such it may be an attractive option for small companies which lack the resources to compete directly against the major players. But there need to be *pockets within the market that provide the opportunity for profitable operations*, and in which a *competitive advantage can be created*. Typical circumstances where these conditions apply are when the major players are underserving a particular group of customers as they attempt to meet the needs of the majority of customers, and where the market niche is too small to be of interest to them.

Strategic focus

A key strategic tool for a niche-orientated company is *market segmentation*. Management should be vigilant in their search for underserved segments that may provide profitable opportunities. The choice will depend upon the attractiveness of the niche and the capability of the company to serve it. Once selected, effort, particularly research and development expenditure, will be focused on serving customer needs. *Focused R&D expenditure* gives a small company a chance to make effective use of its limited resources.[47] The emphasis should be on creating and sustaining a *differential advantage* through

Table 18.4	Hold objectives
Attractive conditions	
Market leader in a mature or declining market	
Costs exceed benefits of building	
Strategic focus	
Monitoring the competition	
Confronting the competition	

Table 18.5	Niche objectives
Attractive conditions	
Small budget	
Strong competitors dominating major segments	
Pockets existing for profitable operations	
Creating a competitive advantage	
Strategic focus	
Market segmentation	
Focused R&D	
Differentiation	
Thinking small	

intimately understanding the needs of the customer group, and focusing attention on satisfying those needs better than the competition. Finally, niche operators should be wary of pursuing growth strategies by broadening their customer base. Often this will lead to a blurring of the differential advantage upon which their success has been built. Indeed, since some niche companies trade on *exclusivity*, to broaden their market base would by definition run the risk of diluting their differential advantage. TVR, which specializes in distinctive, high performance sports cars, is a company that consistently pursues a niche objective. TVR consciously *thinks small* eschewing unsustainable growth in favour of profitability. The emphasis is on high margin not high volume. Table 18.5 summarizes this discussion on niche objectives.

Harvest objectives

A company embarking upon a *harvest objective* attempts to improve unit profit margins even if the result is falling sales. Although sales are falling, the aim is to make the company or product extremely profitable in the short term, generating large positive cash flows that can be used elsewhere in the business (for example, to build stars, and selected problem children, or to fund new product development).

Attractive conditions

Also-ran products or companies in *mature or declining markets* (dogs) may be candidates for harvesting, since they are often losing money, and taking up valuable management time and effort.[48] Harvesting actions can move them to a profitable stance, and reduce management attention to a minimum. In *growth markets* harvesting can also make sense where the *costs of building or holding exceed the benefits*. These are problem children companies or products that have little long-term potential. Harvesting is particularly attractive if a *core of loyal customers* exists, which means that sales decline to a stable level. For example, a Smith Kline Beecham hair product, Brylcream, was harvested but sales decline was not terminal as a group of men who used the product in their adolescence continued to buy it in later life. This core of loyal customers meant that it was profitable to market Brylcream as R&D and marketing expenditure was minimal. More recently Brylcream has been repositioned as a hair gel targeting young men. A final attractive condition is where future breadwinners exist in the company or product portfolio to provide future sales and profit growth potential. Obviously harvesting a one product company is likely to lead to its demise.

Strategic focus

Implementing a harvest objective begins with *eliminating research and development expenditure*. The only product change that will be contemplated is *reformulations* that reduce raw material and/or manufacturing costs. *Rationalization of the product line* to one or a few top sellers cuts costs by eliminating expensive product variants. *Marketing support is reduced* by slashing advertising and promotional budgets, while every opportunity is taken to *increase price*.

Table 18.6 summarizes the attractive con-

ditions and strategic focus for achieving harvest objectives.

Divest objectives

A company may decide to *divest* itself of a strategic business unit or product. In doing so it may stem the flow of cash to a poorly performing area of its business.

Attractive conditions

Divestment is often associated with *loss making products or businesses* that are a drain on both financial and managerial resources. *Low share products or businesses in declining markets* (dogs) are prime candidates for divestment. Other areas may be considered for divestment when it is judged that the *costs of turnaround exceed the benefits*. As such, also-rans in growth markets may be divested, sometimes after harvesting has run its full course. However, care must be taken to examine interrelationships within the corporate portfolio. For example, if a product is making a loss it would still be worth while supporting it if its removal would *adversely affect sales of other products*. In some industrial markets, customers expect a supplier to provide a full range of products. Consequently, even though some may not be profitable, sales of the whole range may be affected if the loss makers are dropped.

Table 18.6   Harvest objectives

Attractive conditions
  Market is mature or declining (dog products)
  In growth markets where the costs of building or holding exceed the benefits (selected problem children)
  Core of loyal customers
  Future breadwinners exist

Strategic focus
  Eliminate R&D expenditure
  Product reformulation
  Rationalize product line
  Cut marketing support
  Consider increasing price

Strategic focus

Because of the drain on profits and cash flow once a decision to divest has been made, the focus should be to *get out quickly so as to minimize costs*. If a buyer can be found then some return may be realized; if not the product will be withdrawn or the business terminated.

Table 18.7 summarizes the attractive conditions and strategic focuses relating to divestment.

Table 18.7 Divest objectives
Attractive conditions
Loss-making products or businesses: drain on resources
Often low share in declining markets
Costs of turnaround exceed benefits
Removal will not significantly affect sales of other products
Strategic focus
Get out quickly: minimize the costs

Summary

Competitive behaviour shapes markets and fuels change. It can comprise conflict, competition, coexistence, cooperation and collusion. Military analogies have been drawn upon to identify strategic options under the conditions of conflict and competition. These have been discussed within the context of the achievement of build and hold objectives. For build objectives the strategies of frontal, flank, encirclement, bypass and guerrilla attacks provide five options for companies wishing to build sales and/or market share. Position, flank, pre-emptive, counter-offensive and mobile defences and strategic withdrawal are options for companies defending sales and/or market share against aggressive competitors.

Other strategic objectives are to niche, harvest and divest. Each requires a specific strategic focus, and the decision regarding which option to choose for a given product or business is dependent on the conditions facing the company. This chapter has highlighted the attractive conditions favouring each option.

Internet exercise

Market strategies

Sites to visit
http://www.waterstones.co.uk
http://www.borders.com
http://www.bertelsmann.dee
http://www.whsmith.co.uk
http://www.amazon.com

Exercise
Discuss the strategies which book publishers and retailers are adopting in the European market.

Study questions

1   Why do many monopolies provide poor service to their customers?

2   Discuss the likely impact of the Single European Market on competitive behaviour.

3   Compare and contrast the conditions conducive to building and holding sales/market share.

4   Why is a position defence risky?

5   Why are strategic alliances popular in Europe? How do they differ from mergers?

6   A company should always attempt to harvest a product before considering divestment. Discuss.

7   In defence it is always wise to respond to serious attacks immediately. Do you agree? Explain your answer.

References

1.   Barratt, F. (1992) Britain Lets Down the Drawbridge, *The Independent*, 19 September, 43.

2.   Easton, G. and L. Araujo (1986) Networks, Bonding and Relationships in Industrial Markets, *Industrial Marketing and Purchasing*, **1** (1), 8–25.

3.   Bronder, C. and R. Pritzl (1992) Developing Strategic Alliances: A Conceptual Framework for Successful Cooperation, *European Management Journal*, **10** (4), 412–21.

4.   Welford, R. and K. Prescott (1996) *European Business: An Issue-based Approach*, London: Pitman, 131–3,

5.   Easton, G. and L. Araujo (1986); Networks, Branding and Relationships in Industrial Markets, *Industrial Marketing and Purchasing*, **1** (1), 8–25.

6.   Welford, R. and K. Prescott (1996) *European Business: An Issue-based Approach*, London: Pitman, 76.

7.   Ries, A. and J. Trout (1986) *Marketing Warfare*, New York: McGraw-Hill.

8.   Kotler, P. and R. Singh (1981) Marketing Warfare in the 1980s, *Journal of Business Strategy*, winter, 30–41.

9.   Sun Tzu (1963) *The Art of War*, London: Oxford University Press.

10. Von Clausewitz, C. (1908) *On War*, London: Routledge and Kegan Paul.

11. Jeannet, J.-P. (1987) *Competitive Marketing Strategies in a European Context*, Lausanne: International Management Development Institute, 101.

12. See Aaker, D. and G. S. Day (1986) The Perils of High-Growth Markets, *Strategic Management Journal*, **7**, 409–21; Wensley, R. (1982) PIMS and BCG: New Horizons or False Dawn?, *Strategic Management Journal*, **3**, 147–58.

13. Anonymous (2000) The Dogfood Danger, *The Economist*, 8 April, 82–6.

14. Taylor, P. (2000) Reshaping the Global Landscape of IT, *Financial Times*, Information Technology Survey, 2 February, 1.

15. Hoggart, S. (1988) President for Slumberland, *Observer*, 6 November, 15.

16. Kotler and Singh (1981) op. cit.

17. Porter, M. E. (1985) *Competitive Advantage*, New York: Free Press, 514–17.

18. Von Clausewitz (1908) op. cit.

19. Hooley, G., J. Saunders and N. Piercy (1998) *Marketing Strategy and Competitive Positioning*, London: Prentice-Hall, 224.

20. Fagan, M. (1991) Unhappy Anniversary for IBM, *Financial Times*, 15 October, 16.

21. Kynge, J. (1997) Malaysia: A Technological Transformation, *Financial Times*, Survey, 19 May, 3.

22. Barksdale, J. (1996) Microsoft World Like to Squash Me Just Like a Bug, *Financial Times*, Special Report on IT, 2 October, 2.

23. Garrett, A. (1997) Wrestling for the Soul of the Internet, *The Observer*, 5 October, 7.

24. Alexander, G. (1999) Shocked Gates Ready to Sue for Peace, *The Sunday Times*, 7 November, 1.

25. Alexander, G. (1999) Humbled Microsoft Ready to Back down, *The Sunday Times*, 28 March, 11.

26. Marsh, H. (1998) Microsoft's Real Trial is Trust, *Marketing*, 3 December, 16–17.

27. Anonymous (2000) After the Verdict, *The Economist*, 8 April, 81–2.

28. Welford and Prescott (1990) op. cit.

29. Lorenz, C. (1992) Take your Partner, *Financial Times*, 17 July, 13.

30. Mitchell, A. (2000) Why AOL/Time Warner Union Will Prove Barren, *Marketing Week*, 20 January, 38–9.

31. Shapinker, M. (2000) Marrying in Haste, *Financial Times*, 12 April, 22.

32. Bronder, C. and R. Pritzl (1992) Developing Strategic Alliances: A Conceptual Framework for Successful Cooperation, *European Management Journal*, **10** (4), 412–21.

33. Lorenz, C. (1992) Take your Partner, *Financial Times*, 17 July, 13.

34. Lorenz, C. (1993) An Affair that Refuses to become a Marriage, *Financial Times*, 19 February, 16.

35. Ohmae, K. The Global Logic of Strategic Alliances, *Harvard Business Review*, March–April, 143–54.

36. Alexander, G. (1999) Alliances Form in Battle to Dominate Mobile Computing, *The Sunday Times*, 14 February, 7.

37. Cane, A. (2000) Playing the Mobile Phone Card, *Financial Times*, 10 February, 13.

38. Lorenz, C. (1992) The Risks of Sleeping with the Enemy, *Financial Times*, 16 July, 11.

39. Bronder, C. and R. Pritzl (1992) Developing Strategic Alliances: A Conceptual Framework for Successful Cooperation, *European Management Journal*, **10** (4), 412–21.

40. Nakamoto, M. (1992) Plugging into Each Other's Strengths, *Financial Times*, 27 March, 21.

41. Hoggart (1988) op. cit.

42. Kotler and Singh (1981) op. cit.

43. Urry, M. (1992) Takeover Put Spark into Battery Maker, *Financial Times*, 14 April, 21.

44. Jeannet (1987) op. cit.

45. James, B. J. (1984) *Business Wargames*, London: Abacus.

46. Peters, T. J. and R. H. Waterman Jr (1982) *In Search of Excellence: Lessons from America's Best-Run Companies*, New York: Harper and Row.

47. Hammermesh, R. G., M. J. Anderson and J. E. Harris (1978) Strategies for Low Market Share Businesses, *Harvard Business Review*, **50** (3), 95–102.

48. Hedley, B. (1977) Strategy and the Business Portfolio, *Long Range Planning*, February, 9–15.

Key terms

competitive behaviour   the activities of rival companies with respect to each other. It can take five forms: conflict, competition, coexistence, cooperation and collusion

strategic alliance   collaboration between two or more organizations through e.g. joint ventures, licensing agreements, long-term purchasing and supply arrangement

strategic focus   the strategies which can be employed to achieve the objective

frontal attack   a competitive strategy where the challenger takes on the defender head-on

flanking attack   attacking geographical areas or market segments where the defender is poorly represented

encirclement attack   attacking the defender from all sides, i.e. every market segment is hit with every combination of product features

bypass attack   circumventing the defender's position, usually through technological leapfrogging or diversification

guerrilla attack   making life uncomfortable for stronger rivals through e.g. unpredictable price discounts, sale promotions, or heavy advertising in a few selected regions

hold objectives   a strategy of defending a product in order to maintain market share

position defence   building a fortification around existing products, usually through keen pricing and improved promotion

flanking defence   the defence of a hitherto unprotected market segment

pre-emptive defence   usually involves continuous innovation and new product development recognising that the best form of defence is attack

counteroffensive defence   a counterattack that takes the form of a head-on counterattack, an attack on the attacker's cash cow or an encirclement of the attacker

mobile defence   involves diversification or broadening the market by redefining the business

strategic withdrawal   Holding on to the company's strengths while getting rid of the weaknesses

niche   objective targeting a small market segment

harvest objective   the improvement of profit margins to improve cash flow even if the longer term result is falling sales

divest   to improve short-term cash yield by dropping or selling off the product

Case 33 Mitsubishi Ireland: The Launch of Black Diamond

Introduction

As the new century commenced, the management of Mitsubishi Electric Europe-Ireland (MEU-IR) couldn't help feeling that their company had moved into a new era. The closing years of the old millennium had been turbulent ones. The inexorable globalization of the consumer electronics industry and the ongoing growth in power of retailers had led Mitsubishi Electric—its parent, to cease production of colour televisions (CTVs) and video cassette recorders (VCRs) at its two plants in the UK. Country subsidiaries throughout Europe were told to exit the CTV and VCR businesses in favour of more profitable products in growth markets such as mobile phones and air conditioners. However, this move presented real problems for the Irish subsidiary. Mitsubishi Ireland had long been a market leader in CTVs and VCRs and these products were the mainstay of its operations. Furthermore, the Irish market was very small relative to other European countries, affording only limited opportunities for other products in the Mitsubishi range. Nevertheless, its response to the crisis was innovative and dramatically successful. The company launched a new brand of CTVs and VCRs called Black Diamond—which are made by Vestel, one of Europe's largest original equipment manufacturers (OEM). Extensive marketing to an initially sceptical dealer base and to the general public resulted in rapid acceptance of the new brand. In one year, the company managed to replace all its Mitsubishi-made CTVs and VCRs with this new range and do so without losing market share but actually increasing it. As he looked into the future, Fergus Madigan, Mitsubishi Ireland's managing director, pondered the strategic implications of the success of Black Diamond. How could the company consolidate its recent successes in a very competitive market and what were the wider implications of having developed a strong brand for products being made by a third party. It was clear that some very important decisions lay ahead.

Mitsubishi Ireland

Mitsubishi Electric has a presence in 39 countries around the world. Most of its key R&D and production activities continue to be in Japan, though the company has significant operations in China, Taiwan and the USA. Mitsubishi Electric Europe's registered office is in the Netherlands with its main corporate office located in London. It has significant operations in the UK, France and Germany as well as offices in Belgium, the Czech Republic, Ireland, Italy, Portugal, the Russian Federation, Spain and Sweden. Mitsubishi's Irish subsidiary (MEU-IR) was established in 1981 as a branch office of Mitsubishi UK. With an initial staff of eight, the company generated over IR£1 million sales in the first year. Since then, its growth rate has been very impressive, peaking at sales levels of IR£44 million in 1995, by which time employment had risen to 42 people (Fig. C33.1). CTVs and VCRs have been the mainstay of MEU-IR's operations over the years. Mitsubishi has a long tradition in television manufacturing, having launched its first television in 1953 and its first colour television in 1960. Though its market share in many European countries was very low, Mitsubishi has been a leading player in the Irish market and its brand is well known and associated with quality, technologically advanced products. When its sales of CTVs and VCRs peaked at over IR£14 million in 1990, these products represented almost three quarters of the company's turnover for that year. Since then, its dependence on this sector has reduced as the company expanded the range of products that it offers on the Irish market and by 1997, CTVs and VCRs accounted for one third of its turnover.

Mitsubishi Ireland currently has 45 employees and it is essentially an integrated sales and marketing company (see Fig. C33.2). The majority of its staff are attached to one of its five support groups, namely, marketing, customer support, logistics and purchasing, distribution and finance. The personnel and capabilities of these groups are then shared across its six major product divisions. Consumer goods, that is CTVs and VCRs, is still its biggest division but is closely matched by its air-conditioning business, which accounts for about 30 per cent of turnover. Equally important is the display products division, which mainly involves the sale of monitors to personal computer companies such as Gateway and its cellular mobile telecommunications division, which primarily markets the Mitsubishi mobile phone brand, Trium. The company also supplies digital security systems such as monitors and time lapse VCRs and some factory automation equipment including programmable logic components, drives and circuit breakers. Therefore, the company has a diversified customer base ranging from manufacturers who need production line equipment to mobile phone network providers to individuals looking for a new television. However, there are also commonalties across these businesses. For example, Mitsubishi's reputation for audio-visual products enhances its competitiveness in display products and security systems as well as in its consumer division. And while some of its businesses involved working directly with industrial customers, its two main divisions—consumer products and air conditioning, require capabilities in managing a dealer network.

1998: a shock for Mitsubishi Ireland

After almost three-quarters of a century of continuous profitability, Mitsubishi Corporation reported heavy losses for the year ending 31 March 1998 in common with a number of other major Japanese corporations. Profits had been rising steadily throughout the 1990s, though the 1997 fiscal year had seen an 86 per cent profit fall to 8.5 billion yen. However, for the first time in its history, Mitsubishi posted a loss in 1998 and it was substantial at 105.9 billion yen (about US$800 million). The fall was attributed to several factors. In terms of products, the bottom had

fallen out of the semiconductor market with the average price of a 16M DRAM dropping to one-third of what it had been twelve months earlier and competition continued to be severe in the audio-visual market. Geographically, the stagnation of the Japanese economy and the economic turmoil that gripped the South East Asian economies of Thailand, South Korea and Indonesia had also adversely affected performance.

On foot of these losses, Mitsubishi undertook an aggressive analysis of product sectors and operations to determine which elements to expand, scale down, spin off or eliminate as a means of streamlining and strengthening its business and improving efficiency. Quick actions were implemented in the USA, including the closure of a semiconductor factory, withdrawal from the analog direct-view television market and the outsourcing of cellular telephone production. Radical measures were also taken in Japan such as the creation of a 'virtual company' internal structure to cut costs and promote competition between internal divisions while in Europe, some lines were closed at its semiconductor assembly and testing facility in Germany. But it was the corporation's decisions with regard to the CTV and VCR business that was to have the most impact on its Irish subsidiary. It was decided to shut down its two CTV and VCR plants in Scotland and instead strengthened its projection television and display monitor operations in Mexico and moved to expand its share of the market for next-generation audio-visual products, including digital

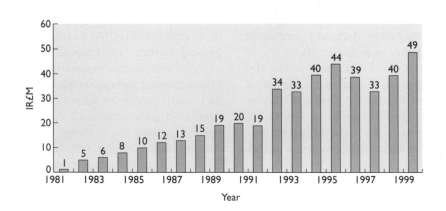

Figure C33.1 Company sales, Misubishi Ireland, 1981–99

televisions, next-generation projection devices and digital broadcasting services. Its strategy was now to focus on the high end of the audio-visual market, manufacturing major items such as colour display systems for public venues like sports stadiums and to exit the consumer end of the business. European sales offices were advised to sell off remaining Mitsubishi stock and the market began to come to terms with the fact that Mitsubishi was withdrawing from the CTV/VCR industry in Europe.

Responding to a crisis: the launch of Black Diamond

The decision to close the two Scottish plants came as a hammer blow to Mitsubishi Ireland. Of all of Mitsubishi's European offices, Ireland more than most depended on the sales of CTVs and VCRs. Mitsubishi CTVs and VCRs had achieved a strong brand recognition, and the Irish branch had a market share in this sector that was the envy of its European counterparts. But now it looked as though all the good work of the previous 20 years was going to be wasted. Fergus Madigan decided that immediate action was necessary. He called together his management team of Denis Boyd (head of sales), Colm Mulcahy (marketing manager) and John Fitzgerald (field sales manager) on several occasions during February 1998 to consider the options. Immediately, it became clear that making a graceful exit from the business was not going to be one of them. Too much effort had been put in for that to be considered. More critically, consumer products were the heart and soul of the Irish branch and the effect on staff morale of having to withdraw from that end of the business would be devastating. The brand was strong, consumer awareness was very high and

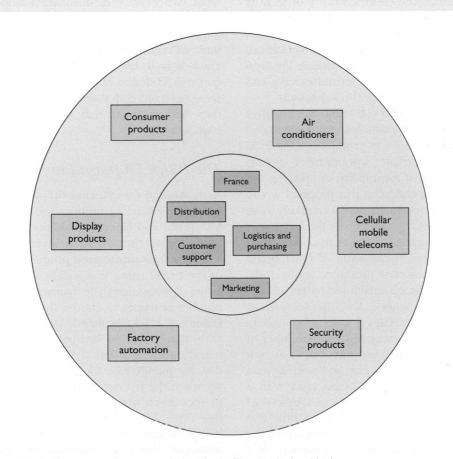

Figure C33.2 Company structure of Mitsubishi Electric Ireland Ltd

relationships with the dealers were very good. With that kind of base, all that was needed was to figure out a way of maintaining the supply of CTVs and VCRs.

The options open to each of the Mitsubishi branch offices were also under consideration at a meeting at head office in London. Though there were several possibilities, none were very palatable. The most straightforward option was to exit the CTV/VCR business and downsize branch offices accordingly. Aside from having to concede defeat in a business sector, this strategy also meant that overheads would have to be allocated to the remaining divisions in each office. Other possibilities involved finding new sources of supply for CTVs and VCRs. One option was for branches to take an agency for brands made by other manufacturers though this was always likely to be unpopular within Mitsubishi given its reputation for product innovation. A second was to have a third party manufacture the products, which would then be branded and sold as Mitsubishi products. Again, given its long history of technological leadership and product quality, this was an option that many Mitsubishi managers were not in favour of. It was then that Fergus Madigan presented his proposed solution, which involved a combination of third-party manufacturing and the development of a Mitsubishi sub-brand.

The development of a sub-brand was clearly a risky strategy. The Mitsubishi brand was renowned for its quality, therefore any product coming from an original equipment manufacturer (OEM) would have to be of top quality. Convincing the dealer base of the merits of this proposal would be critical to its success. Dealers were likely to be very sceptical about the idea given the number of strong brands already on the market. And then there was the very tricky issue of what brand name to use on any new products, as obviously, they were not being manufactured by Mitsubishi. Despite these challenges, MEU–IR decided to progress with the idea. They first set about finding an OEM. During the spring of 1998, a number of alternatives were considered including a French company, an Italian company and two Korean companies. Then Mitsubishi began talks with a Turkish company, Vestel. Initial discussions looked positive. Vestel was a well-established firm that had a lot of experience manufacturing consumer electronics products and had spare capacity in a large production facility at Ismir. They were also one of the largest OEM manufacturers in Europe

and Turkey was also starting to establish a reputation for itself as a producer of consumer products and white goods.

As the discussions progressed, Michael Clancy, Mitsubishi's main technical specialist spent two months in Turkey, where he worked with Vestel's production people to ensure that their product quality matched Mitsubishi's exacting standards. Relations between the two parties during this period were sometimes fraught as Vestel struggled to match the strict criteria set by Mitsubishi. At one stage, Michael Clancy brought the complete production line at the Turkish plant to a halt because he was not happy with the quality of the product. However, both sides persisted and by June 1998, Vestel was manufacturing two colour televisions for Mitsubishi, a 21-inch Text and a 21-inch Nicam. The next step was to ensure that these products presented no problems when in actual use. In terms of television signals, Ireland is a fringe area and the technology required to achieve quality reception is much greater than what is necessary in mainland European areas. Michael Clancy spent a further two months taking the televisions around the country to ensure that they worked well whether they were used in areas served by aerial or cable as reception qualities tended to vary significantly. No problems were detected and Mitsubishi was confident that they had products that matched their quality requirements.

The Black Diamond brand

As it worked on cracking the difficult problem of finding a suitable supplier, the management of Mitsubishi also faced the additional challenge of how to brand the new range given that it was not a Mitsubishi-manufactured product. The selection of the brand name was a difficult one involving hours of discussions. The management team had a number of names to choose from including Blue Diamond, Black Diamond, Diamond Vision and Diva. Blue Diamond had been a Mitsubishi sub-brand during the period 1979 to 1985. In those days the picture tube took a short period to warm up when the television was turned on and again to cool down when it was turned off and during that time the screen had a slight blue tinge— hence the name Blue Diamond. As the technology advanced, this warm-up/cool-down period was virtually eliminated and in 1990, Mitsubishi used the name Black Diamond for its television range as a way of conveying the quality of its products and to describe the sharp visual picture provided by its televisions. The Black Diamond brand name was a registered name of Mitsubishi Ireland but had not been used since 1995 because it was felt then that the use of the sub-brand was confusing customers. Diamond Vision was an attractive proposition as it was the name used on Mitsubishi's range of large outdoor screens and would confer an image of technological advancement on the new range. Diva was a very successful Mitsubishi brand in countries like Singapore, Australia and New Zealand.

The company also considered a two-brand strategy. There was the possibility of having products made by a Japanese OEM, which could be branded Diva and positioned as top of the range while Black Diamond could be used for its mid-market products. But it was felt that as Diva had no brand recognition in Ireland, it would be a very hard sell there. The company finally decided to go with Black Diamond primarily because it had recognition among the employees as well as dealers and customers in the marketplace. And research had shown that it was a name that stood on its own. But there were also important risks. When it was last on the market, Black Diamond had a product association, namely, the Black Diamond tube. But this time it would have to stand on its own as a brand. And then there was the issue of would Black Diamond be too closely associated with CTVs. Discussions led to the consideration of White Diamond for white goods and Red Diamond for audio. At one stage, Fergus Madigan became totally exasperated at a management meeting. They had not even launched the brand and already it seemed that it was being stretched all over the place. A deep breath was taken and the decision was made to go with Black Diamond as the brand. However, it was necessary to make some changes to the logo in order to accommodate the OEM product (see Fig. C33.3). The name Mitsubishi was taken off the top bar, which was now left blank though the words 'TV & Video' were subsequently added to the top bar in 1999 (see Fig. C33.3).

Motivation of the staff was also a critical issue at this time, as they too needed to be assured that the company had a strategy to cope with the closure of two CRV/VCR plants. In January 1999, Fergus Madigan brought all his staff to Paris for their annual conference. It is at this conference that management present their reviews of the past

Figure C33.3 Evolution of the Black Diamond logo

year and budgets and targets for the forthcoming year are outlined. It was essential to show at this stage that the company was in a position of strength while all the uncertainty was going on. This Paris event was repeated in 2000.

In a very short space of time the management of Mitsubishi Ireland were well on their way to turning a potentially disastrous situation around. The closure of the Scottish plants had been announced in February 1998. Yet by June of that year, the company had convinced its corporate office that it still had a future in CTVs and VCRs. It had established a relationship with a third party and was confident that this partner could deliver top-quality products. And it had a brand name that captured the functional and symbolic attributes of the new range. But the strategy was not without significant risks. If Black Diamond failed, reputations would be severely dented and the confidence and morale of employees would take a serious blow. MEU–IR's management knew their credibility was on the line both in terms of the Irish marketplace and within the Mitsubishi corporation. It was now time to take their new strategy to the marketplace, and this was likely to be the most difficult hurdle of them all.

The launch of Black Diamond

The new Black Diamond range was always going to face a difficult birth. The closure of the CTV and VCR plants in the UK had created a great deal of uncertainty among the dealer base, who were concerned about whether there would be adequate service and support available for the existing Mitsubishi stock that they held. At the same time, Mitsubishi's competitors in the Irish market sought to make as much capital as possible out of the unprecedented development. They aggressively targeted dealers, questioning Mitsubishi's commitment to the business and seeking to make the most out of the unexpected opportunity created by the potential withdrawal of one of the dominant firms in the market. So when Mitsubishi launched its new range of Black Diamond televisions at its annual August trade show, it faced a sceptical and worried dealer base.

Members of the Consumer Electronics Distributors Association (CEDA), which includes all the leading brands on the Irish market, each hold an annual trade show usually in August to showcase new products and marketing initiatives. These shows were a particularly important part of the calendar when the dealer base was made up of mostly small, independent brown goods specialists as they created the opportunity to build relationships with a disparate dealer network. Though less important as the dealer base consolidated, the 1998 show was a critical one for Mitsubishi. As usual the show was held at Mitsubishi's premises in Dublin. No effort was spared in convincing dealers of both the quality of the new range of televisions and of Mitsubishi's commitment to the CTV and VCR business. Customers were walked through a display of the entire Mitsubishi consumer product range including CTVs, VCRs, dehumidifiers, monitors, batteries, tapes and so on to demonstrate that Mitsubishi Ireland, far from withdrawing from the consumer market was more committed to it than ever before. The new Black Diamond range was presented at the end of the tour and customers were given a technical demonstration of the product comparing them with other brands to convince them of its quality. They were also invited to have their own engineers take sets away to examine and assess them.

The show was a tremendous success and dealers agreed to stock the two new televisions. As the pre-Christmas period is the most important buying time during the year, Mitsubishi brought out a third Black Diamond CTV—a silver 21-inch Nicam which was also adopted by dealers and well received by the market. The initial positioning of Black Diamond was a central factor in these early successes. Black Diamond was positioned as a Mitsubishi sub-brand. Sub-branding is very popular in the consumer electronics area with brands like Sony's PlayStation being particularly well known. In its other divisions, Mitsubishi Ireland had some strong sub-brands such as Mr Slim and City Multi in air-conditioners and Trium in mobile phones. It pursued a deliberate strategy of keeping a very close association between its new products and the highly credible Mitsubishi name by marketing them as Black Diamond distributed by Mitsubishi. This approach greatly assisted with the acceptance of the new range in the marketplace. Another difficult hurdle—the dealers, had been surmounted and the way was now cleared for a full-scale launch of the Black Diamond range in 1999.

Black Diamond in 1999

1999 saw the full transition to the Black Diamond range as the remaining Mitsubishi stock was sold off. By the end of the year the Black Diamond CTV range had been expanded to include 28-inch and 32-inch televisions as well as a top of the range 42-inch Plasma television. In addition, two new Black Diamond VCRs were added to the four Mitsubishi-made VCR brands offered (see Table 33.1). Across each of the different product categories, the Black Diamond range was positioned as a top quality, competitively-priced product. Prices for each of the different models were in the mid-range, which effectively placed Black Diamond in direct competition with other leading brands like Philips (Table C33.1).

Promotion of the new range was critical in 1999. The major emphasis continued to be on securing dealer loyalty and pushing the product through the channel. In February of that year, Mitsubishi took representatives of 24 of its leading dealers to Paris for a two-day product preview.The main purpose of this event was to unveil the full 1999 Black Diamond range and to demonstrate again the company's commitment to the CTV/ VCR business by showing the promotional support that would be used to drive the brand. It also served as a useful forum for getting dealer feedback from their initial experiences with Black Diamond. These trade efforts proved to be very successful and all the major dealers in Ireland such a Power City, DID Electrical, ESB Retail, the DSG Group and Shop Electric agreed to stock the new range.

A key to building the Black Diamond brand was the advertising concepts used on point-of-sale material and in advertisements targeted at the end user. Two tag lines were used in all the promotional literature, namely 'Quality makes all the difference' and 'See the difference'.The former was used to reinforce the quality image of the products and to convey that Black Diamond was a brand that the consumer could trust. 'See the difference' suggested that the only way televisions

can be evaluated is to look at them, and this tag line showed the company's confidence in its new brand.The main visual used in the advertising was eye-catching and provocative. Rather than showing a television, it showed the body of a woman with a diamond superimposed on it.The message of the visual was simply a reinforcement of the brand name, but the concept did a very effective job of creating awareness in the marketplace (Fig. C33.4). Televisions were shown in some product-specific advertising. For example, its silver 21-inch Nicam television, which was launched for the Christmas 1998 market, showed a Christmas scene on the TV screen, while a sumo wrestler featured on the screen of its 28-inch television to convey the image of size. Some silver 21-inch Nicam CTV sets were offered as prizes on the popular TV programme, *The Late Late Show*, Being the first sets of their kind on the Irish market, they helped to associate the name Black Diamond with innovation.The full Black Diamond range of colour televisions were combined to form a banner line that was included in much of its advertising and point of sale material (Fig. C33.5). The main advertising media used

Table C33.1	The Mitsubishi product line up in 1999		
		Product range	Recommended retail price
Mitsubishi brand	Televisions	C14 M7L—14-inch RC	IR£114.00
		C14 7TL—14-inch text	IR£154.00
		C14 NV1L—combi	IR£349.00
	VCRs	820 V—budget 2HD	IR£142.00
		821 V—mono 2HD	IR£169.99
		841 V—mono 4HD	IR£199.99
		851 V—featured Nicam 4HD	IR£259.99
Black Diamond brand	Televisions	B 14T—14-inch text	IR£119.99
		BD 20T—20-inch text	IR£189.99
		BD 21T—21-inch text	IR£219.99
		BD 21S—21-inch Nicam	IR£249.99
		BDS 21S—21-inch Nicam (silver)	IR£269.99
		BD 28S—28-inch Nicam	IR£359.99
		BD 33S—33-inch Nicam	IR£529.00
		BD 42 WP—42-inch plasma	IR£1000.00
		BD 28WS—28-inch widescreen	IR£599.99
		BD 29S—29-inch Nicam	IR£399.00
		BD 32WS—32-inch widescreen	IR£699.00
	VCRs	BD 100 VS—budget Nicam	IR£199.00
		BD 200 VS—featured Nicam	IR£219.00

during the year were press and point of sale and a schedule for the IR£2 million promotional budget is shown in Fig. C33.6

The performance of Black Diamond

The success of Black Diamond took everyone in the industry by surprise. From a situation of having to consider exiting the business just under two years previously, Mitsubishi Ireland had managed to develop a new line of products and successfully launched them onto the market. But what is perhaps more remarkable is that the transition from Mitsubishi-made products to the Vestel-manufactured range resulted not only in the company maintaining its share of the market, but actually increasing it (see Table C33.2). Market share figures for 1999 show that MEU–IR had significantly strengthened its position as the dominant player in the large screen CTV market.

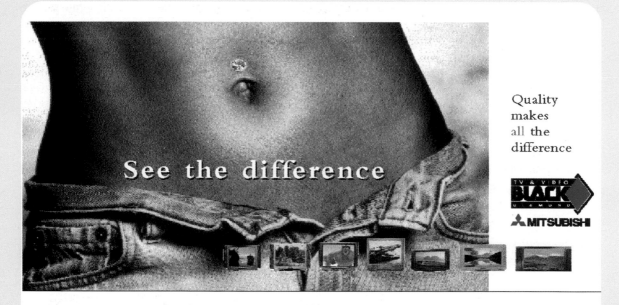

Figure C33.4 Print advertising for Black Diamond television

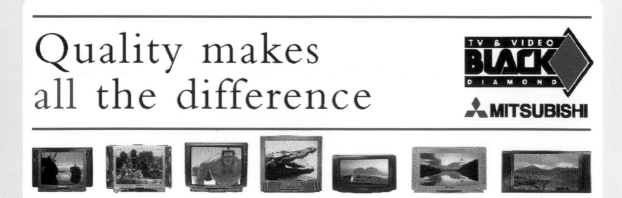

Figure C33.5 The Black Diamond banner line

But it also assumed dominance of the VCR sector and made significant inroads into Philips' leadership of the portable TV sector. By the end of 1999, this success was reflected in the company's dealer-based promotional material which carried the tag line 'From Brand New ... to Brand Leader'. The advertising talked about the success of Black Diamond as well as MEU–IR's support for the brand and invited dealers to join in the success story.

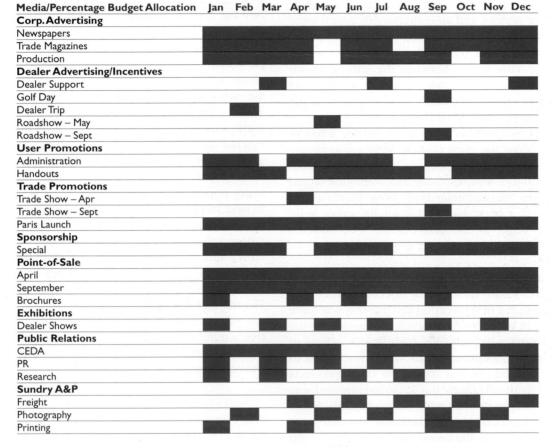

Figure C33.6 Mitsubishi advertising and promotion plan, 1999

Table C33.2   Market shares for TVs and VCRs, 1999

Manufacturer	Portable CTV (%)	Large screen CTV (%)	Total CTV (%)	VCR (%)
Mitsubishi	27	40	32	32
Philips	36	18	30	29
Panasonic	12	12	12	12
Sanyo	12	10	9	11
Sony	5	9	8	7
Grundig	4	4	3	1
Others	4	7	6	8

Building on the success of Black Diamond

The success of the Black Diamond range meant that Mitsubishi Ireland could look forward to the new century with renewed confidence. The brand had solidified its leading position in the important consumer products division and growth was also strong in its other division, particularly mobile phones and air-conditioners, which were benefiting from the thriving Irish economy. But the competitive world of consumer electronics with intense rivalry between the leading brands and continued downward pressure at the retail level meant that Mitsubishi Ireland was not going to have the luxury of being able to rest on its laurels for too long. In the first instance it had to consolidate the gains made in 1999 and continue to build the brand equity of Black Diamond. Expenditure on advertising and promotion would have to be maintained or even increased in view of a likely backlash from the other main competitors in the marketplace who suffered share declines in 1999 at the expense of Black Diamond.

MEU–IR's successful foray into OEM production meant its mode of operations was now evolving in a new direction and one that was quite different to most of its leading competitors in the Irish market. Traditionally, Irish branch offices of consumer electronics firms were closely tied to their UK offices and tended to order products through these offices. But Mitsubishi Ireland was now dealing directly with a manufacturer for its Black Diamond range and building up expertise in this area. And as the brand grew stronger, it could consider dealing in the same direct manner with a range of other potential OEMs.

Further crucial decisions surround whether or not to extend the Black Diamond brand into other consumer electronics products and which of these products might provide the best fit. Most closely related to the current product range would be DVD players, but Mitsubishi could also consider using the brand for a range of audio products and accessories or even white goods. Critical to these decisions would be an understanding of the elasticity of a brand that has just been established in the marketplace. Black Diamond is currently associated with CTVs and VCRs and this is emphasized by the current logo (see Fig. C33.3). Similarly, the red diamond on the logo, while very suitable for print advertising, may pose some problems for product badging, particularly if the brand is extended to white goods. Related to the issue of brand extension is the sensitive question of the extent to which Black Diamond should continue to be associated with Mitsubishi, particularly if the company extends the brand into products such as white goods which have not been part of the Mitsubishi product portfolio. And at the same time there are major opportunities opening up in the Northern Ireland and UK markets given that Mitsubishi UK, who had previously catered for these markets no longer carried CTV and VCR products. Furthermore, due to consolidation in the channel, Mitsubishi Ireland is already supplying a number of the leading British retailers such as DSG, Shop Electric and Lislyn within Ireland. Though it had got off to a great start, Fergus Madigan knew that a number of crucial decisions needed to be made in order to successfully manage the Black Diamond brand into the future.

This case was prepared by John Fahy, Lecturer in Strategic Marketing, University of Limerick, Ireland. It is intended to serve as a basis for class discussion rather than to show either effective or ineffective management. The author gratefully acknowledges the support and assistance of the management and staff of Mitsubishi Electric Ireland Ltd in the development of this case. Copyright © John Fahy, 2001.

Questions

1 Evaluate the launch of the Black Diamond brand. Why was it so successful?

2 Advise the company on whether or not it should seek to extend the Black Diamond brand.

3 Develop a competitive marketing strategy for the Black Diamond brand.

Case 34 Hirefone:
From a Business Concept to an International Player

Early years

The cellular phone market in the UK was effectively created in October 1982 when Vodafone and Cellnet were granted licences to operate the first two mobile phone networks. The mobile phones at that time were 'the size of a briefcase', heavy and with limited application. The networks' signals could cover only limited areas of the country. The coverage in terms of population[1] was a mere 40 per cent, restricted to the southeast of the country. The unit price of £3000 was prohibitive for most private users. Therefore the demand for mobile phones in the early 1980s was relatively limited.

As the coverage offered by the networks gradually increased and the dimensions of the phones improved, sales started picking up. However, the market was still confined to mainly larger business users.

Initial Rental, a car rental company operating in the north of England, noticed that some of its American business clients would ask for phones in the cars they rented. To satisfy this occasional demand for the equipment, Initial Rental acquired nine car phones. This effectively was the beginning of mobile phone rentals, which later would turn into a fast-growing niche industry worth approximately £50 million per annum.

In the 1980s, mobile phones were viewed mainly as car accessories. Avis, the car rental group, for example, bought one of the few phone rental companies operating at that time, in order to improve their car rental service.

As mobile phone technology advanced and handsets became more compact, usage among the business community grew. While unit prices were now coming below the £1000 barrier, phones were still expensive to both business and the public. Continued high cost induced the demand for rental equipment (see Fig. C34.1).

The late 1980s saw the emergence of a small but fast-growing phone rental market. Initial Rental reacted by setting up its own mobile phone rental division separate from their car hire

business. This new division was headed by the newly appointed David Agar.

In its infancy, the mobile phone rental market was chaotic and volume orientated. However, by 1990 distinctive market segments started emerging, the most substantial one being companies with a large headcount of salespeople. Corporate clients were less price sensitive than private individuals and more quality led. Having seen this opportunity, David Agar decided to target the corporate market by positioning Initial Rental as a high-quality, high-service deliverer of mobile phones for hire.

The first challenge was to raise the awareness that Initial Rental offered competitively priced rental equipment for hire. That also meant educating the market that renting mobile phones could be a cost-efficient alternative to buying a fleet of mobile phones for business use. The company started to advertise extensively in regional *Yellow Pages* giving local hotline numbers which diverted the calls to Initial Rental's single call centre. The idea was to create the perception that Initial Rental was a national operator, with an extensive network of offices conveniently located close to their customers. In reality, the firm operated from its northern base, using courier service to deliver the sets. The campaign proved a success and orders started coming in. By the end of 1992, the division was generating £2.5 million worth of sales.

Despite the encouraging figures, Initial Rental's top management began to insist that the division pursued a high-volume, undifferentiated strategy. Their priority was to chase sales instead of employing more focused targeting of corporate users. This was stretching the resources of the division, without properly positioning the product. This contradicted with David Agar's vision of creating a premium brand, which provided communication solutions to business users. This rift between him and Initial Rental's chief executive led to his resignation.

The concept of mobile phone rental

The concept of mobile phone rental mirrors the demand for mobile phones. Business customers

[1] Percentage of the population being able to receive mobile phone signal from a given network.

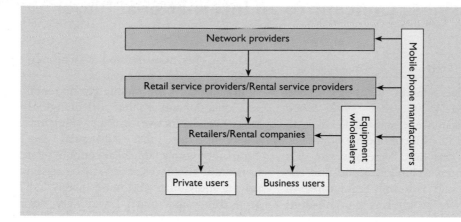

Figure C34.1 The UK cellular phone market

often need a mobile phone, spare batteries, battery charters and various phone accessories to stay connected while away from the company. The rapid changes in mobile phone technology and the unpredictable demand for mobile sets at any certain time often makes it uneconomical for companies to invest in large owned fleets of phones. It is much more cost effective to rent the latest technology for a limited period of time and to get billed just for the airtime and the cost of the service when used.

Hirefone (UK) Limited

Having left Initial Rental, David Agar decided to put his vision to the test by starting his own company. Hirefone (UK) Ltd was set up on 4 January 1993 in York with four employees and a capital of £40 000. Knowledge of the industry and ever-growing demand for mobile phones helped David to steer the company through a successful first year of trading. The company built up a 330 strong fleet of rental units and achieved 70 per cent utilization[2] of its mobile phones in its first year.

The focus of the management team was to position the company as a quality provider of mobile

---

[2] Utilization is the primary measure by which effective rental fleet management can be assessed. It represents the percentage of equipment that is actually with customers (i.e. generating revenue at any time).

communication solutions. Typical customers were multinational companies with a high headcount. While this kind of customer was demanding and had high expectations for levels of customer service, the segment had volume potential and low price sensitivity. This gave scope for the introduction of premium price strategies. If satisfied, such customers offer a high percentage of repeat business. By the end of the first year of trading, 35 per cent of its corporate clients accounted for 60 per cent of Hirefone's revenue and these customers included major banks, consultancy firms and large manufacturers.

Having completed a successful year of business, the team decided to explore opportunities in the south-east and central London in particular. The area had the highest population coverage by the networks and had the highest concentration of large- and medium-sized businesses in the country. Hirefone deliberately set up its office in a prime location not far from the City of London. The exclusive London postcode, EC4, was chosen to project a premium image and proximity to major corporate clients. Initial Rental were already in London and dominated the mobile phone hire market there. Their office was located in the King's Cross area (the main railway station to the north), a choice that reflected logistical considerations rather than being a customer-orientated location.

With the intention of differentiating itself on the basis of customer value, Hirefone commissioned attitude research among companies in

London and the south-east. The research was designed to include market trends analysis, competitor analysis, customer expectations and levels of customer satisfaction. The project covered over 200 large businesses in the capital city and results indicated high levels of awareness and a strong demand for mobile phone rental among big companies. It also highlighted customer dissatisfaction with the quality of services currently available. Main areas of complaints were wrong billing, late delivery and collection, and an overall complacency of existing providers.

For example, Goldman Sachs, the investment bank, complained that one of their rental companies would consistently misspell the bank's name in their correspondence as 'Golden Snacks'. Customer dissatisfaction presented an opportunity for a new entrant such as Hirefone to get noticed and attract business in London. The company actively encouraged City firms to test the quality of their service and by the end of the year Hirefone managed to capture approximately 50 per cent of the London market—a share worth £1 million.

> The great challenge of a service orientated market is the need to steer the company consistently to and above customer expectations. In our business this means a continuous effort to build and sustain relationships and accept that our customers often perceive us to be as good as our last rental.
>
> D. Agar (1999)

Operational efficiency

The rapid growth of the business in 1995 and 1996, of 17 per cent and 25 per cent respectively, required serious attention on issues of efficiency and service quality (see Table C34.1).

> Planning, not knowing what to plan for, reflects the dynamic character of the industry. Very often the demand for phone hire is cyclical and unpredictable. Short-term orders dominate. Careful consideration of fleet size and resources are essential.
>
> D. Agar (1999)

By the end of 1994 the company owned a fleet of 500 mobile phones, by 1999 its fleet exceeded

Table C34.1   Hirefone (UK) Limited

Year	1994 £000	1995 £000	1996 £000	1997 £000	1998 £000
Turnover	1999	1299	1699	1650	1960
Year on year growth in %		16.7	25	3	18.8

Source: The Hirefone Group (2000)

1500 units. One measure of efficiency is the rate of utilization[3] of the fleet. This is the ratio between the number of phones out on hire and those in stock. Optimum utilization is essential for the profitability of the company. From a rate of 70 per cent in 1993, Hirefone managed to achieve rates of utilization of 75 per cent and above (in 1995–96 (see Fig. C34.2). This did not have an adverse effect on the quality of customer service. The 25 per cent included a 'just-in-case' reserve stock of mobile phone packs for emergencies to be able to respond to last minute requests from customers.

Internationalization of the business

Having consolidated its position in the UK market, the company started looking for growth opportunities elsewhere. The company commissioned marketing research, which looked into a number of potential markets on the basis of: market size, GDP per capita, population, network coverage, telecom infrastructure, etc. Over 100 markets were included in the study. Four markets came at the top of the list. They were Germany, the USA, Japan and Italy, two of which, Germany and the USA, looked particularly attractive.

Hirefone then commissioned a team of academics from a university in Germany to do additional research on the German market, this time targeting the mobile phone rental sector. The research came up with a surprising conclusion: 'Although Germany is a huge market for mobile

---

[3] 100 per cent utilization is never possible as equipment may be in transit, under test or undergoing maintenance. Very high utilization is also not advisable as it reduces the ability to service immediate demand. Ideal utilization should be managed between 65 and 80 per cent.

phones, it has no established or recognized rental market'. The recommendations of the research team were that under such circumstances Hirefone should not consider entering the German market.

The company was faced with the dilemma, either to accept the new research recommendations and abandon its plans for market entry, or disregard them and take the risk to view the non-existence of a market as an opportunity, rather. than a threat. The market size and the proximity to the UK tipped the scales of choice towards the second. Germany became the first overseas market for Hirefone. The company intended to capitalize on the well-developed cellular infrastructure and carve out a niche for their services.

In May 1996 Hirefone (Germany) GmbH started business. The subsidiary had three employees who were all trained in the operational delivery of the service with additional support being provided from the UK. The year to follow proved to be particularly difficult. High set up costs, low sales and recruitment problems resulted in an operating loss of DM 250 000 (see Table C34.2). The problem was exacerbated by the non-existence of factoring in Germany, therefore the accumulated loss had to be absorbed entirely by the UK parent company. As a consequence the growth of the UK business was restricted.

Hirefone (USA) Inc.

The portability of phones meant that customers would seek to use them when travelling abroad. However, in 1997 this was not always possible due to the incompatibility of regional network standards. While in Europe and parts of Asia the predominant standard was GSM 900, the USA had three incompatible standards each of them different to GSM (AMPS, D-AMPS and CDMA). This limitation subsequently influenced the development of dual and tri-band mobile phones, which allowed more flexibility in terms of international 'roaming' between countries with different standards.

During 1997, the UK network operator Cellnet introduced its GlobalRoam facility which was the first service to allow GSM users to roam in the USA. It was launched amid a £10 million TV ad campaign which generated considerable demand

Table C34.2   Hirefone (Germany) GmbH

Revenue	Turnover	Profit/loss
1997	DM 0.6 m	DM (0.25 m)
1998	DM 1.8 m	DM 0.11 m
1999	DM 2.7 m	DM 0.41 m
2000 proj.	DM 5.0 m	DM 0.8 m

Source: The Hirefone Group (2000)

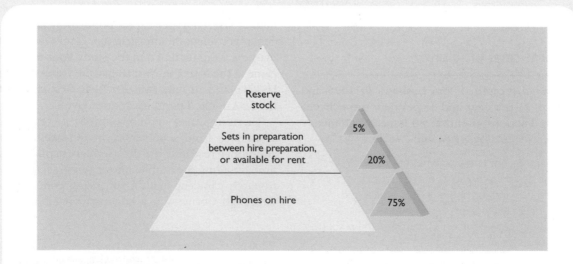

Figure C34.2 Fleet utilization

for the facility among business users. During the planning stage in 1996, Hirefone became aware of this new initiative through an existing business relationship with Cellnet. Since this service targeted the core Hirefone customers, they saw an opportunity to tape into the market of business travellers. This meant considering a strategic partnership with a network operator. Following negotiations with Hirefone, Cellnet also saw such a partnership as a way of rapidly expanding its GlobalRoam service. Since the product was targeting business traffic to and from the USA, Cellnet's key requirement for a partner was that they have a presence in the USA. Already under-resourced due to their recent German start-up, the company had to decide whether to launch an American subsidiary. The prospect of a partnership with a major network tipped the scales towards the launch of Hirefone USA Inc. In January 1997 the company opened their office on Wall Street in New York and became the authorized rental partner for Cellnet. When GlobalRoam was launched in March the same year, Hirefone was instantly servicing 80 per cent of the total demand.

However, things did not work out as expected. GlobalRoam was unstable. At times the failure rate of call connections was 60 per cent. In simple terms, customers renting mobile phones from Hirefone with the intention of using them in the States were unable to do so. The slow system of registration to the service complicated by a long chain of operational partners meant that Hirefone customers were often arriving in New York before being registered on GlobalRoam. Although the technical problems were coming from the network rather than the service provider, customer discontent was always directed towards Hirefone. The company's help-line was inundated with complaints. Senior management had to spend considerable time on the phone, desperately trying to rectify the situation and explain to customers the root cause of the problem. Neither of the operational partners openly accepted responsibility, which aggravated the situation further and had a negative knock-on effect on the rest of Hirefone's services. It put pressure on customer support systems, cash flow and, above all, on relationships with key customers. The net result was a loss of business and damaged reputation as a premium service provider.

The GlobalRoam fiasco triggered additional problems in the US office. Hirefone USA Inc. was

Table C34.3   Hirefone (USA) Inc.

Revenue	Turnover	Profit/loss
1997	$0.18 m	$(0.12 m)
1998	$0.31 m	$(0.13 m)
1999	$0.67 m	$0.05 m
2000 proj.	$1.00 m	$0.12 m

Source: The Hirefone Group (2000)

quickly accumulating losses (see Table C34.3), which led to the resignation of key personnel. Originally staffed in a similar way to Hirefone (Germany), the high level of customer support resulted in people working long hours, often dealing with customer complaints through the night. Despite diverting some of this support to the UK, staff were simply wearing out and the pressures of developing the business at the same time proved too much.

> We chose international growth as our preferred strategy. On the whole the entry into the German market was well planned. And even then we were still on a steep learning curve. Unbelievably we allowed ourselves to enter the US market with negligible research and planning and we had to pay the price. It was time for a strategic review.
>
> D. Agar (2000)

The challenges

Remote outpost syndrome

During 1996 and 1997 the Hirefone Group went through a severe cash crisis and the survival of the business was in question.

> We survived as a result of sheer determination and refusal to accept failure as an option. It took the management team three years to reverse the fortunes of the company. The company had to learn the hard way how important forward planning was. In international markets the cost of getting it wrong is enormous.
>
> D. Agar (2000)

Hirefone had to rethink their international marketing strategy. Market consolidation in the three markets was essential for the survival of the group. The consolidation was possible only if Hirefone could rebuild among customers its reputation for quality and reliability. Standardization of operational procedures across markets was a major challenge. The attempts at standardization were insufficient to prevent subsidiaries working according to localized priorities, with little coordination among themselves. Customer enquiries, rentals, stock control and invoicing in the different markets were effectively run separately. Phone calls, faxes and visits from the head office were not sufficient to ensure consistency in the strategy implementation. Multiple time zones did not help, nor did cultural and employment law differences.

Although English was the company language, it rapidly became clear that there was a lot more to communication than words. For example, reports sent by fax from the UK to the USA often were not dealt with, because American staff did not see a fax communication as urgent. In Germany, on the other hand, an almost obsessive desire to ensure that operational procedures were as correct as possible resulted in valuable resources being diverted from business development activities. The result was an inevitable fall in business generation. Almost from the very beginning, Hirefone had operated to an ISO 9002 Quality Management System and the procedures that this imposed had been very carefully thought through. However, due to limited communication, the satellite offices in Germany and the USA often saw the additional time needed to follow procedures as a head office imposition. Short cuts were common and a vast amount of senior management time became absorbed in correcting the problems that procedural short-cutting created. For instance, large quantities of stock would be held up awaiting maintenance and repair, and therefore would be unavailable to meet high peaks of short-term demand. Accurate operational figures were not always recorded, making planning very difficult and debt recovery systems fell into disarray with the inevitable impact upon cash flow.

The road to recovery

> The problem is that when you find yourself in a downward survival spiral it is very hard to detach yourself from the day-to-day operational issues in order to take a strategic overview. That was the first major challenge.
>
> D. Agar (2000)

Senior management understood the need for change, but they also understood that their hands-on involvement in day-to-day operational issues had become a critical element in Hirefone's survival. All three directors already worked very long hours, and continual international travel had become the routine. In addition, two years of high pressure had taken its toll on the staff.

Although 1997 had seen much inward investment in restructuring and staff recruitment, high staff turnover had resulted in the workforce having good practical skills but little industry experience. It became very difficult to delegate authority to middle management. Yet the directors had to do it so that they could get on with running the business.

> Our operational procedures were robust, when followed and our operational structure was sound. The people were also capable if a little inexperienced. There had to be a leap of faith.
>
> D. Agar (2000)

The year 1998 was one of consolidation and planning. With some freedom to reflect upon the future, each of the group companies was evaluated and the overall objectives were reviewed. Work was also done on refining the products and services and a closer look was taken at operational costs. The limitation and incompatibility of the rental software programs in use to manage stock, finances and customers across the markets had become a major barrier to growth and new product development. This observation underpinned the need for a bespoke, customer management software. Funding new software design became a primary objective in the long-term strategy of the company. Another key development was the recruitment of a human resources professional to help strengthen the team and improve training.

Despite a difficult year, by the beginning of 1999, all the signs were there that the company had turned around. Quality levels were restored, staff training was showing results. More focused marketing and sales activities were taking place in each of the company's markets. Even more promising, cash flow was now under control and profits were being reinvested into the business. All this was happening at a time when many rental competitors were experiencing problems with slowing sales and profit margin pressures.

As 1999 progressed, increasingly more time became available for the directors to concentrate on steering the business. A major strategic objective was to negotiate standardized rental deals with MNCs and network providers, which facilitated longer term planning. Sales levels began to grow. In Germany, for instance, years of sustained investment in educating the market to the benefits of rental began to pay off, with a significant upturn in business. The fortunes of the USA operation also stabilized and it moved into profit (see Table C34.3).

The future

By the beginning of 2000 many of Hirefone's past operational difficulties were over. The high levels of staff turnover experienced during the height of GlobalRoam were a thing of the past due to focused recruitment and training strategies. Operational integrity had been restored and, despite more aggressive competition in all markets, each of the group companies was generating growing levels of sales and profit.

New marketing research in February 2000 among UK customers and competitors confirmed, yet again, that Hirefone was perceived as the premium supplier for cellular rental. While one of the major challenges over the past eight years had been the expensive task of educating the market to the benefits of rental, the emphasis on education now appeared to be over. For the previous 18 months, many companies had started to look for incremental revenue streams and cellular rental had increasingly been identified as such an opportunity. Others had begun to re-evaluate their approach to mobile phone ownership in response to the rapid changes in technology, with short-term rental being seen as a cost-saving solution. The potential for third party[4] and contracted provision[5] of mobile phone rental had grown tremendously. Furthermore, the traditionally sceptical network operators had begun to embrace rental as a serious route to the market. Vodafone had already established Vodafone Rental Services and the others had begun to actively promote rental through independent rental companies (see Fig. C34.2).

With no market information being readily available, estimation of market share within the rental sector is a function of mobile phone fleet sizes, number of customers and sales turnover. This makes accurate estimation difficult. However, under BT Cellnet's rental accreditation scheme, during the first quarter of 2000, Hirefone substantially outperformed all other accredited companies (and yet the company only had the second largest fleet of mobile phones). All signs were, therefore, that Hirefone had become one of the most stable and best performing companies in the sector.

The challenge facing the company was where to go next? The focus on launch was to provide a quality-led, value-added, premium service to the business customer. This strategy led to the development of a range of products reflecting the different levels of customer needs. Hirefone was offering both basic communication solutions and cutting edge technology. Nokia 9000 and satellite phones from a few years ago and most recently WAP phones and personal digital assistants (PDAs) target sophisticated users. During the early years a high proportion of sales were on a one-to-one basis through a dedicated tele-sales team. This costly strategy of constantly prospecting and developing contacts through tele-sales was essential to build up awareness and increase customer base. Now, however, when the market has become more responsive to rental solutions, and the telecommunications industry is showing no signs of slowing down, the company is looking for innovative ways of generating business. One of these is the introduction of an interactive company website across markets, incorporating an automated ordering system.

Growth of the mobile phone market is driven by continued technological developments in the performance, styling and size of the handsets. Just as dual and tri-band technology became the norm during 1999, by the beginning of 2000, Wireless Application Protocol (WAP) phones had begun to appear. WAP has the capability of providing e-mail and limited Internet access. In April 2000, licences for the new generation of mobile phones were being granted in the UK. This new technology has the capacity for high-speed data and video transmission. Falling prices of hardware and reductions in call-tariffs, will accelerate mobile phone penetration in both the business and private

---

[4] To provide services to the customers of another company, on behalf of that company. Either under that company's brand or your own.

[5] Historically, the business sector was resistant to entering into any formal contracts for rental services. Increasing market complexity, cellular awareness and an improved understanding of rental solutions changed this resistance.

consumer sectors. Such developments will almost certainly affect the current structure of the mobile phone rental market. Hirefone has come a long way from a business concept to becoming a true international company. Now that the company is on the wave of market growth, will its success depend on its ability to stay focused? Only time will tell.

This case was prepared by Latchezar Hristov, Senior Lecturer in Marketing and Andy Cropper, Visiting Lecturer, Sheffield Hallam University. The case was made possible by the co-operation of Hirefone (UK) Ltd. The authors wish to thank David Agar, managing director of the Hirefone Group for the help that he provided in preparing this case study.

Questions

1. Define and discuss chronologically the key elements of the marketing strategy pursued by Hirefone sine 1993. How would you characterize their strategy?

2. Fast market expansion was an essential part of Hirefone's marketing strategy in the first five years of their existence. Evaluate the benefits and drawbacks of such an approach.

3. Discuss how Hirefone might sustain and improve its competitive position within the highly dynamic mobile phone market. What challenges might the company face in doing this?

4. What value has marketing research added to Hirefone's ability to maintain its competitive position? Discuss the difficulties they might face in conducting marketing research within a new and highly specialized niche market.

5. Hirefone's substantial growth since 1995 had a significant impact upon its workforce. How may an ambitious marketing strategy be pursued within the limits of the company's existing human resources?

PART FOUR

Marketing Implementation and Application

CHAPTER NINETEEN

Managing Marketing Implementation Organization and Control

*'God grant me the serenity to accept things I cannot change,
courage to change things I can, and the wisdom to know the difference'*

REINHOLD NIEBUHR

*'There is nothing more difficult than to take the lead in the introduction of
a new order of things'*

MACHIAVELLI

Learning Objectives *This chapter explains:*

1 The relationship between marketing strategy, implementation and performance

2 The stages that people pass through when they experience disruptive change

3 The objectives of marketing implementation and change

4 The barriers to the implementation of the marketing concept

5 The forms of resistance to marketing implementation and change

6 How to develop effective implementation strategies

7 The elements of an internal marketing programme

8 The skills and tactics that can be used to overcome resistance to the implementation of the marketing concept and plan

9 Marketing organizational structures

10 The nature of a marketing control system

Designing marketing strategies and positioning plans that meet today's and tomorrow's market requirements is a necessary but not a sufficient condition for corporate success. They need to be translated into action through effective implementation. This is the system that makes marketing happen in companies: it is the face of marketing that customers see in the real world. As we shall see, how implementation is managed has a crucial bearing on business outcomes, and its accompanying process—the management of change—must be accomplished with skill and determination if strategies and plans are to become marketing practice.

This chapter examines the relationship between strategy, implementation, and performance, how people react to change, and the objectives of implementation. It then explores the kinds of resistance that can surface when implementing the marketing concept and strategic marketing decisions. Finally, a framework for gaining commitment is laid out before looking at the skills and tactics that marketing managers can use to bring about marketing implementation and change. A key factor in implementing a change programme is top management support. Without its clear, visible and consistent backing a major change programme is likely to falter under the inertia created by vested interests.[1]

This chapter also examines how companies organize their marketing activities and establish control procedures to check that objectives have been achieved.

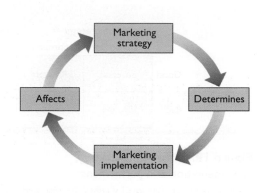

Figure 19.1 Marketing strategy and implementation

is a consequence of strategy, implementation also affects strategy and should form part of the strategy development process. The proposition is straightforward: strategy, no matter how well conceived from a customer perspective, will fail if people are incapable of carrying out the necessary tasks to make the strategy work in the marketplace. Implementation capability, then, is an integral part of strategy formulation. The link between strategy and implementation is shown in Fig. 19.1. Implementation affects marketing strategy choice. For example, a company that traditionally has been a low cost, low price operator may have a culture that finds it difficult to implement a value added, high price strategy. And strategy determines implementation requirements: for example, a value added, high price strategy may require the salesforce to refrain from price discounting.

Marketing strategy, implementation and performance

Marketing strategy concerns the issues of *what* should happen and *why* it should happen. Implementation focuses on actions: *who* is responsible for various activities, *how* the strategy should be carried out, *where* things will happen, and *when* action will take place.

Managers devise marketing strategies to meet new opportunities, counter environmental threats and match core competences. The framework for strategy development was discussed in Chapter 2 on marketing planning. Although implementation

Combining strategies and implementation

Bonoma has argued that combinations of appropriate/inappropriate strategy and good/ poor implementation will lead to various business outcomes.[2] Figure 19.2 shows the four cell matrix, with predicted performances.

Appropriate strategy—good implementation

This is the combination most likely to lead to success. No guarantee of success can be made,

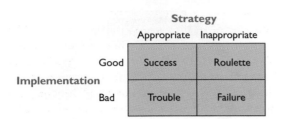

Figure 19.2 Marketing strategy, implementation and performance

Source: adapted from Bonoma, T.V. (1985) *The Marketing Edge: Making Strategies Work,* New York: Free Press, 12. Reprinted with the permission of The Free Press. Copyright © 1985 by The Free Press

however, because of the vagaries of the marketplace including competitor actions and reactions, new technological breakthroughs, and plain bad luck. But with strong implementation backing sound strategy, marketing management have done all they can to build success.

Appropriate strategy—bad implementation

This combination is likely to lead to trouble if substandard performance is attributed to poor strategy. Management's tendency to look for strategy change in response to poor results will result in a less appropriate strategy being grafted on to an already wayward implementation system.

Inappropriate strategy—good implementation

Two effects of this combination can be predicted. First, the effective implementation of a poor strategy can hasten failure. For example, very effectively communicating a price rise (which is part of an inappropriate repositioning strategy) to customers may accelerate a fall in sales. Second, if good implementation takes the form of correcting a fault in strategy then the outcome will be favourable. For example, if strategy implies an increase in sales effort to push a low margin *dog* product to the detriment of a new *star* product in a growing market (perhaps for political reasons), modification at the implementation level may correct the bias. The reality of marketing life is

that managers spend many hours supplementing, subverting, overcoming or otherwise correcting shortcomings in strategic plans.

Inappropriate strategy—bad implementation

This obviously leads to failure which is difficult to correct because so much is wrong. An example might be a situation where a product holds a premium-price position without a competitive advantage to support the price differential. The situation is made worse by an advertising campaign that is unbelievable, and a salesforce who make misleading claims leading to customer annoyance and confusion.

Implications

So what should managers do when faced with poor performance? First, strategic issues should be separated from implementation activities and the problem diagnosed. Second, when in doubt about whether the problem is rooted in strategy or implementation, implementation problems should be addressed first so that strategic adequacy can be more easily assessed.

Major success and profit performance results when marketing implementation reinforces the creation of a superior strategy. Marketing in Action 19.1 shows how Marriott Hotels have executed an outstanding full-service strategy.

Implementation and the management of change

The implementation of a new strategy may have profound effects on people in organizations. Brand managers who discover that their product is to receive less resources (harvested) may feel bitter and demoralized; a salesperson who loses as a result of a change in the payment system may feel equally aggrieved. The implementation of a strategy move is usually associated with the need for people to adapt to *change*. The cultivation of change, therefore, is an essential ingredient in effective implementation.

It is helpful to understand the emotional stages that people pass through when confronted with an adverse change. These stages are known as the ***transition curve*** and are shown in Fig. 19.3.[3]

Numbness

The first reaction is usually shock. The enormity of the consequences lead to feelings of being overwhelmed, despair and numbness. The outward symptoms include silence and lack of overt response. The news that a field salesforce is to be replaced by a telemarketing team is likely to provoke numbness in the field salespeople.

Denial and disbelief

Denial and disbelief may follow numbness leading to trivializing the news, denying it or joking about it. The aim is to minimize the psychological impact of the change. News of the abandonment of the field salesforce may be met by utter disbelief, and sentiments such as 'They would never do that to us'.

19.1   Marketing in Action

Successful Marketing Implementation: Marriott Hotels

Marriott are a US-owned hotel chain whose marketing strategy is to target well-off leisure and business travellers, and provide exceptional levels of service at premium prices. Clearly such a strategy is totally dependent on how their staff implement it in their day-to-day activities. The starting-point of their implementation process is to ensure that their staff are happy, as surly staff mean upset customers. Their basic philosophy, then, is to make sure that their staff (or associates as they are called) enjoy their work so they 'go the extra mile' to take care of their guests.

Management support this philosophy by *empowerment*. Staff are encouraged to solve customer problems even if it means expense to the hotel, without the need to seek approval from management. This might mean anything from lending a customer a pair of cufflinks or an electric shaver to exceptional acts of bravery. When Panama was invaded by US troops in 1989, Marriott staff hid US guests in the laundry-room dryers at considerable personal risk to the former.

Training forms a major element of the implementation programme as might be expected in a service-orientated business. A recent innovation has been to cross-train employees to be able to handle every major customer service. Innovation is encouraged by organizing small discussion groups with staff to identify and solve problems. This is backed up by rigorous customer research. Staff need to be flexible in their attitudes to change: Marriott is always seeking ways of improving customer service. One example was the testing of the 'First 10' scheme which is designed to make the first ten minutes at a hotel more pleasurable. Instead of checking in, which can be tedious and involve queuing, customers are met at the entrance and escorted to their room. Checking in is eliminated as the customer's credit card details are on file.

Technology is also employed to aid marketing implementation. A computer reservation system has been designed to maximize revenue from every hotel room by altering prices according to time of week, location, season, and size and type of booking. Marriott's telecommunications system at their London office is so sophisticated that the country from which an incoming call is made is identified and the call answered in the appropriate language.

Based on: Sambrook (1992)[4]

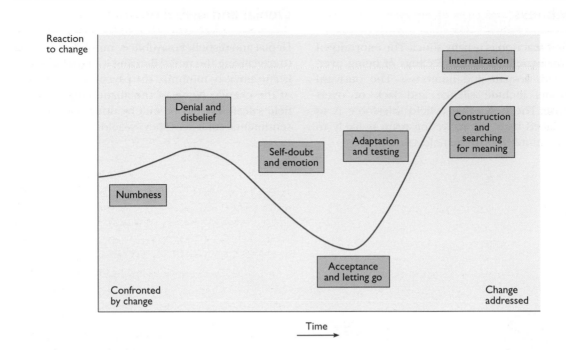

Figure 19.3 The transition curve

Source: Wilson, G. (1993) *Making Change Happen*, London: Pitman, p. 7. Reproduced with kind permission of Pitman Publishing

This is one of a series of advertisements for Marriott Hotels illustrating examples of excellent service based on the idea of empowerment

Self-doubt and emotion

As the certainty of the change dawns, so personal feelings of uncertainty may arise. The feeling is one of powerlessness, of being out of control: the situation has taken over the individual. The likely reaction is one of anger: both as individuals and as a group the salesforce are likely to vent their anger and frustration on management.

Acceptance and letting go

Acceptance is characterized by tolerating the new reality and letting go of the past. This is likely to occur at an emotional low point but is the beginning of an upward surge as comfortable attitudes and behaviours are severed, and the need to cope with the change is accepted. In the salesforce example, salespeople would become accustomed to the fact that they would no longer be calling upon certain customers, and receiving a particular salary.

Adaptation and testing

As people adapt to the changes they become more energetic and begin testing new behaviours and approaches to life. Alternatives are explored and evaluated. The classic case is the divorcee who begins dating again. This stage is fraught with personal risk, as in the case of the divorcee who is let down once more, leading to anger and frustration. The salespeople may consider another sales job, becoming part of the telemarketing team, or moving out of selling altogether.

Construction and searching for meaning

As people's emotions become much more positive and they feel that they have got to grips with the change, they seek a clear understanding of the new. The salespeople may come to the conclusion that there is much more to life than working as a salesperson for their previous company.

Internalization

The final stage is where feelings reach a new high. The change is fully accepted, adaptation is complete and behaviour alters too. Sometimes this is reflected in statements like 'That was the best thing that could have happened to me'.

Implications

Most people pass through all stages although the movement from one stage to the next is rarely smooth. The implication for managing marketing implementation is that the acceptance of fundamental change such as the reprioritizing of products, jobs or strategic business units will take time for people to accept and come to terms with. The venting of anger and frustration is an accompanying behaviour to this transition from the old to the new, and should be accepted as such. Some people will leave as part of the fifth stage—the testing of new behaviours—but others will see meaning in and internalize the changes that have resulted from strategic redirection.

Objectives of marketing implementation and change

The overriding objective of marketing implementation and change from a strategic standpoint is the successful execution of the marketing plan.
   This may include:

1   Gaining the support of key decision-makers in the company for the proposed plan (and overcoming the opposition of others).
2   Gaining the required resources (e.g. people and money) to be able to implement the plan.
3   Gaining commitment of individuals and departments in the company who are involved in front-line implementation (e.g. marketing, sales, service and distribution staff).
4   Gaining the cooperation of other departments needed to implement the plan (e.g. production and R&D).

For some people, the objectives and execution of the plan are consonant with their objectives, interests and viewpoints; gaining support from them is easy. But there are likely to be others who are involved with implementation from whom support is not so readily gained. They are the losers and neutrals. Loss may be in the form of lower status, a harder life, or a reduction in salary. Neutrals may be left untouched overall with gains being balanced by losses. For some losses support will never be forthcoming, for others they may be responsive to persuasion, whereas neutrals may be more willing to support change.

The ladder of support

What does support mean? Figure 19.4 illustrates the degree of support that may be achieved: this can range from outright opposition to full commitment.

Opposition

The stance of direct opposition is taken by those with much to lose from the implementation of the marketing strategy, and who believe they have the political strength to stop the proposed change. Opposition is overt, direct and forceful.

Resistance

With resistance, opposition is less overt and may take a more passive form such as delaying tactics. Perhaps because of a lack of a strong power base, people are not willing to display open hostility but nevertheless their intention is to hamper the implementation process.

Compliance

Compliance means that people act in accordance with the plan but without much enthusiasm or zest. They yield to the need to conform but lack conviction that the plan is the best way to proceed. These reservations limit the length to which they are prepared to achieve its successful implementation.

Acceptance

A higher level of support is achieved when people accept the worth of the plan and actively seek to

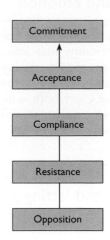

Figure 19.4 The ladder of support

realize its goals. Their minds may be won but their hearts are not set on fire, limiting the extent of their motivation.

Commitment

Commitment is the ultimate goal of an effective implementation programme. People not only accept the worth of the plan but also pledge themselves to secure its success. Both hearts and minds are won, leading to strong conviction, enthusiasm and zeal.

Barriers to the implementation of the marketing concept

In the following pages we shall discuss the various forms of opposition and resistance, and examine the skills and tactics necessary to deal with them. This reflects the growing realism that marketing managers need to be adept at managing the internal environment of the company as well as the external. But first we shall examine some of the barriers to the implementation of the marketing concept mentioned in Chapter 1. This is necessary because the acceptance of marketing as a philosophy in a company is a necessary

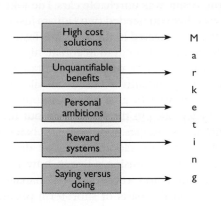

Figure 19.5 Barriers to implementing the marketing concept

prerequisite for the successful development of marketing strategy and implementation.

The marketing concept states that business success will result from creating greater customer satisfaction than the competition. The concept is both seductive and tautological. It is seductive because it encapsulates the essence of business success, and is tautological because it is necessarily true. So why do so many companies score so badly at marketing effectiveness? The fact is that there are inherent *personal and organizational barriers* that make the achievement of marketing implementation difficult in practice. These are summarized in Fig. 19.5.

High cost solutions

Often giving what the customer wants involves extra costs. In today's heavily competitive environment most companies will meet customers' low cost solutions. Therefore many marketing recommendations to beat competition will involve higher costs. Travelworld, a travel agency, were founded on giving better service to their customers. The chief executive recognized that the competition often required customers to queue at peak periods when booking a holiday. This he felt was unacceptable when customers were involved in a major transaction: a holiday is one of the highest expenditure items for families each year. The solution was to hire enough staff at his outlets to ensure that queuing was not a problem. He came from a marketing background and accepted the higher costs involved.

Meeting customer requirements can also conflict with production's desire to gain cost economies of scale, and the finance director's objective of inventory reduction. Customers invariably differ in their requirements—they have different personalities, experiences and lifestyles—and to meet individual requirements is clearly not feasible. A solution to this problem is to group customers into segments that have similar needs and to target one product or service offering to each group. It allows the production manager to reap some economies of scale and marketing to tailor offerings to the marketplace.

It was the failure of Henry Ford to compromise that almost brought his company's downfall.[5] He continued to make the Model T in the face of competition from General Motors, who were making a range of cars in many colours (including pink) because Americans no longer wanted the drab old Model T and could afford something more glamorous. His predilection with economies of scale lost him number one position in the ranking of US car companies, a position that Ford have never managed to regain.

To a finance director stocks mean working capital tied up and interest charges to be made. To the marketing director stocks mean higher service levels and thus higher customer satisfaction. In the retailing of paint, for example, an out-of-stock situation is likely to mean a lost customer. Once more the marketing approach of giving customers what they want is a high cost solution. Clearly, a compromise needs to be reached and target market segmentation can provide its basis. Unipart, a supplier of spare parts to motorists, recognized that inventory cost control procedures meant that competition were holding low stocks. This resulted in customer dissatisfaction when an urgently needed part, say a distributor cap, could not be provided when required. Unipart's strategy was to target those motorists (do-it-yourselfers) who valued instant (or very quick) parts provision and were willing to pay a little more for the service. Their strap-line 'The answer's yes. Now what's the question?' reflected their strategy. They identified a *high price, high service* segment and chose to serve those customers. In other situations, a *low price, low service* segment may be identified, and low stocks and a low price may be the appropriate response.

Unquantifiable benefits

A problem with marketing recommendations is that they are often unquantifiable in the sense that it is very difficult to measure the exact increase in revenue (and profits) that will result from their implementation. A case which illustrates this point is that of a business school faced with a customer problem. The student car park was regularly being raided by thieves who stole radios and cars. One marketing solution was to employ at least one security guard. The extra costs could easily be quantified, not so the economic benefits to the business school, however. On a purely commercial basis, it is impossible to say what the marginal revenue would be. On a similar theme what is likely to be the reduced revenue from removing one platform attendant from a railway station? The cost saving is immediate and quantifiable; the reduced customer satisfaction through not having someone to answer queries is not.

Personal ambitions

Personal ambitions can also hinder the progress of marketing in an organization. The R&D director may enjoy working on challenging, complex technical problems at the leading edge of scientific knowledge. Customers may simply want products that work. Staff may want an easy life which means that the customer is neglected. The teaching of part-time MBA students during the day rather than in the evening is an example of putting personal convenience before customer preferences.

Reward systems

It is a basic tenet of motivation theory that behaviour is influenced by reward systems.[6] Unfortunately organizations are prone to reward individuals in ways that conflict with marketing-orientated action. A problem that Sir John Egan had when he took over at Jaguar was that staff in the buying department were rewarded by the savings they made for their purchases. Consequently the emphasis when negotiating with suppliers was price. In order to meet these demands suppliers were compromising quality

and the result was unreliable cars. The joke in the USA was that you needed two Jaguars just to make sure that one started in the morning. Egan told his purchasing department to negotiate higher prices in return for better quality. Sales staff who are rewarded by incentives based on sales revenue may be tempted to give heavy discounts which secure easy sales in the short term but may ruin positioning strategies and profits. Webster argues that the key to developing a market driven, customer orientated business lies in how managers are evaluated and rewarded.[7] If managers are evaluated on the basis of short-term profitability and sales, they are likely to pay heed to these criteria and neglect market factors such as customer satisfaction that ensure the long-term health of an organization.

Saying versus doing

Another force which blocks the implementation of the marketing concept is the gap between what senior managers say and what they do. Webster suggests that senior management must give clear signals and establish clear values and beliefs about serving the customer.[8] However, Argyris found that senior executives' behaviour often conflicted with what they said, for example they might say 'Be customer orientated' and then cut back on marketing research funds.[9] This resulted in staff not really believing that management were serious about achieving a customer focus.

Implications

The implications are that marketing managers have to face the fact that some people in the organization will have a vested interest in blocking the introduction and growth of marketing in an organization, and will have some ammunition (e.g. the extra costs, unquantifiable benefits) to achieve their aims. Marketing implementation, then, depends upon being able to overcome the opposition and resistance that may well surface as a result of developing market driven plans. The following sections discuss the nature of such resistance, and ways of dealing with it.

Forms of resistance to marketing implementation and change

Opposition to the acceptance of marketing and the implementation of marketing plans is direct, open and conflict driven. Often arguments such as the lack of tangible benefits and the extra expense of marketing proposals will be used to cast doubt on their worth.

Equally likely, however, is the more passive type of *resistance*. Kanter and Piercy suggest ten forms of resistance:[10,11]

1 Criticism of specific details of the plan.

2 Foot-dragging.

3 Slow response to requests.

4 Unavailability.

5 Suggestions that despite the merits of the plan, resources should be channelled elsewhere.

6 Arguments that the proposals are too ambitious.

7 Hassle and aggravation created to wear the proposers down.

8 Attempts to delay the decision hoping the proposer will lose interest.

9 Attacks on the credibility of the proposer with rumour and innuendo.

10 Deflation of any excitement surrounding the plan by pointing out the risks.

Market research reports supporting marketing action can also be attacked. Johnson describes the reaction of senior managers to the first marketing research report commissioned by a new marketing director.[12]

> As a diagnostic statement the research was full, powerful, prescriptive. The immediate result of this analysis was that the report was rubbished by senior management and directors. The analysis may have been perceived by its initiator as diagnostic but it was received by its audience as a politically threatening statement.

In general, there are ten ways of blocking a marketing report.[13] These are described in Marketing in Action 19.2.

Ansoff argues that the level of resistance will depend upon how much the proposed change is likely to disrupt the culture and power structure of the organization and the speed at which the change is introduced.[14] The latter point is in line with our previous discussion about how people adapt to adverse change, requiring time to come to terms with disruptions. The greatest level of opposition and resistance will come when the proposed change is implemented quickly and is a threat to the culture and politics of the organization; the least opposition and resistance will be found when the change is consonant with the existing culture and political structure and is introduced over a period of time. Further, Pettigrew states that resistance is likely to be low when a company is faced with a crisis arguing that a common perception among people that the organization is threatened with extinction also acts to overcome inertia against change.[15]

A major change agent that has appeared on the corporate landscape in recent years is the Internet. New ways of conducting business are emerging as a result of the Internet's capability of reaching millions of consumers and offering them new ways of comparing competing products and prices. e-Marketing 19.1 discusses the way in which newcomers in the car market in the USA are forcing change upon established car manufacturers.

Resistance may also depend on the capability of the organization structure with the proposed change. Marketing in Action 19.3 shows how the introduction of a new system designed to halve delivery times benefited by the organization changes introduced earlier by management at Asea Brown Boveri, the Swedish-Swiss electrical power group.

Developing implementation strategies

Faced with the likelihood of resistance from vested interests, a *change master* needs to develop an implementation strategy that can deliver the required change.[16] A change master is the person who is responsible for driving through change within an organization. This necessitates a structure for thinking about the problems to be tackled and the way to deal with them. Figure 19.6 illustrates such a framework. The process starts with a definition of objectives.

Implementation objectives

These are formulated at two levels: what we would like to achieve (*would like objectives*) and what we must achieve (*must have objectives*). Framing objectives in this way recognizes that we may not be able to achieve all that we desire. Would like objectives are our preferred solution: they define the maximum that the implementer can reasonably expect.[17] Must have objectives define our minimum requirements: if we cannot achieve these then we have lost and the plan or strategy will not succeed. Between the two points there is an area for negotiation, but beyond our must have objective there is no room for compromise.

By clearly defining these objectives at the start we know what we would like, the scope for bargaining and the point where we have to be firm, and resist further concessions. For example, suppose our marketing plan calls for a move from a salary-only payment system for salespeople to a salary plus commission. This is predicted to lead to strong resistance from salespeople and some sales managers, who favour the security element of fixed salary. Our would like objective might be a 60:40 split between salary and commission. This would define our starting-point in attempting

---

19.2   Marketing in Action

Ten Ways of Blocking a Marketing Report

Reports that present critical conclusions or unpopular recommendations to an audience of managers are likely to meet stiff opposition. There are ten devices used by managers to block an undesired report:

1 *Straight rejection*: the report and its writer/commissioner are dismissed without further discussion. This approach requires political strength and self-confidence.

2 *Bottom drawer*: the report is effectively 'bottom drawered' by praising its contents but taking no action on its recommendations. The writer/commissioner, happy to receive praise, does not press the matter further.

3 *Mobilizing political support*: recognizing there is strength in numbers, the opposer gathers support from other managers who are threatened by the report.

4 *Criticizing the details*: a series of minor technical criticisms are raised to discredit the report, such as poor question wording and unrepresentative samples.

5 *But in the future*: the report is recognized as being accurate for today but does not take into account future events and so should not be implemented.

6 *Working on emotions*: make the writer feel bad by asking 'How can you do this to me?'

7 *Invisible man tactic*: the opposer is never available for comment on the report.

8 *Further study is required*: the report is returned for further work.

9 *The scapegoat*: 'I have no problems with this report but I know the boss/head office, etc. will not approve of it.'

10 *Deflection*: an extension of criticizing the details, where attention is directed at areas where the opposer's knowledge is sufficient to contradict some points made by the writer/commissioner and so discredit the whole report.

Based on: Pettigrew (1974)[18]

Figure 19.6 Managing implementation

to get this change implemented. But in order to allow room for concessions, our must have objective would be somewhat lower, perhaps a 80:20 ratio between salary and commission. Beyond this point we refuse to bargain: we either win or lose on the issue. In some situations, however, would like and must have objectives coincide: here there is no room for negotiation, and persuasive and political skills are needed to drive the issue through.

Strategy

All worthwhile plans and strategies necessitate substantial human and organizational change inside companies.[19] Marketing managers, therefore, need a practical mechanism for thinking through strategies to drive change. One such framework is known as *internal marketing*, sometimes called the missing half of the marketing

---

19.1   e-Marketing

The Internet as a Change Agent

It is often the case that the first entry into Internet marketing in an industrial sector is not by a leading company. More usually it is a smaller firm or a complete stranger to the sector who is the first mover in the world of e-commerce. The initial response of larger firms is to monitor the situation and only after some degree of success has been demonstrated, move to counter this growing threat to their future revenue flows.

An example of this process is provided by the car market in America. The first movers offering the consumers the facility of on-line transactions were firms such as Auto-by-Tel and Microsoft Carpoint. These firms tended to bypass the car manufacturers and their dealer networks. Instead they directed the customer to whichever dealer in their respective area was offering the lowest possible price. The response of the Big 3 (General Motors, Ford and Chrysler) was that they realized just using their websites as passive sources of on-line 'brochureware' was an ineffective way of exploiting the new technology. They were forced to move to utilize the Internet as providing much detailed information to customers as the basis for attracting them to visit the manufacturers' dealership network. This is a somewhat different approach to that of firms such as Auto-by-Tel who are clearly positioned as offering the Internet as a market channel through which to obtain the best possible deal. Which of the two models proves to be more effective and whether this evidence will cause the US car manufacturers to revisit their e-commerce marketing strategy will no doubt become clearer in future years.

Based on: Baer (1998)[20]

programme.[21] Originally the idea of internal marketing was developed within the area of services marketing, where it was applied to develop, train, motivate and retain employees at the customer interface in such areas as retailing, catering and financial services. [22] However, the concept can be expanded to include marketing to all employees with the aim of achieving successful marketing implementation. The framework is appealing as it draws an analogy with external marketing structures such as market segmentation, target marketing and the marketing mix. The people inside the organization to whom the plan must be marketed are considered *internal customers*. We need to gain the support, commitment and participation of sufficient of these to achieve acceptance and implementation of the plan. For those people where we fail to do this we need to minimize the effectiveness of their resistance. They become, in effect, our competitors in the internal marketplace.

Internal market segmentation

As with external marketing, analysis of customers begins with ***market segmentation***. One obvious method of grouping internal customers is into three categories:

1   *Supporters*: those who are likely to gain from the change or are committed to the changes.
2   *Neutrals*: those whose gains and losses are in approximate balance.
3   *Opposers*: those who are likely to lose from the change or are traditional opponents.

The three market segments form distinct *target groups* to which specific *marketing mix* programmes can be developed (see Fig. 19.7).

19.3   Marketing in Action

Making Change Happen at Asea Brown Boveri (ABB)

ABB, the world's largest electrical engineering group (with annual turnover exceeding $6 billion), were formed by the merger of Sweden's Asea with Switzerland's Brown Boveri. Driven by a vision of a Single European Market, ABB have been reshaped into a decentralized transnational enterprise capable of operating effectively across borders. A ruthless cost cutter in the pursuit of efficiency, ABB combined growth with job cuts.

A major plank in their drive for effectiveness is their T50 strategy which aimed to halve all lead times by the end of 1993. At the heart of the strategy is the company's desire to implement the key philosophy of marketing: customer satisfaction. Because customers demand orders on time, their systems are being revamped to provide it. For example, the time required to supply standard switch gear has fallen from 3–5 weeks to 3–5 days from receipt of the order to delivery. This is being done by decentralizing work responsibilities and broadening individual worker skills within teams.

The decentralized nature of ABB's operations has made the implementation of the T50 strategy possible. In the old days of stratified management structures there would have been so much resistance it would have been quickly abandoned. Today it is a natural extension of the existing organization.

By changing work practices, upgrading skills through training, and creating a new kind of independent-minded adaptable worker, T50 means higher productivity, higher quality products that are delivered on time, and the prospect of higher profits for ABB.

Based on: Wilson (1993);[23] de Jonquières (1993)[24] Taylor (1993)[25]

Internal marketing mix programmes

Product   this is the marketing plan and strategies that are being proposed together with the values, attitudes and actions that are needed to make the plan successful. Features of the product may include increased marketing budgets, extra staff, different ways of handling customers, different pricing, distribution, advertising, and new product development strategies. The product will reflect our would like objectives; however, it may have to be modified slightly to gain acceptance from our opponents. Hence the need for must have objectives.

Price   the price element of the marketing mix is what we are asking our internal customers to pay as a result of accepting the marketing plan. The price they pay may be lost resources, lower status, fear of the unknown, harder work and rejection of their pet projects because of lack of funds. Clearly, price sensitivity is a key segmentation variable which differentiates supporters, neutrals and opposers.

Communications   this is a major element of the internal marketing mix and covers the communications media and messages used to influence the attitudes of key players. A combination of personal (presentations, discussion groups) and non-personal (the full report,

executive summaries) can be used to inform and persuade. Communication should be two way: we should listen as well as inform. We should also be prepared to adapt the product (the plan) if necessary in response to our internal customers' demands. This is analogous to adaptation of a new product in the external marketplace as a result of marketing research. Communication objectives will differ according to the target group:

1   *Supporters*: to reinforce existing positive attitudes and behaviour, mobilize support from key players (e.g. chief executive).

2   *Neutrals*: the use of influence strategies to build up perception of rewards and downgrade perceived losses; display key supporters and explain the benefits of joining 'the team'; negotiate to gain commitment.

3   *Opposers*: disarm and discredit; anticipate objections and create convincing counter-arguments; position them as 'stuck in their old ways'; bypass by gaining support of opinion and political leaders; negotiate to lower resistance.

Distribution   these are the places where the product and communications are delivered to the internal customers such as meetings, committees, seminars, informal conversations and away-days.

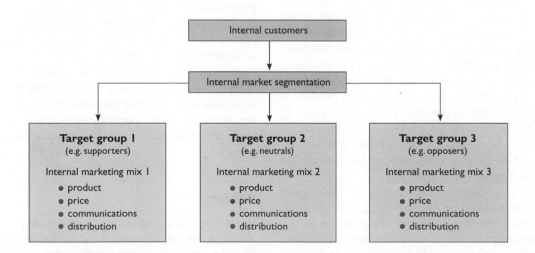

Figure 19.7 Internal marketing

Consideration should be given to whether presentations should be direct (proponents to customers) or indirect (using third parties such as consultants). Given the conflicting viewpoints of the three target segments, thought should be given to the advisability of using different distribution channels for each group. For example, a meeting may be arranged with only supporters and neutrals present. If opponents tend to be found in a particular department, judicious selection of which departments to invite may accomplish this aim.

Execution

In order to execute an implementation strategy successfully, certain skills are required, and tactics need to be employed. Internal marketing has provided a framework to structure thinking about implementation strategies. Within that framework, the main skills are persuasion, negotiation and politics.

Persuasion

The starting-point of persuasion is to try to understand the situation from the internal customer's standpoint. The new plan may have high profit potential, the chance of real sales growth, and be popular among external customers, but if it causes grief to certain individuals and departments in the organization, resistance may be expected. As with personal selling, the proponents of the plan must understand the needs, motivations and problems of their customers before they can hope to develop effective messages. For example, appealing to a production manager's sense of customer welfare will fail if that person is interested only in smooth production runs. In such a situation the proponent of the plan needs to show how smooth production will not be affected by the new proposals, or how disruption will be marginal or temporary.

The implementer also needs to understand how the features of the plan (e.g. new payment structure) confer customer benefits (e.g. the opportunity to earn more money). Whenever possible, evidence should be provided to support claims. Objectives should be anticipated and convincing counterarguments produced. Care

should be taken not to bruise egos unnecessarily (see Chapter 12).

Negotiation

Implementers have to recognize that they may not get all they want during this process. By setting would like and must have objectives (see earlier in this chapter) they are clear about what they want, and have given themselves negotiating room wherever possible. Two key aspects of negotiation are considered now: concession analysis and proposal analysis.

Concession analysis   the key to concession analysis is to value concessions which the implementer might be prepared to make from the viewpoint of the opponent. By doing this it may be possible to identify concessions which cost the implementer very little and yet are highly valued by the opponent. For example, if the must have objective is to move from a fixed salary to a salary plus commission, a salesperson's compensation plan conceding that the proportions should be 80:20 rather than 70:30 may be trivial to the implementer (an incentive to sell is still there) and yet highly valued by the salespeople as they gain more income security, and value the psychological bonus of winning a concession from management. By trading concessions that are highly valued by the opponent and yet cost the implementer little, painless agreement can be reached.

Proposal analysis   another sensible activity is to try to predict the proposals and demands that opponents are likely to make during the process of implementation. This provides time to prepare a response to them rather than relying on quick decisions during the heat of the negotiation. By anticipating the kinds of proposals that opponents are likely to make, implementers can plan the types of counterproposals that they are prepared to make.

Politics

Success in managing implementation and change also depends on the understanding and execution of political skills. Understanding the sources of power is the starting-point so that an assessment of where power lies and who holds the balance can be made. The five sources are reward, expert, referent, legitimate and coercive power.[26]

Reward power this derives from the implementer's ability to provide benefits to members in the organization. The recommendations of the plan may confer natural benefits in the form of increased status or salary for some people. In other cases, the implementer may create rewards for support, for example promises of reciprocal support when required, or backing for promotion. The implementer needs to assess what each target individual values, and whether the natural rewards match those values, or whether created rewards are necessary. A limit on the use of reward power is the danger that people may become to expect rewards in return for support. Created rewards, therefore, should be used sparingly.

Expert power this source of power is based on the belief that implementers have special knowledge and expertise that renders their proposals more credible. For example, a plan outlining major change is more likely to be accepted if produced by someone who has a history of success rather than a novice. Implementers should not be reluctant to display their credentials as part of the change process.

Referent power this occurs when people identify with and respect the architect of change. This is why charismatic leadership is often thought to be an advantage to those who wish to see change implemented.

Legitimate power this is wielded when the implementer insists on an action from a subordinate as a result of their hierarchical relationship and contract. For example, a sales manager may demand compliance with a request for a salesperson to go on a training course or a board of directors may exercise their legitimate right to cut costs.

Coercive power the strength of coercive power lies with the implementer's ability to punish those who resist or oppose the implementation of the plan. Major organizational change is often accompanied by staff losses. This may be a required cost cutting exercise but is also sends messages to those not directly affected that they may be next if further change is resisted. The problem with using coercive power is that, at best, it results in compliance rather than commitment.

Applications of power

The balance of power will depend on who holds the sources of power and how well they are applied. Implementers should pause to consider any sources of power they hold, and also the sources and degree of power held by supporters, neutrals and opposers. Power held by supporters should be mobilized, those neutrals who wield power should be cultivated, and tactics developed to minimize the influence of powerful opposers. The tactics that can be deployed will be discussed shortly, but two applications of power will be discussed first: overt and covert power plays.

Overt power plays this is the visible, open kind of power play that can be used by implementers to push through their proposals. Unconcealed use of the five sources of power is used to influence key players. The use of overt power by localized interest who battle to secure their own interests in the process of change has been well documented.[27]

Covert power plays this is a more disguised form of influence. Its use is more subtle and devious than overt power plays. Its application can take many forms including agenda setting, limiting participation in decision to a few select individuals/departments and defining what is and what is not open to decision for others in the organization.[28]

Tactics

The discussion of overt and covert power plays has introduced some of the means by which implementers and change agents can gain acceptance of their proposals, and overcome opposition. We shall now examine in more detail the array of tactics that can be used to achieve these ends. The discussion so far has described the kinds of resistance and opposition that may arise when trying to implement the marketing concept and, more specifically, marketing plans and strategies. We have also examined the skills that are needed to win implementation battles. We shall now outline the tactics that can be used to apply those skills in the face of some hostile reaction within

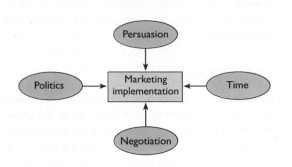

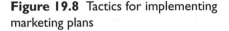

Figure 19.8 Tactics for implementing marketing plans

the organization. These can be grouped into tactics of persuasion, politics, time and negotiation (see Fig. 19.8), and are based on the work of a number of authorities.[29] They provide a wide-ranging checklist of approaches to mobilizing support and overcoming resistance.

Persuasion

Articulate a shared vision the vision—a picture of the destination aspired to and the desired results of the change—needs to be spread to the key players in the organization. For example, if the marketing plan calls for a reduction in staffing levels, the vision that this is required to reposition the company for greater competitiveness needs to be articulated. Without an understanding of the wider picture, people may regard the exercise as 'just another cost drive'.[30] Since most change involves risk and discomfort, a clear vision of its purpose and consequences can make the risk acceptable and the discomfort endurable.

Communicate and train implementation of the marketing concept or a fundamentally different marketing plan means that many individuals have to reorientate, and engage in new activities. To achieve this requires a major commitment to communicating the nature and purpose of the change, and to training staff in the new skills to be mastered. Major changes require face-to-face communication at discussion sessions, and management education seminars. Formal training programmes are needed to upgrade skills and introduce new procedures.

Eliminate misconceptions a major part of the communication programme will be designed to eliminate misconceptions about the consequences of the change. Unfounded fears and anxieties should be allayed. Certain individuals will exaggerate the negative consequences of the proposed changes and their concerns need to be addressed.

Sell the benefits the needs of key players have to be identified and the benefits of the change sold to them on that basis. The benefits may be economic (e.g. increased salary) or psychological (e.g. increased status, enhanced power). Whereas shared vision provides evidence of a wider general benefit (e.g. increased competitiveness) personal benefits should also be sold. This recognizes the fact that individuals seek to achieve not only organizational goals but also personal ambitions.

Gain acceptance by association position the plan against some well-accepted organizational doctrine such as *customer service* or *quality management*. Because the doctrine is heavily backed the chances of the plan being accepted and implemented are enhanced. Another positioning strategy is to associate the plan with a powerful individual (e.g. the chief executive). The objective is to create the viewpoint that if the boss wants the plan, there is no point in opposing it.

Leave room for local control over details leaving some local options or local control over details of the plan creates a sense of ownership on the part of those responsible for implementation, and encourages adaptation to different situations. Thought should be given to the extent of uniformity in execution and the areas where local adoption is both practical and advisable.

Support words with action when implementation involves the establishment or maintenance of a marketing-orientated culture it is vital to support fine words with corresponding action. As we saw when discussing resistance to the marketing concept, it is easy for managers to contradict their words with inappropriate actions (e.g. stressing the need to understand customers, and then cutting the marketing research budget). An illustrative case of how management actions supported the culture that they were trying to create was the story of a regional manager of a US company, United Parcel Service (UPS), who used his initiative to untangle a misdirected shipment of Christmas presents by hiring an entire train and diverting two UPS-owned 727s from their flight plans.[31] Despite the enormous cost (which far exceeded the value of the business) when senior management learned what he had done they praised and rewarded him: their actions supported and reinforced the culture they wanted to foster. As this story became folklore at UPS, their staff knew that senior management meant business when they said that the customer had to come first.

Establish two-way communication it is important that people who are responsible for implementation feel that they can put their viewpoints to senior management; otherwise the feeling of top-down control will spread and resistance will built up through the belief that 'no one ever listens to us'. It is usually well worth listening to people lower down the management hierarchy and especially those who come face-to-face with customers. One way of implementing this approach is through staff suggestion schemes, but these need to be managed so that staff believe it is worth bothering to take part. Marketing in Action 19.4 discusses how Asda's successful scheme works.

19.4   Marketing in Action
Good Ideas Mean Successful Implementation

Asda, the UK supermarket chain acquired by Wal-Mart in 1999, has a policy of tapping into the collective wisdom of its 85 000 staff. It runs two schemes aimed at involving staff in the day-to-day running of the company. The first, entitled Colleague Circles, encourages its staff (Asda calls them colleagues) to put forward suggestions for improved customer service. The best ideas are presented at an annual meeting called the National Circle. The objective is to make it as easy as possible for colleagues to pass on ideas based on their experience with customers. As an off-shoot of this programme, staff representatives talked directly to the president of Wal-Mart via a video-link.

The second scheme, called 'Tell Archie', invites staff to make suggestions direct to Asda's chairman, Archie Norman. A key ingredient is that if someone writes to the chairman they get a reply from the chairman. The scheme reflects the belief in Asda that everyone is equally valued and their contribution respected. It promotes a culture in which everyone takes responsibility for improving the business. In six years, Mr Norman has replied to almost 45 000 suggestions. The most promising are rewarded with a voucher worth up to £20 or 'star points' that can be redeemed against a catalogue of offers including clothes and holidays.

Neither scheme is intended to provide a vehicle for ideas that fundamentally change the strategy of Asda, but to improve Asda's operations in small ways. For example, one suggestion was based on the problem of clearing up litter and trolleys around rose bushes that were used to landscape car parks. The thorns were proving painful and so the roses were replaced with shrubs and trees that made a tiny part of Asda's operations easier and more efficient.

Evidence shows that suggestion schemes only work if people believe that their suggestions will be considered and some implemented. Inviting staff to make suggestions can improve motivation and quality of work including the achievement of high standards of customer service. Staff can never complain that 'no one ever listens to us'!

Based on: White (1999)[32]

Politics

Build coalitions   the process of creating allies for the proposed measures is a crucial step in the implementation process. Two groups have special significance: power sources who control the resources needed for implementation such as information (expertise or data), finance, and support (legitimacy, opinion leadership and political backing); and stakeholders who are those people likely to gain or lose from the change.[33] Discussion with potential losers may reveal ways of sharing some rewards with them ('Invite the opposition in'). At the very least, talking to them will reveal their grievances, and so allow thought to be given to how these may be handled. Another product of these discussions with both potential allies and foes is that the original proposals may be improved by accepting some of their suggestions.

Display support   having recruited powerful allies these should be asked for a visible demonstration of support. This will confirm any statements that implementers have made about the strength of their backing ('Gain acceptance by association'). Allies should be invited to meetings, presentations and seminars so that stakeholders can see the forces behind the change.

Invite the opposition in   thought should be given to creating ways of sharing the rewards of the change with the opposition. This may mean modifying the plan and how it is to be implemented to take account of the needs of key players. So long as the main objectives of the plan remain intact, this may be a necessary step to remove some opposition.

Warn the opposition   critics of the plan should be left in no doubt as to the adverse consequences of opposition. This has been called *selling the negatives*. However, the tactic should be used with care because statements that are perceived as threats may stiffen rather than dilute resistance, particularly when the source does not have a strong power base.

Use of language   in the political arena the potency of language in endorsing a preferred action and discrediting the opposition has long

been apparent. For example, during the Gulf War the following terminology was used:[34]

We (UN) have	*They (Iraq) have*
Army, Navy and Air Force	The War Machine
Reporting guidelines	Censorship
Press briefings	Propaganda
We	*They*
Suppress	Destroy
Eliminate	Kill
Neutralize	Kill
We launch	*They launch*
First strikes	Sneak missile attacks
Pre-emptively	Without provocation
Our men are	*Their men are*
Boys, lads	Troops, hordes

Language can be used as a weapon in the implementation battle with critics being labelled 'outdated', 'backward looking' and 'set in their ways'. In meetings, implementers need to avoid the temptation to *overpower* in their use of language. For people without a strong power base (such as young newcomers to a company) using phrases like 'We must take this action' or 'This is the way we have to move' to people in a more senior position (e.g. a board of directors) will provoke psychological resistance even to praiseworthy plans. Phases like 'I suggest' or 'I have a proposal for you to consider' recognize the inevitable desire on the part of more senior management to feel involved in the decision-making rather than being treated like a rubber stamp.

Decision control   this may be achieved by agenda setting (i.e. controlling what is and is not discussed in meetings), limiting participation in decision-making to a small number of allies, controlling which decisions are open for debate in the organization, and timing important meetings when it is known that a key critic is absent (e.g. on holiday, or abroad on business).

The either/or alternative   finally, when an implementation proposal is floundering, a powerful proponent may decide to use the either/or tactic in which the key decision-maker is required to choose between two documents placed on the desk: one asks for approval of the implementation plan, the other tenders the implementer's resignation.

Time

Incremental steps   people need time to adjust to change, therefore consideration should be given to how quickly change is introduced. Where resistance to the full implementation package is likely to be strong, one option is to submit the strategy in incremental steps. A small, less controversial strategy is implemented first. Its success provides the impetus for the next implementation proposals and so on.

Persistence   this tactic requires the resubmission of the strategy until it is accepted. Modifications to the strategy may be necessary on the way but the objective is to wear down the opposition by resolute and persistent force. The game is a battle of wills, and requires the capability of the implementer to accept rejection without loss of motivation.

Leave insufficient time for alternatives   a different way of using time is to present plans at the last possible minute so that there is insufficient time for anyone to present or implement an alternative. The proposition is basically 'We must move with this plan as there is no alternative'.

Wait for the opposition to leave   for those prepared to play a waiting game, withdrawing proposals until a key opposition member leaves the company or loses power may be feasible. Implementers should be alert to changes in the power structure in these ways as they may present a window of opportunity to resubmit hitherto rejected proposals.

Negotiation

Make the opening stance high   when the implementer suspects that a proposal in the plan is likely to require negotiation, the correct opening stance is to start high but be realistic. There are two strong reasons for this. First, the opponent may accept the proposal without modification; second, it provides room for negotiation. When deciding how high to go, the limiting factor is the need to avoid unnecessary conflict. For example, asking for a move from a fixed salary to a commission only system with a view to compromising with salary plus commission is likely to be unrealistic, and provoke unnecessary antagonism among the salesforce.

Trade concessions   sometimes it may be possible to grant a concession simply to secure agreement to the basics of the plan. Indeed, if the implementer has created negotiating room, this may be perfectly acceptable. In other circumstances, however, the implementer may be able to trade concession for concession with the opponent. For example, a demand from the salesforce to reduce list price may be met by a counterproposal to reduce discount levels. A useful way of trading concessions is by means of the *if . . . then* technique: 'If you are prepared to reduce your discount levels from 10 to 5 per cent, I am prepared to reduce list price by 5 per cent.'[35]

This is a valuable tool in negotiation because it promotes movement towards agreement and yet ensures that concessions given to the opponent are matched by concessions in return. Whenever possible, an attempt to create *win-win* situations should be made where concessions that cost the giver very little are highly valued by the receiver.

Evaluation

Finally, during and after the implementation process, evaluation should be made to consider what has been achieved, and what has been learned. Evaluation may be in terms of the degree of support gained from key players, how well the plan and strategy have been implemented in the marketplace (e.g. by the use of customer surveys), the residual goodwill between opposing factions, and any changes in the balance of power between the implementers and other key parties in the company.

Marketing organization

Marketing organization provides the context in which marketing implementation takes place companies may have no marketing departments; those that do may have functional, product-based market-centred or matrix organizational structures.

No marketing department

As we have seen this is a common situation. Small companies that cannot afford the luxury of managerial specialism, production or financially driven organizations, and companies that eschew marketing because they believe it to be nothing more than glitz, glamour and promotion are unlikely to have a marketing department. In small companies, the owner-manager may carry out some of the functions of marketing such as developing customer relationships, providing market feedback and product development. In larger companies that may use the traditional production, finance, personnel and sales functional division, the same task may be undertaken by those departments, especially sales (e.g. customer feedback, sales forecasting). The classic case of a company that has scorned the popular concept of marketing is Anita Roddick's Body Shop. Despite being based on many of the essentials of marketing (e.g. a clearly differentiated product range, clear, consistent positioning and effective PR) the Body Shop has refused to set up a marketing department. However, the growth of me-too brands led to the need to reappraise the role of marketing through the establishment of a marketing department in 1994.[36]

It should be noted that not all companies that do not have a marketing department are poor at marketing. Nor does the existence of a marketing department guarantee marketing orientation. As we have seen, many marketing departments carry out only a selected range of marketing functions and lack the power to influence key customer-impinging decisions, or to drive through a marketing-orientated philosophy within the business. Marketing should be seen as a company-wide phenomenon, not something that should be delegated exclusively to the marketing department.

Functional organization

As small companies grow, the most likely emergence of a formal marketing structure is as a section within the sales department. As the importance of marketing is realized and the company grows, the status of marketing may rise with the appointment of a marketing manager on equivalent status with the sales manager who reports to a marketing director (see Fig. 19.9a). If the marketing director title is held by the previous sales director, little may change in terms of company philosophy: marketing may subsume a sales support role. An alternative route is to set up *functional structure* under a sales director and a marketing director (see Fig. 19.9b). Both have equal status and the priorities of each job may lead to conflict (see Table 19.1). A study of Fazer, a Finnish confectionery firm, showed that these conflicts can be heightened by the different backgrounds of marketing people who had business training and salespeople who trusted more on personal experience and skills.[37] The preferred

Table 19.1	Potential conflict between marketing and sales	
Area	*Sales*	*Marketing*
Objectives	Short-term sales	Long-term brand/market building
Marketing research	Personal experience with customers/trade	Market research reports
Pricing	Low prices to maximize sales volume	Price set consistent with positioning strategy
	Discount structure in the hands of the salesforce	Discount structure built into the marketing implementation plan
Marketing expenditure	Maximize resources channelled to the salesforce	Develop a balanced marketing mix using a variety of communication tools
Promotion	Sales literature, free customer give-aways, samples, business entertainment	Design a well-blended promotional mix including advertising, promotion and public relations

solution, then, is to appoint a marketing director who understands and has the power to implement marketing strategies that recognize sales as one (usually a key) element of the marketing mix.

Functionalism bring the benefit of specialization of task and a clear definition of responsibilities, and is still the most common form of marketing organization.[38] However, as the product range widens and the number of markets served increases, the structure may become unwieldy with insufficient attention being paid to specific products and markets since no one has full responsibility for a particular product or market.

Product-based organization

The need to give sufficient care and attention to individual products has led many companies (particularly in the fast-moving consumer goods field) to move to a product-based structure. For example, Nestlé moved from a functional to a product management system in 1992. A common structure is for a product manager to oversee a group of brands within a product field (e.g. lagers, shampoos) supported by brand managers who manage specific brands (see Fig. 19.10). Their role is to coordinate the business management of their brands. This involves dealing with advertising, promotion and marketing research agencies, and function areas within the firm. Their dilemma stems from the fact that they have responsibility for the commercial success of their brands without the power to force through their decisions as they have no authority over other functional areas such as sales, production and R&D. They act as ambassadors for their brands, attempting to ensure adequate support from the salesforce, and sufficient marketing funds to communicate to customers and the trade through advertising and promotion.

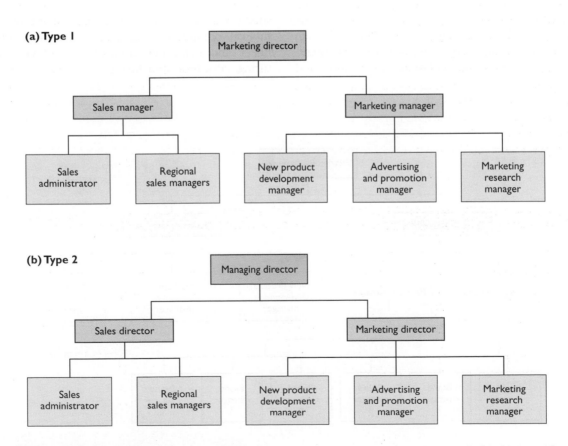

Figure 19.9 Functional marketing organizations

The advantages of a *product-based organization* are that adequate attention is given to developing a coordinated marketing mix for each brand, and assigning specific responsibility means that speed of response to market or technological developments is quicker than relying on a committee of functional specialists. A by-product of the system is that it provides excellent training for young businesspeople as they are required to come into contact with a wide range of business activities.

However, there are a number of drawbacks. First, the healthy rivalry between product managers can sometimes spill over to counter-productive competition and conflict. Second, the system can breed new layers of management which can be costly. For example, brand managers might be supplemented by assistants and as brands are added so new brand managers need to be recruited. Big strides have been taken to reduce inefficiency. A UK study by Booze, Allen and Hamilton, which is reported in Richards,[39] showed that the percentage of brand managers handling just one brand had dropped from 45 per cent in 1990 to 33 per cent in 1994, and the number of brand managers working on more than three brands had jumped from 30 to 46 per cent. Also companies such as Procter and Gamble and Unilever are eliminating layers of management in the face of increasing demands from supermarkets to trim prices (and thus increase efficiency). Procter and Gamble, for example, have eliminated the title of assistant brand manager. Third, brand managers are often criticized for spending too much time coordinating in-company activities and too little time talking to customers. In response to these problems some companies are introducing **category management** to provide a focus on a category of brands. Marketing in Action 19.5 discusses the growth of category management.

Market-centred organization

Where companies sell their products to diverse markets, *market-centred organizations* should be considered. Instead of managers focusing on brands, *market managers* concentrate their energies on understanding and satisfying the needs of particular markets. The salesforce, also, may be similarly focused. For example, Fig. 19.11 shows a market-centred organization for hypothetical computer manufacturer. The specialist needs and computer applications in manufacturing, education and financial services justify a

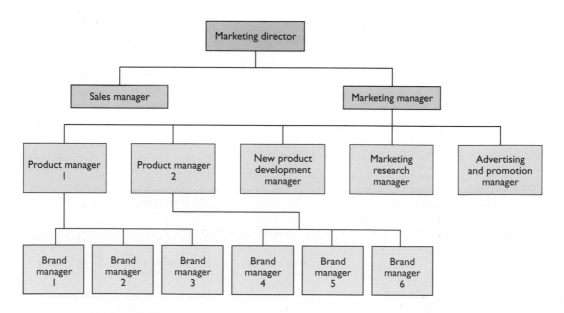

Figure 19.10 Product-based organization

sales and marketing organization based on these market segments.

Occasionally hybrid product/market-centred organizations based on distribution channels are appropriate. For example, at Philips, old organizational structures based on brands or products have been downgraded, replacing them with a new focus on distribution channels. Product managers who ensure that product designs fit market requirements still exist. However, under a new combined sales and marketing director the emphasis has moved to markets. Previously, different salespeople would visit retailers selling different products from the Philips range. This has

19.5   Marketing in Action

The Growth of the Category Manager

The criticism levelled at the brand management system—conflict, cost and inwardly focused—and the demands of the trade have led major marketing organizations to look at category management as an alternative. Instead of separate brand managers, category teams manage several brands, with specialists handling advertising, sales promotion, line extensions and packaging and customizing each category's product mix, merchandising and promotions on a store-by store basis. The result is that brands are managed as a portfolio, thus reducing conflict, the number of management layers are reduced, thus lowering costs, and the customer (or at least the trade) is in sharper focus.

Two additional forces are encouraging the growth of category management. First, retailers are using information technology and databases to manage categories as their unit of analysis. Consequently, they expect their suppliers also to possess a category perspective. Indeed, some multinational retailers are expecting one worldwide contact person for a category to provide the 'big picture' necessary to manage cross-nationally. Second, category management promotes greater clarity in strategy across brands. Brand positions within categories can be more readily defined and resource allocation decisions involving promotional budgets and product innovations can be made strategically. The goal is to make the brands within a category work together to provide the greatest collective impact and reap the maximum operational efficiencies.

Lever Brothers have moved down this route. No longer do they have a marketing director. Two business units—fabrics and homecare—with two core, parallel marketing teams have been set up. A *consumer marketing team* focuses on the consumer/brand marketing, and a new *category marketing team* moulds brand plans to fit the requirements of retailers especially the supermarket chains. For example, if a new brand or extension is being considered, it would be developed only if it makes sense in the trade's vision of the category. The category management team can help retailers determine the best category mix of brands for a given store or a specific community.

An accompanying change is that the old sales department at Lever Brothers becomes a *customer development department*, recognizing the changing role of salespeople as looking to develop business with customers rather than looking for quick sales.

These developments have led to the ideas of three important marketing concepts, the three Cs: *consumers*, *categories* and *customers*. The reorganization is more than a change in the management structure; it reflects a fundamental change of approach to marketing and sales.

Based on: Mitchell (1994);[40] Nielsen (1993);[41] Aaker and Joachimsthaler (2000)[42]

been replaced by dedicated sales teams concentrating on channels such as the multiples, the independents and mail order.[43]

The enormous influence of the trade in many consumer markets has forced other firms, besides Philips, to rethink their marketing organization. This has led to the establishment of *trade marketing* teams who serve the needs of large retailers.

The advantage of the market-centred approach is the focus it provides on the specific customer requirements of new opportunities, and develop new products that meet their customer needs. By organizing around customers, it embodies the essence of the marketing concept. However, for companies competing in many sectors it can be resource-hungry.

Matrix organization

For companies with a wide product range selling diverse markets, a *matrix structure* may be necessary. Both product and market managers are employed to give due attention to both facets of marketing activity. The organizational structure resembles a grid as shown in Fig. 19.12, again using a hypothetical computer company. Product managers are responsible for their group of products' sales and profit performance, and monitor technological developments that impact on their products. Market managers focus on the needs of customers in each market segment.

For the system to work effectively, clear lines of decision-making authority need to be drawn up because of the possible areas of conflict. For example, who decides the price of the product? If a market manager requires an addition to the product line to meet the special needs of some customers, who has the authority to decide if the extra costs are justified? How should the salesforce be organized: along product or market lines? Also, it is a resource hungry method of organization. Nevertheless, the dual specialism does promote the careful analysis of both product and markets so that customer needs are met.

Marketing organization and implementation are inevitably intertwined as the former affects the day-to-day activities of marketing managers. It is important that we understand the organizational world as marketing managers have come to understand it, in particular the activities which constitute their job.[44] Marketing in Action 19.6 describes what marketing managers actually do with their time and how organizational change affects activities.

Marketing control

Marketing control is an essential element of the marketing planning process because it provides a review of how well marketing objectives have been achieved. A framework for controlling marketing activities is given in Fig. 19.13. The

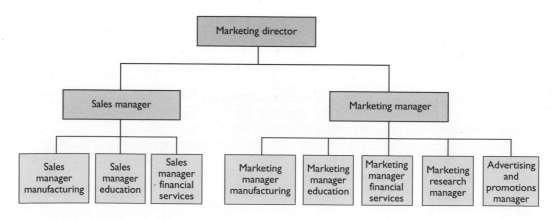

Figure 19.11 Market-centred organization

process begins by deciding marketing objectives leading to the setting of performance standards. For example, a marketing objective of 'widening the customer base' might lead to the setting of the performance standard of 'generating twenty new accounts within twelve months'. Similarly the marketing objective of 'improving market share' might translate into a performance standard of 'improving market share from 20 per cent to 25 per cent'. Some companies set quantitative marketing objectives in which case performance standards are automatically derived.

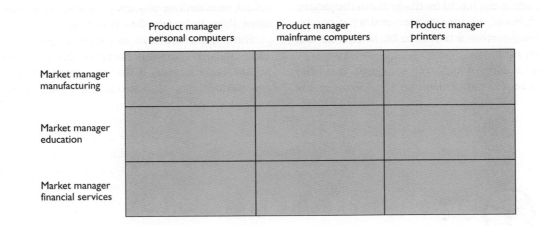

Figure 19.12 Matrix organization

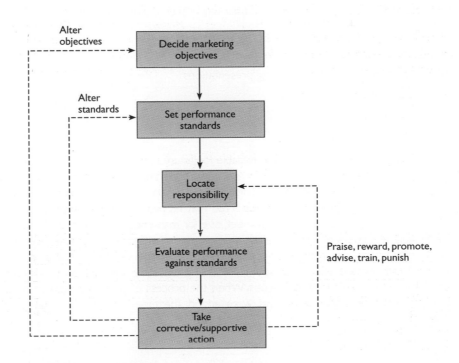

Figure 19.13 The marketing control system

The next step is to locate responsibility. In some cases responsibility ultimately falls on one person (e.g. the brand manager), in others it is shared (e.g. the sales manager and salesforce). It is important to consider this issue since corrective or supportive action may need to focus on those responsible for the success of marketing activity.

Performance is then evaluated against standards which relies on an efficient information system and a judgement has to be made about the degree of success and failure achieved and what corrective or supportive action is to be taken. This can take various forms.

First, failure which is attributed to poor performance of individuals may result in the giving of advice regarding future attitudes and actions, training and/or punishment (e.g. criticism, lower pay, demotion, termination of employment). Success, on the other hand, should be rewarded through praise, promotion, and/or higher pay.

Second, failure which is attributed to unrealistic marketing objectives and performance standards may cause them to be lowered for the subsequent period. Success which is thought to reflect unambitious objectives and standards may cause them to be raised next period.

Third, the attainment of marketing objectives and standards may also mean modification next period. For example, if the marketing objective and performance standard of opening 20 new

19.6 Marketing in Action

What Marketing Managers Really Do

Marketing managers fully recognize their crucial role in planning for the future but the realities of the job often mean that the short-term pressures of dealing with administrative tasks leave little time for strategic planning. One survey of 50 brand and marketing managers found that short-term business accounted for 83 per cent of their day, broken down as follows:

✦ 29 per cent on marketing operations or 'maintenance'.

✦ 23 per cent working with other functions.

✦ 11 per cent preparing and giving presentations.

✦ 8 per cent on administration.

✦ 6 per cent travelling.

✦ 6 per cent training.

This left only 17 per cent of the day available for 'future marketing'.

Organizational structures can influence how much time is spent on various tasks. Virgin, for example, have flattened structures which give individuals more responsibility. As a result there are fewer meetings. One executive reported that he had only three meetings a month: one for manufacturing where all the divisions meet, one for marketing (if needed) and one for sales. Since there were few layers of middle management, work was invigorating because 'you spend your time doing what you are meant to be doing'. This contrasted with his experience at an advertising agency where much wasted effort was spent presenting the same information to different groups of colleagues, clients and their colleagues. When the process of preparing contact reports, monthly updates and three-monthly reviews were added, the time left over for strategic thinking was minimal.

Based on: Leggett (1996)[45]

accounts is achieved, this may mean the focus for the next period may change. The next objective may focus on customer retention, for instance.

Finally, the failure of one achieved objective to bring about another may also require corrective action. For example, if a marketing objective of increasing calls to new accounts does not result in extra sales, the original objective may be dropped in favour of another (e.g. improving product awareness through advertising).

Strategic control

Two types of control systems may be used. The first concerns major strategic issues and answers the question 'Are we doing the right thing?' It focuses on company strengths, weakness, opportunities and threats, and the process of control is through a *marketing audit*. This has been discussed in depth in Chapter 2 in The Process of Marketing Planning, and will not be elaborated upon here.

Operational control

The second control system concerns day-to-day ongoing marketing activities and is called operational control. Key methods of operational control are *customer satisfaction measurement*, *sales and market share analysis*, and *cost and profitability analysis*. Although focused on operational issues, this information can usefully be fed into the marketing audit also.

Customer satisfaction measurement

An increasing common barometer of marketing success is *customer satisfaction measurement*. This is an encouraging sign as customer satisfaction is at the heart of the marketing concept. Although this measure does not appear directly on a company's profit and loss account, it is a fundamental condition for corporate success. The process involves the setting of customer satisfaction criteria, the design of a questionnaire to measure satisfaction on those criteria, the choice of which customers to interview, and the

analysis and interpretation of results. The use of a market research agency is advised to take advantage of their skills, and unbiased viewpoint. One industrial marketing research agency advocates interviewing three customer groups to give a valid picture of customer satisfaction and marketing effectiveness:

+ Ten current customers.
+ Ten lapsed customers (who bought from us in the past but not now).
+ Ten non-customers (who are in the market for the product but hitherto have not bought from us).

Invaluable information can be gained concerning customer satisfaction, how effective the sales-force are, why customers have switched to other suppliers, and why some potential customers have never done business with our company.

Sales and market share analysis

Sales analysis compares actual with target sales. The starting-point is to compare overall sales revenue. Negative variance may be due to lower sales volume, or lower prices. Product, customer and regional analysis will be carried out to discover where the shortfall arose. A change in the product mix could account for a sales fall with more lower priced products being sold. The loss of a major customer may also account for a sales decline. Regional analysis may identify a poorly performing area sales manager or salesperson. These findings would point the direction of further investigations to uncover the reasons for those outcomes.

Market share analysis evaluates a company's performance in comparison to that of its competitors. Sales analysis may show a healthy increase in revenues but this may be due to market growth rather than an improved performance over competitors. An accompanying decline in market share would sound the warning bells regarding relative performance. Again, these findings would stimulate further investigation to root out the causes.

It should be recognized that a market share decline is not always a symptom of poor performance. This is why outcomes should always be compared to marketing objectives and performance standards. If the marketing objective was to harvest a product leading to a performance standard of a 5 per cent increase in profits, its achievement may be accompanied by a market share decline (through the effect of a price rise). This would be a perfectly satisfactory outcome given the desired objective.

Cost and profitability analysis

Cost analysis deals with expenses, and when compared to sales revenue provides the basis for *profitability analysis*.

Profitability analysis provides information on the profit performance of key aspects of marketing such as products, customers or distribution channels. The example given focuses on products. The hypothetical company sells three types of products: paper products, printers and copiers. The first step is to measure marketing inputs to each of these products. These are shown in Table 19.2. Allocation of sales calls to products is facilitated by separate sales teams for each group.

If the sales teams were organized on purely geographic lines an estimate of how much time was devoted to each product, on average, at each call would need to be made. Table 19.2 shows how the costs of an average sales call, advertising insertion and order are calculated. This provides vital information to calculate profitability for each product.

Table 19.3 shows how the net profit before tax is calculated. The results show how copiers are losing money. Before deciding to drop this line the company would have to take into account the extent to which customers expect copiers to be sold alongside paper products and printers, the effect of dropping copiers on paper sales, the possible annoyance caused to customers who already own one of their copiers, the extent to which copiers cover overheads that otherwise would need to be paid for from paper products and printer sales, the scope for pruning costs and increasing sales, and the degree to which the arbitrary nature of some of the cost allocations has unfairly treated copier products.

Table 19.2   Allocating functional costs to products

Products	Salesforce (number of sales calls per year)	Advertising (number of one-page ads placed)	Order processing (number of orders placed)
Paper products	500	20	1000
Printers	400	20	800
Copiers	250	10	200
Total	1150	50	2000
Functional cost per unit	£165 per call	£2600 per ad	£40 per order

Table 19.3   Profitability statement for products (£)

	Paper products	Printers	Copiers
Sales	1 000 000	700 000	300 000
Cost of goods sold	500 000	250 000	250 000
Gross margin	500 000	450 000	50 000
Marketing costs			
Salesforce (at £165 per call)	82 500	66 000	41 250
Advertising (at £2600 per advertisement)	52 000	52 000	26 000
Order processing (at £40 per order)	40 000	32 000	8 000
Total cost	174 500	150 000	72 250
Net profit (or loss) before tax	325 500	300 000	(25 250)

Summary

Developing effective marketing plans requires not only the vision to create strategies that fit the environment but also the ability to translate those plans into action. This requires a knowledge and understanding of how to gain acceptance and commitment to their implementation. An appropriate strategy with bad implementation often means poor performance and an inability to identify the cause of failure; inappropriate strategy coupled with good implementation can lead to a hastening of failure, or success as good implementation patches up the inadequacies of strategy.

Since implementing new plans requires change, implementers need to understand the stages that people go through when confronted with a major disruption. This is called the transition curve and suggests that people require time to come to terms with change.

The objectives of marketing implementation and change were described by means of the ladder of support, which ranges from outright opposition to full commitment. Implementers need the skills to deal with opposition and foster commitment.

For some companies, change means the adoption of the marketing concept for the first time. The five barriers to adoption are marketing's tendency to require high cost solutions, the unquantifiable nature of its benefits, personal ambitions of individuals which may emphasize enjoyment and convenience at the expense of customer satisfaction, reward systems that reflect short-term profitability rather than long-term customer satisfaction, and finally, the inability of managers to support their words with customer-centred actions.

Resistance to change may take the form of direct overt opposition or more passive actions such as foot-dragging, unavailability, delaying the decision and creating hassle to wear the proposer down. Whatever form resistance takes, implementers need a plan of action to manage the process of change. A four-stage plan is outlined: objectives, strategy, execution and evaluation.

A key element of strategy is internal marketing, which likens the development of an internal implementation strategy to creating external marketing strategies. For example, market segmentation provides an analytical tool to analyse internal customers. Execution requires the skills of persuasion, negotiation and politics and the ability to translate those skills into action through the use of tactics. Persuasive tactics include the articulation of a shared vision, communication and training, the elimination of misconceptions, and the ability to support words with actions. Political tactics vary from building coalitions and displaying support to warning critics of the consequences of opposition and the use of language to discredit them. Tactics which are time-related should also be considered, including introducing the change in incremental steps and being persistent in the resubmission of plans. Negotiation tactics involve making the opening stance high and trading concessions. Finally, an evaluation should be made.

Many marketing textbooks are written on the assumption that all companies have a marketing department. This is far from the truth and the majority of those that do are not integrated, full service departments. Marketing organization is important because it affects how marketing strategies are implemented. Different organizational structure have varying potential for creating customer satisfaction. These are functional, product-based, market-centred and matrix organizations. Product-based, market-centred and matrix organizations add management layers and so increase not only resources devoted to the marketing task but also costs.

Marketing control provides a means of checking how well marketing objectives have been achieved. The marketing control system consists of deciding marketing objectives, setting performance standards, locating responsibility, evaluating performance against standards, and taking corrective or supportive action.

Strategic control is carried out through a marketing audit (see Chapter 2). Operational control monitors day-to-day marketing activities and is based on customer satisfaction measurement, sales and market share analysis, and cost and profitability analysis. Although being focused on tactical decisions some of this information can be usefully fed into the marketing audit.

Internet exercise

Service delivery

Sites to visit
http://www.marriott.com/
http://www.careers.marriott.com/extras.asp
http://www.accor.com

Exercise
Discuss how Marriott delivers its services.
Compare Marriott's approach to human resources with Accor's.

Study questions

1 Think of a situation when your life suffered from a dramatic change. Using Fig. 19.3 recall your feelings over time. How closely did your experiences match the stages in the figure? How did your feelings at each stage (e.g. denial and disbelief) manifest themselves.

2 Can good implementation substitute for an inappropriate strategy? Give an example of how good implementation might make the situation worse and an example of how it might improve the situation.

3 What might be the objectives of market implementation and change? Distinguish between gaining compliance, acceptance and commitment.

4 Why do some companies fail to implement the marketing concept?

5 Describe the ways in which people may resist the change that is implied in the implementation of a new marketing plan. Why should they wish to do this?

6 What is internal marketing? To what extent does it parallel external marketing strategy?

7 Describe the skills that are necessary to see a marketing plan through to successful implementation.

8 What tactics of persuasion are at the implementer's disposal? What are the advantages and limitations of each one?

9 Without the use of political manoeuvres, most attempts at marketing implementation will fail. Discuss.

10 Discuss the options available for organizing a marketing department. How well is each form likely to serve customers?

11 Discuss the problems involved in setting up and implementing a marketing control system.

References

1. Johannessen, J.-A., J. Olaisen and A. Havan (1993) The Challenge of Innovation in a Norwegian Shipyard Facing the Russian Market, *European Journal of Marketing*, **27** (3), 23–38.

2. Bonoma, T. V. (1985) *The Marketing Edge: Making Strategies Work*, New York: Free Press.

3. Wilson, G. (1993) *Making Change Happen*, London: Pitman.

4. Sambrook, C. (1992) Marriott: A Name to Contend with, *Marketing*, 3 September, 16–18.

5. Abopdaher, D. (1986) *A Biography of Iacocca*, London: Star.

6. Stanton, W. J., R. H. Buskirk and R. Spiro (1991) *Management of a Sales Force*, Boston, Mass: Irwin.

7. Webster, F. E. Jr (1988) *Rediscovering the Marketing Concept, Business Horizons,* **31** (May–June), 29–39.

8. Webster (1988) op. cit.

9. Argyris, C. (1966) Interpersonal Barriers to Decision Making, *Harvard Business Review*, **44** (March–April) 84–97.

10. Kanter, R. M. (1983) *The Change Masters*, London: Allen and Unwin.

11. Piercy, N. (1997) *Marketing-Led Strategy Change*, Oxford: Butterworth-Heinemann.

12. Johnson, G. (1987) *Strategic Change and the Management Process*, Oxford: Basil Blackwell.

13. Pettigrew, A. M. (1974) The Influence Process between Specialists and Executives, *Personnel Review* **3** (1), 24–30.

14. Ansoff, I. and E. McDonnell (1990) *Implanting Strategic Management*, Englewood Cliffs, NJ: Prentice-Hall.

15. Pettigrew, A. M. (1985) *The Awakening Giant: Continuity and Change in* ICI, Oxford: Basil Blackwell.

16. Kanter (1983) op. cit.

17. Kennedy, G., J. Benson and J. MacMillan (1980) *Managing Negotiations*, London: Business Books.

18. Pettigrew, A. M. (1974) The Influence Process between Specialists and Executives, *Personnel Review*, **3** (1), 24–30.

19. Piercy, N. (1990) Making Marketing Strategies Happen in the Real World, *Marketing Business,* February, 20–1.

20. Baer, W. S. (1998) Will the Internet Bring Electronic Services to the Home? *Business Strategy Review*, **9** (1), 29–37.

21. Piercy, N. and N. Morgan (1991) Internal Marketing: The Missing Half of the Marketing Programme, *Long Range Planning*, **24** (2), 82–93.

22. See Gronroos, C. (1985) Internal Marketing: Theory and Practice, in Bloch, T. M., G. D. Upah and V. A. Zeithaml (eds) *Services Marketing in a Changing Environment*, Chicago: American Marketing Association; Gummesson, E. (1987) Using Internal Marketing to Develop a New Culture: The Case of Ericsson Quality, *Journal of Business and Industrial Marketing*, **2** (3), 23–8; Mudie, P. (1987) Internal Marketing: Cause of Concern, *Quarterly Review of Marketing*, Spring–Summer, 21–4.

23. Wilson, G. (1993) *Making Change Happen*, London: Pitman.

24. Jonquières, G. de (1993) Apocalypse: But Not Just Now, *Financial Times*, 4 January, 30.

25. Taylor, R. (1993) Resetting the Clock, *Financial Times*, 10 February, 14.

26. French, J. R. P. and B. Raven (1959) The Bases of Social Power, in Cartwright, D. (ed.) *Studies in Social Power*, Ann Arbor, Mich: University of Michigan Press, 150–67.

27. See Hickson, D. J., C. R. Hinings, C. A. Lee, R. E. Schneck and J. M. Pennings (1971) A Strategic Contingencies Theory of Intraorganizational Power, *Administrative Science Quarterly*, **16** (2), 216–29; Hinings, C. R., D. J. Hickson, J. M. Pennings and R. E. Schneck (1974) Structural Conditions of Intraorganizational Power, *Administrative Science Quarterly,* **19** (1), 22–44.

28. Wilson, D. C. (1992) *A Strategy of Change: Concepts and Controversies in the Management of Change,* London: Routledge.

29. See Kanter, R. M., B. A. Stein and T. D. Jick (1992) *The Challenge of Organizational Change*, New York: Free Press; Kanter (1983) op. cit.; Piercy (1991) op. cit., Ansoff and McDonnell (1990) op. cit.

30. Kanter, Stein and Jick (1992) op. cit.

31. Bonoma, T. V. (1984) Making your Marketing Strategy Work, *Harvard Business Review*, **62** (March–April), 68–76.

32. White, D. (1999) Good Ideas Come from Little Boxes, *Financial Times*, 15 September, 18.

33. Kanter, Stein and Jick (1992) op. cit.

34. Wilson (1993) op. cit.

35. Kennedy, Benson and MacMillan (1980) op. cit.

36. Hewitt, M. (1994) Body Shop Opens its Doors to Marketing, *Marketing*, 26 May, 20.

37. Eriksson, P. and K. Räsänen (1998) The Bitter and the Sweet: Evolving Constellations of Product Mix Management in a Confectionery Company, *European Journal of Marketing*, **32** (3/4), 279–304.

38. Workman J. P. Jr, C. Homburg and K. Gruner (1998) Marketing Organisation: an Integrative Framework of Dimensions and Determinants, *Journal of Marketing*, **62**, July, 21–41.

39. See Richards, A. (1994) What is Holding Back Today's Brand Managers?, *Marketing*, **3** (3 February), 16–17.

40. Mitchell, A. (1994) Dark Night of Marketing or a New Dawn?, *Marketing*, 17 February, 22–3.

41. Nielsen, A. C. (1993) *Category Management in Europe: A Quiet Revolution*, Oxford: Nielsen Europe.

42. Aaker, D. and E. Joachimsthaler (2000) *Brand Leadership*, New York: Free Press, 10–11.

43. Mitchell, A. (1994) Dark Night of Marketing or a New Dawn? *Marketing*, 17 February, 22–3.

44. Brownlie, D. and M. Saren (1997) Beyond the One-Dimensional Marketing Manager: The Discourse of Theory, Practice and Relevance, *International Journal of Research in Marketing*, **14**, 147–61.

45. Leggett, D. (1996) Hours Not to Reason Why, *Marketing*, 31 October, 26–7.

Key terms

transition curve   the emotional stages that people pass through when confronted with an adverse change

change master   a person who develops an implementation strategy to drive through organizational change

internal marketing   (i) the training, motivating and retention of employees at the customer interface in services (ii) marketing to all employees with the aim of acheiving successful marketing implementation

concession analysis   the evaluation of things that can be offered to someone in negotiation valued from the viewpoint of the receiver

proposal analysis   the prediction and evaluation of proposals and demands likely to be made by someone with whom one is negotiating

reward power   power derived from the ability to provide benefits

expert power   power which derives from an individual's expertise

referent power   power derived by the reference source, e.g. when people identify with and respect the architect of change

legitimate power   power based on legitimate authority, such as line management

coercive power   power inherent in the ability to punish

overt power play   the use of visible, open kinds of power tactics

covert power play   the use of disguised forms of power tactics

category management   the management of brands in a group, portfolio or category with specific emphasis on the retail trade's requirements

trade marketing   marketing to the retail trade

marketing control   the stage in the marketing planning process or cycle when performance against plan is monitored so that corrective action, if necessary, can be taken

marketing audit   a systematic examination of a business's marketing environment, objectives, strategies, and activities with a view to identifying key strategic issues, problem areas and opportunities

customer satisfaction measurement   a process through which customer satisfaction criteria are set, customers are surveyed and the results interpreted in order to establish the level of customer satisfaction with the organization's product

sales analysis   a comparison of actual with target sales

market share analysis   a comparison of company sales with total sales of the product, including sales of competitors

cost analysis   the calculation of direct and fixed costs and their allocation to products, customers and/or distribution channels

profitability analysis   the calculation of sales revenues and costs for the purpose of calculating the profit performance of products, customers and/or distribution channels

Case 35 Hansen Bathrooms (B)

Rob Vincent had taken Susan Clements' advice The coating on the Hansen bathroom furniture created extra value for consumers and should be reflected in a higher price. A market research survey had shown beyond doubt that households valued the benefits that the coating produced: cleaning could be extended from once every two weeks to once every three months.

Accordingly Rob had recommended to the board a consumer price of £470. This was only £5 and £20 more than the main two competitors. After the usual 25 per cent discount the price differential would be even less. But the board remained unconvinced.

The first meeting to discuss pricing strategy for the new Hansen bathroom range featuring a new, patent-protected coating that contained an agent which dispersed grime and grease from basins and washbasins etc. had taken place three weeks ago. No conclusion had been drawn. Consequently, a second meeting had been arranged to thrash out a coherent strategy.

Rob decided to play it tough. At 30 he was considerably younger than anyone else on the board, who were all in their 50s. Rob began:

'I recommended a price of £470 three weeks ago and that recommendation still stands! I hope my arguments have sunk in since our last meeting because quite honestly they are watertight. Let's go through them once again.

1   The new coating provides tangible customer value: cleaning is extended from once every two weeks to once every three months.

2   Marketing research has shown that the customer is delighted with this change.

3   Our bathroom design and quality of fittings match the competition.

4   Our main competitors are priced at £450 and £465. Our price premium reflects the added value that the coating provides.

5   The higher price feeds directly into our bottom-line profit figures.'

'Thank you, Rob,' said Karl Hansen, the chairman of the board, 'we are well aware of the price impact on profit margins, but at £470 we will sell less than if we enter the market at £440 which gives the consumer two incentives to buy: price and value'.

'I totally agree,' opined Jack Sunderland, the sales director. 'The foundation of this company has been built on volume. We need volume to keep our factories working.'

'But you will get volume,' interrupted Rob, 'the market wants this product. What we need to do is to cash in on a major technological improvement.'

'It certainly is that,' agreed Chris Henderson, the technical director, 'the coating has taken five years to develop and is fully protected by patent. But I thought demand fell as price increased. I tend to agree with Karl and Jack.'

'Not necessarily. In this case I feel a price premium is fully justified. The market research proves it,' continued Rob.

'Could we try out two price levels?' said John France, the finance director, 'We have strong ties with Outram Brothers, a major bathroom retailer. I'm sure Bill Outram would agree to a few trials'.

'Absolutely not!' shouted Rob, 'We must act decisively. Every week we wait is lost profit for us.'

'Yes,' said Hansen, 'but your suggestion is too risky, Rob. We need to follow our tried and tested approach. I propose that we launch at £440. If the public like it, we can always raise the price later. Do I have agreement?'

Later that day Rob told Susan about the outcome:

'I cannot believe those old guys could reach a decision like that. They refuse to accept the facts. All they like to do is eat a hearty lunch in the executive dining-room and sleep it off in the afternoon. If they went jogging like me at lunchtime they might realize that work is more than about food and drink. Do you know, Sue, the only time I've been in that dining-room is when old man Hansen took me in there for a drink on my appointment.'

This case was prepared by David Jobber, Professor of Marketing, University of Bradford.

Questions

1 What do you think of Rob Vincent as a manager?

2 How well has he marketed his pricing proposals internally?

3 Can you suggest a better internal marketing approach?

Case 36 Jambo Records

The butterflies in the stomach of Laura Martell this Sunday evening seemed to be a different species to the ones that had been fluttering there a week ago. Last Sunday she had been looking forward to starting her new job as marketing manager at Jambo Records, one of the UK's leading independent record labels. After two years working as a marketing assistant with one of the five 'major' record companies, she had finally landed a dream job. After her first full week at Jambo, the job was beginning to look more like a nightmare, and she was feeling increasingly in limbo and uncertain about how things were likely to develop.

During the week, she had learnt more about the background to her appointment, and it helped to explain why she had got off to a difficult start. The creating of a marketing manager's position at Jambo had been at the bank's insistence as part of a recent refinancing deal. The last twelve months had been a difficult time for Jambo. A protracted court battle with one of the label's leading acts had been resolved in the company's favour, but had left the label facing an unexpectedly large bill for legal costs. The other difficulties surrounded the purchase of a nightclub aimed at building the Jambo brand, and emulating the likes of the Ministry of Sound, Cream and Knitting Factory. This proved to be a disaster, largely blamed on a poor choice of location, and a failure to invest enough in promotion after the club opened late and considerably over its refurbishment budget. Eight months later the club was sold on at a substantial loss in both financial and public relations terms. Industry analysts forecast that Jambo would be the next in a procession of independent labels to be absorbed within one of the majors. However, Chris Rubold, the founder, CEO and largest shareholder of Jambo had gone to the bank in search of refinancing, armed with the company's first-ever business plan. His proposals had ultimately been accepted, but with certain conditions attached, and Laura's job was one of those conditions.

The first day had started promisingly. Chris Rubold had made her feel very welcome, and had introduced her to the rest of the management team. He also kept stressing how her arrival marked a new era for Jambo, since 'they were now really going to take marketing seriously'. The

company seemed to be structured around three areas, each relating to an area of music, and loosely labelled 'hip-hop', 'house/dance' and 'songs/guitars'. Each area had its own product manager responsible for creating the physical product and getting it into the music retailers, and an A&R (artists and recording) manager responsible for finding, signing and generally looking after the recording artists. The finance/purchasing manager and office manager completed the management introductions for the morning. There were two marketing assistants who handled a myriad of logistical tasks, although one seemed largely concerned with artwork and packaging issues, while the other seemed mostly taken up with organizing concerts and personal appearances. Everybody seemed to report directly to Chris.

After a while, Chris had left Laura to her own devices, and to settle into her new office, telling her that he hoped that she would be able to

pick up the marketing ball for Jambo and run with it, because I won't have a lot of time to think about our marketing. I'm going to be much more involved in the technological development of the company. So far we've been slow in picking up the opportunities that the Internet and MP3 provide, but now we're chasing hard to catch up. How we deliver our music to the customer is going to be the key to success in the twenty-first century, and if we can get the technology right, we could be among the winners. But getting it right isn't easy. MP3 has stolen a lead, and you've got over 25 million consumers already swapping MP3 music files for free through the napster community. Now there's Windows Media offering the same kind of audio capabilities, and the AB Music Player from AT&T—who knows what the standard will be in five years' time, but we've got to be ready for it. They we've also got to make decisions about how much product we make available digitally online. Do we try to re-author all our tracks for MP3, LiquidAudio and any other popular format? Or just our current stuff, or just our most popular stuff? It isn't just a question of getting the music to the audience, we've got to work out how we're going to charge for it as well. People have got so used to free MP3 files on the net, that getting them to pay for it could be tricky. So, with all that to worry about, for the next few months I'm going to be up to my eyeballs in the technology, and won't have much time to think about the marketing.

By the second day, things had begun to deteriorate. In a radio interview, Jambo's biggest selling solo artist complained that he had left one of the Big Five to 'escape from the suits and hairdo's—but now they've followed me to Jambo'. Later, he went on to intimate that at the end of his current contract, he would be dispensing with record companies altogether, and would distribute his music direct to fans via the Internet. It also came to light that on the website of one of the label's highest profile guitar bands, the band and their fans had been corresponding on the subject, and postings from members of the band made it clear they were disappointed that Jambo were 'going corporate'.

Most of Tuesday and Wednesday were taken up with more introductions and meetings. Laura met the rest of the staff, a few of the artists, had a tour of the company's recording studio and attended an album launch. Wednesday afternoon was taken up with a sales meeting. The UK market was first on the agenda, and Chris Rubold outlined the situation. 1999 had not been a good year for the UK record industry generally, with album sales down 5.9 per cent from 1998. Overall revenues were only protected by the rise in the trade price of singles of almost 24 per cent. Jambo had underperformed compared to the market with an album decline of almost 7 per cent, and single sales were static compared to 1 per cent overall market growth. More worryingly, none of the new artists broken during the past 12 months had made a significant contribution to overall sales. The major bright spot had been the organization of a new summer festival of Jambo's dance acts in Ayia Napa. This had been a big success, and generated considerable positive media coverage, including some excellent TV coverage. This had fed through into healthy third and fourth quarter sales growth for most of the artists involved.

Next came the USA and Gabriella Roche, product manager for hip-hop, who had recently returned from there, was enthusiastic about Jambo's partnership with US distributor/promoter Sparkle Distribution. She said:

Sparkle really like our stable of artists, and have made a fantastic effort to push them. They have easily exceeded the targets we set for airplay on the college radio circuit for our guitar bands, and they have really exceeded expectations in terms of getting airplay for some of our hip-hop artists in the big metropolitan areas. I know that might not sound like a big deal, but in the US market, getting radio airplay is a big step towards getting an artist to chart. Of course, if we bring it back to actual sales figures, I have to admit they are disappointing, but it isn't for want of trying. With a music market of over fourteen billion dollars, we only need a tiny slice of it to succeed, and it's growing at over 2 per cent compared to pretty flat sales in most of Europe. But America is tough for indie labels to crack, particularly because so much of the distribution into independent record stores is dominated by two big players, Valley and Orchid.

Last came Europe. It was confirmed that industry-wide sales for 1999 across Europe had been 'flat', but the first quarter of 2000 had seen promising growth in the Scandinavian trio of Sweden, Norway and Finland. International Federation of Phonographic Industry figures suggested that these had grown by 30 per cent, 11 per cent and 7 per cent respectively (although the Swedish figure reflected a growth in exports as much as domestic consumption). Denmark, by contrast, remained flat, and more worryingly in terms of its size, so did Germany following a drop in sales value during 1999. Peter Allt, product manager for house/dance said that he was looking into an idea to improve Jambo's position on the continent.

A couple of other independent labels have established small regional offices in Germany, and we could look to follow suit. We could put together a little project team, perhaps one Product Manager, one A&R Manager, and they could go out for six months or a year and try to promote our current artists, and maybe find some new ones.

By this stage Laura felt that she had done a lot of listening and learning, but now the time had come to contribute to a meeting. The safest way to do this to begin with, she thought, was to ask a few intelligent questions. 'Why Germany?' she asked. 'Well', said Peter, 'We know their English is pretty good, which will help, and I've got a few useful contacts out there. It's a big market in which dance is strong, and others have done it, which suggests it's a smart thing to do.' Laura sensed that her question hadn't been entirely welcome, and she lapsed back into silence and listened to the others debating the potential costs and benefits of Peter's idea.

On Thursday morning, Laura decided that it was time to get proactive and make progress on one of several ideas she had brought with her into the job, convinced they could make a positive impact at Jambo. She went to see Phil Stone, A&R Manager for songs/guitars to explain her idea. She began:

> I really appreciate the importance of the A&R Manager's role; given the pace of change in the industry, the whole business depends on you turning up good new artists. The trouble is, there's a limit to how many bands any one individual can get around to meet up with and check out. I know demo tapes are another way of picking people up, but there's a small mountain of incoming demo tapes in reception that seems to be getting bigger every day. Why don't we follow the lead of websites like Dealwithepic.com which the Epic label have put together. It allows bands to upload demos through the website, and they are given a guarantee that it will be given a listen by the A&R staff. It's been pretty successful since they had fifty uploads on the first day the system went live.

Laura waited for a reaction, but it wasn't what she had hoped for. Phil said that it she thought she could replace him with a website, she's 'got another think coming' and that he didn't have time for any more of 'this nonsense' because he had to go and meet up with some 'real people' at an artist's store visit. Over lunch she suggested to the product managers that they could insert customer feedback cards into their CDs. This could help gather some useful information about customers, and would only need a bit of merchandise offered as a draw prize to encourage a response. This idea, like the last, went down like the proverbial Led Zeppelin. 'The music business', one of her new colleagues explained, 'is all about getting the music right. If the music is right, and the radio stations play it, the music markets itself.' Another commented that it was a pity the nightclub had closed down, as that had proved a really good way of finding out about what customers wanted. 'If a new track went down really well at the club, within a couple of weeks you could have it out as a single and moving up the charts.'

Friday, fortunately, was relatively uneventful, and Laura was very glad to get to the weekend. Now, she pondered what she should do and say in the week ahead. She was convinced that Jambo's enthusiasm for trying to break artists into the American market was misplaced. The British presence had been eroding rapidly over recent years to the point where in 1999 no UK artists featured in the 80 US biggest-selling albums. Only Fatboy Slim and Charlotte Church had come even close, by selling just over a million units. Nobody in the current Jambo stable looked likely to take America by storm, and if it happened, they could still capitalize through a licensing agreement with one of the majors. The 'German Project' also looked ill-judged. Jambo's continental business was invaluable, but very fragmented, and she could see little reason why it would be easier to develop further from Berlin as opposed to London. A more effective method might be through joining forces with NetBeat, the multilingual music portal, which specializes in partnerships with independent record labels to promote their artists across the continent. Netbeat sells CDs, MP3 downloads and music merchandise, and provides editorial content slanted towards the different continental music markets. It could prove an ideal way to create continental penetration without excessive costs. It would also sidestep the distribution stranglehold held by a handful of channels in countries like Italy. She dug out some of the market research reports she had salvaged from her last job, and browsed through them. Several of them said the same thing, that Western Europe and North America were not going to see much growth in the near future, it was the Latin American and Asia Pacific markets that were up and coming, but could they really form part of Jambo's future plans?

Laura knew that Jambo, like most of the rest of the industry, was at a turning point. It needed to improve sales, it needed to find good new artists, and it needed to respond appropriately to the changes being ushered in by new technology. Jambo, like other independent labels, faced some real opportunities. The prospect of on-line delivery of recordings could allow them to compete more effectively against the majors' giant production and promotion systems. The merger of EMI and Warner, two of the five majors, could also create opportunities. Analysts were forecasting a shake-out of artists following this merger, and a trend towards the majors increasingly shedding artists viewed as incapable of generating sales on an international scale. Again, this could prove beneficial to the independents. Laura was convinced that as Jambo's marketing manager, she could play a leading role in helping the company grasp these opportunities. First, however, she needed to get them to take marketing a little more seriously.

This case was prepared by Ken Peattie, Professor of Marketing, Cardiff University and James Roberts, InformedSources International. This case is a fictionalized account based around actual events.

Questions

1 Why do you think Laura had such a difficult first week?

2 What can she do to improve things at Jambo?

3 What difficulties might she face in trying to move Jambo towards more formalized marketing?

CHAPTER TWENTY

Marketing Services

'Closed for lunch'

SIGN ON DOOR OF MOSCOW RESTAURANT

Learning Objectives *This chapter explains:*

1 The nature and special characteristics of services

2 Managing customer relationships

3 Managing service quality, productivity and staff

4 How to position a service organization and brand

5 The services marketing mix

6 The major store and non-store retailing types

7 The theories of retail evolution

8 Key retail marketing decisions

9 The nature and special characteristics of non-profit marketing

This chapter discusses the special issues concerning the marketing of services. This is not to imply that the principles of marketing covered in earlier chapters of this book do not apply to services; rather it reflects the particular characteristics of services and the importance of service firms to the economy. In most industrialized economies, expenditure on services is growing. For example, in the European Union figures compiled by the European Commission show that the percentage share of gross domestic product attributable to the services sector rose from 38 per cent in 1970 to almost 50 per cent by 1990. There are a number of reasons for this:[1]

1 Advances in technology have led to more sophisticated products that require more design, production and maintenance services.

2 Growth per capita income has given rise to a greater percentage being spent on luxuries such as restaurant meals, overseas holidays, and weekend hotel breaks, all of which are service intensive. Greater discretionary income also fuels the demand for financial services such as investment trusts and personal pensions.

3 A trend towards out-sourcing means that manufacturers are buying services that are outside the firm's core expertise (such as distribution, warehousing, and catering).

4 Deregulation has increased the level of competition in certain service industries (e.g. telecommunications, television, airlines) resulting in expansion.

Retailing is an important element of services. Because of this some of the special marketing considerations relevant to retailing will be covered later in this chapter. Marketing in the non-profit sector will also be discussed, with hospitals, national television companies, employment services, museums, charities, schools and universities all being service-orientated. First, we shall examine the nature of services.

The nature of services

Cowell states that 'what is significant about services is the relative dominance of *intangible attributes* in the make-up of the "service product". Services are a special kind of product. They may require special understanding and special marketing efforts.'[2] Pure services do not result in ownership although they may be linked to a physical good. For example a machine (physical good) may be sold with a one-year maintenance contract (service).

Many offerings, however, contain an element of the tangible and intangible. For example, a marketing research study would provide a report (physical good) that represents the outcome of a number of service activities (discussions with client, designing the research strategy, interviewing respondents and analysing the results). This distinction between physical and service offerings can, therefore, be best understood as a matter of degree rather than in absolute terms. Figure 20.1 shows a physical goods–service continuum with the position of each offering dependent upon its ratio of the tangible/intangible elements. At the pure goods end of the scale is clothing, as the purchase of a skirt or socks is not normally accompanied by a service. Carpet purchases may involve an element of service if they require professional laying. Machinery purchase may involve more service elements in the form of installation and maintenance. Software design is positioned on the service side of the continuum since the value of the product is dependent on design expertise rather than the cost of the physical product (disk). Marketing research is similarly services-based as previously discussed. Finally, psychotherapy may be regarded as a pure service since the client receives nothing tangible from the transaction.

We have already touched upon one characteristic of services that distinguishes them from physical goods: intangibility. There are, in fact, four key distinguishing characteristics: *intangibility*, *inseparability*, *variability*, and *perishability* (see Fig. 20.2).

Intangibility

Pure services cannot be seen, tasted, touched, or smelled before they are bought, that is they are *intangible*. Rather a *service* is *a deed, performance or effort*, not an object, device or thing.[3] This may mean that a customer may find difficulty in evaluating a service before purchase. For example, it is virtually impossible to judge how enjoyable a holiday will be before taking it because the holiday cannot be shown to a customer before consumption.

For some services, their intangible nature leads to *difficulty in evaluation* after consumption. For example, it is not easy to judge how thorough a car service has been immediately afterwards: there is no way of telling if everything that should have been checked has been checked.

The challenge for the service provider is to *use tangible cues* to service quality. For example, a holiday firm may show pictures of the holiday destination, display testimonials from satisfied holidaymakers and provide details of the kind of entertainment available in a brochure. A garage may provide a checklist of items that are required to be carried out in a service, and an indication

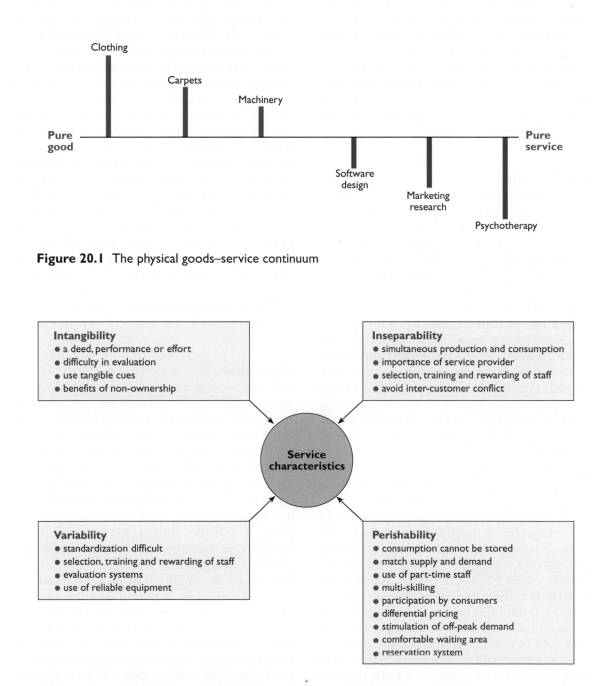

Figure 20.1 The physical goods–service continuum

Figure 20.2 Characteristics of services

that they have been. The task is to provide the evidence of service quality. McDonald's do this by controlling the physical settings of their restaurants and by using the golden arcs as a branding cue. By having a consistent offering, the company has effectively dealt with the difficulties that consumers have in evaluating the quality of a service. Standard menus and ordering procedures have also ensured uniform and easy access for customers, while allowing quality control.[4]

Intangibility also means that the customer cannot own a service. Payment is for use or performance. For example, a car may be hired, or a medical operation performed. Service organizations sometimes stress the *benefits of non-ownership* such as lower capital costs and the spreading of payment charges.

Inseparability

Unlike physical goods, services have ***inseparability***, that is they have *simultaneous production and consumption*. For example, a haircut, a medical operation, psychoanalysis, a holiday, and a pop music concert are produced and consumed at the same time. This contrasts with a physical good which is produced, stored, distributed through intermediaries before being bought and consumed. This illustrates the *importance of the service provider*, who is an integral part of the satisfaction gained by the consumer. How service providers conduct themselves may have a crucial bearing on repeat business over and above the technical efficiency of the service task. For example, how courteous and friendly the service provider is may play a large part in the customer's perception of the service experience. The service must be provided not only at the right time and in the right place but also in the right way.[5]

Often, in the customer's eyes, the photocopier service engineer or the insurance representative *is* the company. Consequently, the *selection, training and rewarding of staff* who are the front-line service people is of fundamental importance in the achievement of high standards of service quality. This notion of the inseparability between production and consumption gave rise to the idea of relationship marketing in services. In such circumstances, managing buyer–seller interaction is central to effective marketing and can only be fulfilled in a relationship with the customer.[6]

Furthermore, the consumption of the service may take place in the presence of other consumers. This is apparent with restaurant meals, air, rail or coach travel, and many forms of entertainment, for example. Consequently, enjoyment of the service is dependent not only on the service provided, but also on other consumers. Therefore service providers need to identify possible sources of nuisance (e.g. noise, smoke, queue jumping) and make adequate provision to *avoid inter-customer conflict*. For example, a restaurant layout should provide reasonable space between tables and non-smoking areas so that the potential for conflict is minimized.

Marketing managers should not underestimate the role played by customers in aiding other customers in their decision-making. A study into service interactions in IKEA stores found that almost all customer–employee exchanges related to customer concerns about 'place' (e.g. 'can you direct me to the pick-up point?') and 'function' (e.g. 'how does this chair work?'). However, interactions between customers took the form of opinions on the quality of materials used in products, advice on bed sizes and how to move around the in-store restaurant. Many customers appeared to display a degree of product knowledge or expertise bordering on that of contact personnel.[7]

Variability

Service quality may be subject to considerable ***variability***, which makes *standardization difficult*. Two restaurants within the same chain may have variable service owing to the capabilities of their respective managers and staff. Two marketing courses at the same university may vary considerably in terms of quality depending on the lecturer. Quality variations among physical products may be subject to tighter controls through centralized production, automation and quality checking before dispatch. Services, however, are often conducted at multiple locations, by people who may vary in their attitudes (and tiredness), and are subject to simultaneous production and consumption. The last characteristic means that a service fault (e.g. rudeness) cannot be quality checked and corrected between production and consumption, unlike a physical product such as misaligned car windscreen wipers.

The potential for variability in service quality emphasizes the need for rigorous *selection, training, and rewarding of staff* in service organizations. Training should emphasize the standards expected of personnel when dealing with customers. *Evaluation systems* should be developed which allow customers to report on their experiences with staff. Some service organizations, notably British Airports Authority, tie reward systems to customer satisfaction surveys which are based, in part, on the service quality provided by their staff.

Service standardization is a related method of tackling the variability problem. For example, a university department could agree to use the same software package when developing overhead transparencies for use in lectures. The *use of reliable equipment* rather than people can also help in standardization, for example, the supply of drinks via vending machines or cash through bank machines. However, great care needs to be taken regarding equipment reliability and efficiency. For example, bank cash machines have been heavily criticized for being unreliable and running out of money at weekends.

Perishability

The fourth characteristic of services is their *perishability* in the sense that *consumption cannot be stored* for the future. A hotel room or an airline seat that is not occupied today represents lost income that cannot be gained tomorrow. If a physical good is not sold, it can be stored for sale later. Therefore it is important to *match supply and demand* for services. For example, if a hotel has high weekday occupancy but is virtually empty at weekends, a key marketing task is to provide incentives for weekend use. This might involve offering weekend discounts, or linking hotel use with leisure activities such as golf, fishing or hiking.

Service providers also have the problem of catering for peak demand when supply may be insufficient. A physical goods provider may build up inventory in slack periods for sale during peak demand. Service providers do not have this option. Consequently alternative methods need to be considered. For example, supply flexibility can be varied through the *use of part-time staff* doing peak periods. *Multi-skilling* means that employees may be trained in many tasks. Super-

market staff can be trained to fill shelves, and work at the checkout at peak periods. *Participation by consumers* may be encouraged in production (e.g. self-service breakfasts in hotels). Demand may be smoothed through *differential pricing* to encourage customers to visit during off-peak periods (for example, lower priced cinema and theatre seats for afternoon performances). *Stimulation of off-peak demand* can be achieved by special events (e.g. golf or history weekends for hotels). If delay is unavoidable then another option is to make it more acceptable, for example, by providing a *comfortable waiting area* with seating and free refreshments. Finally, a *reservation system* as commonly used in restaurants, hair salons, and theatres can be used to control peak demand and assist time substitution.

Managing services

Four key aspects of managing services are *managing customer relationships, managing service quality, managing service productivity, managing service staff,* and *positioning services.*

Managing customer relationships

Relationship marketing in services has attracted much attention in recent years as organizations focus their efforts on retaining existing customers rather than only attracting new ones. It is not a new concept, however, since the idea of a company earning customer loyalty was well known to the earliest merchants who had a saying: 'As a merchant, you'd better have a friend in every town.'[8] Relationship marketing involves the shifting from activities concerned with attracting customers to activities focused on current customers and how to retain them. Although the idea can be applied to many industries it is particularly important in services since there is often direct contact between service provider and consumer, for example, doctor and patient, and hotel staff and guests. The quality of the relationship which develops will often determine its length. Not all service encounters have the potential for a long-term relationship, however. For example, a passenger at an international airport who needs road transportation will probably never meet the taxi driver again, and the choice of taxi supplier will be dependent on the passenger's position in the queue rather than free choice. In this case the exchange—cash for journey—is a pure transaction: the driver knows that it is unlikely that there will ever be a repeat purchase.[9] Organizations, therefore, need to decide when the practice of relationship marketing is most applicable. The following conditions suggest the use of relationship marketing activities:[10]

1 There is an ongoing or periodic desire for the service by the customer, e.g. insurance or theatre service versus funeral service.

2 The customer controls the selection of a service provider, e.g. selecting a hotel versus entering the first taxi in an airport waiting line.

3 The customer has alternatives from which to choose, e.g. selecting a restaurant versus buying water from the only utility company service a community.

Having established the applicability of relationship marketing to services, we will now explore the benefits of relationship marketing to organizations and customers, and the customer retention strategies used to build relationships and tie customers closer to service firms.

Benefits for the organization

There are five benefits to service organizations in developing and maintaining strong customer relationships.[11]

Increased purchases A study by Reichheld and Sasser[12] has shown that customers tend to spend more each year with a relationship partner than they did in the preceding period. This is logical as it would be expected that as the relationship develops, trust would develop between the partners, and as the customer becomes more and more satisfied with the quality of services provided by the supplier so it would give a greater proportion of its business to the supplier.

Lower cost The start up costs associated with attracting new customers are likely to be far higher than the cost of retaining existing customers. Start-up costs will include the time of salespeople making repeat calls in an effort to persuade a prospect to open an account, advertising and promotional costs associated with making

prospects aware of the company and its service offering, operating costs of setting up accounts and systems, and time costs of establishing bonds between the supplier and customer in the early stages of the relationship. Furthermore, costs associated with solving early teething problems and queries are likely to fall as the customer gets used to using the service.

Lifetime value of a customer The lifetime value of a customer is the profit made on a customer's purchases over the lifetime of the customer. If a customer spends £80 in a supermarket per week resulting in £8 profit, uses the supermarket 45 times a year over 30 years, the lifetime value of that customer is £10 800. Thus a bad service experience early on in this relationship which results in the customer defecting to the competition would be very expensive to the supermarket, especially when adding on the costs of bad word of mouth which may deter other customers from using the store.

Word of mouth Word of mouth is very important in services due to their intangible nature which makes them difficult to evaluate prior to purchase. In these circumstances, potential purchasers often look to others who have experienced the service (e.g. a hotel) for personal recommendation. A firm that has a large number of loyal customers is more likely to benefit from word of mouth than another without such a resource.

Employee satisfaction and retention Satisfied, loyal customers benefit employees in providing a set of mutually beneficial relationships, and less hassle. This raises employees' job satisfaction, and lowers job turnover. Employees can spend time improving existing relationships rather than desperately seeking new customers. This sets up the virtuous circle of satisfied customers leading to happy employees who raise customer satisfaction even higher.

The net result of these five benefits of developing customer relationships is high profits. A study has shown across a variety of service industries that profits climb steeply when a firm lowers its customer defection rate.[13] Firms could improve profits from 25 to 85 per cent (depending on industry) by reducing customer defections by just 5 per cent. The reasons are that loyal customers generate more revenue for more years and the costs of maintaining existing customers are lower than the costs of acquiring new customers. An analysis of a credit card company revealed that reducing the defection rate from 20 to 10 years doubled the lifetime value of this customer from $135 to $300.

Benefits for the customer

Entering into a long-term relationship can also reap benefits for the customer.

Risk and stress reduction   Since the intangible nature of services makes them difficult to evaluate before purchase, relationship marketing can benefit the customer as well as the firm. This is particularly so for services that are personally important, variable in quality, complex and/or subject to high involvement buying.[14] Such purchases are potentially high risk in that making the wrong choice has severe negative consequences for the buyer. Banking, insurance, motor servicing and hairstyling are examples of services that exhibit some or all of the characteristics—importance, variability, complexity and high involvement—that would cause many customers to seek an on-going relationship with a trusted service provider. Such a relationship reduces consumer stress as the relationship becomes predictable, initial problems are solved, special needs are accommodated and the consumer learns what to expect. After a period of time, the consumer begins to trust the service provider, can count on a consistent level of quality service and feels comfortable in the relationship[15]

Higher quality service   Experiencing a long-term relationship with a service provider can also result in higher levels of service. This is because the service provider becomes knowledgeable about the customer's requirements. For example, doctors get to know the medical history of their patients and hairstylists learn about the preferences of their clients. Knowledge of the customer built up over a series of service encounters facilitates the tailoring or customizing of service to each customer's special needs.

Avoidance of switching costs   Maintaining a relationship with a service supplier avoids the costs associated with switching to a new provider. Once a service provider knows a customer's preferences and special needs, and has tailored services to suit them, to change would mean educating a new provider and accepting the

possibility of mistakes being made until the new provider has learnt to accommodate them. This results in both time and psychological costs to the customer. Bitner suggests that a major cost of relocating to a new geographic location is the need to establish relationships with unfamiliar service providers such as banks, schools, doctors and hairdressers.[16]

Social and status benefits   Customers can also reap social and status benefits from a continuing relationship with a supplier. Since many service encounters are also social encounters repeated contact can assume personal as well as professional dimensions. In such circumstances, service customers may develop relationships resembling personal friendships. For example, hairdressers often serve as personal confidantes, and restaurant managers may get to know some of their customers personally. Such personal relationships can feed one's ego (status) as when a hotel customer commented, 'When employees remember and recognize you as a regular customer you feel really good'.[17]

Developing customer retention strategies

The benefits of developing long-term relationships with customers mean that it is worthwhile for services organizations to consider designing customer retention strategies. This involves the targeting of customers for retention, bonding, internal marketing, promise fulfilment, building of trust and service recovery (see Fig. 20.3).

Targeting customer for retention   Not all customers are worthy of relationship building. Some may be habitual brand switchers perhaps responding to the lowest deal currently on offer; others may not generate sufficient revenue to justify the expense of acquiring them and maintaining the relationship; and finally some customers may be so troublesome that their attitudes and behaviour cause so much disruption to the service provider that the costs of servicing them outweigh the benefits. Firms need, therefore, to identify those customers with whom they wish to engage in a long-term relationship, those for whom a transactional marketing approach is better suited, and those with whom they would prefer not to do business. This is the classical market segmentation and targeting approach discussed in Chapter 7. The characteristics of those customers who are candidates for a relationship marketing approach are high value, frequent use, loyalty-prone customers for whom the actual and potential service offerings that can be supplied by the firm have high utility.

Targeting customers for retention involves the analysis of loyalty and defection-prone customers. Service suppliers need to understand why customers stay or leave, what creates value for them and their profile. Decisions can then be made regarding which types of customer defectors they wish to try to save (e.g. price or service defectors) and the nature of the value-adding strategy that meets their needs while at the same time maintaining the bonds with loyalty-prone customers.[18]

Bonding Retention strategies vary in the degree to which they bond the parties together. One framework which illustrates this idea distinguishes between three levels of retention strategies based upon the types of bond used to cement the relationship.[19]

l *Level 1*: at this level the bond is primarily through financial incentives, for example higher discounts on prices for larger volume purchases or frequent flyer or loyalty points resulting in lower future prices. The problem is that the potential for a sustainable competitive advantage is low because price incentives are easy for competitors to copy even if they take the guise of frequent flyer or loyalty points. Most airlines and supermarkets compete in this way and consumers have learnt to join more than one scheme, thus negating the desired effect.

2 *Level 2*: this higher level of bonding relies on more than just price incentives and consequently raises the potential for a sustainable competitive advantage. Level 2 retention strategies build long-term relationships through social as well as financial bonds, capitalizing on the fact that many service encounters are also social encounters. Customers become clients and the relationship becomes personalized and the service customized. Characteristics of this type of relationship include frequent communication with customers, providing community of service through the same person or people employed by the service provider, providing personal treatment like sending cards, enhancing the core service with educational or entertainment activities such as seminars or visits to sporting events. Some hotels keep records of their guests' personal preferences such as their favourite newspaper and alcoholic drink. This builds a special bond between the hotel and their customers who feel they are being treated as

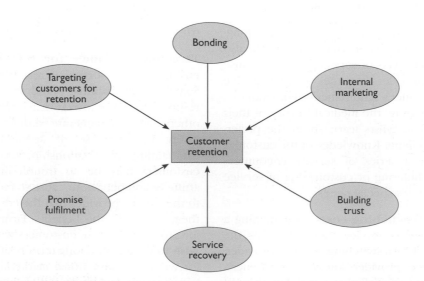

Figure 20.3 Developing customer retention strategies

individuals. Other companies form social relationships with their customers by forming clubs; for example, Harley-Davidson have created the Harley Owners Group fostering camaraderie among its membership and a strong bond with the motorbike, and Nokia has established a club for its mobile phone customers for similar reasons (see advertisement overleaf).

3   *Level 3*: this top level of bonding is formed by financial, social and structural bonds. Structural bonds tie service providers to their customers through providing solutions to customers' problems that are designed into the service delivery system. For example, logistics companies often supply their clients with equipment that ties them into their systems. With combined with financial, and social bonds, structural bonds can create a formidable barrier against competitor inroads and provide the basis for a sustainable competitive advantage.

Internal marketing   A fundamental basis for customer retention is high-quality service delivery. This depends upon high-quality performance from employees since the service product is a performance and the performers are employees.[20] Internal marketing concerns training, communicating to and motivating internal staff. Staff need to be trained to be technically competent at their job as well as to be able to handle service encounters with customers. To do this well, they must be motivated and understand what is expected of them. Service staff act as 'part-time marketers' since their actions can directly affect customer satisfaction and retention.[21] They are critical in the 'moments of truth' when they and customers come into contact in a service situation.

A key focus of an internal marketing programme should be employee selection and retention. Service companies who suffer high rates of job turnover are continually employing new inexperienced staff to handle customer service encounters. Employees who have worked for the company for years know more about the business and have had the opportunity to build relationships with customers. By selecting the right people and managing them in such a way that they stay loyal to the service organization, higher levels of customer retention can be achieved through the build up of trust and personal knowledge gained through long-term contact with customers.

Promise fulfilment   The fulfilment of promises is a cornerstone for maintaining service relationships. This implies three key activities: *making* realistic promises initially, and *keeping* those promises during service delivery by *enabling* staff and service systems to deliver on promises made.[22]

Making promises is through normal marketing communications channels such as advertising, selling and promotion as well as the specific service cues that set expectations such as the dress of the service staff, and the design and decor of the establishment. It is important not to over-promise with marketing communications or the result will be disappointment and customer dissatisfaction and defection. The promise should be credible and realistic. Some companies adhere to the adage 'under-promise and over-deliver'.

A necessary condition for promises to be kept is the enabling of staff and service systems to deliver on the promises made. This means staff must have the skills, competences, tools, systems and enthusiasm to deliver. Some of these issues have been discussed in the previous discussion of internal marketing and are dependent on the correct recruitment, training and rewarding of staff and providing them with the right equipment and systems to do their job.

The final activity associated with promise fulfilment is the keeping of promises. This relies on service staff or technology such as the downloading of software via the Internet. The keeping of promises occurs when the customer and the service provider interact: the 'moment of truth' mentioned earlier. Research has shown that customers judge employees on their ability to deliver the service right the first time, their ability to recover if things go wrong, how well they deal with special requests, and on their spontaneous actions and attitudes.[23] These are clearly key dimensions that must play a part in a training programme and should be borne in mind when selecting and rewarding service staff, not all service encounters are equal in importance, however. Research conducted on behalf of Marriott hotels has shown that events occurring early in a service encounter affect customer loyalty most. Based on these findings they developed their 'First 10 minutes' strategy. It is hardly surprising that first impressions are so important since before

*It's good to belong.

Join Club Nokia. It costs nothing to join and you get valuable benefits.
•Join online, at www.club.nokia.co.uk. You get useful services like information about new Nokia mobile phones and accessories. And assistance if you have a problem with your Nokia mobile phone. •Join Club Nokia and you belong to the international community of Nokia mobile phone owners. Join the club!

Club
NOKIA

Come to the Club Nokia Web site and see all the smileys – there's a face for every situation. www.club.nokia.co.uk

Nokia has established a club for its mobile phone owners

then the customer has had no direct contact with the service provider and will be uncertain of the outcome.

Finally, we need to recognize that the keeping of promises does not solely depend on service staff and technology. Because service delivery is often in a group setting (e.g. listening to a lecture, watching a film or travelling by air) the quality of the experience can be as dependent on the behaviour of other customers as that of the service provider. Lovelock, Vandermerwe and Lewis label the problem customers 'jaycustomers'.[24] These are people who act in a thoughtless or abusive way, causing problems for the organization, its employees and other customers. One particular kind of jaycustomer is the belligerent person who shouts abuse and threats at service staff because of some service malfunction. Staff need to be trained to develop the self-confidence and assertiveness needed to deal with this situation by role-play exercises. If possible, the person should be moved from other customer contact to minimize the latter's discomfort at the situation. Finally, where the service employee does not have the authority to resolve the problem, more senior staff should be approached to settle the dispute.

Building trust   Customer retention heavily relies on building trust. This is particularly so for service firms since the intangibility of services means that they are difficult to evaluate before buying and experiencing them (indeed some, such as car servicing, are hard to evaluate after purchasing them). Purchasing a service for the first time can leave the customer with the feeling of uncertainty and vulnerability particularly when the service is personally important, variable in quality, complex and subject to high-involvement purchasing. It is not surprising that customers who have developed trust in a supplier in these circumstances are unlikely to switch to a new supplier and undergo the uncomfortable feelings of uncertainty and vulnerability again.

Companies who wish to build up their trustworthiness should keep in touch with their customers by regular two-way communication to develop feelings of closeness and openness, provide guarantees to symbolize the confidence they feel in their service delivery as well as reducing their customers' perceived risk of purchase, and to operate a policy of fairness and high standards of conduct with their customers.[25]

Service recovery   Service recovery strategies should be designed to solve the problem and restore the customers' trust in the firm, and to improve the service system so that the problem does not recur in the future.[26] They are crucial because inability to recover service failures and mistakes lose customers directly and through their tendency to tell other actual and potential customers about their negative experiences.

The first ingredient in a service recovery strategy is to set up a tracking system to identify system failures. Customers should be encouraged to report service problems since it is customers who do not complain who are least likely to purchase again. Systems should be established to monitor complaints, follow-up on service experiences by telephone calling, and to use suggestion boxes for both service staff and customers.

Second, staff should be trained and empowered to respond to service complaints. The first response from a service provider to a genuine complaint is to apologise. Often this will take the heat out of the situation and lead to a spirit of cooperation rather than recrimination. The next step is to attempt to solve the problem quickly. Marriott Hotels facilitate this process by empowering front-line employees to solve customers' problems quickly even though it may mean expense to the hotel, and without recourse to seeking approval from higher authority. Other key elements in service recovery are to appear pleasant, helpful and attentive, show concern for the customer, and be flexible. Regarding problem resolution service staff should provide information about the problem, take action and should appear to put themselves out to solve the problem.[27] Marketing in Action 20.1 describes complaint handling at Virgin Trains.

Finally, a service recovery strategy should encourage learning so that service recovery problems are identified and corrected. Service staff should be motivated to report problems and solutions so that recurrent failures are identified and fixed. In this way, an effective service recovery system can lead to improved customer service, satisfaction and higher customer retention levels.

Managing service quality

Intuitively, its makes sense to suggest that improving service quality will increase customer satisfaction leading to higher sales and profits.

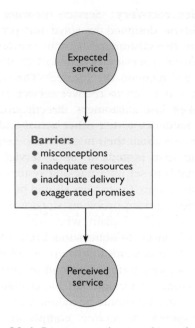

Figure 20.4 Barriers to the matching of expected and perceived service levels

Indeed, it has been shown that companies that are rated higher on service quality perform better in terms of market share growth and profitability.[28] Yet for many companies high standards of service quality remain elusive. There are four causes of poor perceived quality (see Fig. 20.4). These are the barriers that separate the perception of service quality from what customers expect.[29]

Barriers to the matching of expected and perceived service levels

Misconceptions barrier this arises from management's misunderstanding of what the customer expects. Lack of marketing research may lead managers to misconceive the important service attributes that customers use when evaluating a service, and the way in which customers use attributes in evaluation. For example, a restaurant manager may believe that shortening the gap between courses may improve customer satisfaction, when the customer actually values a pause between eating.

Inadequate resources barrier managers may understand customer expectations but be unwilling to provide the resources necessary to

meet them. This may arise because of a cost reduction or productivity focus, or simply because of the inconvenience it may cause.

Inadequate delivery barrier managers may understand customer expectations and supply adequate resources but fail to select, train and reward staff adequately, resulting in poor or inconsistent service. This may manifest itself in poor communication skills, inappropriate dress, and unwillingness to solve customer problems.

Exaggerated promises barrier even when customer understanding, resources, and staff management are in place, a gap between customer expectations and perceptions can still arise through exaggerated promises. Advertising and selling messages that build expectations to a pitch that cannot be fulfilled may leave customers disappointed even when receiving a good service. For example, a tourist brochure that claims that a hotel is 'just a few minutes from the sea' may lead to disappointment if the walk takes ten minutes.

Meeting customer expectations

A key to providing service quality is the understanding and meeting of *customer expectations*. To do so requires a clear picture of the criteria used to form these expectations, recognizing that consumers of services value not only the *outcome* of the service encounter but also the *experience* of taking part in it. For example, an evaluation of a haircut depends on not only the quality of the cut but also the experience of having a haircut. Clearly, a hairdresser needs not only technical skills but also the ability to communicate in an interesting and polite manner. Ten criteria may be used when evaluating the outcome and experience of a service encounter:[30]

1. *Access*: is the service provided at convenient locations and times with little waiting?
2. *Reliability*: is the service consistent and dependable?
3. *Credibility*: can customers trust the service company and its staff?
4. *Security*: can the service be used without risk?
5. *Understanding the customer*: does it appear that the service provider understands customer expectations?

6 *Responsiveness*: how quickly do service staff respond to customer problems, requests and questions?

7 *Courtesy*: do service staff act in a friendly and polite manner?

8 *Competence*: do service staff have the required skills and knowledge?

9 *Communication*: is the service described clearly and accurately?

10 *Tangibles*: how well managed is the tangible evidence of the service (e.g. staff appearance, décor, layout)?

These criteria form a useful checklist for service providers wishing to understand how their customers judge them. A self-analysis may show areas that need improvement but the most reliable approach is to check that customers use these criteria and conduct marketing research to compare performance against competition. Where service quality is dependent on a suc-cession of service encounters (for example a hotel stay may encompass the check-in, the room itself, the restaurant, breakfast and check-out) each should be measured in terms of their impact on total satisfaction so that corrective actions can be taken.[31] Questionnaires have now been developed which allow the measurement of perceived customer satisfaction at distinct stages of the service delivery process (for example, the stages encountered while visiting a museum).[32]

Measuring service quality

A scale called *SERVQUAL* has been developed to aid measurement of *service quality*.[33] Based upon five criteria—reliability, responsiveness, courtesy, competence, and tangibles—it is a multiple-item scale that aims to measure customer perceptions and expectations so that gaps can be identified. The scale is simple to administer with respondents indicating their strength of agreement/

20.1   Marketing in Action

Complaint Handling at Virgin Trains

When customers complain to Chris Green, chief executive, or Richard Branson the owner of Virgin Trains about service failures their complaint is dealt with by a member of a team of three specially assigned to handle the stream of queries, complaints, criticisms and occasionally compliments that are sent or telephoned in. The first step is to assess the complaint carefully. Most customers are wanting an explanation, information and/or reassurance and it is important to under-stand what they are seeking. This is followed by research. For example, if someone complains about a delay, the operational log will be checked to find out why it happened so an explanation can be given. The third step is to find out what action is being taken to improve the situation. This could take the form of increased spending on new trains, and this information would be conveyed to the customer.

As part of their job the team of three get out on the rail network to see the service in action for themselves. It is important for them to experience what people are talking about and meet staff so that they can see what issues need to be dealt with.

Most complaints arrive by letter but occasionally irate customers complain over the telephone. The keys to responding to angry customers are to imagine yourself in their shoes, to be polite and informative. Whether the complaint is by letter or telephone, the response must be fresh. Even though similar complaints occur quite regularly, the temptation to reply with a standard letter needs to be resisted.

Based on: Thorpe (2000)[34]

disagreement to a series of statements about service quality using a Likert Scale.

Managing service productivity

Productivity is a measure of the relationship between an input and an output. For example, if more people can be served (output) using the same number of staff (input), productivity per employee has risen. Clearly there can be conflict between improving service productivity (efficiency) and raising service quality (effectiveness). For example, a doctor who reduces consultation time per patient or a university which increases tutorial group size raise productivity at the risk of lowering service quality. Table 20.1 shows how typical operational goals that seek to minimize costs can cause marketing concerns. Marketers need to understand why operations managers have such goals, and operations managers need to recognize the implications of their actions on customer satisfaction.[35]

Clearly a balance must be struck between productivity and service quality. At some point quality gains become so expensive that they are not worthwhile. However, there are ways of improving productivity without compromising quality. *Technology*, obtaining *customer involvement in production* of the service, and *balancing supply and demand* are three methods of achieving this.

Technology

Technology can be used to improve productivity and service quality. For example, airport X-ray surveillance equipment raises the throughput of passengers (productivity) and speeds the process of checking-in (service quality). Automatic cash dispensers in banks increase the number of transactions per period (productivity) while reducing

Table 20.1 Marketing and operations' views on operational issues

Operational issues	Typical operations goals	Common marketing concerns
Productivity improvement	Reduce unit cost of production	Strategies may cause decline in service quality
Standardization versus customization	Keep costs low and quality consistent: simplify operations tasks; recruit low cost employees	Consumers may seek variety, prefer customization to match segmented needs
Batch versus unit processing	Seek economies of scale, consistency, efficient use of capacity	Customers may be forced to wait, feel 'one of a crowd', be turned off by other customers
Facilities layout and design	Control costs; improve efficiency by ensuring proximity of operationally related tasks; enhance safety and security	Customers may be confused, shunted around unnecessarily, find facility unattractive and inconvenient
Job design	Minimize error, waste, and fraud; make efficient use of technology; simplify task for standardization	Operationally orientated employees with narrow roles may be unresponsive to customer needs
Management of capacity	Keep costs down by avoiding wasteful underutilization of resources	Service may be unavailable when needed; quality may be compromised during high-demand periods
Management of queues	Optimize use of available capacity by planning for average throughput; maintain customer order, discipline	Customers may be bored and frustrated during wait, see firm as unresponsive

Source: Lovelock, C. (1992) Seeking Synergy in Service Operations: Seven Things Marketers Need to Know about Service Operations, *European Management Journal*, **10** (1), 22–9. Reprinted with permission from Elsevier Science Ltd, The Boulevard, Langford Lane, Kidlington OX5 1GB, UK

customer waiting time (service quality). Automatic vending machines increase the number of drinks sold per establishment (productivity) while improving accessibility for customers (service quality). Computerization can also raise productivity and service quality. For example, Direct Line, owned by the Royal Bank of Scotland, is based on computer software that produces a motor insurance quote instantaneously. Callers are asked for a few details (such as how old they are, where they live, what car they drive, and years since last claim) and this is keyed into the computer which automatically produces a quotation.[36]

Retailers have benefited from electronic point of sale (EPOS) and electronic data interchange (EDI). Timely and detailed sales information can aid buying decisions and provide retail buyers with a negotiating advantage over suppliers. Other benefits from this technology include better labour scheduling, and stock and distribution systems.

Customer involvement in production

The inseparability between production and consumption provides an opportunity to raise both productivity and service quality. For example, self-service breakfast bars and petrol stations improve productivity per employee and reduce customer waiting time (service quality). The effectiveness of this tactic relies heavily on customer expectations, and on managing transition periods. It should be used when there is a clear advantage to customers in their involvement in production. In other instances reducing customer service may reduce satisfaction. For example, a hotel that expected its customers to service their own rooms would need a persuasive communications programme to convince customers that the lack of service was reflected in cheaper rates.

Balancing supply and demand

Because services cannot be stored, balancing supply and demand is a key determinant of productivity. Hotels or aircraft that are less than half full incur low productivity. If in the next period, the hotel or airline is faced with excess demand, the unused space in the previous period cannot be used to meet it. The combined result is low productivity and customer dissatisfaction

(low service quality). By smoothing demand or increasing the flexibility of supply, both productivity and service quality can be achieved.

Smoothing demand can be achieved through differential pricing, and stimulating off-peak demand (e.g. weekend breaks). Increasing supply flexibility may be increased by using part-time employees, multi-skilling and encouraging customers to service themselves.

Managing service staff

Many services involve a high degree of contact between service staff and customers. This is true for such service industries as health care, banking, catering, and education. The quality of the service experience is therefore heavily dependent on staff–customer interpersonal relationships. John Carlzon, the head of Scandinavian Airlines System (SAS), called these meetings *moments of truth*. He explained that SAS faced 65 000 moments of truth per day and that the outcomes determined the success of SAS.

Research on customer loyalty in the service industry showed that only 14 per cent of customers who stopped patronizing service businesses did so because they were dissatisfied with the quality of what they had bought. More than two-thirds stopped buying because they found service staff indifferent or unhelpful.[37] Clearly the way in which service personnel treat their customers is fundamental to success in the service industry.

In order for service employees to be in the frame of mind to treat customers well, they need to feel that their company is treating them well. In companies where staff have a high regard for the human resources policy, customers also have a positive opinion of the service they receive.

Selection of suitable people is the starting-point of the process. Personality differences mean that it is not everyone who can fill a service role. The nature of the job needs to be defined and the appropriate personality characteristics needed to perform effectively outlived. Once selected, training is required to familiarize recruits to the job requirements and the culture of the organization. Orientation is the process by which a company helps new recruits to understand the organization and its culture. Folklore is often used to show how employees have made outstanding contributions to the company.

Socialization allows the recruit to experience the culture and tasks of the organization. Usually, the aim is creative individualism whereby the recruit accepts all of the key behavioural norms but is encouraged to display initiative an innovation in dealing with problems. Thus standards of behaviour are internalized, but the creative abilities of the individual are not subjugated to the need to conform.

Service quality may also be affected by the degree to which staff are *empowered* or given the authority to satisfy customers and deal with their problems. For example, each member of staff of Marriott Hotels is allowed to spend up to £1000 on their own initiative to solve customer problems. The company uses some of the situations that have arisen where employees have acted decisively to solve a customer problem in their advertising. The advantage is quicker response time since staff do not have to consult with their supervisors before dealing with a problem.[38] However, empowerment programmes need to recognize the increased responsibility thrust on employees. Not everyone will welcome this, and reward systems need to be thought through (e.g. higher pay or status).

Maintaining a motivated workforce in the face of irate customers, faulty support systems and the boredom which accompanies some service jobs is a demanding task. The motivational factors discussed when examining salesforce management are equally relevant here and include recognition of achievement, role clarity, opportunities for advancement, the interest value of the job, monetary rewards, and setting challenging but achievable targets. Some service companies (e.g. Holiday Inn) give employee-of-the-month awards as recognition of outstanding service. A key factor in avoiding demotivation is to monitor support systems so that staff work with efficient equipment and facilities to help them carry out their job.

Service evaluation is also important in managing staff. Customer feedback is essential to maintaining high standards of service quality. McDonald's continually monitor quality, service, cleanliness and value (QSCV) and if a franchisee fails to meet their standards the franchisee is dropped. The results of customer research should be fed back to employees so that they can relate their performance standards to customer satisfaction. So enlightened companies tie financial incentives to the results of such surveys.

Positioning services

Positioning is the process of establishing and keeping a distinctive place in the market for a company and its products. Most successful service firms differentiate themselves from the competition on attributes that their target customers value highly. They develop service concepts that are highly valued and communicate to target customers so that they accurately perceive the position of the service. For example, Credit Suisse Financial Products position themselves as specialists in risk management products and services.

The positioning task entails two decisions:

1 Choice of target market (where to compete).
2 Creation of a differential advantage (how to compete).

These decisions are common to both physical products and services. Creating a differential advantage is based upon an understanding of target customers' requirements better than the competition. Figure 20.5 shows the relationship between *target customer needs* and the *services marketing mix*. On the left of the figure is an array of factors (choice criteria) that customers may use to judge a service. How well a service firm satisfies those criteria depends on its marketing mix (on the right of the figure). Marketing research can be useful in identifying important choice criteria but care needs to be taken in such studies. Asking customers which are the most important factors when buying a service may give misleading results. For example, the most important factor when travelling by air may be safety. However, this does not mean that customers use safety as a choice criterion when deciding which airline to use. If all major airlines are perceived as being similar in terms of safety, other less important factors like the quality of in-flight meals and service may be the crucial attributes used in decision-making.

Target marketing

The basis of target marketing is **market segmentation**. A market is analysed to identify groups of potential customers with similar needs and price sensitivities. The potential of each of these segments is assessed on such factors as size, growth rate, degree of competition, price sensi-

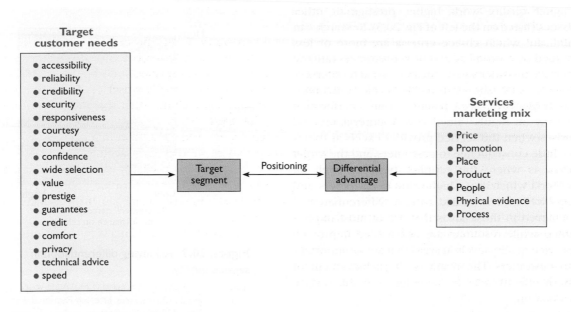

Figure 20.5 Positioning for services

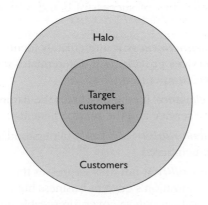

Figure 20.6 Target and halo customers

tivity and the fit between its requirements and the company's capabilities. Note that the most attractive markets are often not the biggest, however, as these may have been identified earlier and have already attracted a high level of competition. There may, however, be pockets of customers who are underserved by companies who are compromising their marketing mix by trying to serve too wide a customer base. The identification of such customers is a prime opportunity during segmentation analysis. ***Target***

marketing allows service firms to tailor their marketing mix to the specific requirements of groups of customers more effectively than trying to cater for diverse needs.

Marketing managers also need to consider those potential customers who are not directly targeted but who may find the service mix attractive. These customers who are at the periphery of the target market are called ***halo customers*** and can make a substantial difference between success and failure (see Fig. 20.6). For example, Top Shop, a UK clothing retailer targeting 16–24 year olds, was very successful in attracting this group to its shops but financial performance was marred by the lack of interest by its halo customers: those who fell out of this age bracket but nevertheless may have found Top Shop's clothing to their taste.

Differential advantage

Understanding customer needs will be the basis of the design of a new service concept which is different from competitive offerings, is highly valued by target customers, and therefore creates a ***differential advantage***. It will be based upon the creative use of marketing mix elements resulting in such benefits as more reliable or faster delivery, greater convenience, more comfort, higher quality work, higher prestige or other issues (listed on the left of Fig. 20.5). Research can indicate which choice criteria are more or less valued by customers, and how customers rate the service provider's performance on each criteria.[39] Figure 20.7 shows three possible outcomes: *underperformance* results from performing poorly on highly valued choice criteria, *overkill* arises when the service provider excels at things of little consequence to customers, and the *target area* is where the supplier performs well on criteria which are of high value to customers, and less well on less valued criteria. Differentiation is achieved in those areas that are of most importance, while resources are not wasted improving service quality levels in areas that are unimportant to customers. The result is the achievement of both effectiveness and efficiency in the service operation.

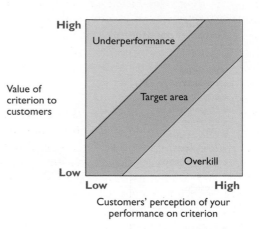

Figure 20.7 Achieving differentiation in service quality.

Source: Christopher, M. and R. Yallop (1990) Audit your Customer Service Quality, *Focus*, June–July. Reprinted with kind permission of Martin Christopher

The services marketing mix

The **services marketing mix** is an extension of the 4-Ps framework introduced in Chapter 1. The essential elements of *product, promotion, price* and *place* remain but three additional variables—*people, physical evidence* and *process*—are included to produce a 7-Ps mix.[40] The need for the extension is due to the high degree of direct contact between the firm and the customer, the highly visible nature of the service assembly process, and the simultaneity of production and consumption. While it is possible to discuss people, physical evidence and process within the original 4-Ps framework (for example, people could be considered part of the product offering) the extension allows a more thorough analysis of the marketing ingredients necessary for successful services marketing. Each element of the marketing mix will now be examined.

Product   physical products can be inspected and tried before buying but pure services are intangible; you cannot go to a showroom to see a marketing research report or medical operation that you are considering. This means that service customers suffer higher perceived risk in their decision-making and that the three elements of the extended marketing mix—people, physical evidence, and process—are crucial in influencing the customer's perception of service quality. These will be discussed later.

The *brand name* of a service can also influence the perception of a service. Four characteristics of successful brand names are as follows:[41]

1   *Distinctiveness*: it immediately identifies the services provider and differentiates it from the competition.

2   *Relevance*: it communicates the nature of the service and the service benefit.

3   *Memorability*: it is easily understood and remembered.

4   *Flexibility*: it not only expresses the service organization's current business but also is broad enough to cover foreseeable new ventures.

Credit cards provide examples of effective brand names: Visa suggests internationality and Access emphasizes easy accessibility to cash and products. Obviously the success of the brand name is heavily dependent on the service organization's ability to deliver on the promise it implies.

Although trial of some services is impossible, for others it can be achieved. For example, some hotels invite key decision-makers of social clubs (for example, social secretaries of pensioner groups) to visit their hotels free of charge to sample the facilities and service. The hotels hope that they will recommend a group visit to their members.

Service providers such as airlines are constantly seeking ways of differentiating themselves from their competitors. The advertisement for Qantas overleaf shows how the quality of physical products that accompany the service can be used as a basis for differentiation.

Promotion   the intangible element of a service may be difficult to communicate. For example, it may be difficult to represent courtesy, hard work and customer care in an advertisement. Once again the answer is to use *tangible cues* that will help customers understand and judge the service. A hotel can show the buildings, swimming pool, friendly staff and happy customers. An investment company can provide tangible evidence of past performance. Testimonials from satisfied customers can also be used to communicate services benefits. Netto, the Danish-based supermarket chain, used testimonials from six customers in their UK advertising to explain the advantages of shopping there.

Advertising can be used to communicate and reinforce the image of a service. For example, store image can enhance customer satisfaction and build store loyalty.[42]

Personal selling can also be effective in services marketing because of the high perceived risk inherent in many service purchases. For example, a salesperson can explain the details of a personal pension plan or investment opportunity, can answer questions and provide reassurance.

Because of the high perceived risk inherent in buying services, salespeople should develop lists of satisfied customers to use in reference selling. Also salespeople need to be trained to ask for referrals. Customers should be asked if they know of other people or organizations who might benefit from the service. The customer can then be used as an entrée and point of reference when approaching and selling to the new prospect.

Word of mouth is critical to success for services because of their experiential nature. For example, talking to people who have visited a resort or hotel is more convincing than reading holiday brochures. Promotion, therefore, must acknowledge the dominant role of personal influence in the choice process and stimulate word of mouth communication. Cowell suggests four approaches:[43]

1   Persuading satisfied customers to inform others of their satisfaction (e.g. American

Express reward customers who introduce others to their service).

2   Developing materials that customers can pass on to others.

3   Targeting opinion leaders in advertising campaigns.

4   Encouraging potential customers to talk to current customers (e.g. open days at universities).

Communication should also be targeted at employees because of their importance in creating and maintaining service quality. Internal communications can define management expectations of staff, reinforce the need to delight the customer, and explain the rewards that follow from giving excellent service. External communications that depict service quality can also influence internal staff if they include employees and show how they take exceptional care of their customers.

Care should be taken not to exaggerate promises in promotional material since this may build up unachievable expectations. For example, Delta Airlines used the advertising slogan 'Delta is ready when you are'. This caused problems because it built up customers' expectations that the airline would always be ready—an impossible task. This led Delta to change its slogan to the more realistic 'We love to fly and it shows'.[44]

The unethical promotion of service products has caused problems in some sectors. A study of senior managers in UK insurance companies revealed an awareness of a range of ethical problems. The design of commission systems which may encourage bias towards products that provide greater returns to the salesperson, and the promotion of inappropriate products were of particular concern.[45]

Price   price is a key marketing tool for three reasons. First, as it is often difficult to evaluate a service before purchase, price may act as an indicator of perceived quality. For example, in a travel brochure the price charged by hotels may be used to indicate their quality. Some companies expect a management consultant to charge high fees, otherwise they cannot be particularly good. Second, price is an important tool in controlling demand: matching demand and supply is critical in services because they cannot be stored. Creative use of pricing can help to smooth demand. Third, a key segmentation variable with

Sorry. We don't *serve* plain food.

Our First Class cuisine is quite unlike any you've experienced on a plane before. Designed by one of Australia's best chefs, Neil Perry, the food is cooked just once, on board the plane, using the best regional and seasonal ingredients available. In short, there's nothing plain about it.

http://www.qantas.com.au

Service firms like Qantas attempt differentiation on the basis of the quality of the physical products that accompany the service

services is price sensitivity. Some customers may be willing to pay a much higher price than others. Time is often used to segment price sensitive and insensitive customers. For example, the price of international air travel is often dependent on the length of stay. Travellers from Europe to the USA will pay a lot less if they stay a minimum of six nights (including Saturday). Airlines know that customers who stay for less than that are likely to be businesspeople who are willing and able to pay a higher price.

Many companies do not take full advantage of the opportunities to use price creatively in the marketing of their services. For example, in the industrial services sector, one study found that firms 'generally lack a customer orientation in pricing; emphasize formula-based approaches that are cost-oriented; are very inflexible in their pricing schemes; do not develop price differentials based on elasticity of different market segments; and rarely attempt to measure customer price sensitivity'.[46]

Some services such as accounting and management consultancy charge their customers fees. A strategy needs to be thought out concerning fees. How far can fees be flexible to secure or retain particular customers? How will the fee level compare to the competition? Will there be an incentive built into fee structure for continuity, forward commitment or the use of the full range of services on offer? Five pricing techniques may be used when setting fee levels:

1 *Offset*: low fee for *core service* but recouping with *add ons*.
2 *Inducement*: low fee to attract new customers or to help retain existing customers.
3 *Diversionary*: low basic fees on selected services to develop the image of value for money across the whole range of services.
4 *Guarantee*: full fee payable on achievement of agreed results.
5 *Predatory*: competition's fees undercut to remove them from the market; high fees charged later.

Place distribution channels for services are usually more direct than for many physical goods. Because services are intangible, the services marketer is less concerned with storage, the production and consumption is often simultaneous, and the personal nature of services means that direct contact with the service provider (or at best its agent) is desirable. Agents are used when the individual service provider cannot provide a sufficiently wide selection for customers. Consequently agents are often sued for the marketing of travel, insurance and entertainment. However, the advent of the Internet means that direct dealings with the service provider are becoming more frequent.

Growth for many service companies means opening new facilities in new locations. Whereas procedures of physical goods can expand production at one site to serve the needs of a geographically spread market, the simultaneous production and consumption of hotel, banking, catering, retailing and accounting services for example means that expansions often means following a multi-site strategy. The evaluation of store locations is therefore a critical skill for services marketers. Much of the success of top European supermarket chains has been their ability to choose profitable new sites for their retailing operations.

People because of the simultaneity of production and consumption in services, the firm's personnel occupy a key position in influencing customer perceptions of product quality.[47] In fact service quality is inseparable from the quality of the service provider. The importance of people is illustrated in the advertisement for IBM overleaf An important marketing task, then, is to set standards to improve the quality of service provided by employees and monitor their performance. Without training and control, employees tend to be variable in their performance leading to variable service quality.

Training is crucial so that employees understand the appropriate forms of behaviour. British Airways train their staff to identify and categorize different personality types of passengers and to modify behaviour accordingly. Staff (e.g. waiters) need to know how much discretion they have to talk informally to customers, and to control their own behaviour so that they are not intrusive, noisy or immature. They also need to be trained to adopt a warm and caring attitude to customers. This has been shown to be linked to customers' perceptions of likeability and service perception as well as loyalty to the service provider.[48] Finally, they need to adopt a customer-first attitude rather than putting their own convenience and enjoyment before that of their customers. The

Creative Technologists

Names:	Mark Andrews, Bhader Singh
Job Description:	Use new computer technologies to help companies create interactive selling tools.
Latest Achievement:	Used HotMedia technology to design an interactive Web site for the Vauxhall Zafira, influencing Web visitors to buy in 40% more cases than non-visitors.
Regrets:	"Not working on commission."
Contact:	Web: www.ibm.com/services/uk e-mail: globserv@uk.ibm.com

IBM Global Services
People who think. People who do.

e business people

People are key to service delivery at IBM

illustration featuring American Express shows how they differentiate themselves based on the quality of their personnel.

Marketing should also examine the role played by customers in the service environment and seek to eliminate harmful interactions. For example, the enjoyment of a restaurant meal or air travel will very much depend upon the actions of other customers. At Christmas, restaurants are often in demand by groups of work colleagues. These can be rowdy affairs that can distract from the pleasure of regular patrons. This situation needs to be managed, perhaps by segregating in some way the two types of customers.

Physical evidence   this is the environment in which the service is delivered and any tangible goods that facilitate the performance and communication of the service. Customers look for clues to the likely quality of a service by inspecting the tangible evidence. For example, prospective customers may gaze through a restaurant window to check the appearance of the waiters, the décor and furnishings. The ambience of a retail store is highly dependent on décor, and colour can play an important role in establishing mood because colour has meaning. For example, black signifies strength and power, whereas green suggests mildness. The interior of jet aircraft is pastel-coloured to promote a feeling of calmness, whereas many nightclubs are brightly coloured with flashing lights to give a sense of excitement.

The layout of a service operation can be a compromise between operations' need for efficiency, and marketing's desire for effectively serving the customer. For example, the temptation to squeeze in an extra table in a restaurant or seating in an aircraft may be at the expense of customer comfort.

Process   this is the procedures, mechanisms and flow of activities by which a service is acquired. Process decisions radically affect how a service is delivered to customers. For example, a self-service cafeteria is very different from a restaurant. Marketing managers need to know if self-service is acceptable (or indeed desirable). Queuing may provide an opportunity to create a differential advantage by reduction/elimination, or making the time spent waiting more enjoyable. Certainly waiting for service is a common experience for customers and is a strong determinant of overall satisfaction with the service and customer loyalty. Research has shown that an attractive waiting environment can prevent customers becoming irritated or bored very quickly even though they may have to wait a long time. Both appraisal of the wait and satisfaction with the service improved when the attractiveness of the waiting environment (measured by atmosphere, cleanliness, spaciousness and climate) was rated higher.[49] Providing a more effective service (shorter queues) may be at odds with operations as the remedy may be to employ more staff.

Reducing delivery time, for example the time between ordering a meal and receiving it, can also improve service quality. As we discussed earlier, this need not necessarily cost more if customers can be persuaded to become involved in the production process as successfully reflected in the growth of self service breakfast bars in hotels.

Finally, Berry suggests seven guidelines when implementing a positioning strategy:[50]

1   Ensure that *marketing* happens at all levels from the marketing department to where the service is provided.

2   Consider introducing *flexibility* in providing the service; when feasible customize the service to the needs of customers.

3   Recruit *high quality staff,* treat them well and communicate clearly to them: their attitudes and behaviour are the key to service quality and differentiation.

4   Attempt to market to *existing customers* to increase their use of the service, or to take up new service products.

5   Set up a *quick response facility* to customer problems and complaints.

6   Employ *new technology* to provide better services at lower costs.

7   Use *branding* to clearly differentiate service offerings from the competition in the minds of target customers.

Retailing

Retailing is an important service industry: it is the activity involved in the sale of products to the ultimate consumer. Retailing employed 17 per cent of the European Union's workforce in 1993 and its international nature is increasing despite laws such as France's Loi Royer, Belgium's Loi

Cadenas and Germany's Baunutzungsverordnung, which restrict retail developments above certain sizes. Many European retailers operate on an international scale. Table 20.2 describes the cross-border activities of four leading European retailers.

The purchasing power of retailers has meant that manufacturers have to maintain high service levels and good relations with them. Many are turning to trade marketing teams to provide dedicated resources to service their needs. Marketing in Action 20.2 describes these developments.

Consumer decision-making involves not only the choice of product and brand, but also the choice of retail outlet. Most retailing is conducted in stores such as supermarkets, catalogue shops and departmental stores, but non-store retailing such as mail order and automatic vending also accounts for a large amount of sales. Retailing provides an important service to customers, making products available when and where customers want to buy them.

Store choice may be dependent upon the buying scenario relevant to consumers in a market. For example, two unique choice situations in Germany are relevant for grocery shopping: shopping for daily household needs (*Normaleinkauf*) and grocery shopping for stocking-up for weekly, or monthly household needs (*Vorratseinkauf*). The stores chosen for the former activity are largely different to those used for the latter.[51]

Many large retailers exert enormous power in the distribution chain because of the vast quantities of goods they buy from manufacturers. This power is reflected in their ability to extract 'guarantee of margins' from manufacturers. This is a clause inserted in a contract that ensures a certain profit margin for the retailer irrespective of the retail price being charged to the customer. One manufacturer is played against another and own-label brands are used to extract more profit.[52]

Major store and non-store types

Supermarkets

These are large self-service stores traditionally selling food, drinks and toiletries, but range broadening by some *supermarket chains* means that such items as non-prescription pharmaceuticals, cosmetics, and clothing are also being sold. While one attraction of supermarkets is their lower prices compared with small independent grocery shops, the extent to which price is a key competitive weapon depends upon the supermarket's positioning strategy. For example, in the UK Sainsbury, Waitrose and Tesco rely less on price than Kwik Save, Aldi or Netto.

Department stores

So-called because related product lines are sold in separate departments such as men's and women's clothing, jewellery, cosmetics, toys, and home furnishings, in recent years *department stores* have been under increasing pressure from discount houses, speciality stores and the move to

Table 20.2 Leading European cross-border retailers

Aldi
Europe's largest discount grocery retailer; over 3800 outlets in Germany, the Netherlands, Denmark, Austria, Belgium, France, Poland and the USA; over 40% of sales outside home country of Germany

Ahold
The Netherland's largest retailer; holds 36% of Dutch grocery market; owns 600 supermarkets in the Netherlands, and 500 outlets in the USA. Over 50% of sales abroad

IKEA
Based in Sweden, it is the world's widest spread international retailer of furniture and furnishings; it operates in 29 countries out of 140 stores; over 75% of business is outside Sweden

Carrefour/Promode's
France's largest quoted food retailer with over 20% of the home market; operates through over 4500 outlets in France, Spain, Germany, Italy, USA, Brazil, Portugal, Greece, South Korea, Indonesia, Argentina, and Taiwan.

Source: European Commission; Jonquières, G. de (1994) Can Europe Compete?, *Financial Times*, 1 March, 14.

out-of-town shopping. Nevertheless, they are still surviving in this competitive arena.

Speciality shops

These outlets specialize in a narrow product line. For example many town centres have shops selling confectionery, cigarettes and newspapers in the same outlet. Many speciality outlets sell only one product line such as Tie Rack and Sock Shop. Specialization allows a deep product line to be sold in restricted shop space. Some *speciality shops* focus on quality and personal service such as butchers and greengrocers.

20.2 Marketing in Action

Trade Marketing

The growing importance of retailers to the success of brand marketing is being reflected in the formation of trade marketing teams to service their needs. The traditional consumer marketing organization of product managers who controlled brands, and a separate salesforce to sell to the trade is gradually being replaced. A combination of the move to key account management on the part of the salesforce, and the brand manager's lack of appreciation of what retailers actually want, has prompted many successful European consumer goods companies to set up a trade marketing organization. Its role is to bridge the gap between brand management and the salesforce.

Trade marketers focus on retailer needs: what kinds of products do they want; in which sizes, with which packaging, at what prices and with what kind of promotion? Supermarkets are demanding more tailored promotions. For example, a large supermarket chain also owned a group of hotels. It demanded from a drinks supplier that the next competition promotion offer holiday breaks in its hotels as prizes (paid for by the manufacturer).

The information on trade requirements is fed back to brand management who develop appropriate products. The trade marketers then brief the salesforce on how best to communicate their value to retailers.

Eventually, trade marketing might provide the integrating force to link the marketing function with key account management under one organizational unit. So far this has proved difficult to achieve because of the different backgrounds and cultures of sales and brand management. For example, sales may be more inclined to support promotions that boost short-term sales whereas brand management may be wary of promotions that may endanger the image of the brand. Most large consumer companies have paused part-way by setting up a hybrid, trade marketing unit with a coordinating role, others, as we have seen, have moved to category management as a means of forging stronger links with the trade.

The key drivers behind the adoption of trade marketing are (i) the need for improved communication and co-ordination between sales and brand marketing so that trade requirements are built into brand plans, (ii) new trade marketing related tasks such as planning trade-orientated promotions, developing expertise in the use of computer models (e.g. space planning or direct product profitability software) and providing information to account handlers on customers, consumers and competitors, and (iii) the move to category management by many retailers which invites a corresponding response from manufacturers in order to improve their trade marketing service and relationships.

Based on: Ohbora et al. (1992);[53] Dewsnap (1997);[54] Nicholas (1999)[55]

Discount houses

These sell products at low prices by bulk buying, accepting low margins and selling high volumes. Low prices, sometimes promoted as *sale prices*, are offered throughout the year. As an executive of Dixons, a UK discounter of electrical goods, commented, 'We only have two sales—each lasting six months.' Many *discounters* operate from out-of-town *retail warehouses* with the capacity to stock a wide range of merchandise.

Category killers

These are retail outlets with a narrow product focus but with an unusually wide width and depth to that product range. *Category killers* emerged in the USA in the early 1980s as a challenge to discount houses. They are distinct from speciality shops in that they are bigger and carry a wider and deeper range of products within their chosen product category, and are distinguished from discount houses in their focus on only one product category. Two examples of the category killer are Toys ' Я ' Us and Nevada Bob's Discount Golf Warehouses.[56] e-Marketing 20.1 discusses how Toys ' Я ' Us operates and gains competitive advantage over traditional toy outlets, while facing a major threat from a new Internet-based competitor eToys.

Convenience stores

These stores offer customers the convenience of close location and long opening hours every day of the week. Because they are small they pay higher prices for their merchandise than supermarkets, and therefore have to charge higher prices to their customers. Some of these stores join buying groups such as Spar or Mace to gain some purchasing power and lower prices. But the main customer need that they fulfil is for top-up buying, for example when short of a carton of milk or loaf of bread. Although average purchase value is low, convenience stores prosper because of their higher prices and low staff costs: many are family businesses.

Catalogue stores

These retail outlets promote their products through catalogues which are either posted or are available in the store for customers to take home.

Purchase is in city-centre outlets where customers fill in order forms, pay for the goods and then collect them from a designated place in the store. In the UK, Argos is a successful *catalogue retailer* selling a wide range of discounted products such as electrical goods, jewellery, gardening tools, furniture, toys, car accessories, sports goods, luggage, and cutlery.

Mail order

This non-store form of retailing may also employ catalogues as a promotional vehicle but the purchase transaction is conducted via the mail. Alternatively, outward communication may be by direct mail, television, magazine or newspaper advertising. Increasingly orders are being placed by telephone, a process which is facilitated by the use of credit cards as a means of payment. Goods are then sent by mail. A growth area is the selling of personal computers by *mail order*. By eliminating costly intermediaries, products can be offered at low prices. Otto-Versand, the Germany mail order company, owns Grattan, a UK mail order retailer, and has leading positions in Austria, Belgium, Italy, The Netherlands and Spain. Its French rival, La Redoute, has expanded into Belgium, Italy and Portugal. Mail order has the prospect of pan-European catalogues, central warehousing and processing of cross-border orders.

Automatic vending

Vending machines offer such products as drinks, confectionery, soup and newspapers in convenient locations, 24 hours a day. No sales staff are required although restocking, servicing and repair costs can be high. Cash dispensers at banks have improved customer service by permitting round-the-clock access to savings. However, machine breakdowns and out-of-stock situations can annoy customers.

Theories of retail evolution

Three retailing theories explain the changing fortunes of different retailing types and how one type is replaced by another. These are the *wheel of retailing*, the *retail accordion* and the *retail life cycle*.

The wheel of retailing

This theory suggests that new forms of retailing begin as cut-price, low cost and narrow profit margin operations. Eventually, the retailer *trades up* by improving display and location, providing credit, delivery and sales services and by raising advertising expenditures. The retailer thus matures as a high cost, high price conservative operator, making it vulnerable to new, lower price entrants.[57] The theory has been the subject of much debate but anecdotal evidence concerning department stores, supermarkets and catalogue stores suggests that many began as low price operators who subsequently raised costs and prices, creating marketing opportunities for new, low price competitors, developments that are consistent with the theory.

The retail accordion

This theory focuses on the width of product assortment sold by retail outlets and claims a

20.1   e-Marketing

New Competition in the Toy Market

The term category killer has been given to a retail format where an outlet specializes in one product category, but with an unusual width and depth of product range which is sold at competitive prices. The term is most commonly associated with Toys 'Я' Us, the world's largest toy speciality retailing chain. The typical store is large, carries around 30 000 toy items, and is situated out of town.

The key to their success is the combination of widest choice, and low, everyday prices. From the customer's viewpoint there is no need to shop around for better prices or alternative products at other toy retailers. By visiting Toys 'Я' Us a customer can feel confident of finding a suitable toy and paying a price which is unlikely to be beaten by a rival outlet.

A new entrant has changed the rules of the game, however. eToys is the first on-line mass market toy store. The eToys concept is to target customers who do not enjoy spending hours searching for their children's toys. To attract these customers eToys positions itself as the place where shoppers can 'save time versus regular retail shopping'. Even at Toys 'Я' Us time is expended travelling to and from their stores. The critical elements affecting the success of any Internet retailer, however, is the company's ability to attract customers to their website.

Attracting these customers can be costly. To launch eToys $3 million was spent to be featured on America Online. Additionally 25 per cent sales commission is offered to customers who direct other people to the eToys website. Other promotional expenses include running advertising in the traditional media such as television and magazines as well as operating an on-line sweepstake. During the 1998 Christmas season, the sweepstake offered potential customers the opportunity to win the toy most in demand, the Furby robotic animal. The objective was to gather the e-mail addresses of entrants so that promotional messages could be sent subsequently.

In today's competitive world even recent success stories like Toys 'Я' Us cannot become complacent. Advances in technology provide the platform for new entrants to challenge existing participants in mature markets.

Based on: Sellers (1999);[58] Davies and Sanghavi (1993)[59]

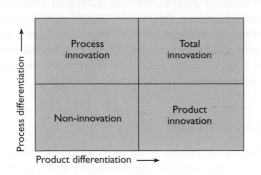

Figure 20.8 Retailing differentiation.

Source: Davies, G. and N. Sanghavi (1993) Is the Category Killer a Significant Innovation?, ESRC Seminar: Strategic Issues in Retailing, Manchester Business School, 1–23

general-specific-general cycle. The cycle begins by retailers selling a wide assortment of goods followed by a more focused range. This, in turn, is replaced by retailers expanding their range.[60] The theory was developed with regard to the evolution of the entire retail system and is broadly in accord with experience in the USA where the general store of the nineteenth century was superseded by the specialist retailers of the early twentieth. These then gave way to the post-1940s mass merchandisers.

The retail life cycle

The concept of a retail life cycle is based upon the well-known product life cycle stating that new types of retailing pass through the stages of birth, growth, maturity, and decline.[61] A retailing innovation enjoying a competitive advantage over existing forms is rewarded by fast sales growth. During the growth stage, imitators are attracted by its success, and by the end of this phase problems arise through over-ambitious expansion. Maturity is characterized by high competition, and is replaced by decline as new retail innovations take over. Evidence suggests that variety stores and counter-service grocery stores evolved in this manner.[62]

Key retail marketing decisions

The three theories of retailing explain the evolution in retailing methods but there is nothing

inevitable about the demise of a given retailer. The key is to anticipate and adapt to changing environmental circumstances. We shall now explore some of the key retailing decisions necessary to prosper in today's competitive climate.

The basic framework for deciding retail marketing strategy is that given earlier in the chapter when we discussed services. However, there are a number of specific issues that relate to retailing, and are worthy of separate discussion. These are *retail positioning, store location, product assortment and services, price* and *store atmosphere*. These decisions are being taken against a background of rapid change in information technology. e-Marketing 20.2 describes some developments and their impact on retail marketing decisions.

Retail positioning

As with all marketing decisions, **retail positioning** involves the choice of target market and differential advantage. Targeting allows retailers to tailor their marketing mix, which includes product assortment, service levels, store location, prices and promotion, to the needs of their chosen customer segment. Differentiation provides a reason to shop at one store rather than another. A useful framework for creating a differential advantage has been proposed by Davies, who suggests that innovation in retailing can come only from novelty in the process offered to the shopper, or from novelty in the product or product assortment offered to the shopper.[63] Figure 20.8 shows that differentiation can be achieved through *process innovation* or *product innovation* or a combination of the two (*total innovation*). The catalogue shop Argos in the UK has offered innovation in the process of shopping, whereas Next achieved success through product innovation (stylish clothes at affordable prices). Toys ' Я ' Us are an example of both product and process innovation through providing the widest range of toys at one location (production innovation) and thereby offering convenient, one-stop shopping (process innovation). By way of contrast, Woolworth by not offering differentiation in either of these dimensions, have lost market share in toys. The customer is offered a limited choice, no price advantage and the risk of having to shop around to be sure of finding a suitable toy.

Store location

Convenience is an important issue for many shoppers, and so store location can have a major bearing on sales performance. Retailers have to decide on regional coverage, the towns and cities to target within regions, and the precise location within a given town or city. Many retailers begin life as regional suppliers, and grow by expanding geographically. In the UK, for example, the Asda

20.2 e-Marketing

Information Technology in Retailing

Retailers are no strangers to information technology developments with electronic point of sale (EPOS) systems allowing the counting of products sold, money taken and quicker service at checkouts. More recent innovations such as loyalty cards, however, have shifted the focus to understanding the customer. By monitoring individual purchasing patterns, direct mail promotions can be targeted at named individuals and adapted to match their known preferences and likely purchases. In-store product assortments can be matched more closely to purchasing patterns. In the USA, retailers are tailoring in-store promotions and discounts to individuals. One supermarket has a scheme where shoppers swipe their loyalty cards through 'readers' as they enter the shop and a list of money-off vouchers, based upon their previous spending patterns, is printed.

A key technological development that is changing the way products are bought is the Internet. On-line shopping is set to soar in the early years of the twenty-first century as more people gain access to the Web, become accustomed to electronic payment, and more companies provide facilities to buy over the Internet. Already e-commerce has made in-roads in books, information technology, hardware and software, travel and music. Many supermarkets are experimenting with on-line shopping and chains such as Ahold and Tesco are claiming to be profitable. Dedicated e-retailers such as Amazon, eToys and Jungle.com are challenging traditional retailers. Two key issues are promotion and fulfilment. New dot.com companies need to spend heavily to gain awareness and drive up traffic to their sites. Delivering the goods is the second challenge. Although the Internet provides a cheap and convenient way of purchasing products, suppliers need to develop fast and reliable delivery systems to ensure customers are not disappointed at the point of receiving the goods.

Multimedia kiosks are also changing the face of retailing. Daewoo, the South Korean car manufacturer, has set up kiosks in its European dealerships. One allows children to 'design a car' while their parents visit a neighbouring kiosk to view the features and prices of the Daewoo car range. In the USA, consumer electronics retailer Best Buy has equipped stores with interactive kiosks offering information on 65 000 CDs, 12 000 videos and 2000 software packages as an alternative to consulting sales assistants.

Information technology is also improving links between manufacturers and retailers. Electronic data interchange (EDI) allows them to exchange purchase orders, invoices, delivery notes and money electronically rather than using paper-based systems.

Based on: Miller (1996);[64] Ody. (1996);[65] Ody (1996);[66] Ody. (1997);[67] Gray (2000);[68] Voyle (2000)[69]

supermarket chain expanded from the north of England, while Sainsbury's original base was in the south of England.

The choice of town or city will depend upon such factors as correspondence with the retailer's chosen target market, the level of disposable income in the catchment area, the availability of suitable sites, and the level of competition. The choice of a particular site may depend on the level of existing traffic (pedestrian and/or vehicular) passing the site, parking provision, access to the outlet for delivery vehicles, the presence of competition, planning restrictions, and the opportunity to form new retailing centres with other outlets. For example, an agreement between two or more non-competing retailers (e.g. Marks and Spencer and Tesco) to site outlets together out-of-town means greater drawing power than could be achieved individually. Having made that decision, the partners will look for suitable sites near their chosen town or city.

Product assortment and services

Retailers have to decide upon the breadth of their product assortment and its depth. A supermarket, for example, may decide to widen its product assortment from food, drink and toiletries to include clothes and toys: this is called *scrambled merchandising*. Within each product line it can choose to stock a deep or shallow product range. Some retailers like Tie Rack, Sock Shop and Toys 'Я' Us stock one deep product line. Department stores, however, offer a much broader range of products including toys, cosmetics, jewellery, clothes, electrical goods and household accessories. Some retailers begin with one product line and gradually broaden their product assortment to maximize revenue per customer. For example, petrol stations broadened their product range to include motor accessories and more recently confectionery, drinks, flowers and newspapers. A by-product of this may be to reduce customers' price sensitivity since selection of petrol station may be based on the ability to buy other products rather than the lowest price.

The choice of product assortment will be dependent on the positioning strategy of the retailer, customer expectations, and ultimately on the profitability of each product line. Slow moving unprofitable lines should be dropped unless they are necessary to conform with the range of products expected by customers. For example, customers expect a full range of food products in a supermarket.

Another product decision concerns *own-label branding*. Large retailers may decide to sell a range of own-label products to complement national brands. Often the purchasing power of large retail chains means that prices can be lower and yet profit margins higher than for competing national brands. This makes the activity an attractive proposition for many retailers. Supermarkets have moved into this area, as have UK electrical giants such as Dixons, which uses the Chinon brand name for cameras and Saisha for brown goods such as hi-fi and televisions, and Currys, which has adopted the Matsui brand name. In both cases the use of a Japanese-sounding name (even though some of the products were sourced in Europe) was believed to enhance their customer appeal.

Finally, retailers need to consider the nature and degree of *customer service*. Discount stores traditionally provided little service but as price differentials have narrowed some have sought differentiation through service. For example, many electrical goods retailers provide a comprehensive after-sales service package for their customers. Superior customer service may make customers more tolerant of higher prices and even where the product is standardized (as in fast-food restaurants) training employees to give individual attention to each customer can arise loyalty to the outlet.[70]

Price

For some market segments price is a key factor in store choice. Consequently some retailers major on price as their differential advantage. This requires vigilant cost control and massive buying power. A recent trend is towards *everyday low prices* favoured by retailers rather than higher prices supplemented by promotions supported by manufacturers. Retailers such as B&Q, the do-it-yourself discounter, maintain that customers prefer predictable low prices rather than occasional money-off deals, three-for-the-price-of-two offers and free gifts. Supermarket chains are also pressurizing suppliers to provide consistently low prices rather than temporary promotions. This action is consistent with the desire to position themselves on a low price platform.

The importance of price competitiveness is reflected in the alliance of European food retailers called Associated Marketing Services. Retailers such as Argyll (UK), Ahold (The Netherlands), ICA (a federation of Swedish food retailers) and Casino (France) have joined forces to foster cooperation in the areas of purchasing and marketing of brands. Their range of activities includes own branding, joint buying, the development of joint brands and services and the exchange of information and skills. A key aim is to reduce cost price since this accounts for 75 per cent of the sales price to customers.[71]

Some supermarkets sell *no-frills products*. These are basic commodities such as bread, sugar and soft drinks sold in rudimentary packaging at low prices. Kwik Save, for example, sell such products in their own-label No Frills range in plain white packaging with black lettering. It appeals to the price conscious shopper who wants standard products at low prices, and helps to position Kwik Save as a low price supermarket. This is important given the competitive threats of Aldi and Netto in the UK.

Retailers need to be aware of the negative consequences of setting artificial 'sales' prices. The use of retail 'sales' by outlets to promote their merchandise can lead to increasing scepticism of their integrity, especially those that 'must end soon' but rarely do, and the 'never to be repeated' bargain offers which invariably were.[72]

Store atmosphere

This is created by the design, colour and layout of a store. Both exterior and interior design affect atmosphere. External factors include architectural

20.3   Marketing in Action

Music and Retailing

Retailers are increasingly using music to influence the mood of customers, the length of time they spend in the store, the service they receive and the amount they spend per visit. Research conducted by Leicester University on behalf of Asda, a UK supermarket chain, showed that consumer spend could be influenced by music: the sales of German and French wines increased when music from those countries was played in the drinks area. Retailers have found that other sounds can increase sales as well. Sports retailers, for example, have found that using commentaries of football and athletic events can boost sales in those product categories.

Music works by influencing the part of the brain responsible for alertness and in the retail environment it can be used to excite or relax customers. For example, it can soothe frustrations associated with queuing. It can have a more general effect of providing a pleasant atmosphere in the store to create the retail theatre that is increasingly necessary to compete with new outlets such as the Internet. Retailers change the type of music they play to appeal to the different types of customer that shop at various times of the day. Asda, for instance, plays music that appeals to a more female and elderly target market during the day but changes the format to appeal to a more male and younger customer in the evening.

Music has also been found to motivate staff. Research by Leicester University for a high street bank found that the productivity at their cheque clearing centre improved by 20 per cent when upbeat music was played in the office.

Based on: Hemsley (2000)[73]

design, signs, window display and use of colour that create an identity for a retailer, and attract customers. Retailers aim to create a welcoming rather than an intimidating mood. The image which is projected should be consonant with the ethos of the shop. The Body shop, for example, project their environmentally caring image through the green exterior of their shops, and window displays that feature environmental issues.

Interior design also has a major impact on atmosphere. Store lighting, fixtures and fittings, and layout are important considerations. Supermarkets that have narrow aisles that contribute to congestion can project a negative image, and poorly lit showrooms can feel intimidating. Colour, sound and smell can affect mood. As we have discussed earlier in this chapter, colour has meaning and can be used to create the desired atmosphere in a store. Supermarkets often use music to create a relaxed atmosphere, whereas some boutiques use pop music to attract their target customers. Departmental stores often place perfume counters near the entrance, and supermarkets may use the smell of baking bread to attract their customers. Marketing in Action 20.3 explains how music is used by retailers to boost sales.

The success of Stew Leonard's supermarket in Connecticut, USA, in projecting a fun atmosphere for shoppers has attracted the attention of European retailers. The Quinn's supermarket chain in Ireland has emulated its success, and other chains, such as Asda in the UK, provide a face-painting service for children at holiday-times to make grocery shopping more fun.

Marketing in non-profit organizations

Non-profit organizations attempt to achieve some other objective than profit. This does not mean that they are uninterested in income as they have to generate cash to survive. However, their primary goal is non-economic, for example to provide cultural enrichment (an orchestra), to protect birds and animals (Royal Society for the Protection of Birds, Royal Society for the Prevention of Cruelty to Animals), to alleviate hunger (Oxfam), to provide education (schools and universities), to foster community activities (community association), and to supply health care (hospitals) and public services (local authorities). Their worth and standing is not dependent on the profits they generate. They are discussed in this chapter as most non-profit organizations operate in the services sector. Indeed, non-profit organizations account for over half of all service provision in most European countries.

Marketing is of growing importance to many non-profit organizations because of the need to generate funds in an increasingly competitive arena. Even organizations who rely on government-sponsored grants need to show how their work is of benefit to society: they must meet the needs of their customers. Many non-profit organizations rely on membership fees or donations, which means that communication to individuals and organizations is required, and they must be persuaded to join or make a donation. This requires marketing skills, which are being increasingly applied. Such is the case with political parties which use marketing techniques to attract members (and the fees their allegiances bring) and votes at elections.[74] Advertising is also used extensively by charities to promote their cause (see opposite).

Characteristics of non-profit marketing

These are a number of characteristics of *non-profit marketing* that distinguish it from that conducted by profit-orientated marketing organizations.[75]

Education v. meeting current needs

Some non-profit organizations see their role as not only meeting current needs of their customers but also educating them in new ideas and issues, cultural development, and social awareness. These goals may be at conflict with maximizing revenue or audience figures. For example, a public broadcasting organization like the BBC may trade-off audience size for some of these objectives, or an orchestra may decide that more esoteric pieces of classical music should be played rather than the more popular pieces.

"Breathe a word to anyone and you're dead"

Supported by *Microsoft*

Cruelty to children must stop. FULL STOP ● NSPCC

Non-profit organizations like NSPCC use advertising to promote their messages

Multiple publics

Most non-profit organizations serve several groups or publics. The two broad groups are *donors*, who may be individuals, trusts, companies, and government bodies, and *clients*, who include audiences, patients, and beneficiaries.[76] The need is to satisfy both donors and clients, complicating the marketing task. For example, a community association may be part-funded by the local authority and partly by the users (clients) of the association's buildings and facilities. To succeed both groups have to be satisfied. The BBC has to satisfy not only the viewers and listeners, but also the government, who decide the size of the licence fee which funds its activities.

Non-profit organizations need to adopt marketing as a coherent philosophy for managing multiple public relationships.[77]

Measurement of success and conflicting objectives

For profit-orientated organizations success is measured ultimately on profitability. For non-profit organizations measuring success is not so easy. In universities, for example, is success measured in research terms, number of students taught, the range of qualifications or the quality of teaching? The answer is that it is a combination of these factors, which can lead to conflict: more students and a larger range of courses may reduce the time needed for research. Decision-making is therefore complex in non-profit orientated organizations.

Public scrutiny

While all organizations are subject to public scrutiny, public sector non-profit organizations are never far from the public's attention. The reason is that they are publicly funded from taxes. This gives them extra newsworthiness as all tax-payers are interested in how their money is being spent. They have to be particularly careful that they do not become involved in controversy, which can result in bad publicity.

Marketing procedures for non-profit organizations

Despite these differences the marketing procedures relevant to profit-orientated companies can also be applied to non-profit organizations.

Target marketing, differentiation and marketing mix decisions need to be made. We shall now discuss these issues with reference to the special characteristics of non-profit organizations.

Target marketing and differentiation

As we have already discussed, non-profit organizations can usefully segment their target publics into donors and clients (customers). Within each group, subsegments of individuals and organizations need to be identified. These will be the targets for persuasive communications, and the development of services. The needs of each group must be understood. For example, donors may judge which charity to give to on the basis of awareness and reputation, the confidence that funds will not be wasted on excessive administration, and the perceived worthiness of the cause. The charity needs, therefore, not only to promote itself but also to gain publicity for its cause. Its level of donor funding will depend upon both these factors. The brand name of the charity is also important. Oxfam suggest the type of work the organization is mainly concerned with—relief of famine—and so is instantly recognizable. Action in Distress is also suggestive of its type of work.

Market segmentation and targeting are key ingredients in the marketing of political parties. Potential voters are segmented according to their propensity to vote (obtainable from electoral registers) and their likelihood of voting for a particular party (obtainable from door-to-door canvassing returns). Resources can then be channelled to the segments most likely to switch votes in the forthcoming election, via direct mail and doorstep visits. Focus groups provide a feedback mechanism for testing the attractiveness of alternative policy options and gauging voters' opinions on key policy areas such as health, education and taxation. By keeping in touch with public opinion, political parties have the information to differentiate themselves from their competitors on issues that are important to voters. While such marketing research is unlikely to affect the underlying beliefs and principles upon which a political party is based, it is a necessary basis for the policy adaptations required to keep in touch with a changing electorate.[78]

Developing a marketing mix

Many non-profit organizations are skilled at *event marketing*. Events are organized to raise funds, including dinners, dances, coffee mornings, book sales, sponsored walks and theatrical shows. Not all events are designed to raise funds for the sponsoring organization.

For example, the BBC has organized Comic Relief and Children in Need *telethons* to raise money for worthy causes.

The pricing of services provided by non-profit organizations may not follow the guidelines applicable to profit-orientated pricing. For example, the price of a nursery school place organized by a community association may be held low to encourage poor families to take advantage of the opportunity. Some non-profit organizations exist to provide free access to services, for example the National Health Service in the UK. In other situations, the price of a service provided by a non-profit organization may come from a membership or licence fee. For example, the Royal Society for the Protection of Birds (RSPB) charges an annual membership fee. In return members receive a quarterly magazine and free entry to RSPB bird watching sites. The BBC receives income from a licence fee which all televisions owners have to pay. The level of this fee is set by government, making relations with political figures an important marketing consideration.

Like most services, distribution systems for many non-profit organizations are short, with production and consumption simultaneous. This is the case for hospital operations, consultations with medical practitioners, education, nursery provision, cultural entertainment and many more services provided by non-profit organizations. Such organizations have to think carefully about how to deliver their services with the convenience that customers require. For example, although the Hallé Orchestra is based in Manchester, over half of its performances are in other towns or cities.

Many non-profit organizations are adept at using promotion to further their needs. The print media are popular with organizations seeking donations for worthy causes such as famine in Africa. Direct mail is also used to raise funds. Mailing lists of past donors are useful here, and some organizations use lifestyle geodemographic analyses to identify the type of person who is more likely to respond to a direct mailing. Non-profit organizations also need to be aware of publicity opportunities which may arise because of their activities. Many editors are sympathetic to such publicity attempts because of their general interest to the public. Sponsorship is also a vital income source for many non-profit organizations as Marketing in Action 20.4 explains.

Public relations has an important role to play to generate positive word-of-mouth communications and to establish the identity of the non-profit organization (e.g. a charity). Attractive fund-raising settings (e.g. sponsored lunches) can be organized to ensure that the exchange proves to be satisfactory to donors. A key objective of communications efforts should be to produce a positive assessment of the fund-raising transaction and to reduce the perceived risk of the donation so that donors

develop trust and confidence in the organization and become committed to the cause.[79]

Summary

Services are a large and growing sector in most European countries. While many of the marketing principles discussed in earlier chapters are applicable to services, their special characteristics and importance mean that they deserve separate consideration. These characteristics of intangibility, inseparability between production and consumption, variability and perishability have implications for the marketing of services. Of considerable note is the management of service quality. The barriers that divide the perception of

20.4   Marketing in Action

Sponsoring the Arts

Arts sponsorship is an activity which offers companies public relations and promotional opportunities, corporate hospitality possibilities and the chance to put something into the community (the 'warm glow' effect). Traditionally, arts sponsorship was easy: if the company chairperson or spouse liked Bach or Bacon, a cheque was written to pay for a concert or an art show. Today it is not so simple. The emphasis is on reciprocal benefits where the arts organization contributes to the welfare of the sponsor and the sponsor improves the efficiency or an often poorly-managed arts organization. For example, during Allied Domecq's sponsorship of the Royal Shakespeare Company, the RSC lighting engineers advised on creating the right atmosphere in the drinks company's pubs and voice coaches gave speech training to improve presentation skills. In the opposite direction sponsors are sending accountants, computer specialists and marketing gurus into arts companies as mentors.

In an age when companies are finding differentiation difficult, some companies are ploughing millions into arts sponsorship as a means of distinguishing themselves from the competition. An example is Orange, UK's largest arts sponsor, which has sponsored the Orange prize for women novelists, filming and film awards, and a Bristol-based project to create museums devoted to science and technology. The last project includes an Imaginarium, a sphere-shaped structure which traces developments in the digital communications revolution through the display of Orange products. The aim is to associate the brand name with technological innovation and to distinguish itself as a cut above its rivals in the intensely competitive mobile phone market.

Based on: Thorncroft (2000)[80] Thorncroft (2000)[81]

service quality from customer expectations need to be recognized and managed. These are the misconceptions, inadequate resources, inadequate delivery, and exaggerated promises barriers. Service marketers need to understand the criteria that customers use when forming expectations. Not only are outcomes valued, but also the experience of taking part in the consumption of the service is important.

Operations managers are responsible for managing services productivity. At times there can be a conflict between giving service quality and achieving high productivity. Service marketers need to recognize the importance of productivity and look for ways of improving productivity without compromising quality. The use of technology, encouraging customer involvement in production, and balancing supply and demand are some of the ways of achieving this.

Staff in service institutions require exceptional training to deal with customers face-to-face. Some companies are recognizing the need for empowerment whereby staff are given authority to deal with customers' problems even at considerable expense.

The positioning of services follows the same guidelines as for physical products but three extra dimensions to the marketing mix have been suggested to take account of their special characteristics. These are people, physical evidence, and process. Differentiation should be based on criteria that are highly valued by customers.

Two important areas of services marketing are retailing and marketing in non-profit organizations. Three theories of retail evolution—the wheel of retailing, the retail accordion and the retail life cycle—are discussed. Retail marketers need to pay special attention to retail positioning, store location, product assortment and services, price, and store atmosphere.

Marketing in non-profit organizations requires an appreciation of the characteristics that distinguish it from profit-orientated marketing. Many non-profit organizations are concerned with educating the public as well as satisfying immediate customer needs, they have to deal with multiple publics, have difficulty in measuring success and have conflicting objectives, and are subject to close public scrutiny. Their objectives may mean that rules that apply in the profit sector may not be relevant to their situation. For example, whereas profit-orientated companies may set a high price to maximize profit, non-profit organizations may set a low price to raise accessibility to the service.

Internet exercise

The service process

Sites to visit
http://www.easyjet.com

Exercise
How has easyJet revolutionized air travel?

Study questions

1 The marketing of services is no different to the marketing of physical goods. Discuss.

2 What are the barriers that can separate expected from perceived service? What must service providers do to eliminate these barriers?

3 Discuss the role of service staff in the creation of a quality service. Can you give examples from your own experiences of good and bad service encounters.

4 Use Fig. 20.7 to evaluate the service quality provided on your university course. First, identify all criteria that might be used to evaluate your course. Second, score each criterion from one to ten, based upon its value to you. Third, score each criterion from one to ten based on your perception of how well it is provided. Finally, analyse the results and make recommendations.

5 Of what practical value are the theories of retail evolution?

6 Identify and evaluate how supermarkets can differentiate themselves from competitors. Choose three supermarkets and evaluate their success at differentiation.

7 Discuss the problems of providing high-quality service in retailing in central and eastern Europe.

8 How does marketing in non-profit organizations differ from that in profit-orientated companies? Choose a non-profit organization and discuss the extent to which marketing principles can be applied.

9 Discuss the benefits to organizations and customers of developing and maintaining strong customer relationships.

References

1. Gross, A. C., P. M. Banting, L. N. Meredith and I. D. Ford (1993) *Business Marketing*, Boston, Mass: Houghton Mifflin, 378.

2. Cowell, D. (1984) *The Marketing of Services*, London: Heinemann, 35.

3. Berry, L. L. (1980) Services Marketing is Different, *Business Horizons*, May–June, 24–9.

4. Edgett, S. and S. Parkinson (1993) Marketing for Services Industries: A Review, *Service Industries Journal*, **13** (3), 19–39.

5. Berry (1980) op. cit.

6. Aijo, T. S. (1996) The Theoretical and Philosophical Underpinnings of Relationship Marketing, *European Journal of Marketing*, **30** (2), 8–18 and Gronoos, C. (1990) *Services Management and Marketing: Managing the Moments of Truth in Service Competition*, Lexington, MA: Lexington Books.

7. Baron, S., K. Harris and B. J. Davies (1996) Oral Participation in Retail Service Delivery: A Comparison of the Roles of Contact Personnel and Customers, *European Journal of Marketing*, **30** (9), 75–90.

8. Grönroos, C. (1994) From Marketing Mix to Relationship Marketing: Towards a Paradigm Shift in Marketing, *Management Decision*, **32** (2), 4–20.

9. Egan, C. (1997) Relationship Management, in Jobber, D. (ed) *The CIM Handbook of Selling and Sales Strategy*, Oxford: Butterworth-Heinemann, 55–88.

10. Berry, L. L. (1995) Relationship Marketing, in Payne, A., M. Christopher, M. Clark and H. Peck (eds) *Relationship Marketing for Competitive Advantage*, Oxford: Butterworth-Heinemann, 65–74.

11. Zeithaml, V. A. and M. J. Bitner (1996) *Services Marketing*, New York: McGraw-Hill, 174–8.

12. Reichheld, F. F. and W. E. Sasser, Jr (1990) Zero Defections: Quality Comes to Services, *Harvard Business Review*, September–October, 105–11.

13. Reichheld and Sasser, Jr (1990) op. cit.

14. Berry, L. L. (1995) Relationship Marketing of Services—Growing Interest, Emerging Perspectives, *Journal of the Academy of Marketing Science*, **23** (4), 236–45.

15. Bitner, M. J. (1995) Building Service Relationships: It's All About Promises, *Journal of the Academy of Marketing Science*, **23** (4), 246–51.

16. Bitner (1996) op. cit.

17. Parasuraman, A., L. L. Berry and V. A. Zeithaml (1991) Understanding Customer Expectations of Service, *Sloan Management Review*, Spring, 39–48.

18. Berry (1995) op. cit.

19. Berry, L. L. and A. Parasuraman (1991) *Marketing Services*, New York: Free Press, 136–42.

20. Berry (1995) op. cit.

21. Gummesson, E. (1987) The New Marketing—Developing Long-Term Interactive Relationships, *Long Range Planning*, **20**, 10–20.

22. Bitner (1995) op. cit.

23. See Bitner, M. J., B. H. Booms and M. S. Tetreault (1990) The Service Encounter: Diagnosing Favourable and Unfavourable Incidents, *Journal of Marketing*, **43**, January, 71–84 and Bitner, M. J., B. H. Booms and L. A. Mohr (1994) Critical Service Encounters: The Employee's View, *Journal of Marketing*, **58**, October, 95–106.

24. C. H. Lovelock, S. Vandermerwe and B. Lewis (1999) *Services Marketing—A European Perspective*, New York: Prentice-Hall, 176.

25. Berry (1995) op. cit.

26. Kasper, H., P. van Helsdingen and W. de Vries, Jr (1999) *Services Marketing Management*, Chichester: Wiley, 528.

27. Johnson, R. (1995) Service Failure and Recovery: Impact, Attributes and Process, in Swartz, T. A., D. E. Bowen and S. W. Brown (eds) *Advances in Services Marketing and Management*, 4, 52–65.

28. Buzzell, R. D. and B. T. Gale (1987) *The PIMS Principles: Linking Strategy to Performance*, New York: Free Press, 103–34.

29. Parasuraman, A., V. A. Zeithaml and L. L. Berry (1985) A Conceptual Model of Service Quality and its Implications for Future Research, *Journal of Marketing*, fall, 41–50.

30. Parasuraman, Zeithaml and Berry (1985) op. cit.

31. Danaher, P. J. and J. Mattson (1994) Customer Satisfaction during the Service Delivery Process, *European Journal of Marketing*, **28** (5), 5–16.

32. De Ruyter, K., M. Wetzels, J. Lemmink and J. Mattsson (1997) The Dynamics of the Service Delivery Process: A Value-Based Approach, *International Journal of Research in Marketing*, 14, 231–43.

33. Zeithaml, V. A., A. Parasuraman and L. L. Berry (1988) SERVQUAL: A Multiple Itemscale for Measuring Consumer Perceptions of Service Quality, *Journal of Retailing*, **64** (1), 13–37.

34. Thorpe, A. (2000) On . . . Handling Complaints, *The Guardian*, 10 April, 3.

35. Lovelock, C. (1992) Seeking Synergy in Service Operations: Seven Things Marketers Need to Know about Service Operations, *European Management Journal*, **10** (1), 22–9.

36. Mudie, P. and A. Cottam (1993) *The Management and Marketing of Services*, Oxford: Butterworth-Heinemann, 211.

37. Schlesinger, L. A. and J. L. Heskett (1991) The Service-Driven Service Company, *Harvard Business Review*, Sept.–Oct., 71–81.

38. Bowen, D. E. and L. L. Lawler (1992) Empowerment: Why, What, How and When, *Sloan Management Review*, Spring, 31–9.

39. Christopher, M. and R. Yallop (1990) Audit your Customer Service Quality, *Focus*, June–July, 1–6.

40. Booms, B. H. and M. J. Bitner (1981) Marketing Strategies and Organisation Structures for Service Firms, in Donnelly, J. H. and W. R. George (eds) *Marketing of Services*, Chicago: American Marketing Association, 47–51.

41. Berry, L. L., E. E. Lefkowith and T. Clark (1980) In Services: What's in a Name?, *Harvard Business Review*, Sept.–Oct., 28–30.

42. Bloemer, J. and K. de Ruyter (1998) On the Relationship Between Store Image, Store Satisfaction and Store

Loyalty, *European Journal of Marketing*, **32** (5/6), 499-513.

43. Cowell (1984) op. cit.

44. Sellers, P. (1988) How to Handle Customers Gripes, *Fortune*, **118** (October), 100.

45. Diacon, S. R. and C. T. Ennew (1996) Ethical Issues in Insurance Marketing in the UK, *European Journal of Marketing*, **30** (5), 67-80.

46. Morris, M. H. and D. Fuller (1989) Pricing an Industrial Service, *Industrial Marketing Management*, **18**, 139-46.

47. Rafiq, M. and P. K. Ahmed (1992) The Marketing Mix Reconsidered, *Proceedings of the Annual Conference of the Marketing Education Group*, Salford, 439-51.

48. Lemmink, J. and J. Mattsson (1998) Warmth During Non-Productive Retail Encounters: The Hidden Side of Productivity, *International Journal of Research in Marketing*, **15**, 505-17.

49. Pruyn, A. and A. Smidts (1998) Effects of Waiting on the Satisfaction with the Service: Beyond Objective Times Measures, *International Journal of Research in Marketing*, **15**, 321-34.

50. Berry, L. L. (1987) Big Ideas in Services Marketing, *Journal of Services Marketing*, fall, 5-9.

51. Thelen, E. M. and A. G. Woodside (1997) What Evokes the Brand or Store? Consumer Research on Accessibility Theory Applied to Modelling Primary Choice, *International Journal of Research in Marketing*, **14**, 125-45.

52. Krishnan, T. V. and H. Soni (1997) Guaranteed Profit Margins: A Demonstration of Retailer Power, *International Journal of Research in Marketing*, **14**, 35-56.

53. Ohbora, T., A. Parsons and H. Riesenbeck (1992) Alternative Routes to Global Marketing, *McKinsey Quarterly*, **3**, 52-74.

54. Dewsnap, B. (1997) Trade Marketing, in D. Jobber (ed.) *The CIM Handbook of Selling and Sales Strategy*, Oxford: Butterworth-Heinemann, 104-25.

55. Nicholas, R. (1999) Thirsty Work, *Marketing Week*, 11 November, 79-83.

56. Davies, G. and N. Sanghavi (1993) Is the Category Killer a Significant Innovation? *ESRC Seminar: Strategic Issues in Retailing*, Manchester Business School, 1-23.

57. Brown, S. (1990) Innovation and Evolution in UK Retailing: The Retail Warehouse, *European Journal of Marketing*, **24** (9), 39-54.

58. Sellers, P. (1999) Inside the First E-Christmas, *Fortune Magazine*, 1 February, 52-5.

59. Davies, G. and N. Sanghavi (1993) Is the Category Killer a Significant Innovation? *ESRC Seminar: Strategic Issues in Retailing*, Manchester Business School, October-November, 1-23.

60. Hollander, S. C. (1966) Notes on the Retail Accordion, *Journal of Retailing*, **42** (2), 24.

61. Davidson, W. R., A. D. Bates and S. J. Bass (1976) The Retail Life Cycle, *Harvard Business Review*, **54** (Nov.-Dec.), 89-96.

62. Knee, D. and D. Walters (1985) *Strategy in Retailing: Theory and Application*, Oxford: Philip Adam.

63. Davies, G. (1992) Innovation in Retailing, *Creativity and Innovation Management*, **1** (4), 230.

64. Miller, R. (1996) IT and Miss, *Marketing*, 14 November, 32-4.

65. Ody, P. (1996) Successful Retailers Compete on Value Not Merely on Price, *Financial Times*, Focus on IT in Retailing, 2 October, 2.

66. Ody, P. (1996) Retailers Jump on the Loyalty Bandwagon, *Financial Times*, Focus on IT in Retailing, 2 October, 7.

67. Ody, P. (1997) Reaching Out to the Individual, *Financial Times*, Special Report on IT, 3 September, 4/.

68. Gray, R. (2000) E-tail Must Deliver on Web Promises, *Marketing*, 2 March, 37-8.

69. Voyle, S. (2000) Food E-tailers Struggle to Get the Recipe Right, *Financial Times*, 15 February, 17.

70. Bloemer, S., K. de Ruyter and M. Wetzels (1999) Linking Perceived Service Quality and Service Loyalty: A Multi-Dimensional Perspective, *European Journal of Marketing*, **33** (11/12), 1082-106.

71. Elg, U. and U. Johansson (1996) Networking When National Boundaries Dissolve: The Swedish Food Sector, *European Journal of Marketing*, **30** (2), 61-74.

72. Betts, E. J. and P. J. McGoldrick (1996) Consumer Behaviour with the Retail 'Sales', *European Journal of Marketing*, **30** (8), 40-58.

73. Hemsley, S. (2000) Sound Advice, *Marketing Week*, 15 June, 43-4.

74. See Lock, A. and P. Harris (1996) Political Marketing—Vive La Difference, *European Journal of Marketing*, **30** (10/11), 21-31 and Butler, P. and N. Collins (1996) Strategic Analysis in Political Markets, *European Journal of Marketing*, **30** (10/11), 32-44.

75. Bennett, P. D. (1988) *Marketing*, New York: McGraw-Hill, 690-2.

76. Shapiro, B. (1992) Marketing for Non-Profit Organisations, *Harvard Business Review*, Sept.-Oct., 123-32.

77. Balabanis, G., R. E. Stables and H. C. Phillips (1997) Market Orientation in the Top 200 British Charity Organisations and its Impact on their Performance, *European Journal of Marketing*, **31** (8), 583-603.

78. For an in-depth examination of political marketing see Butler, P. and N. Collins (1994) Political Marketing: Structure and Process, *European Journal of Marketing*, **28** (1) 19-34.

79. Hibbert, S. A. (1995) The Market Positioning of British Medical Charities, *European Journal of Marketing*, **29** (10), 6-26.

80. Thorncroft, A. (2000) Commerce and the Arts Swap Skills for their Mutual Benefit, *Financial Times*, Business and the Arts Survey, 17 February, 1.

81. Thorncroft, A. (2000) Business Treads a Thinning Line, *Financial Times*, 6 March, 20.

Key terms

intangibility   a characteristic of services, namely that they cannot be touched, seen, tasted or smelled

service   any deed, performance or effort carried out for the customer

inseparability   a characteristic of services, namely that their production cannot be separated from their consumption

variability   a characteristic of services, namely that being delivered by people the standard of their performance is open to variation

perishability   a characteristic of services, namely that the capacity of a service business, such as a hotel room, cannot be stored – if it is not occupied, that is lost income which cannot be recovered

relationship marketing   the process of creating, maintaining and enhancing strong relationships with customers and other stakeholders

misconception barrier   a failure by marketers to understand what customers really value about their service

inadequate resources barrier   a barrier to the matching of expected and perceived service levels caused by the unwillingness of service providers to provide the necessary resources

inadequate delivery barrier   a barrier to the matching of expected and perceived service levels caused by the failure of the service provider to select, train and reward staff adequately, resulting in poor or inconsistent delivery of service

exaggerated promises barrier   a barrier to the matching of expected and perceived service levels caused by the unwarranted building up of expectations by exaggerated promises

positioning   the choice of target market (where the company wishes to compete) and differential advantage (how the company wishes to compete)

market segmentation   the process of identifying individuals or organizations with similar characteristics that have significant implications for the determination of marketing strategy

target marketing   the selection of a segment as a focus for the company's offering and communications

halo customers   customers who are not directly targeted but may find the product attractive

differential advantage   a clear performance differential over competition on factors that are important to target customers

services marketing mix   product, place, price, promotion, people, process and physical evidence

wheel of retailing   a theory of retailing development which suggests that new forms of retailing begin as low-cost, cut-price and narrow margin operations and then trade up until they mature as high price operators, vulnerable to a new influx of low-cost operators

retail accordion   a theory of retail evolution which focuses on the cycle of retailers widening and then contracting product ranges

retail life cycle   a theory of retailing evolution which is based on the product life cycle stating that new types of retailing pass through birth, growth, maturity and decline

retail positioning   the choice of target market and differential advantage for a retail outlet

Case 37 First Direct 2000: The Development of Virtual Banking

In the 1980s, domestic retail banking was mature, static and dominated by price. Kevin Newman, chief executive officer of First Direct bank from 1991 to 1996, describes it as follows:

> The domestic retail bank of the time was like a desert. It needed some rain to bring it back to life. Banking was believed to be a mature sector in which differentiation was only possible on the basis of price. This was not a sustainable means of achieving competitive advantage. Price changes were mirrored by competitors and led to price wars. Eventually all of the banks ended up back at equilibrium, but financially worse-off. The main threat was posed by firms 'new to banking'. Inertia was huge. There was a perception that all banks were the same.

New ways of adding value to customers had to be found if retail banks were to achieve competitive advantage. HSBC, parent company of First Direct, recognized that there was latent dissatisfaction with the traditional branch banking system. Customers, accustomed to the convenience of longer opening hours in the retail sector, were increasingly unhappy at the short opening hours of traditional branches. They were also unhappy at other negative features of the traditional banking system, such as queues and bank charges:

> The remarkable success of the telephone banking system, pioneered by Midland's First Direct, is testimony as much to the unpopularity of conventional branch banks as to the convenience of a 24-hour telephone service.[1]

First Direct arrived at an innovative solution to the weaknesses of the traditional system. By centralizing banking operations and offering direct access by telephone, it was able to significantly reduce overheads. Without an expensive network of branches to run, resources could be devoted to providing a high level of customer service. First Direct offered unrivalled flexibility and convenience through a range of new service features such as 24-hour access, free banking and direct service via telephone. These services were targeted primarily at customers in the ABC1 socio-demographic segments, between the ages of 25 and 45. Peter Simpson, commercial director of First Direct, believes that the most important success factor has been the firm's aims and philosophy. He describes the core concept of the firm as:

> developing intelligent relationships with customers on a one-to-one basis. Use of direct delivery by telephone is simply the means by which this is achieved.

Marketing First Direct

Building customer relationships

Choosing the means of building relationships remotely was one of the first challenges for First Direct. Mike Harris, chief executive officer at the launch of First Direct, explained that market research showed that 85 per cent of people prefer to talk to a person rather than to a computer and, consequently, First Direct opted for telephone.[2] In the late 1980s, the significance of this choice is confirmed by the fate of some of those who opted for higher technology solutions:

> Many of the banks which rushed to offer computer-based services in the late 1980s are giving up on the high-tech approach and going for real people instead.[3]

Potential customers, however, had to be persuaded that 'virtual' banking could work. First Direct's choice of promotional strategy was particularly significant given that without a high street presence the bank was less visible to customers than traditional banks: 'This means that marketing is our only form of visual communication with our customers', said Ms Jan Smith,

---

[1] O'Connor, G., Quarterly Review of Personal Finance, *Financial Times*, 29 April 1994.

[2] Bradshaw, D., Technology: Dial M for Money. Why Improvements in Telephone Banking Should Increase Convenience, *Financial Times*, 15 January 1994.

[3] Hutton, B., 'Finance and the Family: Ringing in the Revolution – A look at the way technology is affecting Financial Services, *Financial Times*, 15 January 1994.

First Direct's marketing director. 'Getting it right from the start was vital'.[4]

In its launch phase, First Direct emphasized the innovative nature of its services with revolutionary launch adverts, designed by advertising agency Howell, Henry, Chaldecott, Lury. These were first shown on television on 1 October 1989. The first advert took the form of a message from 2010 to the current day (see Fig. C37.1). This was followed up by an interactive advert which addressed two possible emotional responses of customers to the First Direct idea. The optimistic and pessimistic views of First Direct were shown simultaneously on different channels. The optimistic highlights the positive features which the service offers, while the pessimistic addresses concerns which potential customers might have (see Fig. C37.2).

Another challenge for First Direct was the fact that its target market was comprised of infrequent television viewers, so a mix of promotional tools had to be developed to reach potential customers. First Direct also communicated its service using direct press advertisements, which featured 'tip-ons', an origami-style envelope stuck to a page showing First Direct's phone number and a business reply card. Every respondent received an explanatory brochure, a 'help-card' giving details of how to open an account and an interest rate card for various types of account. First Direct's distinctive black and white corporate identity (see Fig. C37.3) was used to attract attention and increase readership of the mailshot.

Developing a portfolio of services

Kevin Newman saw the initial services offered by First Direct as falling into categories based on its level of complexity and frequency:

✦ Simple, routine operations would increasingly be automated and handled via automatic telling machines (ATMs).

✦ More complex issues, which would previously have required going to the branch, or even speaking with the bank manager, must be handled with greater sensitivity. The challenge for First Direct was to replicate the trusting relationship that a

Breaks into Audi advert as an announcement from the year 2010:

'Please don't be alarmed. This is a first attempt to communicate across time. This experiment is being sponsored by First Direct to celebrate our 21st anniversary. For us it is the year 2010. To celebrate the 21st anniversary of First Direct we have returned to the year of our launch. We return you now to your own programmes with every best wish for your personal happiness in your own future.

Figure C37.1 First Direct Launch Advertising—An Announcement from the Future: shown 1 October 1989

customer would have had with a bank manager. The more complex financial products, such as mortgages and insurance, with which First Direct would expand its service would require this type of relationship (see Table C37.1).

To support its development of a portfolio of services, First Direct built an in-depth database of its customers. This included demographic facts and details of banking preferences. First Direct Operators could rapidly call up details of previous transactions to provide a consistent and personalized banking service. This database also provided sufficient information for First Direct to decide a customer's propensity to buy additional services. This allows it to use targeted direct mail campaigns to increase the number of services which existing customers use.

Building sustainable advantage

The success of First Direct in virtual banking exceeded all expectations. By late 1996, First Direct had developed well beyond the niche position which it expected to occupy. It had grown to 600 000 and despite ploughing income into further growth, its financial contribution in the year ending 1995 made a significant contribution to the 10 per cent increase in the profits of HSBC.

The pioneering First Direct virtual banking

---

[4] O'Kelly, L., Survey of International Direct Marketing: Banking on Phones—Case Study: First Direct, *Financial Times*, 18 April 1990.

Charlotte Rampling then presents factual information about First Direct's new telephone banking services using an interactive format.

'First Direct is a new banking organisation that does things differently. For example, no branches. What is your reaction?'

'For an optimistic view, stay on this channel, for a pessimistic view, turn to Channel 4 now.'

Optimistic scenario

[Shot as a song and dance act with singer in London street dressed in white.]

'I'm going to have a place for my money, I can call both night and day.
I am going to speak to intelligent people there, who will do anything I say.
They will give me instant decisions. I get an overdraft automatically.
First Direct will be wonderful for you and me.
They don't have any branches. They can spend more on service for me.
First Direct will be wonderful for you and me.'

Charlotte Rampling:
'Because First Direct don't have any branches they can spend more on service and it's free.'

Call 0800 22 2000 for a current account information pack.
First Direct is a division of Midland Bank plc.

Pessimistic scenario

[Shot as a Blues song in London street, with singer dressed in black.]

'You heard about First Direct, mm? Won't work for sure.
They say they're a new kind of banking, huh? No branches no more.
But we have had branches for years, what are they changing it for?
They say you can call their people, 24 hours a day.
They're far too new and different. They'll close down right away (like tomorrow, honey).
They're not an old institution, that's where my money stays.'
[shot of red herrings]

Charlotte Rampling:
'Phone your bank now . . . if nobody answers, ring First Direct instead.'

Call 0800 22 2000 for a current account information pack.
First Direct is a division of Midland Bank plc.

Figure C37.2 Optimistic and pessimistic scenarios

service rapidly became a benchmark for new entrants into the market:

> In setting up the service, executives were careful to learn the lessons of First Direct and similar operations. Rather than providing a huge number of little-used services at high cost, they focused on some 30 operations that were judged the most popular.[5]

This success, however, spawned a variety of imitators, such that a *Which?* survey of home banking in 1996[6] showed most of the virtual banks as offering a similar range of services.

Additionally, retail banking in the late 1990s saw a broad range of new entrants. Players now offering banking services included retailers, such as Sainsbury, Tesco and Marks and Spencer, and others, such as Virgin Direct, expanding their financial services offering to include retail banking provision.

The most significant change to virtual banking came, however, from the growth in Internet banking. As Internet penetration had increased, and consumers had become more comfortable with the technology, a number of standalone Internet banks had entered the market. One of the most visible of these was Egg, the Prudential's Internet banking operation launched in 1998. In response to its offer of an 8 per cent interest rate on its savings the Egg service took £100 million of savings in its first month, despite delays in opening accounts caused by the unprecedented response. Deloitte and Touche consulting group predict more new entrants so that:

> ten years from now [there will be] a massive increase in the number of banking transactions handled from home or office via the Internet[7] and will continue to

Ten years after its launch, First Direct has over a million customers. More are joining at the rate of around 10 000 per month. So rapidly has it expanded that it now has 4000 staff manning telephones in three call centres, two based in Leeds and one in Hamilton, Scotland. It continues to reap rewards for its levels of customer service.

5 See footnote 7.
6 *Which?*, Survey of Home Banking Systems, May 1996, 53. Published by the Consumer Association, 2 Marylebone Road, London NW1 4DF.
7 Anon., First Direct Faces up to Rivals, *Marketing*, 19 November 1998, 19.

Figure C37.3 First Direct corporate identity

Table C37.1 First Direct service portfolio

Type of transaction	Routine transaction	Complex transactions	Complex products
Task	Balances Cash management Simple products Paying in	Queries Bank loans Extend overdrafts	Insurance Mortgages Investment Major complaints
Equivalent in traditional banking system	Automated	Essentially automated but may wish to 'go into branch' or deal with same person	Bank managers

A recent *Guardian* survey of banking rated First Direct as best in customer service overall, best current account provider and best savings account provider.[8] The explanation for its success remains, as *The Guardian* puts it 'refreshingly simple'.[9] Says First Direct Chief Executive Alan Hughes:

> It is our people. Our customers don't want to buy financial services. They want to feel good. They want reassurance that they are in control, that they are known as an individual . . . our people are the difference. In the way we recruit and manage our people we encourage them to treat the customers as their friends and to let their personalities shine through.

First Direct remains the dominant player, but new entrants, such as Virgin Direct and Tesco are growing rapidly. Accordingly the bank has recently announced a number of initiatives to develop a new identity. First, there are new technological advances in service delivery channels. Banking via PC and mobile phone have already been introduced. Internet banking—launching in July 2000—and interactive digital TV will further increase the range of interfaces with customers.

Second, there is an extension of the portfolio of services offered. Using its Octopus personalized research service launched in October 1998, First Direct aims to offer 'life management' services covering major life decisions such as financial services, health care and social activities, like holidays.

Despite its ongoing success, First Direct operates in an increasingly competitive marketplace and must continue to look for ways to sustain its competitive advantage. That First Direct

[8] *The Guardian*, Victory for the Talking Bank on Three Fronts, 18 March 2000, 39.
[9] *The Guardian*, Victory for the Talking Bank on Three Fronts, 18 March 2000, 39.

is committed to do so was clearly signalled on its tenth anniversary when the firm introduced the new brand positioning. Using a 'What next . . .' strapline, First Direct positions itself as the bank that liberates people from the drudgery of financial services.[10]

This case was prepared by Susan Bridgewater, University of Warwick.

Questions

1   What were the differences between the First Direct service and traditional branch banking?

2   What were the marketing mix consequences of developing this type of virtual bank?

3   Evaluate the challenges facing First Direct in sustaining its competitive advantage in the new marketplace.

[10] *Marketing*, First Direct Repositioning with New Image to Mark Decade, 9 September 2000, 3.

Case 38 Club La Santa Lanzarote: A Sporting Experience

Club La Santa is located on the northern coast of Lanzarote in the Canary Islands. The complex was constructed in 1972 by a major bank, La Caja Insular de Ahorros de Canarias. The original intention was to create a self-contained village with accommodation for 6000 people. The initiative was tangential to the bank's core business and this lack of focus probably contributed to economic problems and eventual closure.

In 1978 the attention of Danish tour operator, Tjaaereborg, was drawn to Lanzarote as a potential tourist destination. At that time there was little commercial development of the region, and its beneficial geographic location and climate had not been exploited. The owner of Tjaaereborg, Pastor Eilif Krogager, and a senior executive, Willy Bechman, decided to acquire the complex and develop it as a sport and holiday resort. By 1983, La Santa Sport, now renamed Club La Santa, was accepting guests, although renovations to apartments were ongoing and many of the sports facilities were under construction. The original intention was to operate the whole complex

on the (then) recently introduced timeshare concept, although this was not particularly successful. While the timeshare facility is still available, only approximately 10 per cent of guests are part of the scheme.

Visitors to the complex are diverse in nature and may travel as singles, couples, families or as part of an organized group such as a school, university or swimming club. During off-peak periods Club La Santa arranges a number of special event weeks that focus on, for example,

cycling, running, aerobics, golf and triathlon (Table C38.1). Activities are conducted under the guidance of internationally famous athletes, which brings credibility to the programmes.

The sporting achievements and requirements of visitors may vary considerably. At one extreme are the Olympic and world-class performers who utilize the warm climate and excellent facilities to enhance their training (Table C38.2). Many national teams also use Club La Santa as a training base, as do a broad range of professional and amateur sports clubs. At the other extreme are recreational visitors who seek a relaxing holiday with a variety of sporting options and who have no pretence to perform at a high level.

While visitors to Club La Santa are drawn from all over the world, the clientele is predominantly West European with particularly strong represen-

tation from Denmark (32 per cent), the UK (31 per cent) and Germany (18 per cent)—1999 figures. English is the official language used at Club La Santa, which means that instruction and excursions are conducted in English. However, many of the staff, and the Green Team in particular, are conversant in several languages.

Accommodation

The living accommodation is described as the hotel and comprises approximately 350 apartments configured around a number of towers. Several different layouts are available to cater for between 4 and 10 people. Apartments are also colour coded (yellow, green, red) based on their location. For example, red apartments have views

---

Table C38.1   Examples of event weeks and special events

Date (2001)	Event
5–12 January	Club La Santa Aerobics Week
19–26 January	Walking Week with Lisbeth Matthiesen
27 January	Club La Santa International Duathlon
15 February–1 March	Club La Santa International Bike Week with Tony Doyle
1–15 March	Robin Brew Triathlon Training Camp
2–9 March	Club La Santa International Bike Week with Bjarne Riis
8–15 March	Club La Santa and London Flora Marathon Training Camp

---

Table C38.2   Examples of sports stars who have trained at Club La Santa

Sport	Athlete	Achievements*
Athletics	Linford Christie	Olympic gold metal 100 m
		World champion 100 m
Boxing	Frank Bruno	WBC world heavyweight champion
Cycling	Eddy Merckx	Five times Tour de France winner
	Jan Ullrich	Tour de France winner
Triathlon	Simon Lessing	Five times world champion
	Luc Van Lierde	World ironman champion
	Spencer Smith	Two times world junior champion
		World senior champion
Swimming	Mette Jacobsen	World champion 200 m backstroke
Mountain biking	Henrik Djemis	Three times world champion
Track and field	Lily Anggreny	Gold medal 500 m paralympics
Modern pentathlon	Eva Fjellerup	Four times world champion

*Note: not all achievements listed.

that are more attractive and receive more sun on the balcony area, although these benefits are reflected in a higher price (Table C38.3).

All apartments are fully equipped to allow self-catering. The apartments are cleaned once a week, starting normally on the fourth or fifth day after arrival, and towels are replaced on a daily basis. Daily cleaning can be arranged at an extra charge as can laundry and ironing services.

Sports facilities

Club La Santa prides itself on offering clients 35 sports that, with the exception of scuba diving tours are free at the point of delivery. Sports activities are administered by the Green Team, an enthusiastic group of approximately 30 staff who have experience and expertise in a variety of sport and leisure pursuits. Clients may participate at an individual or group level, or alternatively, join in any of the daily programme of activities organized by the Green Team (Table C38.4).

Instruction in squash, badminton, tennis, beach volleyball, swimming and windsurfing is available for both adults and children. Fitness and weight training programmes for the over 14-year-olds are also available at the Fitness Centre. Sports instruction, which is free of charge, is conducted in small groups and operates on three levels— green (beginners), blue (intermediate) and red (advanced). Professional one-to-one coaching can

also be arranged on a few basis as can massage and physiotherapy services.

Children are not overlooked at Club La Santa and they have a number of activities included in the daily programme. Indeed, many children have been introduced to new sports through the support and guidance of the Green Team members. A range of equipment is available in sizes that are suitable for younger visitors and allows them to participate, either individually or as part of family groups.

Sports facilities (e.g. tennis courts) and equipment (e.g. cycles, windsurfers) are available subject to a booking system. Clients receive a token on arrival at the complex that can be exchanged for specific items. Bookings may be made one day in advance or two days in advance for timeshare owners. To prevent misuse of the system, in the event that a facility or item of equipment is not claimed within 10 minutes of the allotted time it becomes available for general use again.

Social facilities

Shops In addition to a supermarket, there is a range of shops on site including a fashion shop, Fun Sun, a paper kiosk offering newspapers, sweets, souvenirs, etc., a video rental service and the Club La Santa sports shop, selling a variety of leading brands of sports clothing, shoes and

Table C38.3   Examples of differential pricing based on date, location and size of apartment

Prices per apartment per week

Date	AY	AG	AR	BY	CY	Sports
4 May 2000	374	419	536	563	658	986
25 May 2000	311	356	473	468	563	937
6 July 2000	468	514	635	752	820	1171
17 August 2000	572	617	739	847	914	1266
21 September 2000	473	419	536	563	658	986
19 October 2000	468	514	635	752	820	1171
9 November 2000	351	398	538	529	636	1062
28 December 2000	678	730	842	1025	1081	1455

Apartment price codes

AY	:	One bedroom	yellow	(4 max)*
AG	:	One bedroom	green	(4 max)*
AR	:	One bedroom	red	(4 max)*
BY	:	Two bedroom	yellow	(6 max)*
CY	:	Double	yellow	(6 max)*
SPORTS	:	Sports	yellow	(10 max)

*One must be under 15 years old
Based on UK brochure prices

Table C38.4   Examples of the daily programme of activities

Time	Activities/tours	Meeting point
Daily		
08.00	Morning gymnastics	Leisure Pool
08.15	Morning run (2 km, 3 km, 4 km, 5 km)	Stadium
08.15	Morning walk (3 km)	Stadium
08.45–1300***	Diving safari beg./adv.	Dive Centre
09.30***	Scuba diving instruction	Dive Centre
13.30–17.30***	Diving safari beg./adv.	Dive Centre
14.00**	Scuba diving instruction	Dive Centre
17.30	Evening gymnastics	5-a-side
Tuesday		
07.45*	Half marathon	Stadium
09.00*	Badminton tournament, children	Badminton Hall
09.15**	Golf tour to Costa Teguise, adv.	Bike Centre
09.30–14.30**	Excursion: surf safari	Reception
10.00	Bolas tournament	Beach
10.00*	Introduction to self-defence	Boxing Ring
10.00	Step, beg.	5-a-side
10.00–14.00*	Children's Tropical Park	Reception
11.00	Compact gold competition	Minigolf
11.00*	Badminton tournament, blue	Badminton Hall
11.00	Body toning	5-a-side
11.30	Social beach volleyball tournament	Beach
11.30*	Introduction to self-defence	Boxing Ring
15.00*	Badminton tournament, red/green	Badminton Hall
15.00–17.30**	Mountain bike tour 30 km, adv.	Bike Centre
16.00–21.30**	Excursion: El Golfo/Fire Mountain	Reception
17.00	Information tour/German	Sports booking
17.30–19.00	Back school	Physio
17.30*	Body bike, beg.	Fitness
18.00	Evening workout—aerobic, interm.	5-a-side
18.30*	Body bike, intermediate	Fitness
	Entertainment:	
20.30	Movie: Runaway Bride	Cinema
21.30	Green Team Band	Square
Wednesday		
07.45*	Mini Triathlon (400 m swim, 15.2 km bike, 4.8 km run)	Bike Centre
08.15–17.30**	Excursion: MTB tour on the island La Graciosa, all levels	Bike Centre
09.00–13.00***	Snorkel tour	Dive Centre
09.00*	Squash tournament, children/junior	Squash CT 1
09.00	Step, adv.	5-a-side
09.30–16.30**	Excursion: catamaran tour	Reception
10.00	5-a-side football, adults	5-a-side
10.00	Information tour/German	Sports booking
10.00	Aerobic power	Lawn
10.30*	Body bike, beg.	Fitness
11.00	Stretching	Lawn
11.00*	Squash tournament, blue	Squash CT 1
11.30*	Body bike, adv.	Fitness
11.30–13.00*	Introduction to massage	Physio Clinic
12.00	5-a-side football, 5–11 years	5-a-side
12.30	5-a-side football, 12–16 years	5-a-side

Table C38.4 (*cont.*)

Time	Activities/tours	Meeting point
13.15	5-a-side football, Green Team v. Guests	5-a-side
15.00	Windsurf race, beg. and children	Surf Station
15.00	Rehearsal for Children and Guest Show	Square
16.00	Windsurf race, adv.	Surf Station
16.00*	Squash tournament, red/green	Squash CT 1
17.00	Windsurf—fun race for everyone	Surf Station
18.00	Evening workout—step, beg.	5-a-side
18.30	Presentation of diplomas	Square
	Entertainment:	
20.30	Movie: ED TV	Cinema
21.30	Children and Guest Show	Square

*	Book in the Sports booking	beg. =	beginners
**	Book and pay in the Guide Office	int. =	intermediate
***	Please contact the Dive Centre	adv. =	advanced

equipment. A hairdressing salon is located in the square.

Restaurants   Clients have a choice of cuisine at affordable prices.

Atlántico—a self-service restaurant with a breakfast and dinner buffet—open 07.30 to 10.30 and 18.30 to 21.30.

La Bodega—a broad menu catering for all the family—open 19.00–22.00.

La Casa—an à la carte restaurant with a large variety of international dishes including vegetarian and Canarian food—open 19.30 to 22.00

Bars   Three bars are available to visitors in addition to a disco for late night revellers. This operates between 23.00 and 03.00.

Pool Bar—close by the leisure pool and open from 10.00 to 22.00. It also serves a variety of snacks and full meals throughout the day.

Green Bar—open each night between 18.00 and 01.00. It also includes pool tables and television facilities.

Sports Café—in addition to being a bar which opens daily, the Sports Café is a hall of fame containing photo plaques of all the sports champions who have visited the complex. Sports action is broadcast on several television monitors.

Cinema   A film is shown every day between Saturday and Thursday, beginning at 21.00. These are in English, although on occasions Danish subtitles are available.

Entertainment   A programme of live music, games and shows is offered each evening in the square, beginning at around 21.00.

Excursions   Clients can gain an appreciation of Lanzarote through a variety of excursions such as Tequise market, Fire Mountains, cave exploration, mountain bike tour, surf safari, Jeep safari, camel safari.

Playtime   The Green Team provide activities for children between the ages of 2-12 years. This operates under the name of Playtime, which is open every day between 10.00–13.00 and 15.00–18.00. Activities include a visit to a tropical park, treasure hunts, beach days and Olympic sports. Evening babysitting services can also be arranged.

Car hire   A range of vehicles is available at competitive prices to suit different needs, for example Renault Twingo, Opel Corsa, Renault Clio, VX Cabriolet, Jeep Wrangler 4×4, Renault Megane and Renault Minibus.

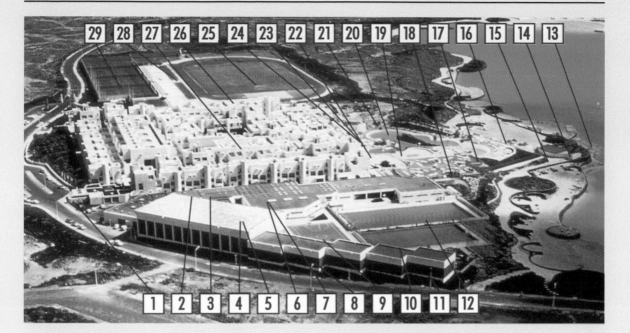

1	Reception	16	Beach area
2	Massage and physiotherapy and conference centre	17	Children's area*
3	Supermarket	18	Mini golf*
4	Sports hall	19	Sun terrace
5	Badminton, volleyball, handball and basketball	20	Leisure pool
6	Sports testing	21	Playground
7	Fitness centre	22	Restaurants
8	Squash courts	23	Sports bar
9	Basketball court	24	Pool bar/disco
10	Football and aerobics	25	Football pitch
11	Table tennis	26	Bike centre
12	Olympic pool, 50 metres	27	Shopping area
13	Windsurfing lagoon	28	Sports stadium
14	Windsurfing station	29	Tennis courts
15	Beach club		

*Some relocation of facilities takes place from time to time.

This case was prepared by Des Thwaite, Senior Lecturer in Marketing, University of Leeds.

Questions

1   Consider the characteristics of services outlined in this chapter and discuss their implications for an organization such as Club La Santa.

2   How might Club La Santa segment its market? Are some potential segments incompatible, in which case, how could be problem be overcome?

3   Given the nature of the service which Club La Santa offers, which forms of communication would be most effective?

CHAPTER TWENTY-ONE

International Marketing

*'I want to be a good Frenchman in France and a good Italian in Italy.
My strategy is to go global when I can and stay local when I must'*

ERIC JOHANNSON   *President of Electrolux*

Learning Objectives   *This chapter explains:*

1   The reasons why companies seek foreign markets

2   The factors that influence which foreign markets to enter

3   The range of foreign market entry strategies

4   The factors influencing foreign market entry strategies

5   The influences on the degree of standardization—adaptation

6   The special considerations involved in designing an international marketing mix

7   How to organize for international marketing operations

oday's managers need international marketing skills to be able to compete in an increasingly global marketplace. They require the capabilities to identify and seize opportunities that arise across the world. Failure to do so brings stagnation and decline, not only to individual companies but also to whole regions.

The importance of international marketing is reflected in the support given by governmental bodies set up to encourage and aid export activities. Such organizations often provide help in gathering information on foreign markets, competitors and their products, and barriers to entry. They disseminate such information through libraries, abstract services and publications. Furthermore, they organize business missions to foreign countries, provide exhibition space at international trade fairs and may give incentives to firms to attend the fairs. Often, they employ trade officers in important foreign markets to help exporters gather marketing research information and find prospective customers for their products.[1] The importance of such government-sponsored activities in assisting exporting performance of firms was supported by the findings of a study of Greek exporters.[2]

The emergence of the international marketplace known as the World Wide Web has the potential to transform international transactions. Suppliers and customers can communicate electronically across the world through sending e-mail messages and setting up interactive websites. Small companies can gain access to global markets without the need for expensive salesforces or retail outlets. Transactions can be accomplished by giving credit card details and clicking a button. Not all markets will be fundamentally changed by Internet marketing because of delivery considerations and the fact that many customers may prefer to buy such things as clothing and furniture after personal contact and viewing. Nevertheless, established players in mature global markets are analysing the potential of the Internet to provide opportunities and threats to their businesses.

The purpose of this chapter, then, is to explore four issues in developing international marketing strategies. First, we address the question of whether to go international or stay domestic; second, we consider the factors that impact upon the selection of countries in which to market; third, foreign market entry strategies are analysed;

finally, we examine the options available for developing international marketing strategies.

Deciding whether to go international

Many companies shy away from the prospect of competing internationally. They know their domestic market better, and they would have to come to terms with the customs, language, tariff regulations, transport systems and volatile currencies of foreign countries. On top of that their products may require significant modifications to meet foreign regulations and different customer preferences. So, why do companies choose to market abroad? There are seven triggers for international expansion (see Fig. 21.1).

Saturated domestic markets

The pressure to raise sales and profits coupled with few opportunities to expand in current domestic markets provide one condition for international expansion. This has been a major driving force behind Marks and Spencer's moves into Europe and the USA, and their interest in expanding their activities into Japan and China.[3] Many of the foreign expansion plans of European supermarket chains were fuelled by the desire to take a proven retailing formula out of their saturated domestic market into new overseas markets.

Figure 21.1 Going international

Small domestic markets

In some industries, survival means broadening scope beyond small national markets to the international arena. For example, Volvo (cars) and Philips and Electrolux (electrical goods) could not compete against the strength of global competitors by servicing their small domestic market alone. For them, internationalization is not an option: it is a fundamental condition for survival.

Low-growth domestic markets

Often recession at home provides the spur to seek new marketing opportunities in more buoyant overseas economies. This was the reason for the international moves of Thornton's, a small company specializing in the refurbishment of commercial premises. Survival in the severe UK recession of the early 1990s was achieved through winning contracts in countries such as Denmark, Sweden and Germany.

Customer drivers

Customer-driven factors may also affect the decision to go international. In some industries customers may expect their suppliers to have an international presence. This is increasingly common in advertising, with clients requiring their agencies to coordinate international campaigns. A second customer-orientated factor is the need to internationalize operations in response to customers expanding abroad.

Competitive forces

There is a substantial body of research that suggests that when several companies in an industry go abroad, others feel obliged to follow suit to maintain their relative size and growth rate.[4] This is particularly true in oligopolistic industries. A second competitive factor may be the desire to attack an overseas competitor which has entered our domestic market, in their home market. This may make strategic sense if the competitor is funding its overseas expansion from a relatively attractive home base.

Cost factors

High national labour costs, shortages of skilled workers, and rising energy charges can raise domestic costs to uneconomic levels. These factors may stimulate moves towards foreign direct investment in low cost areas such as Taiwan, Korea and Central and Eastern Europe. It is suggested that one of the motives behind BMW's take-over of the Rover Group was to establish a low-cost manufacturing base in the UK. Expanding into foreign markets can also reduce costs by gaining economies of scale through an enlarged customer base.

Portfolio balance

Marketing in a variety of regions provides the opportunity of achieving portfolio balance as each region may be experiencing different growth rates. At any one time, the USA, Japan, individual European and Far Eastern countries will be enjoying varying growth rates. By marketing in a selection of countries, the problems of recession in some countries can be balanced by the opportunities for growth in others.

Deciding which markets to enter

Having made the commitment to internationalize, marketing managers require the analytical skills necessary to pick those countries and regions which are most attractive for overseas operations. Two sets of factors will govern this decision: *macroenvironmental issues* and *microenvironmental issues*. These are shown in Fig. 21.2.

Macroenvironmental issues

These consist of *economic*, *socio-cultural*, and *political-legal influences* on market choice.

Economic influences

A country's size per capita income, stage of economic development, infrastructure and exchange rate stability and conversion affect its attractiveness for international business expansion. Small markets may not justify setting up a distribution and marketing system to supply goods and services. Low per capita income will affect the type of product which may sell in that country. The market may be very unattractive for car manufacturers but feasible for bicycle producers. Less developed countries at the early stages of economic development may demand inexpensive agricultural tools but not computers.

The economic changes that have taken place in Central and Eastern Europe have had varying effects on each countries attractiveness. For example, the move from centrally planned to market-based economy of Poland initially caused a rise in unemployment to 400 000 people, and a 40 per cent fall in purchasing power of some households as government subsidies and price controls were abolished.[5] However, these shocks were followed by greater investment by Western countries and a fall in inflation from as high as 250 per cent to 3.4 per cent.[6]

Another economic consideration is a nation's infrastructure. This comprises the transportation structures (roads, railways, airports), communication systems (telephone, television, the press, radio) and energy supplies (electricity, gas, nuclear). A poor infrastructure may limit the ability to manufacture, advertise and distribute goods, and provide adequate service backup. In 1990 there was a 20-year waiting period to have a telephone installed in Poland, and the Romanian telephone network was almost 60 years old. Such conditions may severely hamper the efficiency of international marketing and communications. In other areas of Europe infrastructure improvements are enhancing communications, for example, the ambitious, if costly, Eurotunnel that links the UK with mainland Europe, and the bridge and tunnel that will connect the two main parts of Denmark.

Finally, exchange rate stability and conversion may affect market choice. A country that has an unstable exchange rate or one that is difficult to convert to hard currencies such as the dollar or mark may be considered too risky to enter.

Socio-cultural influences

Differences in socio-cultural factors between countries are often termed *psychic distance*.

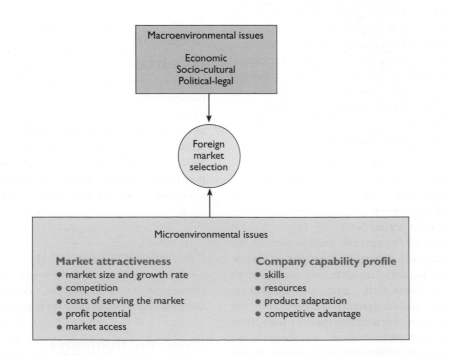

Figure 21.2 Selecting foreign markets

These are the barriers created by cultural disparities between the home country and the host country and the problems of communication resulting from differences in social perspectives, attitudes and language.[7] This can have an important effect on selection. International marketers sometimes choose countries that are psychically similar to begin their overseas operations. This has a rationale in that barriers of language, customs, and values are lower. Johanson and Vahlne, on the basis of four Swedish manufacturing firms, showed that firms often begin by entering new markets which are psychically close (culturally and geographically), gaining experience in these countries before expanding operations abroad into more distant markets.[8] Erramilli states that this is also true of service firms who move from culturally similar foreign markets into less familiar markets as their experience grows.[9] Language, in particular, has caused many well-documented problems for marketing communications in international markets. Marketing in Action 21.1 describes some of the classic mistakes that have been made.

Political-legal influences

Factors that potential international marketers will consider are the general attitudes of foreign governments to imports and foreign direct investment, political stability, and trade barriers. Negative attitudes towards foreign firms may also discourage imports and investment because of the threat of protectionism and expropriation of assets. Positive governmental attitudes can be reflected in the willingness to grant subsidies to overseas firms to invest in its country and a willingness to cut through bureaucratic procedures to assist foreign firms and their imports. The willingness of the UK government to grant investment incentives to Japanese firms was a factor in Nissan, Honda and Toyota setting up production facilities there.

Eagerness to promote imports has not always been a feature of Japanese attitudes, however. Until recently, imports of electrical goods were hampered by the fact that each one had to be inspected by government officials. Also their patent laws rule that patents are made public after eighteen months but are not granted for four to six years. In many Western countries patents remain secret until they are granted. The Japanese system discourages high technology and other

firms who wish to protect their patents from entering Japan.

Countries with a history of political instability may be avoided because of the inevitable uncertainty regarding their future. Countries such as Iraq and Lebanon have undoubtedly suffered because of the political situation.

Finally, a major consideration when deciding which countries to enter will be the level of tariff barriers. Undoubtedly the threat of tariff barriers to imports to the countries of the EU has encouraged US and Japanese foreign direct investment into Europe. Within the Single Market the removal of trade barriers is making international trade in Europe more attractive, as not only tariffs fall but also the need to modify products to cater for national regulations and restrictions is reduced.

Microenvironmental issues

While the macroenvironmental analysis provides indications of how attractive each country is to an international marketer, *microenvironmental analysis* focuses on the attractiveness of the particular market being considered, and the company capability profile.

Market attractiveness

Market attractiveness can be assessed by determining market size and growth rate, competition, costs of serving the market, profit potential, and market access.

Market size and growth rate large, growing markets (other things being equal) provide attractive conditions for market entry. Research supports the notion that market growth is a more important consideration than market size.[10] It is expectations about future demand rather than existing demand which is important, particularly for foreign direct investment.

Competition markets that are already served by strong, well-entrenched competitors may dampen enthusiasm for foreign market entry. Volatility of competition also appears to reduce the attractiveness of overseas markets. Highly volatile markets with many competitors entering and leaving the market and where market concentration is high are particularly unattractive.[11]

Costs of serving the market two major costs of servicing foreign markets are distribution and control. As geographic distance increases, so these two costs rise. Many countries' major export markets are in neighbouring countries, such as the USA whose largest market is Canada. Costs are also dependent on the form of market entry.

Obviously foreign direct investment is initially more expensive than using distributors. Some countries may not possess suitable low cost entry options, making entry less attractive and more risky. Long internal distribution channels (e.g. Japan) can also raise costs as middlemen demand their profit margins. If direct investment is being

21.1 Marketing in Action

Classic Communication Faux Pas

Language differences have caused innumerable problems for international marketers, and can provide a barrier to foreign market entry. The problem is particularly acute in countries like Britain, where one-third of its small and medium-sized companies admit to having communication difficulties abroad. This contrasts with Belgium, where 92 per cent of companies employ foreign language specialists, closely followed by The Netherlands and Luxembourg. It is no excuse to claim that English is a world business language, and consequently there is no need to develop foreign language skills. As the former German Chancellor Willy Brandt once exclaimed, 'If I am selling to you I will speak English, but if you are selling to me dann müssen Sie Deutsch sprechen!'

Here are some classic examples of translations that have gone wrong:

✦ A Thai dry cleaners: 'Drop your trousers here for best results'

✦ A sign in a Hong Kong tailor: 'Ladies may have a fit upstairs'

✦ A Moscow guide to a Russian Orthodox monastery: 'You are welcome to visit the cemetery where famous Russian and Soviet composers, artists, and writers are buried daily, except Thursdays'

✦ A Portuguese restaurant that offers 'butchers' mess from the oven'

✦ A Spanish sports shop called 'The Athlete's Foot'

✦ A French dress shop advertising 'Dresses for street walking'.

The world of advertising is not without its humorous errors in translation:

✦ Come alive with Pepsi: Rise from the grave with Pepsi (German)

✦ Avoid embarrassment—use Parker pens: Avoid pregnancy—use Parker pens (Spanish)

✦ Cleans the really dirty parts of your wash—Cleans your private parts (French)

✦ Body by Fisher: Corpse by Fisher (Flemish)

✦ Chrysler for power: Chrysler is an aphrodisiac (Spanish)

✦ Tropicana orange juice: Tropicana Chinese juice (Cuba)

✦ Tomato paste: tomaco glue (Arabic).

Based on: Halsal (1994);[12] Egan and McKiernan (1994);[13] Cateora et al. (2000)[14]

contemplated, labour costs and the supply of skilled labour will also be a consideration. Finally, some markets may prove unattractive because of the high marketing expenditures necessary to compete in them.

Profit potential some markets may be unattractive because industry structure renders them with poor profit potential. For example, the existence of powerful buying groups may reduce profit potential through their ability to negotiate low prices.

Market access some foreign markets may prove difficult to penetrate because of informal ties between existing suppliers and distributors. Without the capability of setting up a new distribution chain, this would mean that market access would effectively be barred. Links between suppliers and customers in organizational markets would also form a barrier. In some countries and markets, national suppliers are given preferential treatment. The German machine tool industry was a case in point, as was defence procurement in many West European countries.

Company capability profile

Company capability to serve a foreign market also needs to be assessed: this depends on skills, resources, product adaptation, and competitive advantage.

Skills does the company have the necessary skills to market abroad? If not, can sales agents or distributors compensate for any shortfalls? Does the company have the necessary skills to understand the requirements of each market?

Resources different countries may have varying market servicing costs. Does the company have the necessary financial resources to compete effectively in them? Human resources also need to be considered as some markets may demand domestically supplied personnel.

Product adaptation for some foreign markets, local preferences and regulations may require the product to be modified. Does the company have the motivation and capability to redesign the product?

Competitive advantage a key consideration in any market is the ability to create a competitive advantage. Each foreign market needs to be studied in the light of the company's current and future ability to create and sustain a competitive advantage.

Deciding how to enter a foreign market

After a firm decides to enter a foreign market, it must choose a mode of entry, that is select an institutional arrangement for organizing and conducting international marketing activities.

The choice of foreign market entry strategy is likely to have a major impact on a company's performance overseas.[15] Each mode of entry has its own associated levels of commitment, risks, control and profit potential. The major options are indirect exporting, direct exporting, licensing, joint ventures, and direct investment either in new facilities or through acquisition (see Fig. 21.3).

Indirect exporting

Indirect exporting involves the use of independent organizations within the exporter's domestic market. These include the following:

1   *Domestic-based export merchants* who take title to the products and sell them abroad.
2   *Domestic-based export agents* who sell on behalf of the exporter but do not take title to the products; agents are usually paid by commission.
3   *Piggybacking*, whereby the exporter uses the overseas distribution facilities of another producer.
4   *Cooperative organizations*, which act on behalf of a number of producers and are partly controlled by them; many producers of primary products such as fruit and nuts export through cooperative organizations.

Indirect exporting has three advantages. First, the exporting organization is domestically based, thus communication is easier than using foreign intermediaries. Second, investment and risk are lower than setting up one's own sales and marketing facility. Third, use can be made of the exporting organization's knowledge of selling abroad.

Direct exporting

As exporters grow more confident, they may decide to undertake their own exporting task. This will involve building up overseas contracts, undertaking marketing research, handling documentation and transportation, and designing marketing mix strategies. **Direct exporting** modes include export through foreign-based agents or distributors (independent middlemen), a domestic-based salesforce, an overseas sales/ marketing office or subsidiary.

Foreign-based agents or distributors

Most companies use agents or distributors in some or all of their exporting abroad. Over 60 per cent of US companies use them for some or all of their export activity, and for European firms the figure rises to over 70 per cent.[16] *Agents* may be *exclusive*, where the agreement is between the exporter and the agent alone; *semi-exclusive*, where the agent handles the exporter's goods along with other non-competing goods from other companies; or *non-exclusive*, where the agent handles a variety of goods, including some that may compete with the exporter's products.

Distributors, unlike agents, take title to the goods, and are paid according to the difference between the buying and selling prices rather than commission. Distributors are often appointed when after-sales service is required as they are more likely to possess the necessary resources than agents.

The advantages of both agents and distributors are that they are familiar with the local market, customs and conventions, have existing business contracts and employ foreign nationals. They have a direct incentive to sell through either commission or profit margin but since their remuneration is tied to sales they may be reluctant to devote much time and effort towards developing a market for a new product. Also, the amount of market feedback may be limited as the agent or distributor may see themselves as a purchasing agent for their customers rather than a selling agent for the exporter.

Overall, exporting through independent middlemen is a low investment method of market entry although significant expenditure in marketing may be necessary. Also it can be difficult and costly to terminate an agreement with them, suggesting that this option should be viewed with care and not seen as an easy method of market entry.

Domestic-based sales representatives

As the sales representative is a company employee, greater control of activities compared

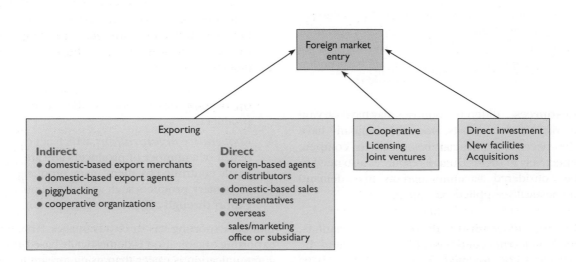

Figure 21.3 Foreign market entry strategies

to independent middlemen can be expected. Whereas a company has no control over the attention that an agent or distributor gives to its products or the amount of market feedback provided, it can insist that various activities be performed by its sales representatives.

Also the use of company employees shows a commitment to the customer that the use of agents or distributors may lack. Consequently they are often used in industrial markets, where there are only a few large customers who require close contact with suppliers, and where the size of orders justifies the expense of foreign travel. This method of market servicing is also found when selling to government buyers and retail chains, for similar reasons.

Overseas sales/marketing office or subsidiary

This option displays even greater customer commitment than using domestic-based sales representatives, although the establishment of a local office requires a greater investment. However, the exporter may be perceived as an indigenous supplier, improving its chances of market success. In some markets, where access to distribution channels is limited, selling direct through an overseas sales office may be the only feasible way of breaking into a new market. The sales office or subsidiary acts as a centre for foreign-based sales representatives, handles sales distribution and promotion, and can act as a customer service centre.

For the company contemplating exporting for the first time, there are many potential pitfalls.[17] Marketing in Action 21.2 discusses ten common mistakes and ways of avoiding them.

Licensing

Licensing refers to contracts in which a foreign licensor provides a local licensee with access to one or a set of technologies or know-how in exchange for financial compensation.[18] The licensee will normally have exclusive rights to produce and market the product within an agreed area for a specific period of time in return for a *royalty* based on sales volume. A licence may relate to the use of patent for either a product or process, copyright, trade marks and trade secrets

(e.g. designs and software) and know-how (e.g. product and process specifications).

Licensing agreements allow the exporter to enter markets that otherwise may be closed for exports or other forms of market entry without the need to make substantial capital investments in the host country. However, control of production is lost and the reputation of the licensor is dependent on the performance of the licensee. A grave danger of licensing is the loss of product and process know-how to third parties who may become competitors once the agreement is at an end.

The need to exploit new technology simultaneously in many markets has stimulated the growth in licensing by small high-tech companies which lack the resources to set up their own sales and market offices, engage in joint ventures or conduct direct investment abroad. Licensing is also popular in R&D-intensive industries such as pharmaceuticals, chemicals and synthetic fibres, where rising research and development costs have encouraged licensing as a form of reciprocal technology exchange.

In Europe, licensing is encouraged by the European Commission (EC), which seeks the mechanism as a way of offering access to new technologies to companies without the resources to innovate and provide a means of technology sharing on a pan-European scale. Licensing activities have been given exemption in EC competition law, which means that companies engaged in licensing cannot be accused of anti-competitive practices, and *tied purchase* agreements whereby licensees must buy components from the licensor have not been ruled anti-competitive since they allow the innovating firm protection from loss of know-how to other component suppliers.

Franchising

Franchising is a form of licensing where a package of services are offered by the franchisor to the franchisee, in return for payment. The two types of franchising are *product and trade name franchising*, the classic case of which is Coca-Cola selling its syrup together with the right to use its trade mark and name to independent bottlers, and *business format franchising* where marketing approaches, operating procedures and quality control are included in the franchise package as well as the product and trade name. Business

21.2   Marketing in Action

Ten Common Exporting Mistakes and Their Solutions

Exporting can be a hazardous activity, particularly for those doing it for the first time. Here are ten common errors and how to avoid them.

1 *Error*: failure to obtain qualified export advice and to develop an international marketing plan before starting exporting activities.
Solution: seek qualified outside counselling.

2 *Error*: inadequate commitment by top management to solve the initial problems and provide the necessary financial requirements of exporting.
Solution: take a long-term view and be prepared to build a solid foundation, or do not get involved.

3 *Error*: careless choice of overseas agents or distributors.
Solution: carry out a personal evaluation of the people handling the account, the distributors' facilities and their management skills.

4 *Error*: chasing orders around the world instead of establishing a base for profitable operations and orderly growth.
Solution: based on market attractiveness and company capability analysis, concentrate efforts in one or two geographic areas at first, then move on to the next selected geographic area.

5 *Error*: neglecting export markets when the home market booms.
Solution: consciously ensure that export markets receive due attention through making a long-term commitment to export business.

6 *Error*: failure to treat international distributors on an equal basis to domestic counterparts.
Solution: create partnerships with all key distributors and extend special discount offers, sales incentives programmes, special credit terms and shared advertising campaigns to them.

7 *Error*: unwillingness to modify products to meet customer preferences or regulations in export markets.
Solution: do not rely on distributors making the necessary changes. Modifications should be made at the factory to maintain distributor goodwill and ensure quality control.

8 *Error*: failure to print services, sales and guarantee messages in local language.
Solution: employ foreign nationals to translate messages into local languages.

9 *Error*: failure to consider the use of an export management company or other marketing intermediary.
Solution: if the exporter does not have the people or capital to employ experienced export staff, engage a qualified intermediary.

10 *Error*: overlooking licensing or joint venture opportunities.
Solution: licensing or a joint venture agreement may be a simple, profitable means of avoiding import restrictions, overcoming inadequate resources, or a too-narrow product line in an otherwise overseas market.

Based on: Anonymous (1987)[19]

format franchising is mainly used in service industries such as restaurants, hotels and retailing where the franchisor exerts a high level of control in the overseas market since quality control procedures can be established as part of the agreement. For example, McDonald's specify precisely who should supply the ingredients for their fast-food products wherever they are sold to ensure consistency of quality in their franchise outlets.

Franchising is also exempt from EC competition law as it is seen as a means of achieving increased competition and efficient distribution without the need for major investment. It promotes standardization which reaps scale economies with the possibility of some adaptation to local tastes. For example, McDonald's include salad in their product range in Germany and France, and Benetton allow a degree of freedom to their franchisees to stock products suitable to their particular customers.[20]

Joint ventures

Two types of joint ventures are contractual and equity joint ventures. In **contractual joint ventures** no joint enterprise with a separate personality is formed. Two or more companies form a partnership to share the cost of an investment, the risks and long-term profits. The partnership may be to complete a particular project or for a longer term cooperative effort.[21] They are found in oil exploration, aerospace and car industries and co-publishing agreements.[22] An **equity joint venture** involves the creation of a new company in which foreign and local investors share ownership and control.

Joint ventures are sometimes set up in response to government conditions for market entry or because the foreign firm lacks the resources to set up production facilities alone. Also the danger of expropriation is less when a company has a national partner than when the foreign firm is the sole owner.[23] Finding a national partner may be the only way to invest in some markets that are too competitive and saturated to leave room for a completely new operation. Many of the Japanese/US joint ventures in the USA were set up for this reason. The foreign investor benefits from the local management talent and knowledge of local markets and regulations. Also, joint ventures allow partners to specialize in their particular areas of technological expertise in a

given project. Finally, the host firm benefits by acquiring resources from their foreign partners. For example, in Hungary host firms have gained through the rapid acquisition of marketing resources which have enabled them to create positions of competitive advantage.[24]

There are potential problems, however. The national partner's interests relate to the local operation while the foreign firm's concerns relate to the totality of its international operations. Particular areas of conflict can be the use made of profits (pay out versus plough back), product line and market coverage of the joint venture, and transfer pricing.

In Europe, incentives for joint research projects are provided through the European Strategic Programme for Research and Development in Information Technology (ESPRIT) so long as the project involves companies from at least two member states. Equity joint ventures are common between companies from Western Europe and Eastern European countries. Western European firms gain from low cost production and raw materials while Eastern bloc companies acquire Western technology and know-how. Eastern bloc governments are keen to promote joint ventures rather than wholly owned foreign direct investment in an attempt to prevent the exploitation of low cost labour by Western firms.

Direct investment

This method of market entry involves investment in foreign-based assembly or manufacturing facilities. It carries the greatest commitment of capital and managerial effort. Wholly owned **direct investment** can be through the *acquisition* of a foreign producer (or by buying out a joint venture partner) or by building *new facilities*. Acquisition offers a quicker way into the market and usually means gaining access to a qualified labour force, national management, local knowledge and contacts with the local market and government. In saturated markets acquisition may be the only feasible way of establishing a production presence in the host country.[25] However, coordination and styles of management between the foreign investor and the local management team may cause problems. Whirlpool, the US white goods (washing machines, refrigerators, etc.) manufacturer, is an example of a company that has successfully entered new international markets using acquisition. The company has successfully entered European markets through its acquisition of Philips's white goods business and its ability to develop new products that serve cross-national Euro-segments. European companies have also gained access to North American markets through acquisition. For example, ABN Amro has built up market presence in the USA through a series of acquisitions to become the largest foreign bank in that country.[26]

Wholly owned direct investment offers a greater degree of control than licensing or joint ventures, and maintains the internalization of proprietary information. It accomplishes the circumvention of tariff and non-tariff barriers, and lowers distribution costs compared with domestic production. A local presence means that sensitivity to customers' tastes and preferences is enhanced, and links with distributors and the host nation's government can be forged. Foreign direct investments can act as a powerful catalyst for economic change in the transition from a centrally planned economy. Foreign companies bring technology, management know-how and access to foreign markets.[27]

Direct investment is an expensive option, though, and the consequent risks are greater. If the venture fails, more money is lost and there is always the risk of expropriation. Furthermore, closure of plant may mean substantial redundancy payments.

The creation of the Single European Market allows free movement of capital across the EU removing restrictions on direct investment using greenfield sites. Foreign direct investment through acquisition, however, may be subject to investigation under EC competition policy. American firms, in particular, sought to acquire European firms prior to 1992 in an attempt to secure a strong position in the face of the threat of *Fortress Europe*.

The selection of international market entry mode is dependent on the trade-offs between the levels of control, resources and risk of losing proprietary information and technology. Figure 21.4 summarizes the levels associated with exporting using middlemen, exporting using company staff, licensing, joint ventures and direct investment.

Considerable research has gone into trying to understand the factors that have been shown to

Factor

Level	Risk of losing proprietary information	Resources	Control
High		Direct investment	Direct investment Exporting (own staff)
Medium	Licensing Joint venture	Joint venture Exporting (own staff)	Joint venture Licensing
Low	Exporting (own staff) Exporting (middlemen) Direct investment	Licensing Exporting (middlemen)	Exporting (middlemen)

Figure 21.4 Selecting a foreign market entry mode: control, resources and risk

have an impact on selection of market entry method. Both external (country environment and buyer behaviour) and internal (company issues) factors have been shown to influence choice. A summary of these research findings is given in Table 21.1.

Developing international marketing strategy

Standardization or adaptation

A fundamental decision that managers have to make regarding their international marketing strategy is the degree to which they standardize or adapt their marketing mix around the world. Many writers on the subject discuss *standardization* and *adaptation* as two distinct options. Pure standardization means that a company keeps the same marketing mix in all countries to which it markets. The commercial reality, however, is that few mixes are totally standardized. The brands that are most often quoted as being standardized are Coca-Cola, McDonald's and Levi Strauss. It is true that many elements of their marketing mixes are identical in a wide range of countries but even here adaptation is found.

First, in *Coca-Cola*, the sweetness and carbonization vary between countries. For example, sweetness is lowered in Greece and carbonation lowered in Eastern Europe. Diet Coke's artificial

---

Table 21.1   Factors affecting choice of market entry method

External variables
Country Environment
+ Large market size and market growth encourage direct investment
+ Barriers to imports encourage direct investment[28]
+ The more the country's characteristics are rated favourable, the greater the propensity for direct investment[29]
+ The higher the country's level of economic development, the greater the use of direct investment
+ Government incentives encourage direct investment
+ The higher the receiving company's technical capabilities, the greater the use of licensing
+ Government intervention in foreign trade encourages licensing[30]
+ Geocultural distance encourages independent modes, e.g. agents, distributors[31]
+ Psychic distance does not favour integrated modes, e.g. own salesforce, overseas sales/marketing offices[32]
+ Low market potential does not necessarily preclude direct investment for larger firms[33]
Buyer behaviour
+ Piecemeal buying favours independent modes
+ Project and protectionist buying encourages cooperative entry, e.g. licensing and joint ventures[34]

Internal variables
Company issues
+ Lack of market information, uncertainty and perception of high investment risk lead to the use of agents and distributors[35]
+ Large firm size or resources encourages higher level of commitment[36]
+ Perception of high investment risk encourages joint ventures[37]
+ Small firm size or resources encourages reactive exporting[38]
+ Limited experience favours integrated entry modes[39]
+ Service firms with little or no experience of foreign markets tend to prefer full control modes, e.g. own staff, overseas sales/marketing offices
+ Service firms who expand abroad by following their clients' expansion plans tend to favour integrated modes[40]
+ When investment rather than exporting is preferred, lack of market information leads to a preference for a cooperative rather than integrated modes[41]

Source: Whitelock, J. and D. Jobber (1994) The Impact of Competitor Environment on Initial Market Entry in a New, Non-Domestic Market, *Proceedings of the Marketing Education Group Conference,* Coleraine, July, 1008–17

sweetener and packaging differ between countries.[42]

Second, *Levi Strauss* uses different domestic and international advertising strategies.[43] As Dan Chow Len, Levi's US advertising manager, commented:

> The markets are different. In the US, Levi's is both highly functional and fashionable. But in the UK, its strength is as a fashion garment. We've tested UK ads in American markets. Our primary target market at home is 16–20 year old, and they hate these ads, won't tolerate them, they're too sexy. Believe it or not, American 16–20 year old don't want to be sexy …When you ask people about Levi's here, it's quality, comfort, style affordability. In Japan, it's the romance of America.[44]

Third, in *McDonald's*, menus are changed to account for different customer preferences. For example, in France and Germany salads are added to the menu. The proportion of meat in the hamburgers also varies between countries.

Most global brands adapt to meet local requirements. Even high tech electronic products have to conform to national technical standards and may be positioned differently in various countries. As the Unilever chairman, Michael Perry, warned, most brands will remain national:

> Global brands are simply local brands reproduced many times. Although it may be true that increasingly we address even larger numbers of consumers we do well to remember that we continue to do that one-to-one.[45]

How, then, do marketers tackle the standardization—adaptation issue? A useful rule-of-thumb was cited at the start of this chapter: go global (standardize) when you can, stay local (adapt) when you must. Figure 21.5 provides a grid for thinking about the areas where standardization may be possible, and where adaptation may be necessary. For a car like the Audi 6 featured in the advertisement opposite, the product elements may be standardized to a high degree, although the positioning of the car may differ in various countries. Standardization is an attractive option because it can create massive economies of scale. For example, lower manufacturing, advertising

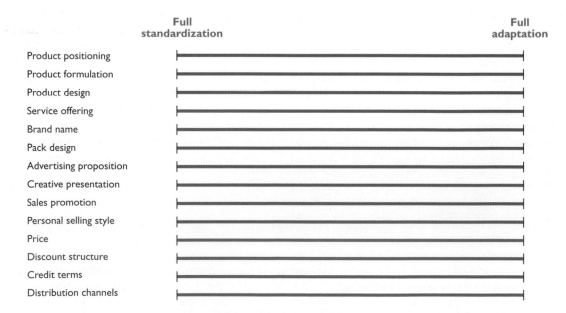

Figure 21.5 Standardization and adaptation of the marketing mix

Audi style and technology cross national borders

and packaging costs can be realized. Also the logistical benefit of being able to move stock from one country to another to meet low stock situations should not be underestimated. This has led to the call to focus on similarities rather than differences between consumers across Europe, and the rest of the world. However, there are a number of barriers to developing standardized global brands. These are discussed in Marketing in Action 21.3.

Developing global and regional brands requires the commitment from management to a coherent marketing programme. The sensitivities of national managers need to be accounted for as they may perceive a loss of status associated with greater centralized control. One approach is to have mechanisms that ensure the involvement of national managers in planning and which encourage them to make recommendations. The key is to balance this local involvement with the need to look for similarities across markets rather than differences. It is the essential differences in consumer preferences and buyer behaviour that need to be recognized in marketing mix adaptation rather than the minor nuances. Managers must also be prepared to invest heavily

and over a long time period to achieve brand penetration. Success in international markets does not come cheaply or quickly. Market research should be used to identify the required positioning in each global market segment.[46]

This discussion has outlined the difficulties in achieving a totally standardized marketing mix package. Rather the tried-and-tested approach of market segmentation based upon understanding consumer behaviour and identifying international target markets which allow the benefits of standardization to be combined with the advantages of customization is recommended. The two contrasting approaches are summarized in Fig. 21.6.

International marketing mix decisions

Once a thorough understanding of the target market has been achieved, marketing managers can then tailor a marketing mix to fit those requirements. We can now explore some of the special considerations associated with developing an effective *international marketing mix*.

21.3   Marketing in Action

Barriers to Developing Standardized Global Brands

The cost of logistical advantages of developing standardized global marketing approaches has meant that many companies have looked carefully at standardizing their approach to the European market. Mars, for example, changed the name of their chocolate bar Marathon in the UK to conform to their Euro-brand name Snickers. Full standardization of the marketing mix is difficult, however, because of five problems:

1   *Culture and consumption patterns*: different cultures demand different types of products (e.g. beer and cheese). Some countries use butter to cook with rather than to spread on bread; people in different countries wash clothes at different temperatures. Consumer electrical products are less affected, though.

2   *Language*: brand names and advertising may have to change because of language differences. For example, the popular French drink PSCHITT would probably require an alteration to the brand name in the UK.

3   *Regulations*: while national regulations are being harmonized in the Single Market, difference still exist, for example with colourings and added vitamins in food.

4   *Media availability and promotional preferences*: varying media practices also affect standardization. For example, wine cannot be advertised on television in Denmark, but in The Netherlands it is allowed. Beer cannot be advertised on television in France, but it is allowed in most other European countries. Sales promotions may have to change because of local preferences. For example, French shoppers prefer coupons and twin packs, whereas their British counterparts favour X per cent extra free.

5   *Organizational structure and culture*: the changes necessary for a standardized approach may be difficult to implement where subsidiaries historically have enjoyed considerable power. Also where growth had been achieved through acquisition, strong cultural differences may lead to differing views about pan-European brand strategy.

The reality is that full standardization is rarely possible. Even brands that are regarded as global such as Sony, Nike, Visa, IBM, Disney, Heineken, McDonald's and Pringles are not as identical globally as may first appear. For example, Visa uses different logos in some countries, Heineken is positioned as a mainstream beer in some countries but as a premium beer in others, Pringles uses different flavours and advertising executions in different countries, and although McDonald's core food items are consistent across countries some products are customized to local tastes. Setting the objective as being to develop a standardized global brand should not be the priority; instead global brand leadership—strong brands in all markets backed by effective global brand management—should be the goal.

Based on: De Chernaton (1993);[47] Aaker and Joachimsthaler (2000)[48]

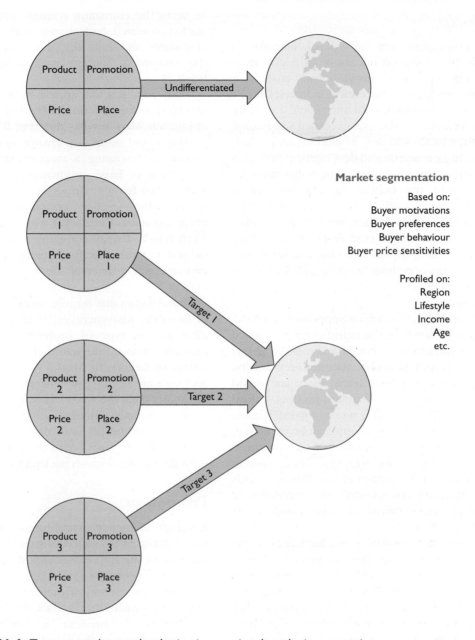

Market segmentation

Based on:
Buyer motivations
Buyer preferences
Buyer behaviour
Buyer price sensitivities

Profiled on:
Region
Lifestyle
Income
Age
etc.

Figure 21.6 Two approaches to developing international marketing strategies

Product

Some companies rely on global markets to provide the potential necessary to justify their *huge research and development costs*. For example, in the pharmaceutical industry, Glaxo's Zantac and Wellcome's Zovirax could not have been developed (R&D costs exceeded £30 million in both cases) without a worldwide market. Canon's huge research and development budget is also justified by the potential of global markets. For example, the bubble jet and laser beam computer printers which it invented formed the bases upon which it has built world market shares of 30 and 65 per cent, respectively.[49] Once developed, the company can offer a standardized product to generate huge positive cash flow as the benefits that these products provide span national boundaries.

A second situation which supports a standardized product is where the brand concept is based on *authentic national heritage* across the globe: Scotch whisky, Belgian chocolate and French wine are relevant examples. Clearly, there are sound marketing reasons for a standard product. A third basis for standardization is where a global market segment of like-minded people can be exploited. This is the basis for the success of such products as Swatch and Rolex watches, Gucci fashion accessories and Chanel perfume. Where brands make statements about people, the *international properties* of the brand add significantly to its appeal.

In other cases, however, products need to be modified. Product adaptations come in two forms, permanent and temporary.[50] A company may make a fairly standard product worldwide but make adaptations for particular markets. For example, the Barbie doll is a standardized product for most countries but in Japan, based on market research, it had to be redesigned by making it smaller, darkening hair colour and giving it smaller breasts. This was a *permanent adaptation*. However, the change may be only a *temporary adaptation* if the local consumer needs time to gradually adjust to the new product. This often occurs with food products. For example, when McDonald's entered Japan they had to alter the red meat content of their hamburgers because Japanese consumers preferred fat to be mixed with beef. Over time the red meat content has been increased making it almost as high as in the USA. Also when Mister Donut was introduced in Japan the cinnamon content was reduced as market research had shown that the Japanese customers did not like the taste. Over time the cinnamon content was increased to US levels.[51]

Many products that appear to be the same are modified to suit differing tastes. For example, the ubiquitous Mars bar has different formulation in northern and southern Europe with northern Europeans favouring a sweeter taste. Also, the movement of large multinational companies to seek global brands winners can provide opportunities for smaller companies to exploit emerging market segments. For example, in The Netherlands, a small company took the initiative to sell environmentally friendly products and captured one-quarter of the household cleaning market.[52]

Brand names may require modification because of linguistic idiosyncrasies. Many companies are alive to this type of problem now. Mars, for example, changed the name of their Magnum ice cream in Greece to Magic. However, in France McVitie's are having problems trying to convince consumers that the word Digestive has nothing to do with stomach disorders. Brand name changes also occur in the UK with Brooke Bond PG Tips being called Scottish Blend in Scotland together with distinctive Scottish packaging.[53]

Promotion

A survey of agency practitioners found that the use of standardized advertising campaigns is set to increase in the future.[54] Standard campaigns can realize cost economies and a cohesive positioning statement in a world of increasing international travel. Standardization allows the multinational corporation to maintain a consistent image identity throughout the world and minimizes confusion among consumers who travel frequently.[55] As with all standardization–adaptation debates the real issue is one of degree. Rarely can a campaign be transferred from one country to another without any modifications because of language difference. The clever use of pop music (an international language) in Levi's advertising is one exception, however. Coca-Cola are also close to the full standardization position with their one-sound, one-sight, one-appeal philosophy. Benetton also succeeded in running a global advertising campaign based on the 'United Colours of Benetton' theme.

Other companies find it necessary to adopt different positions in various countries, resulting in the need for advertising adaptation. In Mexico, Nestlé managed to position the drinking of instant coffee as an up-market activity. It is actually smarter to offer guests a cup of instant coffee than ground coffee. This affects the content of its advertising. When brands are used differently in various countries, the advertising may need to be changed accordingly. For example, Schweppes tonic water is very much a mixer (e.g. drunk with gin) in the UK and Ireland, but is drunk on its own in Spain and France. Marketing in Action 21.4 gives examples of regulations on advertising in various countries.

An analysis of the extent of advertising adaptation that is necessary can be assisted by separating the advertising proposition from the creative presentation of that proposition. The *advertising platform* is the aspect of the seller's product that is most persuasive and relevant to the potential customer: it is the fundamental proposition that is being communicated. The *creative presentation* is the way in which that proposition is translated into visual and verbal statements.[56] Table 21.2 gives some examples. Advertising platforms, being broad statements of appeal, are more likely to be transferable than creative presentations. If this is the case, the solution is to keep the platform across markets but change the creative presentation to suit local demands. In other cases both platform and presentation can be used globally, as was the case with the British Airways campaign shown in Table 21.2.

Advertising can be used to position brands using one of three strategies:[57]

1 *Global consumer positioning*: This strategy defines the brand as a symbol of a given global culture. For example, a jeans brand could be positioned as one worn by adult, upper-middle-class men who are globally cosmopolitan. The objective would be to have consumers identify the brand as a sign of membership in a globally cosmopolitan segment. Real-world examples include Sony ('My First Sony') which positioned one of its brands as appropriate for young people around the world; Philips ('Let's Make Things Better'), whose advertisements featured people from different countries; and Benetton ('The United Colours of Benetton') whose slogan emphasizes the unity of humankind and promotes the idea that people all over the world consume the brand.

2 *Foreign consumer culture positioning*: With this strategy the brand is associated with a specific foreign culture. It becomes symbolic of that culture so that the brand's personality, use occasion and/or user group are associated with a foreign culture. For example, Gucci in the USA is positioned as a prestigious and fashionable Italian product and Singapore Airlines' use of the 'Singapore Girl' in its global advertising campaign and the positioning of Louis Jadot wine as a 'taste' of France are two further examples.

3 *Local consumer culture positioning*: This involves the association of the brand with local consumer culture. The brand is

Table 21.2   Adapting advertising for global markets

Product category	Advertising platform	Creative presentation
Four-wheel-drive vehicles	Off-the-road technology	Jeep's 'We wrote the book on 4-wheel drive'
Toothpaste	Cosmetic benefits	Colgate's 'ring of confidence'
Airline travel	In-flight service quality	British Airways 'It's the way we make you feel that makes you fly British Airways. The World's Favourite airline'
Washing detergent	Heavy duty cleaning	Procter and Gamble's 'Tide gets out the dirt kids get into'

associated with local cultural meanings, reflects the local culture's norms and identities, is portrayed as consumed by local people in the national culture and/or is depicted as locally produced for local people. For example, Dr Pepper soft drinks is positioned in the USA as part of the 'American' way of life. In international advertising, it could be used when a good is produced or a service supplied locally.

Selling styles may also require adaptation because of cultural imperatives. Various cultures have different *time values*: In Latin America cultures salespeople are often kept waiting a long time for a business appointment and in Spain delay in answering correspondence does not mean the matter has low priority but may reflect the fact that close family relatives take absolute priority and no matter how important other business is, all other people are kept waiting. In the West deadlines are common in business but in

21.4   Marketing in Action

Global Advertising Taboos

Standardized advertising campaigns are hampered by the rules and regulations in various countries around the world. These prevent certain types of advertising from appearing. Here are some examples:

France	ban on alcohol advertising
Eastern Europe	alcohol advertising banned or heavily restricted; for example, in the Czech Republic drink cannot be poured, and ads cannot show people enjoying it; in Bulgaria no bottles, glasses, or any actors drinking can be shown
Sweden	no TV advertisements of toys to children under 12
Nordic countries	strict regulations on tobacco advertising
Finland	children may not sing or speak the name of a product
UK	TV tobacco ads banned
Austria	children not allowed to appear in an ad unless accompanied by a parent or comparable adult figure
Lithuania	petfood ads banned before 11p.m.
Malaysia	cannot wear baseball caps worn back to front (claimed to be indicative of gang influences and the undesirable side of Western society); blue jeans cannot appear in ads (other colours are acceptable)
Asia	men with long hair banned from ads
Muslim countries	women can appear only if suitably attired; certain parts of the body (e.g. armpits) are not allowed to be shown for religious reasons
Korea	all models, actors and actresses in ads have to be Korean.
Belgium, Luxembourg and Germany	ban on comparative advertising
Kuwait	ban on advertising cigarettes, lighters, pharmaceuticals, alcohol, airlines and chocolates

Based on: Richmond (1994);[58] Cateora et al. (2000)[59]

many Middle Eastern countries a deadline is taken as an insult and may well lose the overseas salesperson business.

The concept of space, also, has different meaning in different cultures. In the West the size of an executive's office is often taken to indicate status. In the Arab world this is not the case: a managing director may share the same office with clerks. In Western cultures business is often conducted at a distance, say six feet or more. In the Middle East and Latin America business discussions are often carried out in close proximity, involving physical contact to which the Western salesperson needs to get accustomed.

The unwritten rules of doing business are often at variance too. In the West business may be discussed over lunch or at dinner in the businessperson's home. In India, this would violate hospitality rules. Western business relies on the law of contract for sales agreements but in Muslim culture a person's word is just as binding. In fact a written contract may be seen as a challenge to his or her honour.[60] Salespeople need to adapt their behaviour to accommodate the expectations of customers abroad. For example, in Japan sales presentations should be low key with the use of a moderate, deliberate style reflecting their preferred manner of doing business. Salespeople should not push for a close of sale; instead they should plan to cultivate relationships through sales calls, courtesy visits, the occasional lunch and other social events.

A study by Campbell, Graham, Jolibert and Meissner suggests that sales negotiation outcomes may depend on country factors in the West.[61] In Germany the *hard sell* approach was positively related to negotiation success; in France similarity (in terms of background and personality) was important; in the UK the role of the negotiator had a significant bearing on outcomes with buyers outperforming sellers; and in the USA adapting a problem-solving approach was related to negotiation success.

The Internet is creating opportunities for companies to advertise globally by setting up a website. Persuading consumers to visit the site is not as easy, however, and top dot.com companies such as Amazon, Ebay, eToys and Jungle spend vast sums promoting their presence on the Web. Using electronic media as a promotional tool may be hampered by the need to set price lists, however. Where prices are currently very different across national borders some companies like the Millipore Corporation discussed in e-Marketing 21.1 may decide that the risks of establishing a global Internet presence may outweigh the advantages.

Country images may have a role to play in the selection of goods in overseas markets. For example a negative image of a country may influence a consumer's attitudes towards products originating from that country. Country of origin is sometimes used to promote products abroad when associations are believed to be favourable and the extent to which the national image is considered suitable for the specific type of product being marketed. For example, the product categories most often promoted by means of the Danish image are foodstuffs and dairy produce, design goods and products related to agriculture.[62]

A clear instance of the power of country images is the case of the Toyota Corolla which is built on the same assembly line as the near identical GM Prism in the USA. However, because of the added value of Japanese origin, the Corolla commands a 10 per cent price premium.[63]

Price

Price setting is a key marketing decision because price is the revenue-generating element of the marketing mix. Poor pricing decisions can undermine years of toil on fashioning strategy and pruning costs. As Leszinski states:

> As Europe moves towards a single market, lack of attention to pricing is a serious problem. The stakes are unusually high. . . . On average, a 1% increase results in a 12% improvement in a company's operating margin. This is four times as powerful as a 1% increase in its volume. But the sword cuts both ways. A price decrease of 5 to 10% will eliminate most companies' profits. As the single market develops, decreases of this magnitude can easily happen: the existing price differentials across Europe for some products are in the region of 20 to 40%.[64]

In the face of more intense global competition, international marketers need to consider six issues when considering cross-national pricing decisions:

I   Calculating extra costs and making price quotations.

2   Understanding the competition and customers.

3   Using pricing tactics to undermine competitor actions.

4   Parallel importing.

5   Transfer pricing.

6   Countertrade.

Each of these special considerations will now be explored.

Calculating extra costs and making price quotations   the extra costs of doing business in a foreign market must be taken into account if a profit is to be made. *Middlemen and transportation costs* need to be estimated. Distributors may demand different mark-ups and agents may require varying commission levels in different countries. The length of the distribution channel also needs to be understood, and the margins required at each level before a price to the consumer can be set. These can sometimes almost double the price in an overseas market compared to at home. Overseas transportation may incur the additional costs of insurance, packaging, and shipping. *Taxes and tariffs* also vary from country to country. Although there are moves to standardize the level of value added tax in the Single Market there are still wide variations. Denmark,

21.1   e-Marketing

Obstacles to Global Web Marketing

As early as 1995, Millipore Corporation in Bedford, Massachusetts, began to contemplate how to exploit the World Wide Web as a marketing tool. The company, which has annual sales of $600 million, makes filtration products for tasks such as purifying water for laboratories and detecting contaminants in the gases used to manufacture semiconductors. Customers in the US include firms such as Eli Lilly, Genetech, Intel and Motorola. The company has a similar list of 'blue chip' corporations in virtually every other developed national economy around the world. Given the global nature of the company's sales base, the Internet clearly offered an effective medium through which to both communicate information and support the customer purchase process.

The speed with which Millipore has been able to achieve its Internet ambitions has repeatedly been affected, however, by a series of unforeseen complications. One problem was how to integrate the firm's existing Oracle-based internal databases with the Internet system. Also some of the outside contractors brought into the project were unable to offer secure sites or had problems rapidly up-dating the price bulletins issued by Millipore. The biggest complication is that, similar to most multinational corporations, Millipore charges higher overseas prices in order to cover the additional costs of supporting the delivery of support services in countries outside of North America.

Once a website is established which has an on-line purchase facility, there is the risk that overseas customers will want to cut out the local in-market distributor, place orders electronically and demand price discounts. Having examined the potential dilemmas associated with intercountry pricing differentials, Millipore has decided to postpone the decision of offering an on-line ordering facility and for now, to restrict their website to providing information associated with supporting pre- and post-purchase service activities.

Based on: Cronin (1997)[65]

especially, is a high tax economy. A tariff is a fee charged when goods are brought into a country from another country. Although tariff barriers have fallen among the member states of Europe, they can still be formidable between other countries. Companies active in international business need to protect themselves against the costs of *exchange rate fluctuations*. Nestlé, for example, lost $1 million in six months due to adverse exchange rate moves.[66] Companies are increasingly asking that transactions be written in terms of the vendor company's national currency, and *forward hedging* (which effectively allow future payments to be settled at around the exchange rate in question when the deal was made) is commonly practised.

Care should be taken when *quoting a price* to an overseas customer. The contract may include such items as credit, who is responsible for the goods during transit, and who pays insurance and transportation charges (and from what point). As we have seen, the currency in which payment is made can have a dramatic effect on profitability. This must be spelled out. Finally, the quantity and quality of the goods must be defined. For example, the contract should specify whether a ton is a metric or an imperial ton. Quality standards to be used when evaluating shipments should be agreed so that future arguments regarding returned-as-defective products are minimized. The price charged, then, in a quotation can vary considerably depending on these factors.

Understanding the competition and customers as with any pricing decision these factors play a major role. The difference is that information is often more difficult to acquire for exporters because of the distances involved. When making pricing moves, companies need to be aware of the present *competitors' strategic degrees of freedom,* how much room they have to react, and the possibility of the price being used as a weapon by companies entering the market from a different industry. Where prices are high and barriers to entry are low, incumbent firms are especially vulnerable.

Companies also need to be wary of using **self-reference criteria** when evaluating overseas customer's perceptions. This occurs when an exporter assumes that the choice criteria that are important to his overseas customers are the same as those used by his domestic customers. The viewpoints of domestic and foreign consumers

to the same product can be very different. For example, a small Renault car is viewed as a luxury model in Spain, but utilitarian in Germany. This can affect the price position *vis-à-vis* competitors in overseas markets.

Using pricing tactics to undermine competitor actions four tactics can be used in the face of competitor activity:[67]

1 *Disguise price reductions*: rather than reduce advertised list price, which is visible to competitors and may lead to a downward price spiral, cuts should be communicated directly to customers via the salesforce or direct mail by such methods as changes in the terms of sale (training included), reduced service charges, or revised discount structures.

2 *Abolish printed lists*: quote price directly on a customer-by-customer basis. This creates uncertainty in the market as competitors are less confident of knowing what to quote against.

3 *Build barriers to price switching*: try to build up switching costs. For example, in the mobile phone market, the problems involved for users in changing numbers and acquiring a new handset limit switching between providers such as Vodafone and raise their price flexibility.

4 *Respond to competitor attacks decisively*: for example, an electrical components supplier who held market leadership was successfully attacked by a competitor on price. The situation was not helped by the leader's policy of strictly following a printed price list along with predictable discounts for large accounts. A major plank of the leader's response was to target the aggressor's largest account with massive discounts. Although the customers stayed loyal the aggressor understood the message and refrained from continuing their price attack.

International marketers need to understand how to use such pricing tactics in the face of increasingly fierce global competition.

Parallel importing a major consideration in international markets is the threat of parallel imports. These occur when importers buy products from distributors in one country and sell them in another to distributors who are not part of the manufacturer's normal distribution system. The motivation for this practice occurs when there are large price differences between countries, and the free movement of goods between member states means that it is likely to grow. Companies protect themselves by:

1 Lowering price differentials.

2 Offering non-transferable service/product packages.

3 Changing the packaging; for example, a beer producer by offering differently shaped bottles in various countries ensured that the required recyclability of the product was guaranteed only in the intended country of sale.[68]

Transfer pricing this is the price charged between profit centres (e.g. manufacturing company to foreign subsidiary) of a single company. Transfer prices are sometimes set to take advantage of lower taxation in some countries than others. For example, a low price is charged to a subsidiary in a low tax country and a high price in one where taxes are high. Similarly low transfer prices may be set for high tariff countries. Transfer prices should not be based solely on taxation and tariff considerations, however. For example, transfer pricing rules can cause subsidiaries to sell products at higher prices than the competition even though their true costs of manufacture are no different.

Countertrade not all transactions are concluded in cash; goods may be included as part of the asking price. Four major forms of countertrade are the following:

1 *Barter*: payment of goods with goods with no direct use of money; the vendor then has the problem of selling the goods that have been exchanged.

2 *Compensation deals*: payment using goods and cash. For example, General Motors sold $12 million worth of locomotives and diesel engines to former Yugoslavia and received $8 million in cash plus $4 million worth of cutting tools.[69]

3 *Counterpurchase*: the seller agrees to sell a product to a buyer and receives cash. The deal is dependent on the original seller buying goods from the original buyer for all or part of the original amount.

4 *Buy-backs*: these occur when the initial sale involves production plant, equipment or technology. Part or all of the initial sale is financed by selling back some of the final product. For example, Levi Strauss set up a jeans factory in Hungary that was financed by the supply of jeans back to the company.

A key issue in setting the countertrade 'price' is valuing the products received in exchange for the original goods and estimating the cost of selling-on the bartered goods. However, according to Shipley and Neale it forms 20–30 per cent of world trade with yearly value exceeding $100 billion.[70]

Place

A key international market decision is whether to use importers/distributors or the company's own personnel to distribute a product in a foreign market. Initial costs are often lower with the former method and so it is often used as an early method of market entry. For example, Sony and Panasonic entered the US market by using importers. As sales increased they entered into exclusive agreements with distributors, before handling their own distribution arrangements by selling directly to retailers.[71]

International marketers must not assume that overseas distribution systems resemble their own. As we have mentioned, Japan is renowned for its long, complex distribution channels; in Africa distribution bears little resemblance to that in more developed countries. An important consideration when evaluating a distribution channel is the power of its members. Selling directly to large powerful distributors such as supermarkets may seem attractive logistically but their ability to negotiate low prices needs to be taken into account.

Customer expectations are another factor bearing on the channel decision. For many years, in Spain yoghurt was sold through pharmacies (as a health product). As customers expected to buy yoghurt in pharmacies, suppliers had to use them as an outlet. Regulations also affect the choice of distribution channel. For example, over-the-counter pharmaceuticals are sold only in pharmacies in Belgium, France, Spain and Italy, whereas in Denmark, the UK and Germany other channels (notably grocery outlets) also sell them.

As with domestic marketing, the marketing mix in a foreign market needs to be blended into a consistent package that provides a clear position for the product in the marketplace. Furthermore, managers need to display high levels of commitment to their overseas activities as this has been shown to be a strong determinant of performance.[72]

Organizing for international operations

The starting-point for organizing for international marketing operations for many companies is the establishment of an export department. As sales, the number of international markets and the complexity of activities increase so the export department may be replaced by a more complex structure. Bartlett and Ghoshal describe four types of structure for managing a worldwide business enterprise: international, global, multinational and transnational organization.[73]

International organization

The philosophy of management is that overseas operations are appendages to a central domestic operation. Subsidiaries form a coordinated federation with many assets, resources, responsibilities and decisions decentralized but overall control is in the hands of headquarters. Formal management planning and control systems permit fairly tight headquarters–subsidiary links.

Global organization

The management philosophy is that overseas operations should be viewed as delivery pipelines to a unified global market. The key organizational unit is the centralized hub which controls most strategic assets, resources, responsibilities and decisions. The centre enforces tight operational control of decisions, resources and information.

Multinational organization

A multinational mentality is characterized by a regard for overseas operations as a portfolio of independent businesses. Many key assets, responsibilities and decisions are decentralized. Control is through informal headquarters–subsidiary relationships supported by simple financial controls.

Transnational organization

This organizational form may be described as a complex process of coordination and cooperation in an environment of shared decision-making. Organizational units are integrated with large flows of components, products, resources, people and information among interdependent units. The transnational organization attempts to respond to an environment that is characterized by strong simultaneous forces for both global integration and national responsiveness.[74]

Centralization v. decentralization

A key determinant of the way international operations are organized is the degree to which the environment calls for global integration (centralization) versus regional responsiveness (decentralization). *Centralization* reaps economies of scale and provides an integrated marketing profile to channel intermediaries who themselves may be international, and customers who are increasingly geographically mobile. Confusion over product formulations, advertising approaches, packaging design and labelling, and pricing is eliminated by a coordinated approach. (However, too much centralization can lead to the *not invented here syndrome* where managers in one country are slow to introduce products that have been successful in others, or fail to fully support advertising campaigns that have been conceived elsewhere.)

Decentralization maximizes customization of products to regional tastes and preferences. Since decentralized decision-making is closer to customers, speed of response to new opportunities is quicker than with a centralized organizational structure. Relationships with the trade and government are facilitated by local decision-making.

Many companies feel the pressure of both sets of forces, hence the development of the transnational corporation. European integration has led many companies to review their overseas operations with the objective of realizing global economies wherever possible. European centralized marketing teams carry the responsibility for looking at the longer-term strategic picture alongside national marketing staff who deal less with advertising theme development and brand positioning and more with handling retailer relationships.[75] The result is loss of responsibility and power for national marketing managers. This is a sensitive issue and many companies are experimenting with the right blend of centralization and national power.[76] Desire to preserve national identity and resentment of centralized European interference can run deep. One British company, owned by a German parent for more than a decade, still battled to preserve its national identity by holding its own formal board meetings and publishing its own separate annual report.[77] When Pampers was launched across Europe by Procter and Gamble, an employee found that 'as soon as it was known that I was from the European Technical Centre . . . my local support dried up'.[78] Marketing in Action 21.5 describes how some European companies have approached the task of moving towards a more global approach to their marketing operations.

Summary

In the face of severe global competition and untapped foreign markets, international marketing skills are at a premium. With saturated home markets that may be small and offer little prospects for growth, the need to find customers abroad, competitor and cost factors that demand a global presence, and the need to achieve portfolio balance, companies may seek new opportunities abroad.

Market selection depends upon economic, socio-cultural and political-legal influences (macroenvironmental factors) and market attractiveness and company capability profile issues (microenvironmental factors). After selecting a market a company must decide upon entry mode. Exporting can be indirect using independent agents or organizations in the exporter's domestic-based sales representatives or an overseas sales office. Some companies prefer licensing or joint ventures, both methods involving collaboration with another organization. Finally, direct investment involves setting up a wholly owned subsidiary either through acquisition of a foreign partner or by building new facilities.

A key issue in developing international marketing strategies is the degree of standardization or adaptation of the marketing mix. Standardization reaps cost economies, while adaptation tailors the mix more closely to customer requirements. Marketing managers need to identify target markets, and by understanding customer requirements develop an appropriate marketing mix. Adaptation should focus on significant differences in customer motivations, preferences, behaviour and price sensitivities rather than minor nuances.

Four types of structure for organizing international operations have been identified: international, global, multinational and transnational organization. A key influence on the way international operations are organized is the degree to which global integration (centralization) versus regional responsiveness (decentralization) is needed. Centralization reaps economies of scale, presents an integrated profile, reduces marketing mix confusion. A disadvantage is that regional managers may be demotivated by too central an approach to strategy and tactics. Decentralization permits customization to local requirements, promotes rapid response and facilitates the building of local relationships with the trade and government.

21.5   Marketing in Action

Managing the Process of Globalization

The fact that national marketing managers often lose responsibility and power in moves to a more centralized marketing approach means that simply preaching the virtues of globalization will not gain their commitment. Compelling business logic is unlikely to remove their opposition.

One approach to developing support is through the creation of *taskforces*. A business area is selected where the urgency of need is most clear, and where positive early results can begin a ripple effect, creating champions for change within the company. Procter and Gamble, for example, created a taskforce of national product managers to decide upon common brand requirements. A freight company, under intense pressure from international buying groups, set up a pricing taskforce to thrash out a coordinated European pricing strategy. One by-product of the taskforce approach is that it provides top management with a forum for identifying potential Euro-managers.

For some intransigent national managers, removing them from office may be the only effective solution. But there are less blatant methods. One approach is to put responsibility for planning prospective changes in the hands of the individual managers most threatened by them. For example, the roles of national marketing managers most threatened by them. For example, the roles of national marketing managers could be expanded to include responsibility for developing brands across Europe. Another way forward is to establish an accountability and compensation system for national marketing managers that reflects their new situation. When a centralized approach is needed, they are more willing to give up power in return for what makes them succeed.

To minimize conflict, some companies are trying to build tiered systems where the marketing decisions that are centrally determined and those that are subject to local control are clearly defined. For example, the brand positioning and advertising theme issues may be determined centrally but the creative interpretation of them is decided locally.

Whichever approach is used a system that shares insights, methods and best practices should be established. The system should provide a global mechanism to identify first-hand observations of best practices, communicate them to those who would benefit from them, and allow access to a store of best practices when required. To do this, companies need to nurture a culture where they are communicated. This can be helped by rewarding people who contribute. Tracking employees who post insights and best practices and rewarding them during annual performance reviews is one method. Regular meetings can also aid communication especially when they include workshops that engage the participants in action-orientated learning. Sometimes the sharing of information at these meetings is less important than the establishment of personal relationships that foster subsequent communications and interactions. Technological developments can also make communication easier and quicker such as the formation of Intranets that allow global communication of best practice, competitor actions and technological change. Of more lasting use, however, is the sending of teams to see best practice at first hand to allow the depth of understanding not usually achieved by descriptive accounts.

Based on: Blackwell et al. (1992);[79] Mazur (1993);[80] Aaker and Joachimsthaler (2000)[81]

Internet exercise

Global marketing

Sites to visit
http://www.thecoca-colacompany.com/

Exercise
Discuss how Coca Cola is using the web as part of its global marketing strategy.

Study questions

1 What are the factors that drive companies to enter international markets?

2 Joint ventures are a popular method of entering markets in Europe. Choose an example (many are given in this book) and research its background (and outcomes if any).

3 For a company of your choice research its reasons for expanding into new foreign markets, and describe the moves that have been made.

4 Using information in this chapter and Chapter 16 on distribution, describe how you would go about selecting and motivating overseas distributors.

5 Why are so many companies trying to standardize their global marketing mixes? With examples, show the limitations to this approach.

6 What are the factors that influence the choice of market entry strategy?

7 Select a familiar advertising campaign in your country, and examine the extent to which it is likely to need adaptation for another country of your choice.

8 Describe the problems of pricing in overseas markets and the skills required to price effectively in the global marketplace.

References

1. Cuyvers, L., P. de Pelsmacker, G. Rayp and I. T. M. Roozen (1995) A Decision Support Model for the Planning and Assessment of Export Promotion Activities by Government Export Promotion Institutions—the Belgian case, *International Journal of Research in Marketing*, **12**, 173-86.

2. Katsikeas, C. S., N. F. Piercy and C. Ioannidis (1996) Determinants of Export Performance in a European Context, *European Journal of Marketing*, **30** (6), 6-35.

3. Laurence, B. (1994) M&S Plans £1 Billion Investment, *Guardian*, 25 May, 14.

4. See Aharoni (1966) *The Foreign Investment Decision Process*, Boston, Mass: Harvard University Press; Aagarwal, S. and S. N. Ramaswami (1992) Choice of Foreign Market Entry Mode: Impact of Ownership, Location and Internalisation Factors, *Journal of International Business Studies*, spring, 1-27; and Knickerbocker, F. T. (1973) *Oligopolistic Reaction and Multinational Enterprise*, Boston, Mass: Harvard University Press.

5. Borrell, J. (1990) Living with Shock Therapy, *Time*, 11 June, 31.

6. Tully, S. (1990) Poland's Gamble Begins to Pay Off, *Fortune*, 27 August, 91-6.

7. Litvak, I. A. and P. M. Banting (1968) A Conceptual Framework for International Business Arrangements, in King, R. L. (ed.) *Marketing and the New Science of Planning*, Chicago: American Marketing Association, 460-7.

8. Johanson, J. and J.-E. Vahlne (1977) The Internationalisation Process of the Firm: A Model of Knowledge Development and Increasing Foreign Market Commitments, *Journal of International Business Studies*, **8** (1), 23-32.

9. Erramilli, M. K. (1991) Entry Mode Choice in Service Industries, *International Marketing Review*, **7** (5), 50-62.

10. Knickerbocker (1973) op. cit.

11. Whitelock, J. and D. Jobber (1994) The Impact of Competitor Environment on Initial Market Entry in a New, Non-Domestic Market, *Proceedings of the Marketing Education Group Conference*, Coleraine, July, 1008-17.

12. Halsall, M. (1994) Nova means 'does not go' in Spanish: Why British Firms Need to Learn the Language of Customers, *The Guardian*, 11 April, 16.

13. Egan, C. and P. McKiernan (1994) *Inside Fortress Europe: Strategies for the Single Market*, Wokingham: Addison-Wesley, 118.

14. Cateora, P. R., J. L. Graham and P. J. Ghauri (2000) *International Marketing*, London: McGraw-Hill, 377.

15. Young, S., J. Hamill, C. Wheeler and J. R. Davies (1989) *International Market Entry and Development*, Englewood Cliffs, NJ: Prentice-Hall.

16. West, A. (1987) *Marketing Overseas*, London: Pitman.

17. For a comprehensive coverage of the problem faced by exporters see Katsikeas, C. S. and R. E. Morgan (1994) Differences in Perceptions of Exporting Problems based on Firm Size and Export Market Experience, *European Journal of Marketing*, **28** (5), 17-35.

18. Young, Hamill, Wheeler and Davies (1989) op. cit.

19. Anonymous (1987) Twelve Most Common Mistakes of New-to-export Firms, *Business America*, 7 December, 14-15.

20. Welford, R. and K. Prescott (1996) *European Business*, London: Pitman.

21. Wright, R. W. (1981) Evolving International Business Arrangements, in Dhawan, K. C., H. Etemad and R. W. Wright (eds) *International Business: A Canadian Perspective*, Reading, MA: Addison Wesley.

22 Young, Hamill, Wheeler and Davies (1989) op. cit.

23. Terpstra, V. and R. Sarathy (1996) *International Marketing*, Fort Worth, Tex: Dryden.

24. Hooley, G., T. Cox, D. Shipley, J. Fahy, J. Beracs and K. Kolos (1996) Foreign Direct Investment in Hungary: Resource Acquisition and Domestic Competitive Advantage, *Journal of International Business Studies*, (4), 683-709.

25. Terpstra and Sarathy (1996) op. cit.

26. Smit, B. (1996), Dutch Bank Moves Deeper into the Mid West, *The European*, 28 November-4 December, 25.

• 27. Ghauri, P. N. and K. Holstius (1996) The Role of Matching in the Foreign Market Entry Process in the Baltic States, *European Journal of Marketing*, **30** (2), 75-88.

28. Buckley P. J., H. Mirza and J. R. Sparkes (1987) Foreign Direct Investment in Japan as a Means of Market Entry: The Case of European Firms, *Journal of Marketing Management*, **2** (3), 241-58.

29. Goodnow, J. D. and J. E. Hansz (1972) Environmental Determinants of Overseas Market Entry Strategies, *Journal of International Business Studies*, **3** (1), 33-50.

30. Contractor, F. J. (1984) Choosing between Direct Investment and Licensing: Theoretical Considerations and Empirical Tests, *Journal of International Business Studies*, **15** (3), 167-88.

31. Anderson, E. and A. T. Coughlan (1987) International Market Entry and Expansion via Independent or Integrated Channels of Distribution, *Journal of Marketing*, **51** (January) 71-82.

32. Klein, S. and J. R. Roth (1990) Determinants of Export Channel Structure: The Effects of Experience and Psychic Distance Reconsidered, *International Marketing Review*, **7** (5), 27-38.

33. See Agarwal and Ramaswami (1992) and Knickerbocker (1973) op. cit.

34. Sharma, D. D. (1988) Overseas Market Entry Strategy: The Technical Consultancy Firms, *Journal of Global Marketing*, **2** (2), 89-110.

35. Johanson and Vahlne (1977) op. cit.

36. Johanson, J. and J.-E. Vahlne (1990) The Mechanisms of Internationalisation, *International Marketing Review*, **7** (4), 11-24.

37. Buckley, Mirza and Sparkes (1987) op. cit.

38. Sharma (1988) op. cit.

39. Klein and Roth (1990) op. cit.

40. Erramilli (1991) op. cit.

41. Buckley, Mirza and Sparkes (1987) op. cit.

42. Quelch, J. A. and E. J. Hoff (1986) Customizing Global Marketing, *Harvard Business Review*, May-June, 59-68.

43. Banerjee, A. (1994) Transnational Advertising Development and Management: An Account Planning Approach and a Process Framework, *International Journal of Advertising*, **13**, 95–124.

44. Mayer, M. (1991) *Whatever Happened to Madison Avenue? Advertising in the '90's*, Boston, Mass: Little, Brown, 186–7.

45. Mitchell, A. (1993) Can Branding Take on Global Proportions? *Marketing*, 29 April, 20–1.

46. Chernatony, L. de (1993) Ten Hints for EC-wide Brands, *Marketing*, 11 February, 16.

47. De Chernatony, l. (1993) Ten Hints for EC-wide Brands, *Marketing*, 11 February, 16.

48. Aaker, D. A. and E. Joachimsthaler (2000) *Brand Leadership*, New York: Free Press, 303–9.

49. Dawkins, W. (1996) Time to Pull Back the Screen, *Financial Times*, 19 November, 14.

50. Dudley, J. W. (1989) *1992: Strategies for the Single Market*, London: Kogan Page.

51. Ohmae, K. (1985) *Triad Power*, New York: Free Press.

52. Mitchell (1993) op. cit.

53. Harris, P. and F. McDonald (1994) *European Business and Marketing: Strategic Issues*, London: Chapman.

54. Duncan, T. and J. Ramaprasad (1993) Ad Agency Views of Standardised Campaigns for Multinational Clients, *Conference of the American Academy of Advertising*, Chicago, IL, 17 April.

55. Papavassiliou, N. and V. Stathakopoulos (1997) Standardisation versus Adaptation of International Advertising Strategies: Towards a Framework, *European Journal of Marketing*, **31** (7), 504–27.

56. Killough, J. (1978) Improved Pay-offs from Transnational Advertising, *Harvard Business Review*, July–August, 58–70.

57. Alden, D. L., J.-B. E. M. Steenkamp and R. Batra (1998) Brand Positioning Through Advertising in Asia, North America, and Europe: The Role of Global Consumer Culture, *Journal of Marketing*, **63**, January, 75–87.

58. Richmond, S. (1994) Global Taboos, in World Advertising, *The Campaign Report*, 13 May, 19–21.

59. Cateora, P. R., J. L. Graham and P. N. Ghauri (2000) op. cit., 376.

60. Jobber, D. and G. Lancaster (2000) *Selling and Sales Management*, London: Pitman.

61. Campbell, N. C. G., J. L. Graham, A. Jolibert and H. G. Meissner (1988) Marketing Negotiations in France, Germany, the United Kingdom and the United States, *Journal of Marketing*, **52** (April), 49–62.

62. Niss, N. (1996) Country of Origin Marketing Over the Product Life Cycle: A Danish case study, *European Journal of Marketing*, **30** (3), 6–22.

63. See Powell, C. (2000) Why We Really Must Fly the Flag, *The Observer, Business Section*, 25 April 1999, 4 and Yip, G. (1994) *Total Global Strategy*, Englewood Cliffs, NJ: Prentice-Hall, 88.

64. Leszinski, R. (1992) Pricing for the Single Market, *McKinsey Quarterly*, **3**, 86–94.

65. Cronin, M. J. (1997) To Sell or Not to Sell on the World Wide Web, *Fortune*, 9 June, 144–6.

66. Cateora, P. R. (1998) *International Marketing*, Homewood, Ala: Irwin.

67. Garda, R. A. (1992) Tactical Pricing, *McKinsey Quarterly*, **3**, 75–85.

68. Leszinski (1992) op. cit.

69. Cateora (1998) op. cit.

70. Shipley, D. and B. Neale (1988) Countertrade: Reactive or Proactive, *Journal of Business Research*, June, 327–35.

71. Darlin, D. (1989) Myth and Marketing in Japan, *Wall Street Journal*, 6 April, B1.

72. Chadee, D. D. and J. Mattsson (1998) Do Service and Merchandise Exporters Behave and Perform Differently? *European Journal of Marketing*, **32** (9/10), 830–42.

73. Bartlett, C. and S. Ghoshal (1991) *Managing across Borders: The Transnational Solution*, Cambridge, Mass: Harvard Business School Press.

74. Ghoshal, S. and N. Nohria (1993) Horses for Courses: Organizational Forms of Multinational Corporations, *Sloan Management Review*, Winter, 23–35.

75. Mazur, L. (1993) Brands sans Frontières, *Observer*, 28 November, 8.

76. Ohbora, T., A. Parsons and H. Riesenbeck (1992) Alternative Routes to Global Marketing, *McKinsey Quarterly*, **3**, 52–74.

77. Blackwell, N., J.-P. Bizet, P. Child and D. Hensley (1992) Creating European Organisations that Work, *McKinsey Quarterly*, **2**, 31–43.

78. Bartlett, C. (1991) Procter and Gamble Europe, Cambridge, Mass: Harvard Business School Case, no. 9-384-139.

79. Blackwell, N., J.-P. Bizet, P. Child and D. Hensley (1992) Creating European Organisations that Work, *McKinsey Quarterly*, **2**, 31–43.

80. Mazur, L. (1993) Brands sans Frontières, *Observer*, 28 November, 8.

81. Aaker, D. A. and E. Joachimsthaler (2000) *Brand Leadership*, New York: Free Press, 310–14.

Key terms

macroenvironment   a number of broader forces that affect not only the company but the other actors in the environment, e.g. social, political, technological and economic

microenvironment   the actors in the firms immediate environment that affect its capability to operate effectively in its chosen markets, namely, suppliers, distributors, customers and competitors

indirect exporting   the use of independent organizations within the exporter's domestic market to facilitate export

direct exporting   the handling of exporting activities by the exporting organization rather than by a domestically-based independent organization

licensing   a contractual arrangement in which a licensor provides a licensee with certain rights, e.g. to technology access or production rights

franchising   a form of licensing where a package of services is offered by the franchisor to the franchisee in return for payment

contractual joint venture   two or more companies form a partnership but no joint enterprise with a separate identity is formed

equity joint venture   two or more companies form a partnership which involves the creation of a new company

direct investment   market entry which involves investment in foreign-based assembly or manufacturing facilities

standardized marketing mix   an international marketing strategy for using essentially the same product, promotion, distribution, and pricing in all the company's international markets

adapted marketing mix   an international marketing strategy for changing the marketing mix for each international target market

global consumer culture positioning   positioning a brand as a symbol of a given global culture (e.g. young cosmopolitan men)

foreign consumer culture positioning   positioning a brand as associated with a specific foreign culture (e.g. Italian fashion)

local consumer culture positioning   positioning a brand as associated with a local culture (e.g. local production and consumption of a good)

self-reference criteria   the use of one's own perceptions and choice criteria to judge what is important to consumers. In international markets, the perceptions and choice criteria of domestic consumers may be used to judge what is important to foreign consumers

parallel importing   when importers buy products from distributors in one country and sell them in another to distributors who are not part of the manufacturer's normal distribution; caused by big price differences for the same product between different countries

transfer pricing   the price charged between profit centres of the same company, sometimes used to take advantage of lower taxes in another country

countertrade   a method of exchange where not all transactions are concluded in cash; goods may be included as part of the asking piece

centralization   in international marketing it is the global integration of international operations

decentralization   in international marketing it is the delegation of international operations to individual countries or regions

Case 39 Eurocamp: Going International 1983–97

Introduction

Eurocamp is a tour operator specializing in self-drive camping and mobile home holidays in Europe. The company is the acknowledged market leader in its sector and has been operating for 25 years.

When the company started in 1975, the self-drive camping holiday was very much in its infancy. The principal player was the aptly named Canvas Holidays. Alan Goulding, a Cheshire-based entrepreneur, had seen the Canvas product while on holiday in France with his family. The product seemed to represent an exciting business opportunity and he was very much aware that others would have similar thoughts—indeed, by 1977 there were half a dozen UK-based operators.

Goulding started Eurocamp with the aim of developing a company more professional and more profitable than Canvas, to become, little by little, a new market leader.

In 1976, the company carried 4000 people to seven camp sites in France, principally in Brittany, a favourite for English holiday-makers. As the decade progressed, more destinations were added initially along the west coast of France, but subsequently on the Mediterranean and English Channel coasts as well. By the turn of the decade the company had introduced sites in inland France (Loire Valley and Dordogne) and in the first non-French destinations, the alpine regions of Germany and Switzerland.

Growth was rapid and by 1983 the company carried 45 000 people to 50 sites which now included Austria, Italy and Spain. It was a highly profitable organization with margins well above the travel industry average. Goulding was keen to realize his investment, and in 1981 he sold the company to Combined English Stores, a retail sector holding company which included high street names such as Harry Fenton, Collingwood Jewellers and Salisbury Handbags. Traditionally, its period of poorest cash flow was the period January to March, just when Eurocamp was bringing in substantial deposit income.

The time under CES ownership was a positive one which saw many new developments including international marketing and UK travel agency sales. Market share increased organically and through the acquisition of competitive companies, Sunsites and Carefree Camping. In 1988, CES was itself purchased, this time by Next, the high street retailer hungry for additional retail space. This was very much Next's calm before the storm and by 1989 it was massively divesting itself of subsidiaries in order to stay afloat. In that year, the four Eurocamp directors, backed by institutional investor money, purchased Eurocamp for £32 million in a classical management buyout.

Expansion continued and, in 1992, the company floated on the UK stock market and became Eurocamp plc. Despite some lean years in the mid-1990s, the company has maintained its undisputed position as market leader. It has acquired its biggest competitor, Keycamps, and also diversified through the purchase of UK short breaks market leader, Superbreak and adventure operator Explore Worldwide. In 1999, the holding company was renamed Holidaybreak plc. Today the group carries over 1 000 000 people, turns over £142 million and makes profits of £17 million.

The Eurocamp product

So what of the core product itself?

The self-drive camping and mobile home holiday is a classic lifestyle product. Customers drive themselves to nice holiday destinations. There is plenty of freedom, lots of choice and flexibility, lots for the children to do and a solid middle-class clientele to befriend.

A convenient way of describing the Eurocamp product is through the use of product attributes, benefits and marketing support services.

Product attributes

Accommodation Six-berth tents or eight-berth mobile homes. The former, equipped with beds, fridge, cooker, saucepans, crockery and cutlery, electric lights and a wide range of garden furniture. The latter, almost mini self-catering lodges, with bedrooms, shower, toilet, proper kitchen, etc. Bedlinen is not included, but the tent or mobile home is always cleaned and prepared prior to the customer's arrival.

Reception service Couriers speak a local language and the language(s) of the customer. Their principal role is that of cleaning, welcoming, informing and being on hand should any problems arise. Self-drive customers are by and large independent and do not have need of the traditional 'rep'.

Camp sites Not holiday camps but good-quality camp sites by the coast, inland, in the mountains, near historic towns. Facilities include pools, restaurants, activity areas and very clean washing facilities. Eurocamp does not own the sites but rents out areas on which to site its accommodation.

Travel service Principally for UK-based customers and includes full range of ferry, motor rail and Eurotunnel services and overnight stops. These are complemented by route plans, detailed travel information and local facility information.

Product benefits

The product benefits are both tangible and intangible. The product itself, accommodation and site, is of the highest quality. Choice of location, accommodation, start or finish dates and method of travel are all highly flexible. Great emphasis is placed on personal service, from the initial reservation to the return home questionnaire.

Marketing support services

Principal among these is the attention paid to children. '*If the children are happy, then so are the parents*' has always been important. Special Children's Couriers, facilities for very young children, baby packs, junior tents, children's travel packs are all provided.

Moving international

Eurocamp traditionally sold its holidays direct to the UK market. Through the first half of the 1980s, growth was very strong. The entrepreneurially focused management was not, however, one to bask in the comfort of recent success. By 1983, there was a recognition that new market opportunities needed to be researched, for a SWOT analysis at the time would have shown some potentially damaging weaknesses (see Fig. C39.1).

The company had one micromarket—UK/direct sell. The company had just one product. The period for taking Eurocamp holidays was highly skewed towards the school holidays: late May/late July–August.

For Eurocamp there were four potential courses of action which can be best illustrated through an Ansoff Matrix as shown in Fig. C39.2.

The most accessible course of action was to increase penetration of the UK market through the introduction of sales to travel agents. The company had purchased Inn Tent, a competitor with a presence in the agency sales market. This was developed and entry into a UK market sector achieved. Product development or diversification was considered only very briefly—the company had a long way to go with its core product and had little expertise elsewhere.

It was market development, however, that became the object of most activity. Eurocamp had always tried to innovate and its management were becoming increasingly aware of the many Dutch campers on its sites, increasing numbers of whom were approaching its couriers for information. The Dutch market was an obvious one to look at, its 'psychic' distance or market synergies/culture being very close to the UK.

A little desk research showed that the Dutch were great travellers to France, great campers and, highly significantly, their key summer school holidays were in July rather than August, which would result in an extension of Eurocamp's high season. So, the company decided to take a proper

Strengths
+ UK penetration
+ Market leadership
+ Reputation
+ Brand
+ Niche market
+ Cash
+ Profitability

Weaknesses
+ Seasonal holiday pattern
+ One market
+ One product

Opportunities
+ New markets
+ New camping markets
+ Poorly served family holiday market

Threats
+ More sophisticated competition
+ Product life cycle

Figure C39.1 SWOT analysis for Eurocamp

look at the Dutch market through a combination of talking to travel/advertising industry people and desk/qualitative research. The result was that a new market with quite some potential existed.

Holland 1994

A formal Dutch market agency agreement followed and Eurocamp Holland was up and running for the 1984 season. The company collaborated with a vice-president of advertising agency J. Walter Thompson, Amsterdam (JWT was Eurocamp's UK advertising agency), who was keen to leave his secure, highly paid but ultimately not satisfying job and develop a new, innovative travel business. The agent paid for all administration and office costs and Eurocamp paid for the product and marketing. The agent received an income based on holiday sales.

The key difference to other similar agency agreements was that the agent actually created and operated the marketing campaign while the 'parent' paid for it. Eurocamp UK had recruited a marketing rather than operational expert because it was very apparent that simply translating the UK marketing concept was hardly innovative or for the long term—especially when the product itself would be brand new. From an early stage, the new agent had identified not a camping market but rather a middle-class family market who would not normally see themselves as campers! In fact this market felt that camping was very much 'a poor man's holiday'. The marketing approach would be focused on projecting an image of quality time, freedom and enjoyment for both parents and children.

Distribution differed from the UK through a 50/50 direct sell/travel agency split—in Holland, the travel agency system was very important and offered the opportunity for rapid market penetration and pursuit of critical mass volume. Eurocamp's agent wanted exclusivity of distribution to match the new product's positioning. Accordingly, he chose to sell through just two chains of travel agencies, Holland International (the leading brand) and ANWB (the Dutch Automobile Association).

At the end of the 1984 season, 1500 bookings (families not individuals) had been made, 13.5 per cent of Eurocamp's total.

An early and welcome benefit to this new marketing activity was the Eurocamp name. Eurocamp's UK forerunner, *Canvas Holidays*, had chosen a very English name which would prove very difficult to translate when it decided to test international sales. '*Eurocamp*', however, met a number of classical criteria for successful branding, as applicable to international marketing as national marketing—it suggested benefits, was easy to pronounce, recognise and remember and was distinctive and meaningful.

	Present products/services	New products/services
Present markets	Market penetration ✦ Selling through travel agents	Product/service development ✦ Introduce a family focused winter holiday
New markets	Market development ✦ Selling through entirely new markets (international expansion)	Diversification ✦ Develop a completely new product

Figure C39.2 The four potential courses for Eurocamp

The Dutch market saw steady growth. The 'theme' approach was developed, direct sell techniques improved and a third and final agency distribution partner, RABO Bank, very strong in small rural towns and villages, recruited. By 1992, bookings had grown to over 18 000 or 26 per cent of Eurocamp's total. That was a peak and the proportion settled down at around 25 per cent through the mid-1990s.

Germany 1988

As the Dutch market grew, so arrived the competition. Eurocamp had taken the prudent decision to start and make a success of one international market. For Eurocamp UK management the time was right to stay ahead and look at another one. Germany appeared as the obvious next step. Serious approaches had been made by a number of German companies wishing to start a Eurocamp tour operation. German campers and caravanners were also to be seen in large numbers on many of Eurocamp's sites, especially those in more southerly and westerly locations.

Initial research found two potential joint partners, both with the necessary Eurocamp strengths—marketing and entrepreneurial drive. One agent was the managing director of the Dusseldorf office of a Swedish advertising agency. The other, marketing manager of Seiko in Germany. The agents undertook detailed qualitative and quantitative research and a market potential was established. The positive holiday-taking pattern in early May and July well complemented that of the UK and Holland.

In Germany, much of the Dutch 'model' was replicated. The agency agreement was similar as was the family focused positioning, with the slogan '*If the children are happy, the parents have time to relax*', aimed at higher income earners aged 25 to 45 with children. Both product and positioning were unique in Germany, especially as the market was, as originally in Holland, very much a non-camping one. Promotion was primarily direct sell and, due to the size of the country, focused on two key regions, Rheinland Westphalia and Bavaria.

1988 was a respectable first year and saw 1530 bookings (about the same as the first year in Holland) equating to 4.5 per cent of the total Eurocamp market (as compared to 13.5 per cent

in the first Dutch year, reflecting how Eurocamp as a whole had grown).

In subsequent years, while the core positioning remained much the same, the scope offered by Germany's huge population ensured that new markets could be developed 'simply' by promoting the Eurocamp brand within new regions. A new innovation, however, was the introduction of a dynamic sales promotion strategy. Eurocamp's agents identified the then growing IKEA chain as a perfect lifestyle partner. Eurocamp became IKEA's selected tour operator. Full page advertisements were taken in IKEA catalogues and brochure distribution/bookings outlets set up in many of IKEA's German stores. This was partnership rather than classical agency promotion.

Bookings grew dramatically in the early 1990s with 2015 bookings in 1989 rising to 14 378 in 1992. The percentage of Eurocamp's German business levelled out at around 22 per cent.

Other countries

As the Dutch and German markets grew, the individual agents realized that a homogeneous expansion policy '*expanding out of the nation state to countries with a similar culture/ language*' could be adopted. For Holland, the Flemish-speaking Belgian market was culturally a good fit, but far too small to warrant a standalone marketing operation. A sales promotion strategy through VTB, the Flemish motoring association, was launched using a customized Dutch brochure. PR was used to pull customers into VTB retail outlets. The Belgian market grew to account for some 15 per cent of total Dutch bookings.

In the German speaking market, Austria and Switzerland also exhibited a good cultural fit. Initial promotion was through IKEA stores, but a separate sales office was eventually set up in Switzerland to focus on developing an important September market. Between them, the two markets eventually accounted for around about 15 per cent of total German business.

Other markets were also tested. In 1992, Eurocamp developed a sales operation in Sweden, hoping to capitalize on its important June high season. However, difficulties in the Swedish economy and the distance from Sweden to Eurocamp camp sites resulted in an unsustainable level of business and the operation was discontinued in 1994. Coincidentally, a Danish sales operation was started in 1994 through an existing Danish tour operator, Larsen Rjeisen. Again, early summer high season business was important but much closer proximity to mainland Europe ensured a successful outcome.

Product adaptation

Customizing the marketing according to individual market was what attracted international consumers to the Eurocamp product. But the product itself also had to satisfy new requirements. While the core product was essentially standardized, elements were tailored, within reason, according to demand. On-site couriers were recruited who spoke Dutch and German as well as English. Travel documentation was specifically produced for each market. For Dutch customers, coffee filters, not really a priority for English customers, larger beds (the Dutch are taller than the English), and more sites in inland France were introduced. For German customers, site capacity was increased on Mediterranean islands and in Italy and Scandinavia.

International bookings growth

By 1997, overseas markets accounted for over 50 per cent of the total Eurocamp business and the initial UK high seasons of late May, late July and August had been extended to include early May, part June, all July and early September. Quite a success story and one that has not been replicated by other operators (Table C39.1).

This case was prepared by Julian Rawel, managing director, The Julian Rawel Consultancy Ltd.

Table C39.1	Eurocamp—international bookings growth				
	UK	Holland	Germany	Other	International total
1983	100	—	—	—	—
1984	87	13	—	—	13
1985	84	16	—	—	16
1986	79	21	—	—	21
1987	77	23	—	—	23
1988	72	24	4	—	28
1989	74	22	4	—	26
1990	64	23	13	—	36
1991	57	26	17	—	43
1992	54	26	17	2	46
1993	57	23	19	1	43
1994	56	21	20	3	44
1995	56	21	20	3	44
1996	46	25	24	5	54
1997	47	24	22	7	53
	Includes Ireland	Includes Belgium	Includes Austria/Switz.	Includes Denmark/Sweden	

Questions

1   There are many classical reasons for companies wishing to adopt an international approach. In the mid-1980s, which of these were applicable to Eurocamp and why?

2   Eurocamp used agents as its preferred method of market entry. What do you believe to be the advantages of this approach and could other options have been considered? Please note, agents in this question are not travel agents.

3   Could the Eurocamp concept be successfully sold to incoming long-haul tourists to Europe? Explain why or why not.

4   International marketing can frequently be a recipe for failure. What do you consider to be the principal reasons for Eurocamp's success?

Case 40 British Airways World Cargo

British Airways

British Airways is the world's biggest international airline, carrying more passengers from one country to another than any of its competitors. In 1999–2000, more than 41 million people chose to fly on the 538 000 flights that it operated. Some 30 million of those passengers flew internationally, representing around 1 in every 15 people flying from one country to another worldwide.

British Airways operates 321 aircraft, covering a worldwide route network of 233 destinations in 96 countries. The group employs more than 60 000 people in over 100 countries worldwide. London's Heathrow Airport (the world's largest international airport) and Gatwick Airport are the main operating bases. The company's spectacular, purpose-built headquarters are at Waterside, near Heathrow Airport.

British Airways' stated corporate mission is: '*To be the undisputed leader in world travel*'.

British Airways World Cargo

British Airways World Cargo (BAWC) is the fifth largest international cargo airline. In 1999–2000, the airline carried 897 000 tonnes of freight, mail and courier shipments across a global network spanning more than 160 destinations in over 80 countries, generating revenues of £556 million.

Cargo is a core business activity for British Airways, 90 per cent of all cargo is carried in the holds of passenger aircraft, supplemented with additional outsourced freighter capacity on key routes in Asia, the Americas, Africa and the Indian Sub Continent. The airline transports a wide variety of products, including fresh fruits, flowers and vegetables, pharmaceuticals, a vast range of high-tech products, spare parts for cars and ships, textiles and fashion goods, and even family pets relocating overseas with their owners. BAWC was also the largest carrier of Beaujolais Nouveau to markets all over the world in November 1999. The airline's freighter and passenger services carried more than 1800 tonnes of 1999 'Beaujo' to destinations in the USA, Japan and Australia.

Customers include freight forwarders such as BAX Global, Danzas AEI and Expeditors; integrators such as FedEx and DHL; and niche forwarders such as Jag Freight.

British Airways World Cargo's services aim to combine speed and flexibility with value for money. The organization has undertaken a five-year, £250 million-plus global change programme which is nearing completion. The programme has included investments in facilities, new technology and training. The aim is to make BAWC the first choice cargo airline for customers transporting goods anywhere in the world.

British Airways introduce a corporate service style

British Airways takes great pride in seeking to deliver the highest levels of innovative customer service. In January 2000, it unveiled £600 million worth of new customer services and products, to be introduced during the next two years. This is the biggest investment of its kind in airline history. It includes flat beds in the Club World long-haul business cabin, and a fourth cabin, World Traveller Plus, for full-fare Economy passengers on longhaul flights.

In further efforts to improve the quality of service delivery British Airways recently introduced a 'corporate service style'. Employees across the airline, both those in customer-facing roles and those in support functions, were encouraged to adopt this service style when interacting with customers and with their colleagues.

The development of the service style included qualitative research with BA passengers and staff in the UK and in key overseas markets. The research identified customer needs which BA's brand management team translated into 'service style standards' or attributes of the service style. Service style behaviours, or behaviour intended to support those service style attributes, were also defined.

Service style for British Airways World Cargo

Then in the spring of 2000 a project was carried out to consider whether British Airways service style could be adapted for British Airways World Cargo.

BAWC operates as an autonomous contribution centre within BA. All central functions are located at the World Cargo Centre in Heathrow and not at the airline's Waterside headquarters. The BAWC commercial and operational offices throughout the world are on the whole separate from British Airways' passenger operations.

Some important branding issues were raised. The British Airways' brand lends a significant amount of brand value to the BAWC brand. As a result, the BAWC brand character has traditionally mirrored that of British Airways. On an operational level, BAWC is dependent upon BA aircraft and flight crew to facilitate the delivery of its products and services.

On the other hand BAWC operates in a predominantly business-to-business market, and currently occupies a different position in that marketplace (a follower not a leader). The passenger side of British Airways is pursuing a strategy of product leadership, whereas BAWC is pursuing a strategy of operational excellence.

The project was to focus on formulating a service style for BAWC. It was identified that the service style needed to strike a balance between being appropriate to national cultures around the world and maintaining consistency across those cultures. The air cargo market in which BAWC operates is becoming increasingly global, and building a 'global brand' and ensuring its customers experience similar service regardless of where they are was viewed as vital to the organization.

The process of developing a service style for British Airways World Cargo

The initial question was whether BAWC should seek to adapt the existing British Airways service style, or create a completely new service style for BAWC. There was some debate. One argument was that an adaptation of the existing British Airways service style might be inappropriate, because the research for it was conducted in a passenger, rather than a cargo, context. Others argued that as the BAWC brand derives significant brand equity from the BA brand, it could be important that the BAWC service style mirrors that of BA. This

approach, it was argued, would encourage consistency of experience when customers interact with BA and BAWC. It was also pointed out that a number of key decision-makers within BAWC's customers are known to be frequent flyers with the airline. In the meantime British Airways had taken the decision that the whole of its organization would be embracing the new service style across all its operations and all the countries where it operates. On balance it was concluded that BAWC should now develop a service style by adapting the existing British Airways service style to reflect the differences between the passenger and cargo operations.

Questions were raised about the development of a specifies service style. Three approaches were considered:

1   A global set of service style standards and behaviours, developed centrally and consistently implemented across the world.

2   A global set of service style standards and behaviours, centrally developed and adapted to different national cultures.

3   A global set of service style standards and behaviours, centrally developed and locally adapted to different national cultures.

To explore these issues an extensive research exercise was carried out within British Airways and BAWC. A draft BA service style for BAWC was produced, and feedback obtained from overseas managers and BAWC service delivery teams. Proposals were evaluated in the light of a number of models taken from the management literature on culture and cultural differences.

The service style attributes, which emerged from the research, were:

Recognition
What does the customer experience?
I feel that BAWC people recognize me as an individual.

Customer focus
What does the customer experience?
When I am with BAWC people, I feel as though I am their number one priority.

Effective action
What does the customer experience?
BAWC people take accountability and deliver.

Being proactive
What does the customer experience?
BAWC people focus on what they can do, not what they can't.

Delivering on our promises
What does the customer experience?
BAWC people understand my requirements and deliver a solution of standard processes and services.

Teamwork
What does the customer experience?
I see BAWC people across the world work as a team to deliver for me.

The recommended approach was the third option; to articulate the BA service style for BAWC through the eyes of the customer and provide the local BAWC offices with a menu of behaviours intended to create that customer experience. The local offices could define how they will create that customer experience by selecting the behaviours appropriate to the national culture and agree 'their' service style with the BAWC Brand Management team in London. The objective was to maintain a consistency of brand throughout the world, while delivering a customer experience appropriate to the national culture.

Example of a BA service style for BAWC menu:

Recognition
What does the customer experience?
I feel that BAWC people recognize me as an individual.

How can you do it?
Approach customers who may require assistance.
Give immediate attention to approaching customers.
Acknowledge and greet each customer.
Be welcoming.
Introduce yourself by name.
Use the customer's name.
Smile.
Establish eye contact.
Maintain open body language.
Maintain a confident and friendly tone of voice.
Maintain a smart appearance—exceed the uniform standards.
Wear your name badge.
Be calm and in control.
Acknowledge all customer 'thank-yous'.
End each customer interaction with a pleasant close.
On farewell, ask if any further assistance is required.

What is it not?
Displaying low energy levels.
Not making eye contact.
Being uncertain about the task or the next steps.
Being aloof.
Being indifferent.
Having a lack of pride.

Customer focus
What does the customer experience?
When I'm with BAWC people, I feel as though I'm their number one priority.

How do you do it?
Show empathy.
Demonstrate respect.
Show care and consideration.
Listen to customers' needs and concerns.
Treat all customers' concerns and issues as a priority.
Maintain a presence at all customer facing points.
Maintain a welcoming and approachable posture.
Face the customer.
Have an optimistic attitude.
Keep personal items out of sight.
If still finishing a task from the last customer, do not ignore approaching customers; greet them and explain when you will be available.
Clarify your understanding of the problem or issue directly with the customer. On no account should a customer be expected to repeat themselves to one or your colleagues.
Ask all incoming calls if you can put them on hold until your current transaction is over (unless the call concerns the current transaction).
Politely ask all interruptions (including other customers) to kindly wait until your current transaction is over.

What is it not?
Leaving the customer contact point unmanned.
Having your back to the customer.
Hiding in the office!
Having newspapers or magazines on desks or counters.
Talking to colleagues while customers are present.
Ignoring customers.
Dismissing or invalidating customers' questions and concerns.

'I hear what you say but . . .'

Justifying your actions.

Picking an argument.

Not deliberately making the situation worse.

Interrupting the customer.

Using inappropriate language.

Believing that customers are an irritation or inconvenience.

This case was prepared by Eleanor Hamilton, Director of the Entrepreneurship Unit, Lancaster University Management School and Sion O'Connor, Brand Manager, British Airways World Cargo

Questions

1   Why would an organization like BAWC consider introducing a corporate service style?

2   What difficulties might be encountered implementing a common service style across a global organization spanning different cultures?

3   Evaluate the advantages and disadvantages of the approach finally recommended to BAWC.

Glossary

Above-the-line advertising advertising in the mass media, including press, radio, television, and posters

ACORN stands for A Classification of Residential Neighbourhoods, which is a system of UK geodemographic segmentation provided by the CACI company

Acquisition usually, the purchase of a company by another company

Adapted marketing mix an international marketing strategy for changing the marketing mix for each international target market

Ad-hoc research a research project which focuses on a specific problem collecting data at one point in time with one sample of respondents

Administered vertical marketing system a channel situation where a manufacturer who dominates a market through its size and strong brands may exercise considerable power over intermediaries even though they are independent

Advertising any paid form of non-personal communication of ideas or products in the prime media, i.e. television, the press, posters, cinema and radio, the internet and direct marketing

Advertising agency an organization which specializes in providing services such as media selection, creative work, production and campaign planning to clients

Advertising allowance money paid to a retailer by a manufacturer for featuring its brands in the retailer's advertising

Advertising clutter the confusion caused by the presence of many advertisers using the same media

Advertising message the use of words, symbols and illustrations to communicate to a target audience using prime media

Advertising platform the aspect of the seller's product that is most persuasive and relevant to the target consumer

Agent (1) generally, a representative of a company (2) an organization which acts for another usually in an intermediary role and paid on commission

AIDA awareness, interest, desire, action—the stages through which a consumer is believed to pass before purchasing a product

Ambush marketing originally referred to activities of companies who try to associate themselves with an event (e.g. the Olympics) without paying any fee to the event owner; now meaning the sponsoring of the television coverage of a major event, national teams and the support of individual sportspeople

ATR awareness, trial, reinforcement—the stages a consumer is said to pass through when buying a product in a low involvement situation

Attitude the degree to which a customer or prospect likes or dislikes a brand

Automatic vending machines retailing products in convenient locations 24 hours a day

Awareness set the set of brands that the consumer is aware may provide a solution to the problem

Banded pack offer a free sample of one brand banded to another

Barter payment for goods with goods with no direct use of money

Beliefs descriptive thoughts that a person holds about something

Below-the-line advertising point-of-purchase material, direct mail, exhibitions—i.e. non-mass-media advertising

Benefit segmentation   the grouping of people based upon the different benefits they seek from a product

Benefits   the advantages which customers seek from buying a particular brand or product

Bonus   an additional amount paid to e.g. a salesperson on top of salary and commission in recognition of exceptional performance

Bonus pack   giving a customer extra quantity at no additional cost

Brainstorming   the technique where a group of people generate ideas without initial evaluation. Only when the list of ideas is complete is each idea then evaluated

Brand   a distinctive product offering created by the use of a name, symbol, design, packaging, or some combination of these intended to differentiate it from its competitors

Brand assets   the distinctive features of a brand

Brand domain   the brand's target market

Brand extension   the use of an established brand name on a new brand within the same broad market

Brand equity   the good will associated with a brand name which adds tangible value to a company through the resulting higher sales and profits

Brand heritage   the background to the brand and its culture

Brand personality   the character of a brand described in terms of other entities such as people, animals and objects

Brand reflection   the relationship of the brand to self-identity

Brand stretching   the use of an established brand name for brands in unrelated markets

Brand values   the core values and characteristics of a brand

Branding   the process by which companies distinguish their offerings from the competition

Brands   the distinctive identity of a product

Break-even analysis   the calculation of the quantity needed to be sold to cover total costs

Breaking bulk   usually an activity performed by a wholesaler by buying in bulk and breaking the quantities down into smaller quantities for further distribution

Broadcast sponsorship   a form of sponsorship where a television or radio programme is the focus

Build   a strategy of managing a product for sales and share growth

Bundled prices   the pricing of a number of separable products as one package, usually effectively lowering the price

Business analysis   a review of the projected sales, costs and profits for a new product to establish whether these factors satisfy company objectives

Business format franchising   a franchising method whereby marketing approaches, quality control and operating procedures are offered to the franchisee

Business mission   the organization's purpose, usually setting out its competitive domain, which distinguishes the business from others of its type

Buy-back   where part of e.g. a sale of production plant is financed by buying back some of the final product

Buy class   a category of organizational purchase, generally of three kinds, namely, new task, straight re-buy or modified re-buy

Buy-response method   a study of the value customers place on a product by asking them if they would be willing to buy it at varying price levels

Buyer   those who have the authority to negotiate and execute the contractual arrangements

Buyer behaviour   the reasons why customers buy, their choice criteria, when, how and where they buy

Buying centre   a group who are involved in the buying decision (also known as a decision-making unit)

Buying signal   a statement by a buyer which indicates she is interested in buying

Buying situation   extended problem solving, limited problem solving and habitual solving

Bypass attack   circumventing the defender's position, usually through technological leapfrogging or diversification

Call frequency   the frequency with which a salesperson calls on a customer

Campaign   usually refers to a planned marketing or advertising activity designed to achieve certain commercial objectives

Campaign objectives   goals set by an organization in terms of e.g. sales, profits, customers won or retained or awareness creation

Cannibalization   a situation where a new brand gains sales at the expense of another of the company's brands

Cash cows   high-share products in low-growth markets

Catalogue marketing   the sale of products trough catalogues distributed to agents and customers, usually by mail or at stores

Catalogue stores   retail outlets promoting their products through catalogues which are either posted or are available in the store for customers to take home

Category killer   retail outlets with a narrow product focus but with an unusually wide breadth and depth to that product range, for example Toys 'Я' Us

Category management   the management of brands in a group, portfolio or category with specific emphasis on the retail trade's requirements

Cause-related marketing   the commercial activity by which businesses and charities or causes form a partnership with each other to market an image, good or service for mutual benefit

Centralization   in international marketing it is the global integration of international operations

Change master   a person who develops an implementation strategy to drive through organizational change

Channel integration   the way in which the players in the channel are linked together

Channel intermediaries   organizations which facilitate the distribution of products to customers

Channel of distribution   the means by which products are moved from the producer to the ultimate consumer

Channel strategy   the selection of the most effective distribution channel, the most appropriate level of distribution intensity and the degree of channel integration

Choice criteria   the various attributes (and benefits) people use when evaluating products and services

Classical conditioning   the process of using an established relationship between a stimulus and a response to cause the learning of the same response to a different stimulus

Coercive power   power inherent in the ability to punish

Cognitive dissonance   post-purchase concerns of a consumer arising from uncertainty as to whether a decision to purchase was the correct one

Cognitive learning   the learning of knowledge and development of beliefs and attitudes without direct reinforcement

Commission   a method of payment based on the achievement of sales results and usually expressed as a percentage of the value sold

Communications mix   advertising, personal selling, sales promotion and publicity, public relations and direct marketing

Compensation   a form of exchange where payment involves using both goods and cash

Competencies   the skills and resources which a company has

Competitive advantage   the attempt to achieve superior performance through differentiation to provide superior customer value or by managing to acheive lowest delivered cost

Competitive behaviour   the activities of rival companies with respect to each other. It can take five forms: conflict, competition, coexistence, cooperation and collusion

Competitive bidding   drawing up detailed specifications for a product and putting the contract out for tender

Competitive scope   the breadth of a company's competitive challenge, e.g. broad or narrow

Competitive strategy   the strategy a firm adopts in relation to the competition

Competitor analysis   an examination of the nature of actual and competitor analysis and their objectives and strategies

Competitor audit   a precise analysis of competitor strengths and weaknesses, objectives and strategies

Competitor targets   the organizations against which a company chooses to compete directly

Concept testing   testing new product ideas with potential customers

Concession analysis   the evaluation of things that can be offered to someone in negotiation valued from the viewpoint of the receiver

Concession close   an attempt to convince an indecisive buyer to close a deal by offering a concession, e.g. a discount

Consultative selling working with customers to discover their needs and work out an acceptable business solution

Consumer behaviour the reasons why customers buy, their choice criteria, when, how and where they buy

Consumer decision-making process the stages a consumer goes through when buying something, namely, problem awareness, information search, evaluation of alternatives, purchase and post-purchase evaluation

Consumer panel data a type of continuous research where information is provided by household consumers on their purchases over time

Consumer pull the targeting of consumers with communications (e.g. promotions) designed to create demand that will pull the product into the distribution chain

Continuous research repeated interviewing of the same sample of people

Contractual joint venture two or more companies form a partnership but no joint enterprise with a separate identity are formed

Contractual vertical marketing system a franchise arrangement (e.g. a franchise) tying producers and resellers together

Control the stage in the marketing planning process or cycle when the performance against plan is monitored so that corrective action, if necessary, can be taken

Convenience stores retail outlets offering customers the convenience of close location and long opening hours every day of the week

Core competencies the principal distinctive capabilities possessed by a company—what it is really good at

Core strategy the means of achieving marketing objectives, including target markets, competitor targets and competitive advantage

Corporate goals the overall objectives of an entire organization

Corporate identity the ethos, aims and values of an organization, presenting a sense of its individuality which helps to differentiate it from its competitors

Corporate plan a document which contains the strategy for the corporate entity usually for a one-year time horizon

Corporate vertical marketing system a channel situation where an organization gains control of distribution through ownership

Cost analysis the calculation of direct and fixed costs and their allocation to products, customers and/or distribution channels

Cost focus strategy with this strategy a firm seeks a cost advantage with one or a small number of segments

Cost leadership the achievement of the lowest cost position in an industry, serving many segments

Counteroffensive defence a counterattack that takes the form of a head-on counterattack, an attack on the attacker's cash cow or an encirclement of the attacker

Counterpurchase the seller agrees to sell a product to a buyer and receives cash, subject to the seller buying goods from the buyer for all or part of the original amount

Countertrade a method of exchange where not all transactions are concluded in cash; goods may be included as part of the asking piece

Country of origin the country in which a product is substantially manufactured

Covert power play the use of disguised forms of power tactics

Credit scoring a system used by financial service and mail order companies to help predict credit or loan default rates based on customer profiles

Credit terms the basis (usually the number of days delay in payment) on which goods are released to the customer before payment is received

Critical success factors those factors which an organization needs to control if it is to succeed

Cross-selling persuading an existing customer to buy another product from the company

Cultural distance the degree to which norms and values or working methods between two companies differ because of their separate national characteristics

Culture the traditions, taboos, values, and basic attitudes of the whole society in which an individual lives

Custom targeting treating each customer as a separate segment

Customer analysis a survey of who the customers are, what choice criteria they use, how they rate competitive offerings and on what variables they can be segmented

Customer benefits   those things that a customer values in a product. Customer benefits derive from product features

Customer database   a system which records details about the organization's customers

Customer satisfaction   the fulfilment of customers' requirements or needs

Customer satisfaction measurement   a process through which customer satisfaction criteria are set, customers are surveyed and the results interpreted in order to establish the level of customer satisfaction with the organization's product

Customer value   perceived benefits minus perceived sacrifice

Customized marketing   the market coverage strategy where a company decides to target individual customers and develops separate marketing mixes for each

Data   the most basic form of knowledge, the result of observations

Database marketing   an interactive approach to marketing which uses individually addressable marketing media and channels to provide information to a target audience, stimulate demand and stay close to customers

Data warehousing (or mining)   the storage and analysis of customer data gathered from their visits to websites for classificatory and modelling purposes so that products, promotions and price can be tailored to the specific needs of individual customers

Decentralization   in international marketing it is the delegation of international operations to individual countries or regions

Decider   a person who has the authority to select the supplier

Decision-making unit   a group of people within an organization who are involved in the buying decision (also known as the buying centre)

Decision-making process   the stages which organizations and people pass through when purchasing a physical product or service

Demographic variable   attributes of consumers such as age, gender and life cycle

Department stores   retail outlets where related product lines are sold in different departments

Depth interviews   the interviewing of consumers individually for perhaps one or two hours with the aim of understanding their attitudes, values, behaviour and/or beliefs

Derived demand   demand for a particular product which is driven by demand for a different product, e.g. the demand for joinery is at least partly derived from the demand for new housing

Descriptive research   research undertaken to describe customer's beliefs, attitudes, preferences, behaviour

Differential advantage   a clear performance differential over competition on factors that are important to target customers

Differentiated marketing   a market coverage strategy where a company decides to target several market segments and develops separate marketing mixes for each

Differentiated targeting   offering different products to different segments

Differentiation focus   where a firm aims to differentiate within one or a small number of targeted segments

Differentiation strategy   the selection of one or more customer choice criteria and positioning the offering accordingly to achieve superior customer value

Diffusion of innovation   the process by which a new product spreads throughout a market over time

Direct cost pricing   the calculation of only those costs which are likely to rise as output increases

Direct exporting   the handling of exporting activities by the exporting organization rather than by a domestically-based independent organization

Direct investment   market entry which involves investment in foreign-based assembly or manufacturing facilities

Direct mail   material sent through the postal service to the recipient's house or business address promoting a product and/or maintaining an ongoing relationship

Direct marketing   (1) acquiring and retaining customers without the use of an intermediary; (2) the distribution of products, information and promotional benefits to target consumers through interactive communication in a way which allows response to be measured

Direct response advertising   the use of the prime advertising media such as television, newspapers and magazines to elicit an order, enquiry or a request for a visit

Discount houses Retailers selling products at low prices by bulk buying, accepting low margins and selling high volumes

Discount policy the extent to which reductions from list prices is permitted

Discount structure the system of rebates off the list price

Display allowance money paid to a retailer by a manufacturer for promotional facilities in store

Distribution analysis an examination of movements in power bases, channel attractiveness, physical distribution and distribution behaviour

Distribution centres warehouses operating as central locations for the fast movement of goods

Distribution push the targeting of channel intermediaries with communications (e.g. promotions) to push the product into the distribution chain

Distributor an intermediary which takes title to goods and sells them on to a third party

Distributor brands brands created and owned by distributors or retailers

Diversification the development of new products for new markets

Divest to improve short-term cash yield by dropping or selling off the product

DMU see Decision-making unit

Dogs weak products in low-growth markets

DRTV direct response television, a method of direct marketing

Early adopters customers who are willing to buy a new product quite soon after launch

E-commerce the use of technologies such as the Internet, electronic data interchange, e-mail and electronic payment systems to streamline business transactions

E-commerce marketing mix the extension of the traditional marketing mix to include the opportunities afforded by the new electronic media such as the intranet

Economic order quantity the quantity of stock to be ordered where total costs are at the lowest

Economic value to the customer (EVC) the amount a customer would have to pay to make the total life cycle costs of a new and a reference product the same

EDI electronic data interchange, electronic links between suppliers and retailers allowing purchase orders, packing lists, delivery notices, invoices and remittance advices, as well as self-billing by retailers

Effectiveness doing the right thing, making the correct strategic choice.

Efficiency a way of managing business processes to a high standard, usually concerned with cost reduction; also called 'doing things right'

Ego drive the need to make a sale in a personal way, not merely for money

Electronic data interchange a pre-Internet technology which was developed to permit organizations to use linked computers to exchange information rapidly

Empathy to be able to feel as the buyer feels, to be able to understand customer problems and needs

Encirclement attack attacking the defender from all sides, i.e. every market segment is hit with every combination of product features

Enquirers people who have contacted the organization and shown interest in one or more products but, as yet, have not bought

Entry barriers barriers which act to prevent new firms from entering a market, e.g. the high level of investment required

Entry into new markets (diversification) the entry into new markets by new products

Environmental scanning the process of monitoring and analysing the marketing environment of a company

Equity joint venture two or more companies form a partnership which involves the creation of a new company

Ethics the moral principles and values that govern the actions and decisions of an individual or group

Event sponsorship sponsorship of a sporting or other event

Everyday low prices a retailers' policy of keeping prices low every day rather than through sales promotions

Evoked set the set of brands that the consumer seriously evaluates before making a purchase

Exaggerated promises barrier a barrier to the matching of expected and perceived service levels caused by the unwarranted building up of expectations by exaggerated promises

Exchange the act or process of receiving something from someone by giving something in return

Exclusive distribution an extreme form of selective distribution where only one wholesaler, retailer or industrial distributor is used in a geographical area to sell products of a supplier

Exhibition an event which brings buyers and sellers together in a commercial setting

Exit barrier the barriers to leaving an industry, e.g. the cost of closing down plant

Experience curve the combined effect of economies of scale and learning as cumulative output increases

Experimental research research undertaken in order to establish cause and effect

Experimentation the application of stimuli (e.g. two price levels) to different matched groups under controlled conditions for the purpose of measuring their effect on a variable (e.g. sales)

Expert power power which derives from an individual's expertise

Exploratory research the preliminary exploration of a research area prior to the main data collection stage

Export merchant an organization which takes title to products and sells them abroad

Extended problem-solving a high degree of information search, close examination of alternative solutions using many choice criteria

Facelift a minor product change with little or no change to the rest of the marketing mix or target market

Family brand name a brand name used for all products in a range

Features attributes of a product which may or may not confer a customer benefit

Fighter brands low-cost manufacturers' brands introduced to combat own-label brands

Flanking attack attacking geographical areas or market segments where the defender is poorly represented

Flanking defence the defence of a hitherto unprotected market segment

Focus group a group normally of 6–8 consumers brought together for a discussion focusing on an aspect of a company's marketing

Focused marketing a market coverage strategy where a company decides to target one market segment with a single marketing mix

Focused targeting Competing in one segment only (also known as niche targeting)

Folder techniques a press advertising pre-testing method in which proposed advertisements are placed in a folder of competing displays in order to test unaided recall

Foreign consumer culture positioning positioning a brand as associated with a specific foreign culture (e.g. Italian fashion)

Foreign direct investment (FDI) investment in a foreign-based assembly or manufacturing facility

FRAC stands for frequency, recency, amount and category and forms the transactional information on a customer's purchases in a direct marketing database

Franchise a legal contract in which a producer and channel intermediaries agree each other's rights and obligations. Usually the intermediary receives marketing, managerial, technical, and financial services in return for a fee

Franchising a form of licensing where a package of services is offered by the franchisor to the franchisee in return for payment

Freephone a special telephone number which customers can call without incurring any expense

Frontal attack a competitive strategy where the challenger takes on the defender head-on

Full cost pricing pricing so as to include all costs and based on certain sales volume assumptions

Full-service marketing departments departments which show a high degree of integration of marketing functions, control or influence all marketing decisions

Gatekeeper those who control the flow of information, e.g. secretaries who may allow or prevent access to a DMU member, or a buyer whose agreement must be sought before a supplier can contact other members of the DMU

Generic competitors products which solve a customer's problem or eliminate it in a dissimilar way

Geodemographic segmentation the segmentation of consumers on the combined basis of location and certain demographic and socio-economic data

Geodemographics the process of grouping households into geographic clusters based upon such information as type of accommodation, occupation, number and age of children and ethnic background

Global branding achievement of brand penetration worldwide

Global consumer culture positioning positioning a brand as a symbol of a given global culture (e.g. young cosmopolitan men)

Going-rate pricing pricing at the rate generally applicable in the market, focusing on competitors' offerings rather than on company costs

Group discussion a group usually of 6–8 consumers brought together for a discussion focusing on an aspect of a company's marketing

Guarantee a promise by a manufacturer that if a product fails within a certain period it will make good the defect for free under certain conditions

Guerrilla attack making life uncomfortable for stronger rivals through e.g. unpredictable price discounts, sale promotions, or heavy advertising in a few selected regions

Habitual problem solving a consumer purchase which involves a repeat buy with little or no evaluation of alternatives

Hall tests bringing a sample of target consumers to a room that has been hired so that alternative marketing ideas (e.g. promotions) can be tested

Halo customers customers who are not directly targeted but may find the product attractive

Harvest objective the improvement of profit margins to improve cash flow even if the longer term result is falling sales

High-involvement purchase purchase decisions in which the customer becomes highly involved and seeks detailed information

Hold objectives a strategy of defending a product in order to maintain market share

House list a company's list of its own customers

Image repositioning keeping product and target market the same, but changing the image of the product

Implementation the stage of the marketing planning process when the plan is put into operation

Impulse purchasing a consumer's decision to buy which is taken on the spur of the moment

Inadequate delivery barrier a barrier to the matching of expected and perceived service levels caused by the failure of the service provider to select, train and reward staff adequately, resulting in poor or inconsistent delivery of service

Inadequate resources barrier a barrier to the matching of expected and perceived service levels caused by the unwillingness of service providers to provide the necessary resources

Indirect exporting the use of independent organizations within the exporter's domestic market to facilitate export

Individual brand name a brand name which does not identify a brand with a particular company

Industrial market companies which purchase inputs for further processing or their own use

Industry a group of companies that market products which are close substitutes for each other

Information Combinations of data which provide decision-relevant knowledge

Information framing the way in which information is presented to people

Information processing the process by which a stimulus is received, interpreted, stored in memory and later retrieved

Information search the identification of alternative ways of problem solving

Innovation the commercialization of an invention by bringing it to market

Innovators the first customers willing to buy a new product after launch

In-or-on-pack gifts gifts which are given away free with brands

Inseparability a characteristic of services, namely that their production cannot be separated from their consumption

Inside order-taker usually a retail sales assistant whose task is simply to take payment and hand over the products

In-supplier a competitor who is already supplying to a target account and therefore has the 'inside track'

Intangible repositioning targeting a different market segment with the same product

Intangibility a characteristic of services, namely that they cannot be touched, seen, tasted or smelled

Integrated marketing communications
the concept that companies co-ordinate their
marketing communications tools to deliver a
clear, consistent, credible, and competitive
message about the organization and its
products

Intensive distribution the aim is to provide
saturation coverage of the market by using all
available outlets

Interaction approach an approach to
buyer–seller relations which treats the
relationships as taking place between two
active parties

Intermediaries distributors or resellers

Internal marketing (i) the training,
motivating and retention of employees at
the customer interface in services (ii)
marketing to all employees with the aim of
acheiving successful marketing
implementation

Internet a vast global computer network that
permits instant global communication such as
the gathering and sharing of information and
the ability of users to communicate with each
other

Internet and on-line marketing the
distribution of products, information and
promotional benefits to consumers through
electronic media

In-the-mail offer a promotion involving the
collection of packet tops, labels or ring-pulls
which are sent in the mail as proof of
purchase to claim a free gift or money
voucher

Invention the discovery of new methods and
ideas

Joint venture co-operation by two or more
parties on a business project, which may or
may not involve the creation of a separate
company

Journey routing the planning of a
salesperson's route when calling on prospects
or customers

Junk mail mail which is sent to a prospect
who is not a suitable target

JIT the just-in-time (JIT) concept aims to
minimize stocks by organizing a supply
system which provides materials and
components as they are required

Key account management an approach
to selling which focuses resources on
major customers and uses a team selling
approach

Ladder of support the spectrum of the
degree of support which can be expected
when introducing change

Laggards those who are the last to buy a new
product

Lead time the time gap between one event
and another

Legitimate power power based on legitimate
authority, such as line management

Licensing a contractual arrangement in which
a licensor provides a licensee with certain
rights, e.g. to technology access or production
rights

Life cycle the stage people have reached in
their life, from single at home through young
parents to solitary retired

Life cycle costs all the components of costs
associated with buying, owning and using a
physical product or service

Lifestyle the pattern of living as expressed in a
person's activities, interests and opinions

Lifestyle segmentation the grouping of
people according to their pattern of living as
expressed in their activities, interests and
opinions

Lifetime value the lifetime value of a
customer is the profit made on a customer's
purchases over the customer's lifetime

Limited problem solving information search
which may be mainly internal through
memory

List broker an organization which acts as an
intermediary in the supply of lists of names
and addresses for direct mail purposes

List owner an organization which own a list
of customers or prospects

List price the price quoted by a company
before any discounts

Local consumer culture positioning
positioning a brand as associated with a local
culture (e.g. local production and
consumption of a good)

Location gap the geographic separation of
producers from the customers they serve

Low involvement purchase a purchase
decision in which the customer does not
become highly involved and does not seek
detailed information

Loyalty card usually a plastic card which is
issued by a company to a customer and is
used to record the frequency of the
customer's purchases and calculate resulting
discounts, rewards or allowances

Loyalty scheme an arrangement whereby customers apply for a loyalty card which entitles them to discounts for continued purchases

Macroenvironment a number of broader forces that affect not only the company but the other actors in the environment, e.g. social, political, technological and economic

Macrosegmentation the segmentation of organizational markets by size, industry and location

Mail order catalogue usually a colour catalogue featuring products and prices sent through the mail and from which customers can select and order

Mail order a non-store form of retailing using catalogues or other media as a promotional vehicle

Manufacturer brands brands which are created by producers and bear their chosen brand name

Marginal cost pricing the calculation of only those costs which are likely to rise/fall as output increases/decreases

Market the people who represent the actual or potential demand for a product

Market development to take current products and sell them in new markets

Market expansion the attempt to increase the size of a market by converting non-users to users of the product and by increasing usage rates

Market intelligence information on present and future customer needs

Market penetration to continue to sell an existing product in an existing market

Market segmentation the process of identifying individuals or organizations with similar characteristics that have significant implications for the determination of marketing strategy

Market share analysis a comparison of company sales with total sales of the product, including sales of competitors

Market testing the limited launch of a new product to test sales potential

Marketing audit a systematic examination of a business's marketing environment, objectives, strategies, and activities with a view to identifying key strategic issues, problem areas and opportunities

Marketing concept the achievement of corporate goals through meeting and exceeding customer needs better than the competition

Marketing control the stage in the marketing planning process or cycle when performance against plan is monitored so that corrective action, if necessary, can be taken

Marketing environment the actors and forces that affect a company's capability to operate effectively in providing products and services to its customers

Marketing information system a system in which marketing information is formally gathered, stored, analysed, and distributed to managers in accord with their informational needs on a regular, planned basis

Marketing mix a framework for the tactical management of the customer relationship, including product, place, price, promotion (4Ps). In the case of services three other elements to be taken into account are: process, people and physical evidence.

Marketing objectives there are two types of marketing objectives—strategic thrust, which dictates which products should be sold in which markets, and strategic objectives, i.e. product-level objectives, such as build, hold, harvest and divest

Market-oriented pricing an approach to pricing which takes a range of marketing factors into account when setting prices

Marketing orientation companies with a marketing orientation focus on customer needs as the primary drivers of organizational performance.

Marketing planning the process by which businesses analyse the environment and their capabilities, decide upon courses of marketing action and implement those decisions

Marketing research the gathering of data and information on the market

Marketing strategy the approach a firm takes to securing and retaining profitable relationships with its customers, generally involving segmentation, targeting and positioning choices as well as adaptation of a suitable marketing mix

Marketing structures the marketing frameworks (organization, training and internal communications) upon which marketing activities are based

Marketing systems sets of connected parts (information, planning and control) which support the marketing function

Media class decision the choice of prime media, i.e. the press, cinema, television, posters, radio, or some combination of these

Media coverage mention of a particular event, product or organization in the media

Media relations communications about a product or organization by placing news about it in the media without paying for the time or space directly

Media vehicle decision the choice of the particular newspaper, magazine, television spot, poster site, etc.

Mega-marketing lobbying political power and public opinion

Member-get-member a programme of customer recruitment incentivizing existing customers or members to recruit others

Merger the amalgamation of two or more organizations

Microenvironment the actors in the firm's immediate environment that affect its capability to operate effectively in its chosen markets, namely, suppliers, distributors, customers and competitors

Microsegmentation segmentation according to choice criteria, DMU structure, decision-making process, buy class, purchasing structure and organizational innovativeness

Misconceptions barrier a failure by marketers to understand what customers really value about their service

Missionary salespeople order-creators whose task is not to close the sales but to persuade the customer, e.g. a medical practitioner, to specify the seller's products

Mobile defence involves diversification or broadening the market by redefining the business

Modified re-buy where a regular requirement for the type of product exists and the buying alternatives are known but sufficient (e.g. a delivery problem) has occurred to require some alteration to the normal supply procedure

Moments of truth staff-customer contacts

Money-back guarantee a promise by a retailer or manufacturer that if a customer is not happy with the purchase he or she may return the product in good condition and get a full refund

Money-off a sales promotion that discounts the normal price

Motivation the process involving needs that set drives in motion to accomplish goals

Nano-relationships relations between internal customers, internal markets, divisions and business areas within organizations

National account large and important customers who may have centralized purchasing departments that buy or co-ordinate buying for decentralized, geographically dispersed business units

New business salespeople salespersons whose task is to win new business by identifying and selling to prospects

New task refers to the first time purchase of a product or input by an organization

Niche objective targeting a small market segment

Niche targeting competing in one segment (niche) only

No-frills products basic commodities such as bread, sugar and soft drinks sold in rudimentary packages at low prices

Non-profit organization an organization which attempts to achieve an objective other than profit, for example relief of famine, animal rights, or public service

Omnibus survey a regular survey usually operated by a market research specialist company which asks questions of respondents

Operant conditioning the use of rewards to generate reinforcement of response

Opportunity a situation favourable to the achievement of the organization's objectives, usually characterized by unfulfilled customer demand, the organization being in a position to meet that demand and the relative weakness or total absence of competition.

Opportunity cost that which is foregone in the pursuit of a given strategy

Order point the level of inventory at which re-ordering is advisable to avoid stock-outs caused by the lead-time to resupply

Order-creators salespeople who do not receive orders directly as they talk to specifiers rather than buyers

Order-getters salespeople who attempt customers to place an order directly

Order-takers salespeople who respond to already committed customers

Organizational salespeople salespersons whose role is to maintain close long-term relationships with organizational customers, often involved in team selling

Overt power play   the use of visible, open kinds of power tactics

Own label   retailer's own brand

Own-label brands   brands created and owned by distributors or retailers

4 Ps   product, place, price, promotion

7 Ps   product, place, price, promotion, process, people, physical evidence

Parallel importing   when importers buy products from distributors in one country and sell them in another to distributors who are not part of the manufacturer's normal distribution; caused by big price differences for the same product between different countries

Parent company   a company which owns another

Penetration strategy   a low-priced new product launch designed to achieve maximum market share

Perception   the process by which people select, organize and interpret sensory stimulation into a meaningful picture of the world

Perceptual mapping   a useful tool for determining the position of a brand as seen by customers

Perishability   a characteristic of services, namely that the capacity of a service business, such as a hotel room, cannot be stored—if it is not occupied, that is lost income which cannot be recovered

Personal selling   oral communication with prospective purchasers with the intention of making a sale

Personality   the inner psychological characteristics of individuals that lead to consistent responses to their environment

Physical distribution   a set of activities concerned with the physical flows of materials, components and finished goods from producer to channel intermediaries and consumers

Physical evidence   that part of the services marketing mix which refers to the environment in which the service is delivered and tangible goods which facilitate the communication and performance of the service

PIMS   Profit Impact of Marketing Strategy

Place   the distribution channels to be used, outlet locations, methods of transportation

Portfolio planning   managing groups of brands and product lines

Position defence   building a fortification around existing products, usually through keen pricing and improved promotion

Positioning   the choice of target market (where the company wishes to compete) and differential advantage (how the company wishes to compete)

Positioning chart   a useful tool for determining the position of a brand as seen by customers (also known as a perceptual map)

Post-testing   the evaluation of the effectiveness after a campaign

Pre-emptive defence   usually involves continuous innovation and new product development recognising that the best form of defence is attack

Premiums   any merchandise offered free or at low cost as an incentive to purchase

Press relations   communications about a product or organization by placing news about it in the press without paying for the time or space directly

Pre-testing   the testing of advertisements before screening

Price   (1) the amount of money paid for a product; (2) the agreed value placed on the exchange by a buyer and seller

Price unbundling   pricing each element in the offering so that the price of the total product package is raised

Price waterfall   the difference between list price and realized or transaction price

Private label   retailer's own brand

Problem children   Low share products in high growth markets

Process   procedure, flow of activities, sequence of tasks

Product   a good or service offered or performed by an organization or individual which is capable of satisfying customer needs

Product champion   an individual who takes on or is given responsibility to promote a particular product or project within an organization and bring it to a successful conclusion

Product churning   a continuous spiral of new product introductions

Product development   increasing sales by improving present products or developing new products for current markets

Product differentiation the process of making a product distinctive along a factor or set of factors important for customer choice

Product features the characteristics of a product that may or may not convey a customer benefit

Product form competitors technically similar competing products

Product life cycle a four-stage cycle in the life of a product illustrated as a curve representing the demand, the four stages being introduction, growth, maturity and decline

Product line a group of brands which are closely related in terms of the functions and benefits they provide

Product line pricing taking account of the prices of the existing products when introducing a new product

Product manager the person responsible for co-ordination of functional areas to support the success of the product

Product mix the total set of products marketed by the company

Product portfolio the total range of products offered by the company, cf. Product mix

Product positioning the creation of a unique image of the company's product in the minds of the customer

Product repositioning modification of the product to make it more acceptable to its present market

Product substitutes products which customers regard as fulfilling the same needs although they are technically dissimilar

Product type products can be classified into four main types, namely, materials, components, plant & equipment and maintenance/repair/operation (MRO)

Production orientation a business approach that is inwardly focused either on costs or on a definition of a company in terms of its production facilities

Profile segmentation the grouping of people in terms of profile variables such as age and socio-economic group so that marketers can communicate to them

Profitability analysis the calculation of sales revenues and costs for the purpose of calculating the profit performance of products, customers and/or distribution channels

Project teams the bringing together of staff from such areas as R&D, engineering, manufacturing, finance, and marketing to work on a project such as new-product development

Promotional mix advertising, personal selling, sales promotions, public relations and direct marketing

Proposal analysis the prediction and evaluation of proposals and demands likely to be made by someone with whom one is negotiating

Prospect An individual or organization who is a possible buyer of a product

Prospecting searching for and calling upon potential customers

Psychographic segmentation the grouping people according to their lifestyle and personality characteristics

Public relations the management of communications and relationships to establish goodwill and mutual understanding between an organization and its public

Publicity communication about a product or organization by placing news about it in the media without paying for the time or space directly

Pull strategy Direct communication by manufacturers or service providers with consumers to draw them into channel intermediaries, usually using advertising and consumer promotions

Push strategy an attempt to sell into channel intermediaries using personal selling and sales promotions

Qualitative research exploratory research which aims to understand consumers' attitudes, values, behaviour and beliefs

Reasoning a more complex form of cognitive learning where conclusions are reached by connected thought

Reference group a group of people that influences an individual's attitude or behaviour

Referent power power derived by the reference source, e.g. when people identify with and respect the architect of change

Referrals people who have been recommended to the organization as potential customers

Relationship marketing the process of creating, maintaining and enhancing strong relationships with customers and other stakeholders

Remerchandising a modification of name, promotion, price, packaging and/or distribution while maintaining the basic product

Repositioning Changing the target market or differential advantage or both

Research brief written document stating the client's requirements

Research proposal a document defining what the marketing research agency promises to do for its client and how much it will cost

Reseller market organizations which buy products to resell, e.g. mail order companies and supermarkets

Respondent a person who answers questions in a marketing research exercise

Retail accordion a theory of retail evolution which focuses on the cycle of retailers widening and then contracting product ranges

Retail audit a type of continuous research tracking the sales of products through retail outlets

Retail life cycle a theory of retailing evolution which is based on the product life cycle stating that new types of retailing pass through birth, growth, maturity and decline

Retail positioning the choice of target market and differential advantage for a retail outlet

Retailing the activity involved in selling products to the ultimate consumer

Reverse marketing the process whereby the buyer attempts to persuade the supplier to provide exactly what the organization wants

Reward power power derived from the ability to provide benefits

Rote learning the learning of two or more concepts without conditioning

Safety (buffer) stocks stocks or inventory held to cover against uncertainty about re-supply lead-times

Sales analysis a comparison of actual with target sales

Salesforce evaluation the measurement of salesperson performance so that strengths and weaknesses can be identified

Salesforce motivation the motivation of salespeople by the process involving needs that set encouraging drives in motion to accomplish goals

Sales lead information on a potential purchaser

Sales promotion incentives to customers or the trade that are designed to stimulate purchase

Sampling process a term used in research to denote the selection of a sub-set of the total population in order to interview them

Satellite conferencing conferences by satellite transmitting of messages from one location to many sites

Secondary research data which has already been collected by another researcher for another pupose

Segment a group of customers or potential customers who share certain common characteristics

Segmentation (1) the identification of groups of individuals or organizations with characteristics in common that have significant implications for the development of marketing strategy; (2) the process of dividing the total market into homogeneous groupings or segments

Selective attention the process by which people screen out those stimuli that are not meaningful to them nor consistent with their experiences and beliefs

Selective distortion the distortion of information received by people according to their existing beliefs and attitudes

Selective distribution the use of a limited number of outlets in a geographical area to sell products of a supplier

Selective retention the process by which people only retain a selection of messages in memory

Self-liquidating offer an offer where consumers are asked to pay to cover the promoter's costs of the promotional merchandise plus administration and postal charges

Self-reference criteria the use of one's own perceptions and choice criteria to judge what is important to consumers. In international markets, the perceptions and choice criteria of domestic consumers may be used to judge what is important to foreign consumers

Sensitivity analysis the running of alternative scenarios with changed input variables (price, cost, consumer acceptance) to see the impact on sales and profits

Service any deed, performance or effort carried out for the customer

Services marketing mix product, place, price, promotion, people, process and physical evidence

Simultaneous engineering the involvement of manufacturing and product development engineers in the same development team in an effort to reduce development time

Skimming strategy a high-priced new product launch designed to recover research and development expenditure

Skunkworks a new product development team separated from other employees to work on a project free from bureaucratic interference

Social distance the extent to which both the individuals and organizations in a relationship are unfamiliar with each other's way of working

Social responsibility the ethical principle that a person or an organization should be accountable for how its acts might affect the physical environment and general public

Socialization within an organization, a process whereby a new entrant experiences the culture and tasks of the organization

Speciality shops retail outlets specializing in a narrow product line

Specifier an individual in an organization who is responsible for determining the specification of a product which is to be bought

Sponsorship A business relationship between a provider of funds, resources or services and an individual, event, or organization which offers in return some rights and association that may be used for commercial advantage

Stakeholders individuals or groups having a stake in the organization's well-being, e.g. shareholders, employees

Standardized marketing mix an international marketing strategy for using essentially the same product, promotion, distribution, and pricing in all the company's international markets

Stars market leading products in high-growth markets

Storage warehouse warehouses which store goods for moderate or long time periods

Straight re-buy refers to a purchase by an organization from a previously approved supplier of a previously purchased item

Strategic alliance collaboration between two or more organizations through e.g. joint ventures, licensing agreements, long-term purchasing and supply arrangement

Strategic business unit a business or company division serving a distinct group of customers and with a distinct set of competitors, usually strategically autonomous.

Strategic degrees of freedom how much room a company has to react

Strategic focus the strategies which can be employed to achieve the objective

Strategic intent a driven focused objective of winning such as encircle Caterpillar (Komatsu) or beat Xerox (Canon)

Strategic issue analysis an examination of the suitability of marketing objectives and segmentation bases in the light of changes in the marketplace

Strategic objectives product level objectives relating to the decision to build, hold, harvest, or divest products

Strategic options ways of increasing sales volume and/or profitability

Strategic profile a summary of the organization's chosen strategy, including strategic objective, core strategy, market type, marketing attitudes and performance

Strategic thrust the decision concerning which products to sell in which markets

Strategic withdrawal Holding on to the company's strengths while getting rid of the weaknesses

Strong theory of advertising the notion that advertising can change people's attitudes sufficiently to persuade people who have not previously bought a brand to buy it. Desire and conviction precede purchase

Subsidiary a company which is owned by another

Supermarket large self-service stores traditionally selling food, drinks and toiletries, but now increasingly selling a wider range of items, including clothing, books, pharmaceuticals

Supply chain the means by which products are moved from the producer to the ultimate consumer

Switching costs the costs to a buying organization of changing from one supplier to another

SWOT analysis a structured approach to evaluating the strategic position of a business by identifying its strengths, weaknesses, opportunities and threats

Synergy   when the power of the whole is greater than the sum of the parts

Tangible repositioning   when the target market and product are changed

Target accounts   organizations or individuals whose custom the company wishes to obtain

Target audience   the group of people at which a direct marketing campaign is aimed

Target marketing   the selection of a segment as a focus for the company's offering and communications

Targeting   selecting a segment or segments in which to compete

Team selling   the use of the combined efforts of salespeople, product specialists, engineers, sales managers and even directors to sell products

Technological distance   the difference between two companies' product and process technologies

Telemarketing   a marketing communications system whereby trained specialists use telecommunications and information technologies to conduct marketing and sales activities

Television viewership panel   a sample of TV viewers which measures audience size

Test marketing   the launch of a new product in one or a few geographic areas chosen to be representative of the intended market

Threat   a situation or trend which is unfavourable to the achievement of organizational objectives, for example a government regulation, competitor initiative or technological development

Time distance   the time which must elapse between establishing contact or placing an order and the actual transfer of the product or service involved

Time gap   the discrepancy between when a manufacturer wants to produce goods and when consumers wish to buy

Time-to-market   the time it takes for a company to develop a new product and turn it into a product which people can buy

Toll-free number   a special telephone number which customers can call without incurring any expense

Total quality management   the set of programmes designed to constantly improve the quality of physical products, services and processes

Tracking studies   usually retail audits which track sales across retail counters or research which tracks consumer awareness and/or attitudes over time

Trade marketing   marketing to the retail trade

Trade-off analysis   a measure of the trade-off customers make between price and other product features so that their effects on product preference can be established

Transactional information   information on a customer database which indicates which customer has bought what products, how often and how recently

Transfer pricing   the price charged between profit centres of the same company, sometimes used to take advantage of lower taxes in another country

Transition curve   the emotional stages that people pass through when confronted with an adverse change

Trial   the sampling, tasting or test consumption of a product by a consumer

Undifferentiated marketing   a market coverage strategy where a company decides to ignore market segment differences and develops a single marketing mix for the whole market

Undifferentiated targeting   offering the same product to the entire market without regard to differences in the customer profiles

Up-sell   persuading an existing customer to buy more valuable product from the firm's portfolio

User   a member of a decision-making unit who will actually be using the purchased item

Value analysis   a method of cost reduction in which components are examined to see if they can be made more cheaply

Value chain   the set of the firm's activities that are conducted to design, manufacture, market and distribute and service its products

Value-added   the difference between the selling price achieved and the company's costs.

Variability   a characteristic of services, namely that being delivered by people the standard of their performance is open to variation

Vicarious experience   the opportunity to experience situations or lifestyles to which an individual would not otherwise have access

Vicarious learning learning from others without direct experience or reward

Video conferencing two-way communication of both words and pictures via telephone lines

Video magazine a video which disseminates a corporate message

Video news release video coverage of a public relations event sent to television news departments via cassette, vision circuits or satellite

Warranty a guarantee by a manufacturer that if a product fails within a certain period it will make good the defect for free under certain conditions

Website a www file that contains text, pictures and/or sound

Weak theory of advertising the notion that advertising can first arouse awareness and interest, nudge some consumers towards a doubting first trial purchase and then provide some reassurance and reinforcement. Desire and conviction do not precede purchase

Wheel of retailing a theory of retailing development which suggests that new forms of retailing begin as low-cost, cut-price and narrow margin operations and then trade up until they mature as high price operators, vulnerable to a new influx of low-cost operators

Word-of-mouth a form of product promotion generated by consumers to consumers

Workload approach a method for deciding the number of salespeople required

World wide web a collection of computer files that can be accessed via the Internet allowing documents containing text, images, sound and video to be used

Author Index

Companies and Brands Index

Page numbers in **bold** indicate main references/case histories. Page numbers in *italics* indicate illustrations. Company names are in parenthesis to brand names where they appear in the text.

Subject Index